Sara Steele

Blueprints for Paradise

The Watercolor Paintings of Sara Steele

Published by Tide-mark Press, Ltd.
P.O. Box 20, Windsor, Connecticut 06095-0020

Archival Photography: Rich Genga, Joe Mikuliak, Jack Ramsdale
Photo Credits: Nick Kelsh, Steve Hebden
Design: Paul Rasid

Library of Congress Control Number: 2005924657

ISBN 1-59490-117-1

First Edition/First Printing
Printed in Korea

Contents

Acknowledgements 2
Contributors 4
Preface: Composing toward Compassion—*Anne Mugler* 5
Sara Steele, An Introduction—*Lisa Tremper Hanover* 6
Uniting Forms—*Nancy Post, Ph.D.* 8
A Conversation with Sara Steele 10
Wholly One—*Patricia Pearce* 28

水 Water 30
木 Wood 80
火 Fire 122
土 Earth 176
金 Metal 224

List of Plates and Attributions 276
Chronology: Personal Events 284
Chronology: Professional Highlights 285
Index of Plates 287

Acknowledgements

Creative acts are collective endeavors, whether they appear to be or not. Inevitably then, and with appreciation, *Blueprints for Paradise* benefited from the care of many hearts and minds.

My thanks to Lisa Tremper Hanover, Director of the Philip and Muriel Berman Museum of Art, for the invitation to exhibit *Blueprints for Paradise*, and to Sue Shifrin and Sue Calvin who ably assist her, and to Scott Kaeser, my publisher, for his commitment to quality and his ability to read between the lines despite existential crises. Thanks to everyone at Tide-mark for being a pleasure to work with.

Seeds in the desert may wait a long time for conditions conducive to germination. I thank Dom Reale for a conversation twenty-some years ago that seeded a vision of wider possibilities. Anne Mugler and I have had many extended conversations over the years, and I thank her for her relentless pursuit of the right words, and for walking this life-labyrinth with such grace and care. Patricia Pearce's solid, steady presence, her practicality and her creativity are among the gifts she shares generously with me for which I am deeply grateful. To Kathleen Kler, fellow traveler, thanks for pinch-hitting. Special thanks to Davia "La Buena Diva" Wilson who helped me in numerous ways, and to Ann Marie, Janice, and Patricia for their willingness to listen deeply and "transform the story."

Thanks to Pam Pittenger, Emily Gavin, and Davia Rivka for sharing their talents with me, and Eliza Callard for all that, her enduring good nature and humor, and her fulfillment skills. Thanks to Holly Phares, transcribing Diva; to Kip Leitner, tech Guru; to Sara Allen for suggesting a scaffolding; to Bob Musil for web-work; to Janine and Mike Zaikowski at Profiles; and to Harold Kellar and Gloria Klein for crafting beautiful frames for so many years.

To Terry Tempest Williams who inspires me through her relentless leaps and her passionate activism; Barbara Kingsolver, whose writings cheer me and egg me on; Mary Oliver, who manages to say with words some of the things I attempt to say with color; Wendell Berry for his feisty perseverance and plain-speaking; and to all those writers, sculptors, dancers, painters, musicians, gardeners, peacemakers and creatures who make my heart beat faster and my soul feel like a hawk in flight — my immense gratitude to you for sharing your gifts. Special thanks to Dorothy Allison for her patient listening and clarifying questions; to Ellen Bass for sharing her poems, warmth, and generosity; and to Beth Van Vleck for introducing me to Dr. Jane Goodall and Mary Lewis.

Huge hugs to many who hold me in the light of their big hearts and who help to keep the flow going with loving support of all kinds (including dark chocolate), especially Meg, Judd "The Germinator", Lillaby, Nini, the QAF Crew: Heinz, Sue O., and YuPing, and the Durango clan for being home. Special thanks to Deets for planting seeds long ago of Deep Ecology and The Way. *Mi corazón à Maria and Domingo y mi familia española.* A deep and affectionate bow to Teya, Susan, Patricia, Andy Kraft Scott, and Kathleen Kler—my soul sisters in and out of The Cauldron—and to Patranna for helping me to remember elusive core truths when I forget them again and again.

Thanks to Donna Allender for help untangling the skeins; to Janice MacKenzie for balance and stamina; to Barry Belt, Bill Harvey, Rebecca Carli-Mills, and Linda Good for being wonderful healers. I have had the privilege of being the student of several remarkable teachers: Sara Allen, Gladys Bloch, Andy Benjamin, Anne Pinkenson, and Nancy Post have all influenced my thinking and my work. Thanks to Barry and Oi Fan Chan Peters for bringing me and my paintings to Bainbridge Island. Chris Sickles Merchant and Judy McFadden have been steadfast friends and have always encouraged me in my creative endeavors.

I am grateful to my mother for her sense of social justice and for encouraging me to take risks, and to my father for his loving heart, his steadfast support, and his willingness to forgive.

The Leeway Foundation and Friends of Steele provided essential support throughout the work on this project, and this affirmation was a special gift.

My thanks to Linda Lee Alter, Martha Anderson, Susan Balder, Shari Basom/Small Changes, Fay Bullitt, Martha and Jim Bywater, Anne Dranginis, Rosalind Dutton, Linda and Michael Dzuba, Anne and William Ewing, Kate and Joel Feldman, Jane Fortune, Marilyn Frazer, Laurentine Fromm, Barbara Furman, Linda Good, Kathy Harris and Joe DiAndrea, Fritz and Deetsie Herbine, Connie Hershey, Rita Shaughnessy and Rick Josiassen, Connie and Sam Katz, Signe Wilkinson and Jon Landau, Manon Floquet and Rebecca Lee, Melissa Manix, Dorothy Manou, Meg Wallace and Tim McDermott, Janice McKenzie, Betsy and Tom Melvin, Anne Mugler, Robert and Caryn McTighe Musil, Sue Osthoff, Peter Pakradooni, Lois Pearce, Patricia Pearce, Kelley Phillips, Project H.O.M.E., Carrie Rickey, Sachiyo Searles, Teya Sepinuck, Abby Stamelman Hocky, Steeleworks, Jim and Lynn Stillman, Swan Stull and Marty Gates, Patty Sundberg, Marni Sweet, Susan Tobias, Beth Van Vleck, Cathy Weber, Murray Weidenbaum, Janice Williams, and Maureen Wood.

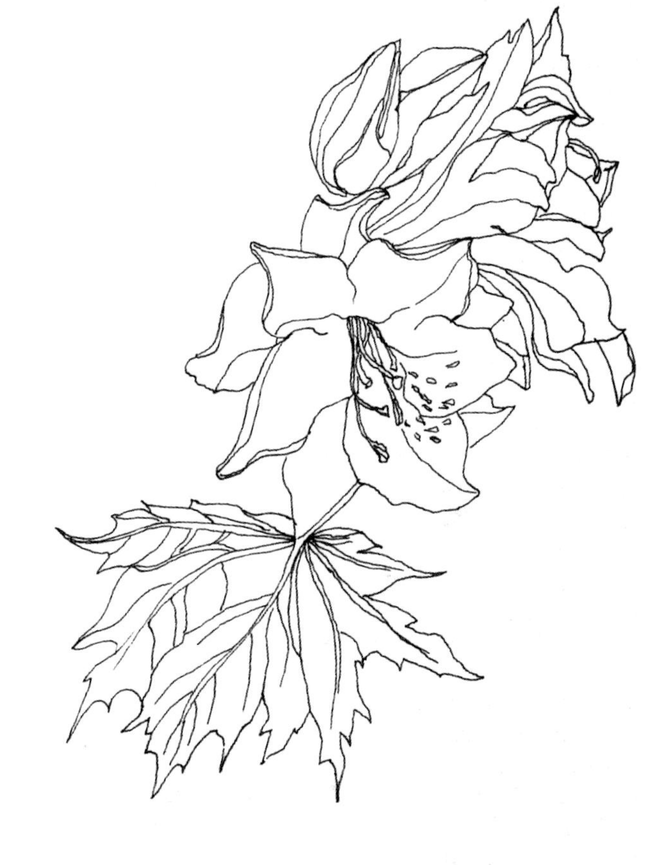

In memory of Jean Miller Bullock and Geneva Miller,
and dedicated to Harriet Heaney and Ralph Allen,
who lived Deep Ecology.

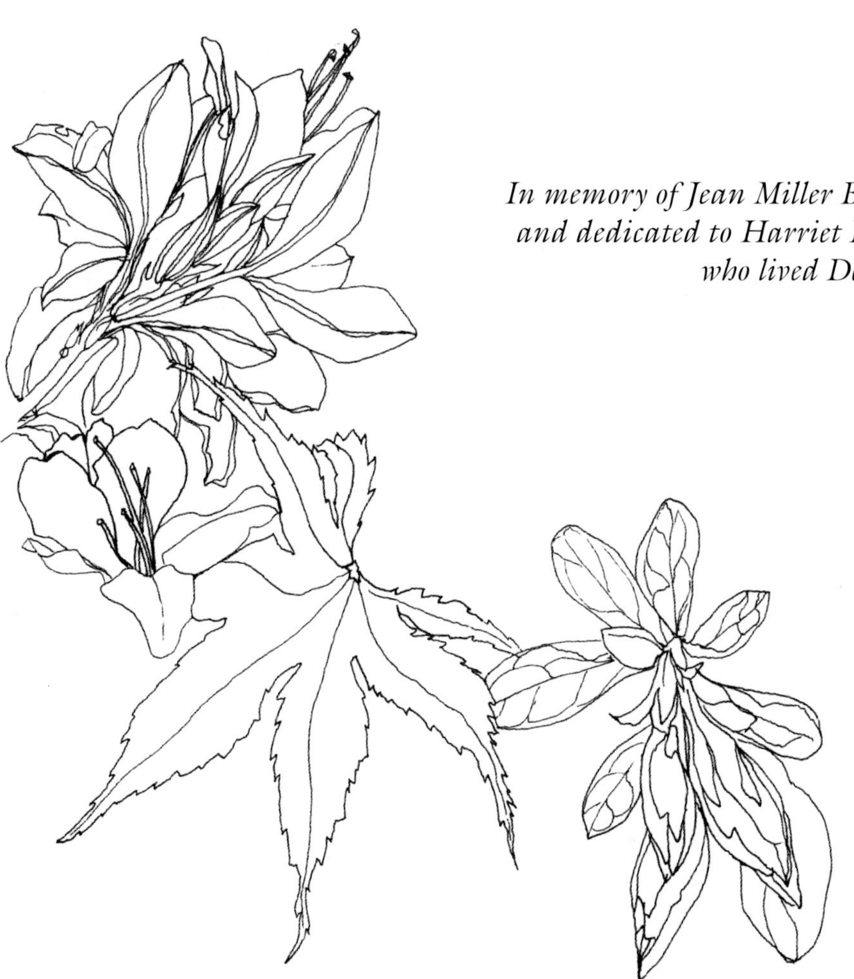

Contributors

Anne Mugler

Anne Mugler, MSW, is a psychotherapist, poet, equestrienne, and rug hooker living in Arlington, Virginia.

Patricia Pearce

Patricia Pearce is pastor of Tabernacle United Church and co-founder of the Arts & Spirituality Center in Philadelphia. She served as a Peace Corps Volunteer in Ecuador, South America, and holds a Master of Divinity degree from San Francisco Theological Seminary. Her interests include nonviolence, energy healing, ecology, quantum physics, religion, and the interplay of creativity and spirituality.

Nancy Post, Ph.D.

Dr. Nancy Post is an expert in the areas of strategic planning, organizational change, and energy management. As a consultant she has advised large and small organizations on the benefits of strategic development, organization, and leadership training, with a client list that includes Kaiser Permanente, General Motors, Bellsouth Wireless, the states of Delaware, Vermont, and Massachusetts, and the University of Maryland. She has held a variety of teaching positions at the University of Pennsylvania in the Organizational Dynamics program and at Wharton's Aresty Institute for Executive Development as well as at Temple University's Executive MBA program.

She lives in Philadelphia with her husband, an Englishman, and her eight-year-old son.

Preface

Composing toward Compassion

In the presence of work by Sara Steele, it is difficult to move away. The color and form allow our eyes little choice but to train their sight on her paintings. We are startled by and drawn into the vision in front of us.

Art of any sort is language, potentially producing both an internal and external dialogue. It is most assuredly a way of telling one's story. No artist can write or paint or compose without imbuing the composition with his or her own historical landscape. Additionally, the artist is influenced by the conversation he or she has with other artists who place their stories in public arenas with the courage and audacious hope that this conversation occurs. Finally, the reception of a composition is dependent upon generating some part of the tale belonging to the viewer. Thus, art allows us to tell by composing or by being drawn into compositions, which, consciously or unconsciously, tell what we know.

This process is not always easy or simple. We construct containers to hold our stories. The containers we develop for ourselves are often safe and seemingly life-sustaining. Breaking them can be shattering, creating openings to new thoughts both terrifying and inspirational. A beautiful painting can break our containers, a crisis can break them, falling in love can break them—perhaps bringing forth grief and terrible knowledge, perhaps unlocking our fears and hatreds. At these moments, as theologian Michael Dwinell puts it, we as humans are called to bear witness to the truth that, no matter how shattering, there is something out there beyond our containers, beyond the boundaries, "that is calling for our attention, that demands to be validated, and finally requires to be embraced on its own terms, drawing us into its own mystery."

Perhaps it is in these moments that we, as witnesses to our own truth or another's truth, are given access to our own kindness and compassion. It is this conversation between the artist, the viewer, and the witness that is sacred. The artwork, be it a painting, a poem, a symphony, or a landscape of Creation, becomes the medium of possibility, and we may develop, as poet Wendell Berry states, "our imagination to the point that permits sympathy to happen."

Nature knows this at a deep cellular level. Healthy development depends upon the building of channels between cells, keeping these channels well-maintained, unclogged, and flexible, and in sending messages through them, one cell to another, that are clear and specific. The geometric structure of these cellular channels is dazzling. What nature knows is that to live we must communicate—we must tell our story. As poet William Stafford writes,

> the signals we give—yes or no, or maybe—
> should be clear: the darkness around us is deep.

Sara Steele's paintings give us an opportunity. Her work is informed by classical structures that edit what we take in and that allow such dazzling intensity of color. They give us an experience of light through color that holds us, communicates its depth and touches us. We inhale, we go deeply, we say yes, we say no, we say maybe. And the light through color gives meaning to the possibilities of the dark.

Anne Mugler

Sara Steele, An Introduction

Sara Steele is passionate. With the intensity of her watercolor palette, she boldly articulates a deep knowledge of the natural world. Rising from the rich earth of her personal beliefs, her visual messages reflect a life devoted to understanding social conditions, cultural chasms, ecological dilemmas, and the political processes that complicate, and even hasten destruction of, the natural course of planetary life. Her artistic gifts and social activism flow from her conviction that our choices alter both inner and outer environments, affecting our human neighbors and other species. This is the philosophy behind *Blueprints for Paradise*, which seeks to codify with paper, brush, pigment, and water, how flora and terra firma, by their intrinsic natures, are imprinted to regenerate and change in order to survive. In the midst of this extravagantly coded drive to live, we humans can reflect on the intense beauty of life on earth, and thus draw on a passion to preserve the planet that we inhabit.

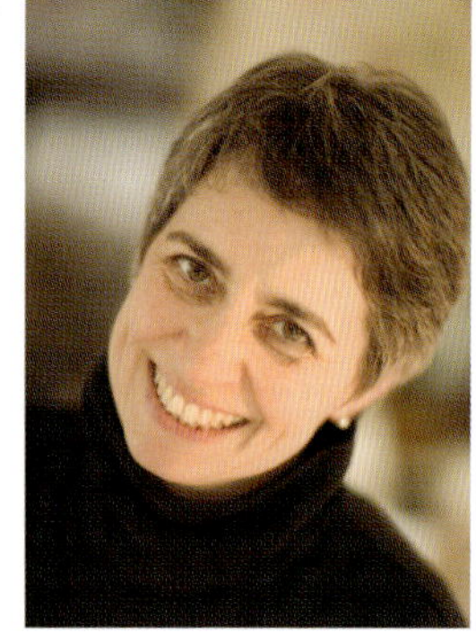

Steele chooses to contemplate her passions and concerns in a visual way. One might expect a riotous and energetic assault on a canvas that would reveal discontent and possible solutions. This is not the case. She uses her paintings to explore her inner world, yet they work on a different level to document the landscape accessible to public perspective. In addition to capturing great beauty, her sublime watercolor compositions carry a message of reflection, and are powerful sources of inspiration. The audience need not know the multilayered process that drives the artist in order to appreciate and respond to these lush images.

While it is illuminating to know that the artist has used her talent, from an early age, to process and gain deeper awareness of violence and disorder, this is but one context for the strength of her imagery. Her activism in the arenas of domestic abuse and environmental desecration flows back and forth from the cloister of her studio to her lively urban neighborhood and the world. (See Patricia Pearce's introductory dialogue with the artist.)

Steele has been drawn to and studied numerous twentieth-century artists and their works—from the metaphysical automatic writings of Paul Klee to the saturated color fields of Mark Rothko. If there is a physical reference stylistically, and indeed philosophically, it is the work of Helen Frankenthaler, whose abstractions are grounded in the structure of the landscape.

Steele is self-taught; however, it would be a mistake to consider her an "outsider" artist. Though she does not hold a degree from an academy of learning, it is clear that the Steiglitz group, John Marin, Arthur Dove, Georgia O'Keeffe, and Charles Demuth, in particular, opened her eyes to the possible, and her work proceeds in this lineage. That said, Steele's is as individual a voice as any of these, and evidences a radical and nontraditional education. An untrained artist does not choose watercolor as a vehicle of expression. The unforgiving nature of the watercolor medium requires focus, a deep knowledge of how layers of transparent color will interact, and a quick sense of how the composition will unfold. Her working vocabulary of technique is broad. There is an innate touch of the brush to paper that reveals itself in Steele's work—from the delicate tendrils and petal spines in her orchid and iris images to the saturated brilliance in the color combinations of her Hawaiian and Southwestern desert landscapes.

Like the Hudson River School of painters, Steele is capturing a moment in our ecological continuum and, at the same time, using her particular visual perspective and color choices to elicit an intangible feeling. The low horizon line in *Cathleen's Mountain* puts the viewer in a position to appreciate the majesty of the rock face, dappled with pigment that itself reflects a range of natural, unforced colorations. The attitude of the plants in *Setting Sunflowers*, a portrait of dying set in a stark white background, communicates the essence of a particular time in the cycle of life.

Ashes and *Tod* both illustrate how Steele incorporates written language to complement visual imagery, reinforcing each in an explicit way. The artist has spoken of this interaction as one that she has always used "privately" and that has come into her formal work in the last decade. This direction allows her to communicate with both the gesture of calligraphy and that of the brush stroke. This approach has precedents in the work of mid-twentieth-century artists such as Robert Rauschenberg and Larry Rivers, but it relates more specifically to Japanese and Chinese scrollwork that uses landscape elements in tandem with the characters of the language.

Steele's oeuvre, at mid-career, can now be viewed as nonsequential, yet ongoing, distinct series that continue to express the concerns of the artist. As *Nuclear Family Holocaust* shows, some cycles were a deliberate, focused progression; others, such as *Endangered Orchids*, demonstrate a concern with delicate ecosystems.

A key philosophical underpinning of Steele's work is the Tao as expressed in traditional Chinese medicine, which Steele has studied and embraced as a holistic source of wisdom and physical well-being. In this tradition there are five elements that correspond to seasons and therefore the life cycle. Water, wood, fire, earth, and metal are translated by Steele into recognizable subjects that, taken at face value, convey a powerful message. They are also a comment on the enduring corollaries to ancient connections made between ecological rudiments and our physical state of being.

Water, the fundamental element necessary to life, is literally represented as liquid, solid, and vapor in such works as *Na Pali Coast, Kaua'i*, *From Wellfleet at Night*, *LavaFlow/Alaska*, and *Mist Rising Near Big Sur*. It is also represented in the lush foliage of *Plume Poppy* and *Cyclamen*. The seascapes, uninhabited by human or animal life, are tranquil, touched only by wind, light, and gravity. The water has carved the coastline and rock outcroppings in a subtle manipulation. *Cycla-*

men twists itself from its ground of plump leaves like a wave being pulled by the moon.

The *Forces of Attraction* goes beyond the literal to convey the essence of the laws of physics, while simultaneously expressing emotional dynamics in human relationships. Deep purples clash with a rainstorm of red, orange, and blue, taking our sight line beyond the horizon to deep space. *The Point II* suggests the cervix of a womb, the point of origination in human geography. Where *The Point I* depicts a crisply defined wedge of energy, we see the frenzied opposition of water and fire in *The Point IV*. Combining these two elements illustrates how the natural dynamics of the world collide and fuse, seemingly chaotic and discordant. And so it is with the dynamics of the human race where none truly live in isolation. The portrait of a weed in *May Storm* echoes the movement of "The Point" series, with its wedgelike composition and tension between elements in the foreground and background.

A metaphor for growth and the rhythms of organized structures, wood is also analogous to the fresh growth of plants and new life blooming in spring. The garden serves as inspiration and as a physical source of subject matter for Steele. A rich variety of lilies, irises, poppies, and exotics vie with leaves and plant architecture for the artist's attention. These optimistic portraits, such as *Riots of Spring* and *Amazon Botanicals*, are depicted with bold color, the staple of her palette, and speak to an annual rebirth that confirms the natural cycle of the seasons. Even *Fan Coral*, which examines the spiny structure of submerged animal life, relates to the strong, skeletal foundation that parallels the cellular organization of wood.

Reds, oranges, and yellows signify fire and its nature: random, enthusiastic, warming. The glowing sunsets of summer and vibrant fields of tulips inspire a sense of unity as Steele uses these images to impart a sense of community. Vibrant reds play against blues and yellows in *Migration* and *Hollyhocks*, but it is the shape of the Birds of Paradise plant that plays out in the physical image of fire; points of yellow and red and blue slash toward the sky with power much like the abstract *Oh! Karen*... with its tendril flashes arcing skyward in the same fashion.

Steele calls the visible landscape "the skin of the planet," and it is our endangered Earth that supports all life forms. She uses this arena to comment on other endangered subjects in works such as her "Orchid Series." The earth aspect of Chinese thought equates to late summer and the harvest, and it is this element that envelops all of the others. As we prepare for a time when the ground is not producing the products necessary to sustain us, the landscape is celebrated and the bounties of the rich earth are depicted out of their environment in still-life repose. Peppers, eggplants, tomatoes, and pears are shown ripe and ready, with their shapes and colors rendered much like a landscape such as *Abiquiu Dam I* or *Alizarin Wing*.

Metal represents the end and beginning anew of the life cycle, and it is here that we see the artist exploring themes of dying and grief. *Storm Lilies* shows late season blooms set against a volatile sky that can be interpreted as dangerous and something to be feared. With delicacy and precision Steele articulates death's proximity to truth, choosing as subject matter the beautiful forms of dying blossoms. In *Lake Visions* she holds a prism to the crystalline structure that both grief and inspiration share. *Alterpiece*, an intentional play on words, is a powerful composition that communicates a state of mind and perhaps the conclusion of a period of great emotional distress; it is not only an homage to the death of that turmoil, but an expression of willingness to open to the new.

There is eloquent consistency in Sara Steele's vocabulary as it has matured; however, the artist's prolific compositions, spanning more than thirty years, could not be considered repetitive. Her impassioned vision remains fresh, her technique sophisticated, and her imagery approachable—yet charged with layered messages both personal and global.

Lisa Tremper Hanover
Director
Philip and Muriel Berman Museum of Art
Ursinus College

Uniting Forms

When I was sixteen, I flew from New York to visit my cousins who lived in Minnesota. It was 8 degrees Fahrenheit in February when I arrived, and Minneapolis was deeply blanketed in snow. I had never seen snow so deep that it covered cars and created small, sparkling white mountains at the entrances to driveways. And such quiet...in a big city...amazing! Nature ruled an urban landscape, and I was entranced.

Eventually, I visited the Minnesota Museum of Art and took a tour of the building. That proved to be a pivotal experience in my life, one that permanently altered my future.

While the tour group assembled in the lobby, the guide explained that the museum, designed by Japanese architect Kenzo Tange, reflected a deep-seated value of Minnesotans: that man and nature must live in balance. From the earliest Native Americans to the Scandinavian immigrants who came later, Minnesotans have prided themselves on inspired, direct, clear thinking, and valued living in harmony with nature. The guide then described aspects of the building's materials and architectural plan, showing us how the use of materials, placement of windows, doors, and structural forms helped unite the building with the world outside. This concept of unity came as a transforming revelation to me.

For a moment, I stopped hearing the guide. All sound disappeared and, for me, the room was exquisitely quiet. The white forms, vast windows, and luxurious play of light captivated me. I felt a sense of deep joy and quiet peace. This feeling came to me again, years later, when I stood at the edge of the Grand Canyon and, later still, in Thailand while gazing up a mountaintop at a smiling white Buddha.

Penetrating this experience, like a gentle breeze, the voice of the guide whispered, "The main design principle used by Tange was to integrate the inside with the outside." At that moment I understood my life's work. I came to understand that I needed to create forms that integrate the inside with the outside. Do this, and you will feel joy. The outside was nature. The inside was the beliefs, feelings, sensations, thoughts, perceptions, and meaning created from life experience. Find a way to integrate them. My mission was clear.

The Work of Balance

The insights I gained led me to become a city planner—to learn to use form—on a mass scale to create integrated, balanced environments in urban areas. Through that work I saw that when people related well to each other and their contexts, energy was generated. When dynamics were not harmonious no energy was created. Balance generated energy and supported life. Imbalance drained resources and was unsustainable over the long term.

During years as a planner, I found that "balance" was not a very popular principle. Companies prefer to dominate environments, rather than living in harmony with them. Domination requires lots of energy, however—often more than the organization has to spare. Leaders seem unaware of the human and economic costs of striving to be dominant. Often they treat people in their organizations (their lifeblood) as expendable commodities to be used to achieve organizational goals. Companies use people to achieve these aims, but give no thought to replenishing them. People are treated as "nonrenewable resources." They often appear tired and driven, relying increasingly on coffee and fear to keep themselves pumped up in work environments that promise less and less reward.

I frequently saw these hardworking people become sick—sometimes physically, but inevitably in the soul. When you give more than you receive, you burn out. Nature and man were out of balance in the workplace.

In these early years of working with organizations, I grappled with my clients' propensity for excess while I attempted to facilitate balance. How could I help organizations use their energy more wisely? How could they use and replenish energy in order to find sustainable patterns? Planning education helped, as did group and systems dynamics theory, but a piece was still missing. Eventually, I turned again to the East for guidance, and found principles and practices of energy management in its purest form—designed directly for creating balance in people.

The Five Phases

Perhaps the oldest continuously practiced form of medicine in the world, Chinese medicine offers a complex diagnostic system that relates imbalances of natural energy to the manifestation of illness. Medical conditions are considered "imbalances" of energy that can be "excess" or "deficient." Diagnostic methods help doctors determine, very specifically, which of fourteen main channels (meridians) have adequate energy or are deficient. Treatment, diet, lifestyle, and exercise are commonly altered to regain balance. The closer to balance, the less severe the symptoms. It's elegantly simple. You can only use the energy you have. If you consume too much you will become deficient, which eventually leads to being symptomatic. Genetics also plays a part in health history, but smart lifestyle and diet choices can help build energy if you need it.

This made sense to me. I saw examples of deficiency; for example, tired people are sick more often. Sleep-deprived people feel pain more acutely. People worn down by chronic pain may not have the energy needed to heal quickly.

Examples of excess also abound. Overzealous organizations have established unattainable goals that prompted inefficient behavior from people who struggled to reach targets before thinking about the best ways to work. Adrenaline-driven organizations create a proliferation of projects, leading managers to race from meeting to meeting without time to think or prepare. As driven people stay later to finish their work, excess leads to inefficiency, which, in turn, results in deficiency. The energy metaphor makes sense. It also works. Recently, the World Health

Organization endorsed Chinese medicine as an efficacious system of primary care. It is the mostly widely used system of medicine in the world.

Balance is often described as what we find in nature, where seasons show us different types of energy and when they are best employed. Winter, the season in which water (as snow) blankets much of the landscape, is a good time for reflection, for storage, for being still. Spring is a time for energetic activity—a good time to build, to plan, to grow. Summer, a hot time, adds fullness and blossoming to the beginnings made in spring, bringing maturity along with growth. Late summer's humidity brings abundance, harvest, and the chance to stabilize. Finally, autumn distills the best, ending the cycle of growth and offering a chance to give thanks.

In addition, each of these phases reveals different forms and light. Winter's blue light, reflected on water and snow, emphasizes swirls and reflections. More defined (yet organic) forms—with clearer borders—take shape in spring's bright light. Full summer sun shows reds and orange better than at any other time of the year, but also reveals upward movement towards light as plants (and humans) arch toward the sun. The descent starts in late summer, as full fruit emerges and plants grow heavy. The white light, autumn's gift, shows the brilliance of all colors. Vivid hues are sharply revealed each fall, like crystals.

This cycle of Five Phases corresponds to five seasons. But the phases apply to all levels of human and natural functioning. People evolve through the seasons of their lives. Organizations, too, go through cycles. Even products have life cycles. Unifying the laws of nature with social systems, we can (and do) apply these phases to achieve balance in many types of human endeavor.

Along with me, Sara Steele found this model of Five Phases a compelling one. We both understand the five energies as the animating force of life, but we apply that understanding in different ways. I work in a private practice that brings insight and understanding to individuals and organizations about ways to use energy consciously. Sara inspires equanimity by enticing her viewers into a loving relationship with the natural world. I had the privilege of being Sara's first teacher of this model in the mid-1980s. I have since enjoyed twenty years viewing the manifestation of her understanding of it, expressed through her glorious paintings.

Sara Steele

Perhaps the first of many bonds I have with Sara is that we chose to make our homes in the same neighborhood. We both share the need to integrate our daily lives with our environment. We live in a neighborhood of Philadelphia that was home to European Quakers more than 300 years ago, when the new settlers met the Lenape Indians and lived peacefully with them. Peace and dignity are cherished attributes of our neighborhood, which also, quietly, was a main station on the underground railroad. The town watch says that we live in the most continuously peaceful, integrated neighborhood in North America.

The streets are lined with homes built from locally quarried stone. Much of the outdoor activity centers on the city's largest park, which provides seven miles of hills, streams, and middle-Atlantic woodlands. Parkland seeps into the neighborhood. Grand trees are everywhere, as are spectacular displays of azaleas in spring, irises in late spring, lilies in summer, dogwoods and red maples in autumn, and plays of light on snow and ice reflecting on the river in winter. We live this way. Anyone observant enough to look sees beauty and balance.

Sara looks with a keener eye than most. Painting, as you know, starts with an acute sense of sight.

When you look at Sara's early work, you will find many elements of our neighborhood carefully observed. Irises, gladiolas, lilies, and squash blossoms abound where we live. If you enjoyed a gallery exhibit of Sara's work before 1985, and you lived in this region, you would have found elements that you recognized but had never appreciated so fully. Even in her early days, Sara's great gift was her ability to entice a viewer into a more loving relationship with the natural world, finding exquisite natural forms in the heart of a city.

Unlike many artists, Sara wants her work to have social impact, hoping that viewers are inspired to action. Some of the most famous of her early works, the orchid series, were used by the group Women's Resources as a motivating logo. Later works became motivating visuals for countless environmental and feminist organizations. The National Wildlife Federation commissioned her to paint its endangered orchids. SANE, the Committee for Sane Nuclear Policy Alternatives, showed three versions of *Dutch Iris*, which, as you may know, can look entirely different depending on the angle of view. "Consider the Alternatives," said the poster. "See how nature generates options," said the painter Sara Steele.

When the feminist collective in Cincinnati decided to mark the tenth anniversary of their bookstore with a new logo, Sara gave them *Winged Victory*. Cincinnati's Crazy Ladies Bookstore, a thriving feminist institution, evolved in 2002 to become the Greater Cincinnati Women's Resource Center.

Using concepts of balance learned from the Chinese system, Sara does not turn away from the chaos or illness of the world. Rather, she chooses, again and again, to remind us that there are natural forms—the shape of life around us—that can help us heal our fractured lives.

Look carefully at her work. You will find repetition, newness, life, death, maturity, youth, pain, and gladness. You will feel more integrated with Sara Steele as your tour guide, as she shows you how to use form to create harmony and celebrate the glorious gem that is our planet.

Nancy Post, Ph.D.

A Conversation with Sara Steele

Beginnings and Early Influences

Patricia Pearce (P.P.): Okay—where shall we begin?

Sara Steele (S.S.): "Anywhere," said the Mad Hatter.

P.P. How old were you when you started painting? What got you started painting?

S.S. The first actual painting that I remember making . . . I think I was ten or eleven, and somebody had given me a small watercolor box. I made a little painting of an iris near the side of our house. I remember drawing a lot. I was really into mushrooms for awhile. I'd walk in the woods and find fungus and make pencil drawings of them. That was an extended phase. And I went through a rocks and stones phase.

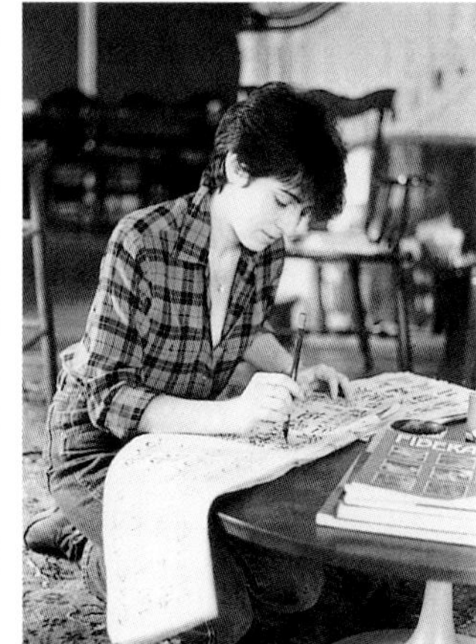

P.P. Were you always drawn to natural world subject matter?

S.S. Yes. Always. The only things apart from natural forms that intrigued me were geometrical . . . architectural things. I must have been in my late teens when the East Wing of the National Gallery opened, and my teacher and friend Sara Allen and I went down there. I walked into that space and fell in love as soon as I saw it. It's such a temple! I. M. Pei considered every angle in the space, every surface, and it all harmonizes. It's a truly beautiful space.

P.P. Who encouraged you [in your art] along the way?

S.S. Some teachers. My mother encouraged me. And my dad. My father was a Sunday painter. He made me a painter's box. I still have it: my own little box that holds a palette and tubes of paint and brushes. I remember when I was 11, I fell madly in love with Toulouse Lautrec's work. There was a store on Sansom Street where I think I bought every Toulouse Lautrec poster they had. I plastered them all around my room, and even changed the fabrics of my bedroom so they would match the posters. For my birthday my mother got me a book of Toulouse Lautrec's work, my first real art book.

P.P. Now you are, for the most part, self-taught?

S.S. Well, more or less.

P.P. What does that mean?

S.S. Well, although I've had some really incredible teachers in my life, I did not attend art school and I've only taken a handful of art classes.

P.P. Was that a conscious choice?

S.S. No. It was a fear-based choice. When I was college-age I didn't think I was good enough to apply to art school, and I had so little self-esteem that I could hardly write a college application essay. During the years when my friends were in college, I was dealing with a suicidal depression —in and out of institutions.

P.P. Were you still painting?

S.S. I drew a lot. I always kept notebooks and sketchbooks. I took an art course here or there. I don't know how it actually happened that I decided I was going to be an artist. It was almost an act of will—I just set myself to it. I created exercises for myself, did color studies, went to museums, read art books. I bought good watercolor paints and papers and brushes and just practiced . . . for about twenty years! I always liked to look at art a lot. I still do. I can't stop looking.

P.P. What [other] artists have you been drawn to, that have influenced you?

S.S. Early on I really liked Paul Klee. I love Mark Rothko's work. When I first started studying the Abstract Expressionists with Sara Allen, Rothko's work spoke to me most directly. His work seemed the most pure. When we first went to the East Wing for that big exhibit of the Abstract Expressionists, his work moved me the most.

P.P. Do you know why?

S.S. Yes. It's so direct. It's essence. It's just color . . . color in space. I think he really understood, in a very deep way, how a resonant color vibration goes into your body and induces a powerful sensation, a physical emotion. When I sit in the Rothko room in the Phillips Gallery looking in one direction, aware of the other two paintings in my peripheral vision, and then turn and look at a different one with those others in my peripheral vision, my sensation completely changes. I think he was working way out on the edge.

I always loved Bosch's work. In my late teens and early twenties I steeped myself in his paintings. Helen Frankenthaler. I love her work—it's beautiful and free and expressive and complex. Lately I've been taken with Chillida, whose work I fell in love with during my first trip to Spain, and Jean-Paul Agosti, a French watercolorist. Matisse's cut-outs. Kandinsky. O'Keeffe, John Marin, Dove, Ansel Adams, that whole Steiglitz group.

When I met their work it felt to me like I had met my forebears, my art great-grandparents. Their visual ideas really resonated with me.

Because I never had formal training, I feel my encounters with "Great Art" have been sort of hit or miss, but I've always discovered work that I love. In Raphael Peale's still lifes of fruit, there's a painting of raspberries and blackberries that look so luscious you just want to pluck and eat them.

Particular paintings grab me. When I first saw the Van Der Weyden in the Prado of taking Christ down off the cross, I just fell to the floor and sat there weeping. I can't even tell you why, because I don't know much about Christian religion. But there's something about that painting. When Queen Elizabeth II's collection of DaVinci drawings was shown at the Art Museum in Philadelphia, there were pages of his notebooks under glass so that you could see both sides. If *Gray's Anatomy* had been illustrated by Leonardo it would've been a much better book! There are so many! Have you ever read Kandinsky's book *On The Spiritual in Art*?

P.P. No.

S.S.: Matta—I think you would appreciate Matta. Very spacious paintings, very expressive. He is Chilean. Actually, he died recently. For years I sought pieces of his to look at, and I'd find *one*. Then, the last time I was in Madrid, there was a huge retrospective of Matta's at the Reina Sofia. It was like a dream come true: the whole first floor of the museum!

I have love affairs with artists' work. Wolf Kahn. Charles Burchfield. Mary Frank. Martin Puryear. Andy Goldsworthy. Oscar Bluemner. Ed Ruscha. Barbara Kruger. Alice Aycock. There's so much amazing work out there. I think it's impossible not to keep falling in love with different artists. The last time I was at the Prado there was an exhibit of Vermeer and his contemporaries, more Vermeers than have ever been gathered in one place at one time. I'd never seen any in person before. Until I saw that show I didn't really understand what it was about Vermeer, but in each room, his paintings jumped right out at you. They so surpassed the work of his peers.

Process

P.P. How would you describe your creative process?

S.S. Of course it's different at different times. When inspiration is playing "hide and seek," I lean on discipline. I don't mean discipline in a harsh way. I mean practicing things, like musical scales. I make up exercises for myself. I work on technical challenges. I may have a color in mind, or a series of colors I want to learn about. So, I'll practice mixing colors, and inevitably mixing colors leads me somewhere. Sometimes I'll be journaling and something that has been on my mind will congeal into a word or an image, so I'll follow it to see where it leads. I'll look it up in the O.E.D. [*Oxford English Dictionary*] or the Chinese dictionary. I'll play with the components of the Chinese characters. I'll play with the etymology. And in the process of doing things that feel "playful" to me, other information in my psyche starts to reveal itself. Or it might begin with a quote or a passage that I've been reading.

P.P. I'm thinking about language as a portal into the creation of something visual. Would that happen with a floral painting or would that tend to be a painting that was more abstract?

S.S. Well, with more abstract paintings, it's definitely a component, as well as in paintings where I've started to incorporate language. I guess I've gotten braver about exposing my process, and also more interested in having the process as available to the viewer as the endpoint. It's visible in a painting like *Ashes* or *Tod*.

With floral paintings, let's say I'm in the garden making a study or drawing of a particular plant or flower—for example when I was drawing bloodroot. Things occur while I'm making the drawing. I try to keep my attention very focused on my subject so that my eye and my hand are connected in a way that bypasses my conscious mind. But things happen. A bee or butterfly flies by, or a breeze . . . something may start a chain of thought. And it tends to loop back to the subject matter so that those things get almost woven together. It's like watching a metaphor sculpt itself. So, I might be watching this bloodroot and thinking about both "blood" and "root"—because those words are such rich, charged words. How did it come to have that name? Was it because someone discovered that its root produced a nice brownish-red dye stuff? And I notice the structures of the plant. I observe how it grows. I become aware of what some Buddhists call the "monkey mind" because when I'm working my mind leaps and jumps all over the place. In a less judgmental vein, perhaps, it's "mercurial"—it's mischievous—sometimes it amuses me.

There's also the physical sensation of the pencil or the brush on paper, or mixing color on a palette. It has a feeling of resonance for me. It will bring up emotions and it's also an in-the-body sensation. And those sensations may evolve into other things on the paper. I watch them generating themselves. It's like watching something give birth to itself on the paper. Then a dialogue begins to happen. When a mark is made on the paper, I respond, and it becomes a conversation with the composition. There are so many levels to it. It's a wonder that I ever leave the studio because it really is the best place to be!

P.P. You talked about how when the muse is hiding or playing "hide and seek," you rely on discipline. And, what about when that's not the case? What about when it's just coming?

S.S. Then it's like riding a wild horse . . . without a saddle or reins. You just grab on for dear life. I think it was Chuck Close who said, "Inspiration is for amateurs." And I knew exactly what he meant because inspiration is joyous. It's a lucky break. But if I waited around to be inspired all the time, I'd do very little work. Sometimes inspiration comes in the doing of the work. It's like the practice of meditation: not every meditation is a blissful, prayerful, energetic experience. Sometimes it's just being aware that my stomach is growling or my heart is beating faster or a mosquito is singing in my ear. In meditation, the discipline is calling your attention back to the center, it's a grounding process. I think in painting, it's returning to the not-so-simple act of painting. Just making a picture—making a painting—is coming back to that center point. And sometimes the inspiration will expose itself to you through doing that. It took me a long time to understand that inspiration is a lucky break. It's a gift.

P.P. There's nothing one can do to encourage that?

S.S. Well, I'm not sure I would want to mess with that, in part because many things that have become inspiration for me have been experiences I would not have chosen to have.

P.P. Tell me about your relationship with color.

S.S. I think of it as a nutrient. You know how you could be B-vitamin deprived? I could be Scarlet Lake deprived. I made a big painting once, trying to encompass my peripheral vision, and the whole painting was Scarlet Lake . . . because I needed an infusion of Scarlet Lake. It sounds silly, but it's true.

There's a juxtaposition of Cadmium Yellow Deep and French Ultramarine Blue . . . and certain color combinations . . . an orange made from Cadmium Yellow Deep and Scarlet Lake, and the corresponding blue-purple from French Ultramarine and Violet, and the combination of those two together sets up a vibration that just makes my eyes feel happy! Different colors of turquoise, different blue-green colors . . . even when I was a little kid, the blue-green crayons, the magenta crayons, the red-purple crayons would be down to the nubs before any others. I wouldn't go near the browns but those crayons would be gone. One of the luxuries of being a grown-up was allowing myself to buy as many large boxes of crayons as I wanted, and to have scissors in every room.

P.P. A rite of passage . . .

S.S. Yeah. I don't know why, but for some reason, I remember scissors and Scotch tape being sacred items when we were growing up.

Indigo was another great crayon. And it turned out to be an even better paint. It's almost black at full strength, and it's a beautiful blue-gray when it's pale. It mixes well with other colors. It's a wonderful paint.

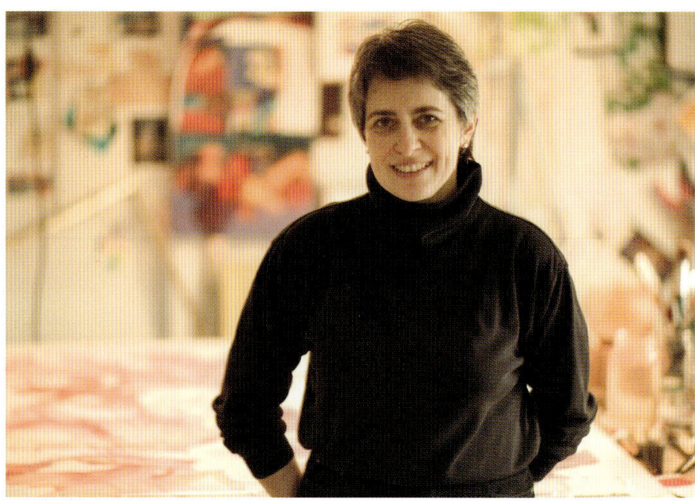

I think if I could only have a few colors they would be: Scarlet Lake, French Ultramarine, Indigo, Cadmium Yellow Deep, Permanent Rose (Quinacridone Rose). The Quinacridone colors are great. It's a good thing I was born after the Industrial Revolution because otherwise I wouldn't have the Quinacridones, and the Phthalocyanines to mix blue-greens. Oh, and Cobalt Teal, and . . .

P.P. When you do landscapes, oftentimes the colors are not what we would necessarily see if we look at a mountain or sky. How do you select the colors, or how do the colors select you when you're painting a landscape?

S.S. Selecting me is a good way to say that. It's different at different times. Sometimes, if you look down the street in a certain light and squint, you notice that the gray of the asphalt doesn't look gray—it actually looks almost purple. Or the sky, or the light coming through the trees doesn't actually look pale yellow, it looks pale lavender or pale blue or pale apricot. It's seeing the colors behind the colors, under the colors. If we look right now, for example, at that hemlock tree outside, the different greens in some places look almost orangy-red, and right along the very edges it looks white, and then right next to that it's almost purple.

P.P. So do you have the feeling or the experience that your subject matter is inviting you to see it in a deeper way than we might see it?

S.S. Maybe what I'm doing is exaggerating what I see there. I'm exaggerating it partly because it makes me happy, and partly because other people might not be looking quite as closely and noticing it, and so I can amplify it, make it more available for them to see, and see in a different way.

There are other times when I'm painting landscape and I'm just borrowing the form of the landscape.

Painting is a conversation: once you make a mark on a white piece of paper, it becomes a dialogue with the composition because that one mark changes the whole thing. Now what is the composition asking, what does it require? So you respond and then that changes it again, so it's a constant dialogue with the composition.

Sometimes when that happens in a landscape painting, it's very surprising. There was one of the Hawai'i paintings where the sky wanted to be very red. I remember thinking, "Skies aren't red! Not that color red." But that was what was required in that composition, so it became red. I'm not a realist. I don't paint to re-create the way something looks. I paint because I'm interested in the process of the conversation with the painting.

P.P. Is it a conversation with the painting or with the subject matter, or both?

S.S. It feels more like a conversation with the painting than with the subject matter.

P.P. So in your creative process the subject matter is a catalyst?

S.S. The subject matter feels like a starting point. It's almost as if the subject matter is the skeleton of the composition, but once that dialogue starts to happen, it moves into very different realms. I think that's why even some of my most straightforward still lifes or flower paintings feel very abstract to me—they move beyond the realm of representational work. I'm not trying to paint a picture of eggplants and peppers. I'm interested in the shapes and colors of the eggplants and peppers, the sculptural qualities of them. I'm interested in those organic forms, in the way light moves around something that's three-dimensional and sculpts it, and how you portray that in two dimensions.

I think that's why the "portraits" I've done aren't recognizable as portraits to most people. If you looked at them you would say, "That's an orchid." And I would say, "No, that's a portrait of Karen." Because to me it so clearly has the feeling in color, in the way it's organized in space: it feels like Karen . . . it has qualities she has.

P.P. You've talked about color, and you've also mentioned form . . . the eggplant, the shape of it, how light falls on it. You've also spoken to me about the way that you see things—that the way you see the world is in the repetition of patterns and forms. Can you talk about that?

S.S. I credit Mrs. Bloch, my art teacher in high school, with this. She taught me how to see the underlying geometries that were all around me. Look at the triangles created in space, for example, by your elbow bending. It's a process of looking out and seeing the space and the things in it, not just as things, but as shapes carving up space in different ways. I see geometry—the most primitive geometric forms, the circle, the triangle in particular—as the building blocks of every other form. The way that they tessellate—the way that they set themselves into structures—creates all the other forms. And because those primary shapes are contained, or are the building blocks of all the other forms, those larger forms echo the primary geometries. Just like the way our cells assemble themselves . . .

P.P. So there's a holographic nature to it? Would you describe it that way?

S.S. I hadn't thought of that word. The way I think of it is the repetitions of forms on different scales.

P.P. How does that sense of repetition of form find its way into your paintings?

S.S. I think it sets up rhythm in compositions. If color is the sound equivalent of mood, the tone of the piece—it might be major, it might be minor, it sets up the emotional quality—then the patterns are rhythm, they're the time signatures in a piece, not that they set up time in a composition per se. Visually this keeps your eye moving around a piece so that you keep taking it in in different ways, it allows your brain to perceive more. If you focus on the center of something and stare at it, you can have a meditative, hypnotic experience, and may absorb things at a very deep level. Another way to absorb at a deep level is to keep moving around a given composition. In this way you discover many inner relationships within the composition.

Sacred Play, Sacred Spaces

P.P. You've used the term sacred play. What is that?

S.S. Well, you and I have talked about sacred time and sacred space as a deep way of inhabiting time and space, a way of slowing oneself down to a point of expanded awareness. I think of the best work that I do in my studio as play because it has that childlike aspect of curiosity and discovery and pleasure and excitement. And it's very quiet and calm and sacred. It has a resonance, a vibrational quality. If you walk into an old cathedral in Europe, you can feel that worship has been going on in that space for hundreds of years—the stones hold it. I feel my studio holds that energy. And when I come in there, if I can calm myself down enough to enter into its vibrational level, if I can take off those outer layers of cultural debris, I can enter into it and it's the most delicious thing! It happens late at night when I'm playing with my Chinese dictionary. I will have read a hexagram or a poem or I'll be thinking of a word, and I'll wonder what "paradox" looks like in Chinese. So I'll look it up in various Chinese dictionaries. In a Chinese dictionary it's not simple. It may be three different root characters making up a complex character containing the idea, and then it may have all these other relationships that make the idea go off in different directions. That's the best kind of play!

P.P. And what makes it feel sacred?

S.S. When I am engaged at that level of attention, which is pretty much undivided, I am also aware of being a speck of dust in an enormous and complex universe. I don't necessarily walk around in that awareness every day at every given moment. The times I can enter into that awareness feel profoundly pleasurable to me. It's as if every cell in my body feels ecstatic. That's what I mean by that experience.

P.P. You referred to being in your garden and drawing. And you've gardened for how long?

S.S. I don't really know. For a long time I was not a gardener and then suddenly I was. When I moved back into the house that I grew up in, the yard and gardens had been neglected for quite a long time.

When I was little, my cousin Amy and I would be in the woods, or under pine trees in her backyard, or under the magnolia tree in our backyard—and we would build little houses for elves and fairies. We'd make little miniature furniture out of walnut hulls and magnolia pods, with moss cushions for them to sit on and pine needle carpets. We knew they wouldn't come while we were there because they were shy. We made it really comfy so that they could have a nice place to be.

One afternoon I was outside my house feeling very tender toward the plant material there, and wondering why this place had become such an abandoned lot. I was in a nostalgic mood, so I had an imaginary conversation with the nature spirits and I made a little pledge to them. I invited them to return, and pledged to them that I would make as hospitable a welcome for them as I could. I pledged that I would do no harm in the yard and that I would try to provide whatever nurturing I could. It was all layers of metaphor of what I was giving to myself psychologically, too. And I just got very interested in the dirt—and the creatures—in what life was there. I found a few plants that had been there, as far as I know, from when my grandparents lived there. There were a few old German irises and some of the original plantings: a spirea, a Bridal Veil bush, some hydrangeas, and a very, very old climbing rose. I started tending them without knowing anything about gardening. I observed how seeds and plants occur in nature without being tended, how it seems they have the desire to grow. And perhaps I could assist that arrangement. I could put something where it might be a little happier if, for instance, it seemed to want more sun. Over the years I absorbed gardening information from all over the place. The more I had my fingers in the dirt, the more the garden taught me about how to tend it. And that's really what it feels like—that I am being instructed by the garden. I am not a book learner about that kind of stuff. I absorb information from people who have knowledge: if it has specific usefulness to me then it sticks.

I started experimenting with composting because it seemed to me that "compost happens," and it turns out that compost doesn't quite just "happen." You can refine the process, and for a while, composting got to be a big theme in my metaphorical universe. I was composting a lot of negative emotions, digesting things, and by disassembling that material into small enough particles, it was made available to nourish something new.

For a while, I was battling a particularly nefarious weed that kept crossing into my yard from under my neighbor's fence. It became clear to me that following the root threads of this particular weed was really the spiritual discipline of the moment. It lasted for several summers. I would run my fingers through the dirt, following this gout weed as far as it stretched. At first I was mentally cursing my neighbor for letting it grow under the fence, but then did I really want to be thinking about my neighbor that way? Just rooting out the tendrils of my own nastiness while I had my fingers in the dirt was very good medicine.

So, lots and lots of different things have happened in the garden. What's been amazing to me over the years, as I've learned more, is the amount of life that has come into the space. Hummingbirds and butterflies and goldfinches and squirrels, of course, and lots of snakes, an occasional toad, spiders, praying mantises, and salamanders . . . all kinds of things! When I first found a praying mantis egg case I was thrilled, and now the juniper bushes are full of them. I often find them when they emerge—they're about a quarter of an inch high and are perfect miniatures of their adult selves. Then I watch them growing over subsequent weeks. There's an endless parade of life. And when I started vegetable gardening and growing fruits, it increased even more. Gardening's a magical activity. It has truly enriched my life.

P.P. It's remarkable that this oasis exists in the city. I'm pondering what that teaches us about possibilities for those of us who live in urban places.

S.S. You know, at one point, I was very unhappy with the neighborhood dogs who were taking advantage of that little strip between the sidewalk and the street. So I started taking extra perennial divisions and planting them out there. Now the whole strip is full of flowers and fragrant mints.

When I first started gardening in the front of my house, because I didn't want to mow grass anymore, there was very little gardening visible on the block. Now more and more people are gardening. There are flowers up and down the block, and more and more creature life has shown up: varieties of birds, butterflies, bees.

P.P. Imagine if all the lawns in the city were converted to organic flower gardens . . .

S.S. Yes, lawns and vacant lots. When I have extra tomato seedlings, I plant them out front. This began to be a way to teach the neighborhood kids who were walking to and from school. Some of these kids have no clue that a tomato grows on a vine that grew from a seed. I let them pick tomatoes, I show them the seeds inside. I give them different kinds of mint leaves to rub between their fingers and smell. I show them you can chew it. There are so many opportunities to make change at almost no expense. The earth is so willing to help.

P.P. . . . and so ready—waiting for the opportunity.

S.S. Yes! Right now I'm gathering oak leaves. I have an oak tree that's taller than the house, grown from an acorn I planted. Oak trees now sprout up all around my house because of squirrel Alzheimer's—they bury acorns everywhere so that when they dig, they'll always find something. I'm gathering the oak leaves for my compost heap, which has really heated up in the last few weeks. I put the finished compost on the vegetable gardens when I put them to bed for the winter. What was once horrible, hard-to-dig soil that didn't hold moisture is now loamy, fertile, dark, rich soil.

P.P. So, speaking of transformations, tell us about the house that you live in.

S.S. Oh, my house was my grandparents' house—they bought it in the 1930s and gave it to my parents when we were young. My mother and her sister grew up there, and I grew up there with two of my siblings. I loved it. It's a very special house. My grandparents made some good changes to it—added more windows so it has a lot of light. I always wanted to live in it and, as an adult, had an opportunity to buy it. The house had fallen into pretty serious disrepair. So, I've been very slowly restoring and renovating, and also making changes that suit me. I've taken out walls and expanded the studio space. I've "re-plumbed" the house and brought a number of systems up to healthy functioning.

P.P. And is the house a metaphor through this transformation?

S.S. It's such a metaphor! You know how houses are in dream-life? This house has always appeared in my dreams, although the structure is slightly different in the dream version. There are consistent alterations in the dream version that don't actually exist in the physical structure. There is an extra floor in between the second and third floor in the dream architecture. Isn't that interesting?

P.P. Interesting . . . the transitional space between living and studio space . . .

S.S. Yes. And certainly there are metaphors about making it my own. I realized that in some ways, as a child, the house felt more like family to me than my actual family. So coming home to the house has also been connected with coming home into my own center. And altering the house to be a place that suits me, that nourishes me, that I feel happy in, has paralleled some of the work that I've done in my own emotional life. You know, mending wounds, repairing things that were damaged, making things sturdy and strong. I've taken a lot of care to do the repairs and restorations in ways that are very sturdy and solid and well built. There is something about making the structure sound that has absolutely been part of my own internal journey.

P.P. You know, Jung talked about the house being a symbol of the psyche, so it's interesting that your psychological and emotional processes have also manifested themselves in very tangible ways.

S.S. And the process continues to unfold. Any number of times people have said to me, " I can't believe that you live in the house that you grew up in." There have been times I've thought it would be good for me to leave. But lately, I've been deeply appreciating my roots here, and that my roots go back generations: roots in the life of the community, the "greening" of the community, the diversity of the community, and the cooperativeness of it. It feels really good to me. It feels like the right place to be, so I guess I'll stay here as long as it feels that way.

P.P. Where you live is also very close to the Wissahickon woods, and you grew up going to the woods a lot as a child. How do you think that formed you or informed you?

S.S. Well, we spent an inordinate amount of time in the woods when I was a kid. We had all kinds of games that we played, and there was a great imaginative life that occurred in the woods. I wonder about kids' lives now because they're not allowed to run free in the way that we did. We were always outside, always observing. We'd collect frogs' eggs. We'd hatch tadpoles. We'd find snakes and toads. We'd collect leaves and insects. It was our laboratory. We were very close to it. We were in the creek all the time. Even the mica in Wissahickon schist is a specific part of my inner life. One of my childhood friends now lives in a place that doesn't have what she calls "sparkling dirt." We're so used to the earth sparkling from the mica schist. We knew those woods inside out—where to hide from each other—where to hide from grown-ups. I think this intimate relationship with the natural world is a really important part of the imagination's life. There's a hillside covered with very tall, old pine trees, and the ground is thick with many layers of fallen pine needles. Lying there is like being on a cushion. We spent hours there lying on our backs looking up at the sky through the trees. And I wonder, do kids still do that? I still am quite capable of being mesmerized by a creek. I can sit at the edge and watch the water for hours, looking at the little eddies, watching how water flows and makes patterns, listening to how the sound of the creek changes at different places, feeling the quality of the air in different places: cooler or warmer, or more humid or more dry. There'll be certain kinds of bugs in one place or certain kinds of toads in another. A snake will slither in and swim away.

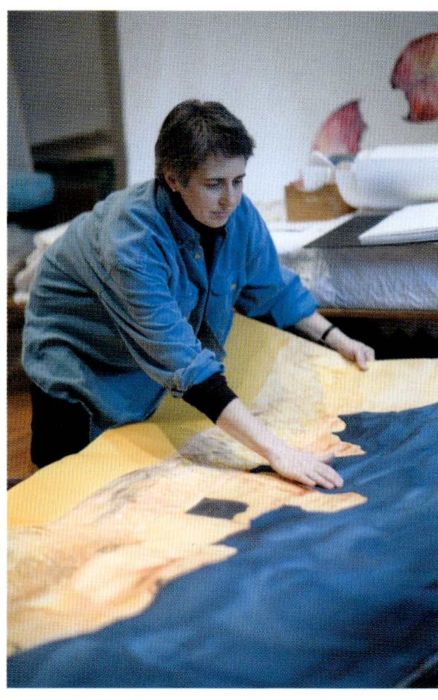

There was a children's geography of the woods, with names like "The Big Pine-ees" and "Devil's Pool," different places where we would meet our friends. "Meet me at the ruins below the canoe club." Or, "I'll be on the other side of the dam, down by the third stepping stone." It was a big space to inhabit as a kid, a very generous space. We would be out in every kind of weather. Did the Wissahickon freeze? Can you ice skate on it or would you fall in? Was Surprise Lake squishy or solid?

P.P. So you really grew up having an intimate relationship with the natural world—which a lot of people don't.

S.S. And with the unnatural world. We used to go down to the woods on Sundays with my Dad and clean debris out of the dam. In those days it was very polluted, and there was a lot of trash in it. The detergents in the water made huge amounts of soap bubble foam, and it smelled horrible. But we played there on Sunday afternoons, cleaning out the creek.

P.P. So you observed both sides, the natural world and the human impact on the natural world. And I'm thinking about how caring for the environment has become such a passion of yours.

S.S. I never made that connection—that it came very directly out of loving being in it. All those places in the woods—the secret trails and the not secret trails. It seems funny to say it this way, but it hurts when they're damaged. It feels like this special place has been wounded or mistreated.

P.P. And it makes me wonder how the alienation from the natural world that's part of our culture not only wounds the earth but also wounds us.

S.S. Absolutely. I think that when we don't have access to those connections—are not aware of them—it harms us and we behave badly.

Cats

P.P. We haven't yet talked about your cats. You've had cats in your life and you currently have two. And I sense that, like the garden and the house and the woods, they are also your teachers. So, what role do your cats play in your life?

S.S. Well, I'll work backward from the current cats. Geneva showed up "fully loaded," unbeknownst to me, and produced three kittens. Two of the kittens have moved on and Gus stayed. Gus is a love bug and a clown. He'll eat anything. He just wants to be where the action is. Everything in his universe is a toy! He's teaching me about being a child. His mother Geneva is a more complex cat, very sweet and gentle. She likes to sit in my lap when I'm meditating. And she's an excellent huntress. She has her own little bird blind in the garden where she'll sit perfectly still until she pounces. So, she now has bells on her neck to protect the bird population.

These two are so different from the two cats I had before. Pud came to me as an itty-bitty kitty, and he was with me for almost twenty years. I was unkind to him earlier in his life in ways that I didn't understand. I didn't realize what I was doing. I got insight into that when I was doing my own therapy, and I had such remorse—I felt so awful that I could have done anything unkind to this really loving, gentle creature. I spent all the rest of the years with him apologizing and appreciating him and being very, very gentle and loving with him. He was extraordinarily gracious with me. He never became afraid of me and was always willing to accept my kindness. He was like a sage, a very wise cat, and as he got elderly and infirm, it was an honor to be able to care for him.

Very gradually over a period of about five years, he lost more and more capacity to be an active creature. By the time he was near the end, he took up residence in a box on my kitchen table (where, of course, he had been forbidden to be all of his life). His universe got very small. I felt I was in a grieving process with him for the last couple years of his life. I knew he was leaving, and he seemed to be doing it in a very slow way so that I had time to adjust to him not being there anymore. When he finally died, and he died in my arms, I spent the day making him a little coffin and burying him, and it felt like a release. I was extremely sad, missing him. And I was very glad that he was no longer suffering. The last couple days of his life, he was clearly suffering, and that made me so sad. I didn't want him to be in pain at all.

I felt so grateful that he spent all that time with me. I actually lived with him longer than any other living being in my life, and I'm so glad that

I got to spend that time with him. I don't mean to get all weepy. He taught me a lot about autonomy. He never tolerated anything that he didn't want to tolerate. He accepted love and affection completely on his own terms. It was impossible to impose anything on him, and I'm still learning from that instruction. And he was always glad to see me when I came home. He was a very loving cat, a sponge for love—he would just soak it up. I would rub his belly as long as I wanted to, and he would just lie there and purr. I learned a lot about the pleasures of simply giving to another creature.

And then there was Natalie, the teenager—the punk rocker! Natalie wandered into my life when she was about five or six months old. She followed me home and camped out on my back porch for two weeks, protesting the whole time. I told her she couldn't live with me. I gave her away twice and she bounced back both times. She was determined to be my cat. Natalie was a very feisty girl. She wanted what she wanted when she wanted it. She cracked me up. She was a total teenager. Last year I went to France, and the day after I left, Natalie left. And knowing Natalie, she's having a good time somewhere else. I imagine her thinking "Well, you went to France . . . and left me home?!" When I got home from France, I put up bulletins all over the neighborhood with her picture: "Have you seen this cat?" I searched and searched, and many people called, but it was never Natalie.

P.P. And that's how Geneva came.

S.S. Yes. Some people were walking in the woods on New Year's Day. They found a tame cat in the woods, and on their way home saw the poster —these things had been posted since September!—and called me right away. They brought her over, and it wasn't Natalie. She jumped into my arms, and I spent a week trying to find her owners, but she adopted me. Yes—the history of cats.

P.P. Well, onto a very different tack. Probably one of the ways that a lot of people know of your work is through the calendars that you've been creating for twenty-five years. How did that get started?

S.S. It was a fluke. Some little entrepreneurial tic that I have. I was doing some freelance graphic design work for a women's non-profit organization that needed name recognition, and I wanted my images to get some exposure. At the time I had this little thing stuck in my craw. I would go to bargain stores and see awful pieces of "art" and home decor and packaging that offended me. I knew it didn't have to be this way! You shouldn't have to be wealthy to afford something beautiful! So I decided to create a poster that would sell for $5, so that anyone could afford to have something pretty to look at. Well, that poster, because of the organization's name, which was Women's Resources, took off. It was the right thing at the right time. So, I created several more. One year at holiday time, I was looking at the Sierra Club calendar and wondered why most calendars around were from your local garage, and the only beautiful ones were the Sierra Club calendar or calendars by dead male artists. So, I made a calendar of my pictures using the model of the Sierra Club calendar. And I've been doing it ever since. I don't have a clue why this has continued to be something that the world responds to. But, it's been a good discipline for me to have to create a certain number of new works every year. And it's been a very nice opportunity for me to put new work out into the world to be seen. It's one of those graceful accidents.

P.P. And how did Chinese writing and Chinese poetry find its way into the calendars?

S.S. Well, in the first calendar, I put the days and months in four languages just because I wanted to. I'd been interested in Chinese thought like the Tao and the I Ching since I'd been a teenager. A friend of mine gave me a Chinese dictionary when I was seventeen or eighteen, and to this day, it's one of my favorite toys. I just love the language. I don't speak it or really even read it. I just love it visually and in terms of meaning making—it's very beautiful and complex. As I got more and more interested in it, I found out about the Chinese traditional calendar and thought, why not make it a Chinese traditional calendar as well as a regular Western calendar? Then I started to study calligraphy a little, and read more Chinese poetry. Now, I have a really wonderful Chinese playmate, and we have a lot of fun working on the poetry every year.

Five Elements

P.P. And how did you get interested in Chinese medicine?

S.S. My first inkling of Chinese medicine was in my early twenties when I attended a holistic health conference in Philadelphia, and Jack Worsley was there. Worsley's the Englishman who, along with Père Larre and Elisabeth Rochat de la Vallée, did the work of bringing Five Elements/ Traditional Chinese Medicine (TCM) to the West in an accessible way. And that's the line of it that I've gotten into. That was my first encounter with it. I was introduced to the I Ching back when I was fourteen or fifteen, and I'd always been reading Taoist stuff. I was always drawn in that direction. The I Ching hit the spot for me—the Wilhelm translation. So I was somewhat grounded in those ideas before I encountered Traditional Chinese Medicine. I don't remember precisely when I met Nancy Post for the first time. I remember we met for dinner, and in conversation she started explaining Systems Energetics as it related to organizations and physical systems and human beings' bodies and TCM. And I felt she had just given me the missing link. Everything that I was trying to make sense of, in terms of organizing the ways that I had been thinking—about health, about healing, how energy flows, nature, color, sound, medicine—diagnosis and prescription . . . all of these ideas that

I had been working with . . . Here was a system that had already put all of them together in a way that made absolutely perfect intuitive sense to me. So I started studying with her, and Père Larre and Elisabeth. And then I studied pulse diagnosis with Janice MacKenzie, who became my acupuncture practitioner. It has continued to be the most elegant organizational structure that I've found yet.

P.P. Do you think it informs your painting? When you look at the work, can you use that as a framework?

S.S. I don't know if I can say that it informs the painting. In some ways it may translate aspects of my paintings to me. Perhaps to other people too. It's a way that I can look at the work and see it in a larger whole.

P.P. So when you are creating the work itself, you're not conscious of the Five Elements, but afterward you can look at the painting through that lens?

S.S. I might look at it and analyze it using that system. The only time I would say that it's intentional is when I'm making a painting with some specific purpose in mind. If I'm making a painting that I intend to give to someone in a prescriptive way, for them to work with energetically, then I might do something intentional, both with color and with shape, as well as with the amount of activity that's in a composition—calm and peaceful composition, or very active. I think of a painting like *Canary in a Coal Mine*, which has incredible, active energy, as different from *Eclipse*, which is a very contemplative piece.

In the paintings, in terms of the Five Elements, I'm investigating subtle aspects that I've taken to calling dynamic balance, the Kô cycle in TCM, which has been translated as the control cycle, the way one element controls another. I tend to think the idea of controlling is a Western overlay. The actual relationship of those two energies may be that they're pushing against one another. It might be that they're counterbalancing one another, or that one is outweighing the other or not permitting the other one to have its say, its way. I'm interested in those seemingly oppositional forces. Perhaps they need each other to define themselves. I'm interested in how those relationships are set up in the paintings. If I look at *The Point I*, I see a tension between Fire and Water—the water is pushing down, the fire is pushing up, but they're also flowing one into another. It's a language that contains an exponential number of metaphors. It takes the symbols and metaphorical language that I feel steeped in and organizes them into a connected cycle of flow, one into the next into the next into the next. It's a really great tool.

Recurring Themes

P.P. Would you talk about the series of works that you've done, and why?

S.S. I do series for different reasons. I'll get intrigued with a given thing, and I grow to know it by looking at it. When I got interested in French irises—the shapes that they have, the different shapes of the petals—I drew them for years, again and again. I would draw different parts close-up: leaves, or petals, or interior views. It was the way I got to intimately know the structure of that particular flower. Sometimes I'll get hooked on a certain color, or I'll need a way to work out a relationship with colors that I'm interested in understanding more deeply, so I'll use them over and over again with tiny variations to see if I can get the particular effect that I'm after. I may have it in my mind in a certain way and I won't quite get it, and I'll do it over and over again until I've got it.

P.P. And once you've got it, then it's on to something else?

S.S. Yes.

P.P. What are some of the series?

S.S. Well, there are series that I think of more as recurring gestures. "The Point" series is a recurring gesture. It's a shape-form gesture. I don't know a better way to describe it. I'm trying to do that in paint. It feels like a gesture that I have done as far back as I can remember. If I put my hands together in a prayer pose but not quite touching, and then I push them up like doing a breast stroke in the air, and then move them up and out, like making a funnel. It's that gesture. I'll be standing, looking down, and then gradually looking up, so that my rib cage opens as I raise my arms. It feels like wings to me. There's the up and out motion of it, and then there's a similar, simultaneous, downward motion of the point that goes down where the two sides are not quite parallel. They're coming together toward a point, but never actually reach the point where the two lines touch and close. That's the descending aspect, sort of the yin and the yang of that same movement. I used to doodle that incessantly in school. It's all over the edges of my school notes. And I've done it purposefully in "The Point" series. There are lots and lots of those—some that are numbered, but others that just got made and are out in the world somewhere. I'm still working with that gesture. I think that, in the way that Scarlet Lake is an essential primary nutrient color for me, this shape is a primary shape gesture for me. It feels like core information, core material. And the longer that I work with it, the more deeply it expands for me.

P.P. Do you have a sense that the shape or the form is trying to convey something to you? Communicate something to you?

S.S. I don't know that I would use that language, but yes. Not that it's trying to: it actually does. At the same time that it's a shape I'm drawing or painting, it's also a form that I'm experiencing. I'm living in it. There is a physical way in which I experience that form. Physical and beyond physical. Energetic. It's a way I feel energy becoming available to me from outside—both from above, coming down—and from below, coming up. It is also a way I feel energy coming from within me going out. It's all those things at once. And I think the reason I make them in paint is because they are so tricky to describe in language. There's something very direct about them. Some paintings, for example *Solar Plexus* or *The Struggle to Remember*, come directly out of bodily experience, energetic experience. They feel very specific. There's a physicality to them and a lot of metaphorical resonance. "The Point" series information doesn't feel as specific or as connected to anything recognizable.

P.P. One of your interests is deep ecology. Can you talk about how you would describe deep ecology, first of all, and then how you became interested in that?

S.S. The way I think about deep ecology probably differs somewhat from what others have written about. I think of it as practicing an awareness of myself as an ecosystem, of my relationships as ecosystems, of my community as an ecosystem, and of the planet as an ecosystem. I work on maintaining an awareness of that and having my movements be in harmony with the healthy balance of all those things. So, it has to do with conscious integrity, constantly learning about the different individual components of the ecosystems. The more I know, the more I can align my movements and my behavior with the systems in which I participate to do so in a harmonious way. For me it starts with "first do no harm," and it radiates out from there.

When I was fourteen, I happened one day upon a copy of *The Meat Cutters Trade Journal* and was flabbergasted to read it! They were very nonchalant about butchering and different machines for slaughtering cows and herding animals into slaughterhouses—all the different aspects of the production of meat. I had some awareness of nonviolence at the time, but I had no idea about what was involved in bringing hamburger to my kitchen in a little Styrofoam package. I stopped eating meat right then and there.

P.P. You were fourteen?

S.S. I was fourteen and I was blown away. I couldn't bear to participate in that. I wasn't willing to participate in that. When I was in my twenties, I met a woman in Montana who had grown up on a farm in Idaho. Where she lived, on the outskirts of Missoula, she raised all kinds of animals. She had rabbits and chickens and guinea hens and goats and horses . . . all kinds of animals and they all had names. And she did eat meat and she slaughtered her own animals. She took complete responsibility for tending to her animals, caring for them, and killing them when it felt appropriate. And she was the first meat-eater I'd ever met where I understood her relationship to eating meat, because she had so much integrity about it. She knew the creatures she was eating. She had raised them. She honored them. She tended to them in a thorough way. It felt wholesome to me. It didn't feel ignorant or without awareness.

I know sometimes I cause harm by being unaware. I'm sure I do it all the time, in more ways than I can probably imagine. So, I'm always trying to refine that awareness of how many resources I am using. Am I balancing my use of resources with my replenishment of them? How can I improve that? How can I be a part of a more sustainable world in terms of global economics? How do the dollars that run through my life take away from the harmony of the planet, including all beings—human beings, other beings—trees? And how much am I helping by the ways in which I choose to spend my resources? It's an ongoing education and awareness process for me.

P.P. I think your example of the meat arriving in a Styrofoam package is really emblematic of our culture's disconnect with our participation in the natural world and the natural order of things. Does your work speak to that disconnect between our society and the way that we order our lives and the rest of life on the planet?

S.S. There are times that I have spoken to that very intentionally and directly. When I was doing the "Endangered Orchids" project, it was specifically to document those endangered species and to illustrate how orchids, because of their very specific relationships to their very tiny eco-niches, act as canaries in a coal mine in their ecosystems. If the pH balance of the soil is changed so that the microorganisms in the soil that allow them to take in nutrients is disturbed in any way—or if their pollinator disappears—they vanish. They're gone, they're the first to go. We used to have cypripedia—Lady Slipper orchids—here in the woods.

P.P. Here, in Philadelphia?

S.S. Yes. Orchids are very site specific. So, documenting them and telling their stories felt like a direct attempt to do some of that work.

P.P. What was it like for you to be painting and bearing witness to these flowers that are endangered?

S.S. It was actually alarming. There was one species I learned about, and I found a really beautiful, healthy specimen of it at Longwood Gardens. It's a stunning plant, a remarkable looking creature. Orchids have complex ways of attracting their pollinators: that's often why they look and smell the way they do. Well, the one I saw at Longwood came from Sumatra—North Borneo. It is one of the few endangered species of orchids ever that, wiped out in the wild at the turn of the century, was propagated from one or two specimens and has been somewhat, possibly successfully, reintroduced into its native habitat. But there are well over

50,000 species of orchids in the world, and some 20,000 haven't even been identified yet. They are disappearing before they are being identified. And orchids provide us with things. Vanilla is an orchid—it comes from the pod of a particular cattleya. Orchids could hold the next great medicine. And that is just one tiny example of something that's going on all over the planet on so many levels. We are losing things—mostly due to interference by human beings—myriad varieties of fruits, vegetables and grains . . . because of monoculture [large-scale] agriculture and genetic manipulation. And in the loss of the variety is a loss of the ability

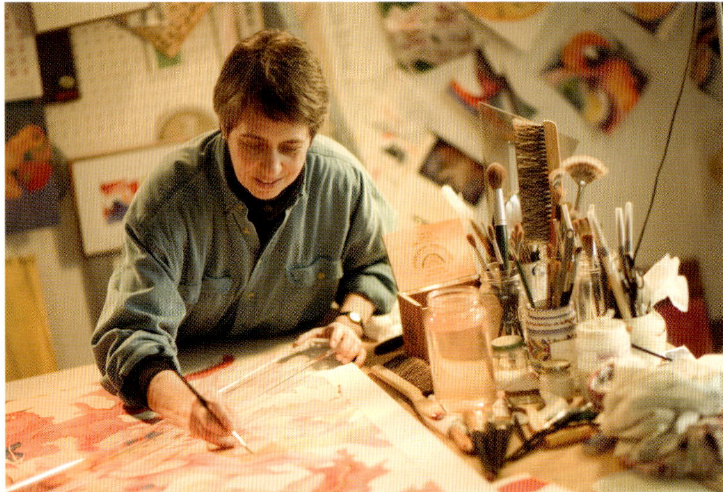

of any particular species to survive, because, built into genetic variation, is the ability to withstand all kinds of changes that occur naturally in any given 10,000-year period. When we engineer plants to make something resistant to a particular pest, or to Round-Up, we're also weakening the variations in that gene pool which permit the wider population of that species to keep on keeping on. So, if we're down to—and, I'm making this up—ten varieties of rice on this planet, and we used to have 300, we've whittled down the ability of rice to support us, the hungry human population. I think it's dangerous. Clearly we already know how bad it is for the land. Monoculture is terrible for the land. Monoculture farming of animals is leading to ammonia and nitrates running off into feeder streams, polluting watersheds and rivers, and ruining the ecology of important estuaries and wetlands. I feel hyper-aware of this interconnectedness almost minute by minute. Sometimes I have to let go because it is too painful to walk around. I would make myself unable to function. I see the devastation—the destruction—all around me all the time. And I feel I don't have enough energy, ability, or talent to make enough noise to save everything that I see needs saving—or to help restore it. That's where I have to work on my own ecology and be part of an ecosystem of human relationships that helps me to maintain my own energy in a healthy way.

P.P. Which brings us back to Chinese medicine and the flow of energy and healthy systems. When you look at Western culture through the lens of Chinese medicine, what do you see in terms of the flow of energy or the blockage of energy, and how that creates societal dysfunction?

S.S. Well, I don't know if I can speak to all Western culture, but I think in this country we started out in a Water place and quickly moved to Wood. We landed here and there was abundance—abundance! We were blown away by the amazing productiveness of this land and the creatures that inhabited it.

P.P. "We" being the Europeans?

S.S. The Europeans. There were cultures here for many years before that, but we Europeans don't seem to know much about that or be very interested. Mostly, Europeans brought a lot of disease that wiped out a lot of native populations and then stomped on the rest of them, usurped lands, you know, the whole sad history of Native American culture and the natural world. There was all of this amazing, resource-rich land. Hardwood trees and fertile land, natural life and plant life—plant medicines, edible plants, streams full of fish—abundance, abundance, abundance! So we prospered and moved across this territory, and I think either came with or got into and got stuck in a "go – go – go, grow – grow – grow!" mentality, a way of thinking about resources as boundless. We were not good stewards of them.

P.P. So, that "disconnect" already was happening?

S.S. I think that we almost came with it. It seems like there were groups—Shakers, Quakers, some of the original settlers—who had some idea of stewardship, and it either didn't last or didn't maintain itself as we fanned out across the county and moved west. Then came the Industrial Revolution, and again, our huge load of natural resources: iron ore, coal, minerals of every kind. We had the capacity and the energy and the ingenuity to make use of that stuff, which we did in a big, big way. I don't think we've been doing a very good job of moving beyond that. The way that I see it, we started with this abundance of resources, of Water energy —and moved very easily into Wood—that ascending yang, the upward movement of building, creating, planning, creating structures—and then didn't move particularly well into Fire. We started to, but somehow we interrupted ourselves.

P.P. And Fire being . . . ?

S.S. Fire being community, communication, love, joy, the harmonic interaction of many diverse parts as a healthy whole. I think we have inclinations toward that and a desire for it, and we don't do very well at it. Now we are moving into a phase—almost a Fire phase culturally—where we have an incredible explosion of ways of communicating, but the content seems to be lacking. At the same time, we still see a consciousness of endless resources, where there no longer are endless resources. Some of us see that they are finite, a disequilibrium in distribution of resources that is getting more and more and more extreme, and in part, I think that has to do with the fact that we haven't allowed ourselves culturally to move the rest of the way around the cosmic wheel.

P.P. The downward cycle . . .

S.S. . . . the downward cycle, the yin . . .

P.P. . . . the letting go and the grieving . . .

S.S. Well, even before that—the downward cycle requires that once you get into that Fire place of communication and joy, celebration, laughter, community, then you move into a place of appreciation of the abundance, of appropriately harvesting and distributing the abundance. Nourishment—that's what Earth is about.

P.P. Does gratitude play any role in that?

S.S. Yes, gratitude. That's how Thanksgiving began, when harvest time was more challenging. It was gratitude for an abundant harvest, gratitude to the land for providing, gratitude to the people who worked the land to make it provide. We've become separated from that.

P.P. It almost seems like a taking for granted rather than gratitude.

S.S. Absolutely. I think part of that comes actually from the disconnect we discussed. When you harvest apples—take them in and cut out the "wormy" spots, put up applesauce, make apple butter, make pies—when you eat those pies and that applesauce several months later, the deliciousness of it extends beyond the flavors on the tongue. It extends to the knowledge of remembering the smells in your kitchen, the smell of ripe fruit on the tree—the beauty of all those red apples on that green tree, the sound of the bees and the birdsong and the wind. It's a very full appreciation. I find this in a small way from vegetable gardening. When we start seeds in March, and those little seedlings get their first set of leaves, it's so exciting to watch all that potential being born. When we plant them in May or June, they look so lonely in that big garden plot. But I know that by July it's going to look like a jungle! And now, here I am, I can't harvest fast enough. There's almost too much sauce to put up. I'm giving tomatoes away. That's the distribution of nourishment, both harvesting and keeping what's appropriate to keep. Keeping what I need and distributing the rest of it so nothing gets wasted, so that it does get appreciated.

That then moves into the "letting go" phase, when the trees die back and the garden goes to sleep and you put things away for the winter rest. There is sadness—grieving the last perfectly ripe tomato I will eat until next summer because I know how good a Brandywine tastes coming right off the vine and choose not to eat tasteless ones from the grocery store. This allows me to participate in the cycle of the seasons in a different way: the loss of those things—and, at a larger level, grieving lots of losses of lots of things. But truly experiencing that grief is what allows me to move into a replenishment of my own inner resources, going all the way down, so that I can re-emerge in the spring, come back and grow again.

In terms of cultural imbalance, when I see substance abuse, process abuse, bad behavior, violence, etc., I would describe it broadly as people not being able to move from notions of progress, competition, growth, expansion (Wood energy) to notions of loving, supportive, nourishing community (Fire and Earth energies). I think there is almost a biological impulse toward Fire and Earth, and when people don't experience them, they become angry and sad, or try to get them any way they can. Unfilled needs do not necessarily engender discernment or good decision-making skills, so people may move toward artificial forms of Fire and Earth, forms of self-medicating, drug abuse, excessive consumption, or overdoing what, on the surface, seems pleasurable or easy to attain. But these things don't satisfy in a deep way. Often that awareness of being deeply unsatisfied is preceded by an addictive cycle.

Perhaps one of the reasons why Twelve-Step programs seem to work better for people with addictions than other methods is that they are encouraged to experience their grief and sadness in the presence of a community of witnesses. They share their woundedness, and can grieve and be held throughout the process by a loving community. They are encouraged to really experience their woundedness in as deep a way as possible, to go all the way down. People in Twelve-Step programs talk about "bottoming out," and how it's not until they really bottom out that they start to truly recover. Their entire process is carefully supported and encouraged.

I feel we have a real resistance to grief in our culture. We give it very short shrift. But deep grieving is the beginning of an appreciation of the true value of what has been lost, and this engenders good stewardship. A loving community encourages people to rebalance themselves, to rebalance their relationships with others and with the world. If we're going to continue living on this planet in a good way—in a sustainable way—I think that process has to occur on a massive scale.

P.P. That's very countercultural—I'm thinking about the individualism of our culture. It does not support the kind of community that you are talking about—that is really needed for that kind of healing and transformation. You know the mentality of "pull yourself up by your own bootstraps."

S.S. Right, tough guy stuff—John Wayne!

P.P. Right, isolation, an attitude that everyone is expected to fend for themselves. There is no place to go with that grief—no place for it to be held or heard.

S.S. And now we've extended that into another dimension. We've taken this notion of "terror" as an opportunity to frighten ourselves into even more self-sufficiency, as if that ever worked to begin with. Not that a certain amount of being able to tend to oneself and to one's own needs isn't important, but we also need to remember that we're all part of a connected web. If I choose to hoard in preparation for the next terror attack, what good will it do me after the first couple of weeks of holing up in my basement? What good will it do me when I come out to the street? How will it help me to relate to my neighbors and the rest of the world? I think we made a really tragic mistake in this country after 9/11, which was to perceive it as a threat, as a "shot over the bow" of our boat, rather than hear it as an incredibly distressing and really horrifying call of dismay from worlds that we don't listen to and don't really comprehend. Our response has been almost exactly the opposite of what I think would have been useful and productive. I heard George Ellis ask, "What if leaders in the West, after 9/11, put out a global call through the media saying, 'We're so full of sorrow. We don't understand why you have done this to us. We want to understand your grievances with us. Is there a safe place where we can sit down and listen to you—truly listen?' " All around me I hear lots of rhetoric, and I feel like asking everybody, "Do you know what the words you are saying mean? Is that what you truly feel deep in your heart?"

P.P. In Chinese medicine—in this cycle that you talk about—where does fear enter in?

S.S. Fear—and courage—are associated with Water—with resources. As I understand it, fear occurs when one is lacking sufficient resources.

P.P. It seems—in this post 9/11 time—people have spoken of two paths: one, the path of fear—of living in fear and playing on the fear and reacting out of fear. And the other one is more what you are describing in terms of reaching out and attempting to understand, of finding paths to peace and to listening—the path to love, you might say. So there's the fear response and the love response. When you look at the fear that seems to be an undercurrent in our culture right now, how do you see that related to resources?

S.S. Well—very directly in several ways. One way, and this might be less apparent but more germane, is if we are perceived by the rest of the world as having so many more resources and using so many more resources than the rest of the world, then I can see anger being directed at us for our thoughtless use of resources—for our lack of good stewardship. In Chinese medicine the preceding season—the preceding element—is considered the parent of the following one. If you follow the cycle backward, what precedes Water, or a state of fear, is Metal. And Metal is that ability to grieve deeply as well as the ability to value appropriately and receive inspiration. I see those things as intricately—intricately linked together. My own experience is that when I can't find inspiration, it is often because it's blocked by incomplete grieving. And when I can move myself into a place of truly grieving my losses, it seems that once I do that sufficiently, inspiration just follows naturally like the tide: the tide of grieving going out and the tide of inspiration coming back in. Once inspiration starts to fill me, I feel my own inner resources filling, and I am more able to have courage—not to feel full of fear or anxiety. I can feel more solid in my balance internally and be rooted in my own center—so that I don't get buffeted about and reactive when external things are coming at me. But grieving takes time. It cannot be artificially terminated, just as inspiration can't be artificially induced.

P.P. Is Water also associated with vision—with inspiration-vision—or is that something different?

S.S. I would say mission more than vision. I think of it in the amorphous sense of drive. Inspiration might be an "Ah-hah!" sort of experience, of being awestruck by something from without. I've heard the word "ambition" used in relation to Water, and it doesn't feel completely accurate to me. It's like a force from behind—at one's back—propelling you forward.

P.P. Purposefulness?

S.S. Purpose—yes! Mission. That, then, moves into a more specific vision. Once the feeling of an urge to go forward occurs, then vision can occur. Vision sees a wide horizon of possibilities, then makes decisions and crafts the best path forward.

P.P. Well, as I think about that in terms of 9/11—what I experienced was that one of the opportunities that was lost—and I think you might have already said this, was the opportunity to grieve. I think we had an opportunity for collective national grieving—deep grieving. We had an opportunity to set aside a week of mourning. Or to designate this as a time for us to grieve this horrendous display of what humans are capable of—the loss of life, and the anger that lies behind the attack—and to grieve all of that. And we didn't. We jumped to the way we've always reacted to threats and, because of that, we lost the opportunity to look at a broader horizon of possibilities. Out of that grief—to receive some sort of inspiration for how things might be done differently—how we might, as a human family, interact in new ways. It seems like this door of opportunity was open . . .

S.S.: It felt like that.

P.P. . . . and we didn't go through it . . . we didn't step through it. It was a time for us to descend—to experience the yin, to reflect, to go inward, to go deeply into the darkness. And we didn't, so we just stay on the other side of the cycle, which doesn't generate new cultural possibilities.

S.S. In the same way, we turn away from death in our culture. We don't like to look at it—it's too distasteful—too messy. Little inroads have been made in hospice over the last ten years and have been a really positive movement. But, when 9/11 happened—just watching those images—for those of us who saw them—like when Kennedy was shot—they forever are in us. If that isn't awesome, I don't know what is. Think about the horrible things in myths. Joseph Campbell talked about needing new myths to move us forward into the next cycle of cultural life in this world—seen through a certain lens, 9/11 could be part of a new myth. And what happened in Chechnya, when children and adults were taken hostage in a school and many killed, seems to be cropping up a lot right now. It reminds me of the ogre in fairy tales—the distressing energy. We're seeing it all over the place. And, as in fairy tales, there's first the foolish brother who doesn't make the right response, and so suffers the same fate as the ones who came before. And then the slightly wiser sibling, who figures out a little bit but doesn't go quite far enough. We're still waiting for the third one—the third way—which is taking that opportunity to either love the beast—befriend the beast—or to go into the dark scary place, examine our shadow side, our negative projections . . .

P.P. . . . and to let go of the things that we've held to so firmly for so long that they are no longer working.

S.S. They're not working. They haven't been working for a long time. Imagine what might have happened. It would have been physically dangerous for people to descend into the area of destruction in New York after 9/11. But what if more people had simply filed past for months—made pilgrimages to Ground Zero and silently filed past?

P.P. . . . while it was still smoldering . . .

S.S. Yes—to take it in—to experience that scale of destruction, the awe that flows from a witnessing experience like that. When I listened to people who were in New York, even for several months after that, I heard the kind of grieving, the kind of descent that seemed accurate to me, that seemed appropriate to me. And what I heard coming out of that felt very hopeful.

P.P. Yes—and this idea of people making pilgrimages there. I went to Ground Zero to accompany a friend whose father had been killed—and it was still smoldering and was off limits to the public. When I entered that space and saw the devastation, I was overcome with grief. And although it was grief for these particular lives, it was truly a much larger grief.

S.S. . . . for all of us . . .

P.P. For all of us. For all of us. For the ways that human beings have been living—or not living together. I know that other people who visited that sight reacted with intense anger. So, observing these different sorts of responses to witnessing, where does anger fall within the cycle, how would you translate that in terms of Chinese medicine?

S.S. Well, anger is associated with Wood—Wood follows Water. I see the angry response, in a situation like that, as a child of fear. In my imagination—because I don't know what the actual experience is for someone else: "This could happen to me. How dare you do that!"

P.P. So it's an attempt to perhaps not go into the fear—but to react in a way that feels more powerful or maybe not vulnerable.

S.S. You see it in the displays animals put on when they're in danger or threatened. I see my cat do this. When a big dog comes down the street, the cat magnifies itself, pushes all its hair out, and becomes three times its size, which says, "I'm fierce! Don't mess with me!" I think there is something natural about that response, autonomic. But humans have the ability to think about how we respond, and we can choose a different response. And I think the crux of deep change is that choice. Deep ecology is making and remaking those choices—over and over and over again.

P.P. So, I'm going to bring us back to your painting. How has art been a healing influence in your life?

S.S. In so many ways. It's healing for me to go to a museum and look at paintings, or to sit down with an art book. It feels like my eyes have been washed clean. Even more, making things that feel beautiful to me feels healing. The process itself is very slow most of the time. It allows me to put myself back in better order. It calms whatever frenzy or distraction I'm concerned about. It moves me away from anxiety toward a more contemplative, calm awareness that helps me stay rooted. It helps me attend to what I choose to focus on rather than the myriad things offered to me continually from without. There are also very specific ways that I've used work as a healing practice.

Making paintings is, for me, a very intuitive process in which my insight occurs faster and in many more aspects than in language processes like talking. In other words, it's not a linear, phonetic addition, like the structure of an English sentence. Rather—you used the word holographic before—it's a holographic way of experiencing a penetrating understanding. My awareness may be concentrated within my body, experiencing a particular sensation, and I put onto paper the way it feels to me and then feel it changing through the process, and I come to understand something deep. It could be a deep wound that's locked in my musculature, or a very old emotion that's been troubling to me that I haven't been able to disperse. The process has been very useful for me.

P.P. And you feel that something in you shifts when you do that, when you enter into that process?

S.S. It's a way that I've used for a long time to understand things that are elusive for me. Sometimes through making a painting, I'll discover patterns within the composition that allow me to understand on a metaphorical level a pattern, say, a dynamic of behavior in my family system. Or, making a piece like *Canary in a Coal Mine*, which was an actual nightmare that I had . . . by making the painting I understood the dream and the metaphors within the dream on many levels, and then looking at the painting over time it continued to unfold and explain more to me. It's dialogue: one dialogue is of making, and one is of looking.

P.P. There is one series that I think really speaks to letting go, of the descent of the yin into Metal, and grieving until grief has expressed itself and can move then into Water. That series is "Nuclear Family Holocaust." Can you talk about that body of work and what it meant to create it, and how it helped you in terms of healing?

S.S. Before doing work in therapy on some of the really deep, almost ancient wounds in myself and my family system—wounds from emotional violence and sexual violence, generations and generations of sorrow and pain that had never been adequately addressed or grieved—these wounds manifested, in my particular system of self, in a very distressed, depressed teenager, who tried to commit suicide multiple times. When I finally began working on that material, when I felt strong enough to do that work, I was lucky enough to have a therapist who understood that a lot of my deepest processes are intuitive, non-verbal, and visual, who suggested that I do a lot of that work on paper in my studio. We were also working in a therapeutic setting, but I was doing much of the work in my studio—sometimes taking it in to sessions—but not always. At times, just making the work was enough for me to integrate the information I needed to understand.

Then I started "mining" my own work. I started going back through old notebooks, and through drawers of old drawings and paintings. I unearthed things, and they began to make sense to me as a coherent body of work, rather than just as individual pieces—both the older pieces and new work I was making. I also, at that time, started to integrate into the new pieces something I had been doing all along privately in my journals and notebooks, which was a lot of language play. I started to let the process come into the work itself, as though the integration that was occurring in my psyche was also occurring in my art making. It was a very strenuous period—very, very sorrowful—difficult some days even to get up in the morning. And it went on for several years. I was also doing body work at the time—and some of the memories I had were deep in my musculature—in my physical structure. When I attempted to make paintings to express those sensations, it was extremely difficult to stay in my art making and my physical experience simultaneously. The process was very thorough. It was so consuming I could hardly do anything else. And when it started to resolve itself, it was quite amazing to me.

A very synchronous thing happened toward the end of that work. Women Against Abuse asked me to do a benefit exhibit for them, and I knew what they wanted was to show the paintings from the calendars. The work I was making at that time was very, very different from that, so I asked them if they would let me show this body of work instead. They were supportive beyond my wildest dreams. They embraced the idea. They embraced the work itself. They were encouraging and supportive and really held me through that process. We ended up exhibiting those pieces at the opening of the new Philadelphia Electric Company headquarters. PECO was also very supportive. PECO had two employees who had been murdered by abusive partners, and so had made a commitment, as a company, to educate their entire 10,000-member workforce about issues of domestic violence, which I thought was a startlingly wonderful response. The process of pulling that work together to display it publicly was very challenging for me, including the fact that a lot of publicity came with it. It was also a great opportunity to shift out of my own personal experiences and discover their resonance in a larger universe, to discover that the work seemed to have usefulness beyond my own process and seemed to resonate with many people.

I started to be much more public with the work, to exhibit it, and speak about it—and that led me to working with battered women. A revolution was occurring in my own psyche and the work came to a natural end point. Any time I've been in a deep grieving process, it feels as if it will never end. My fear is that it will never end, and yet there is nothing else to do but grieve, so I surrender to it. I'm always stunned to find out that it does end. It always is so surprising. It feels almost miraculous. One day I wake up and feel different and my gaze turns to other things. With "Nuclear Family Holocaust," that came, in part, from the gift of feeling useful to other people. That made a huge difference—not just sharing my experiences with other people, but sharing the process of mending my own heart. It was very helpful. And, as that restorative process occurred, the paintings started to change and become spontaneously joyous. They moved into a different realm, and I felt a chapter close. It sounds almost trite to say that I felt "reborn," and that wouldn't be accurate either, but I certainly felt renewed and much, much more free. That process taught me a tremendous amount about the value of grief. Grief would have been a hard sell to me before that—and I don't think

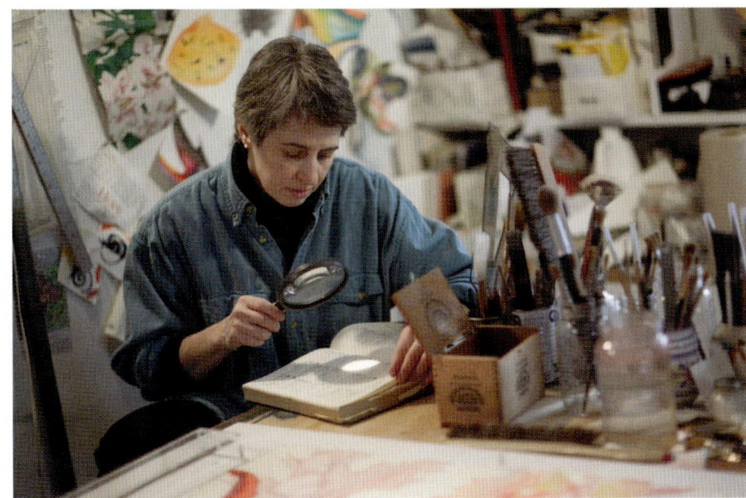

anybody could have told me that it was the cure for what was ailing me.

P.P. . . . and the doorway to transformation . . .

S.S. . . . and I understand culturally that it's a really hard sell.

P.P. Well, we've talked about your personal experience of art as being a healing influence for you or a modality for healing. I'd be interested to hear your reflections on whether you think art could also facilitate cultural healing.

S.S. How could it not? I have a fantasy that, at some point in time, people will no longer need to work as much as they do now, and so many, many more people will express themselves creatively. Used as a way to compost negative emotions, creative expression can not only heal the person doing it, but can provide opportunities for dialogue with people who experience the work. Then those emotions don't have to go out and generate harm. If people were free to be expressive of themselves creatively—whether through dance, or theater, or puppetry, or sculpture, or ceramics, or music, or painting—there could be a museum or house of culture on every corner of every street. It would be such a wonderful thing! What if you had a house of culture on every street corner, available for people to share their expressions and their performances? It seems like it could be done so easily, especially in a city, where you see abandoned properties on so many blocks. Turn the trashed-up vacant corner lot into a garden. Dream on.

P.P. So, what is it like to be a woman artist in the U.S. at this time?

S.S. I may not be the best person to answer that question. I don't feel I'm a part of the "legit" art world. Still, it seems to me when I go to galleries and exhibitions and museums, I see far fewer examples of the works of women than I do of men. And when I read art magazines and go to the library looking for art books, there is just not as much information as I would like about women artists. I know we're here making art. And I know in my own limited interactions with other women artists, we seem to share similar experiences and concerns, many of which have to do with feeling that we're not good enough, or that our work isn't good enough. I never encounter that from the male artists that I know. And that seems to me to be very much societally and culturally introjected, and very, very hard to exorcize. It's really an impediment, Virginia Woolf's "Angel in the House."

P.P. Do you see any signs of hope on the horizon?

S.S. I don't know. I really don't know. Maybe in this little time period right now I'm not feeling particularly hopeful. On the other hand, I see women doing tremendous amounts of creative work all over the world. Look at Wangari Maathai winning the Nobel Peace Prize! There are powerfully creative women, with unique voices, and messages that are worth hearing and seeing.

P.P.: Maybe even critical and essential, especially in this time.

S.S. Yes, definitely. You know, that kind of change is slow. Think about when women's studies started happening in the university world. I'm sure women have always been writing literature, but their work has been a relatively recent addition to the canon. I think in so many fields we could benefit from more women—from the full range of their voices and experience. I think we both edit and censor ourselves, and have it done for us. I know I certainly have introjected plenty of those messages. It's hard to pull those threads out of my fiber, to remain aware of them. They feel like handicaps at times.

Blueprints for Paradise

P.P. When I walk into a room that's filled with your paintings, there is an energetic quality that I experience. It's as if the paintings set up a palpable resonance in the space. It goes right into me at a cellular level. There's something about your use of color and form and the joy that you're talking about that comes through the work. Oftentimes I experience your work as healing—I'm aware of more than just your individual process of making art as a healing or transforming experience. There's something about witnessing it—that something comes through at an energetic level. Is that something that you are conscious of in your work? Do you know what I'm talking about, first of all?

S.S. Yes—absolutely. It is absolutely my intention to create images that generate a response in people, and hopefully a positive response. It is a healing energy—that's the intention behind the work. There are times when that's a very specific intention, for example, if I'm making a piece that is to be looked at by someone for a particular reason—for a particular specific ailment, or soul ailment. That's what I love so much about certain music, or the works of Rothko. When I encounter it, it can fill me with energy—with joy—sometimes with awe—sometimes with grief. But it fills me with feeling. I don't think it's bad for us to feel what we feel: that's where a lot of the good information is. So, yes, I hope that I make work that connects with people in an energetic way and at the level of their feelings. I know that I make some work that people resist. It's been interesting to observe—there are certain pieces that some people turn away from. Sometimes it's hard to look at things that are frightening or that make you feel things you might generally avoid. But in my own life, every time I've encountered my own resistance and have consciously made the choice to turn toward it instead of away from it, I've almost always benefited from the experience.

P.P. When you look to where you are headed with your work in the future, do you have any sense of what you want to explore?

S.S. I'm full of ideas I want to explore right now. I want to integrate language even more into my images. One of these days I'm going to be brave enough to explore sculpture, which, I think for about ten years, has been winking at me. It seems daunting. Not just learning a whole new vocabulary—but all the technical things and the tools and massive boulders of stone. One of these days I'd like to learn how to weld. There are just so many things to do! I want to be more playful in my work. I want to do more collaborative work. I have a lot of fun collaborating, especially with people in other media. I get really jazzed—it sends me off in directions that I wouldn't think of myself. In my mind I create in other media. I just don't have the real skills to do it. I choreograph in my head and I write music in my sleep. But it may take my whole life just to be a good enough painter. Really—I've hardly started as a painter.

P.P. In the realm of painting, what things do you still want to explore?

S.S. I've felt drawn to portraiture recently, and I really have no clue what to do about that. And big pieces. I really love working large and I want to work even larger.

P.P. When you say "large," what do you mean?

S.S. Well, you know—a whole room! The size of a wall panoramically around a room.

P.P. And what challenges and surprises do you find when you are working on pieces that large?

S.S. Oh, it's incredibly difficult to work large in watercolor, because you have problems with saturation and evaporation. How do you keep an area eight feet away wet enough, so that when you pull your paint across it absorbs it in the way you intend? Scale has problems I had no comprehension of until I started working large. I couldn't find brushes big enough to hold enough pigment yet allow me to paint in a controlled way. There was a period where I found myself carefully studying huge paintings—like Monet's *Water Lilies* at the Met—just to try to understand how you could be that close making it, and then step away and have it look the way you want it to. "How did you do that? How did you know when you stepped away that it was going to look that good?!" And with watercolor it's even harder. With an oil painting you can actually step back—

P.P. . . . because the work is on an easel.

S.S. Yes. With watercolor you have to wait till it's dry before you can do that! I just love what watercolor does, especially on a large scale. Working on *Moon Over Montana*, the paint just did the most incredible things.

P.P. Things that wouldn't have occurred to you—the paint did it?

S.S. Yes – the paint did it for me. That also happened when I was working on *Point Lobos*. I was painting in the Sanctuary Studio when Janice Williams and I had our program at Friends' Hospital. There was a patient in the room who was working on her own painting on the floor beside me. She had tremendous energy and focus on her painting, and I felt her energy leap into me and then leap into my painting—this is what it physically felt like. And suddenly I was doing things in that painting that I had never done or imagined myself doing. I was so grateful to her for that. It was as if she gave me a new technique.

P.P.: And is that the "parallel play" that you talk about? That creating in the same space with someone else does something?

S.S.: Yes, it's incredible. We were both completely focused on our own work, and I was aware of her in my periphery, but I was not paying attention to her. I really felt her excitement about her painting infected me. And it absolutely improved my piece. I love that!

P.P.: So, there's that interplay . . . it's collaboration that just happens.

S.S. It's collaboration, but it's not collaboration . . .

P.P. It's not conscious collaboration.

S.S. Right—it's not like a conversation. It's more like a dance.

P.P. An energetic dance. A dance of two people's creativity expressing itself in its own way.

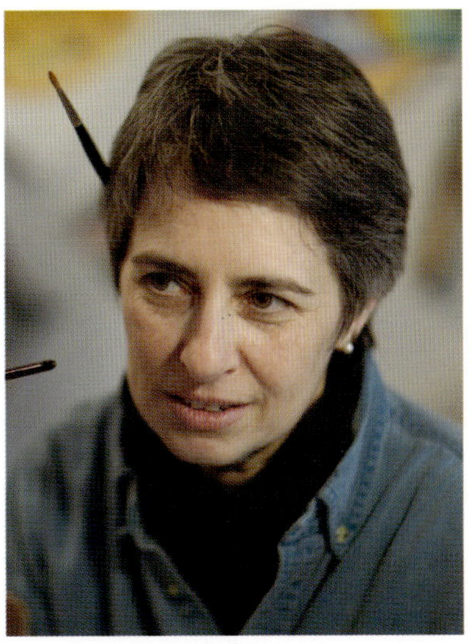

S.S. It can be more than two people. I find that exhilarating. I love it. I think that's almost like paradise for an introvert. You know, I get to be in my own sacred space and have company, but I'm not required to engage with them.

P.P. So, speaking of paradise . . . the title of your museum exhibit is "Blueprints for Paradise." Can you talk about that title, how it came to you, what it says to you?

S.S. It came out of a journaling session, and it struck me as being full of hubris! Or naivete. I look out at the natural world and am amazed all the time. I'm amazed at the little miniature feathers within a feather. Or the little tiny powdery scales on a butterfly's wing, the iridescence of it, and how that creature flies 3,000 miles to Mexico on a set of very fragile wings that crumble when you touch them. Those things astonish me. And they're all over this whole planet. When I look at these things, I sense, embedded in them, the instructions for how human beings can live on this planet and have it be paradise. I think the various myths about paradise were instructions to us, that paradise is an actual possibility, although we're very far from it right now. And I feel one of the ways that people can be encouraged to move toward living on this planet as paradise is to fall in love with it, fall in love with the myriad amazing aspects of it in evidence everywhere. That's what I'm attending to when I'm making my work.

January 2005

Wholly One

When a country is in harmony with the Tao,
the factories make trucks and tractors.
When a country goes counter to the Tao,
warheads are stockpiled outside the cities.

There is no greater illusion than fear,
no greater wrong than preparing to defend yourself,
no greater misfortune than having an enemy.

Whoever can see through all fear
will always be safe.

Tao te Ching
translation by Stephen Mitchell

One need not be a student of the Tao or of Chinese medicine to know that the world we live in is out of balance. We find ourselves inhabiting a planet that is experiencing the dramatic impact of human "progress." The destruction of ecosystems, the prevalence of warfare, and the extent of human suffering are symptoms of a fundamental failure in humankind's relationship to the rhythms and cycles of life. Even as these imbalances grow to unprecedented extremes, there is also an awakening within humanity's consciousness, a growing sense that we are at a historic turning point—a time that demands urgent transformation. Above all else, such a transformation requires profound changes in the way we see the world.

In the midst of our global crisis, the new emerging worldview recognizes that the fundamental reality of the cosmos is relational, that nothing exists in isolation, and that all life is interdependent and sacred. It is an understanding that nothing—no individual or race or nation or species—exists outside the web of life that sustains us all. It is this worldview of sacred oneness which offers us the way into our future.

Fortunately for us, sacred oneness is not a construct we have to invent, but a reality we need only recognize and step into. The blueprints are already at hand, embedded in the natural world itself, which thrives in harmonious and interdependent balance within the cycles of life, death, and regeneration.

It is toward this understanding of sacred oneness that Sara Steele's work points. Her intuitive knowledge of the interconnectedness of all life and her insights into the energetic cycle of creation—insights which also find articulation within the teachings of Chinese medicine—give us a lens through which to view the world. Her work invites us into a sense of wonder at the spiritual essence that inhabits all matter and all life, and it reawakens us to something that as children we knew intuitively but have forgotten: that reality itself is magical. Her paintings open our eyes to the mystical essence of a desert mesa or the fragile beauty of an endangered orchid; they invite us to marvel at these "ordinary" expressions of nature and, in that marveling, to be changed. She invites us, as she says, to fall in love with the Earth and all these myriad expressions of the creativity of nature and to see ourselves as part of this vast enterprise of life. Through her paintings, Sara calls us back to a relationship of awe and wonder at the wisdom and the beauty of the natural world, back to the portal of reverence through which human consciousness is reintegrated with the consciousness of the Earth.

The beauty of Sara's work pierces the soul; it is profoundly healing, and to experience it fully one must open oneself to its energetic presence and potency. One must do more than see her paintings. One must look into them, meditate on them, breathe them in, and allow them to penetrate one's imagination and spirit. Like a skilled acupuncturist, but one whose needles are color and form, Sara, through the beauty of her art, sparks the imagination of the viewer and awakens in us a deep awareness of the reality of new possibility. Her work invites us to discover the dimension of energy and consciousness that exists beneath the surface of things—the realm of love—that gives rise to and permeates the material world. Through her insights into the regenerative cycles of nature and her artistic talent, the process of dying and death also becomes beautiful. She wisely and skillfully depicts the release of life as a numinous, sacred transition, an occasion to be revered and blessed rather than feared.

The crumbling paradigm of domination and its narrative of fear suggest that we are headed inexorably toward an apocalypse. Sara's work draws our eyes to another possibility, an alternative future that is ours to choose. She invites us to envision the human species living in balance with the web of life and yielding to the natural cycles that are at its core. She points toward that web of life and the regenerative energy that pulsates within it. She reassures us that what we need for our survival is already at hand if we will only open our eyes to see.

The experience of sacred oneness is the experience that mystics have spoken of for millennia. It is the experience of seeing the timelessness, the complexity, the beauty, and the vastness of all that is and knowing that all is wholly one. It is a reality that is reached through the gateways of blessing and compassion, beauty and joy, kindness and gratitude—and sometimes through grief. In the awareness of sacred oneness, the mystic apprehends that paradise is indeed at our doorstep and that the isolation, fear, and despair that so influence human actions and choices are only illusions. We are fortunate that Sara Steele is such a mystic, and that through her art we may share her vision.

Patricia Pearce

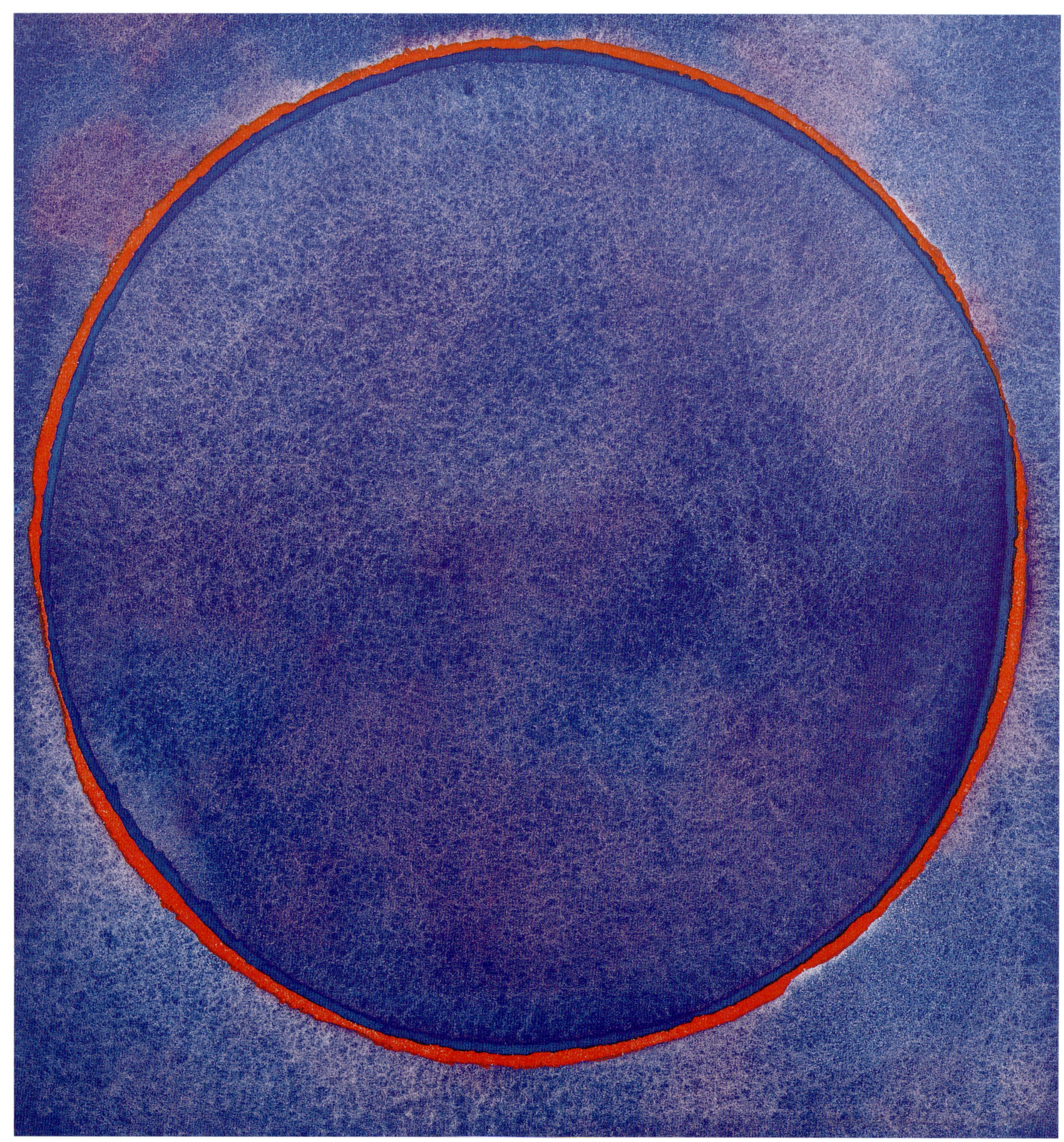

Eclipse/Plane Dream, 1981

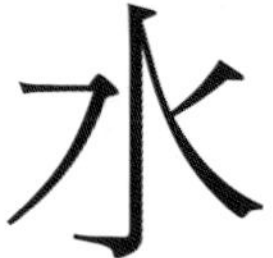

Water

We begin the cycle where the creative process itself begins: in the realm of fluidity, of gestation, of that which is silently stirring but still without form. Water is the amorphous primordial element that precedes defined structure, the abundant source of all possibilities, and the boundless resource out of which life emerges. In the season of winter all that will burst forth into the new growth of spring still lies unseen and waiting beneath the surface, beneath the level of consciousness.

In this collection of paintings the generative element of Water is reflected in images with a primordial and fluidic quality. The profoundly simple elegance of *Eclipse* unites Water with its dynamic opposite, Fire, etching a circle containing infinite potentiality. Here also are *The Point II* and *The Point IV*, images suggesting the in-breaking of something newly conceived, the mysterious flow of energy into matter and back again. *La Frontera* conveys the permeability of the boundary between the dream state and the waking state, while *Leaf Skeleton* depicts the fluidity of the transition between life, death, and rebirth. *Bioluminescence* captures the stunning beauty of marine life that dwells hidden beneath the water's surface. Here too are images of oceanic bodies of water, and representations of plant life and flowers evolving from concept into form. In *Forces of Attraction* we see the power of atomic and erotic energy that precedes the emergence of life and matter, forces holding the boundless possibilities that exist within the quantum void. Finally, in the "Hawaii" series, Sara reimagines the pre-Colonial beauty of the Hawaiian islands, a pristine paradise rising up out of the ocean's depths.

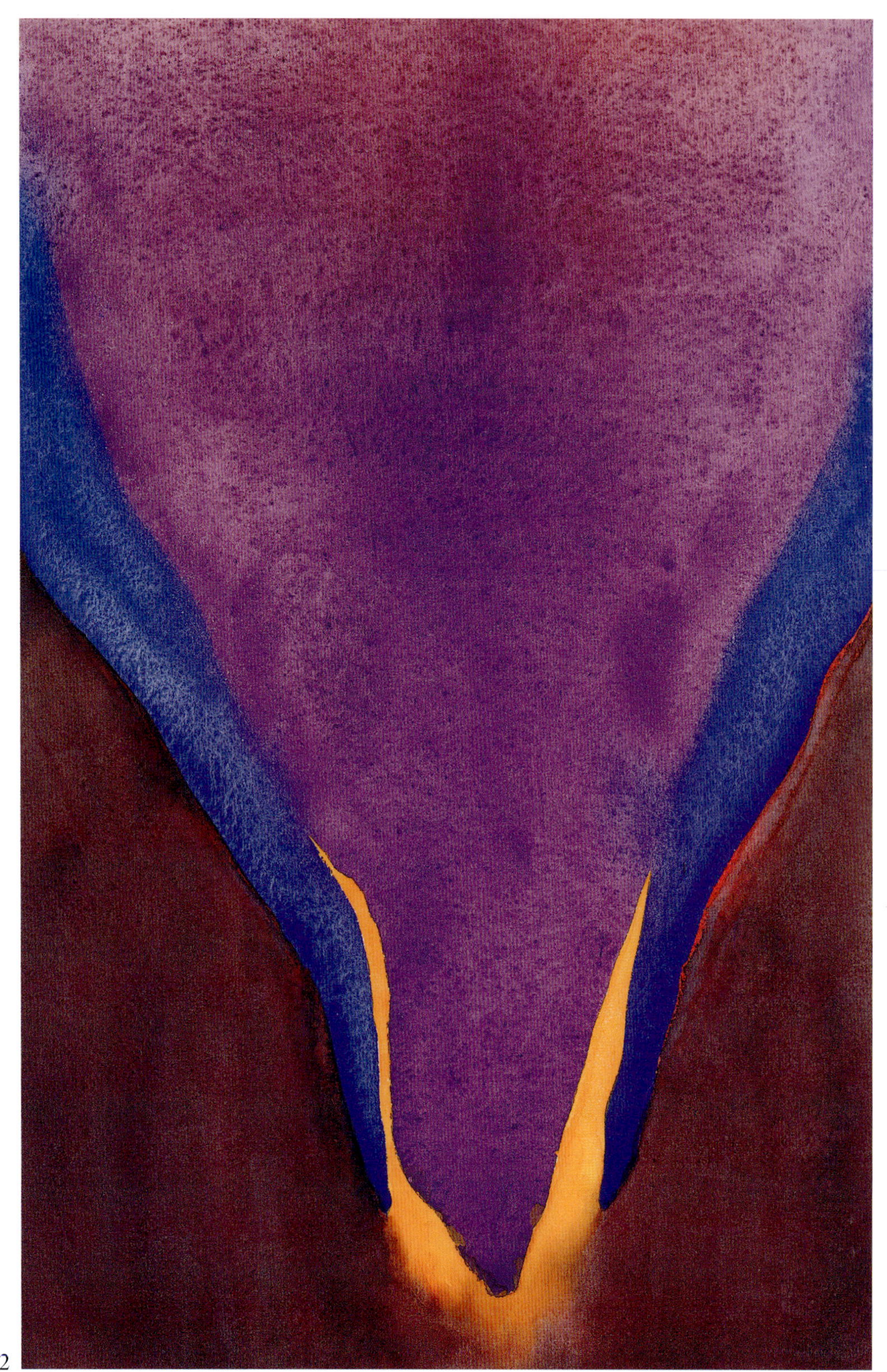

The Point II, 1992

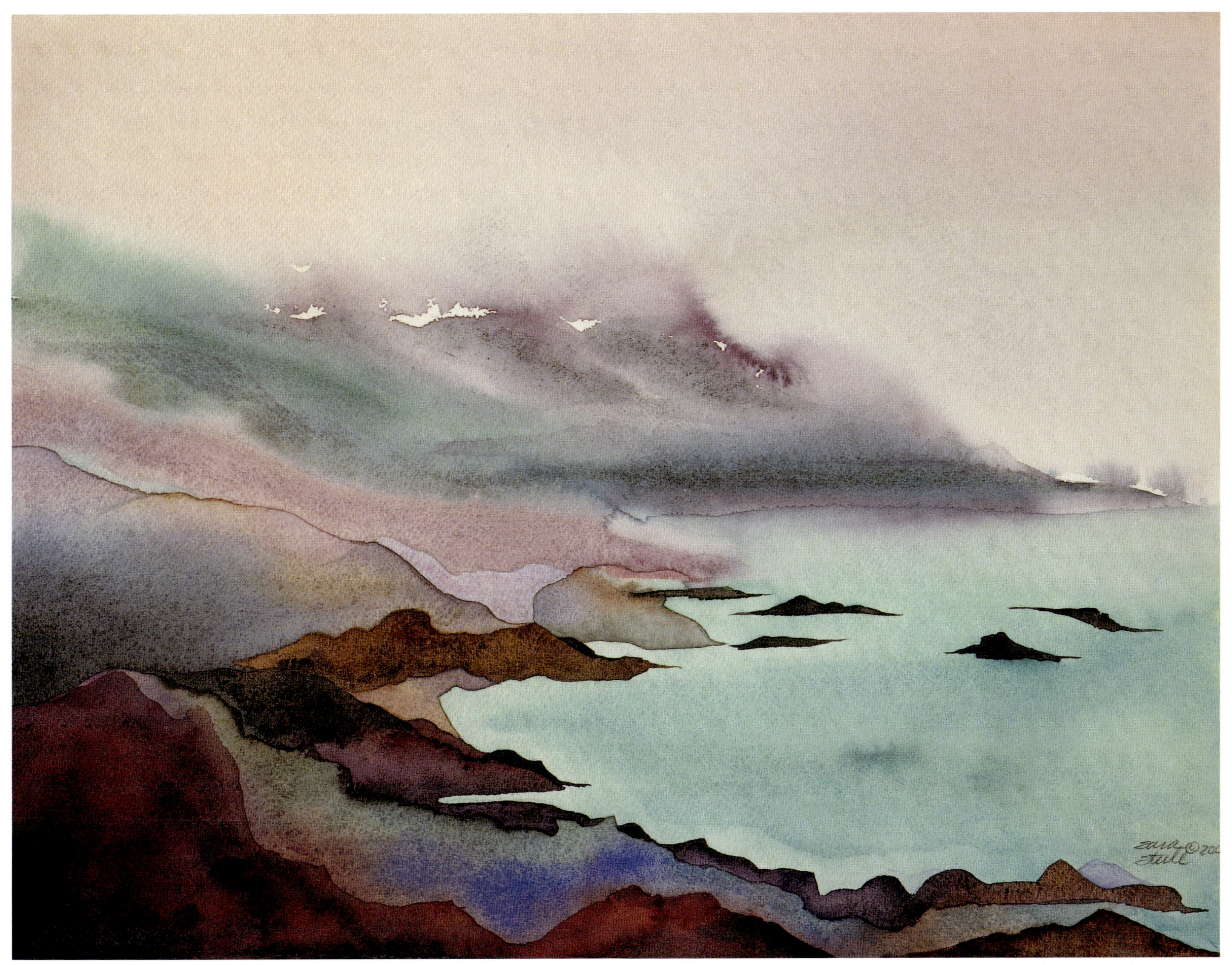

Mist Rising Near Big Sur, 2000

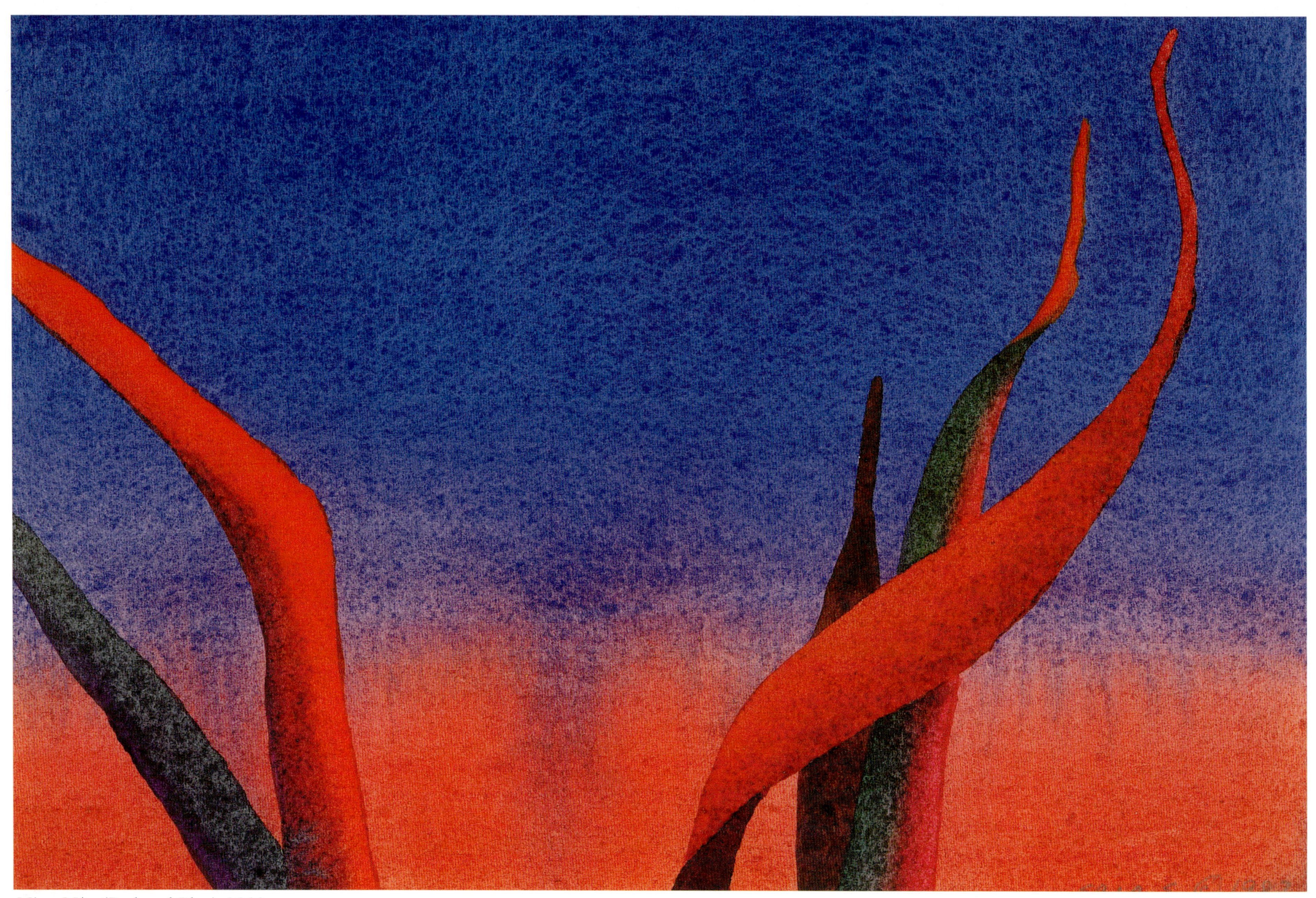

Ming Mên (Red and Blue), 1982

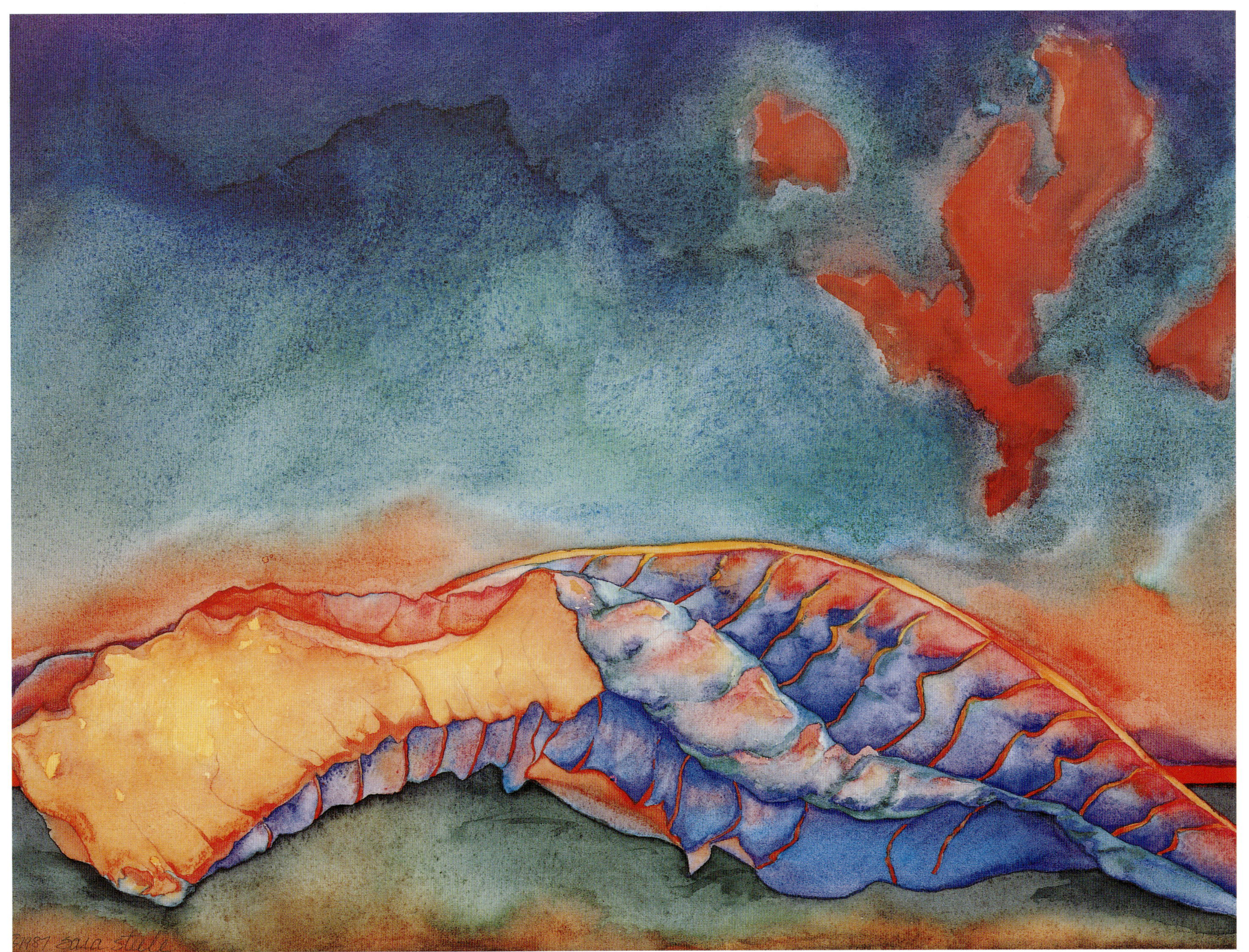

Leaf Skeleton/Spirit Leaves, 1987

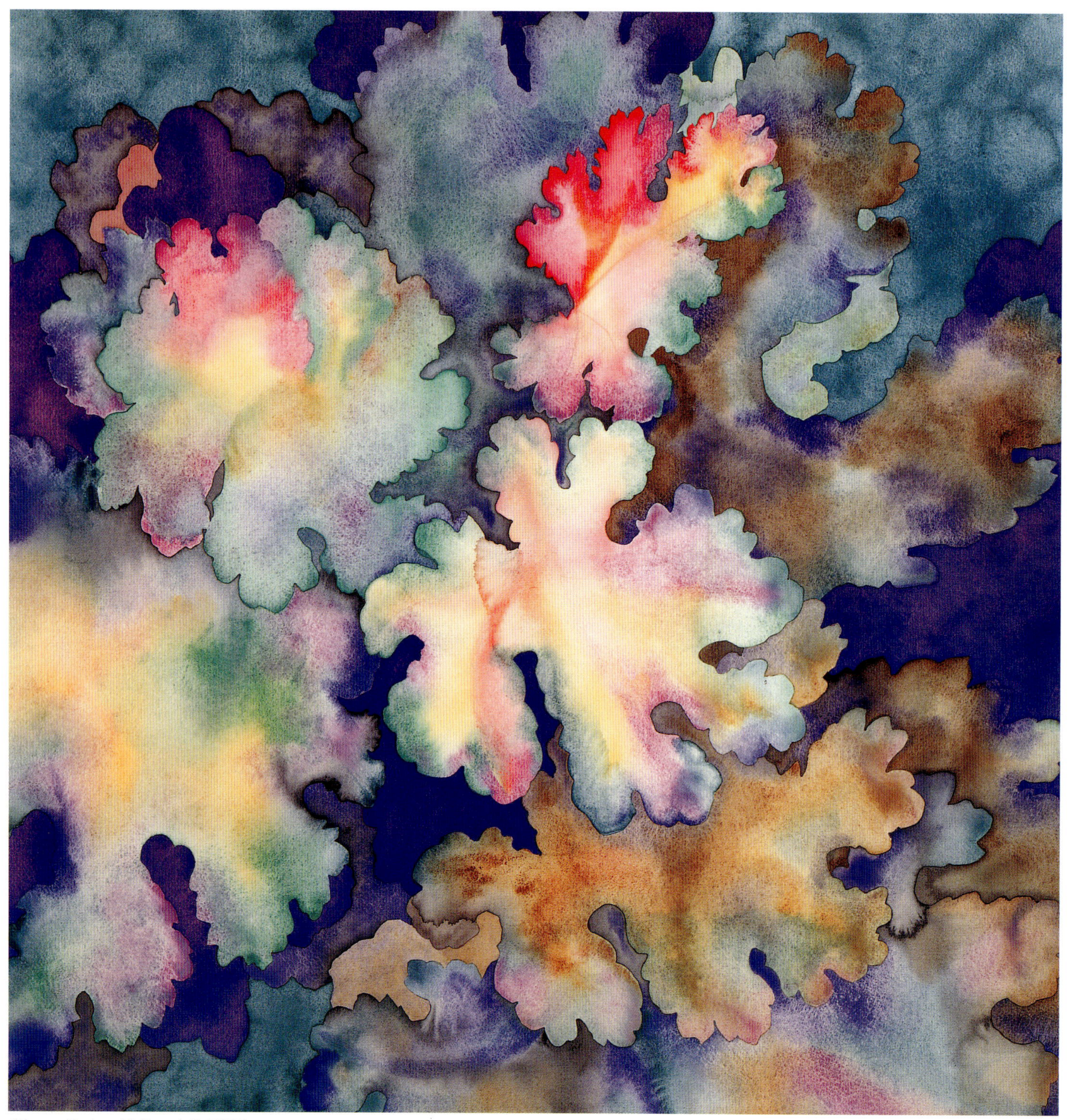

Plume Poppy (foliage) I, 1993

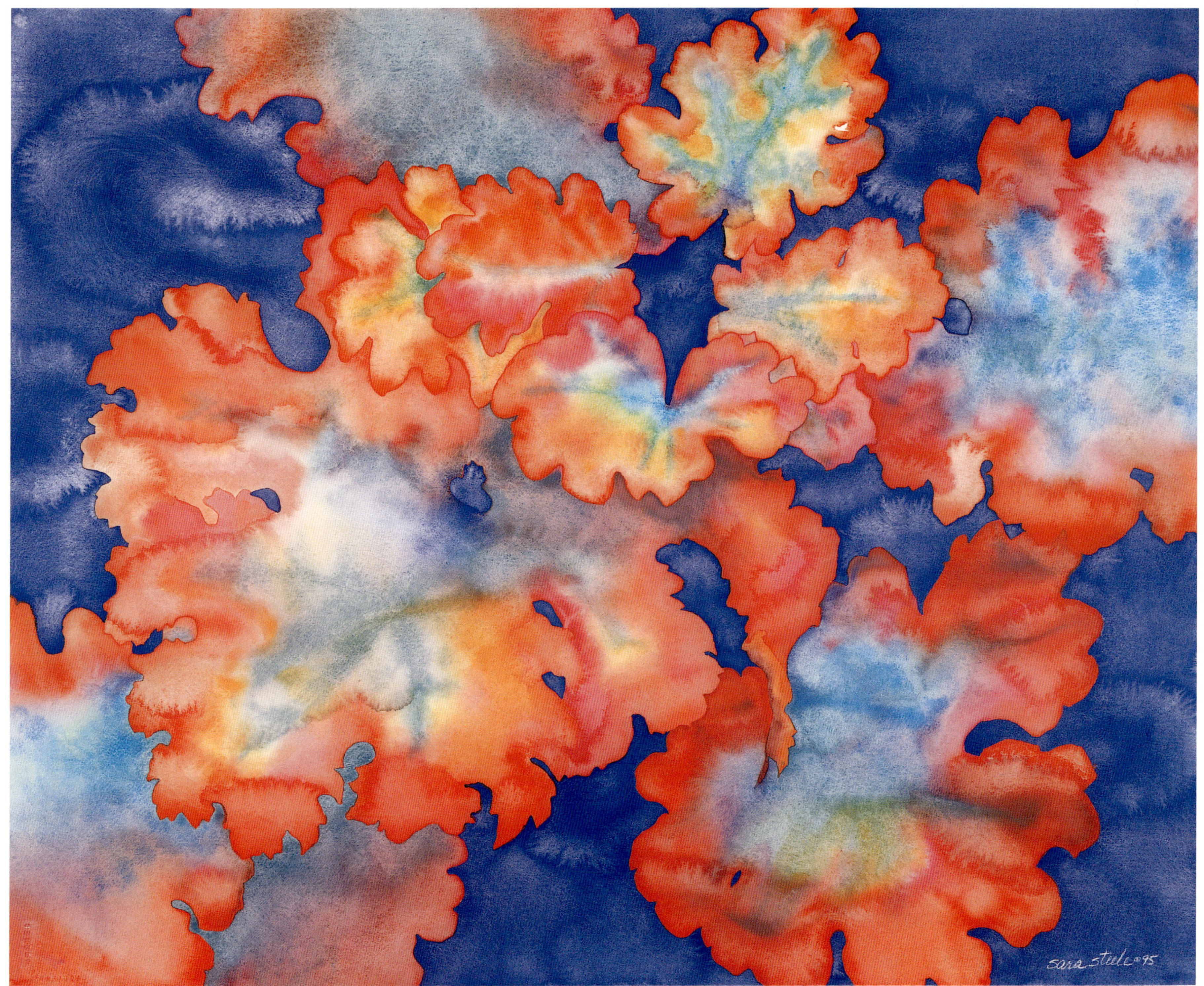

Plume Poppies (foliage) II, 1995

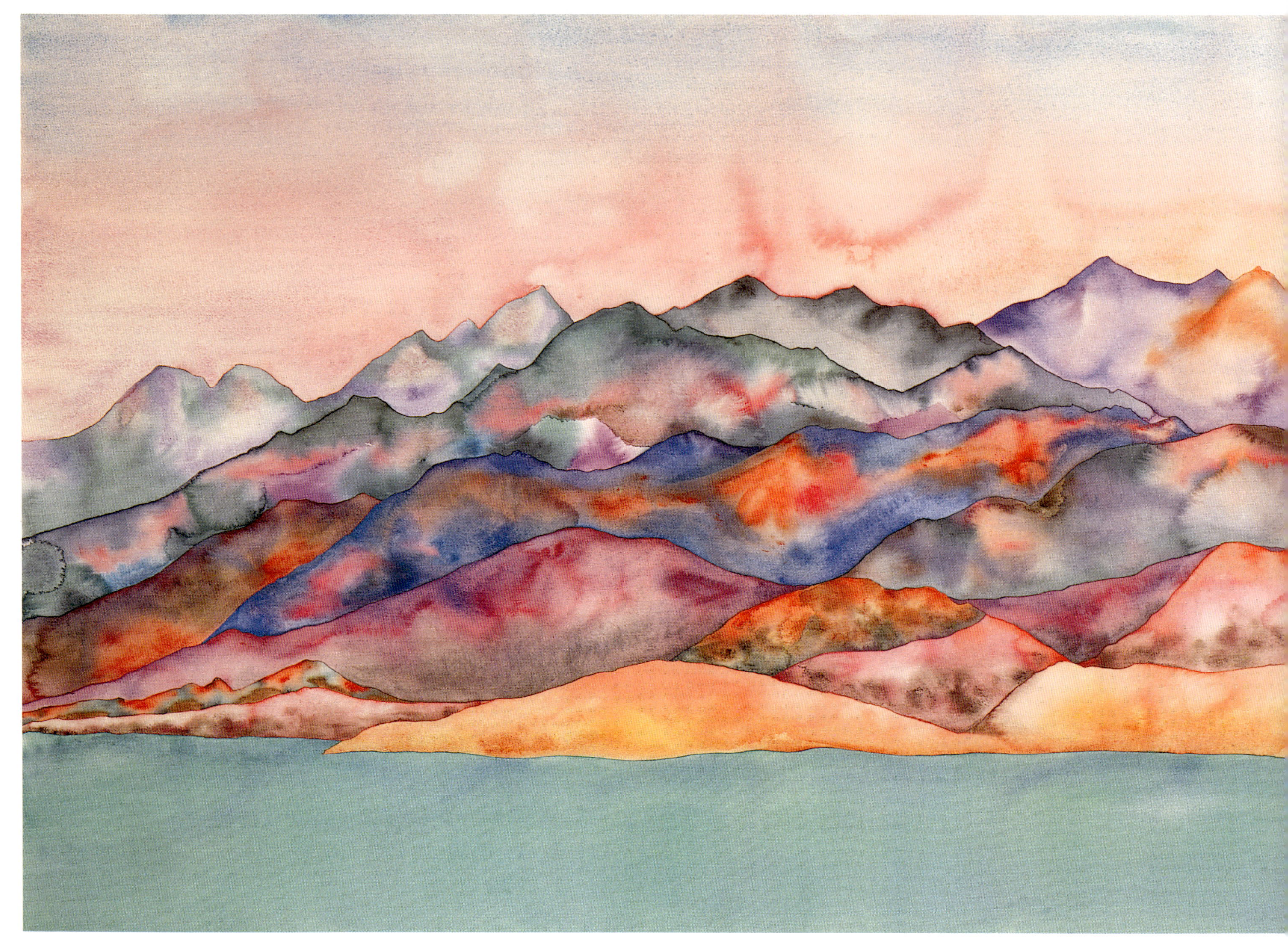

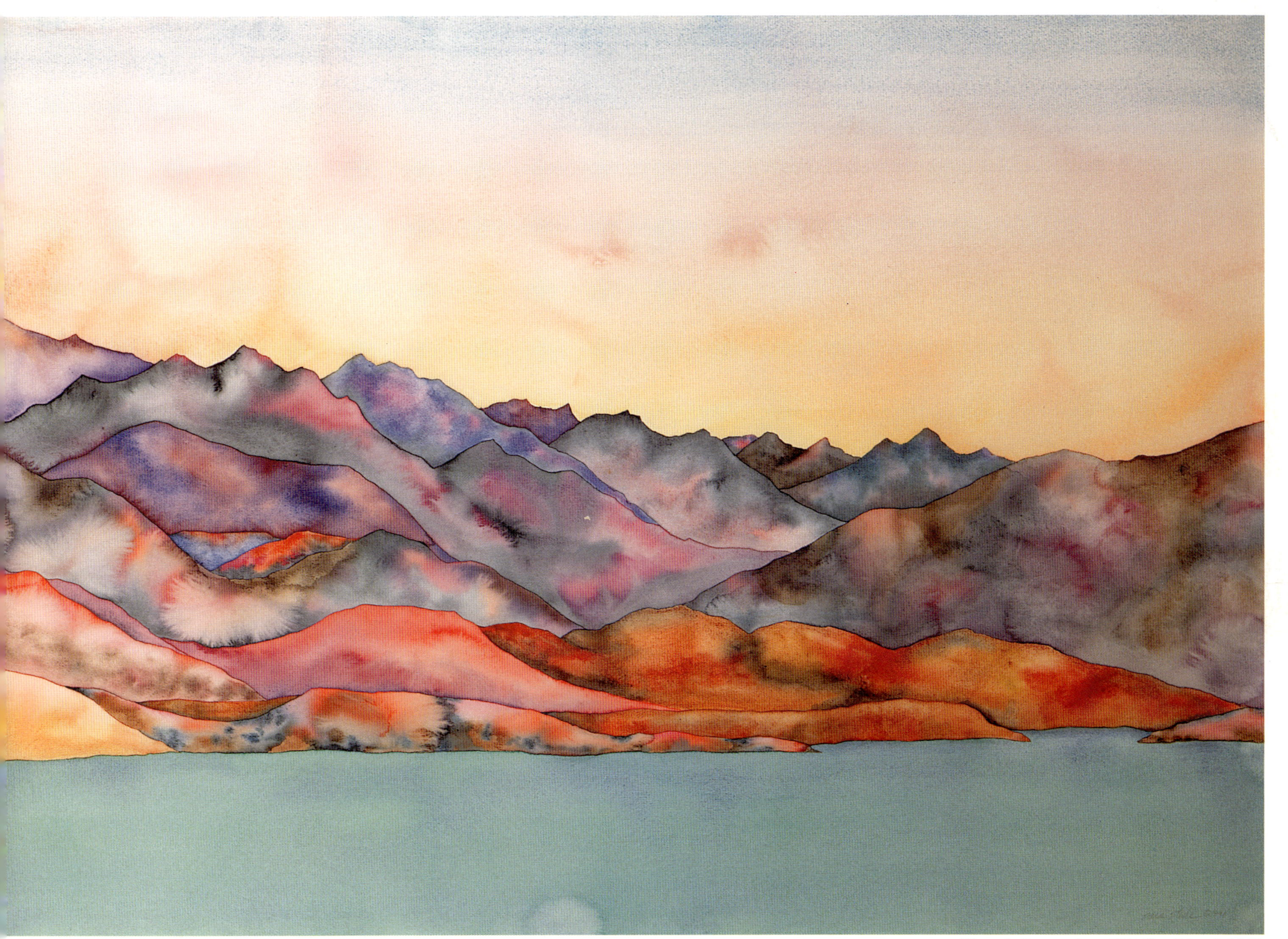

Olympic Range from Whidbey Island, 1991

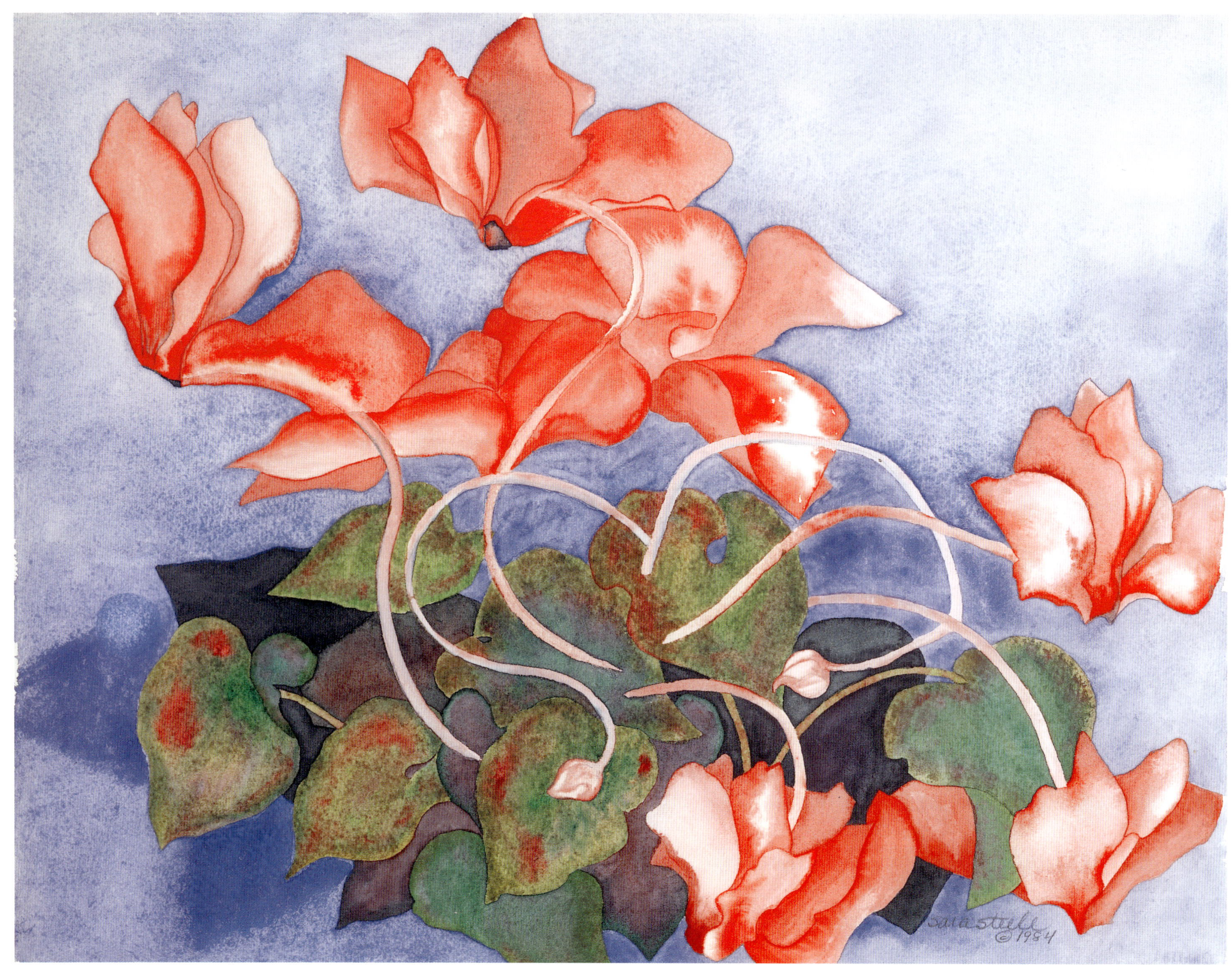

Cyclamen (seeing blue), 1984

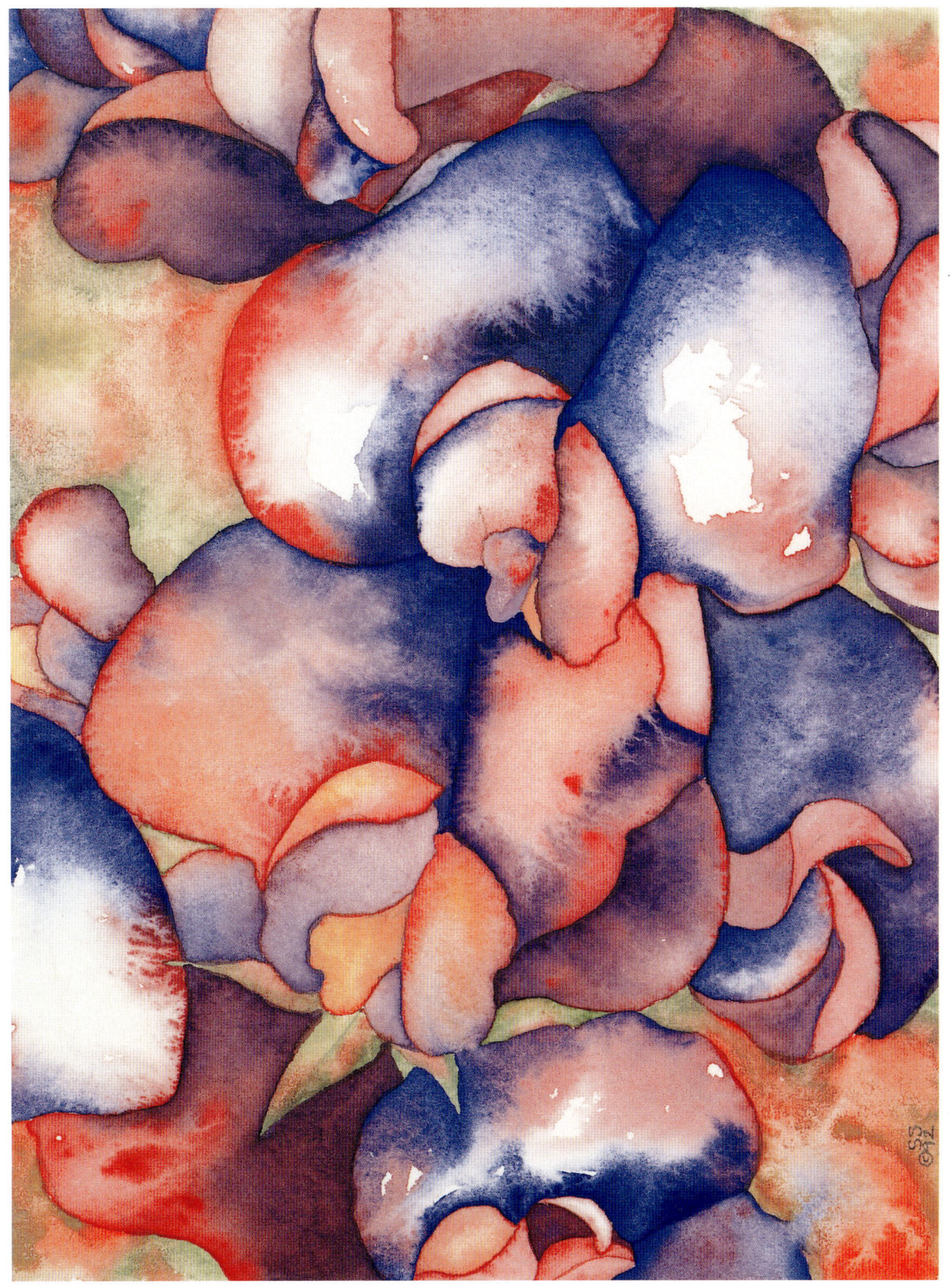

Whidbey Island Vetch, 1992

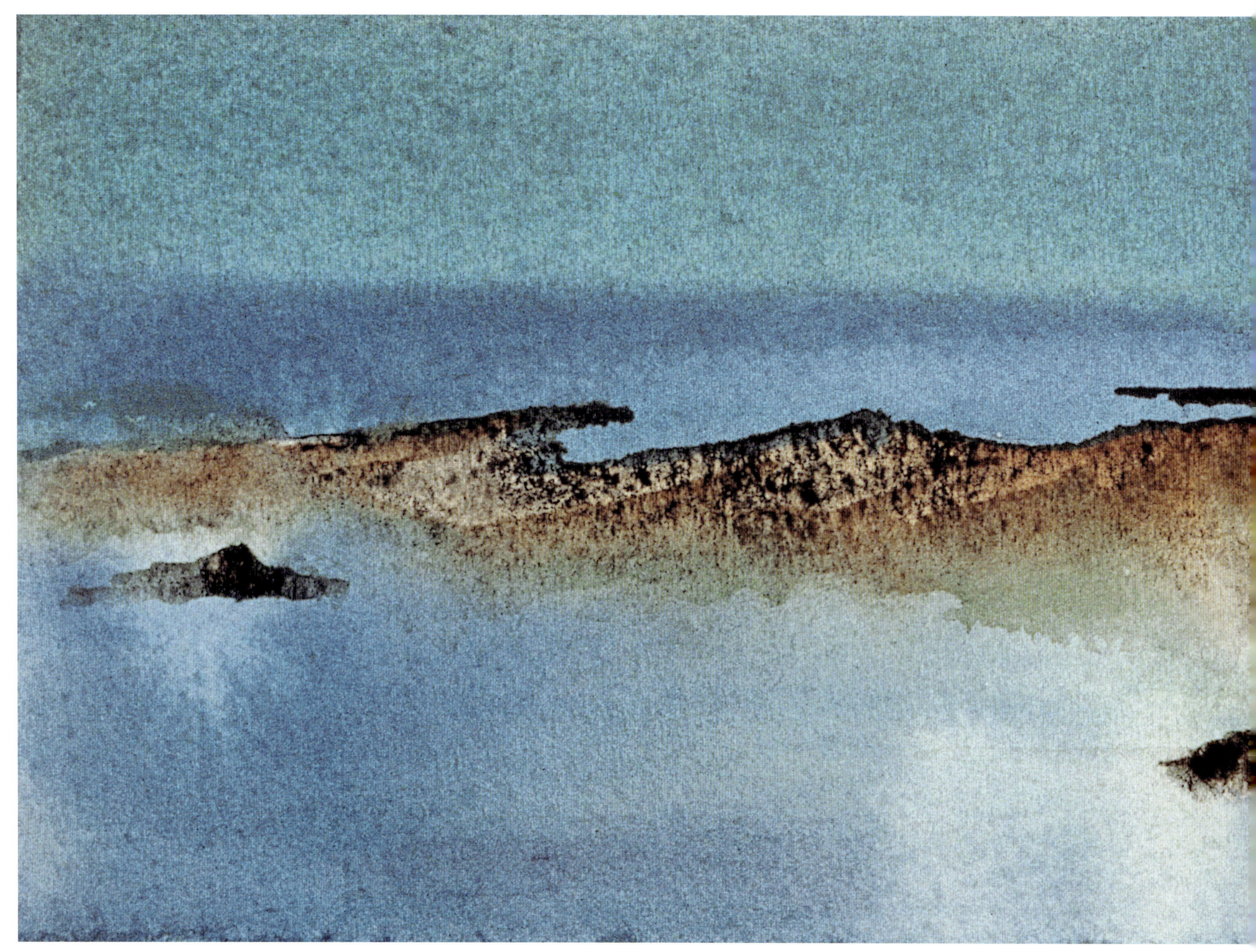

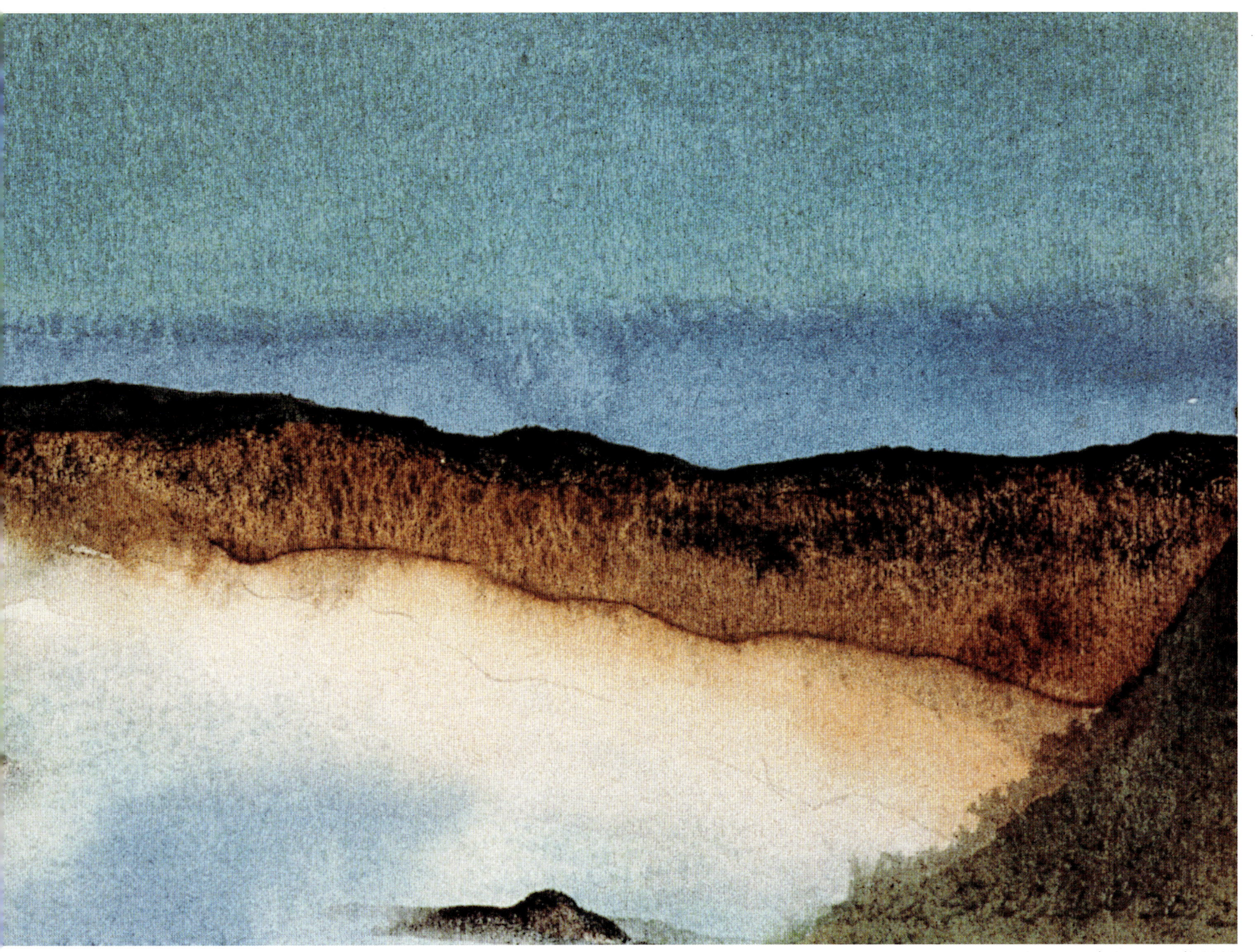

Near Manele Bay, Lana'i, 2002

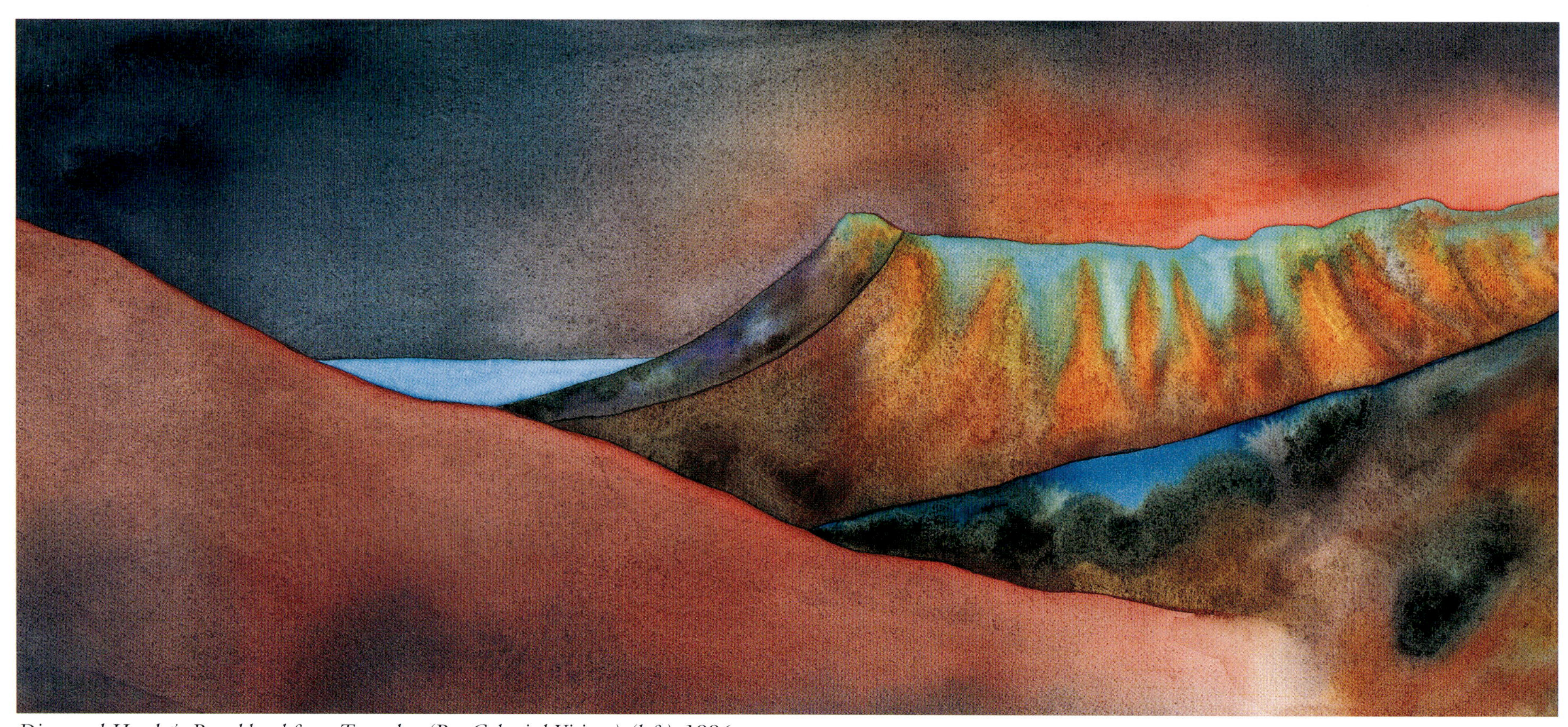

Diamond Head & Punchbowl from Tantalus (Pre-Colonial Visions) (left), 1996

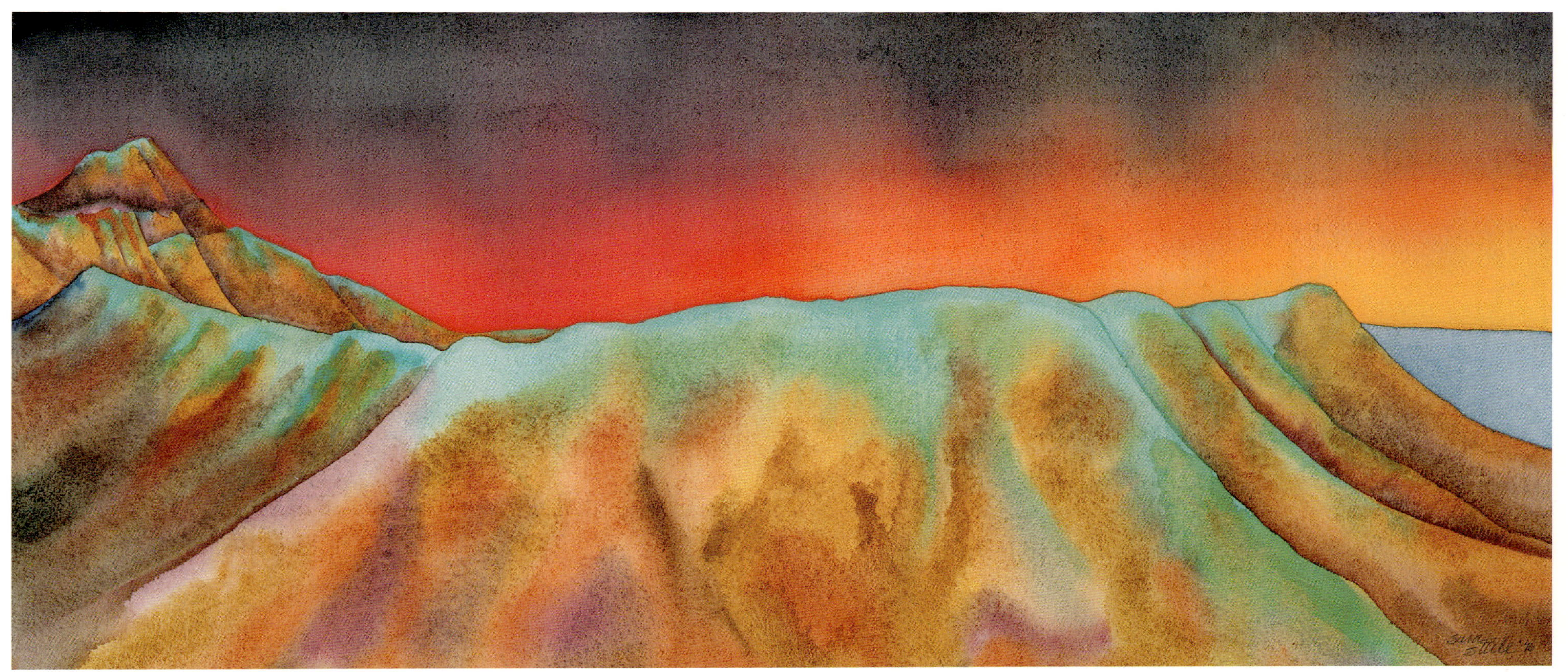

Diamond Head & Punchbowl from Tantalus (Pre-Colonial Visions) (right), 1996

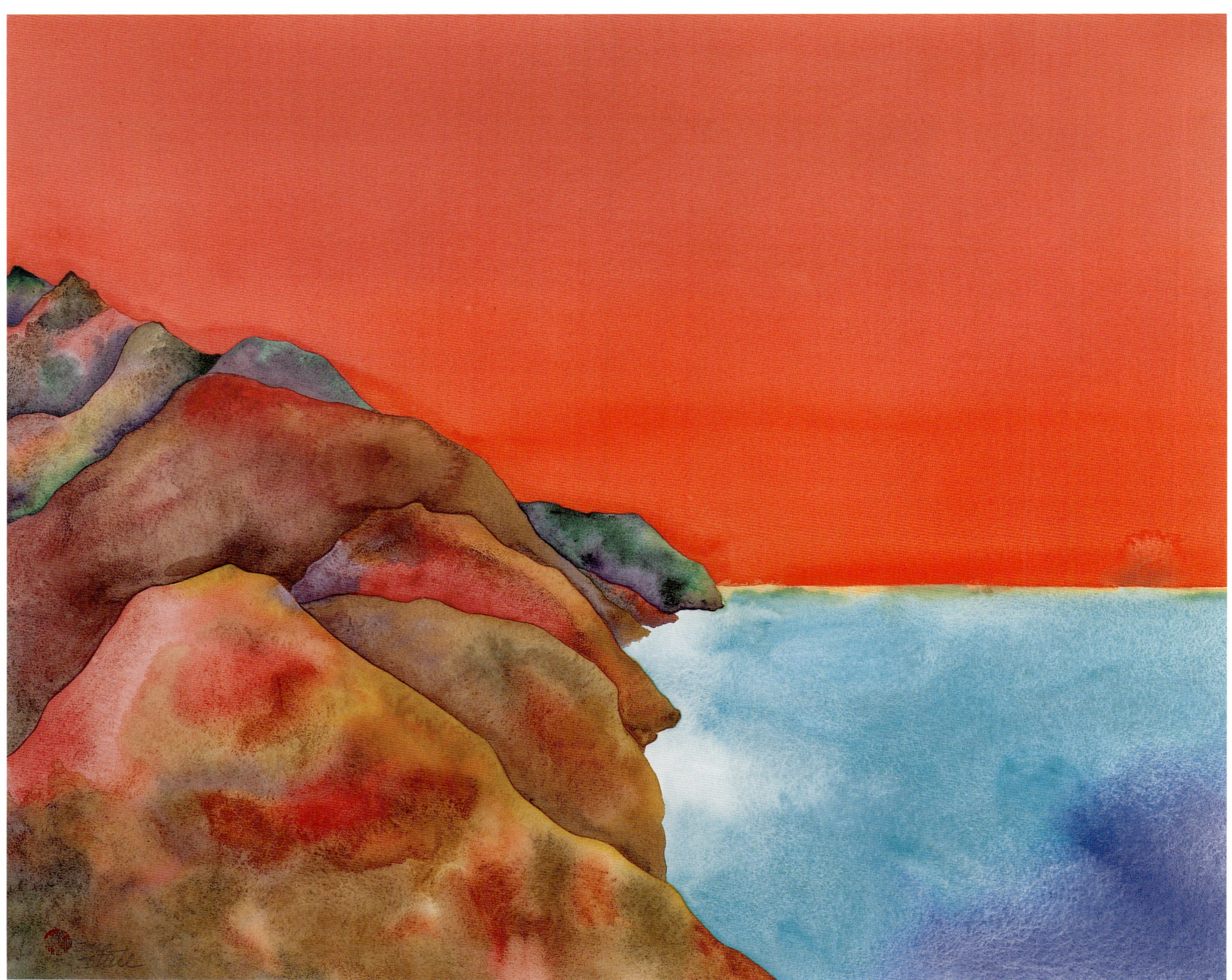

Na Pali Coast V, 1999

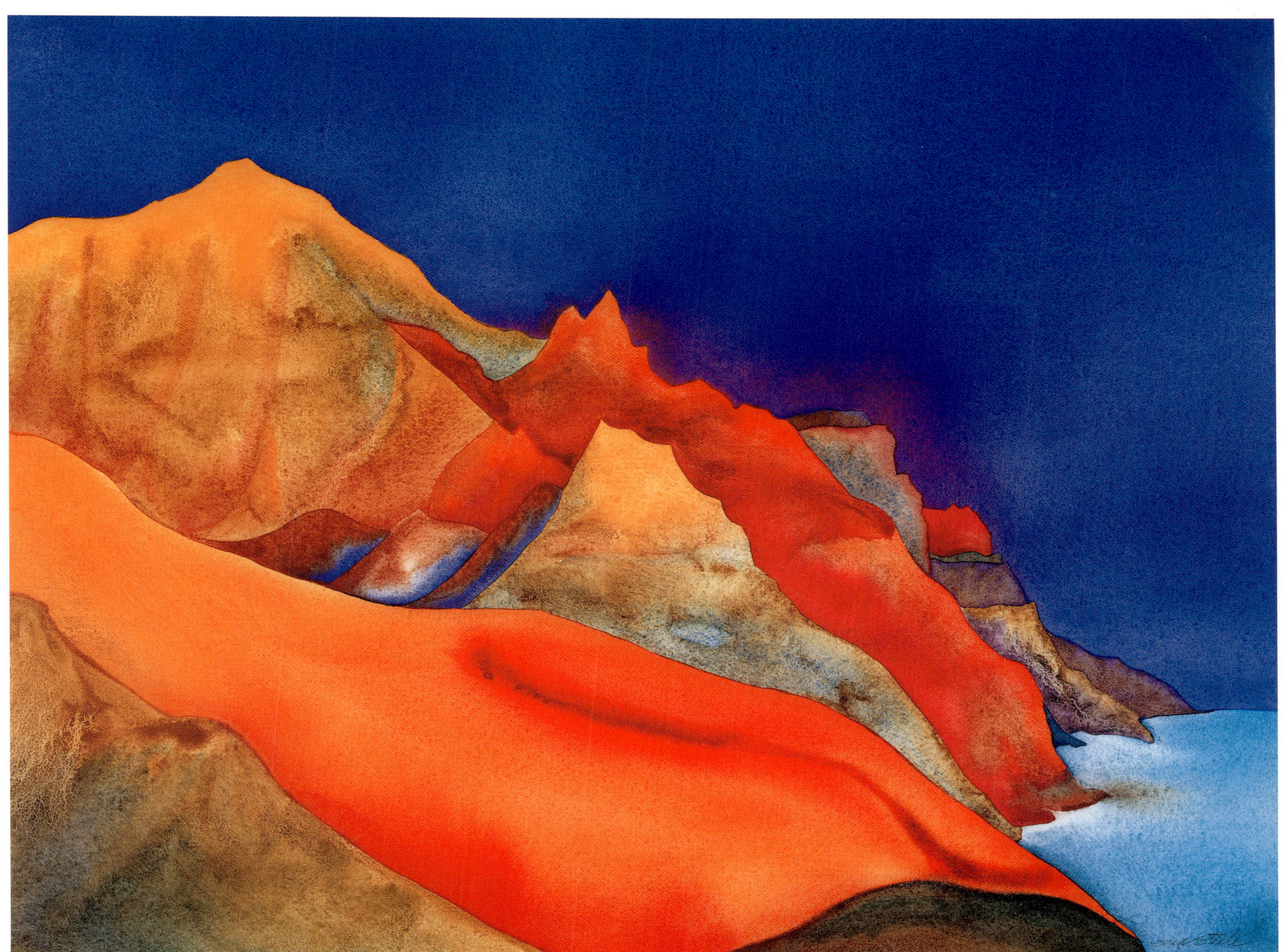

Na Pali Coast IV, 1998

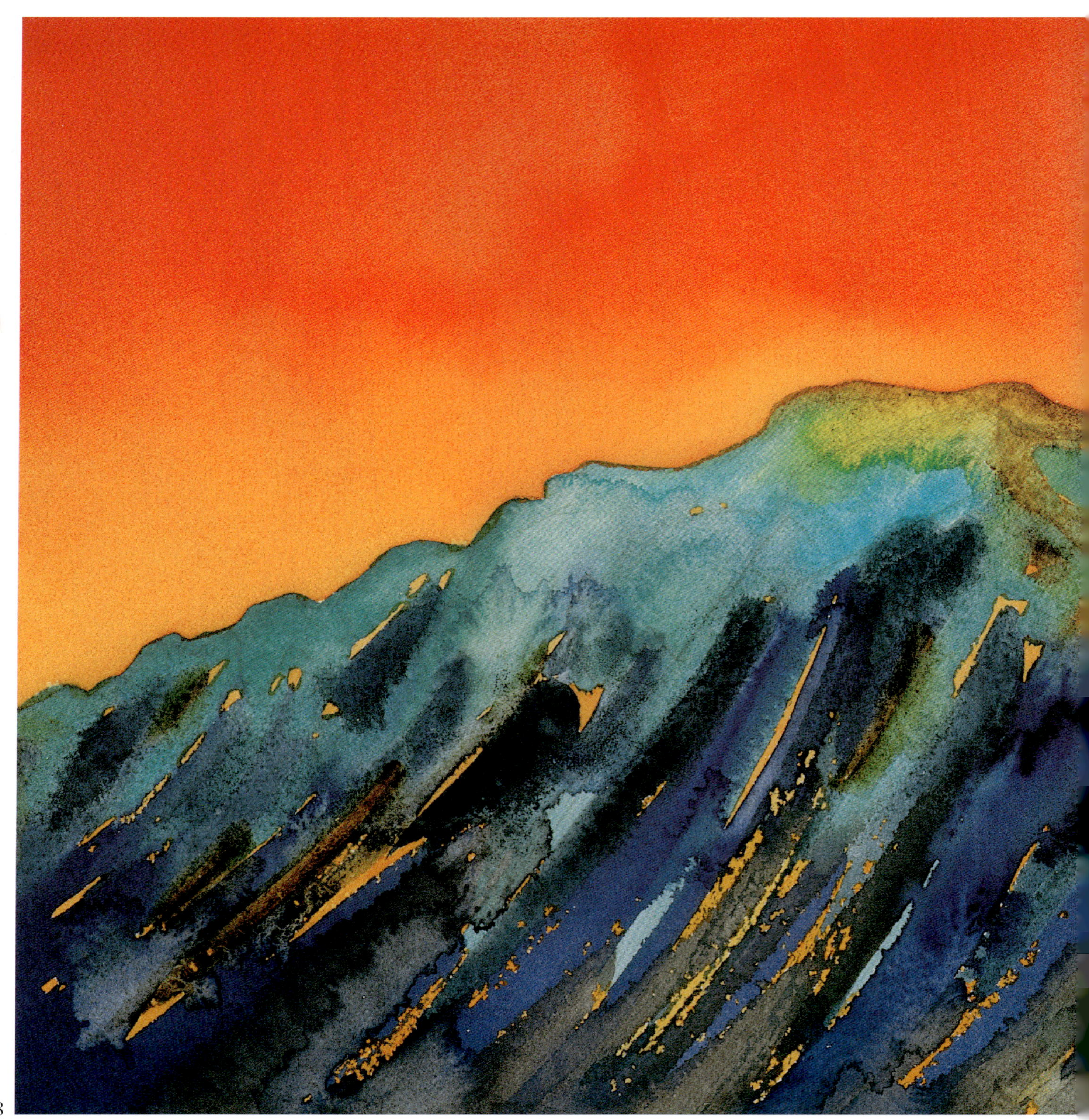

Sunset Diamond Head, 1998

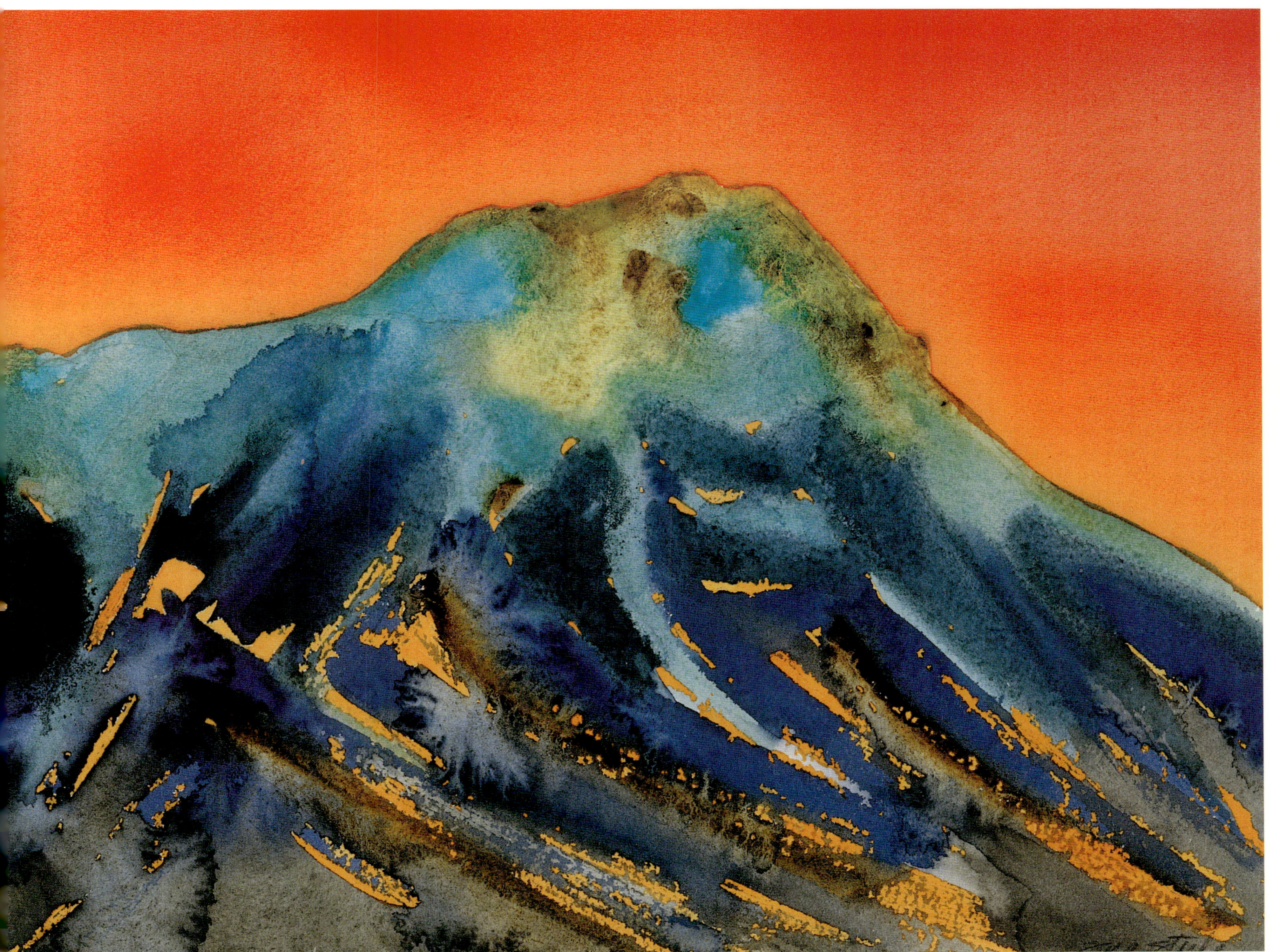

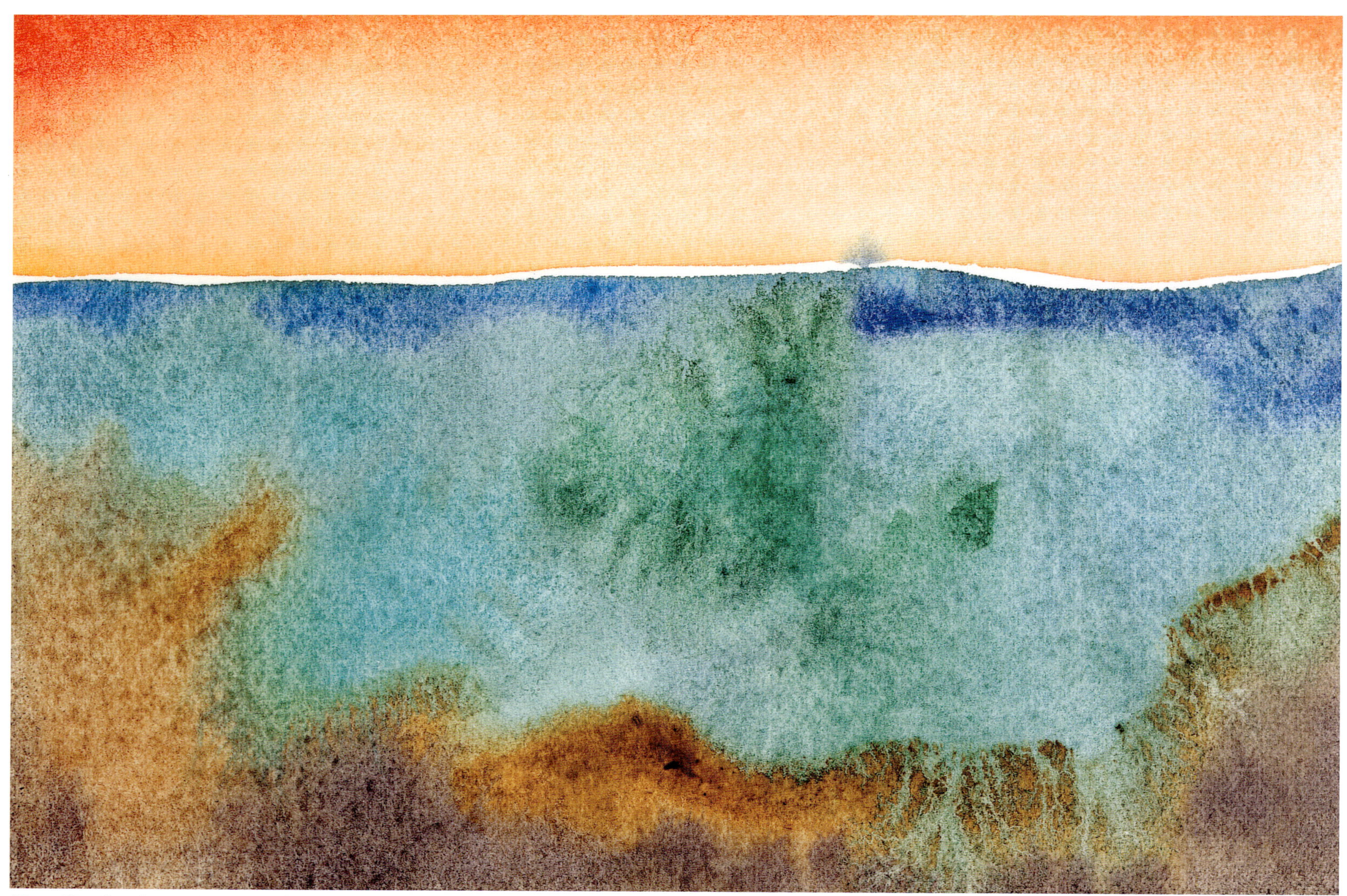

Hawai'ian Landscape: Rose Dore Sky, 1998

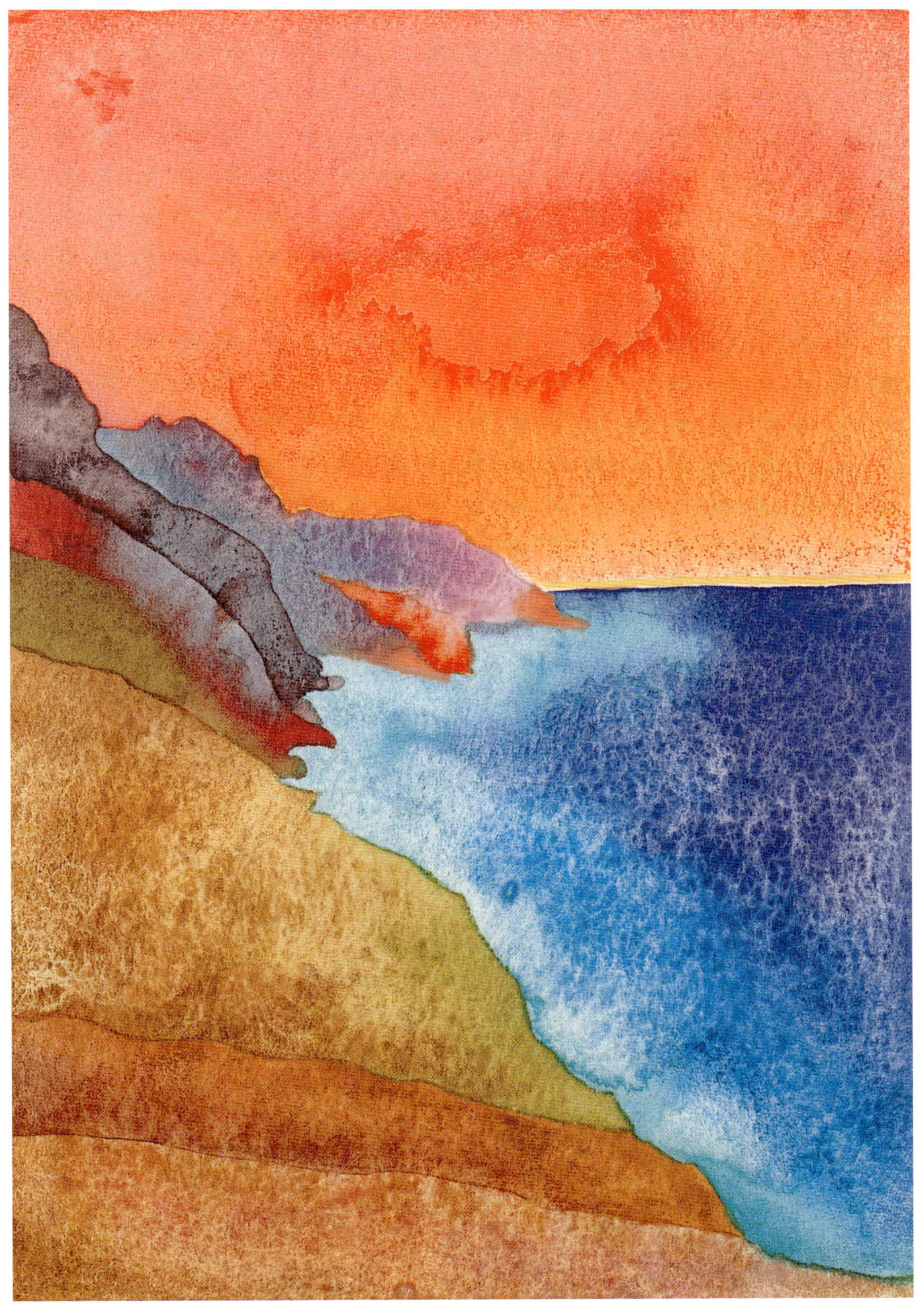

Na Pali Coast II, 1998

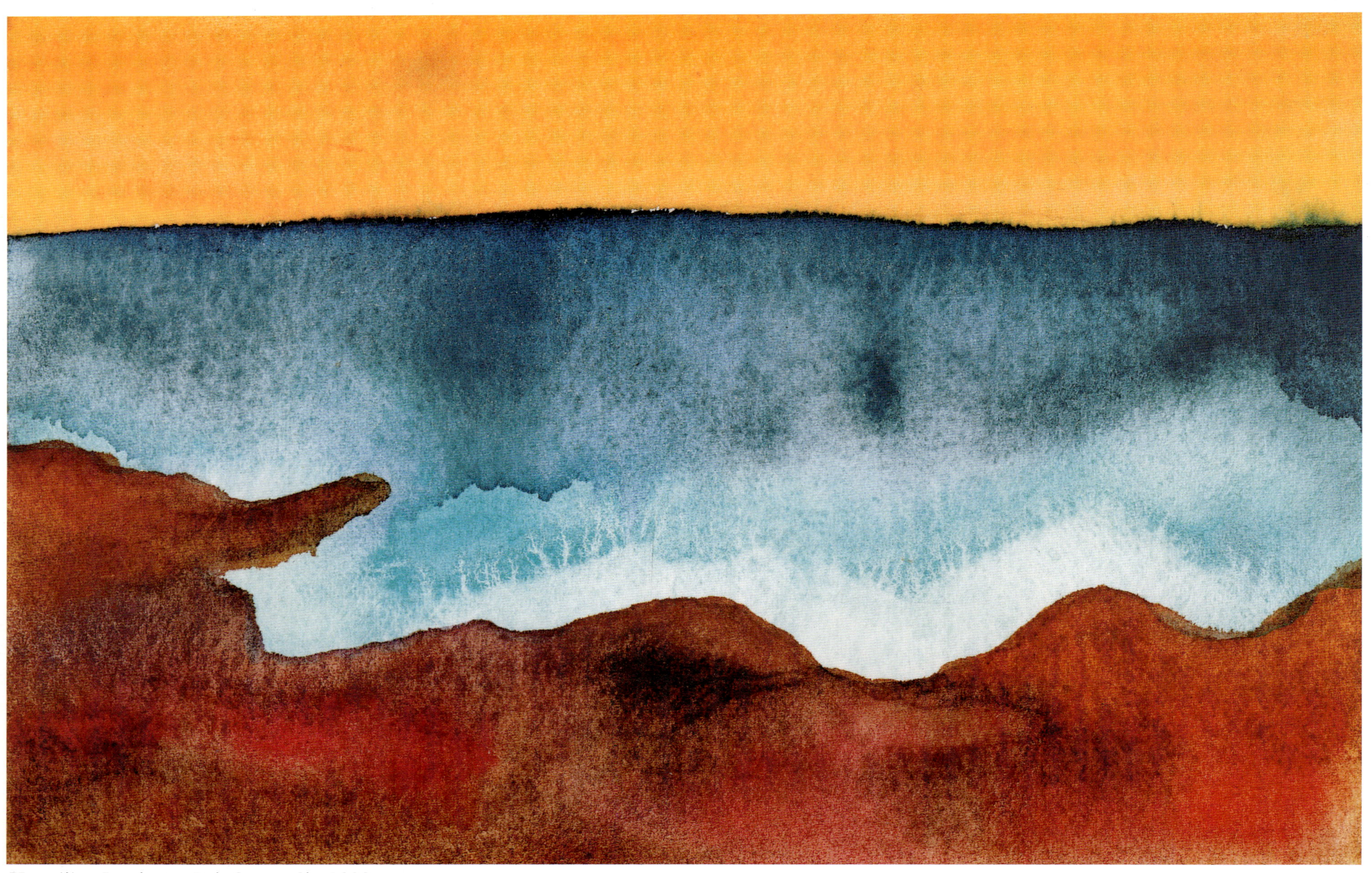

Hawai'ian Landscape: Pale Orange Sky, 1998

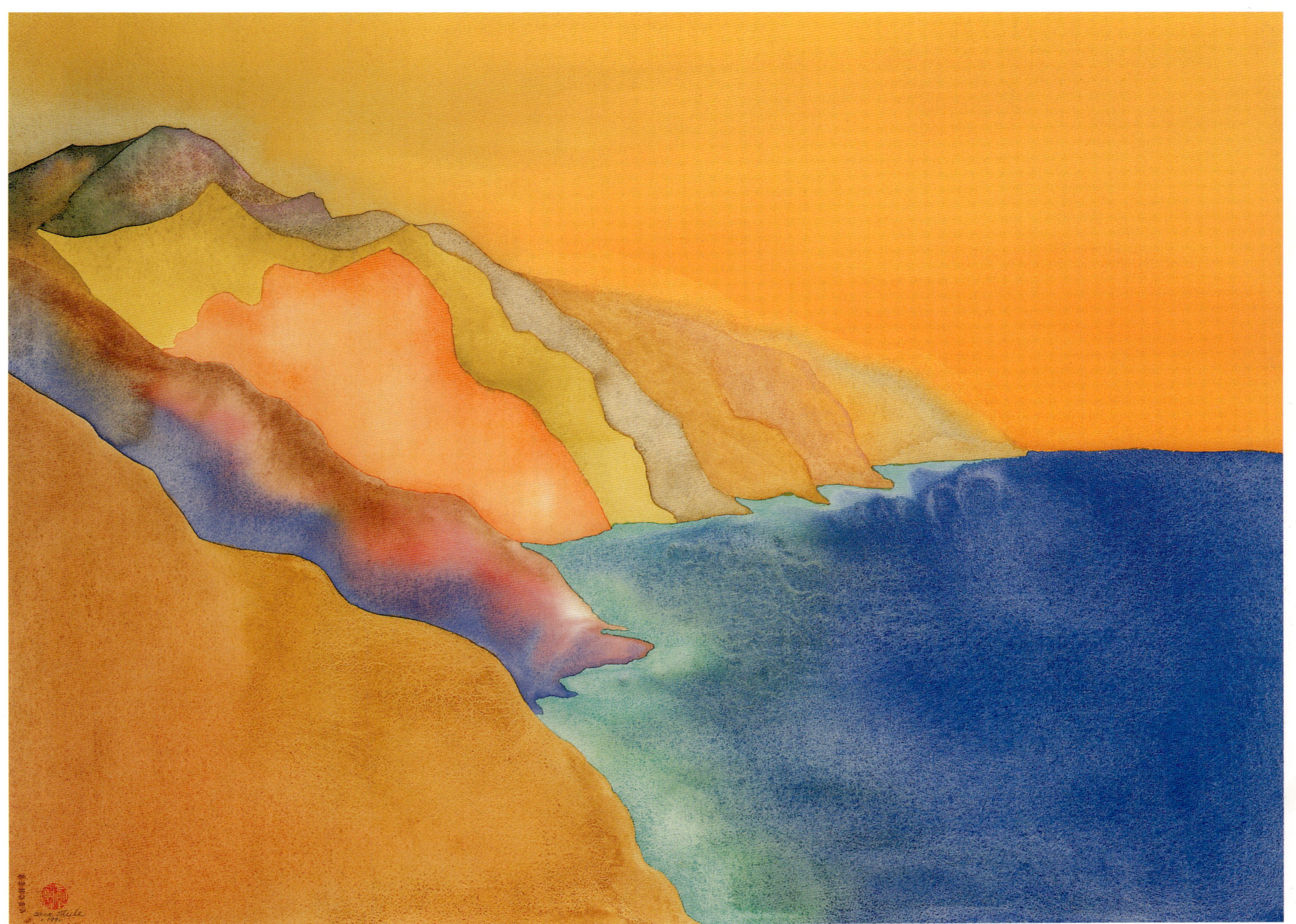

Na Pali Coast, Kaua'i, 1996

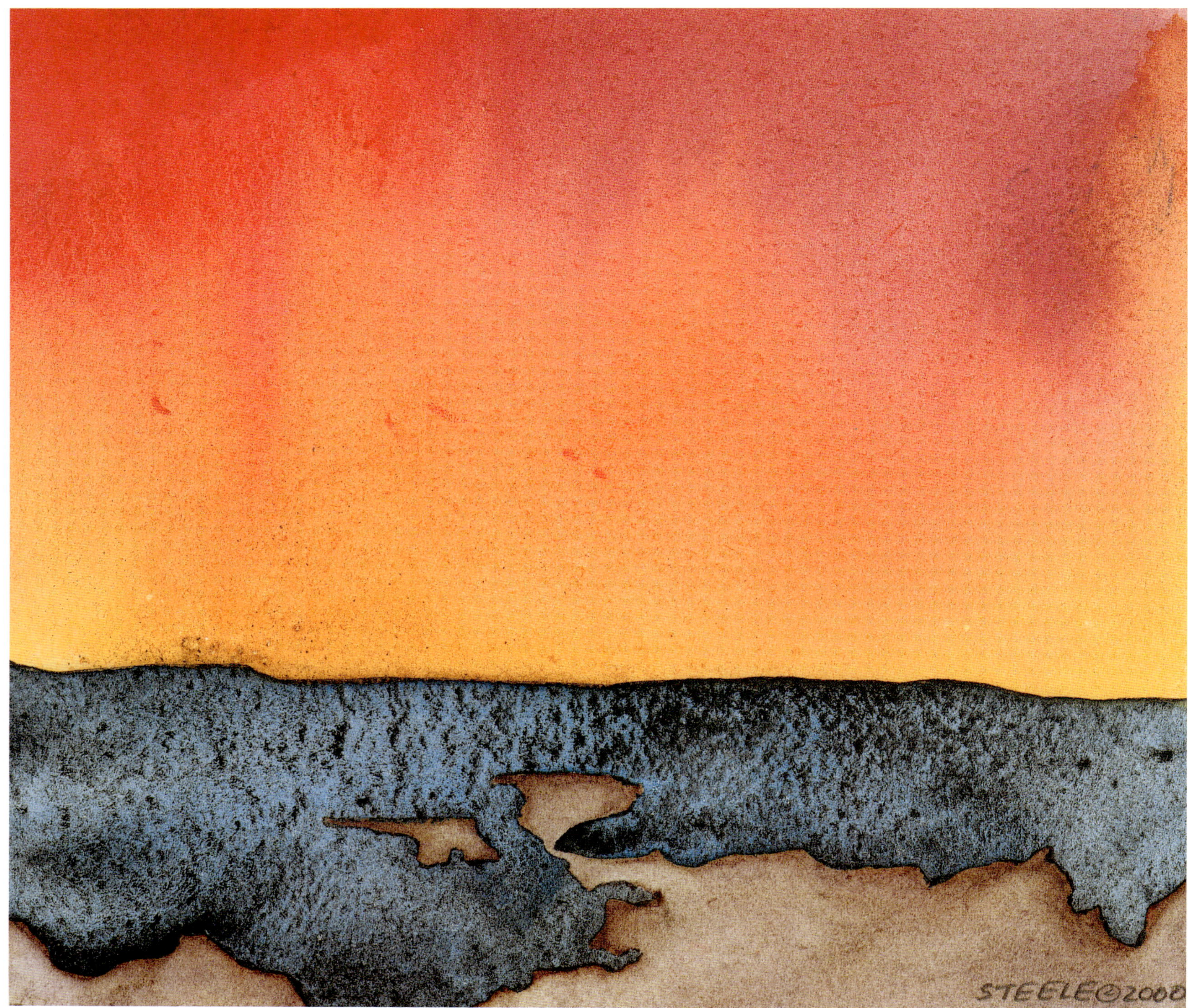

Poipu, Sunset, 2000

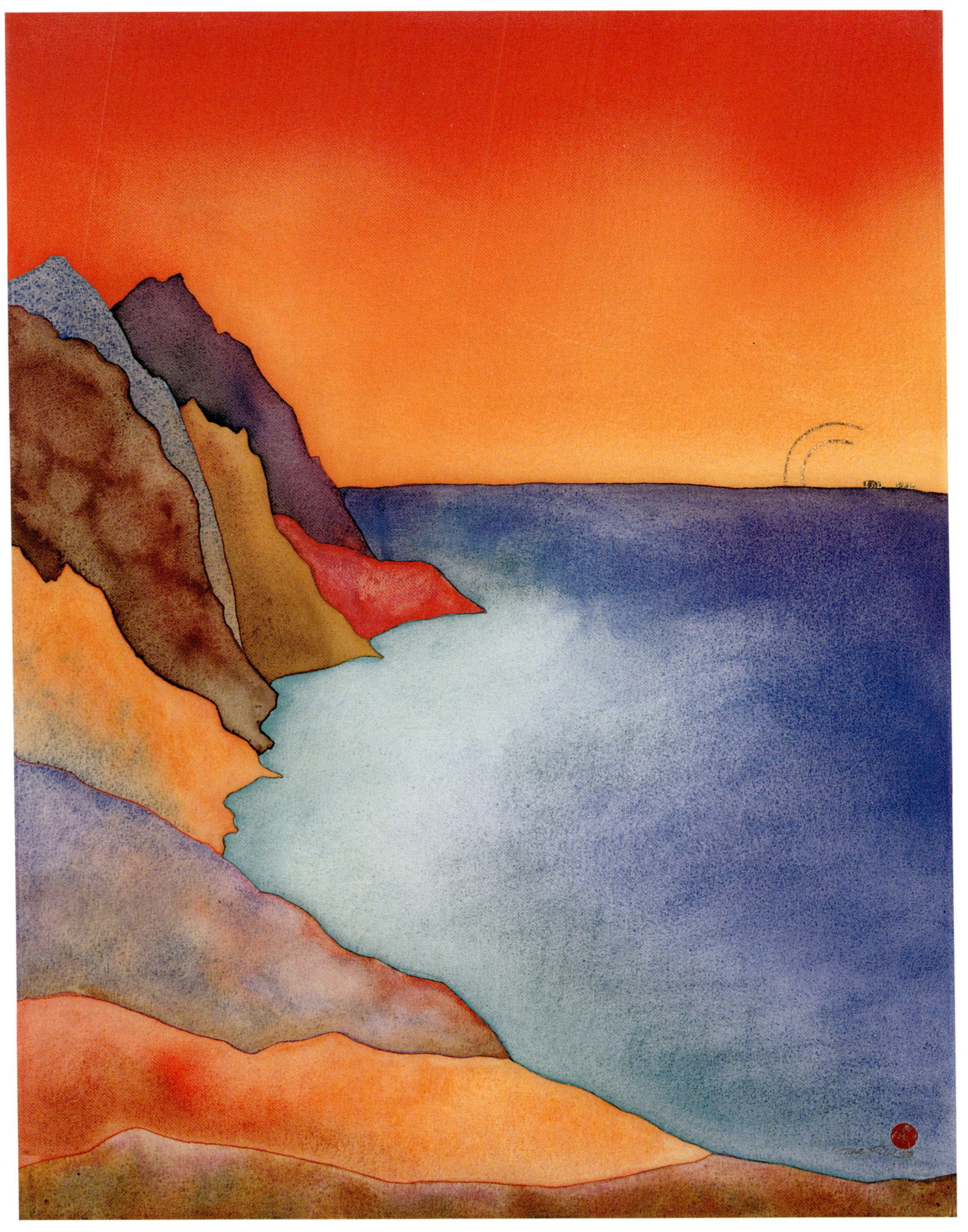

Na Pali Coast III, 1998

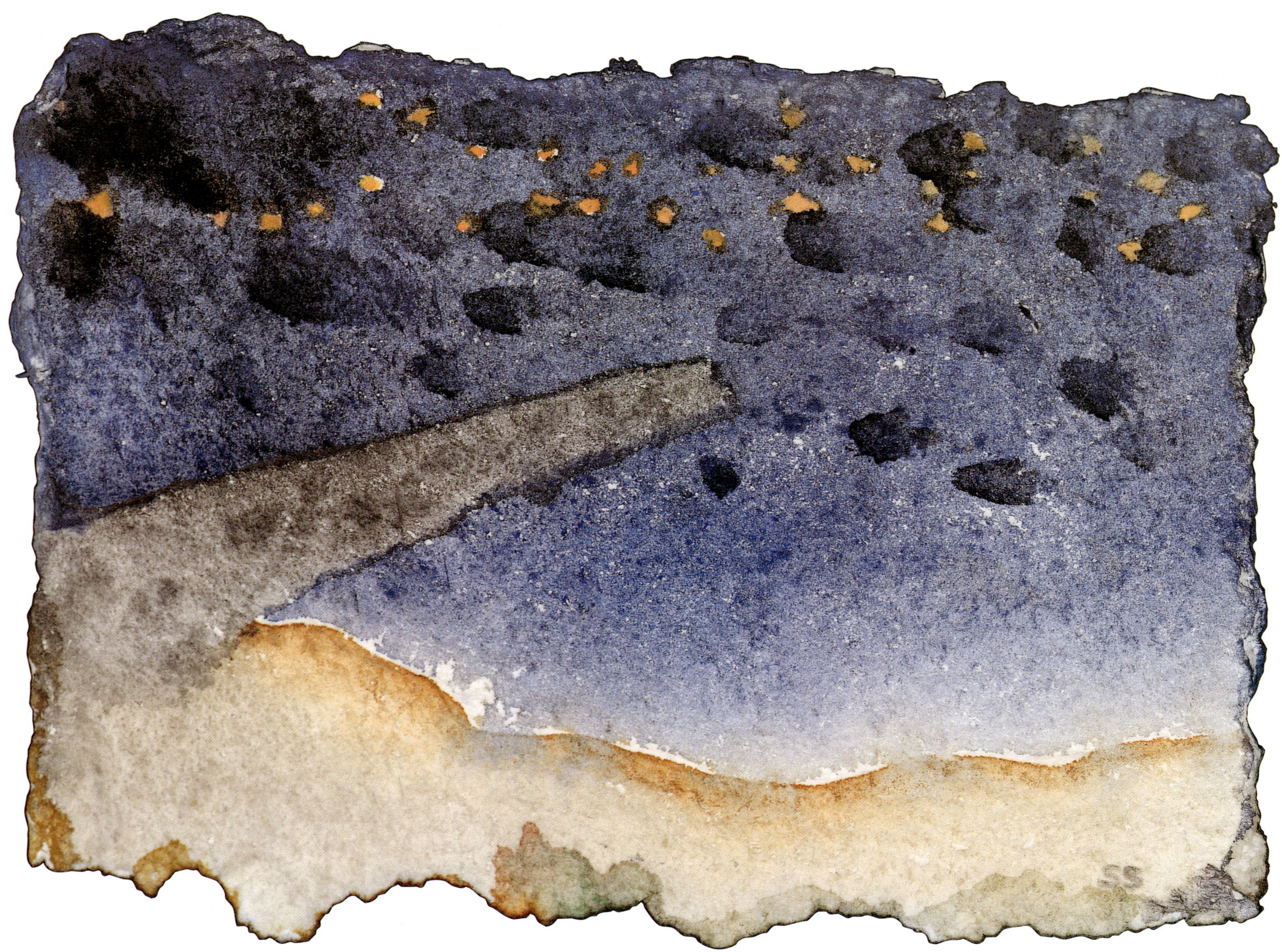

From Wellfleet at Night (RECTO), 1998

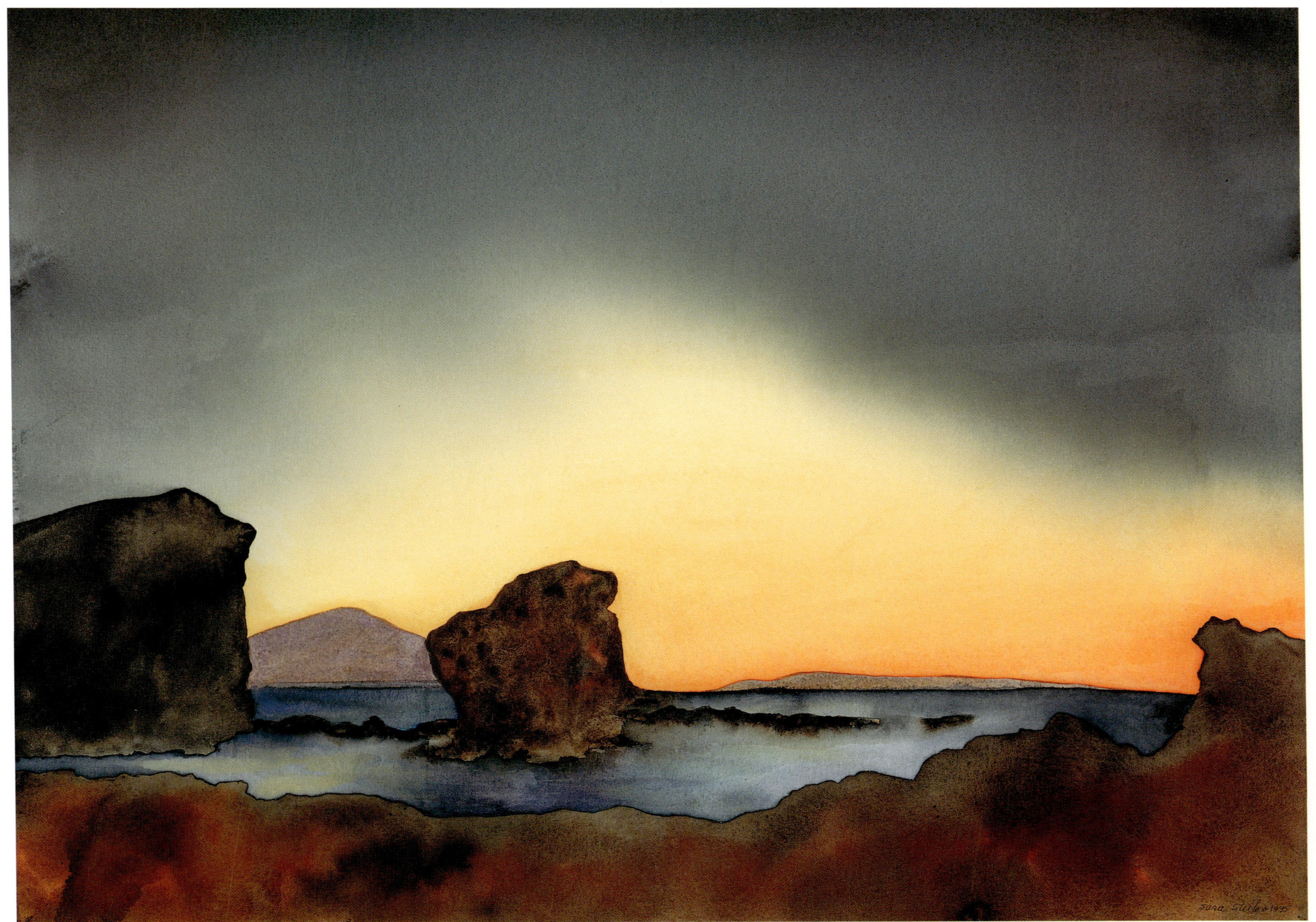

From Pu'u Pehe Cove, Manele Bay, Lana'i, 1995

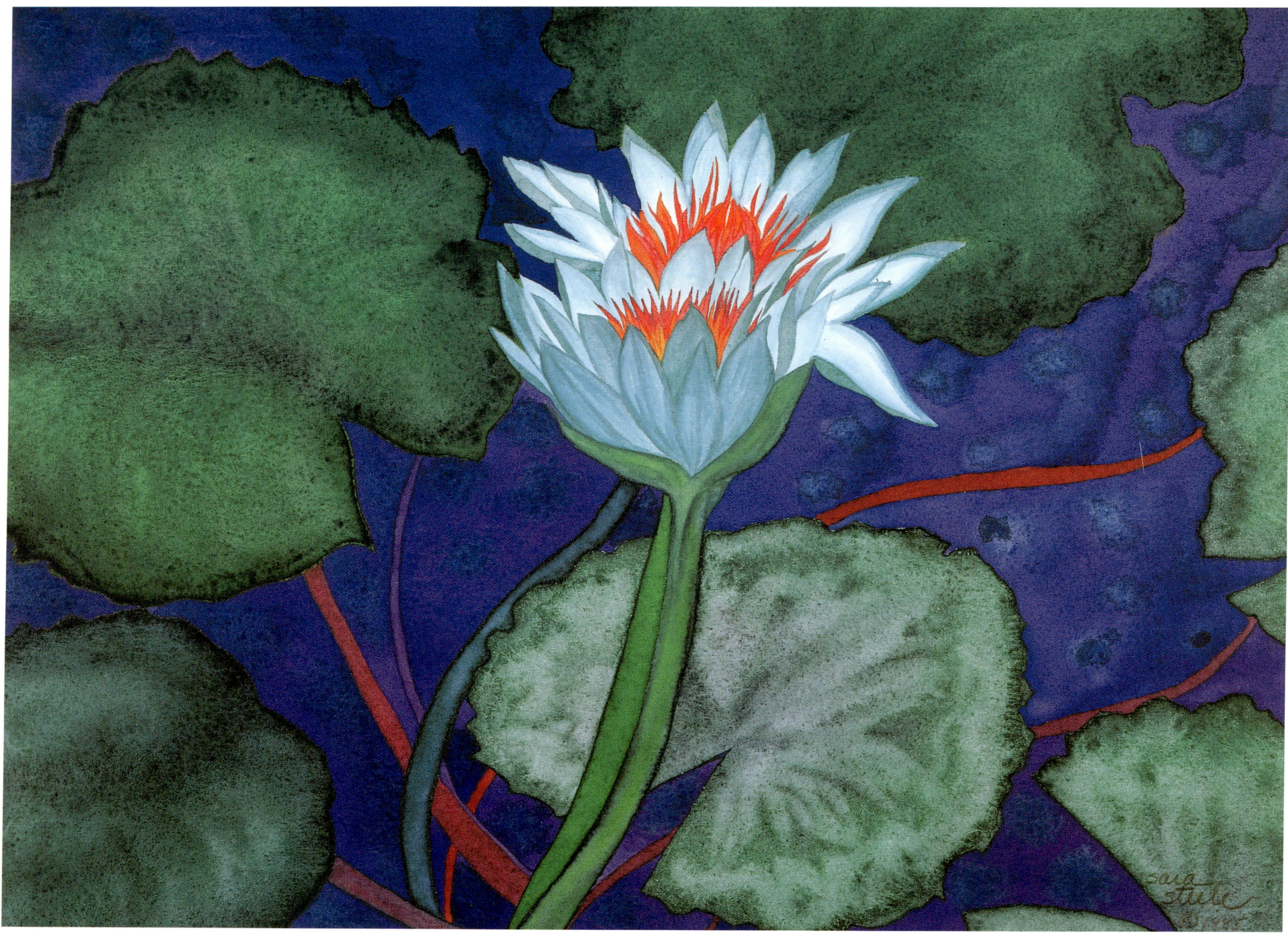

Halcyon Waterlilies, 1985

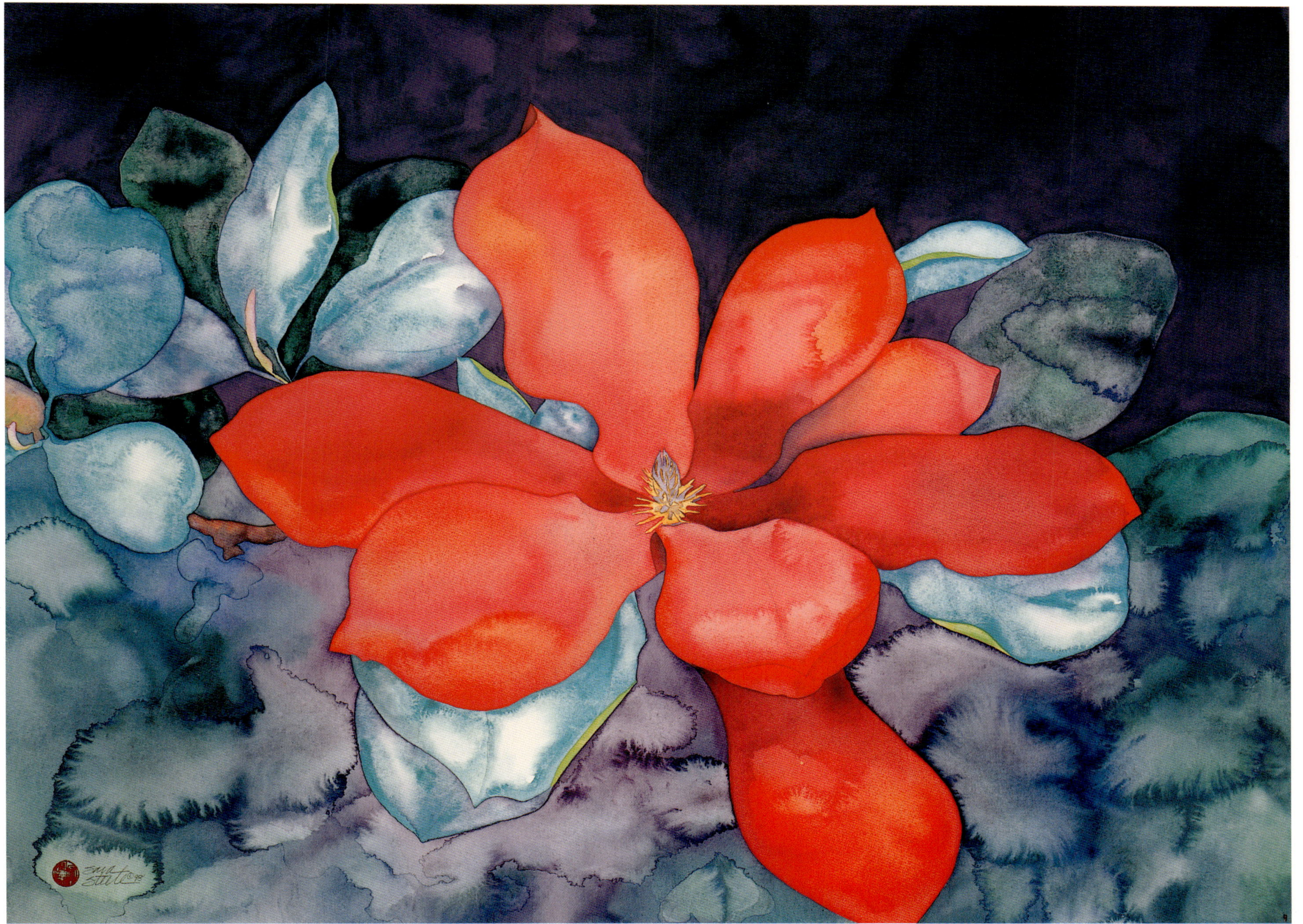

Fuchsia Magnolia, 1998

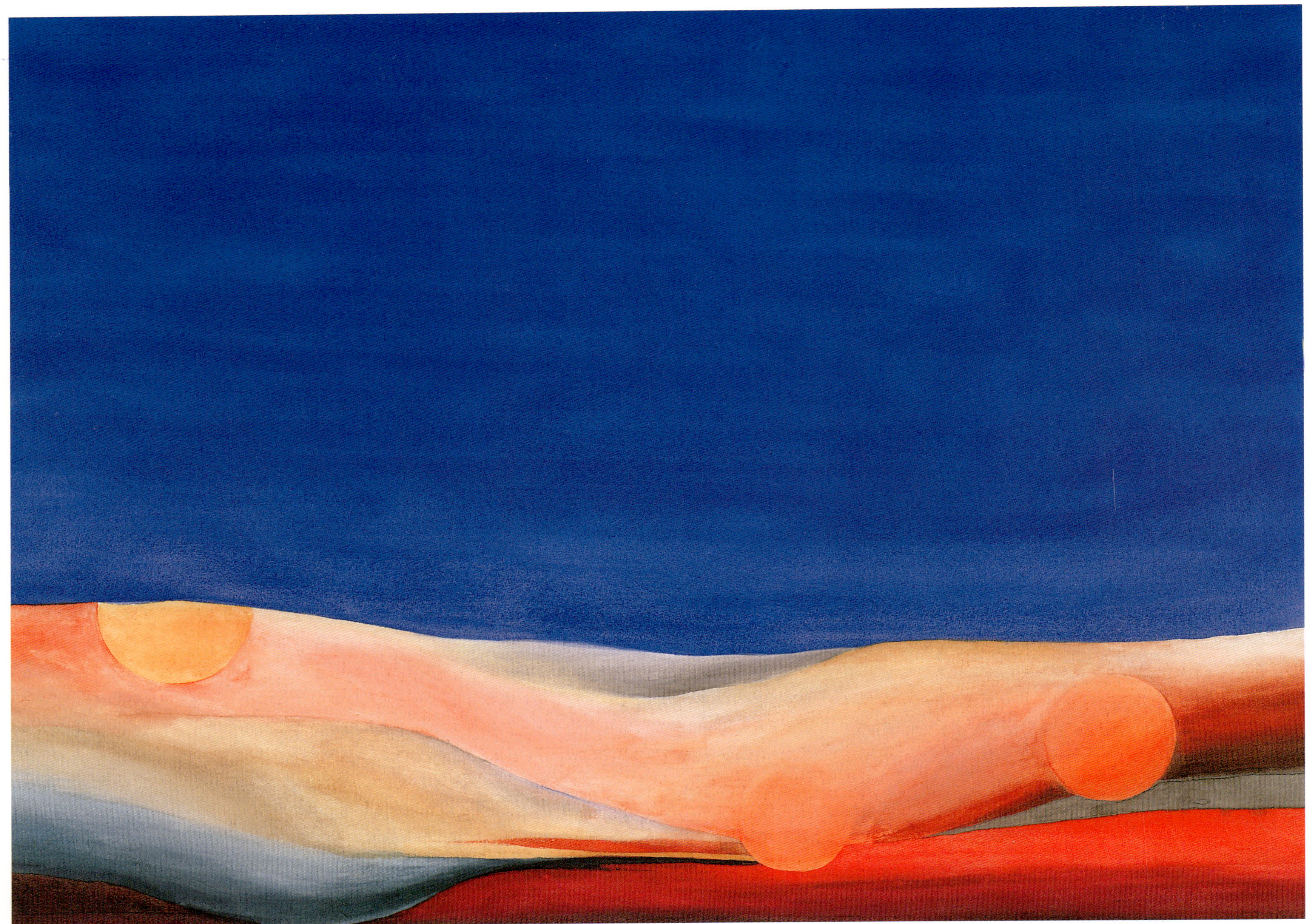

La Frontera/Seamless Dream, 1988

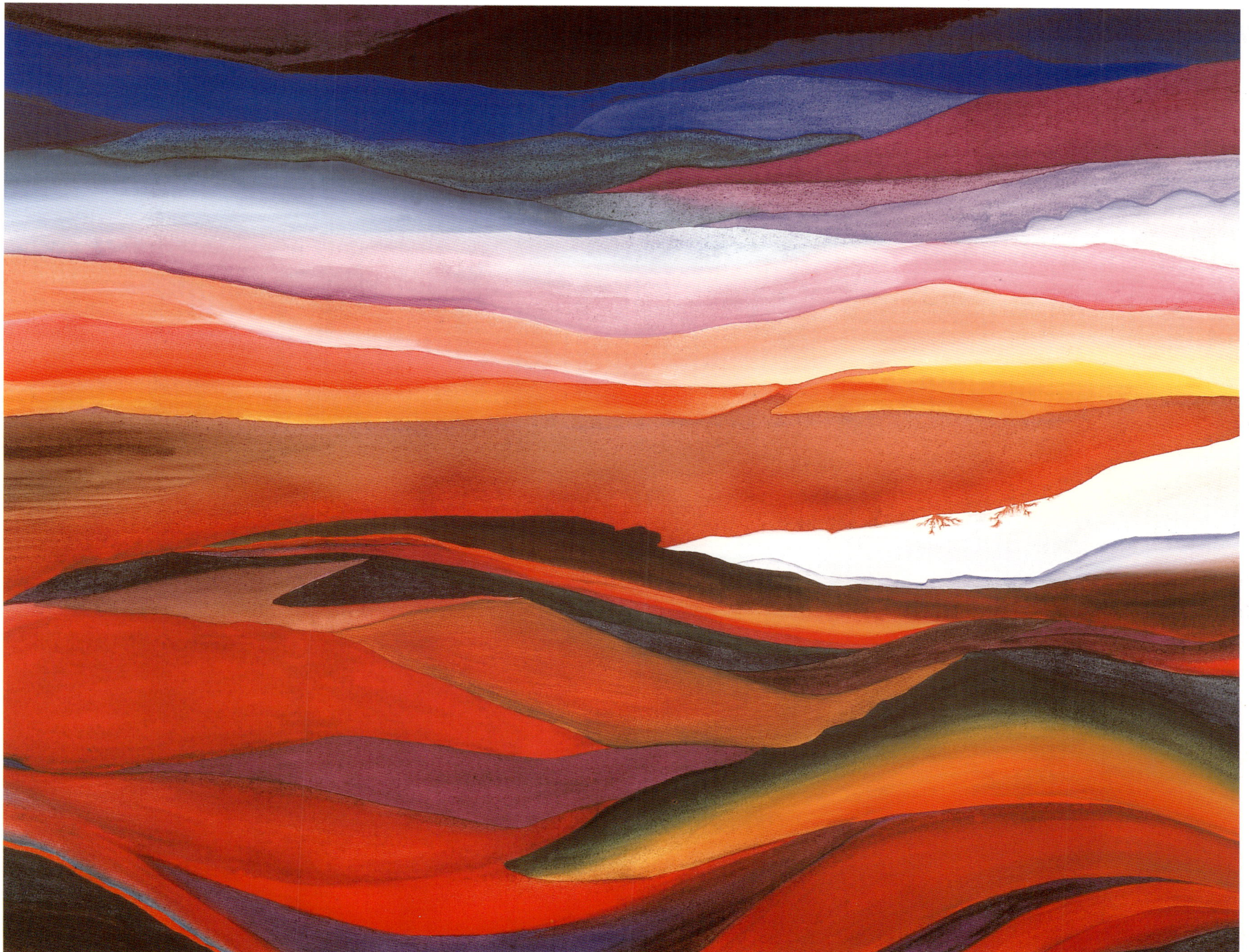

River of Fire, 1982

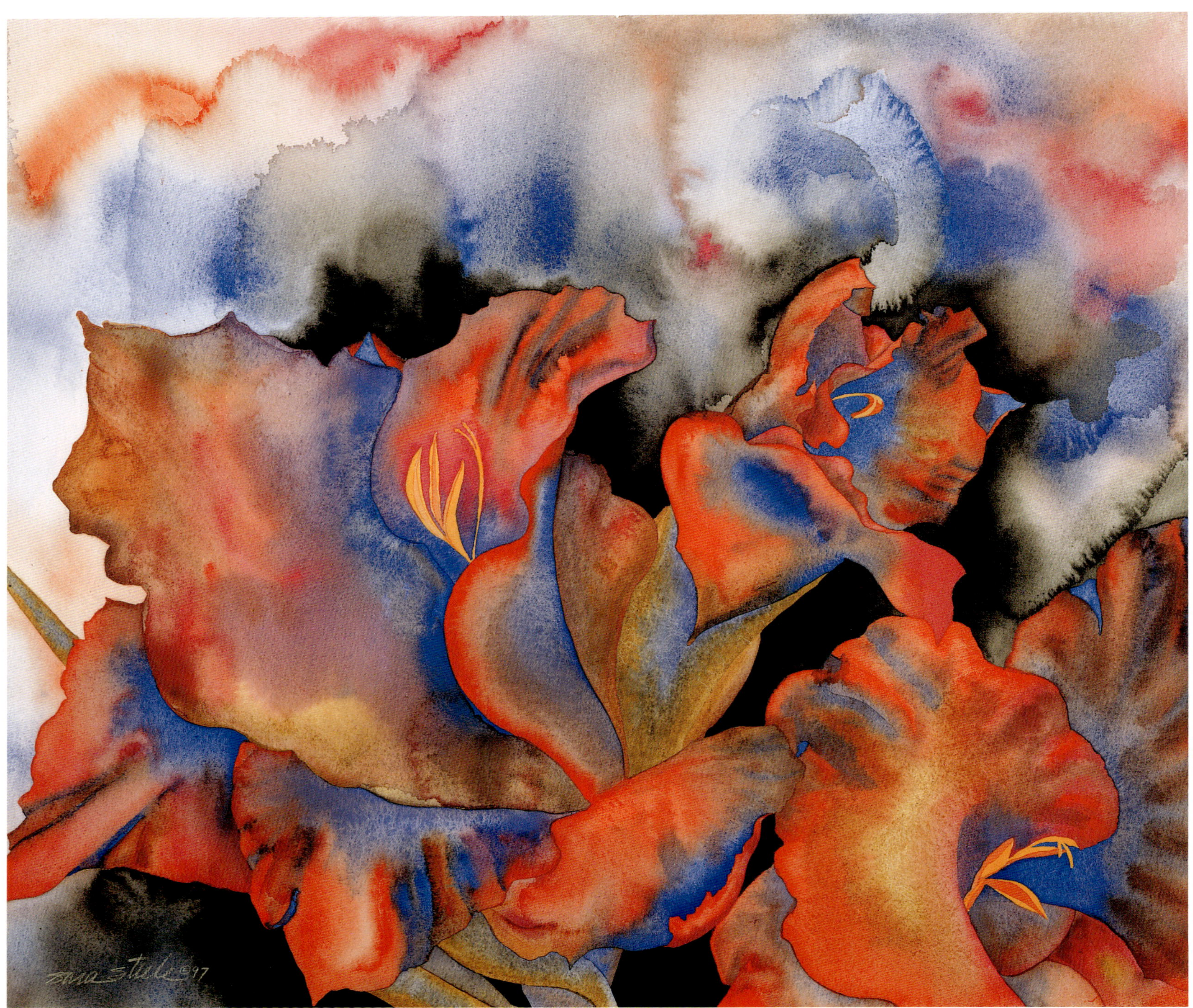

Wild Red Glads, 1997

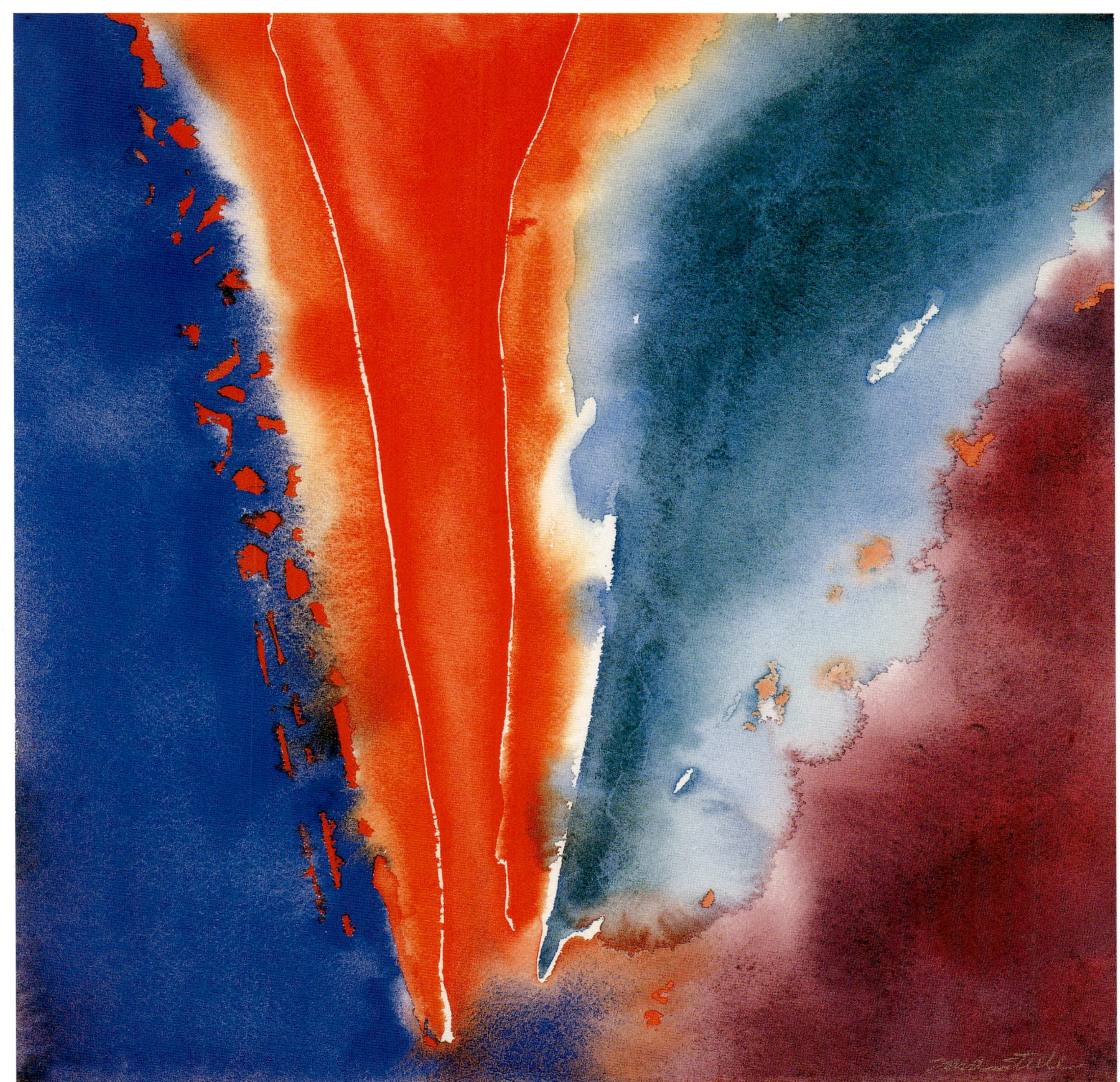

The Point IV,
1998

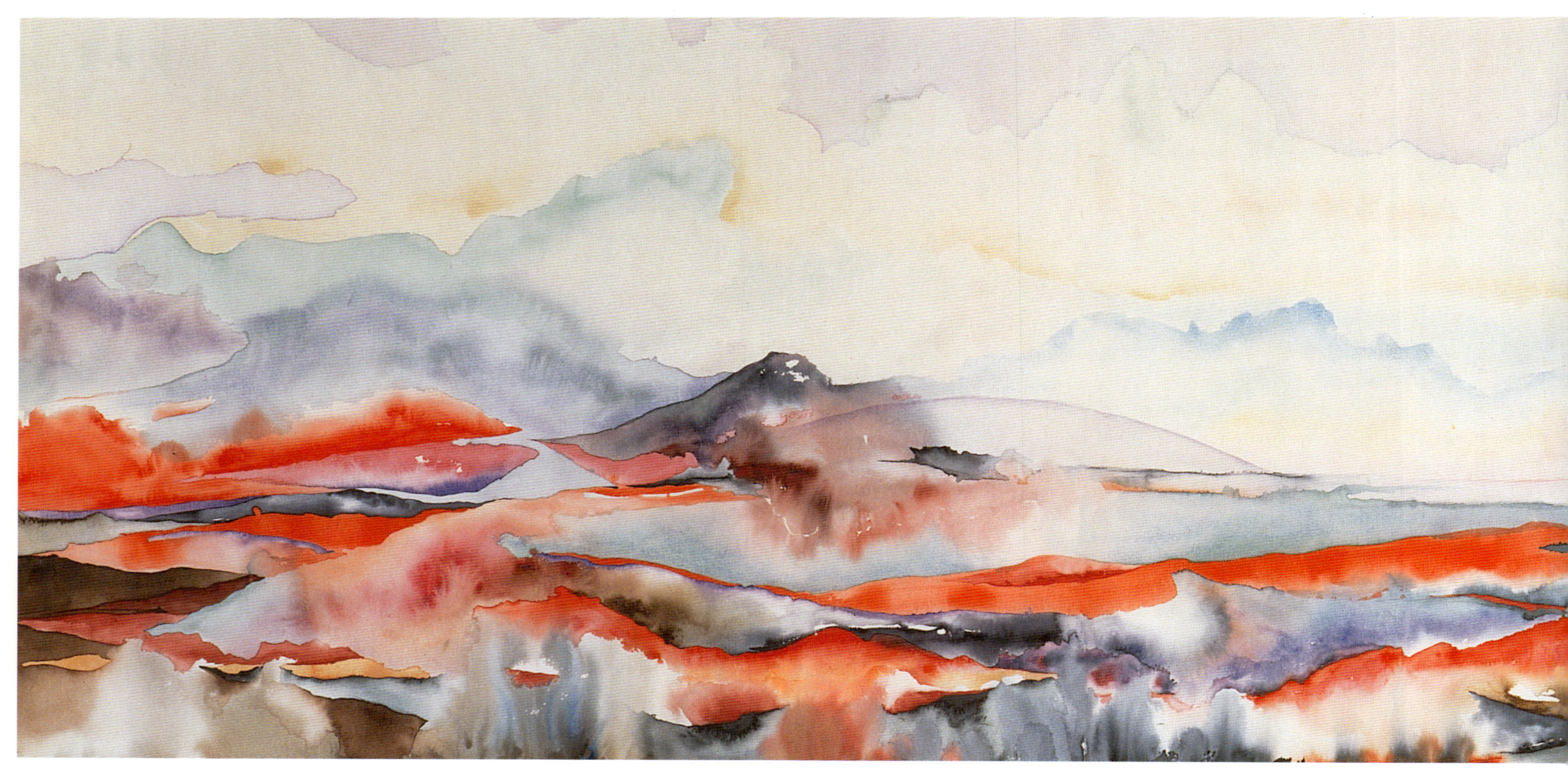

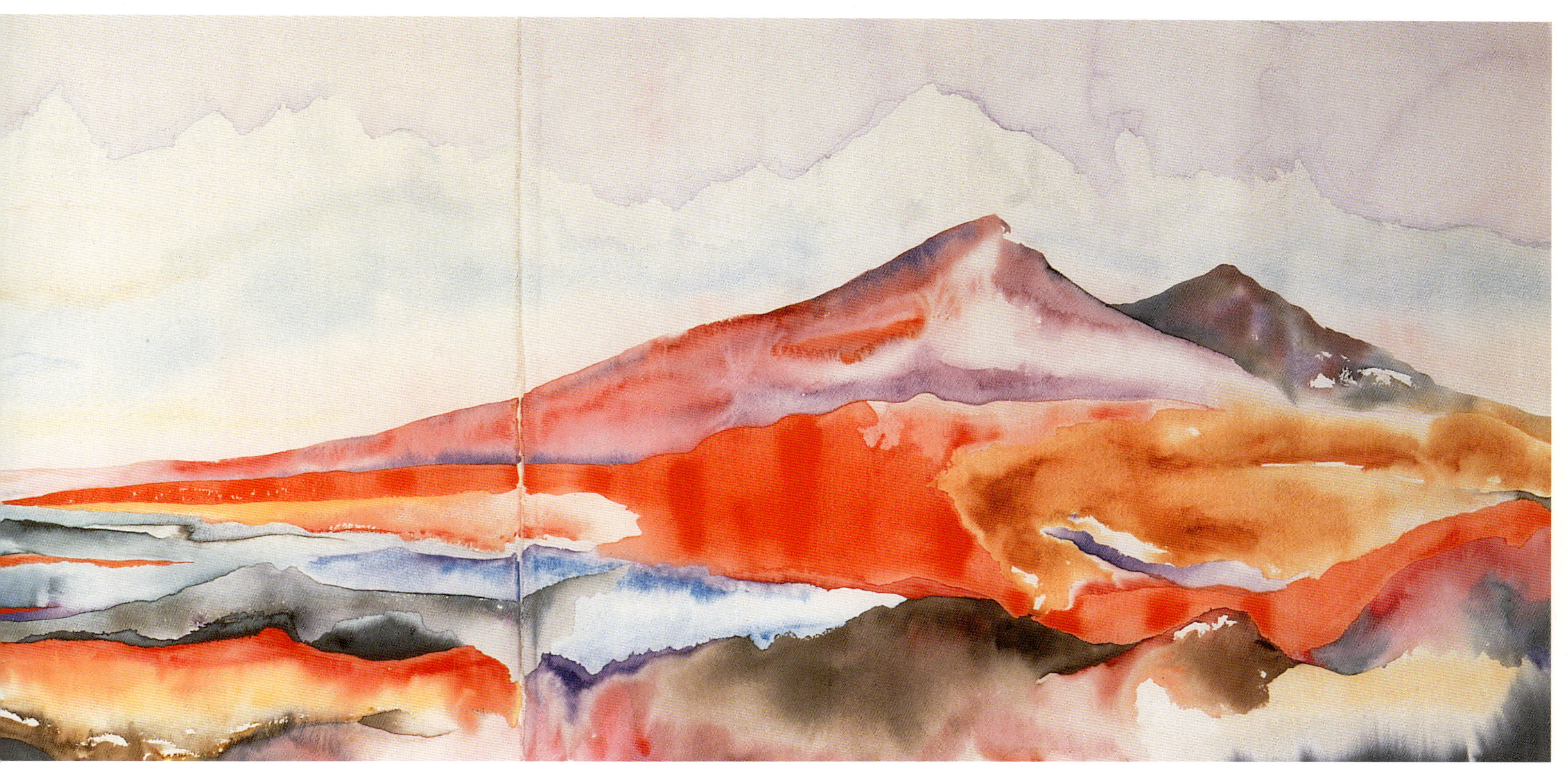

Lava Flow/Alaska, 1986

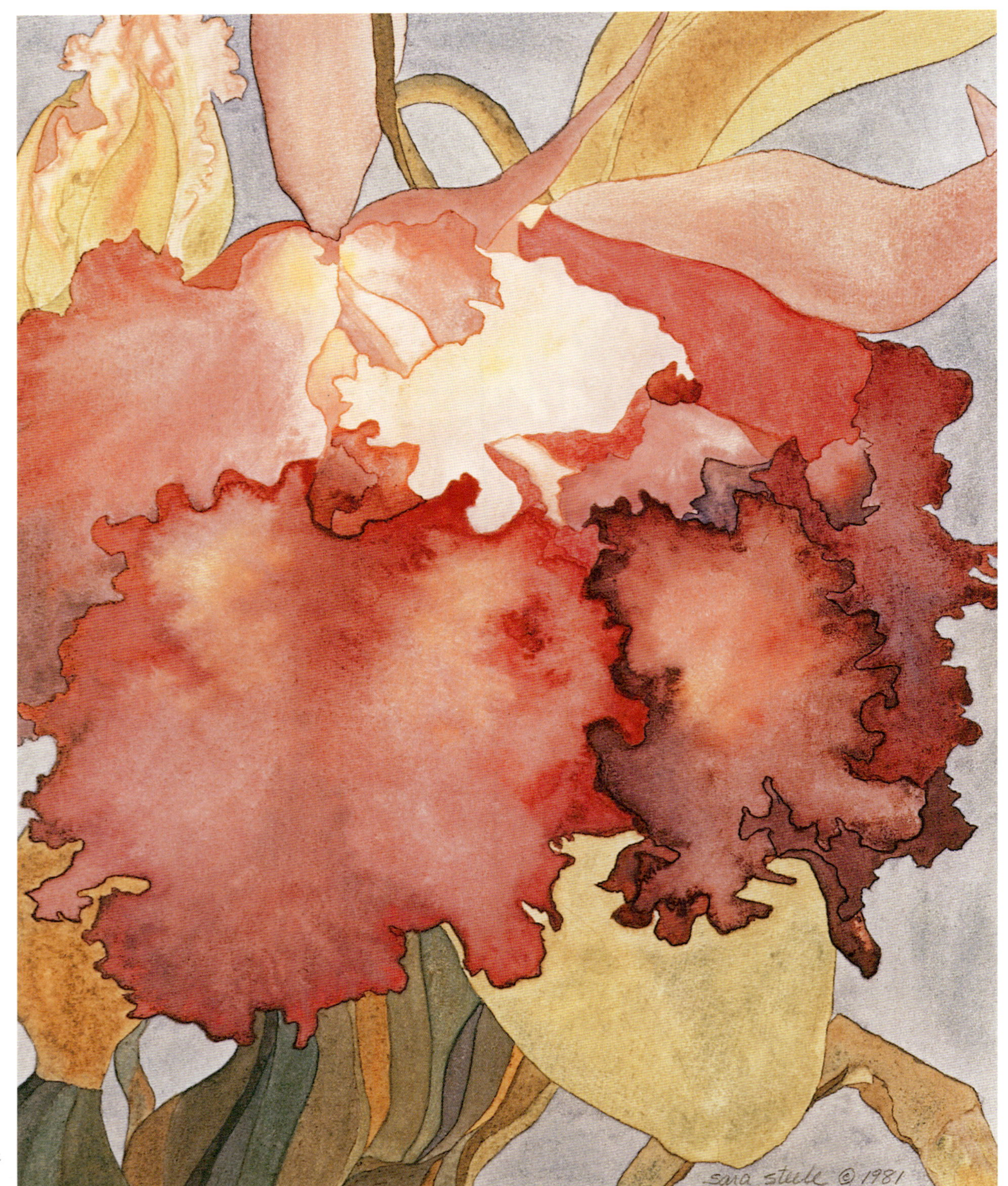

Brassolaeliocattleya
Cliftonia 'Magnifica', 1981

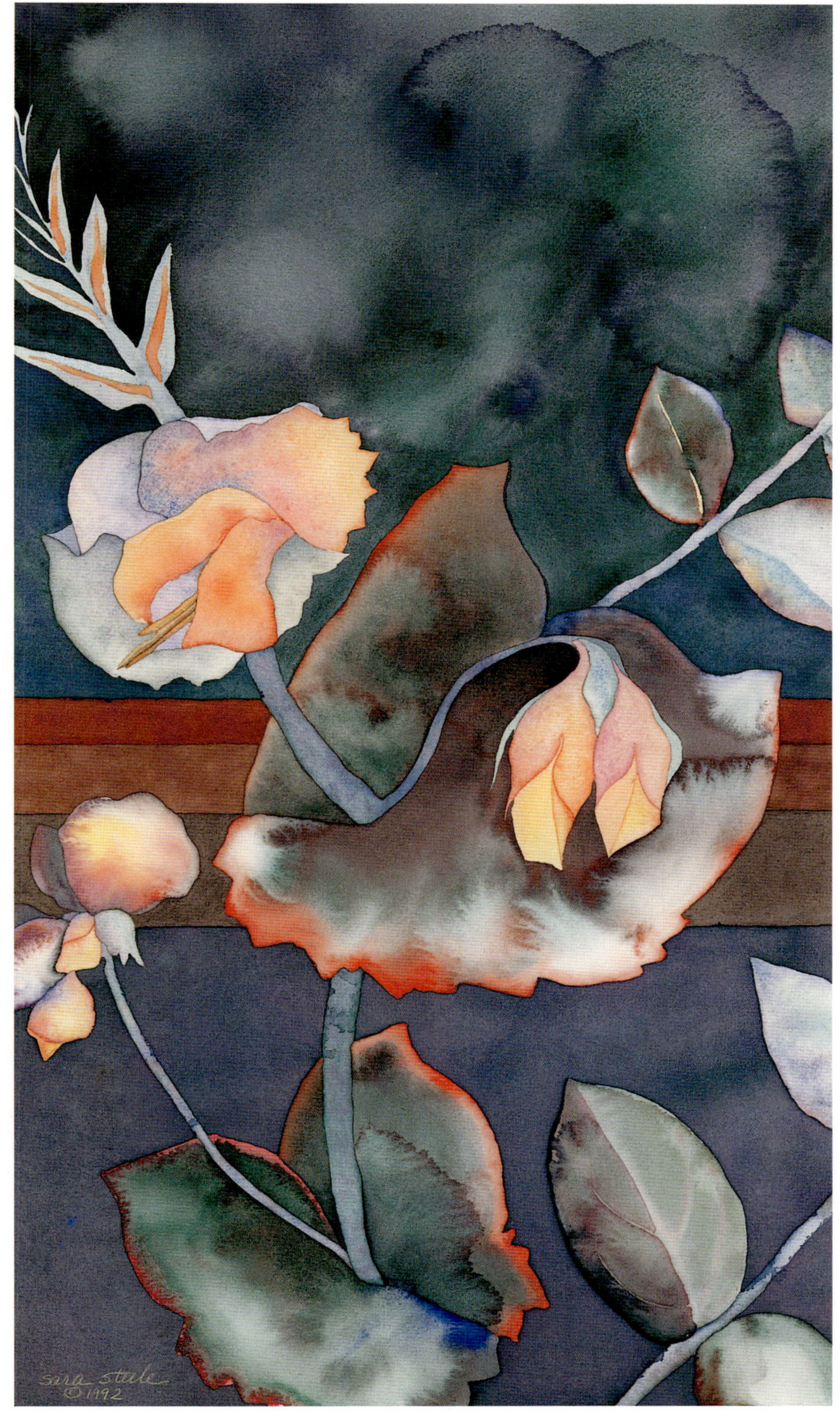

Tornado Sweet Pea, 1992

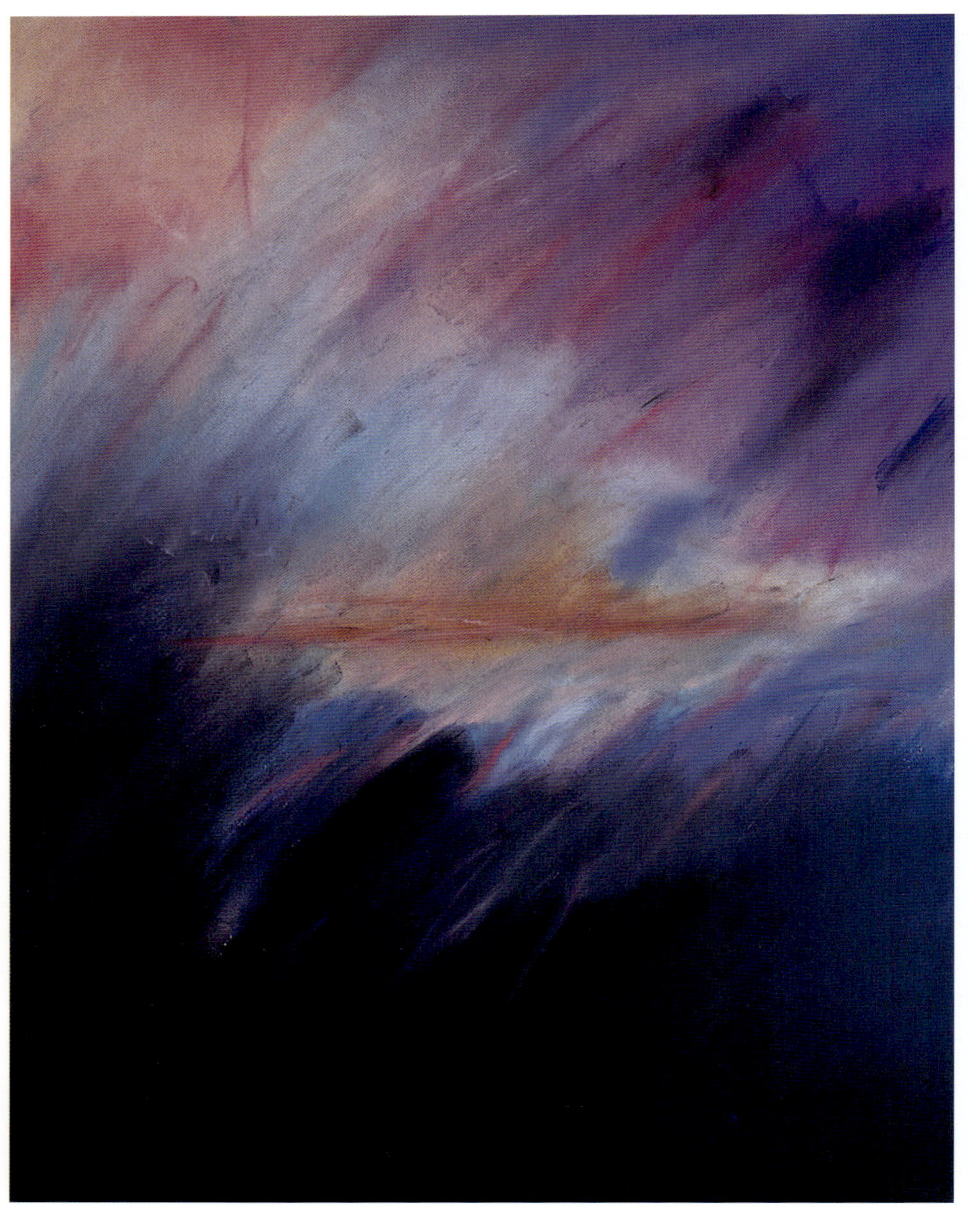

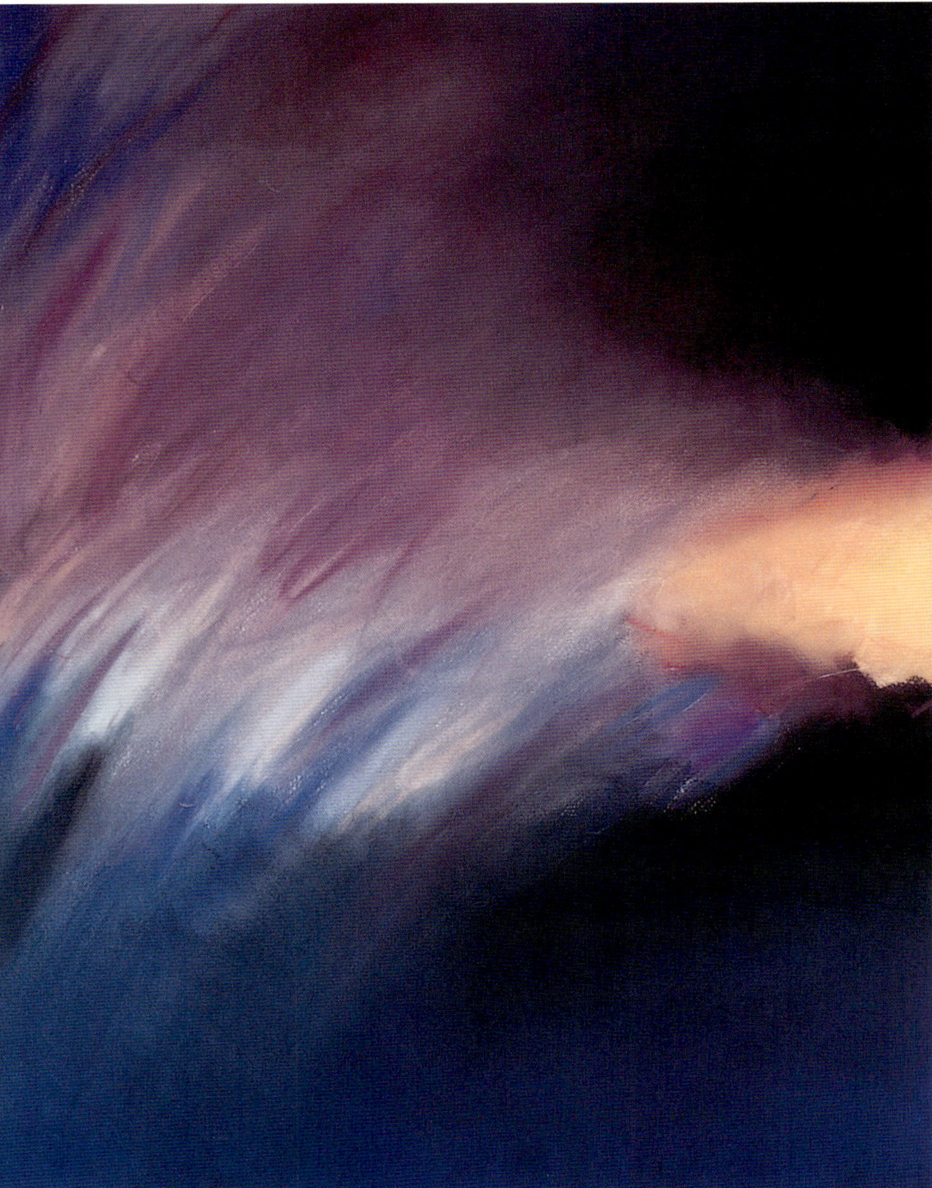

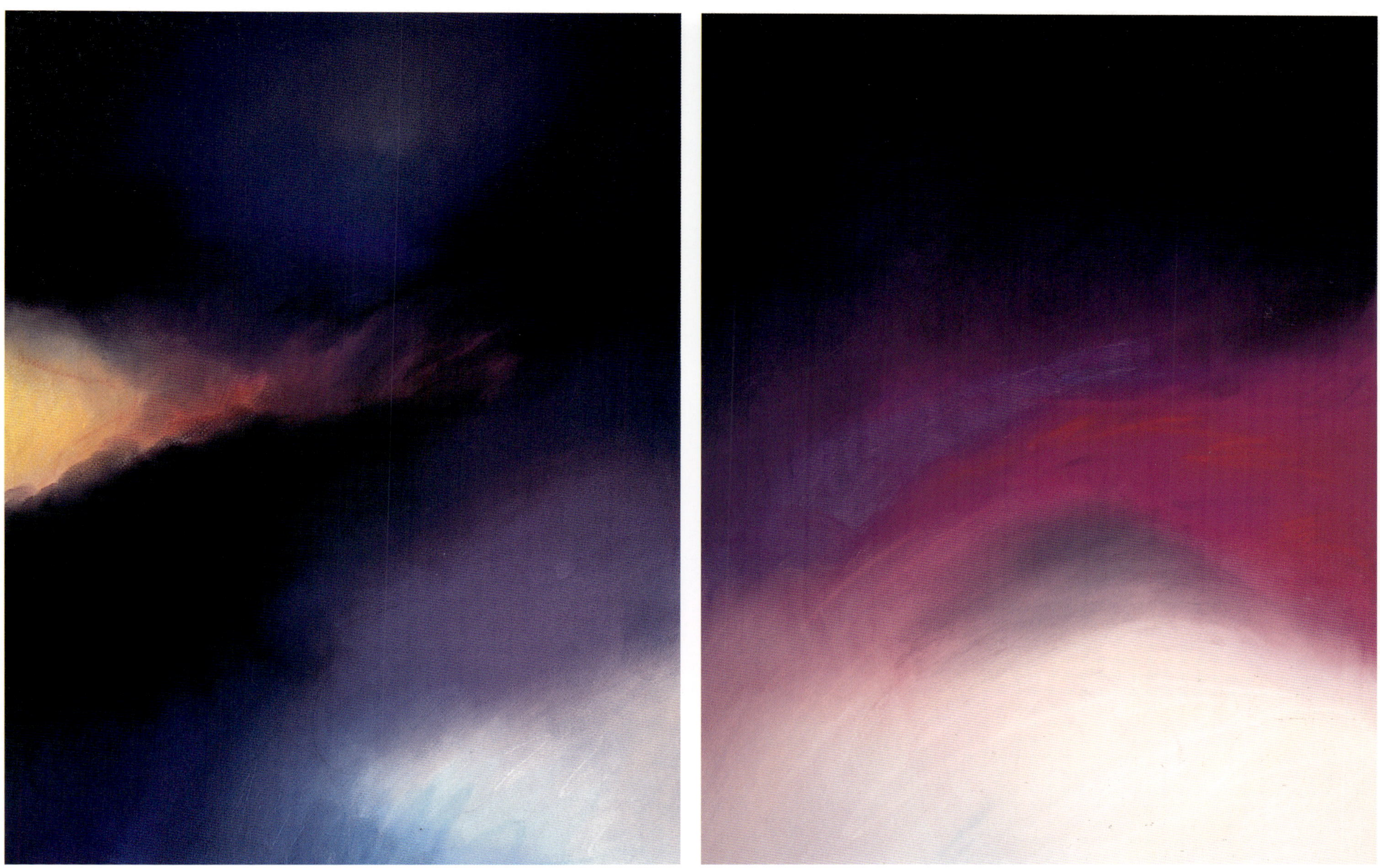

The Forces of Attraction, 1984

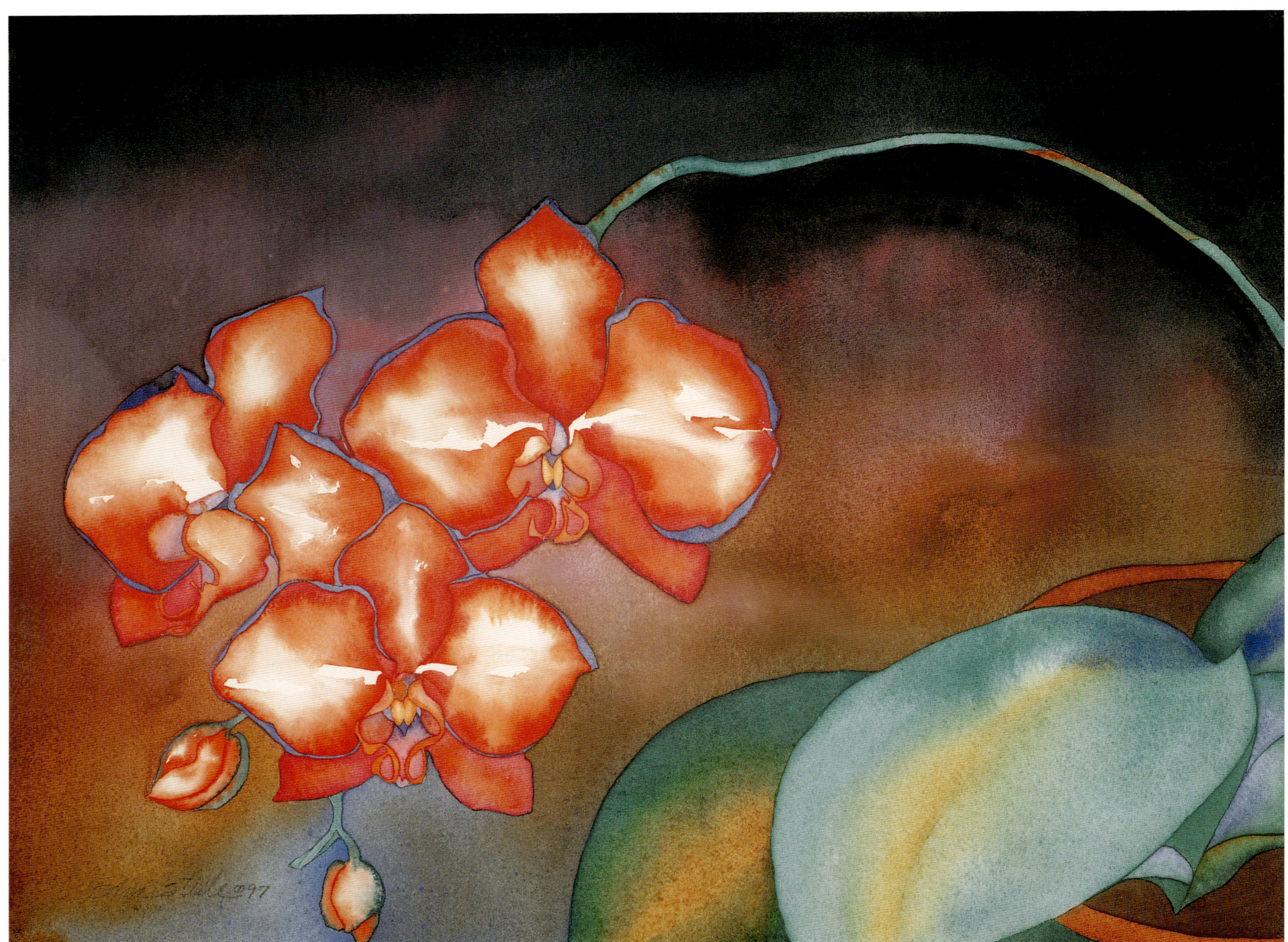

Stormy Phalaenopsis, 1997

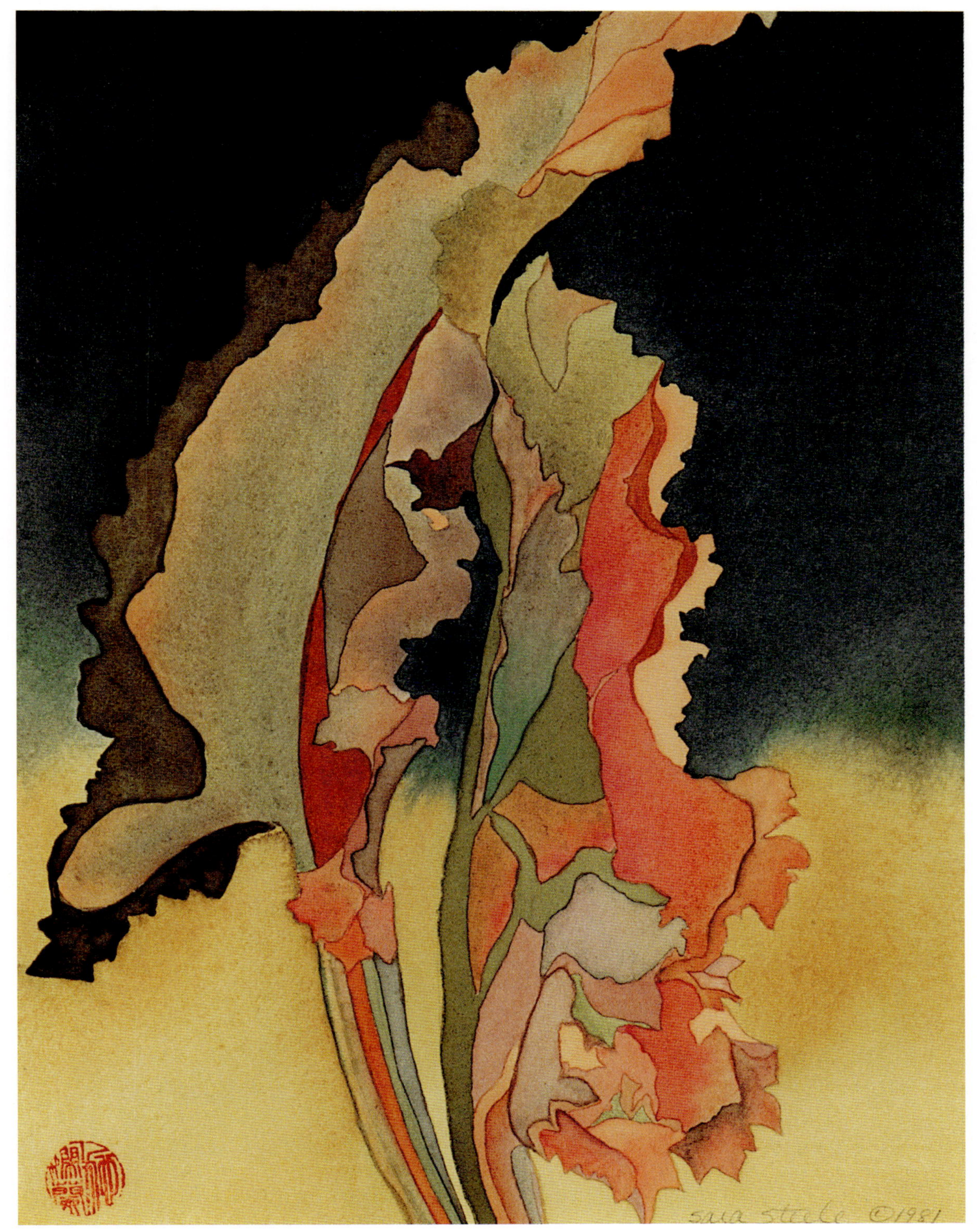

May Storm in Johnstown, 1981

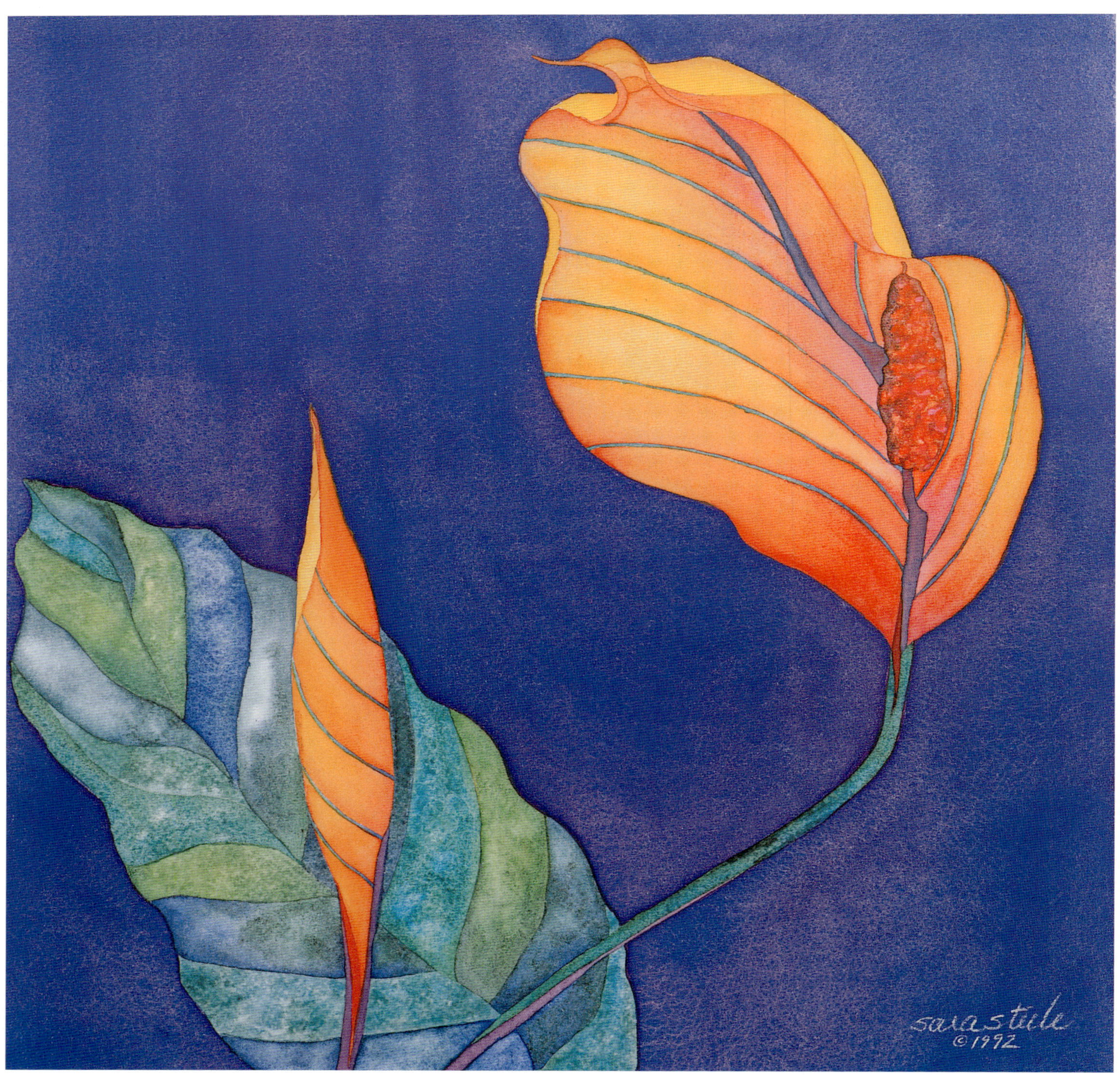

Spathiphyllum, 1992

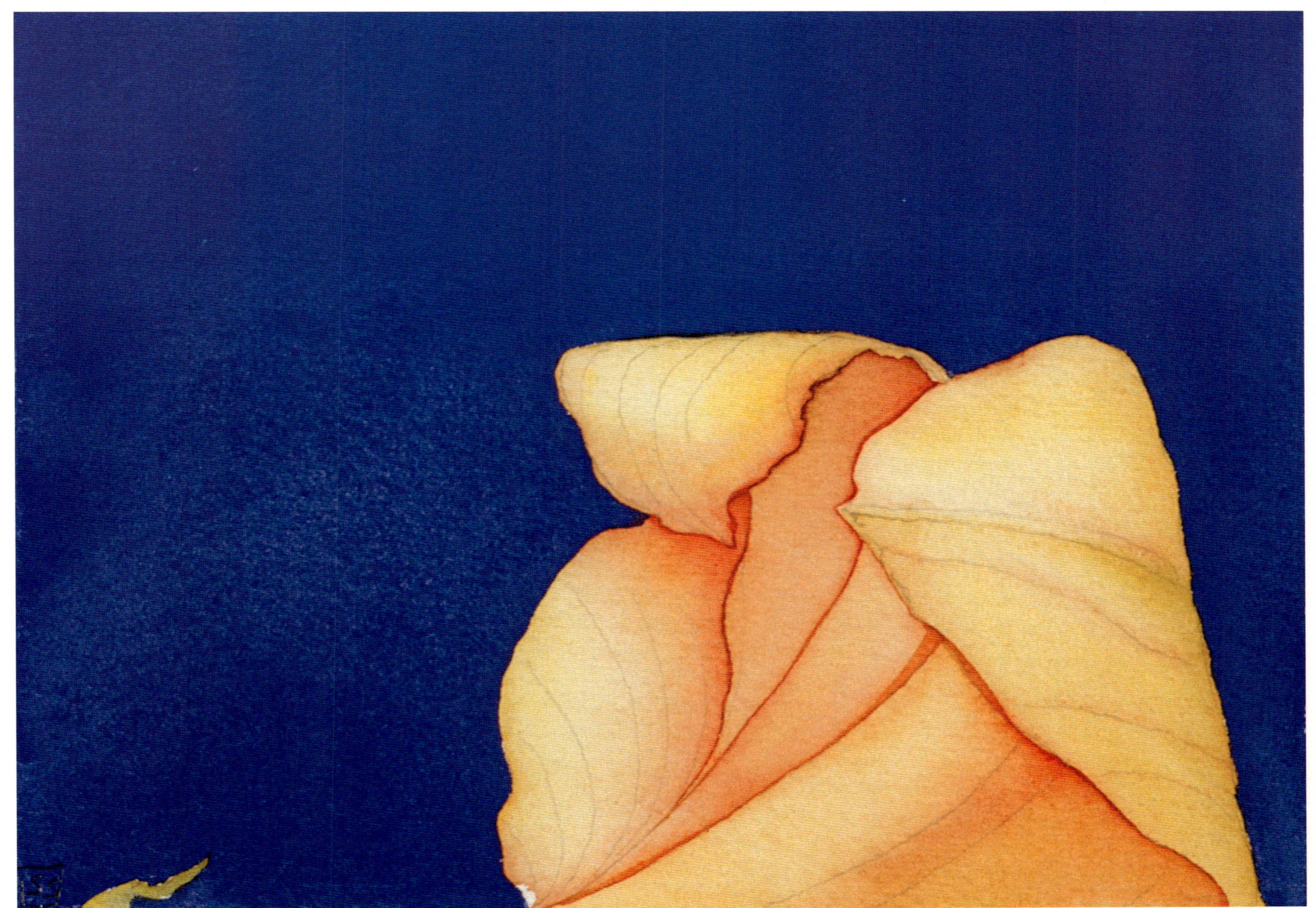

Lily Petals (1), 2002

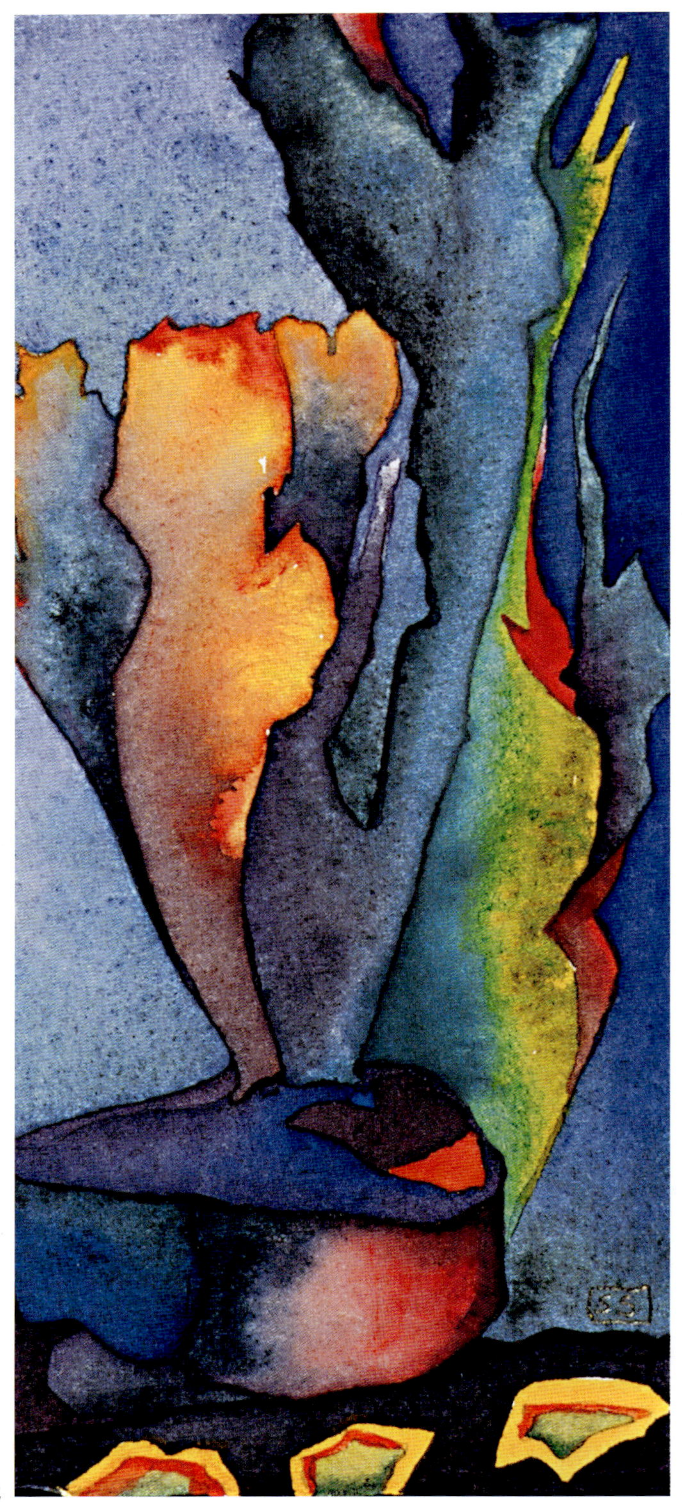

Coral, 2002

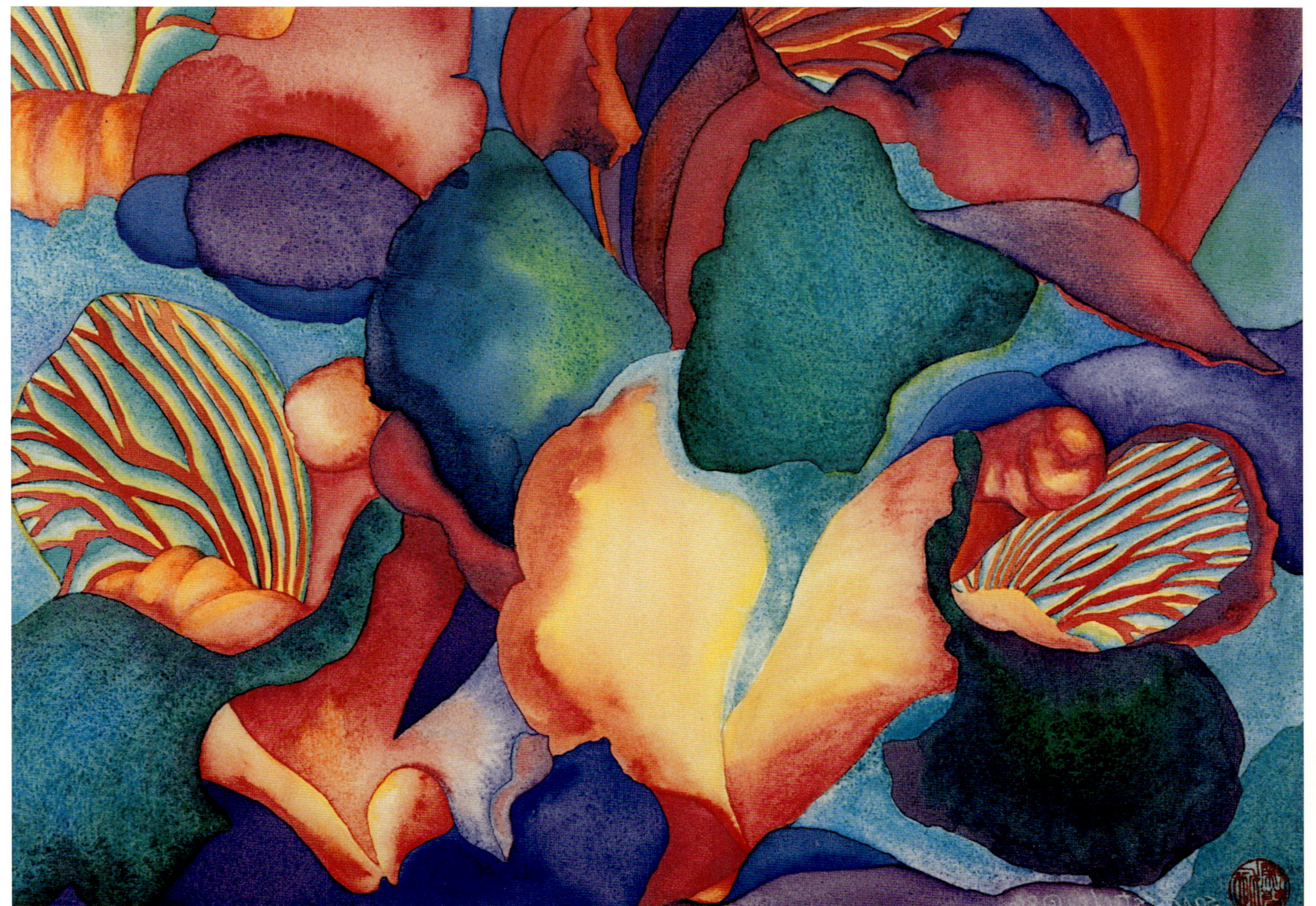

Bioluminescence, 1986

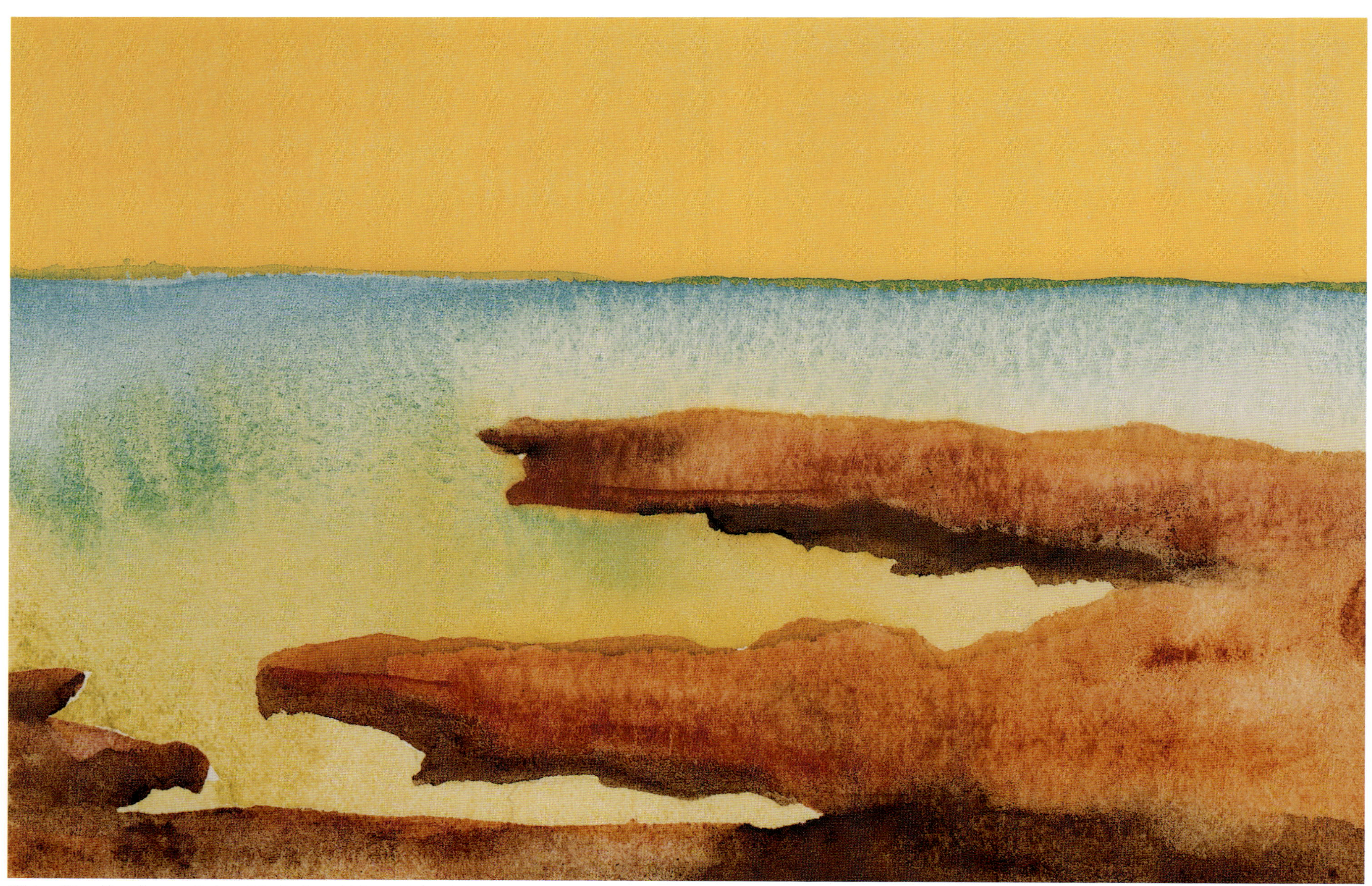

Hawai'ian Landscape: Poipu (Cadmium Yellow Light Sky), 1998

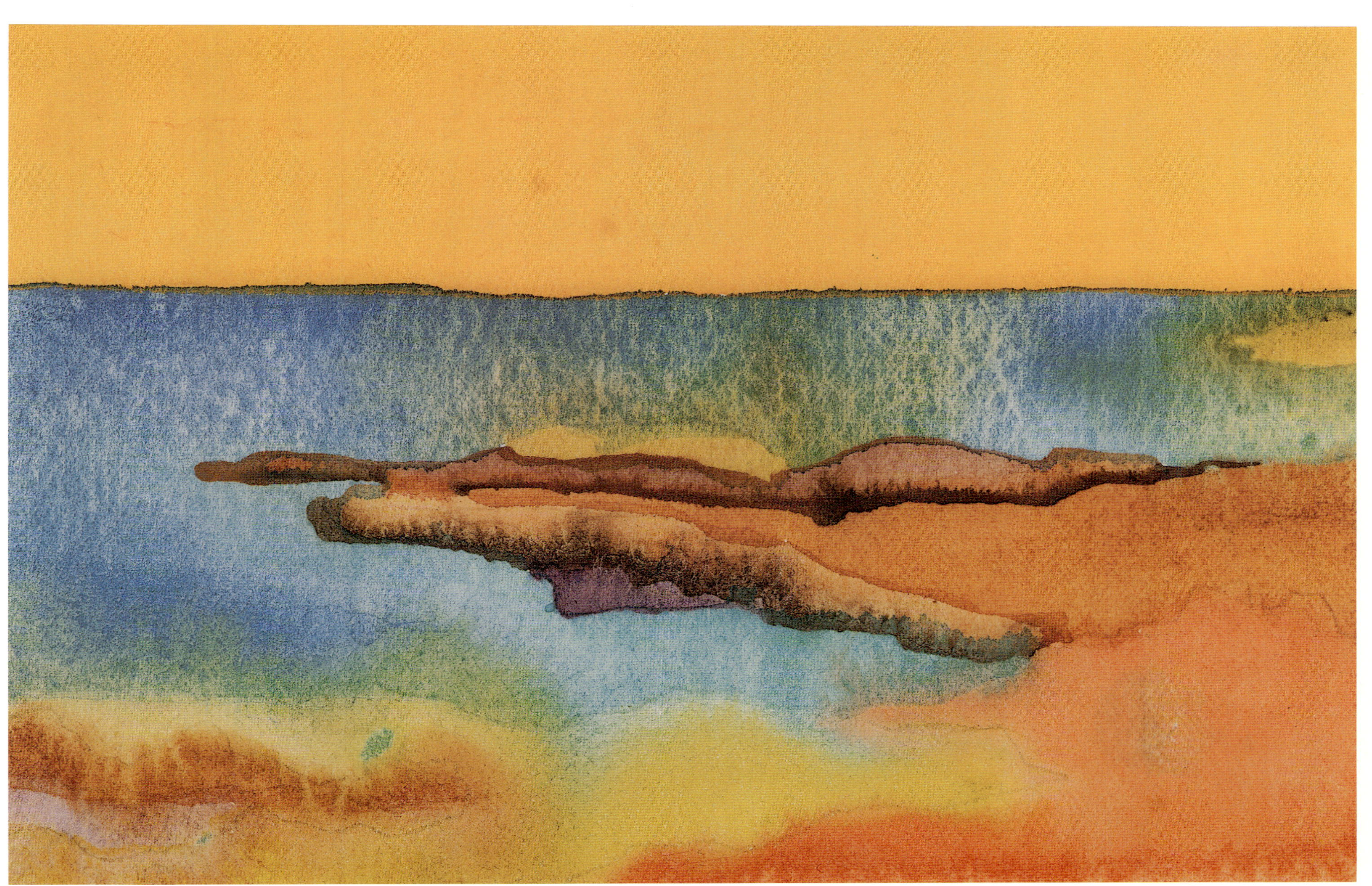

Hawai'ian Landscape: Poipu (Cadmium Yellow Deep Sky), 1998

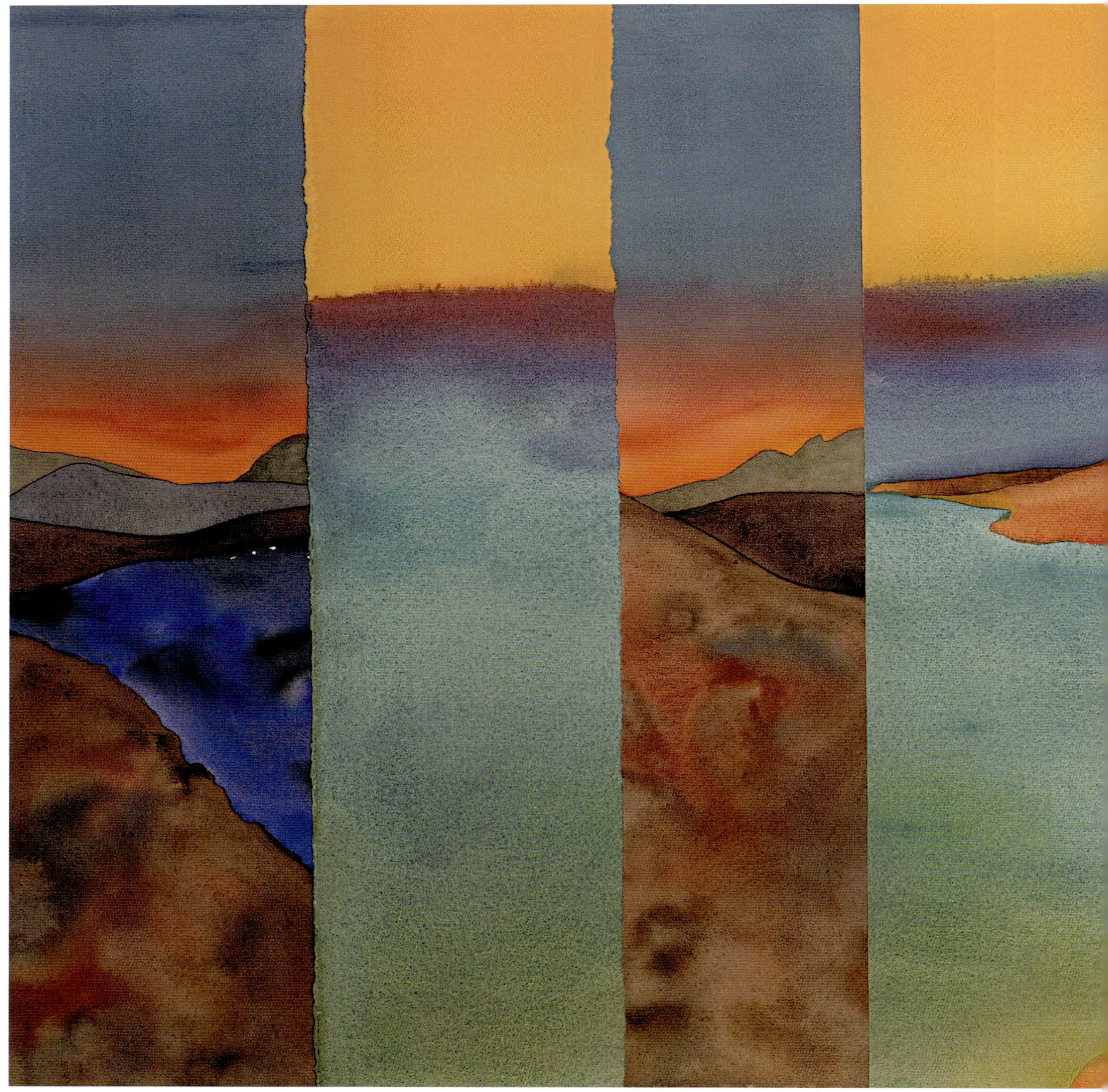

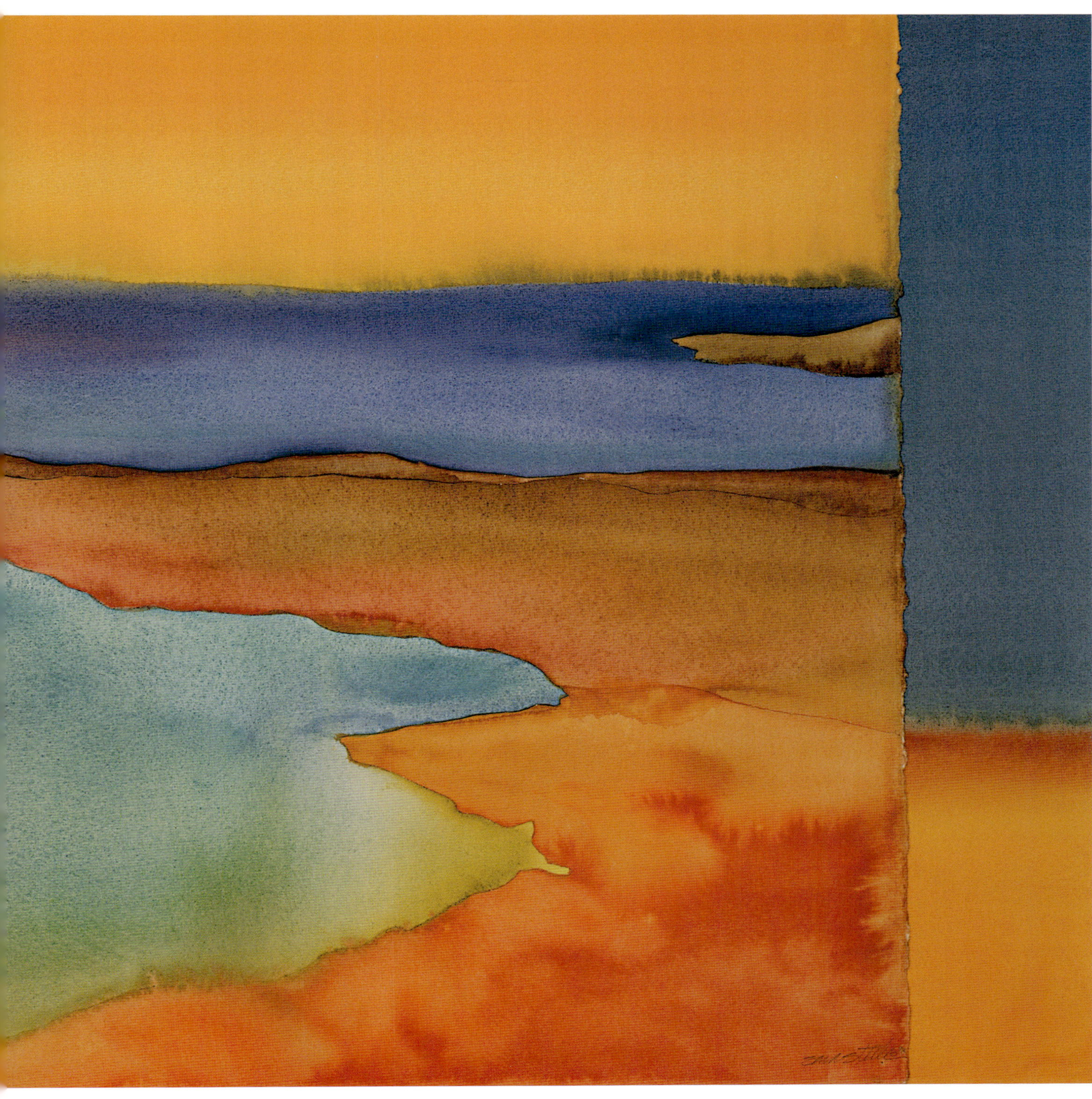

Pacific Pieces, 1998

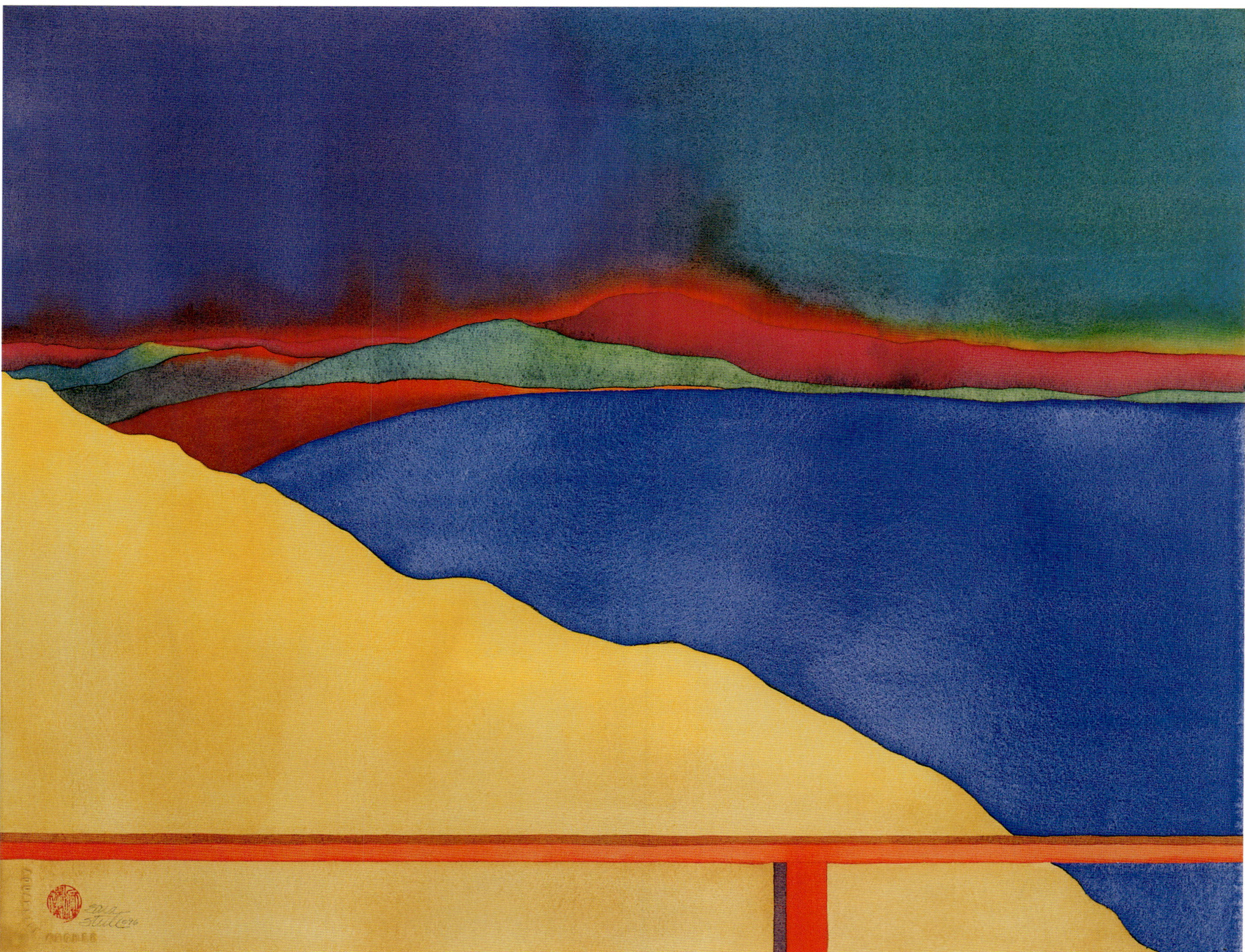

From Big Rock, 1996

木

Wood

Gestating in the dark depths of winter, the seeds of new life begin to stir. Roots thread their way into the moist, replenished Earth, nourishing tender shoots that break though the surface of the soil, growing toward the light. Spring has arrived, and the life that existed within Water's translucent realm begins to coalesce and grow, gaining structure and form. As the sap rises, the growing Wood element of spring provides the organic, living framework upon which life thrives and moves toward its full blossoming. Buds and butterflies emerge, colors and patterns burst forth, and the upward cycle of the yang movement has begun.

The paintings gathered here explore patterns and structures, a literal emergence of life, as well as the life of emerging ideas. *Sacred Gate* portrays the pelvic bones whose opening allows new life to pass from the womb into the world. *Winged Victory* presents a bold display of life pushing up through death and decay and bursting out of the confines of former structures. *Chemistry of Feeling* depicts the bones of the skull, which encase the network of neurotransmitters, making possible the interaction of physiological and chemical structures that enable human emotional experience. *Amish Quilt* is a colorful exploration into the highly complex, dancing geometry of a kaleidoscope.

In this collection too is the painting *Canary in a Coal Mine*, based on Sara's nightmare imagining a devastated city. This image is an illustration and a warning of what can occur when the element of Wood is out of balance. When structure and progress are not united with justice and compassion, the imbalance expresses itself in anger and rage, resulting in devastation.

The floral paintings in this section emphasize the upward reaching of stalks and blossoms, and the collection concludes with *Riots of Spring*, an explosion of growth and beauty that leads to the full flowering of summer.

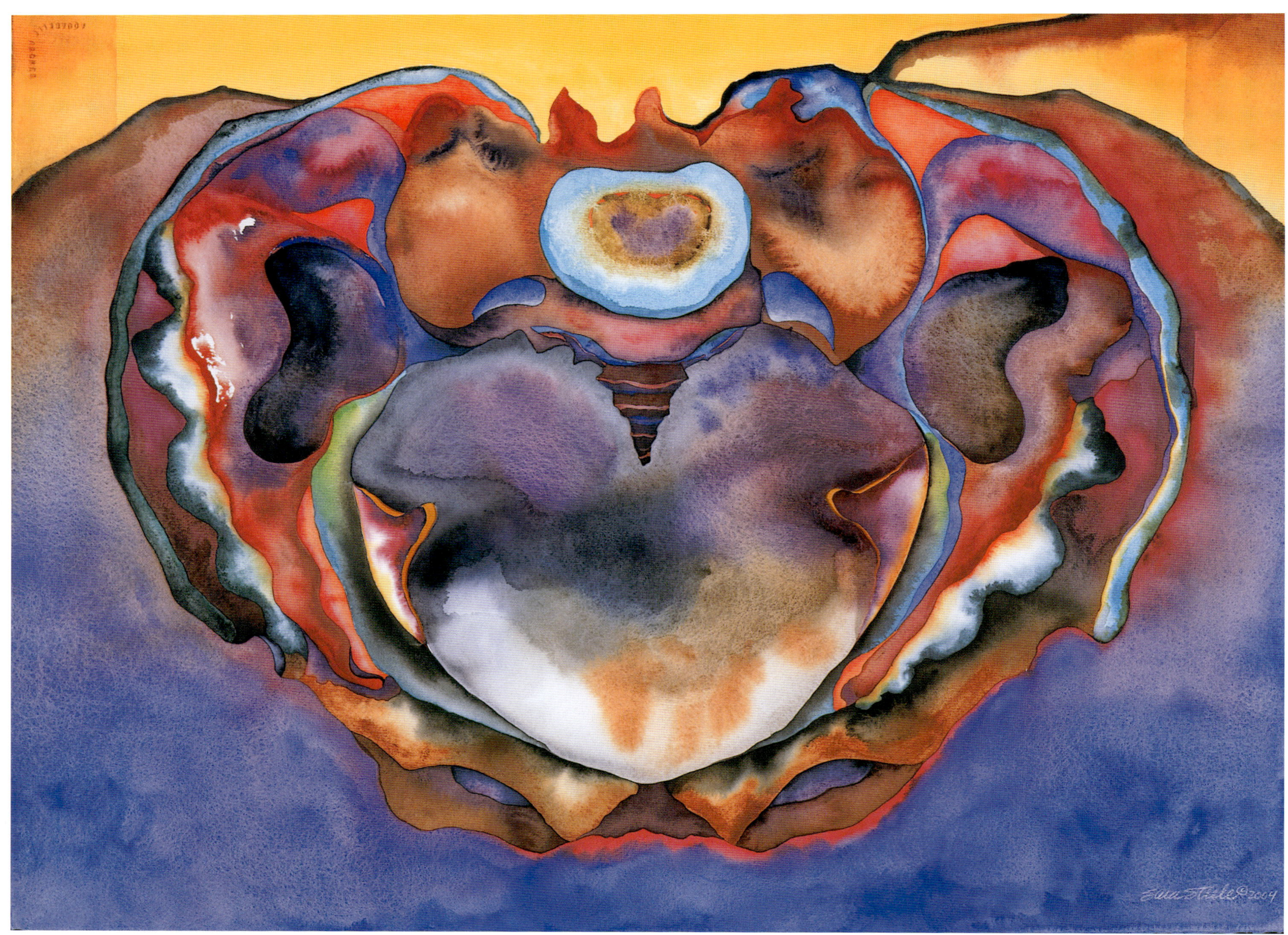

Sacred Gate, 2004

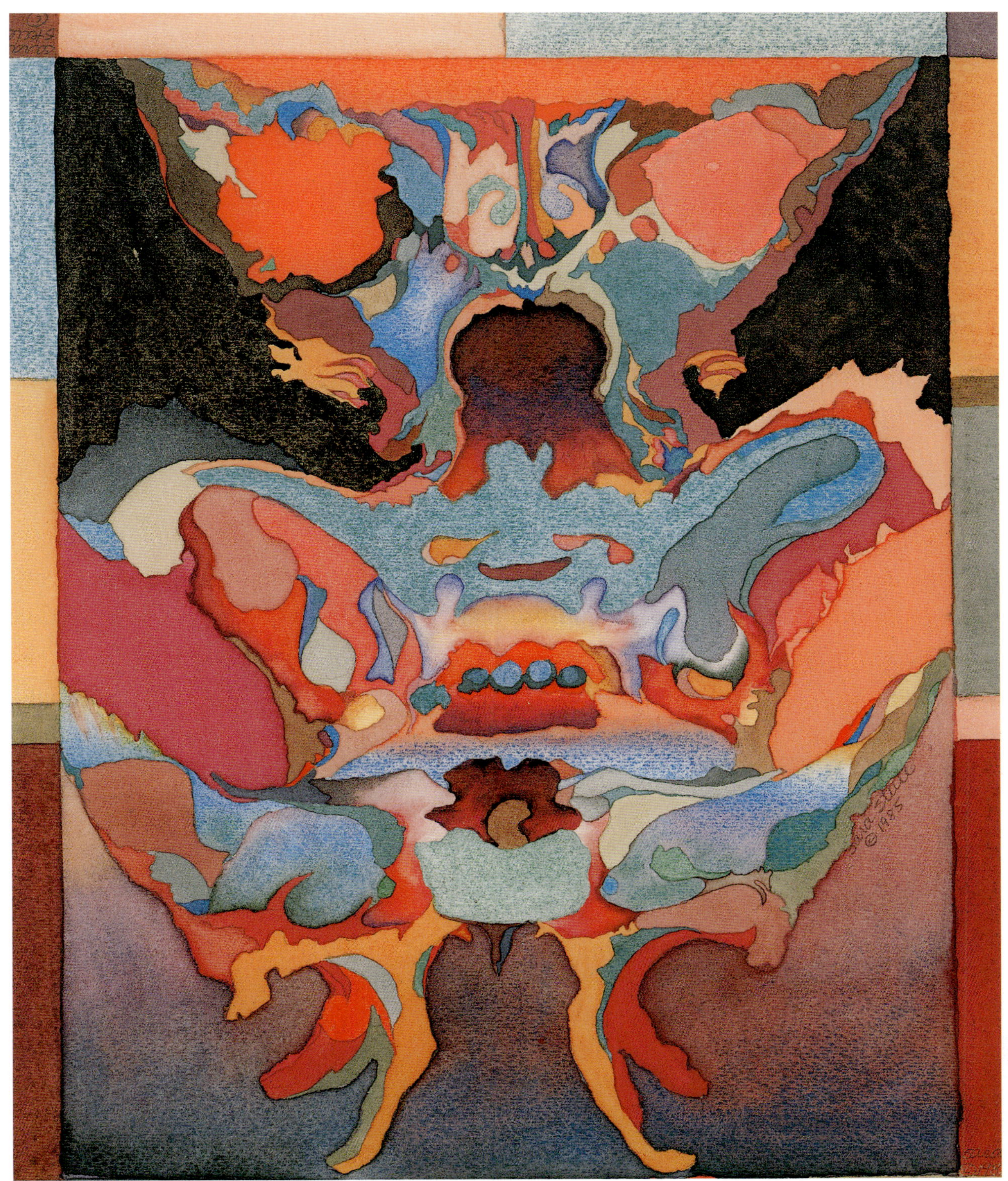

Sphoenix (Sphenoid Totem), 1985

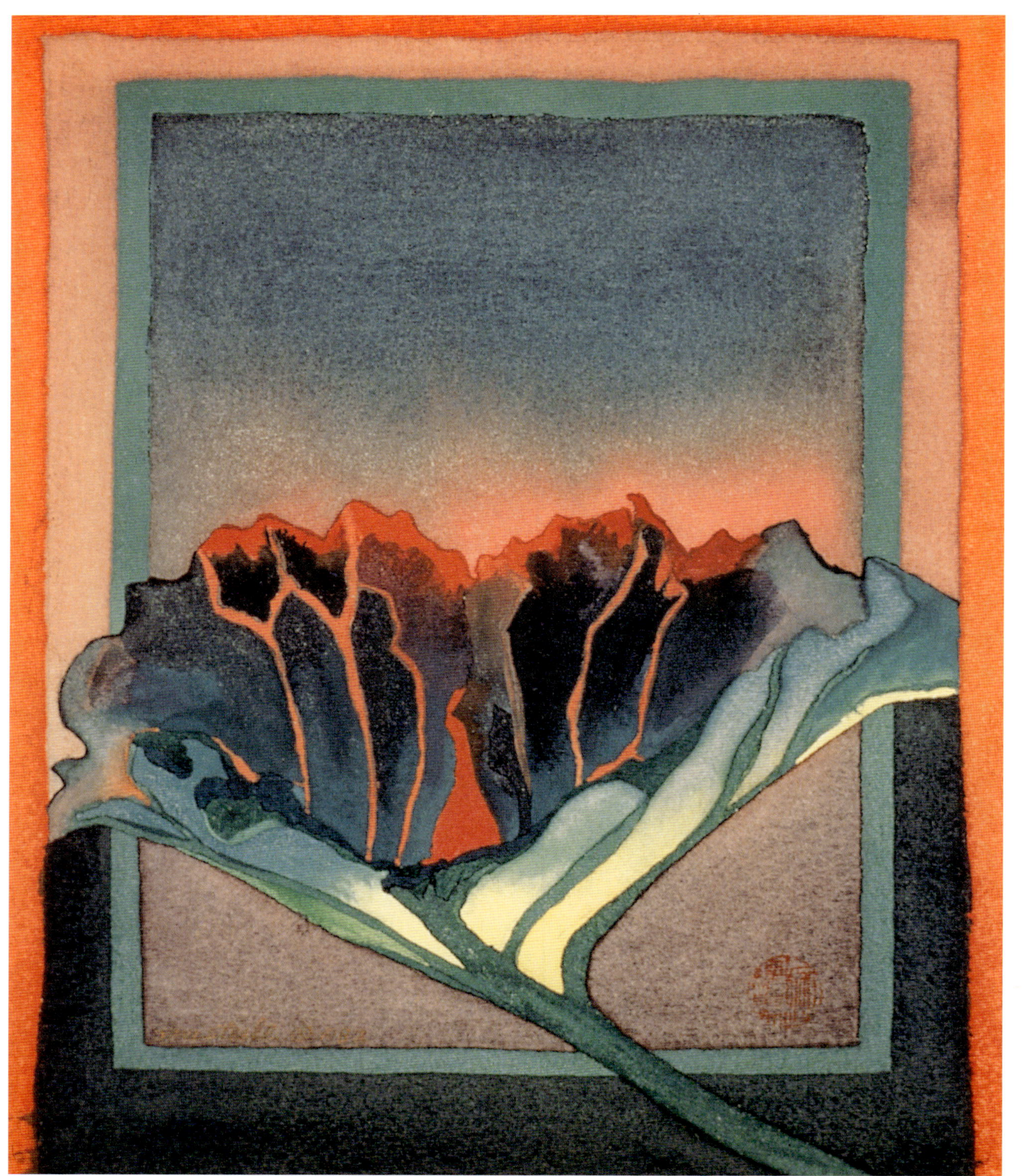

Winged Victory, 1986

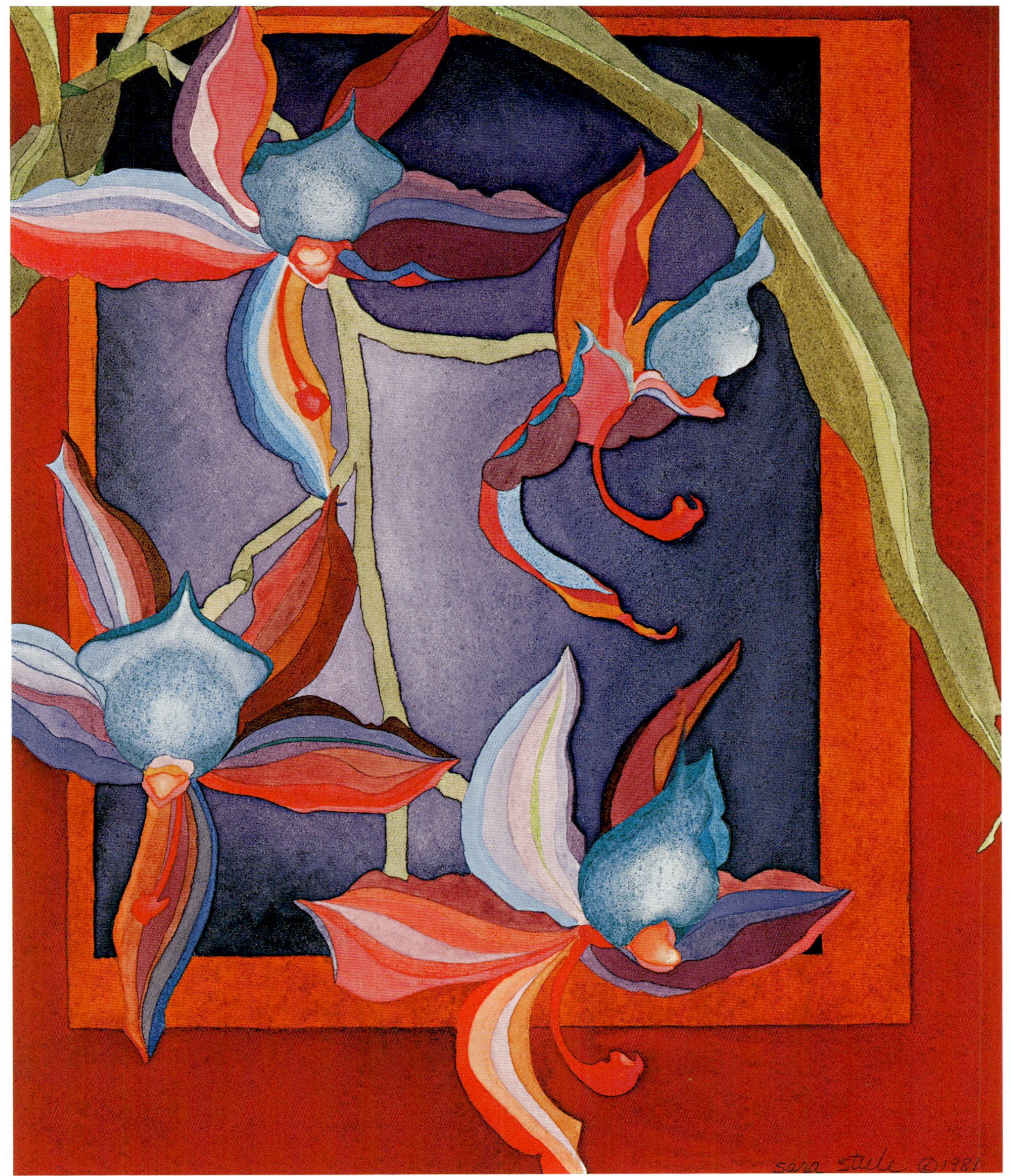

Cynoches chlorichilorii, 1981

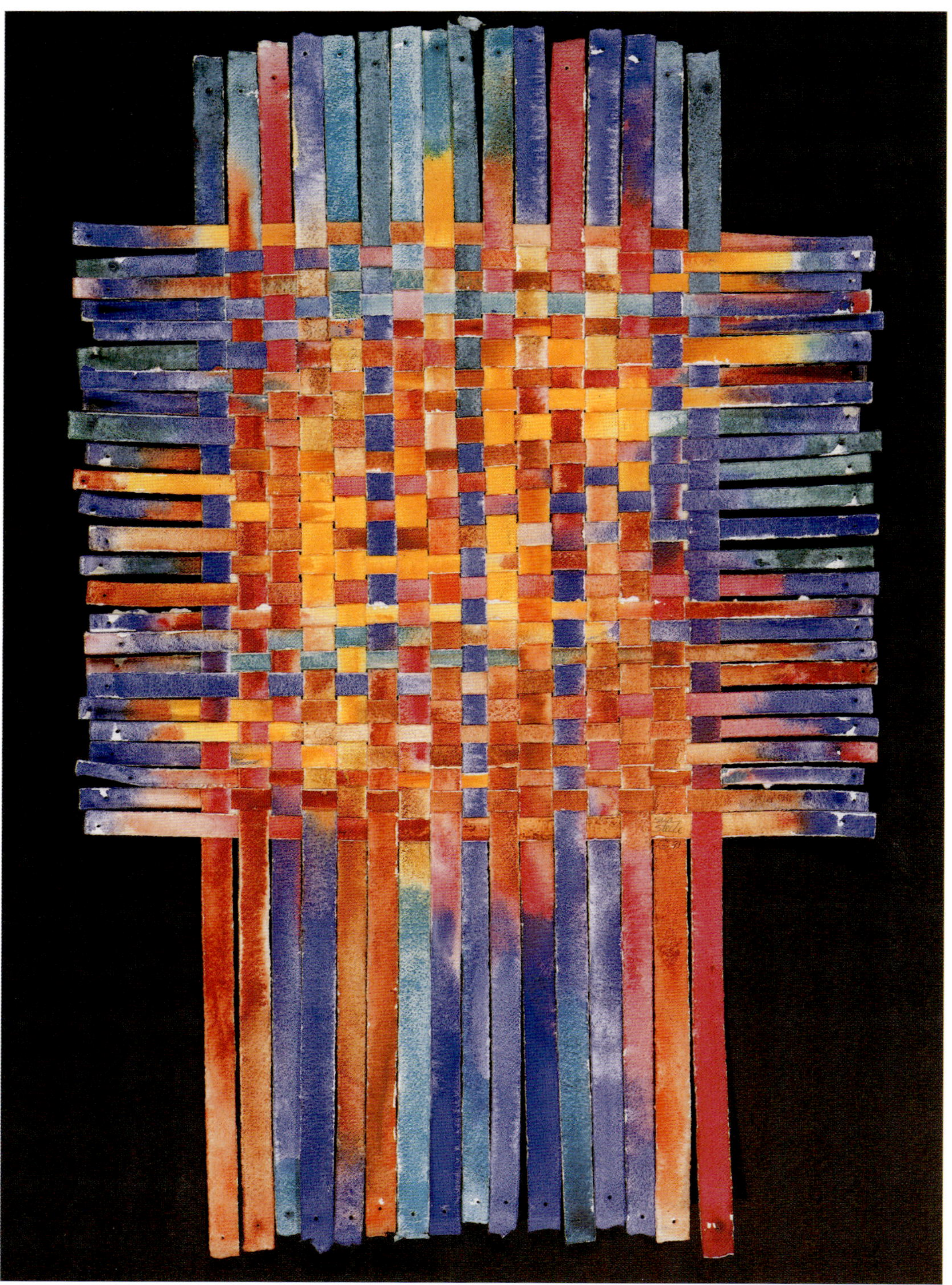

Heritage Ceramics, 1991

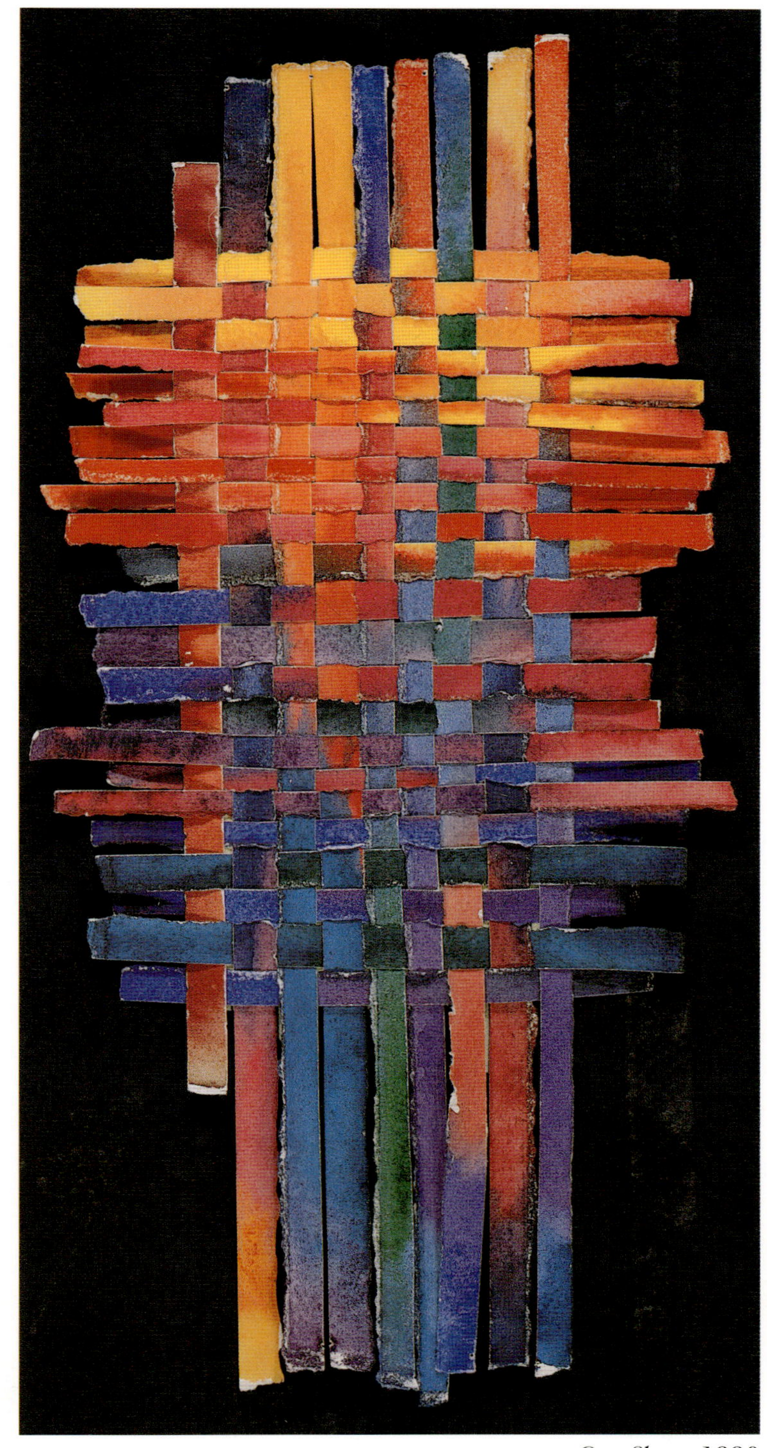

One Short, 1990

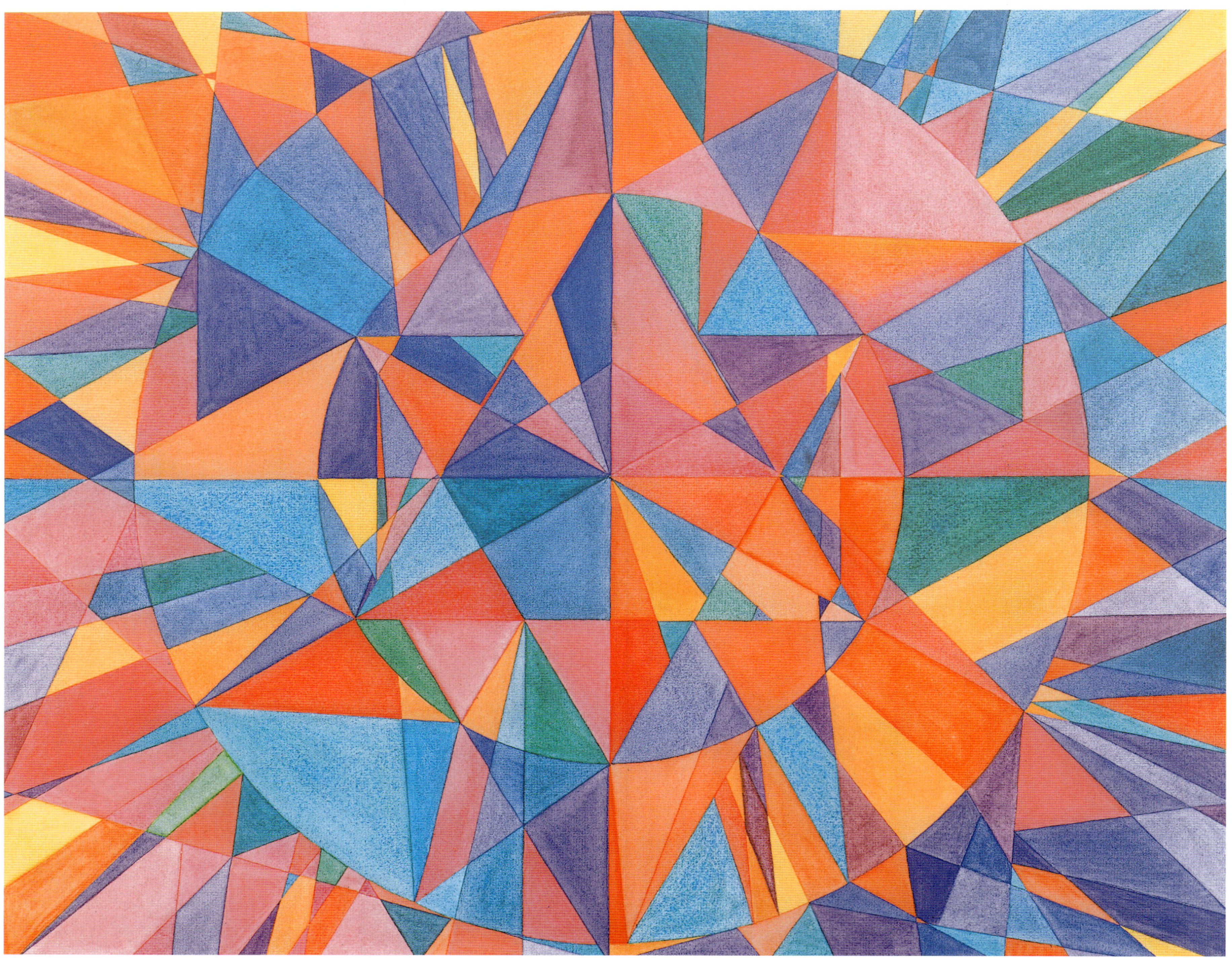

Song of Four/Amish Quilt, 1988

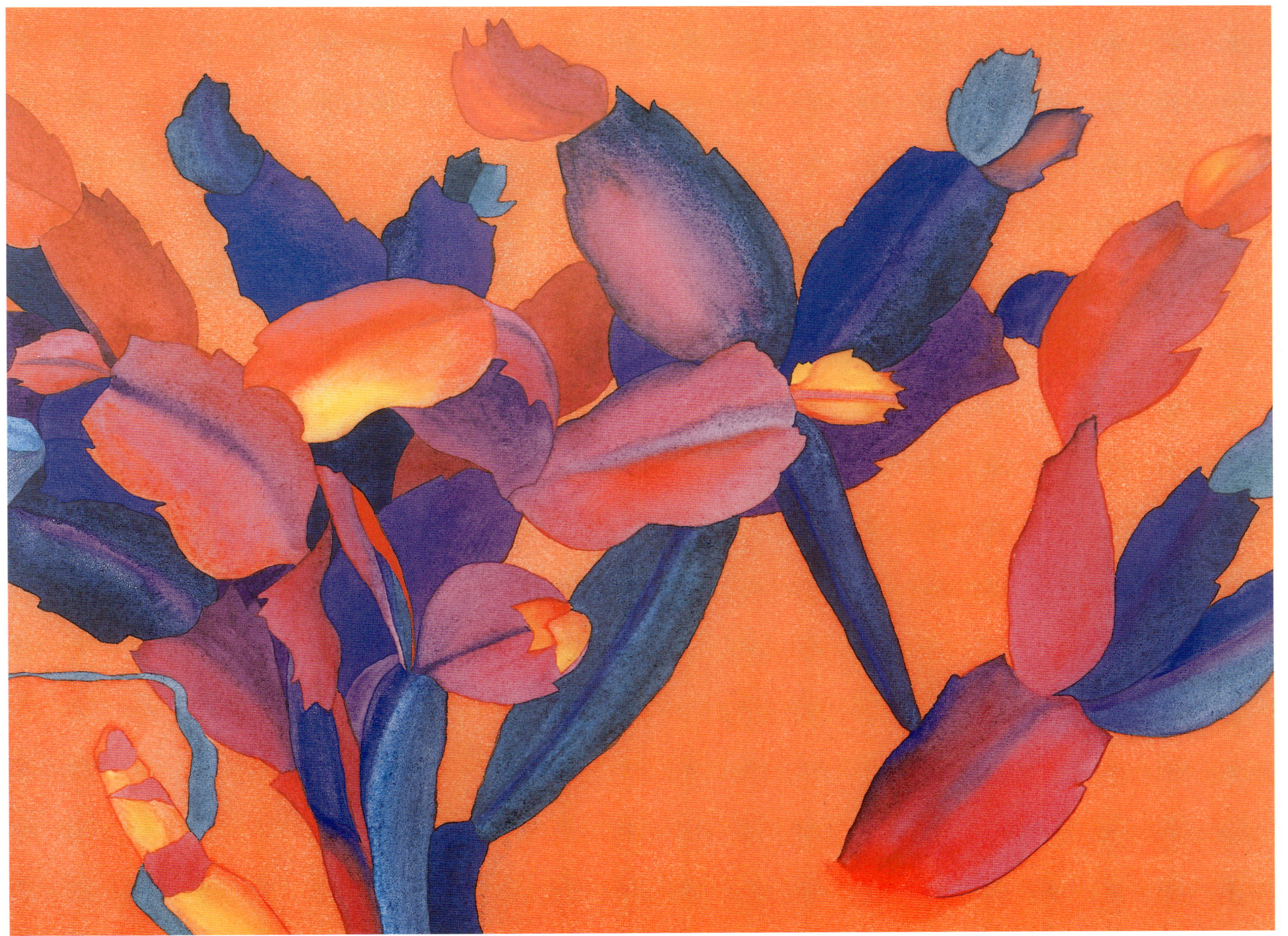

XYGO, 1983

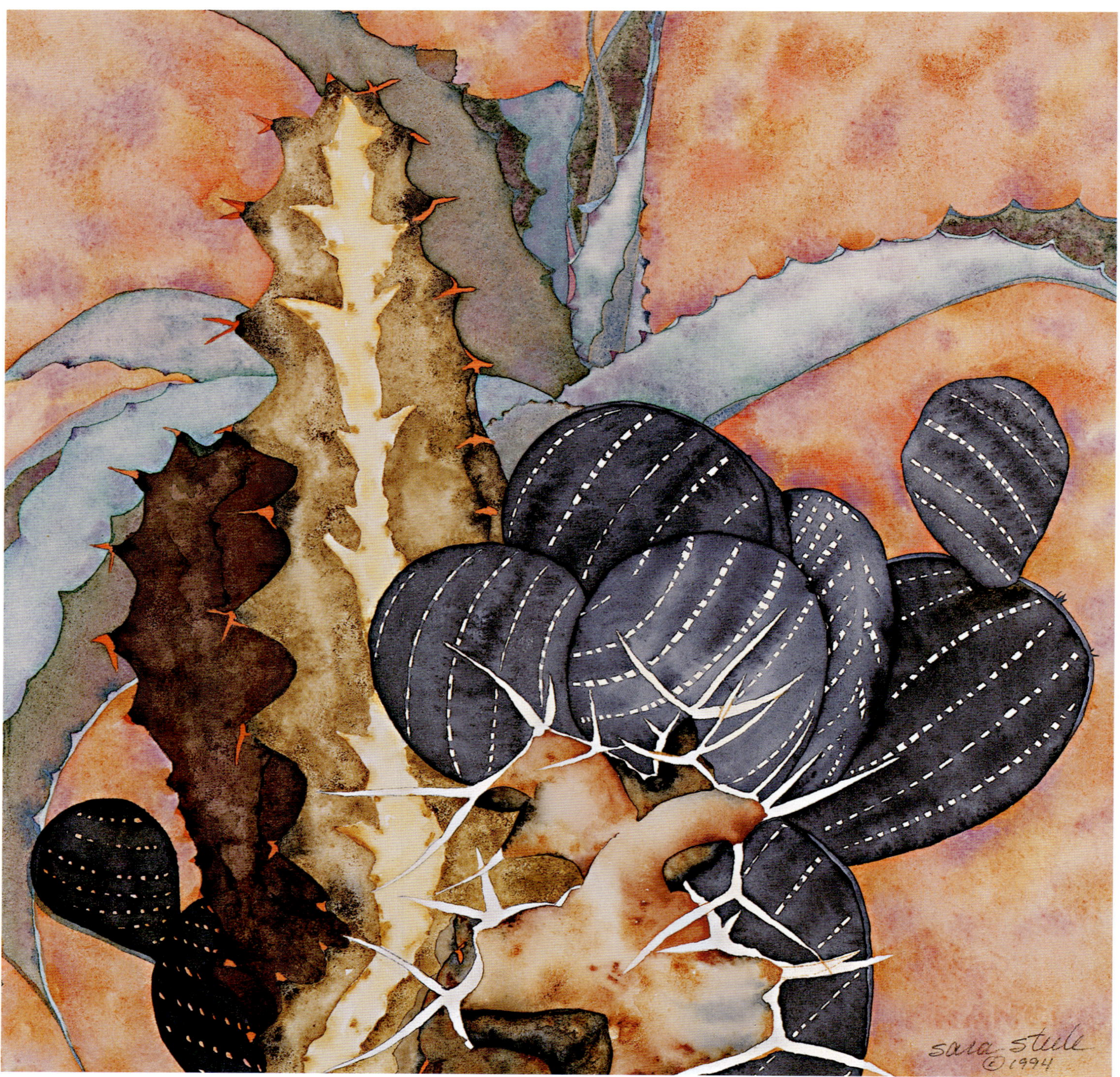

Cacti and Agave, 1994

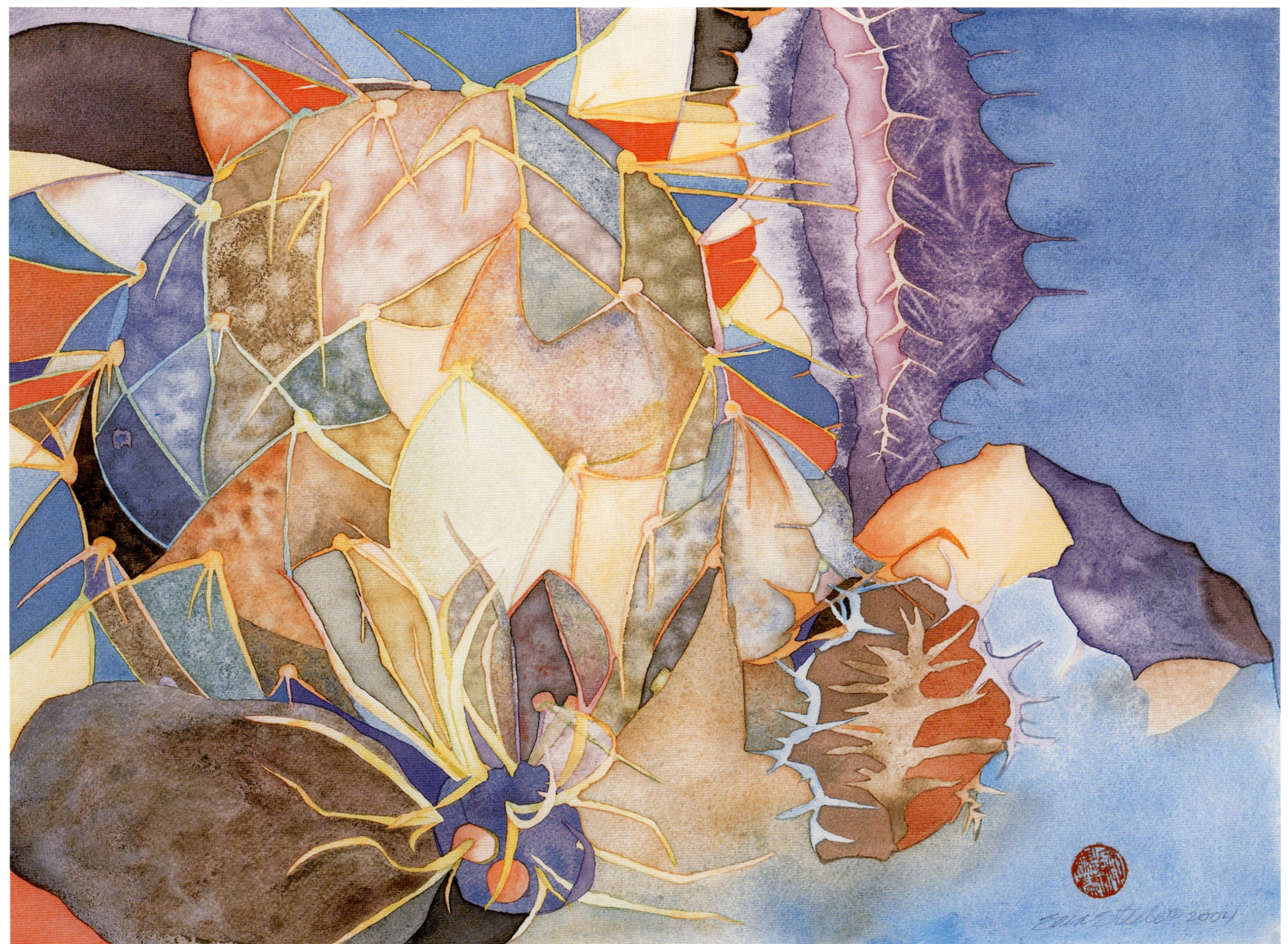

Xeriscape, 2004

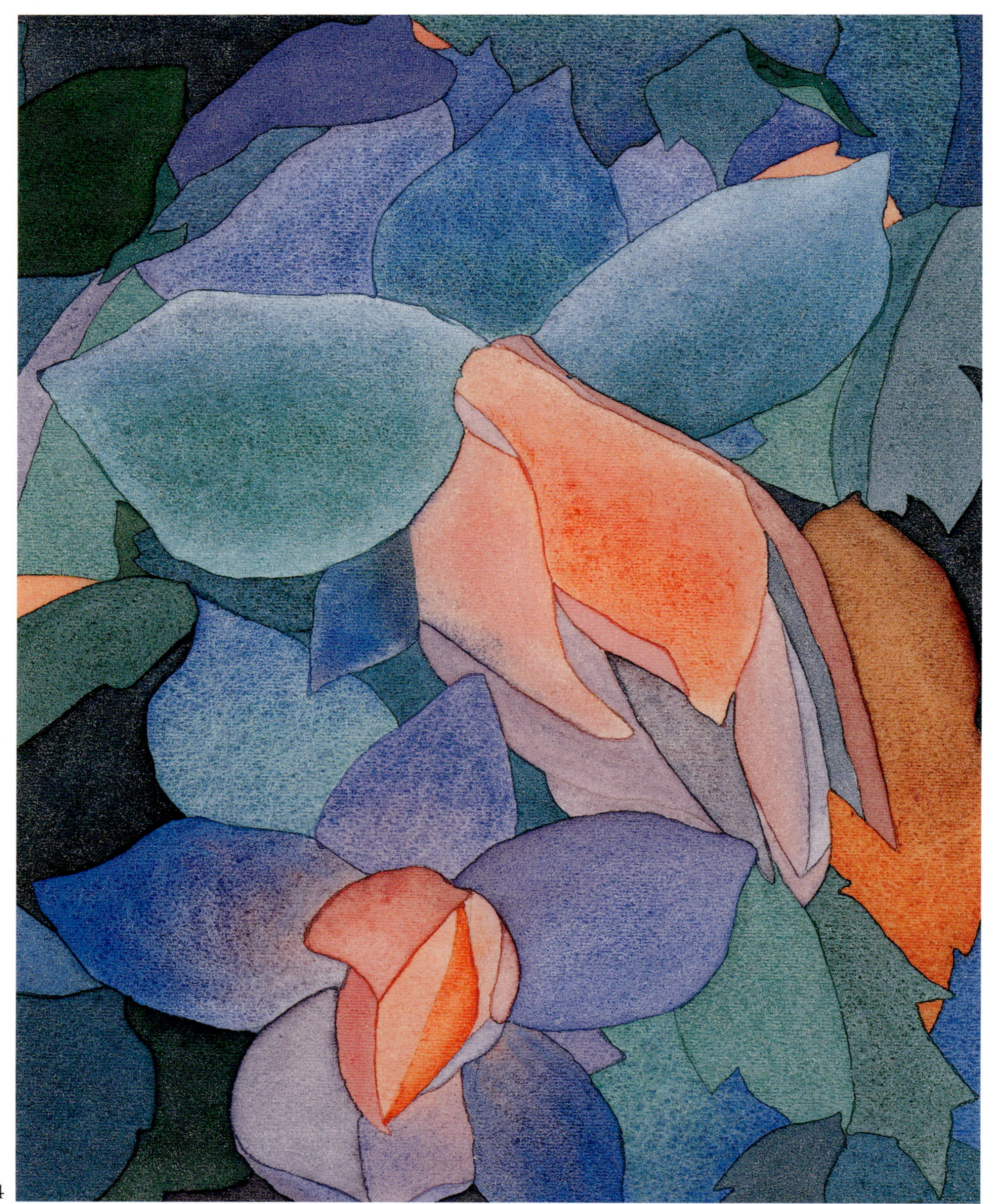

Xygo Blooming, 1984

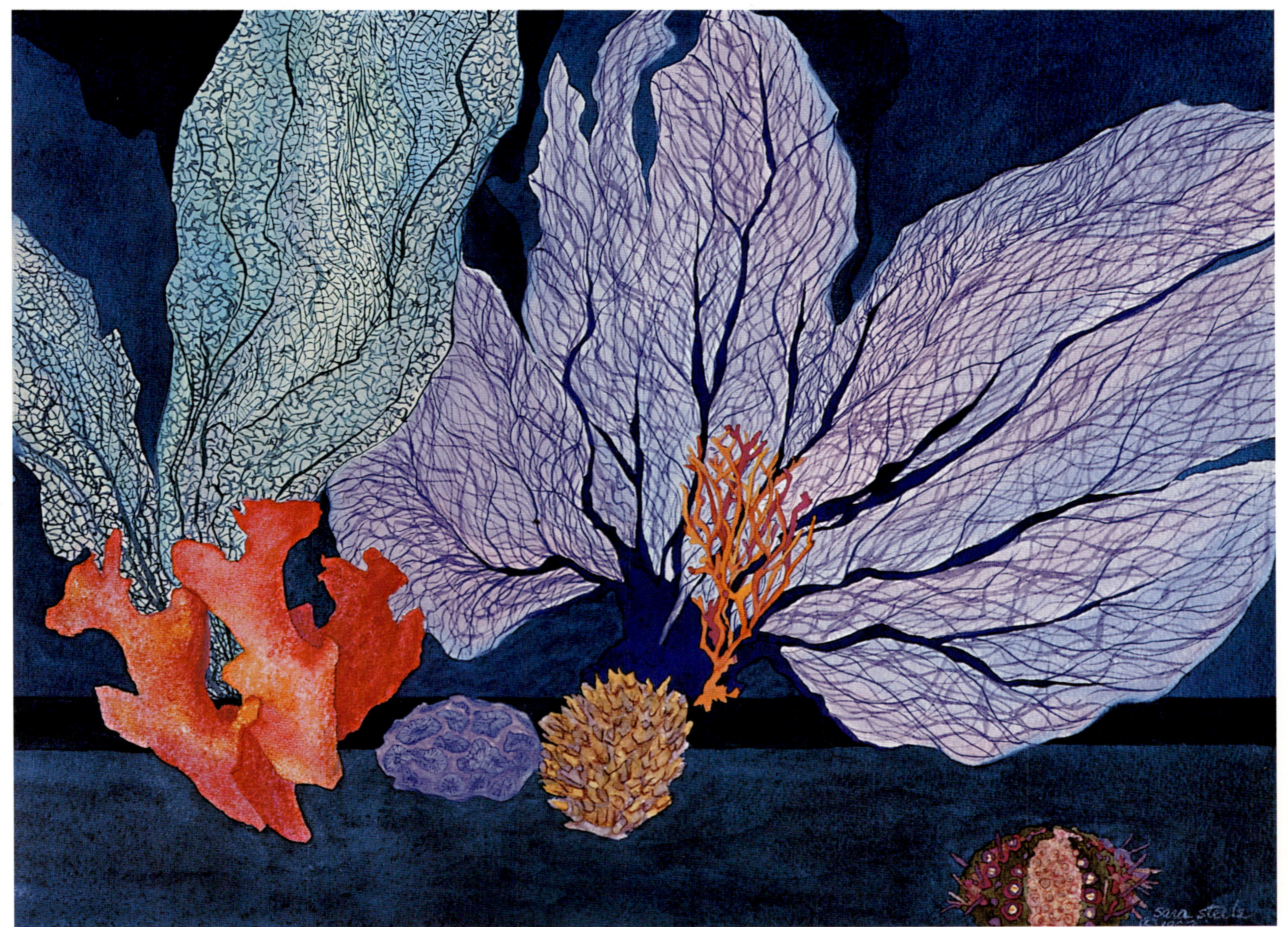

Fan Coral, 1983

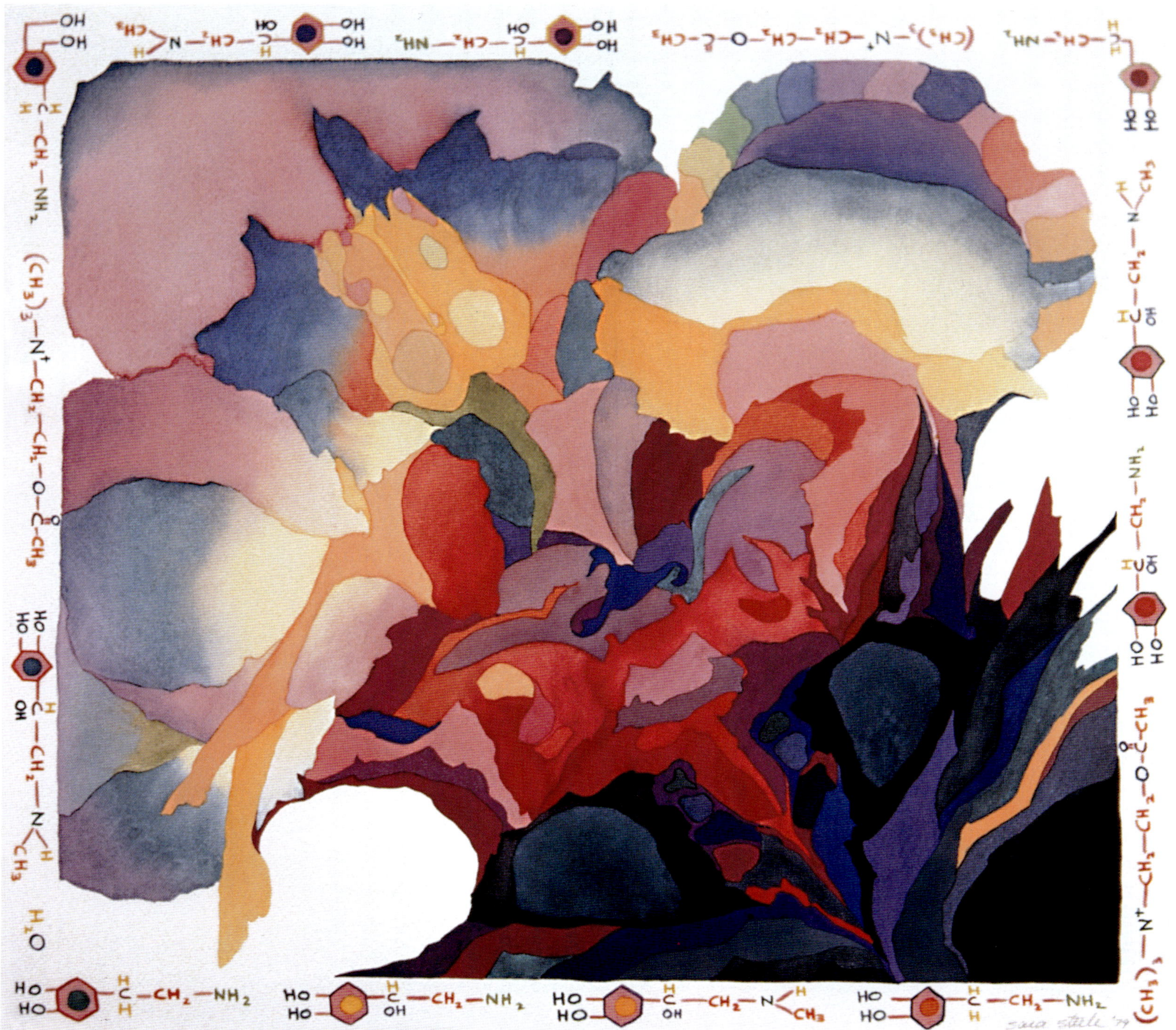

The Chemistry of Feeling, 1979

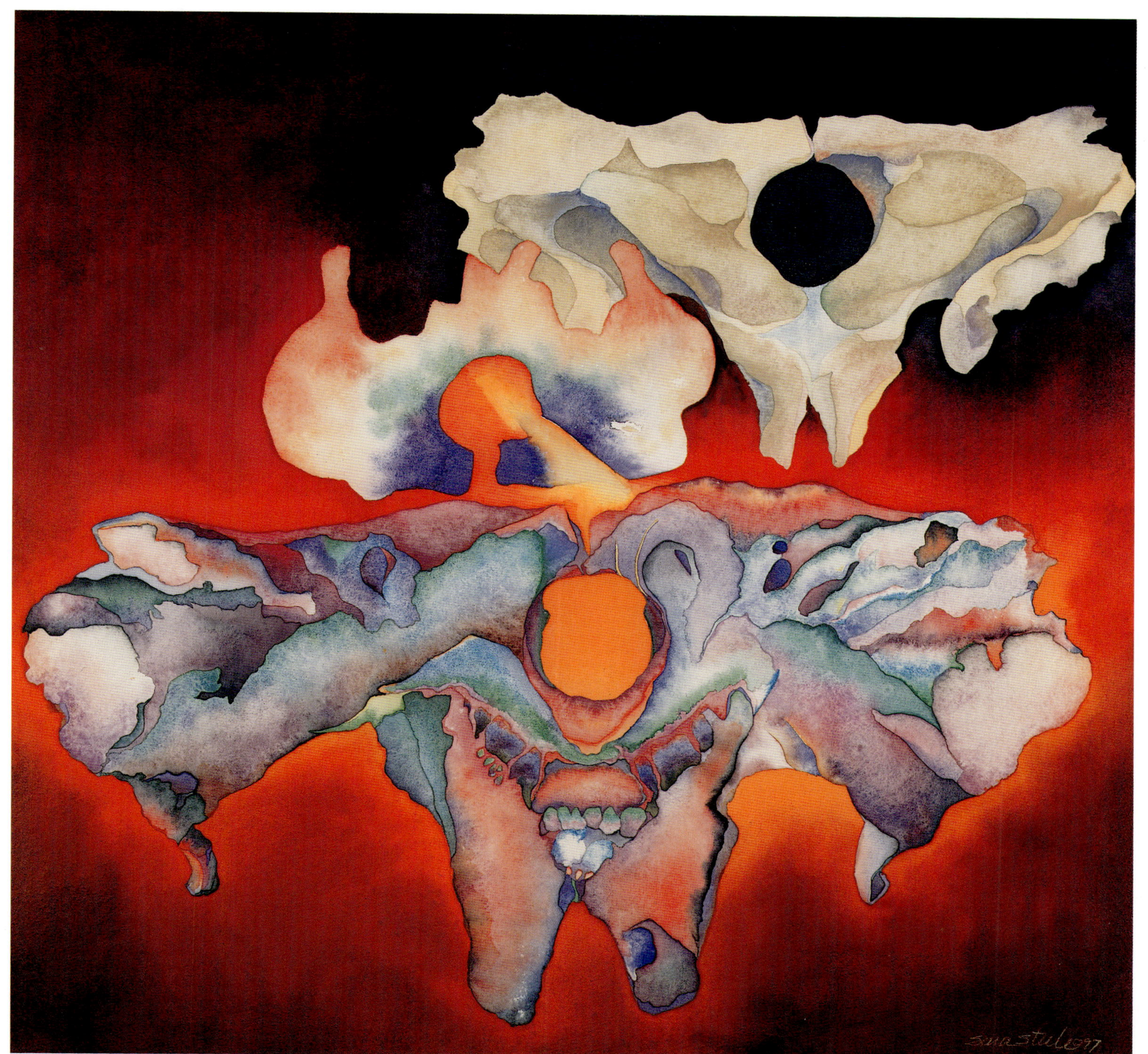

Holy Cow / Shape Shifter, 1997

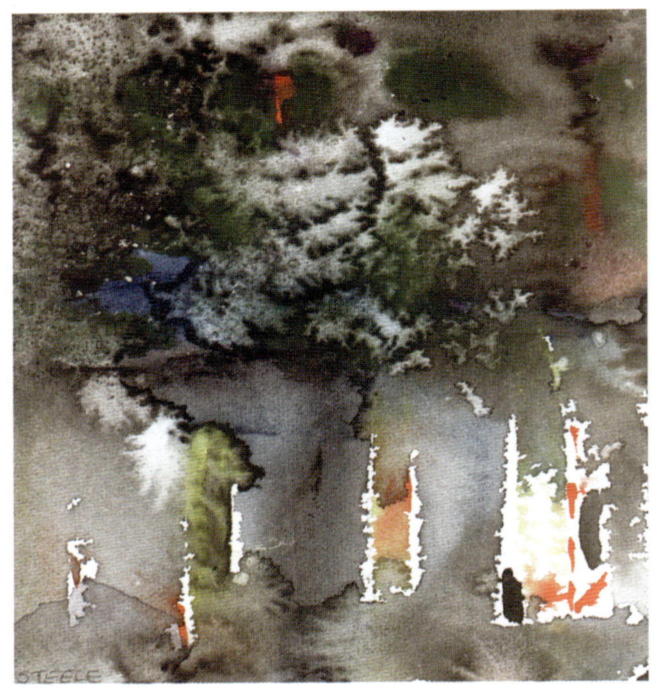

The Towers Go Down, 2001

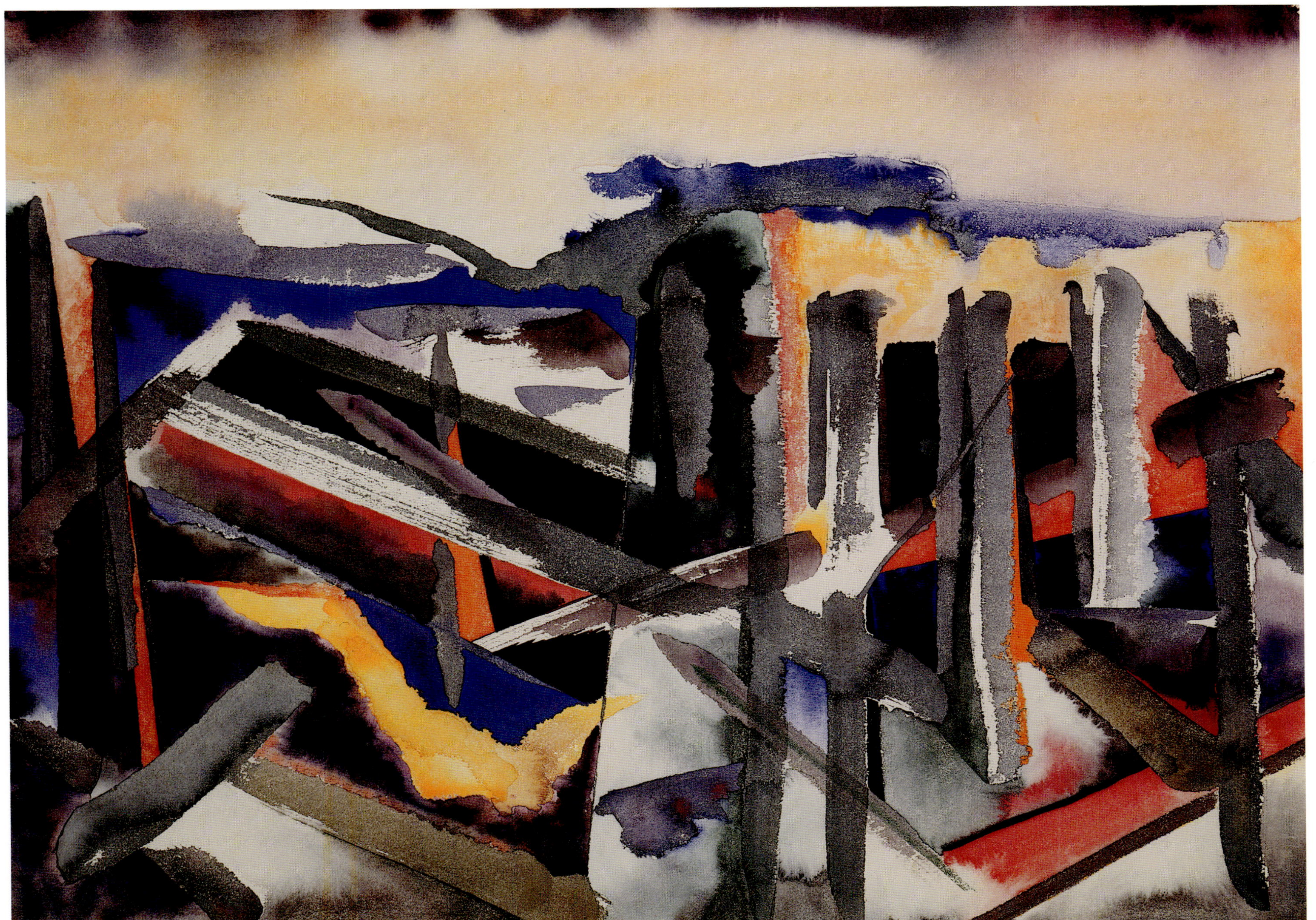

Canary in a Coal Mine, 1998

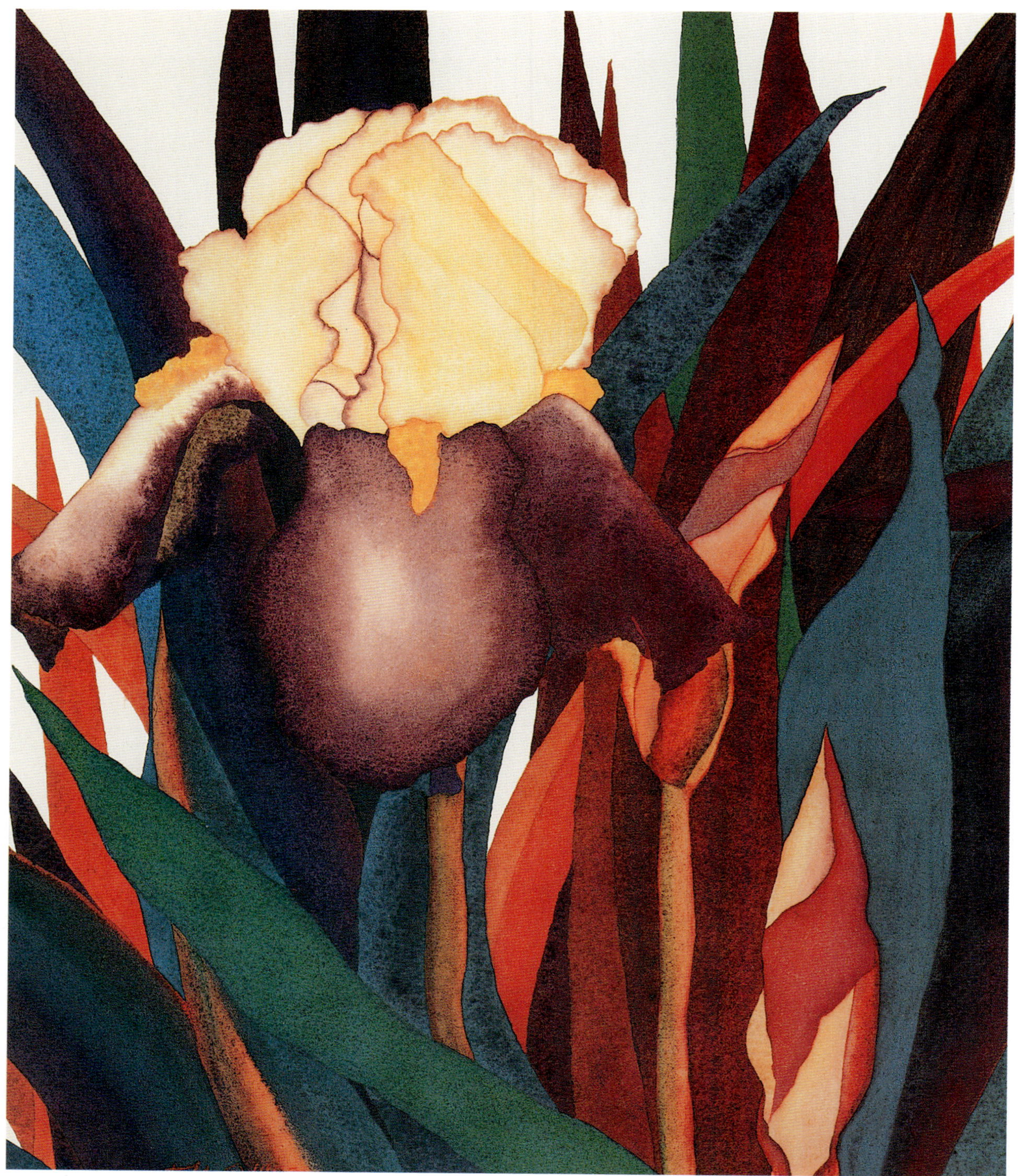

Iris Unfolding, 1982

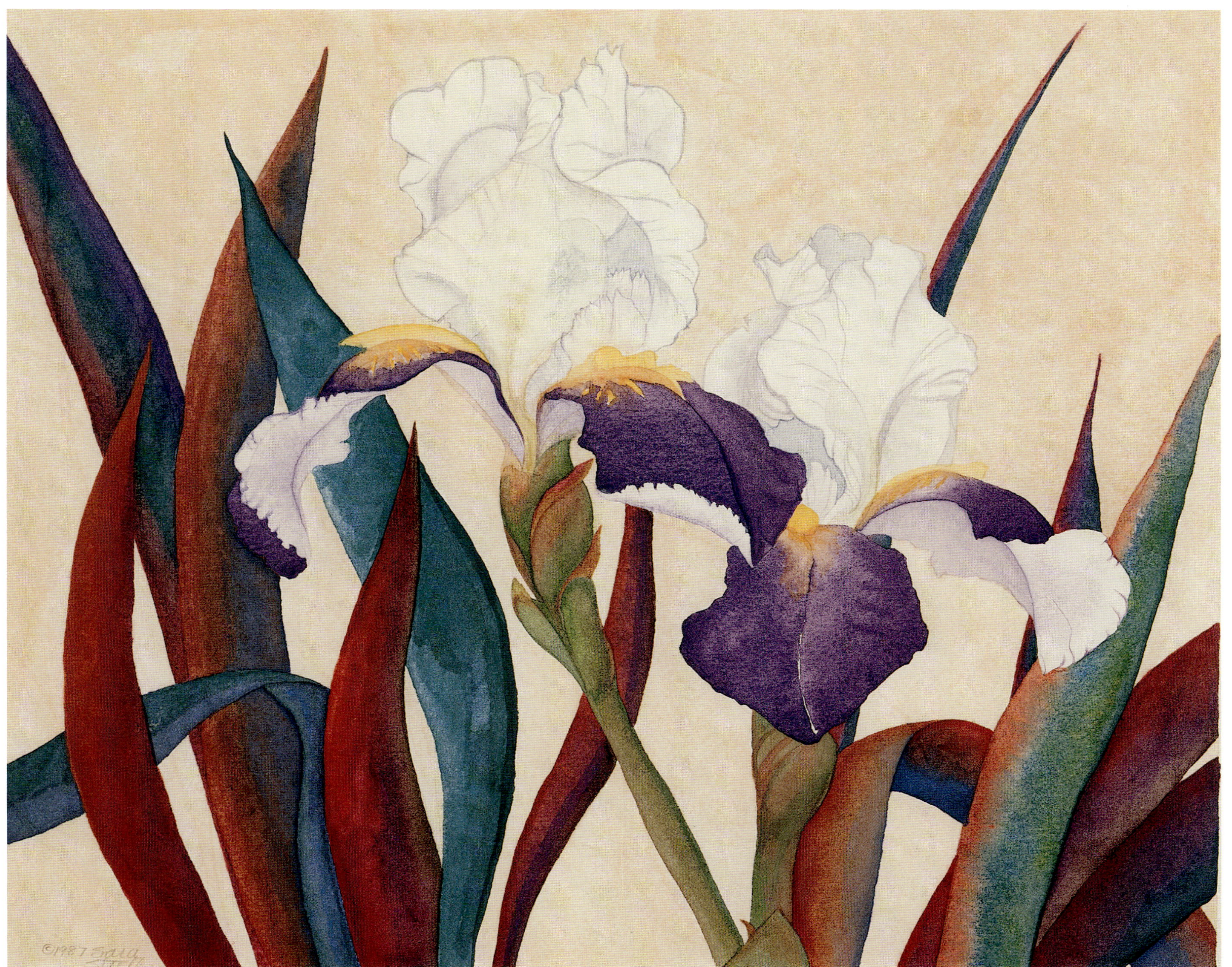

Royal Velvet Irises, 1987

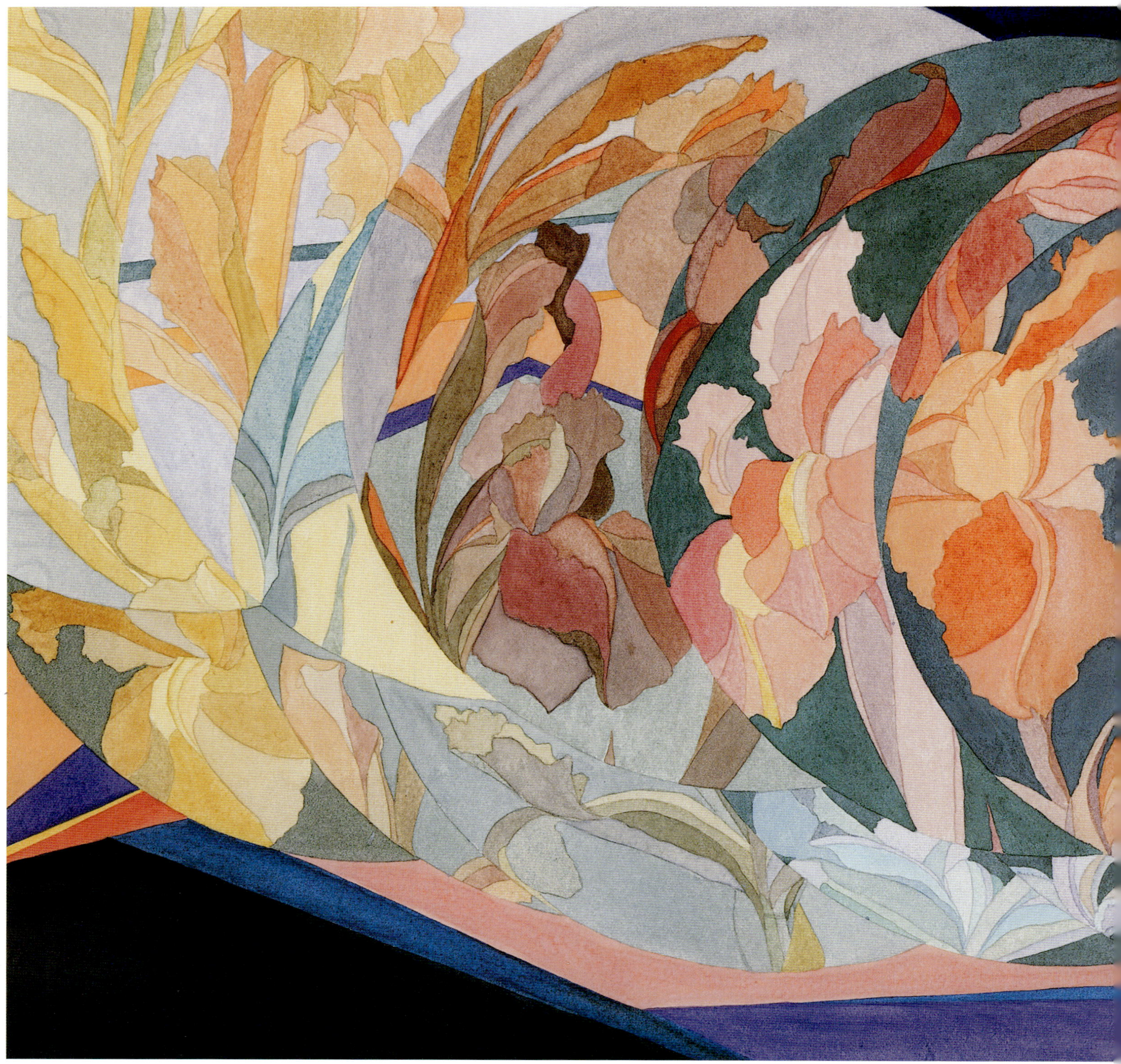

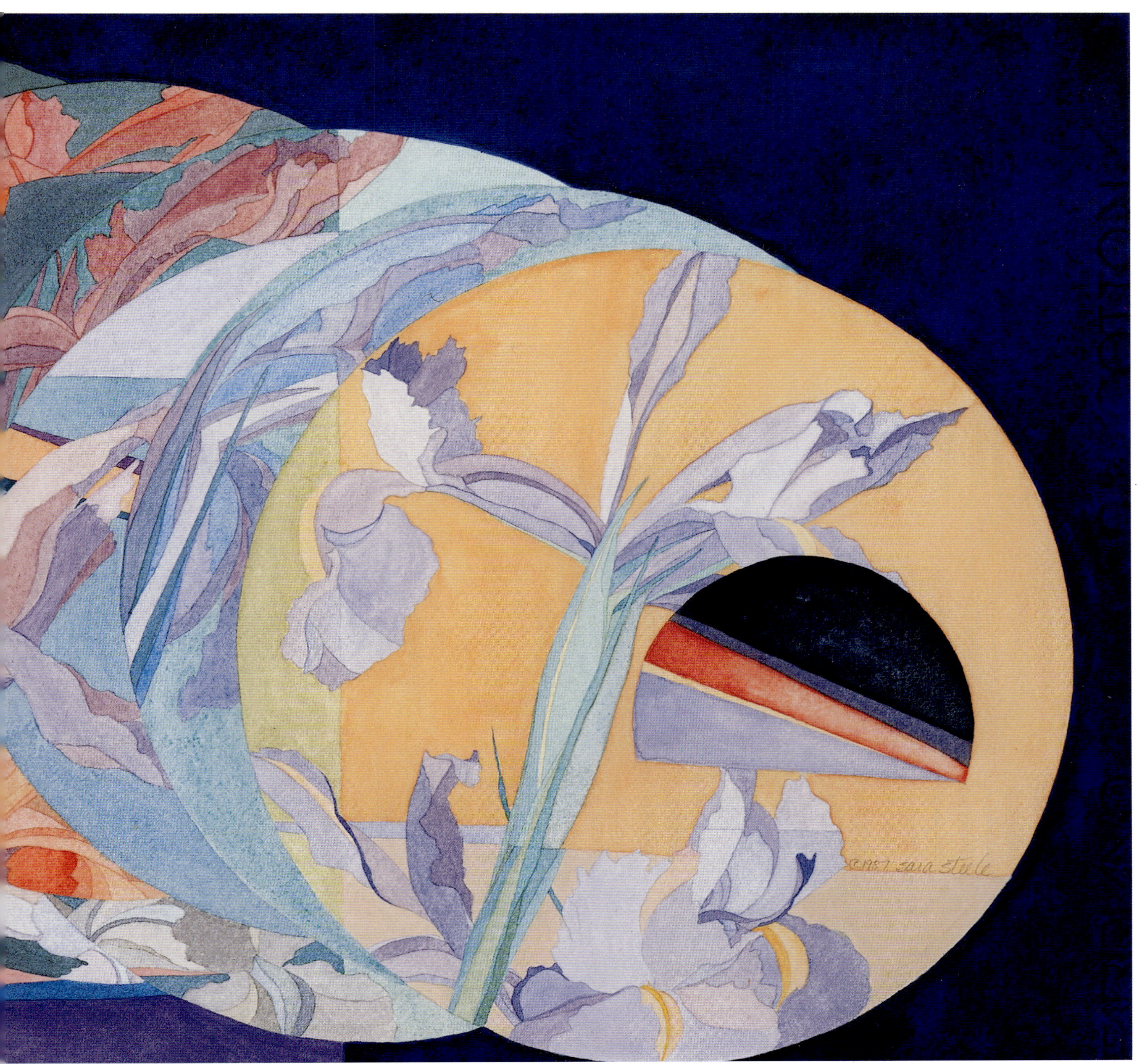

The Layers of the Mind, 1987

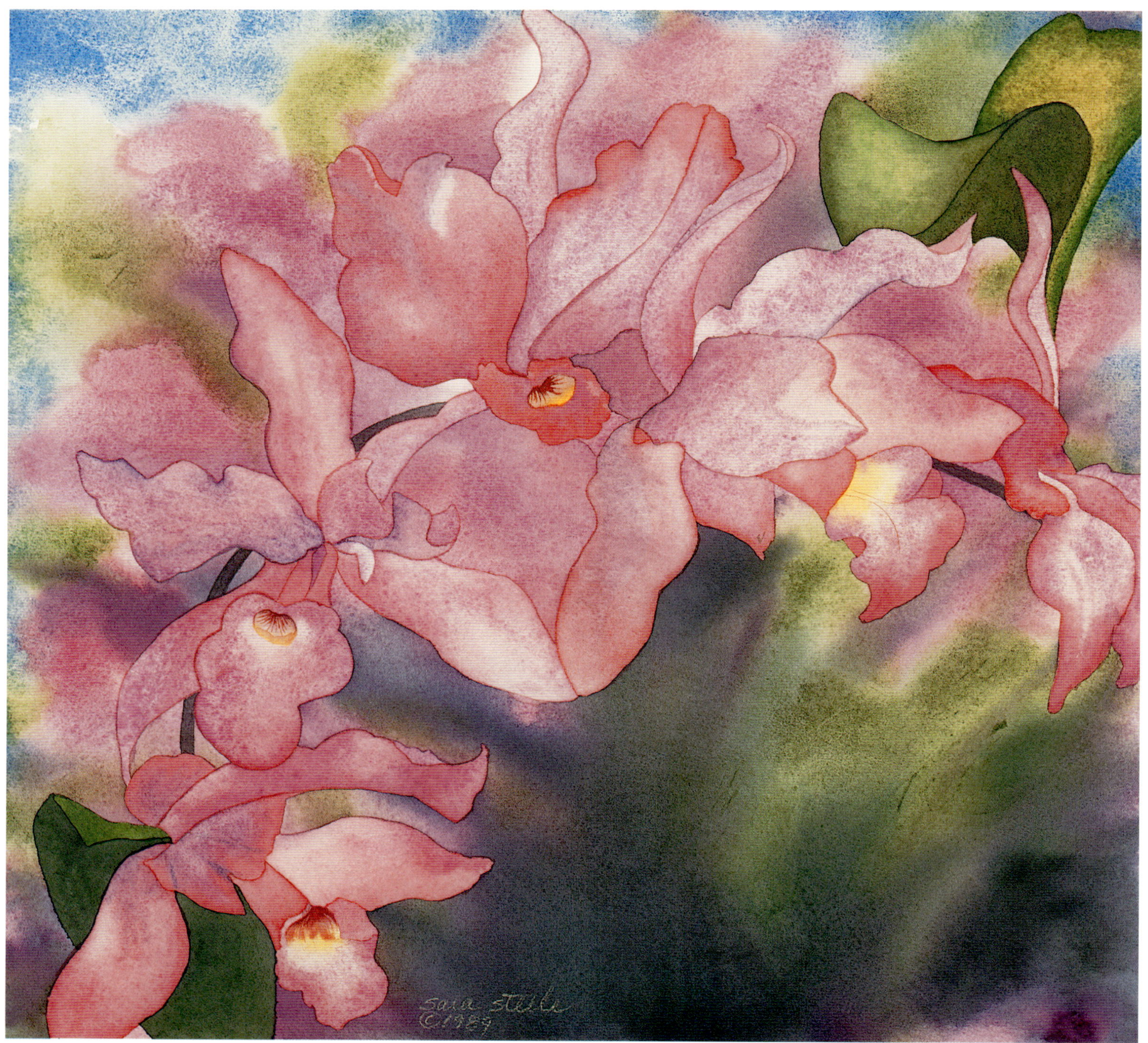

Cattleya Skinnerii, from the Endangered Orchids series, 1989

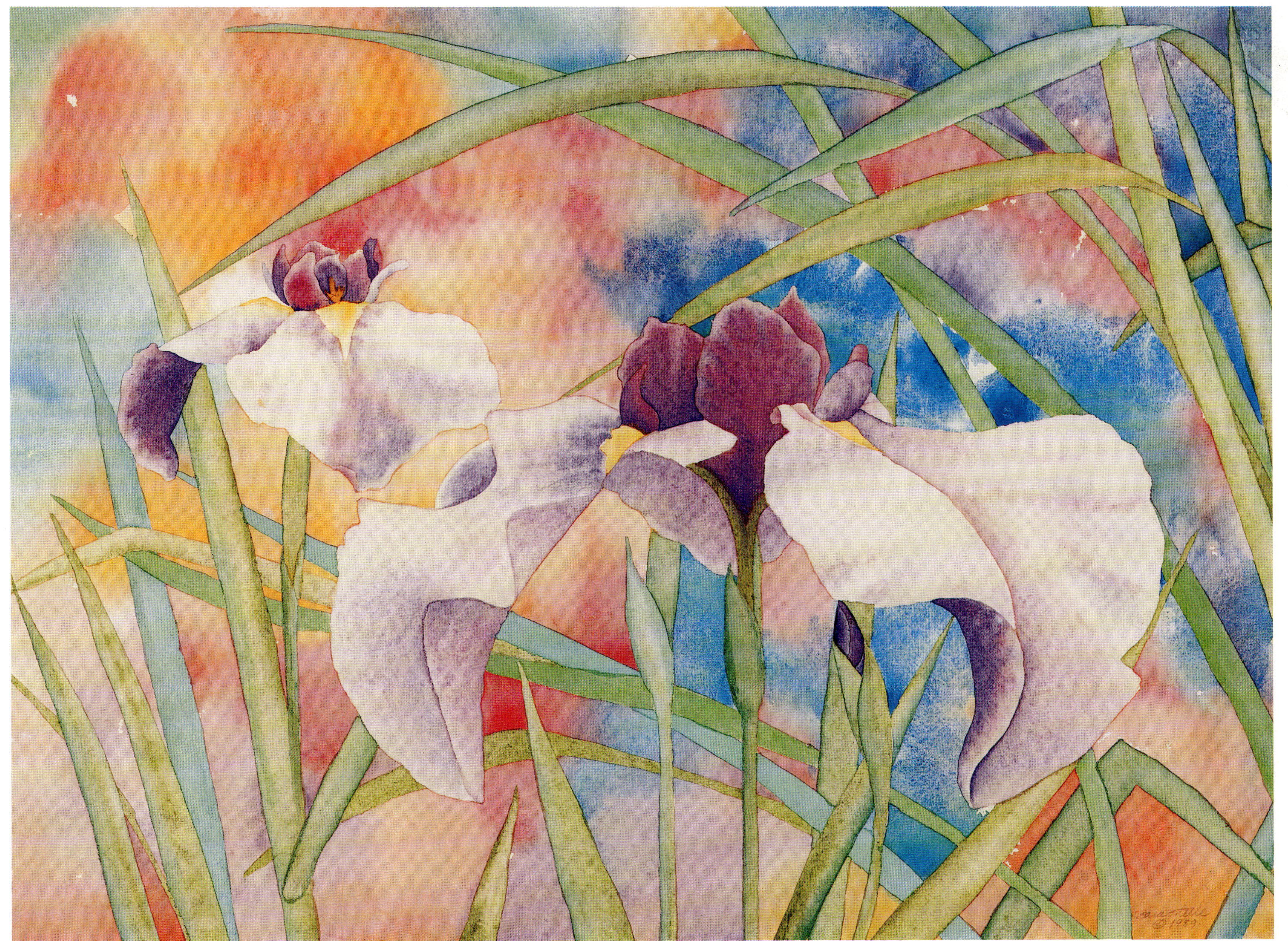

Higo Irises, 1989

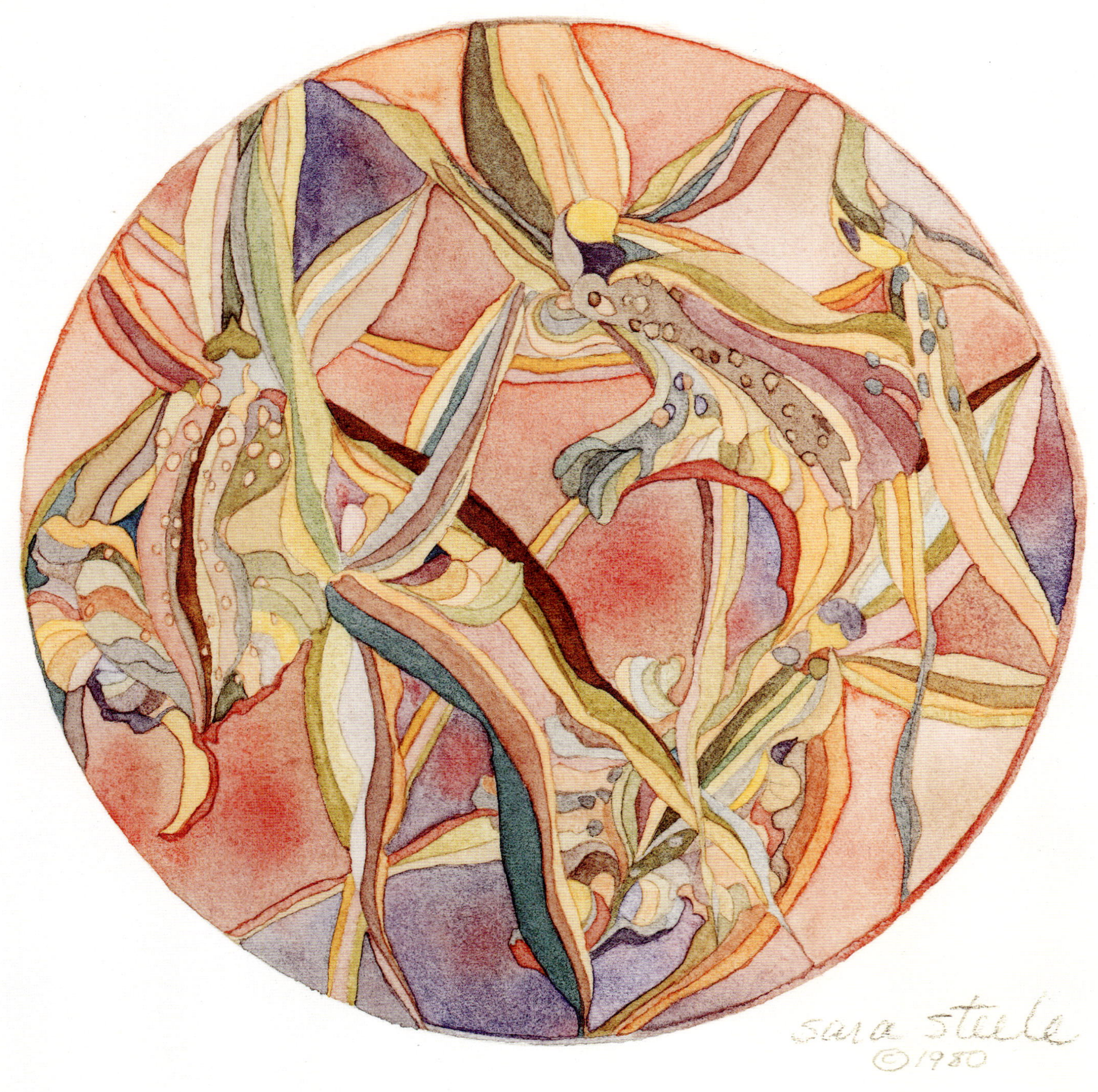

Brasil, 1980

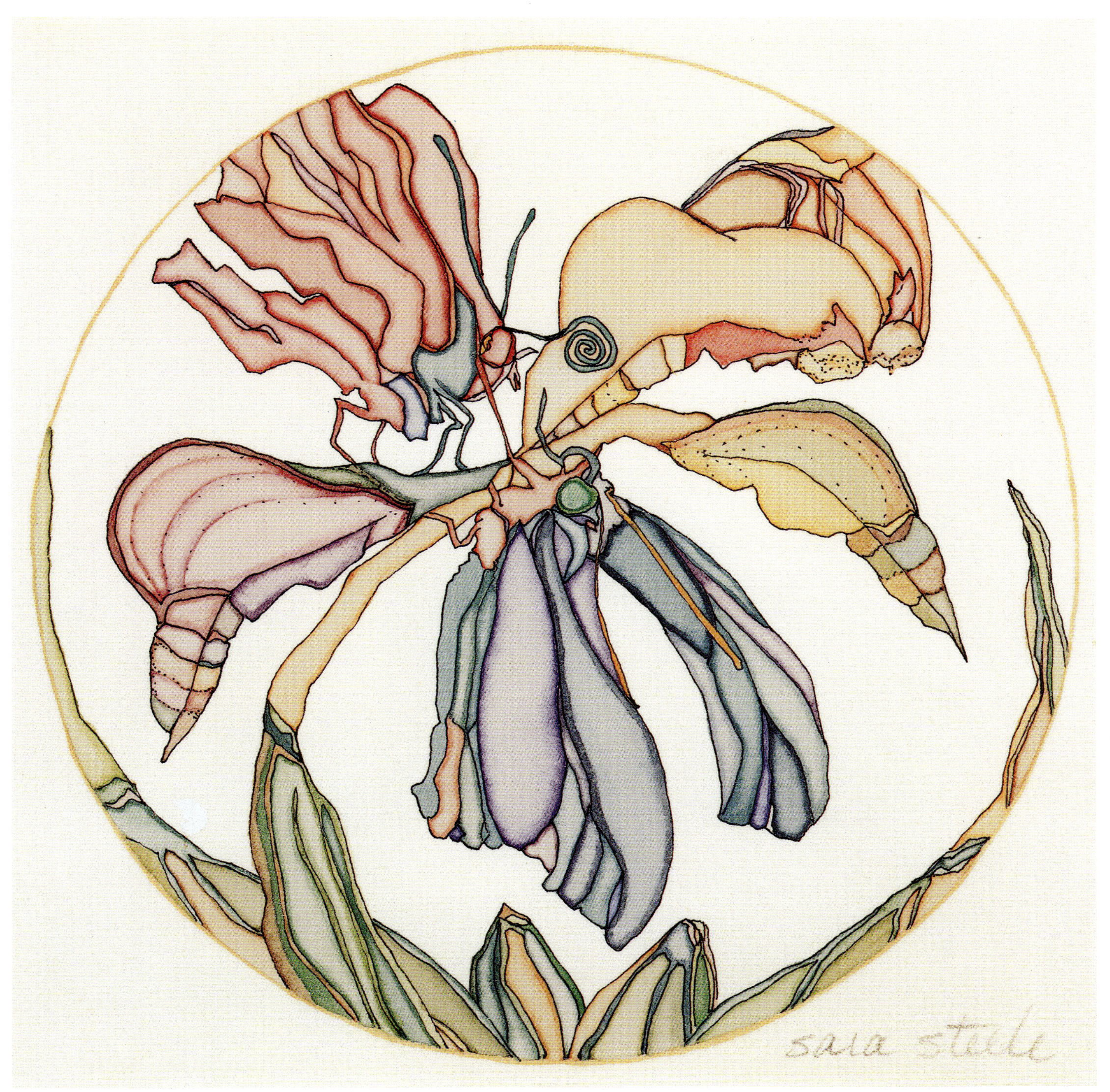

Kô/Molting, 1980

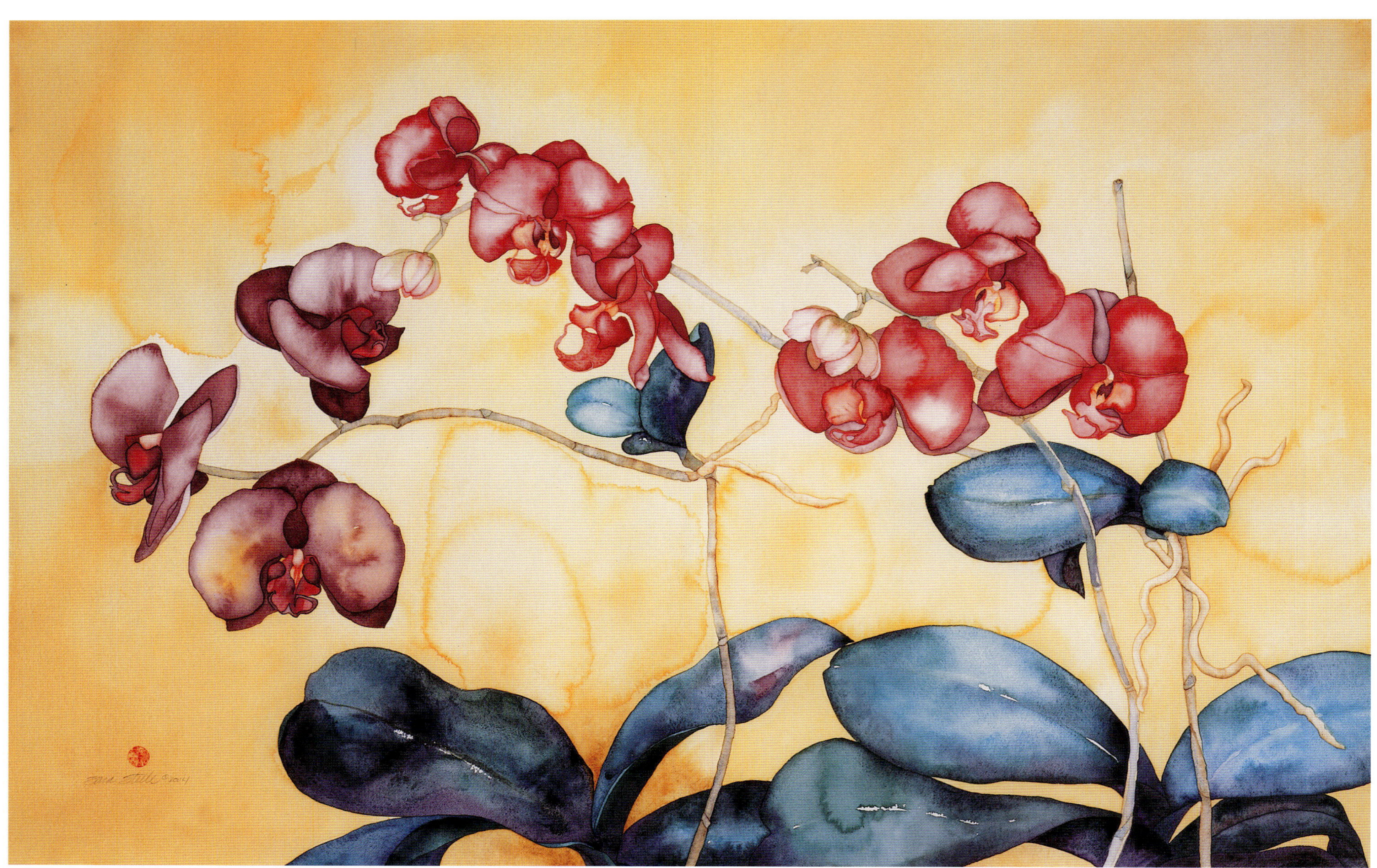

Phals for Patranna, 2004

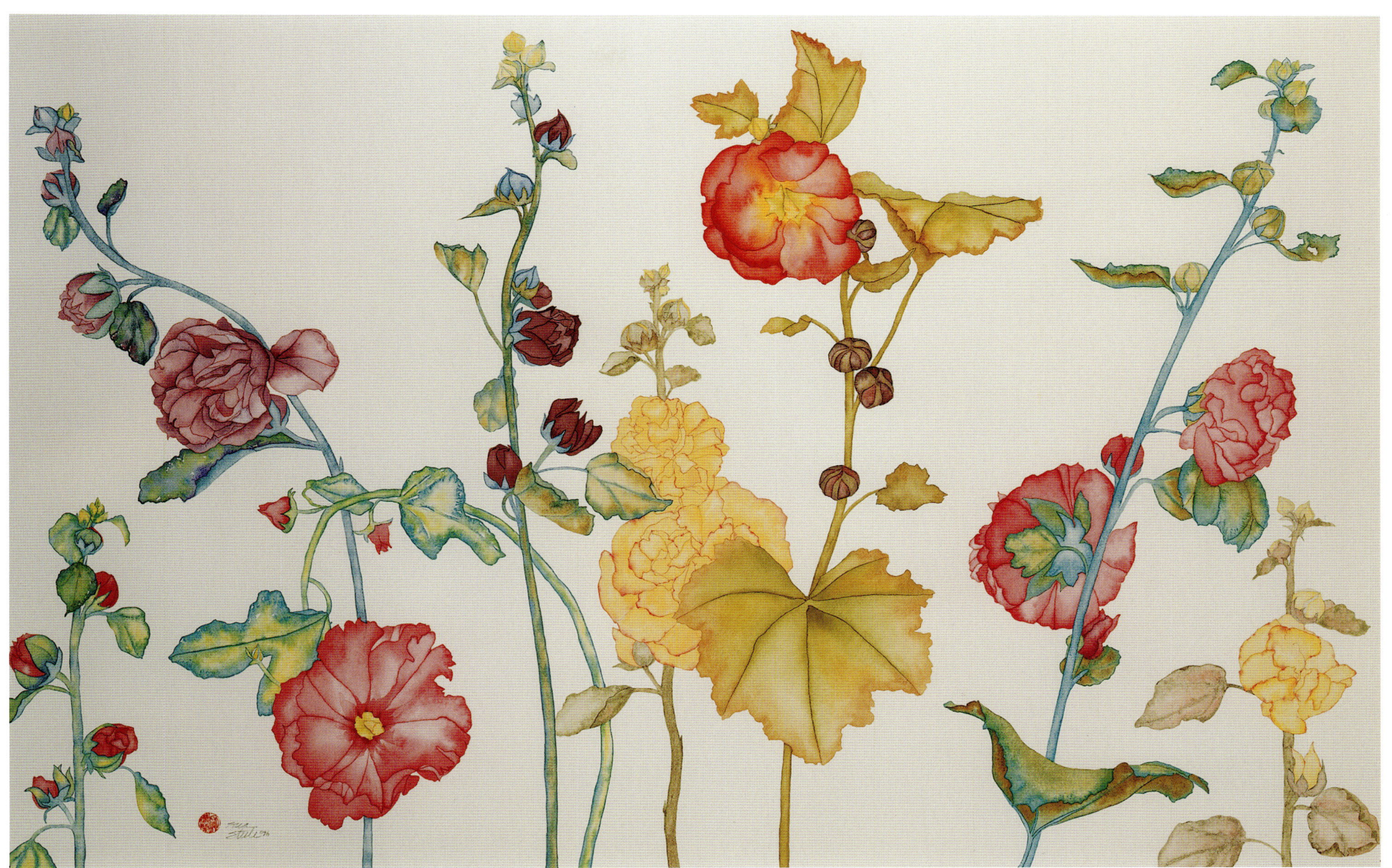

Hollyhocks, 1996

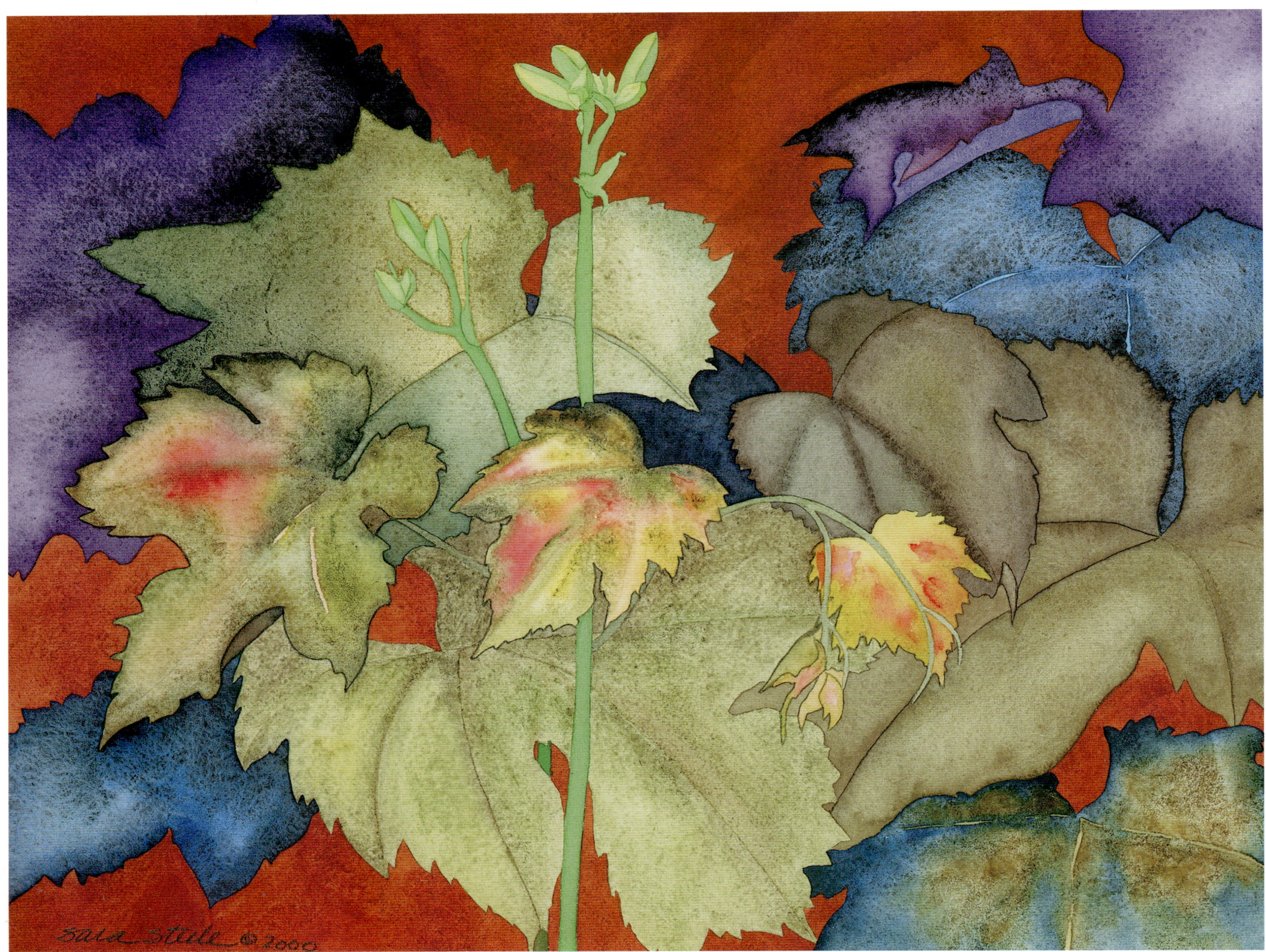

Grape Vine and Daylily Buds, 2000

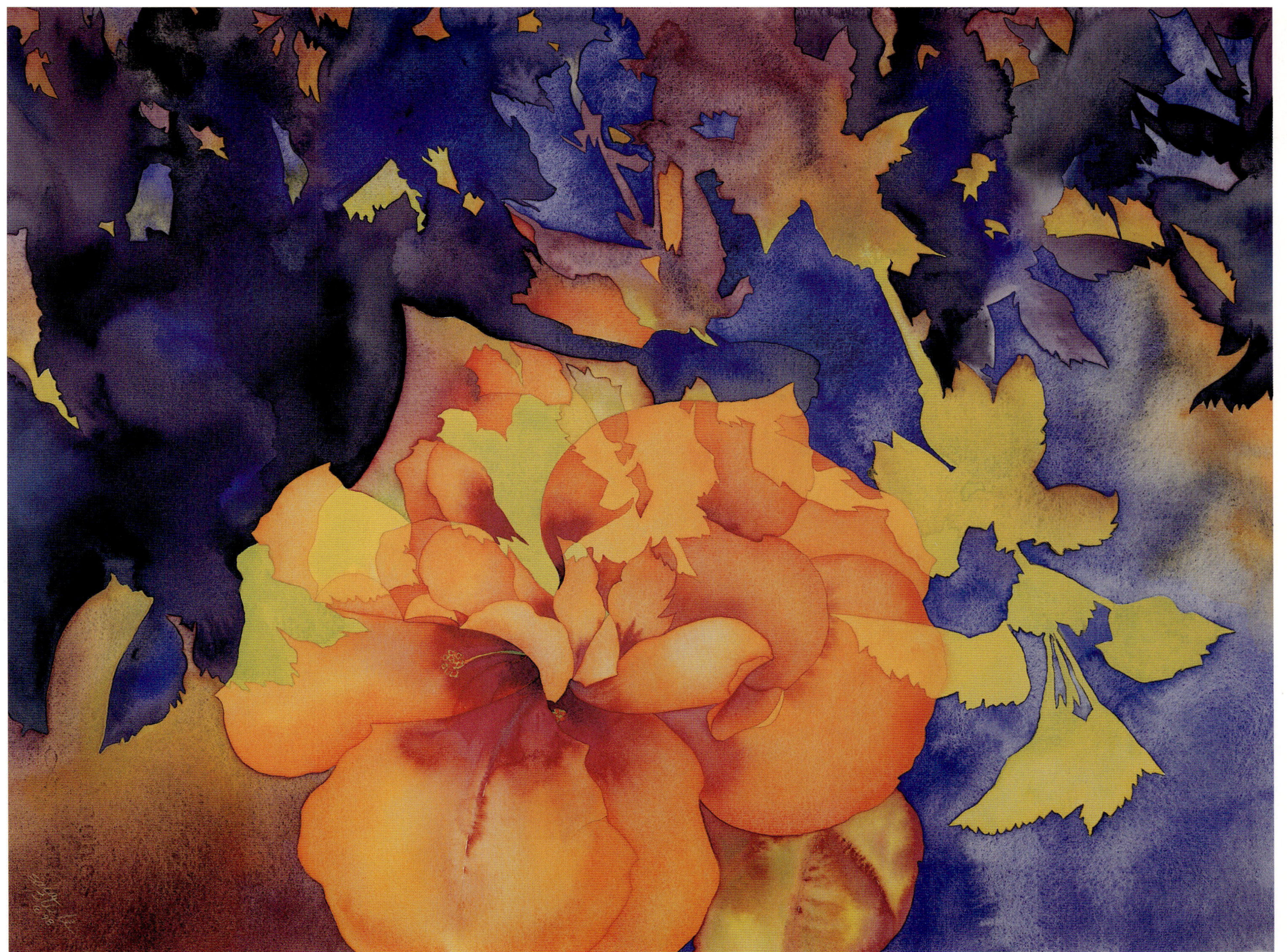

Shadows at Sandy's (Seeing Patterns), 1998

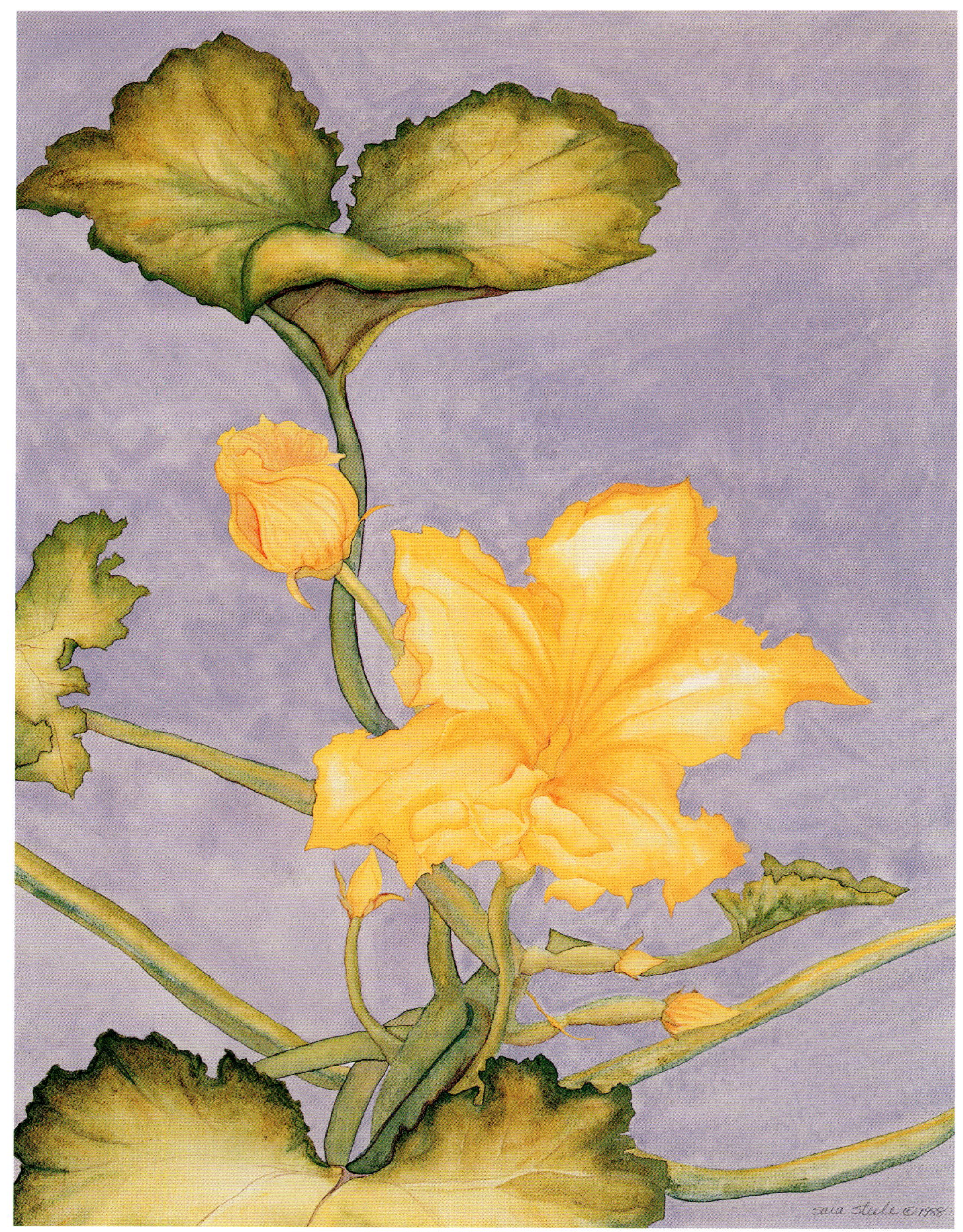

Squash Blossoms, 1988

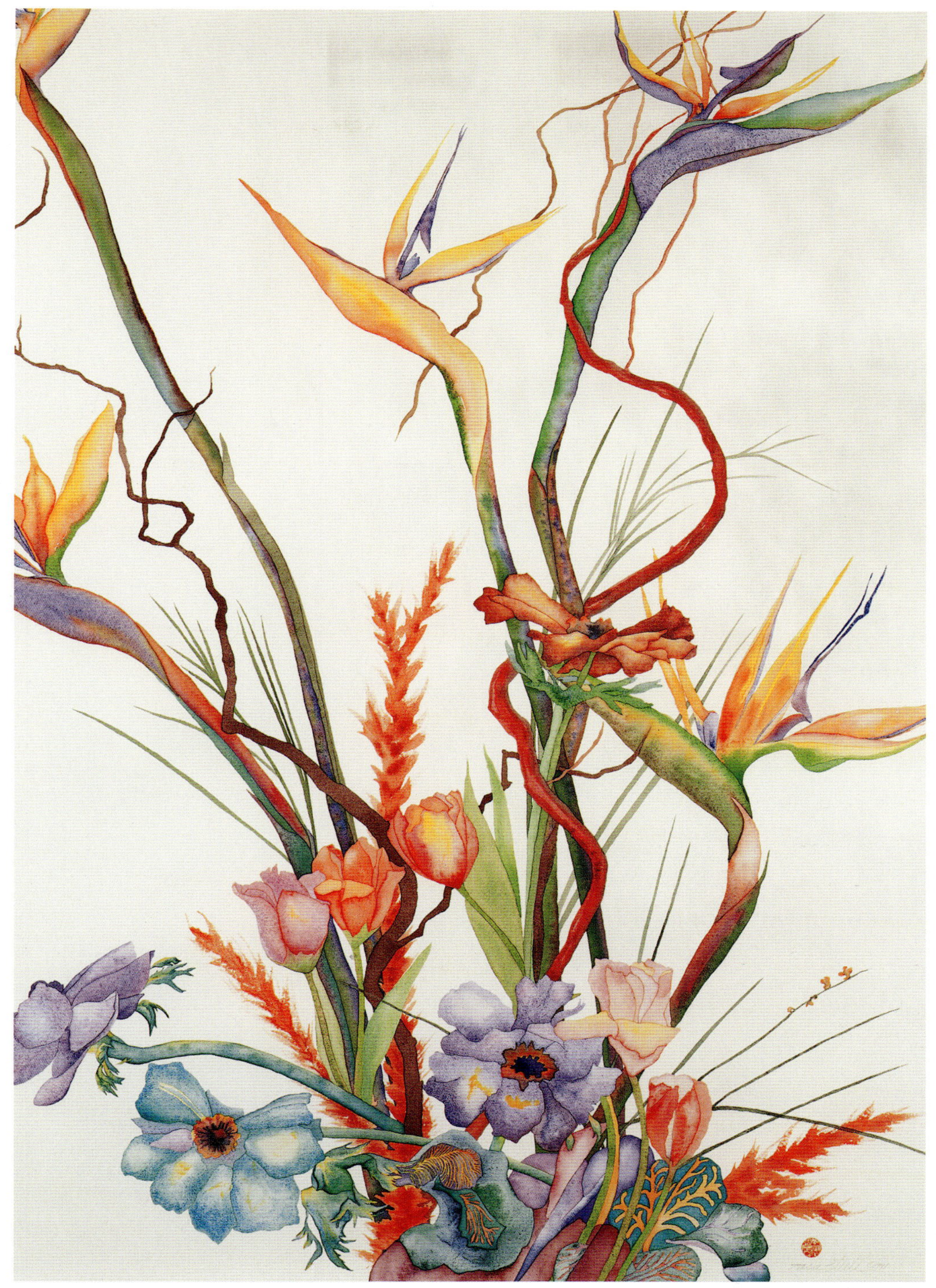

Amazon Botanicals, 1991

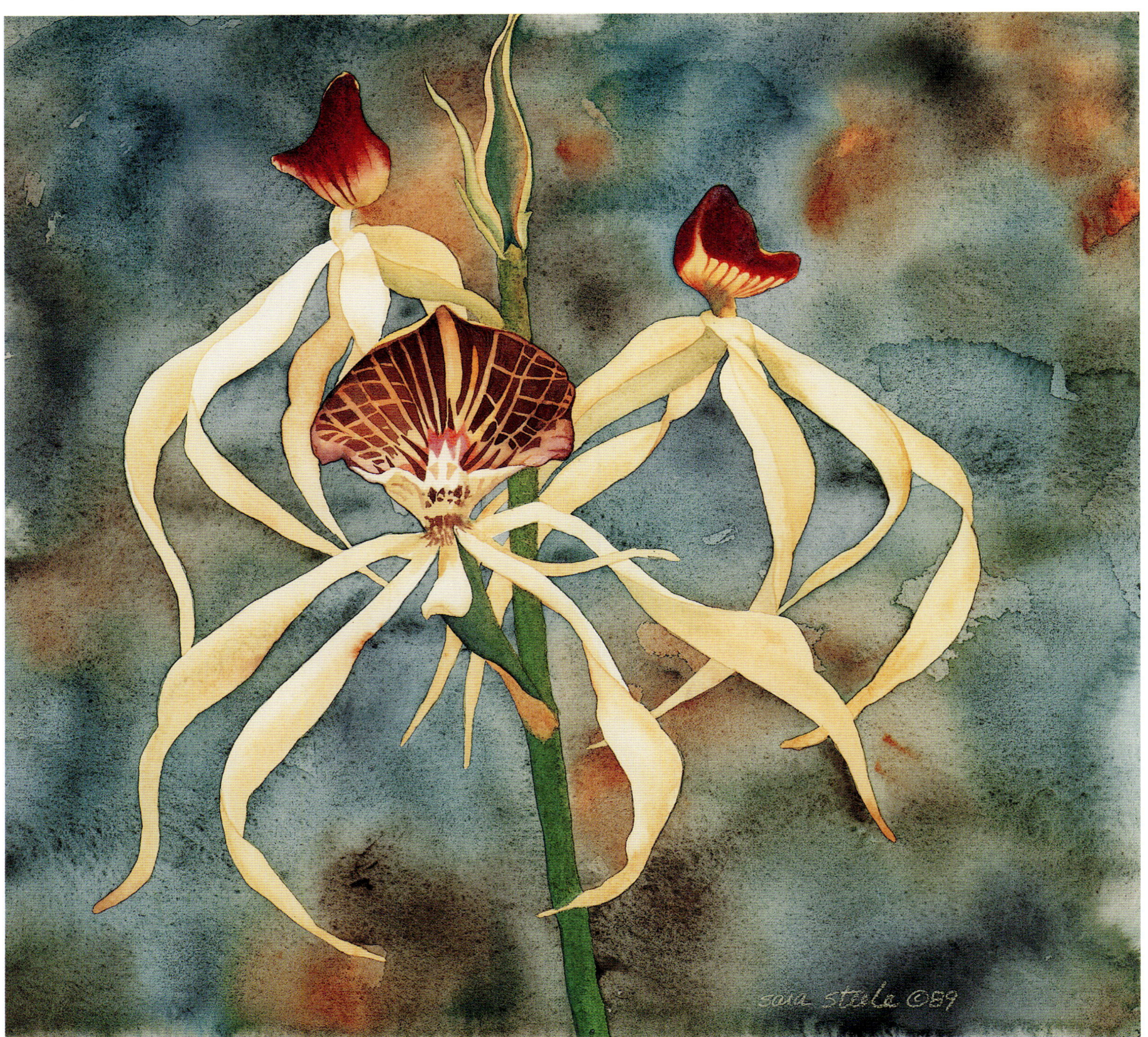

Encyclia cochleata, from the Endangered Orchids series, 1989

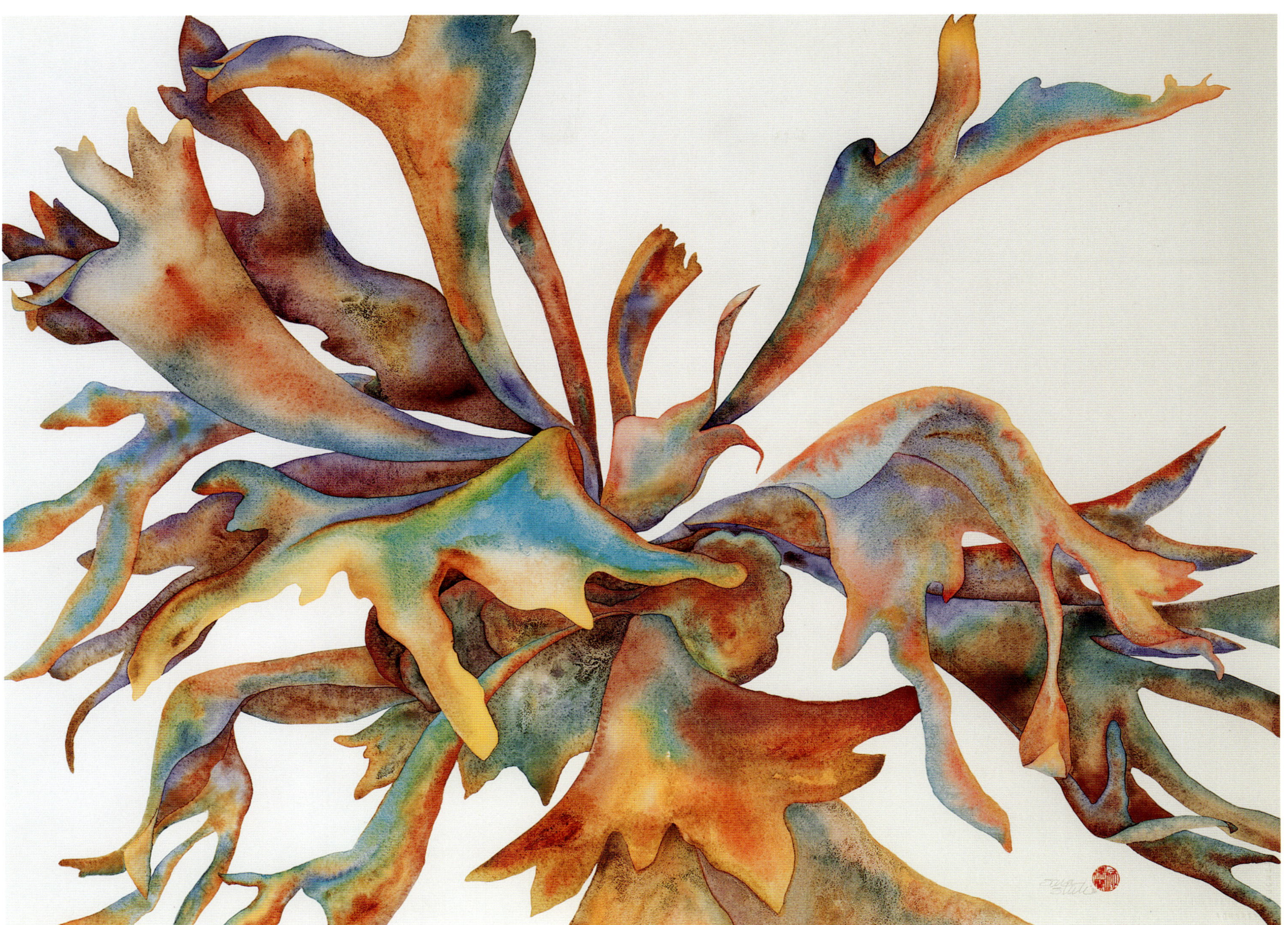

Staghorn Fern, 1996

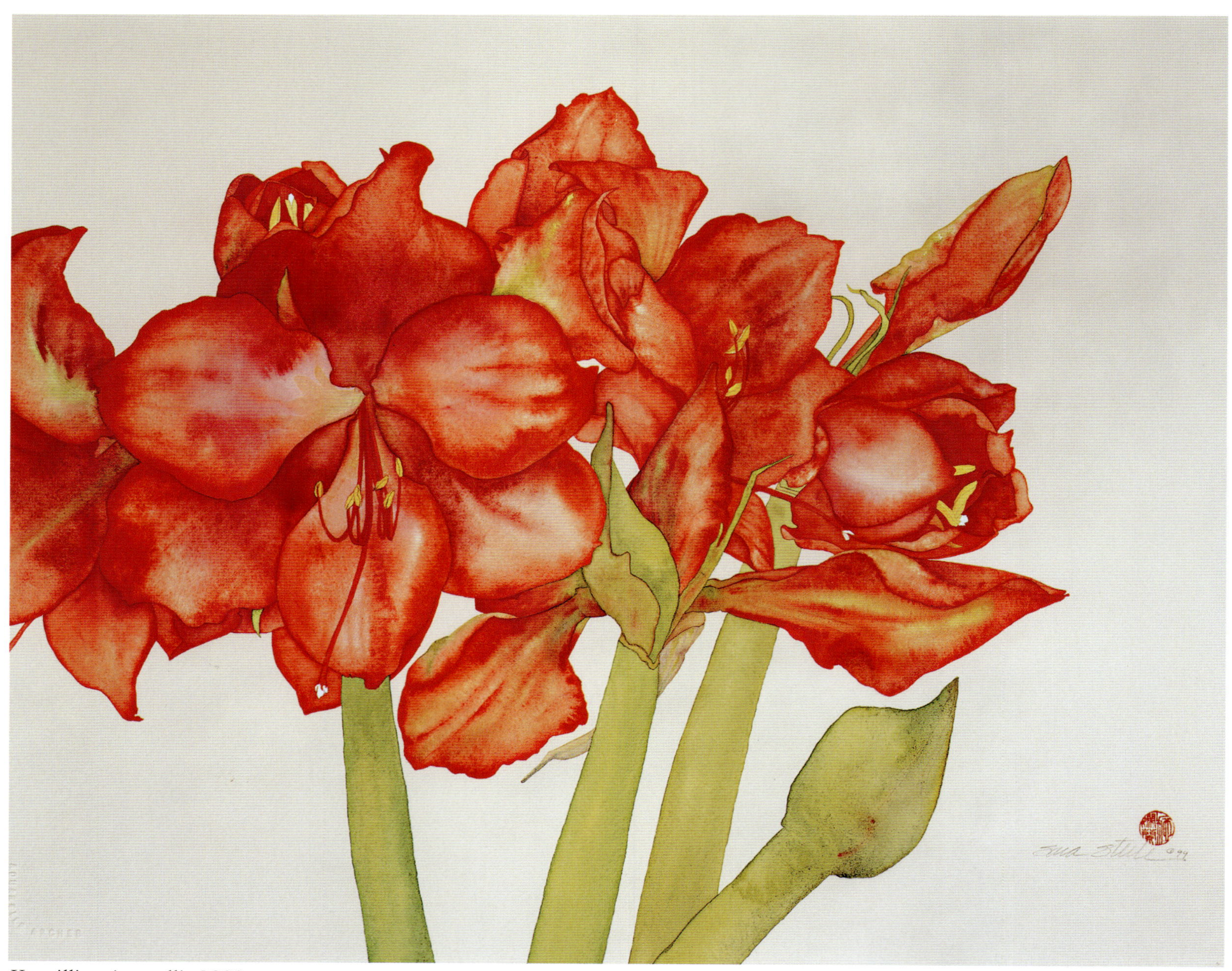

Vermillion Amaryllis, 1999

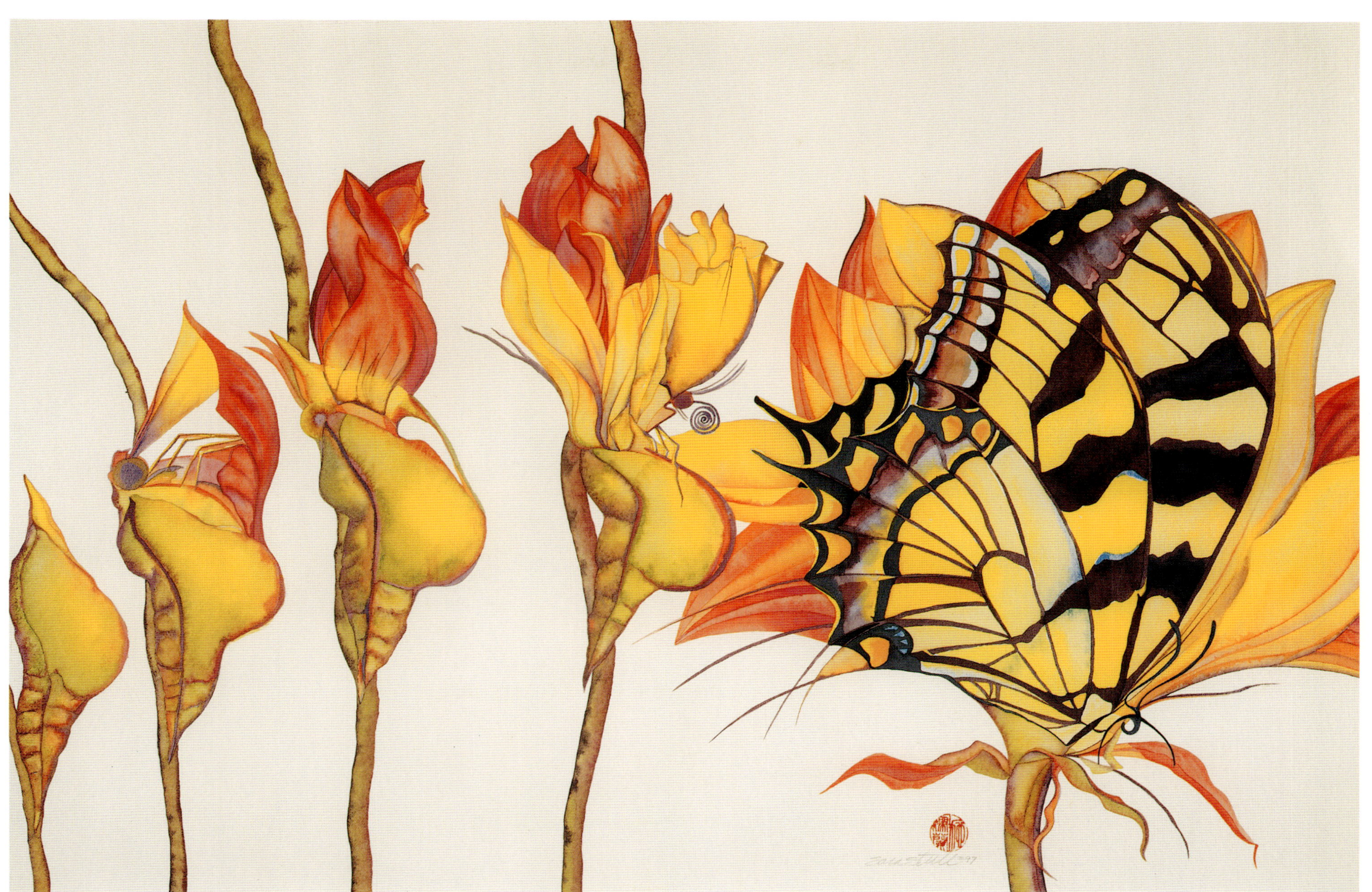

Metamorphogenesis: Nascimiento, 1997

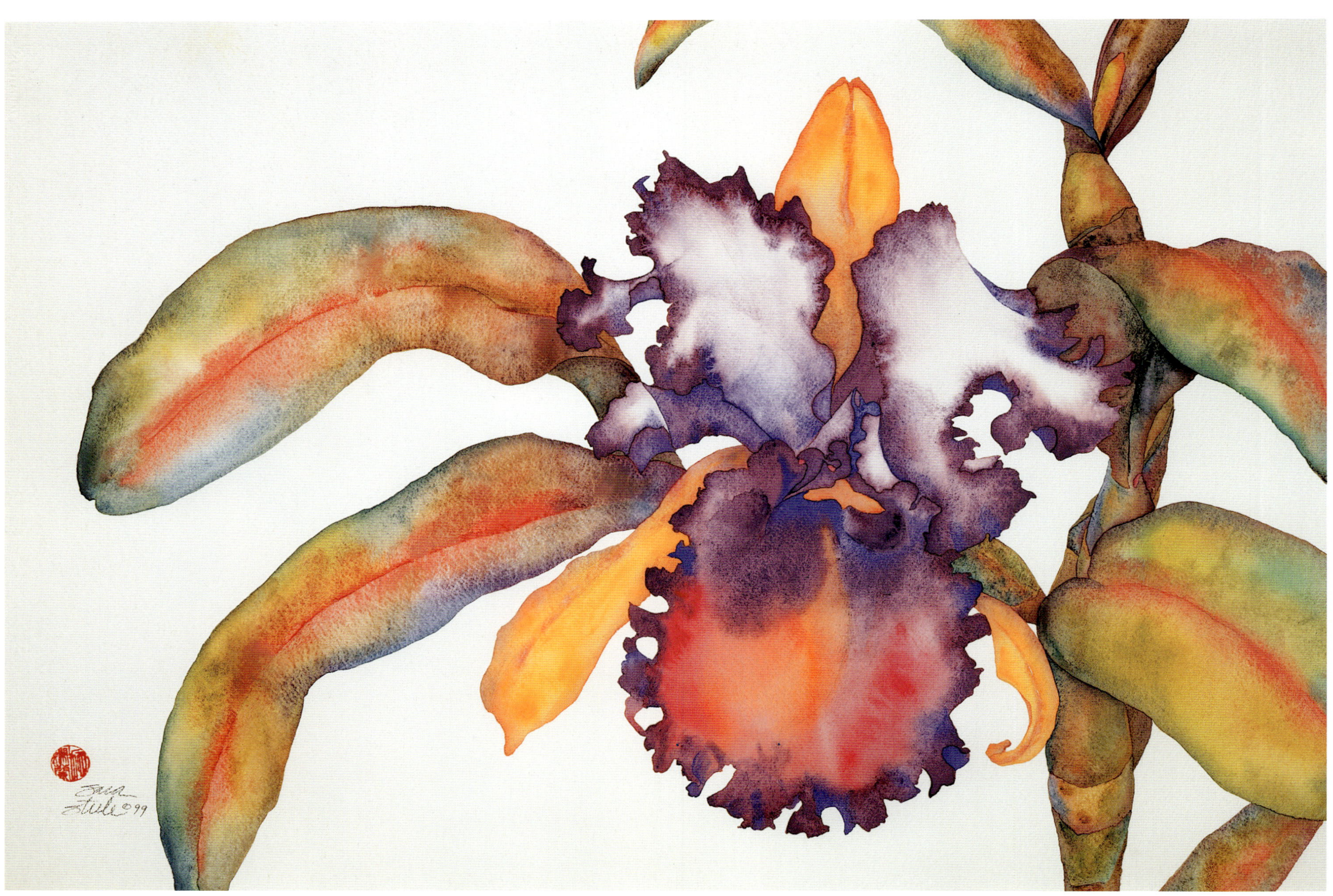

Cattleya Creatura, 1999

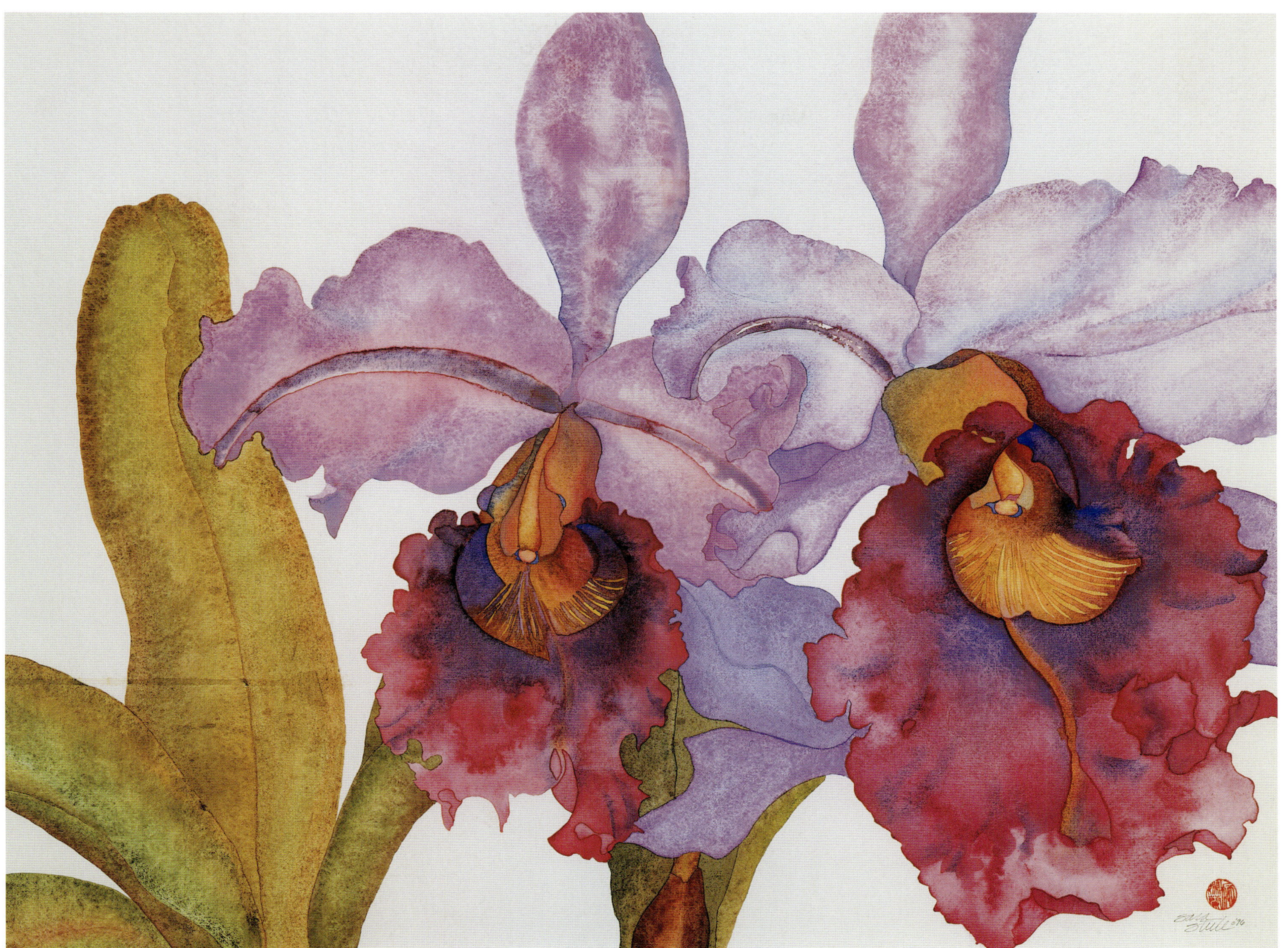

Laeliocattleya Moonwind, 1996

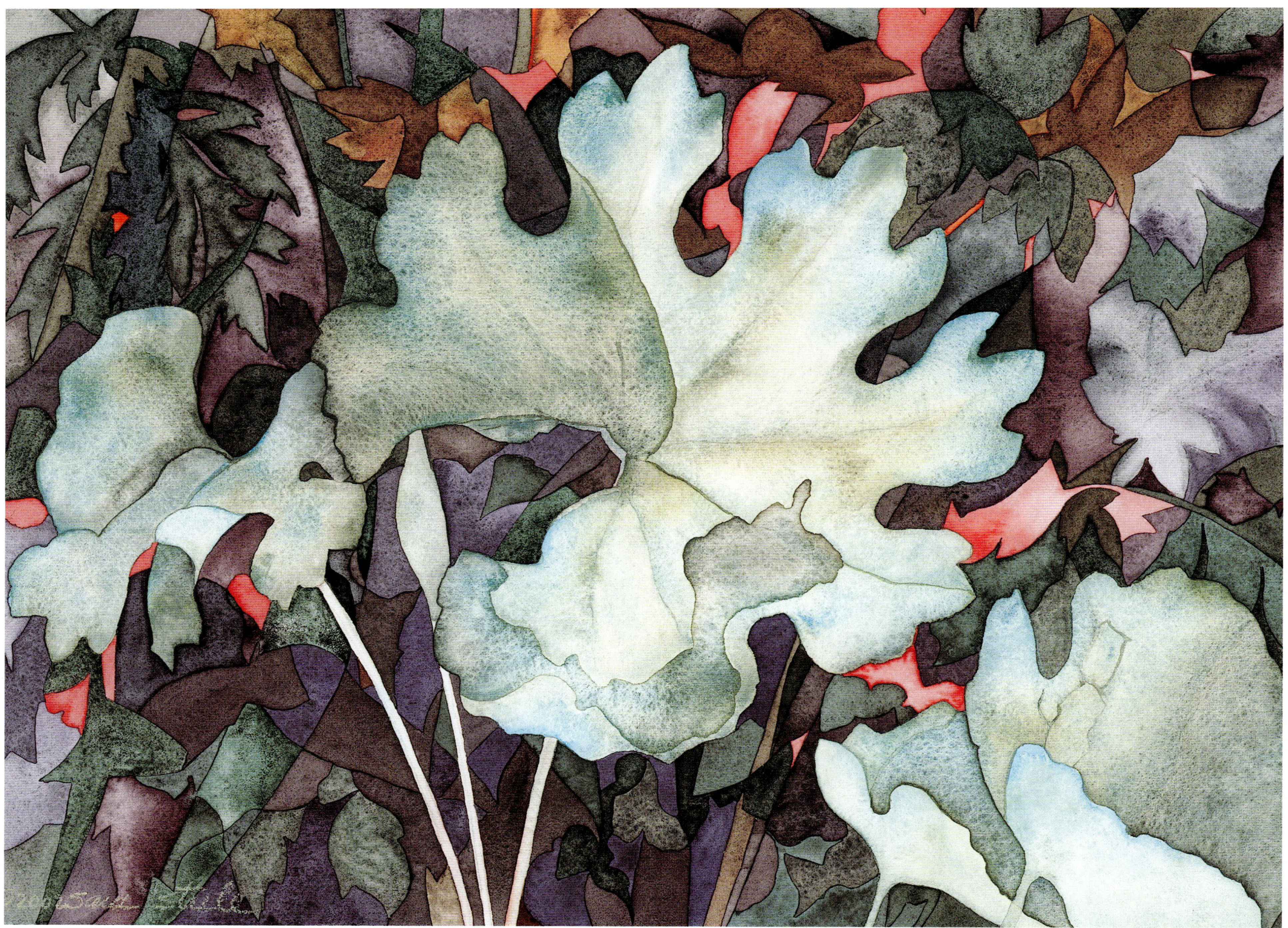

Bloodroot, 2002

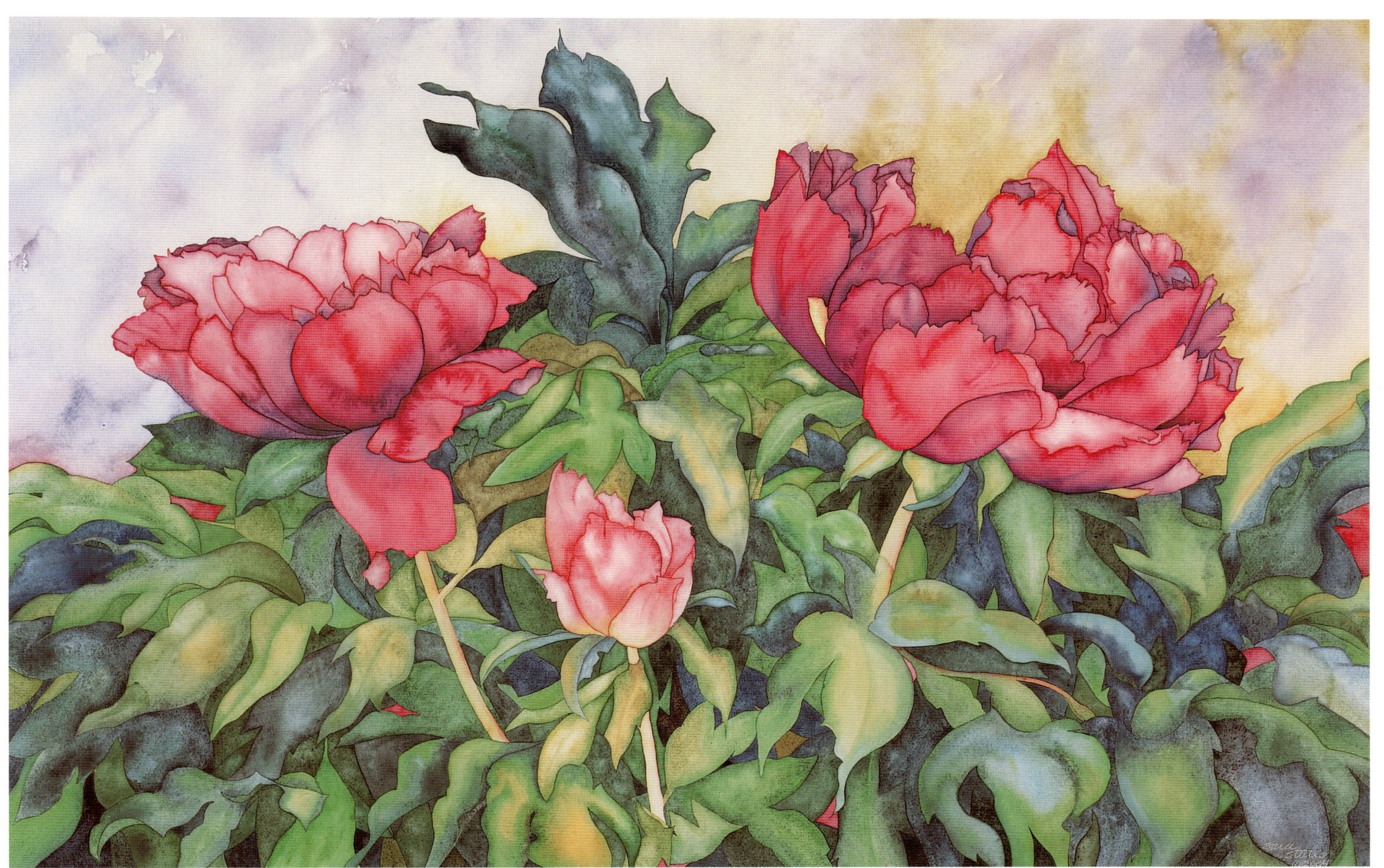

Scott's Tree Peonies, 2004

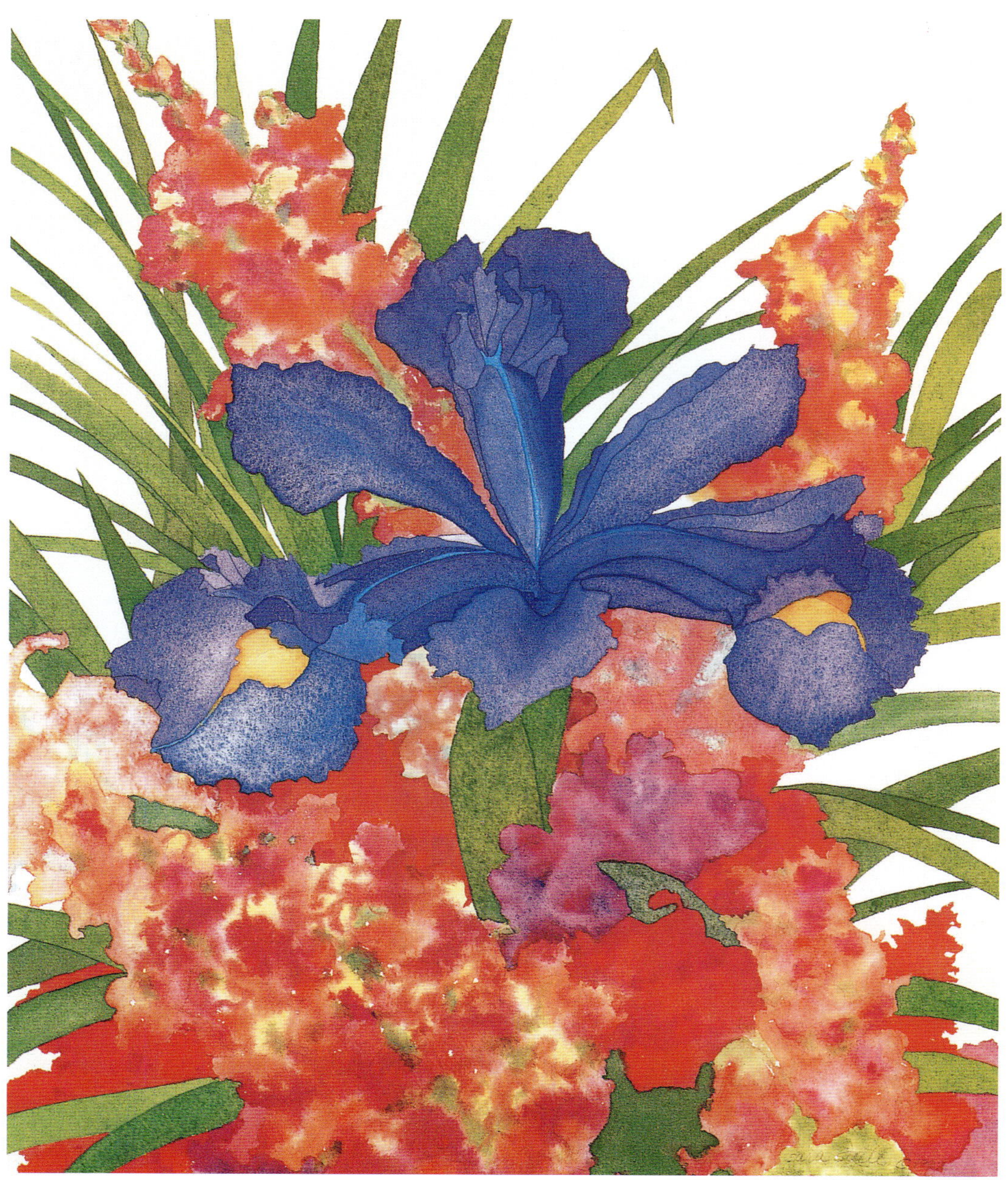

Sarah's Bouquet, 1982

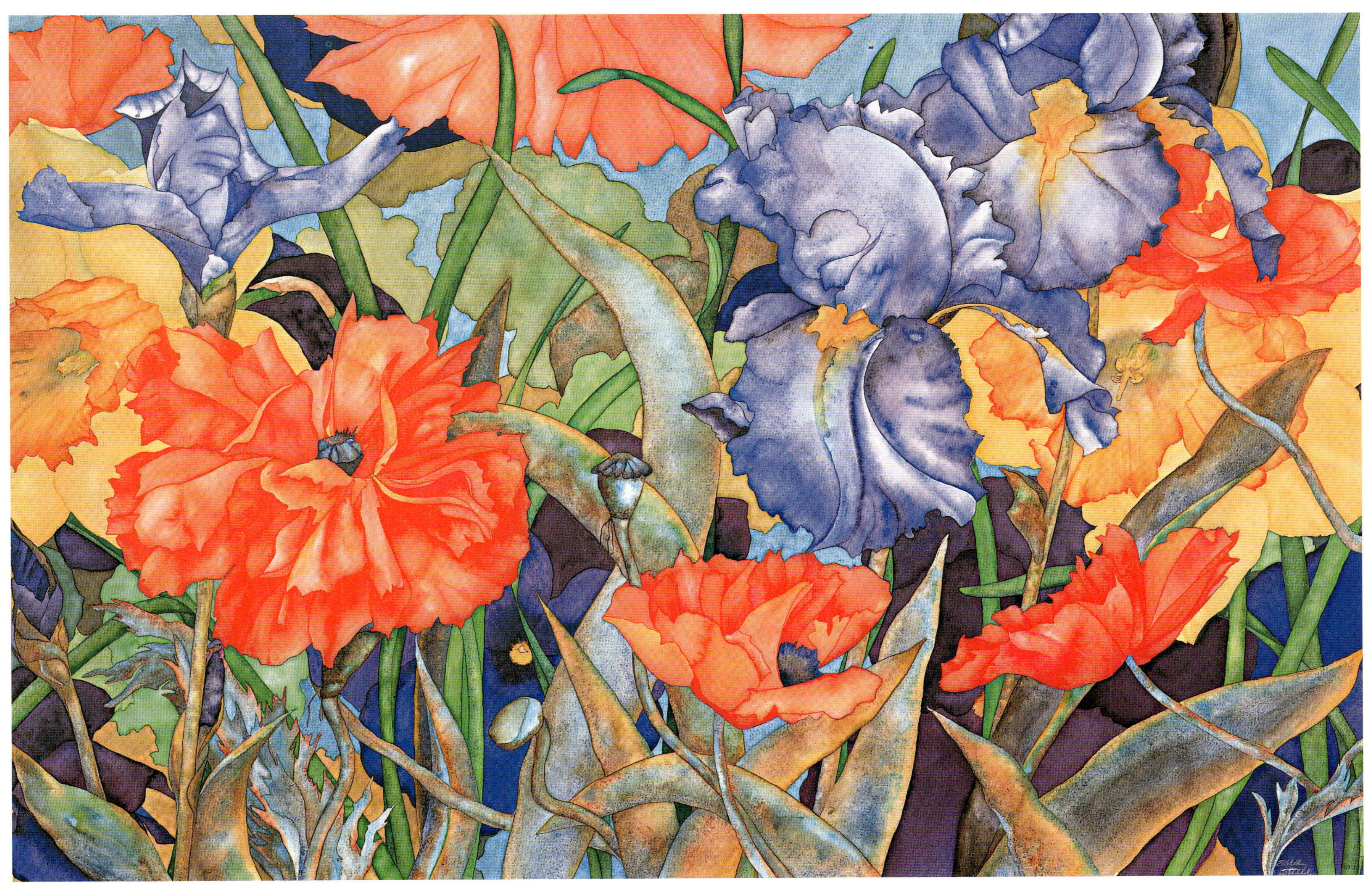

The Riots of Spring, 2004

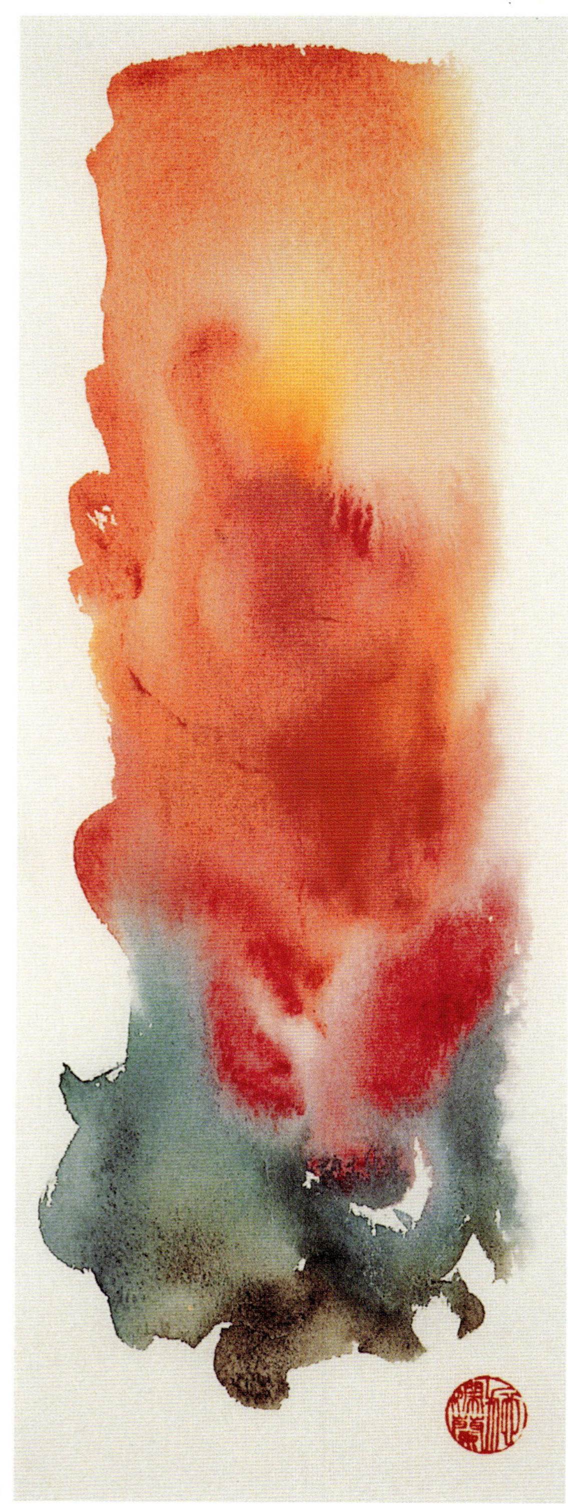

Flame, 1986

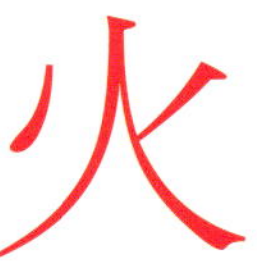

Fire

With summer, life reaches its zenith in an outpouring of exuberance and joy as the creative process of growth is fully realized. It is a time of celebration and connection, a season during which all of life is united into joyful community. The energetic element of Fire erupts into love and beauty as the upward cycle of the yang attains its creative and joyful climax.

The pieces in this collection pulsate with the random, upward, celebratory energy of Fire, which is highlighted in the abstract form of the opening painting, *Flame*, as well as in *Abstract #7* and *The Point I*. The floral still lifes in this section express an appropriately vibrant energy. *Magic Tulip* shows the effects of refracted light landing on a tulip's petal, bringing with it an awareness of the resilience of life. *Cereus* captures the graceful, elusive beauty of a plant with fragrant blossoms that last for only one night. *Oscoda* renders the visual effect of a distant forest fire reflected on the surface of a lake. *Heart Healing*, part of the "Nuclear Family Holocaust" series, depicts the creative and healing transmutation of anger into love and compassion. The final painting in the collection, *Sunflowers*, points toward the seasonal shift of earth and sun into late summer, when many plants create the seeds of future generations.

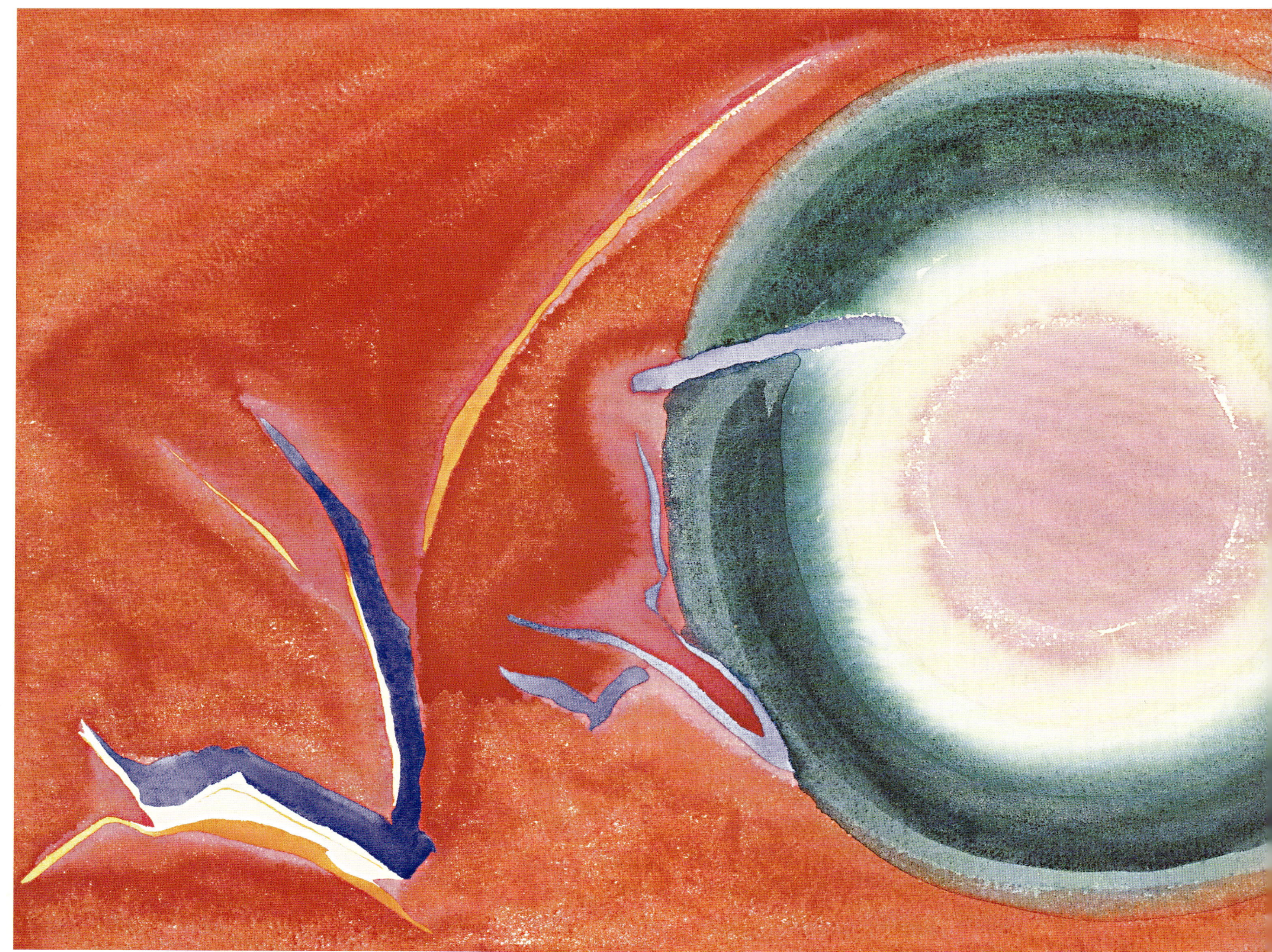

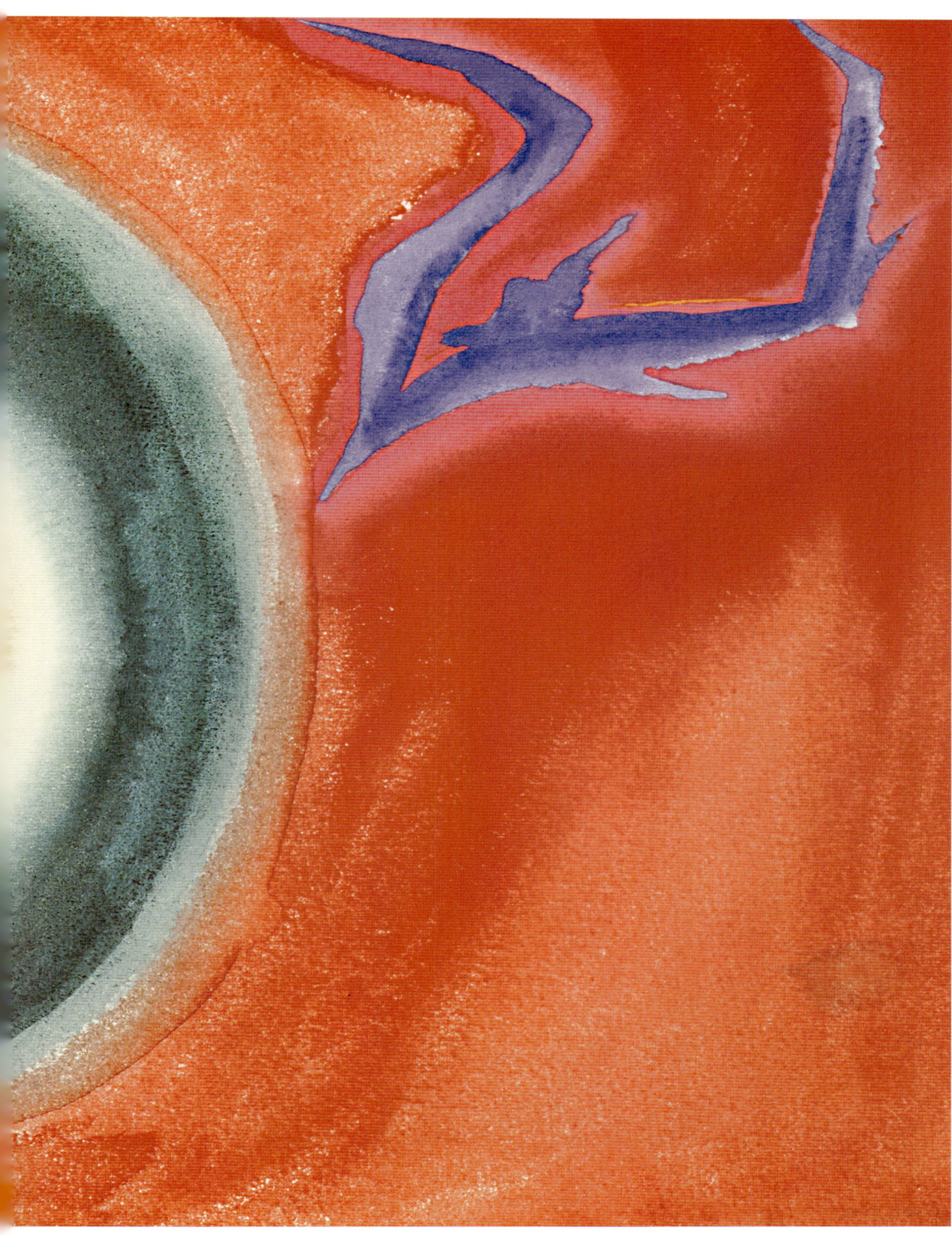

Heart Healing, 1983

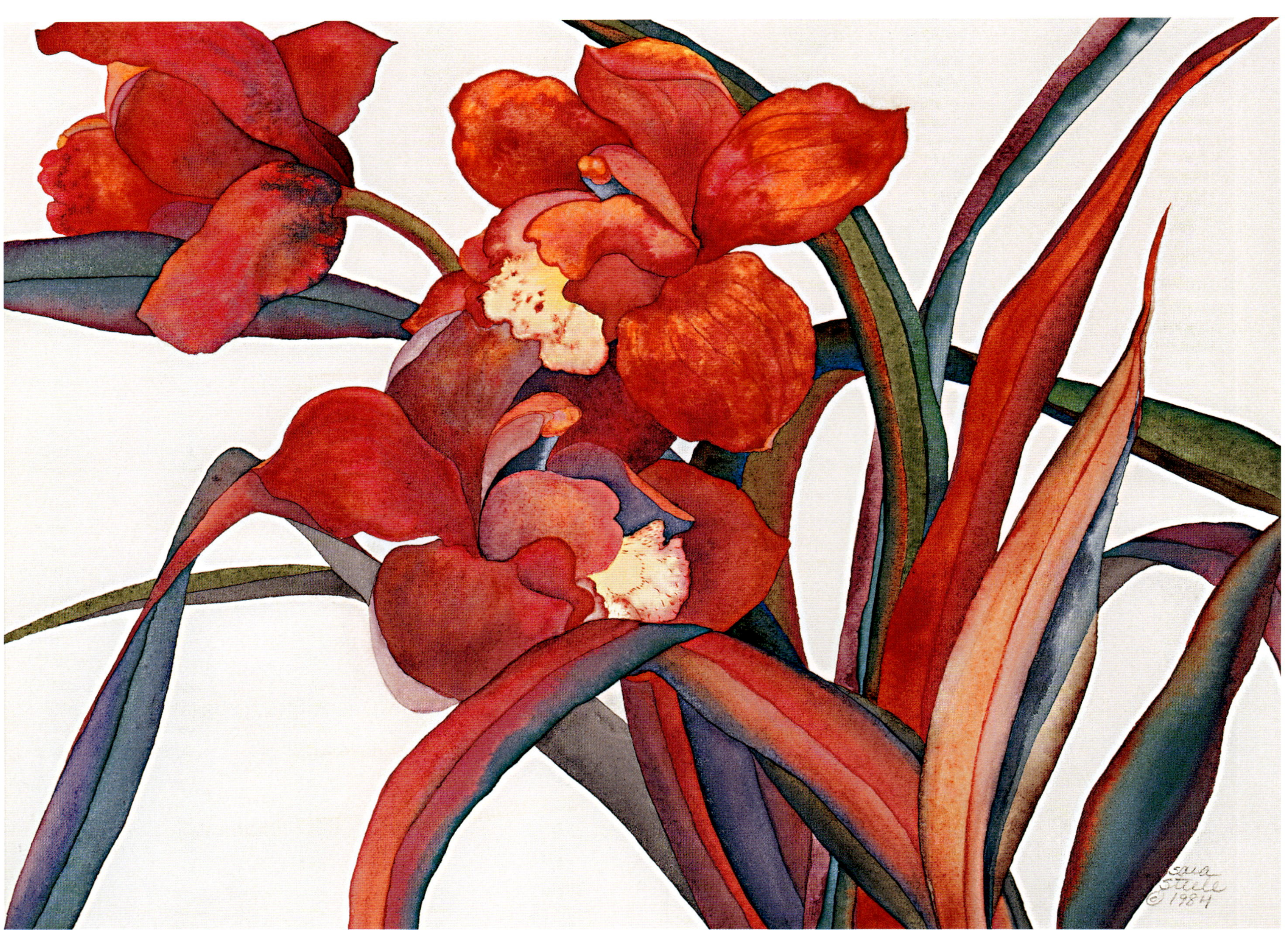

Cymbidium Anna Marie Sunshine, 1984

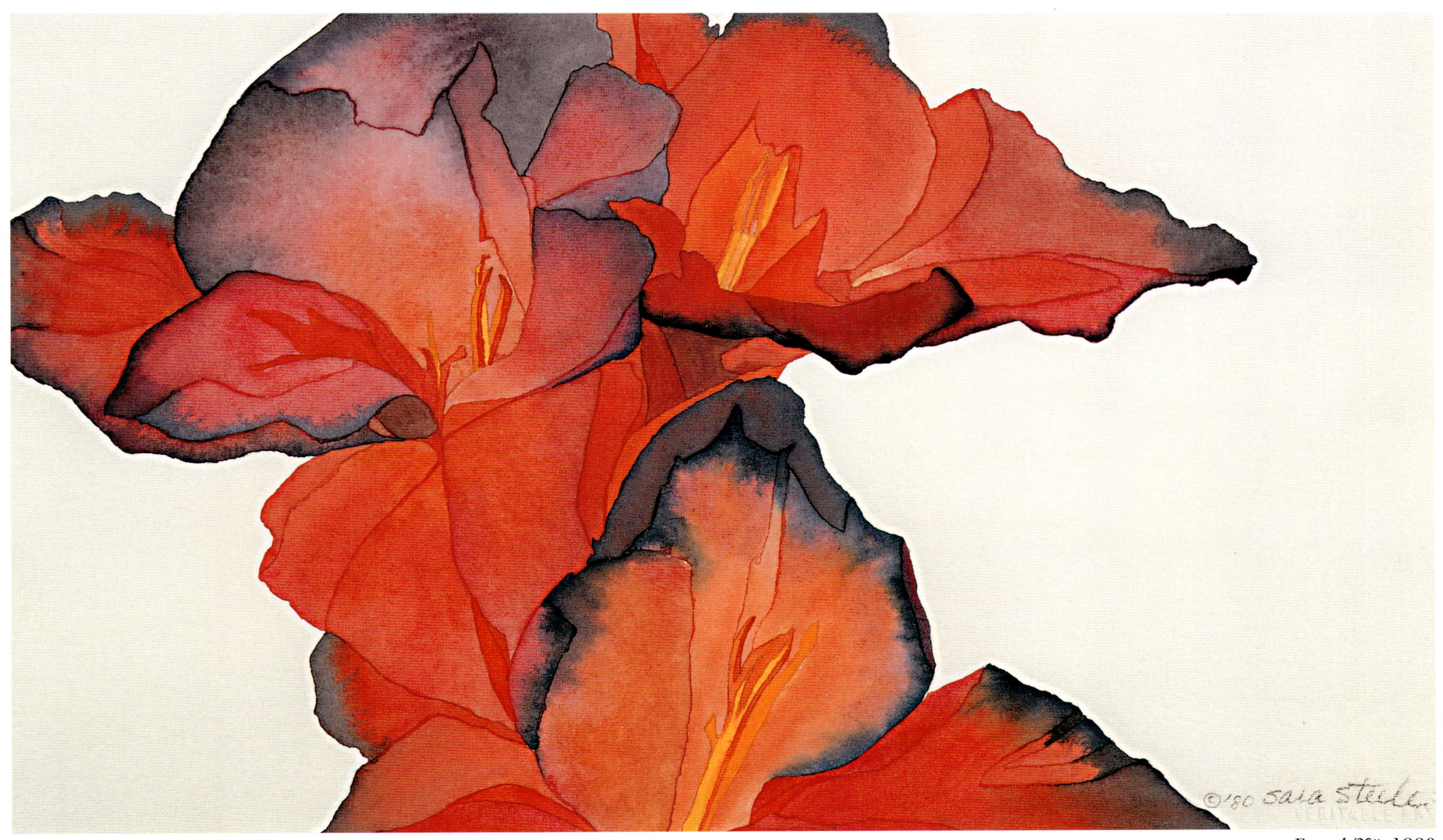

Found/Yü, 1980

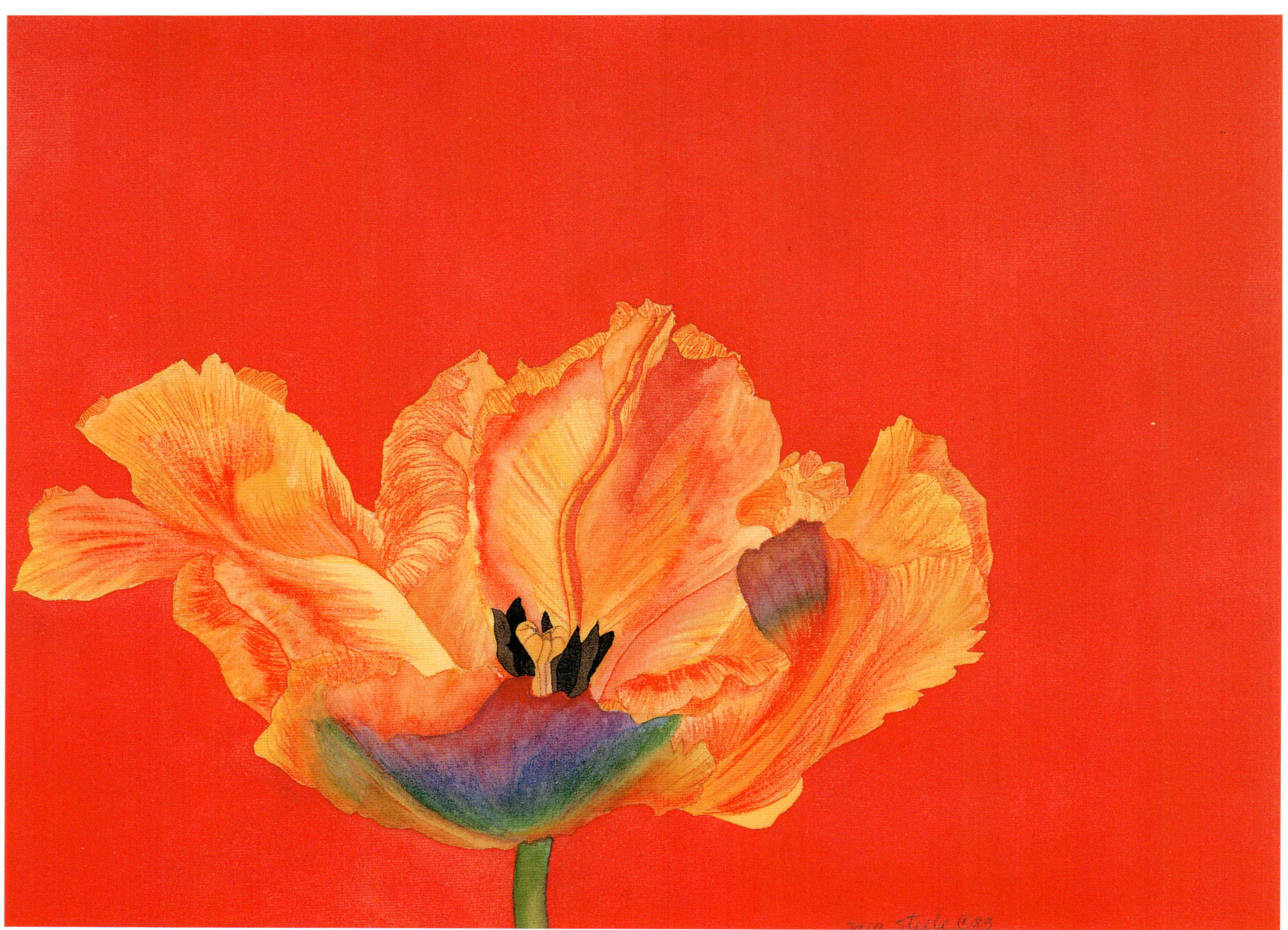

Magic Tulip, 1983

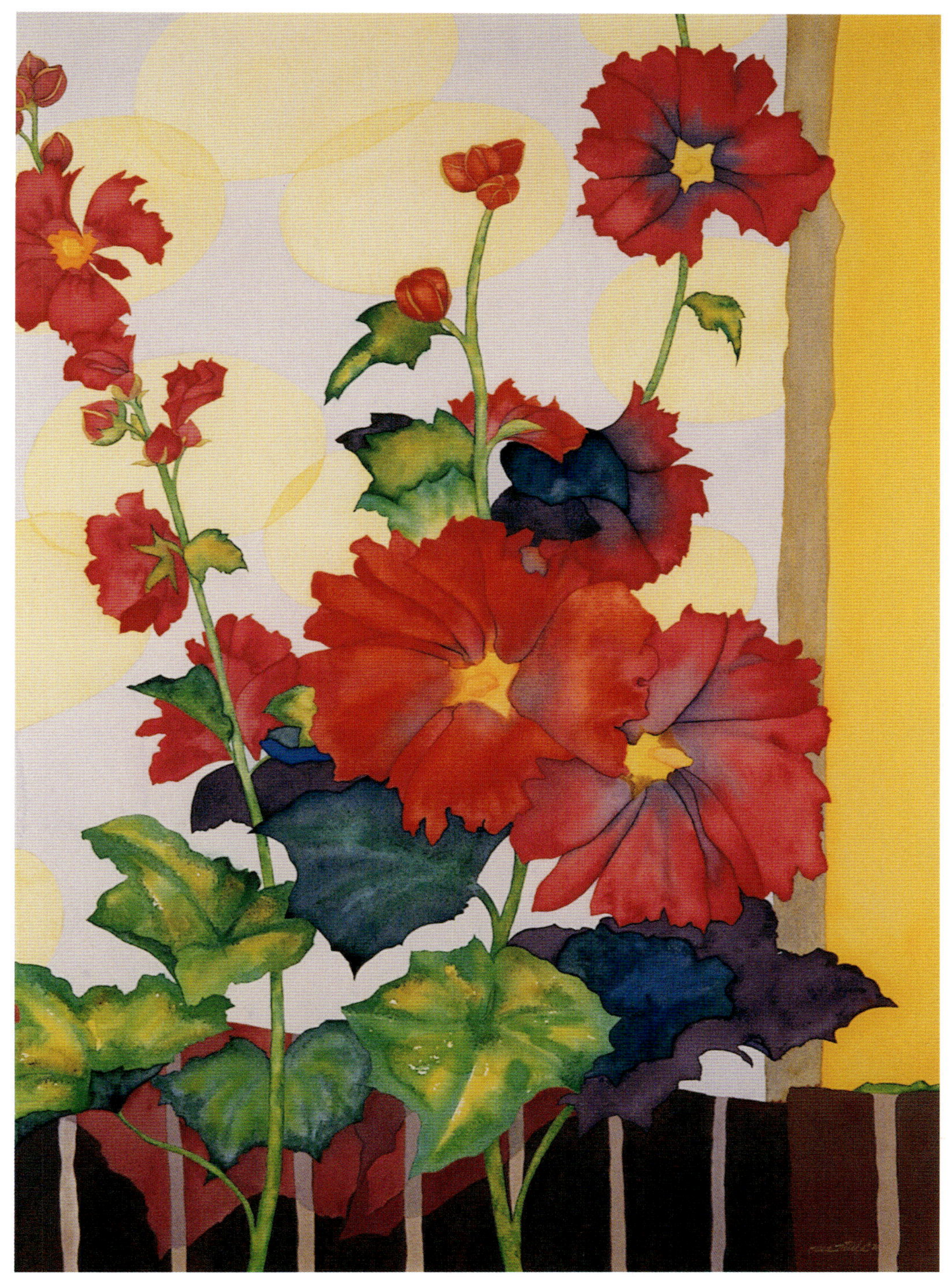

Hollyhocks with Sunspots/Freedom Flowers, 1998

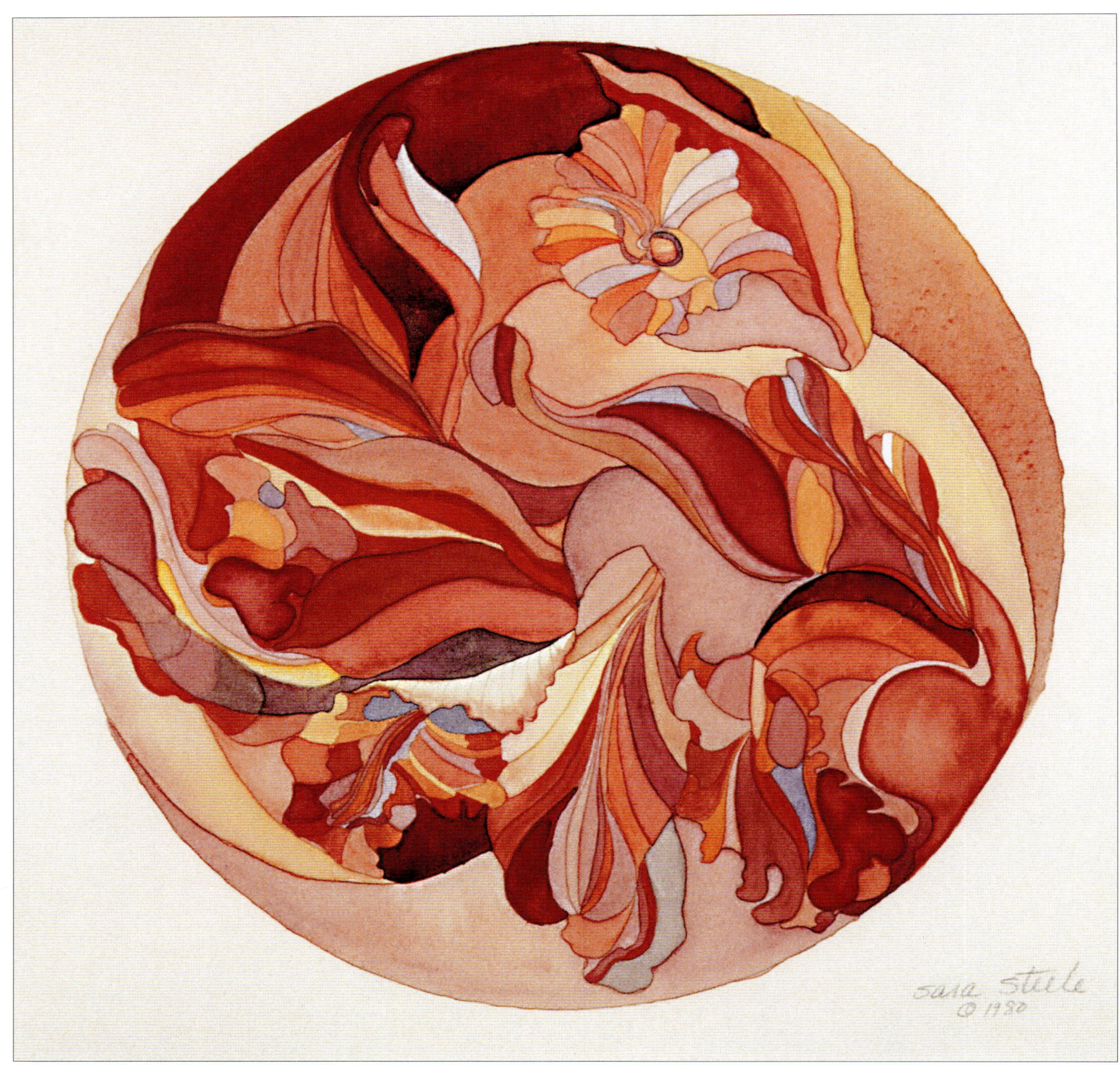

Neptune's Daughter, 1980

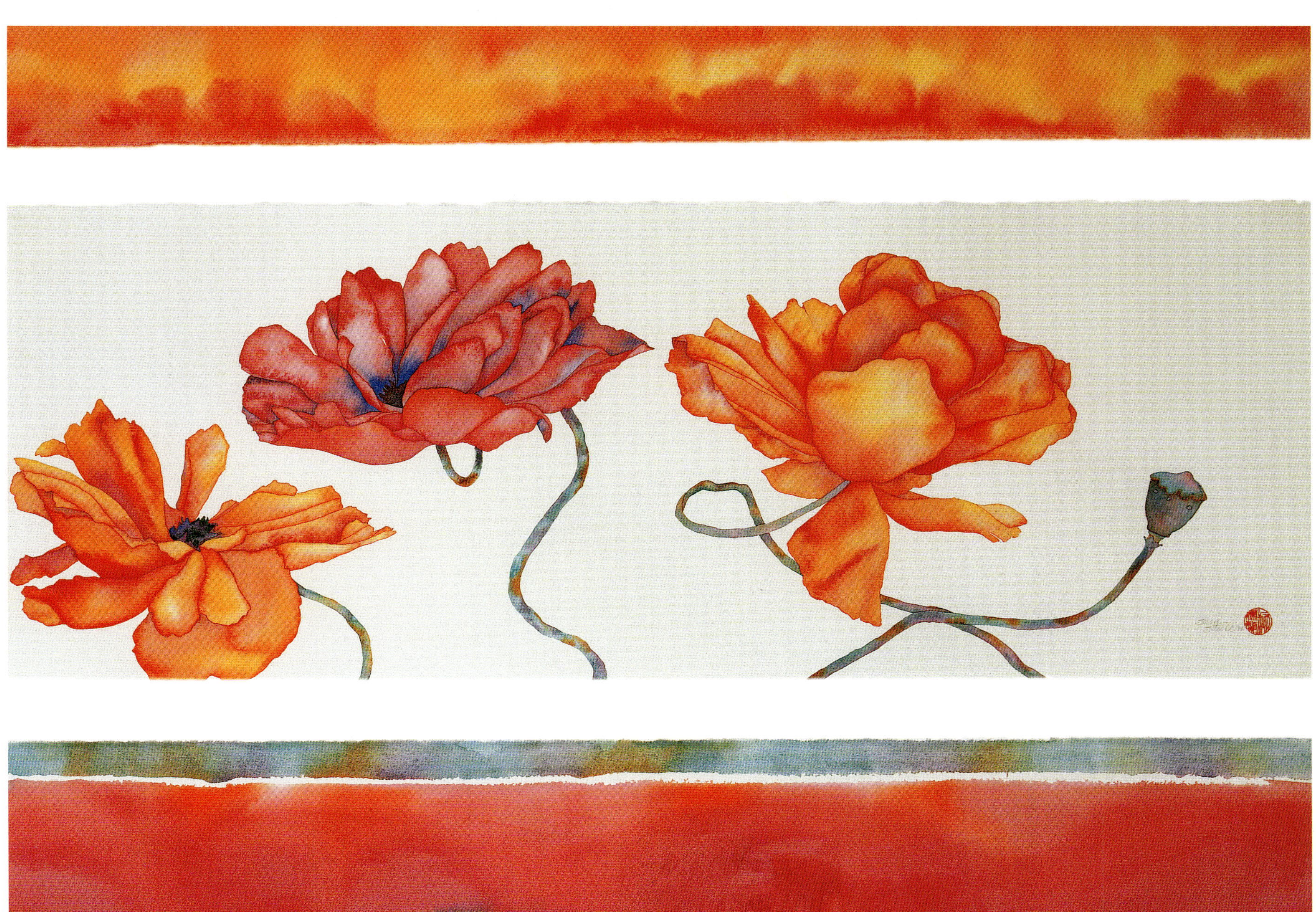

Poppies, 1996

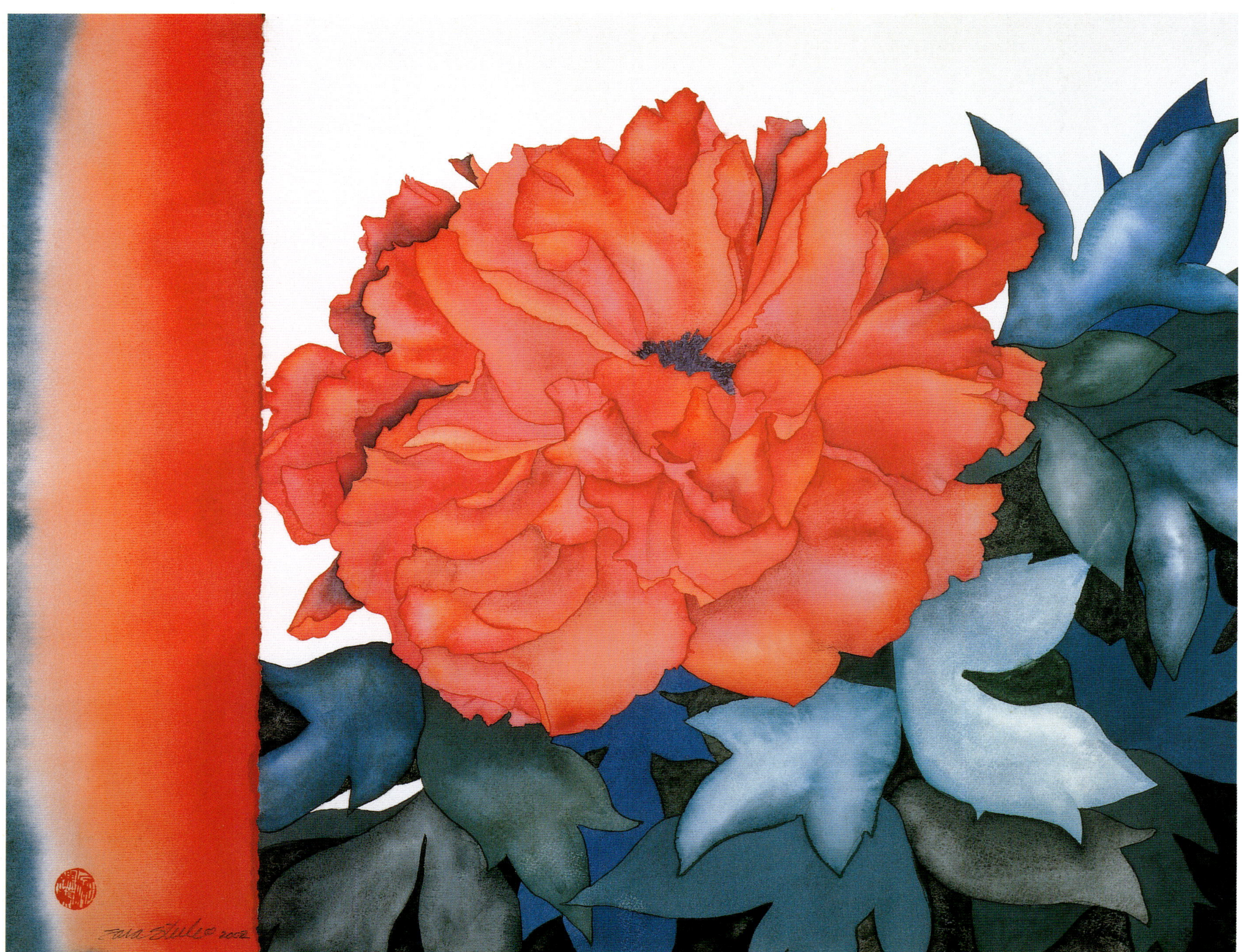

Tree Peony, 2002

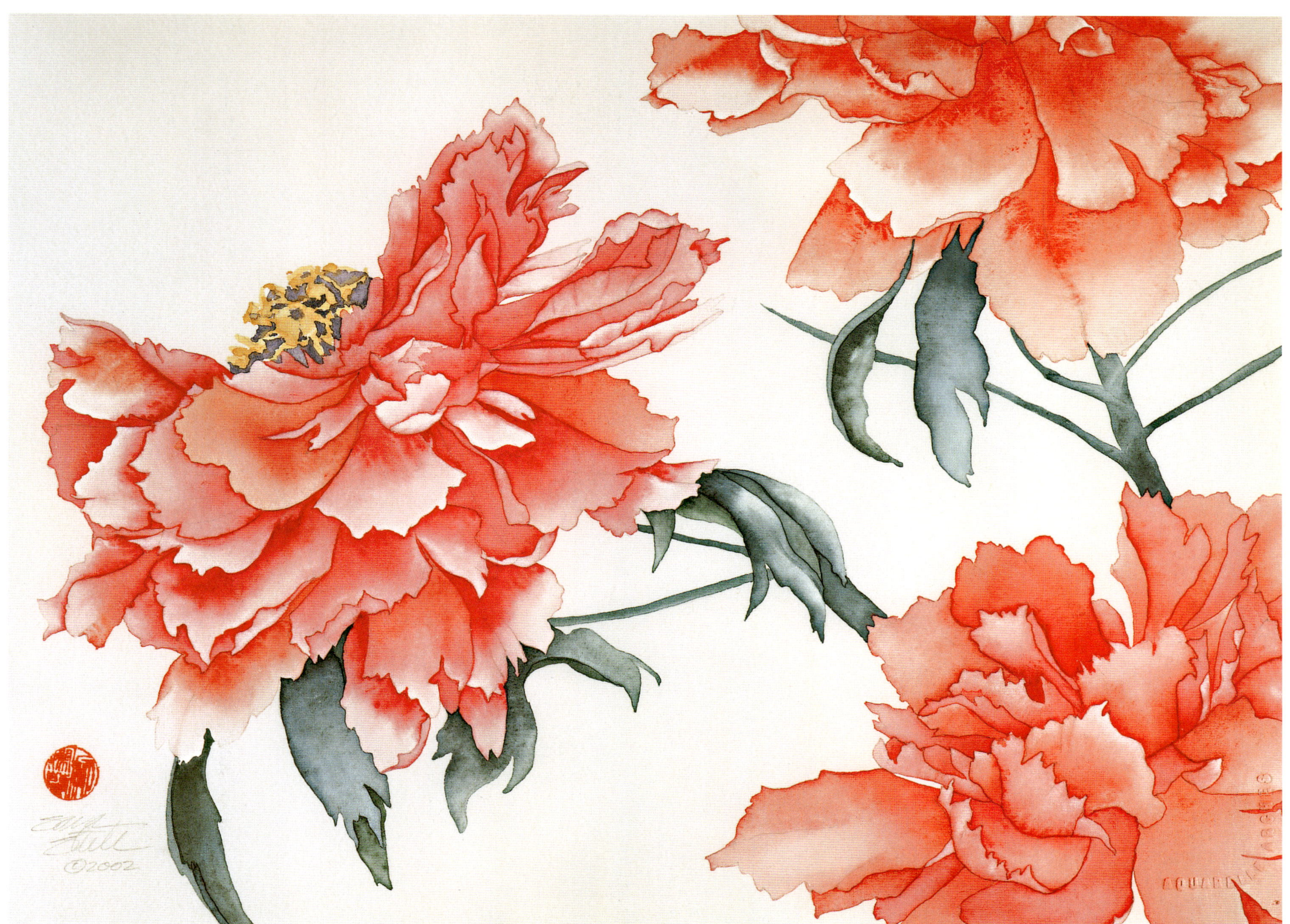

Three Tree Peonies (Allen's Lane), 2002

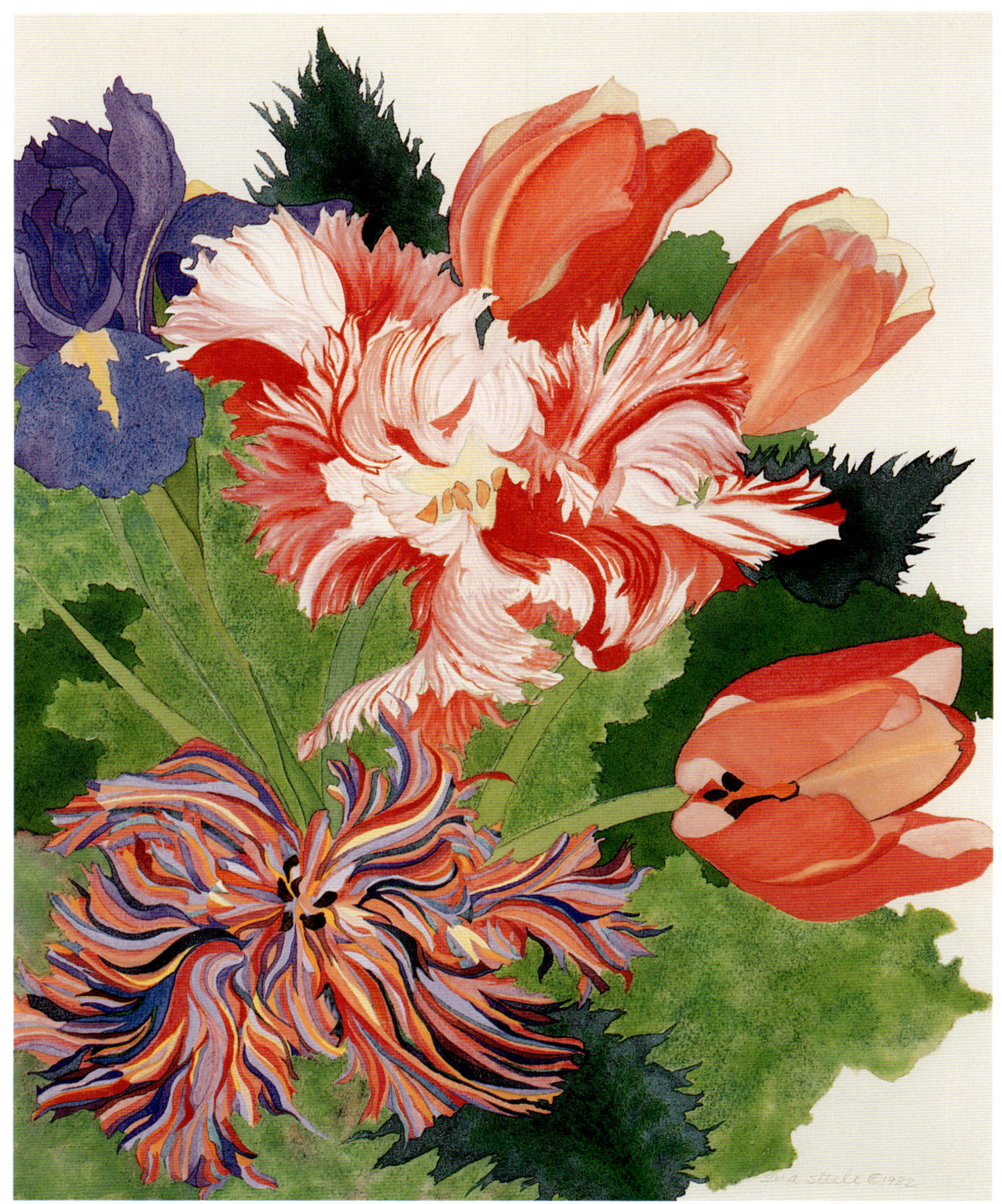

Parrot Tulips, 1982

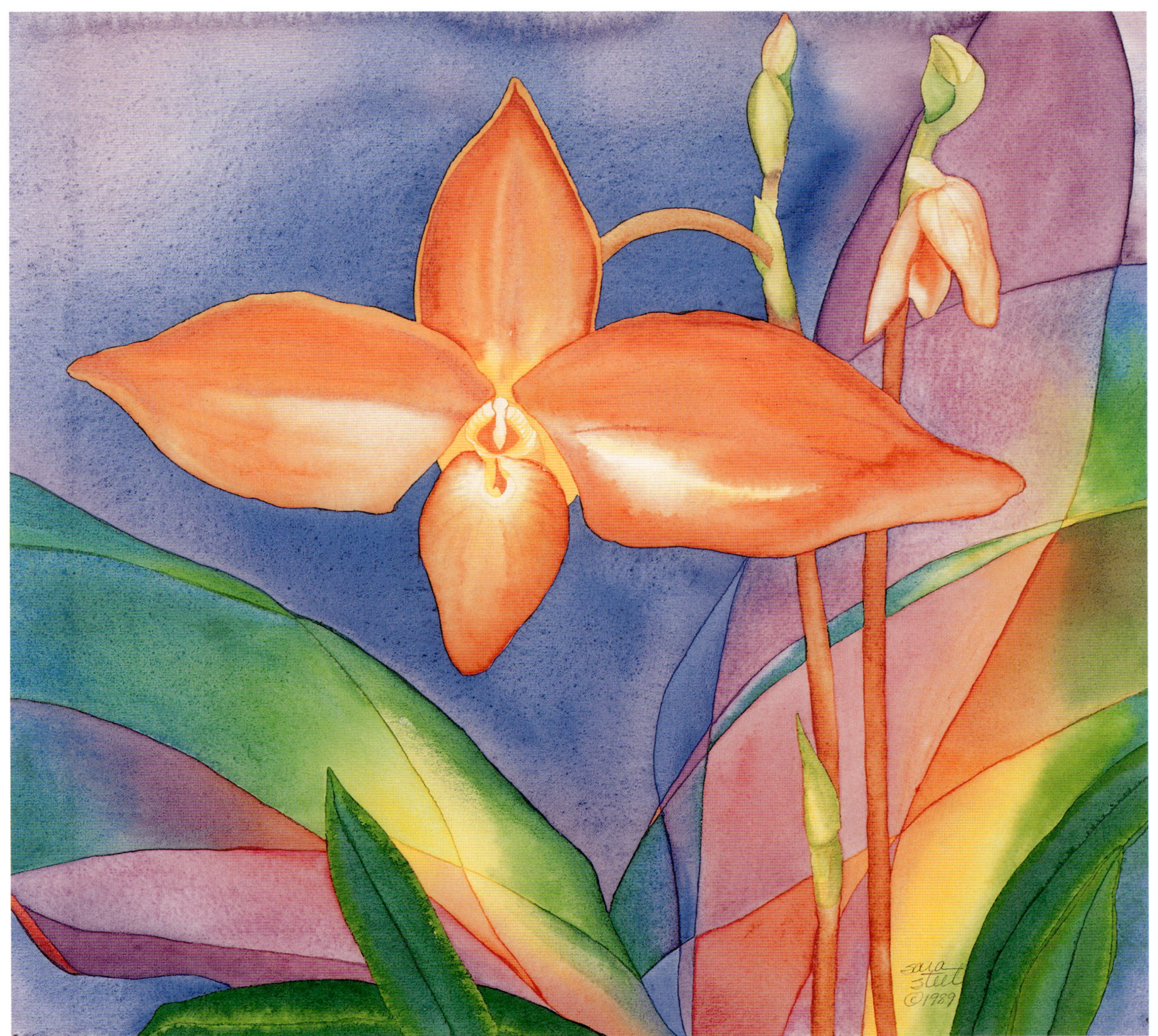

Phragmepedium besseae, from the Endangered Orchids series, 1989

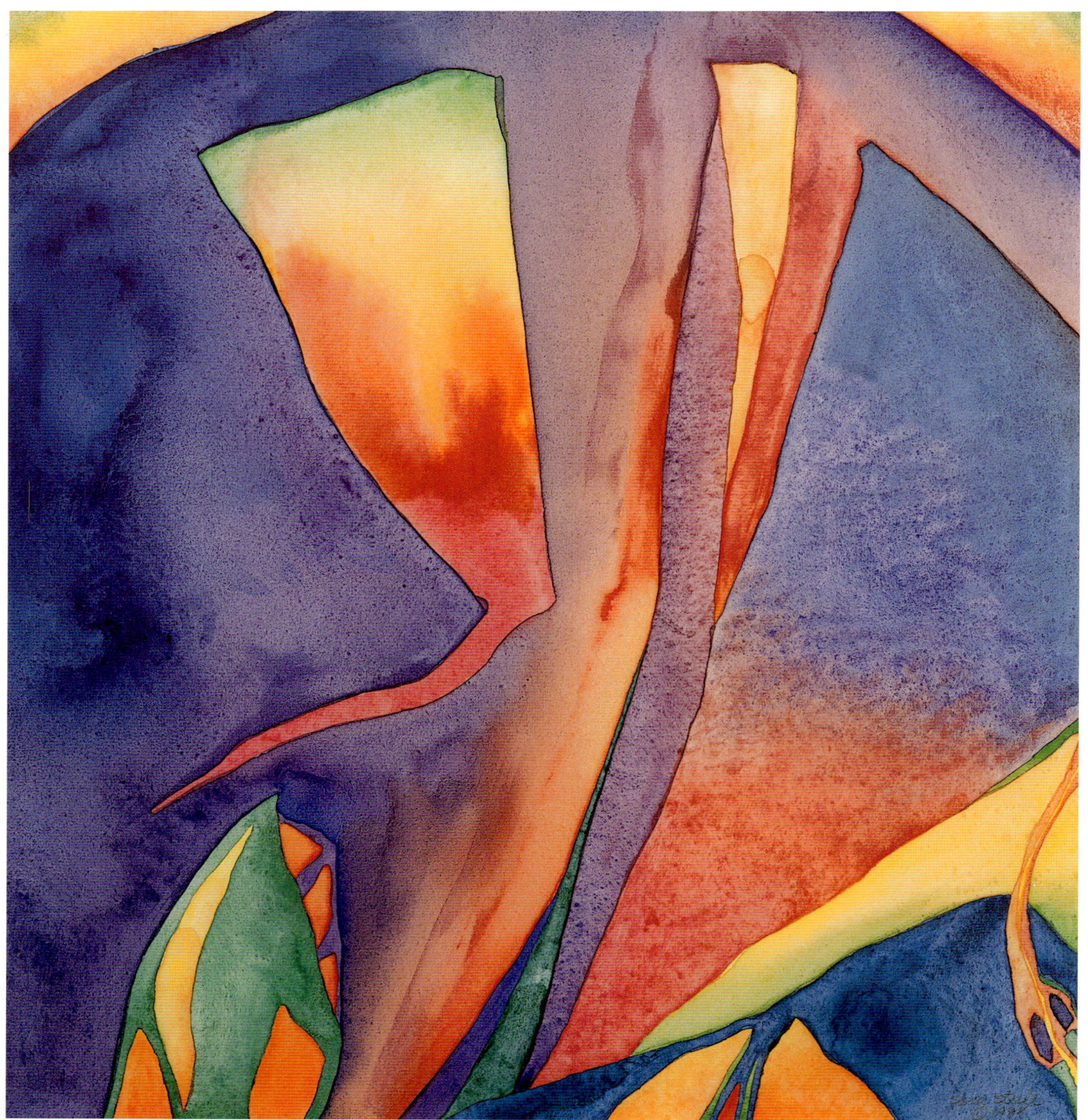

Gekkos in Paradise, 1988

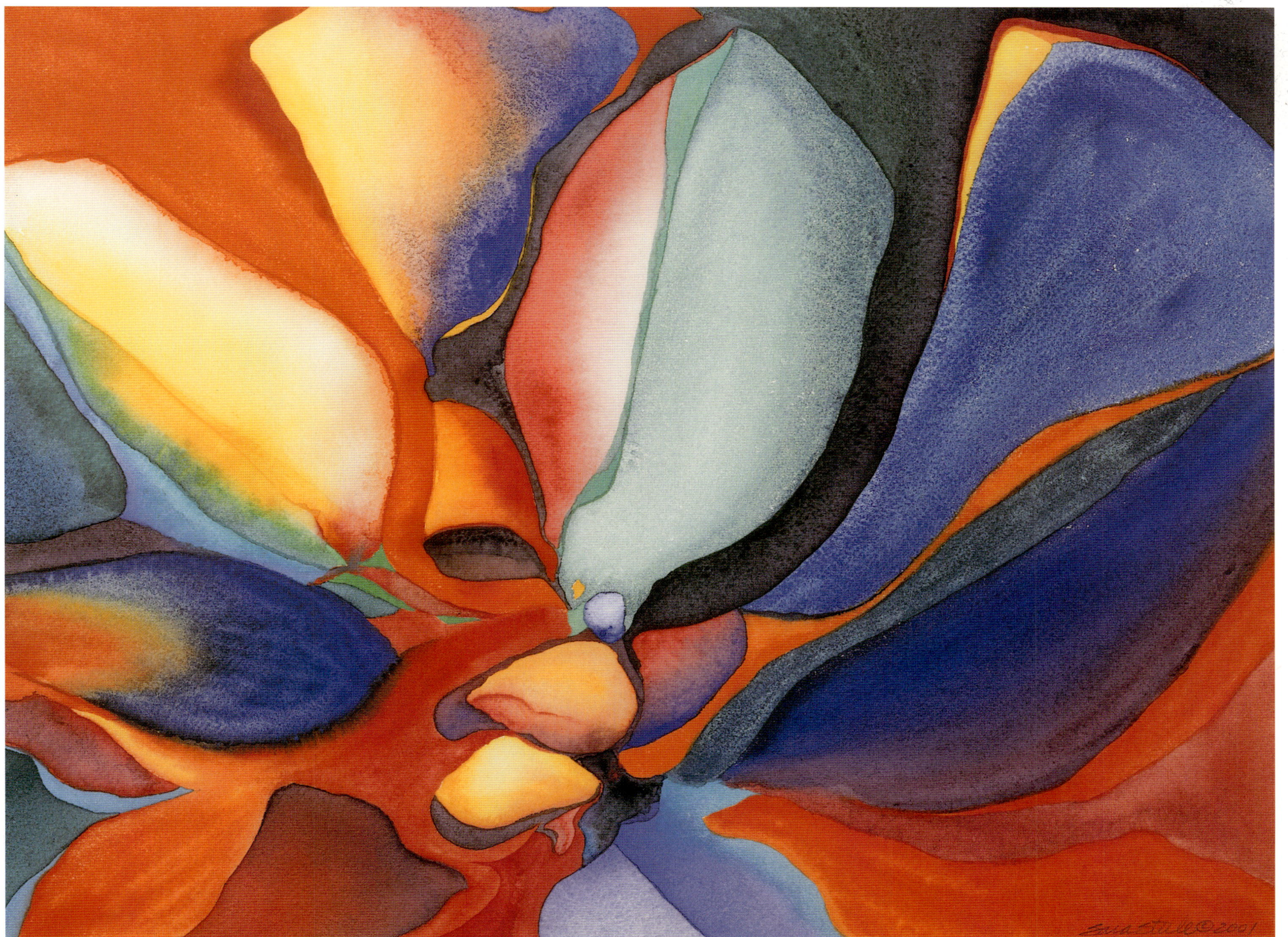

Migration, 2001

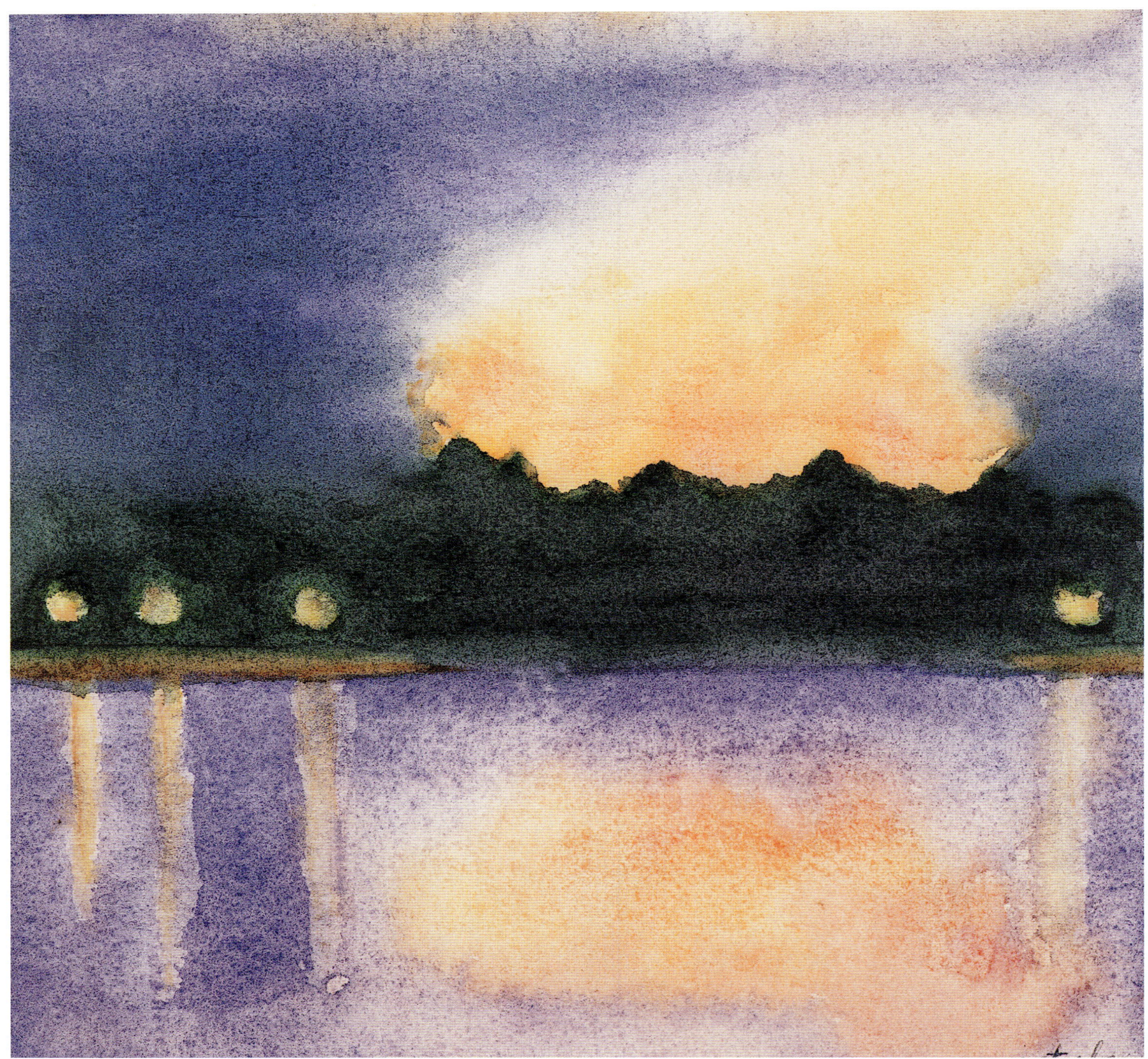

Forest Fire, Oscoda, 1978

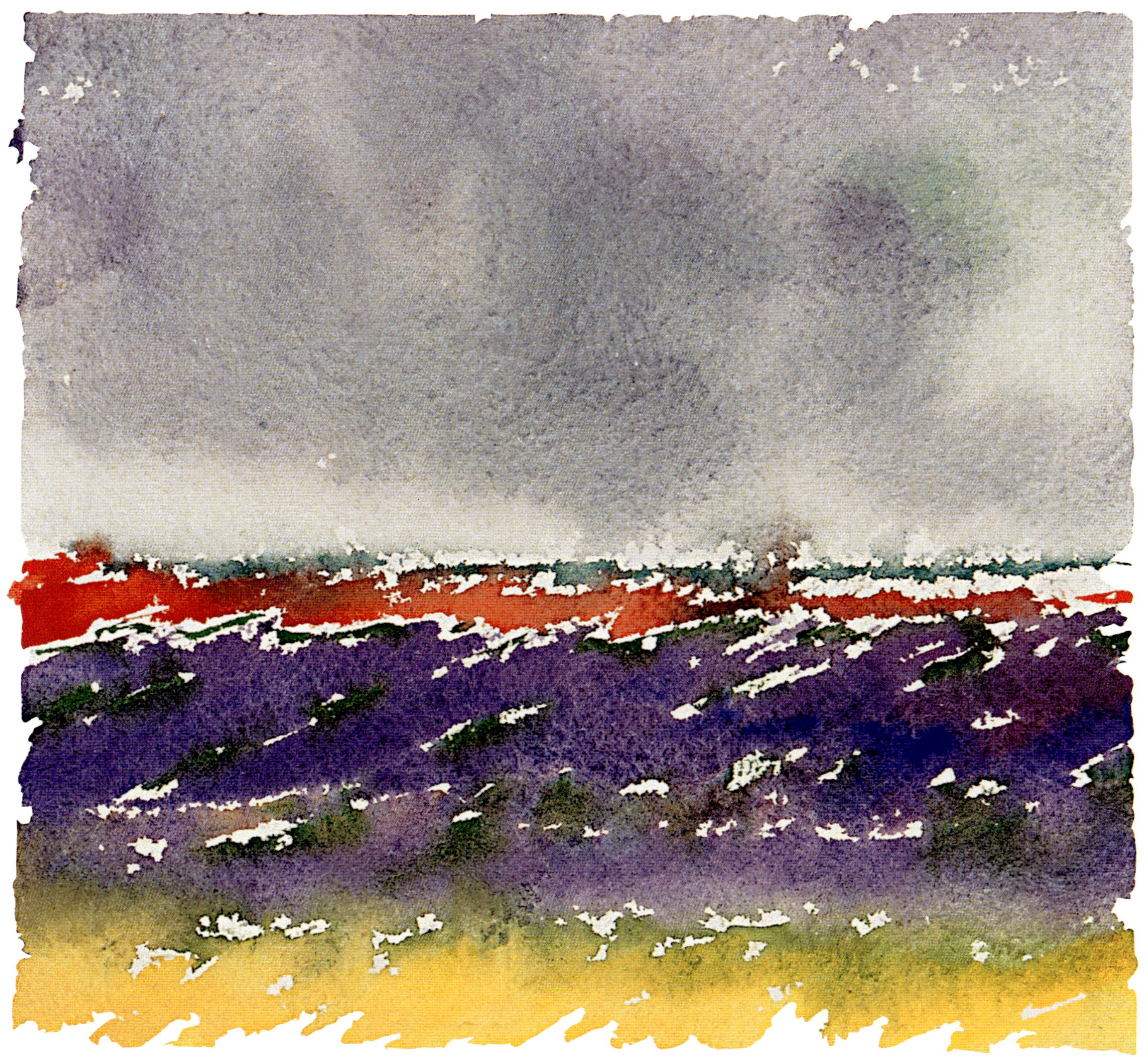

Tulip Fields, 1985

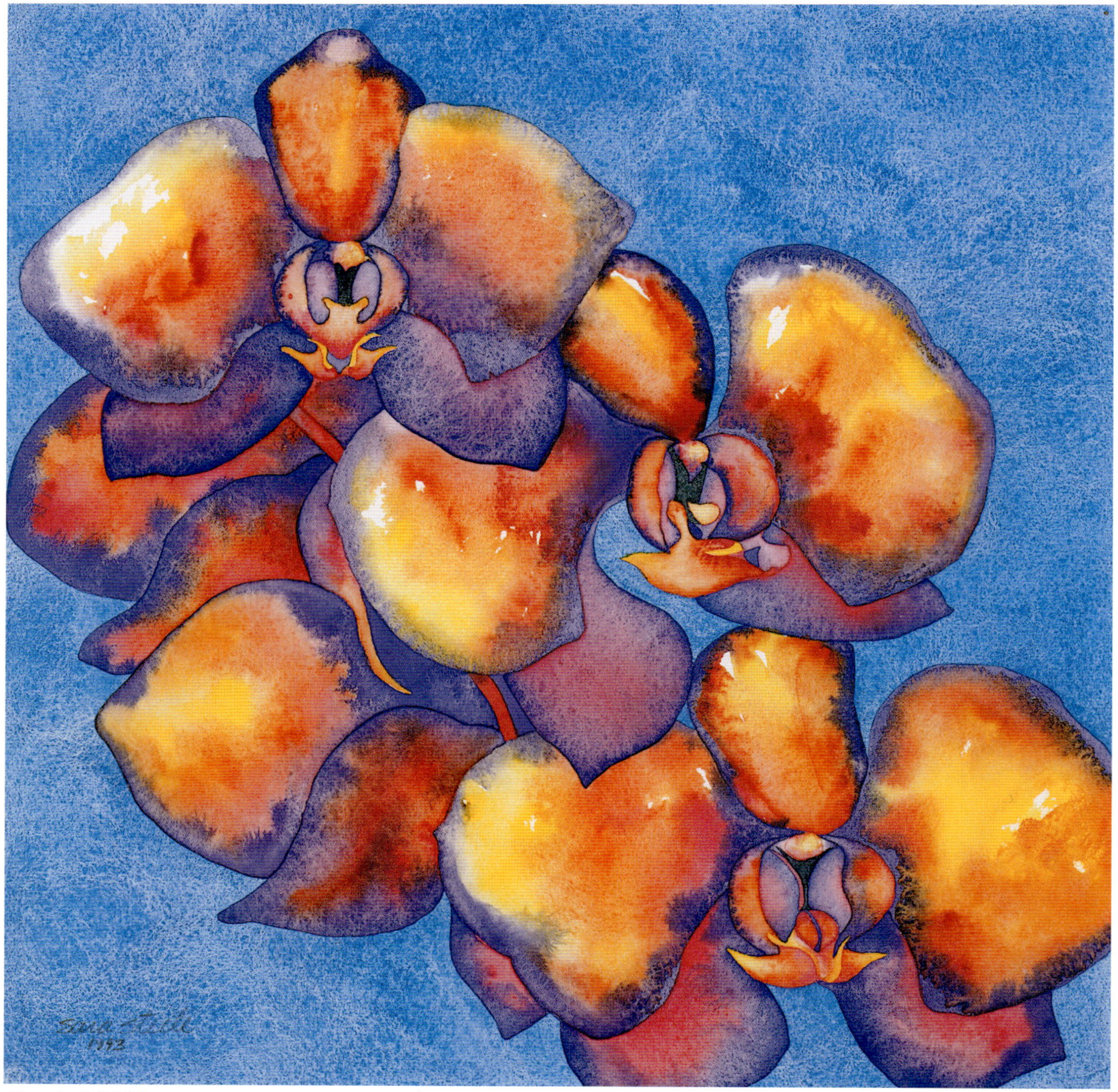

Firephal, 1993

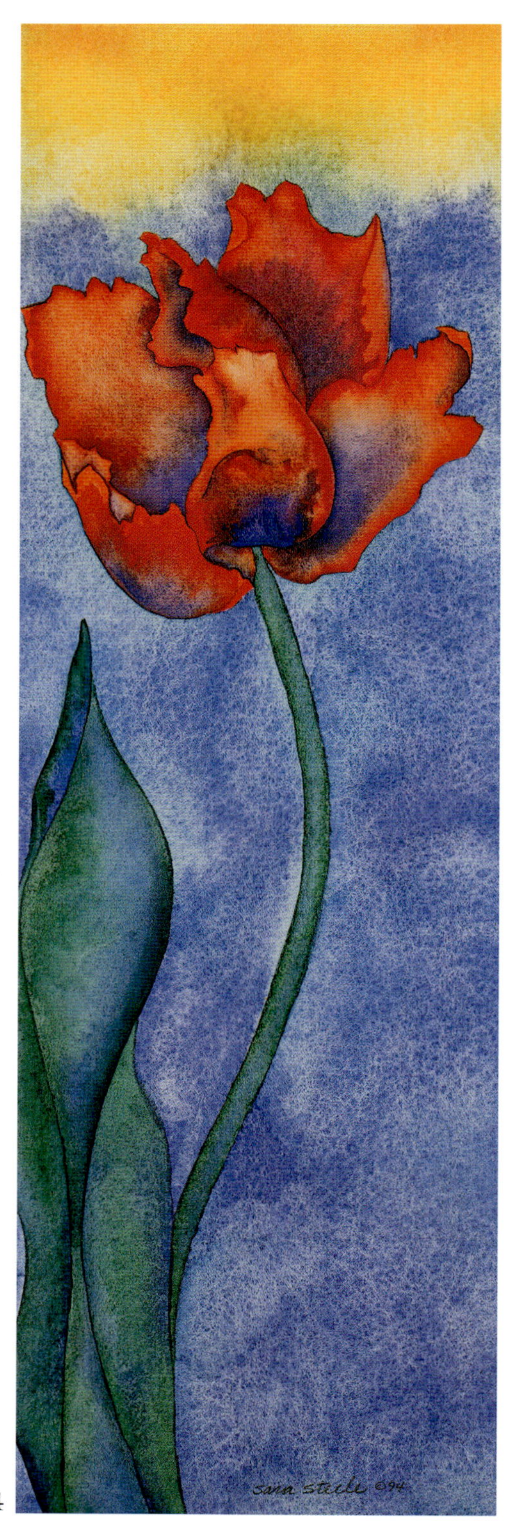

Long Relaxed Tulip, 1994

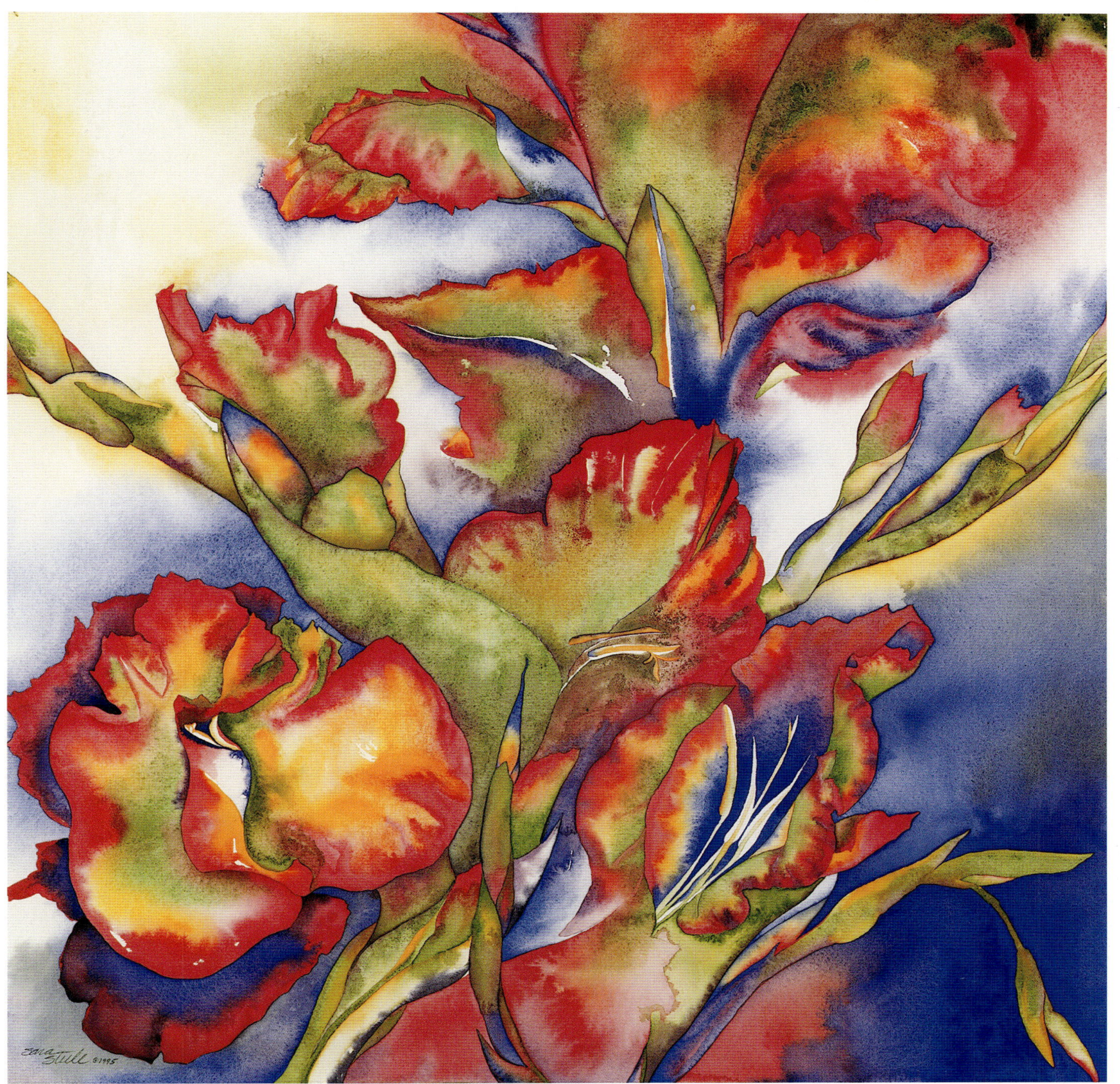

Wild Glads, 1995

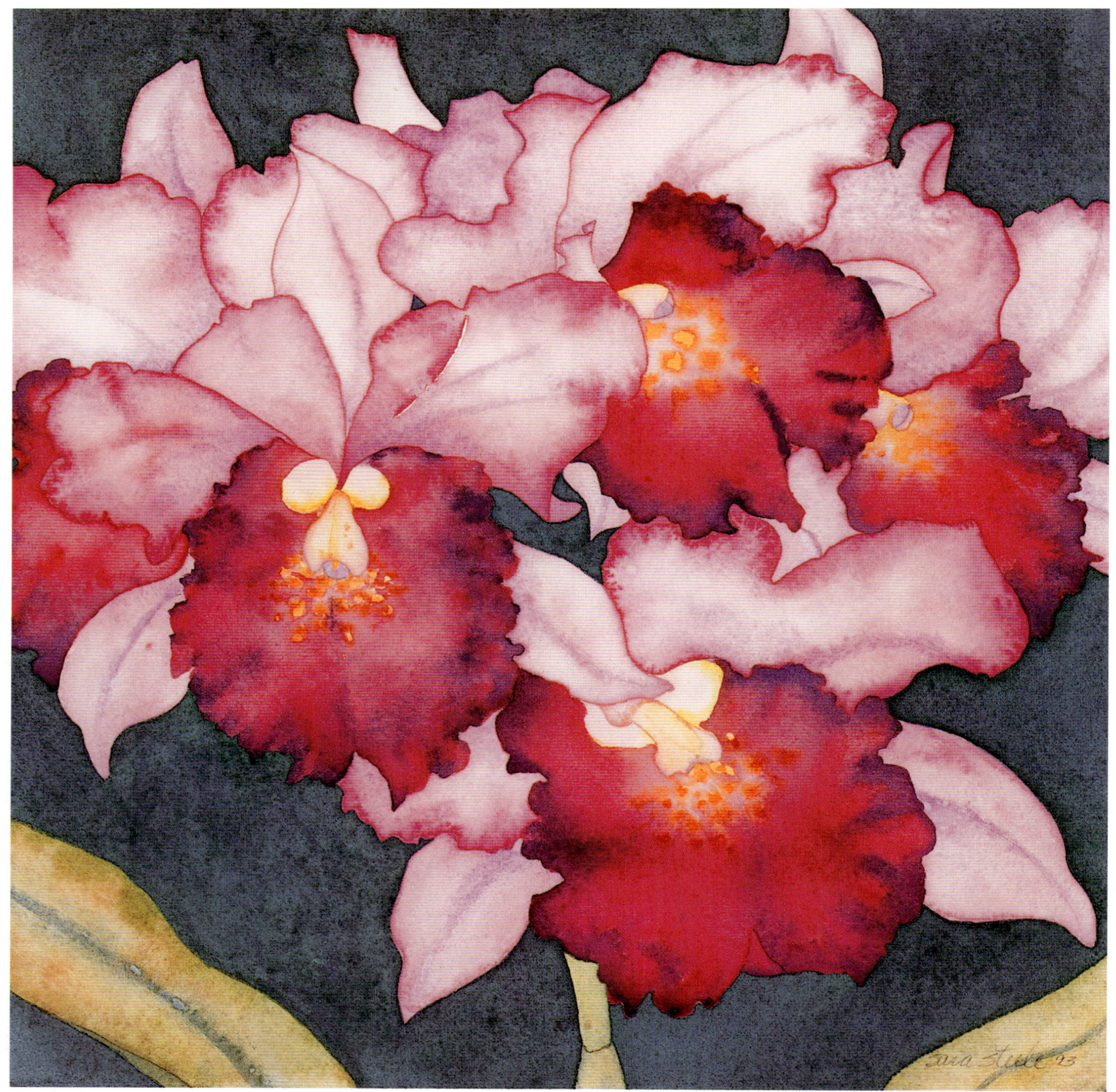

Cattleya Quintet, 1993

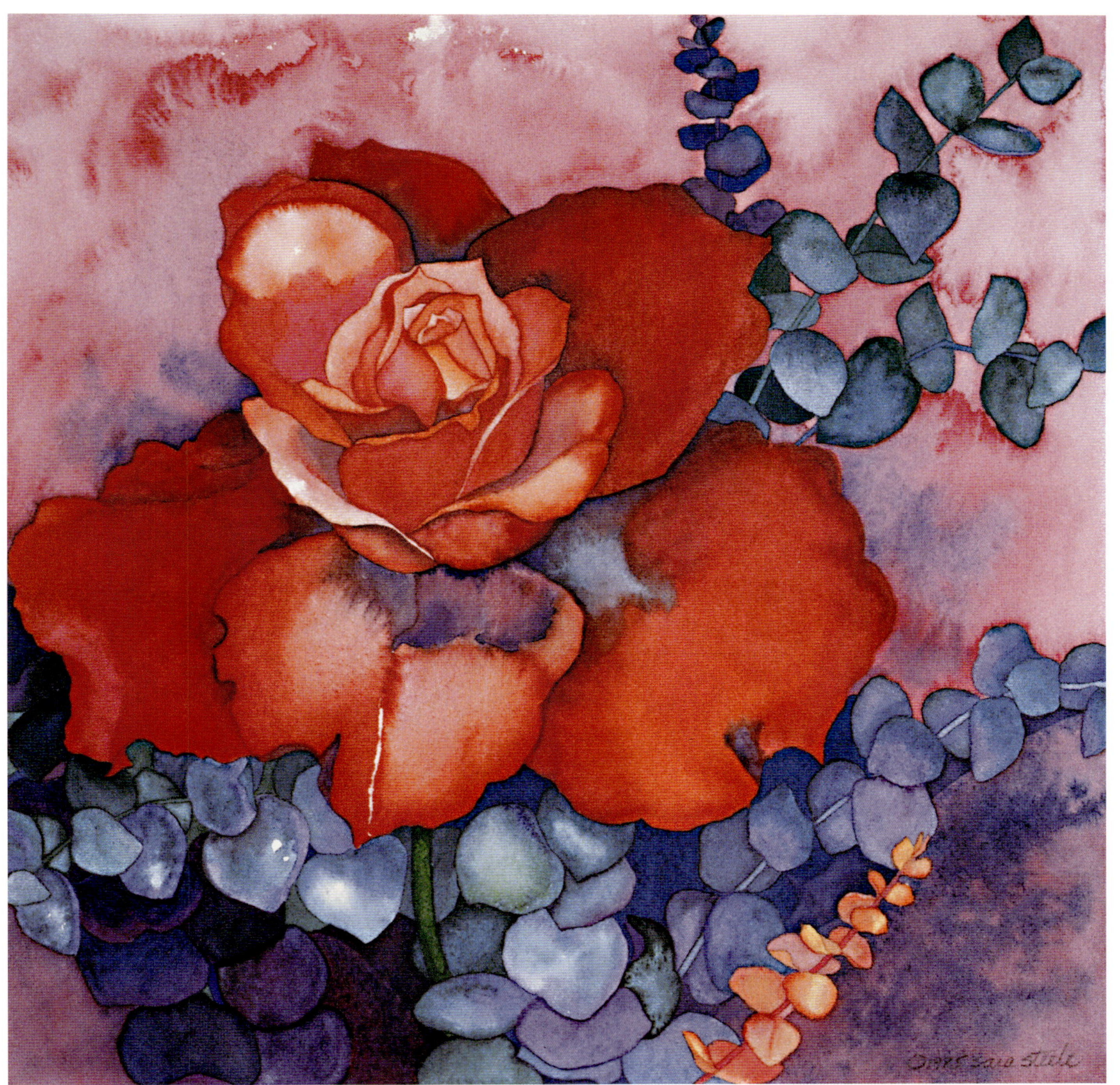

Rose and Eucalyptus, 1985

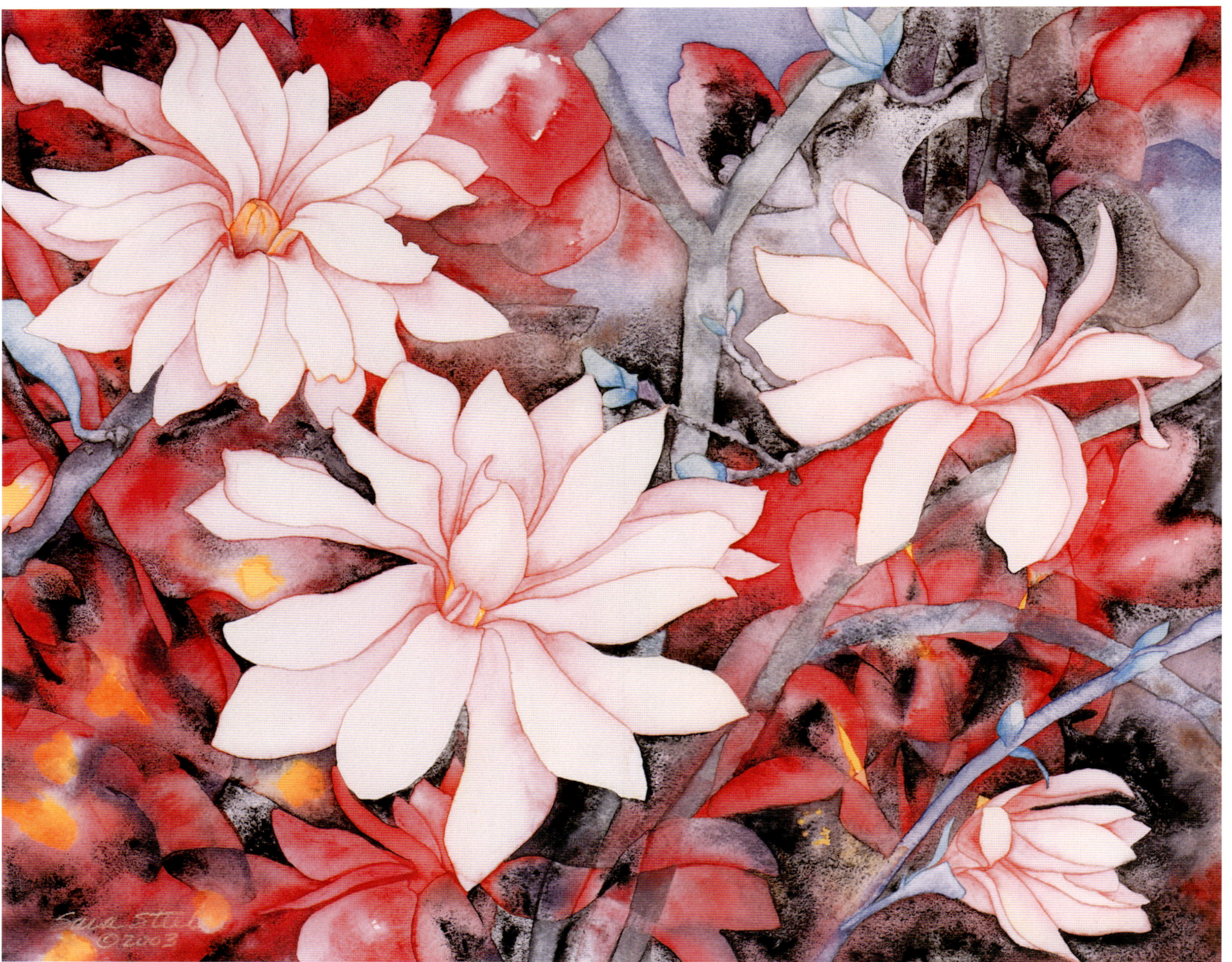

Star Magnolias, 2003

On the first day of the week, the twenty-fourth day of the month of Tammuz in the year 5754 corresponding to July 3, 1994, here in Orlando, Florida

The bride **Karen** daughter of Martin Leventhal & Marilyn Leventhal said to the groom Mark Wolman "Be my husband according to the law of Moses and Israel.

The groom **Mark** son of Samuel Wolman & Esther Wolman said to the bride Karen Leventhal "Be my wife according to the law of Moses and Israel.

I will work diligently to fill our home with love and commitment. I will provide sustenance and honor to our family and our community. I will cherish you and hold precious the holiness you bring to my life. I will give thanks for the gift of our union through my words and my deeds. I will nourish you mind, body and soul. I will comfort you and encourage your spiritual and intellectual growth. I will support you with a secure home and shelter; a place of intimacy, refuge and light. I will sustain our Jewish home and community through celebration, learning and the observance of mitzvot. I will do this in accordance with the custom of Jewish husbands and wives who work for, cherish, nourish and support each other in truth."

באחד בשבת בארבעה ועשרים יום לחודש תמוז שנת חמשת אלפים ושבע מאות וחמישים וארבע לבריאת עולם למנין שאנו מונין כאן באורלנדו, פלורידה

איך הכלה **קרן** בת משה הלל ומיכלה פעריל אמרה לחתן מארק היה לי לאיש כדת משה וישראל.

איך החתן **מארק** בן שמואל ואסתר אמר לכלה קרן היה לי לאשתי כדת משה וישראל.

אעבוד בשקידה בבנית בית עתיר אהבה ומסירות. אפעל להשגת פת-לחם אהבה וכבוד לתא משפחתנו וקהלתנו המצומצם והרחב ואשמור קיומם. אוקיר ואאצר את הרוח שמשרה את.ה בחיי. מילותי ומעשי הן הן מתנתי כהוכחה לאסירות-תודתי לזוגן זה. אזינך ברוח נפש וחומר. אהיה לך מקור בלתי נלאה לעדוד ולנחמה למיצוי שאיפותיך אפרנסך ואגן עליך מכל צר. ביתנו יהא לנו מפלט בפני כל צרה שלא תבוא עלינו. ביתנו יהא סמל לאחדותנו מקורובותנו יהודנו ואורנו. מהות ביתנו היהודי וקהילתנו בה הוא שוכן יאופין על ידי למידת הבנת וקיום מסרת מועדי ישראל ושמירת מצוות. כל הכתוב לעיל יעשה בהתאם להלכות ומנהגי כלה יהודיה אשר תשקד תוקיר ותזין ותפרנס את אישה באמונה וחתן יהודי אשר ישקד יוקיר יזין ויפרנס את אשתו באמונה.

Bride:
כלה

Groom:
חתן

Witness:
עד

Witness:
עד

Rabbi
רב

זהכל שריר וקים.

It is valid and binding.

Q'tuba, 1994

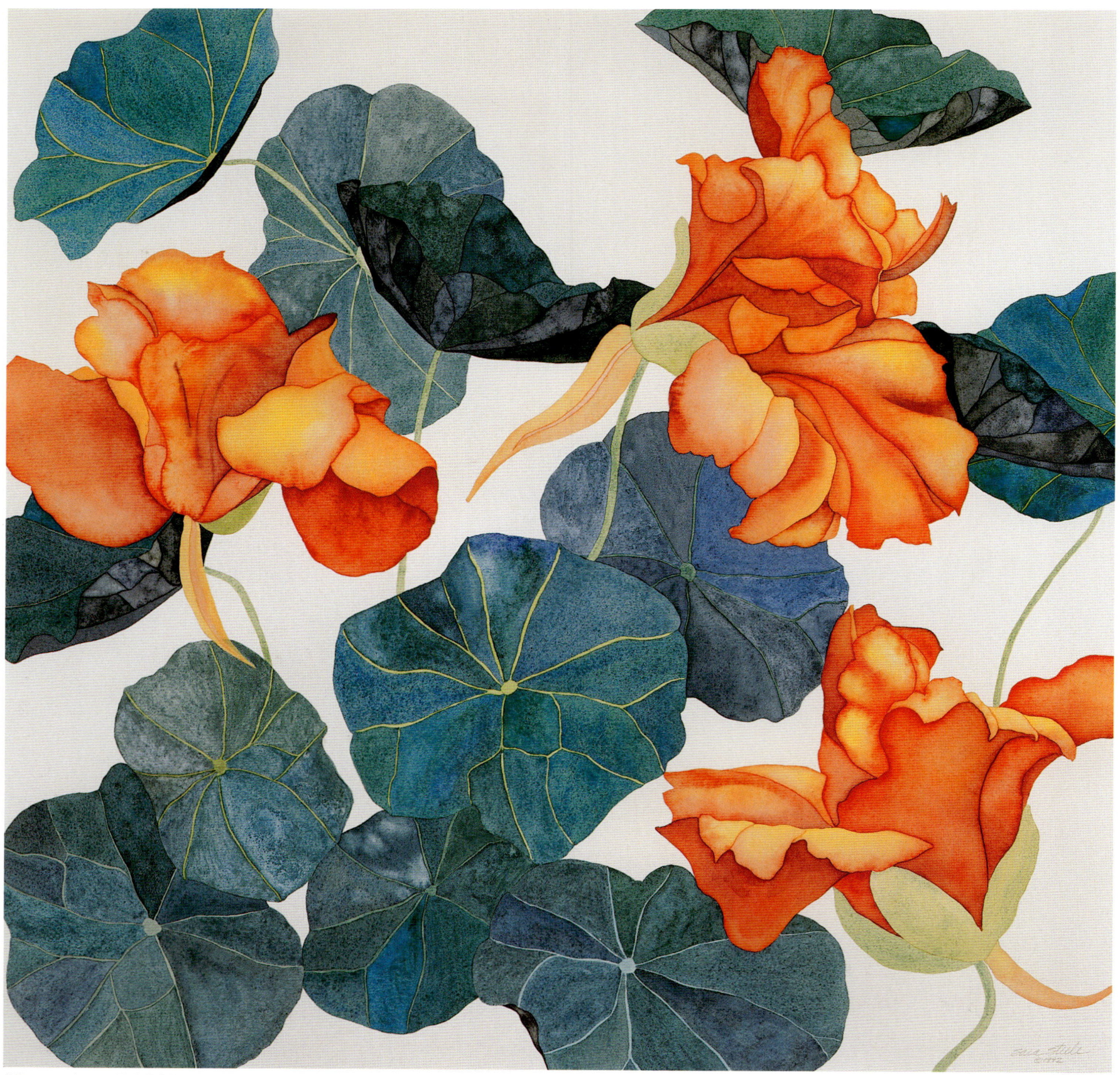

Nasturtiums I, 1992

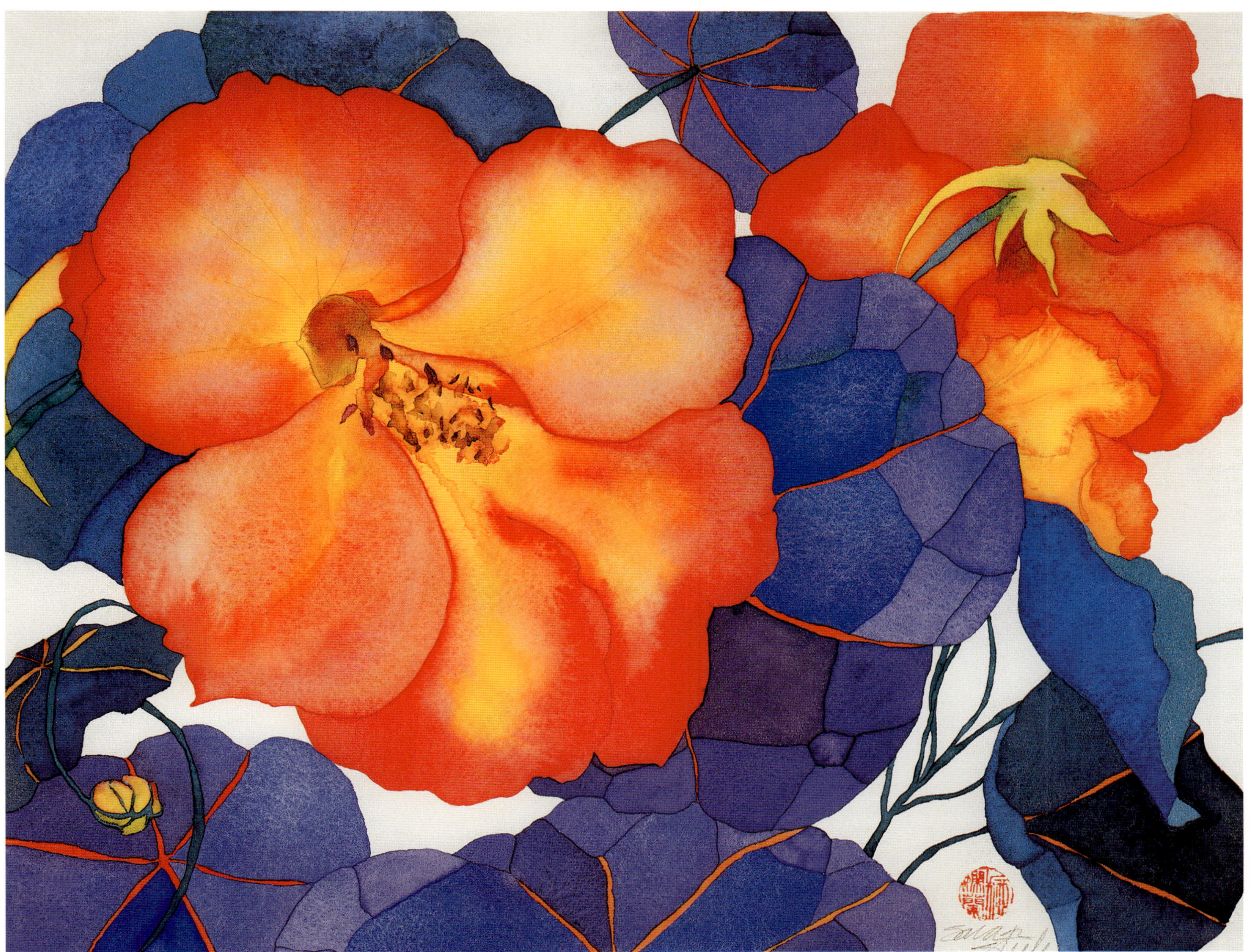

Nasturtiums III, 1998

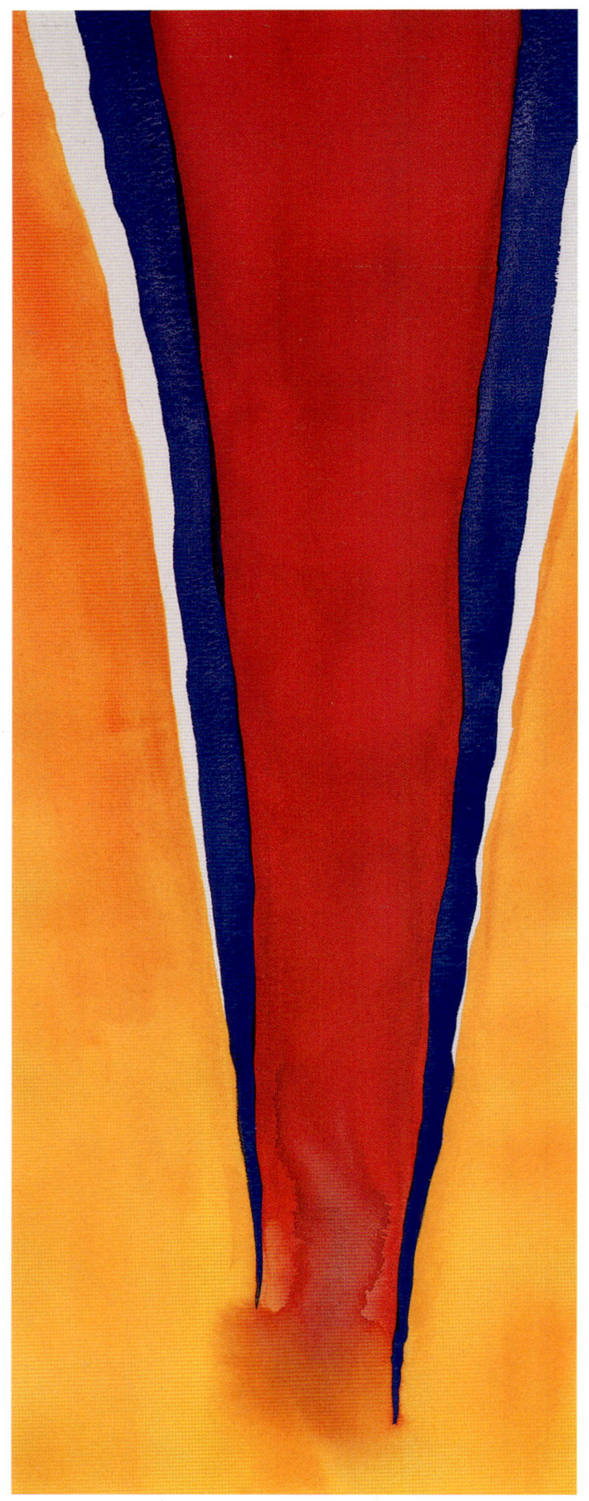

The Point I, 1992

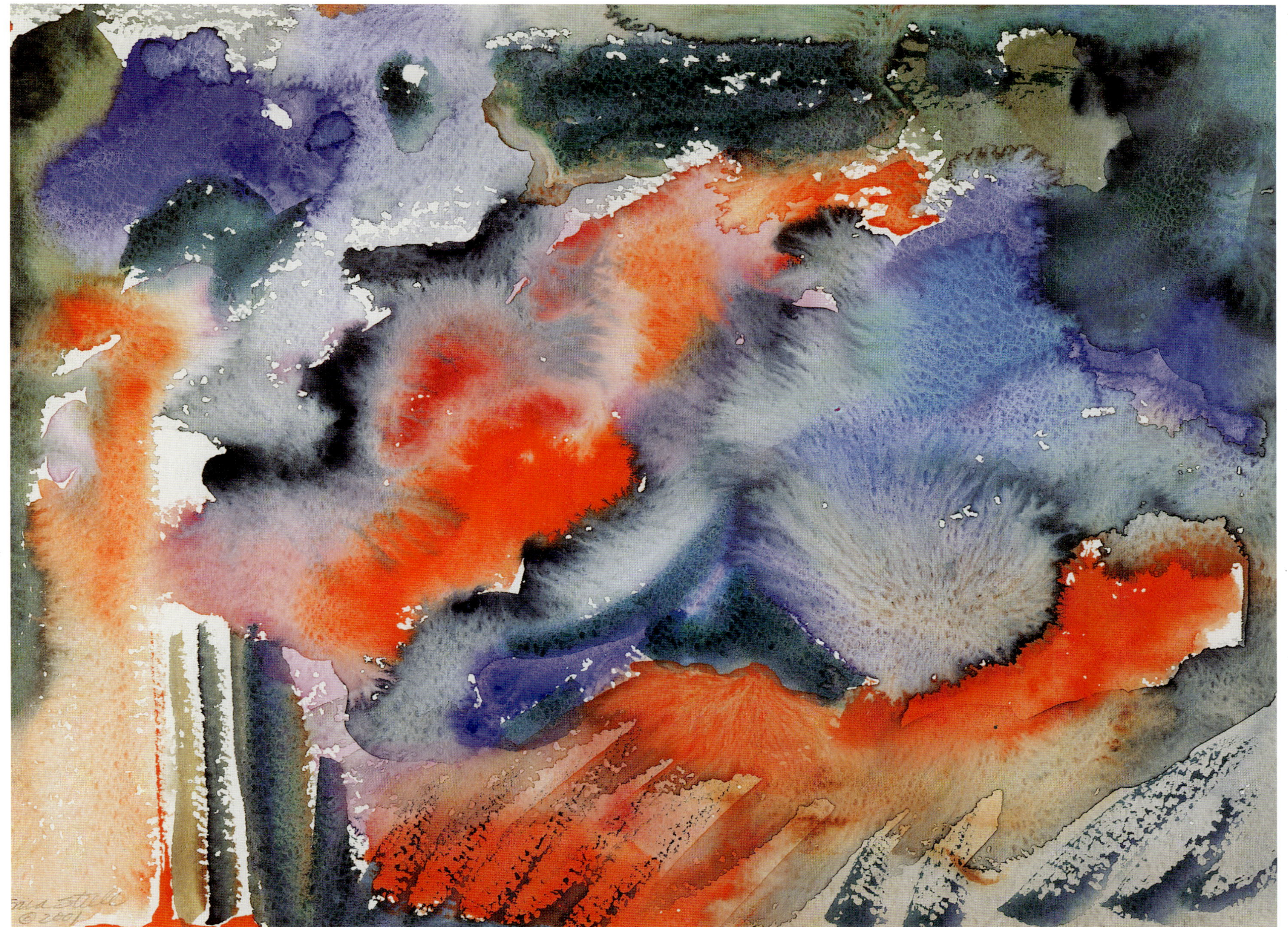

Madrid, 2001

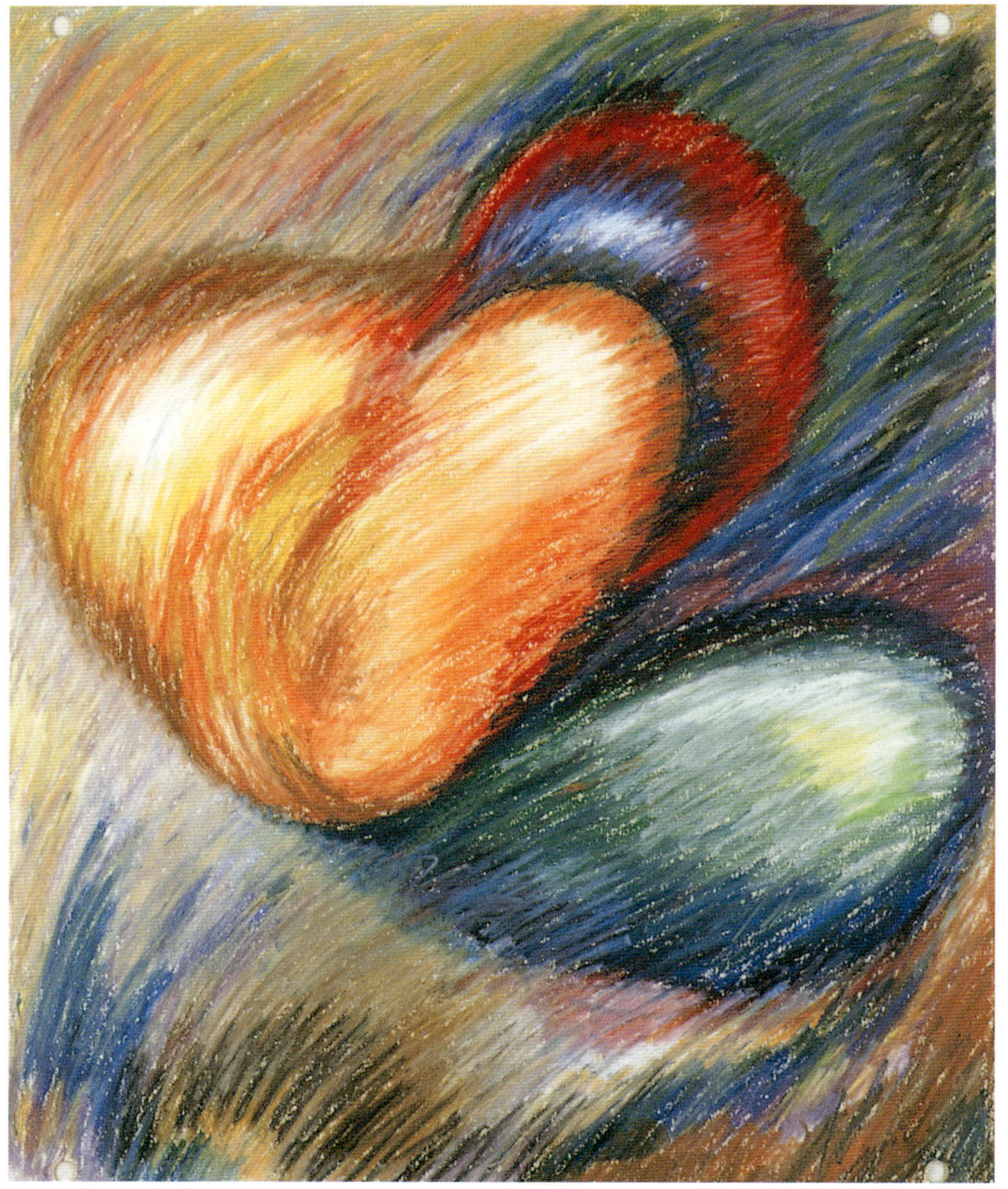

1970 (Sweet Sixteen), 1970

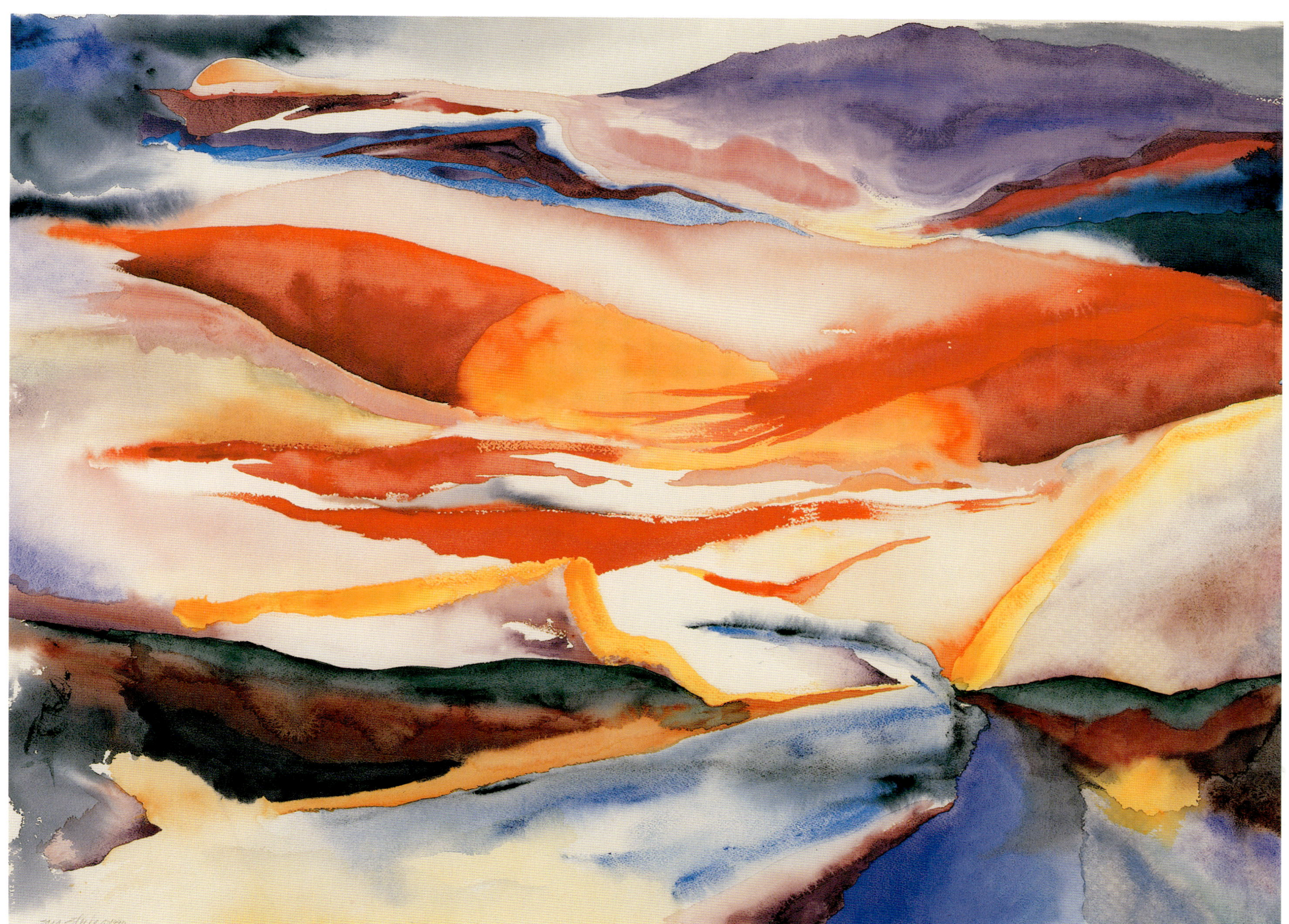

Arianna (longing like Icarus, seeing like Hawk), 1990

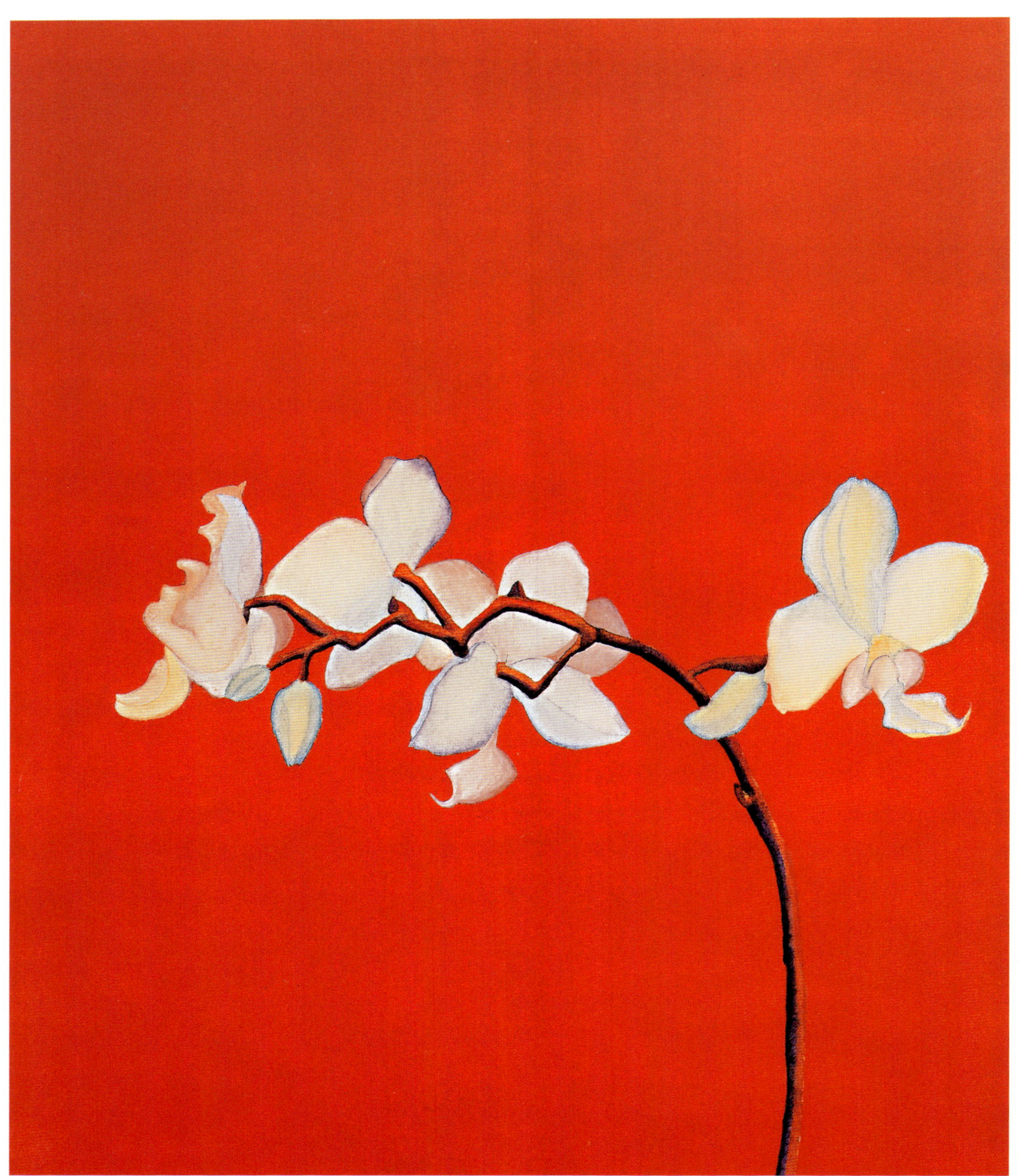

Gerald's Phalaenopsis, 1982

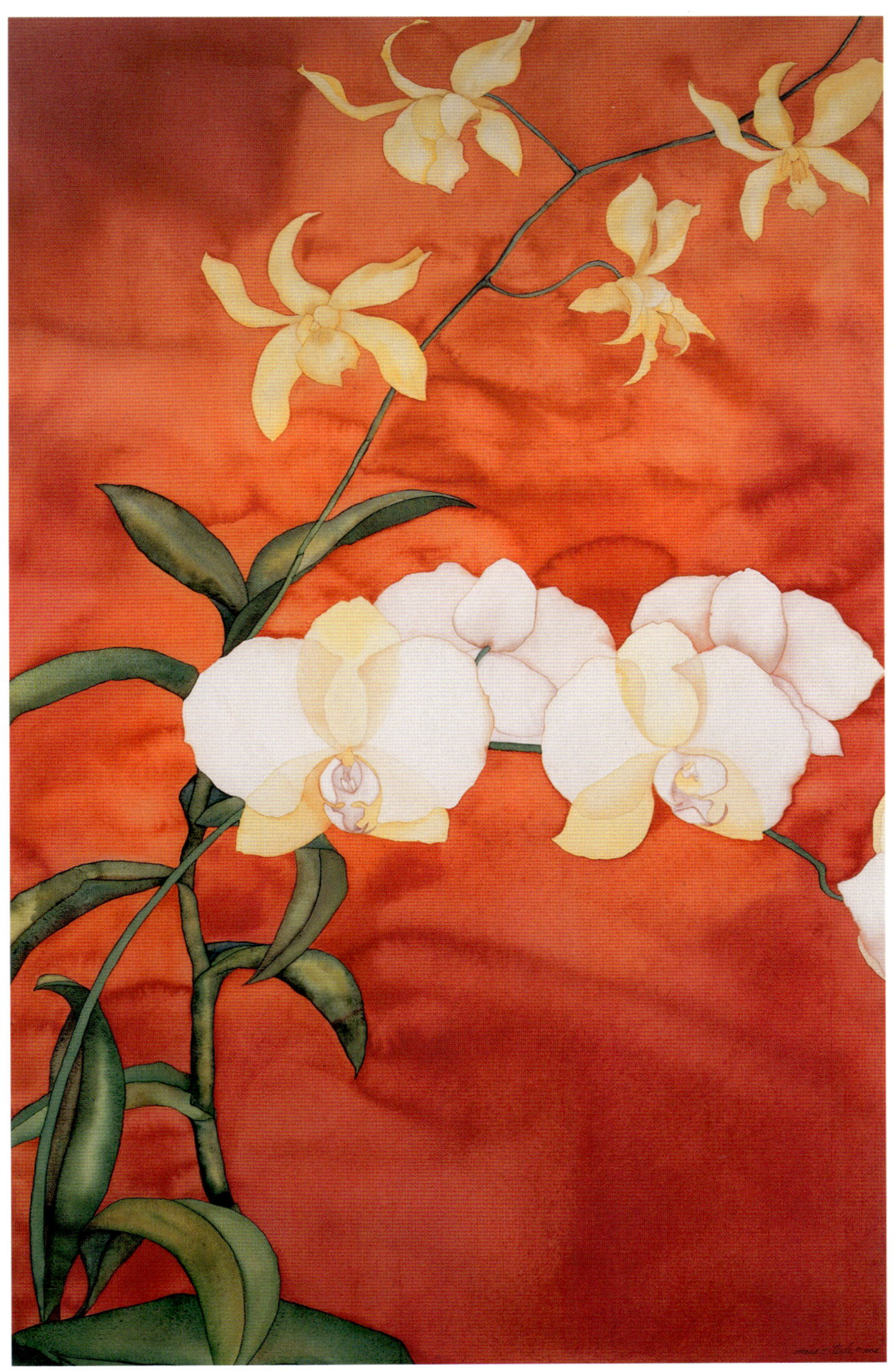

Dendrobiums, Phalaenopsis, 2002

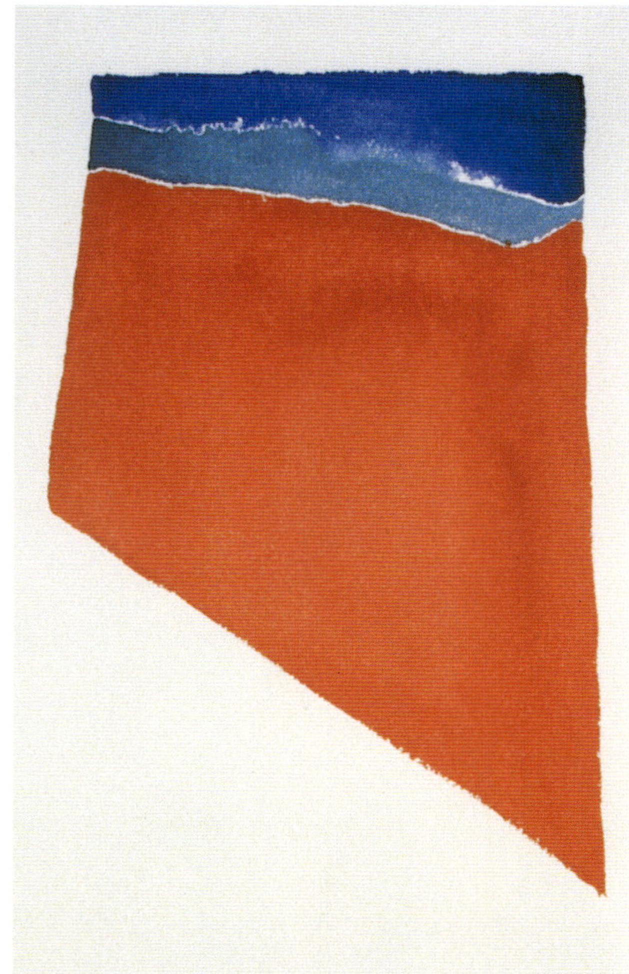

Oh! Karen…II, 1985

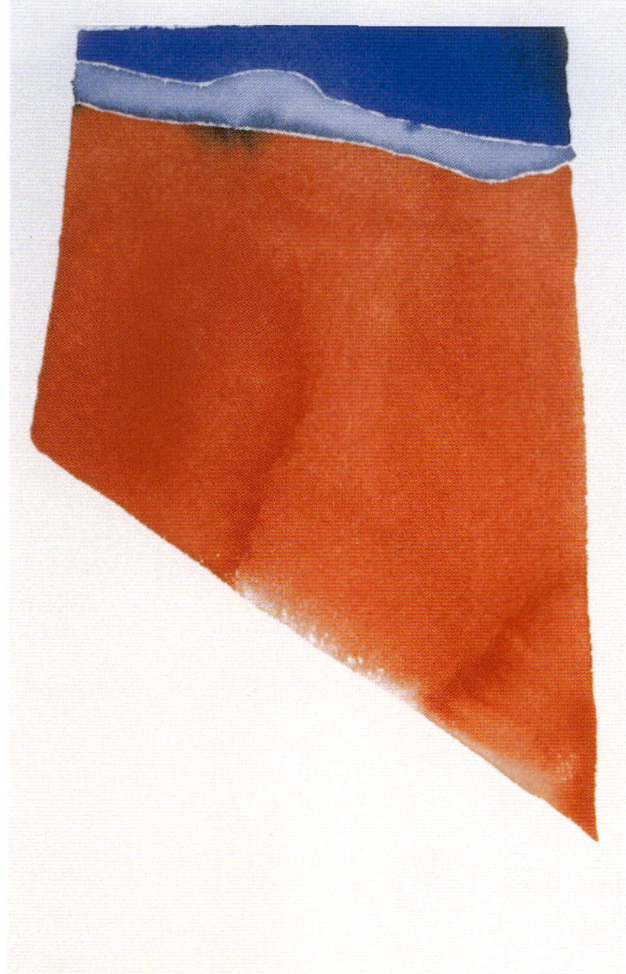

Oh! Karen…III, 1985

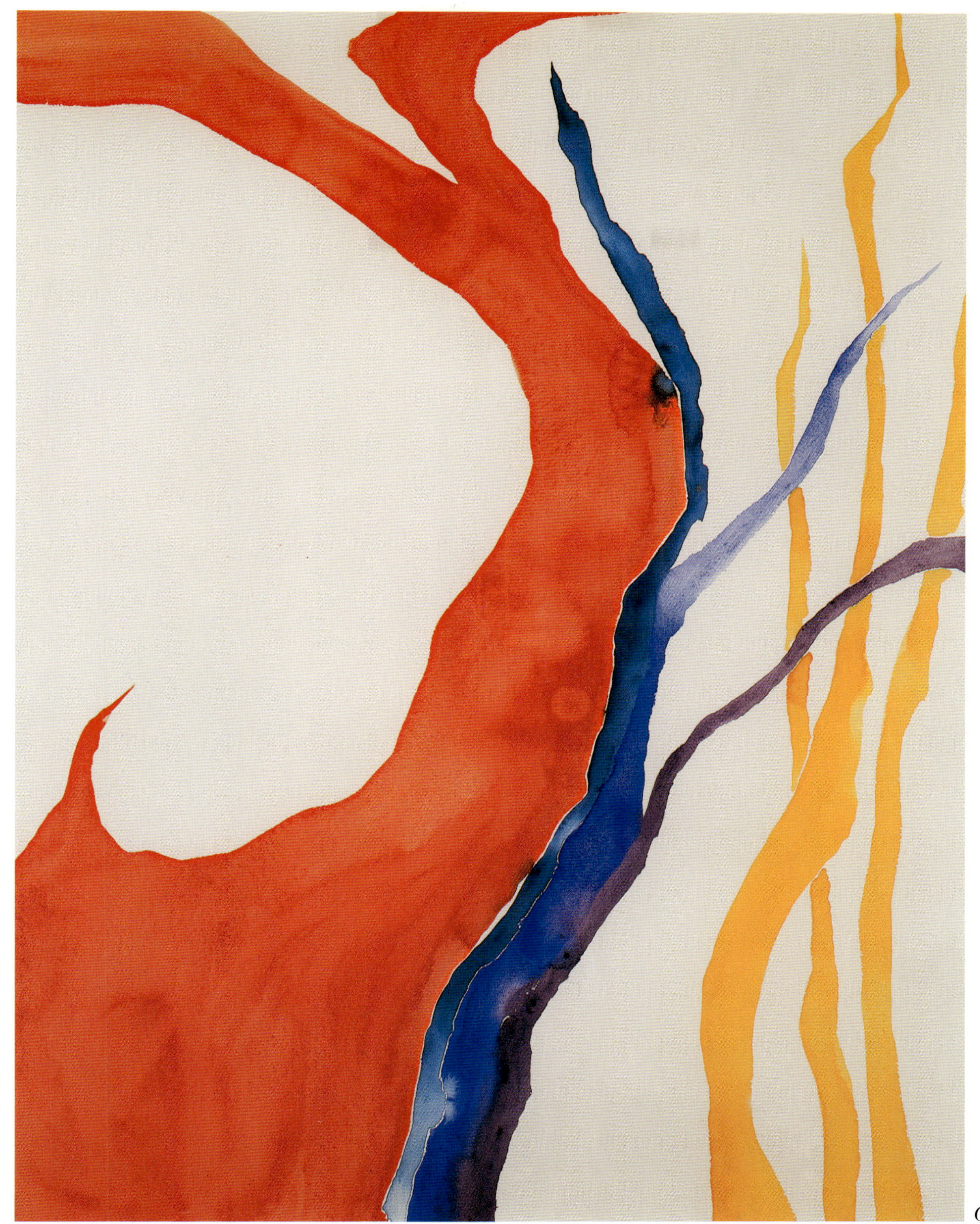

Oh! Karen..., 1985

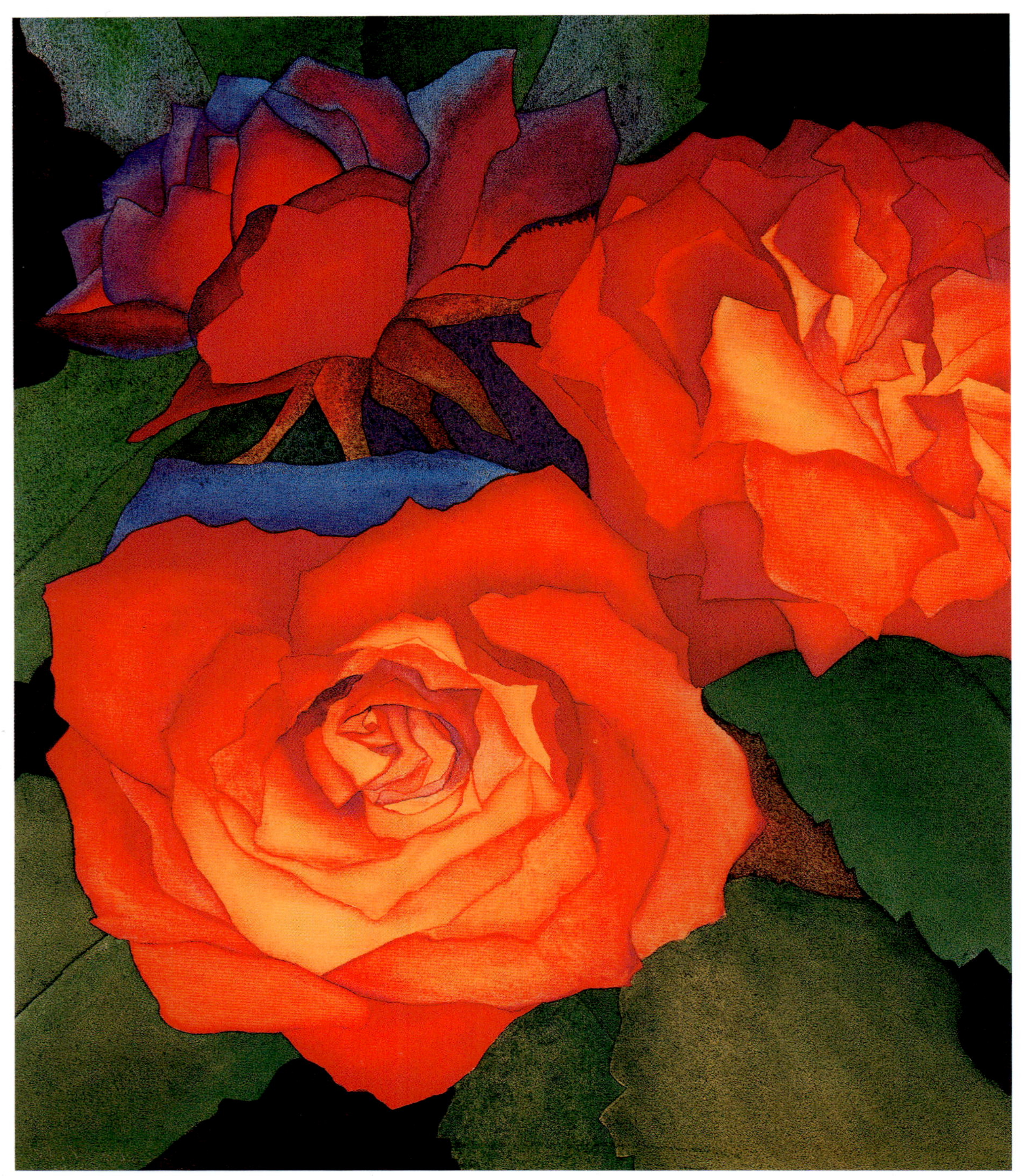

Bertha's Birthday Roses, 1982

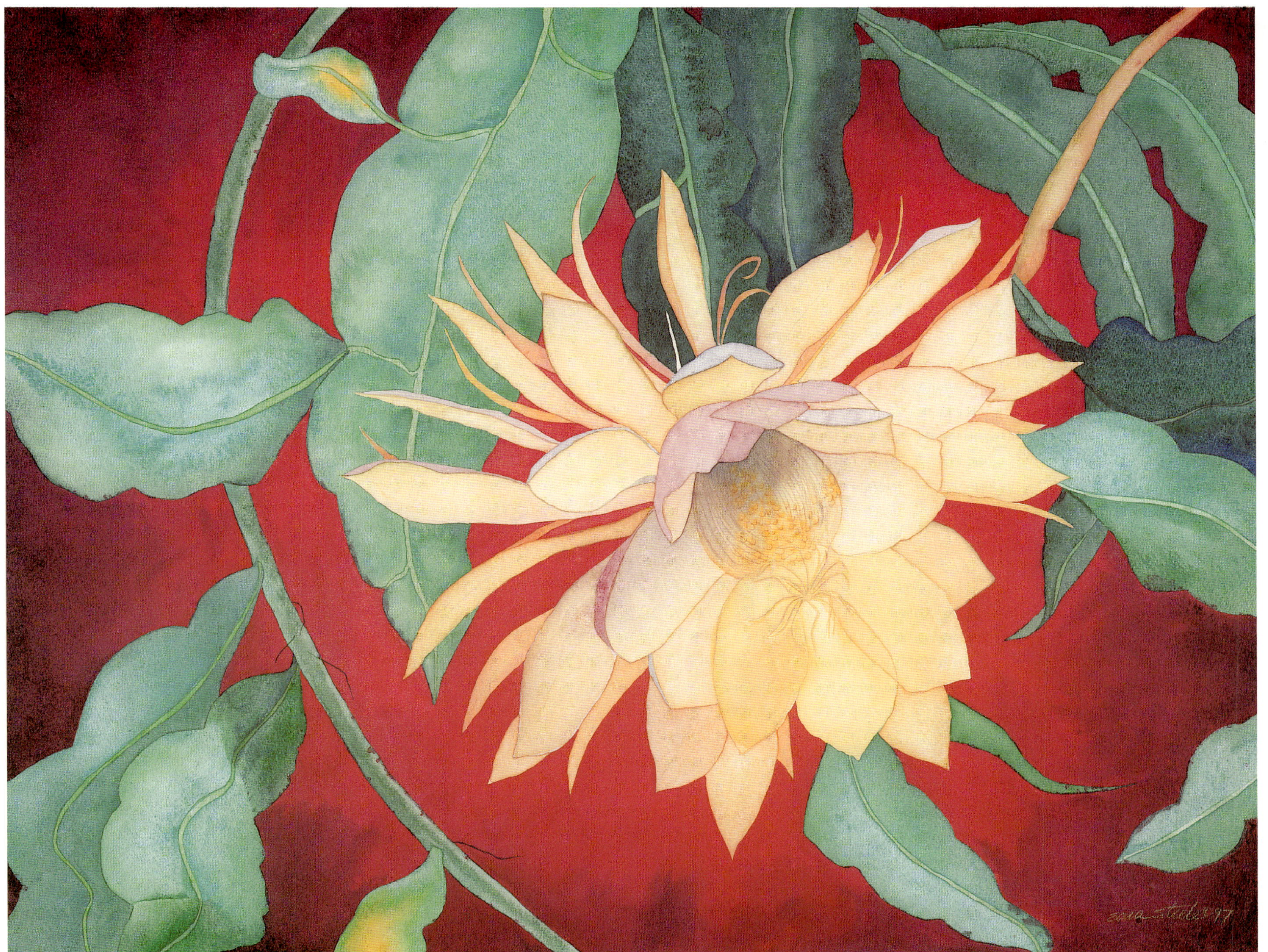

Night-blooming Cereus, 1997

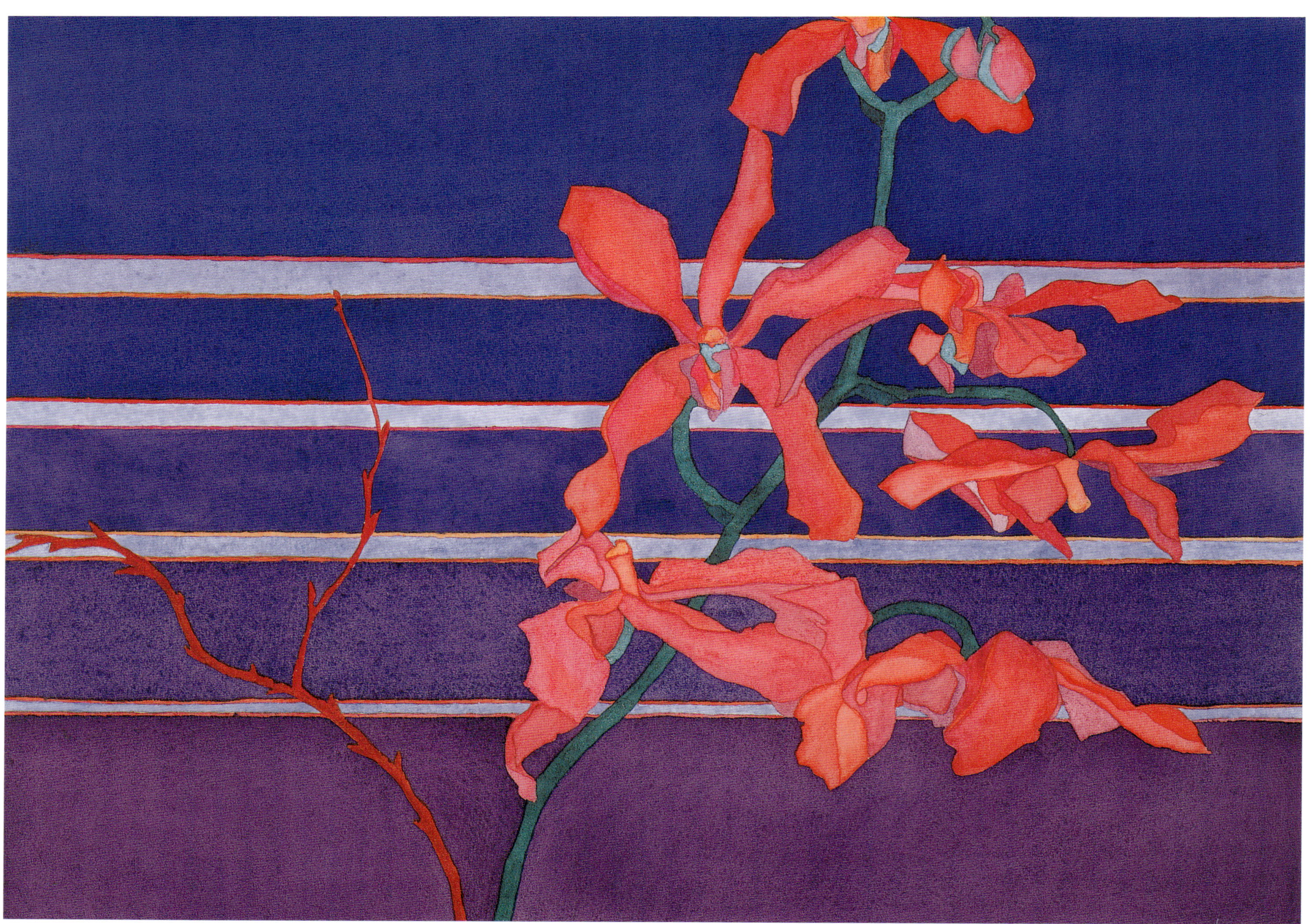

Fractured Light/Night, 1983

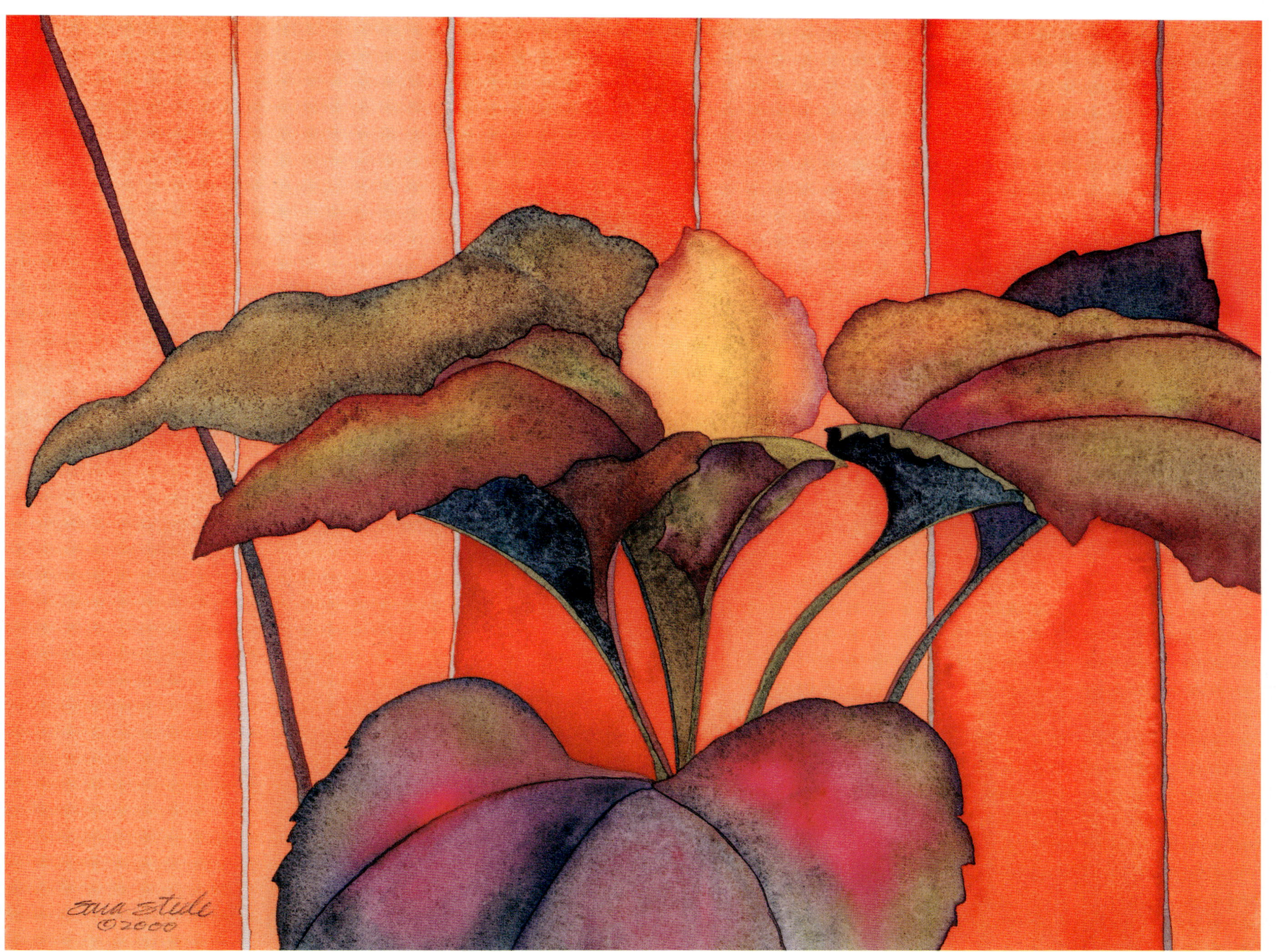

Sunflower Leaves at Dusk, 2000

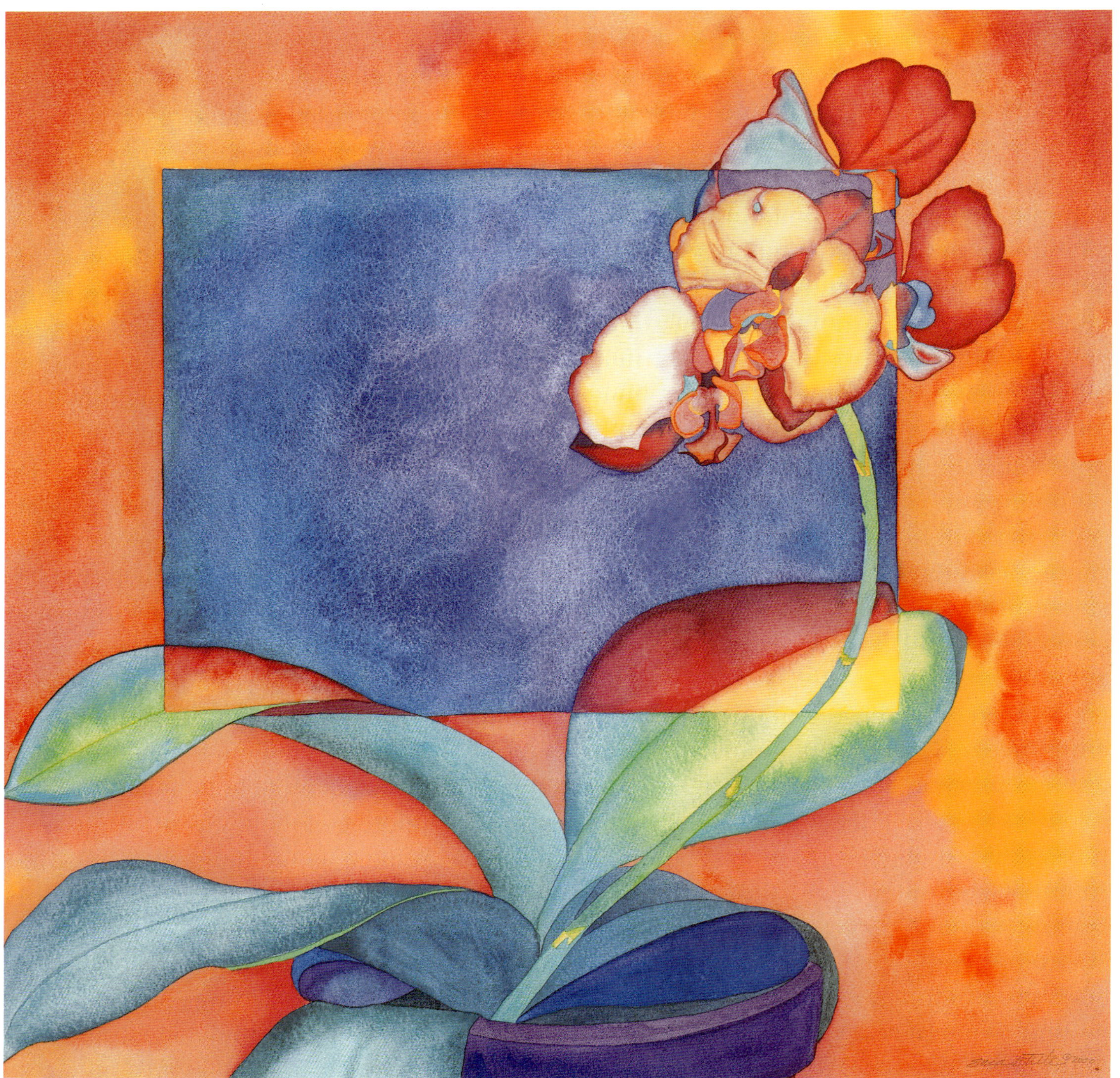

Phalaenopsis Revival, 2000

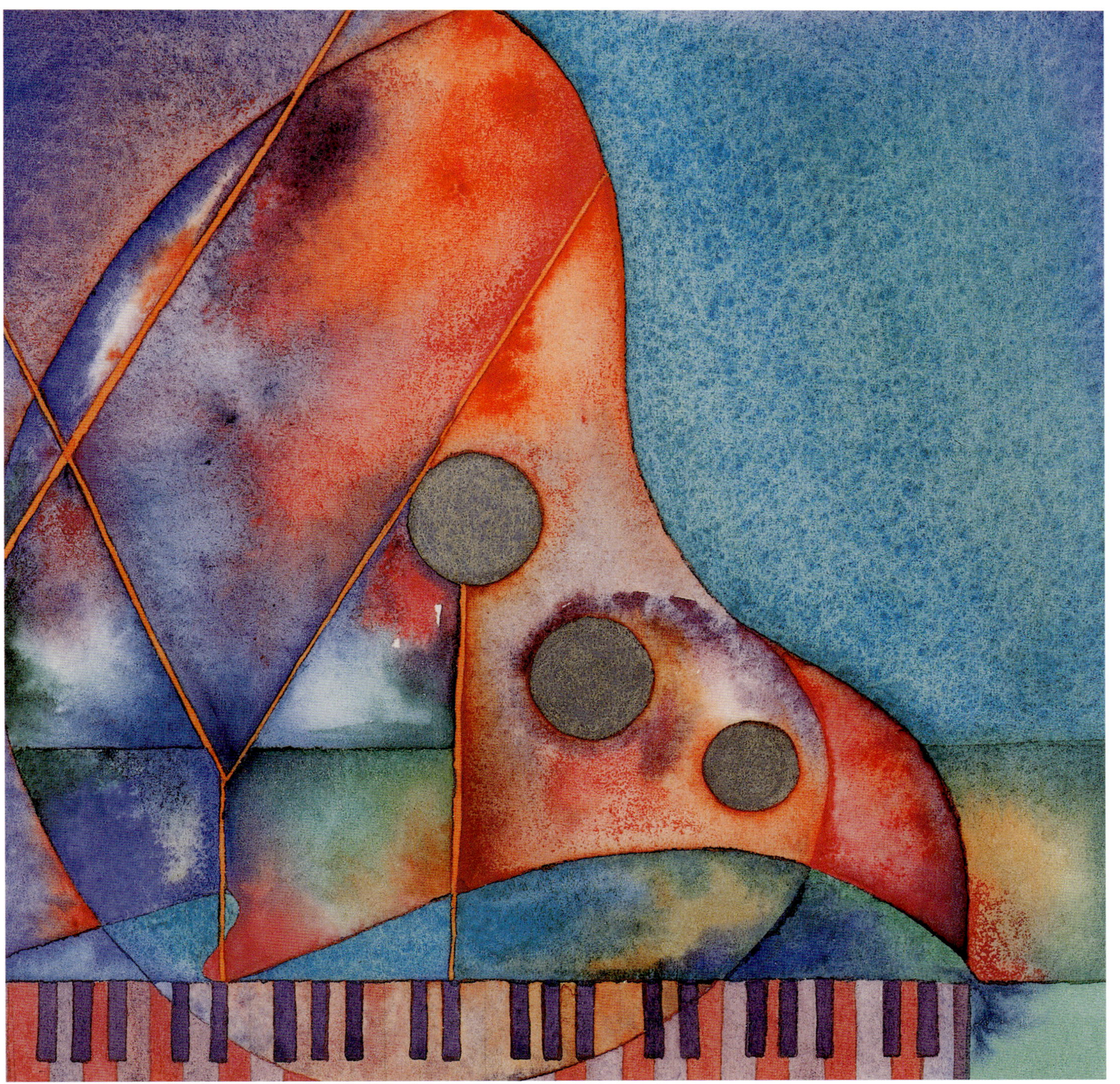

Love Propaganda, 1994

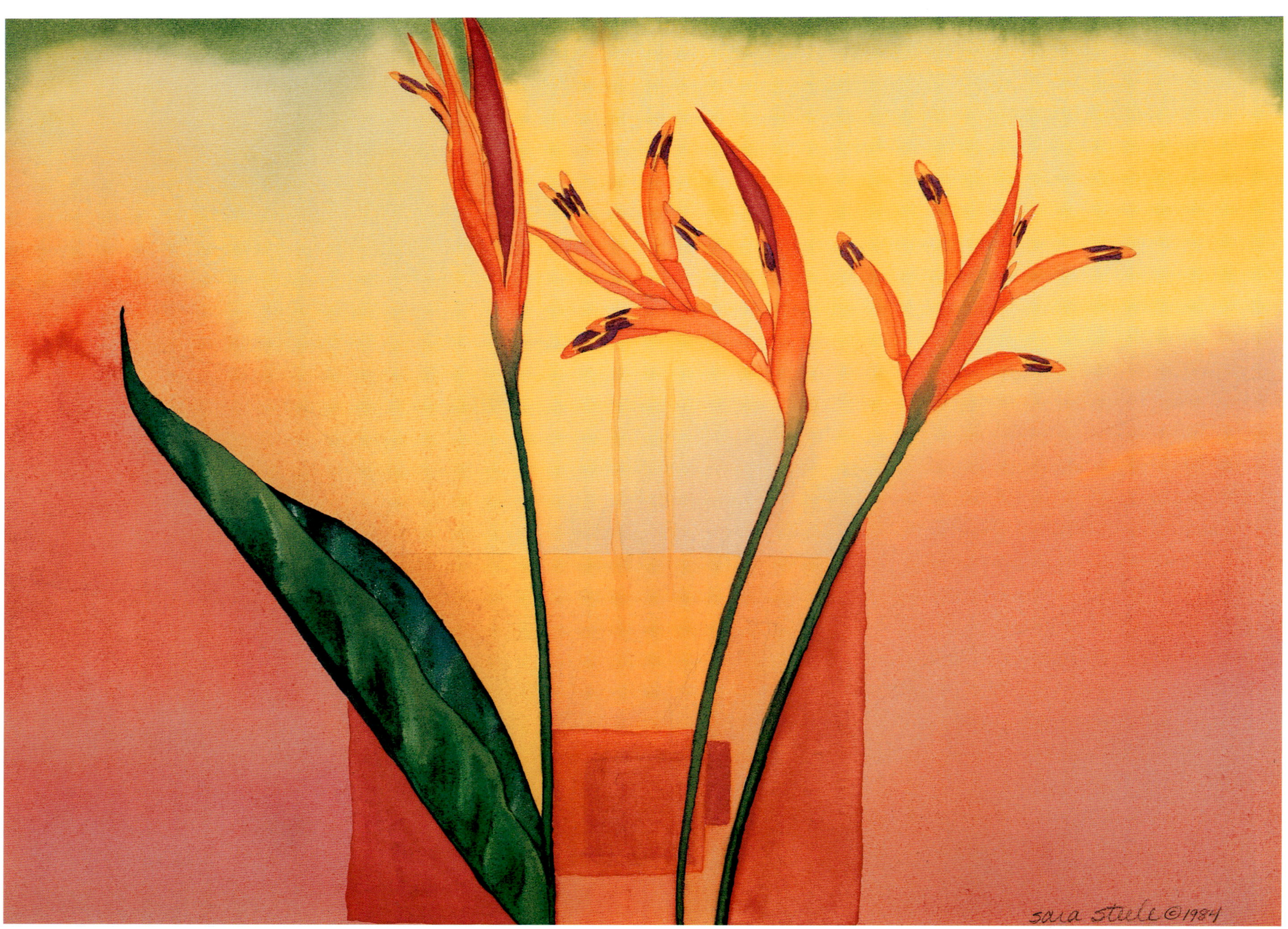

Christina's Flowers, 1984

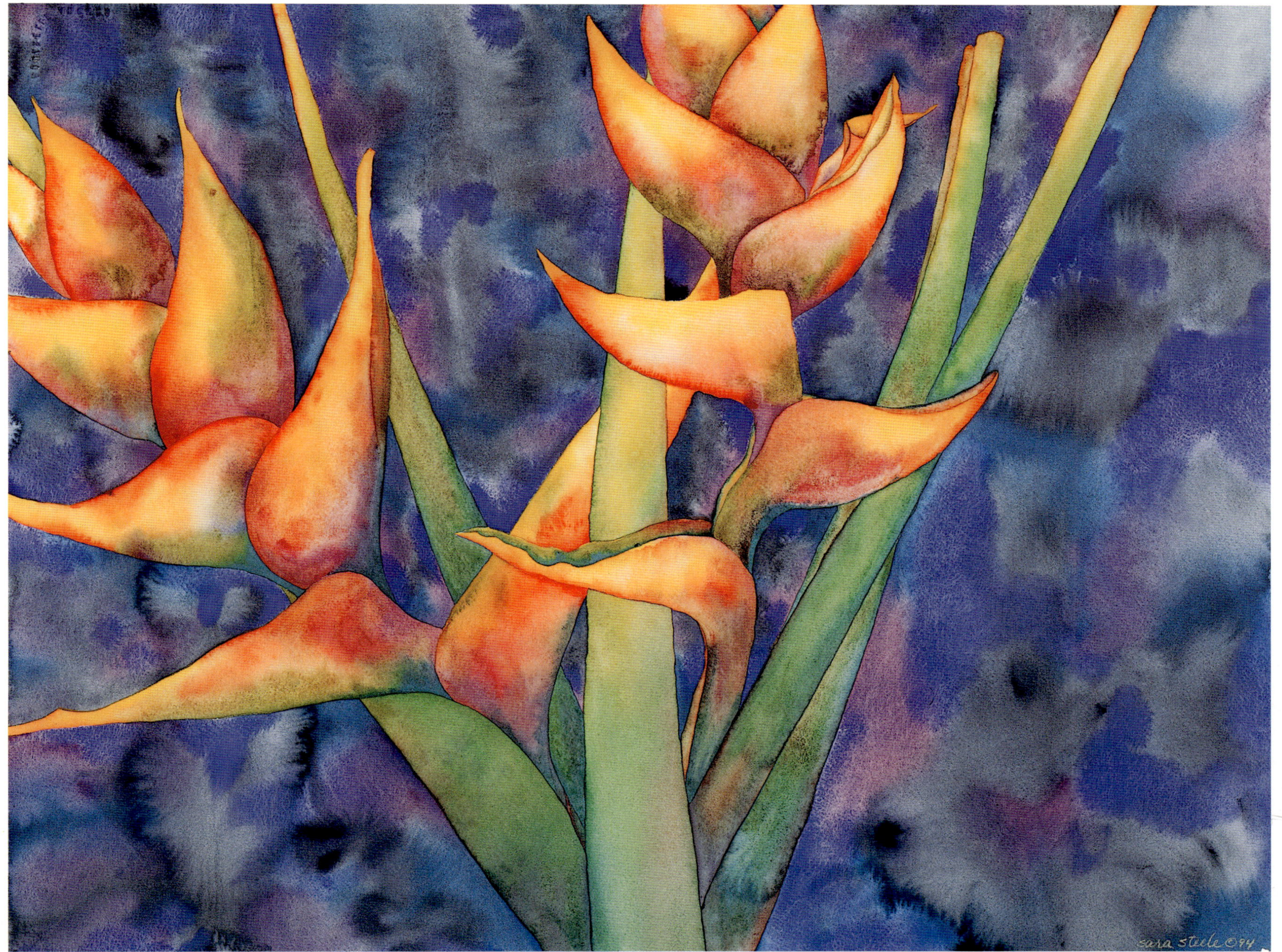

Heliconia, 1994

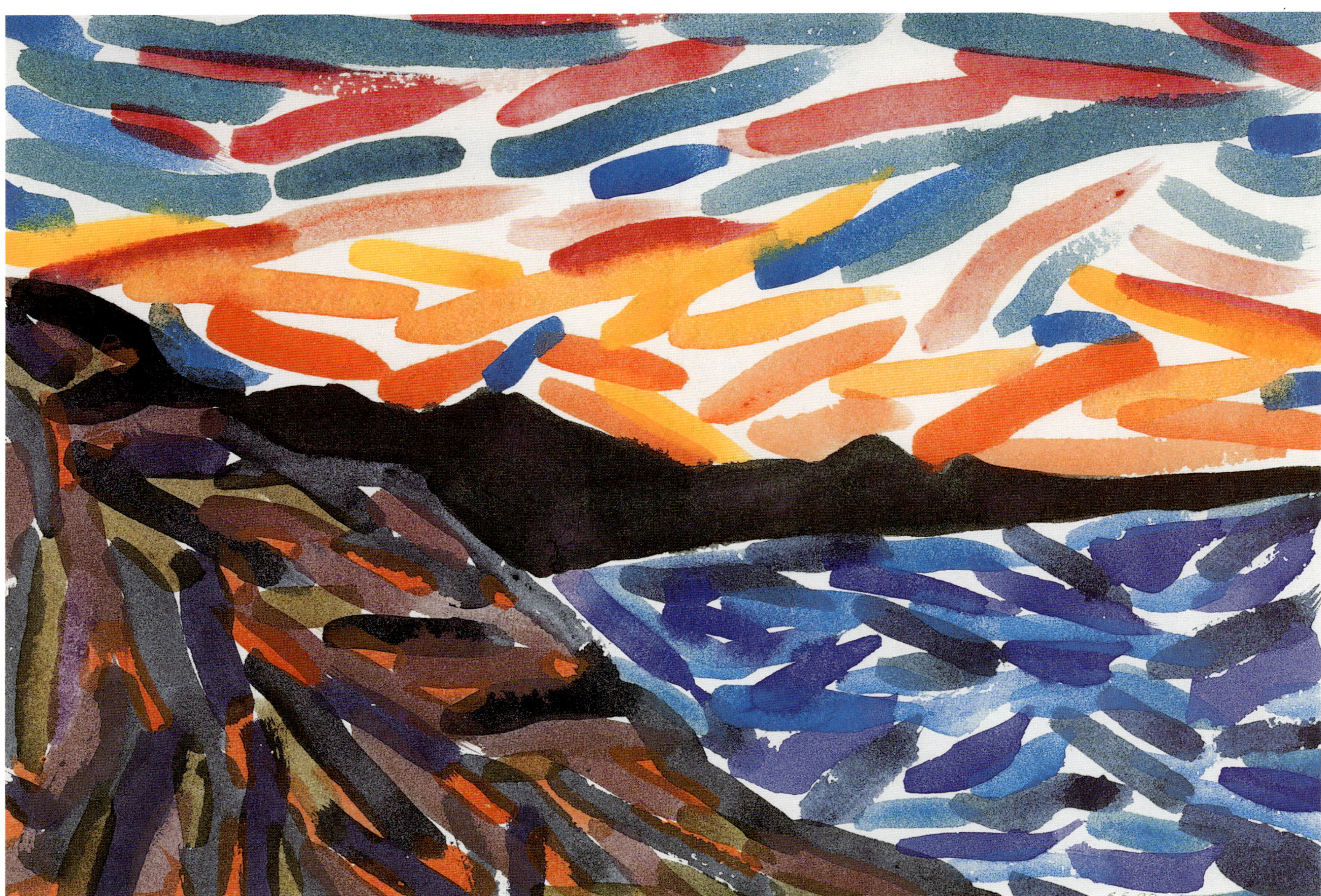

Big Rock Dawn I, 1990

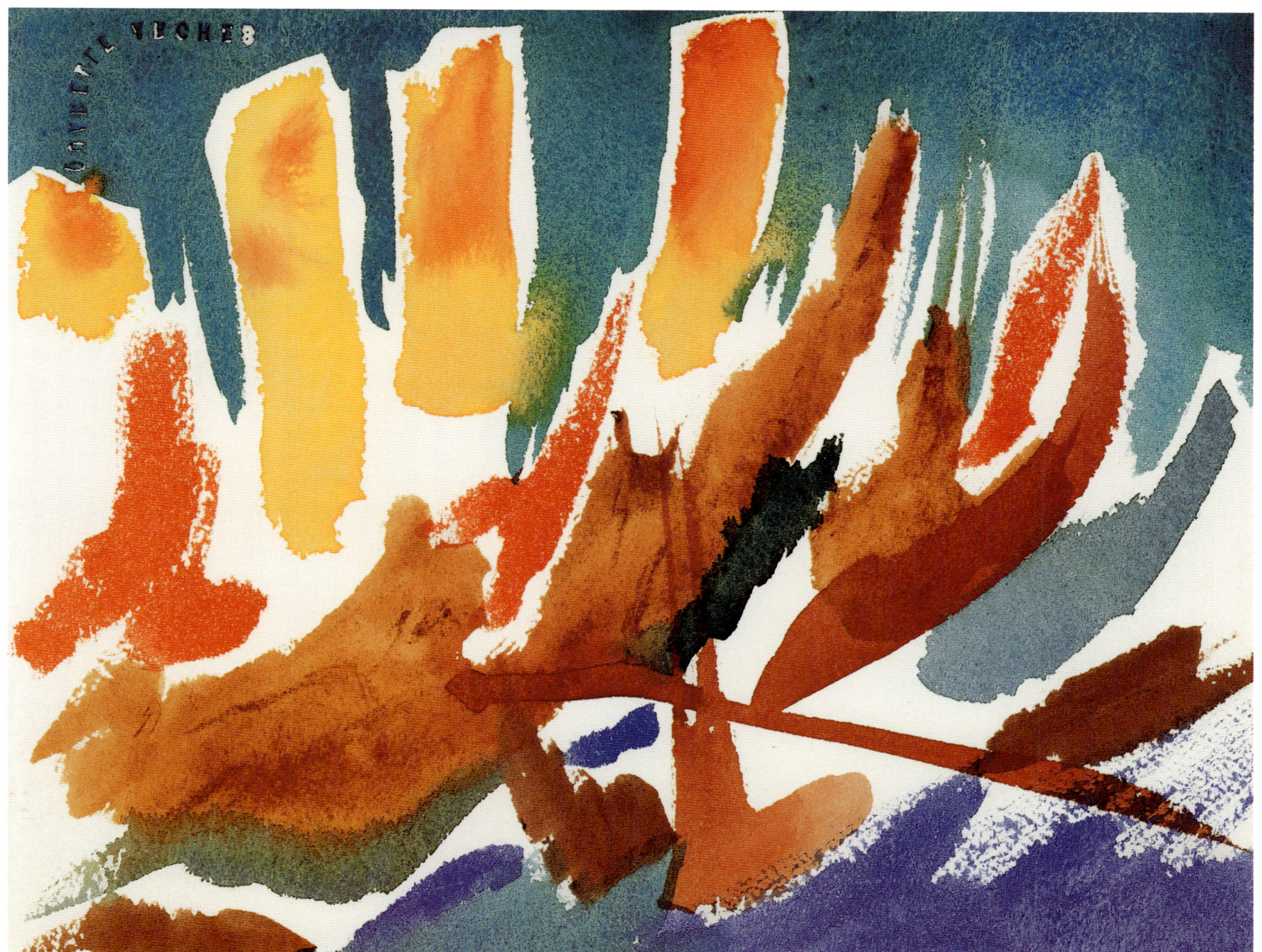

Abstract #7, 1993

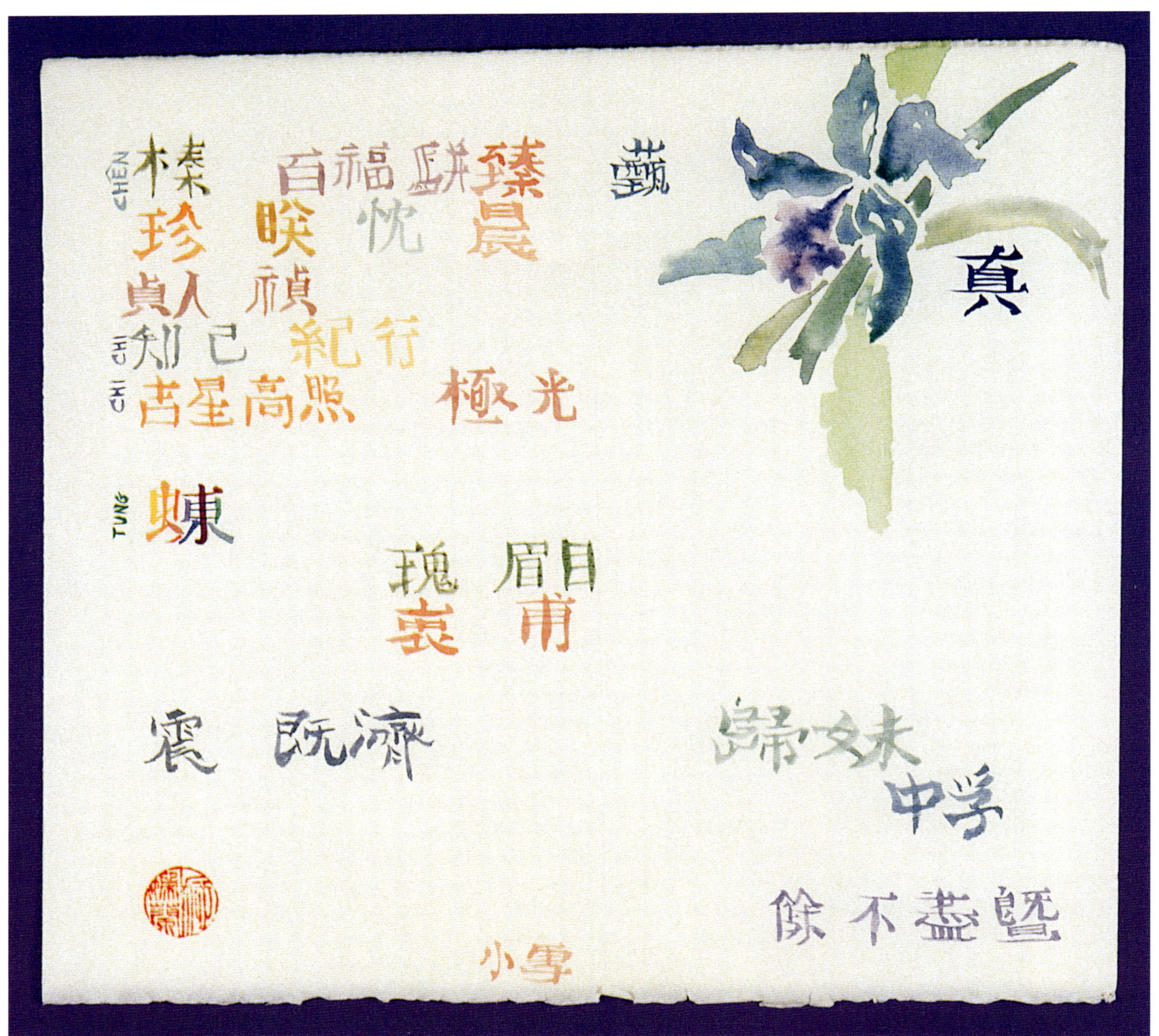

Love Letter Blue Orchid, 1983

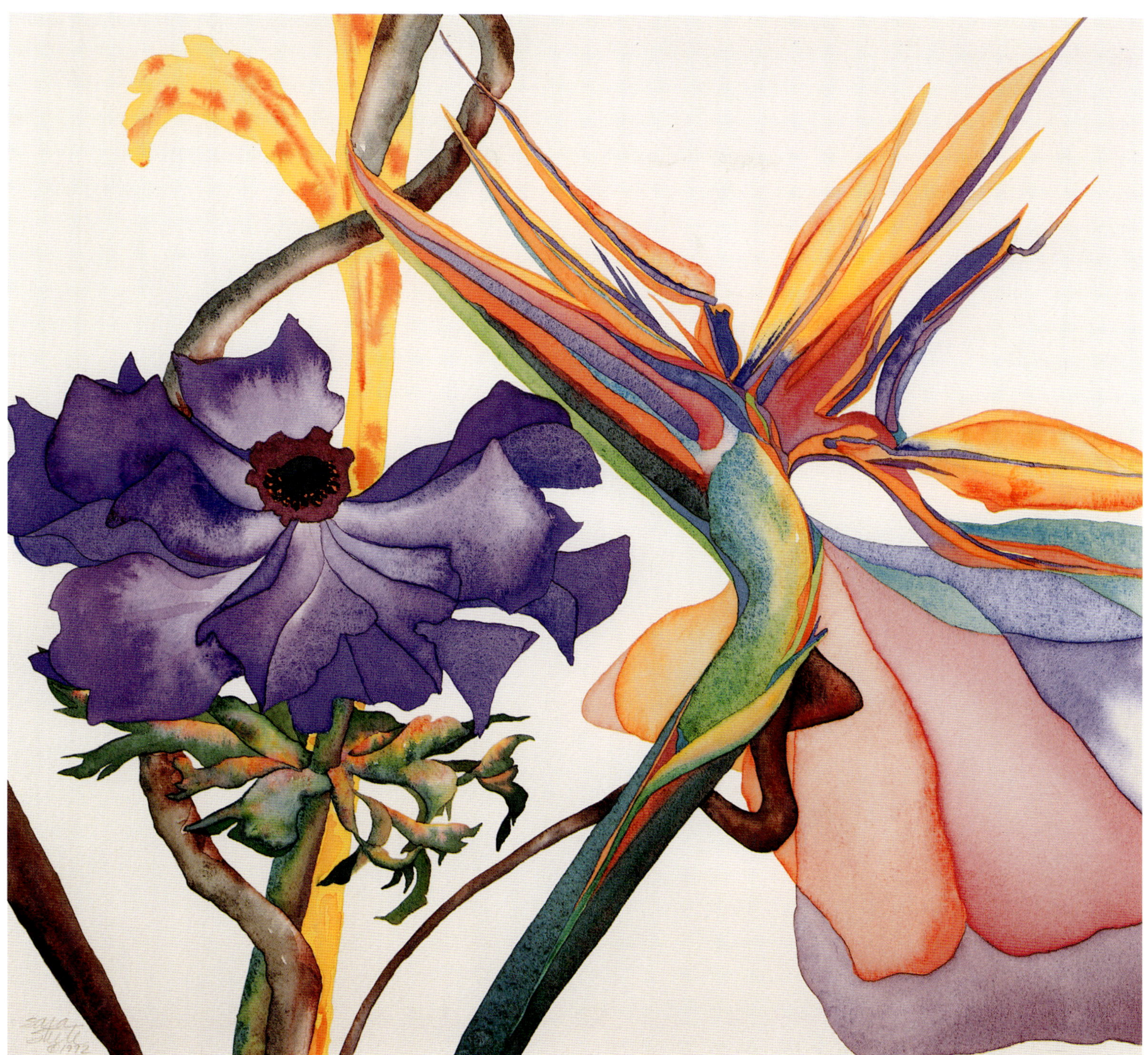

Anemone & Bird of Paradise, 1992

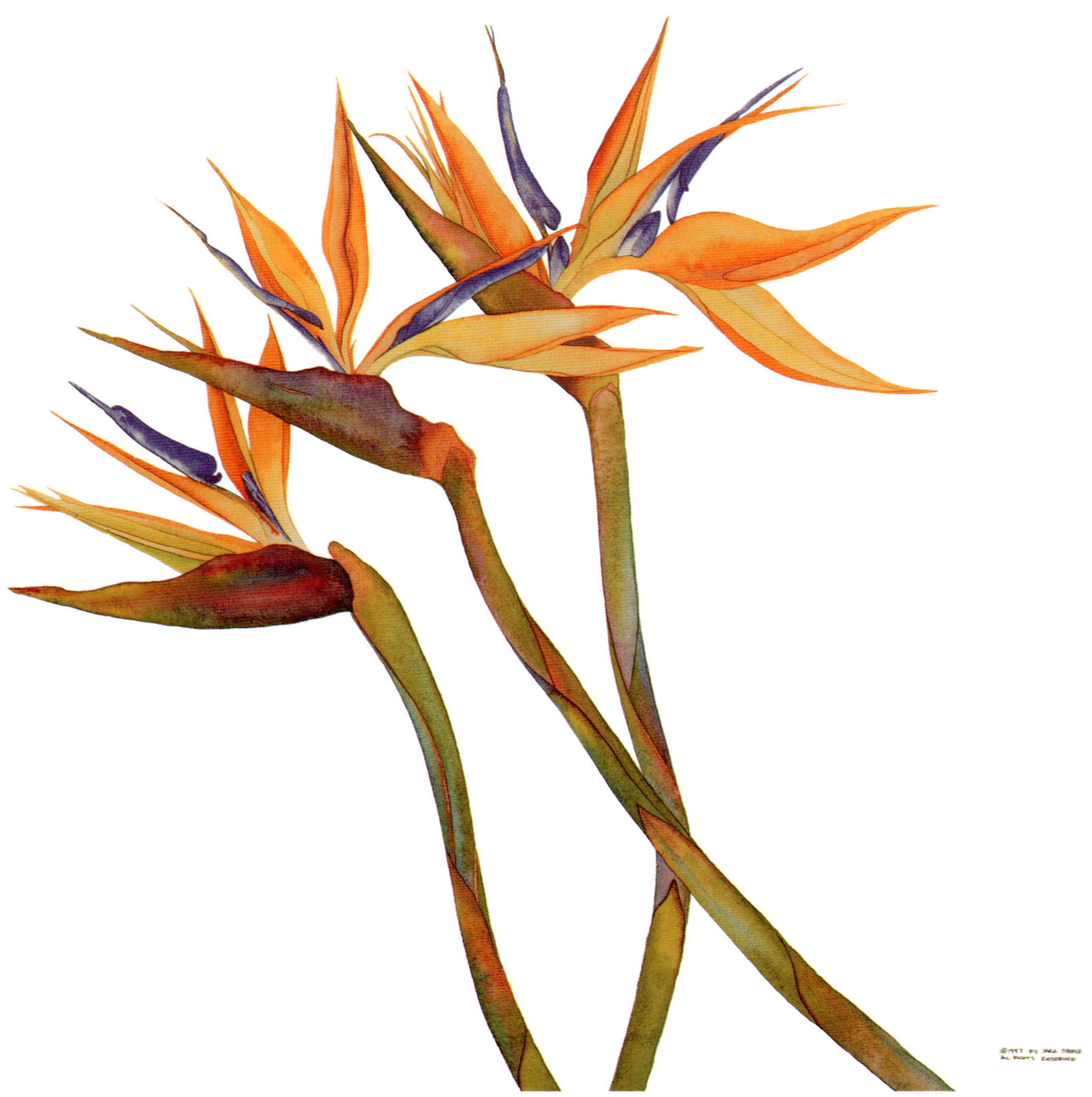

Birds of Paradise I (Plate Series), 1997

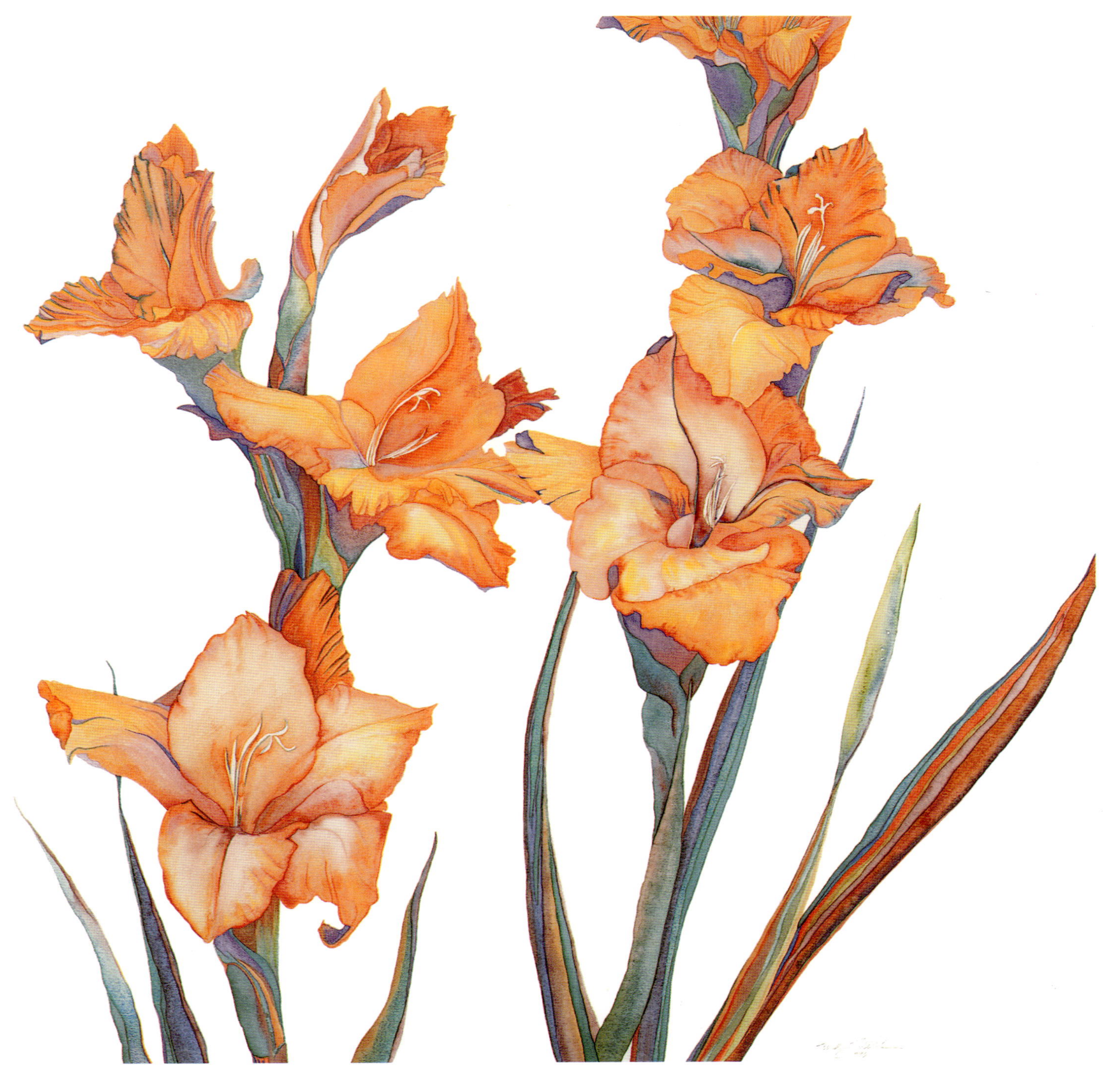

Orange Gladiolas, 1990

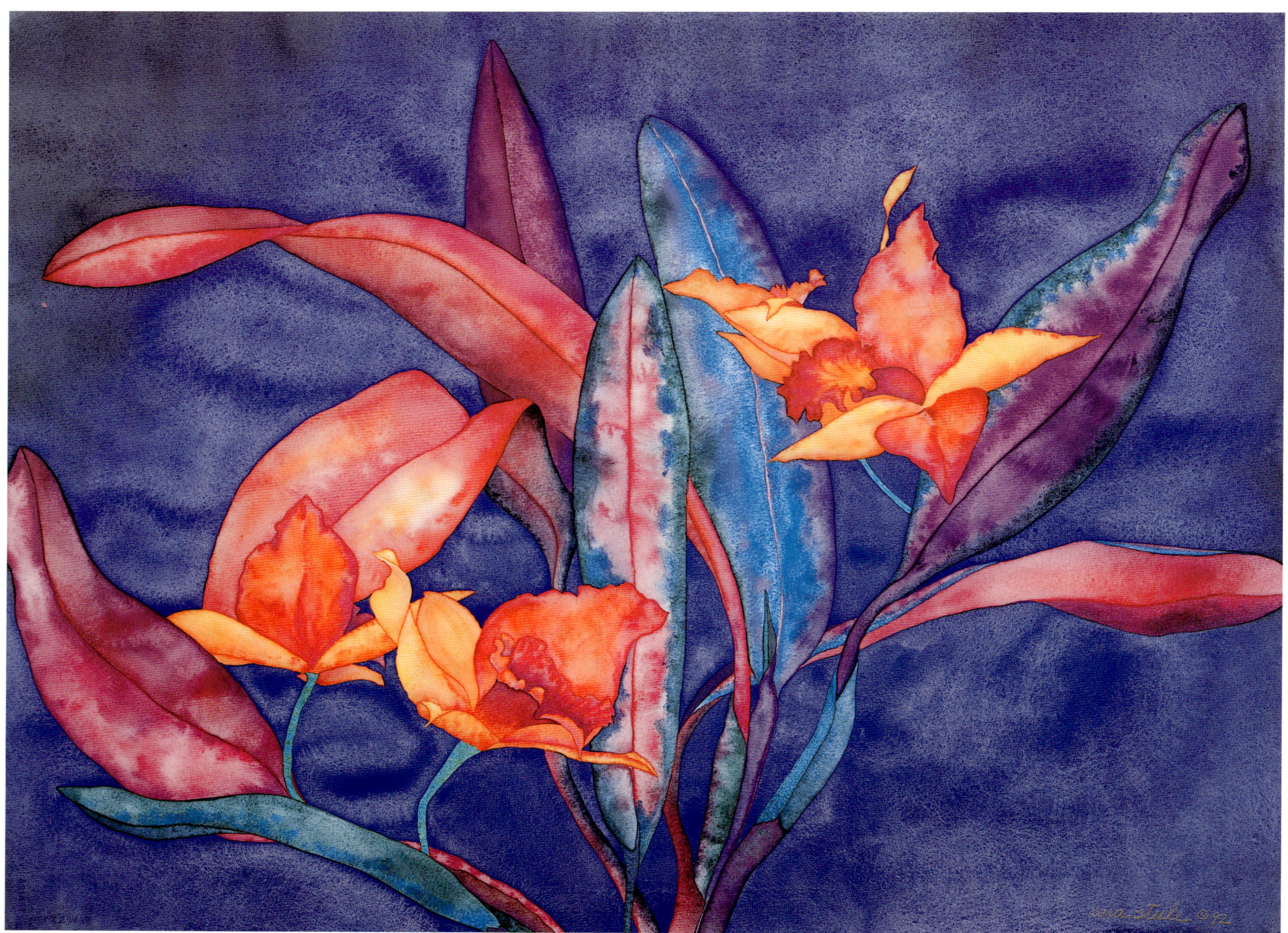

Slc. Redzac Carteria Flame, 1992

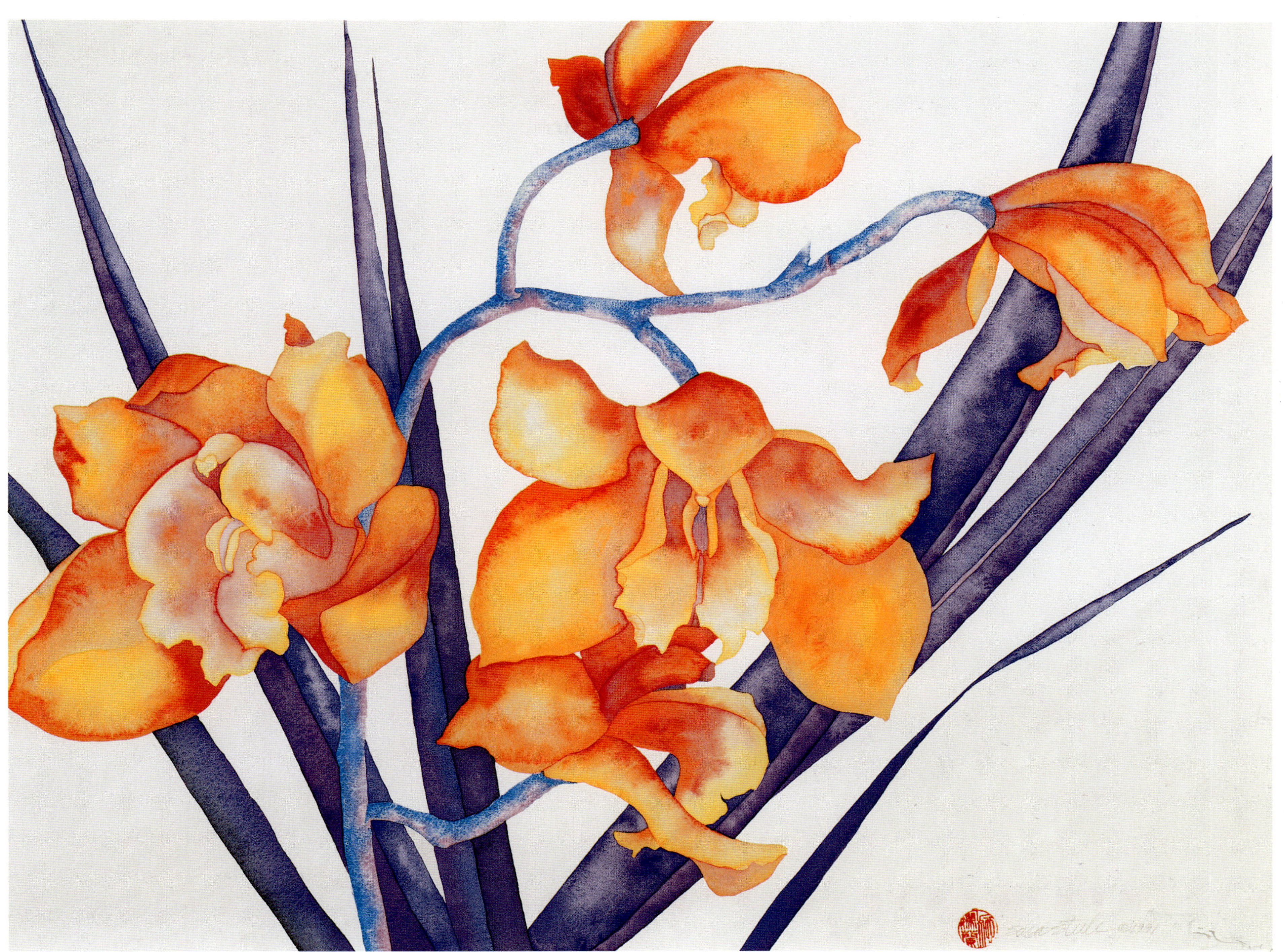

Study in Orange & Blue, 1991

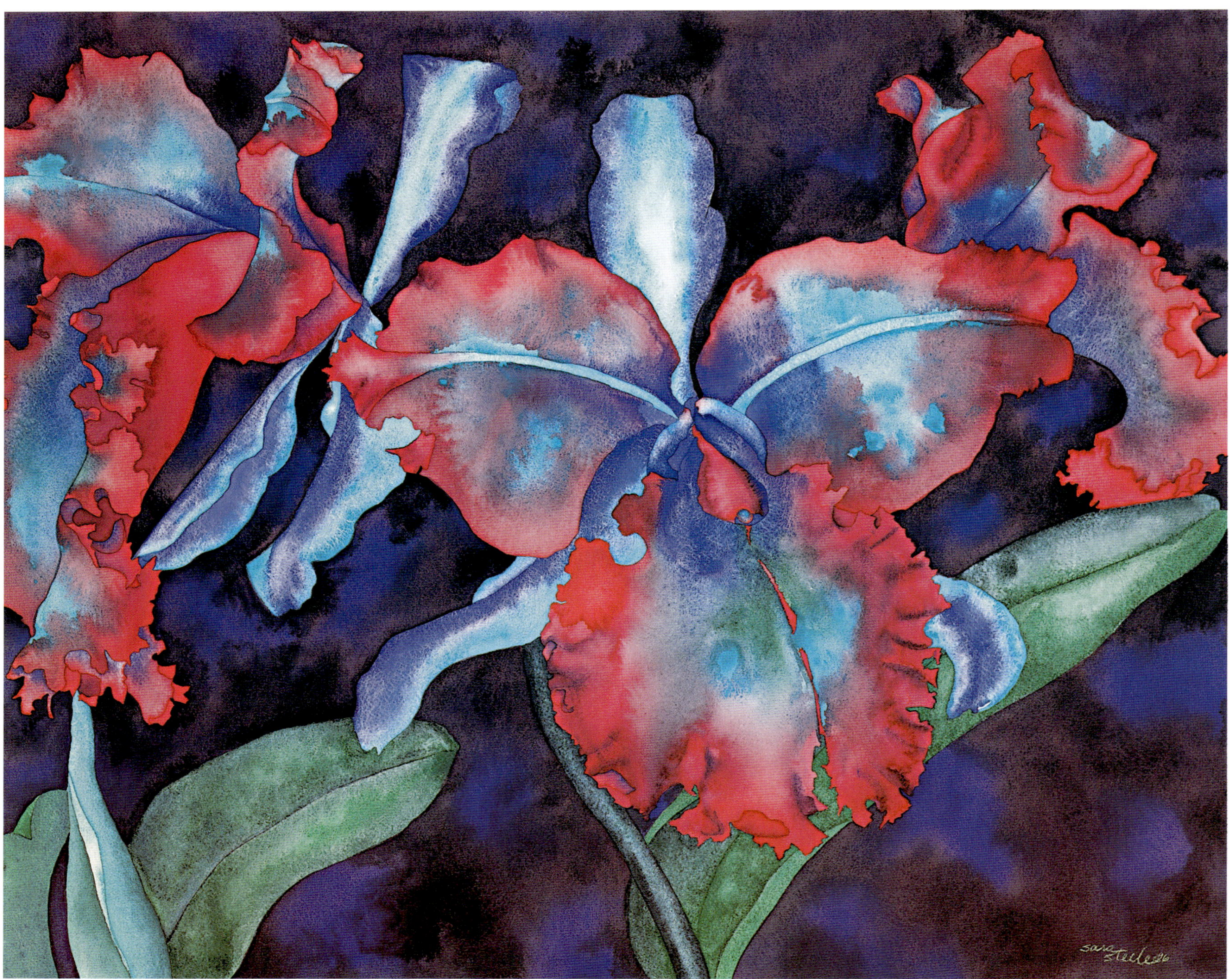

Dark Laeliocattleya, 1996

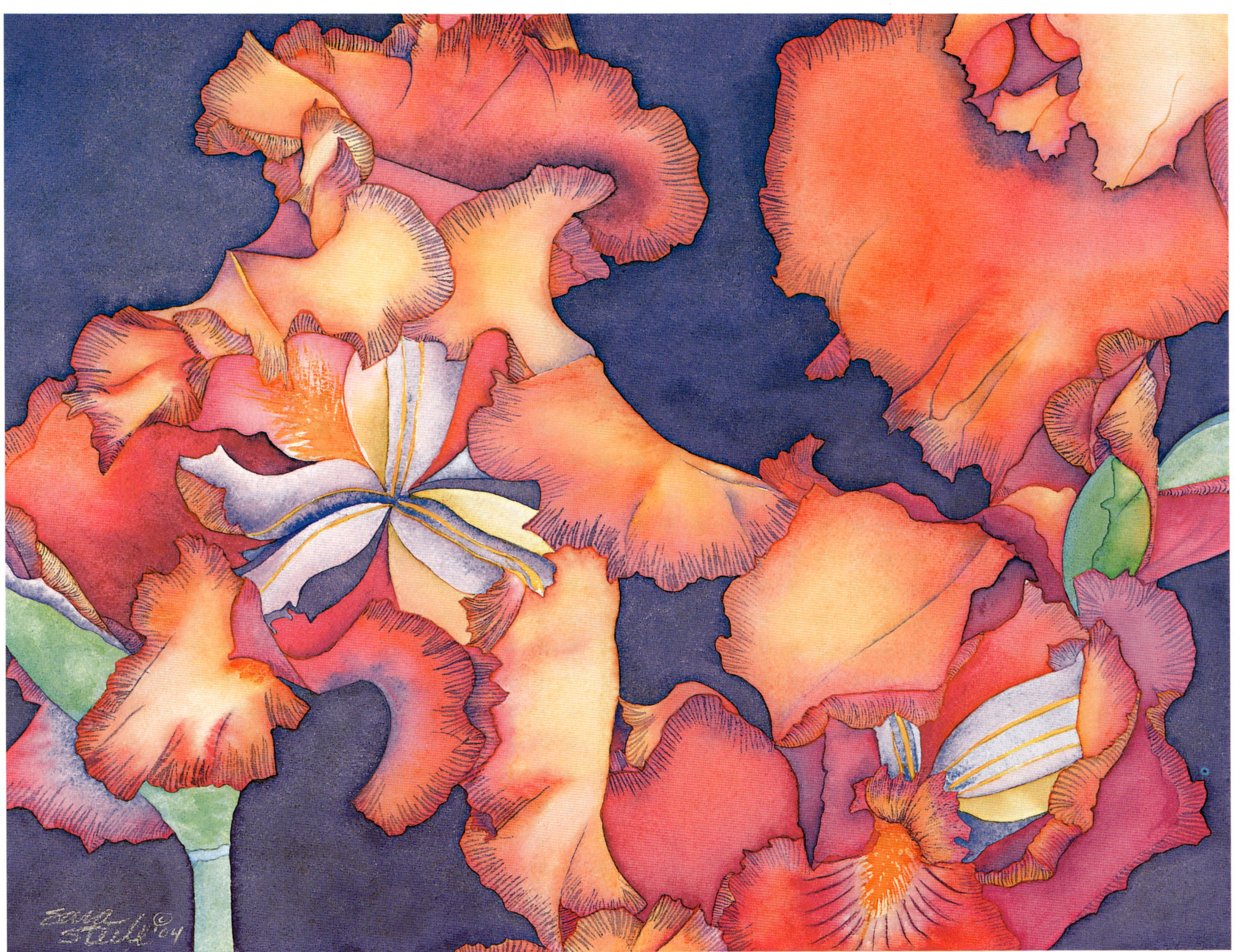

Modern Classic Celebration, 2004

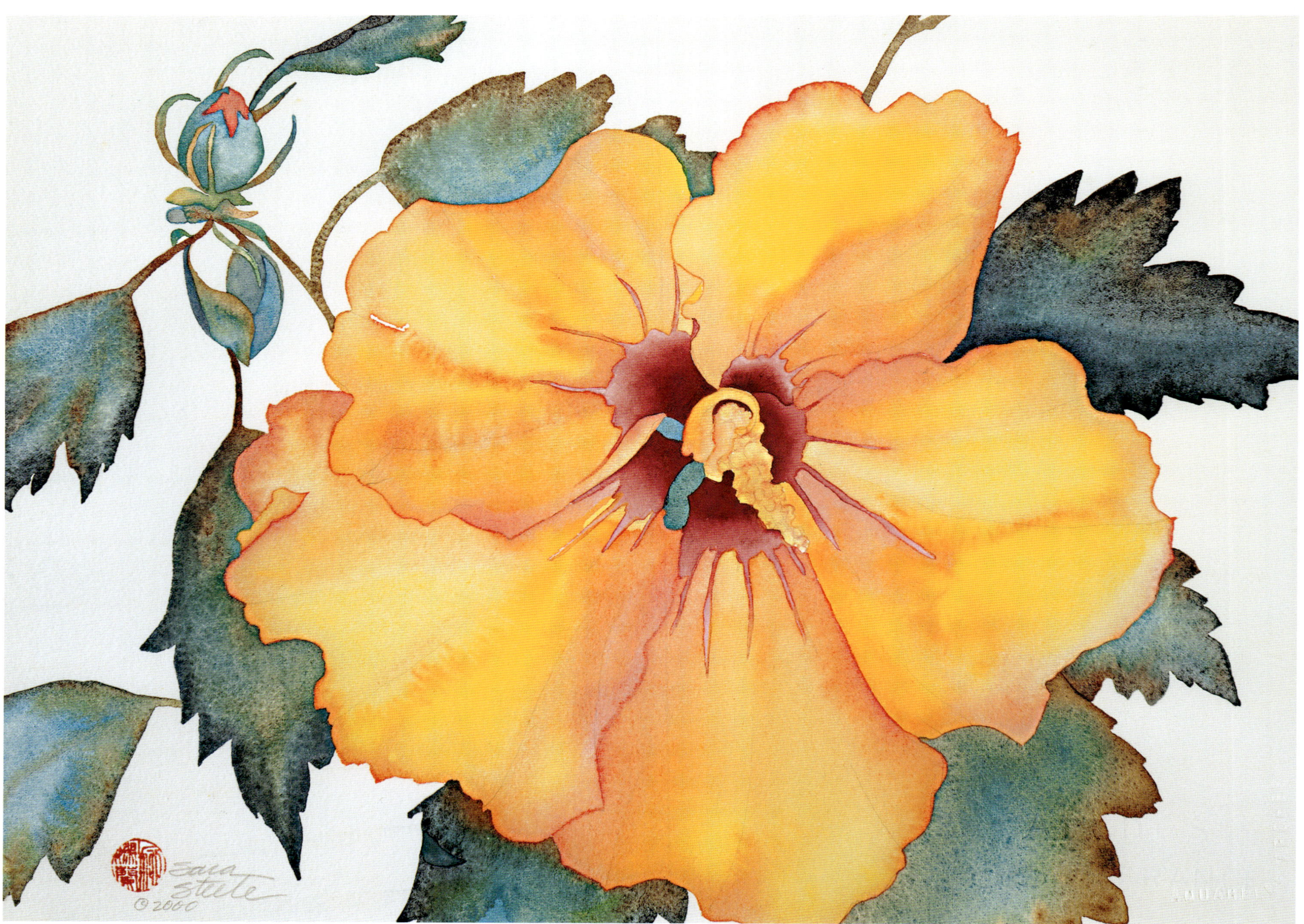

Rose of Sharon II, 2000

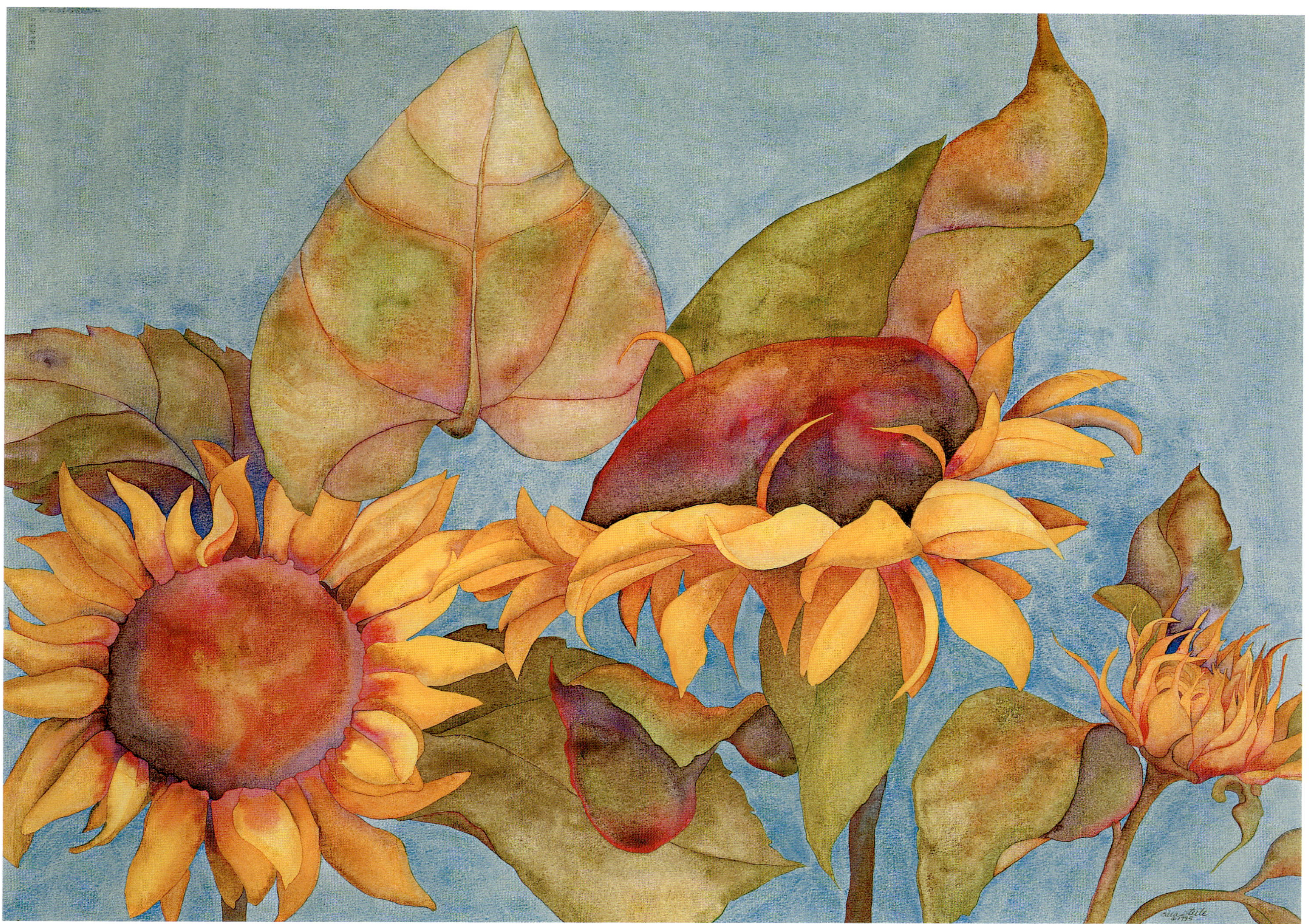

Sunflowers, 1995

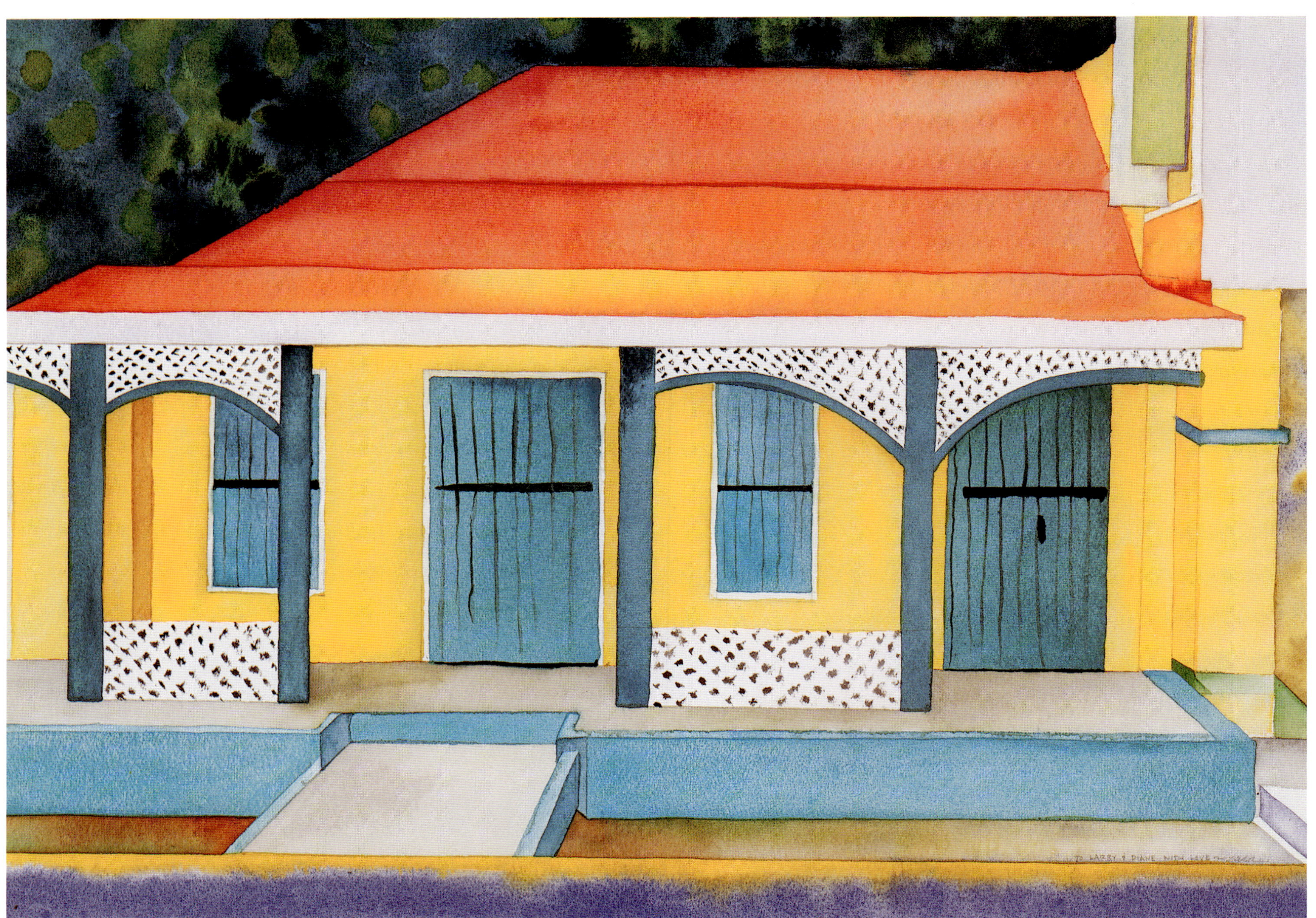

Shop in Christianstad, St. Croix, 1998

土

Earth

As summer's exuberant and fiery energy begins to settle into a serene fullness, we share the element of Earth and the season of late summer. Plants that once reached outward and upward now bow to the earth, weighed down with plentiful fruits ready for the harvest. The loving and joyful community that found expression in the element of Fire has ripened into the experience of gratitude and belonging. Life is now embraced and replenished by the bounteous, nurturing sustenance of Earth, as the cycle relaxes into the downward movement of the receptive yin.

The paintings in this collection are characterized by a sense of nurture, stability, and bounty. *St. Croix*, the initial painting, captures that feeling of home and hearth. *Mellonhead Tea* is a still life composed using heirlooms and other objects connected to the stability of the home. Other paintings portray the abundant fruits of the harvest. *Mormodes*, *Rothschildianum*, and *Paphiopedilum*, the endangered orchids in this collection, are terrestrial orchids that grow from the soil and receive their nutrients directly from the earth.

Also in this collection are landscapes that convey the peaceful, nurturing qualities of Earth. In *Mesa Lands* we are given a glimpse of Sara's imaginative landscape of the Southwestern desert where her spirit finds replenishment, while *Abiquiu Dam I* shows the precious element of Water in the desert being protected and contained by the Earth. This collection concludes with the graceful serenity of *Alizarin Hills*.

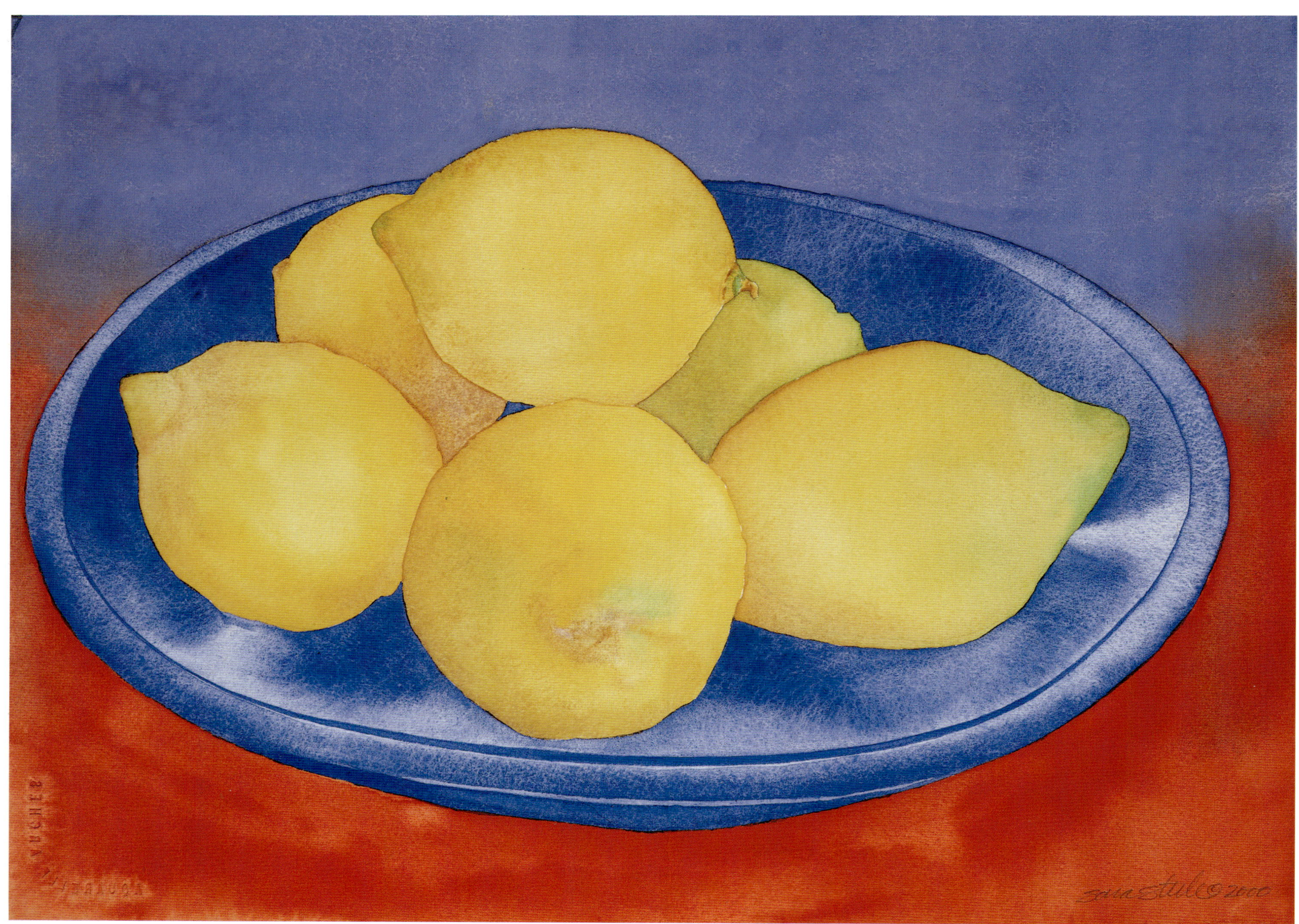

Lemons in Blue Bowl, 2000

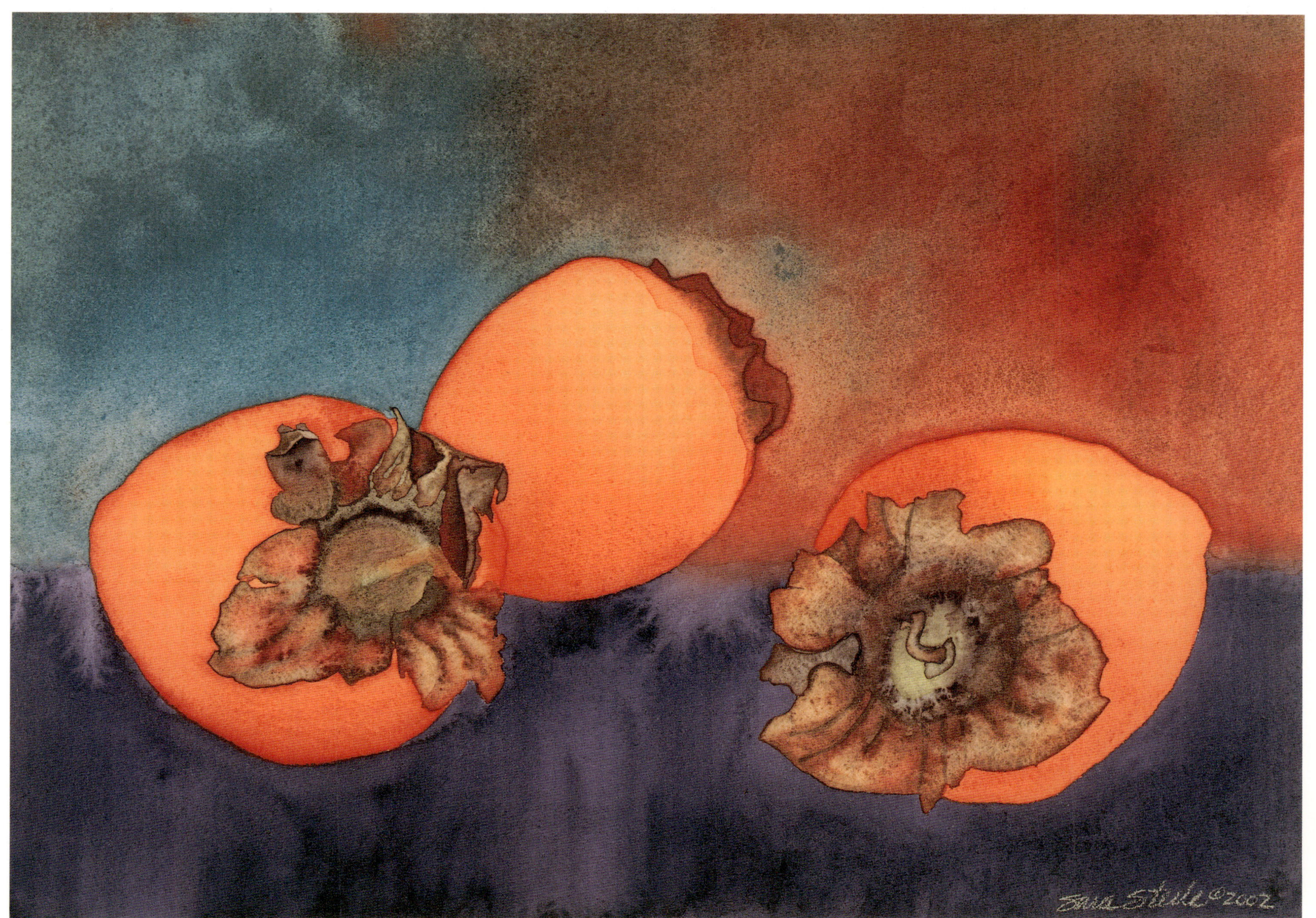

Hachiya Persimmon, 2002

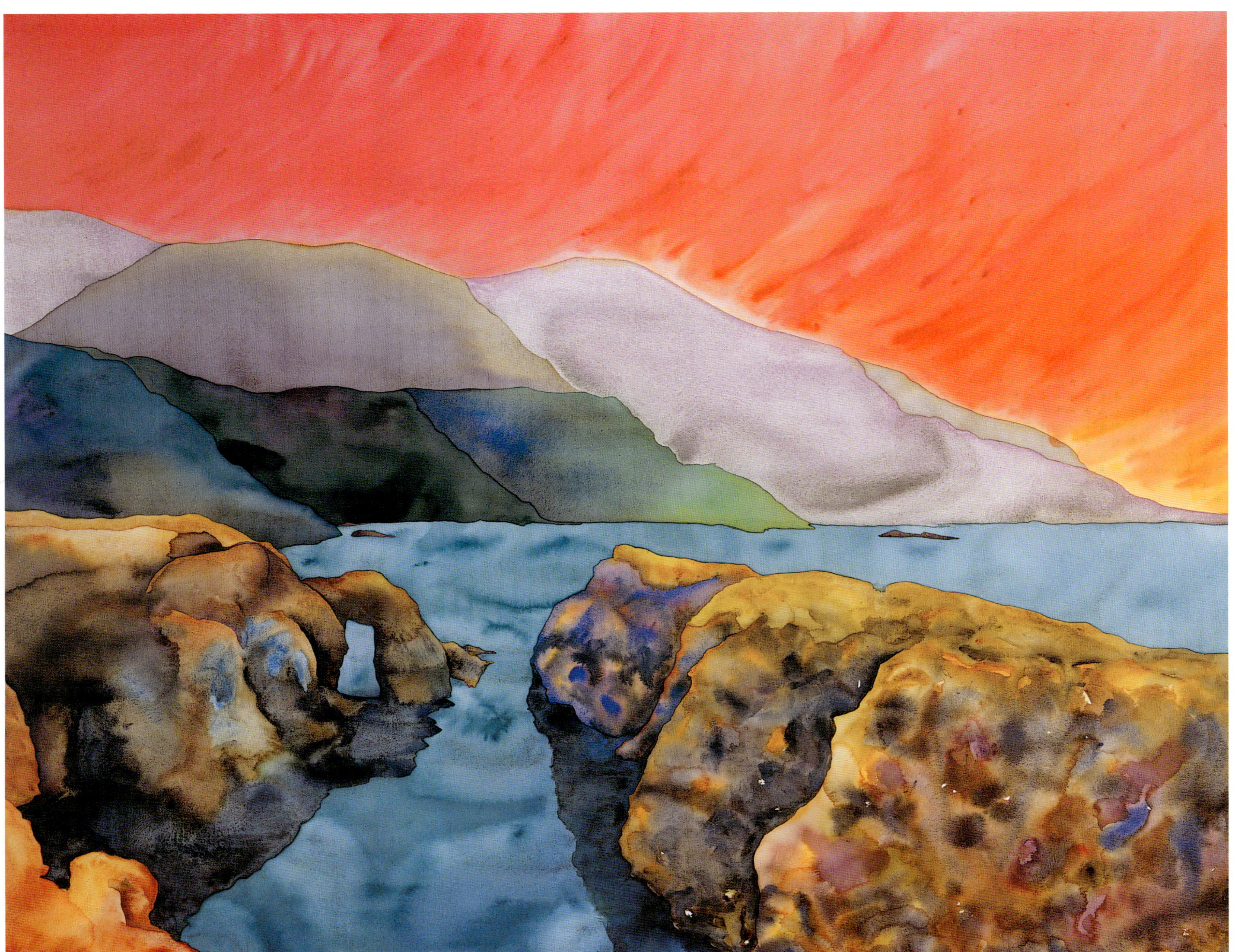

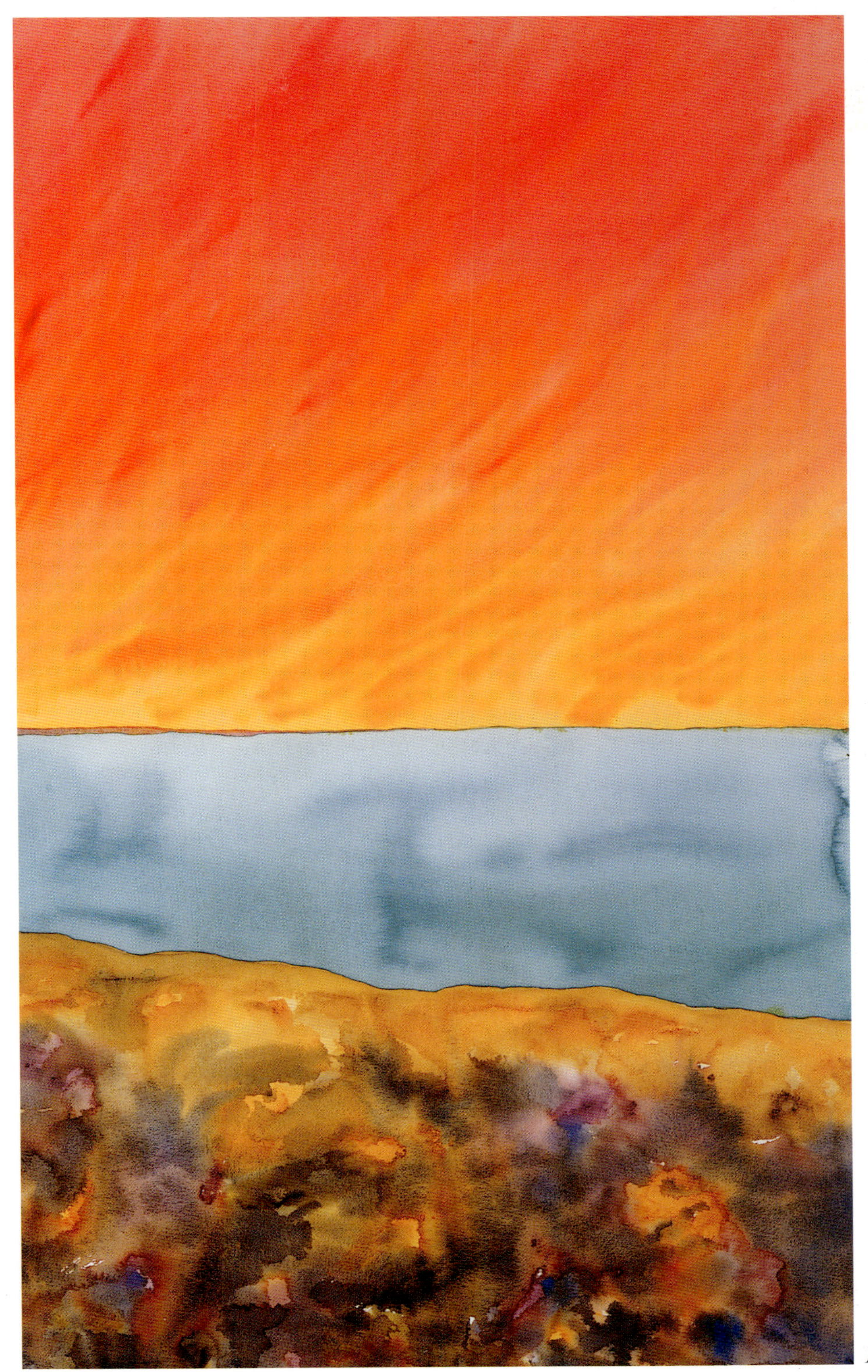

Point Lobos, Carmel I, 1998

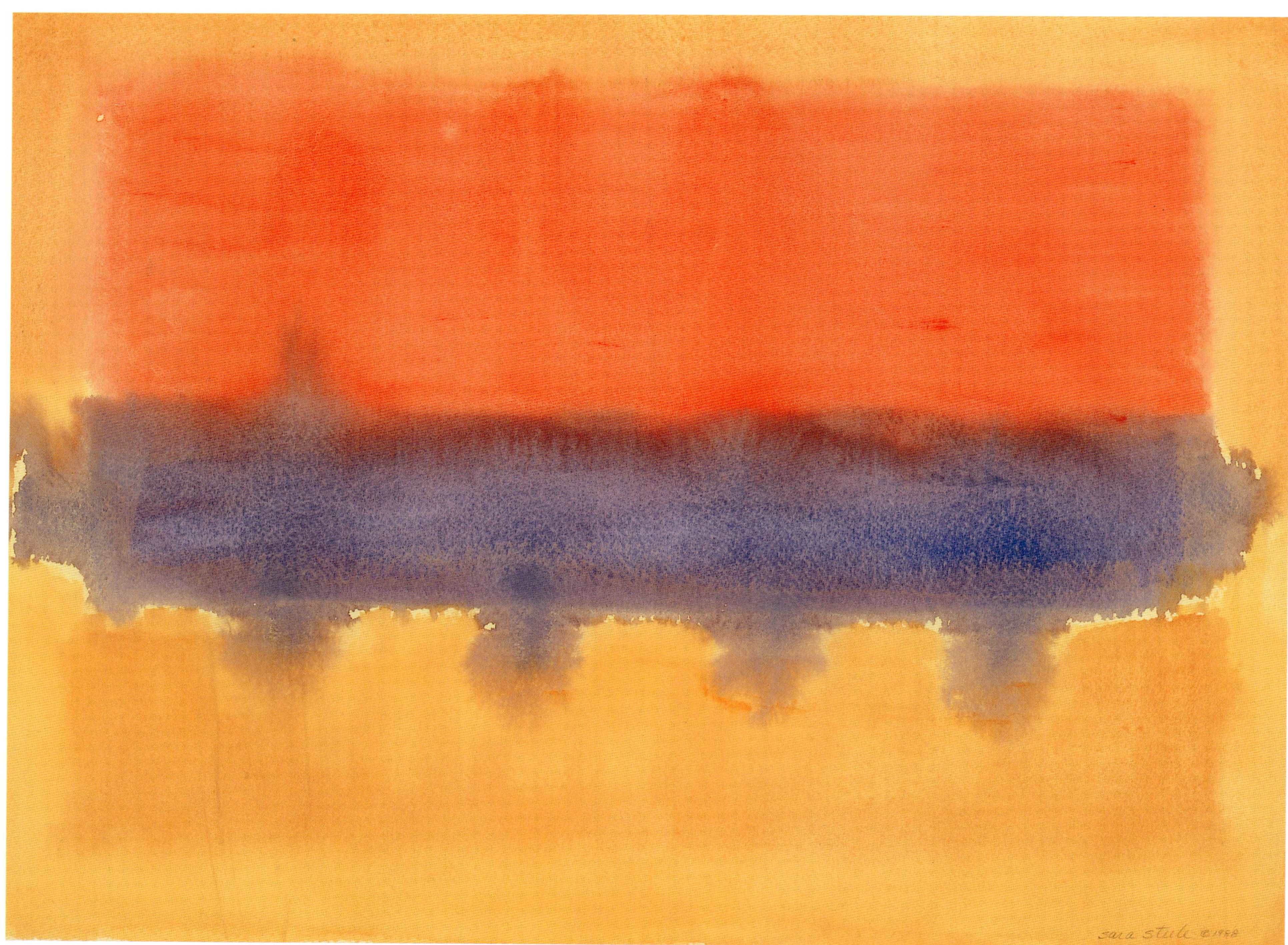

Remembering (M.R.), 1988

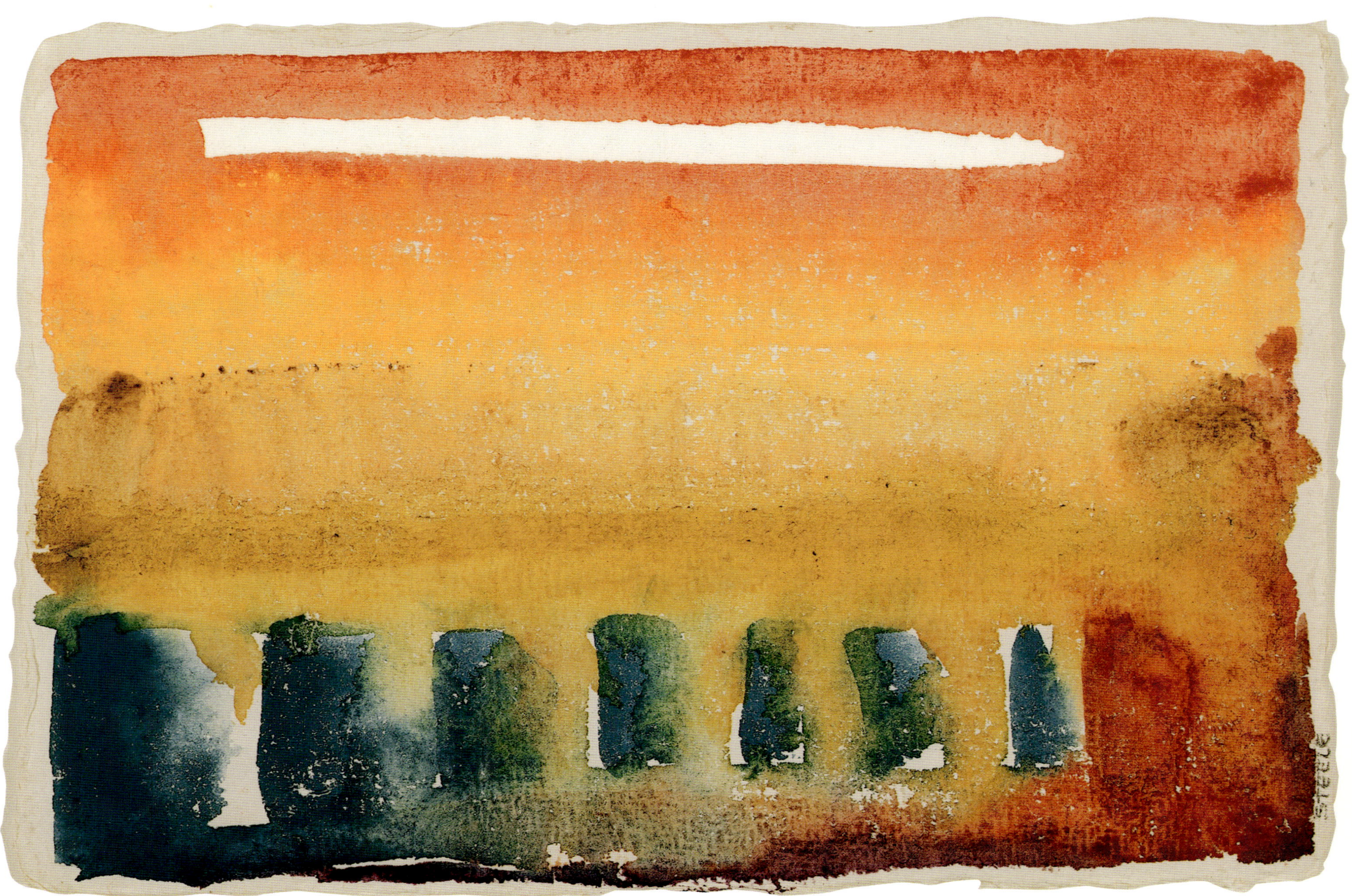

Teal Columns II, 1998

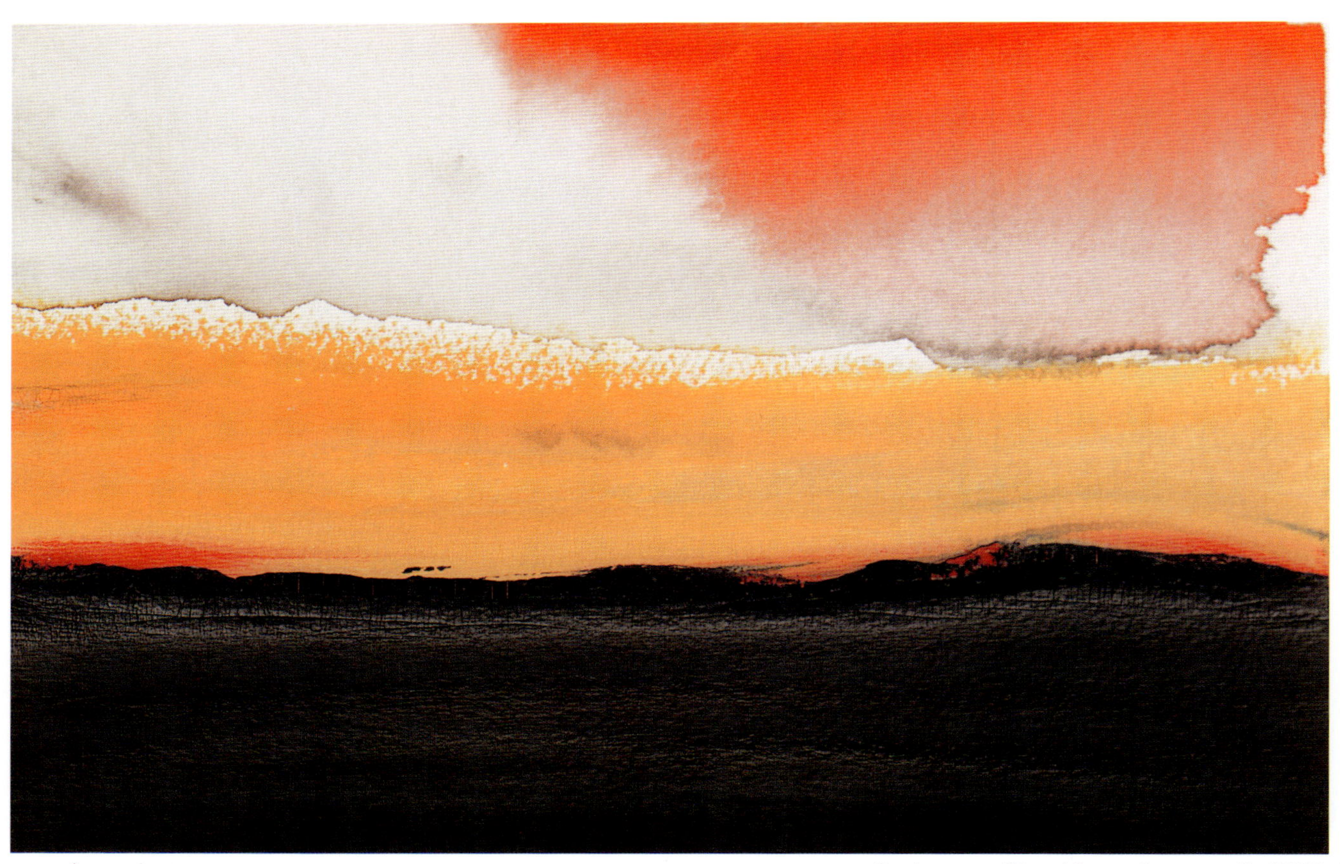

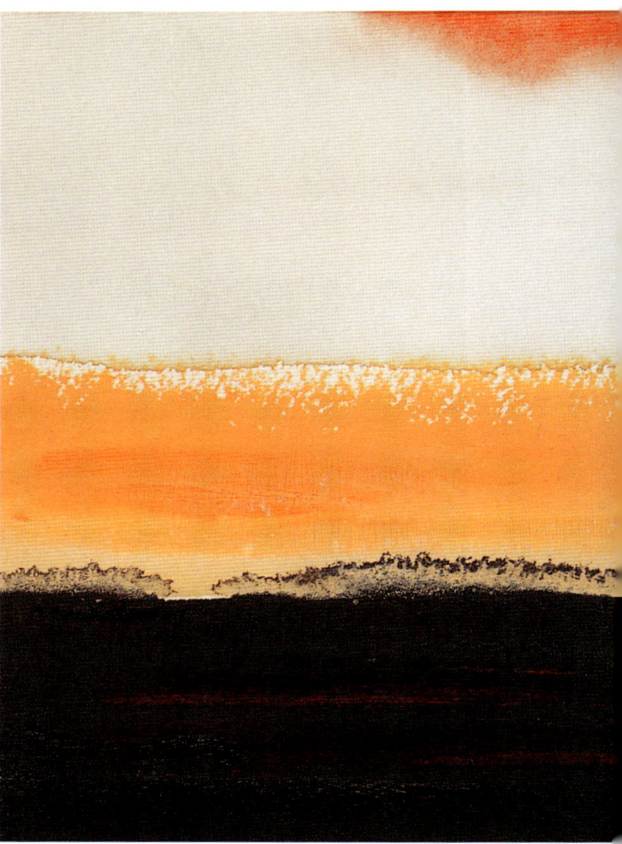

Sepiascapes/Providence (top panel), 1981

Sepiascapes/Providence (middle panel), 1981

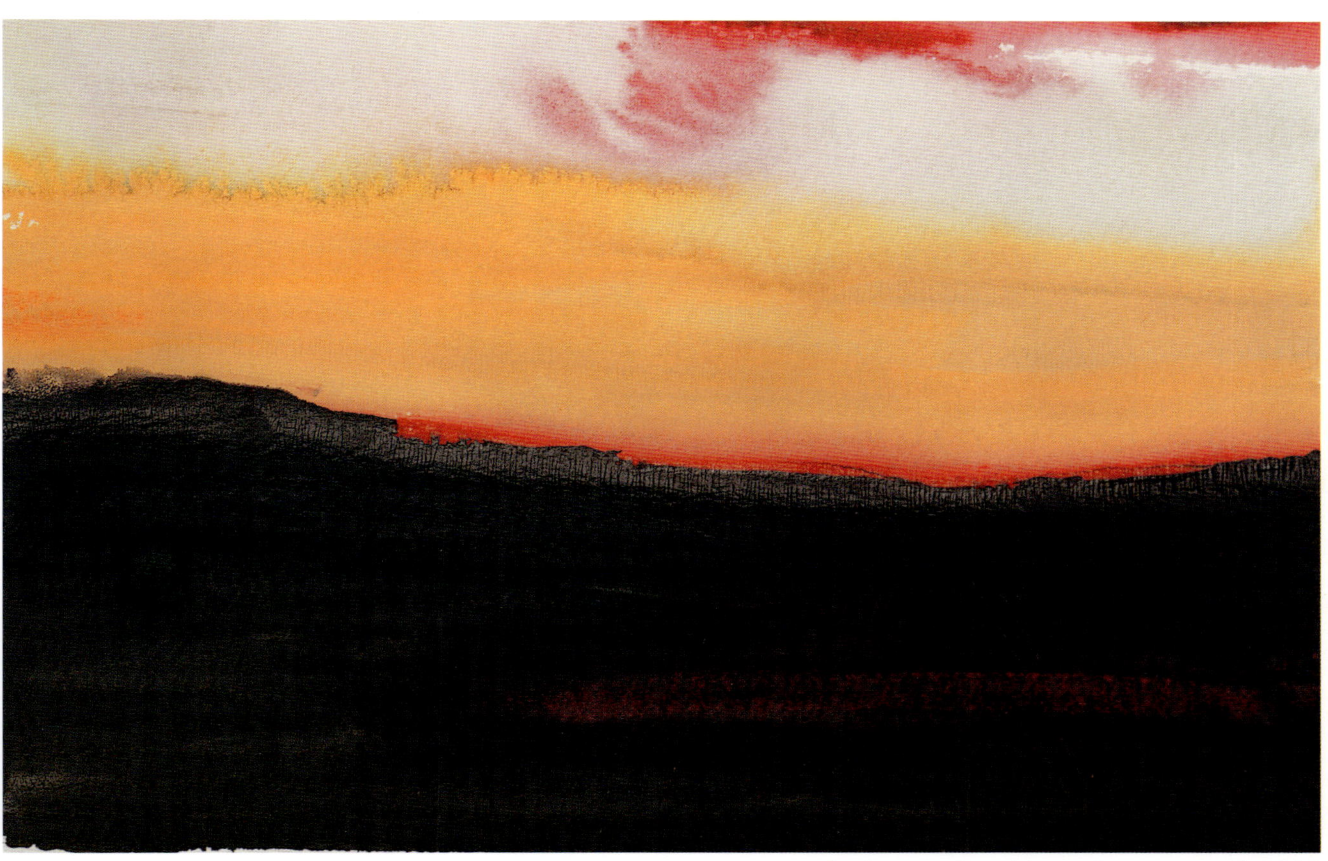

Sepiascapes/Providence (bottom panel), 1981

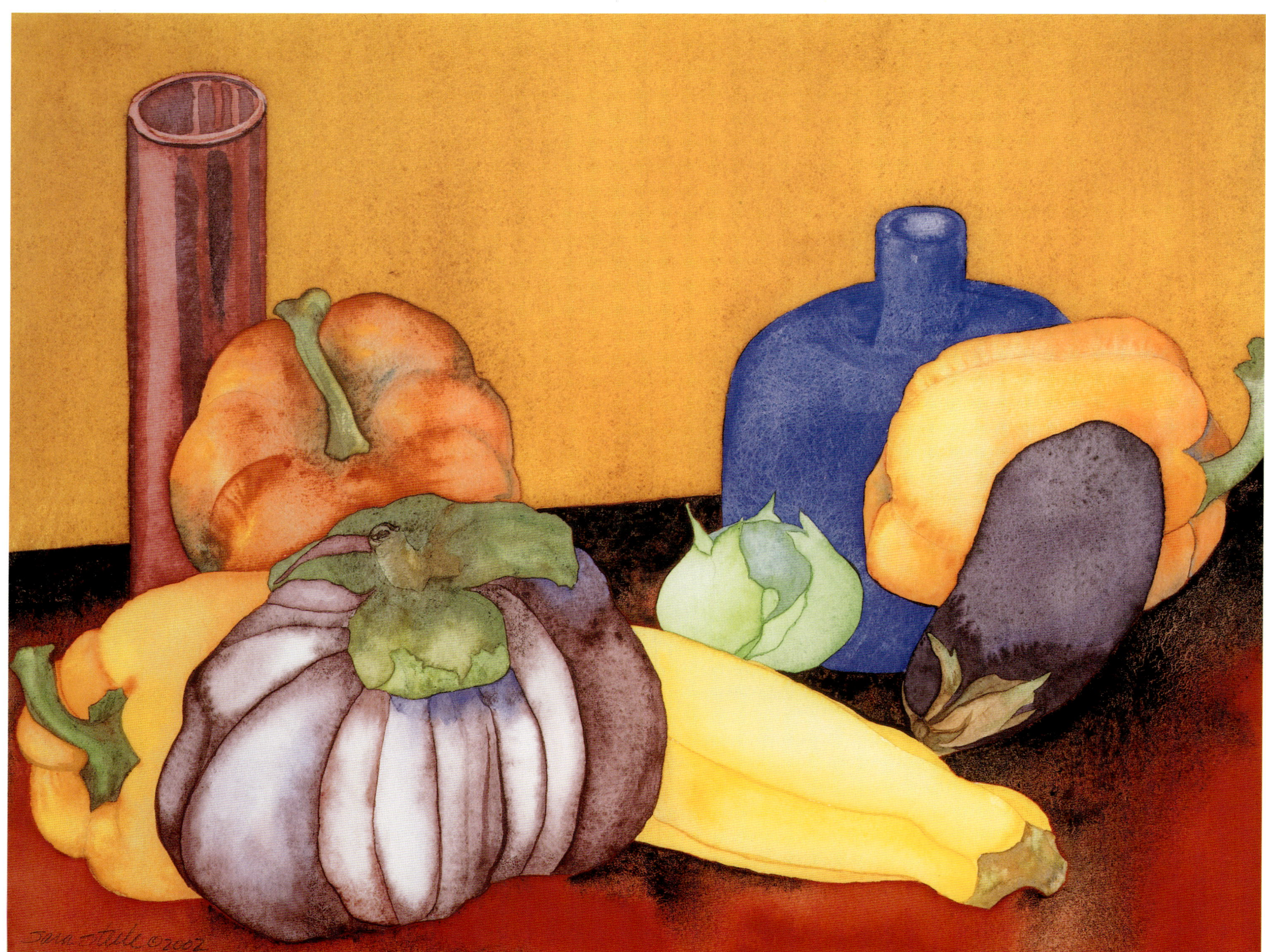

Still Life with Tomatillo, 2002

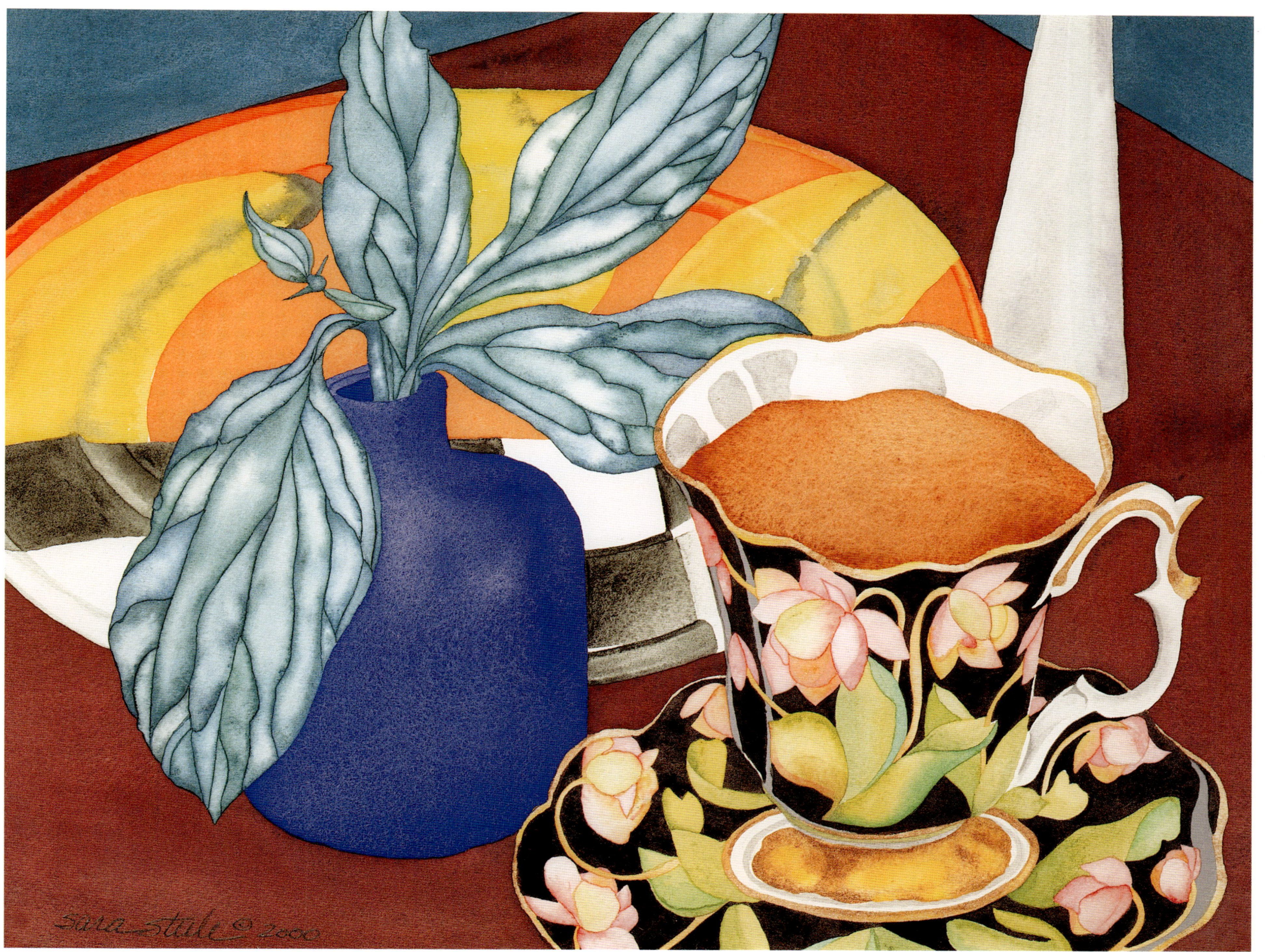

Mellonhead Tea, 2000

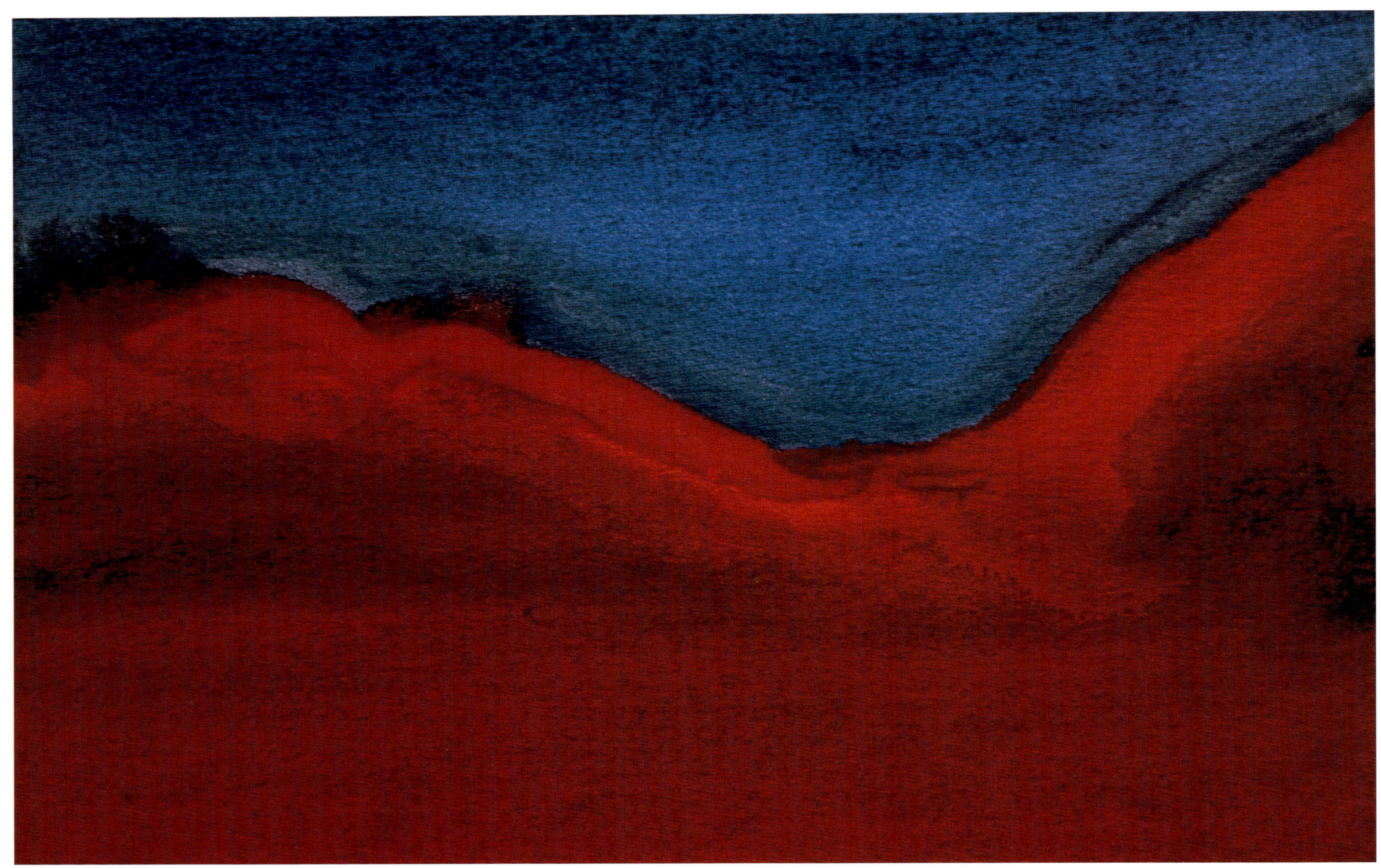

Alizarin Wing, 1981

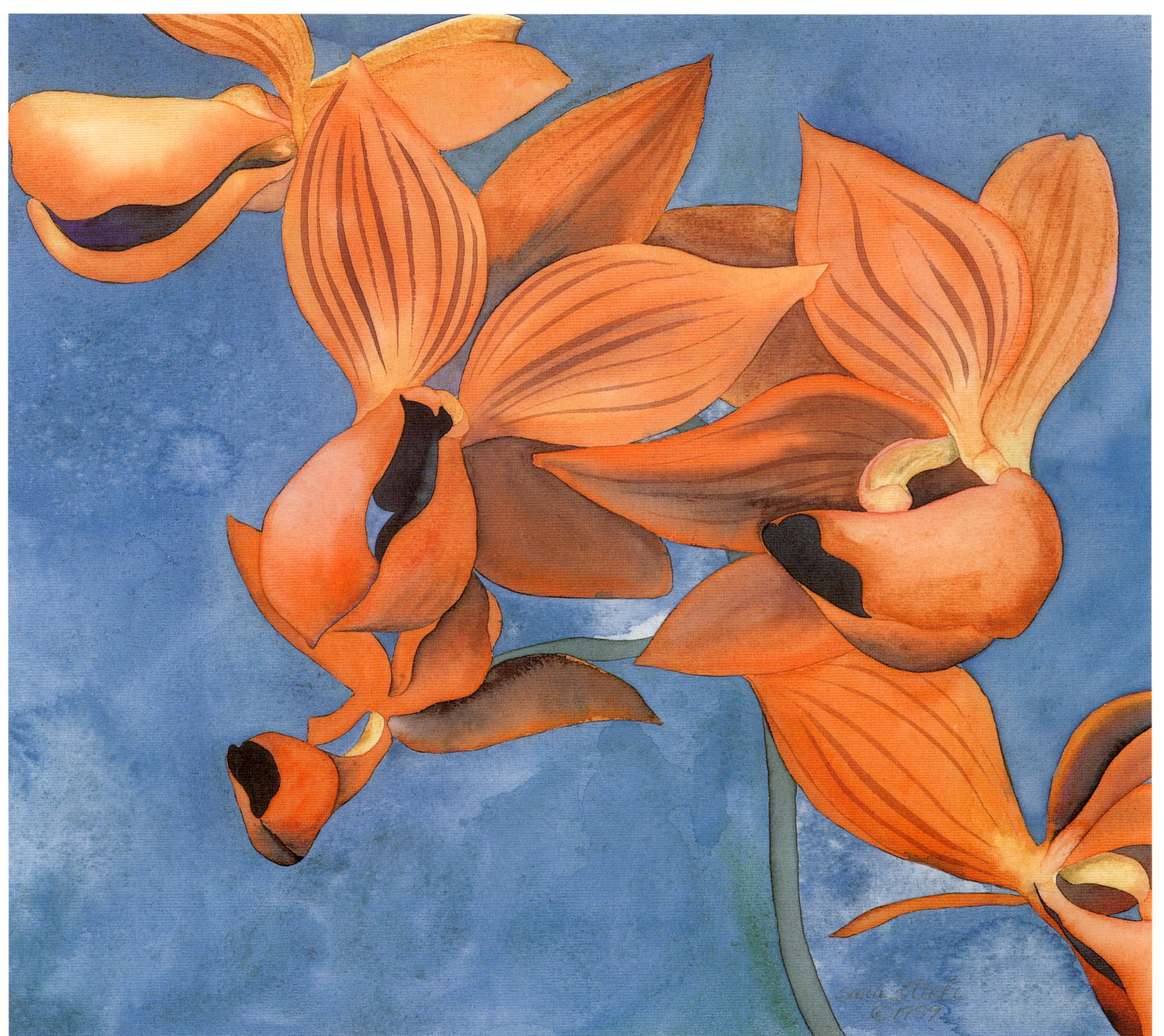

Mormodes species, from the Endangered Orchids series, 1989

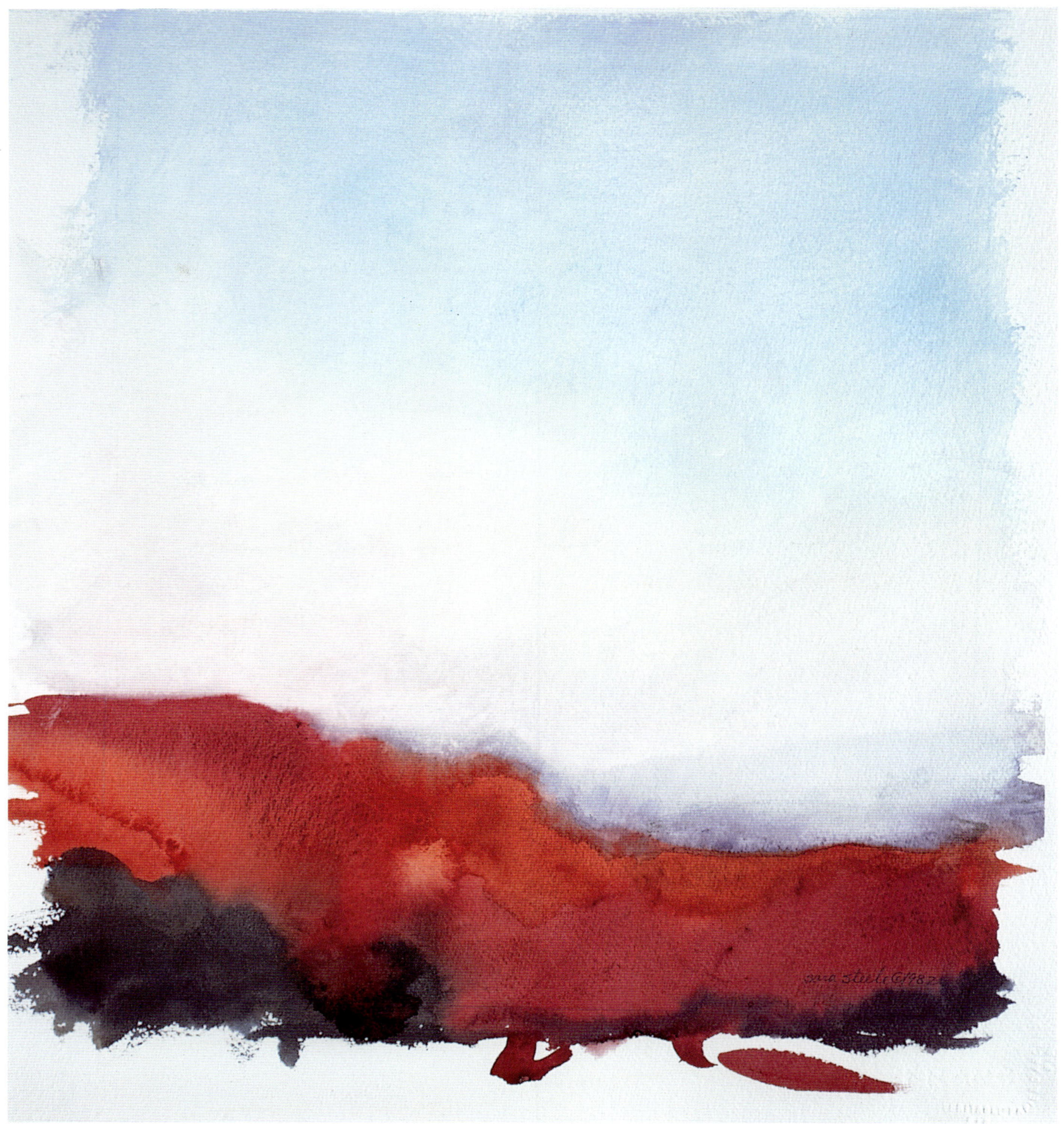

New Land, 1983

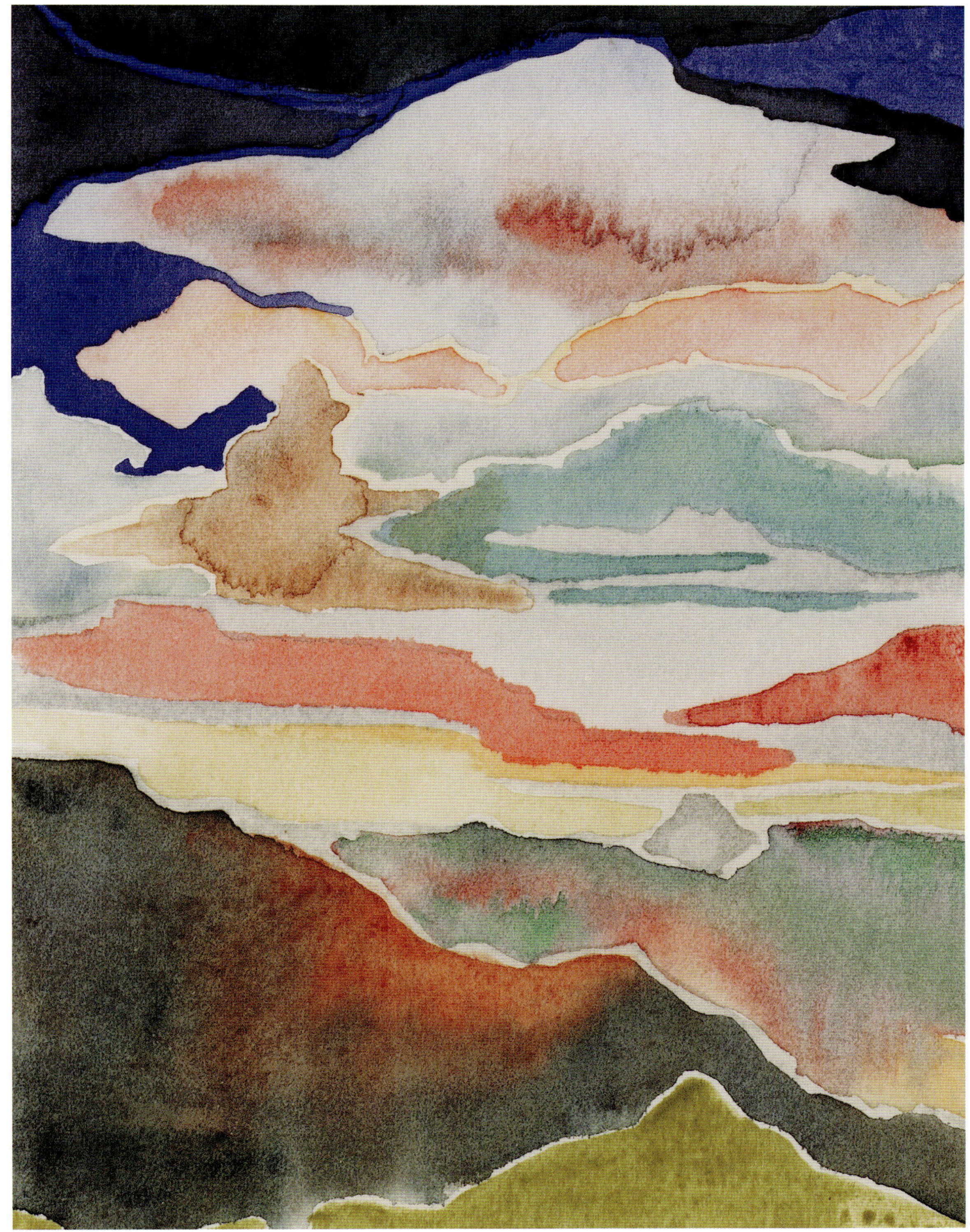

RE-scape, 1979

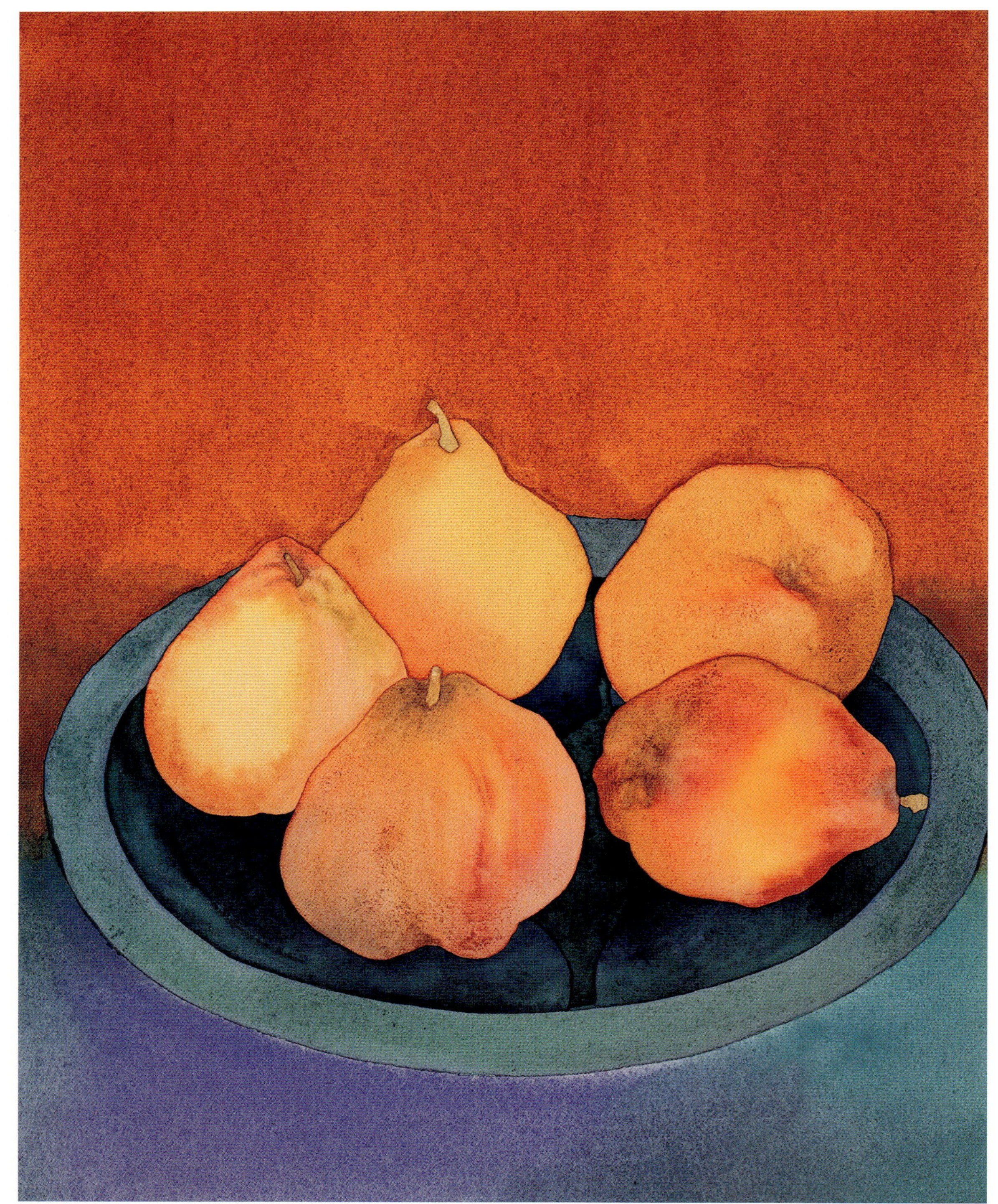

Comice Pears III, 1998

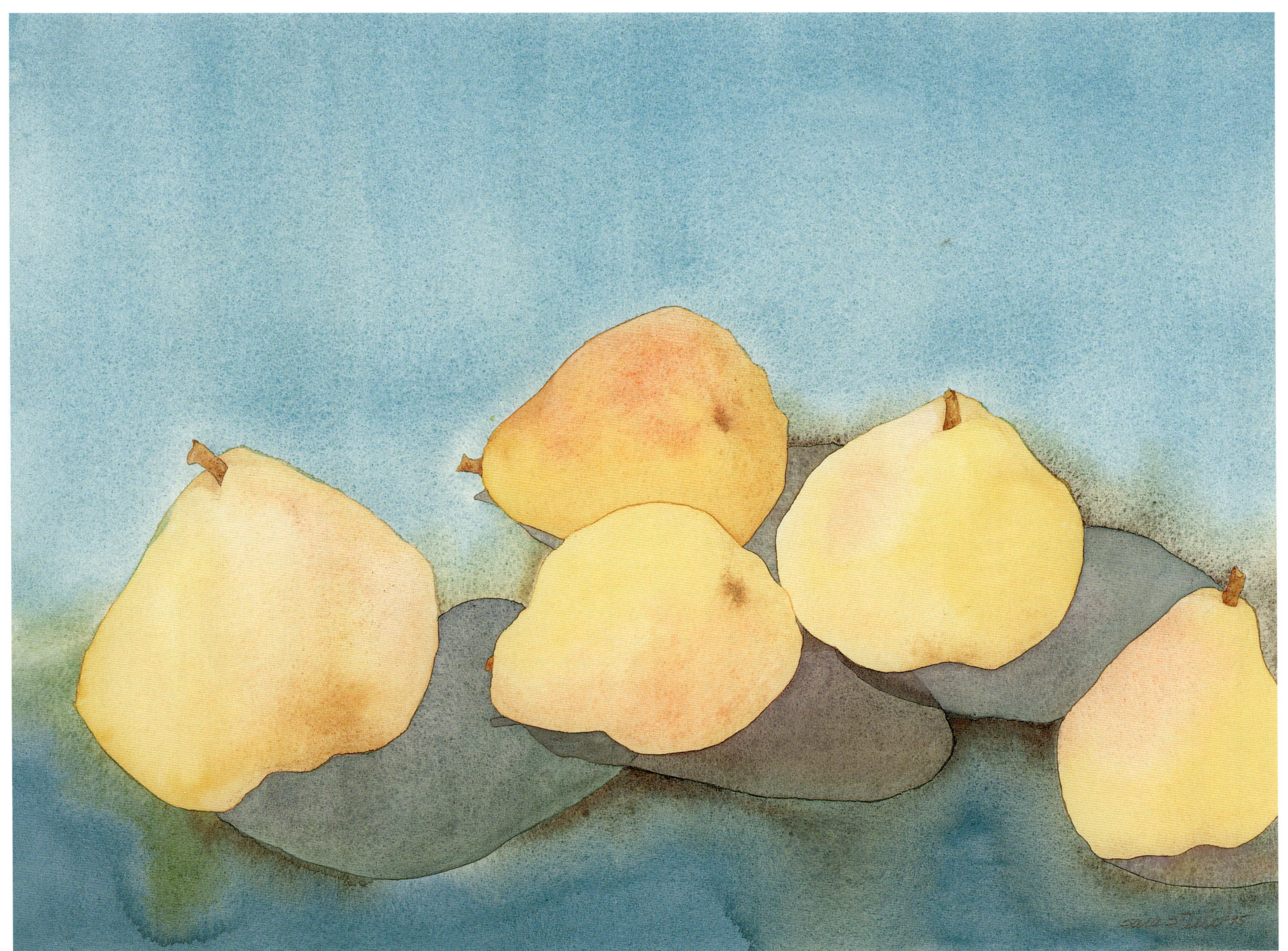

Comice Pears I, 1995

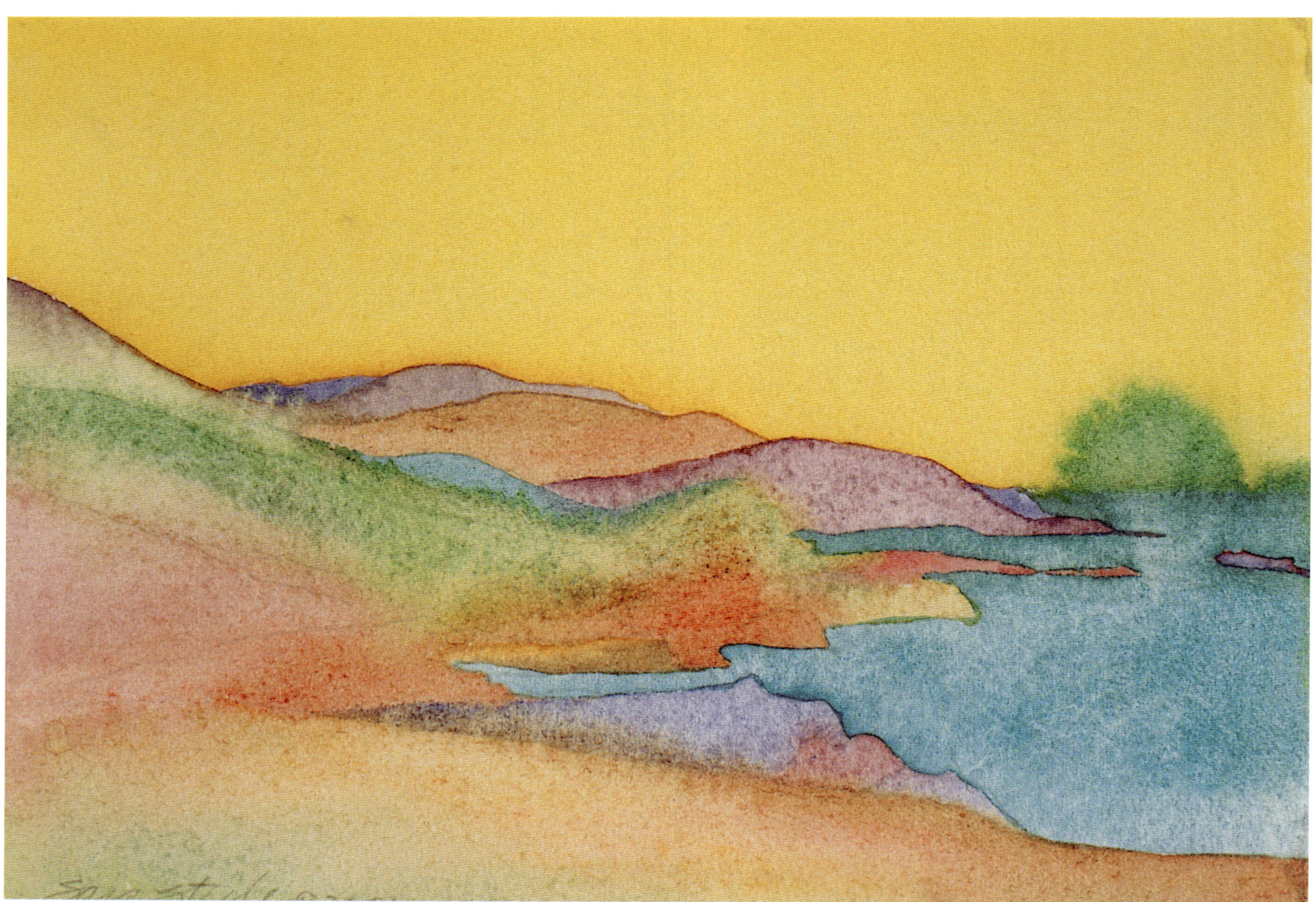

Big Sur (Lemon Sky), 2002

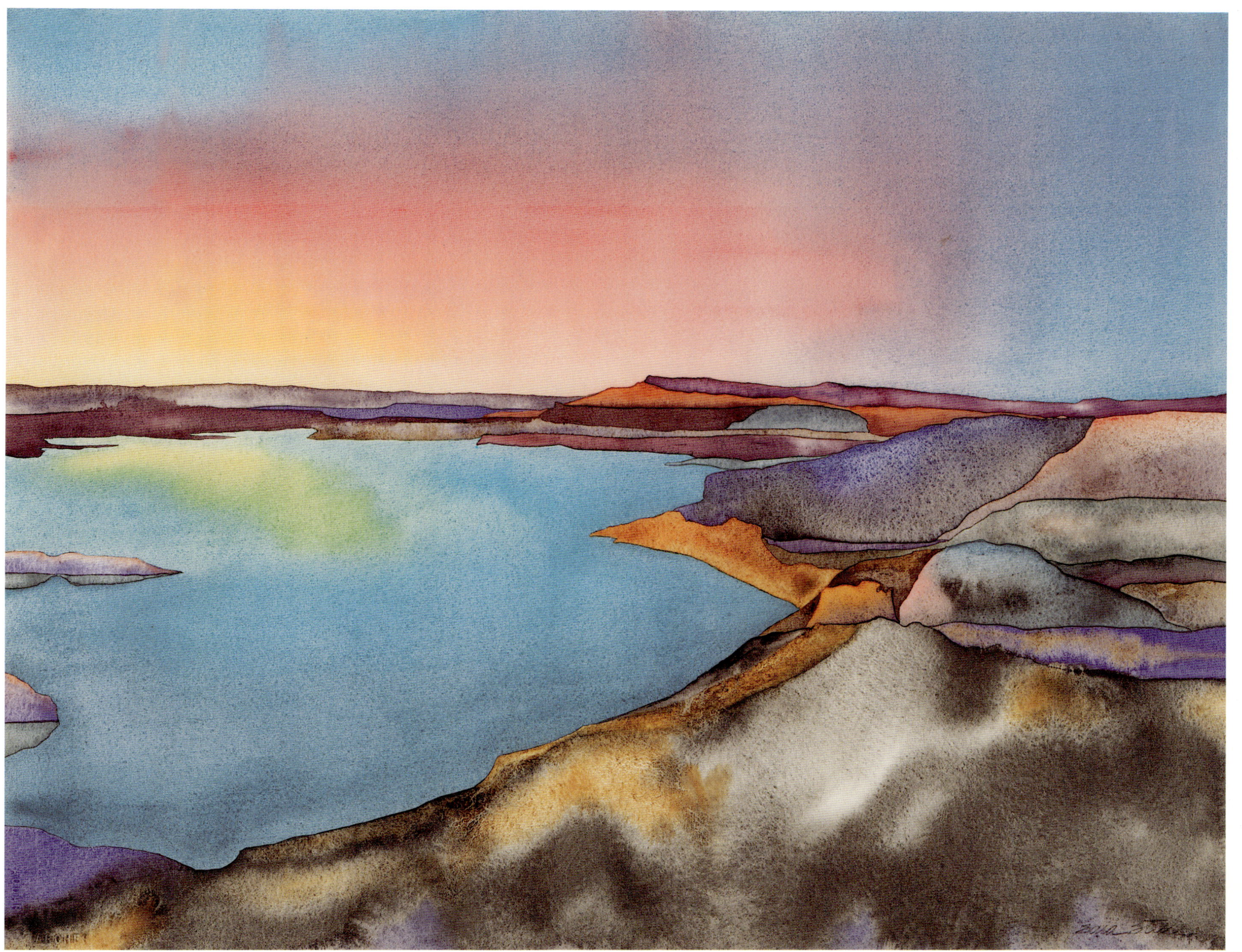

Abiquiu Dam II, 1998

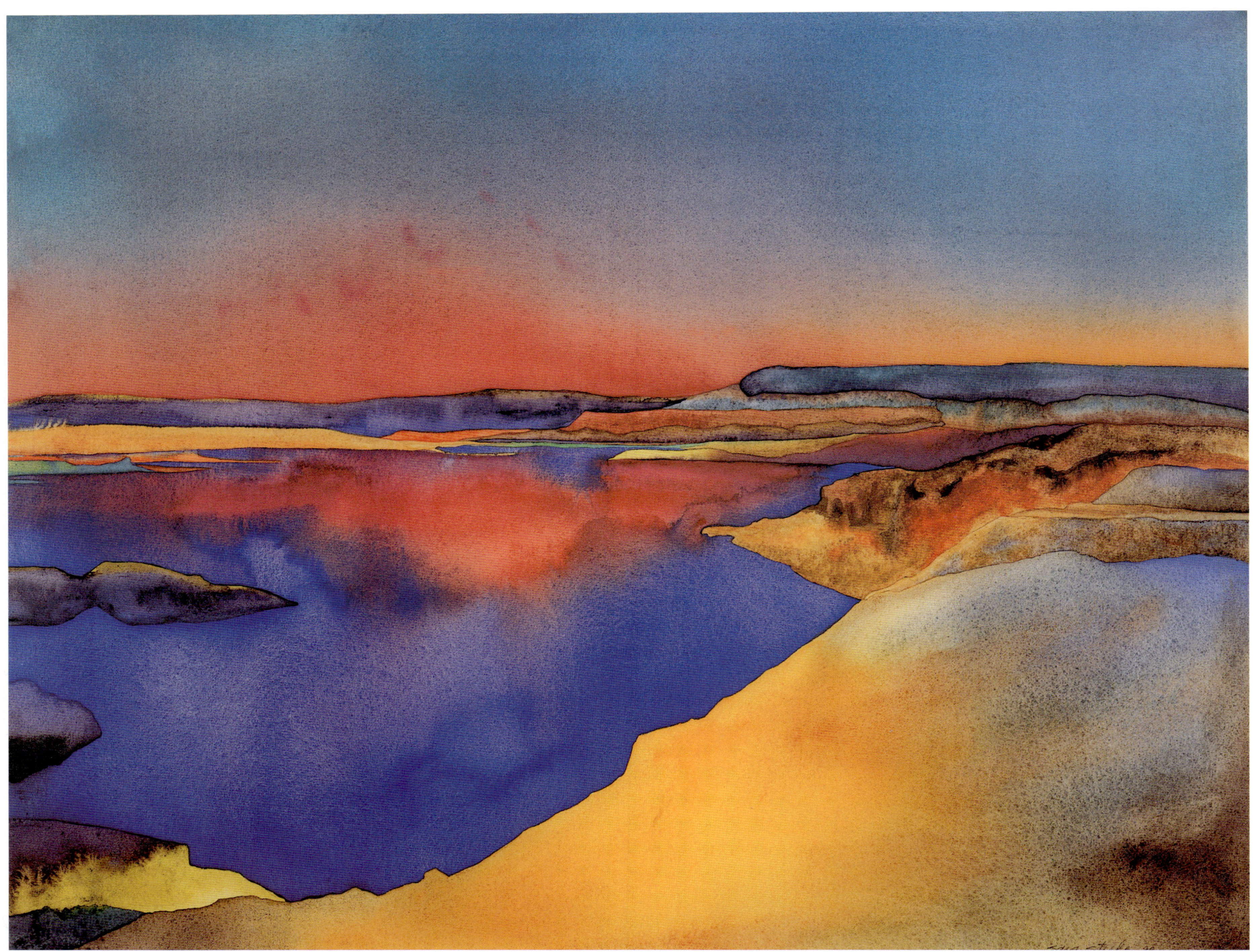

Abiquiu Dam I, 1998

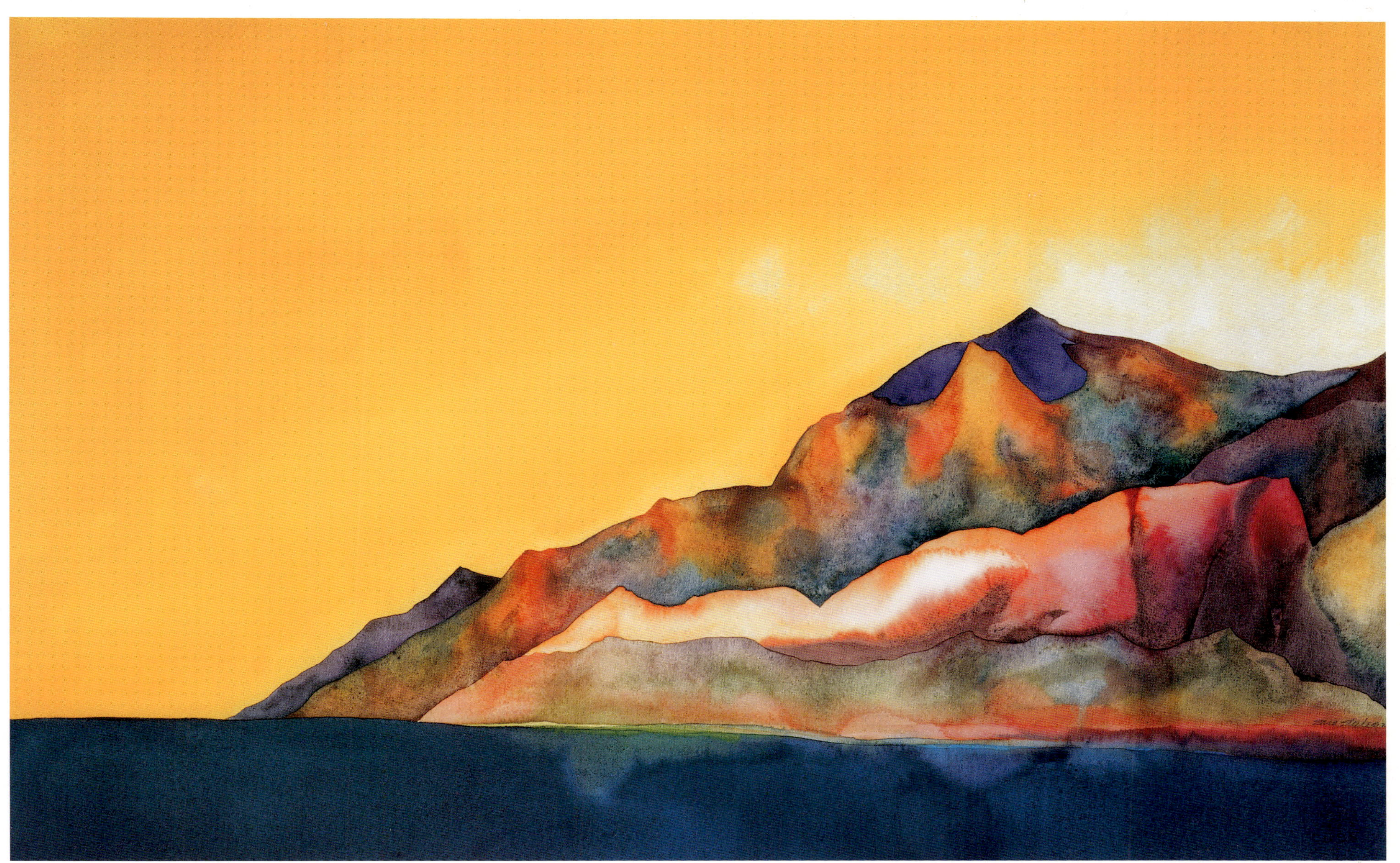

Cathleen's Mountains, 2002

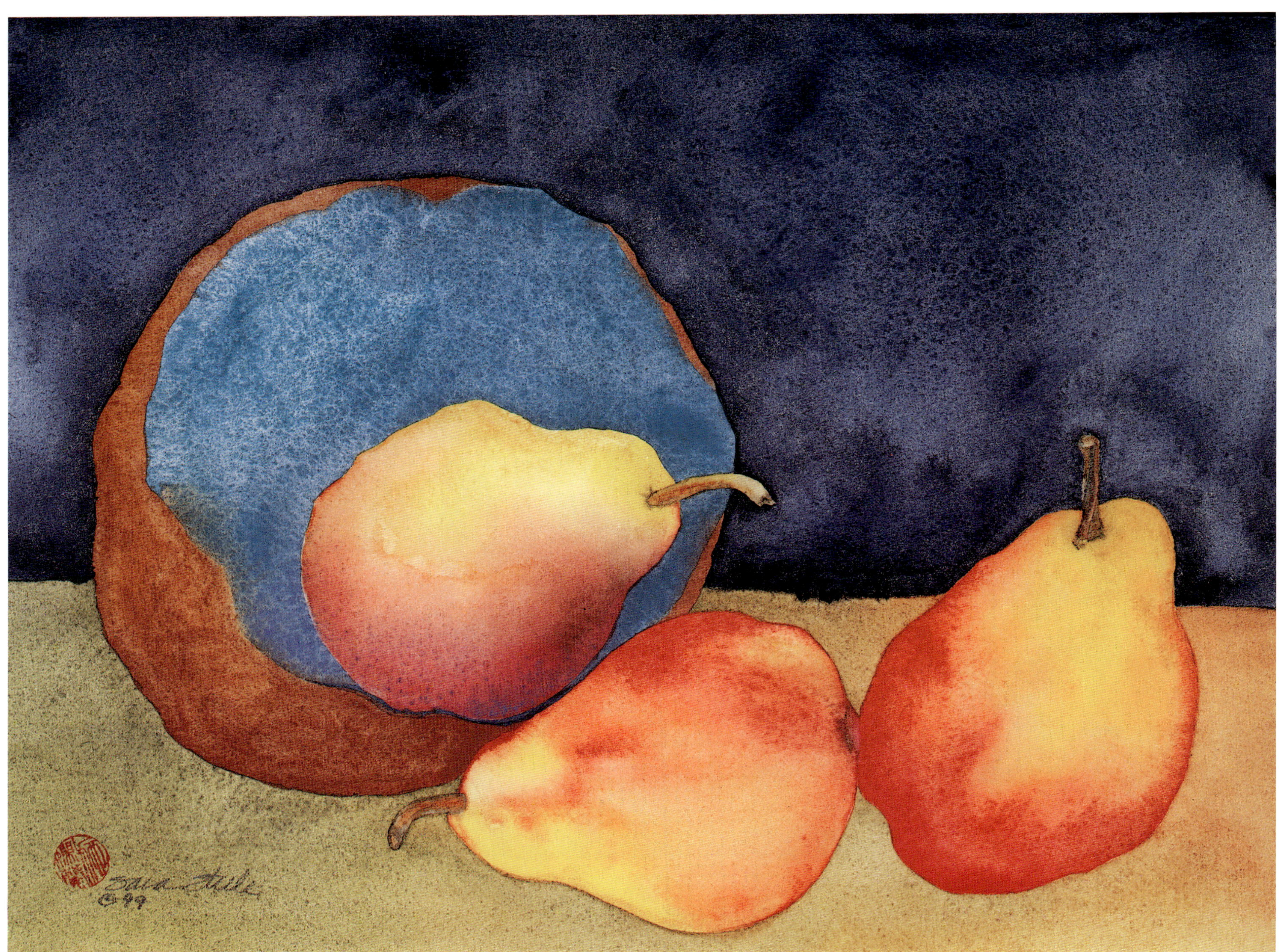

Pears with Cast Paper Bowl, 1999

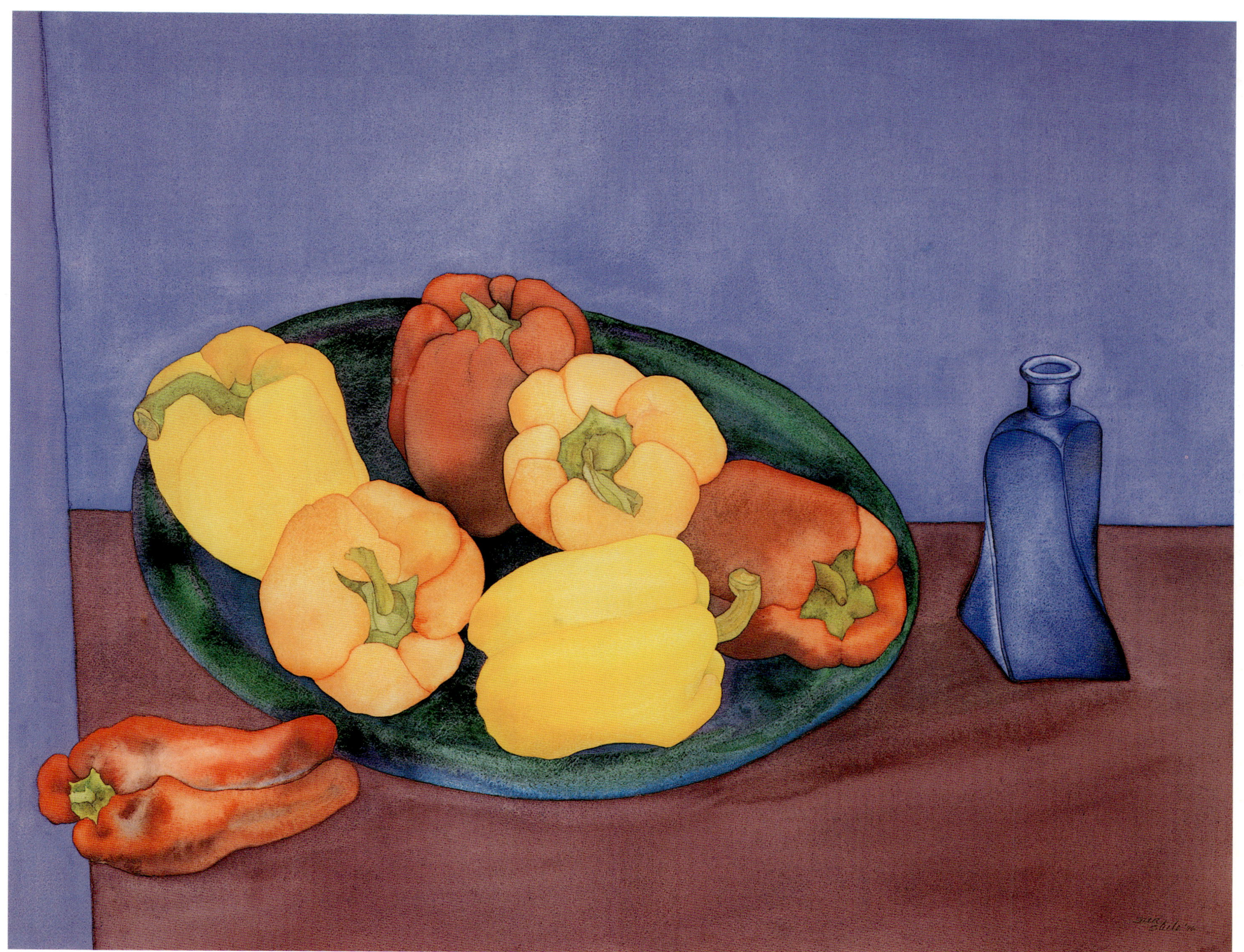

Peppers, Green Plate, Blue Bottle, 1996

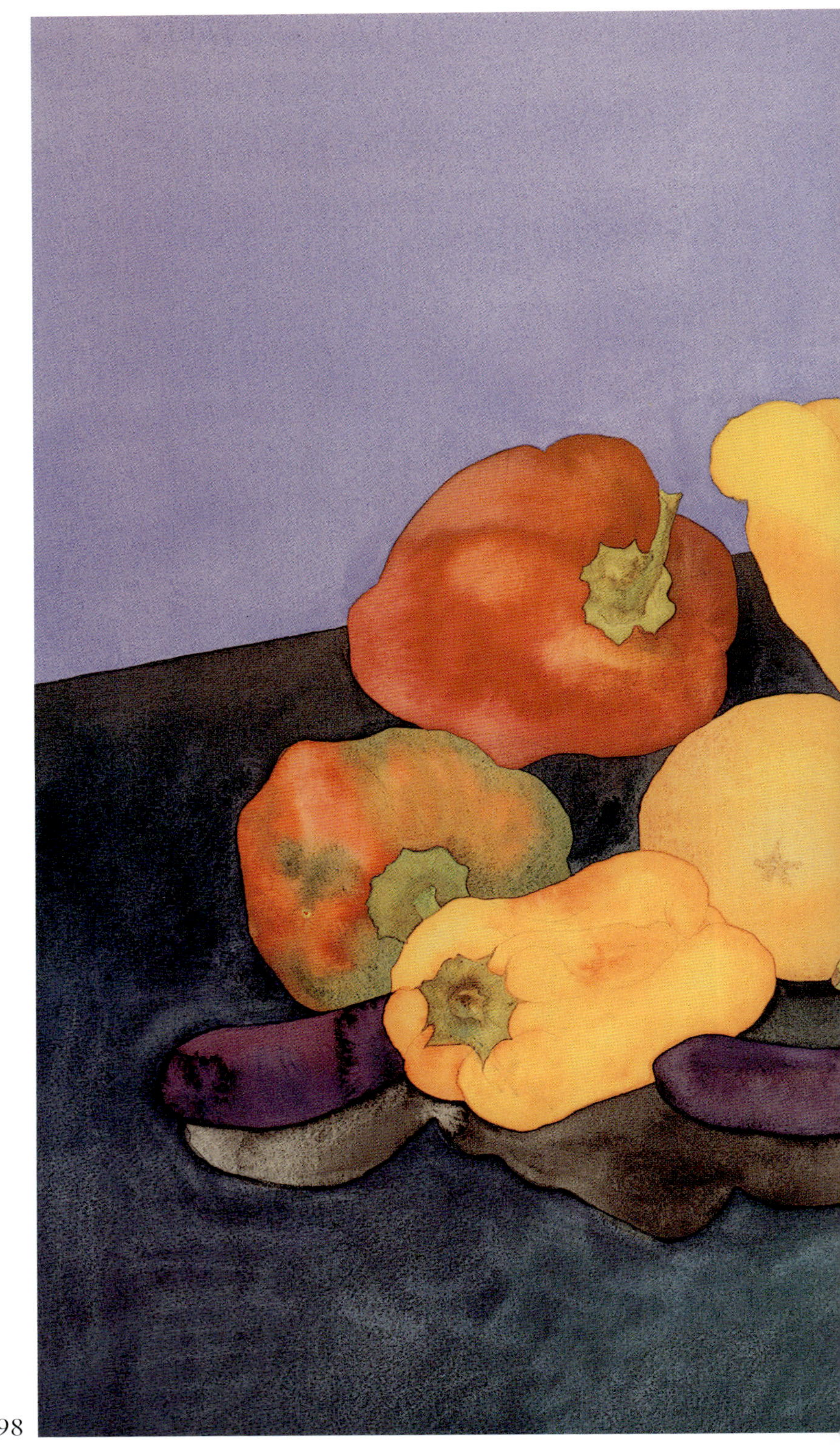

Peppers, Eggplants & Honey Tangerines, 1998

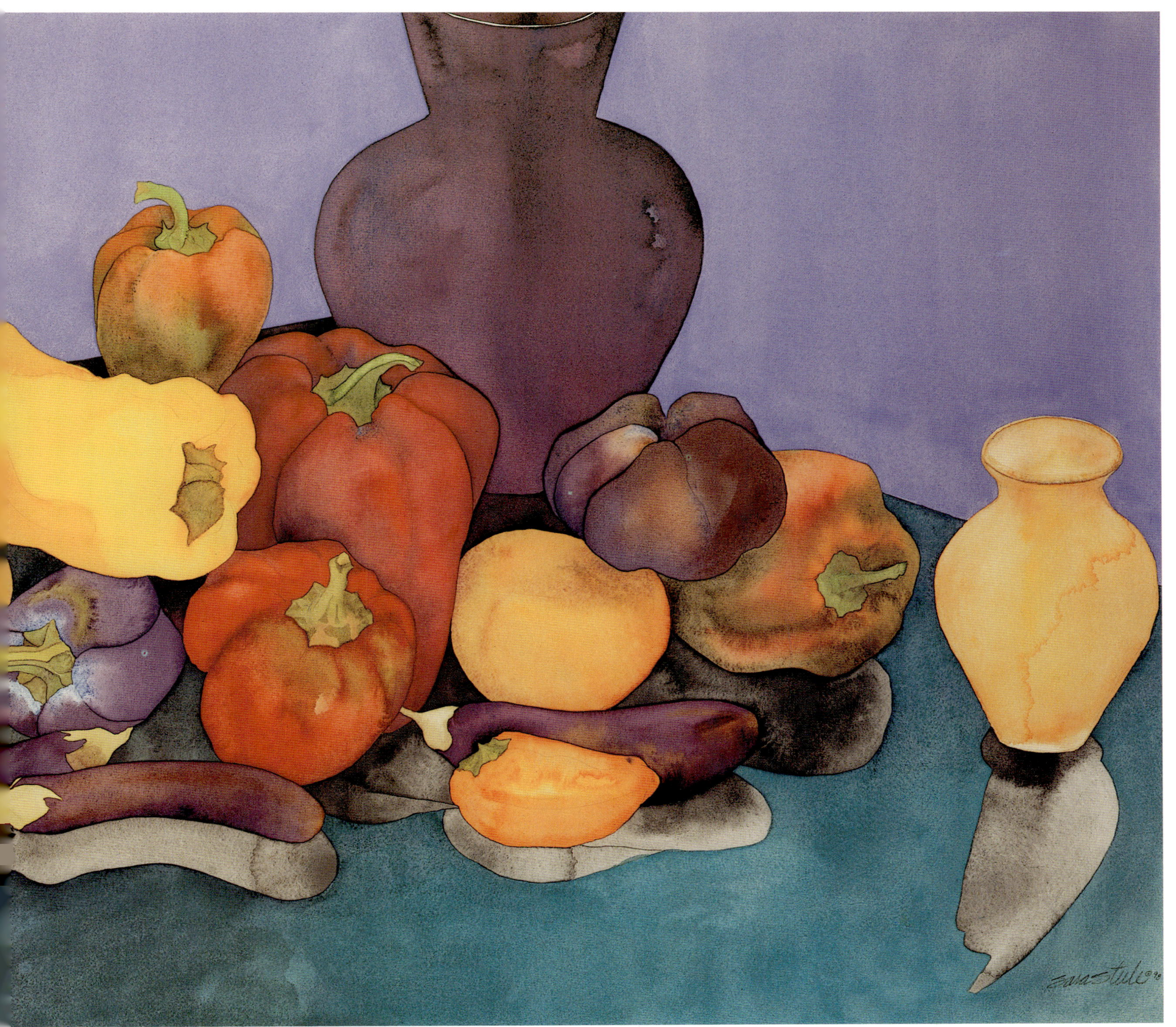

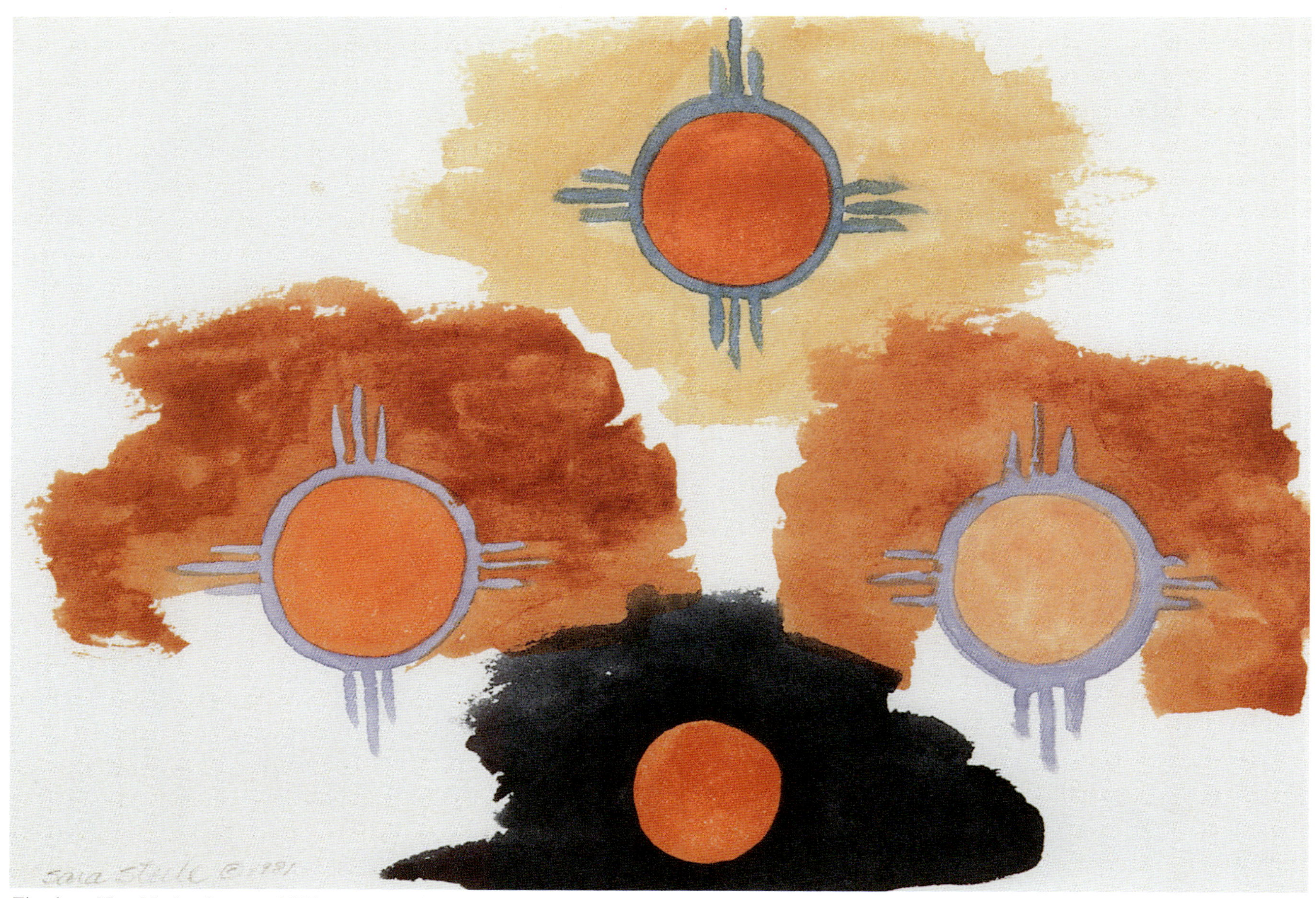

Zia, from New Mexico Quartet, 1981

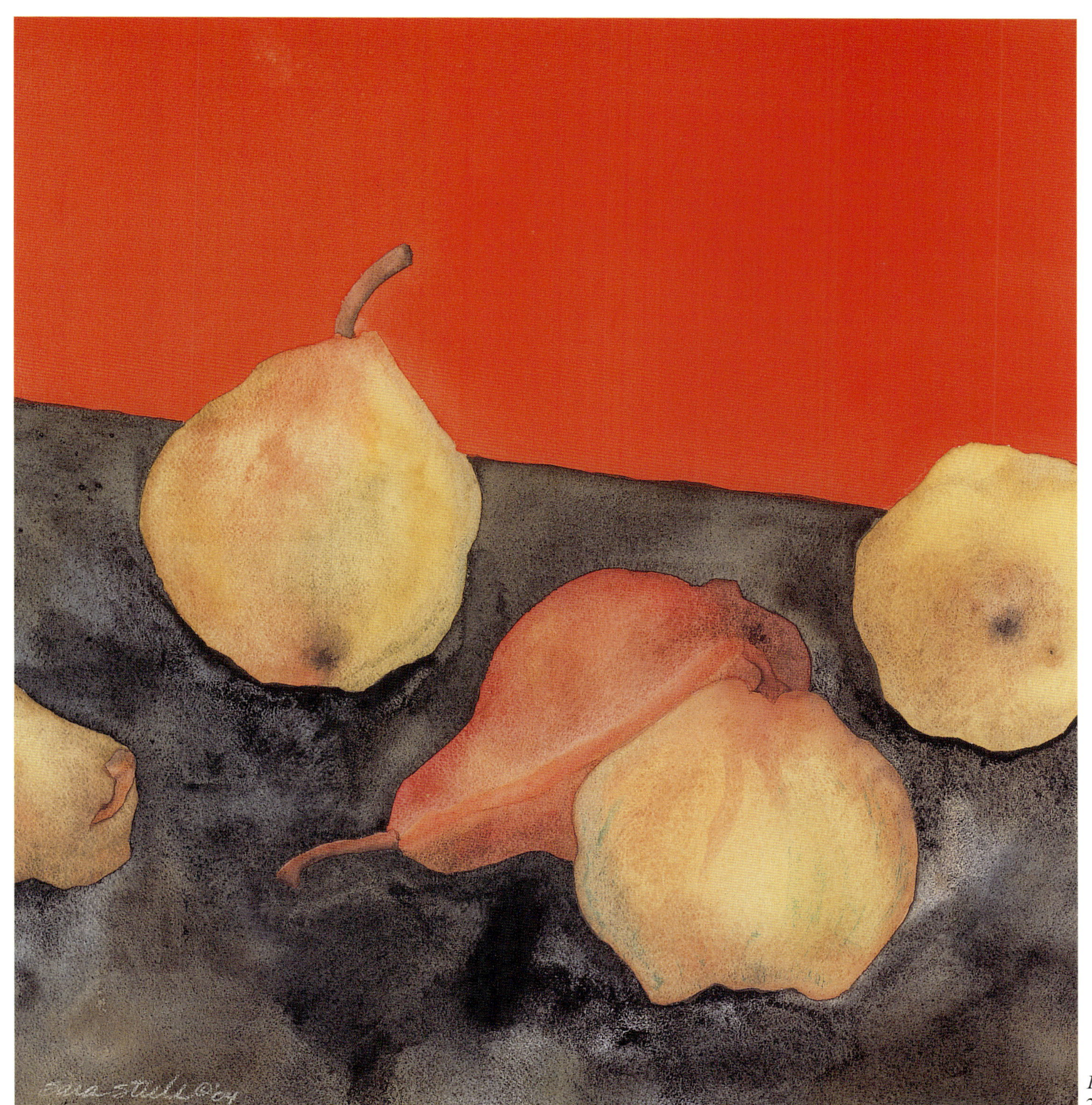

Red Bartlett Pears,
2004

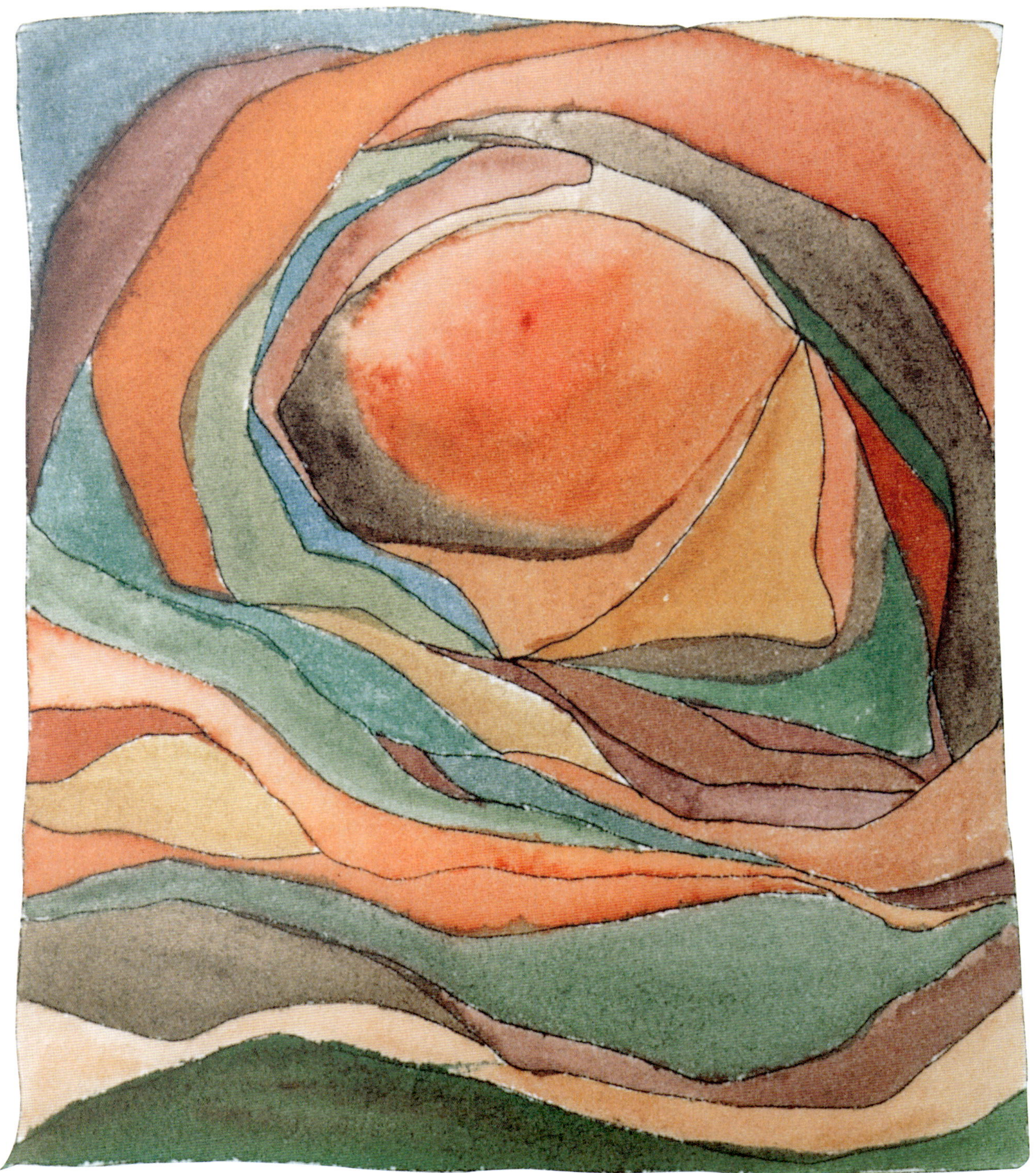

Ingrid's Quilt, 1978

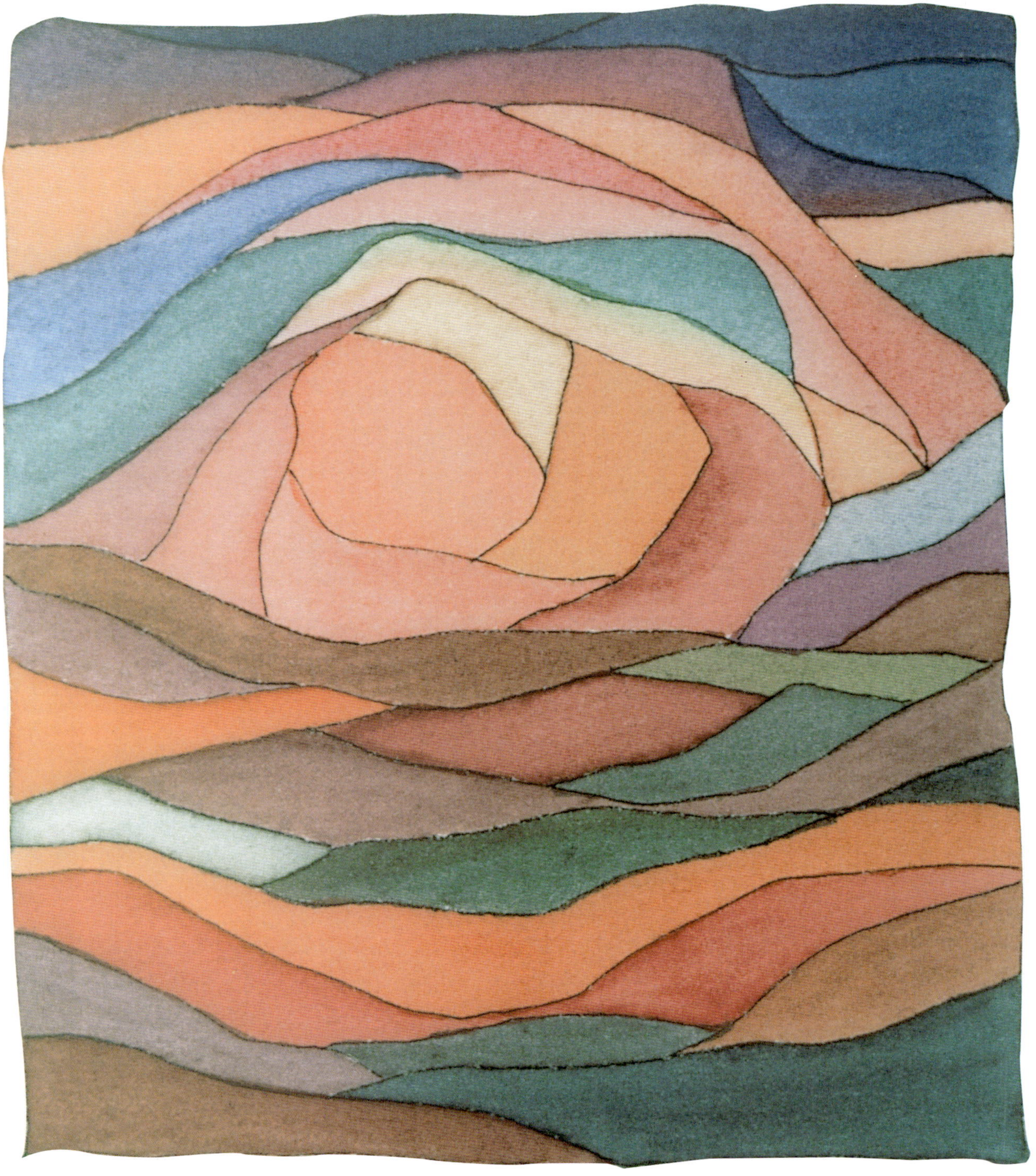

Tenerife, 1980

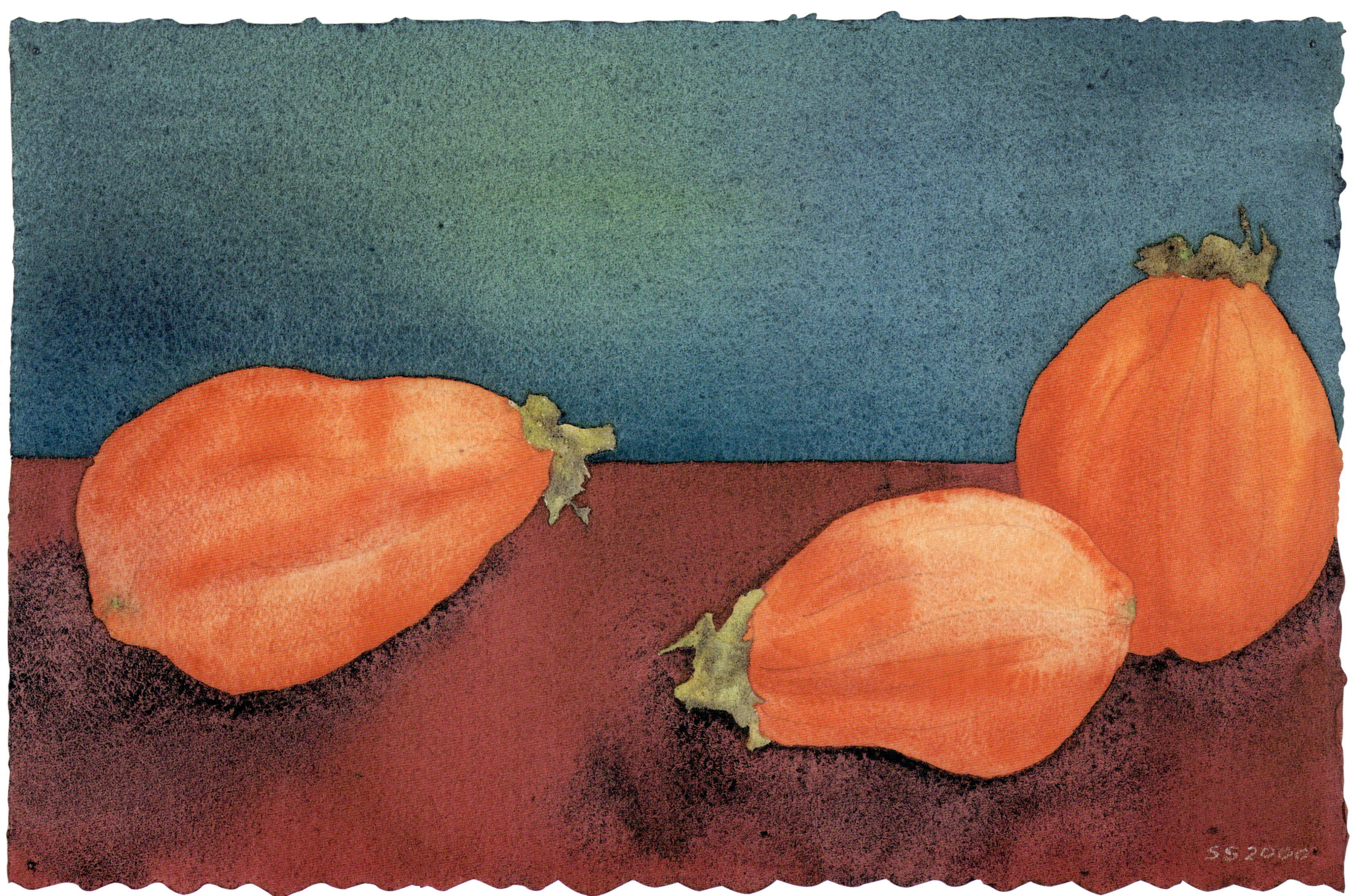

Jamaican Eggplants I, 2000

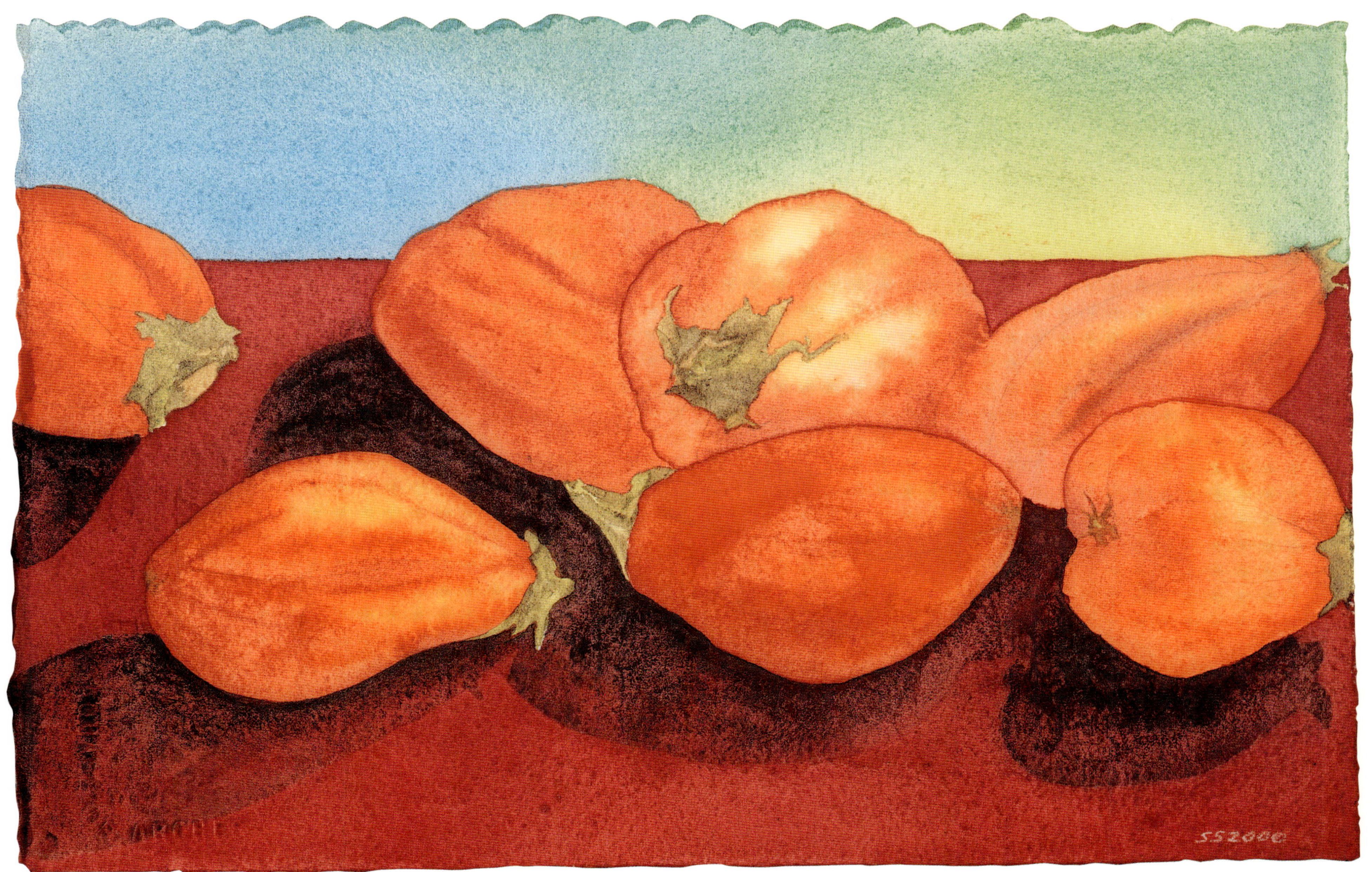

Jamaican Eggplants II, 2000

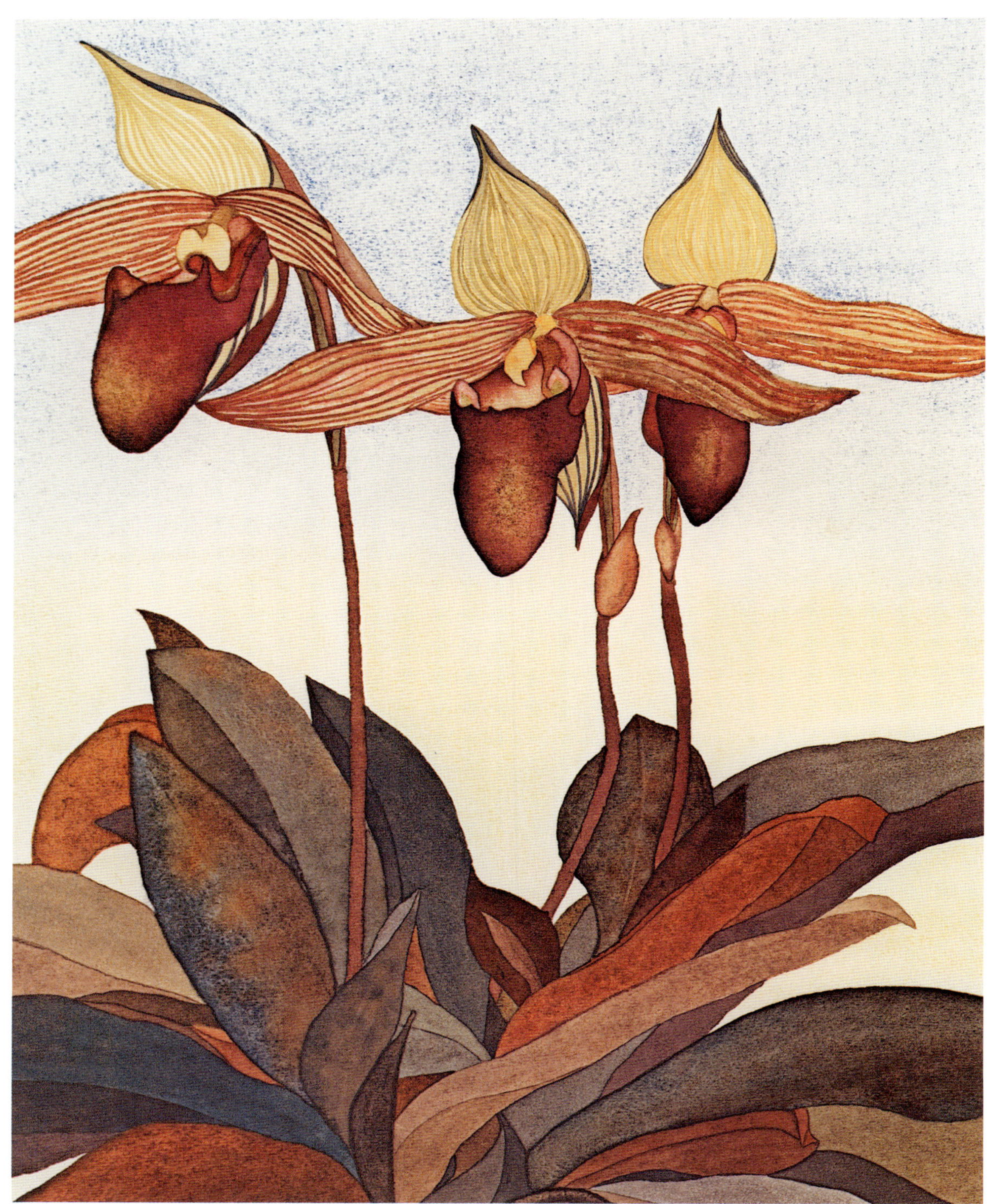

Paphiopedilum Sukhakulii (KAK), 1981

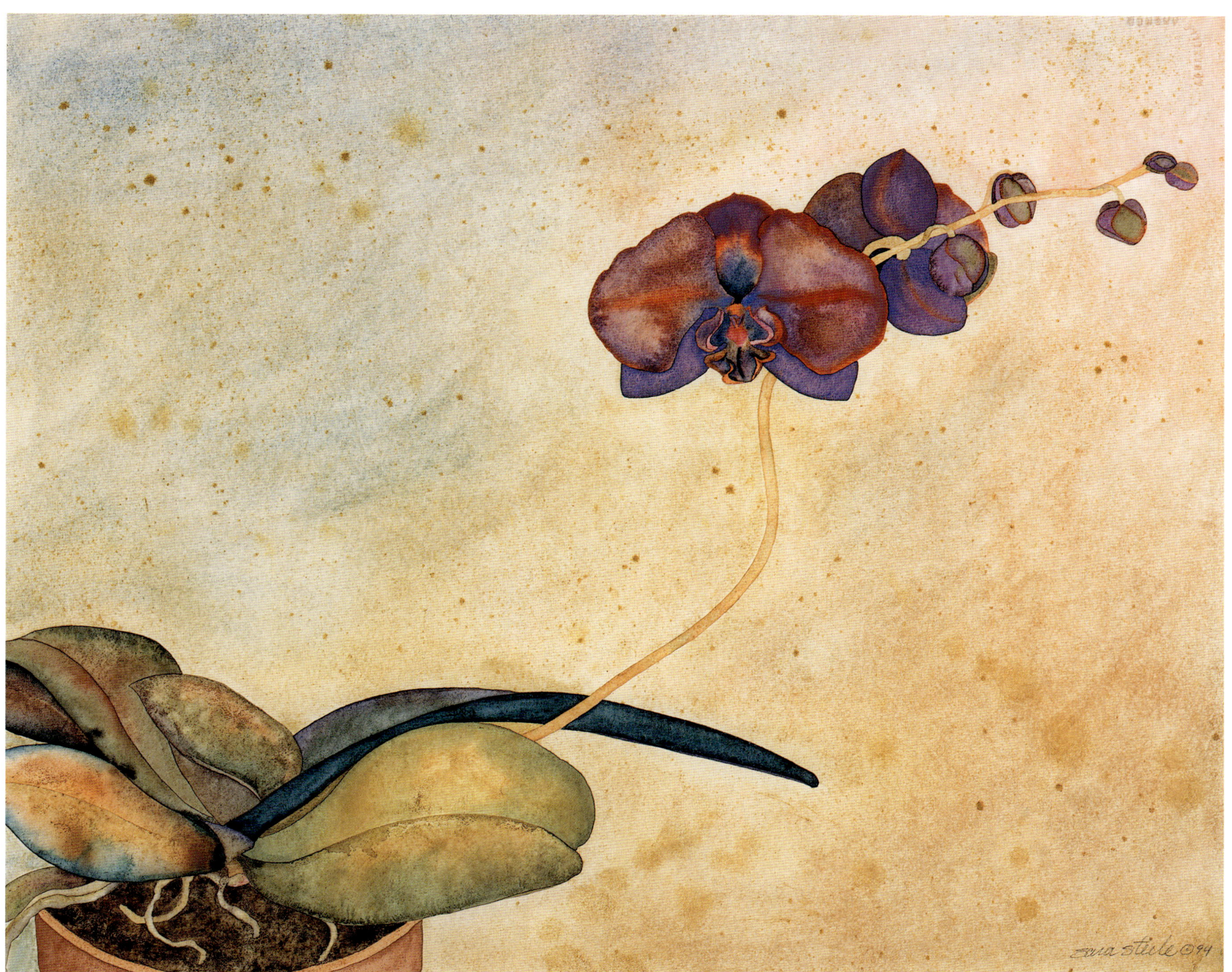

Phalaenopsis, 1994

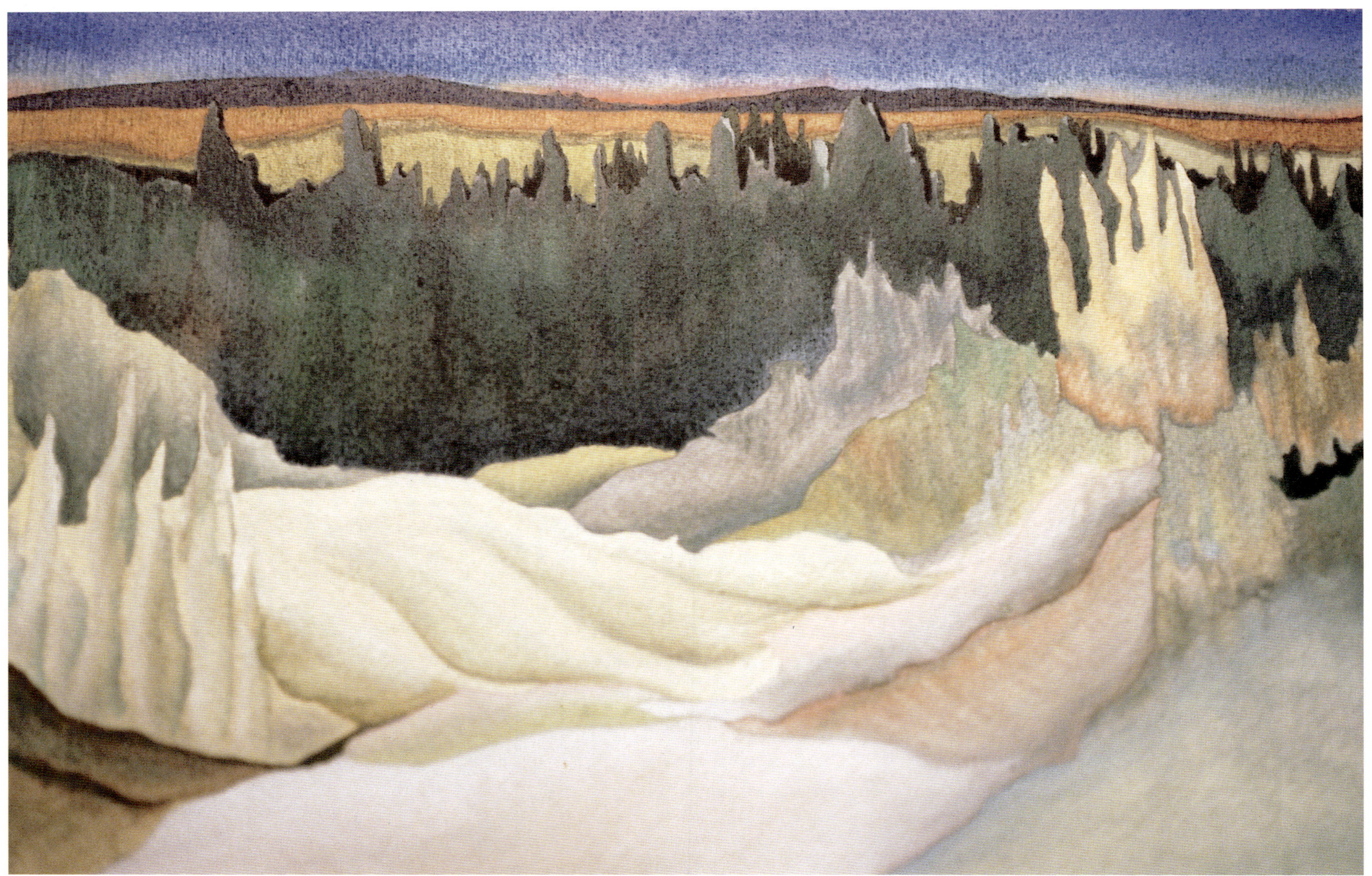

Bryce Canyon, 1981

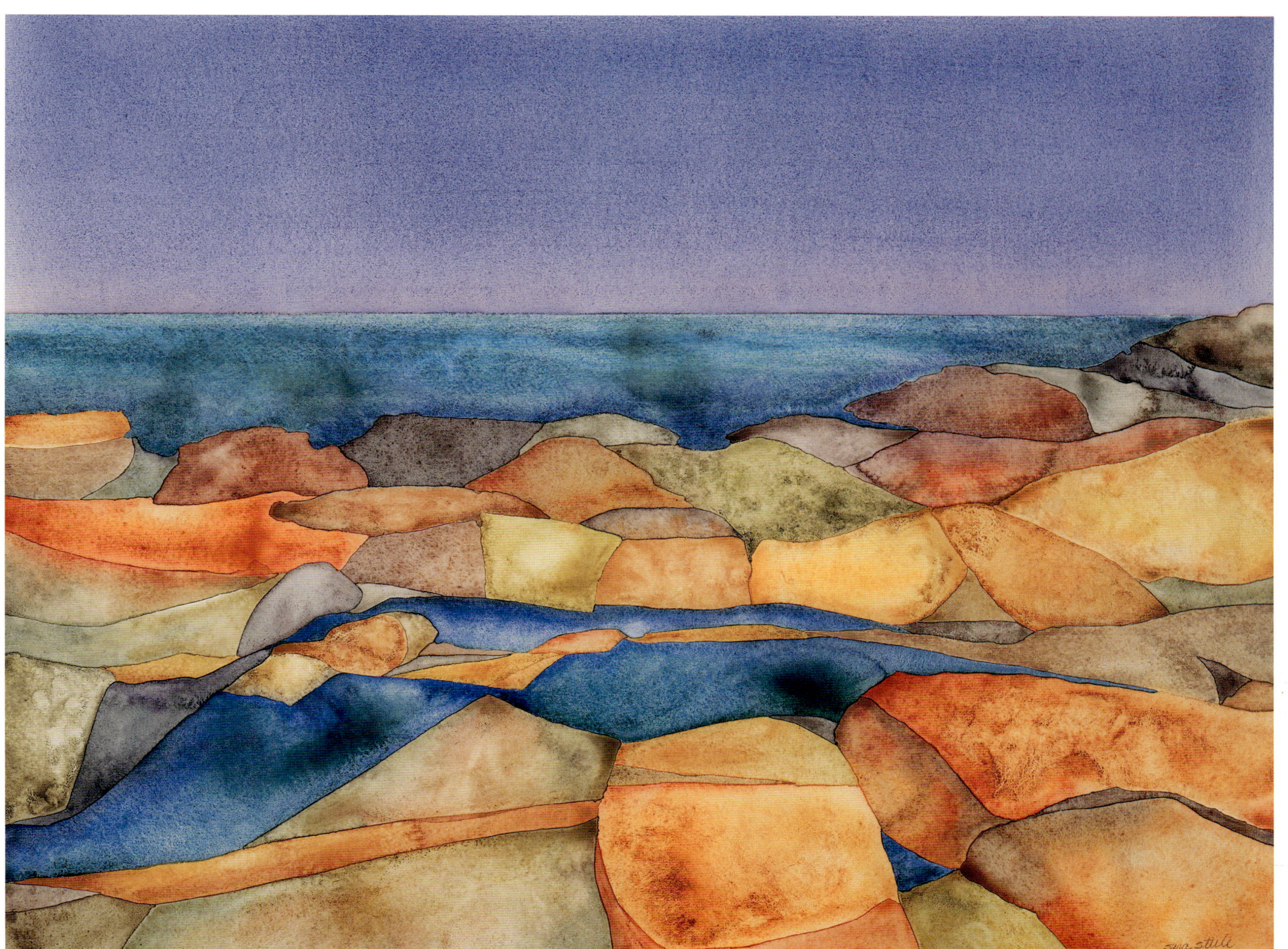

Halibut Point I, from the Quarry series, 1992

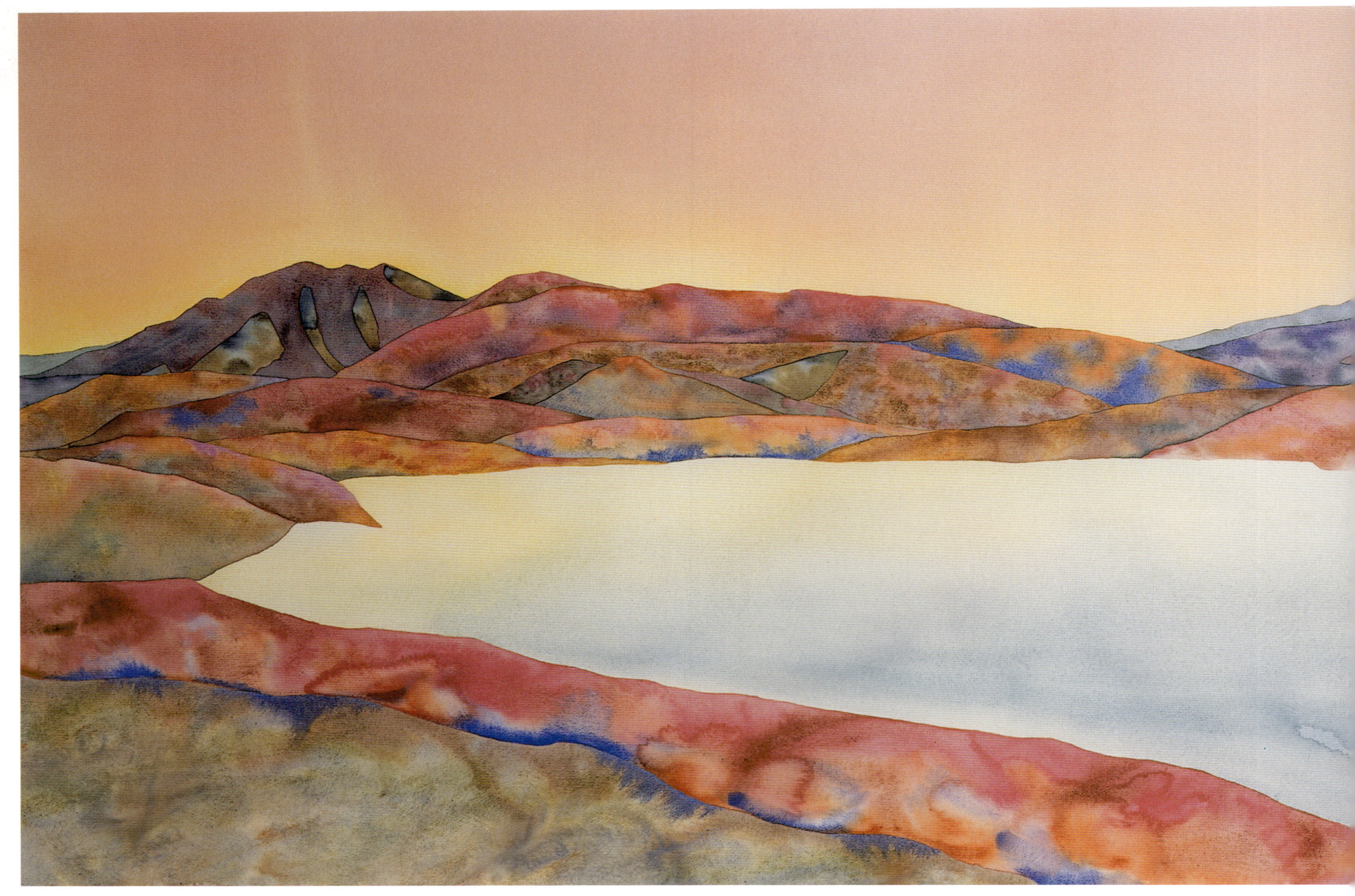

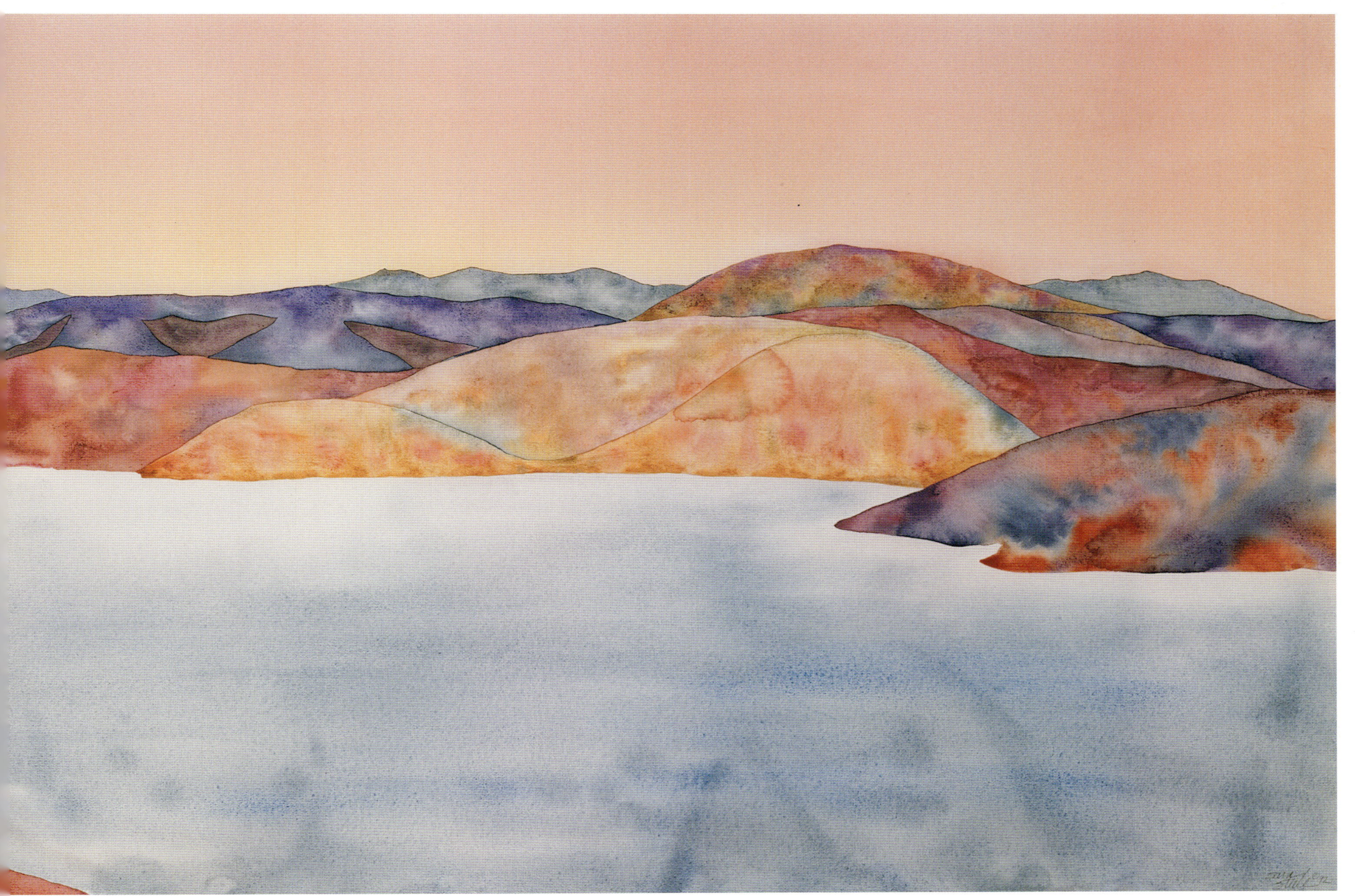

Drake's Bay, Point Reyes, 1992

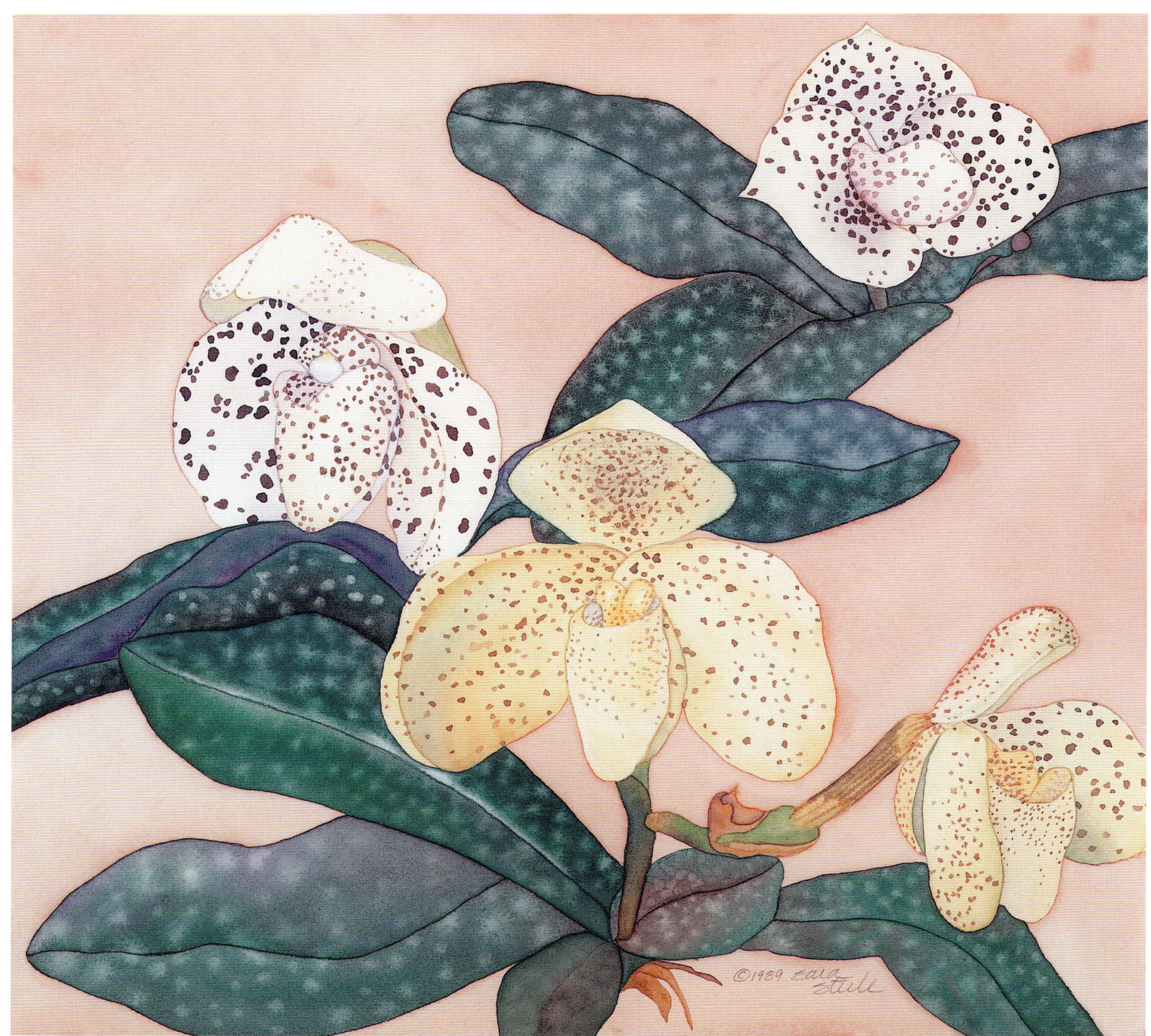

Paphiopedilum concolor & P. bellatulum, from the Endangered Orchids series, 1989

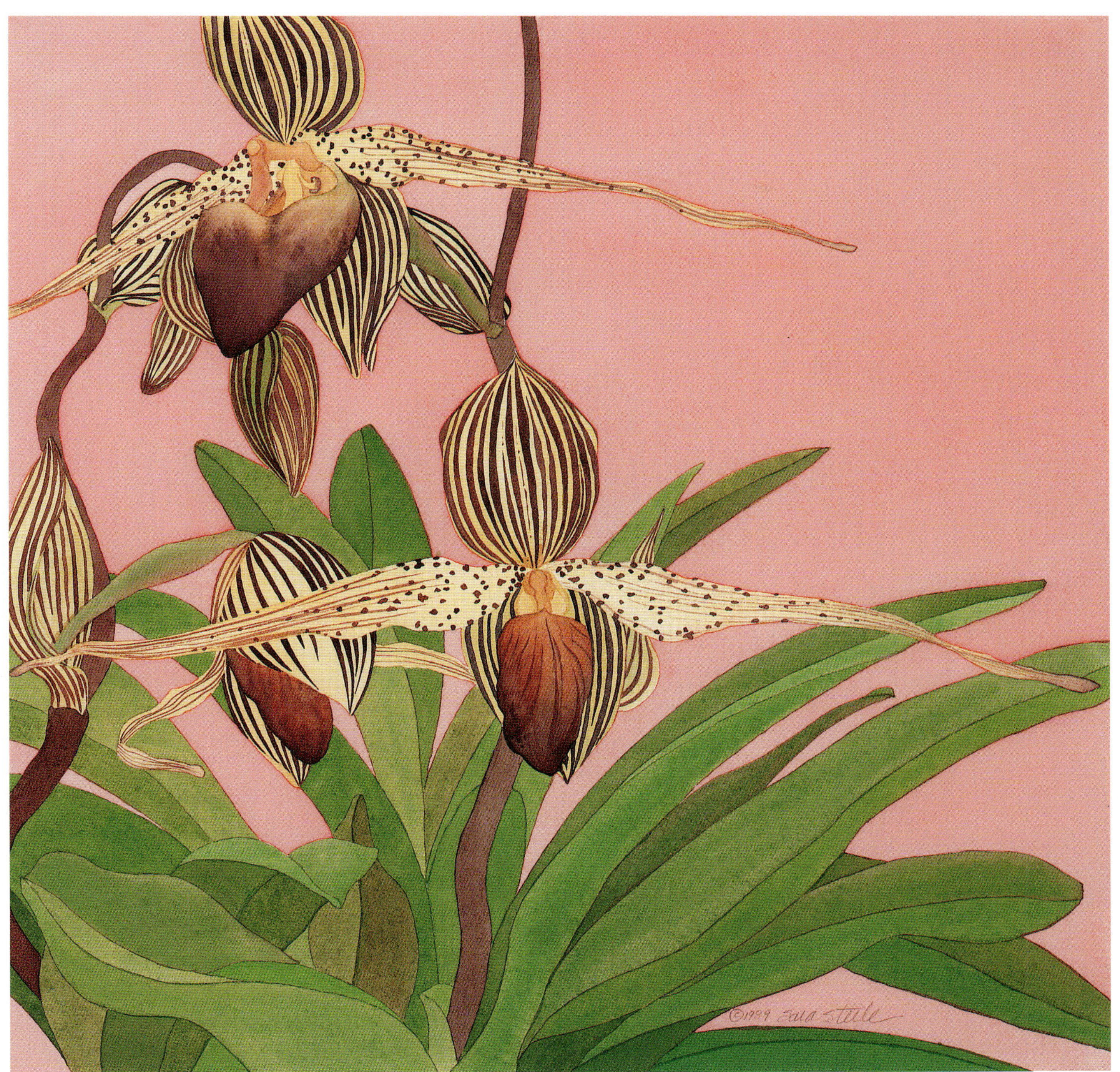

Paphiopedilum Rothschildianum, from the Endangered Orchids series, 1989

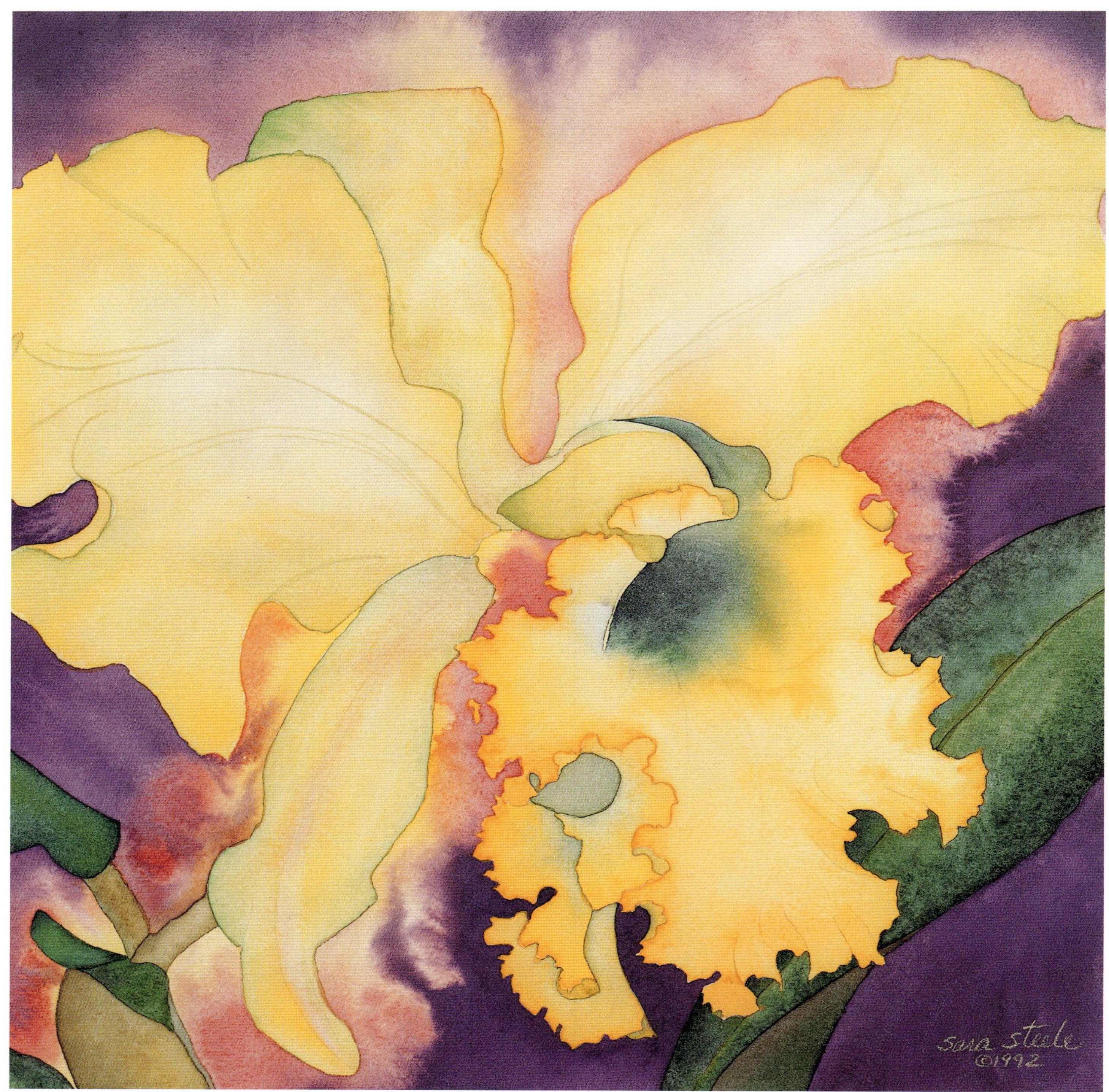

Yellow Cattleya, 1992

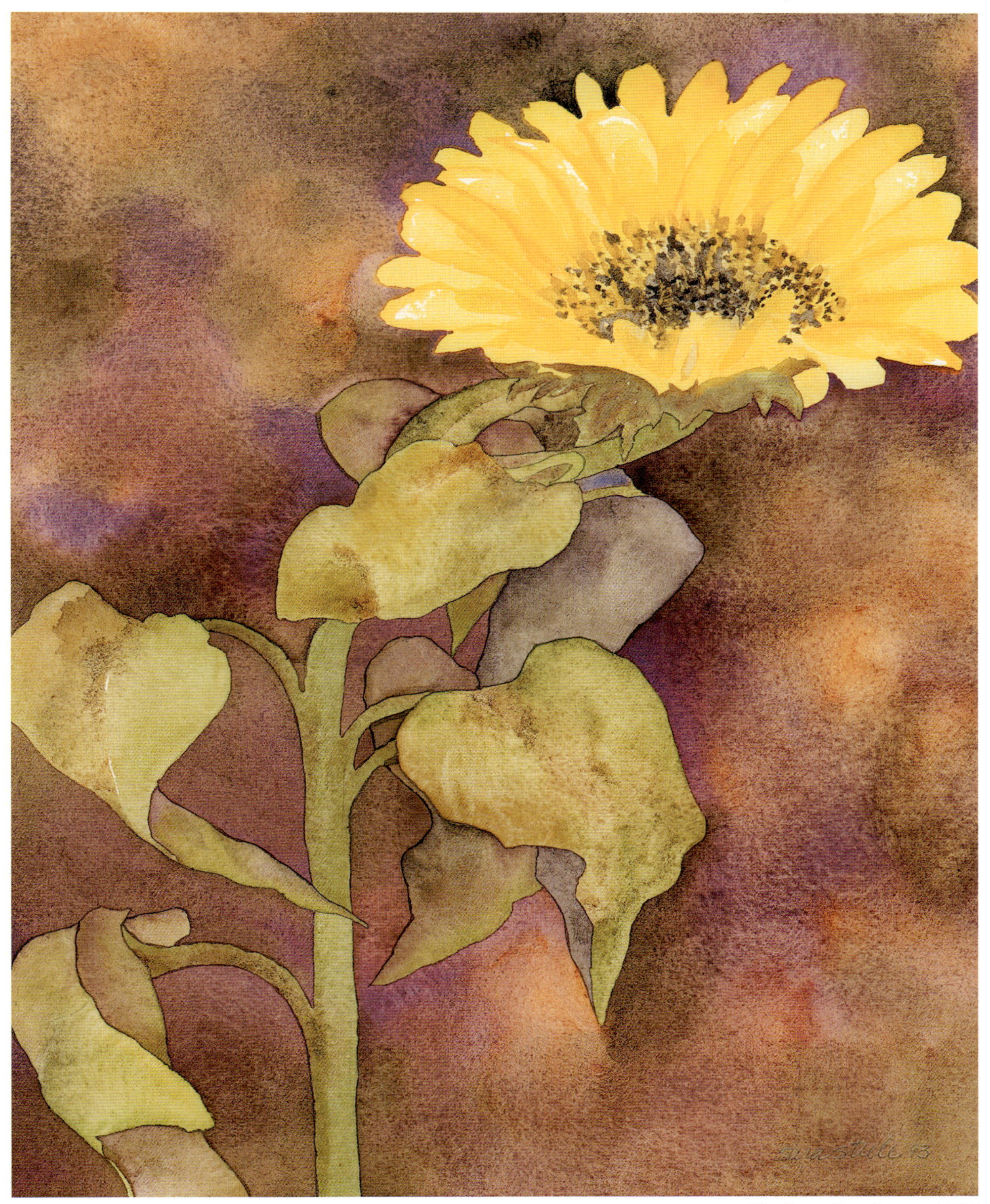

The Last Sunflower, 1993

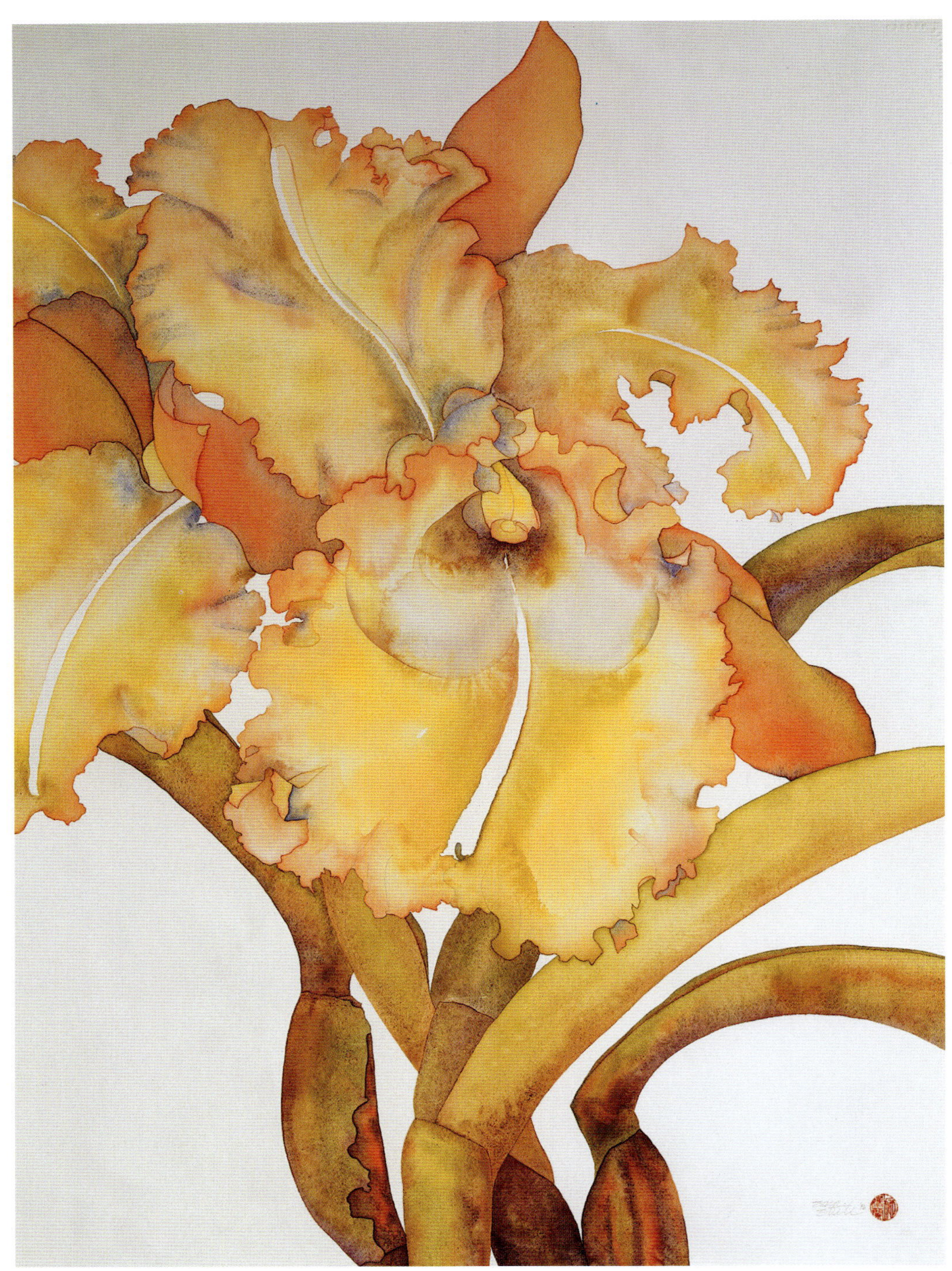

Cattleya Nancy Off, 1996

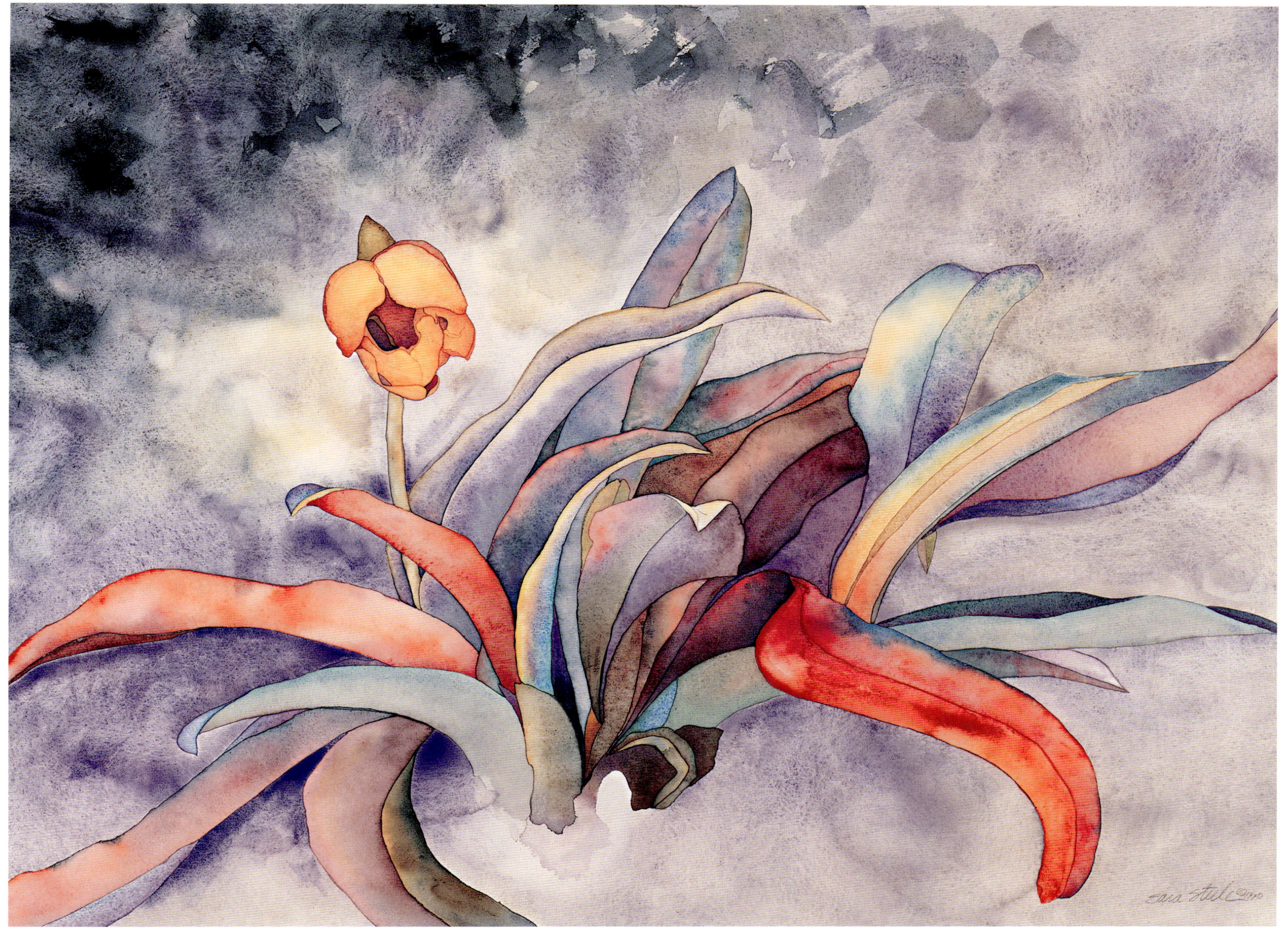

Terrestrial, 1990

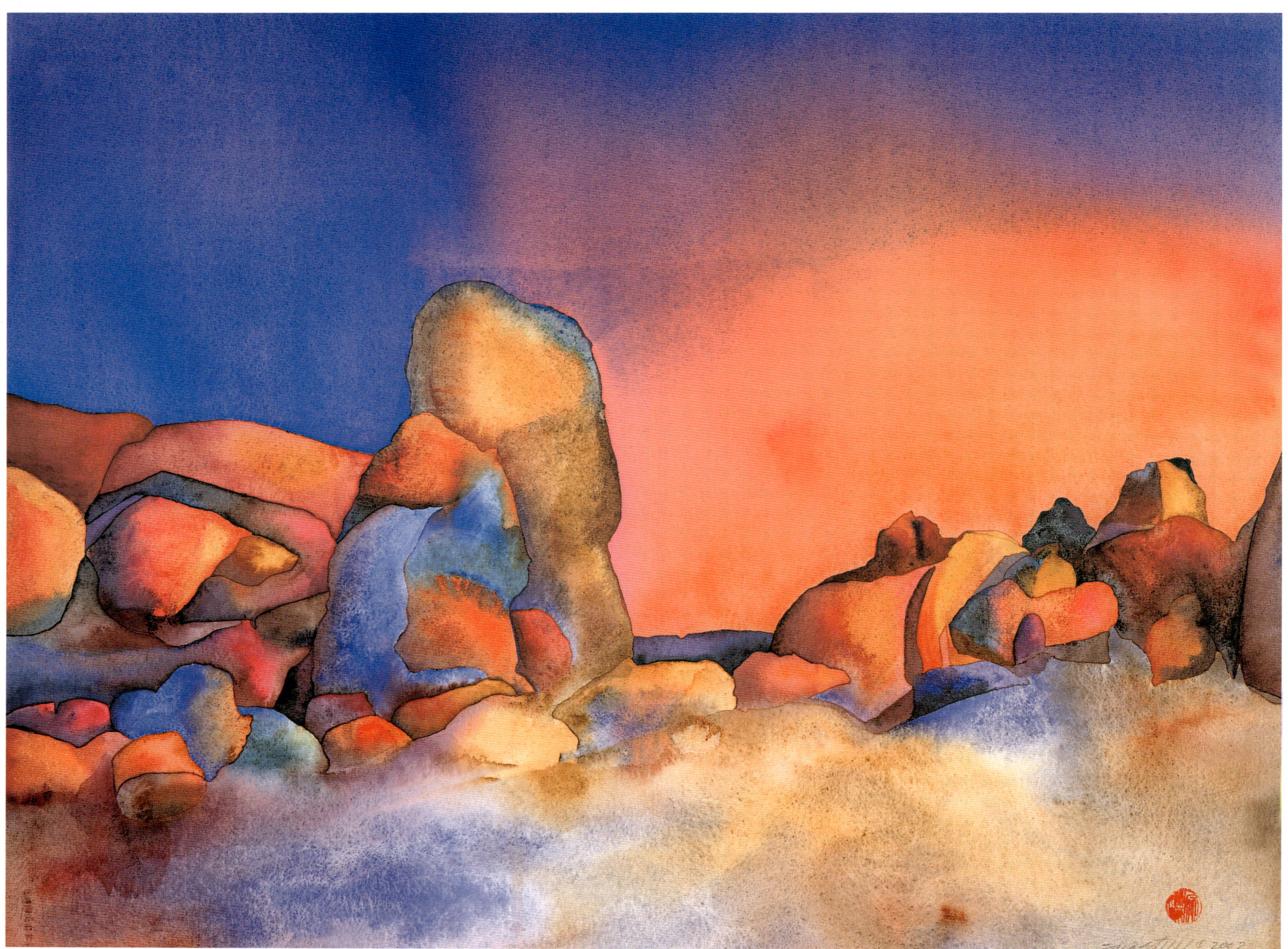

Song for Bilbao, 2002

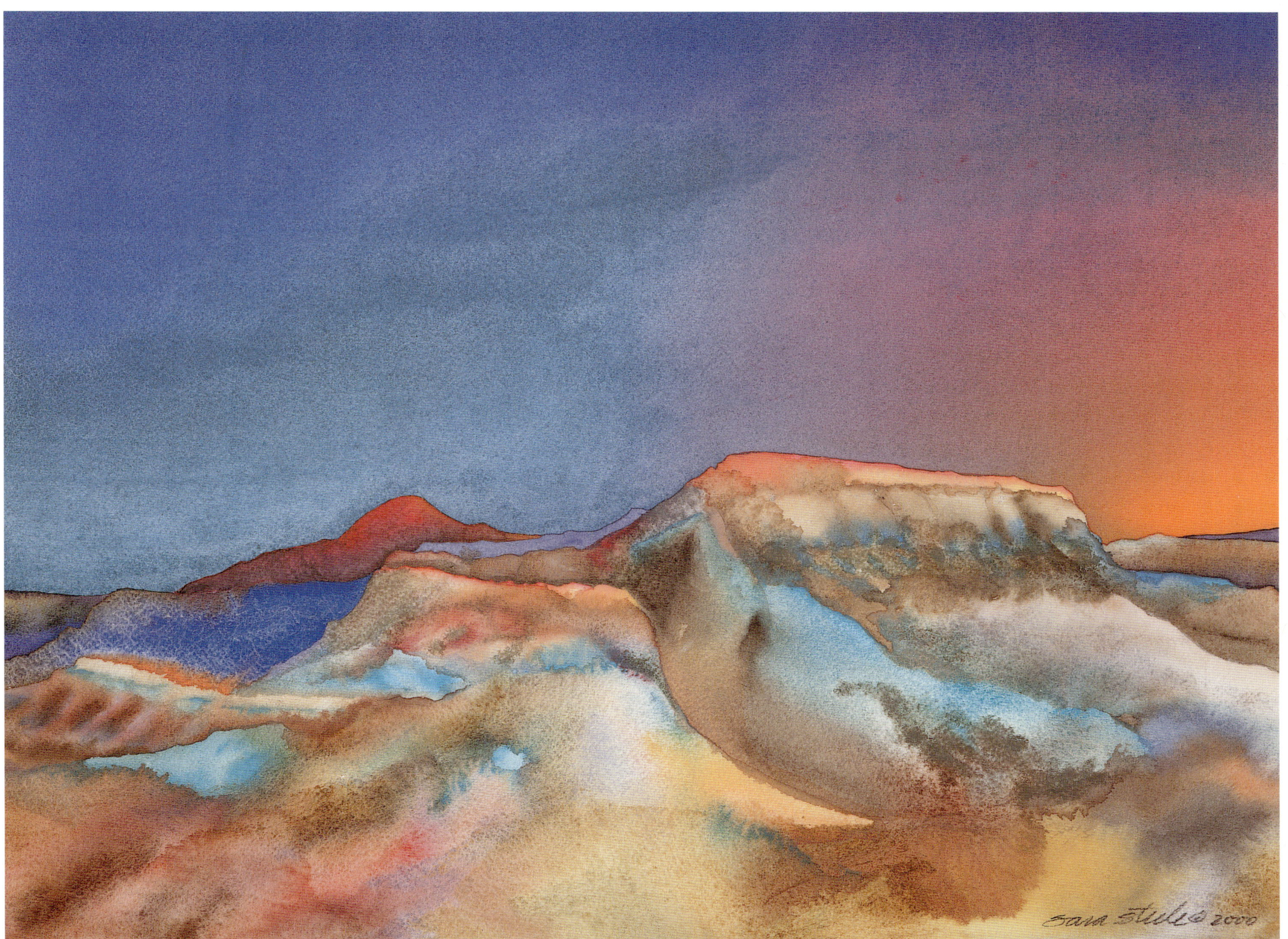

Mesa Lands, New Mexico, 2000

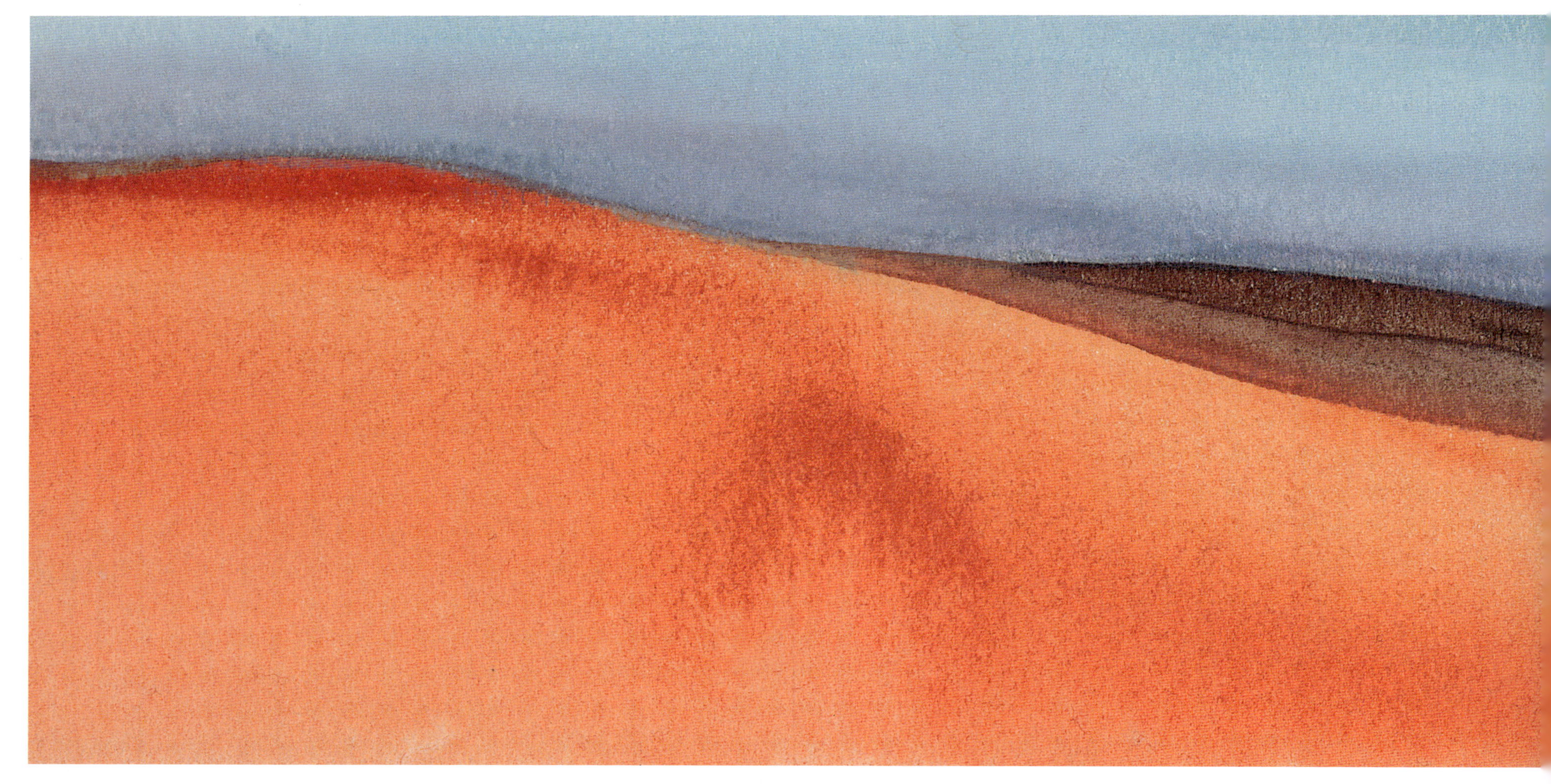

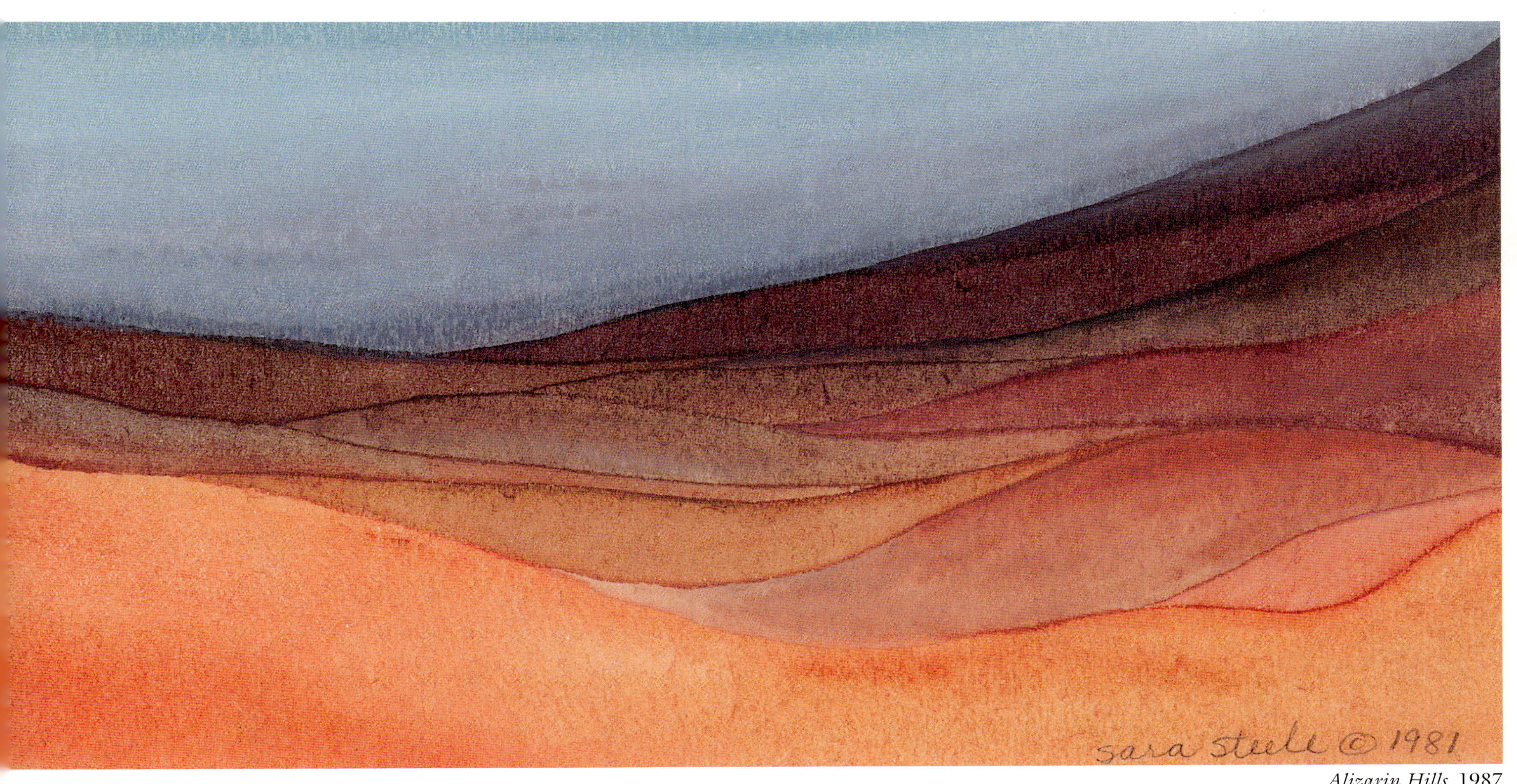

Alizarin Hills, 1987

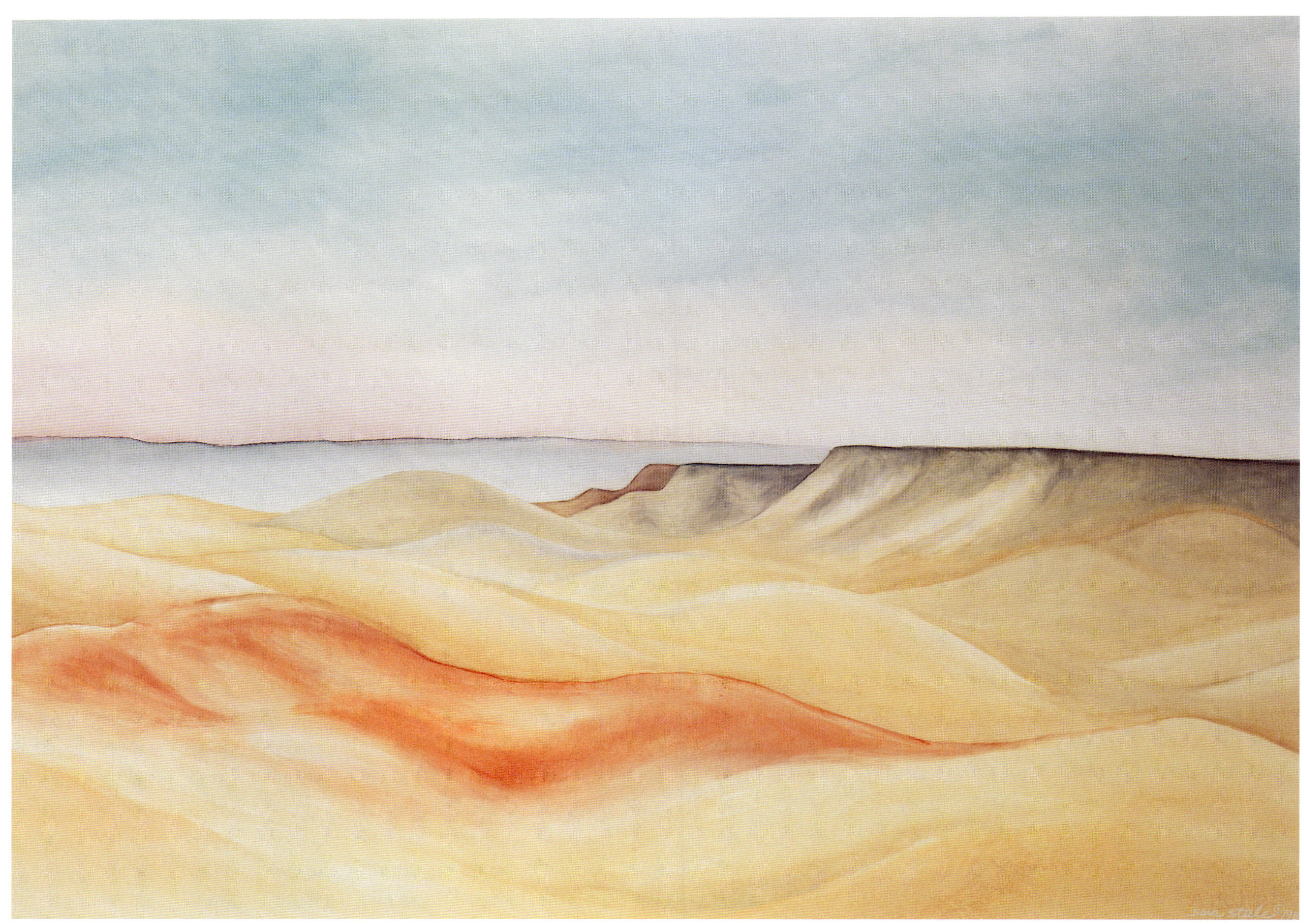

Along the Road to Santa Fe, 1981

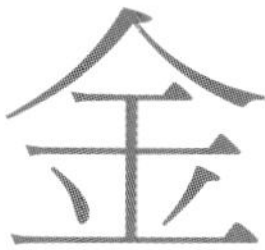

Metal

The harvest concluded and nature's nourishment realized, the Earth's cycle moves into autumn, symbolized by the element of Metal. The clarity of this season's light brings a time for reflection and the distilling of ideas, a time for evaluating what has come before, and a time for letting go in order to make way for new inspiration. Stems and structures, having served their purpose, now wither and die, returning fundamental nutrients to the soil that will sustain future growth. Leaves released from their branches swirl in brilliant displays of color. Nature, shedding the last remnants of summer growth, descends into the quiet dark of winter, where unforeseen possibilities find new life.

The paintings compiled here are characterized by a spacious, refined, and ethereal quality. A number of paintings explore the emotions of grief, an aspect of the element of Metal. The collection opens with *Along the Road to Santa Fe*, a work that conveys the vastness and subtlety of the desert landscape. This piece, inspired by Sara's first visit to the Southwest, initiated her exploration of landscape painting and prompted the expansion of her palette to include the region's earth tones. *Lake Visions* considers the ethereal effect of refracted light. *Tod* delves into the nature of grief, bringing together scenes of vanishing farmland, visual language through the portal of Chinese characters, and the image of the mythical kachina. *Magnolias* shows the final blossoms of the backyard tree of Sara's childhood, which uprooted itself in full bloom when her grandmother died.

This collection includes several paintings from the "Nuclear Family Holocaust" series, Sara's exploration into personal pain and grief. Among them is *Halibut Point II*, where land dug open as a quarry enjoys healing renewal through the cycles of nature. The painting reminds us of the regeneration of the human spirit that is possible after suffering loss. *Struggle to Remember* represents the concept of body memory. *Ashes* combines poetry, Chinese calligraphy, and a representation of biochemical molecular structure. It also includes a symbolic representation of the bat, which signifies double happiness in Chinese, and is a Native American symbol of rebirth.

The autumn collection culminates in the painting *Alterpiece*. This pivotal work represents the re-emergence of hope following grief. It combines allusions to animal life—the swimming tail and the flying wings—with the light of dawn breaking over a horizon. Here too are echoes of *The Point* paintings, the breaking in and rising up of energy that transforms rigid structures into a living, organic, and interdependent whole.

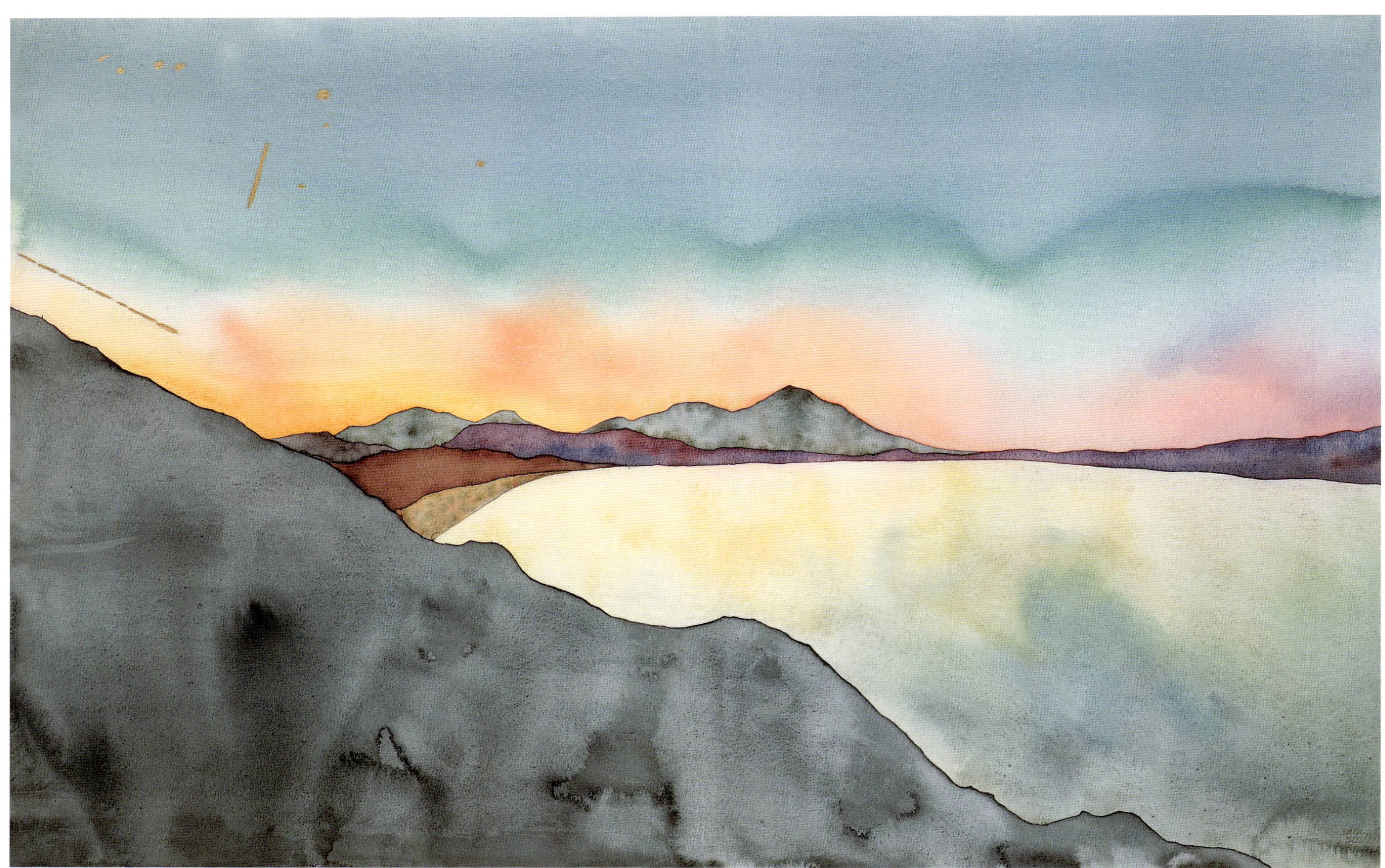

Big Rock Dawn III, 1991

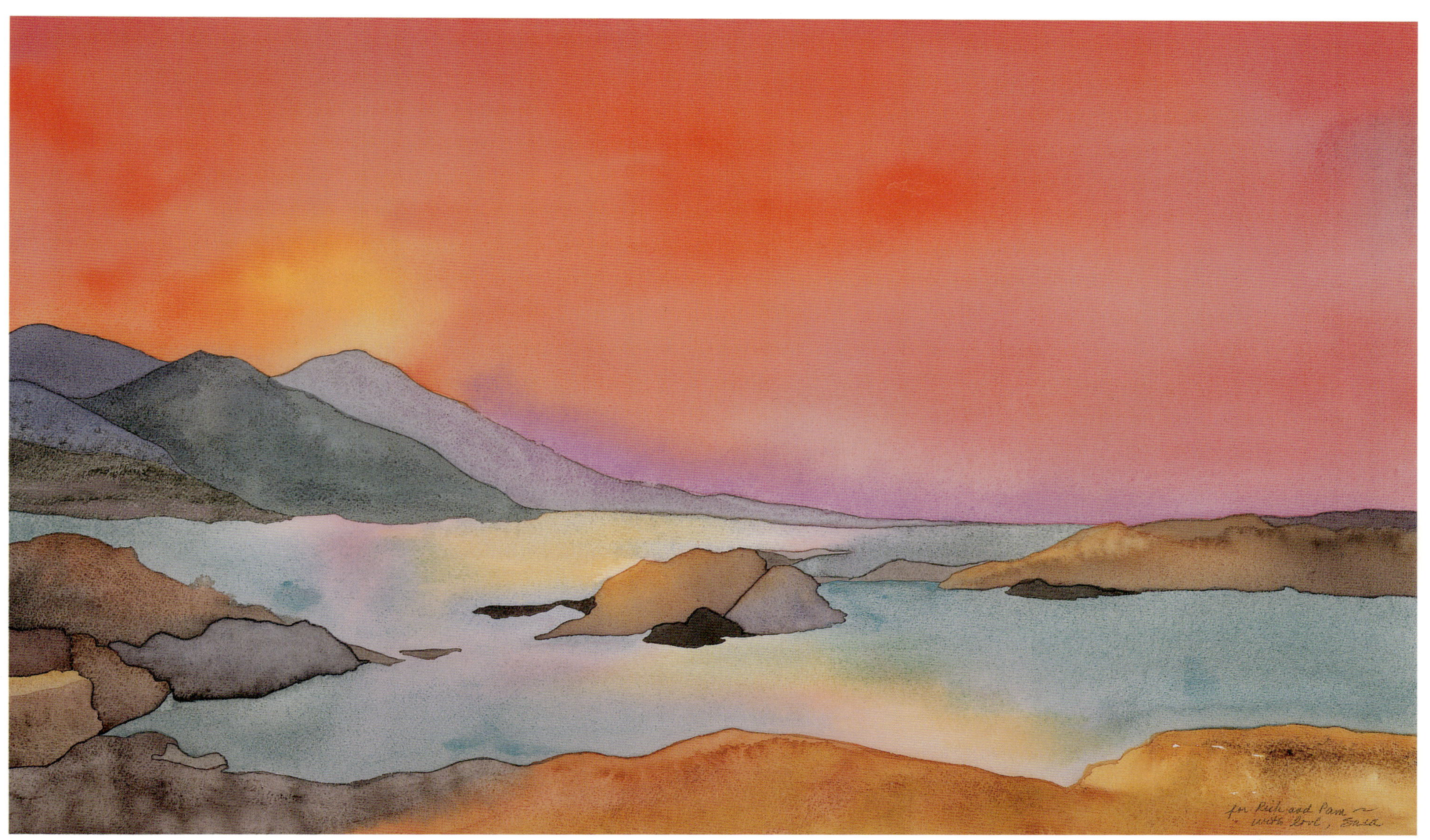

Point Lobos, Carmel II, 1998

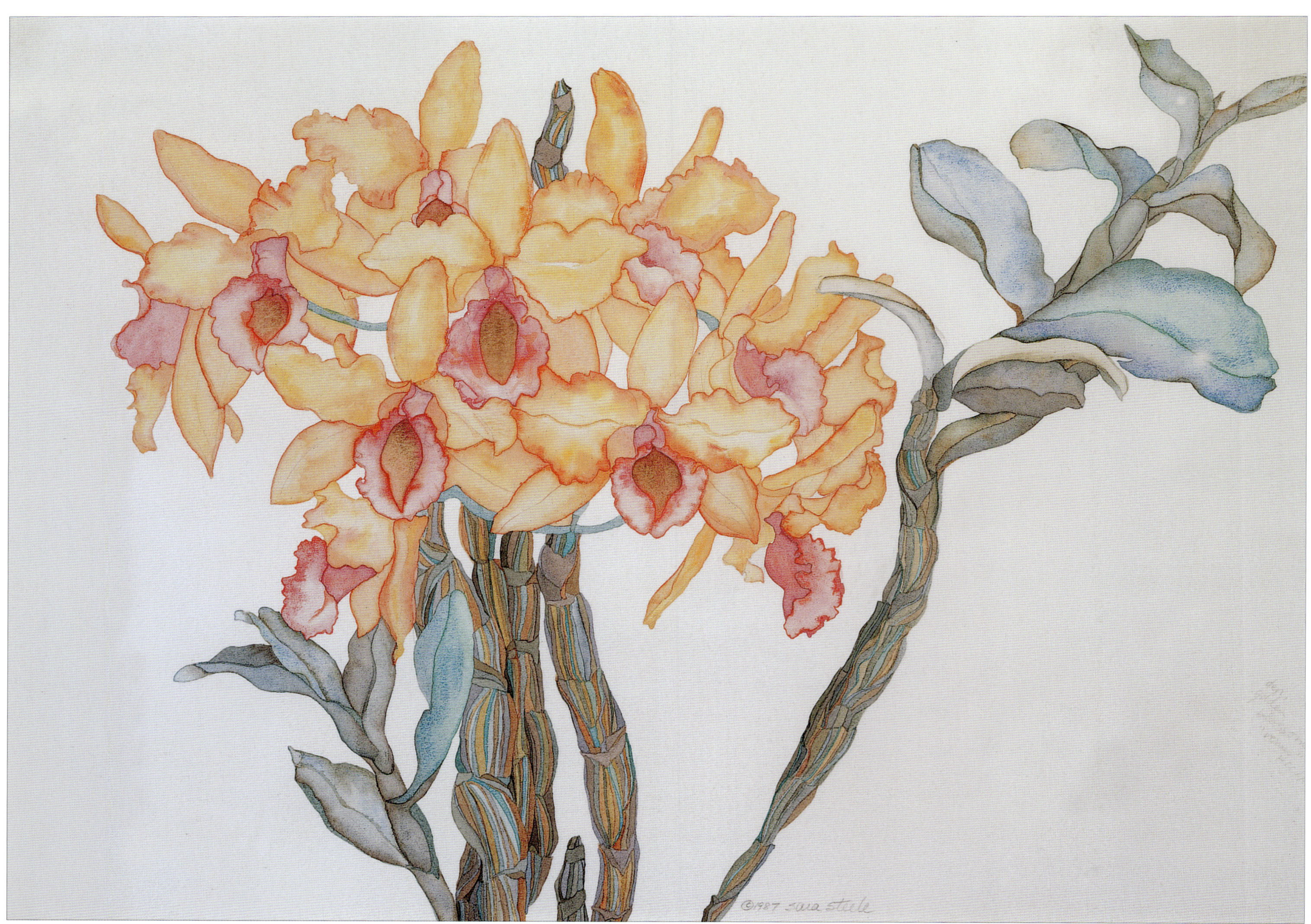

Dendrobium Golden Blossom 'Venus', 1998

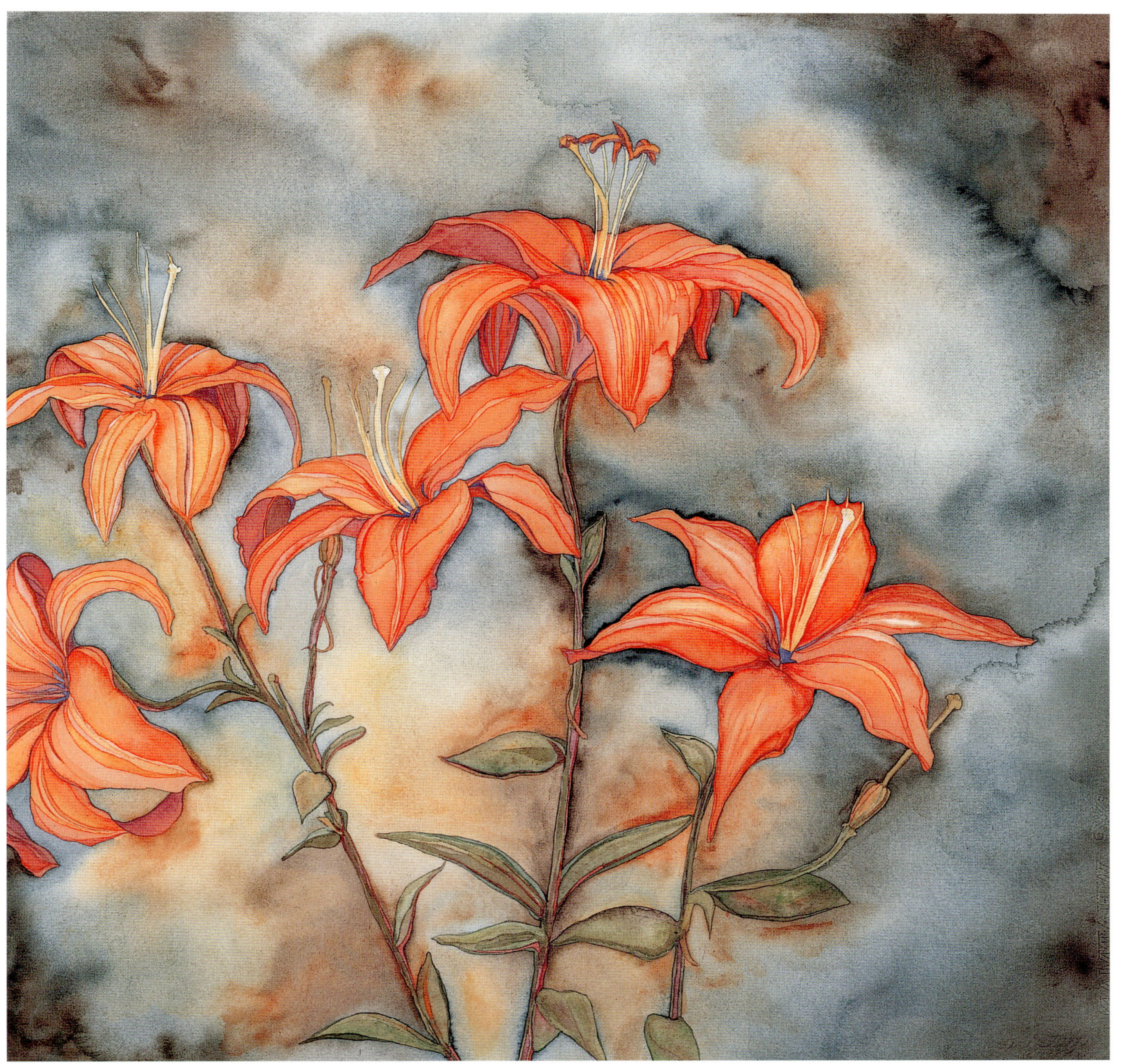

Storm Lillies (Bittersweet Slow Burn), 1988

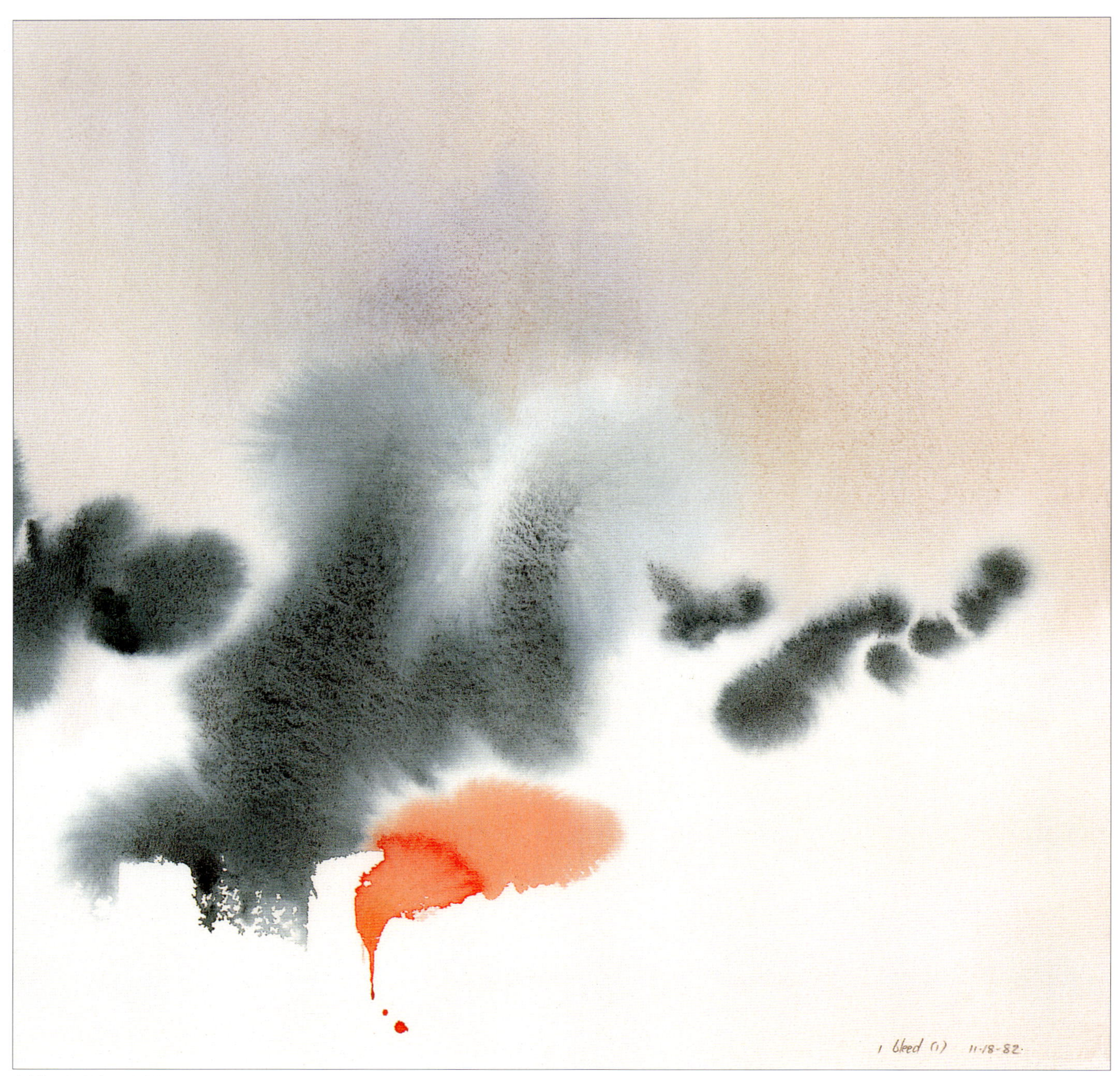

i bleed (1), 1982

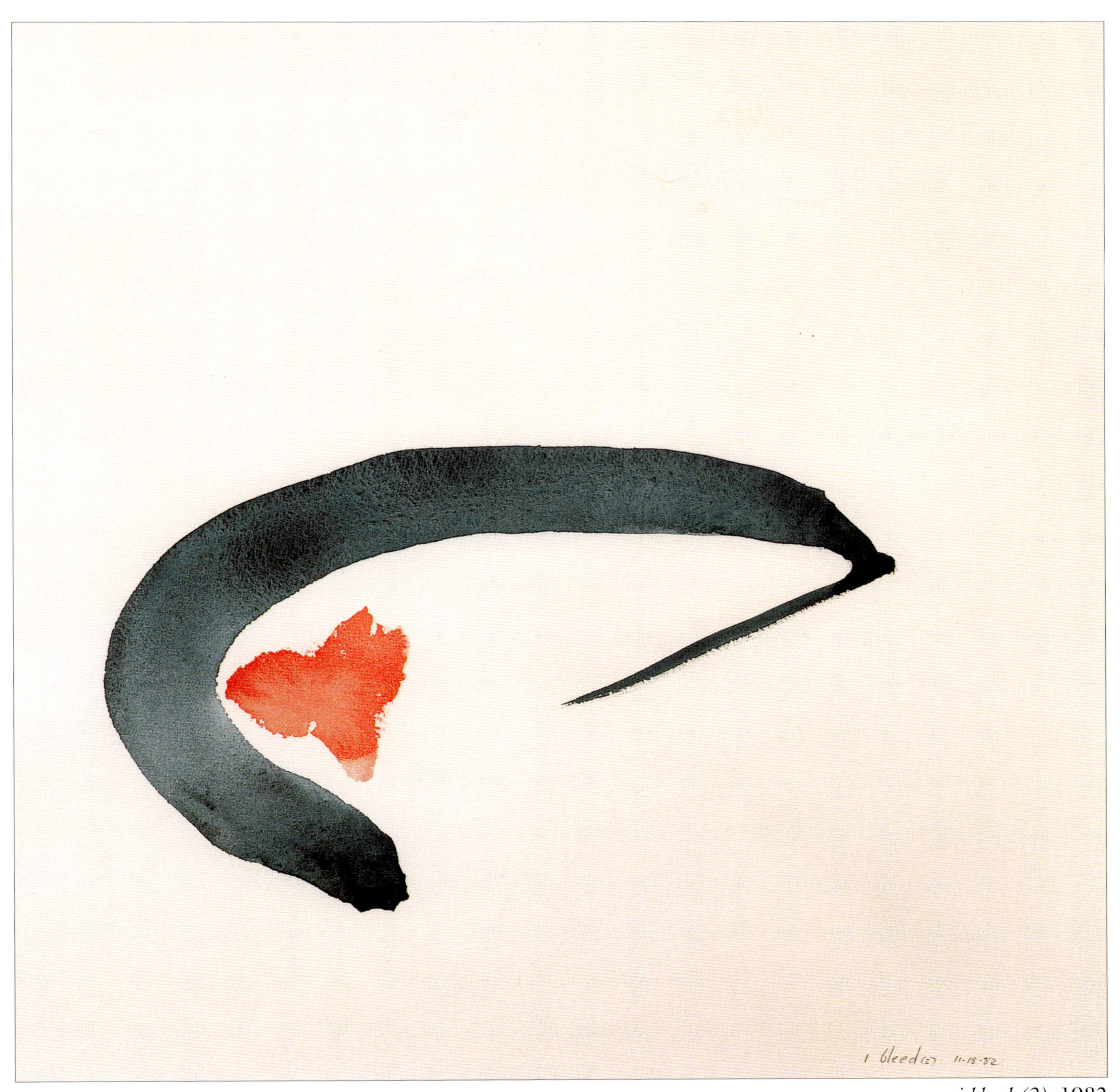

i bleed (2), 1982

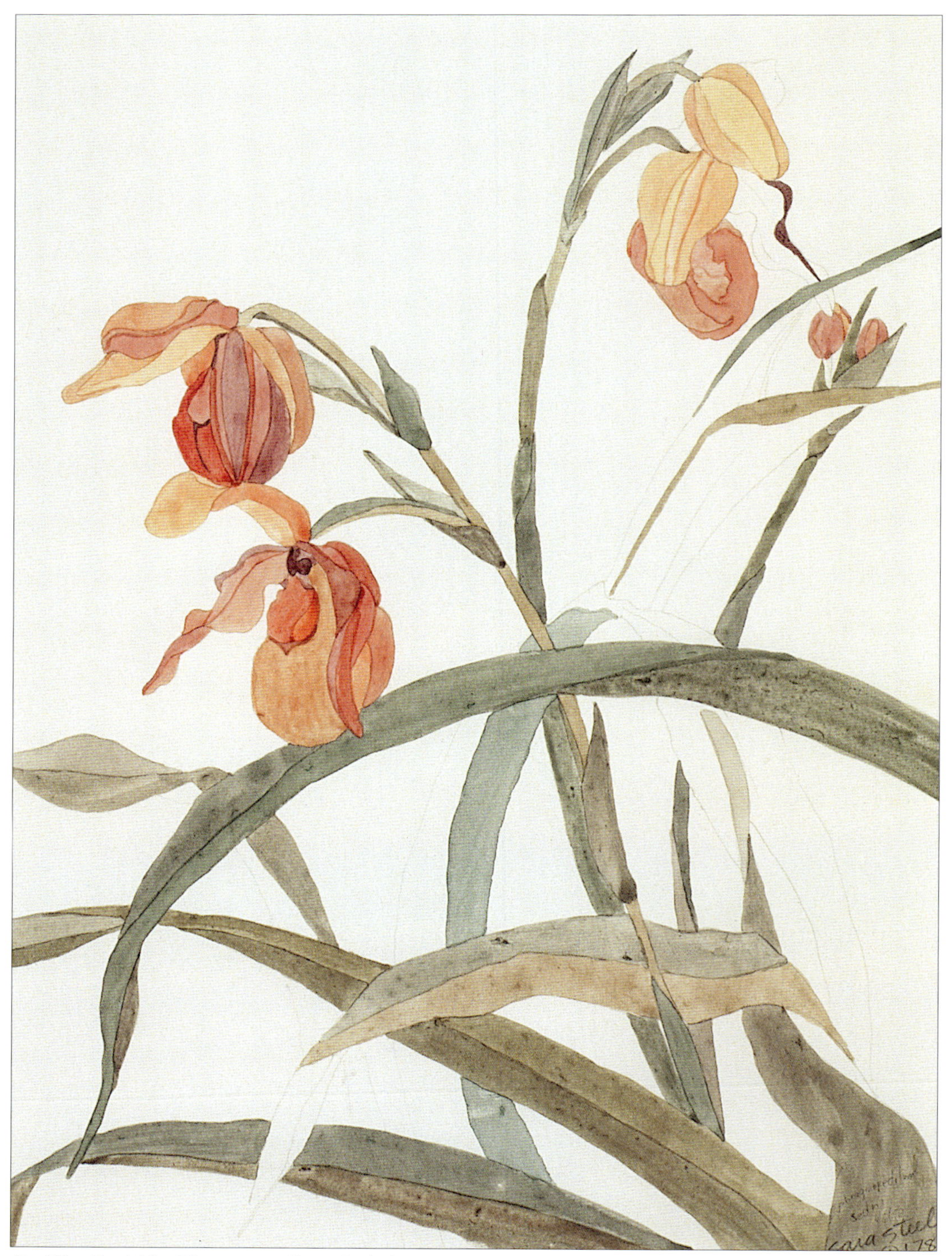

Dublin Orchids: Phragmepedium Sedni, 1978

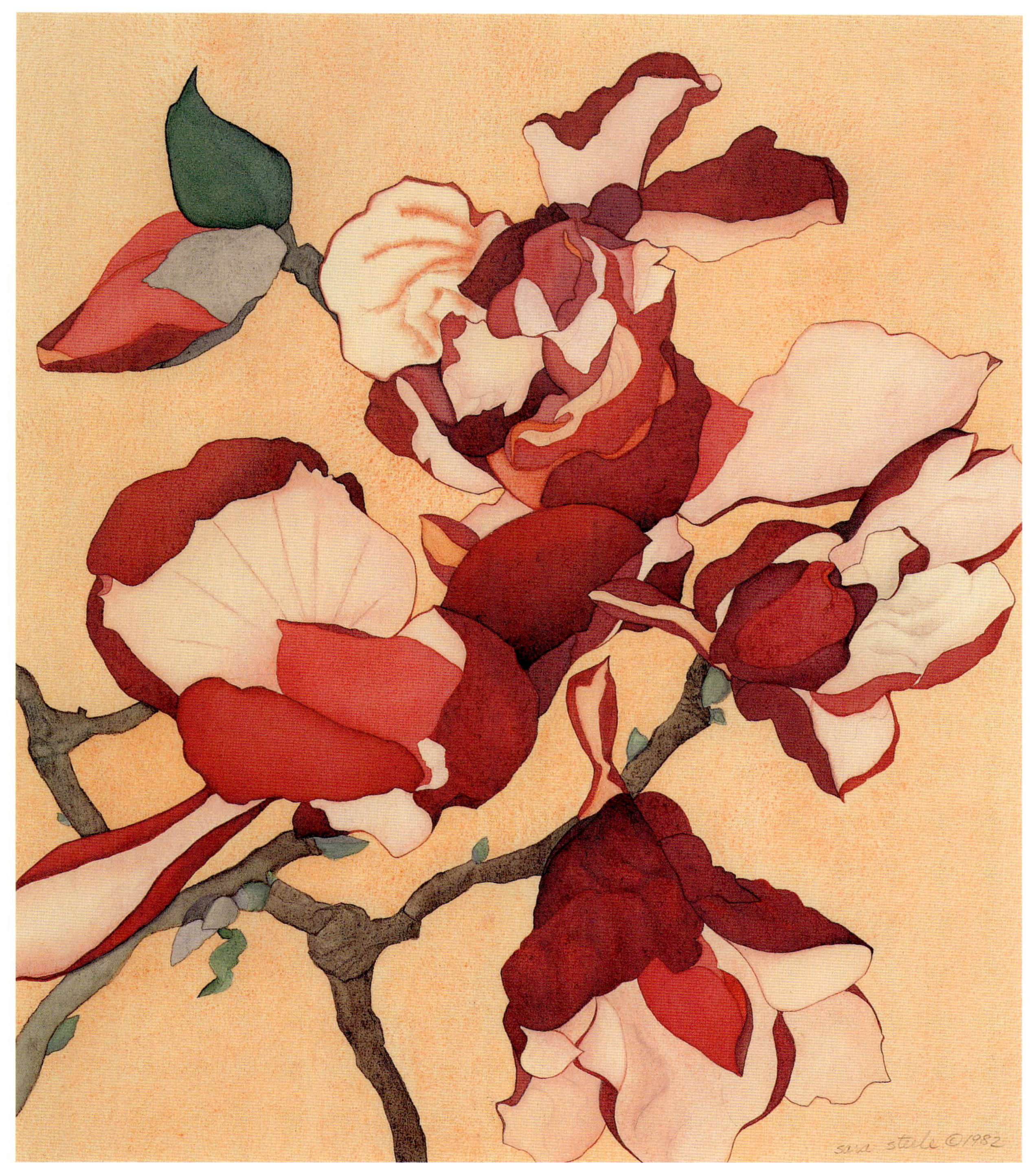

Magnolia (A Season of Mourning), 1982

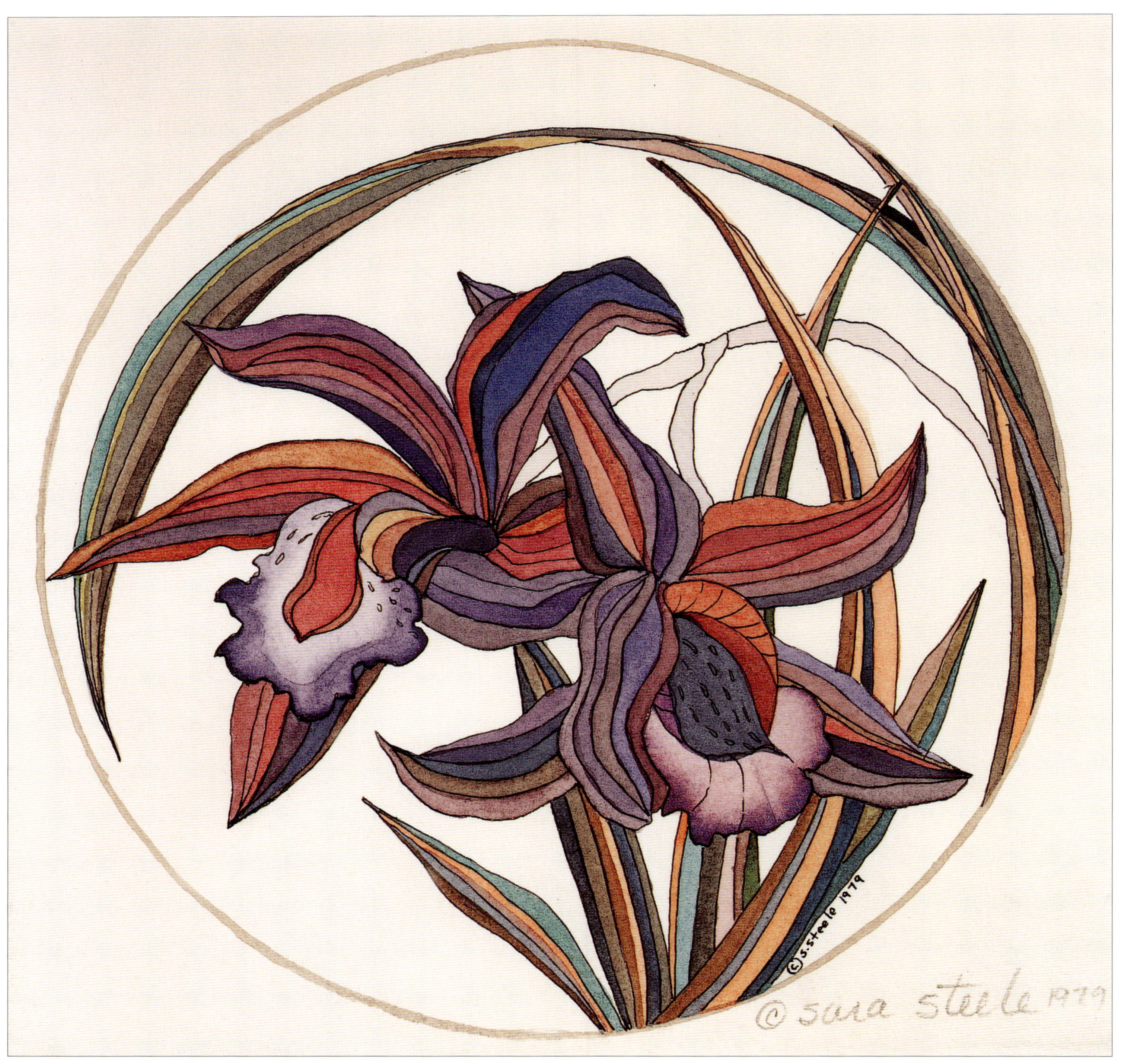

Orchid Poster - LL, 1979

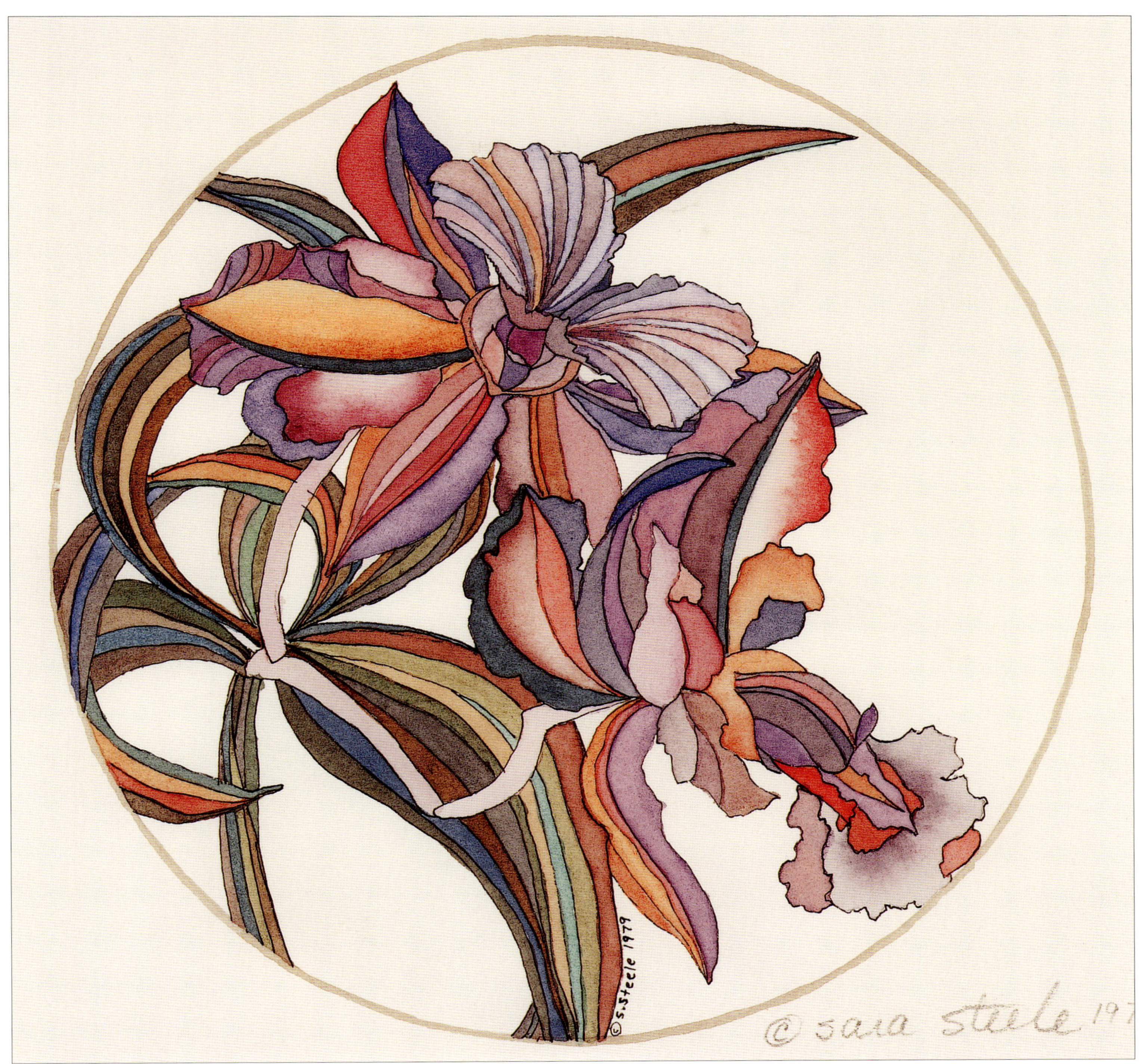

Orchid Poster - LR (Laeliocattleya Erin), 1979

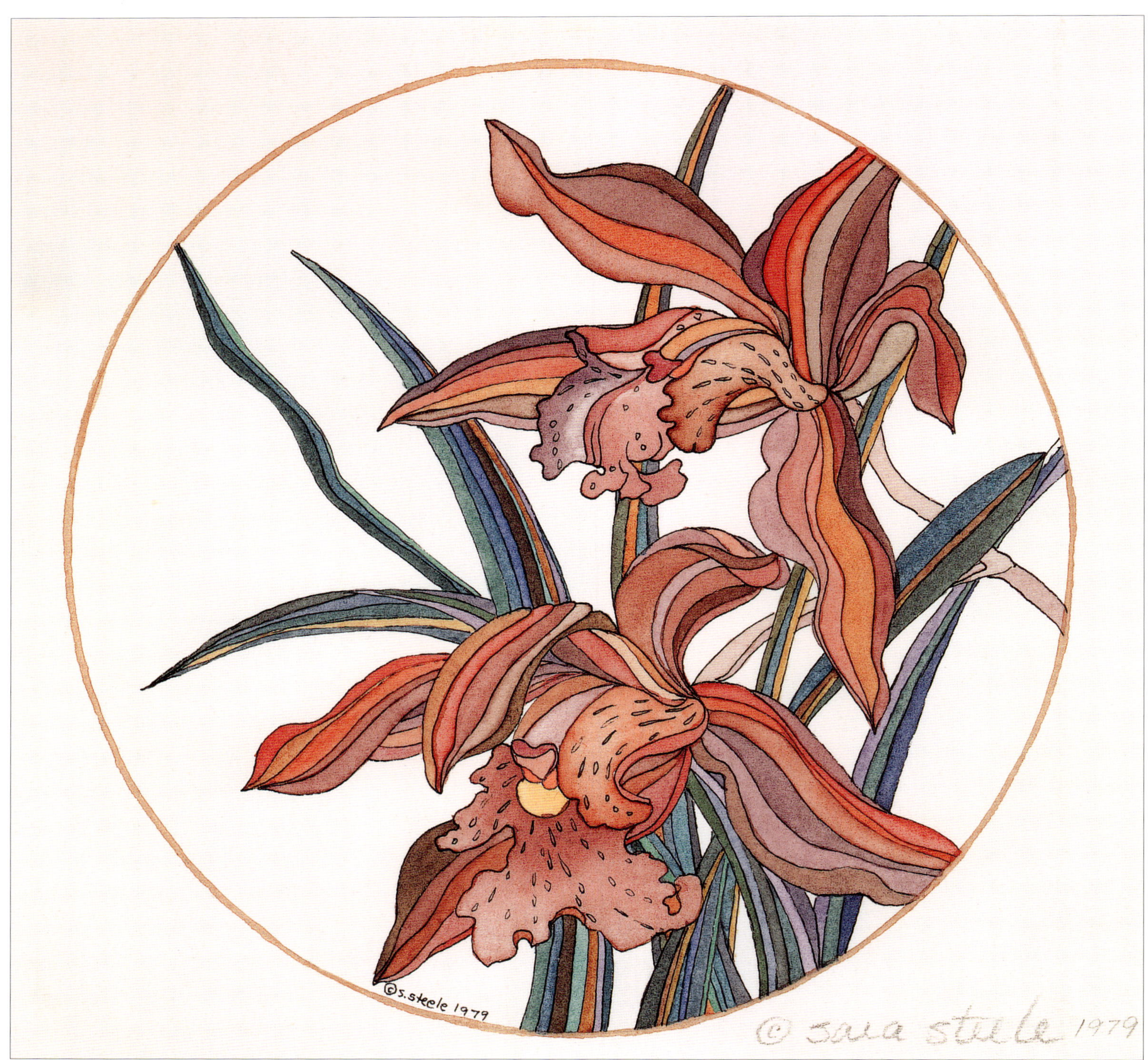

Orchid Poster - UL (Cymbidium Nicolansianum II), 1979

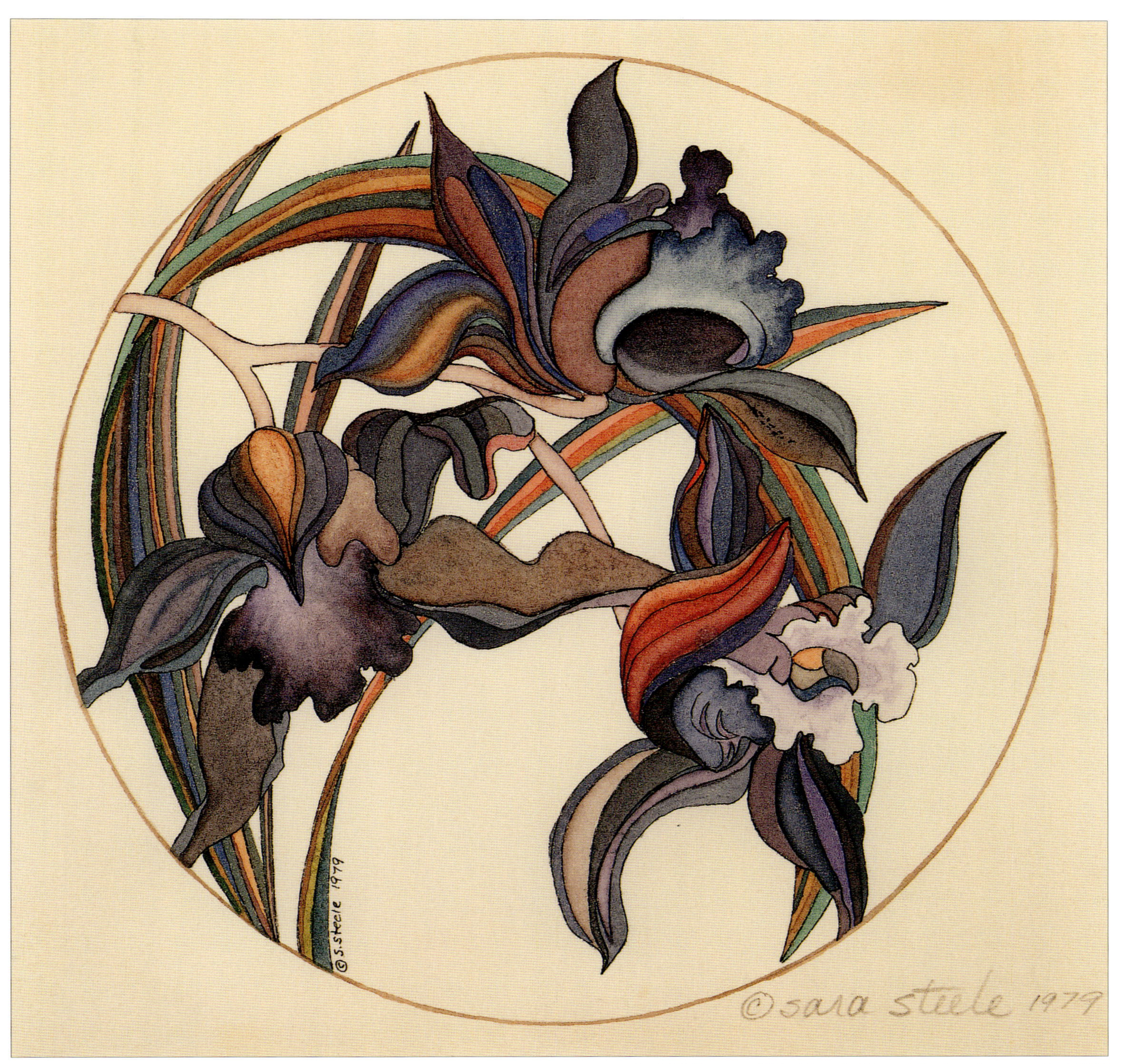

Orchid Poster - UR (Cymbidium Nicolansianum I), 1979

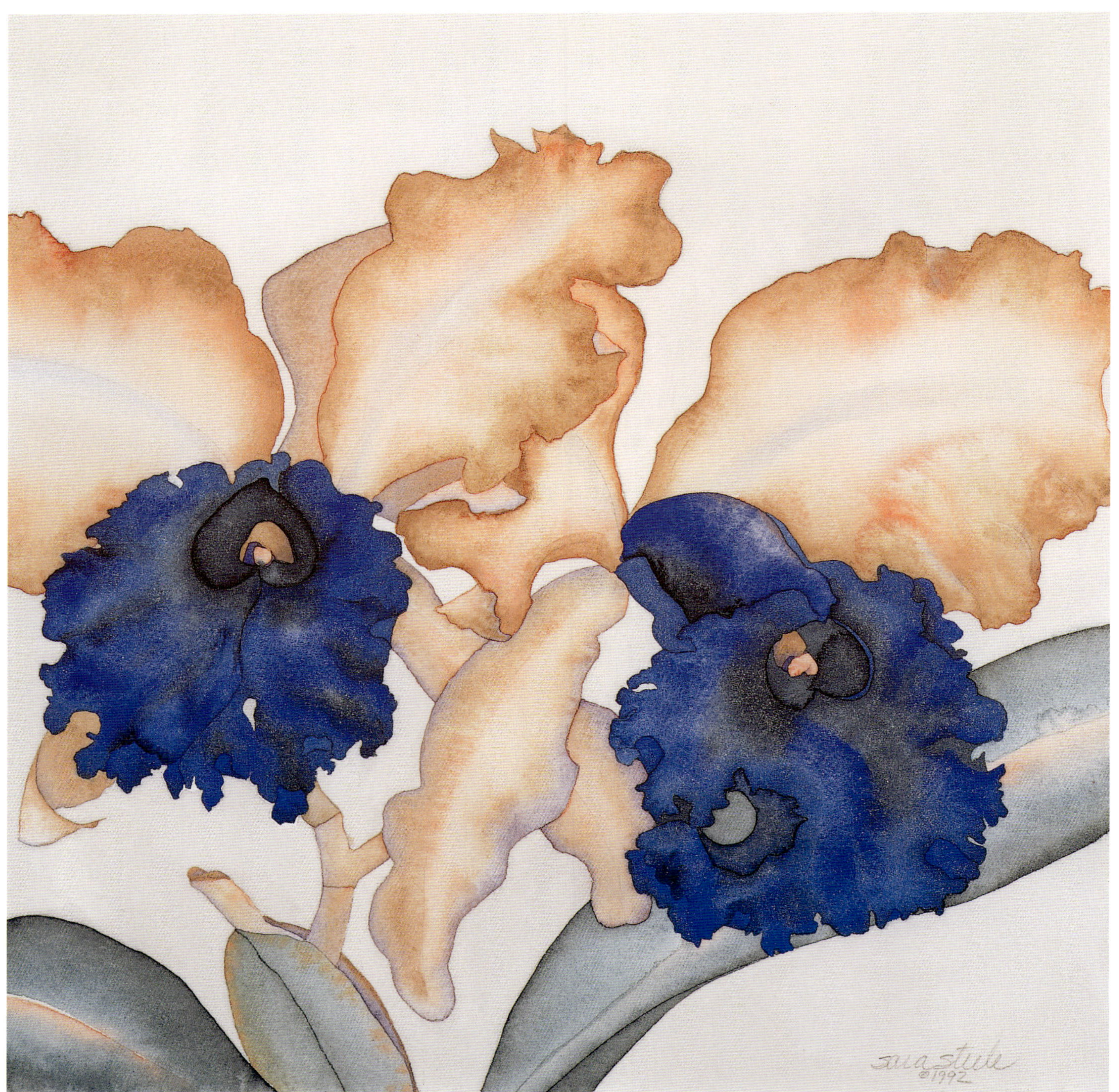

Blue-lipped Cattleya, 1992

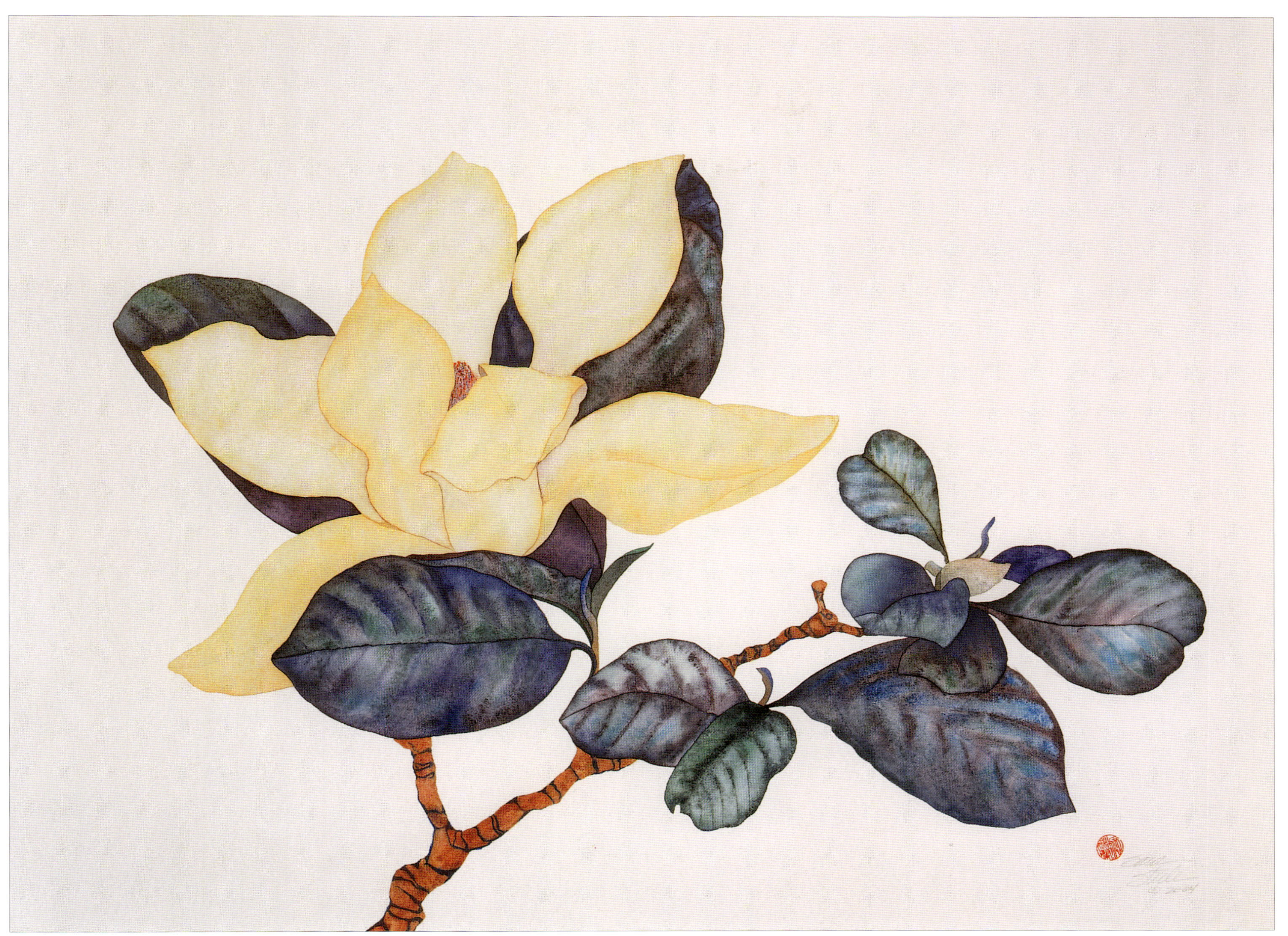

Pale Magnolia, 2004

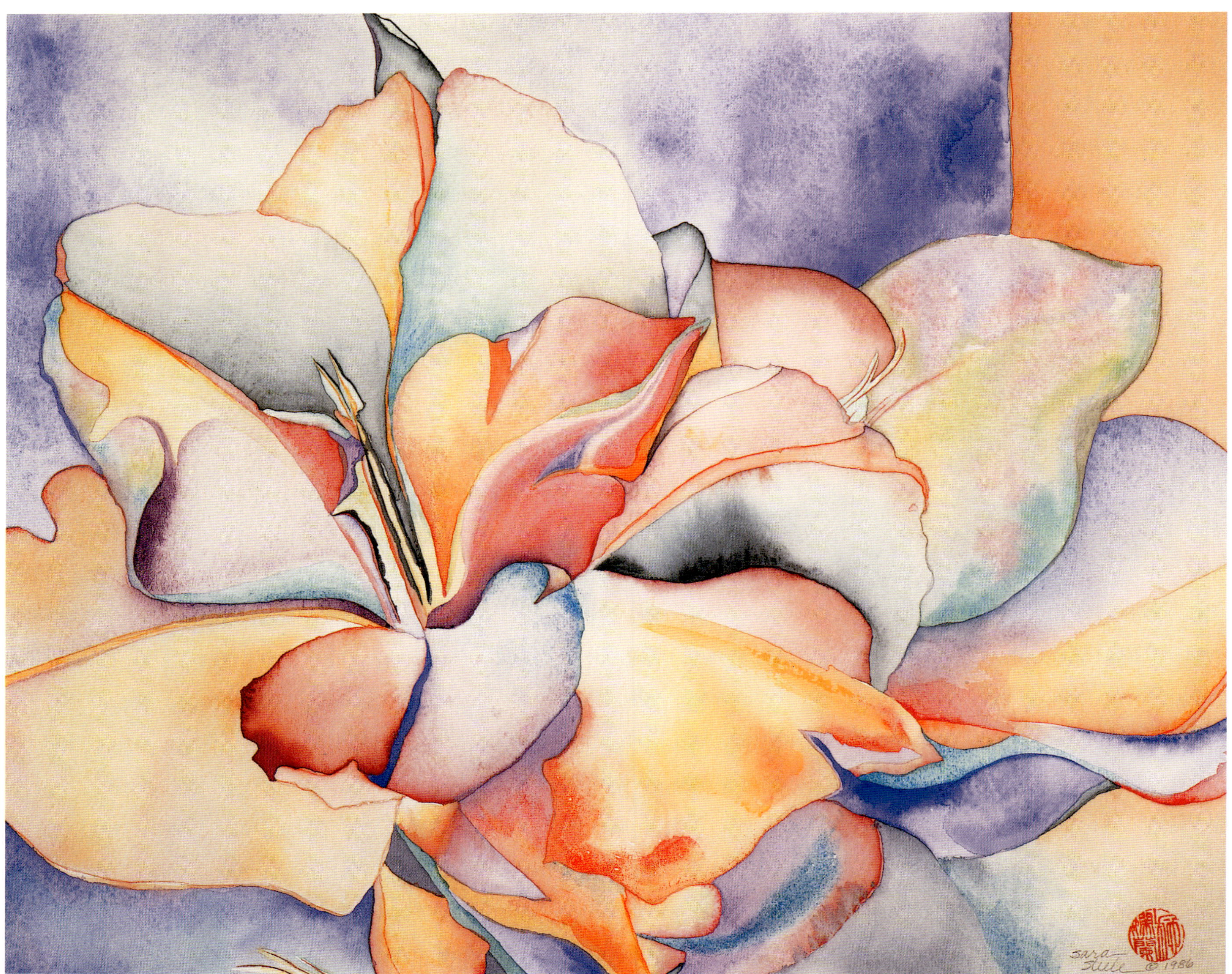

Fêng/Abundance of Light, 1986

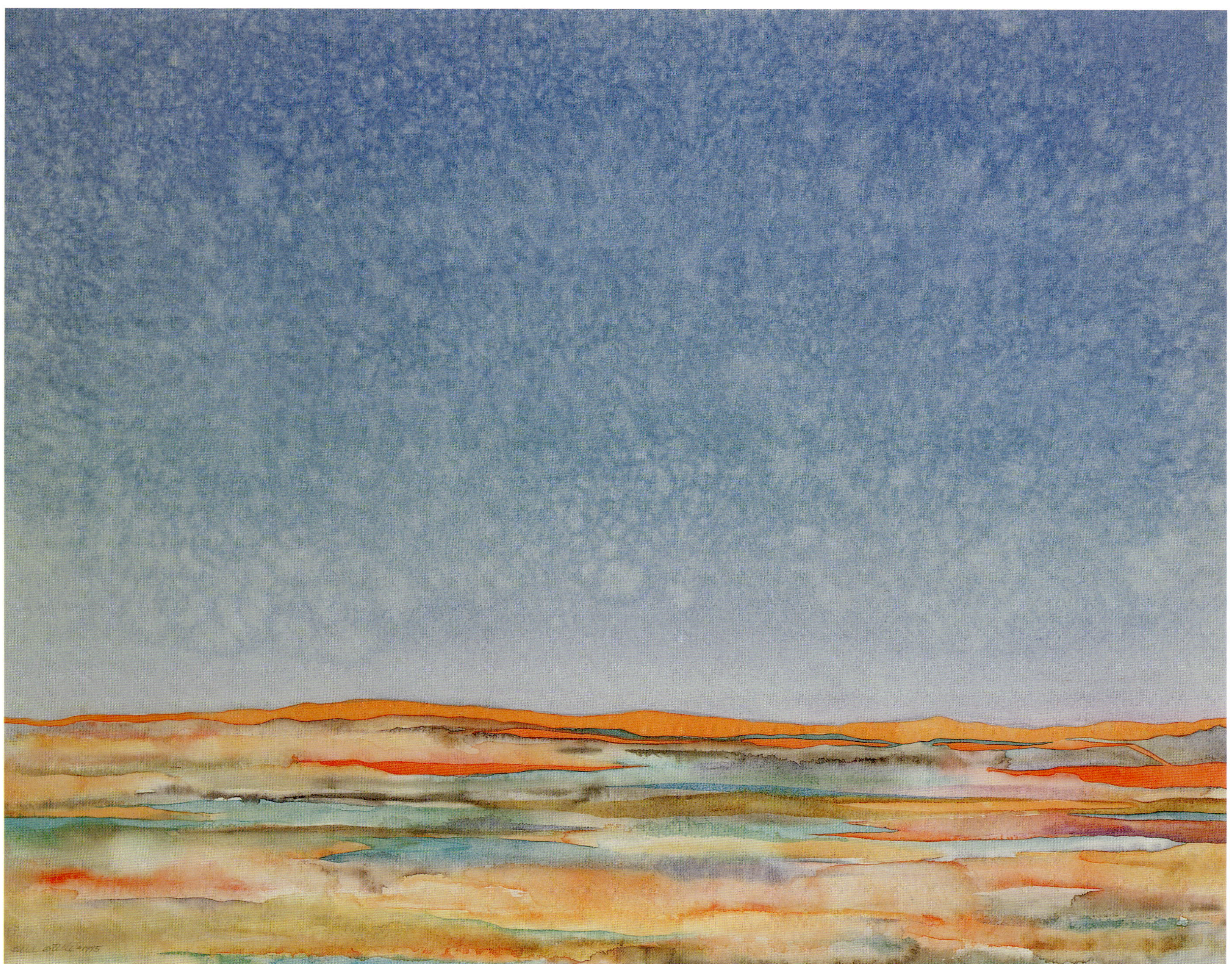

Beloved Aire, 1995

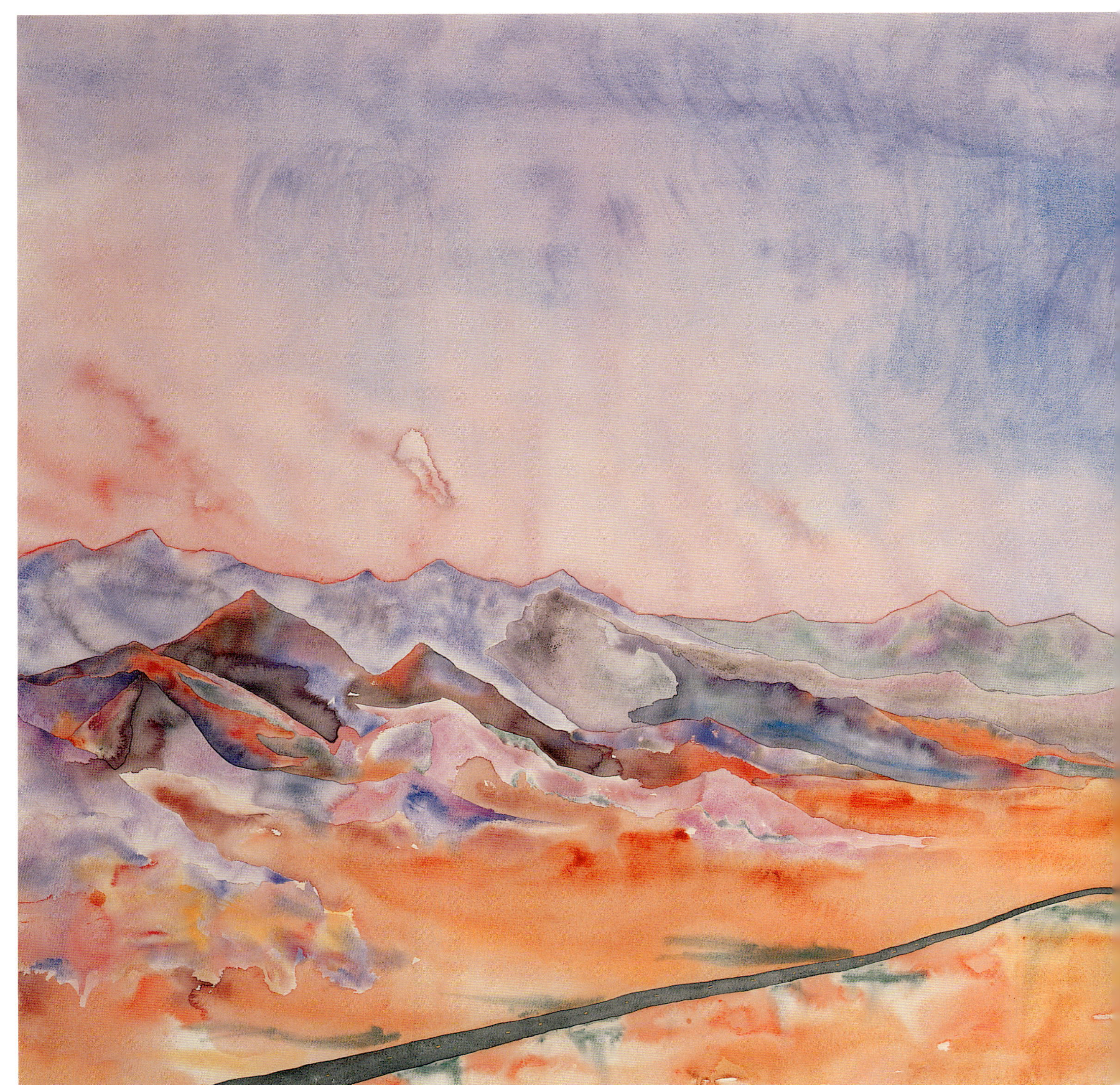

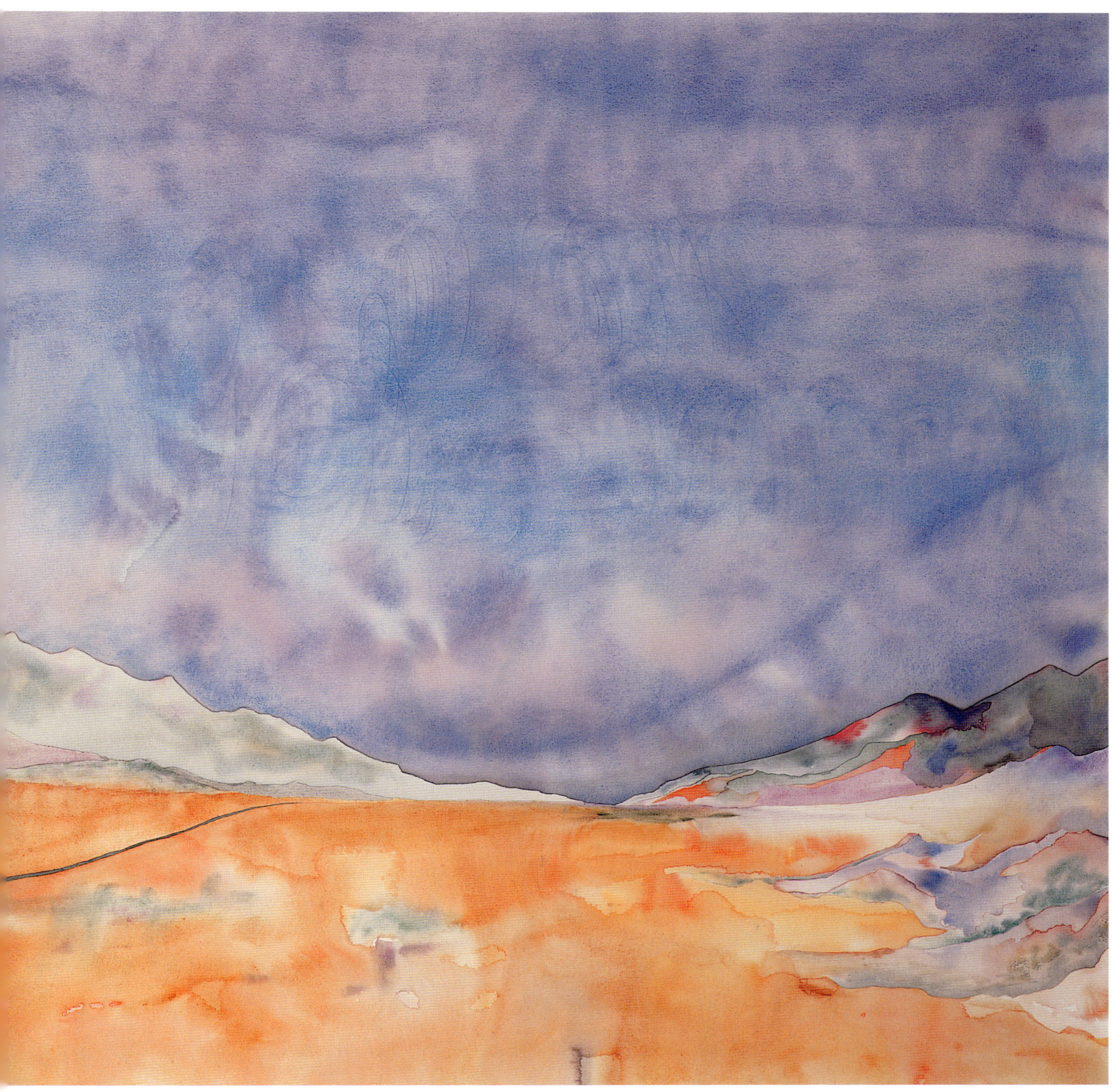

Moon Over Montana, 1989

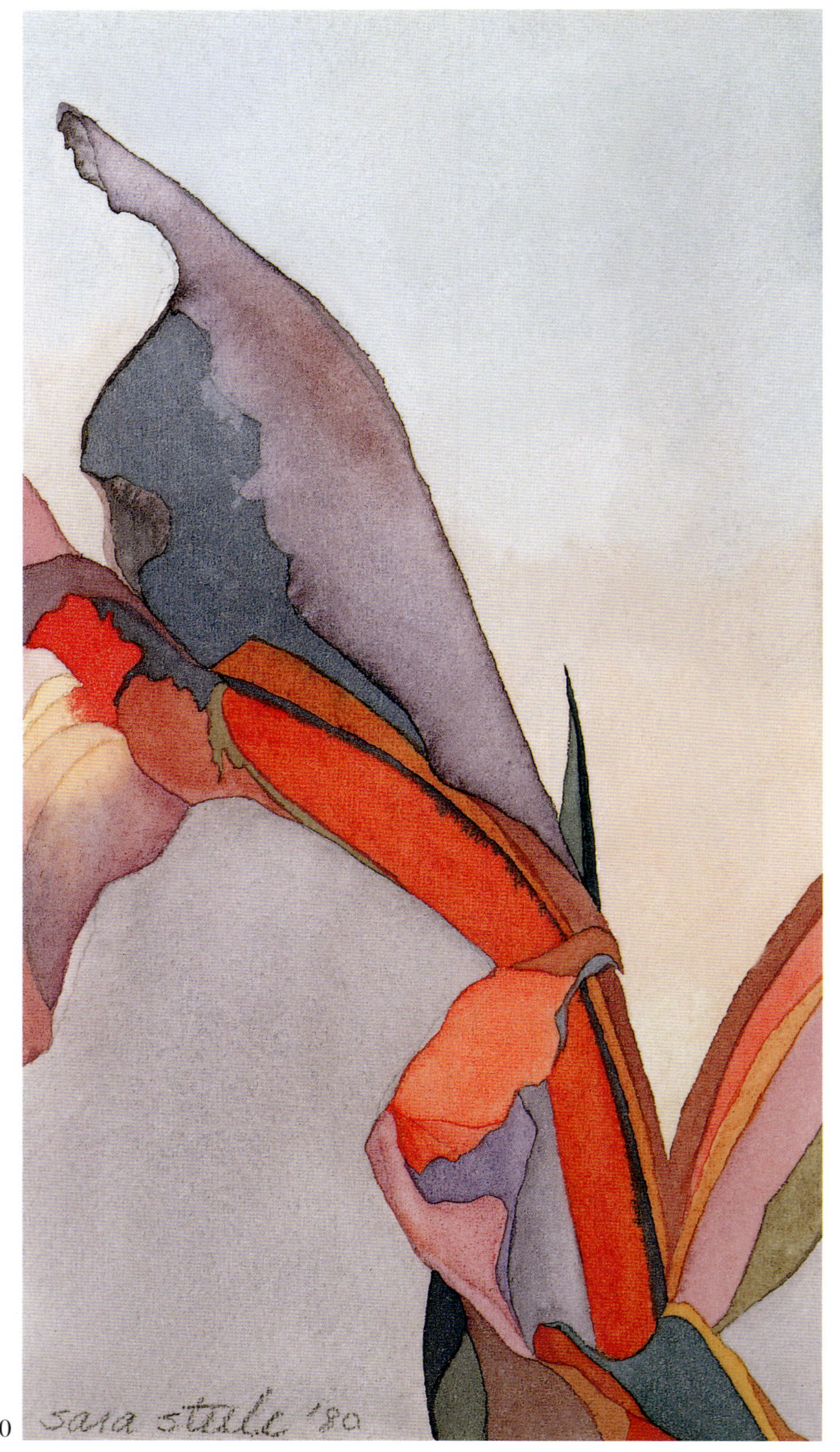

Artless Blossom, 1980

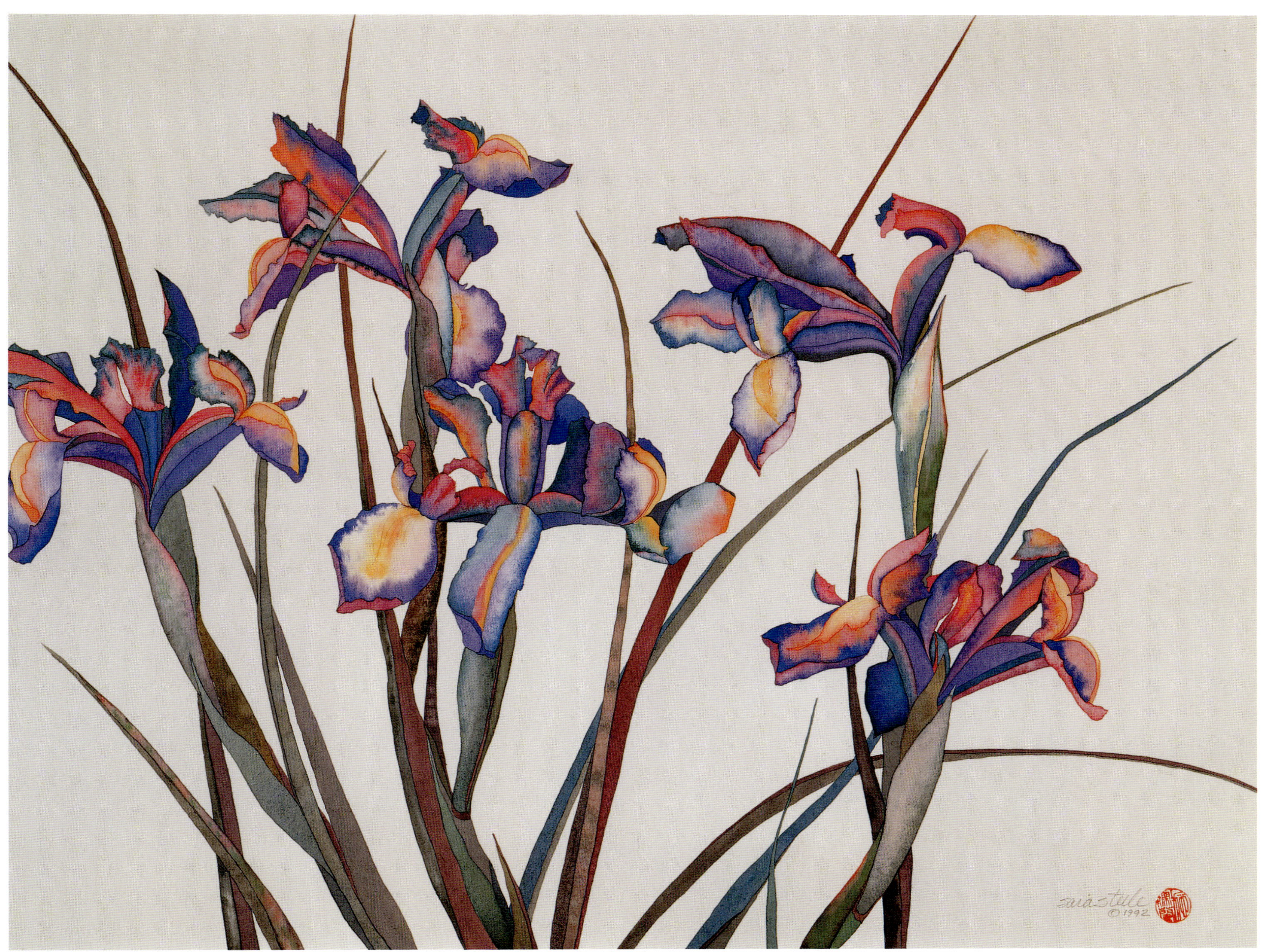

French Irises, 1992

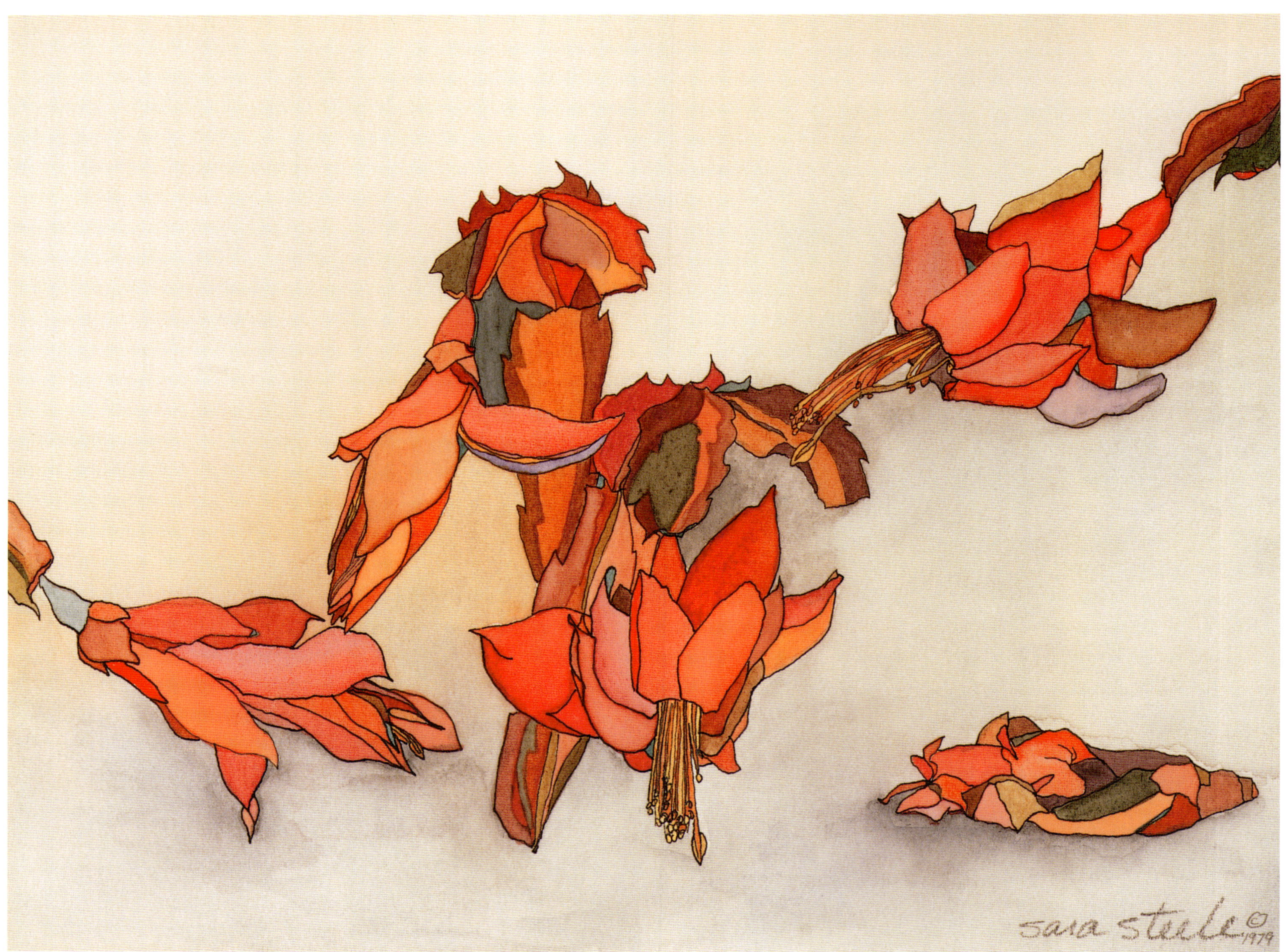

Dying Blossoms, 1979

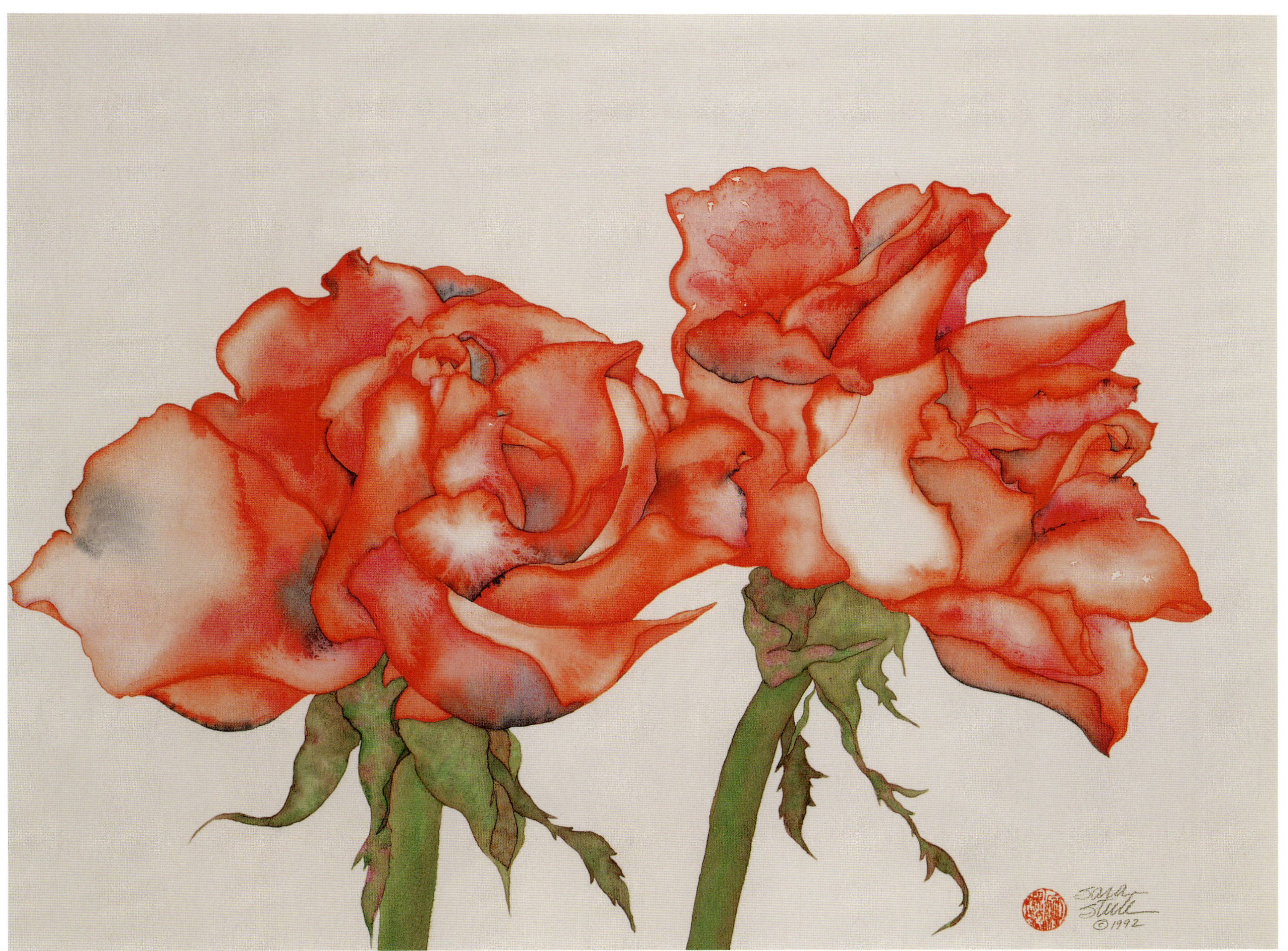

Turkey Roses, 1992

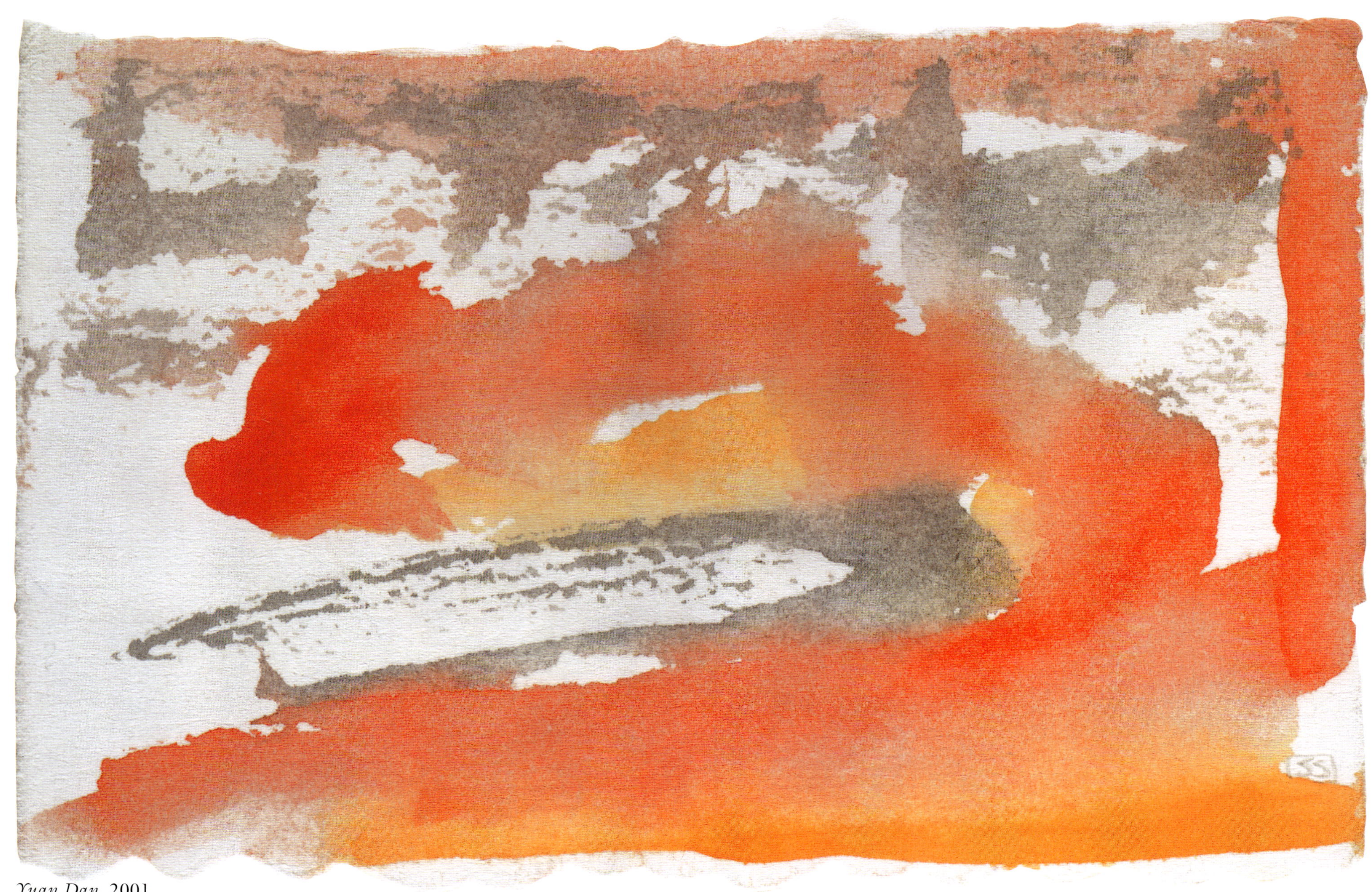

Yuan Dan, 2001

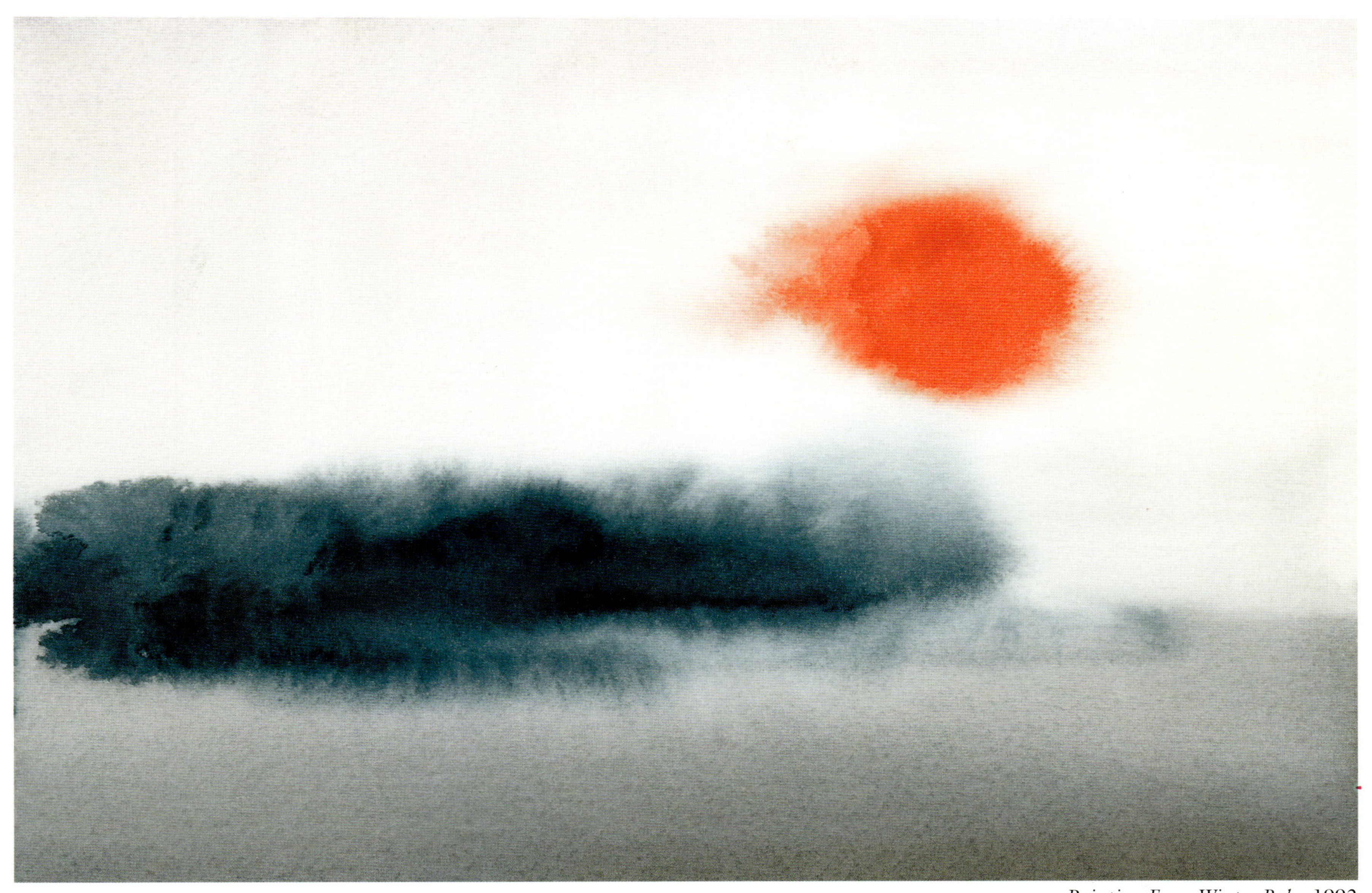

Painting For a Winter Baby, 1992

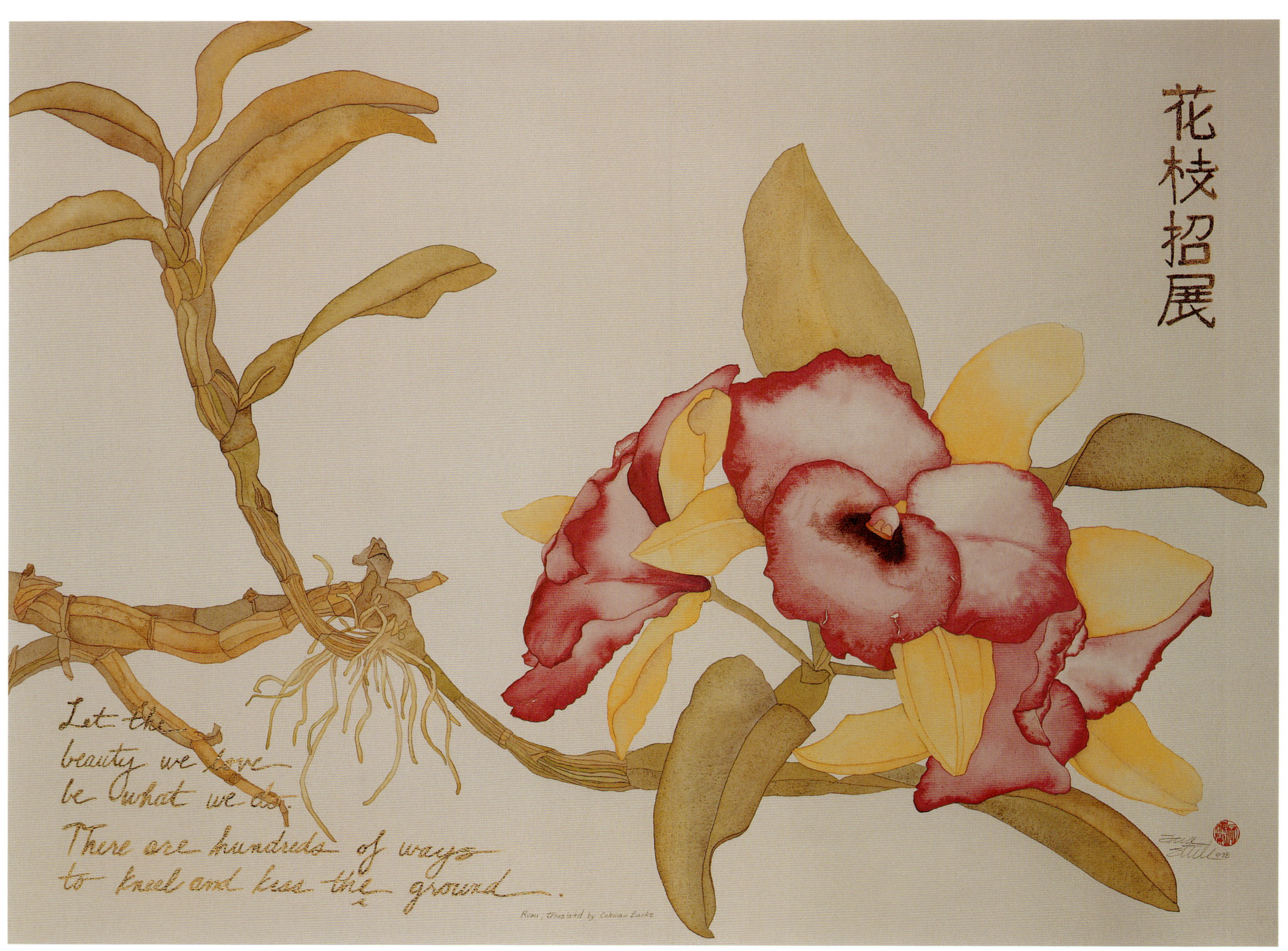

Dendrobium Small Dowan, 1998

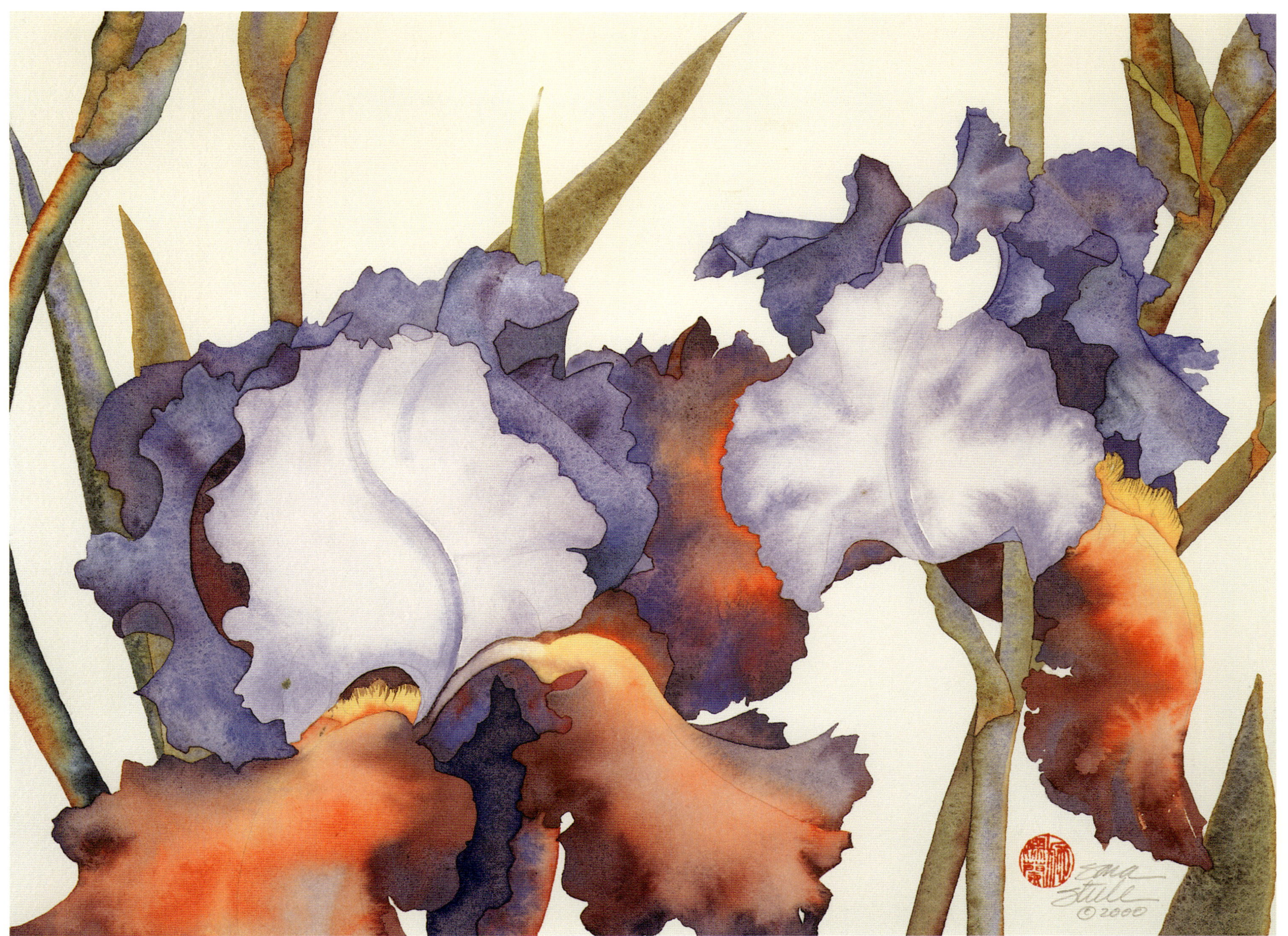

Irises from D.K., 2000

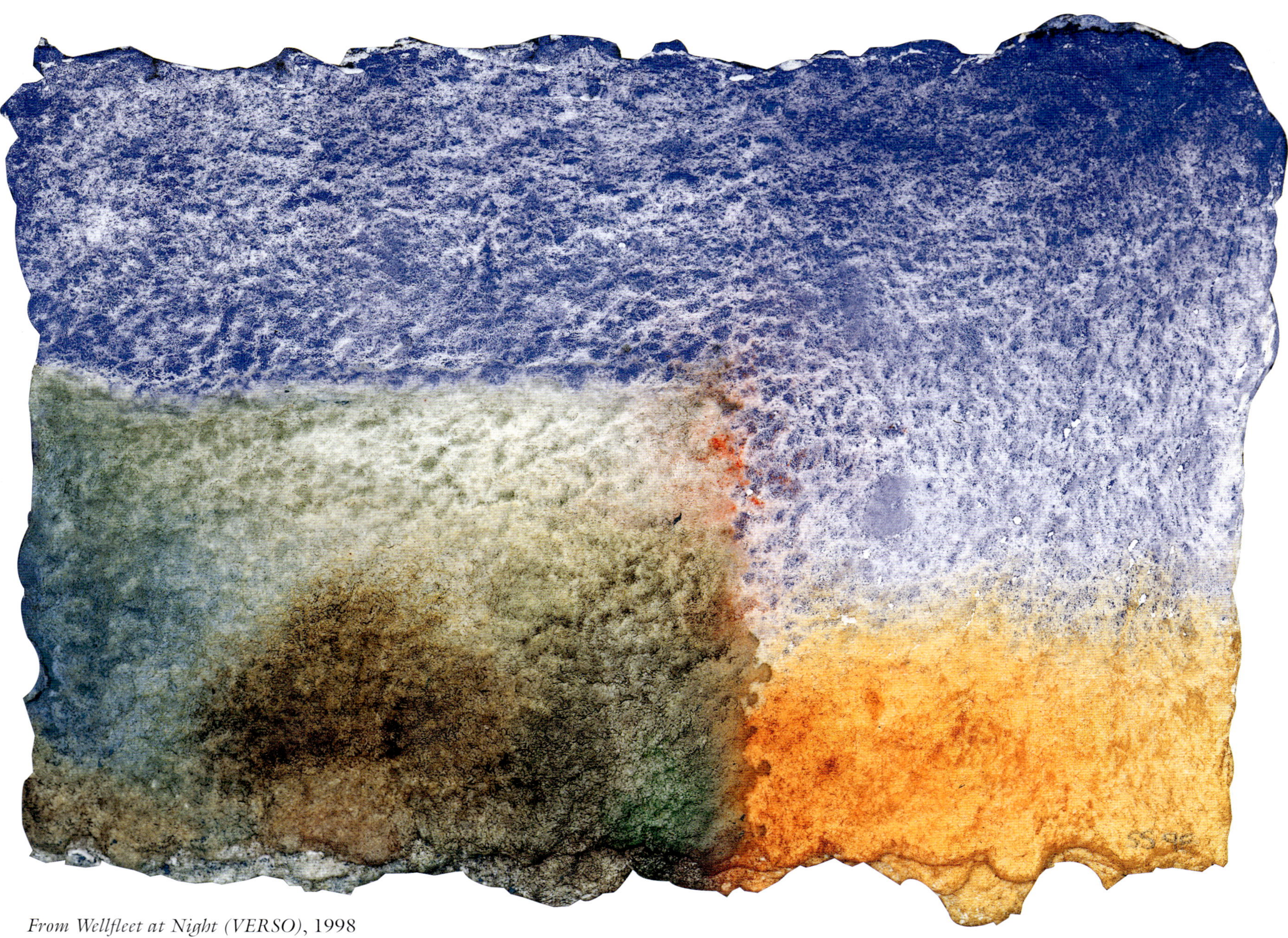

From Wellfleet at Night (VERSO), 1998

Landscape # 21, 1994

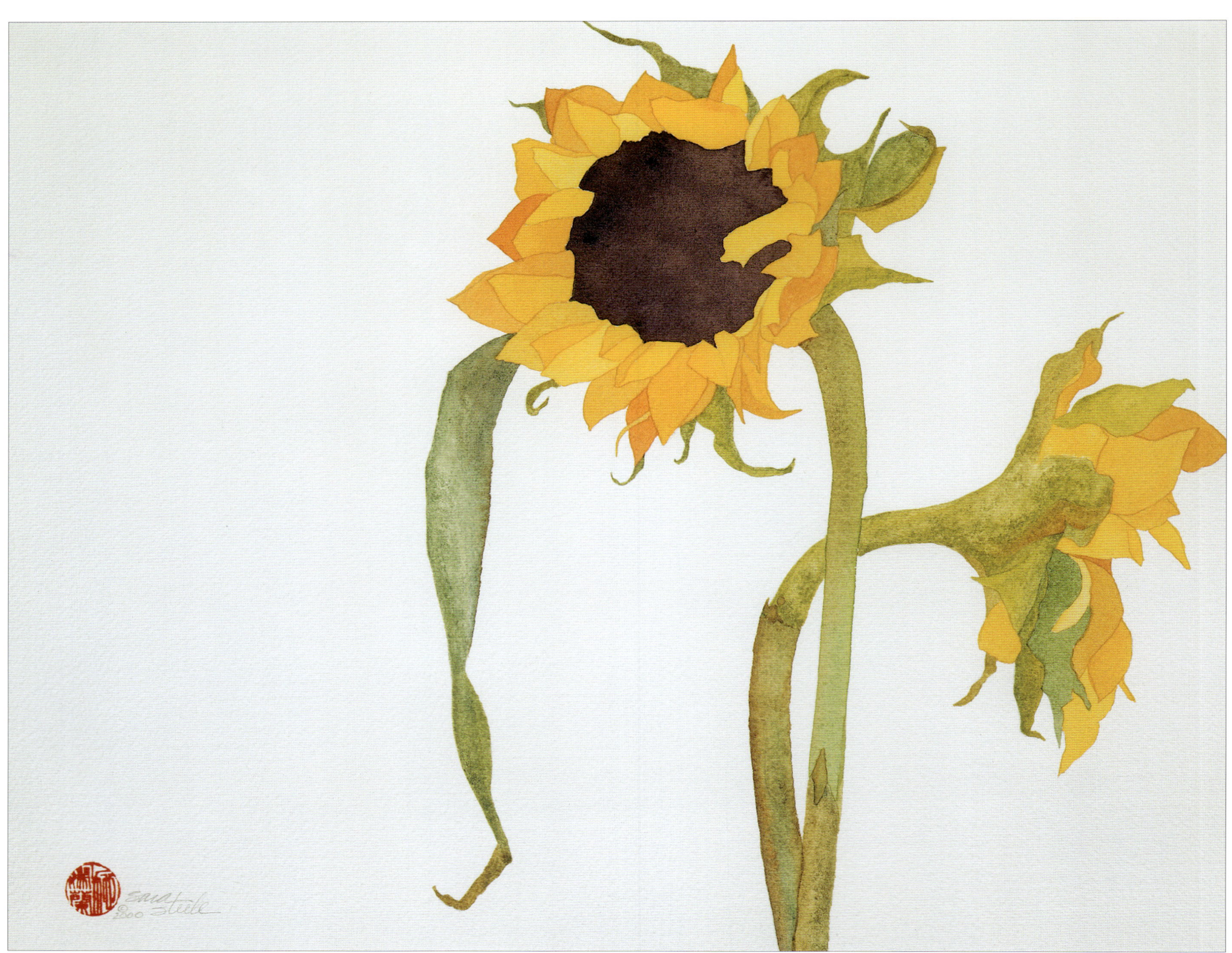

Setting Sunflowers from Lisa, 2000

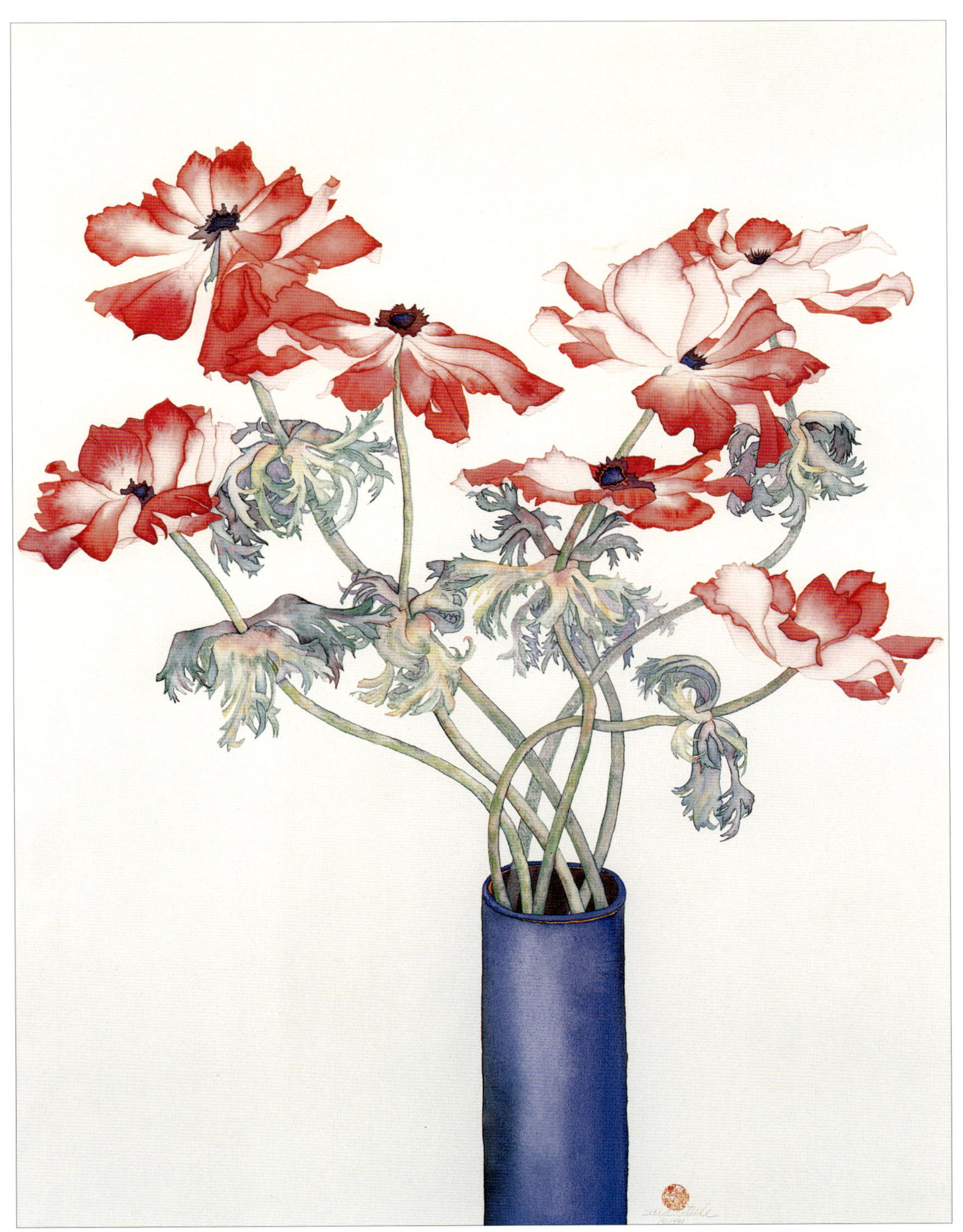

Red Anemones, 1991

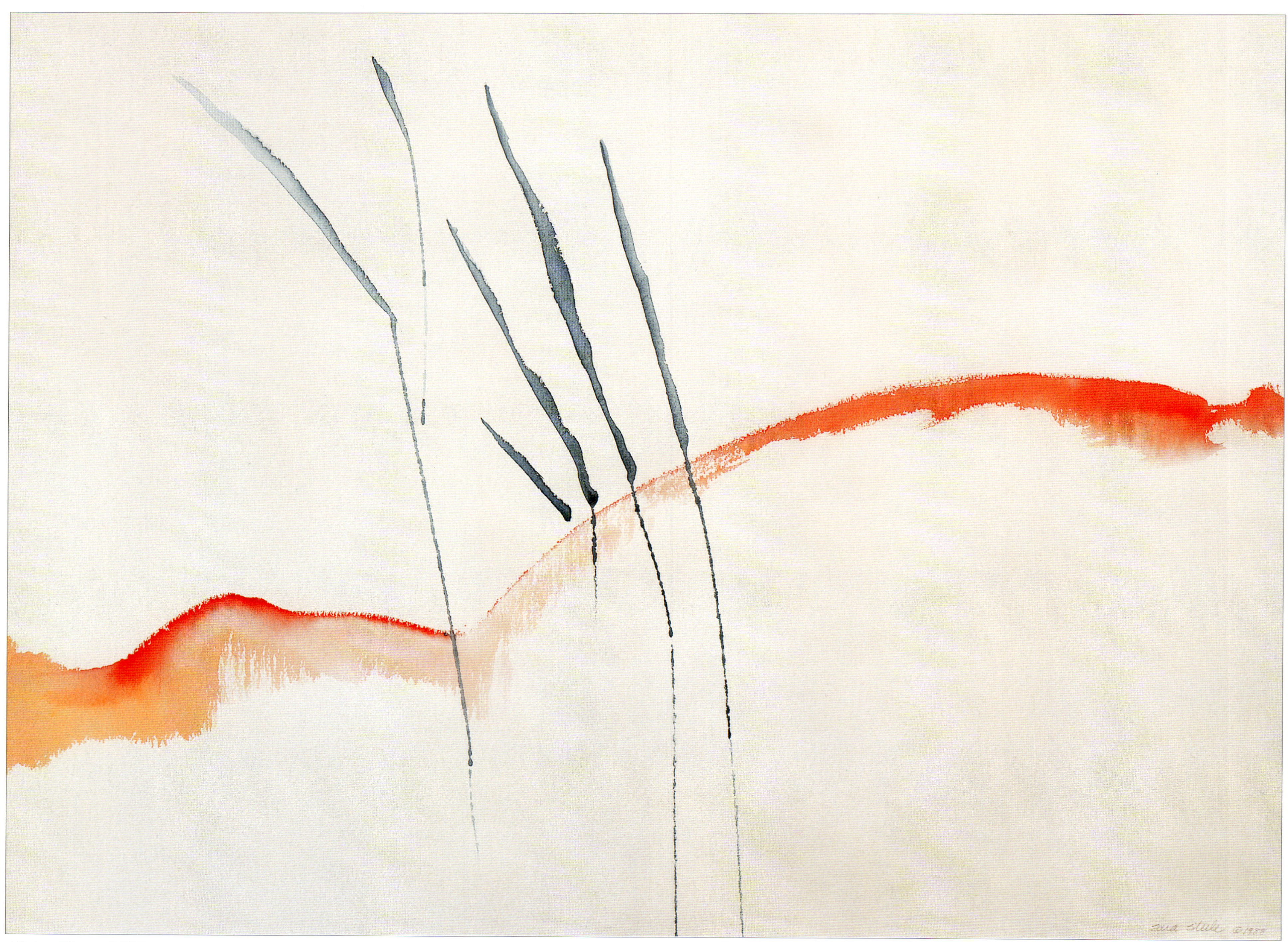

Maine Tears, 1988

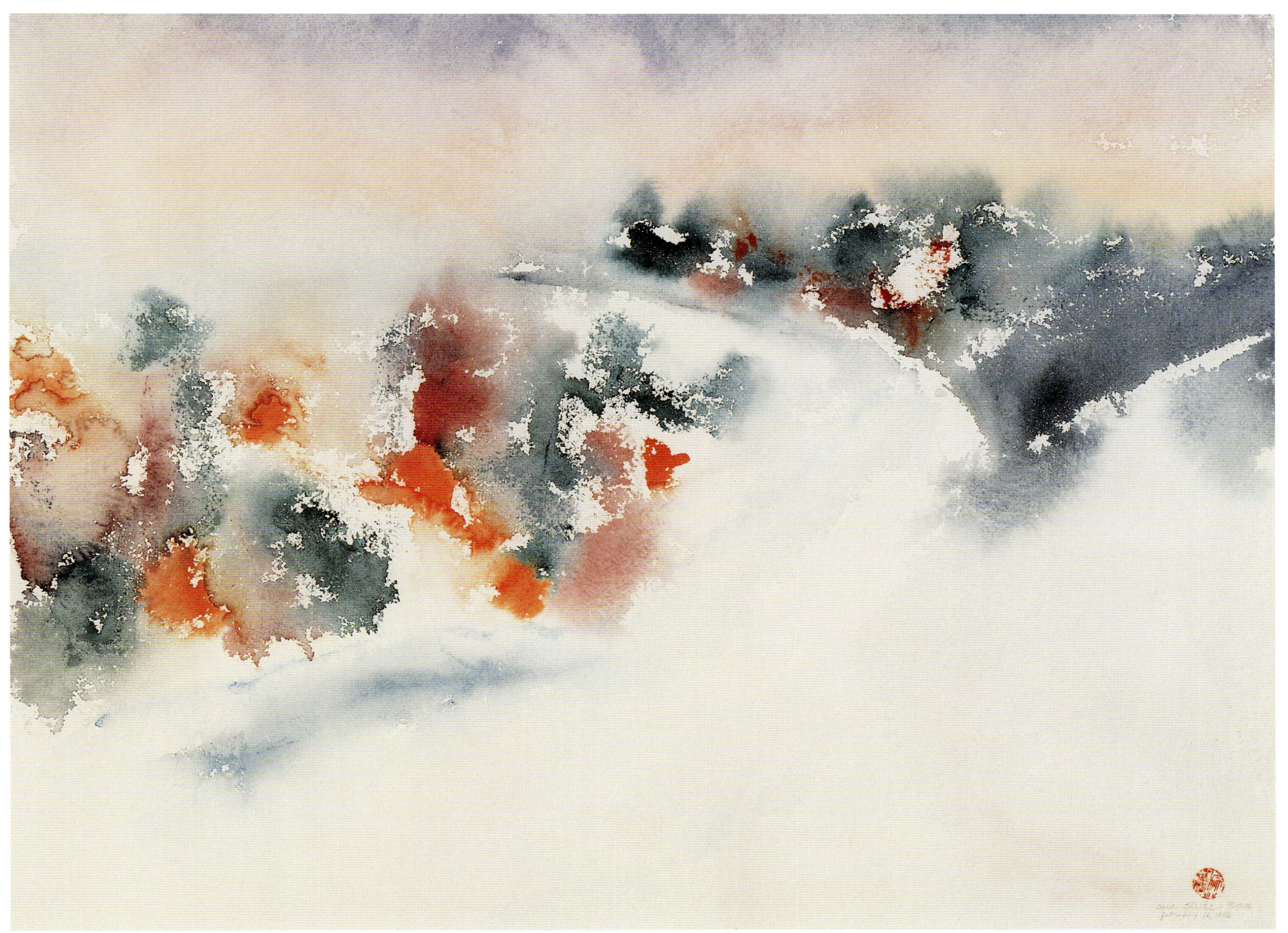

Arianna (River of Silver), 1986

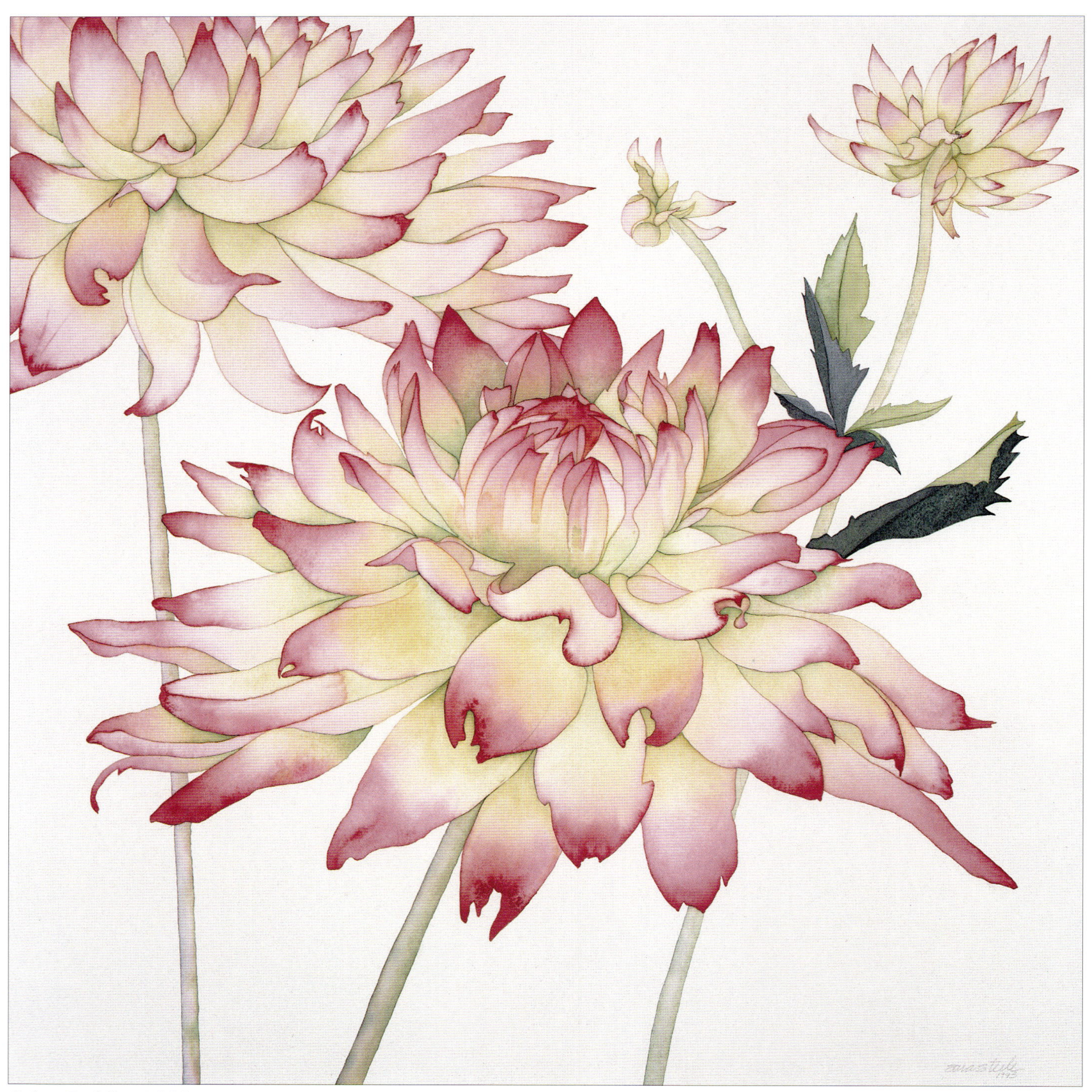

Salem Dahlias, 1993

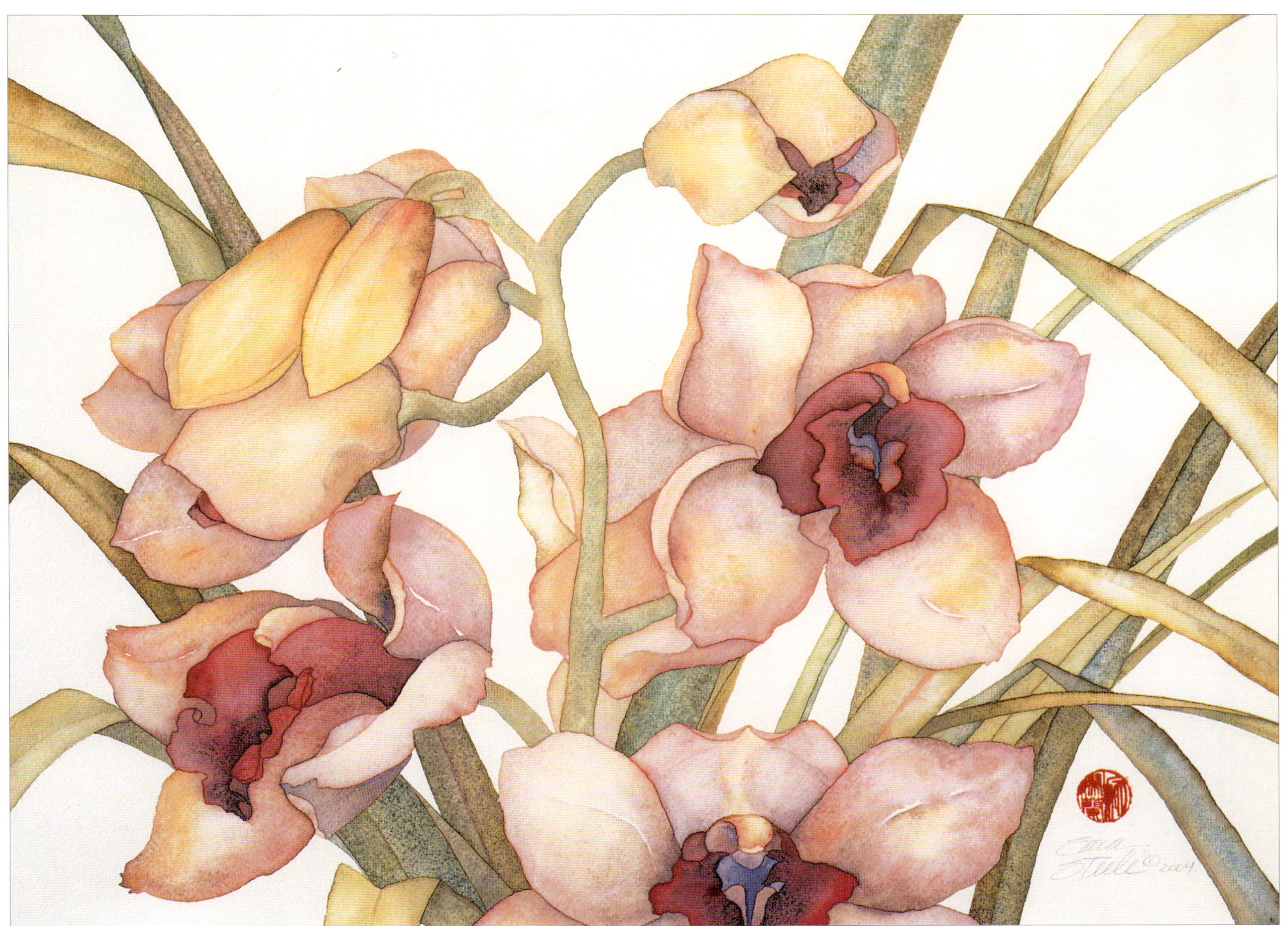

Castaway Cymbidium, 2004

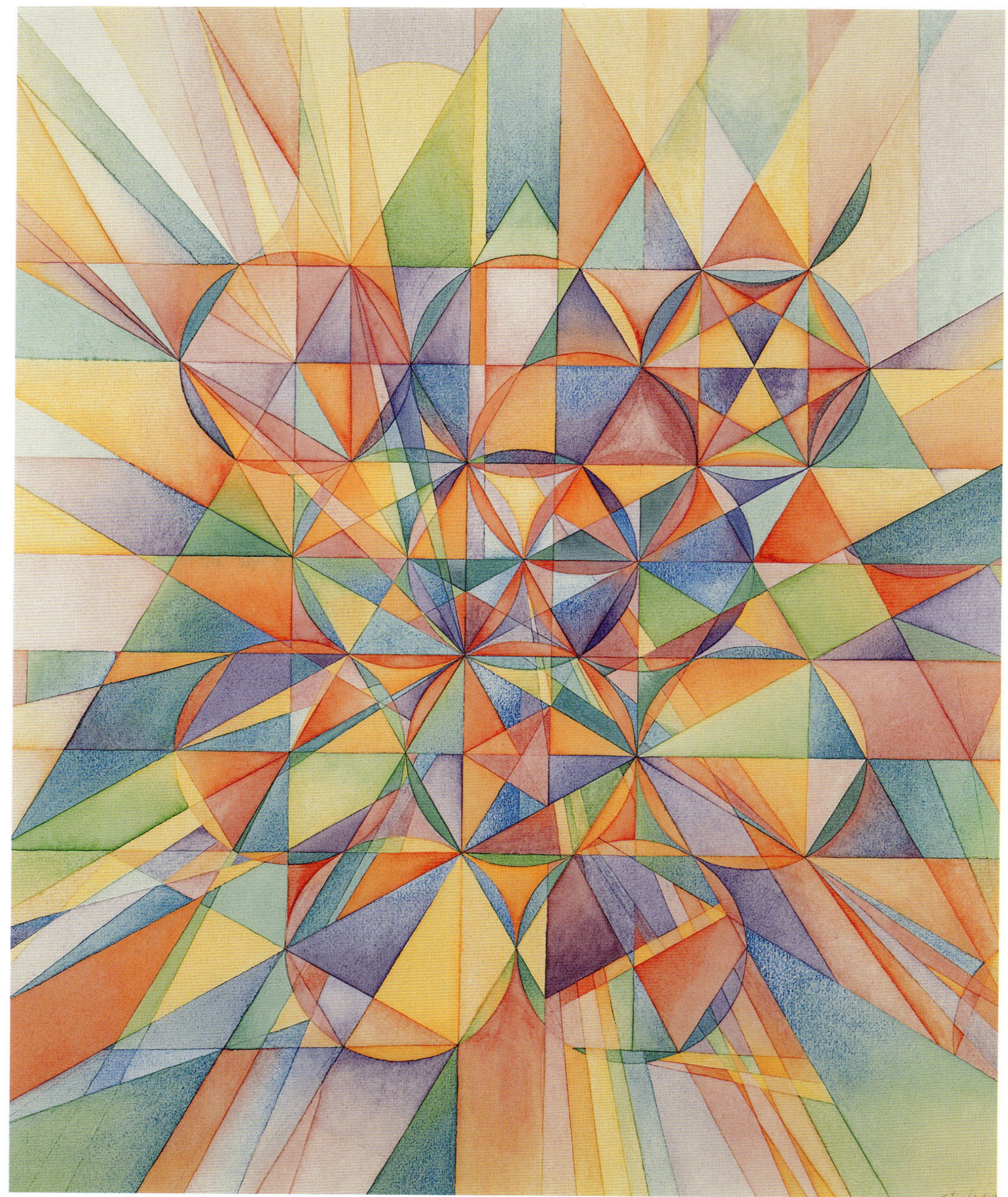

Lake Visions (No Soap Radio), 1988

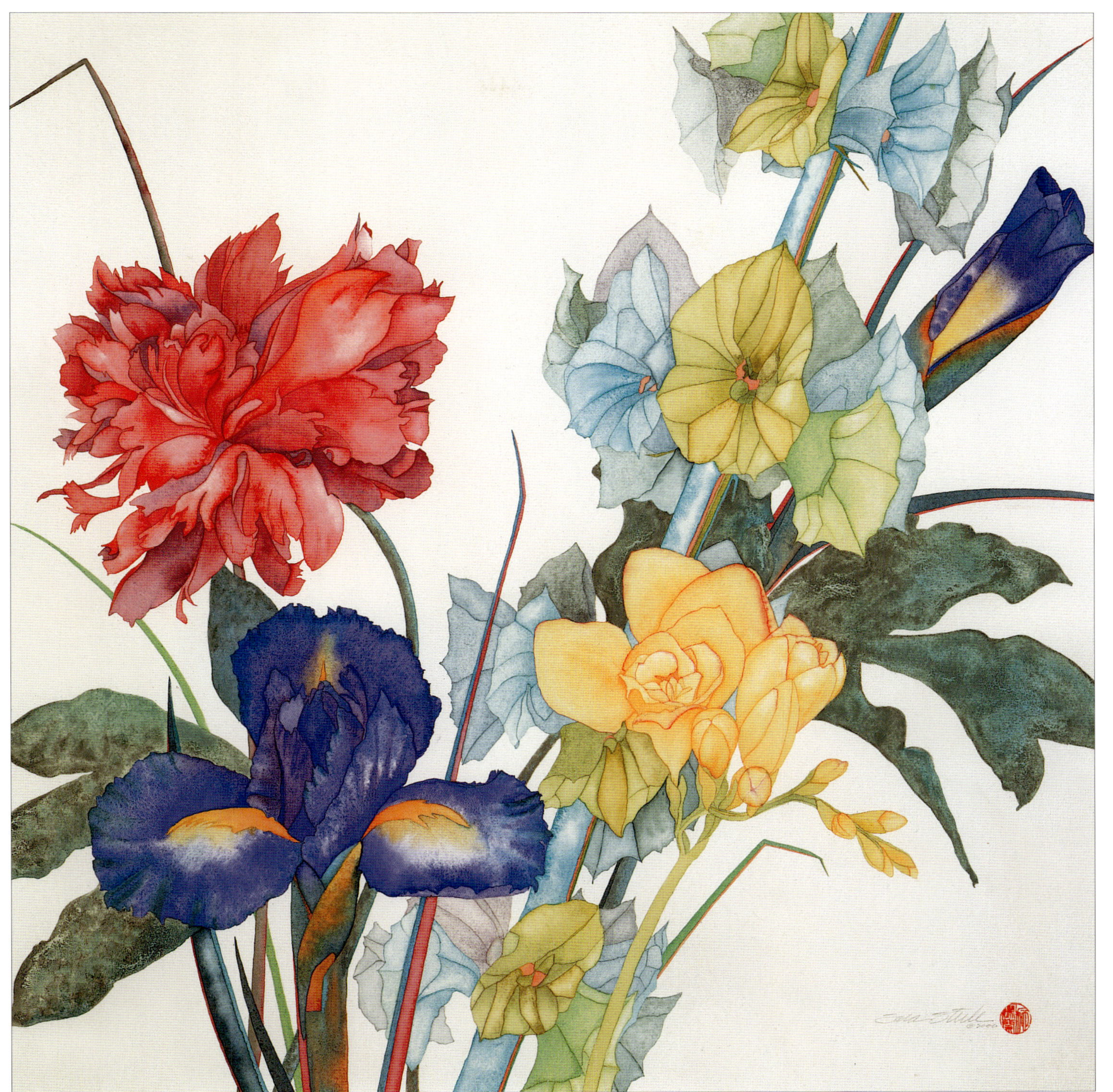

Peony, Freesia, Irises and Bells of Ireland, 2000

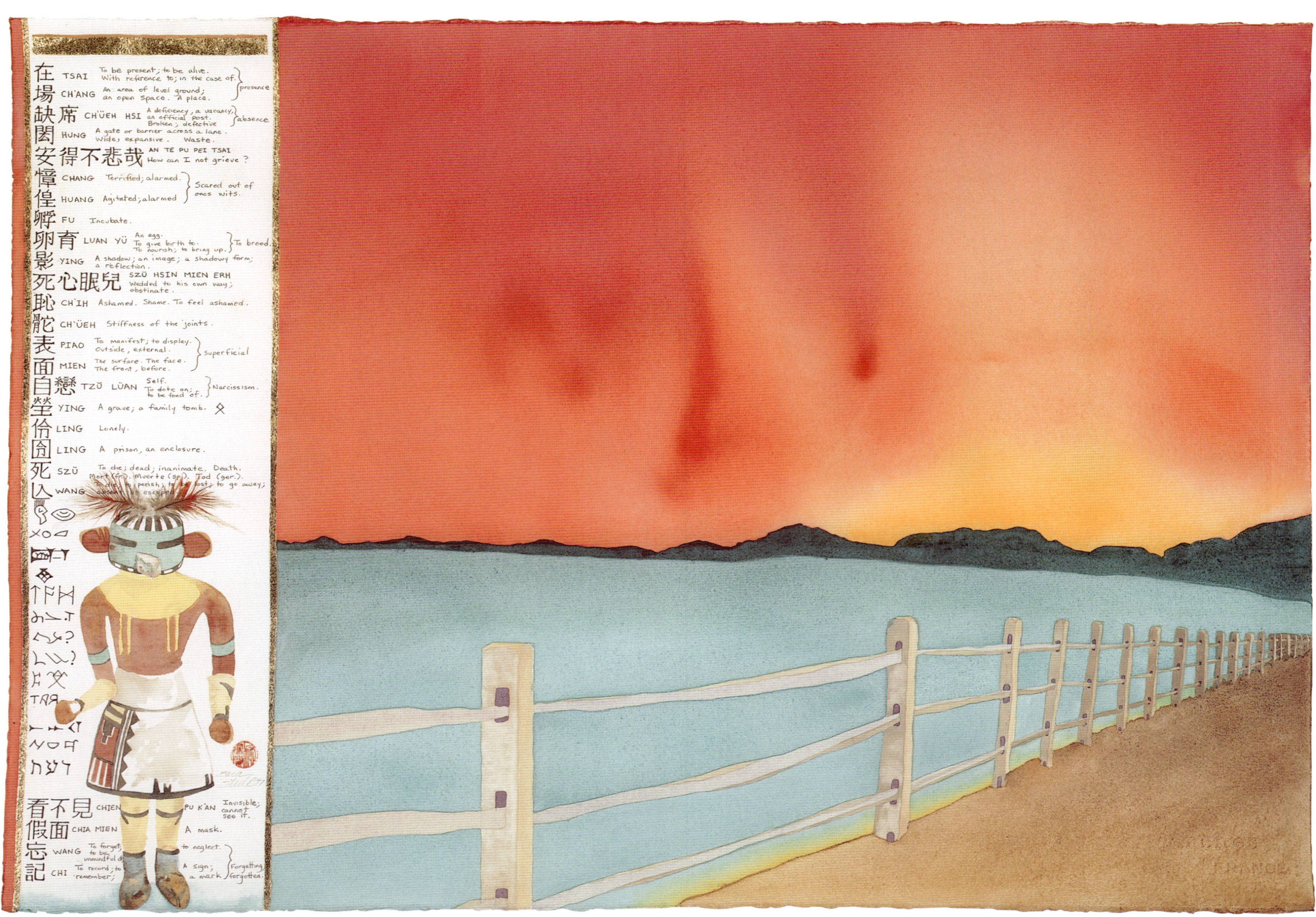

Tod: The Presence of Absence, 1997

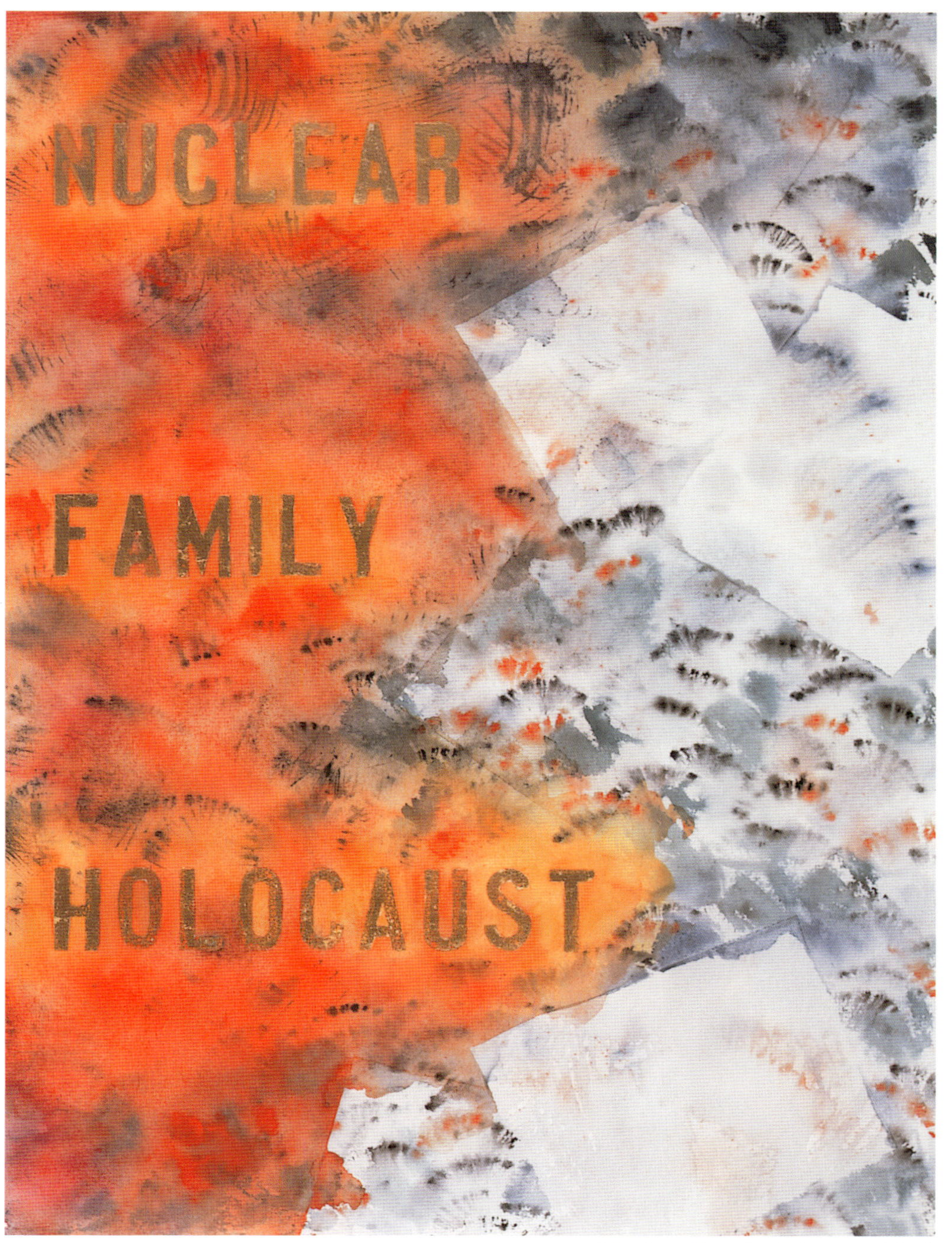

Nuclear Family Holocaust, 1992

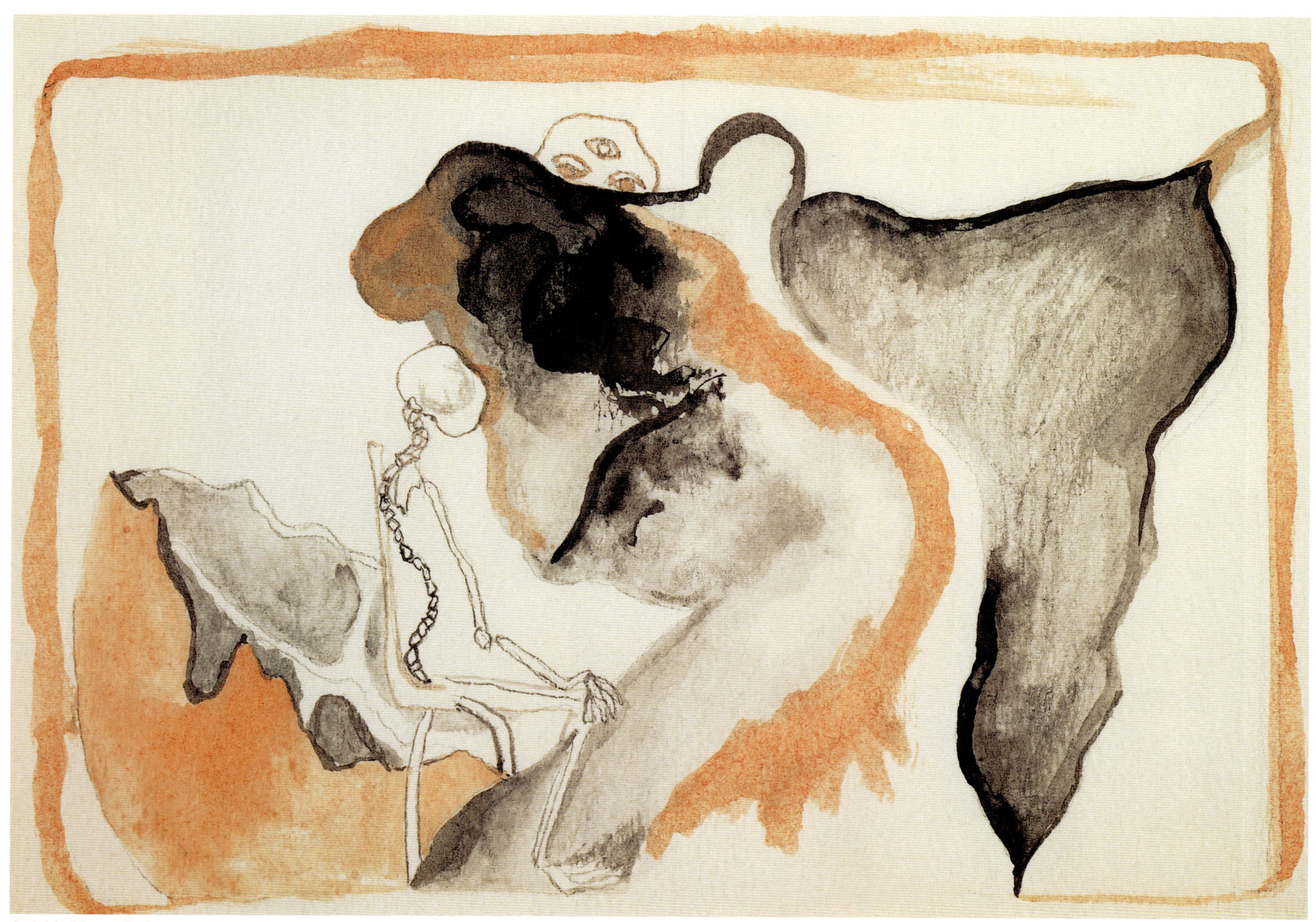

Suicide Note, 1970

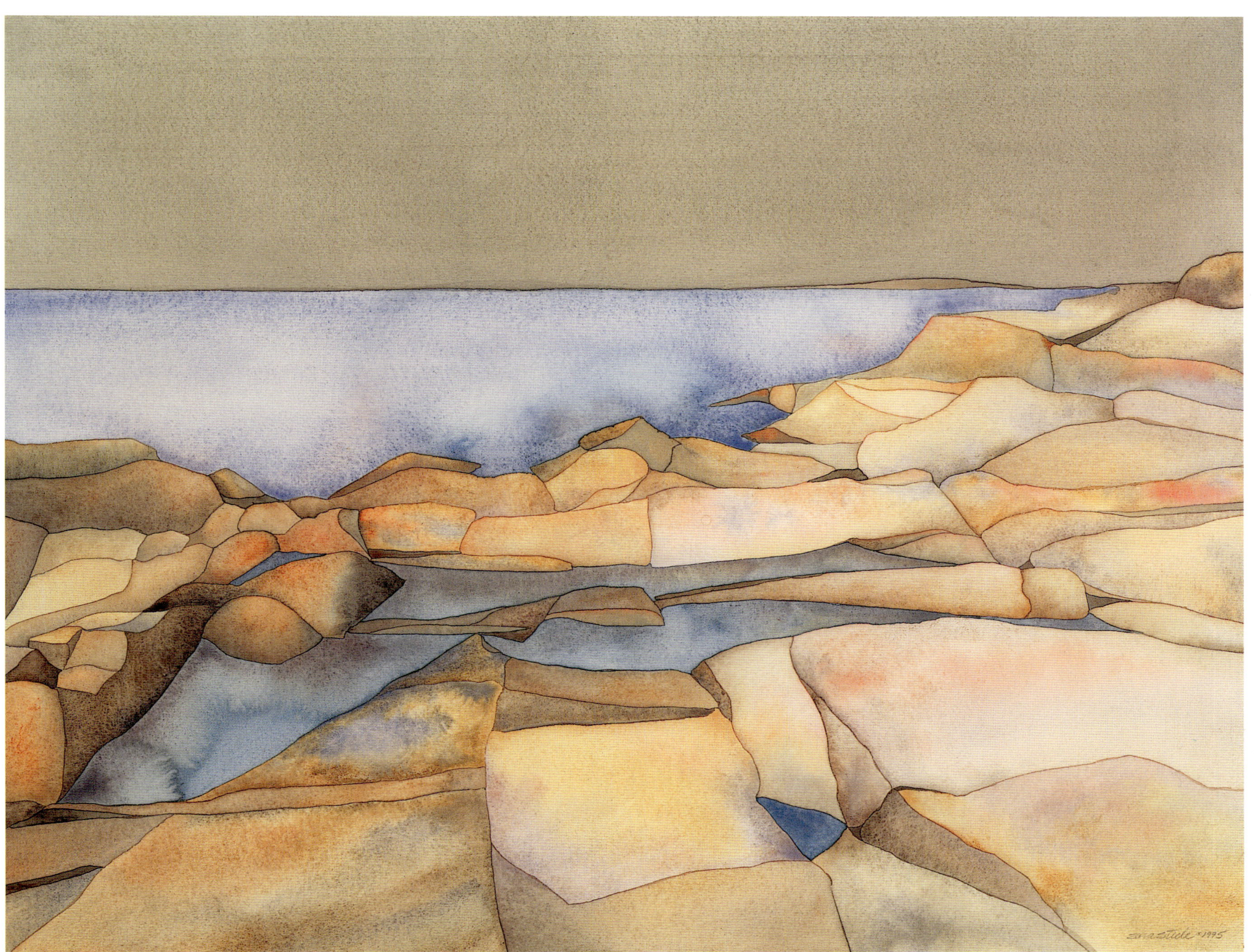

Halibut Point II, from the Quarry Series, 1995

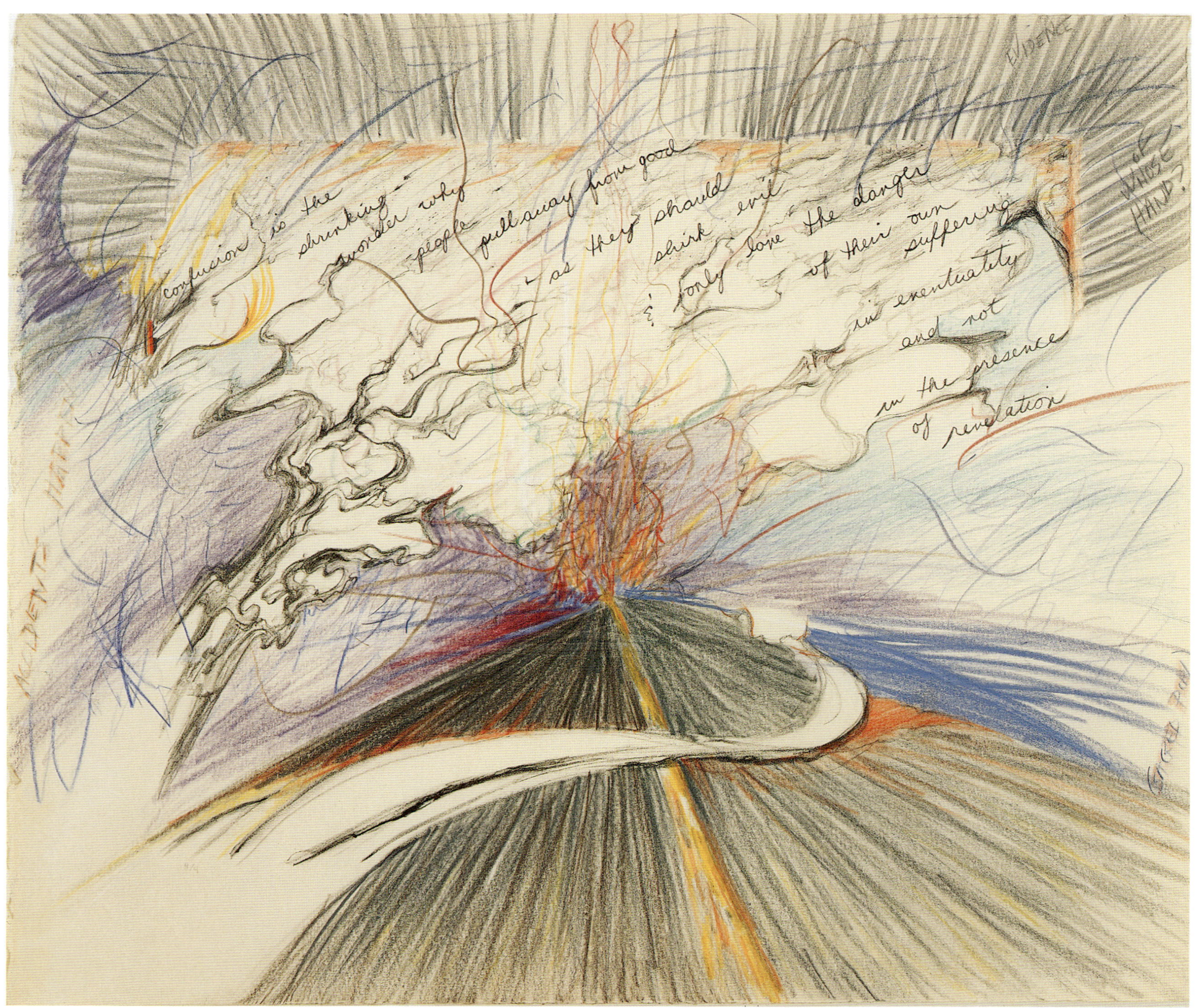

Spirited Charger/Accident, 1991

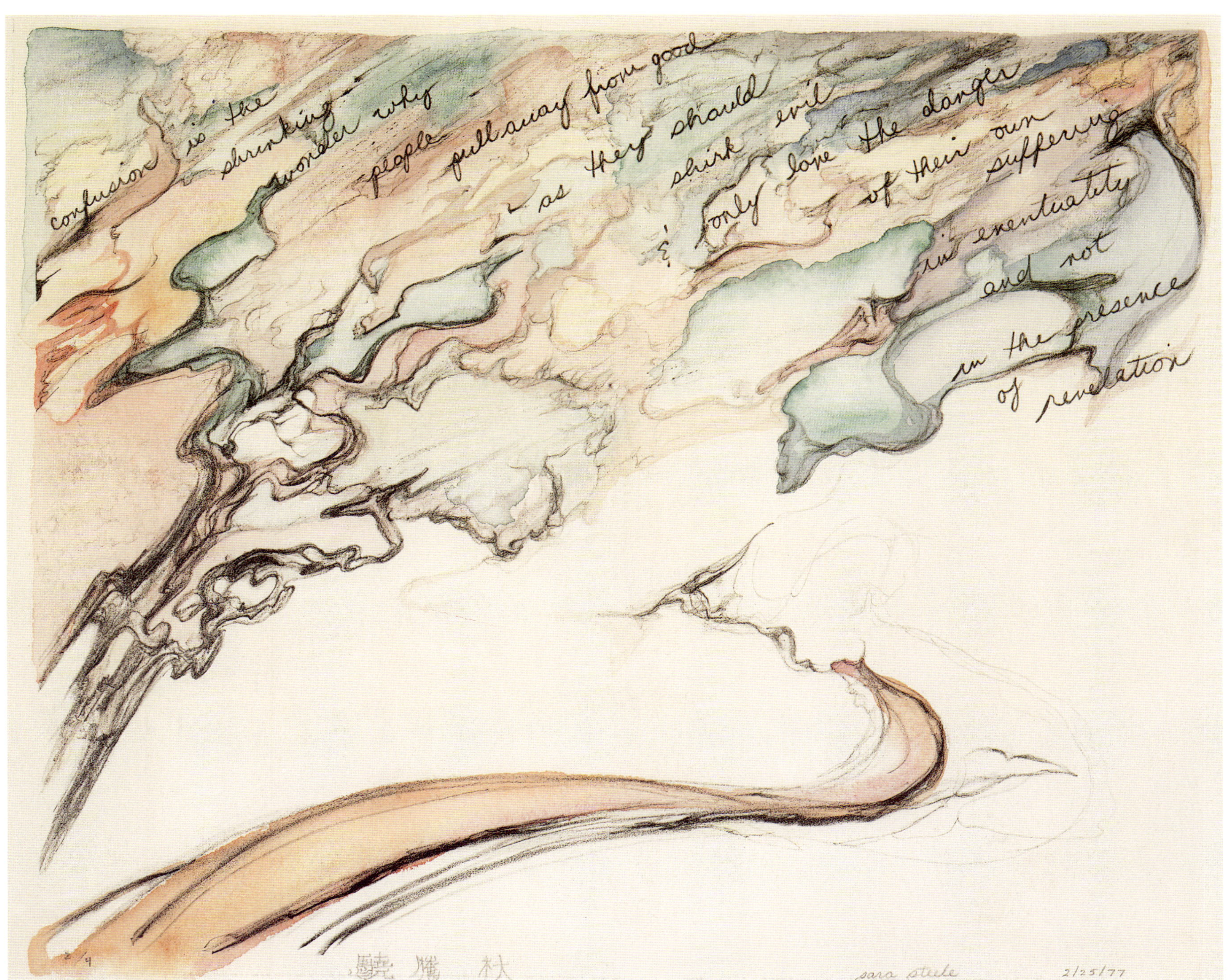

Spirited Charger/Standing Alone, 1977

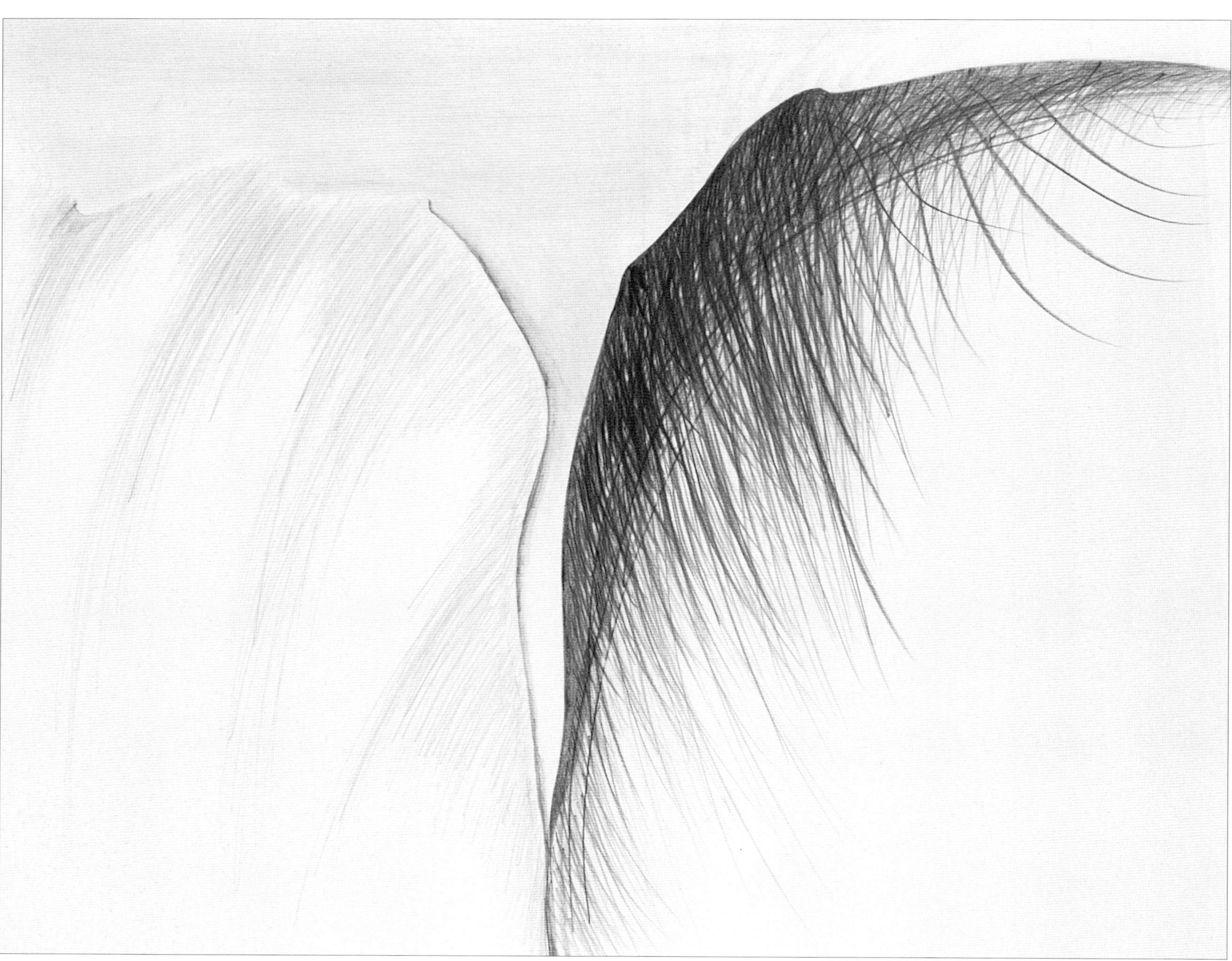

Winged Form I, 1991

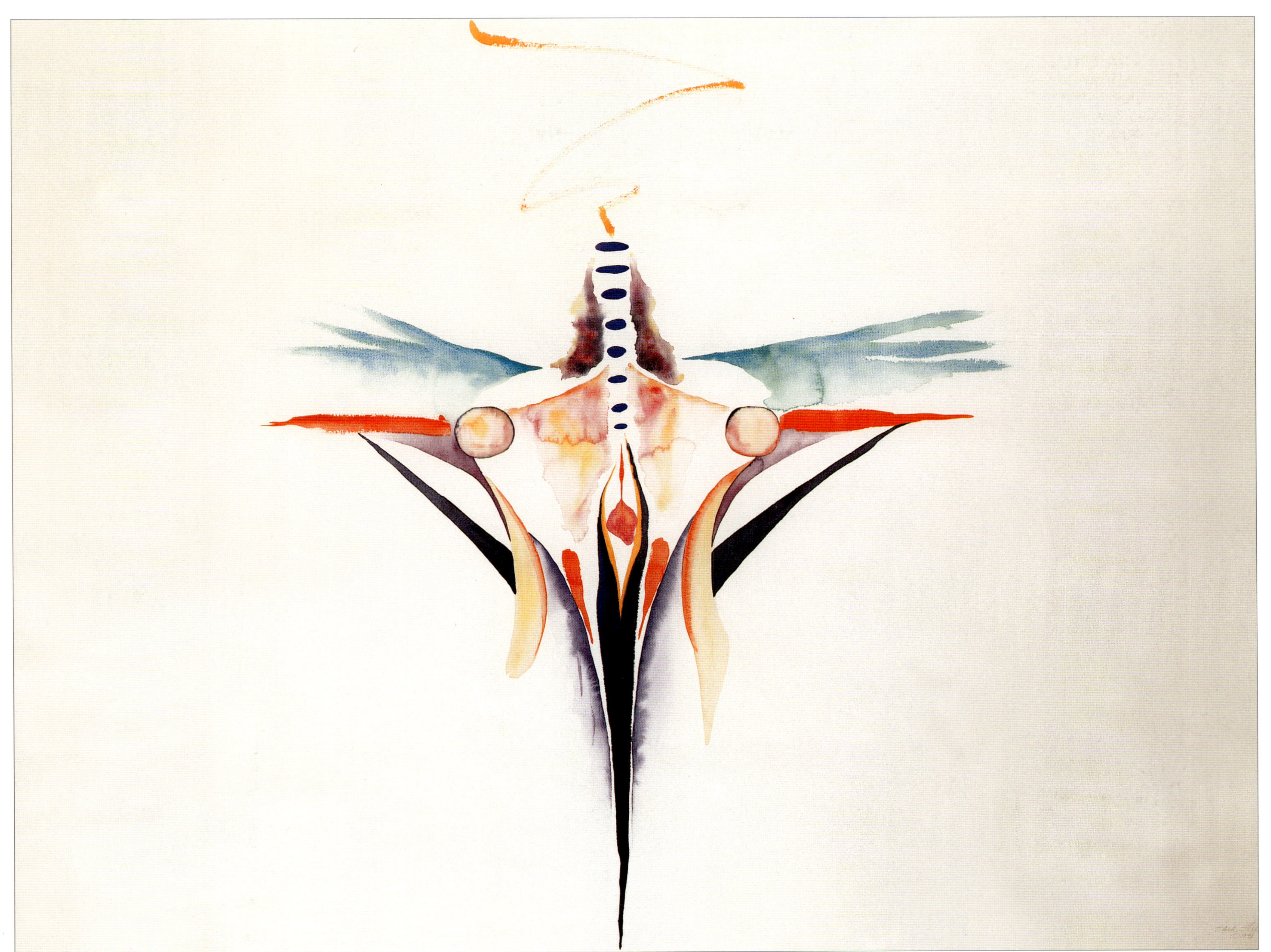

The Struggle to Remember, 1991

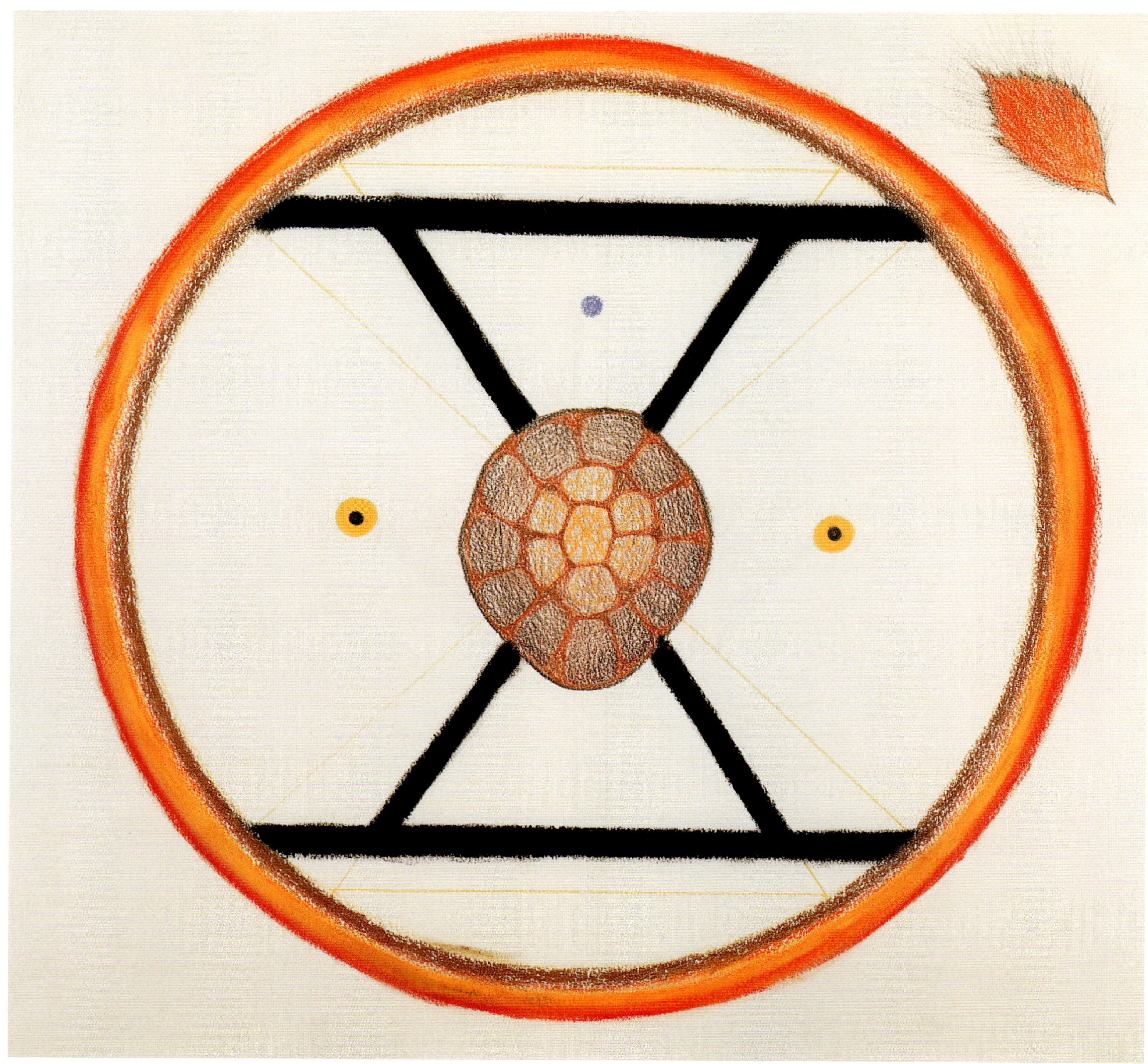

Hex Sign, 1991

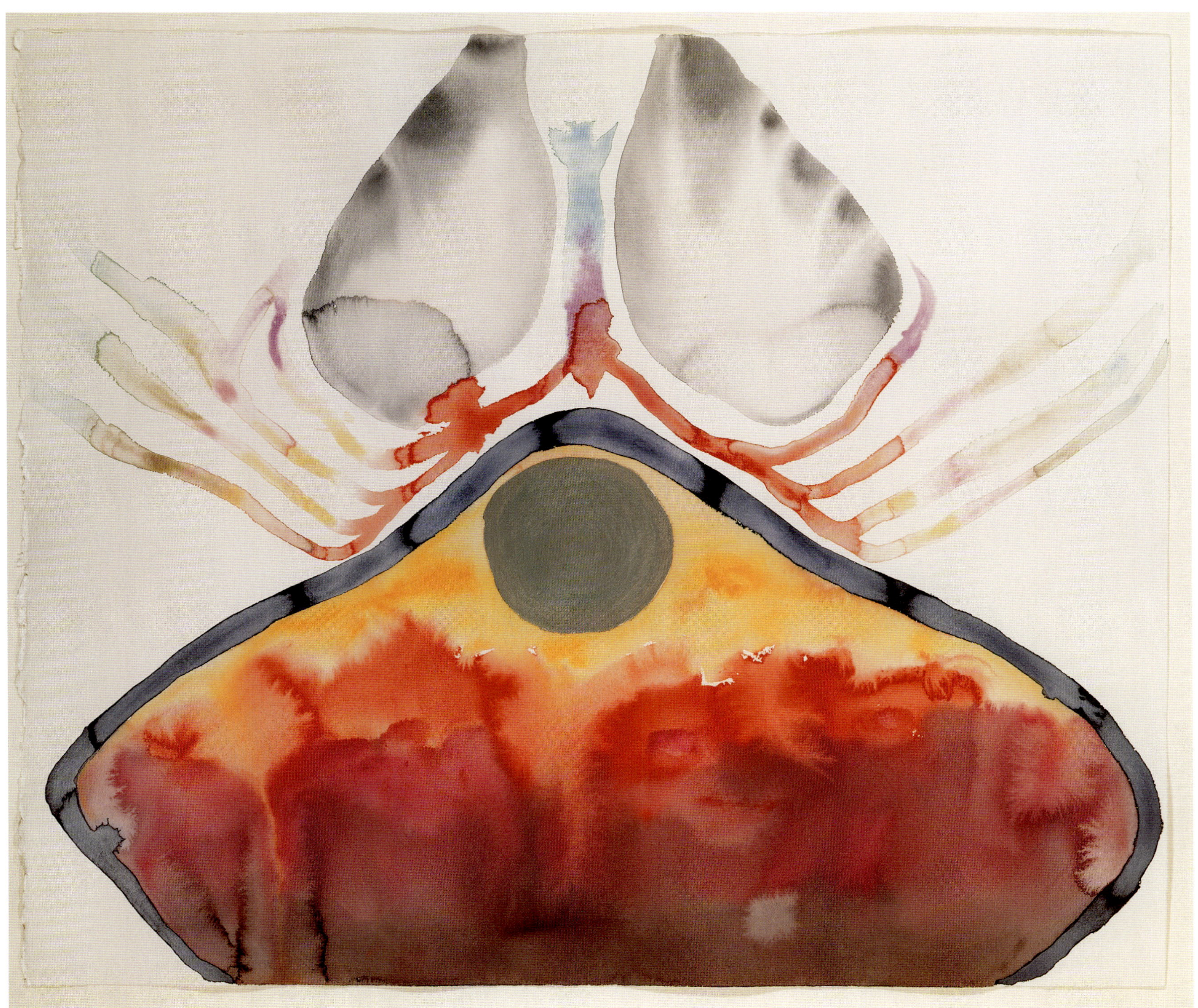

Solar Plexus/Iron Ball, 1992

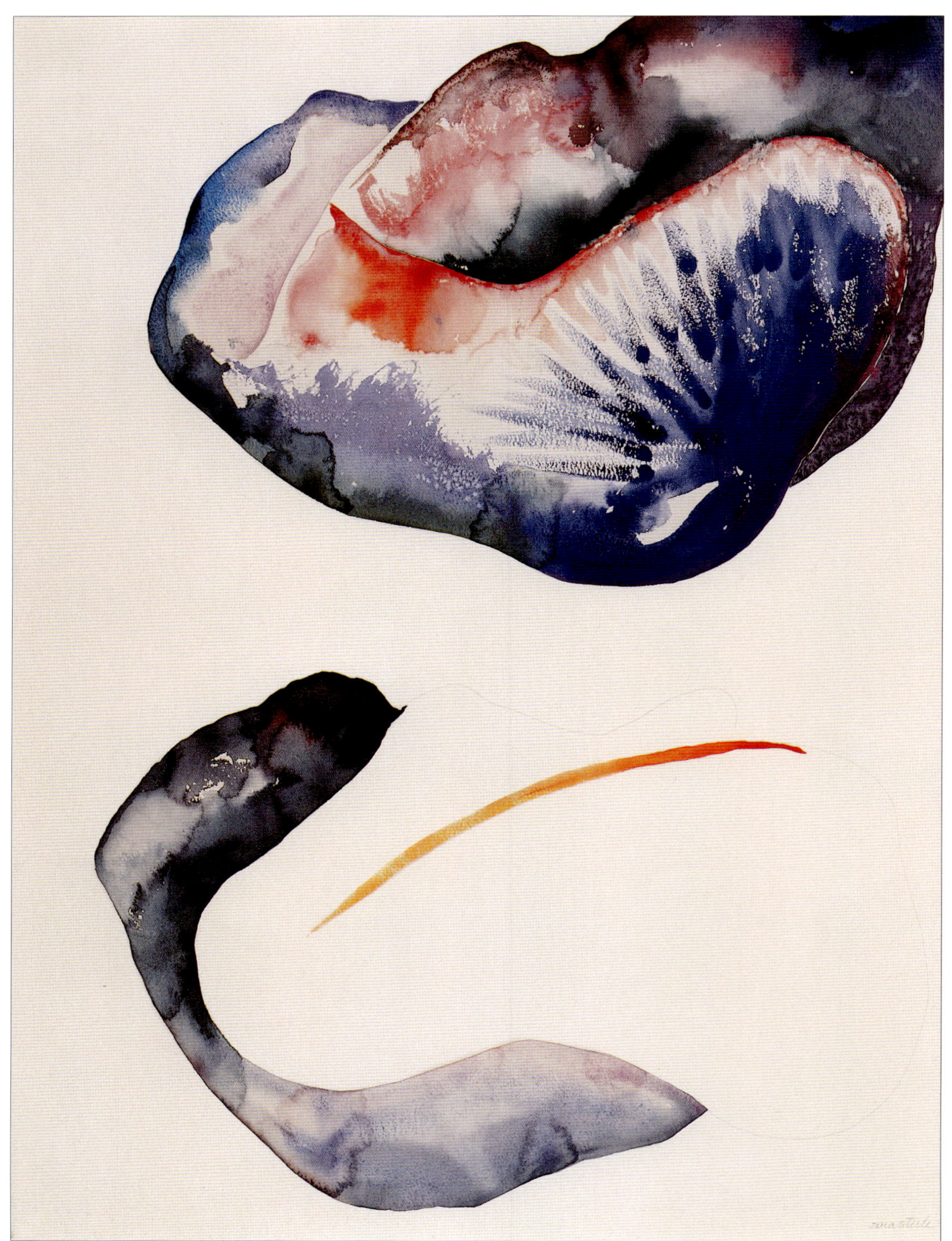

Imperfect Fit (The Kiss), 1991

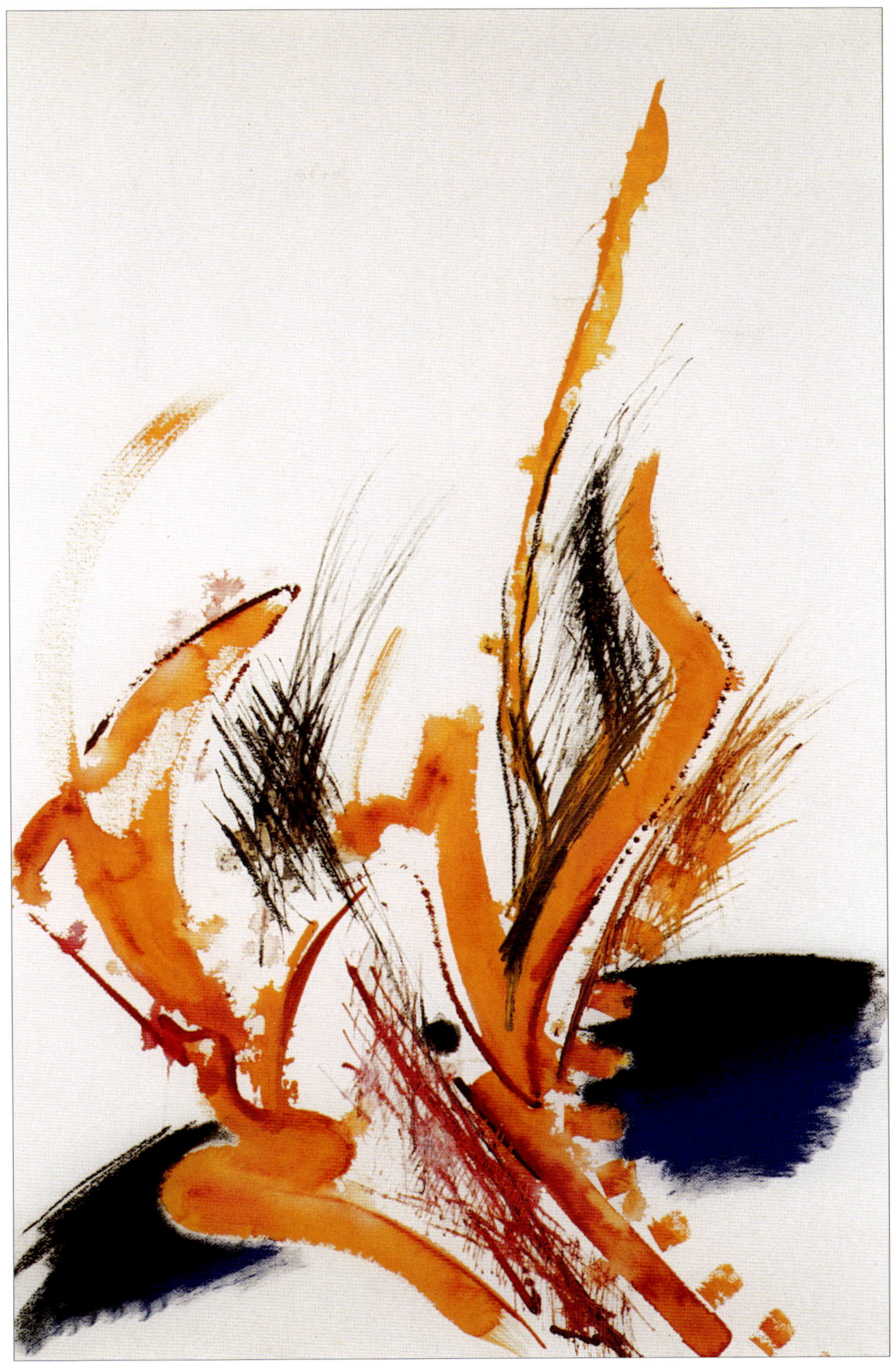

Untitled (Dancer), 1991

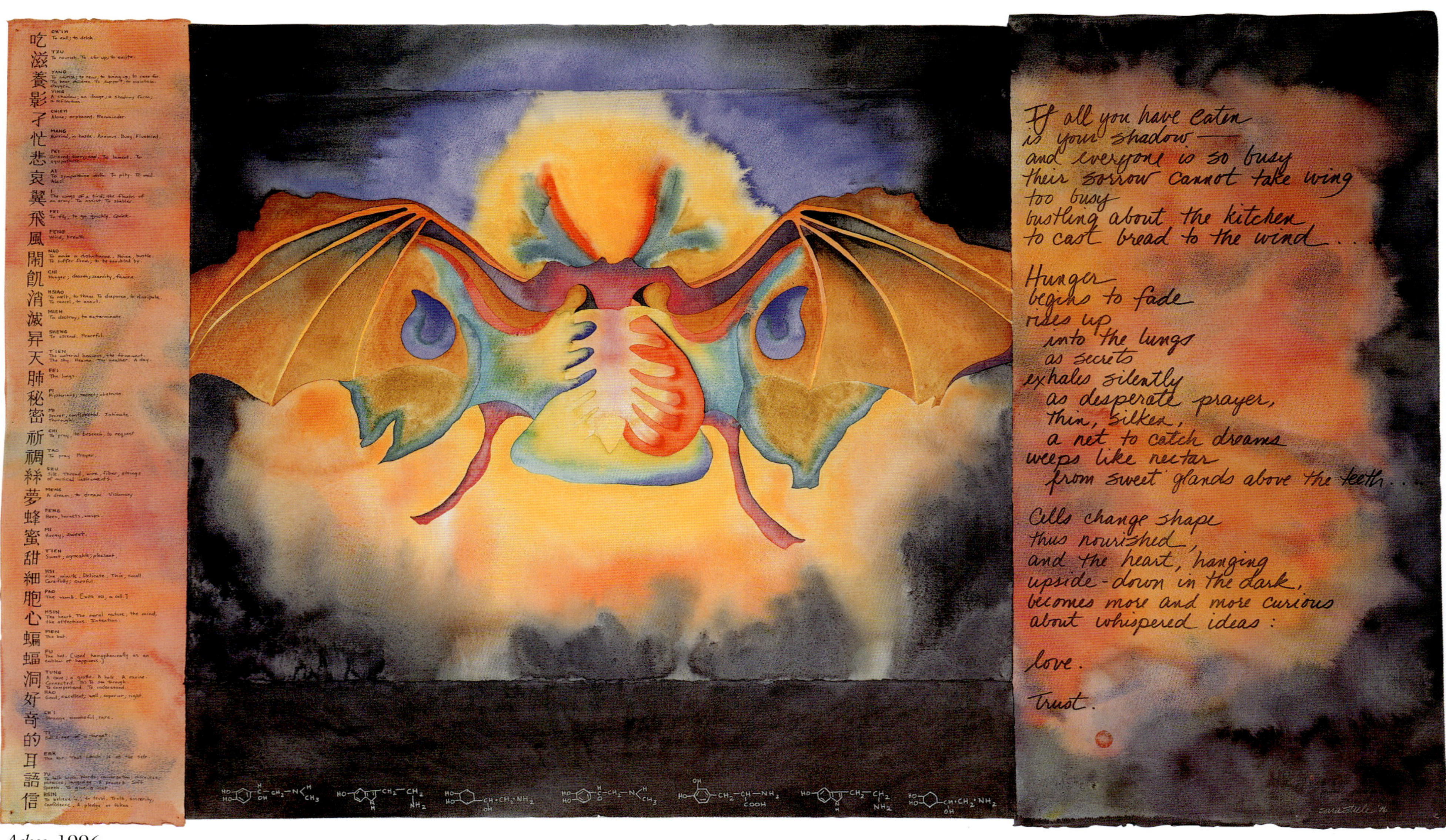
吃滋養影子忙悲哀翼飛風鬧飢消滅昇天肺秘密祈禱絲夢蜂蜜甜細胞心蝙蝠洞好奇的耳語信
If all you have eaten
is your shadow —
and everyone is so busy
their sorrow cannot take wing
too busy
bustling about the kitchen
to cast bread to the wind . . .
Hunger
begins to fade
rises up
into the lungs
as secrets
exhales silently
as desperate prayer,
thin, silken,
a net to catch dreams
weeps like nectar
from sweet glands above the teeth . . .
Cells change shape
thus nourished,
and the heart, hanging
upside-down in the dark,
becomes more and more curious
about whispered ideas:
love.
Trust.

Ashes, 1996

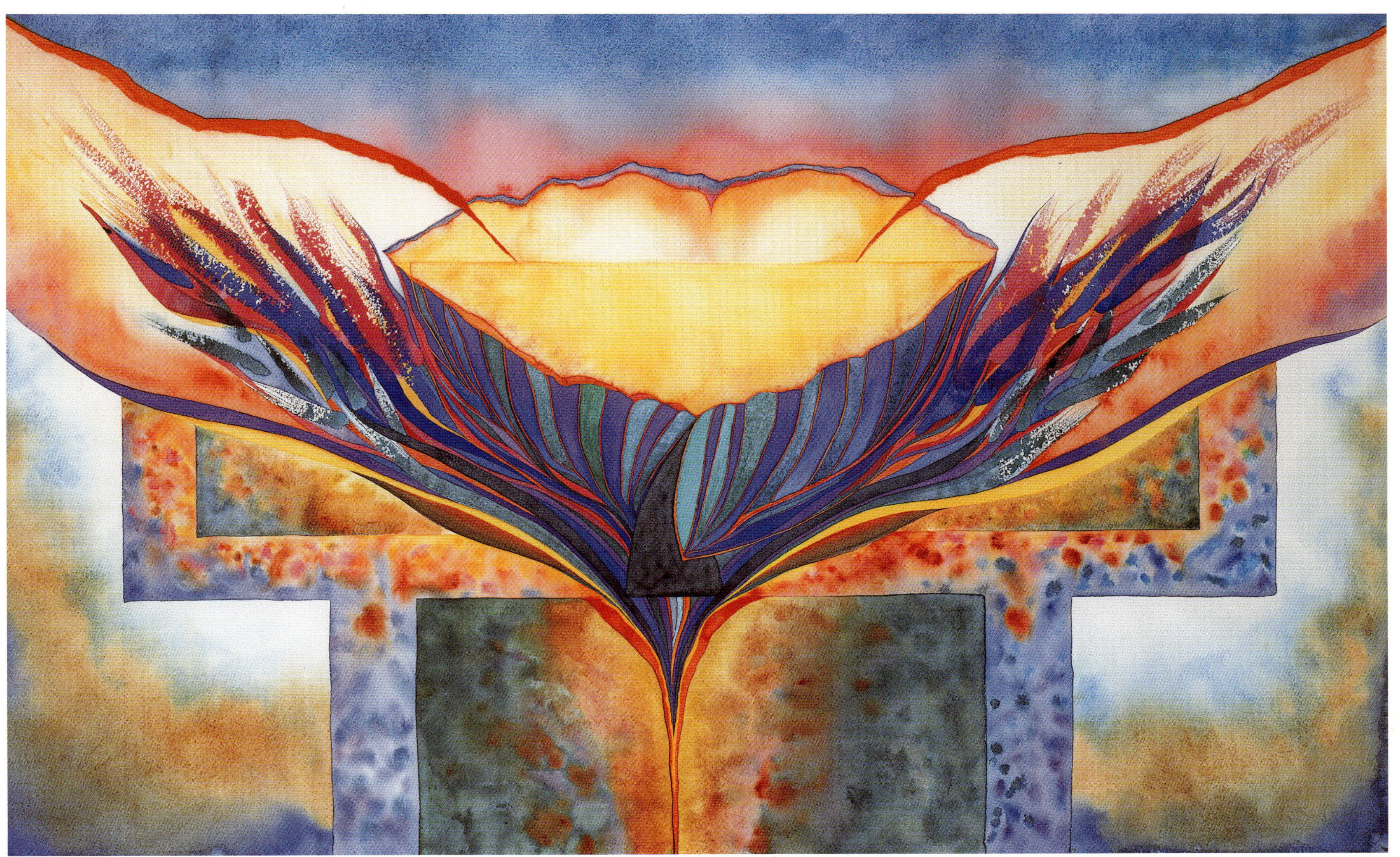

Alterpiece, 1991

List of Plates and Attributions

All paintings are watercolor unless otherwise noted.

1970 (Sweet Sixteen)
1970, oil pastel on board
19.875h x 15.25w
Collection of the Artist
Philadelphia, PA

Abiquiu Dam I
1998, 22.375h x 17.625w
Collection of Ted and Emily Warm
Boulder, CO

Abiquiu Dam II
1998, 18h x 22w
Collection of Z. and R. Gepner
Philadelphia, PA

Abstract #7
1993, 7.25h x 9w

Alizarin Hills
1987, 3.25h x 13w
Collection of the Artist
Philadelphia, PA

Alizarin Wing
1981, 7h x 9.5w
Collection of Christina Sickles Merchant
Bloomfield, NJ

Along the Road to Santa Fe (the Skin of the Planet)
1981, 21.25h x 28.75w
Collection of the Artist
Philadelphia, PA

Alterpiece
1991, 25.5h x 40.25w
Collection of Lauren Grammar
Tucson, AZ

Amazon Botanicals
1991, 40h x 29.5w
Collection of Janet and Woody Dries
Wilmington, DE

Amish Quilt/Song of Four
1988, 12h x 15w

Anemone and Bird of Paradise
1992, 13h x 13w
Collection of Francis Guarnaccia
Philadelphia, PA

Arianna (longing like Icarus, seeing like Hawk)
1990, 22h x 30w
Collection of Daniel Gottlieb
Cherry Hill, NJ

Arianna (River of Silver)
1986, 20h x 26.5w
Collection of Bill Harvey
Philadelphia, PA

Artless Blossom
1980, 8h x 4.5w
Collection of the Artist
Philadelphia, PA

Ashes
1996
watercolor, colored pencil and ink on mortised paper
30.25h x 52w
Collection of Rhoda Toperzer
Philadelphia, PA

Beloved Aire
1995, 22.375h x 27.875w
Collection of Janet and Woody Dries
Wilmington, DE

Bertha's Birthday Roses
1982, 11h x 13w
Collection of Charles N.K. Cluxton
Baltimore, MD

Big Rock Dawn I
1990, 7h x 10w
Collection of Dr. Judith McFadden
Philadelphia, PA

Big Rock Dawn III
1991, 25.5h x 40w
Collection of Janice Williams
Haverford, PA

Big Sur (Lemon Sky)
2002, 4.25h x 6.25w

Bioluminescence
1986, 10h x 13.375w
Collection of Dr. Judith McFadden
Philadelphia, PA

Birds of Paradise I
1997, 22.5h x 22w

Bloodroot
2002, 11h x 15w
Collection of Beth Van Vleck
Philadelphia, PA

Blue-lipped Cattleya
1992, 11.5h x 11.5w
Collection of Sharon Tennyson
Narberth, PA

Brasil
1980, 6.5h x 6.625w

Brassolaeliocattleya Cliftonia 'Magnifica'
1981, 10.5h x 12.75w
Collection of Gerald Paul Leube
Glenside, PA

Bryce Canyon
1981, 8.75h x 14.875w
Collection of Dr. Hubertus Wohl
Freiburg, Germany

Cacti and Agave
1994, 11h x 11.25w
Collection of Donna M. Foster
Mullica Hill, NJ

Canary in a Coal Mine
1998, 22.25h x 30.25w

Castaway Cymbidium
2004, 11.25h x 15w

Cathleen's Mountains
2002, 25.625h x 40.25w

Cattleya Creatura
1999, 14.875h x 22.375w
Collection of Dr. Jeanne L. Sebaugh
and Diane M. Booth
Columbia, MO

Cattleya Nancy Off
1996, 29.875h x 22.375w
Collection of Fay Bullitt
Philadelphia, PA

Cattleya Quintet
1993, 11.5h x 11.25w
Collection of Pat Piro
Lafayette Hill, PA

Cattleya Skinneri,
from the Endangered Orchids series
1989, 15h x 14w
Collection of Nini Melvin
Wendell, MA

Christina's Flowers
1984, 14h x 10.5w
Private Collection

Comice Pears I
1995, 14.875h x 19.125w
Collection of Janice Williams
Haverford, PA

Comice Pears III
1998, 19.25h x 15w
Collection of James P. and Nancy Julian
Philadelphia, PA

Coral
2002, 9.5h x 3w
Collection of Amy Weissman and Pat Martin
Bainbridge Island, WA

Cyclamen (seeing blue)
1984, 10.25h x 13.5w
Collection of Connie and Sam Katz
Philadelphia, PA

Cymbidium Anna Marie Sunshine
1984, 13.5h x 10.5w
Collection of Ann Marie Donohue
Glenside, PA

Cynoches chlorichilorii
1981, 10.5h x 12.75w
Collection of Rich Rudin
Elkins Park, PA

Dark Laeliocattleya
1996, 18h x 22.375w
Collection of Manon Floquet
Moorestown, NJ

Dendrobium Golden Blossom 'Venus'
1987, 15h x 22.5w

Dendrobium Small Dowan
1998, 22.5h x 30.25w
Collection of Cathy Barlow and Susan Karol Martel
Philadelphia, PA

Dendrobiums, Phalaenopsis
2002, 51h x 32.5w

Diamond Head & Punchbowl from Tantalus
(pre-Colonial Visions) (diptych)
1996, 10h x 44w
Collection of Lyndra J. Bills
Lancaster, PA

Drake's Bay, Point Reyes
1992, 24.5h x 72w
Provenance: Pamela Bogle, San Jose, CA
Jennifer Fox, Montrose, CO

Dublin Orchids: Phragmepedium Sedni
1978, watercolor and pencil, 9h x 12w
Private Collection
Philadelphia, PA

Dying Blossoms
1979, 6.5h x 8.5w
Collection of Jonathan Harrington
Philadelphia, PA

Eclipse/Plane Dream
1981, 11h x 10w
Collection of Eileen Courtney
Media, PA

Encyclia cochleata,
from the Endangered Orchids series
1989, 14h x 15w
Collection of Barbara G. Taylor
Fayetteville, AR

Fan Coral
1983, 9.25h x 13.25w
Collection of David and Jennifer Robkin
Philadelphia, PA

Fêng/Abundance of Light
1986, 14.75h x 21w
Collection of Cynthia Lacy-Stallworth
Philadelphia, PA

Firephal
1993, 11.25h x 11w
Private Collection

Flame
1986, 11h x 4.375w
Collection of Bill Harvey
Philadelphia, PA

Found/Yü
1980, 12.5h x 7.5w
Collection of the Artist
Philadelphia, PA

Fractured Light/Night
1983, 10.5h x 13.5w
Collection of Frank and Terry Foster
Chester Springs, PA

French Irises
1992, 17.5h x 22w
Collection of Meg Wallace & Timothy McDermott
Herndon, VA

From Big Rock
1996, 23h x 18.25w
Collection of Elizabeth Harrington
Potomac, MD

From Pu'u Pehe Cove, Manele Bay, Lana'i
1995, 21h x 28w
Collection of Gary Gottlieb and Derri Shtasel
Chestnut Hill, MA

From Wellfleet at Night (RECTO) and (VERSO)
1998, 6.25h x 8.5w
Collection of Cathleen Crain and Niel Tashima
Turlock, CA

Fuchsia Magnolia
1998, 22.625h x 30.125w
Collection of Liberty Property Trust
Malvern, PA

Gekkos in Paradise
1988, 15.5h x 14.75w
Collection of Meg Wallace
Herndon, VA

Gerald's Phalaenopsis
1982, 10.5h x 12.75w
Collection of Jane Mastro
San Diego, CA

Grape Vine and Daylily Buds
2000, 11.25h x 14.25w
Collection of Beth and Don Mittica
Lafayette Hill, PA

Hachiya Persimmons
2002, 11.25h x 14.875w
Collection of Joanna and Robert Robinson
Philadelphia, PA

Halcyon Waterlilies
1985, 15h x 12.5w
Private Collection

Halibut Point, from the Quarry series
1992, 20h x 25.5w
Collection of Lisa Shalett
Chappaqua, NY

Halibut Point II, from the Quarry series
1995, 20.25h x 25.75w

Hawai'ian Landscape: Pale Orange Sky
1998, 6h x 4w
Private Collection

Hawai'ian Landscape: Poipu (cadmium yellow deep sky)
1998, 6h x 4w

Hawai'ian Landscape: Poipu (cadmium yellow light sky)
1998, 4h x 6w
Collection of Jill Davidson and Kevin Eberman
San Francisco, CA

Hawai'ian Landscape: Poipu (turquoise sky)
1998, 4h x 6w
Collection of Jill Davidson and Kevin Eberman
San Francisco, CA

Hawai'ian Landscape: Rose Dore Sky
1998, 6h x 4w
Private Collection

Heart Healing
1983, 14h x 28.5w
Collection of Michelle Castiglioni
Hatfield, PA

Heliconia
1994, 17.5h x 22.25w
Collection of Claudette and Jim Leyden
Malvern, PA

Heritage Ceramics
1991, 16.875h x 10.375w
Collection of Leah Buturain and Dr. Edward Schneider
Los Angeles, CA

Hex Sign
1991, mixed media on paper
20.25h x 22w

Higo Iris
1989, 15h x 20w
Collection of Jolyn Kucko
Duluth, GA

Hollyhocks
1996, 20.25h x 40.5w

Hollyhocks with Sunspots/Freedom Flowers
1998, 29.75h x 41.75w

Holy Cow/Shape Shifter
1997, 20.5h x 21w
Collection of Michelle Castiglioni
Hatfield, PA

i bleed (1)
1982, 14.75h x 14.5w
Collection of Davia L. Wilson
Reston, VA

i bleed (2)
1982, 14.75h x 14.5w

Imperfect Fit (The Kiss)
1991, watercolor and pencil
29.75h x 22.25w

Ingrid's Quilt
1978, watercolor and ink
6.75h x 5.875w
Collection of Ingrid Brown
Flourtown, PA

Iris Unfolding
1982, 10.5h x 12.75w
Collection of Jane Mastro
San Diego, CA

Irises from D.K.
2000, 11h x 15w
Collection of Marilyn and John Anthony
Philadelphia, PA

Jamaican Eggplants I
2000, 7h x 10.5w
Collection of Kathy Harris
Chalfont, PA

Jamaican Eggplants II
2000, 7.375h x 11.375w
Collection of Monica R. Fread
Philadelphia, PA

Kô/Molting
1980, 6.25h x 6.25w
Collection of Janet Stribling
Knoxville, TN

La Frontera/Seamless Dream
1988, 21.25h x 28.75w
Collection of Suzanne Walsh
Bryn Mawr, PA

Laeliocattleya Moonwind
1996, 20.75h x 27.375w
Collection of Fay Bullitt
Philadelphia, PA

Lake Visions (No Soap Radio)
1988, 22.25h x 17.75w
Collection of Marilyn Leventhal Fraser
Scottsdale, AZ

Landscape #21
1994, 4h x 6w
Collection of Gisha and Ray Berkowitz
Philadelphia, PA

Lava Flow/Alaska (triptych)
1986, 17.75h x 21.5w
Collection of David and Jennifer Robkin
Philadelphia, PA

Leaf Skeleton/Spirit Leaves
1987, 10.5h x 14w
Collection of the Artist
Philadelphia, PA

Lemons in Blue Bowl
2000, 11h x 15w
Collection of Swan S. Stull and Marty Gates
Lewisburg, PA

Lily Petals (1)
2002, 5.5h x 7.5w
Collection of Davia L. Wilson
Reston, VA

Long Relaxed Tulip
1994, 18h x 6w
Private Collection
Nederland, CO

Love Letter/Blue Orchid
1983, 8.5h x 9w

Love Propaganda
1994, 5.25h x 5.25w
Collection of Drs. Roz Warner and
W. Michael Hogan
Thousand Oaks, CA

Madrid
2001, 11.25h x 15w

Magic Tulip
1983, 9.5h x 13w
Collection of Sarah Wunsch
Brookline, MA

Magnolia (A Season of Mourning)
1982, 11h x 13w
Collection of the Artist
Philadelphia, PA

Maine Tears
1988, 22h x 30w
Collection of Harold and Claudia Goodman
Philadelphia, PA

May Storm in Johnstown
1981, 11.5h x 9w
Collection of Bernadette Gallen
Berwyn, PA

Mellonhead Tea
2000, 11.25h x 14w
Collection of Janice Williams
Haverford, PA

Mesa Lands, New Mexico
2000, 11h x 15w
Collection of Stacey Meadows
Elkins Park, PA

Metamorphogenesis: Nascimiento
1997, 15h x 22.5w
Collection of Fay Bullitt
Philadelphia, PA

Migration
2001, 11h x 15w
Collection of Dana Parnes and Moshe Engelberg
San Diego, CA

Ming Mên (Red and Blue)
1982, 6.5h x 9w
Collection of Bernadette Gallen
Berwyn, PA

Mist Rising Near Big Sur
2000, 11.25h x 14w
Collection of Drs. Maria Garcia-Alegré and
Domingo Guinea
Madrid, Spain

Modern Classic Celebration
2004, 11.125h x 14w

Moon Over Montana
1989, 51.5h x 97w
Collection of Pat Gozemba
Salem, MA

Mormodes species,
from the Endangered Orchids series
1989, 14h x 15w
Collection of Dr. Judith McFadden
Philadelphia, PA

Na Pali Coast II
1998, 6.5h x 4.5w
Private Collection

Na Pali Coast III
1998, watercolor and gold leaf
22.75h x 30w
Private Collection
Philadelphia, PA

Na Pali Coast IV
1998, 19.375h x 25.125w
Collection of Niel Tashima and Cathleen Crain
Turlock, CA

Na Pali Coast V
1999, 26.5h x 22.25w
Collection of Janis and David Glusman
Merion, PA

Na Pali Coast, Kaua'i
1996, 22.25h x 30w
Collection of Janice Williams
Haverford, PA

Nasturtiums I
1992, 23h x 23w
Collection of Janice Mackenzie
New Hope, PA

Nasturtiums III
1998, 11h x 14w
Private Collection
Malvern, PA

Near Manele Bay, Lana'i
2002, 4h x 11.1875w

Neptune's Daughter
1980, 10.125h x 10.5w
Collection of Michelle Castiglioni
Hatfield, PA

New Land
1983, 13.5h x 11.5w
Collection of David and Jennifer Robkin
Philadelphia, PA

New Mexico Quartet: Zia
1981, 6h x 8.5w
Collection of Susan and Neil Greenberg
Langhorne, PA

Night-blooming Cereus
1997, 17h x 22w
Collection of Mary Ann Malhame
Longboat Key, FL

Nuclear Family Holocaust
1992, watercolor, ink, gold leaf
30h x 22.25w

Oh! Karen...
1985, 24.375h x 30w
Collection of David and Jennifer Robkin
Philadelphia, PA

Oh! Karen... II
1985, 9.625h x 6.375w
Private Collection

Oh! Karen... III
1985, 9.625h x 4.125w
Private Collection

Olympic Range from Whidbey Island
1991, 32h x 81w
Collection of Bob Inman & Margie Linn
Swarthmore, PA

One Short
1990, 11h x 5.5w
Collection of Judy Berkman
Philadelphia, PA

Orange Gladiolas
1990, 22h x 21w
Collection of Marjorie Wetherill
Bala Cynwyd, PA

Orchid Poster - LL
1979, watercolor and ink
6h x 6w
Collection of the Artist
Philadelphia, PA

Orchid Poster - LR - (Laeliocattleya Erin)
1979, watercolor and ink
6.75h x 6.325w
Collection of the Artist
Philadelphia, PA

Orchid Poster - UL - (Cymbidium Nicolansianum II)
1979, watercolor and ink
6h x 6.125w
Collection of the Artist
Philadelphia, PA

Orchid Poster - UR - (Cymbidium Nicolansianum I)
1979, watercolor and ink
6.325h x 6.25w
Collection of the Artist
Philadelphia, PA

Oscoda Forest Fire
1988, 5h x 5.5w

Pacific Pieces
1998, watercolor on mortised paper
22.25h x 45w
Collection of Lillian H. Young
Fairfax, VA

Painting for a Winter Baby
1992, 6h x 8w
Collection of The Pinkenson-Feldman Family
Bala Cynwyd, PA

Pale Magnolia
2004, 22.75h x 30.25w

Paphiopedilum concolor and P. bellatulum, from the Endangered Orchids series
1989, 15h x 14w
Collection of Mark A. McClurg
and Keith H. Watanabe
Philadelphia, PA

Paphiopedilum Rothschildianum, from the Endangered Orchids series
1989, 14h x 14w
Collection of Mark A. McClurg
and Keith H. Watanabe
Philadelphia, PA

Paphiopedilum Sukhakulii (KAK)
1981, 10.5h x 12.75w
Collection of Karen Kelly
Pittsburgh, PA

Parrot Tulips
1982, 10.5h x 12.75w
Collection of Elizabeth Jacobs Klatzkin
Yardley, PA

Pears with Cast Paper Bowl
1999, 11.25h x 14.875w
Collection of Dayle Friedman
and David Ferleger
Philadelphia, PA

Peony, Freesia, Irises and Bells of Ireland
2000, 22.75h x 22.25w
Collection of Dorothy Ernst
Doylestown, PA

Peppers, Eggplants and Honey Tangerines
1998, 24h x 41.25w
Collection of Dr. Jeanne L. Sebaugh
and Diane M. Booth
Columbia, MO

Peppers, Green Plate, Blue Bottle
1996, 22.375h x 28.125w
Collection of Sandra L. Bloom, MD
Philadelphia, PA

Phalaenopsis
1994, 18.5h x 22.5w
Collection of Mimi Rose
Philadelphia, PA

Phalaenopsis Revival
2000, 20.125h x 20.5w
Collection of Leonard M. Jensen
Wyndmoor, PA

Phals for Patranna
2004, 26h x 40.75w

Phragmepedium besseae, from the Endangered Orchids series
1989, 15h x 14w
Collection of Barbara Lanning
Santa Fe, NM

Plume Poppies (foliage) II
1995, 22.375h x 28.25w

Plume Poppy (foliage) I
1993, 22.5h x 22.5w
Collection of Laurentine Fromm
Philadelphia, PA

Point Lobos, Carmel I (diptych)
1998, 51h x 92w
Collection of Gary Pickens and Patricia Riskind
Wilmett, IL

Point Lobos, Carmel II
1998, 14.625h x 21w
Collection of Rich and Pam Genga
Philadelphia, PA

Poipu, Sunset
2000, 7.75h x 9w
Collection of Susan L. Lytle
Philadelphia, PA

Poppies
1996, 3.125h x 29.875w
Collection of Ellie and Stuart Fine
Bryn Mawr, PA

Q'tuba for Karen
1994, watercolor; ink calligraphy by Betsy Teutsch
22h x 30w
Collection of Karen Leventhal and Mark Wolman
Orlando, FL

Red Anemones
1991, 30h x 22w
Collection of Mel M. Steele
Delray Beach, FL

Red Bartlett Pears
2004, 17h x 16w

Remembering (M.R.)
1988, 12h x 16w
Collection of Janice and Dick Williams
Haverford, PA

RE-scape
1979, 5.625h x 6.5w
Private Collection

River of Fire
1982, 22h x 30w
Collection of Barry Belt
Yardley, PA

Rose and Eucalyptus
1985, 12h x 12w
Collection of Maureen Abbott
Oreland, PA

Rose of Sharon II
2000, 11.25h x 15.125w
Collection of Dr. Jeanne L. Sebaugh
and Diane M. Booth
Columbia, MO

Royal Velvet Irises
1987, 11h x 13w
Collection of Gerald Paul Leube
Glenside, PA

Sacred Gate
2004, 22.25h x 30w

Salem Dahlias
1993, 22.5h x 22.75w
Collection of Pat Gozemba
Salem, MA

Sarah's Bouquet
1982, 10.5h x 12.75w
Collection of Paul Korshin
Wyncote, PA

Scott's Tree Peonies
2004, 26h x 40.75w

Sepiascapes/Providence (three panels)
1981
Collection of Rachel Smith
Lexington, NC

Setting Sunflowers from Lisa
2000, 11.25h x 14.25w
Collection of Lisa DiNardo
Wayne, PA

Shadows at Sandy's (Seeing Patterns)
1998, 17.5h x 22.5w
Collection of David A. Berkowitz
Somerville, MA

Shop in Christianstad, St. Croix
1998, 11h x 15w
Collection of Diane and Larry Loebell
Philadelphia, PA

Slc. Redzac Carteria 'Flame'
1992, 22h x 29.5w
Collection of Carole King
Lake Toxaway, NC

Solar Plexus/Iron Ball
1992, watercolor, metal powders
25.5h x 30w

Song for Bilbao
2002, 17.5h x 22.5w

Spathiphyllum
1992, 11.5h x 11.5w
Collection of Gary Gottlieb
Chestnut Hill, MA

Sphoenix (Sphenoid Totem)
1985, 10.5h x 9w
Collection of the Artist
Philadelphia, PA

Spirited Charger/Accident
1991, hand-colored lithograph
12h x 14.5w

Spirited Charger/Standing Alone
1977, hand-colored lithograph
12h x 14.5w

Squash Blossoms
1988, 23.5h x 17.75w
Collection of Nancy Post, Ph.D.
Philadelphia, PA

Staghorn Fern
1996, 22.25h x 29.75w
Collection of Margaret Krebs
Palo Alto, CA

Star Magnolias
2003, 12.375h x 15w

Still Life with Tomatillo
2002, 12.625h x 16w
Collection of Ann Homan
Philadelphia, PA

Storm Lillies (Bittersweet Slow Burn)
1988, 14.5h x 15w
Collection of Janice Shinholster
Philadelphia, PA

Stormy Phalaenopsis
1997, 16.125h x 12.125w
Collection of Jill Heppenheimer
Sante Fe, NM

Study in Orange and Blue
1991, 16h x 20w
Collection of Sandra Tomita and Larry Berkowitz
San Diego, CA

Suicide Note
1971, ink on paper
5.5h x 7.625w
Collection of the Artist

Sunflower Leaves at Dusk
2000, 11h x 14w
Collection of David A. Berkowitz
Somerville, MA

Sunflowers
1995, 22.375h x 29.785w
Collection of Melinda Fudge and Timothy Smith
Rydal, PA

Sunset, Diamond Head
1998, 10h x 22.375w
Collection of Debra L. Rappaport
Philadelphia, PA

Teal Columns II
1998, 4.125h x 6.125w
Collection of Leonard M. Jensen
Wyndmoor, PA

Tenerife
1980, watercolor and ink
7h x 4.325w
Collection of Barry Belt
Yardley, PA

Terrestrial
1990, 22h x 30w
Collection of Christina Sickles Merchant
Bloomfield, NJ

The Chemistry of Feeling
1979, 22.375h x 17.875w
Collection of Joel Elkes and Jo Rhodes
New Albany, IN

The Forces of Attraction (four panels)
1984, pastel on paper
31h x 96w
Collection of Rick Josiassen and Rita Shaughnessy
Philadelphia, PA

The Last Sunflower
1993, 13.75h x 11w
Collection of Fred and Joy Stocke Young
Stockton, NJ

The Layers of the Mind
1987, 19h x 29.5w
Collection of Maureen Abbott
Oreland, PA

The Point I
1992, 22h x 8.5w

The Point II
1992, 15h x 9.875w
Collection of Amy Williams
New York, NY

The Point IV
1998, 11.75h x 11.75w

The Riots of Spring
2004, 26h x 40.75w

The Spectrum Range
1983, 15.25h x 7.75w

The Struggle to Remember
1991, 38.5h x 51.5w

The Towers Go Down
2001, 4.5h x 4w
Collection of John Riebow
Hatfield, PA

Three Tree Peonies (Allen's Lane)
2002, 11.125h x 15w
Collection of Joyce King
Long Beach, CA

Tod: The Presence of Absence
1997, watercolor, ink, gold leaf, parrot feathers
21h x 30w

Tornado Sweet Pea
1992, 12.5h x 22.5w
Collection of Susan and Neil Greenberg
Langhorne, PA

Tree Peony
2002, 15.25h x 19.125w

Tulip Fields
1985, 7.75h x 6.75w
Collection of Larry Loebell
Philadelphia, PA

Turkey Roses
1992, 18.5h x 14w
Collection of Gail Birnbaum
Jamaican Plain, MA

Untitled (dancer)
1991, watercolor, pastel, charcoal
40.25h x 25.75w
Collection of Davia L. Wilson
Reston, VA

Vermillion Amaryllis
1999, 17.75h x 22.375w
Collection of Rudolf and Linda Staroscik
Jenkintown, PA

Whidbey Island Vetch
1992, 5.5h x 7.5w
Collection of Dorsey Donovan
Philadelphia, PA

Wild Glads
1995, 22.5h x 22.5w
Collection of Catherine Joyce
Peru, NY

Wild Red Glads
1997, 19.375h x 22.375w
Collection of the Philip and Muriel Berman
Museum of Art

Winged Form
1992, pencil and graphite
22.5h x 29w

Winged Victory
1986, 11.5h x 9w
Collection of Dr. Judith McFadden
Philadelphia, PA

Xeriscape
2004, 11.375h x 15w

XYGO
1983, 13.5h x 10w
Collection of Jane Axelrod
Andover, MA

Xygo Blooming
1984, 7.5h x 9.5w

Yellow Cattleya
1992, 11.5h x 11w
Collection of Drs. Roz Warner & W. Michael Hogan
Thousand Oaks, CA

Yuan Dan
2001, 3.25h x 5.25w

Chronology

Personal Events

1954 Born on November 25, Thanksgiving Day, in Champaign, Illinois. Family moved soon after to New York where brother Michael was born.

1959 Shortly after birth of sister Janet, family is given grandparents' home and moves to Philadelphia.

1963 Parents divorce. President Kennedy assassinated.

1966 Youngest sister, Sandy, is born.

1967 Involved with committee to start Parkway Program, the first alternative public high school in Philadelphia.

1969 Attended Girls' High School and studied art with Gladys Bloch.

1970 Left Girls' High in frustration. Studied independently with Sara Allen, who introduced her to twentieth-century American artists including Dove, Marin, O'Keeffe, Rothko, Demuth, and the Abstract Expressionists.

1971 Saw Georgia O'Keeffe exhibit at Bryn Mawr College.

1972 Selected by lottery to attend Parkway Program for final months of high school. Studied American history with curatorial staff at Independence National Park. Summer job restoring Peale portrait frames for Second Bank of the U.S. Volunteered as elementary school art teacher.

1973–4 Hospitalized for severe suicidal depression. An artist friend is murdered. Rape and several attempted rapes are endured. Committed to a psychiatric hospital again, for several months, and spent most of that time in seclusion.

1975–6 Attended a vocational school. Teacher Anne Pinkenson encouraged her to begin drawing again. Studied cranial anatomy with Dr. Andy Benjamin. Created series of hand-colored orchid prints on parchment. Later, returned to the school to teach.

1978 Traveled to England, Ireland, and Tenerife in the Canary Islands. At the National Botanical Gardens in Dublin, found scores of blooming Coelogyne cristata and made many drawings of orchids.

Visited "American Abstract Expressionists" show with Sara Allen during the opening of the East Wing of the National Gallery. Attended an holistic health conference in Philadelphia and met British acupuncturist Jack Worsely. Entered therapy.

1979 Did freelance graphic design work for Women's Resources and co-published "The Orchid Poster," which was well-received.

1980 Created two more posters and first calendar with Women's Resources. Attended workshop with Judy Chicago in NYC and met artist Cathy Weber. Worked on costumes for choreographer/dancer Nini Melvin of Sybil Dance Company. Made drawings at Foxcatcher Orchids and Longwood Gardens. The resulting paintings published as "The Orchid Calendar" in 1982.

1981 Traveled to Germany to deliver several commissioned paintings. Studied textile design at Philadelphia College of Textiles and Sciences. Traveled through the southwestern U.S. for the first time.

1982 Costume design for choreographer/dancer Mady Cantor of Anne Vachon Dance Conduit.

1983 Designed award-winning Philadelphia Flower Show exhibit for the Greater Philadelphia Orchid Society. Collaborated with furniture designer Peter Korn and other craftspeople to create several "hand-crafted spaces." Continued publishing posters and calendars with Ars Femina, an offshoot of Women's Resources. Began laying the foundation for Steeleworks, her publishing company.

1984 Commissioned to create "Consider the Alternatives" poster for SANE/Committee for a Sane Nuclear Policy. Traveled to St. Lucia and made drawings in the primary rain forest.

1985 Traveled to Paris and met architect and sculptor Jean Weinfeld during his exhibition, "Fonics." Commissioned to create poster for the National Women's Studies Association that led to a multi-year involvement with the organization. Began studying Chinese calligraphy with Cecilia Chiang.

1986 Collaborated with kaleidoscope-maker Carolyn Bennett. Moved to southern Maine and set up a studio where she created her first large landscape, "LavaFlow/Alaska."

1988 Commissioned by National Wildlife Federation to create paintings that became the "Endangered Orchids" series. Invited by Peter Korn to teach watercolor workshop at Anderson Ranch. Traveled to Montana for the first time.

1989 Created poster for feminist bookstore in Cincinnati and met community organizer Maureen Wood. Met Nancy Post and began studying systems energetics and traditional Chinese medicine. Entered therapy for a second time and began exploring her experiences of incest and trauma through her paintings.

1990–1 Taught workshops in Whidbey Island, Washington, and San Diego, California. Publishing company sold. Purchased her family home in Philadelphia.

1992 Invited by Women Against Abuse to exhibit "Nuclear Family Holocaust" for the first time. Other invitations to show and speak about the work followed. Began working with The Clothesline Project. Invited by the Women's Board of the Pennsylvania Academy of the Fine Arts (PAFA) to lead workshops for women living in shelters (lasted through 1999). Saw Martin Puryear's work.

1993 Created series of book and album covers, and the posters "Alterpiece" and "Springside." Twenty-year retrospective show, and artist-in-residence at Springside School. Large piece, "My Fortress is the Sun," is destroyed by roof leak at exhibition. Invited to create CD-ROM screensaver for the Nature Conservancy.

1994 Monograph *In Bloom* published. Collaborated with poets Anne Mugler and Daniel Moore to create chapbooks. Also worked on chapbooks for Working Writers Group and Meridian Writers Group.

1995 Traveled to the Hawaiian Islands. Saw David Nash's work. Organized public display of the Clothesline Project at the Philadelphia City Hall courtyard.

1997 Created two-year artist's residency at Friends Hospital and worked collaboratively with Janice Williams, MSW, and trauma unit in-patients. Invited to design china for Lenox. Created 10th anniversary poster for The National Clearinghouse for the Defense of Battered Women.

1998 Created *Extraordinary Art: Beyond the Museum*, two national juried shows for artists with special needs, as part of USArtists' annual exhibition of the Women's Board of PAFA. Exhibited in Carmel, California, and visited Point Lobos and Big Sur. Participated in making the video, "Somewhere Inside is the Survivor Spirit."

1999 Commissioned to create series of ecclesiastical paraments. Traveled to Spain and saw retrospective of Matta, and the works of Eduardo Chillida and Jean-Paul Agosti. Attended mosaic workshop led by Isaiah Zagar. Invited to return to Spain to exhibit in 2000.

2001 Work shown on Bainbridge Island, Washington. Began association with Seattle Children's Hospital's family violence prevention program. Commissioned to create series of digital posters for non-profit organizations. Created series of digital broadsides with poet Susan Windle. Led Art in Healing workshop for Domestic Abuse Project of Delaware County. Met TOVA/Theater of Witness founder Teya Sepinuk.

2003 Attended ARCO, the Spanish international art fair, in Madrid and visited Barcelona with artist Kathleen Kler.

2005 Mid-career retrospective exhibit at the Philip and Muriel Berman Museum of Art, Ursinus College, Collegeville, Pennsylvania; publication of *Sara Steele, Blueprints for Paradise.*

Selected Solo Exhibitions

1974 The Ambler Theater, Ambler, PA
1982 The Faculty Club of the University of Pennsylvania, Philadelphia
1983 The Hahn Gallery, Philadelphia
1984 La Salle University, Philadelphia
1984 The University of Delaware, Newark
1988 La Salle University, Connelly Library, Philadelphia
1989 Hillel Gallery, University of Cincinnati, OH
1990 *Endangered Orchids*, National Wildlife Federation Headquarters, Vienna, VA
1991 Off the Avenue Gallery, Cincinnati, OH
1992 *Nuclear Family Holocaust*, Philadelphia Electric Company Headquarters, Philadelphia
1993 *Retrospective: 20 Years*, McNeil Center for Creative Arts, Springside School, Philadelphia
1993 GRACE/Greater Reston Art Center, Reston, VA
1996 *Inside/Out*, Friends Hospital, Philadelphia
1997 *Fêng/Abundance of Light*, Raab Gallery, Chestnut Hill, PA
1997 University of Pennsylvania Women's Center, Philadelphia
1998 *Solstice: The Victory of Light*, Raab Gallery, Chestnut Hill, PA
2000 Allens Lane Art Center, Philadelphia
2000 Casa de Cultura, San Lorenzo de El Escorial, Spain
2002 Allens Lane Art Center, Philadelphia
2005 *Blueprints for Paradise*, The Philip and Muriel Berman Museum, Ursinus College, Collegeville, PA

Selected Juried, Invitational and Group Exhibitions

1979 Zoma Gallery, New York, NY
1979 Rocky Mountain National Watermedia Exhibition, Golden, CO
1980 *Groundworks*, The Philomathian Society, University of PA, Philadelphia
1981 *Method and Madness: American Watercolor Painting*, University of Delaware, Newark
1981 Springville Museum of Art, Springville, UT
1982 42nd Annual Juried Exhibition, Woodmere Art Museum, Philadelphia
1983 *National Poster Art/Images of Our Time*, Local 1734 Gallery, Washington, D.C.

1986 *A Riot of Color*, The Gallery, Chestnut Hill, PA
1988 Clark-Fork Gallery, Missoula, MT
1990 WILPF at the Painted Bride Gallery, Philadelphia
1990 *Art at the Armory*, Philadelphia
1991 Woodmere Art Museum, Philadelphia
1992 *Art at the Armory II*, Philadelphia
1994 Amos Enos Gallery, New York, NY
1995 Sutton West Gallery, Missoula, MT
1995 *Global Focus: Women in Art & Culture*, U.N. 4th World Conference on Women, Beijing, China & National Museum of Women in the Arts, Washington, D.C.
1998 Textura Gallery, Carmel, CA
1998 *Extraordinary Art: Beyond the Museum*, USArtists'98, PAFA
1999 *Extraordinary Art: Beyond the Museum II*, USArtists'99, PAFA
2000 Woodmere Art Museum 60th Annual Juried Exhibition
2002 *From the Heart of the Valley*, The Packwood House Museum, Lewisburg, PA
2002 60th Annual Awards Painting Exhibition, Cheltenham Center for the Arts, PA
2003 Main Line Art Center, Haverford, PA
2004 *Parallel Lives*, Mural Arts Program Headquarters, Philadelphia

Selected Grants and Awards

1983 *Distinguished Alumna Award*, Citizens' Committee on Public Education, Philadelphia
1988 *Peace & Freedom Award*, Women's International League for Peace and Freedom
1990 *First Place Award* and *Special Award for Art*, Southeastern Pennsylvania Orchid Society
1997 Major grant for Living Sanctuary Artist-in-Residency, Friends Hospital, Philadelphia
1998 *The Brandt F. Steele Aesthetic Award for the Promotion of Peace & Prevention of Violence*, Primary Children's Medical Center, Salt Lake City, UT
2000 *The Crystal Stair Award*, University of Pennsylvania School of Social Work
2003 *Window of Opportunity Grant*, The Leeway Foundation, Philadelphia

Shows Curated

1980 *Groundworks*, The Philomathian Society, University of PA, Philadelphia
1986 *A Riot of Color*, The Gallery, Chestnut Hill, PA
1988 *Women in the Arts Festival*, La Salle University, Philadelphia
1997 Carpenter Gallery, Springside School, Philadelphia, for Women's Caucus for Art's 25th National Conference
1998 *Extraordinary Art: Beyond the Museum*, USArtists'98, PAFA
1999 *Extraordinary Art: Beyond the Museum II*, USArtists'99, PAFA

Selected Teaching and Residencies

1989 Anderson Ranch Arts Center, Snowmass Village, CO
1990 Coupeville Arts Center, Whidbey Island, WA
1991 San Diego Watercolor Society, San Diego, CA
1993 Artist-in-Residence, Springside School, Chestnut Hill, PA
1995 *Art and Trauma*, Bryn Mawr College School of Social Service & Social Research, Bryn Mawr, PA
1997 Guest Lecturer in Art Therapy, Arcadia University, Glenside, PA
1997–8 Living Sanctuary Artist-in-Residence, Friends Hospital, Philadelphia
2001 *Art in Healing: Finding Our Voice*, Domestic Abuse Project of Delaware County, Neumann College, Aston, PA

Selected Articles and Interviews

1987 *Woman of Power*, Caryn Musil, Ph.D., Spring
1989 *Endangered Orchids*, Earth Talk, Michael Weilbacher, WHYY-FM Philadelphia, December 16
1992 *The Philadelphia Inquirer*, Julia M. Klein, March 18
1992 *Radio Times*, Marti Moss-Coane, WHYY-FM Philadelphia, February 5
1993 *Soujourner*, Janet Melvin, February, Vol. 18, No. 6
1994 *Soujourner*, Diane M. O'Donoghue, November, Vol. 20, No. 3
1995 *The Philadelphia Inquirer*, Marie McCullough, September 21
1997 *Chestnut Hill Local*, Rita Beyer, February 20
1998 *"Extraordinary Art: Beyond the Museum,"* Peter Clowney, WHYY-FM Philadelphia, October
1998 *Chestnut Hill Local*, Rita Beyer, December 10
1998 *The Power of Art*, Voices in the Family, Dr. Dan Gottlieb, WHYY-FM Philadelphia, September 14
1999 Daria Hertzig, "Art and Personal Violence," National Public Radio, August, November
1999 Palaestra, *"Extraordinary Art: Beyond the Museum,"* Vol. 15. No. 1, Winter
2000 *Contemporary Master of Watercolor*, WorldofWatercolor.com, online magazine, Gloria Angelino, Nov.'99–Jan.'00
2004 American Artist's Watercolor Magazine, *"A Love Affair with Color,"* Linda Price, Spring 2004

Index of Plates

1970 (Sweet Sixteen), 150
Abiquiu Dam I, 196
Abiquiu Dam II, 195
Abstract #7, 165
Alizarin Hills, 222–23
Alizarin Wing, 188
Along the Road to Santa Fe, 224
Alterpiece, 275
Amazon Botanicals, 111
Anemone & Bird of Paradise, 167
Arianna (longing like Icarus, seeing like Hawk), 151
Arianna (River of Silver), 257
Artless Blossom, 244
Ashes, 274
Beloved Aire, 241
Bertha's Birthday Roses, 156
Big Rock Dawn I, 164
Big Rock Dawn III, 226
Big Sur (Lemon Sky), 194
Bioluminescence, 75
Birds of Paradise I (Plate Series), 168
Bloodroot, 118
Blue-lipped Cattleya, 238
Brasil, 104
Brassolaeliocattleya Cliftonia 'Magnifica', 66
Bryce Canyon, 210
Cacti and Agave, 90
Canary in a Coal Mine, 97
Castaway Cymbidium, 259
Cathleen's Mountains, 197
Cattleya Creatura, 116
Cattleya Nancy Off, 218
Cattleya Quintet, 1993
Cattleya Skinnerii, 102
Chemistry of Feeling, The, 94
Christina's Flowers, 162
Comice Pears I, 193
Comice Pears III, 192
Coral, 74
Cyclamen (seeing blue), 40
Cymbidium Anna Marie Sunshine, 126
Cynoches chlorichilorii, 85
Dark Laeliocattleya, 172
Dendrobium Golden Blossom 'Venus', 228
Dendrobium Small Dowan, 250
Dendrobiums, Phalaenopsis, 153
Diamond Head & Punchbowl from Tantalus (Pre-Colonial Visions) (left), 44
Diamond Head & Punchbowl from Tantalus (Pre-Colonial Visions) (right), 45
Drake's Bay, Point Reyes, 212–13
Dublin Orchids: Phragmepedium Sedni, 232
Dying Blossoms, 246
Eclipse/Plane Dream, 30
Encyclia cochleata, 112
Fan Coral, 93
Fêng/Abundance of Light, 240
Firephal, 140
Flame, 122
Forces of Attraction, The, 68–69
Forest Fire, Oscoda, 138
Found/Yü, 127
Fractured Light/Night, 158
French Irises, 245
From Big Rock, 80
From Pu'u Pehe Cove, Manele Bay, Lana'i, 57
From Wellfleet at Night (RECTO), 56
From Wellfleet at Night (VERSO), 252
Fuchsia Magnolia, 59
Gekkos in Paradise, 136
Gerald's Phalaenopsis, 152
Grape Vine and Daylily Buds, 108
Hachiya Persimmon, 179
Halcyon Waterlilies, 58
Halibut Point I, 211
Halibut Point II, 265
Hawai'ian Landscape: Pale Orange Sky, 52
Hawai'ian Landscape: Poipu (Cadmium Yellow Deep Sky), 77
Hawai'ian Landscape: Poipu (Cadmium Yellow Light Sky), 76
Hawai'ian Landscape: Rose Dore Sky, 49–50
Heart Healing, 124–25
Heliconia, 163
Heritage Ceramics, 86
Hex Sign, 270
Higo Irises, 103
Hollyhocks with Sunspots/Freedom Flowers, 129
Hollyhocks, 107
Holy Cow/Shape Shifter, 95
i bleed (1), 230
i bleed (2), 231
Imperfect Fit (The Kiss), 272
Ingrid's Quilt, 204
Iris Unfolding, 98
Irises from D.K., 251
Jamaican Eggplants I, 206

Jamaican Eggplants II, 207
Kô/Molting, 105
La Frontera/Seamless Dream, 60
Laeliocattleya Moonwind, 117
Lake Visions (No Soap Radio), 260
Landscape #21, 253
Last Sunflower, The, 217
Lava Flow/Alaska, 64–65
Layers of the Mind, The, 100–101
Leaf Skeleton/Spirit Leaves, 35
Lemons in Blue Bowl, 178
Lily Petals (1), 73
Long Relaxed Tulip, 140
Love Letter Blue Orchid, 166
Love Propaganda, 161
Madrid, 149
Magic Tulip, 128
Magnolia (A Season of Mourning), 233
Maine Tears, 256
May Storm in Johnstown, 71
Mellonhead Tea, 187
Mesa Lands, New Mexico, 221
Metamorphogenesis: Nascimiento, 115
Migration, 137
Ming Mên (Red and Blue), 34
Mist Rising Near Big Sur, 33
Modern Classic Celebration, 173
Moon Over Montana, 242–43
Mormodes species, 189
Na Pali Coast II, 51
Na Pali Coast III, 55
Na Pali Coast IV, 47
Na Pali Coast V, 46
Na Pali Coast, Kaua'i, 53
Nasturtiums I, 146
Nasturtiums III, 147
Near Manele Bay, Lana'i, 42–43
Neptune's Daughter, 130
New Land, 190
Night-blooming Cereus, 157
Nuclear Family Holocaust, 263
Oh! Karen . . . , 155
Oh! Karen . . . II, 154
Oh! Karen . . . III, 154
Olympic Range from Whidbey Island, 38–39
One Short, 87
Orange Gladiolas, 169
Orchid Poster – LL, 234
Orchid Poster – LR (Laeliocattleya Erin), 235
Orchid Poster – UL (Cymbidium Nicolansianum II), 236
Orchid Poster – UR (Cymbidium Nicolansianum I), 237
Pacific Pieces, 78–79
Painting For a Winter Baby, 249
Pale Magnolia, 239
Paphiopedilum concolor & P. bellatulum, 214
Paphiopedilum Rothschildianum, 215
Paphiopedilum Sukhakulii (KAK), 208
Parrot Tulips, 134
Pears with Cast Paper Bowl, 198
Peony, Freesia, Irises & Bells of Ireland, 261
Peppers, Eggplants & Honey Tangerines, 200–201
Peppers, Green Plate, Blue Bottle, 199
Phalaenopsis Revival, 160
Phalaenopsis, 209
Phals for Patranna, 106
Phragmepedium besseae, 135
Plume Poppies (foliage) II, 37
Plume Poppy (foliage) I, 36
Point I, The, 148
Point II, The, 32
Point IV, The, 63
Point Lobos, Carmel I, 180–81
Point Lobos, Carmel II, 227
Poipu, Sunset, 54
Poppies, 131
Q'tuba, 145
Red Anemones, 255
Red Bartlett Pears, 203
Remembering (M.R.), 1988
RE-scape, 191
Riots of Spring, The, 121
River of Fire, 61
Rose and Eucalyptus, 143
Rose of Sharon II, 174
Royal Velvet Irises, 99
Sacred Gate, 82
Salem Dahlias, 258
Sarah's Bouquet, 120
Scott's Tree Peonies, 119
Sepiascapes/Providence (three panels), 184–85
Setting Sunflowers from Lisa, 254
Shadows at Sandy's (Seeing Patterns), 109
Shop in Christianstad, St. Croix, 176
Slc. Redzac Carteria Flame, 170
Solar Plexus/Iron Ball, 271
Song for Bilbao, 220

Song of Four/Amish Quilt, 88
Spathiphyllum, 72
Spectrum Range, The, 289
Spectrum Range, The, (detail), 1
Sphoenix (Sphenoid Totem), 83
Spirited Charger/Accident, 266
Spirited Charger/Standing Alone, 267
Squash Blossoms, 110
Staghorn Fern, 113
Star Magnolias, 144
Still Life with Tomatillo, 186
Storm Lillies (Bittersweet Slow Burn), 229
Stormy Phalaenopsis, 70
Struggle to Remember, The, 269
Study in Orange & Blue, 171
Suicide Note, 264
Sunflower Leaves at Dusk, 159
Sunflowers, 175
Sunset Diamond Head, 48
Teal Columns II, 183
Tenerife, 205
Terrestrial, 219
Three Tree Peonies (Allen's Lane), 133
Tod: The Presence of Absence, 262
Tornado Sweet Pea, 67
Towers Go Down, The, 96
Tree Peony, 132
Tulip Fields, 139
Turkey Roses, 247
Untitled (Dancer), 273
Vermillion Amaryllis, 114
Whidbey Island Vetch, 41
Wild Glads, 141
Wild Red Glads, 62
Winged Form I, 268
Winged Victory, 84
Xeriscape, 91
Xygo Blooming, 92
XYGO, 89
Yellow Cattleya, 216
Yuan Dan, 248
Zia, from New Mexico Quartet, 202

The Spectrum Range, 1983

"Today we are faced with a challenge that calls for a shift in our thinking,
so that humanity stops threatening its life-support system . . .
We are called to assist the Earth to heal her wounds, and in the process to heal our own—
indeed to embrace the whole of creation in all its diversity, beauty and wonder."

Wangari Maathai of Kenya,
Winner of the 2004 Nobel Peace Prize

MW01626298

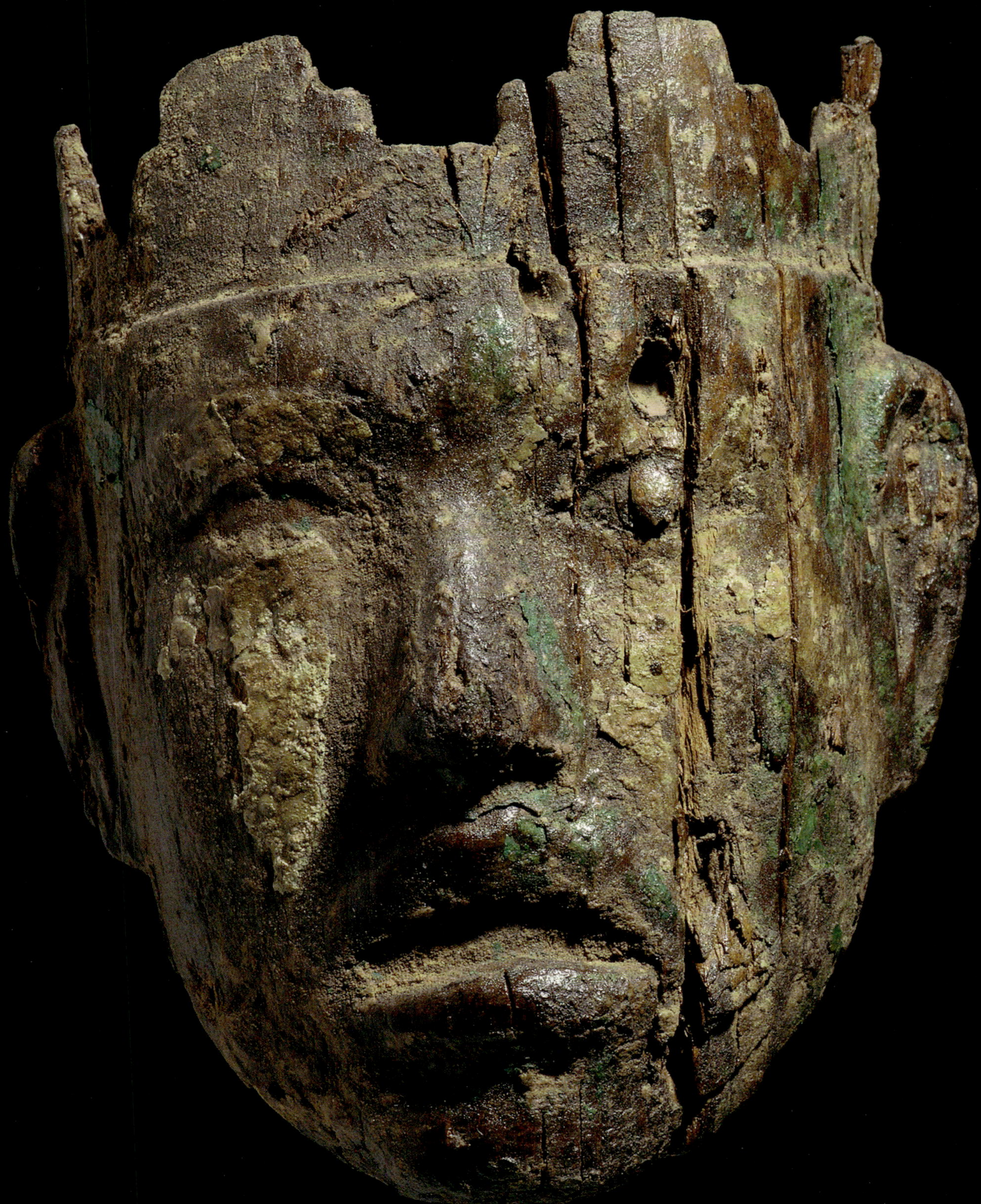

Hero, Hawk, and Open Hand

Townsend, general editor
Robert V. Sharp, editor

with essays and contributions by
Garrick Bailey
Joyce and Turner Bear
James A. Brown
Carol Diaz-Granados
David H. Dye
Stacey Halfmoon
Robert L. Hall
Ruthe Blalock Jones
Adam King
Vernon J. Knight, Jr.
George E. Lankford
Bradley T. Lepper
David W. Penney
F. Kent Reilly III
Mark F. Seeman
Vincas P. Steponaitis
Timmy Thompson
Richard F. Townsend
and Chester P. Walker

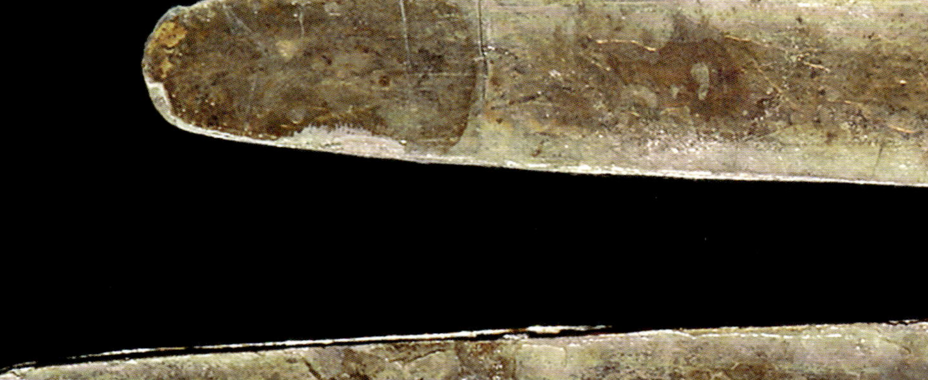

INSTITUTE OF CHICAGO
in association with
YALE UNIVERSITY PRESS
New Haven and London

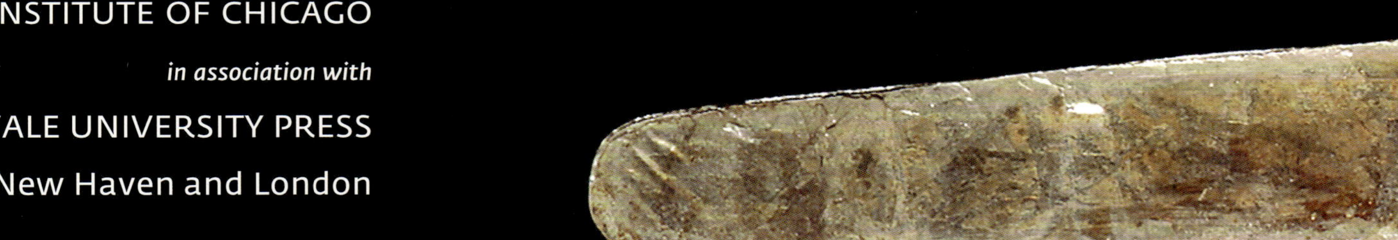

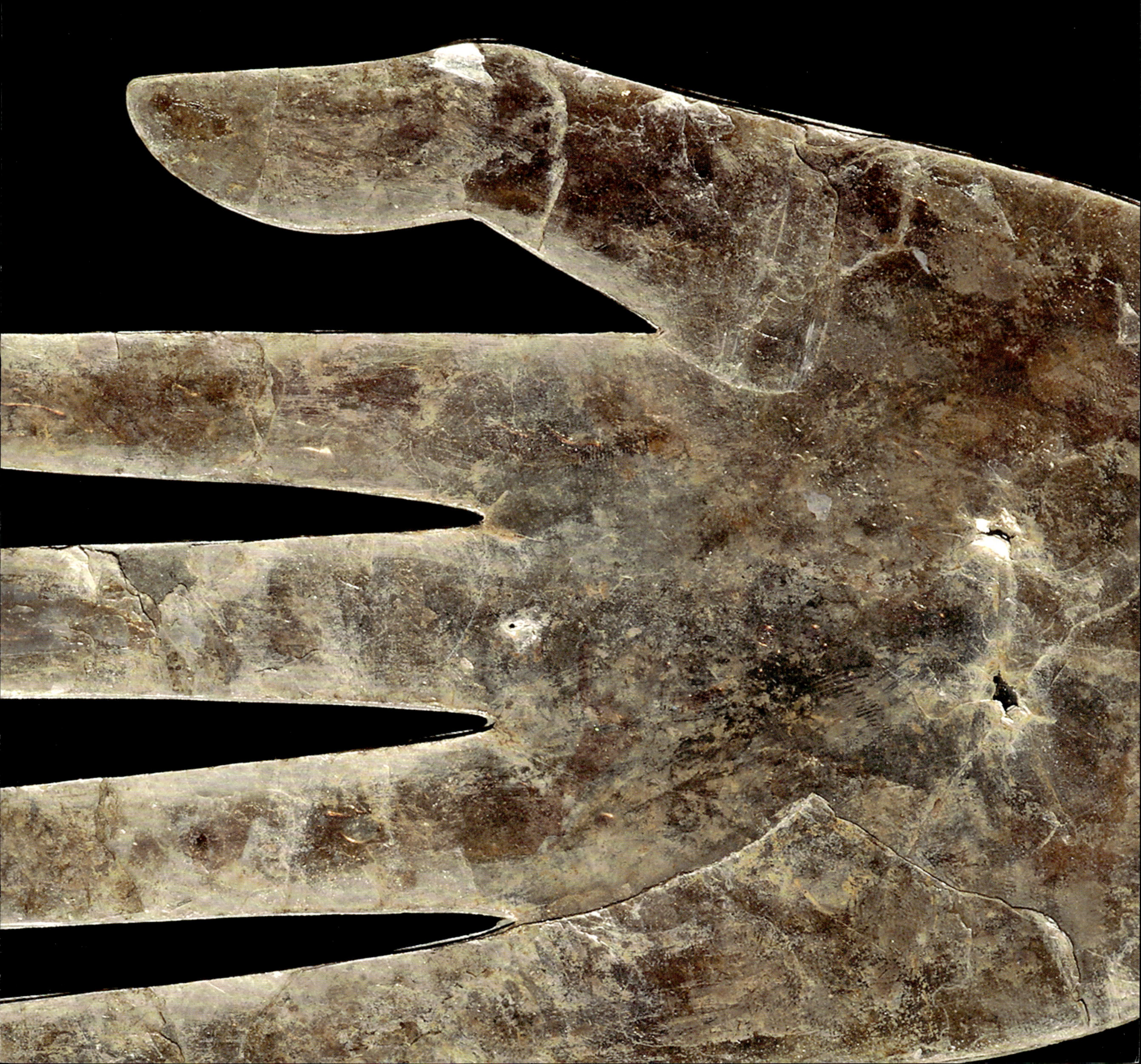

This book was published in conjunction with the exhibition *Hero, Hawk, and Open Hand: American Indian Art of the Ancient Midwest and South*, organized by The Art Institute of Chicago and presented from November 20, 2004, to January 30, 2005. The exhibition was also presented at The Saint Louis Art Museum and at the Smithsonian Institution, National Museum of Natural History, Washington, D.C.

The exhibition was made possible by major funding from the National Endowment for the Humanities, expanding our understanding of the world.

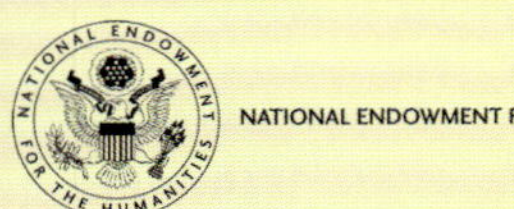

The Chicago presentation of *Hero, Hawk, and Open Hand* was generously sponsored by The Boeing Company.

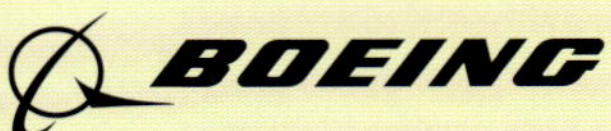

This project was supported by an award from the National Endowment for the Arts, which believes a great nation deserves great art. Additional support was provided by the Community Associates of The Art Institute of Chicago, and a generous grant from the Thaw Charitable Trust.

FIRST EDITION
Printed in England
09 08 07 06 05 04 9 8 7 6 5 4 3 2 1

Published by
The Art Institute of Chicago
111 South Michigan Avenue
Chicago, Illinois 60603-6110
www.artic.edu

Trade edition published by
Yale University Press
New Haven and London

Produced by the Publications Department of The Art Institute of Chicago, Susan F. Rossen, Executive Director

Edited by Robert V. Sharp, Associate Director of Publications, and Lisa Meyerowitz, Special Projects Editor

Production by Sarah E. Guernsey, Production Coordinator

Photography research by Annie Feldmeier, Photo Editor, assisted by Shaun Manning

Designed by Jeff Wincapaw and typeset by Jennifer Sugden of Marquand Books, Seattle, Washington

Principal photography by John Bigelow Taylor and Dianne Dubler, New York

Separations by Professional Graphics, Inc., Rockford, Illinois

Printed and bound by Butler and Tanner, Ltd., Frome, England

Front cover: Copper repoussé plate depicting Birdman; one of the two so-called Rogan plates; Georgia, Bartow County, Etowah, Mound C, 13th century; copper; Smithsonian Institution, National Museum of Natural History, Washington, D.C. Cat. no. 110. *Back cover:* Deer mask; Oklahoma, LeFlore County, Spiro, Craig Mound, A.D. 1200–1400; red cedar and marine shell; Smithsonian Institution, National Museum of the American Indian, Washington, D.C. Cat. no. 272. *Half-title:* Wooden maskette; Illinois, Fulton County, Emmons site, A.D. 1200–1350; red cedar; Illinois State Museum, Springfield. Cat. no. 273. *Frontispiece:* Hand cutout; Ohio, Ross County, Hopewell site, Mound 25, A.D. 1–400; sheet mica; Ohio Historical Society, Columbus. Cat. no. 46. *Credits page:* Human face effigy; Kentucky, Gallatin County, Warsaw, 200 B.C.–A.D. 400; stone; Smithsonian Institution, National Museum of the American Indian, Washington, D.C. Cat. no. 55.

Library of Congress Control Number: 2004108743
ISBN 0-300-10467-7 (cloth)
ISBN 0-300-10601-7 (paper)

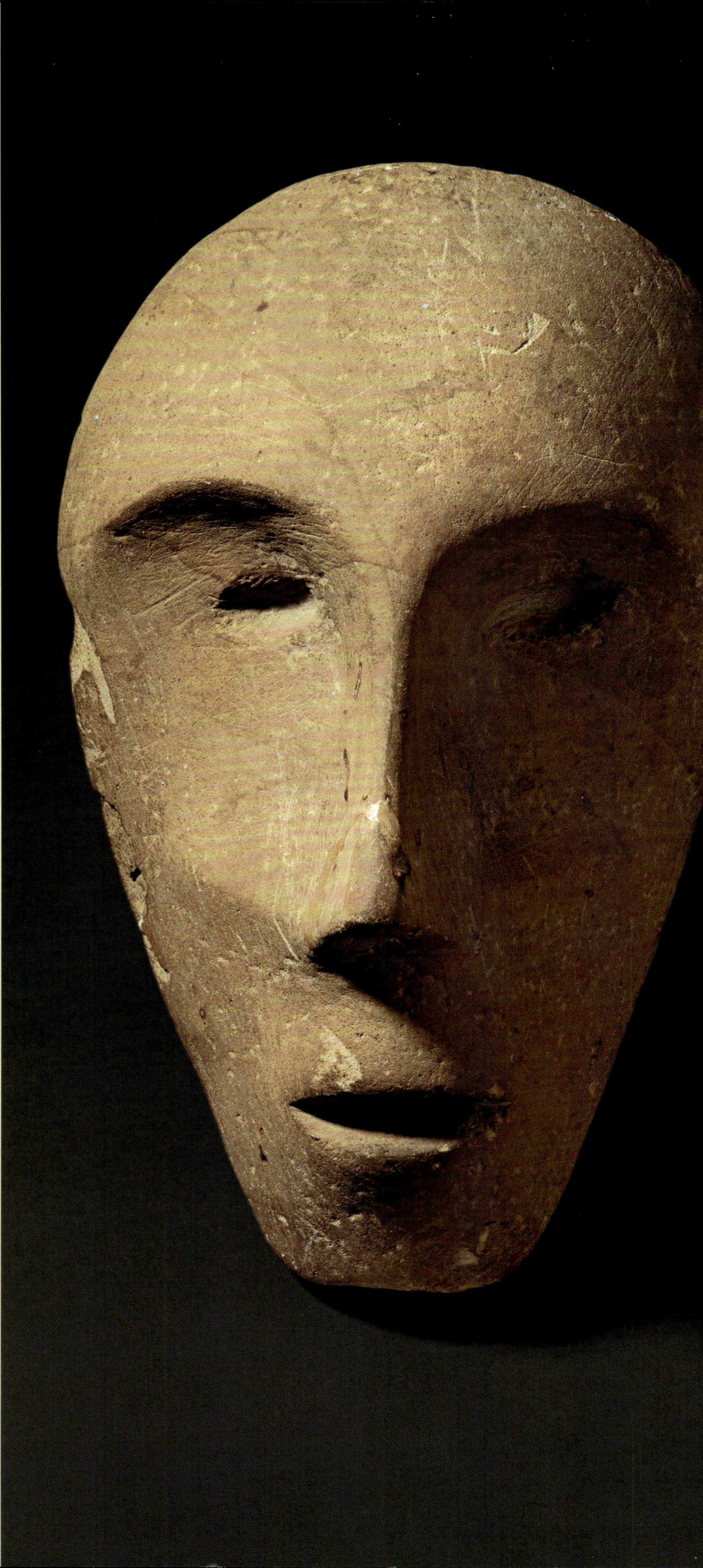

Contents

6 Foreword
James Cuno

8 Acknowledgments
Richard F. Townsend

12 Chronological Chart

13 Map of the Midwest and South

15 American Landscapes, Seen and Unseen
Richard F. Townsend

37 Thoughts on the Preservation of Traditional Culture: An Interview with Timmy Thompson
F. Kent Reilly III

43 The Archaeology of Aesthetics
David W. Penney

57 Hopewell Art in Hopewell Places
Mark F. Seeman

73 The Newark Earthworks: Monumental Geometry and Astronomy at a Hopewellian Pilgrimage Center
Bradley T. Lepper

83 Continuity and Change in Mississippian Civilization
Garrick Bailey

93 The Cahokia Site and Its People
Robert L. Hall

105 The Cahokian Expression: Creating Court and Cult
James A. Brown

125 People of Earth, People of Sky: Visualizing the Sacred in Native American Art of the Mississippian Period
F. Kent Reilly III

139 Marking Stone, Land, Body, and Spirit: Rock Art and Mississippian Iconography
Carol Diaz-Granados

151 Power and the Sacred: Mound C and the Etowah Chiefdom
Adam King

167 Moundville Art in Historical and Social Context
Vincas P. Steponaitis and Vernon J. Knight, Jr.

183 Thoughts on the Preservation of Traditional Culture: An Interview with Joyce and Turner Bear
F. Kent Reilly III

191 Art, Ritual, and Chiefly Warfare in the Mississippian World
David H. Dye

207 World on a String: Some Cosmological Components of the Southeastern Ceremonial Complex
George E. Lankford

219 Prehistoric Art of the Central Mississippi Valley
Chester P. Walker

231 The Ancient Art of Caddo Ceramics
Richard F. Townsend and Chester P. Walker

247 Caddo Art: A Personal Perspective
Stacey Halfmoon

253 The Bread Dance: A Shawnee Ceremony of Thanks and Renewal
Ruthe Blalock Jones

260 Catalogue of the Exhibition

271 Bibliography

280 Contributors

282 Photography Credits

283 Index

Foreword

To all but a few individuals, the works of art featured in this book and the exhibition *Hero, Hawk, and Open Hand: American Indian Art of the Ancient Midwest and South* will be almost entirely unknown. Yet, as with masterpieces from more familiar ancient traditions, the objects strike us with a sense of surprise, wonderment, and puzzled interest. They appear to have a family affinity with the arts of Mesoamerica and other regions of the Americas where early societies arose and flourished, but the imagery is subtly distinct and is also different from that of the well-known arts of nineteenth- and twentieth-century Native American peoples. There are implements of minimal shapes carved in rare and colorful stone, ceramic vessels ornamented with bold graphic designs, and sculptures of animals and composite creatures rendered in keenly observed detail, as well as magical human-animal figures, admirably modeled portraits of individuals, and images of rulers, mythical heroes, and deities, created in wood, shell, stone, and copper.

To many it will be a revelation that these evocative forms are in fact from our midwestern and southern heartlands, where hundreds of archaeological sites attest to the formation of a major branch of Amerindian civilization between 5000 B.C. and A.D. 1500. These sites dot the great river valleys from the Scioto River to the Ohio and the Tennessee; from the Illinois River down the Mississippi to the Arkansas and Red rivers; in addition to the many waterways that traverse the southern piedmont and plain and the Florida peninsula. The larger ruins are locally known and protected in state or national parks, but scores of smaller sites remain on privately owned land.

Birdstone; Ohio, Wood County, southeast of Grand Rapids, 1500–1000 B.C.; greenstone, l. 20.8 cm; American Museum of Natural History, New York. Cat. no. 23.

The earthen cones, pyramidal platforms, geometric precincts, and animal forms of the ancient architectural monuments and settlements commanded much interest in the late eighteenth, nineteenth, and early twentieth centuries, when they were widely surveyed, mapped, and sometimes scientifically excavated—or looted—and published in handsomely illustrated volumes by the Smithsonian Institution, the American Antiquarian Society, the Academy of Natural Sciences of Philadelphia, and others. During the past fifty years, archaeologists have continued explorations and have sought to protect many important sites from destruction. In addition to the archaeological literature there are abundant ethnological and historical sources from the sixteenth century to the present. Why, then, has knowledge of this early form of civilization and its art failed to make its way more decisively into our public system of education and our sense of cultural heritage?

At present we can only point to some obvious factors: the forced removal of Indian tribes beginning in the 1830s from their homelands in the Midwest and South; the doctrine of cultural assimilation and the erosion of traditional indigenous cultures; the myth of the wilderness; the rapid creation of a vast new gridded landscape of farmlands, railroads, highways, and cities answering the idea of limitless progress; and the strong tendency for archaeological information to be primarily written for a specialized academic audience. In addition, the Midwest and South held no colorful romantic allure comparable to that of the scenic Southwest, with its ancient cliff dwellings and traditional Pueblos, Navajos, and other distinctive indigenous peoples, as well as those of Hispanic descent. At the beginning of the twentieth century, the Santa Fe Railway and the Harvey Company hotels successfully opened a thriving southwestern tourism industry with strong stimulating economic effects on the indigenous arts and crafts. From that time to the present the region's diverse history and its cultural and artistic patrimony have figured prominently in our larger cultural landscape. But things have been different in the case of the old midwestern and southern traditions. Although a highly significant exhibition, *Ancient Art of the American Woodland Indians*, was formed at the Detroit Institute of Arts in 1985, knowledge of this part of the indigenous cultural achievement has yet to find its place in our collective imagination.

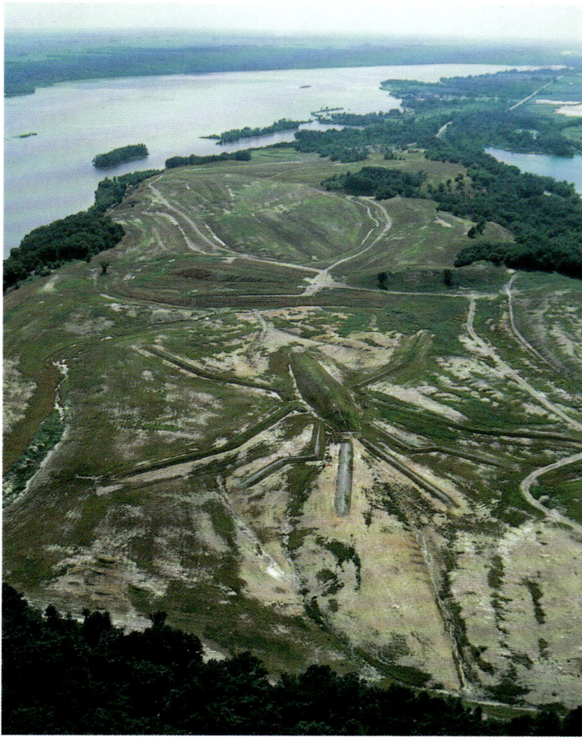

Michael Heizer (American, born 1944), *Effigy Tumuli: Water Strider, Frog, and Catfish*, 1983–85. Buffalo Rock State Park, on the Illinois River, near Ottawa, Illinois.

In 1999, when Dr. Richard F. Townsend proposed the idea of the present exhibition and catalogue to James N. Wood, who was then Director and President of the Art Institute, it was with the notion of working closely with Native American cultural authorities and tribal officials, scholars from several disciplines, museum curators, and private collectors to bring diverse voices and interests together in a project of national significance. From the outset the project began to evolve in a profoundly cooperative way, with participants joining in many meetings held in tribal government offices, ceremonial grounds, museums, universities, and private homes. As the new Director and President of the Art Institute of Chicago, I am especially pleased to express my deepest thanks to everyone who has engaged in this innovative endeavor, finding ways to learn of each other's outlooks, knowledge, and expertise, and developing the ability to work creatively together on many matters of common interest. The project has evolved in a time when the movement of cultural preservation is gathering strength across the land, when the National Museum of the American Indian has opened its new home on the Mall in Washington, D.C., and when, as in many other countries throughout the continent, we are acknowledging and valuing an older, deeper, and more complex indigenous history.

Hero, Hawk, and Open Hand: American Indian Art of the Ancient Midwest and South seeks to recover and bring to public attention the antiquity and character of a Native American aesthetic and symbolic domain, approaching deep-seated cultural themes connecting ancestral societies with tribes of today. Our primary points of reference are works of art of the highest quality, generously lent by many institutions and individuals. The imagery of these objects traces an ancient way of speculative thought, an almost visionary mode of understanding and explaining the active role of human society engaged in maintaining the order of life seen and experienced in the rhythms of the natural environment. Yet, in selecting and presenting the finest works of art, we also call attention to them not just as specimens, symbols, or admirable artifacts, but also as objects for contemplation: expressive forms whose special virtue lies in their power to affect the spirit of the individual viewer. Such exceptional pieces speak for themselves, reaching beyond cultural boundaries and historical circumstances, calling for an intuitive response that carries a sense of personal recognition, pleasure, and restoration.

Finally, we are reminded that ideas explored centuries ago have also informed modern artists, from the paintings and sculptures of Barnett Newman and Ellsworth Kelly to the earthworks of Robert Smithson and Michael Heizer; their innovative syntheses deepen a dialogue in which our search for the present is also a poetic recovery of the past.

James Cuno, *Director and President*
The Art Institute of Chicago

Acknowledgments

In many countries throughout the Americas, movements of cultural recovery and restoration are taking form in the creation of historical districts, the establishment of nature conservancies, and the preservation of archaeological sites. Projects of cultural renewal are also encouraging the teaching of indigenous languages and customs in peril of extinction. The work of museums plays another role in this vital collective endeavor: at the Art Institute of Chicago, our special interest concerns the conservation, presentation, and interpretation of works of art of the highest quality, as expressive and symbolic forms embodying the ethos of many traditions. Our permanent collections and special exhibitions preserve basic visual documents in the history of the imagination, masterpieces of aesthetic achievement that also portray the deeper patterns of thought, values of life, and visions of human society in the cosmos. *Hero, Hawk, and Open Hand: American Indian Art of the Ancient Midwest and South* seeks to approach the visual arts of early indigenous societies, to recover basic themes of the worldview they portray, and to trace ancient strands of perception and communication and their possible links to traditional life among Native American tribes today.

The appeal of these ancient arts first touched my imagination upon reading Miguel Covarrubias's classic book *The Eagle, the Jaguar, and the Serpent: Indian Art of the Americas* in the 1950s as a young man in Guadalajara, Mexico. But it was not until the 1980s that the idea of a future exhibition began to germinate. The civil engineer and surveyor James Marshall had called my attention to the geometric enclosures of Ohio, and we began to commission updated site plans from his survey data, in a long-range project generously supported by Mary Carol Fee. Other museum projects and exhibitions claimed my attention, yet the notion of forming a major exhibition on the ancient Midwest and South gathered strength when, in the spring of 1999, art historian F. Kent Reilly III and archaeologist James A. Brown came to the Art Institute to discuss possible ideas and approaches. These scholars portrayed fresh and imaginative approaches to the field that were being explored in an annual workshop directed by Dr. Reilly at Texas State University. Their ideas have proved fundamental in shaping this project. Our first thanks therefore go to these early participants and supporters.

Our immediate perception was that an exhibition of national significance was really only conceivable in terms of partnerships with people committed to cultural preservation among the Native American communities. At this point anthropologist Garrick Bailey joined the conversation, and volunteered to open the prospect by inviting friends and acquaintances from Oklahoma tribes to meet with us and explore the issues involved in developing a meaningful project. We are deeply grateful for this enthusiastic offer, and for the generous and idealistic support of James N. Wood, former Director and President of the Art Institute, who advanced museum funds to hold a meeting at the University of Tulsa. At this gathering we reviewed earlier Art Institute exhibitions on the ancient arts of the Americas and discussed issues related to the Native American Graves Protection and Repatriation Act (NAGPRA), as well as matters of political and cultural significance. The vast lack of knowledge about the early Midwest and South among the public and among the tribes was noted by many. It began to emerge that the project presented an opportunity to develop areas of positive communication and creative action among museum professionals, academic scholars, and tribal preservationists, and it was recommended that further steps be taken to explore these findings. We remain deeply grateful to all who helped shape the project's inception: Martha Moore Barker (Quapaw/Osage); Turner and Joyce Bear (Creek); Ruthe Blalock Jones (Peoria/Delaware/Shawnee); Durbin Feeling (Cherokee); Stacey Halfmoon (Caddo); Marianne Long (Iowa); Frederick Morris Lookout (Osage); Cindy L. Martin (Choctaw); Archie (Osage/Cherokee) and Ramona Mason (Creek); Henrietta Massey (Sac & Fox); Sandra Kaye Massey (Sac & Fox); Dewayne Mathews (Cherokee/Chickasaw); Ardina Revard Moore (Quapaw/Osage); Anahwake Nahtanaba (Caddo/Choctaw/Chickasaw); Jereldine (Caddo/Potawatomi) and Charles Redcorn (Osage); Knokovtee Scott (Creek/Cherokee); Kevin Smith (Cherokee); Fayetta Glenn West (Choctaw); Olin Williams (Choctaw); and Carrie V. Wilson (Quapaw).

Encouraged by the meeting, we began a series of visits to various tribal headquarters to talk with chiefs, tribal councils, and cultural preservation officials, while also extending invitations and hosting them as visitors to the Art Institute, in order to confer with our director and staff members in the departments of Publications, Conservation, Protection Services, Museum Education, and African and Amerindian Art. These travels and visits continued over the next four years, enabling all participants to understand diverse cultural approaches, requirements, goals, and capabilities. Our special thanks for their valuable council, patience, and optimism go to Stacey Halfmoon and Bobby Gonzalez, NAGPRA Officers, and LaRue Martin Parker, Chairperson, Caddo Nation of Oklahoma; Carrie V. Wilson, NAGPRA Officer, and Tamara Martin, Chairperson, Quapaw Tribe of Oklahoma; Joyce Bear, NAGPRA Officer, Turner Bear, Timmy Thompson, Cultural Advisor, A.D. Ellis, Principal Chief, R. Perry Beaver, former Principal Chief, William E. Freeman, Executive Director, Wilbur Gouge, Speaker, and Patricia Wind, Director, Division of Human Development, Muscogee (Creek) Nation; Tarpie Yargee, Principal Chief, and Bill Fife, Tribal Administrator, Alabama-Quassarte Tribal Town; Wesley Lowell, Town Mekko, Delores Herrod, Cultural Preservation Officer, Melissa Harjo, Heritage and Cultural Director, and Corky Allen, Kialegee Tribal Town; Ellis Tillis, Chair, Gail Thrower, Historian-Cultural Preservation, and Robert Thrower, Department of Natural Resources, Poarch Band of Creek Indians; Brian McGertt, Town Mekko, and Charles Coleman, Cultural Preservation Officer, Thlopthlocco Tribal Town; Chad Smith, Principal Chief, Cherokee Nation; Bill Anoatubby, Governor, and Kirk Perry, Administrator, Division of Heritage Preservation, Chickasaw Nation of Oklahoma; Gregory Pyle, Chief, Terry D. Cole, Director, and Fayetta Glenn West, Admission Counselor, Heritage Resources Technician, Choctaw Nation of Oklahoma; and Jerry Haney, Chief, Seminole Nation. Although the Wichita and Affiliated Tribes chose not to participate in the project, we were courteously received in their Anadarko, Oklahoma, headquarters by Garry MacAdams, President, Stratford D. Williams, Vice President, and Virgil Swift, NAGPRA Officer; and are also grateful to Kathryn Redcorn Lynn, Director, Osage Tribal Museum, Pawhuska, Oklahoma.

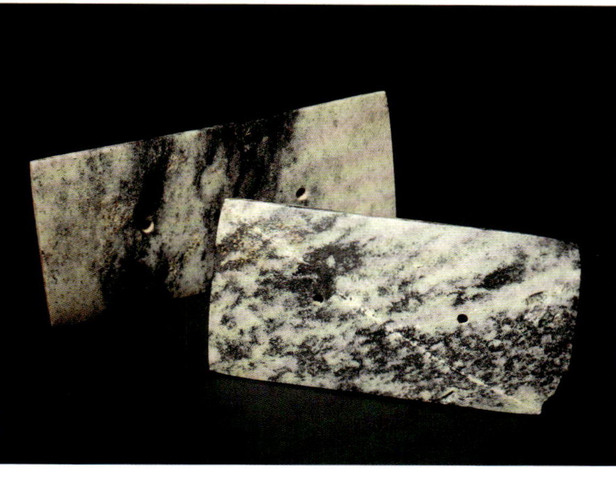

Two rectangular gorgets; Illinois, Brown County, Hemphill site, 1000–500 B.C.; quartz, l. 15.9, 14.9 cm; Gilcrease Museum, Tulsa, Oklahoma. Cat. no. 27.

With these visits in progress and the support of tribal authorities, we applied to the National Endowment for the Humanities for a planning grant to fund a conference at the Art Institute. The success of this application enabled us to convene a group of distinguished scholars, Native American cultural officials, and staff members from the museum in October 2001. The scholars were already participating in the annual workshop on ancient Mississippian art and culture at Texas State University. The innovative objective of this adventurous group was to explore art historical methods for the interpretation of the imagery as an opening field of inquiry. Their ideas were complemented by the cultural perspectives of the Native American participants, who described the effects of government boarding-school education, the repression of indigenous languages, the erosion and loss of traditional culture, and the urgency of preservation efforts. At this planning conference, museum staff members also portrayed the process of catalogue editing and production, the design and presentation of exhibitions, security measures, and the handling, transportation, and conservation of objects requested as loans. Our special thanks to all who contributed to the success of this planning conference go to Dr. Garrick Bailey, University of Tulsa; Turner and Joyce Bear, Muscogee (Creek) Nation; Ruthe Blalock Jones (Peoria/Delaware/Shawnee), Bacone College; Dr. James A. Brown, Northwestern University; Dr. Carol Diaz-Granados, Washington University; Dr. David H. Dye, University of Memphis; Stacey Halfmoon, Caddo Nation; Dr. Robert L. Hall, University of Illinois at Chicago; Dr. Adam King, University of South Carolina; Dr. Vernon J. Knight, Jr., University of Alabama; Dr. George E. Lankford, Lyon College; Dr. Bradley T. Lepper, Ohio Historical Society; James Marshall, registered professional engineer; Dr. David W. Penney, the Detroit Institute of Arts; Dr. F. Kent Reilly III, Texas State University; Stephanie Sick, Choctaw Nation of Oklahoma; Dr. Mark F. Seeman, Kent State University; Dr. Vincas P. Steponaitis, University of North Carolina; Timmy Thompson, Muscogee (Creek) Nation; Chester P. Walker, University of Texas at Austin; and Carrie V. Wilson, Quapaw Tribe of Oklahoma.

The third group to which we owe a special debt of gratitude are the curators, conservationists, and staff from museums, state archaeological parks, and national historical monuments who have generously lent the objects featured in this catalogue and exhibition: Dr. Richard A. Diehl, Director, Alabama Museum of Natural History; Dr. David Thomas, Curator, and Kristen Mable, Registrar, American Museum of Natural History; Dr. Barbara Sirmans, Director, and Yvonne Crumpler, Librarian, Special Collections, Birmingham Public Library; Dr. Jonathan King, Curator, North American Indian Collection, British Museum; Dr. Susan Kennedy Zeller, Assistant Curator, Arts of the Americas, Liz Reynolds, Registrar, Dottie Canady, Assistant Registrar, and Ruth Janson, Rights and Reproductions Manager, Brooklyn Museum of Art; Dr. David W. Penney, Curator, and Michelle S. Peplin, Associate Registrar, the Detroit Institute of Art; Dr. Jonathan Haas, Curator, American Indian Collections, and Dorren Martin-Ross, Registrar, Department of Anthropology, the Field Museum; Lonice D. Barrett, Commissioner, Becky Kelley, Director, Parks, Recreation, and Historic Sites Division, Linda W. Bitley, Curator of Collections, Lawrence Blankenship, Dr. Debbie Wallsmith, Dr. John Morgan, and Dr. David Crass, Georgia Department of Natural Resources, State Parks and Historic Sites; Dr. Randy Ramer, Curator of Anthropology, Dr. Daniel Swan, former Senior Curator, and Joan Thomas, Registrar, Gilcrease Museum; Bill Long, Museum Coordinator, Hampson Museum; Dr. Steven A. LeBlanc, Director of Collections, Genevieve Fisher, Registrar, Peabody Museum of Archaeology and Ethnology, Harvard University; Dr. Terrance J. Martin, Curator of Anthropology, Illinois State Museum Research and Collections Center; Dr. Michael D. Wiant, Director, Dickson Mounds Museum, and Dr. Karen Poulson, Senior Staff Archaeologist/Cultural Resource Manager, Archaeological Research Inc.; Dr. Alex W. Barker, Curator of North American Archaeology and Chair, Milwaukee Public Museum; Quintus H. and Mary H. Herron, Founders, and Dr. Henry Moy, Director, Museum of the Red River; Dr. Deborah Edmond Scott, Chief Curator, and Julie Mattson, Associate Registrar for Loans and Exhibitions, the Nelson-Atkins Museum of Art; Dr. Martha Potter Otto, Curator of Archaeology, Ohio Historical Society; Susan M. Taylor, Director, and Maureen McCormick, Chief Registrar, Princeton University Art Museum; Brent R. Benjamin, Director, Dr. John Nunley, Curator, Department of African, Oceanic, and American Indian Art, and Jeanette Fausz, Registrar, Saint Louis Art Museum; Dr. Carol J. Valenta, Senior Vice President, and Melinda Frillman, Collections Manager, St. Louis Science Center; Superintendent Woody Harrell, Shiloh National Military Park; W. Richard West, Director, Dr. Bruce Bernstein, Assistant Director for Cultural Resources, and Erik Satrum, Assistant Registrar-Loans, Smithsonian Institution, National Museum of the American Indian; Dr. Cristían Samper, Director, Dr. Bruce D. Smith, Director, Archaeobiology Program, Deborah Hull-Walski, Collection Manager, Susan Crawford, Registrar, David Rosenthal, Museum Specialist/Archaeology, and Amy Putnam, Program Assistant, Collections & Archives Program, Department of Anthropology, Smithsonian Institution, National Museum of Natural History; Dr. Stephen Cox, Senior Curator, and Ronald M. Westphal, Registrar, Tennessee State Museum; Dr. Johnnie L. Gentry, Jr., Director, Dr. Michael Hoffman, Curator of Anthropology, and Mary Suter, Curator of Collections, University of Arkansas Museum; Dr. Thomas E. Emerson, Director, Dr. Laura Kozuch, Curator, and Dr. Kenneth B. Farnsworth, Senior Research Editor, Illinois Transportation Archaeological Research Program, University of Illinois at Urbana-Champaign; Dr. Jefferson Chapman, Director, Frank H. McClung Museum, University of Tennessee; Professor Mark S. Weil, Director, and Sara Rowe Hignite, Registrar, Washington University Gallery of Art; Dr. Richard Burger, Director and Professor of Anthropology, and Dr. Roger H. Colten, Collections Manager, Anthropology Division, Peabody Museum of Natural History, Yale University.

Museums are not the only sources of important objects featured in this project. There are also many private lenders, who by enthusiastically explaining their collections to us, brought years of expertise to bear in the selection of works. Theirs has been an activity of searching for and selecting the finest pieces; and scholarship in this group is also not lacking, as seen in Dr. Kent Westbrook's *Legacy in Clay: Prehistoric Ceramic Art of Arkansas*, Roy Hathcock's *The Quapaw and Their Pottery* and *Ancient Indian Pottery of the Mississippi River Valley*, and David Lutz's monumental *The Archaic Bannerstone: Its Chronological History and Purpose from 6000 B.C. to 1000 B.C.* Among the collectors to whom we owe special thanks are the Charles L. Adam Family, Missouri; Tommy Beutell, Tuckasegee, North Carolina; Tommy W. Bryden, Springfield, Illinois; James F. Cherry, M.D., Fayetteville, Arkansas; Arthur Cushman, M.D., Old Hickory, Tennessee; Steve and Susan Hart, Huntington, Indiana; Edward Harvey, Lompoc, California; Roy Hathcock, West Plains, Missouri; James and Elaine Kinker, Hermann, Missouri; David Lutz, Newburgh, Indiana; Terry W. McGuire, Chicago; Maury Meadows, Bethany, Missouri; Bobby Onken, Edwardsville, Illinois; Anthony Patano, Chicago; Jonnie and Kent C. Westbrook, M.D., Little Rock, Arkansas; the Willis Family, Tennessee; and an anonymous collector.

Other scholars contributed their expertise to the project in diverse ways, and we are especially grateful in this respect to Dr. Eugene M. Futato, University of Alabama Office of Archaeological Research; Dr. Timothy Perttula, Archaeological and Environmental Consultants, LLC; Dr. N'omi B. Greber, Curator of Archaeology and Supervisor of Archaeology Collections, Cleveland Museum of Natural History; Kelvin Sampson, Exhibits Department, Dickson Mounds Museum; Julie Droke, Registrar/Repatriations Specialist, and Dr. Don Wyckoff, Associate Curator, Archaeology, Sam Noble Oklahoma Museum of Natural History, University of Oklahoma; Dr. Barbara Purdy, University of Florida; Dr. Mark Norton, Pinson Mounds; Dr. Steve Black, Dr. Darrell

Creel, T. Clay Schultz, Dr. Dee Ann Story, Dr. Pauline Turner Strong, and Dr. Samuel Wilson, University of Texas. We thank Melinda Blustain and Dr. James Bradley for their effort on our behalf, although the Phillips Academy at Andover, Massachusetts, decided against lending objects from Etowah to the exhibition.

New photographs were needed for almost every object in this catalogue, and we must express our admiration and thanks for their excellent work to John Bigelow Taylor and Dianne Dubler, New York City; Dr. David H. Dye, Memphis, who also took admirable views of Cahokia, Moundville, and Etowah; John Pafford, Eva, Tennessee; and Robert Hashimoto of the Art Institute's Imaging Department. Special thanks also go to Ann S. Merritt, Chicago, for the preparation of maps.

It is especially important to note our appreciation to funders without whose major support the exhibition and this book would have been impossible: the National Endowment for the Humanities, the National Endowment for the Arts, the Boeing Company, the Community Associates of the Art Institute, and the Thaw Charitable Trust. The exhibition and catalogue proposals could never have been successfully prepared without the highly competent and purposeful help of Karin Victoria, Emilie DeAngelis, and Jennifer Hamilton of the museum's Department of Government and Foundation Relations. I am also extremely grateful to Lisa Key, Vice President for Development, and to Amy K. Radick of the museum's Corporate and Foundations Relations office.

Also at the Art Institute, my special thanks go to the exceptional staff of our Publications Department under Susan F. Rossen, Executive Director. Taking an extraordinary interest in this subject, Associate Director Robert V. Sharp was inspired to read extensively in the field and to travel to relevant sites and collections. This more than prepared him to coordinate and edit the contributions of our nineteen authors. His impressive knowledge proved invaluable to the shaping of this book from the overarching issues to the smallest details. I am deeply grateful to him and to those colleagues who assisted him: Sarah E. Guernsey, who applied the highest standards in overseeing this book's production; Annie Feldmeier, who coordinated the photo editing with patience and care, assisted by Shaun Manning; and Lisa Meyerowitz, who ably assisted in the demanding editorial process. Thanks also to Gigi Bayliss and Elizabeth Reese Baloutine for their drawings; to Jeff Wincapaw of Marquand Books for his elegant book design; to the staff of Mapping Specialists in Madison, Wisconsin; and to Pat Goley of Professional Graphics, Rockford, Illinois. We are also grateful for the support of our copublishers at Yale University Press. We are delighted with the original watercolors of five major archaeological sites by Steven Patricia, and are grateful for plans of many other sites by James Marshall and Tom Goeke. In our Department of Conservation, Barbara Hall, Suzanne Schnepp, and Emily Dunn Heye brought their highest skills to the inspection and care of objects on loan from many sources. Nenette Luarca, Leah Bowe, and R. Maria Marable-Bunch of the Museum Education Department traveled to Oklahoma to work with educators from many tribes in preparing our school educational booklet and materials; the creation of this illustrated text for wide distribution in schools and community centers is one of our most important project achievements. Mary Sue Glosser also imaginatively organized presentations by notable Native American authors and artists during the exhibition in Chicago. Julia Perkins ably assisted with her customary good humor, optimism, and idealism in the early stages of this project, as did Clare Kunny. Essential audience evaluations and focus group meetings were skillfully conducted by Judith Krajnak. We also owe heartfelt thanks to the experienced financial management and advice brought to bear throughout our preparations by Dorothy Schroeder, Assistant Director for Exhibitions and Budget. Due to the bottomless patience and long experience of Mary Solt, Darrell Green, John Molini, and the Packing Staff, and of Craig Cox and the Installation Staff of the Registrar's Department, arrangements were made for the safe transport and presentation of the works of art. Our special thanks for excellent design go to Lyn DelliQuadri, Joe Cochand, and the staff of Graphic Design and Communication Services. To Eileen Harakal, Vice President for Audience Development and Public Affairs, and her staff; to Ray Van Hook, Executive Director of Protection Services, and his staff; and to William D. Caddick, Director of Physical Plant, and his staff, we also express our very warm thanks. Our audiovisual staff member Jim Currie traveled to Oklahoma to obtain camera interviews, festival scenes, and other film footage, working with Bill Foster to produce a vital exhibition video.

In our Department of African and Amerindian Art, I wish to thank Dr. Kathleen Bickford Berzock, whose sound advice has been invariably supportive; Barbara Battaglia, who has managed the office and so ably attended to its myriad and exacting tasks, including typing of manuscripts, organizing and meticulous ordering of files, reminders of appointments, general efficiency, and invariable courtesy with the many who have worked with us during the past five years on this project; Chester P. Walker, Special Projects Exhibition Assistant, who brought special knowledge and skills as a doctoral candidate in archaeology to bear in organizing the diverse information required for this complex project; and Raymond Ramírez, Departmental Specialist, who patiently and with inexhaustible good humor and admirable foresight oversaw the demanding process of installing and deinstalling the exhibition.

Finally, I especially wish to thank my wife, Pala, for all her invaluable artistic insight, encouragement, and unyielding support in Chicago and on our various travels in quest of the ancient Midwest and South.

Richard F. Townsend, *Curator*
Department of African and Amerindian Art

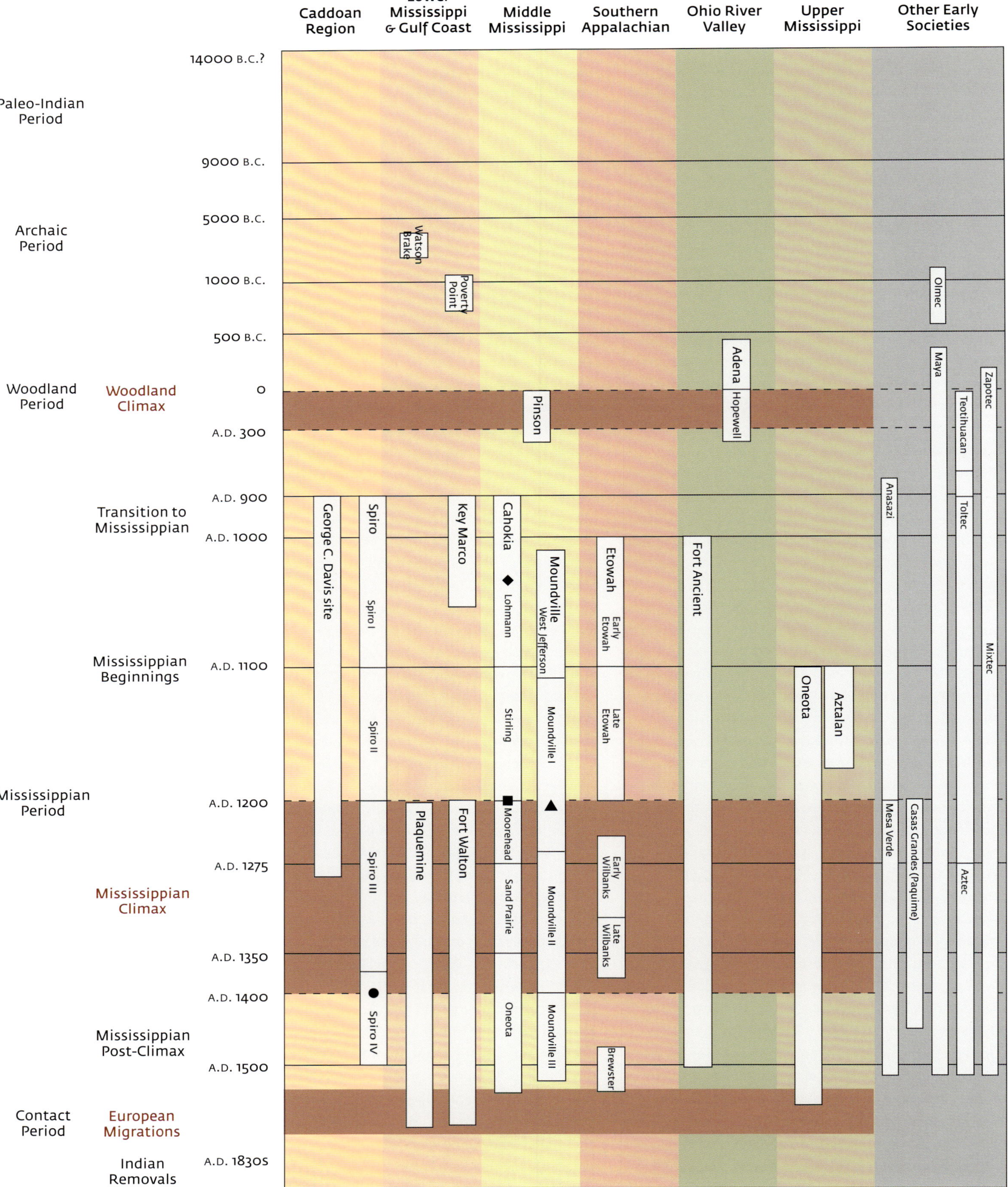
Caddoan Region
Lower Mississippi & Gulf Coast
Middle Mississippi
Southern Appalachian
Ohio River Valley
Upper Mississippi
Other Early Societies
14000 B.C.?
Paleo-Indian Period
9000 B.C.
5000 B.C.
Archaic Period
1000 B.C.
500 B.C.
Woodland Period
Woodland Climax
0
A.D. 300
A.D. 900
Transition to Mississippian
A.D. 1000
Mississippian Beginnings
A.D. 1100
Mississippian Period
A.D. 1200
A.D. 1275
Mississippian Climax
A.D. 1350
A.D. 1400
Mississippian Post-Climax
A.D. 1500
Contact Period
European Migrations
Indian Removals
A.D. 1830s
Watson Brake
Poverty Point
Olmec
Adena
Hopewell
Pinson
Maya
Zapotec
Teotihuacan
Toltec
Anasazi
Mixtec
George C. Davis site
Spiro
Spiro I
Spiro II
Spiro III
Spiro IV
Key Marco
Cahokia
Lohmann
Stirling
Moorehead
Sand Prairie
Oneota
Moundville
West Jefferson
Moundville I
Moundville II
Moundville III
Etowah
Early Etowah
Late Etowah
Early Wilbanks
Late Wilbanks
Brewster
Fort Ancient
Oneota
Aztalan
Plaquemine
Fort Walton
Mesa Verde
Casas Grandes (Paquime)
Aztec
◆ = Cahokia designed as a paramount regional capital
▲ = Moundville designed as a major regional center
■ = Southeastern Ceremonial Complex synthesis
● = Major offerings at Craig Mound

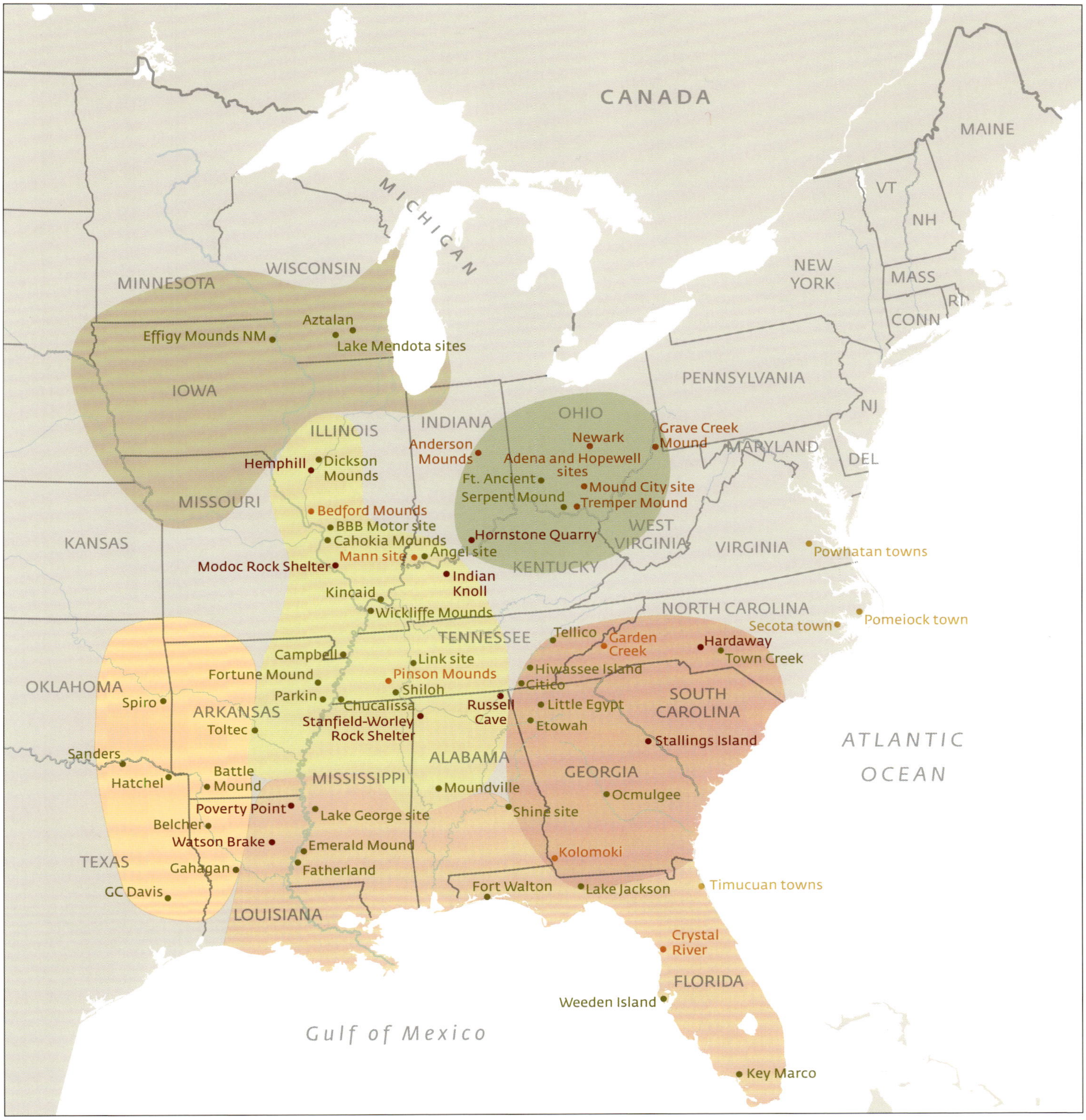

CANADA
MAINE
MICHIGAN
VT
NH
NEW YORK
MASS
RI
CONN
MINNESOTA
WISCONSIN
Aztalan
Effigy Mounds NM
Lake Mendota sites
IOWA
PENNSYLVANIA
NJ
OHIO
Grave Creek Mound
ILLINOIS
INDIANA
Newark
Anderson Mounds
Adena and Hopewell sites
MARYLAND
DEL
Hemphill
Dickson Mounds
Ft. Ancient
Serpent Mound
Mound City site
Tremper Mound
MISSOURI
Bedford Mounds
BBB Motor site
Cahokia Mounds
KANSAS
Hornstone Quarry
WEST VIRGINIA
VIRGINIA
Powhatan towns
Mann site
Angel site
Modoc Rock Shelter
KENTUCKY
Indian Knoll
Kincaid
Wickliffe Mounds
NORTH CAROLINA
Secota town
Pomeiock town
TENNESSEE
Tellico
Garden Creek
Hardaway
Town Creek
Campbell
Link site
Hiwassee Island
Fortune Mound
Pinson Mounds
Citico
OKLAHOMA
Shiloh
SOUTH CAROLINA
Spiro
Parkin
ARKANSAS
Chucalissa
Russell Cave
Little Egypt
Toltec
Stanfield-Worley Rock Shelter
Etowah
Stallings Island
ATLANTIC OCEAN
Sanders
ALABAMA
Battle Mound
GEORGIA
Hatchel
MISSISSIPPI
Moundville
Ocmulgee
Poverty Point
Lake George site
Shine site
Belcher
Watson Brake
Emerald Mound
Kolomoki
TEXAS
Gahagan
Fatherland
GC Davis
Fort Walton
Lake Jackson
Timucuan towns
LOUISIANA
Crystal River
FLORIDA
Weeden Island
Gulf of Mexico
Key Marco

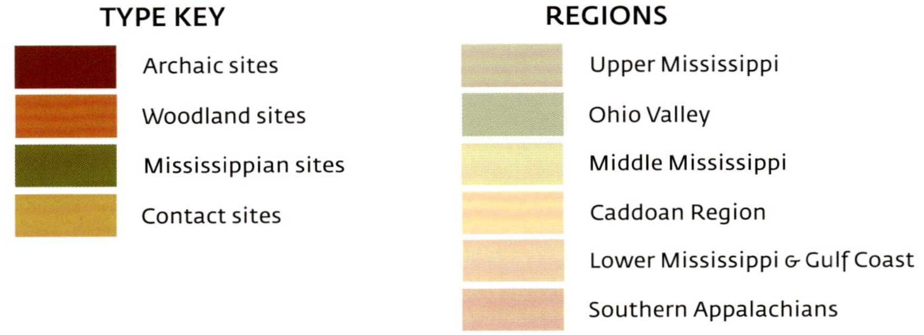

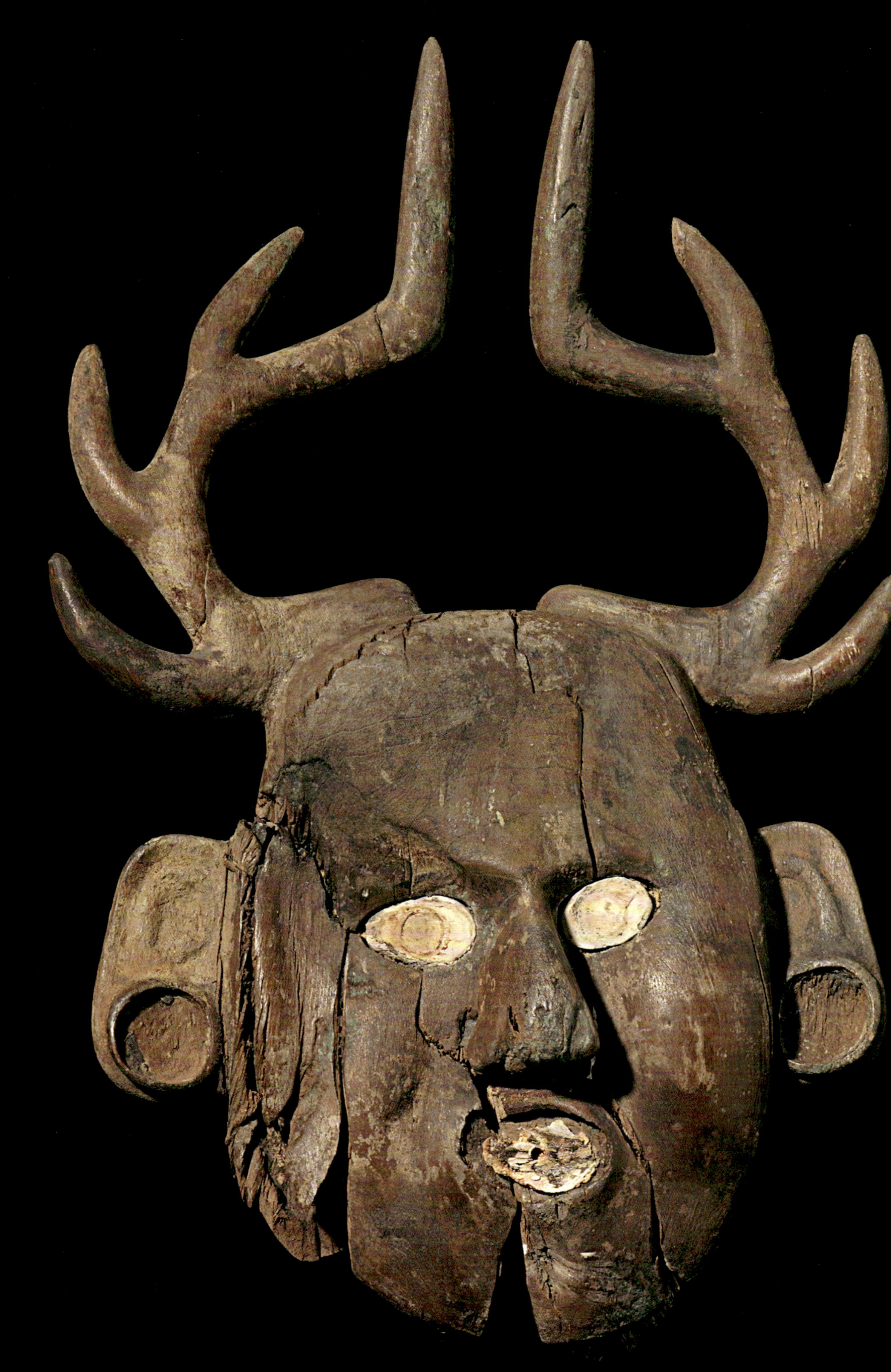

American Landscapes, Seen and Unseen

Richard F. Townsend

Fig. 1 Deer mask; Oklahoma, LeFlore County, Spiro, Craig Mound, A.D. 1200–1400; red cedar and marine shell, 29.2 × 15.9 cm; Smithsonian Institution, National Museum of the American Indian, Washington, D.C. Cat. no. 272. In their search for food and valued materials, humans formed covenants with the animals of prey and acknowledged their wisdom and communion with the all-powerful forces of nature. Art and ritual affirmed these connections in symbolic form, expressing veneration, reconciliation, and participation in the sacred cycle of birth, death, and renewal.

Few notions have so strongly affected the American imagination as the idea of the Untamed Wilderness. The perception of a vast continent, covered with forests and traversed by long rivers and mountain ranges, with immense inland lakes and sweeping prairies with limitless animals; the adventure of exploration and the complex tensions that arose in the fierce battle for North America among the competing French, English, and Spanish, and the many indigenous Indian nations; the formation of the American republic and the wars and tragedies of Indian removal during the nineteenth-century westward migration—all of these have contributed to making the challenge of the wilderness a unique, determining theme in shaping our national ethos. Even today, traveling through the Midwest and South, it is possible to glimpse fragments of what was once perceived as a primeval expanse: a glittering river between wooded banks, flights of snow geese on their annual migration, a dark storm sweeping over the plain. Our passage also offers other, half-noted impressions, presented by things seen but unrecognized, or heard as familiar words of American English, yet stemming from tongues rooted in an earlier time. Such fleeting sensations are prompted by the latent presence of an old, yet almost unknown, cultural dimension of our landscape, embracing the record of ancient societies that once flourished in the woodlands, prairies, and riverine valleys. Names of hundreds of places and geographical features, signs pointing to scattered archaeological sites, and many routes of overland travel testify to the fact that there never really was an untamed wilderness here—or at least not since the time of the mastodon and saber-toothed cat: for North America had been in the process of being explored, populated, and exploited for thousands of years before the European migrations began. The creation of early forms of civilization by Native American peoples between the Atlantic seaboard and the reaches of the Mississippi basin is another aspect of the human adaptive experience that also took place at different times in Mesoamerica, in the Andes of South America, and in Mesopotamia and China, as societies evolved from tiny bands of hunters and gatherers to sedentary villagers, urban agriculturists, and complex dynastic states.[1] The story of this process in the Midwest and South, its connections to Native American life today, and its wider significance in our collective history have yet to be recognized as a vital part of the American experience.

Leading westward from the coastland dunes through Piedmont farmlands and over the Appalachian passes, interstate highways run unimpeded across the breadth of the midwestern basin. Yet our speed of travel is so fast and topographic changes are so gradual between the mountains and the Mississippi, that our sense of space becomes ever less defined by the sequence of natural features than by the sights of the roadway corridor itself—our dominant visual environment. Many will find it hard to imagine that it was barely a hundred and fifty years ago, in the decades that followed the Civil War, that a new enterprise rapidly took form, drastically and permanently changing the face of the continent. Preeminently utilitarian yet not without aesthetic intention, a new environment began to be laid out by surveyors, engineers, urban planners, businessmen, journalists, farmers, and ranchers. The movement was unprecedented in scale, designed to serve a vision of economic growth without discernible limits.[2] Yet the land was not to be organized solely for the exploitation of abundant natural resources: cities and towns were also designed with zones for commercial districts, residential suburbs, and industrial areas as places with specialized functions. Urban settings were beautified with healthful parks and grids of tree-lined streets equipped with public lighting, while the the landscape became an immense mosaic of fields bordered with hedges and rows of windbreak trees. A new kind of space was called into being, designed, remade, and controlled to conduct an uninterrupted, endless flow of energy, people, and materials.[3] It has been called "the largest, most rapidly constructed human artifact on the planet."[4]

Even so, these transformations never entirely stripped away the memory of earlier inhabitants and their ways of perceiving and using the landscape. Every region is filled with names of major topographical formations, local features, small towns, cities, counties, and states that carry the memory of an indigenous American past. From the Pamlico Sound to the Michigan shores, from Chicago to Minnesota, from Tallahassee to Tishomingo and across the Chattahoochee, Tombigbee, and Mississippi rivers to Arkansas, Oklahoma, Missouri, and Iowa, hosts of names reflect Algonquian, Atakapan, Caddoan, Iroquoian, Siouan, Tunican, and Muskhogean speech. Such terms are now so embedded in our national idiom that their origins are barely recalled, their meanings long unremembered. Many highways are also superimposed on roads traveled since early Colonial times, which in turn followed centuries-old Indian trails and, perhaps remotely, the paths of seasonal animal migrations. The vast river network by which goods and people were principally transported before railroads and interstate highways was also well known long before the seventeenth-century French explorers, *voyageurs*, and *coureurs de bois*, whose Indian guides led them from the Great Lakes to the mouth of the Mississippi.

In contrast to the Southwest where the Indian heritage is so visibly rooted, its archaeological monuments visited by thousands, or to Mexico, Guatemala, Peru, and Bolivia, where the Indian present and magnificent past are everywhere manifested, our historical awareness of an earlier indigenous Midwest and South barely reaches into the sixteenth- and seventeenth-century explorations by De Soto, Champlain, La Salle, and Marquette, the lost Jamestown colony, or the fearsome wars waged by the Iroquois against the Huron, Miami, Potawatomi, and Illinois. As to what was there before, the term "moundbuilders" may evoke images of mysterious earthen constructions: tall, conical burial barrows, broad circular or square enclosures bounded by massive earthen berms, or mounds in the shapes of animals and flat-topped earthen pyramids, built by peoples whose achievements and ancestral connections to present-day tribes are at best only vaguely surmised.

Many will therefore be surprised to know that during the past one hundred and fifty years, archaeological explorations have charted thousands of sites—ranging from primitive rock shelters used by migrant hunters and gatherers 15,000 years ago, to early villages and a succession of towns, ceremonial centers, and fortified capitals of chiefdoms and statelike societies that evolved during the past 2,500 years—whose tribal descendants were seen and described by European explorers in the sixteenth and seventeenth centuries (see chronological chart, p. 12). Excavations have shown that each phase of cultural development was marked by distinctive ways of subsistence, patterns of settlement, assemblages of artifacts, and styles of art and architecture: evidence of a succession of diverse societies and the adaptation, transmission, and readaptation of deep-seated cultural themes over thousands of years.

The archaeological record begins with hunting and gathering peoples of the late Pleistocene epoch during the last phases of continental glaciation. Their quarry included the largest of the now-extinct fauna—mammoths and great bisons—in addition to more familiar game; and they collected a wealth of fruits

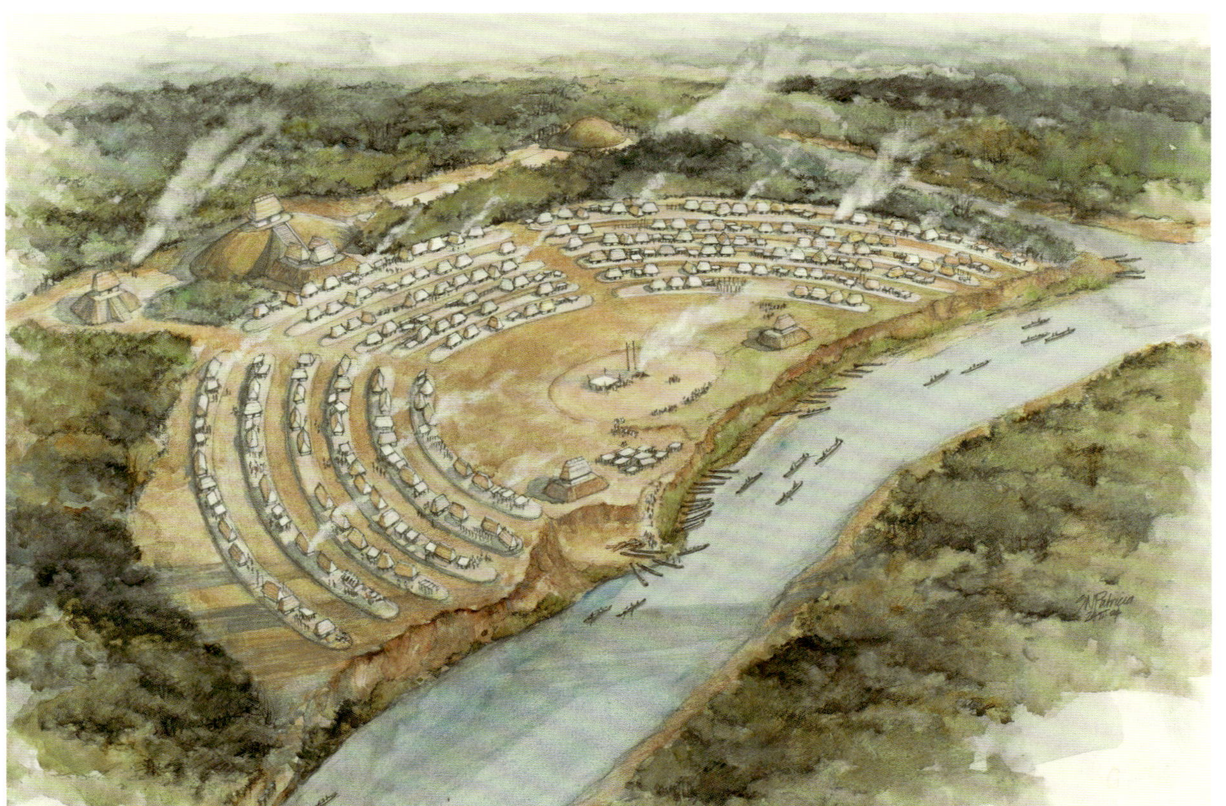

Fig. 2 Poverty Point was constructed around 1500 B.C. along the western bank of the river Bayou Maçon in northeastern Louisiana. The path of the sun bisects the semicircular design of Poverty Point, from the open plaza on the east to the monumental earthen pyramid due west. This alignment linked the rhythms of ritual and communal life to the cosmos, expressing a dominant theme of the Amerindian worldview represented in art, architecture, and ritual performance from Archaic times to the present. Rendering by Steven Patricia.

and plants in season. They possessed an impressive body of empirical knowledge, transmitted for millennia, but of their artistic and symbolic world direct evidence is presently lacking. Certainly the early stone implements such as Clovis or Dalton points often attain a level of perfection that brings them into the larger orbit of art. They were precursors of a long tradition of artful stone blades and weapons (figs. 27–28 and 45). We may only suppose, by analogies drawn from the life of hunters and gatherers of more recent times, that they also engaged in symbolic activity. Far from wandering perpetually in virgin environments these early bands surely formed cultural bonds with their habitat through signs, symbols, and ritual actions. Long before architecture was imagined, sacred geographies were created with systems of ceremonial places in caves, by waterholes or lakesides, in secluded groves and upon mountaintops, or near routes of animal migrations.[5] Marked with special signs or objects, these were places where rites were periodically held to propitiate the animal powers and the deified forces of nature, and to initiate young men and women with dances and songs of creation myths and dramatic legends of heroes and heroines.

By the Archaic period (c. 6000–500 B.C.), hunting, gathering, and fishing peoples were still engaged in age-old lifeways; yet a new family of forms—the subtly shaped objects known as bannerstones, birdstones, and boatstones, which all served as weights for atlatl spear-throwers—made their appearance as the earliest works of art thus far identified in the ancient Midwest and South (see figs. 11–25). The Archaic period also saw construction of the first architecturally defined ceremonial centers, in the teeming forests of Louisiana. At Watson Brake, for example, an unexcavated ring of earthen mounds marked a place of special spiritual importance.[6] By 1500 B.C. at Poverty Point, overlooking the river Bayou Maçon, a town was designed in a roughly semicircular plan, commanded by an imposing earthen pyramid 50 feet high by 500 feet long (15.2 × 152 meters), aligned to the east-west path of the sun (fig. 2). Perhaps inhabited by as many as 1,000 people, this was the largest settlement in North America, formed well before such elaborate sites appeared in southern Mexico.[7] Around 500 B.C. a new form of culture began to take shape as the focus of major activity shifted to the central Ohio River valley in the vicinity

Fig. 3 Parakeet effigy bead; Arkansas, Lafayette County, Badlow Creek, J. T. Lee site, c. 3000 B.C.; red jasper, l. 6 cm; Gilcrease Museum, Tulsa, Oklahoma. Cat. no. 18.

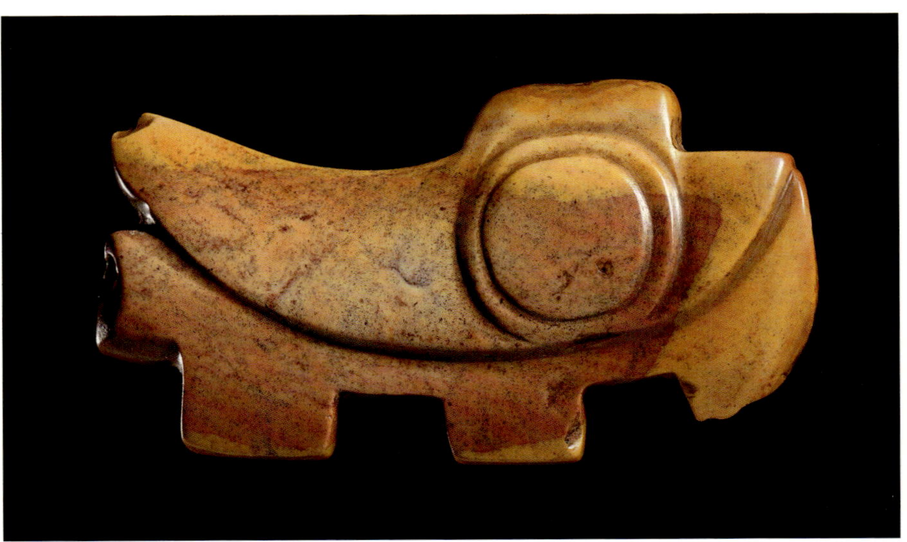

of the modern states of Ohio, West Virginia, and Kentucky. Between roughly 400 B.C. and A.D. 100, peoples participating in Adena ceremonialism were building tall conical burial mounds in commemoration of local leaders (fig. 4). These were followed by the Hopewell sites of c. A.D. 1–400: an impressive series of open circles, hexagons, and squares, defined by high earthen berms, some covering up to 50 acres (20 ha) and linked by long processional ways, were constructed along the course of the Scioto River (fig. 5).[8] By this time the artistic repertoire included a spectrum of specialized forms and a range of exotic materials: shell traded from the Gulf of Mexico, copper from upper Michigan, mica from North Carolina, obsidian from far Wyoming. Woodland subsistence economy still rested strongly on hunting, gathering, and fishing; yet plant foods were also painstakingly cultivated: maize, squash, gourds, sunflowers, chenopodium, maygrass, marsh elder, and little barley. Hopewell culture reached westward into the Illinois River valley, and its influence was evident at Pinson Mounds in west Tennessee (fig. 6).

The next major cultural florescence, known as Mississippian, began taking form between A.D. 800 and 900. The new synthesis was most powerfully expressed at the city of Cahokia, built near the confluence of the Missouri and the Mississippi and the nearby mouths of the Illinois and Ohio rivers. At the pivot of the four quarters, Cahokia became a cosmopolitan capital with monumental flat-topped pyramids, burial mounds, and a vast ceremonial concourse enclosed by formidable defenses and surrounded by residential zones, workshops, a marketplace, and outlying agricultural zones (fig. 7).[9] A center of far-reaching trade and a theocratic seat of political, religious, and military authority, perhaps inhabited by 15,000 to 20,000 people, Cahokia set standards that remained prestigious long after its thirteenth-century decline. In this period, there are suggestive indications of contact with Gulf Coast peoples of Mesoamerica, but substantial archaeological proofs have proven elusive, and this major issue remains to be fully investigated. Important regional centers flourished in Cahokia's orbit: at Spiro, Oklahoma, a rich trove of Cahokia-related works of art and ritual paraphernalia was interred with the provincial nobility as tokens of rank, status, and political and religious legitimacy.[10] The legacy and prestige of Cahokia continued into the late fourteenth and fifteenth centuries, when new "paramount" chieftaincies arose at Etowah, Ocmulgee, and elsewhere in Georgia;[11] at Moundville in western Alabama;[12] and at many lesser sites along the Tennessee River and throughout the Southeast. These were seats of warrior elites that vied for ascendancy over far-ranging polities. A time of disintegration—perhaps due to a cycle of drought—began after 1400, and these centers, like Cahokia before them, were eventually abandoned. Yet Hernando de Soto's expedition of 1539–43 found chiefdoms of the late Mississippian world still flourishing from Florida to the Carolinas, Tennessee, Arkansas,

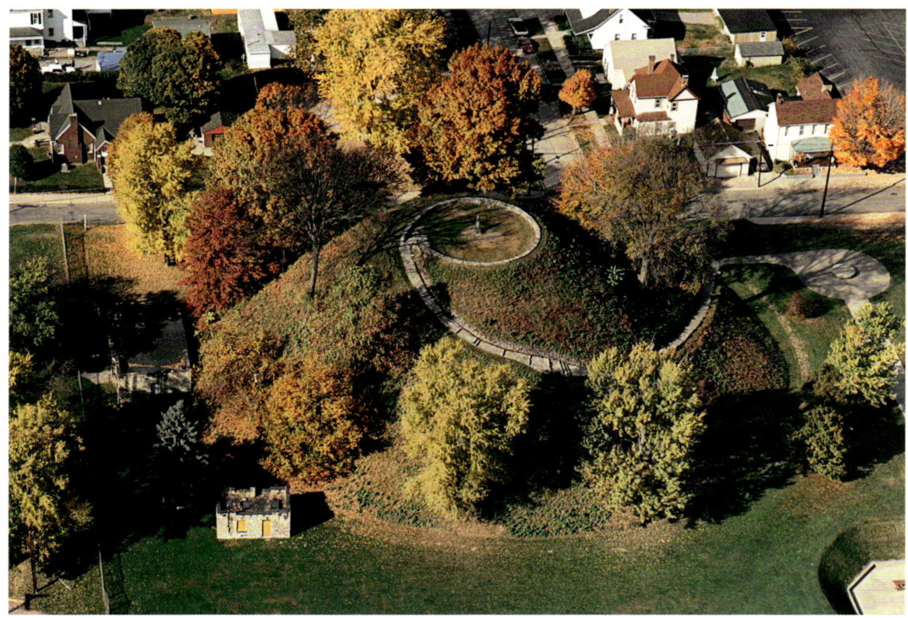

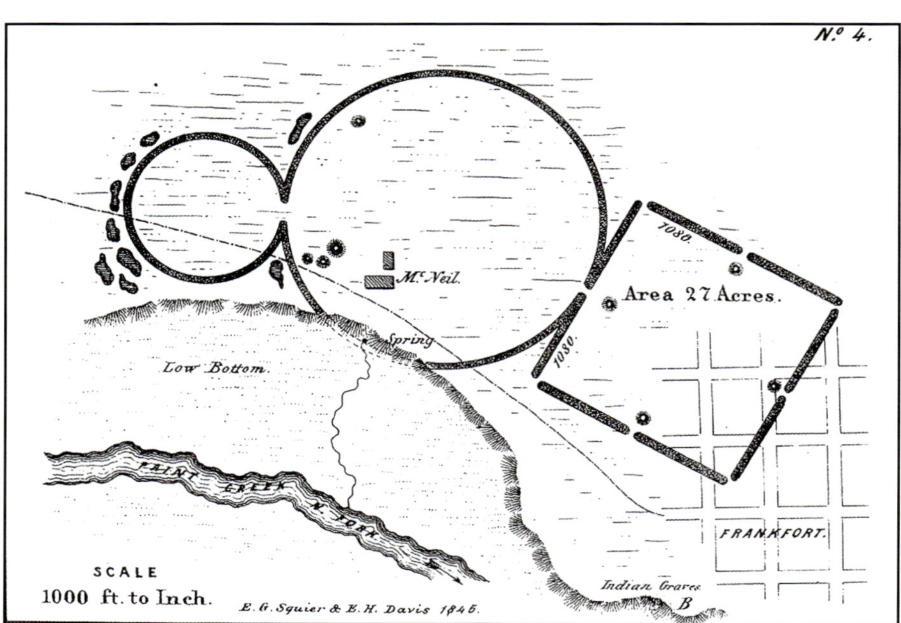

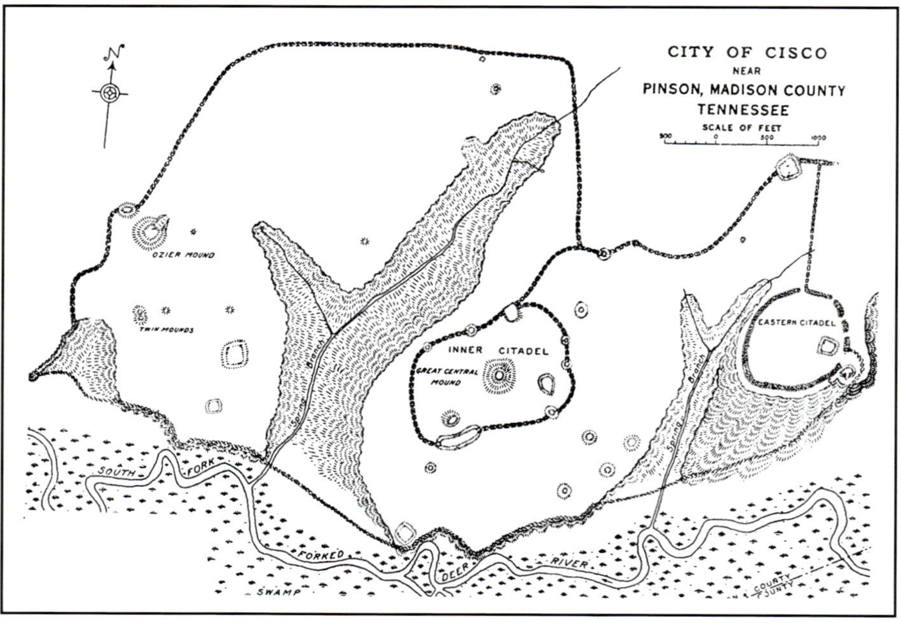

and east Texas.[13] By the seventeenth century, French traders and colonial authorities on the lower Mississippi River traded with the Natchez kingdom, a last manifestation of the old "moundbuilder" tradition.[14]

Devastated by smallpox and other sweeping epidemics from the Old World for which they had no immunity, the indigenous populations were being reduced by as much as two-thirds and by 90% in some instances—a factor contributing to the "empty landscape" found by incoming European and American settlers. Survivors reformed into new tribal groups that held their own through the turbulent Colonial period, only to face forced removal to the Oklahoma Territory by decree of President Andrew Jackson in the 1830s.[15] The fearful disasters of the Trails of Tears, disruptive patterns of resettlement, an enforced government boarding school program that lasted until the 1960s, and the suppression of traditional religion and the widespread acceptance of Christianity and the Native American Church, all resulted in massive losses to native languages and ancient ways of thought and life. Nonetheless, many tribes continue to trace ancestral connections to former homelands of the late Mississippian world, and many also actively maintain forms of belief and ceremonial life stemming directly from the old traditions.[16]

Approaching the Ancient Visual Systems

Hero, Hawk, and Open Hand: American Indian Art of the Ancient Midwest and South seeks an understanding of the way different societies defined themselves and their environment through the symbolism and expressive power of art, architecture, and ritual performance. Our intention is to identify and interpret the dominant forms of symbolic and aesthetic expression, outlining patterns of thought and the determining force of ideas and visual imagery in the formation and maintenance of ancient societies. This approach to the visual arts is relatively new in investigations of the ancient Midwest and South. The first major exhibition to outline such issues was formed in 1985.[17] Since 1994, annual seminars on Mississippian imagery have been held at Texas State University in San Marcos, gradually expanding the area of inquiry. The approach complements information developed thus far by archaeology, which has correlated a great mass of material evidence ranging from the analysis of pollen, fragments of foods, ceramics, implements, dwellings, monuments, settlement patterns, and items of trade. Such remains, meticulously charted, show that improved methods of food production were fundamentally linked to the emergence of ever more stratified and specialized societies with elaborate administrative, religious, and military organizations; long-distance trade; manufacturing; and communities with ceremonial architecture and widespread political, economic, and cultural influence.

The present book and the exhibition it represents acknowledge this achievement while taking up the no less demanding and critical problem of understanding the crucial role of intellectual, spiritual, and artistic life in the evolution of social complexity in the Midwest and South. As a point of departure, our approach takes into account a singular contrast between the way civilizations took form in the Americas as opposed to the Old World. In the ancient Middle East and Mediterranean basin, diverse peoples and conflicting cultures continually interacted and clashed: Mesopotamians, Hittites, and Egyptians; Persians and Greeks; Romans and Carthaginians; and Mongols, Afghans, and Arabs. An essential reality of this experience was one of contact between strange races and different ways of life, dissimilar gods, technical accomplishments, visions of this world and the next. By comparison, New World civilization grew up in an immense historical isolation. In Mesoamerica, for example, the earliest Olmec societies were followed by Maya and Teotihuacan city-states, and those of the Zapotecs, Totonacs, Mixtecs, and others before the Aztec empire took shape. To be sure, the archaeological record is replete with evidence of war, trade, intermarriage, and forms of cultural exchange, as happened in the ancient Middle East and Europe; but for all the Mesoamerican ethnic and linguistic diversity, its distinctive regional history, and the splendor and variety of its art and architecture and the range of its socioeconomic characteristics, these societies were linked in time and space by a fundamental similarity and display a shared cultural tradition. It was not until the sixteenth-century Spanish conquest that the peoples of Mesoamerica and elsewhere on the continent encountered a radically alien, *other*, form of society and culture.

While a set of basic Mesoamerican characteristics was initially identified by 1952, it was not until the late 1960s and 1970s that investigations began to focus intensively on the Mesoamerican worldview and the function of ideas and the visual arts in shaping the life of its peoples.[19] It is now understood that the diverse

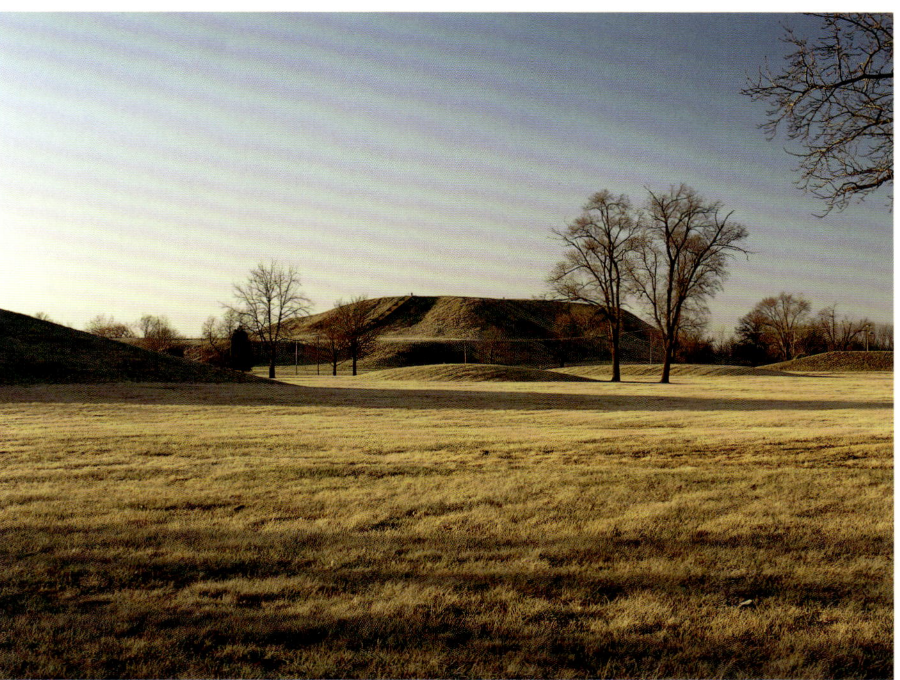

Fig. 7 View looking north toward Monks Mound at Cahokia, the largest Mississippian settlement, located largely in St. Clair County, Illinois, between Collinsville and East St. Louis. The upper platform of this immense earthen pyramid once supported the tall, thatched residence of the principal chief. With duties and obligations embracing the religious, military, and economic spheres, the rulers of Cahokia governed a stratified society and a network of connections reaching across the vast midwestern and southeastern landscape.

facing page

Fig. 4 Grave Creek Mound, an Adena burial mound in Moundsville, West Virginia.

Fig. 5 Ephraim G. Squier and Edwin H. Davis, Map of Hopewell earthworks near Frankfort, Ohio, on North Paint Creek in Ross County; from Squier and Davis 1848, pl. 21, no. 4.

Fig. 6 Plan of Pinson Mounds, Madison County, Tennessee; plan from Myer 1922, with additional information by Mark Norton, Pinson Mounds State Park archaeologist.

peoples of this major cultural tradition participated in a cosmological mode of thought that found order, coherence, and meaning in the integration of human society and the larger structure seen and experienced in the natural environment.[20] The way these societies were organized and functioned followed the way they perceived the design and rhythms of the world around them. In this communal vision of the universe, leaders had the vital obligation to play an active role, by means of religious practices, in ensuring the regular progression of the seasons, the fertility of the soil, the abundance of plants and animals, and the prosperity and integrity of their people. Reflected in the symbolism of art, architecture, and ritual performance, these essential principles were transmitted and adapted by the succession of chieftaincies, states, and empires, each giving rise to its own distinct visual system. Even today among indigenous peoples in remote areas of Mexico or Guatemala, traditional patterns of life may vividly display the intimate relationship between man and nature in notions of sacred geography and concepts of time and space stemming from this ancestral heritage.[21] Such patterns of cultural continuity are also apparent in the Andean and Amazon regions of South America and in the U.S. Southwest.[22]

No systematic attempt has yet been made to outline a comparable structure of unifying factors in the ancient Midwest and South; nevertheless, the archaeological record does suggest a cultural matrix similar to that of Mesoamerica and other regions where early New World civilizations flourished. Here too in the woodlands and prairies a succession of different societies evolved, responding to diverse historical circumstances and ecological conditions yet also seeming to share a broad family resemblance. It therefore seems possible to advance the idea of an analogous history of shared cultural themes, transmitted and adapted from Archaic times through the Woodland period and into the Mississippian centuries, continuing in modified form into the Colonial period and even lasting substantially in a few tribes down to the present time. It is a remarkable fact that in the United States there exists an exceptional wealth of historical documents and ethnographic records of the highest quality, many written by native speakers or prepared in close cooperation with them. These sources, in addition to traditional knowledge still kept among the tribes today, form an extraordinary record of cultural continuity and change that can be effectively linked to the archaeological data and works of art as a means of recovering

facing page, top

Fig. 9 Effigy of a mythic horned animal; Ohio, Hamilton County, Turner site, Mound 3, A.D. 1–400; petrified wood, h. 7.6, l. 25.4 cm; Harvard University, Peabody Museum of Archaeology and Ethnology, Peabody Museum Expedition 1882, F. W. Putnam and Dr. C. L. Metz, Directors. Cat. no. 33. This fearsome, composite creature, at once reptilian and insectlike, is one of the earliest visual metaphors portraying the dangerous, menacing power of rivers and other forms of groundwater.

Fig. 10 Fragment of an engraved whelk shell with an Underwater Panther or piasa; Craig B style; Oklahoma, LeFlore County, Spiro, Craig Mound, A.D. 1200–1400; marine shell, h. 19.7 cm; University of Arkansas Museum, Fayetteville. Cat. no. 128.

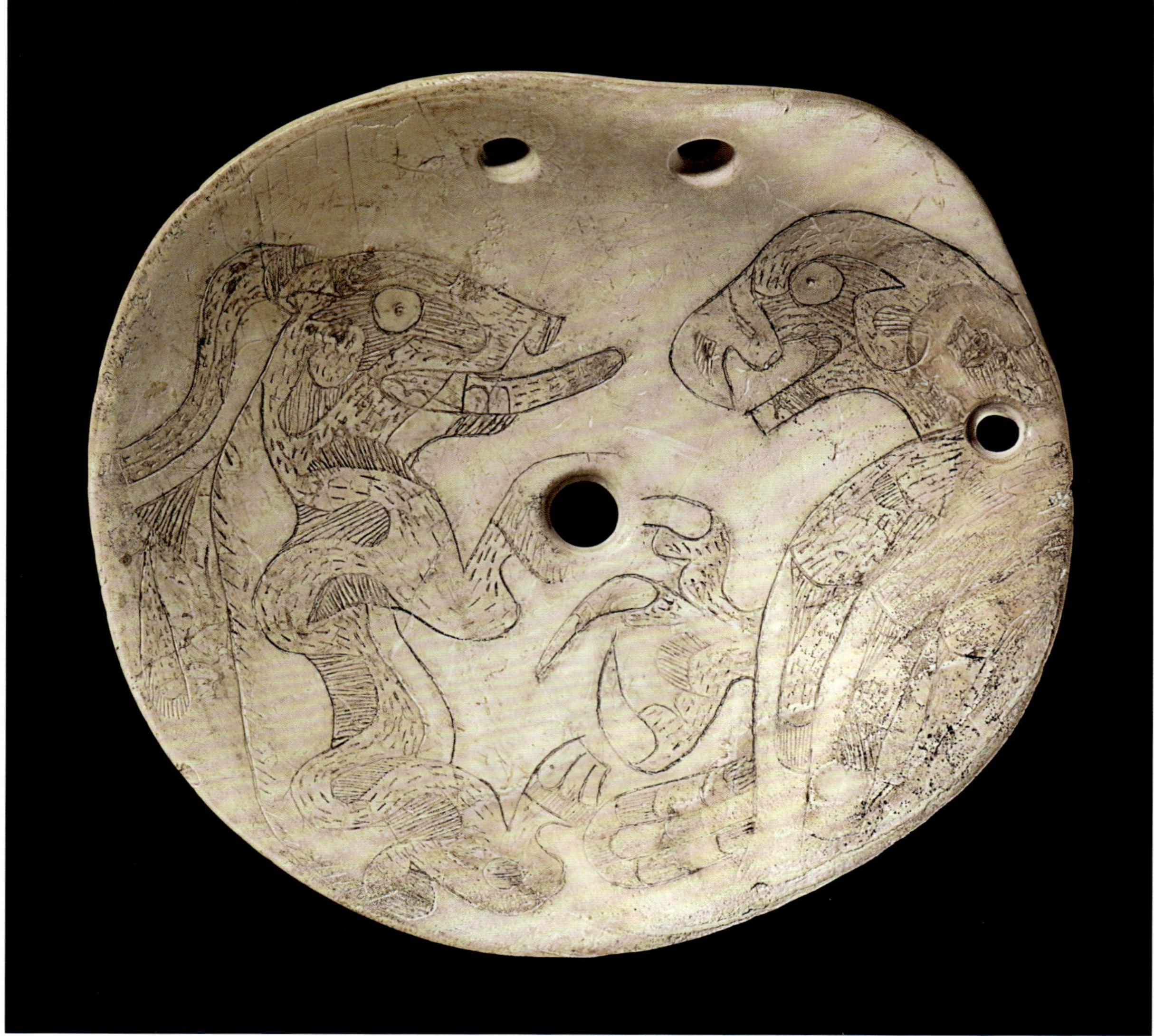

Fig. 8 Engraved shell gorget with feline and hawk; Fairfield style; Texas, Bell County, near Oenaville, A.D. 300–700; marine shell, diam. 14 cm; Smithsonian Institution, National Museum of the American Indian, Washington, D.C. Cat. no. 35. Worn as a badge of high office, this depiction of a confronted feline and hawk may well symbolize the duality of earth and sky, and also allude to corresponding alternations of "winter" and "summer" parts of the year and a two-part division of human society as a moiety system.

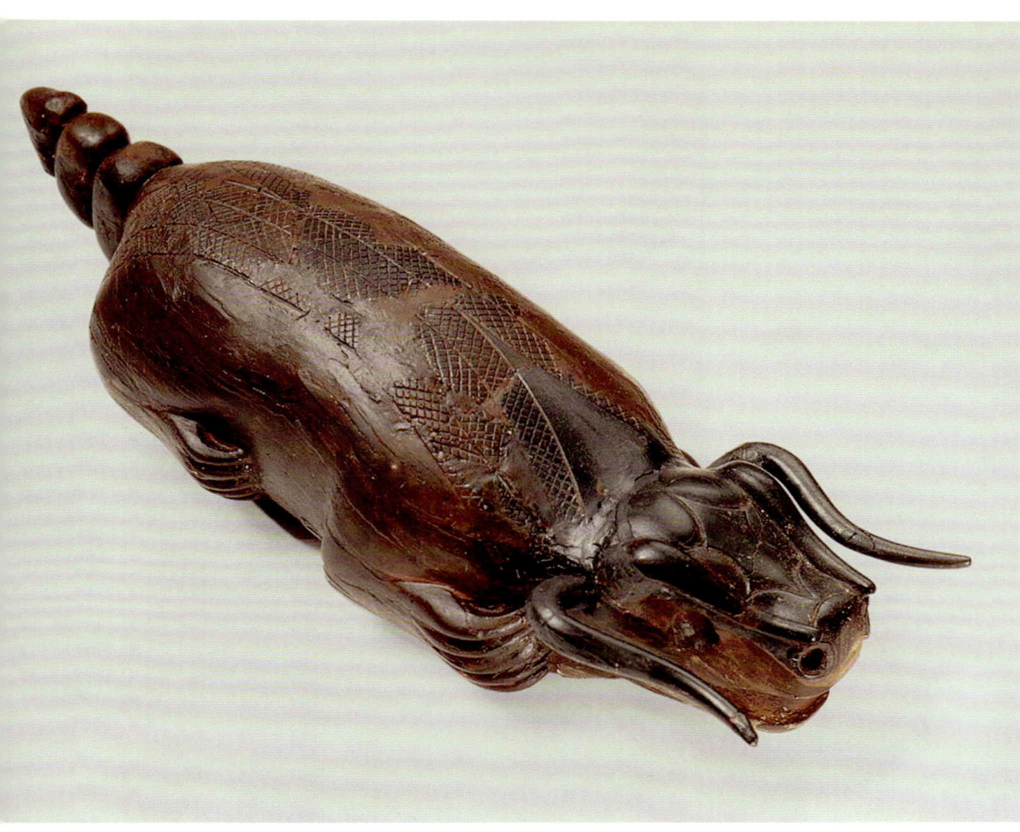

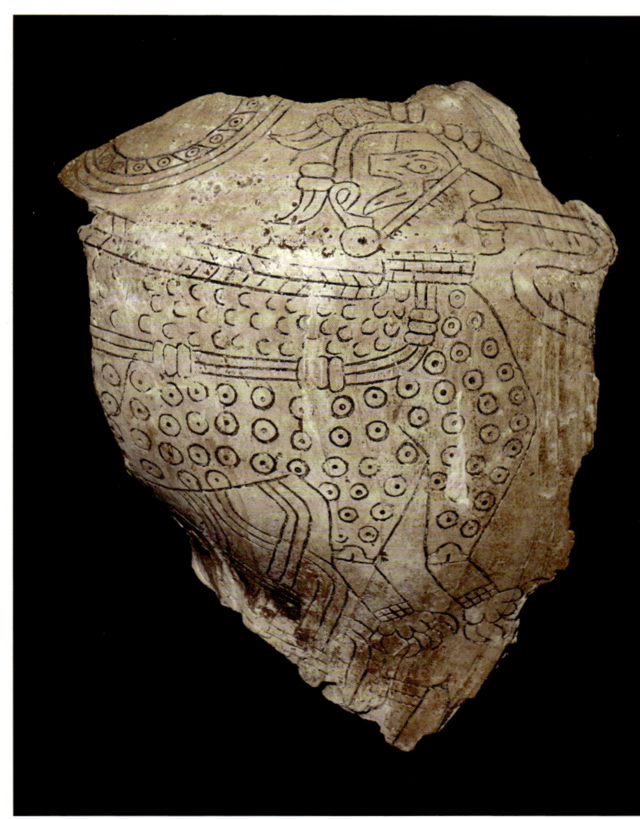

their unfamiliar imagery, identifying their possible meanings and functions, and approaching the mind of the ancient user and beholder.[23] We must not forget that works of art, architecture, and ritual also have their own visual "texts," often speaking of themes that may not be recorded in written records. Drawing upon such information, and with the Mesoamerican example in mind, the essays in this book explore a framework of themes outlined in the visual arts of the ancient Midwest and South over a three-thousand-year span of time. These themes are proposed below.

Cosmic and Social Order. Our initial premise holds that, as elsewhere around the world where old cosmological religions prevailed, the peoples of the ancient Midwest and South considered themselves to be participating in a network of connections that spread outward from their communities into the life of animals and plants, leading to the powers inherent in rivers, rocks, mountains, and other phenomena of the earth and sky, and the remote, immaterial, all-powerful forces of life, death, and renewal. The organization and activities of human society were intimately bound to this web of life-forces residing in the natural environment. The structure of the natural world was abstractly expressed in terms of a celestial dome, the earthly plane surrounded by a primordial sea, and the watery underworld (see the essays by George Lankford and Kent Reilly in this volume). The horizontal disk of the earth, generally conceived in circular shape, was marked with cardinal and intercardinal points, emphasizing the overarching east-west line of the sun. A vertical axis connected the zenith of the heavens to the nadir of the world below. Each day the sun unfailingly rose in the east, traversed the sky, and set below the western horizon, continuing around beneath the dark underworld before rising again on the morrow. This concept was symbolically represented by a circle enclosing a cross corresponding to the four directions, sometimes including a diadem as the sun in its zenith position.

Fig. 11 Birdstone; Georgia, Floyd County, near Rome, 1500–1000 B.C.; greenstone, l. 12 cm; American Museum of Natural History, New York. Cat. no. 22.

Fig. 12 Birdstone; Ohio, 1500–1000 B.C.; stone, l. 8.9 cm; Gilcrease Museum, Tulsa, Oklahoma. Cat. no. 26.

Fig. 13 Birdstone; Ohio, 1500–1000 B.C.; stone, l. 16 cm; Peabody Museum of Natural History, Yale University. Cat. no. 25.

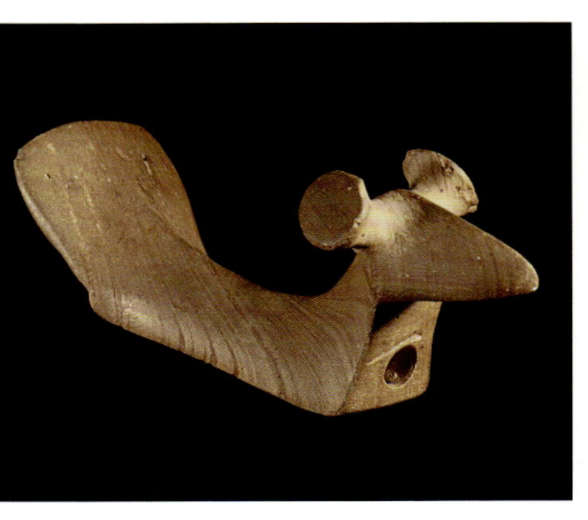

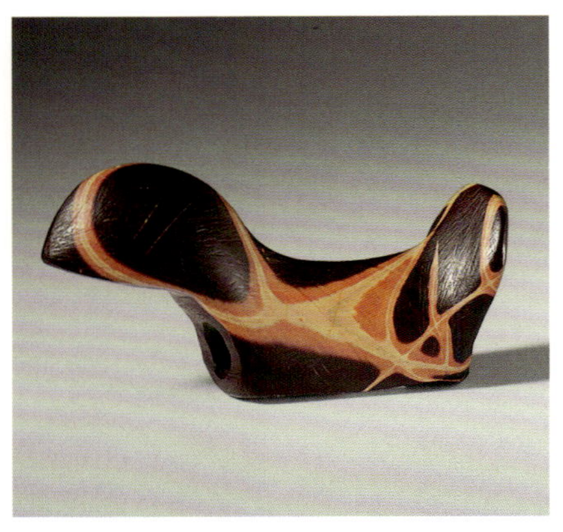

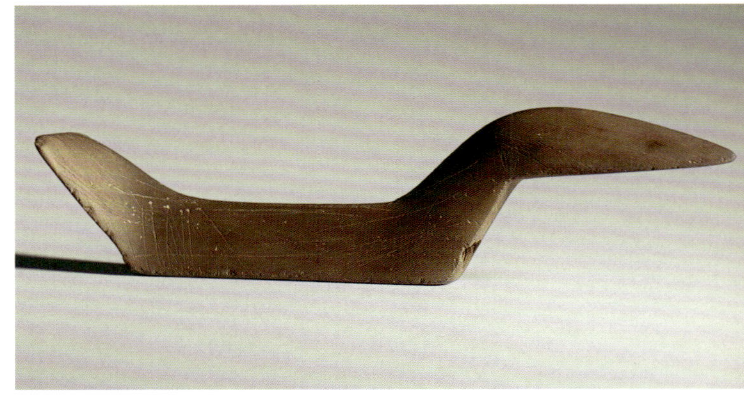

The periodic cycles of the sun, moon, planets, and stars were observed as the most regular, predictable, and reliable natural phenomena on which to base the construction of calendars and the annual round of ceremonies marking the "summer" season for planting, cultivation, and harvest, and the "winter" season for hunting, long-distance trading, and war. Historical and ethnographic data describe how many societies in North America and Mesoamerica were correspondingly divided in halves, or moieties, with "summer" and "winter" people responsible for conducting the governmental and ritual activities according to their assigned half of the year.[24] There is reason to suppose that similar correspondences between cosmological and social categories obtained in the organization of ancient societies as well. Such correspondences could also be symbolically expressed through animal imagery, as in a Woodland shell gorget engraved with the confrontation of a feline and hawk: the cat is associated with the earth and winter "fur" people, while the hawk is associated with the noonday sun, "feather" people, and summer activities (fig. 8). The sun was revered as a supreme deity by the Natchez and others of the ancient Southeast. Even down to the present, the sun's earthly representative, fire, is kept and annually renewed in the Creek ceremonial grounds, where four logs are cardinally placed, around which the elders and notables are seated in arbors, encompassed by the circular boundary of an earthen circle (see figs. 4–5 in the interview with Timmy Thompson in this volume).[25] Other forces of nature were represented by fantastic, metaphorical creatures, the most celebrated of which are piasas—beings that may take the form of "underwater panthers," sometimes with human faces, or horned serpents—personifying the dangerous, yet life-progenitive powers of the abyss, underground water, rivers, and lakes (figs. 9–10). Related creatures, depicted as plumed or winged serpents, become symbols of the sweeping energy of thunderstorms that rise up from the earth in spring and summer.[26] Frogs, too, as heralds of rain and springtime renewal, were rendered in sculptural form (see fig. 21 in the essay by Kent Reilly).

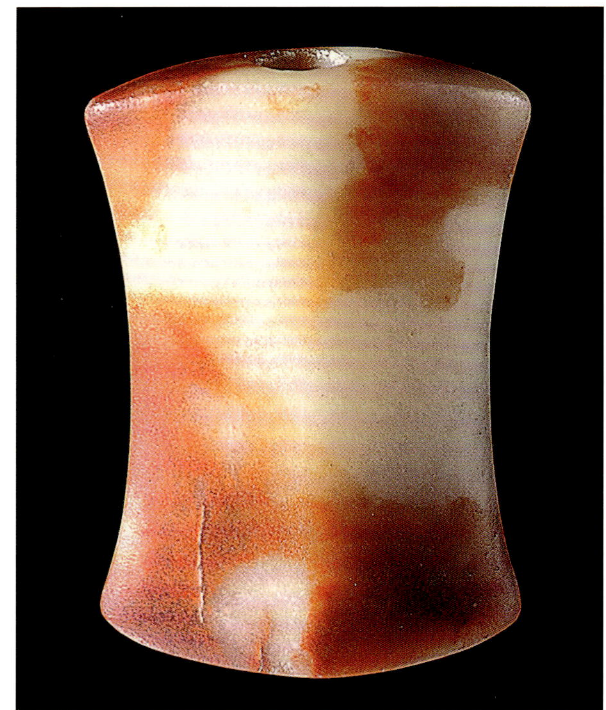

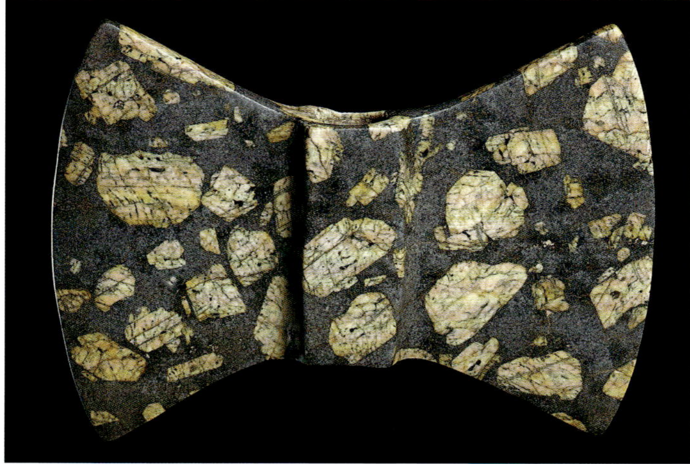

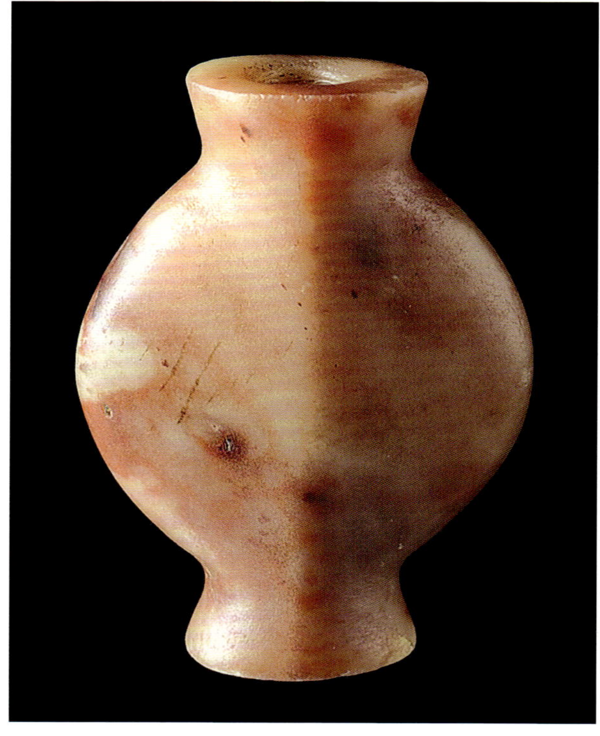

Domains of the Hunt and the Animal Powers. The psychological uncertainties and physical dangers of daily life among early hunters and gatherers were faced by sharpening their skills in the chase and performing rites that imbued them and their implements with magical and religious properties. Such preoccupations may account for the enigmatic archaic atlatl weights—bannerstones, birdstones, and boatstones—widely found from the Appalachians to Iowa, from Florida to the Great Lakes (figs. 11–25). The significance of these objects cannot be conclusively proven, yet may be approached by analogies drawn from weaponry use and symbolism among tribal peoples of historical times. Made of subtly shaped and polished quartzes, banded claystones, and other colorful lithic materials often imported from faraway sources, these minimal geometric forms were

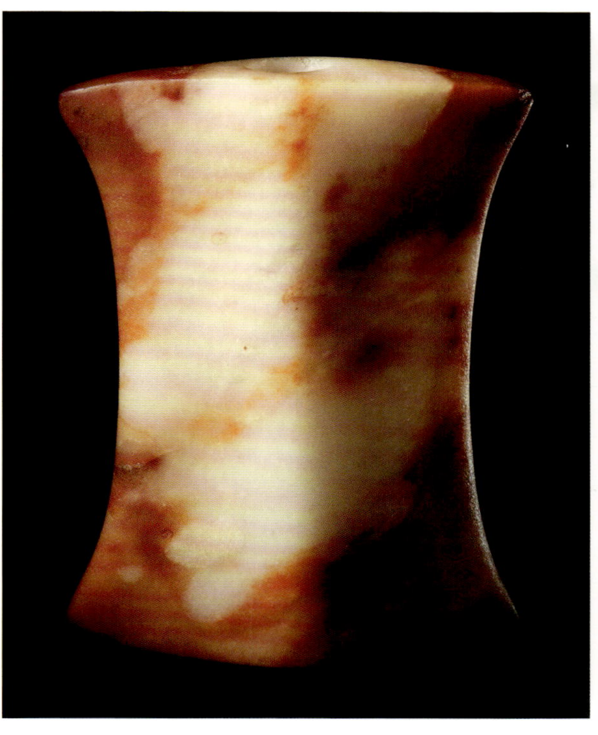

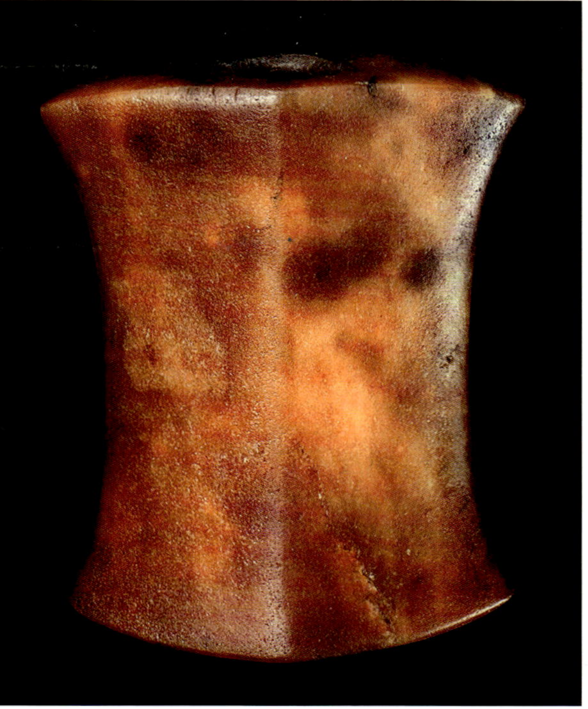

Fig. 14 Hourglass-shaped bannerstone; Indiana, Daviess County, near Plainville, c. 2000 B.C.; ferruginous quartz, h. 8.7, w. 5.9 cm; Maury Meadows Collection, Bethany, Missouri. Cat. no. 14.

Fig. 15 Hourglass-shaped bannerstone; Kentucky, Christian County, c. 2000 B.C.; carnelian, h. 11.4 cm; Gilcrease Museum, Tulsa, Oklahoma. Cat. no. 15.

Fig. 16 Hourglass-shaped bannerstone; Arkansas, Desha County, Boltwier, c. 2000 B.C.; ferruginous quartz, h. 9.5, w. 7.5 cm; Bobby Onken Collection. Cat. no. 16.

Fig. 17 Bowtie bannerstone; Iowa, 5000–3000 B.C.; porphyry granite, h. 8.7, w. 11.6 cm; Tommy Beutell Collection. Cat. no. 2.

Fig. 18 Double-edged bannerstone; Tennessee, Madison County, 5800–4000 B.C.; banded claystone, h. 4.6, w. 10.3 cm; T. W. McGuire Collection. Cat. no. 1.

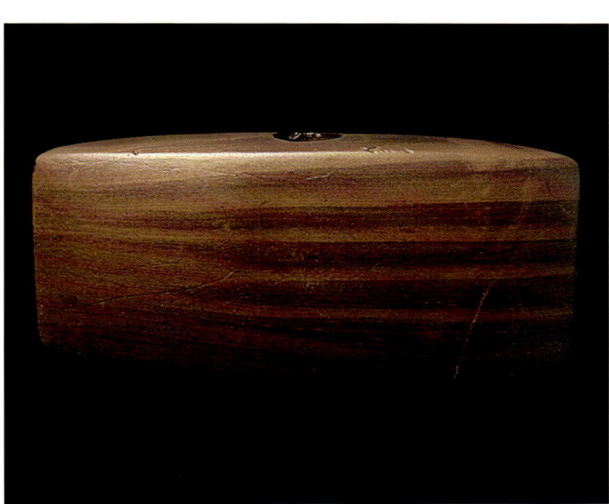

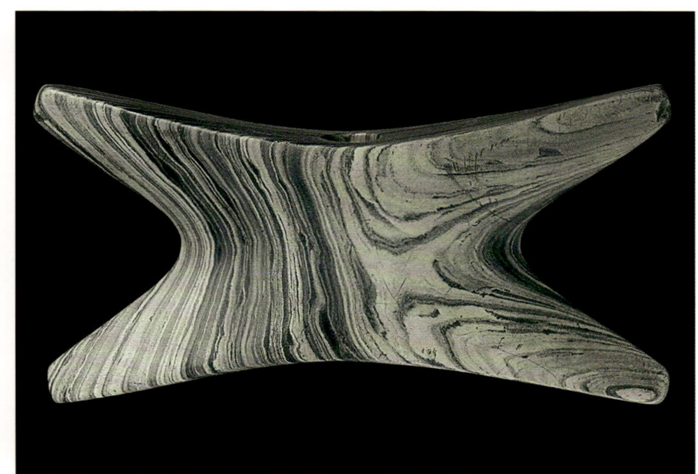

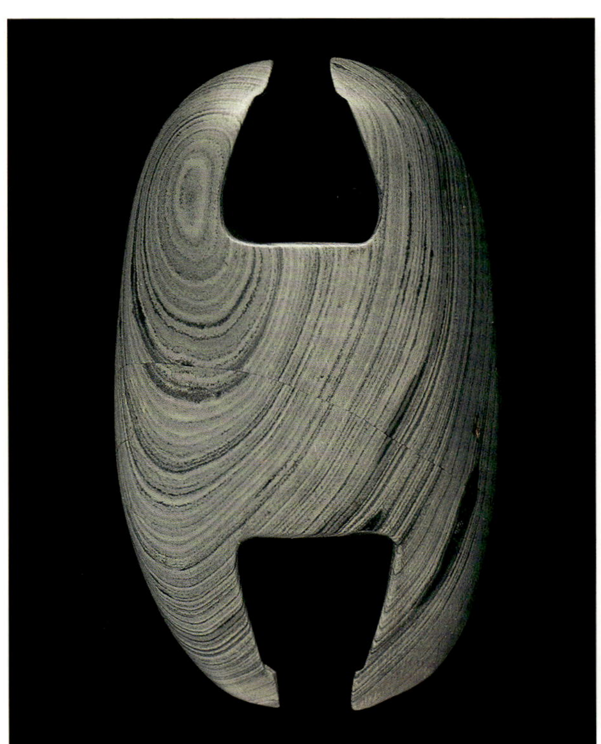

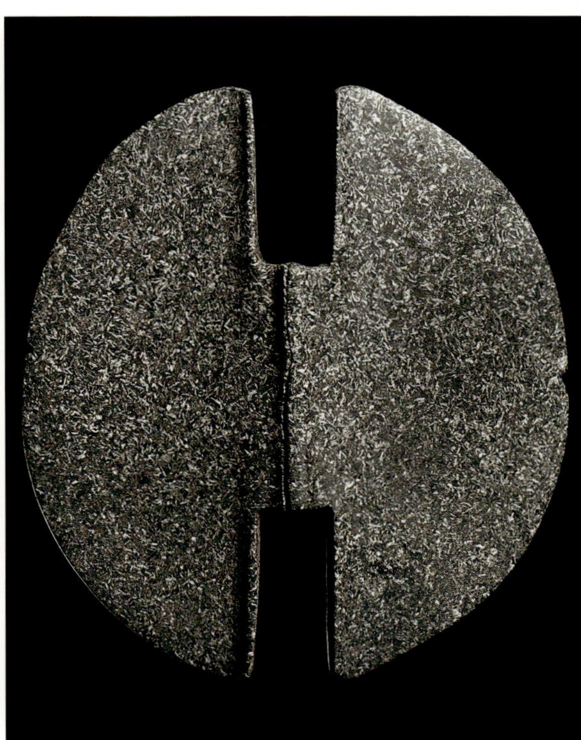

Fig. 19 Reel-shaped bannerstone; Ohio, Ross County, D.J. Jones Farm, south of Bourneville on Paint Creek, 5000–3000 B.C.; banded slate, h. 7.5, w. 13.5 cm; Edward Harvey Collection, California. Cat. no. 3.

Fig. 20 Bottle-shaped bannerstone; Kentucky, Union County, c. 3000 B.C.; ferruginous quartz, h. 8.6, w. 6.4 cm; Maury Meadows Collection, Bethany, Missouri. Cat. no. 10.

Fig. 21 Notched ovate bannerstone; Ohio, Union County, along Bokes Creek, c. 4800 B.C.; banded slate, h. 14.5, w. 8.3 cm; Edward Harvey Collection, California. Cat. no. 6.

Fig. 22 Bannerstone; Florida, Suwannee River, c. 4500 B.C.; granite, h. 11.4, w. 10.2 cm; Tommy Beutell Collection. Cat. no. 7.

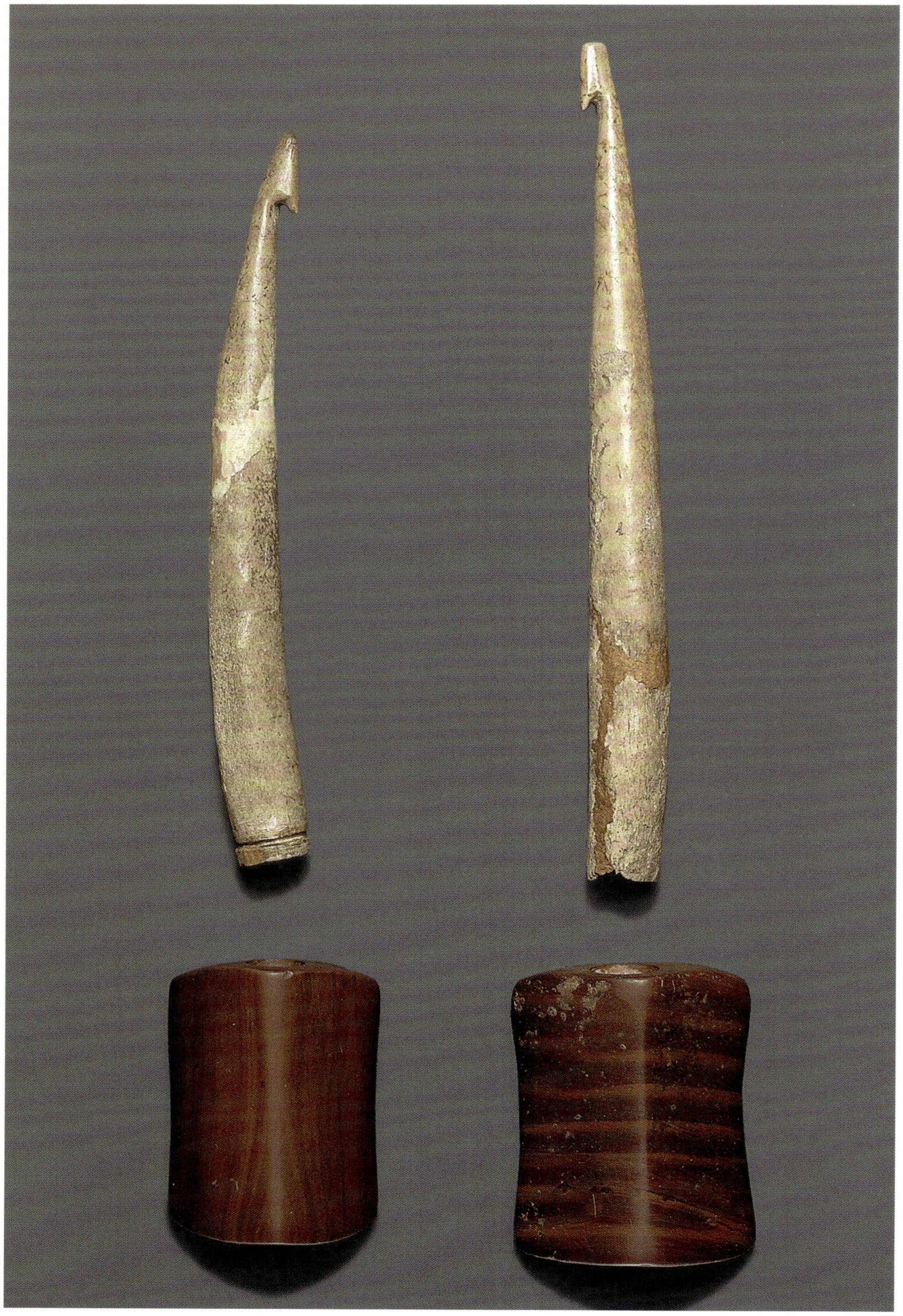

Fig. 23 Two atlatl hooks and weights; Indiana, Spencer County, Crib Mound, c. 3000 B.C.; left: saddle-shaped bannerstone; claystone, l. 7 cm; antler atlatl, l. 18.1 cm; right: saddle-shaped bannerstone; banded claystone, l. 7.6 cm; antler atlatl, l. 21 cm; David Lutz Collection, Newburgh, Indiana. Cat. no. 11. As weights fitted between the hooked end and the shaft of a spear-thrower (atlatl), bannerstones gave the implement a longer potential throwing distance, increased its chances of accuracy, and imparted greater force to the spear. Bannerstones appear to have become emblems of status and perhaps social affiliation, and they were made of prized and rare materials in an array of subtle, abstract, minimal shapes.

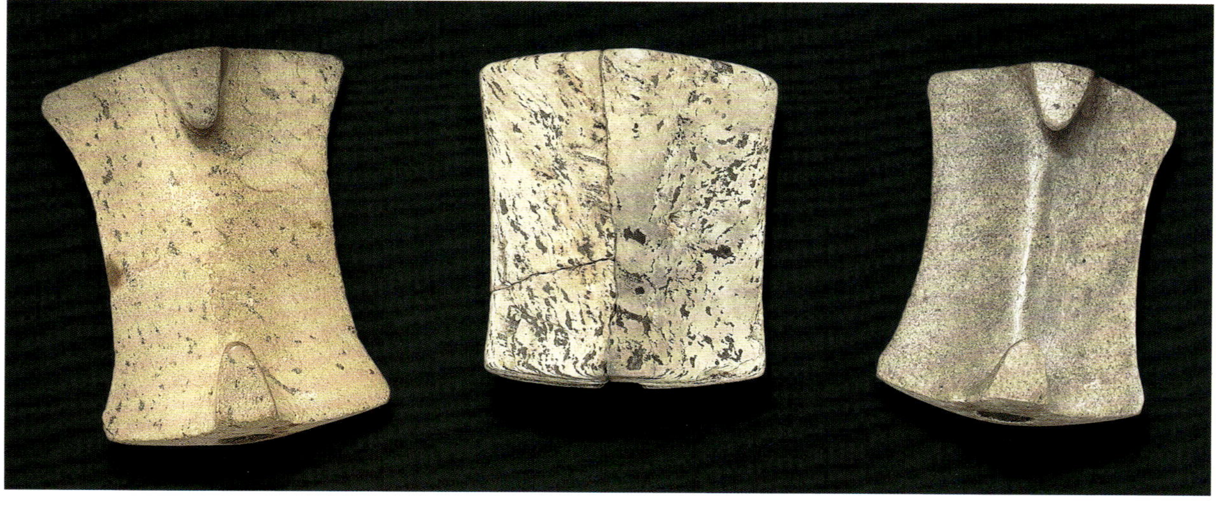

Fig. 24 Cache of three bannerstones (two hooked type; one hourglass-shaped); Indiana, Spencer County, Rockport site, c. 2300 B.C.; left: gneiss, l. 10.5 cm; center: gneiss, l. 9 cm; right: granite, l. 9.5 cm; David Lutz Collection, Newburgh, Indiana. Cat. no. 12.

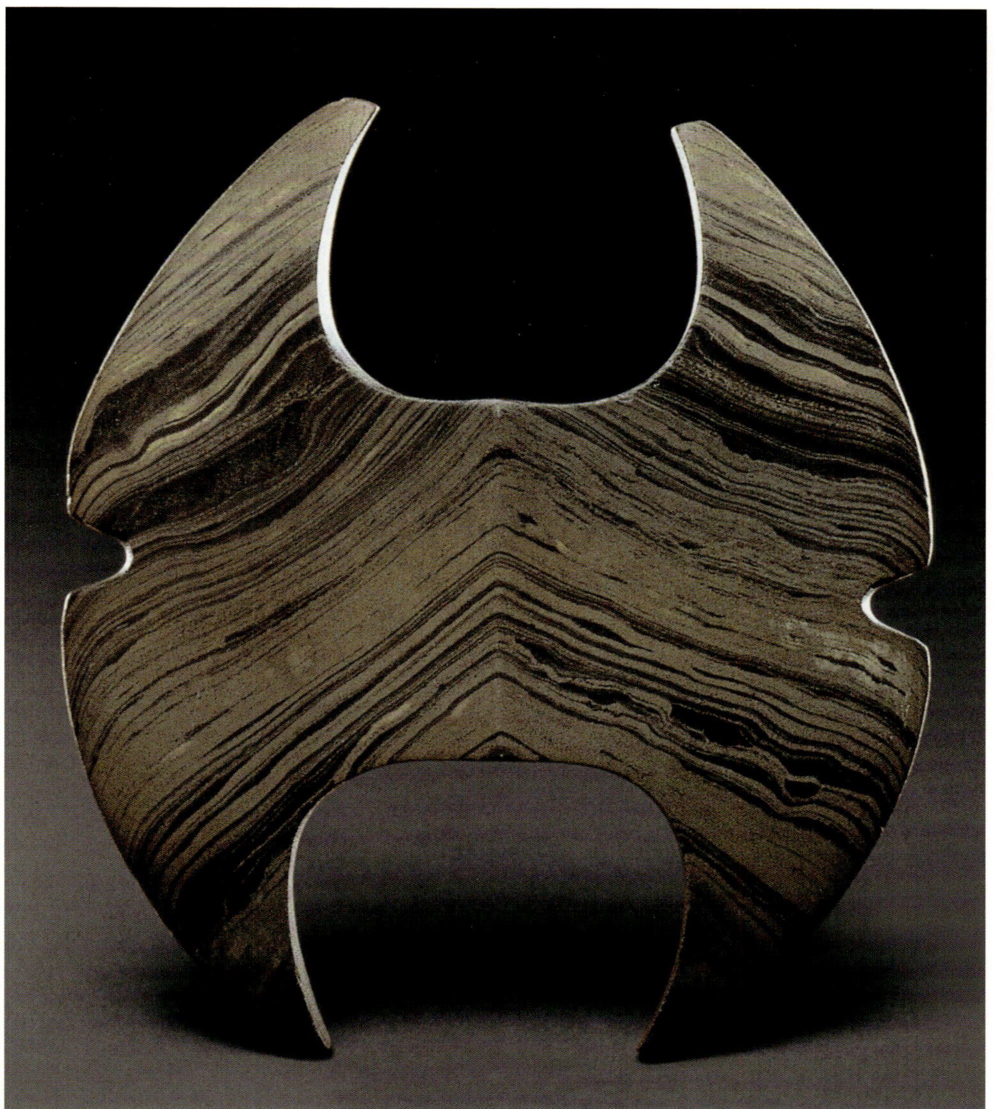

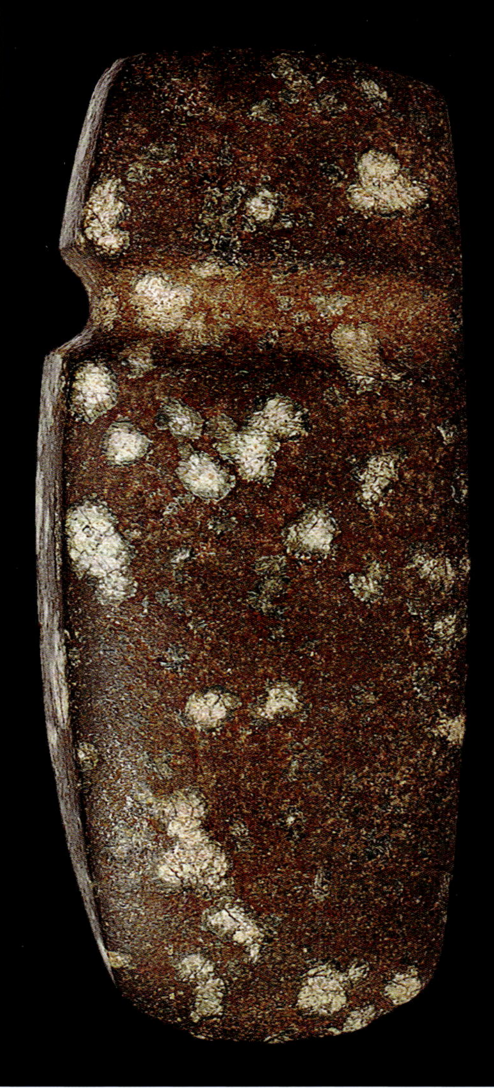

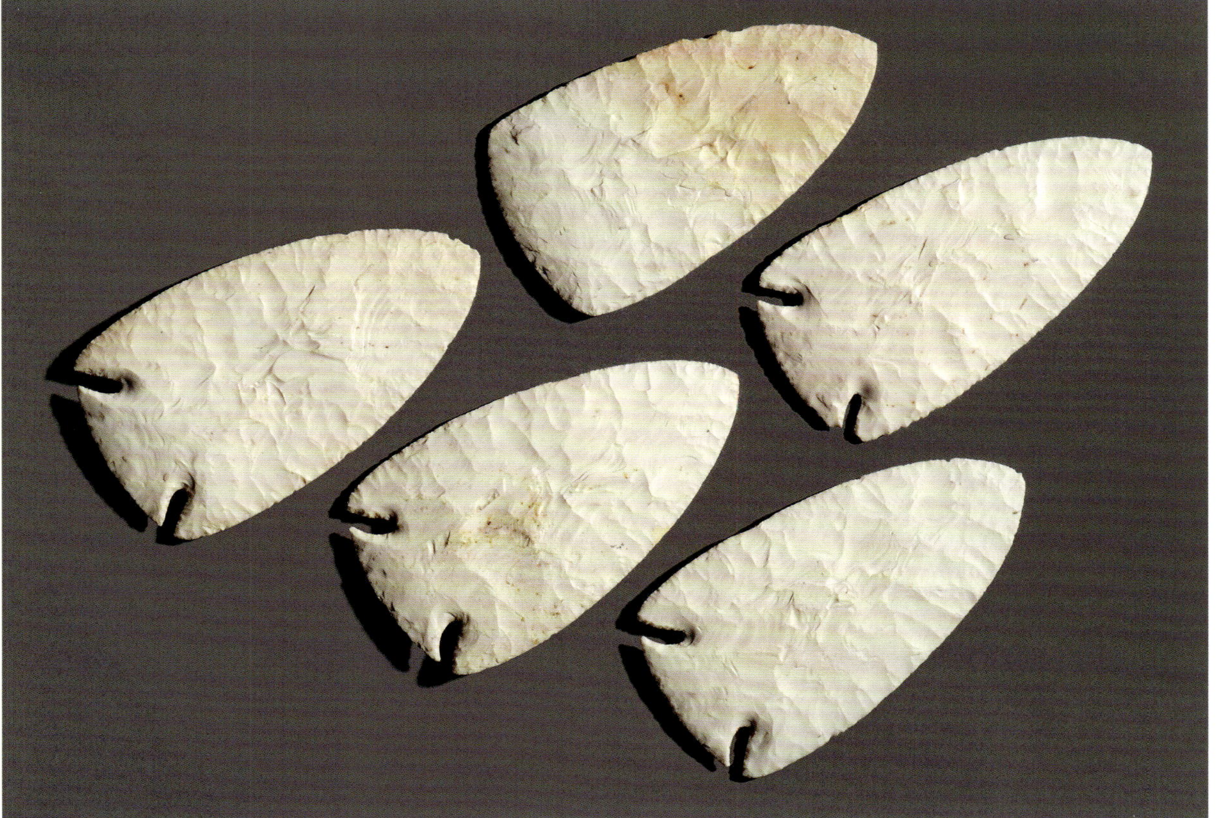

Fig. 25 Notched ovate bannerstone; Michigan, c. 4800 B.C.; banded slate, h. 12.7 cm; Steve and Susan Hart Collection, Huntington, Indiana. Cat. no. 5. The design of this famous piece features a symmetrical convex and concave outline, with a natural pattern of banded slate rising in chevrons across the central axial ridge.

Fig. 26 Axe head; Nebo style; Missouri, Andrew County, south of Savannah, c. 2000 B.C.; porphyry, l. 24.1 cm; Maury Meadows Collection, Bethany, Missouri. Cat. no. 19. Axe heads acquired more than utilitarian functions as emblems of chiefly authority and power during the Archaic period. Valued materials such as porphyry were subtly shaped and finished as ceremonial objects with strong symbolic and visual appeal.

Fig. 27 Cache of 32 bifacial blades; Illinois, Tazewell County, near Mackinaw, Hopewell, A.D. 1–400; Burlington chert, l. 12.7–13.5 cm; Illinois State Museum, Springfield. Cat. no. 38. The manufacture of stone points and blades for offerings and gifts achieved high levels of refinement, as is evident in this cache of 32 nearly identical, exceptionally thin, lanceolate blades.

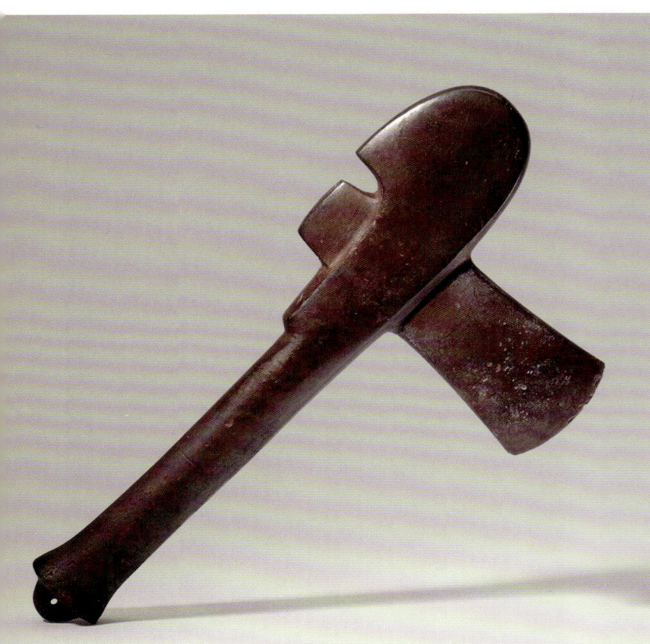

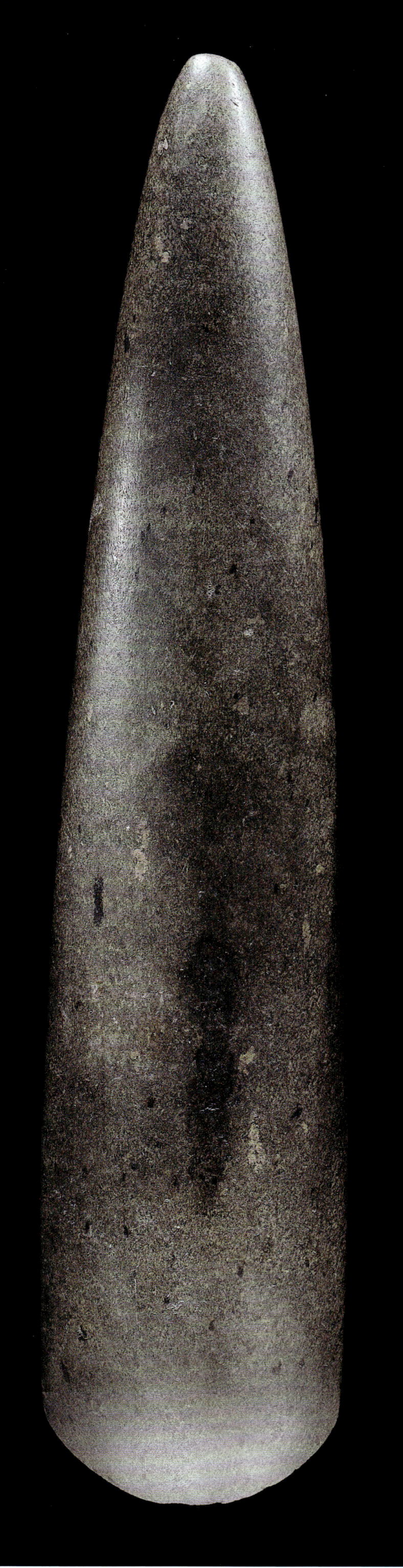

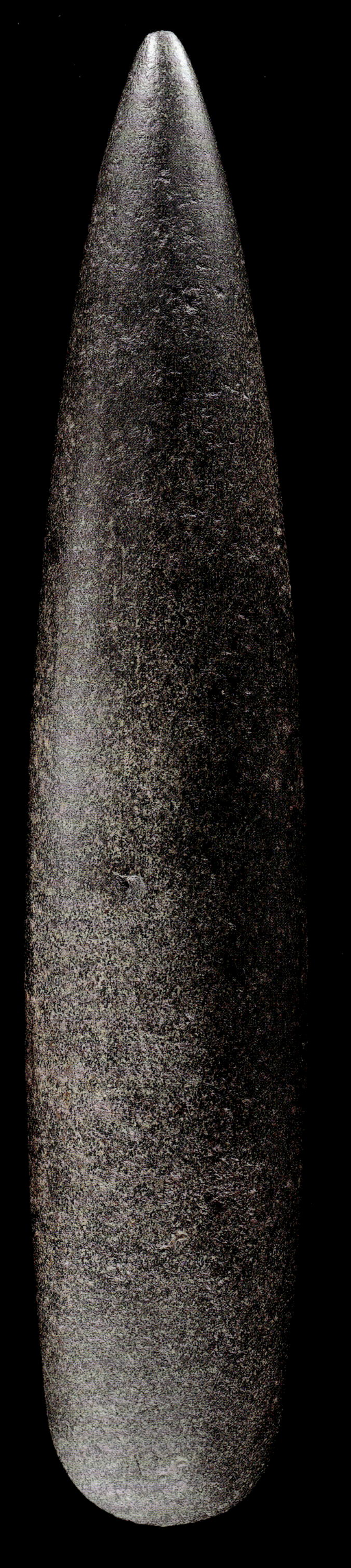

clearly highly valued. They functioned as weights for spear-throwers (atlatls), the primary weapon used for millennia before the bow and arrow (fig. 23).[27] But their craftsmanship and materials suggest that they also served as emblems of prestige and status conferred upon hunters coming of age, and as supernatural talismans for increasing the spear-thrower's efficacy. They may also have served as emblems of clans or other social units. The making of weapons for symbolic use remained a feature of Woodland and Mississippian art, in the form of finely flaked points, blades, and "swords," and beautifully shaped celts, maces, and model hafted axes, as ritualistic implements for the display of authority and power (figs. 26–30).

In the world of hunters and gatherers and among the town-dwelling peoples that followed, animals were seen as more than sources of food and useful materials. Because they have special instincts and properties that humans do not possess, and because they inhabit wild landscapes beyond the familiar, settled environment, animals were correspondingly perceived to be closer, in the continuum of sacred space, to the most distant, dangerous, all-powerful forces upon which life and death depended. Intersecting the sacred and the everyday, animals acted as intermediaries for humans. Diverse myths speak of a time when the earth was still unfinished and many people could understand animal languages, and could talk to reptiles, furred creatures, birds, or butterflies; animals could also change themselves into people, and people

Fig. 28 Monolithic axe; Caddoan; Oklahoma, LeFlore County, Spiro site, A.D. 1200–1350; stone, l. 33 cm; Gilcrease Museum, Tulsa, Oklahoma. Cat. no. 182.

Figs. 29–30 Two ceremonial celts; Tommy Bryden Collection, Springfield, Illinois. Cat. nos. 175–76. The unusual size, subtle proportions, and high finish of these celts suggest that they held important ritualistic significance, perhaps forming part of ceremonial bundles.

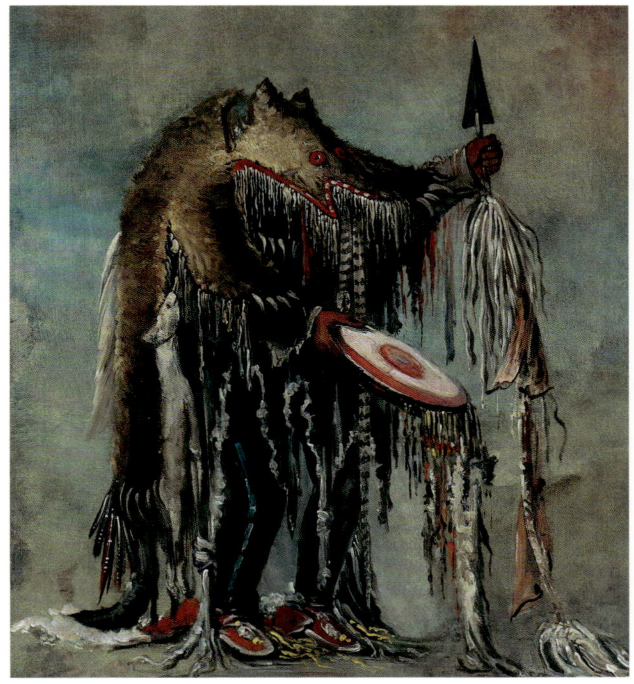

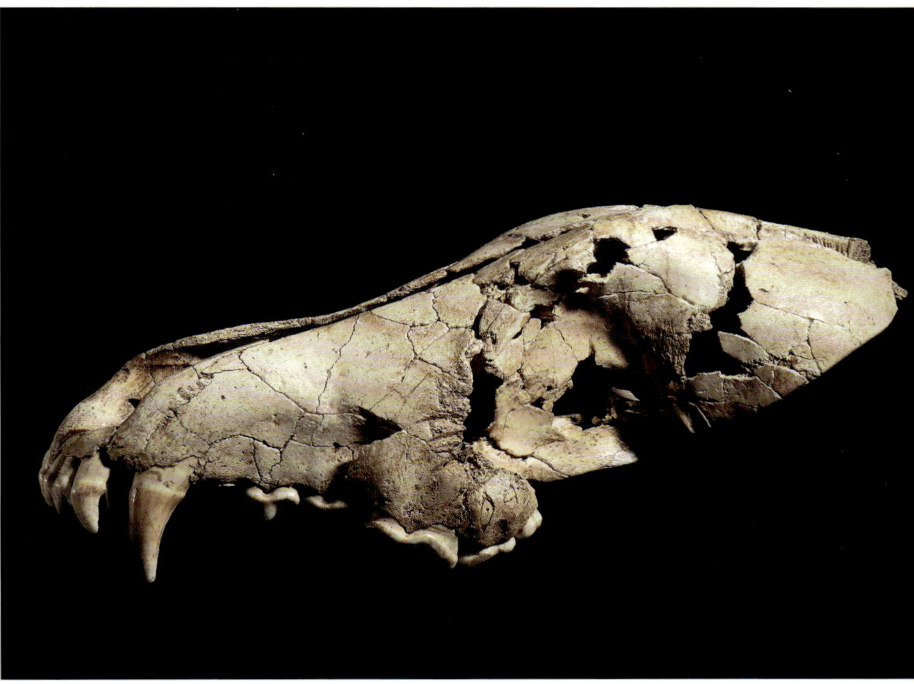

Fig. 31 George Catlin (American; 1796–1872), *Blackfoot Medicine Man, Performing His Mysteries over a Dying Man*, 1832; oil on canvas, 29 × 24 in.; Smithsonian American Art Museum, gift of Mrs. Joseph Harrison, Jr., 1985.66.161.

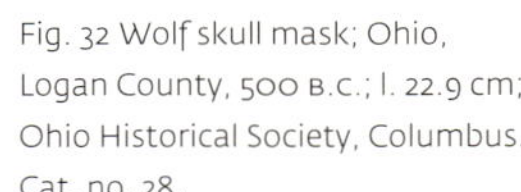

Fig. 32 Wolf skull mask; Ohio, Logan County, 500 B.C.; l. 22.9 cm; Ohio Historical Society, Columbus. Cat. no. 28.

Fig. 33 Aerial view of the great Serpent Mound, set along Ohio Brush Creek in Adams County, Ohio. Although all scholars are not in agreement, the best available evidence suggests that this effigy mound was constructed around A.D. 1000. High on a promontory between winding watercourses, this effigy mound mirrors the sinuous pattern of local topography. The three lower undulations point to the eastern horizon where the solstice and equinox sunrises mark pivotal times of the year.

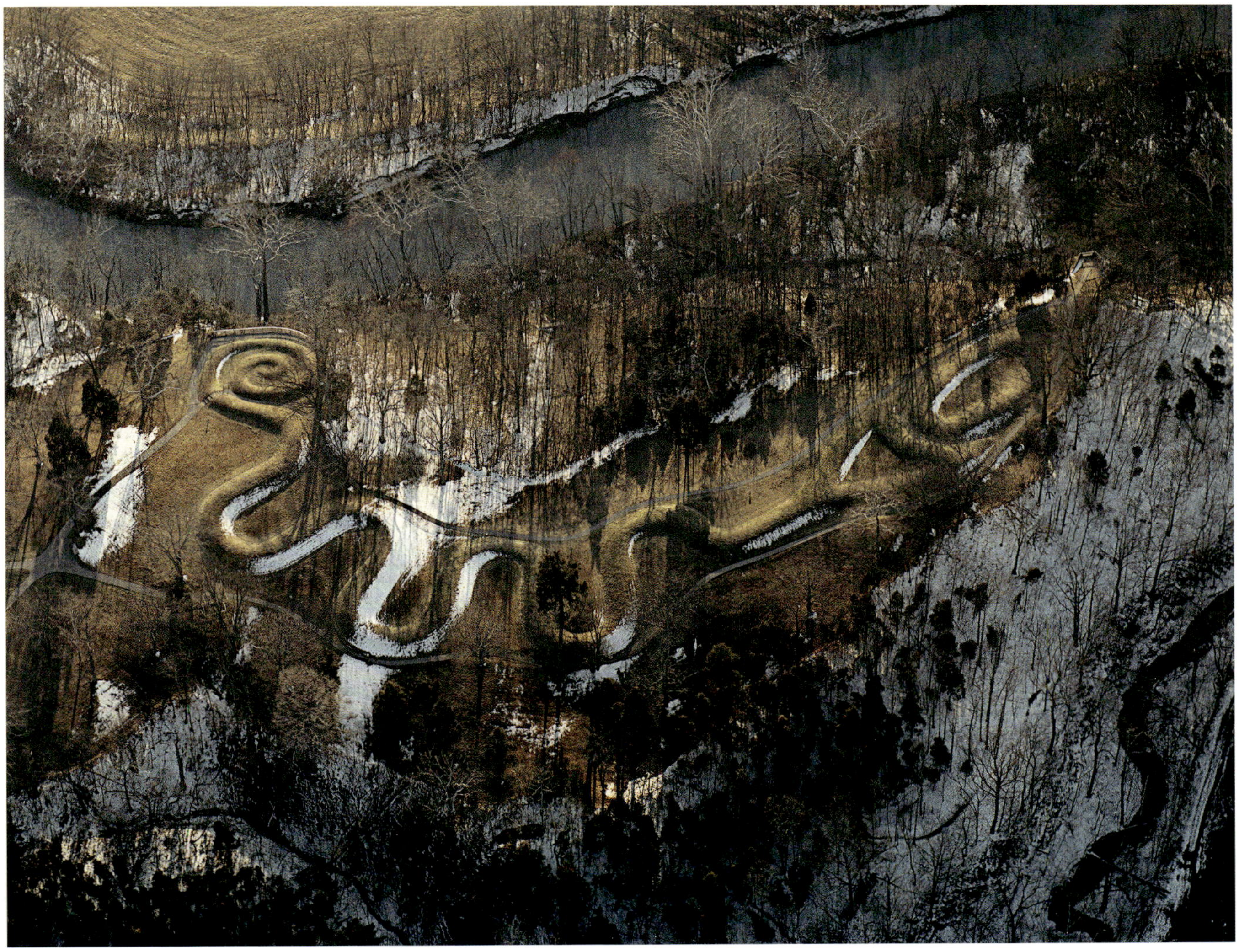

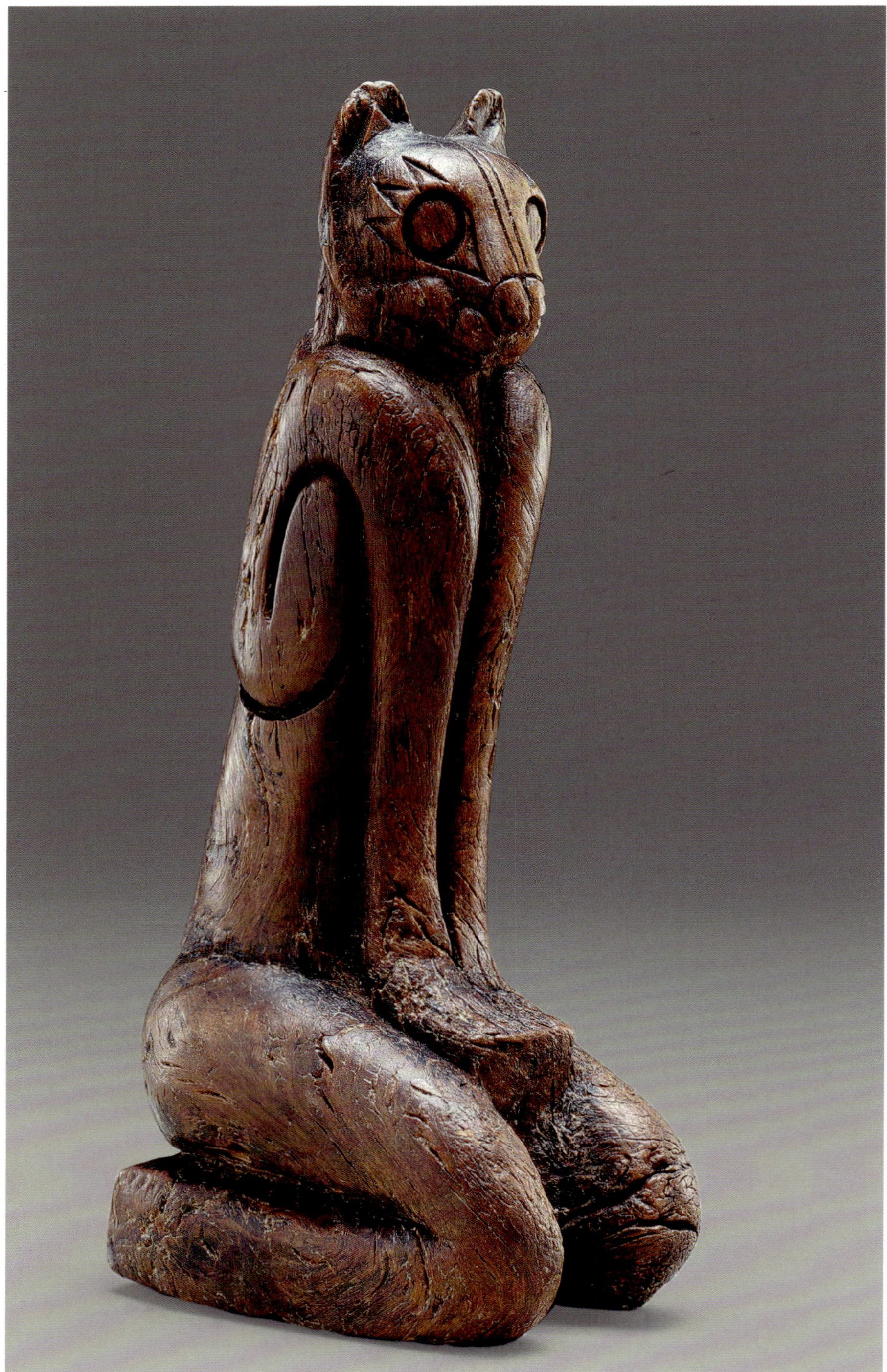

Fig. 34 Kneeling human-feline effigy figure; Florida, Collier County, Key Marco, A.D. 1400–1500; wood, h. 15 cm; Smithsonian Institution, National Museum of Natural History, Washington, D.C. Cat. no. 271.

facing page
Fig. 35 I. A. Lapham, Map of earthworks at Crawfordsville, Wisconsin; from *The Antiquities of Wisconsin*, Smithsonian Institution, Washington, D.C., 1855, pl. 16.

Fig. 36 Ephraim G. Squier and Edwin H. Davis, Map of the earthworks at Mound City, north of Chillicothe, in Ross County, Ohio; from Squier and Davis 1848, pl. 19.

Fig. 37 Hawk effigy platform pipe; Illinois, Naples, A.D. 1–400; pipestone, h. 8.6, l. 11 cm; Anonymous loan to the Brooklyn Museum of Art. Cat. no. 61.

Fig. 38 Owl effigy pipe; Illinois, Shawneetown, A.D. 700–1200; steatite, h. 23.5, l. 18 cm; Peabody Museum of Natural History, Yale University. Cat. no. 74.

into animals. People therefore propitiated animals in order to become more effective in hunting, warfare, and healing. The practice of calling animal spirits through dreams, trances, and vision-quests is recalled in a nineteenth-century painting by George Catlin that depicts a shaman of the Blackfoot tribe on the Upper Missouri wearing a bear-skin robe and headdress bedecked with magical token pieces (fig. 31). The antiquity of such imagery is attested by an Archaic wolf skull from Ohio, shaped and drilled with small holes to serve as a mask, and a Hopewell figurine of a bear-robe-clad shaman (fig. 32; see also fig. 9 in the essay by Bradley Lepper in this volume). Another mask evoking animal-human transformation is carved with spreading antlers and a human face set with shell eyes, and ears shaped for circular plugs denoting high office (fig. 1). This extraordinary work was found in the Spiro Mounds in eastern Oklahoma, a seat of Cahokia-affiliated rulers during the thirteenth and early fourteenth centuries. Perhaps the attire had by then become emblematic of a ruling lineage; but its ancestry is surely traced to customs rooted in a more distant time, when masters of the hunt impersonated the deer to the cadence of drums, chants, and the movement of dancers enacting the stalking, pursuit, and kill of the prey, with prayers of thanks offered to the animal spirit thereafter.

No figure illustrates more poetically the spiritual world of animal-human correspondences than a small wooden effigy from the Key Marco site in southern Florida (fig. 34). The lower, human half of the figure

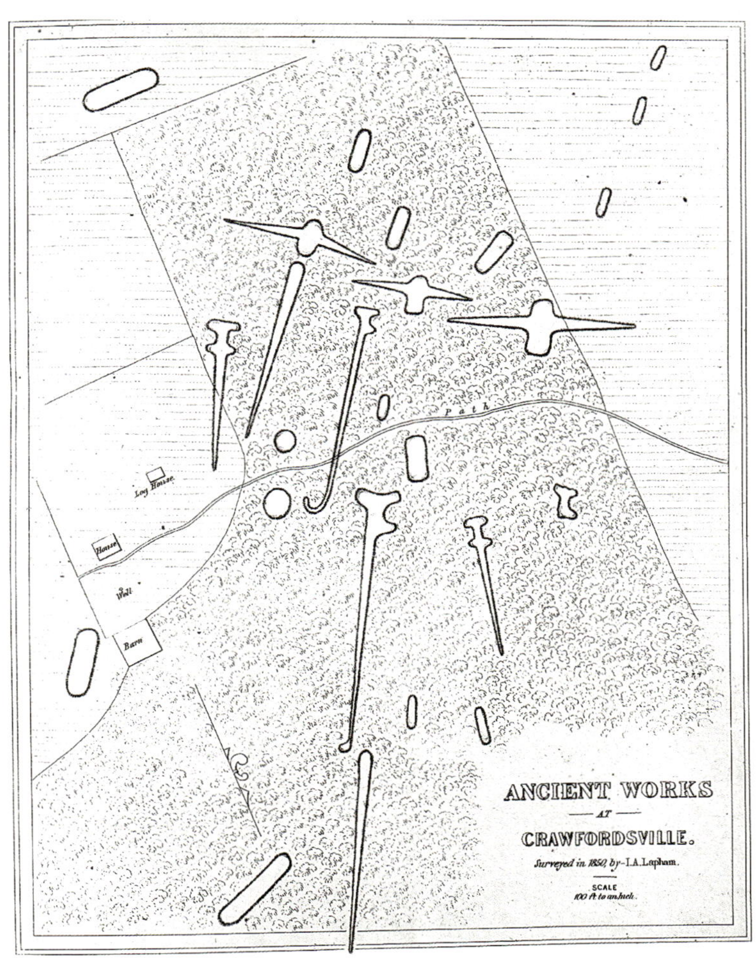
Path
Log House
House
Well
Barn
ANCIENT WORKS
AT
CRAWFORDSVILLE.
Surveyed in 1850, by I.A. Lapham.
SCALE
100 ft. to an Inch.

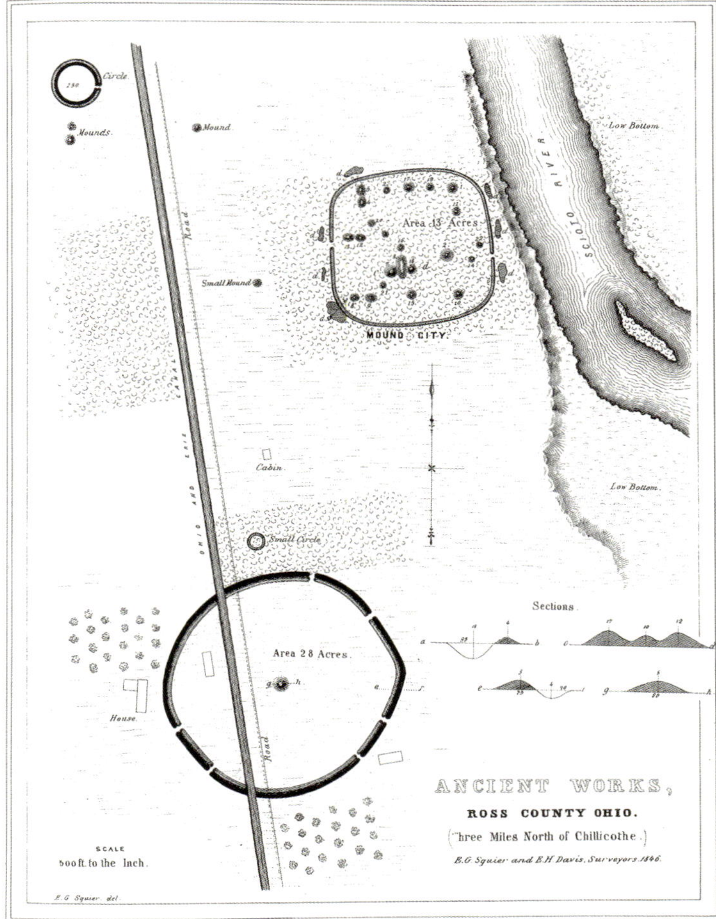
Circle
Mounds
Mound
Low Bottom
SCIOTO RIVER
Area 13 Acres
Small Mound
MOUND CITY
Cabin
Low Bottom
Small Circle
Sections
Area 28 Acres
House
Road
SCALE
500 ft. to the Inch.
ANCIENT WORKS,
ROSS COUNTY OHIO.
(Three Miles North of Chillicothe.)
E.G. Squier and E.H. Davis, Surveyors 1846.
E.G. Squier del.

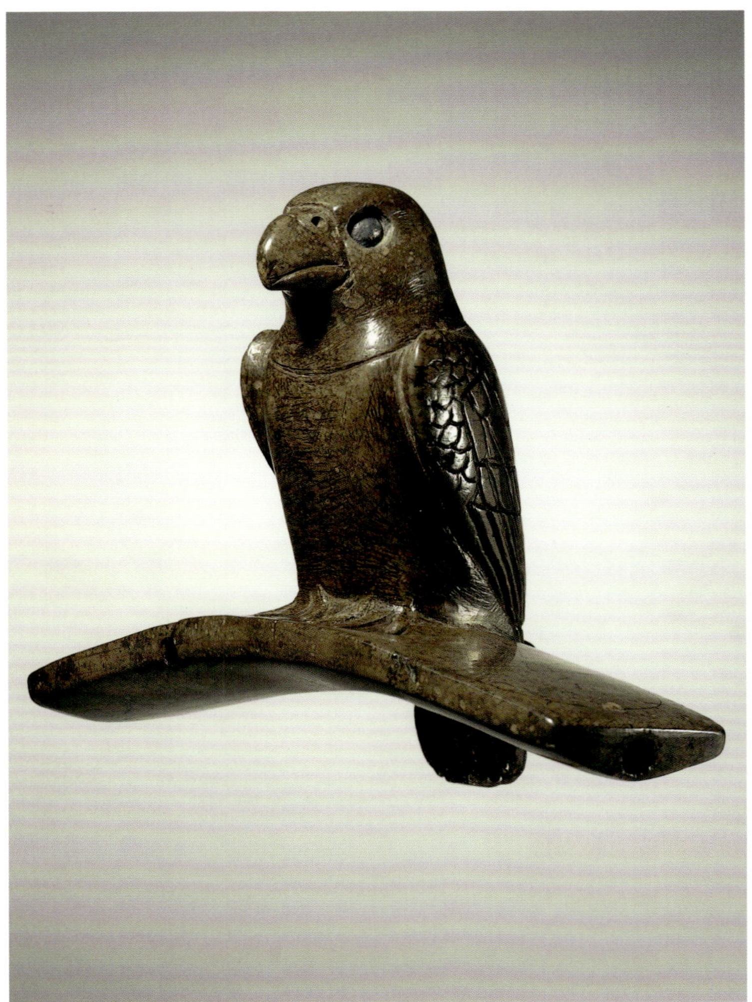

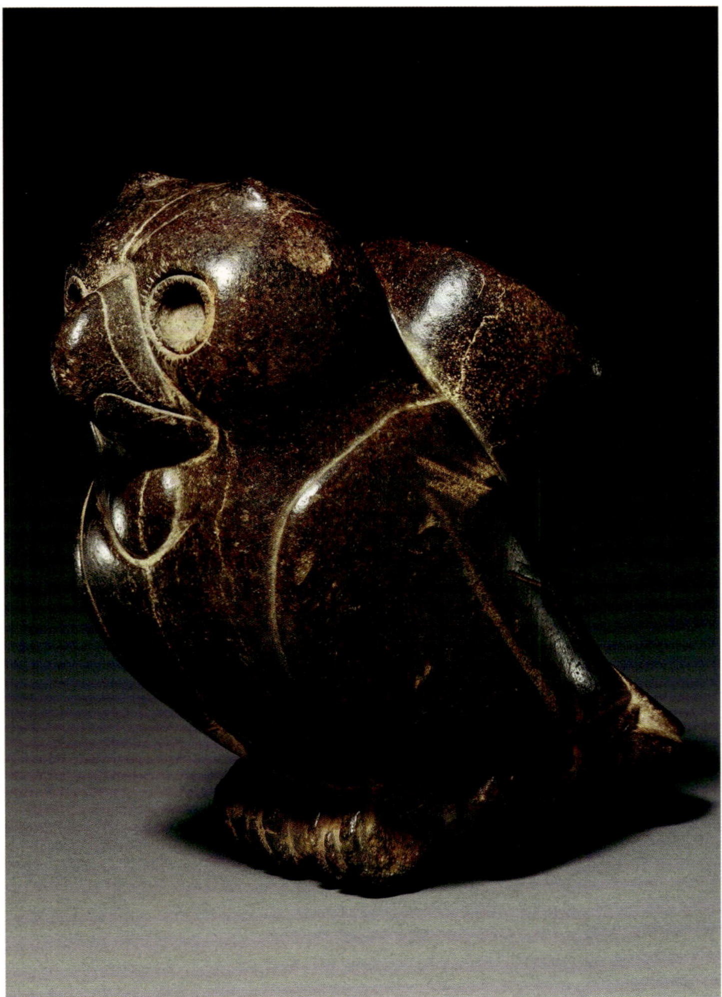

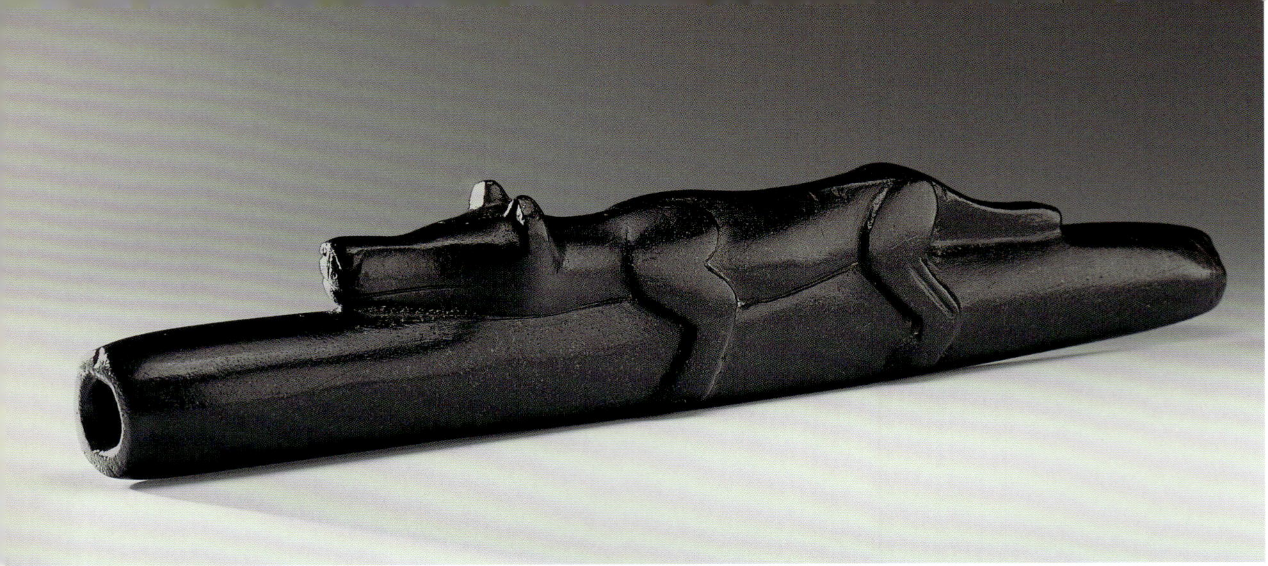

Fig. 39 Blind wolf pipe; Tennessee, Macon County, A.D. 1–400; steatite, l. 56.5 cm; Willis Family Collection. Cat. no. 57. Plowed up in a field in north-central Tennessee in 1940, this major tube pipe is unrivaled in size and mysterious appearance. The streamlined, abstract figure of the wolf embracing the tube conveys a sense of poised attention and the invocation of a powerful spiritual presence.

facing page
Figs. 41a–b Human effigy pipe; Ohio, Ross County, Adena Mound, 100 B.C.–A.D. 100; pipestone, h. 20 cm; Ohio Historical Society, Columbus. Cat. no. 32. Special attention is given to the carved details of the elaborate headdress, prominent earspools, and kilt with its feathered (?) bustle, as features denoting high status. The white and red colored stone may be natural or the result of exposure to fire. The pipe probably represents a fabled hero and would have been used to invoke spiritual bonds between a living ruler, his lineage, and the ancestral figure.

kneels with legs folded under the upright torso. Above, the shoulders narrow abruptly and come oddly forward, the front legs—not arms—extending down straight into the lap. The delicate feline features of the face are not carved as a mask, but fully belong to the lifelike head. Surely this magical effigy signals the transformation of a shaman into an animal, with the corresponding ability to travel closer, in the continuum of social and sacred space, to the great sources of power residing in the natural environment.[28]

Other bonds between animals and humans are portrayed by animal effigy mounds—whether like the great Serpent Mound in southern Ohio or the numerous other effigy sites across the upper Midwest (figs. 33, 35–36)—or in effigy pipes from the tombs of Hopewell chieftains. As in historic times, pipes were undoubtedly smoked for pleasure; but their fundamental purpose was religious, for offering smoke was and still is a form of prayer, giving thanks and asking for power in connection with healing, peacemaking, affirming friendships, or consecrating bonds between people upon undertaking an important communal endeavor.[29] Hopewell "platform" pipes are each carved with a miniature animal in anatomical detail, standing on flat, slightly arched bases (fig. 37). "Great Pipe" effigies, on the other hand, are carved as standing figures or on massive tubular stems (figs. 38 and 40). The menagerie includes birds of many species, bears, raccoons, otters, wolves, felines, and other mammals, as well as a range of reptiles. They almost certainly represent family lineages or clans. The extraordinary "blind wolf pipe" from Tennessee is a massive piece nearly two feet long, weighing some eleven pounds (fig. 39). This monumental pipe, ornamented with sacred feathers and other spiritually related objects, may well have been presented and communally smoked to unify the warriors and pledge them, upon singing war songs, to heroic deeds and risks of battle.

Gods and Heroes. The rich mythic heritage of tribes today and the recent historical past is filled with accounts of origins, the adventures of deities and supernatural heroes and heroines, animal tricksters, vision quests, and the remaking and end of the world. Supernatural characters and events are also represented in the ancient visual arts. Yet the identity of some figures, particularly those from the earliest periods, remain a mystery. One such figure, carved as a magnificent Adena pipe, represents a standing youth with a carefully dressed coiffure and circular earspools denoting high status (figs. 41a–b). The stone was carefully chosen and worked: white on the front, red on the back, colors that in later times have cosmological implications.[30] On the other hand, archaeological monuments at Cahokia and Spiro, as well as Shiloh, Tennessee, and other Mississippian locations, have yielded images that are identifiable through historically recorded myths. Corn Mother, a Cahokian figure carved from flint clay, kneels with open hands from which ripe corn plants grow, while sunflowers cover her shoulders in back. She is described in myths as the mother of all people; the soil is her flesh, rocks are her bones, the wind is her breath, trees and grass her hair. A great goddess, Corn Mother personifies the earth's cycle of fertility (see fig. 1 in the essay by Kent Reilly). A whelk shell is engraved with a representation of the hero Twins, who appear in different guise almost universally throughout North America as well as Mesoamerica (figs. 42–43). They are shown springing into

Fig. 40 Wolf tube pipe; Tennessee, Williams Island, 4th century; greenstone, l. 23.2 cm; Smithsonian Institution, National Museum of Natural History, Washington, D.C. Cat. no. 58.

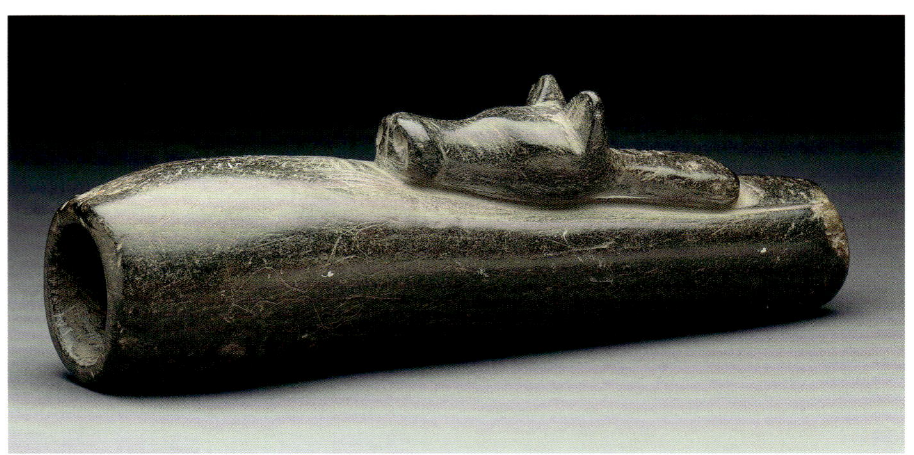

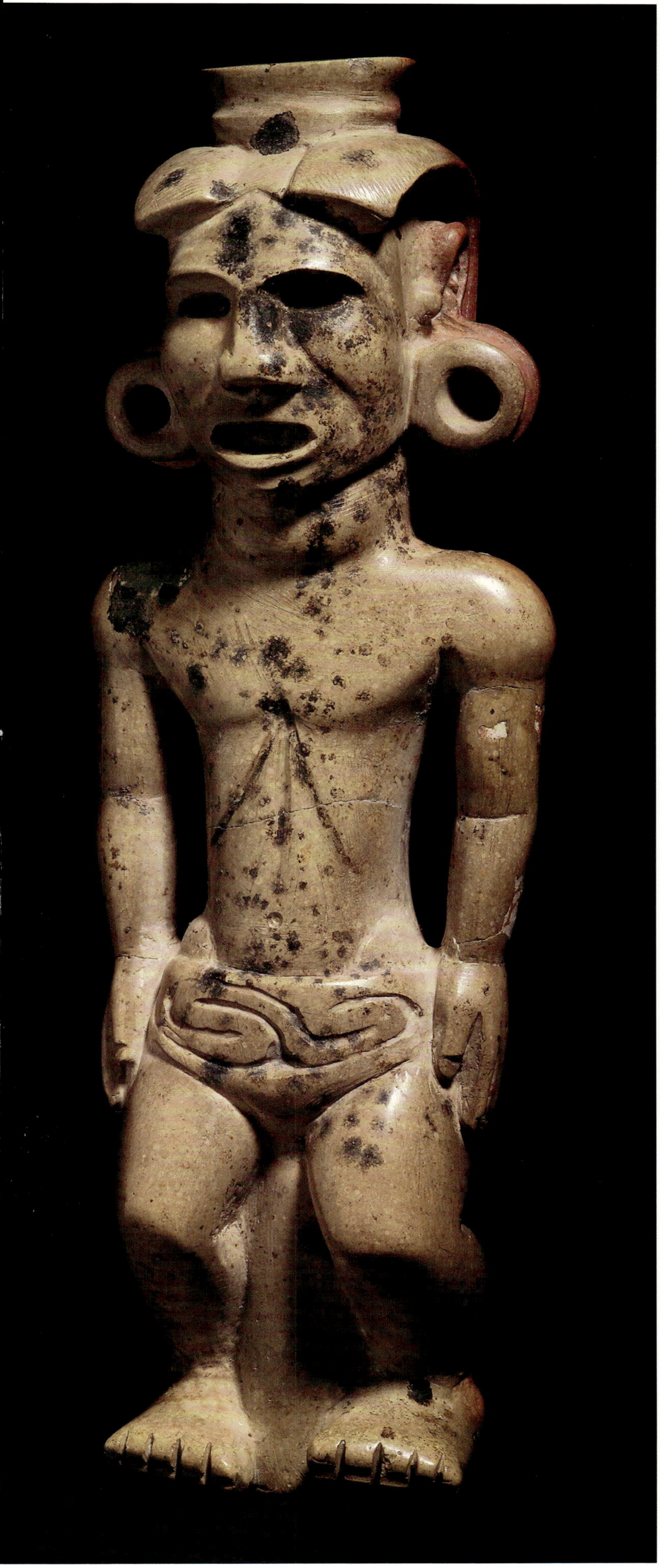

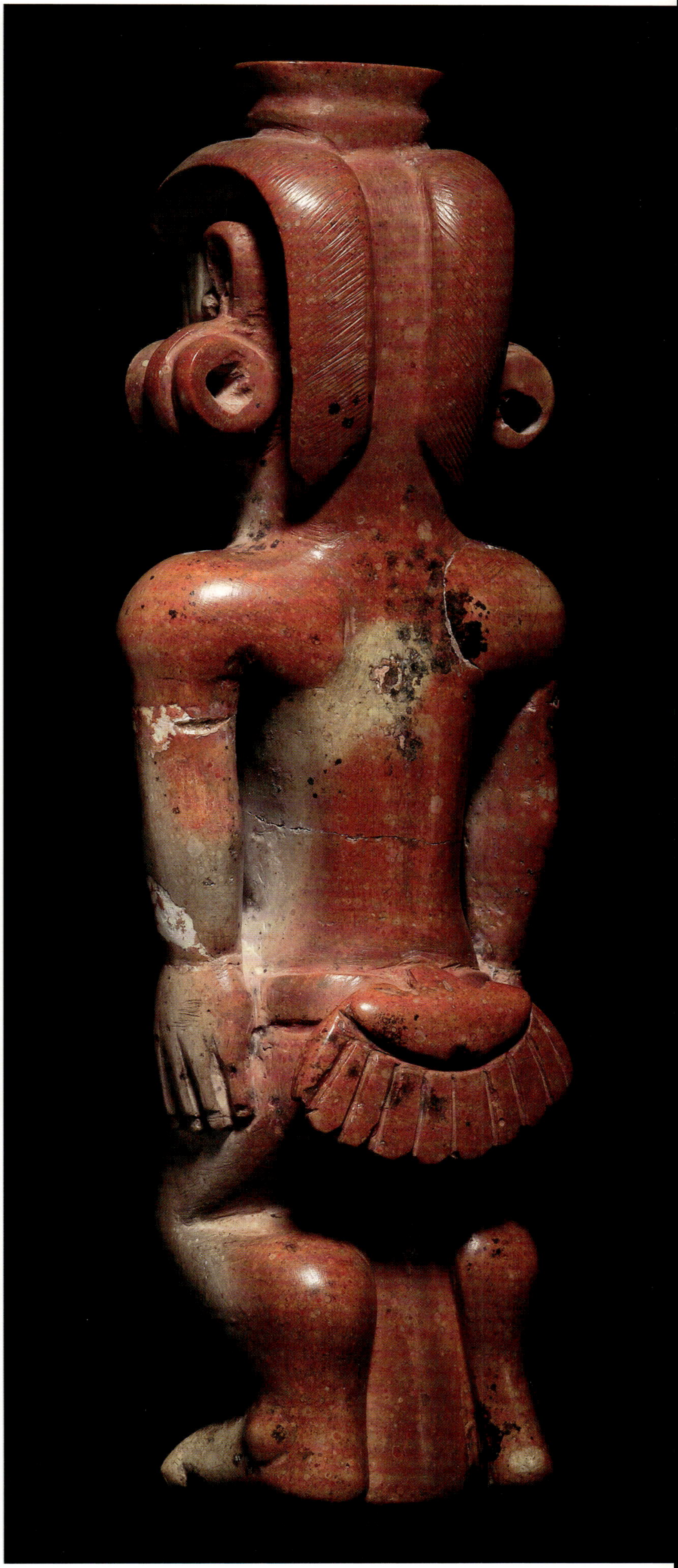

Fig. 42 Engraved whelk shell with two intertwined snake-men; Craig B style; Oklahoma, LeFlore County, Spiro, Craig Mound, A.D. 1200–1400; marine shell, l. 33 cm; Smithsonian Institution, National Museum of the American Indian, Washington, D.C. Cat. no. 126. This engraved whelk shell depicts twin figures with intertwined serpent tails, springing from a coiled serpent/raccoon that symbolizes the earth. The mythical scene surely illustrates an event in the time of origins (see also fig. 43).

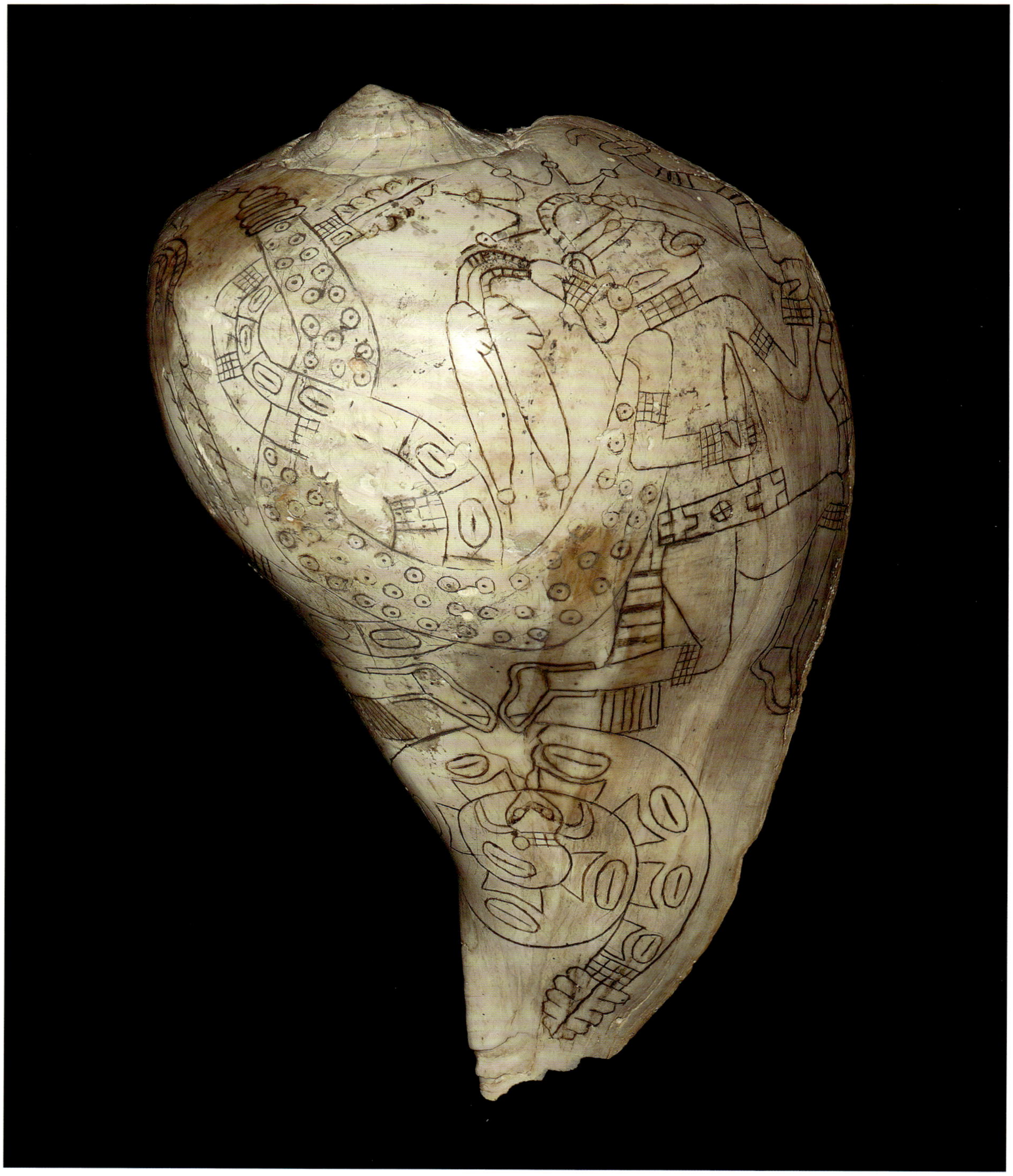

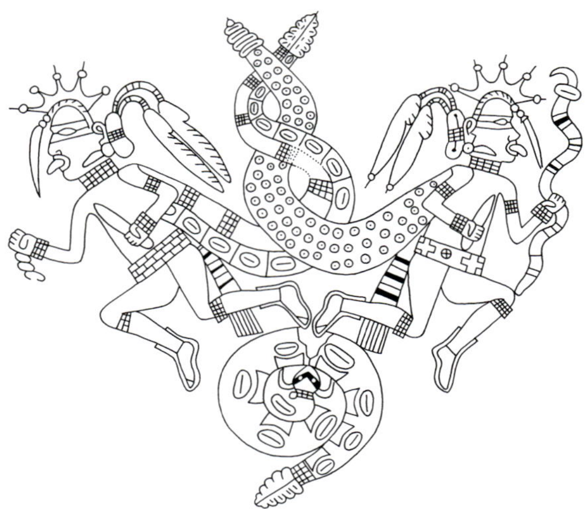

Fig. 43 Drawing of two intertwined snake-men from the engraved whelk shell shown in fig. 42; from Phillips and Brown 1984, pl. 192.

the sky to become Thunderers, rising from a split in the body of a coiled rattlesnake with a raccoon face—*sinti shaui*, in a Choctaw dictionary, a metaphor for the earth itself. The hero Red Horn is portrayed with a long braided tassel and earrings of tiny winking faces, so described in a Winnebago myth (see Reilly, figs. 13a–b).[31] Heroes are characters whose adventures take them beyond the everyday world, into the supernatural realm and encounters with fabulous creatures and forces, to win a gift and return to benefit humankind. Descriptions of deities, heroes, and heroines occur in the mythic accounts of such tribes today as the Winnebago, Cherokee, Caddo, Creek, Choctaw, Chickasaw, Shawnee, and many others.[32] Yet no single set of myths describes all the figures together as a single, coherent pantheon. Can they have once formed a unified group, a family of gods, in a lost legend or epic of the Cahokian world? Or were they even then drawn together from the cults and traditions of diverse peoples and faraway places within the Cahokian orbit? No answers exist at present.

The Worship of Ancestors. In societies where clans and lineages are important units of the social structure, the worship of ancestors is of primary importance in keeping unity and continuity between present generations and their forebears. The residing place of ancestral spirits varies among different peoples throughout the Americas. Some hold this location to be within mountains or beneath the surface of lakes or ponds, while others think of the sky. The constellation Orion, conceived as an open hand among southeastern tribes, was seen as a gathering place for souls of the dead on their way to join others as stars in the Milky Way (see fig. 10 in the essay by George Lankford). The aristocratic ruling lineage of the Natchez knew themselves to be descended from the sun, progenitor of a primordial creator-couple, and they worshipped the sun as the ultimate, sacred source of energy.[33] Early European accounts by Garcilaso de la Vega and Thomas Hariot describe temples in the Southeast where the remains of ancestors were kept, presided over by human effigies.[34] Part of the symbolic program of late Mississippian capitals (see figs. 6–8a–b in the essay by Adam King in this volume), some of these effigies look at us with a wide-eyed impersonal stare, their stylized features representing idealized ethnic types, their bodies seated in tense upright poses; these may be mythic creator couples. Other figures look up with individualized faces and curious, personal expressions: these are portraits of more immediate forebears with closely remembered personalities and actions. From the Archaic through Mississippian times the most imposing archaeological sites feature mortuary monuments containing offerings with imagery attesting to the status, office, and achievements of important historical ancestors and legendary founders of clans or lineages. Such monuments stood in representation of continuity and were periodically visited for commemorative gatherings and feasts, as reminders that the community did not consist of the living alone, but the living and dead together in making up the clan or lineage identity. It is not surprising that such ancestral monuments contain the most elaborate sumptuary objects expressing the impressive presence, prestige, and obligations of chiefs, destined to continue to speak for their people in the land of the spirits.

The Office of Chiefs. The funerary monuments so prominent in ceremonial centers of all periods in the Midwest and South contained objects and paraphernalia attesting to the office and obligations of the deceased (figs. 44–45). Part of the equipment of rulership, these symbolic works accompanied the leaders on their posthumous journey to join the ancestor spirits. Some of the themes to which these objects allude have been touched on in previous pages: cosmological settings within which all significant action unfolded; the world of the hunt and connections with animal powers; the natural elements and deities embodying the cycle of the earth's fertility, to which rites of seasonal passage were unfailingly addressed; the veneration of mythic creators and clan or lineage ancestors. To these themes we must add an ever-present imagery of war in the form of ceremonial weaponry, depictions of prisoners, warriors in ritualized encounters, head-hunting displays, and exultant victory dances (see the essay by David Dye in this volume). Such images are engraved on shell gorgets, carved on figures, and embossed on copper plaques. It also seems likely that the names of mythic heroes were taken as titles by rulers, as is

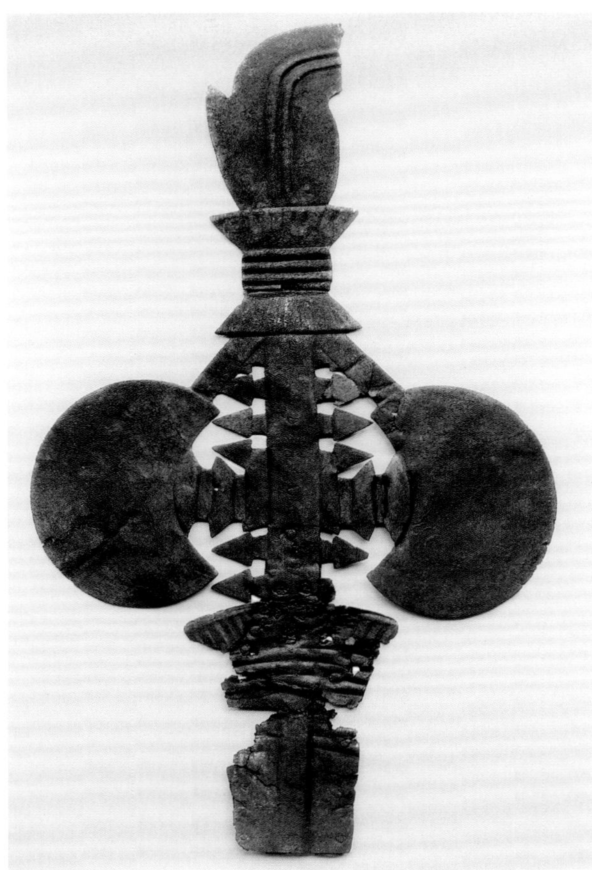

Fig. 44 Bilobed-arrow headdress; Tennessee, Hamilton County, Citico Mound, A.D. 1200–1400; copper, h. 29.2 cm; Smithsonian Institution, National Museum of the American Indian, Washington, D.C. The bilobed-arrow headdress is part of the ceremonial attire of chiefs. Such headdresses display semicircular lobes flanking the central shaft of an arrow. The lobes represent the lungs of a deer, expressing a title given to the legendary hero Red Horn, He-Who-Is-Hit-with-Deer-Lungs.

suggested by copper headdresses curiously adorned with arrows, crossed by a bar holding twin rounded crescentlike objects (fig. 44) This appears to represent He-Who-Is-Hit-with-Deer-Lungs, a youth name of the hero Red Horn—the arrows refer to his hunting activities, the twin crescents representing the lungs of a deer with which he was teasingly hit by his sister-in-law.[35] The famous copper Rogan plates and others depicting a winged dancing chieftain show this kind of headdress, as well as the long braid of hair that was emblematic of Red Horn himself.

A systematic exploration of the points of engagement between art, architecture, and the themes here outlined with the system of seasonal rites and the official rites of passage by which rulers marked their transition from one stage of life or occupation to another, will more fully explain how the peoples of the ancient Midwest and South employed the visual arts and ritual performance as vital elements in maintaining order, coherence and continuity from one generation to the next.[36]

The Idea of a Cultural Continuum

While serving as Mexico's ambassador to India, Nobel laureate Octavio Paz noted that the national project in both countries might be defined as the effort to create a nation out of a conglomeration of peoples whose customs, languages, and rivalries reach back many centuries, even thousands of years before the Spanish viceroyalty or the British Raj. In both countries the past holds an ambiguous position: at once an obstacle to overcome on the path to modernity, yet also to be exalted and salvaged. In these nations, modernity thus carries an extended, ongoing critique of the past.[37] This contrasts with the trajectory of the United States, where the idea of nationhood was from the start bound to the notion of departing from tradition. The founding of this country was not a revolution as in France, where an old regime was changed but the historical reality of France and its culture continued. The beginning of the United States was instead a genuine birth, an act of creation that profoundly broke with the past. The idea of the *future* is a dominant theme, embodying the vision and achievement of modernity. Nowhere is this idea and impulse more profoundly and physically expressed than in the way the American landscape has been transformed and shaped. Nevertheless, in bits and pieces, almost unseen, the record of earlier human occupation is still there: in the location of archaeological sites, the physiognomy of monuments, the countless artifacts and works of art, and the names of a multitude of locations. These relics reach beyond written records, but the vision and worldview they express is not extinct. A cultural continuum also extends forward, partially identified in Colonial documents, more completely described in nineteenth- and twentieth-century records, and despite irreparable losses and fragmentations, cherished in tribal traditions today. Throughout the history of this mode of thought and perception, visual art and ritual performance played

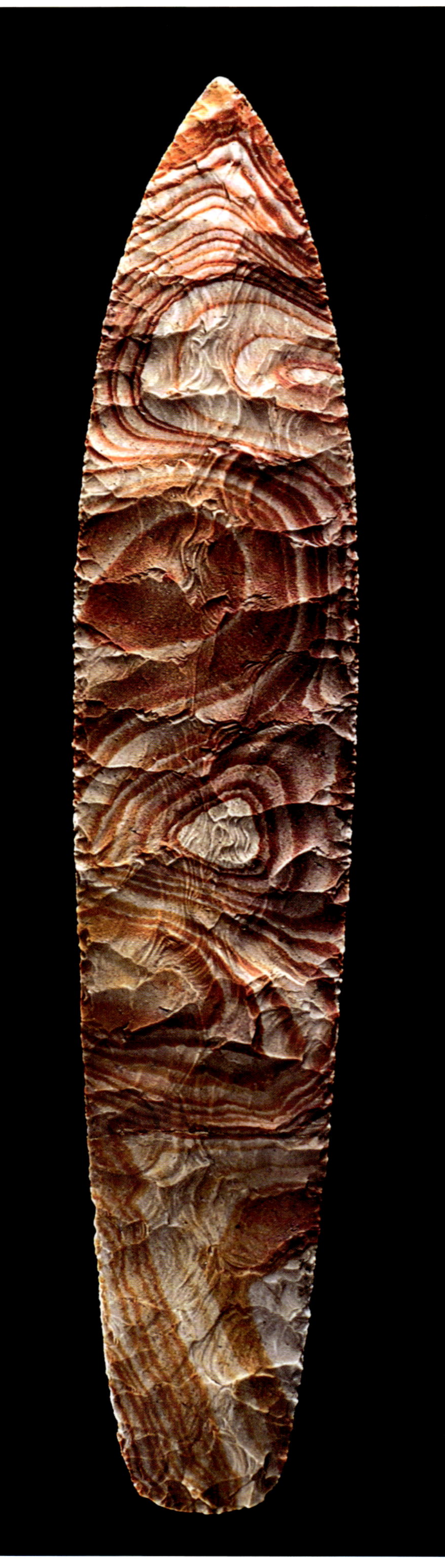

Fig. 45 Ceremonial blade; Oklahoma, LeFlore County, Spiro site, A.D. 1200–1400; Kaolin flint, l. 33.7 cm; Bobby Onken Collection. Cat. no. 188. The brilliant relationship between the blade shape and the swirling pattern and natural coloration of the flint suggests symbolic affinities between the implement, lifeblood, serpents, and rulers.

a critical role in preserving a relationship of reciprocity: the workings of nature are affected by human participation, and the well-being of the community depended on maintaining a steady, equivalent balance within the structures and forces of the natural environment. This is the line of our ancient indigenous heritage. Yet it is also much more. Since the experience of modernity appears not, after all, to be so closely tied to the possibility of limitless expansion as was once widely believed, and inasmuch as life must be lived amidst that which was made before, the unifying pattern and wholeness underlying the diverse and fragmentary archaeological evidence of the early Midwest and South emerges as a contribution of universal significance, a touchstone for a uniquely American critique of the past.

Notes

1. Haas 1982; Redmond 1978.
2. Jackson 1972, pp. 18–38.
3. Jackson 1972, pp. 238–40.
4. Keegan 1996, p. 7.
5. Townsend 1992.
6. Gibson and Carr 2004.
7. Gibson 2000.
8. Lepper 1996; Squier and Davis 1848.
9. Milner 1998; Pauketat and Emerson 1997.
10. Phillips and Brown 1978.
11. King 2003a.
12. Knight and Steponaitis 1998a.
13. Hudson 1997.
14. Swanton 1911.
15. Foreman 1932.
16. Swanton 1946.
17. Brose, Brown, and Penney 1985.
18. Kirchoff 1952.
19. Willey 1973.
20. Townsend 1979.
21. Vogt 1969.
22. Ortiz 1969; Basten 1978.
23. Bailey 1995; Echo-Hawk 2000; Hall 1997a.
24. Becker 1975.
25. Swanton 1928.
26. Emerson 1989.
27. Lutz 2000.
28. Eliade 1964, pp. 96–109.
29. Hall 1987.
30. Lankford 1993.
31. Radin 1948, p. 117.
32. Swanton 1929; Erdoes and Ortiz 1984.
33. Swanton 1911.
34. Vega 1951.
35. Radin 1948, p. 117.
36. Vann Gennep 1960.
37. Paz 1990.

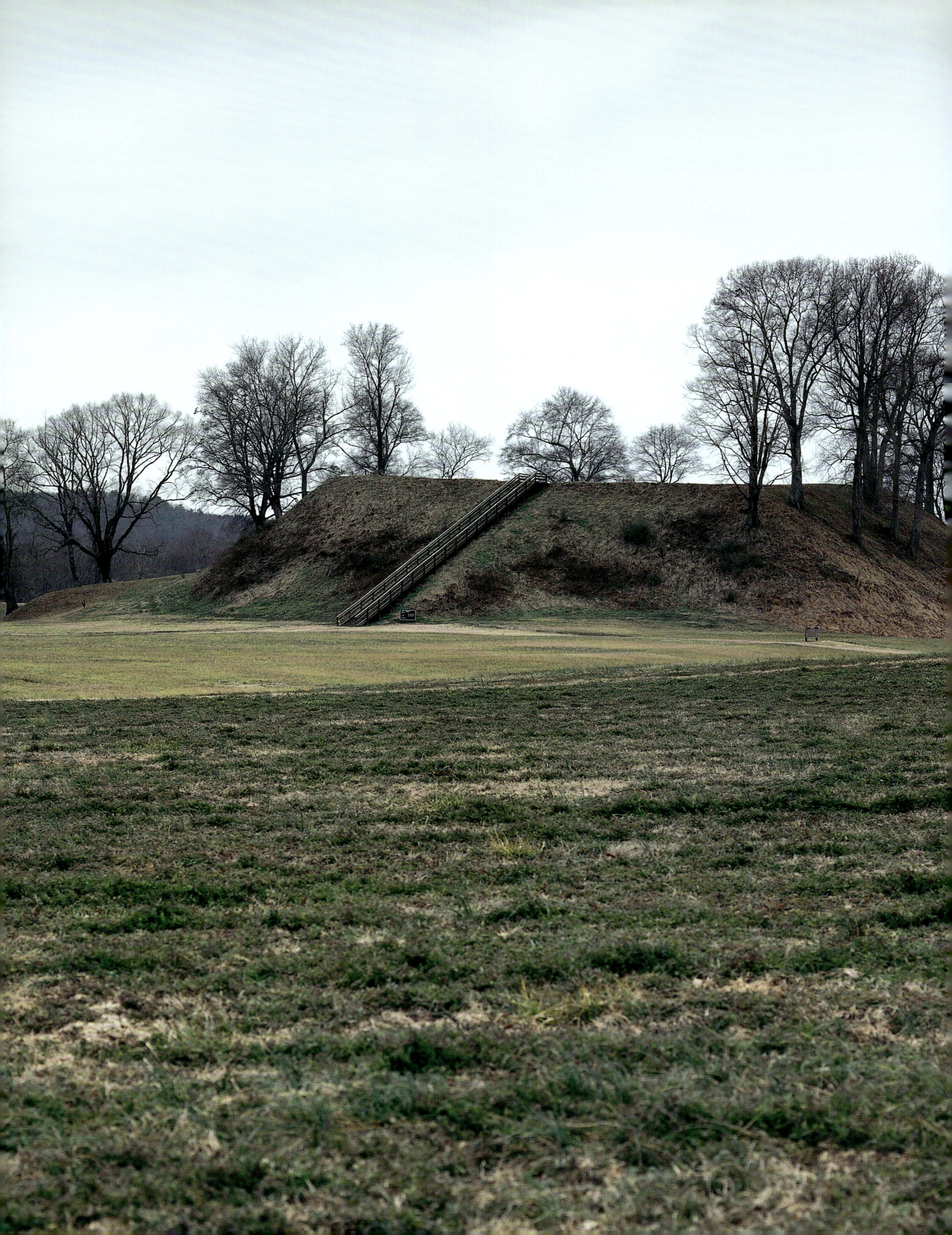

Thoughts on the Preservation of Traditional Culture

F. Kent Reilly III

An Interview with Timmy Thompson

Fig. 1 View of Etowah, Bartow County, Georgia.

December 28, 2002

Kent Reilly: I'd like to start by asking you, as a traditional Muscogee person, and as a Medicine Man at the Hickory Ground near Henryetta, Oklahoma, to talk about growing up traditional and about how you became so fluent in the Muscogee language.

Timmy Thompson: Well, my father was the chief at one of the ceremonial grounds and my mother was active in ceremonial traditions, too. A lot of traditions were passed down from my grandparents on either side, father's side, mother's side. I lost my father when I was just about five years old. Even then, we still kept going with the ceremonial traditions at my mother's tribal grounds. And at the ceremonial grounds people spoke the Creek language. The language spoken in my home was Creek. My grandmother, my uncles—I had about six—were very instrumental in keeping me on my toes in terms of speaking the language and in learning the traditional ways. My family medicine line goes back probably close to one hundred and fifty years. When I was about seventeen years old, I was selected as a candidate for a Medicine Man. But, as I was growing up, I tended to get off track because there were too many other activities going on that interrupted my learning of the traditional ways. I went into the military service at eighteen—had to sooner or later—and as soon as I got out of the service, I went back to school, which also took time away from learning the traditional ways. But, fortunately, I kept my language intact. Creek language was my first language. So when the time came to learn the traditional ways—the customs, medicines, and the songs—for the ceremonial grounds, I had the language to back me up and was able to understand the songs and traditions.

KR: Was your family always associated with the Hickory Ground?

TT: My family was associated with another ground. Due to some strict laws and a lot of people swaying off to Christianity, they decided to break away and went to Hickory Ground.

KR: We've had several conversations outside this interview about the importance of language survival for the preservation of Muscogee culture and of the traditional religious system. Would you like to share your thoughts about language preservation?

TT: One way of preserving language begins with the traditions. But even there, learning the language is hard. We don't have the kind of elders we used to have back when I was growing up. Back then, people in their seventies were considered elders, but people in their sixties were considered men. Anybody below that was considered a boy. And it was always kind of difficult, especially if you were a young kid, trying to hang around these elders—they didn't always want you around. Back then, the language was intact. As years went by, more and more people attended Christian churches, and some of the grounds actually suffered from the Christian influence. But my whole family was always into the traditional culture, so the language was mainly kept through the traditions. Many churches didn't have many elders that spoke the language, but the ones that did were really fluent, they were probably people over the age of seventy-five. Today, there are not that many elders around in that age bracket. There are people in their sixties in some of these churches who can't even speak the language. They understand what I'm saying, but they can't respond back to me.

KR: How many traditional grounds (figs. 4–5) are left?

TT: Out of forty-four, there are only fourteen original grounds—all Upper Creek towns. The Upper Creek towns were mainly traditional, and they're the only ones that are active. The Lower Creeks were pretty much Christianized people, so their fires are no longer active.[1]

KR: I know that you spend a great deal of your time preparing language programs for elementary and secondary schools in this area. Do you see a process where young Muscogee people are learning the language? Do you see good results from these language programs? Do you see the desire among young Muscogee people to maintain their language?

TT: We have some language programs in the communities for which we provide the curriculum if they need it. Although the interest in language classes is there, the desire to try and keep it going is not, because with the young people there are too many outside activities

Fig. 2 On a warm morning in early July the Green Corn festival begins, as a new fire is rekindled in the center of a Creek ceremonial ground. The women's Ribbon Dance moves in a counterclockwise direction to the rhythmic sound of turtle-shell ankle rattles, as the dancers drive each step forcefully into the earth.

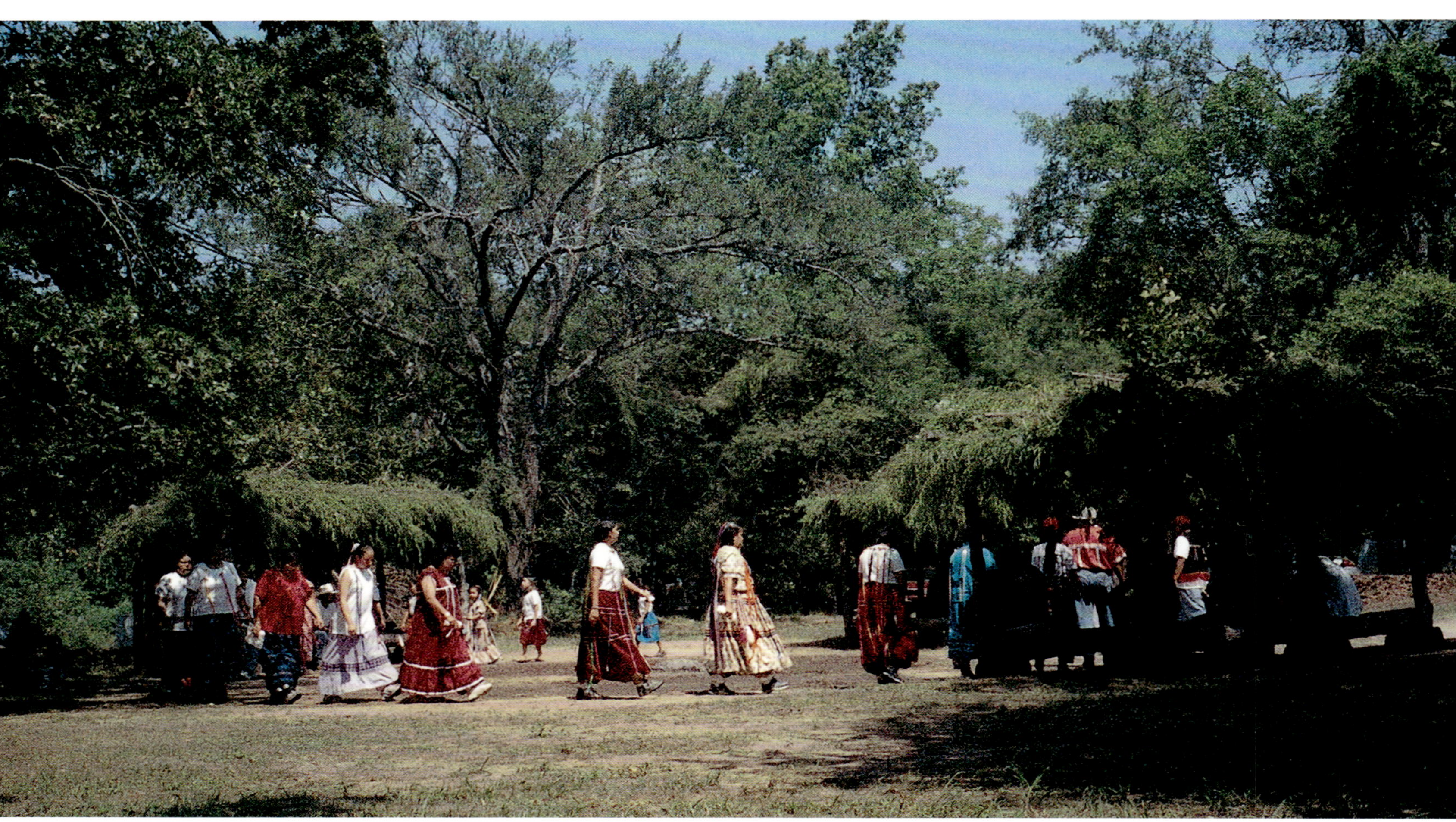

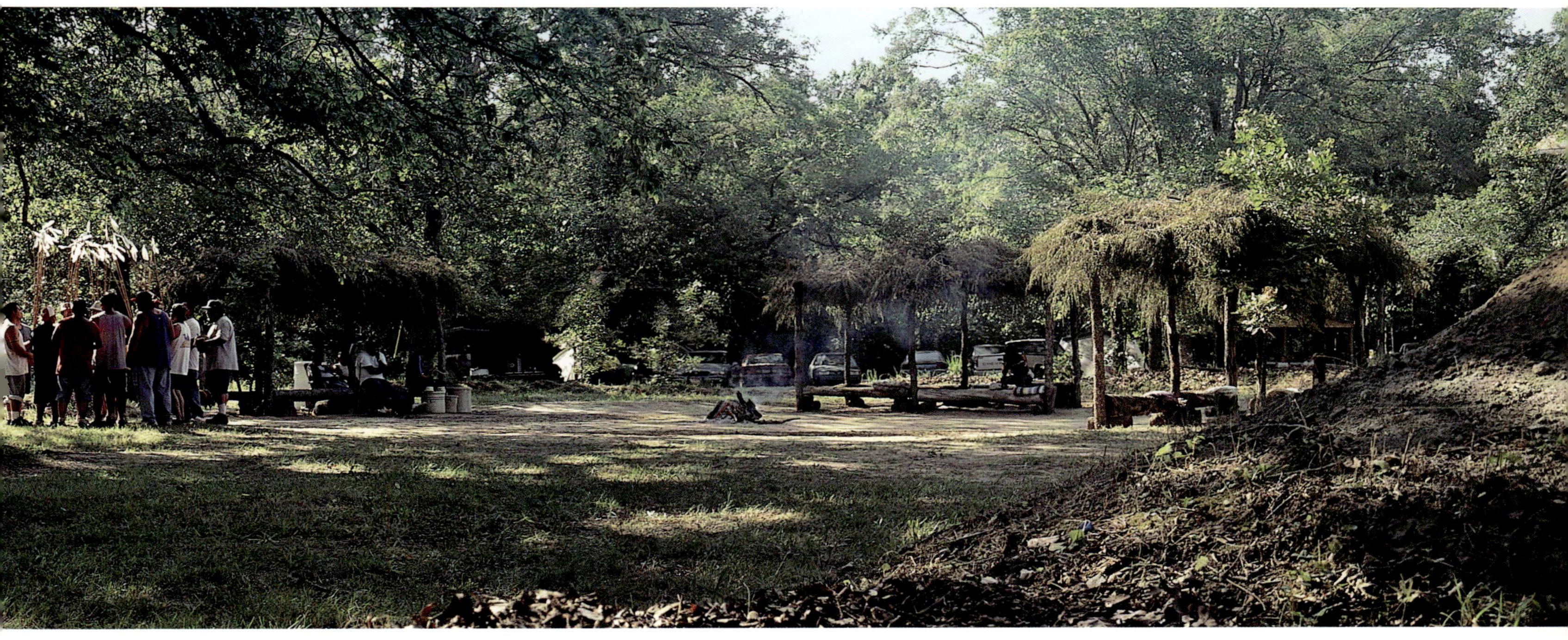

that interfere. When you're trying to teach a language, regardless of what kind, but especially a Native Indian language, it's hard to hold anybody's interest. Because this kind of language was never a written language to begin with. The language is part of the culture, and culture, to me, is something that you can't teach—you have to live it in order to learn it. And when somebody else tries to teach it, it's not going to go anywhere. I realize there are individuals trying to enhance it and trying to preserve it. But some of the teachers aren't fluent, or don't have the ability to read and write. Even the alphabet was written by missionaries. How can they tell us this is the correct alphabet? The only way an individual can become fluent is to start learning at an early age.

KR: During our exhibition meetings both in Oklahoma and at the Art Institute of Chicago, we've emphasized that the exhibition should be of equal value to Native Americans and non-Native American communities. Currently there are Native American religious restrictions on the display and handling of ancient objects that have an association with the honored dead. How, in your opinion, can these objects be respectfully handled and displayed in our exhibition so that they become the voices of those honored ancestors, speaking to and educating modern populations?

TT: Some objects probably wouldn't be allowed to be exhibited today by the elders because most were used in ceremonial situations and therefore were not displayed, except only to them. Personally, I don't have a problem with exhibiting them now. Of course, that depends on what kind of object is being exhibited. I couldn't really say without seeing the object how it should be displayed.

KR: May I name an object, one that we know—well, actually, two: the great marble statues from Etowah (fig. 1). I know you've seen them and been in NAGPRA discussion concerning their eventual location and ownership. Should there be special situations for the display of those marble statues?

TT: Not knowing the background of the objects themselves, and not knowing what it was used for—I can't say at this time.

KR: You mentioned in our previous discussion that objects were displayed during ceremonials. You also mentioned that now there's no longer the time to display them. To your knowledge and in your opinion, in the old ways, how long were they displayed?

TT: Objects were probably displayed for a period from four to seven days. Some grounds would have their ceremonies for seven full days. But, in contemporary times, just four days. It was only when they were being utilized that objects were displayed.

KR: Would it be incorrect for me to ask you—when they're not being displayed, were they kept bundled, or did they have a special place, without asking where that place is, were they kept in a special place and then eventually handled? Were they covered up?

TT: We keep them in a special place away from the circle, covered.

KR: I see. Were there people who understood what these things meant?

TT: Yes, the elders told us that in the old days there were specialists who understood what these objects meant. They would stand up at ritual occasions and tell everybody what each object meant.

KR: In your opinion, Timmy, how does the proposed exhibition reinforce your personal connection to the distant history of the Muscogee people?

TT: The objects tell me that my ancestors were in the Southeast.

Fig. 3 In the waning afternoon hours, as the new fire continues to smolder in the middle of the enclosure, men gather to perform the Feather Dance. Each participant holds a wand with white feathers as the group moves counterclockwise, led by a singer tapping a pottery drum. The songs rise up with each set, ending in an imitation of the call of a wild turkey-cock.

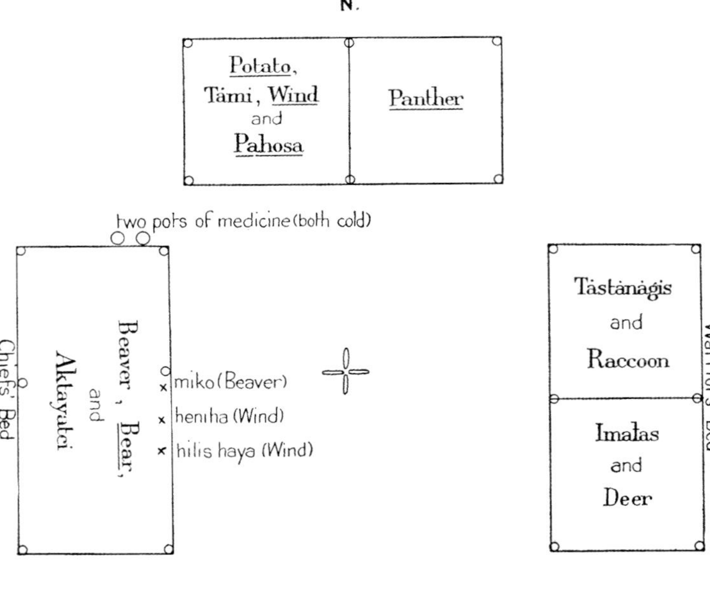

Fig. 4 Plan of the Ocevpofv square ground, a traditional Creek ceremonial site in eastern Oklahoma, as recorded by John R. Swanton of the Bureau of American Ethnology; from Swanton 1928, p. 211. The assigned locations of different clans are shown in the three roofed sheds around the fire.

KR: Do they speak to the high level of sophistication of the religious leaders of those days?

TT: Yes, they do.

KR: Do you think that these objects have the ability, as arranged in an exhibition, perhaps to inspire current Muscogee people to have a stronger interest in their past?

TT: I believe the display of the objects could probably stimulate the younger generation to learn more about their Creek heritage and history.

KR: Timmy, in your capacity as a traditional person and religious leader of the Hickory Ground people, do you feel that these objects, the ones that will be displayed in the exhibition, have a direct liturgical or ceremonial connection to your current religious ceremonies?

TT: Again, it depends on what kind of object it is—since so many objects were only used within the circle, and some were displayed, or probably not, within the circle. I do feel that some objects I've seen do have some connections with our current-day ceremonial objects. Some of the objects have changed physically, or the design of it, or materialwise—they had to. Yet they still serve the same purpose as the authentic, earlier objects.

KR: And you have told us earlier in this interview that your uncles were the source of much of your knowledge. Today, in your position, do you look for young Muscogee people that you can initiate into this very important body of knowledge, in the same way that you were nominated as a potential leader?

TT: I do have some people in mind, but they're not very active in ceremonies. Maybe later on they will mature into it. I have been looking, but at this time I don't envision anyone that would be a good choice or have the potential to be a traditional Medicine Man.

KR: Do you feel that the study of these objects can serve to strengthen modern Muscogee identity in that they will act as a focus not only for language revival but possibly also encourage greater participation in traditional ceremonial life by young Muscogee people (see figs. 2–3)?

TT: Hopefully, observing objects will stimulate them enough to see that this way of life was important at one time.

KR: As a final question, do you feel that the connection of the Muscogee people with the ancient past can be a positive connection that will help at least slow down the process of assimilation that seems to have progressed so rapidly within the last few years?

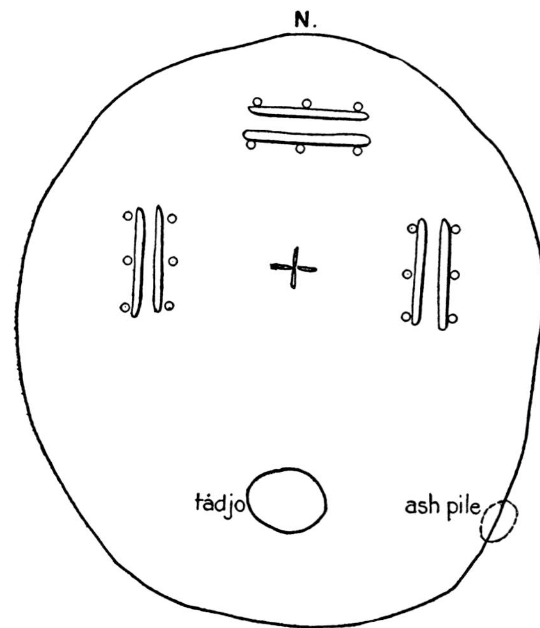

Fig. 5 Plan of the Ocevpofv Green Corn ground as recorded by Swanton in 1912; from Swanton 1928, p. 212. Arbors with log benches are indicated around the fire within a circular enclosure.

TT: I feel that a positive connection between the Muscogee people and the ancient past can help to stem the loss of culture that has occurred through assimilation. It is possible that such a connection can be a positive element. In preserving culture, it can serve to inform the general public about the ancient culture from which the Muscogee people descended.

KR: Do you have any ideas about how we could incorporate the language?

TT: One way is to describe the objects in both Muscogee and English. This way visitors to the exhibition can hear the language and realize its vitality today. It is one aspect of culture that has provided some continuity from the past to today. It can stimulate an interest in where we come from, how our ancestors lived, and what they held in high esteem.

One more thing I want to say is that to learn something about another culture is to go ask the people of that culture. Do not rely on the written history if possible.

KR: That's right. Well, who do you think are the holders of that oral history? It's the Medicine People, right?

TT: Medicine People, the Miccos (the chiefs), and the great warriors at these ceremonial grounds, they should have some knowledge.

Note

1. A fire is the heart of the ceremonial ground; ultimately it represents the generative power of the sun on earth. It is rekindled every year from the embers of the previous year's fire, which has been kept going as a sign of renewal. This New Fire ceremony is an essential part of the yearly Green Corn ceremony performed in June in the Creek communities. The fire symbolizes the life of the community and the world around it.

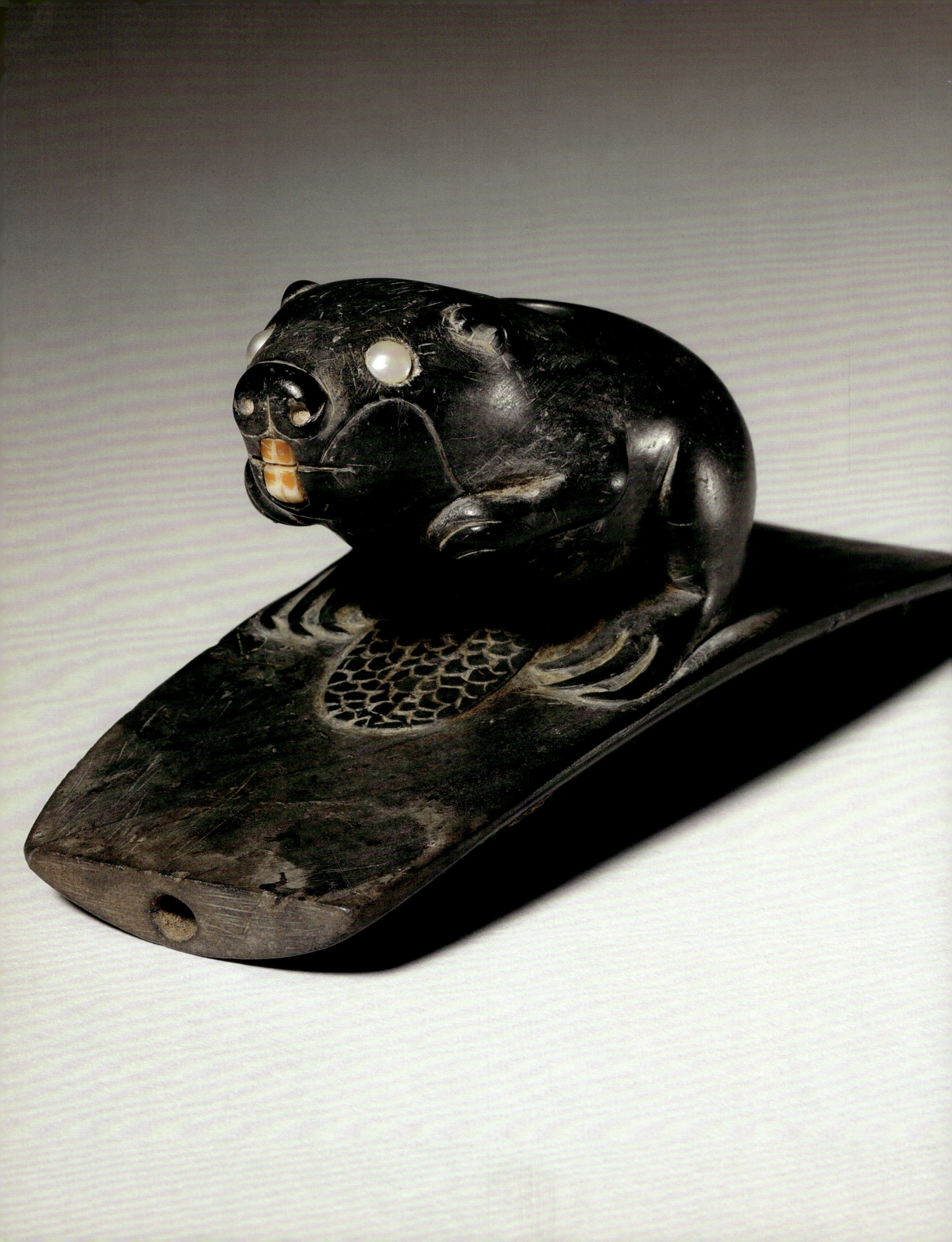

The Archaeology of Aesthetics

David W. Penney

On occasion someone will ask me how I became interested in American Indian art. Perhaps they expect to hear a story about childhood fascination with Indians, Boy Scout merit badges, and the like. But mine is, actually, a very different tale: while an undergraduate studying art history at New York University, I took a reading course with the late Howard Winters, an archaeologist peripherally linked to the early 1970s "New Archaeology" movement identified with Lewis Binford. I discovered that I loved reading archaeological literature, particularly the site reports and regional syntheses from that generation of American archaeologists who worked during what Gordon Willey and Jeremy Sabloff called "the Classificatory-Historical Period" of American archaeology, the span of years between 1914 and 1940. William Webb and William Ritchie's voluminous, workhorse surveys of the Midsouth and New York State, for example, enthralled me.[1] Lacking the more sophisticated technical and statistical analyses of later generations (which for me made for far more rocky reading), Webb and Ritchie relied upon spare, descriptive prose, diagrammatic renderings of trench profiles and floors, and unembellished illustrations of artifacts. Their photographic plates on stiff and glossy paper presented artifacts in stark, black-and-white relief, laid out row by row with the obligatory checkered ruler for scale. This literature, it seems to me today, stripped the basic premise of archaeology down to its barest essentials: what can we know of people when considering only what is

Fig. 1 Beaver effigy platform pipe; Illinois, Pike County, Bedford site, A.D. 200–400; pipestone, river pearl, and bone, l. 11.1 cm; Gilcrease Museum, Tulsa, Oklahoma. Cat. no. 67. Eyes of river pearl and teeth of inlaid shell highlight the lifelike, attentive crouch of this beaver, a masterpiece of Hopewell sculptural naturalism.

left of their lifeless bodies, the remains of objects they made, and the traces of their activity left impressed upon the earth?

It bears repeating that some are offended by the archaeological method of objectifying the body as an artifact. The practice tends to sever the body from any sense of an individual and reconfigures it as part of a sample, reduced to statistics of gender, age, enumerations of physical pathologies, and so forth. The same might be said about objects: described, classified, and grouped in orders of seriation, their patterns of manufacture convert the untidiness of an archaeological site into the neater outline of "component," "focus," "tradition," or "culture." The artifact becomes a cultural product—"an Adena pipe" or "Montgomery stamped" pottery, for example—and thereby a "diagnostic" trait of Adena culture. William Webb attempted to define the "Adena people," as he titled his book of 1945, by tabulating archaeological features and artifacts found at 173 sites scattered throughout southern Ohio, northern Kentucky, and western West Virginia.[2] Webb's list totaled 218 Adena traits. The Adena people, an ancient North American culture whose traces dim from the archaeological record nearly two thousand years ago, could be described for the purposes of archaeological analysis, he reasoned, as the sum total of this list of site features and artifact types.

With the sensibility of an art historian, I found myself increasingly interested in the objects, but an approach that employed objects to define culture led me to a trap of circular reasoning. If objects define culture, how then could I find a plausible cultural context for study of the objects? Furthermore, the objects that interested me seemed in many ways unique. "Engraved tablets, rectanguloid" is trait number 143 on Webb's list, and to support this designation he described nine small tablets, eight of sandstone and the last of "hard clay," each engraved with astonishing images. Eventually I was able to find fifteen such tablets and I prepared a brief study of them under the auspices of Howard Winters's class. Looking back at the essay today, I see that with an art historian's attention to provenance I researched the unique circumstances of their respective excavations, archaeological contexts, and post-excavation histories.[3] That did not get me very far, however. Most of the essay was given over to "functional analysis"—how were the tablets used? Functional analysis of artifacts had been Winters's breakthrough methodology in his study of a series of Late Archaic-period sites located in the central Wabash River valley which he described as "the Riverton Culture."[4] Thus, I performed some experiments with plaster casts of the engraved tablets and established, to my satisfaction, that is was possible to use them to print their images on different pliable media, woven textiles, for example, or deerskin. But the concentrated consideration of these things left me with other questions that I wrestled with in the essay, less than satisfactorily, and that remain with me today.

The fifteen engraved tablets came from nearly as many different sites, some separated by hundreds of miles. The image engraved on each is unique, and yet nearly all share a common visual lexicon (figs. 2–4). In some a fragment of the design in one engraving is reproduced in another but in a different composition and combined with other design fragments that might be

Fig. 2 Wilmington tablet; Adena culture; Ohio, Clinton County, Sparks Mound, 400 B.C.–A.D. 1; sandstone, w. 12.4 cm; Ohio Historical Society, Columbus. Cat. no. 29.

Fig. 3 Berlin tablet; Adena culture; Ohio, Jackson County, 400 B.C.–A.D. 1; sandstone, w. 14.3 cm; Ohio Historical Society, Columbus. Cat. no. 30.

Fig. 4 Low tablet; Adena culture; West Virginia, Wood County, 400 B.C.–A.D. 1; sandstone, l. 12.1 cm; Ohio Historical Society, Columbus. Cat. no. 31.

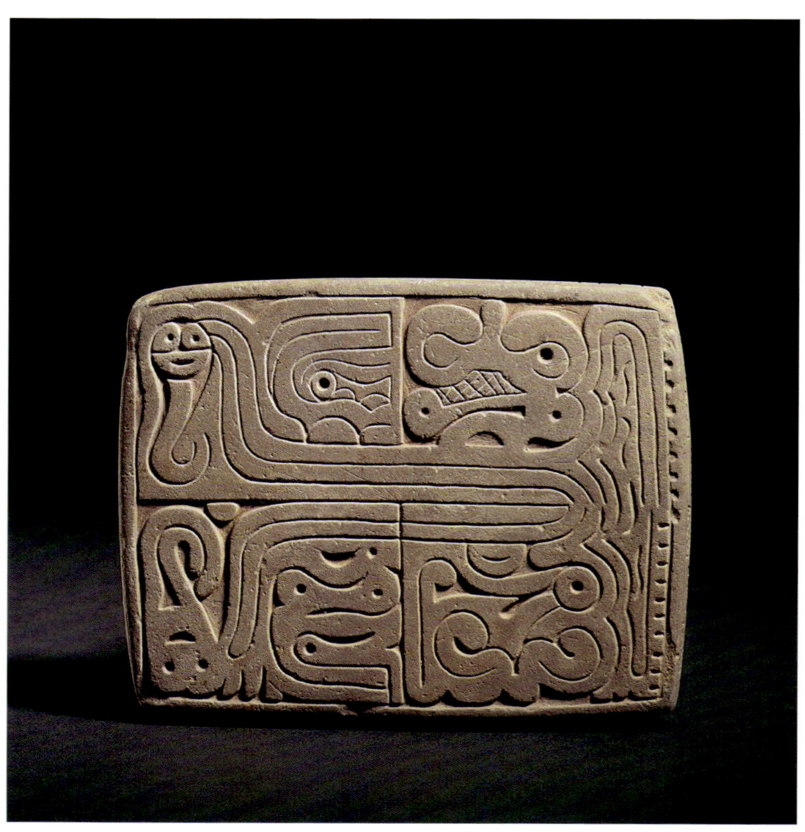

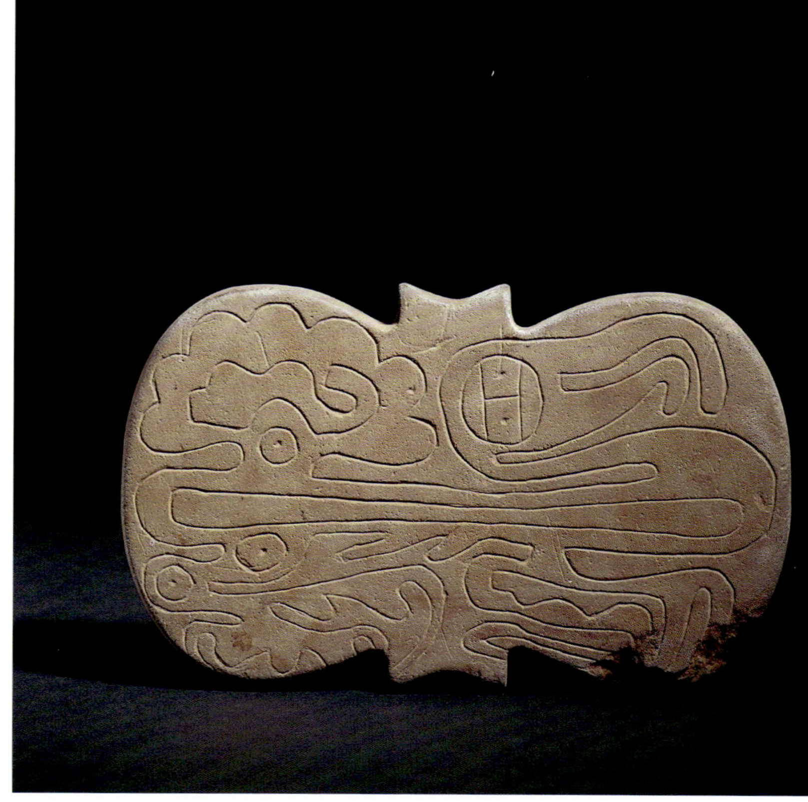

found in a third or fourth engraving of the set. There is no unified hand or style visible throughout them, so it seemed certain that several different people had engraved them. Yet there are three pairs of compositions among six of the tablets, each pair corresponding closely in detail though wildly different in technical and stylistic execution. Using the dispassionate tone of archaeological reportage, I stated my conclusion: "A picture develops of geographically isolated centers of artistic activity sharing a system of ideas and beliefs that is reflected in common imagery."[5]

During the twenty-five years since I wrote that statement, I have become much more sensitive to the fact that Native American art history is hard-pressed to recover the names and identities of artists. Part of this is due to the circumstances of how and why objects made by Native artists had been collected and preserved. When the large natural history museums of America's cities sent ethnographers into the field during the decades before and after 1900, they collected with the belief that Native American cultures were destined to disappear. The artifacts they selected, just like the artifacts excavated by archaeologists, were intended to preserve, document, and represent some remnant of Native American culture. Their very notion of *culture* (borrowed, by the way, by archaeologists) was a construct of traits, beliefs, and practices, including the beaded moccasins, painted pottery, and woven baskets made by individual artists. But their individuality counted less, in the minds of the ethnographers, than did their ability to reproduce accurately a distinctive cultural trait. When the artists did so, it was sufficient for the researchers to identify the objects for the purposes of museum display as "Sioux moccasins," "Zuni pottery," or "Pomo basketry." The extent to which artists asserted an individuality not corresponding to the trait perplexed ethnographers and museum curators, and still does today. I am reminded of an anecdote told by a basket weaver during a conference in 1981. She said she had created a rather eccentric basket, even for her, and a would-be buyer questioned her about it. "Is that a Pomo basket?" he asked, referring to her tribe. "Well, I am Pomo," she answered.

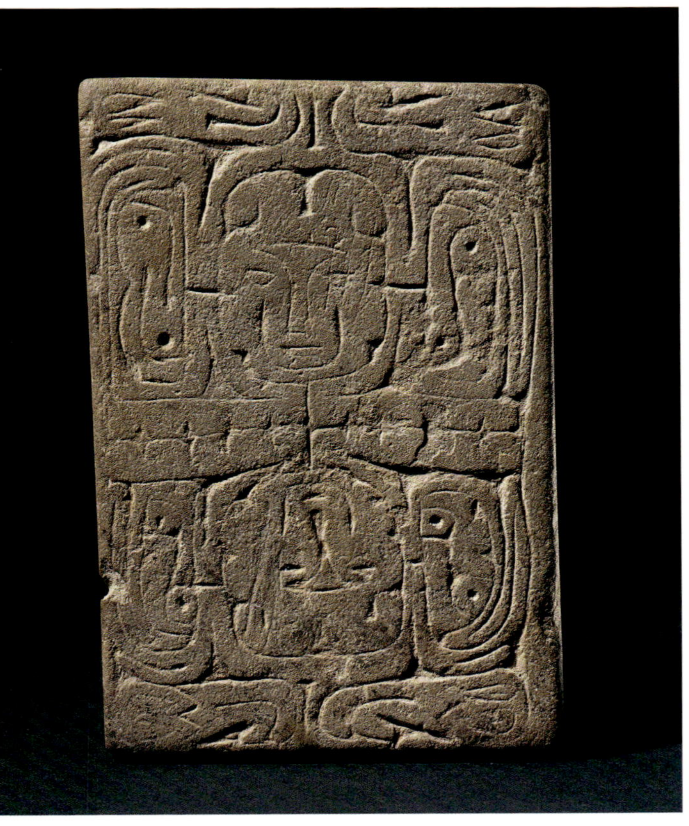

I can see now that the Adena engraved tablets had been created by a small group of artist individuals, awkwardly characterized in my essay as "centers of artistic activity." What really interested me then and now is how the imagery reproduced by different hands might be seen as evidence of relationships between the individuals who created these works. Can a map of the locations where the tablets were found be read as a map of the social relationships between the individuals who shared knowledge about how to make them, how to use them, and the significance of doing so? What was the nature of these social relationships? What was the role of the object, the engraved tablet, or the concept of the object, in nurturing them? And what kinds of special knowledge did these individuals share about the significance of the tablets and their engraved imagery?

These kinds of questions, vaguely formed in my mind at the time, stimulated my dissertation research at Columbia University in the 1980s, the same period during which I organized the special exhibition *Ancient Art of the American Woodland Indians* for the Detroit Institute of Arts.[6] For the dissertation, I looked at effigy smoking pipes, human figurines, and decorated pottery of Middle Woodland period cultures (200 B.C.–A.D. 400) that followed historically on the heels of the Adena culture of the Early Woodland period. Archaeologists had recovered most of these objects from burial sites, earthen mounds that covered the remains of wooden structures where the dead had been gathered for lavish and lengthy mortuary rituals. In many instances, both then and in later periods, the dead had been accompanied by broad inventories of artistically fabricated objects: beads and ornaments made of river pearl and cut shell, blades of chipped stone, and carvings and cutouts of claystone, copper, and mica (figs. 5–11). The raw materials for such objects had been gathered from all across North America: obsidian from Wyoming, marine shell from the Gulf of Mexico, and copper from nuggets garnered among the glacial till of Michigan and Wisconsin. Their inclusion in mortuary ritual was the last chapter in the social lives of such objects. But I wondered about the roles of these things prior to burial (the identity Howard Winters sought with his "functional analysis").

I chose smoking pipes for my study because of the greater weight of evidence regarding their preburial function and cultural significance. At the most basic level of inquiry, a pipe is a tool for smoking, and simple, tubular smoking pipes made of stone had entered the

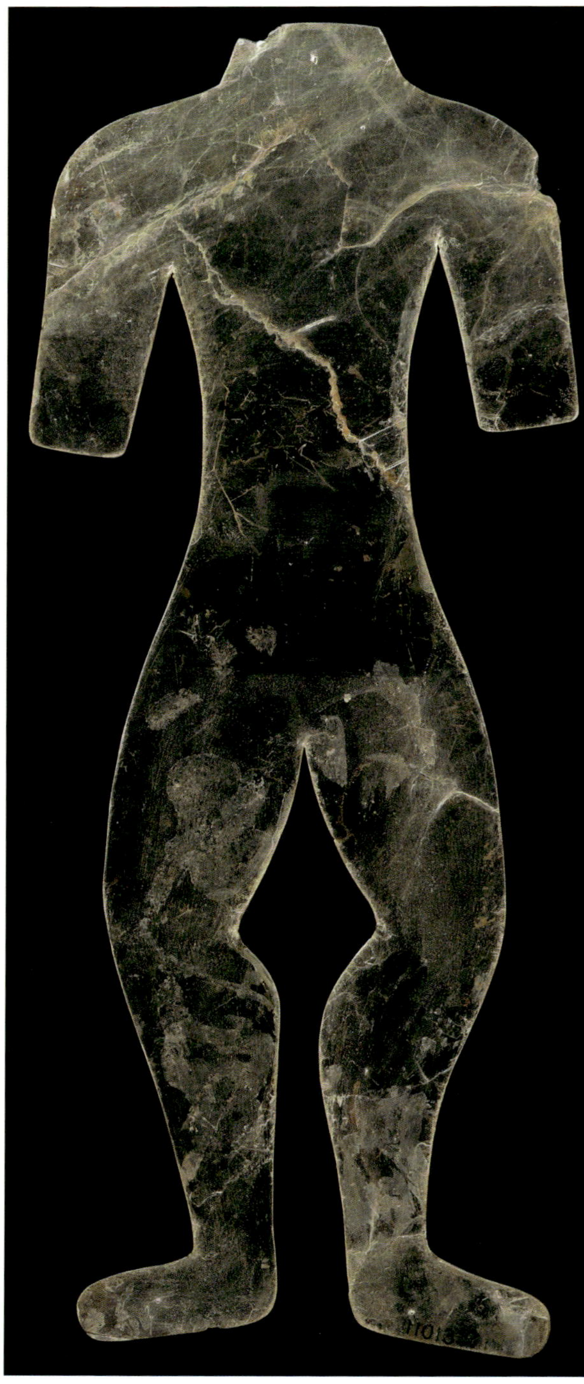

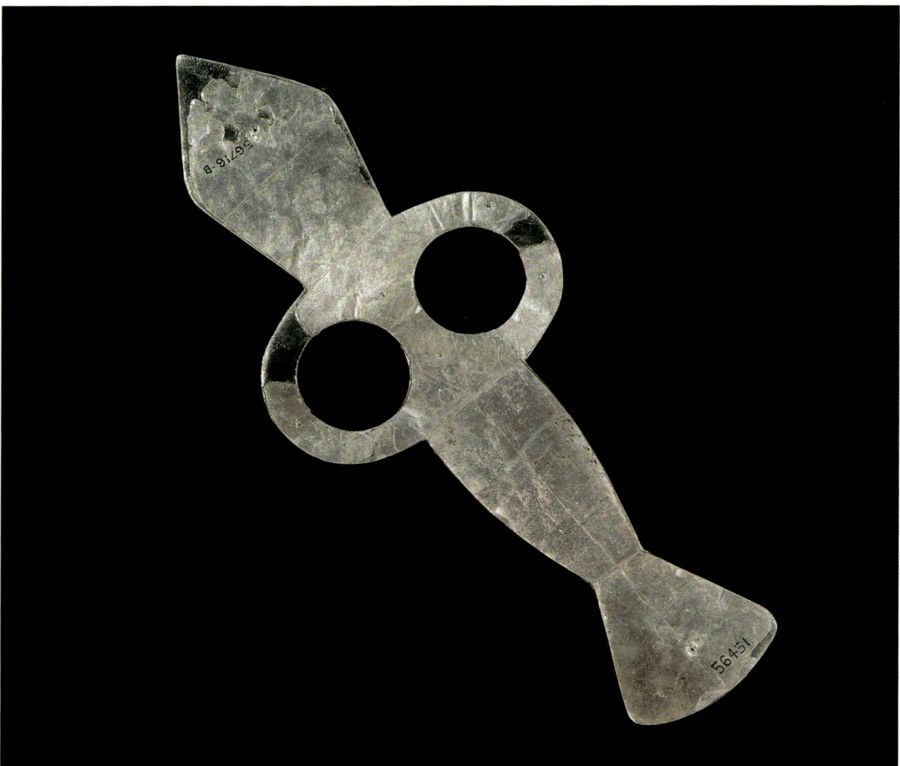

Fig. 5 Headless torso; Ohio, Ross County, Hopewell site, Mound 25. A.D. 1–400; sheet mica, h. approx. 20.3 cm; The Field Museum, Chicago. Cat. no. 44.

Fig. 6 Atlatl effigy; Ohio, Ross County, Hopewell site, Mound 25. A.D. 1–400; sheet mica; The Field Museum, Chicago. Cat. no. 43.

archaeological record in North America as early as 1500 B.C. There is little doubt that early smoking pipes were used to smoke tobacco, more specifically *Nicotiana rustica*. Carbonized seeds of *Nicotiana* sp. have been recovered from Middle Woodland period sites in Illinois (200 B.C.) and, more recently, residue preserved in a tubular pipe from the Cresep Mound (c. 400 B.C.), an Adena mortuary site, tested positive for nicotine.[7] Tobacco was first domesticated in ancient Peru, perhaps as early as 2500 B.C., and came to North America by some means much later. As a domesticated plant, it required cultivation and evidently some individuals in North America cultivated tobacco long before similar knowledge and skills were applied to food plants.

Throughout the history of indigenous North America, smoking pipes and tobacco have remained tied to core religious values and ritual practice. Tobacco is a sacred substance, the origin stories say, given to human beings by the Creator to offer in thanks for spiritual assistance. In some ways, tobacco smoking is analogous to prayer. Over the past two decades, my museum colleagues and I have noted increasing expressions of discomfort from a broad range of Indian people about the museum practice of displaying American Indian smoking pipes as art. In the fall of 1992 Evan Maurer, director of the Minneapolis Institute of Art, felt obligated to withdraw smoking pipes from the exhibition *Visions of the People*, after a series of discussions with members of the Native American community in Minneapolis. I see it as the persistence of age-old values, however adjusted to present circumstances, that have emerged recently due to increasingly assertive Native voices critical of museum practices.

Not surprisingly, smoking pipes represented for William Webb another rather distinctive and rare trait of Adena culture (numbers 117–20 on his list, depending upon their design). Be that as it may, one object in the collection of the Ohio Historical Society in Columbus, the so-called "Adena effigy pipe," is unique in the history of North American Indian art (see figs. 41a–b in the essay by Richard Townsend in this volume). Standing about 7¾ in. (20 cm) tall and carved of pinkish stone, this standing male figure, his legs slightly crouched and his arms held at his sides, wears two crescent-shaped ornaments in his hair, massive circular earspools, and a wrapper around his waist fitted with a bustle like a bird's tail at the back. The cylindrical form is hollow so that tobacco could be inserted at the foot of the pipe and smoked through a slightly flared mouthpiece located above the head. William C. Mills, curator of the Ohio

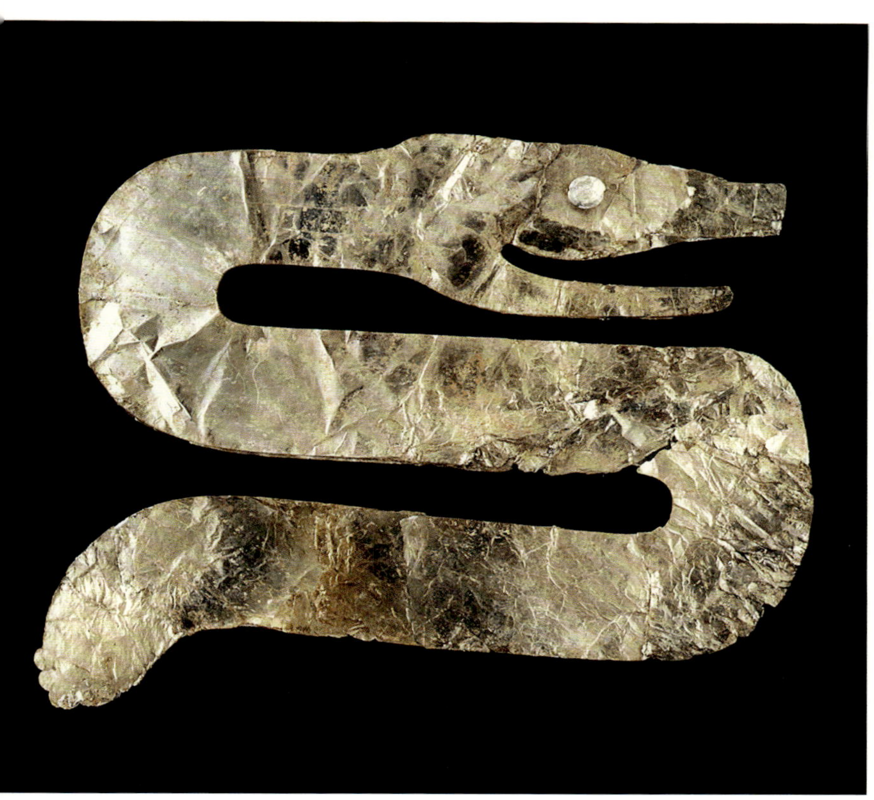

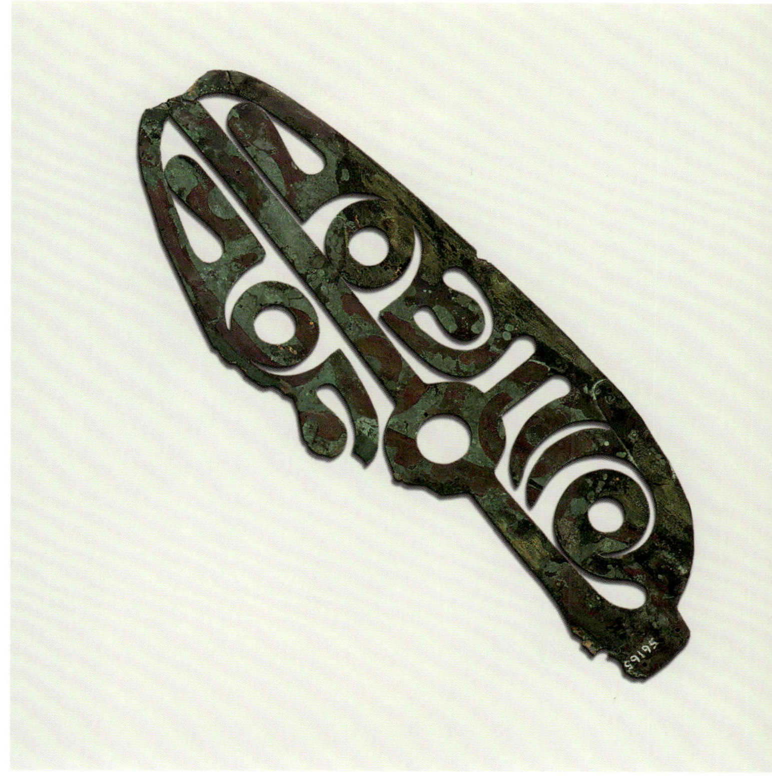

Archaeological and Historical Society, discovered it during the summer of 1901 while excavating a mortuary site known as the Adena Mound near Chillicothe, Ohio.[8] On the floor of the mound, having excavated through it, Mills unearthed a tomb constructed of logs, the interior lined with sheets of bark. Inside he found the body of a man draped with necklaces of shell beads and river pearls and wearing a textile garment with beaded ornament around his waist. The pipe had been placed near his left hand.

Most other Adena smoking pipes are not sculpted with effigy images but are no less carefully crafted: these sleek tubes of immaculately finished pipestone feature either beveled facets at one end for the mouthpiece or their chambers constrict inside to allow a mouthpiece with elegantly flared lips (like the mouthpiece of the Adena effigy pipe). Few Adena people possessed smoking pipes and those who did were highly regarded, if their treatment at the time of burial is any indication. What kind of special knowledge did these individuals possess? We can imagine a list, starting with a knowledge of tobacco and its cultivation; knowledge of its sacred properties; knowledge of where to procure the appropriate materials to fabricate smoking pipes and how to create them; and knowledge of how to activate tobacco's sacred potential through ritual.

Throughout indigenous North America, sacred knowledge is a possession belonging only to those

Fig. 7 Serpent effigy; Ohio, Hamilton County, Turner site, Mound 3, A.D. 1–400; sheet mica, river pearl, and pigment, w. 35.6 cm; Harvard University, Peabody Museum of Archaeology and Ethnology, Peabody Museum Expedition 1882, F. W. Putnam and Dr. C. L. Metz, Directors. Cat. no. 42.

Fig. 8 Ornamental deer ear; Ohio, Ross County, Hopewell site, Mound 25, A.D. 1–400; copper, l. 50.8 cm; The Field Museum, Chicago. Cat. no. 40. Long regarded as an effigy of a serpent's head, because of its mistaken association with a separately made, copper forked tongue, this object is now thought to represent a deer's ear. Although its mate was never found, the pair would presumably have been attached to an item of ceremonial regalia.

Fig. 9 Scroll ornament; Ohio, Hamilton County, A.D. 1–400; copper, w. 21 cm; Harvard University, Peabody Museum of Archaeology and Ethnology, Peabody Museum Expedition 1882, F. W. Putnam and Dr. C. L. Metz, Directors. Cat. no. 39.

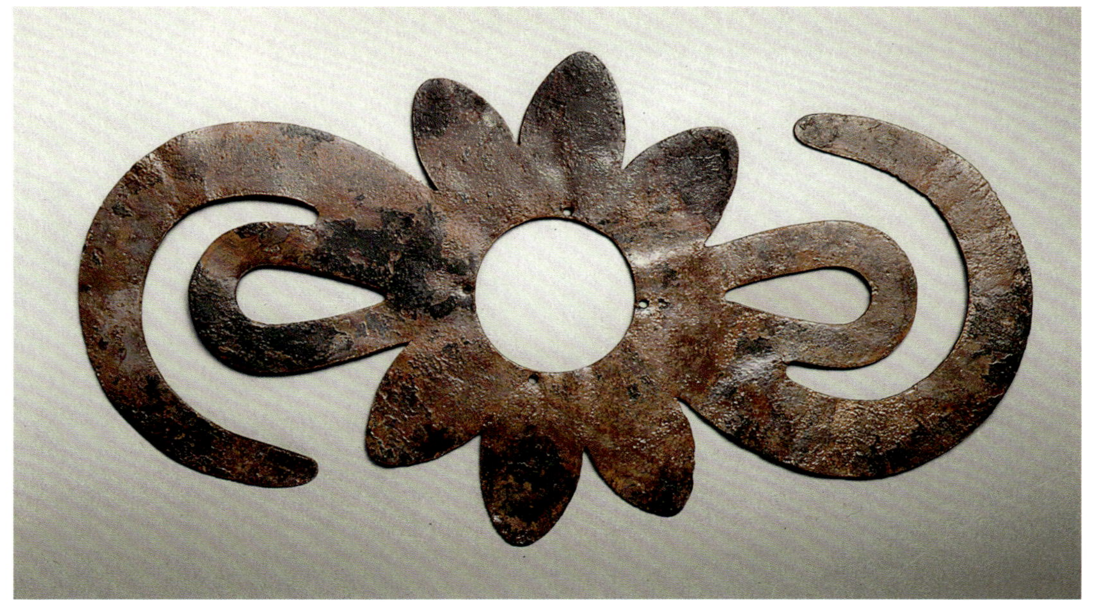

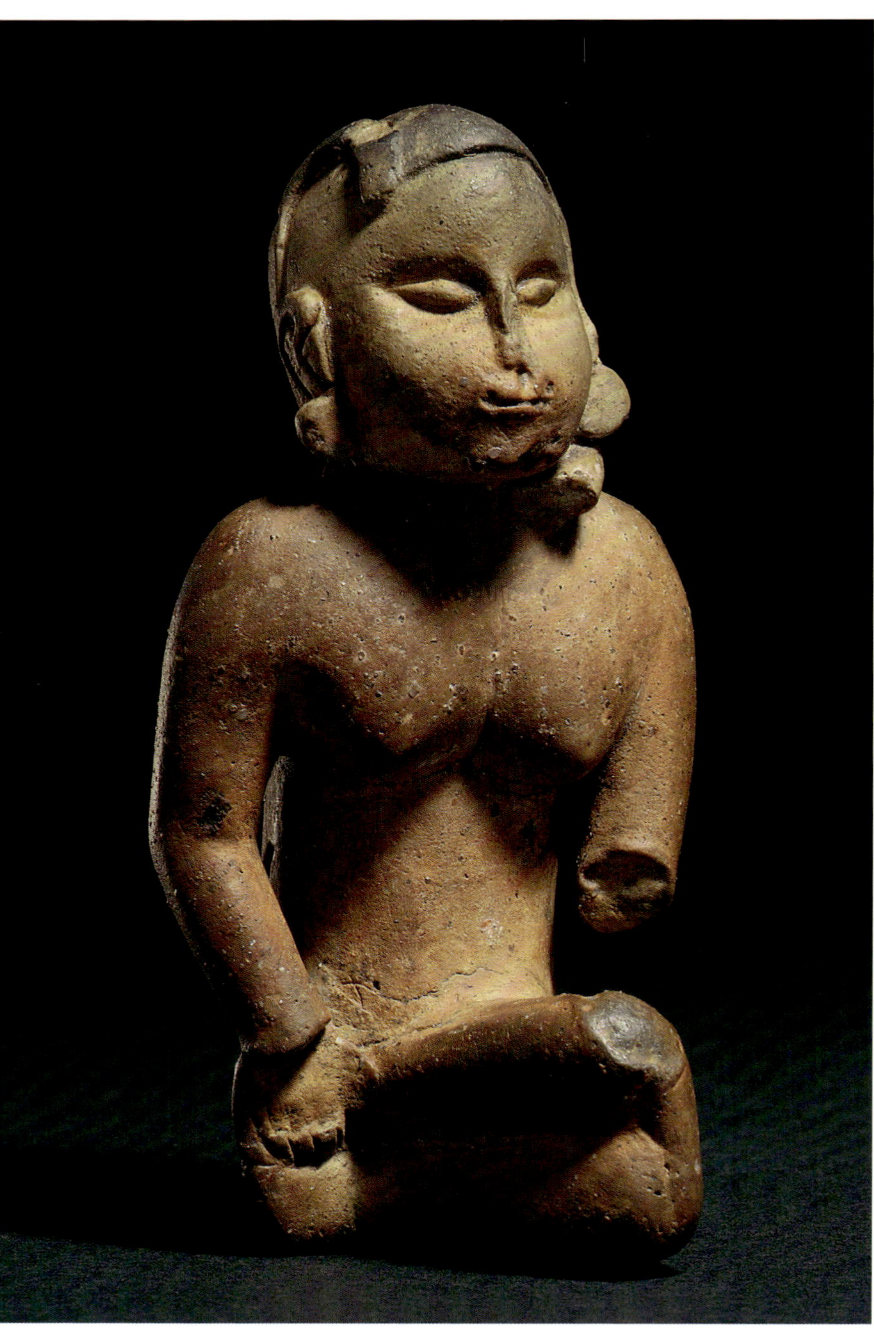

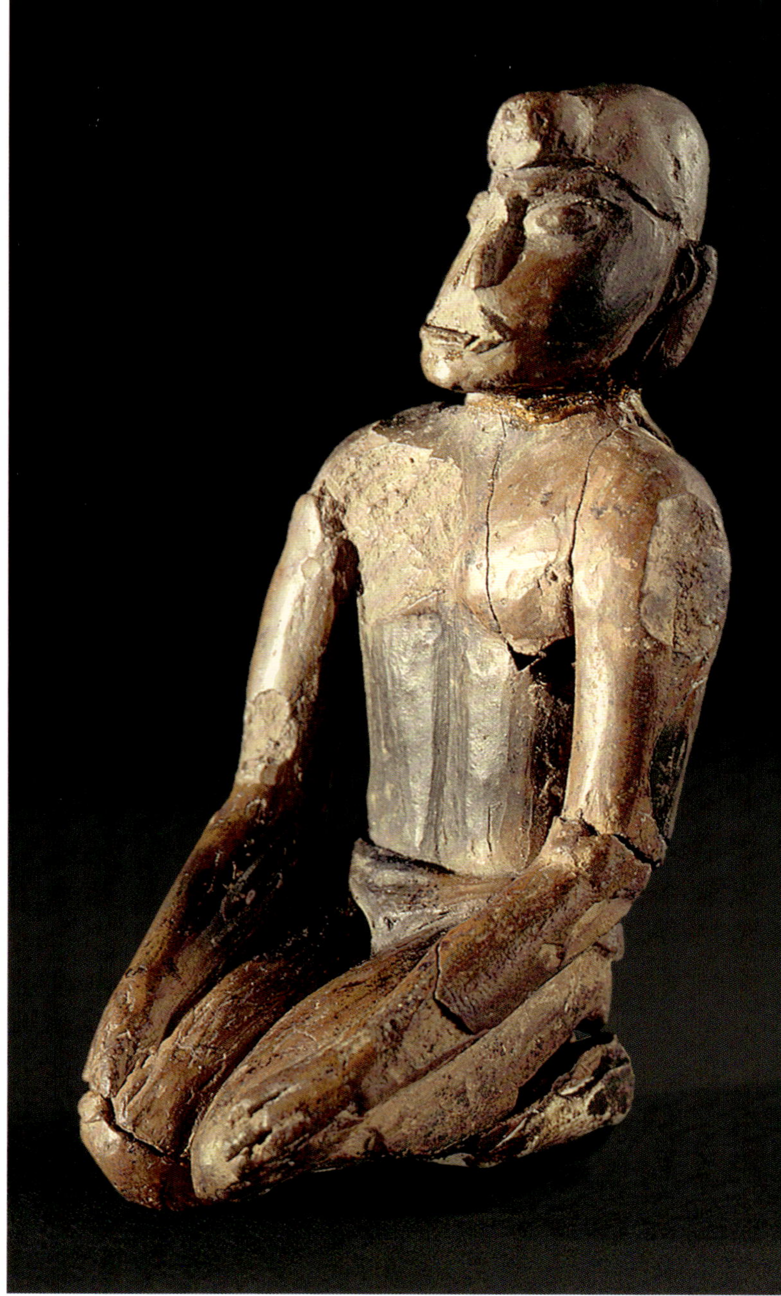

Fig. 10 Seated female figurine; Hopewell culture; Illinois, Jackson County, Twenhafel site, A.D. 200–400; ceramic, h. 8 cm; Illinois State Museum, Springfield. Cat. no. 52.

Fig. 11 Kneeling male figurine; Ohio, Hamilton County, Turner site, Mound 4, A.D. 1–400; ceramic, h. 8.3 cm; Harvard University, Peabody Museum of Archaeology and Ethnology, Peabody Museum Expedition 1882, F. W. Putnam and Dr. C. L. Metz, Directors. Cat. no. 53.

who procure unchallengeable rights to it. I like particularly the term used by anthropologist Franz Boas when he described the rights to perform various kinds of masquerades and ceremonies among the Kwakiutl of British Columbia. Boas referred to such privileges as "prerogatives." If, as the archaeological evidence suggests, we posit that the Adena smoking pipe ritual represented such sacred knowledge—a possession or prerogative—then we are led to speculate about how individuals procured the rights to possess pipes and the rituals attendant to them and the kinds of relations necessary to pass these things from one individual to another. Among the Kwakiutl, ceremonial prerogatives passed down through genealogical relations and spread by gifts of prerogatives between families joined by marriage. Elsewhere sacred prerogatives could be exchanged between individuals through payment and instruction.

The prerogative of owning Adena tubular pipes clearly spread far across the eastern continent of North America, for archaeologists have found them accompanying prominent burials in the vicinity of the St. Lawrence River and Chesapeake Bay, both of which are hundreds of miles away from the core Adena homeland in the central Midwest. For decades they have also debated whether the export of Adena tubular pipes and other finely crafted categories of objects on Webb's list of traits represented the expansion of Adena culture or some kind of trade, although here the relationship between a list of specialized material traits and some kind of cultural or ethnic identity seems particularly tenuous.[9] I suspect that the spread of interest in Adena pipe ritualism among prominent members of communities dispersed across eastern North America two thousand years ago had more to do with the cultural and social values that such objects

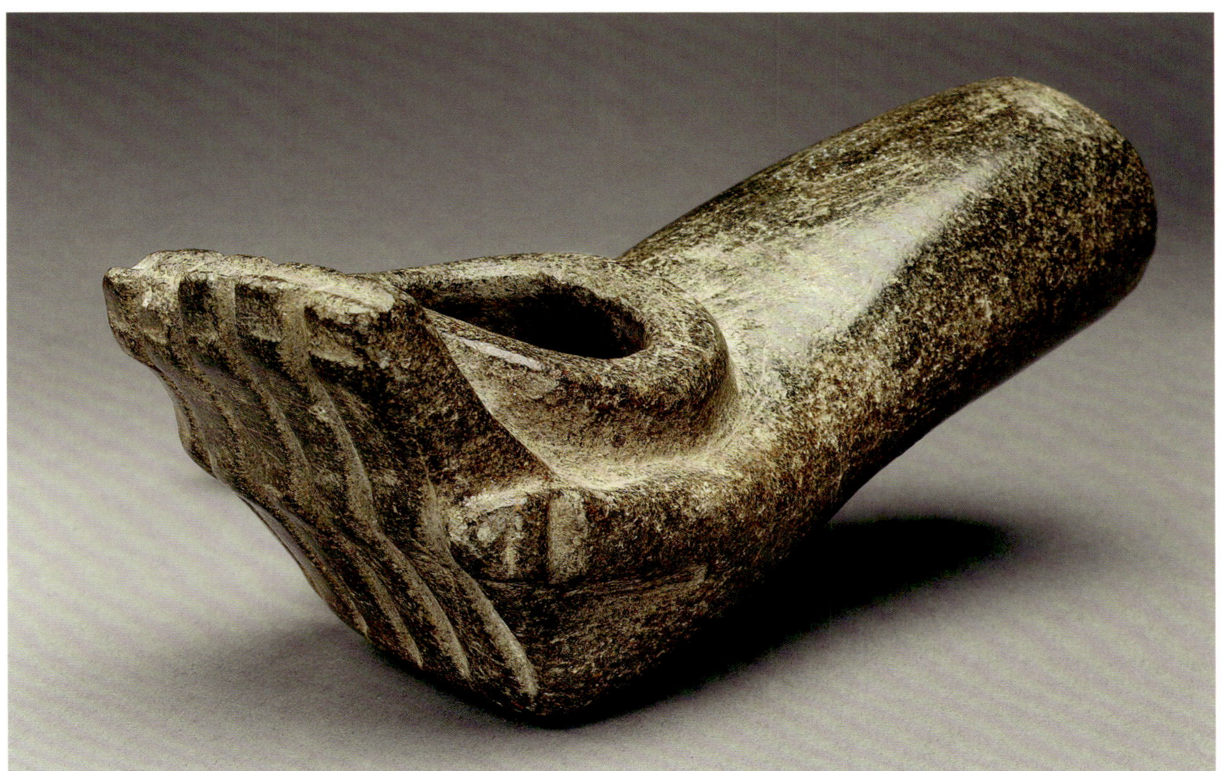

Fig. 12 Six-fingered-hand pipe; Ohio, A.D. 1–400; greenstone, l. 15.2 cm; Smithsonian Institution, National Museum of Natural History, Washington, D.C. Cat. no. 82.

possessed and the knowledge inexorably linked to them (figs. 12–17).

My thinking about values, both collective and individual, has been profoundly influenced by Steven Leuthold's discussion of "aesthetic systems" in his book *Indigenous Aesthetics: Native Art, Media, and Identity*.[10] Frankly, I had felt suspicious and dismissive of the term "aesthetics" when applied to studies of ethnic arts: it seemed so laden with judgmental assumptions from the privileged viewpoint of the outsider connoisseur. Leuthold, however, builds upon anthropologist Edmund Leach's insight that aesthetic and ethical thought inform qualitative judgments underlying all cultural thought and social practice: what is good and what is bad, what has value and what does not. Western connoisseurship values the *formal* aspects of objects, building upon modern, formalist art theory and privileging the informed and practiced eye. The formalist definition of an expert is someone who has seen possibly a hundred examples of a certain kind of object. The educated eye surveys the range of their formal distinctions, while the mind and emotion distinguish their qualitative value. Awkwardly put, this is the "aesthetic system" that informs a great deal of

Fig. 13 Bird and fish effigy pipe; Ohio, Ross County, Hopewell site, Mound 25, A.D. 1–400; steatite, l. 6 cm; The Field Museum, Chicago. Cat. no. 80.

Fig. 14 Double goose pipe; Ohio, Ross County, Hopewell site, Mound 17, A.D. 1–400; steatite, l. 16.5 cm; Ohio Historical Society, Columbus. Cat. no. 73.

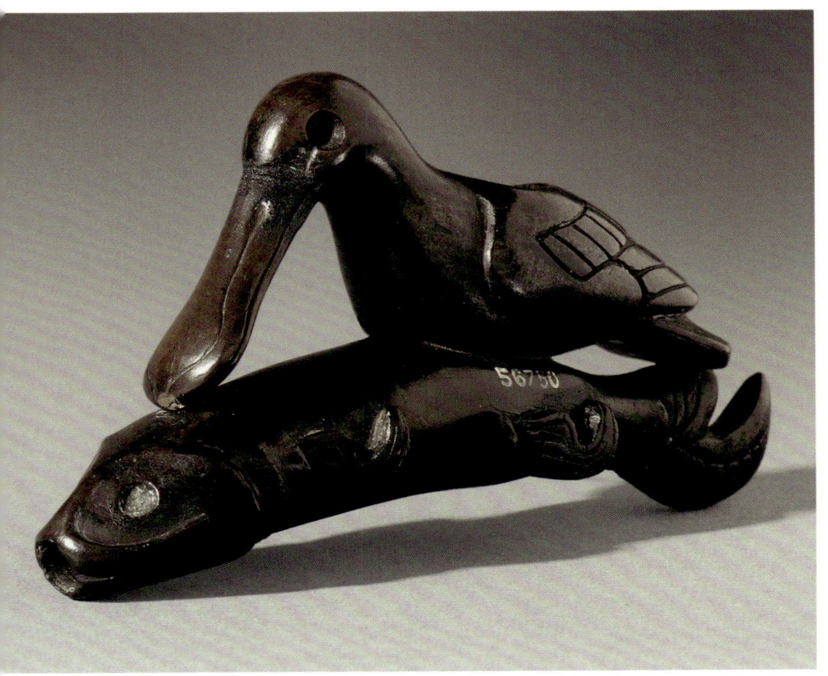

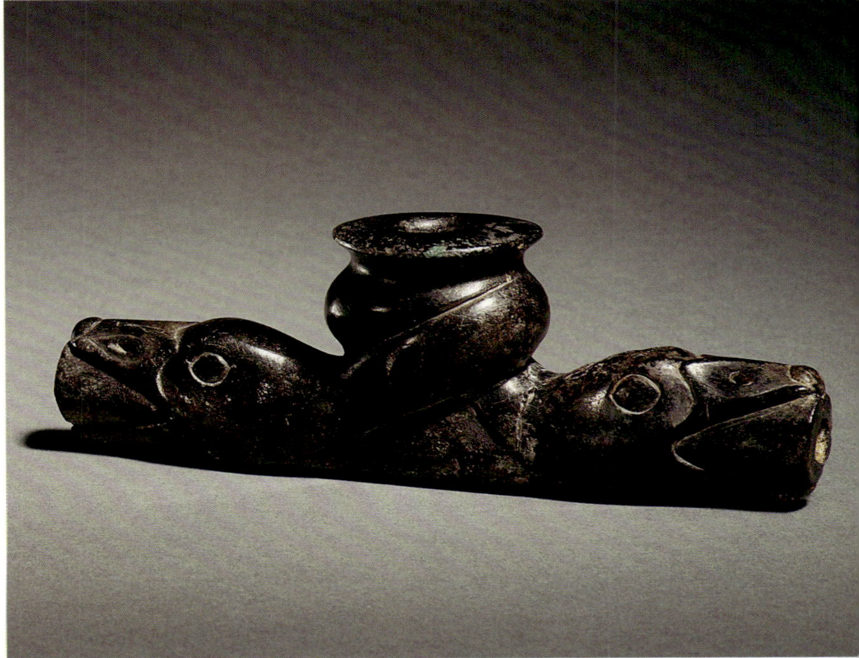

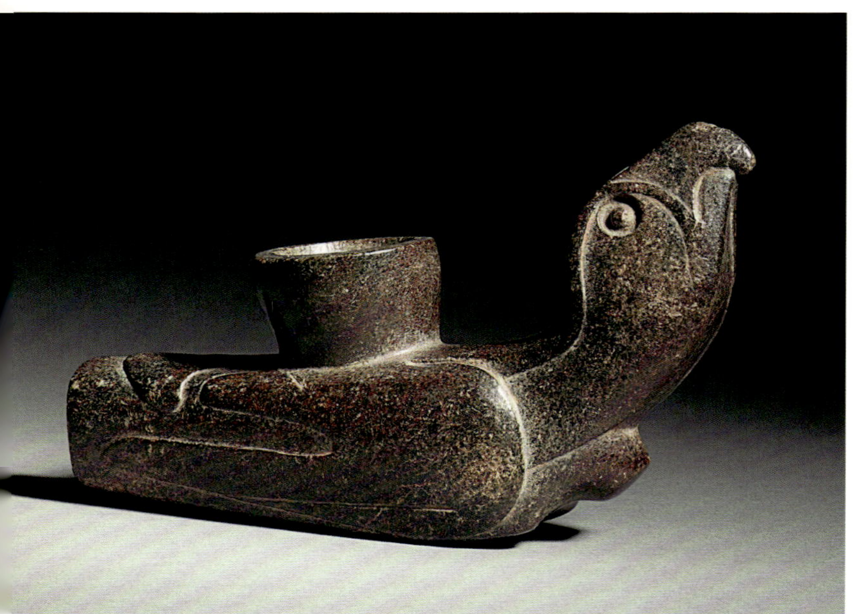

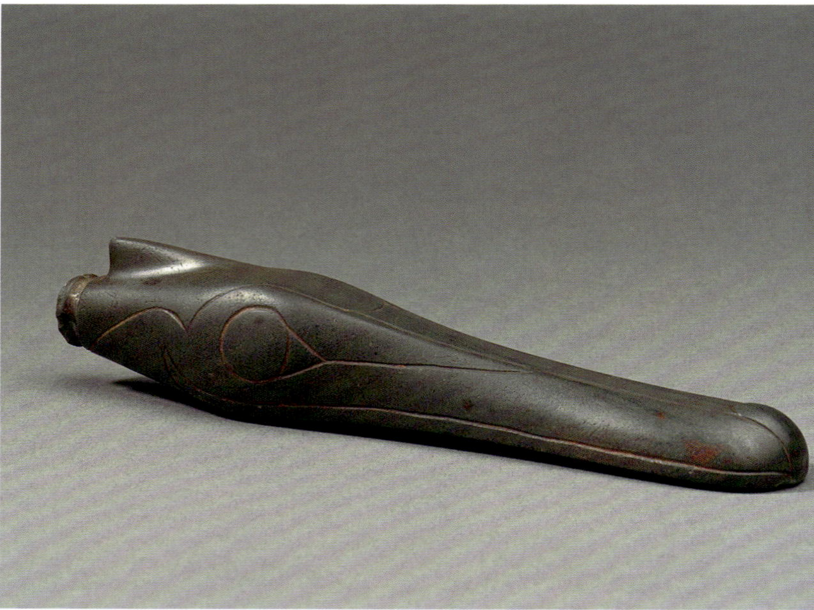

Fig. 15 Raptor effigy pipe; Tennessee, Coffee County, A.D. 600–900; steatite, l. 18.4 cm; Smithsonian Institution, National Museum of the American Indian, Washington, D.C. Cat. no. 76.

Fig. 16 Elongated bird head; Florida, Brevard County, Turkey Creek Mound, south of Melbourne, A.D. 200–500; greenstone, l. 13.6 cm; American Museum of Natural History, New York. Cat. no. 87.

collecting and expertise in the field of American Indian art today. Leuthold argues, quite sensibly, that very different kinds of qualitative, ethical, and aesthetic judgments inform the evaluation of objects within indigenous communities.

When I selected Middle Woodland–period smoking pipes for dissertation study, I did so in part out of respect for their formal properties, privileging these objects because their sculptural qualities corresponded to my training as an art historian. And I do not mean to suggest that those who made and possessed them did not value their qualities of form, craft, and imagery. So far as it goes, perhaps, this is where respective aesthetic systems overlap, creating a point of contact, of entry, for those of us who wonder about these things.

A large number of smoking pipes for my study came from the Tremper Mound, located near present-day Portsmouth, Ohio, and identified with the Ohio Hopewell culture dating sometime between A.D. 1 and A.D. 400. I was particularly attracted to them because their marvelous and masterfully carved images of animals—birds, otters, raccoons, and others—each perched on a small tabular platform that functioned both as a handle and mouthpiece. William C. Mills, once again, excavated the Tremper Mound during the summer of 1915.[11] He found the remains of a large, multichambered structure built of wooden posts set upright in the ground with wickerwork walls of saplings intertwined horizontally among them. The structure measured 61 meters (200 feet) in length with a smooth floor covered in some places with fine sand. It was roughly oblong in plan with entrances at one end and alcoves along one long side that evidently included a kitchen, or at least a location where abundant amounts of food had been prepared, if the large numbers of deer, raccoon, bear, elk, and turkey bones are any indication. Three roughly circular rooms stood at the far end. One, isolated in access and standing to one side, contained three basins where the underlying earth had been baked hard red by fires that evidently had cremated the bodies of human beings. Their cremated remains—Mills estimated over 300 individuals—filled a carefully prepared basin with beveled sides in the far room on the other side. In the center chamber, dominated by a large open fireplace, lay a pile of intentionally broken artifacts—beads, stone ornaments, textiles, ground cones made of galena and quartz crystal, and the fragments of 136 exquisitely crafted smoking pipes.

Mills speculated that the pipes had been broken to prevent theft, reasoning that unbroken artifacts might have proven too much a temptation to those who assembled at the site to perform the activities evidenced there. Without any acknowledgment of irony, Mills had his assistant Henry C. Shetrone piece the fragments back together, restoring 106 of them that are now cared for by the Ohio Historical Society. When the pipes were broken, they were removed from any further social use, a notion underscored by the fact that after all was said and done at Tremper, the structure was burned to the ground and covered with a large mound of earth. Shetrone found that some of the pipes had been broken once before and repaired with narrow bands of copper. But when brought to the structure at Tremper, broken to pieces, and added to what Mills called the "great cache," their social lives were over, just like the individuals whose bodies had been reduced to ashes and placed in the basin in the chamber next door. I dwell on this because I believe it plays to the notion of privilege and exclusivity and suggests that pipe ownership was a prerogative that extended beyond life.

If it is plausible to think of the three hundred plus individuals whose cremated ashes mingled together in the basin at Tremper as a community of the dead, in what manner were they a community while living? Their bodies and presumably some category of their possessions, such as the smoking pipes, had been

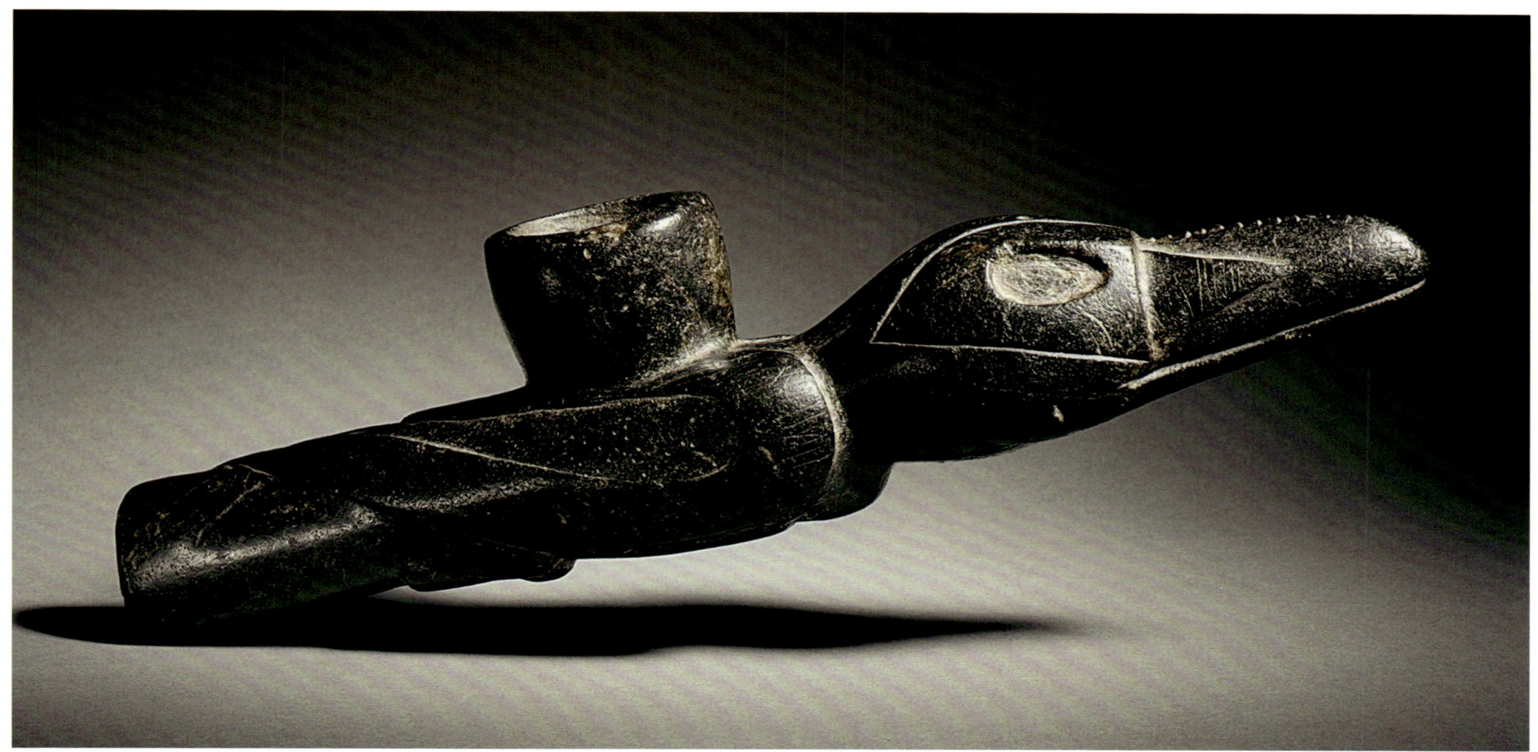

Fig. 17 Raven effigy pipe; Hopewell culture; Tennessee, Cumberland County, A.D. 1–400; steatite, h. 9.2, l. 34.3 cm; Tommy Beutell Collection. Cat. no. 78.

brought to that spot upon their death. How were these individuals related? What aspects of their social lives, their genealogical identities, or some other characteristic, distinguished them for inclusion in these events at Tremper? And what role, if any, did the smoking pipes play in distinguishing such identities?

Effigy platform pipes, like those from the Tremper Mound, are rare among Ohio Hopewell sites. Of the thirty-eight Ohio Hopewell mound sites catalogued by Mark Seeman, effigy platform pipes were found at only a handful, most notably at Mound City where two other large caches like the one at Tremper were found. Mound City, part of the Hopewell Culture National Historical Park, lies north of Chillicothe, about 64 km (40 miles) to the north of Tremper, up the Scioto River. Unlike Tremper's single structure and mound, there are at least twenty-four mounds at Mound City, constructed sequentially in all likelihood, and each containing evidence of a structure housing remains of the dead and a wide assortment of highly crafted objects. A bundle of almost 200 broken pipes and numerous other artifacts had been placed near a crematory basin in Mound 8, another bundle in Mound 13, and eight unbroken pipes, five of them carved with animal effigies, had been placed near a single individual in Mound 18.[12]

Looking at all of these miniature sculptures, I was struck with their myriad similarities and differences, although detailed comparison is challenged by the

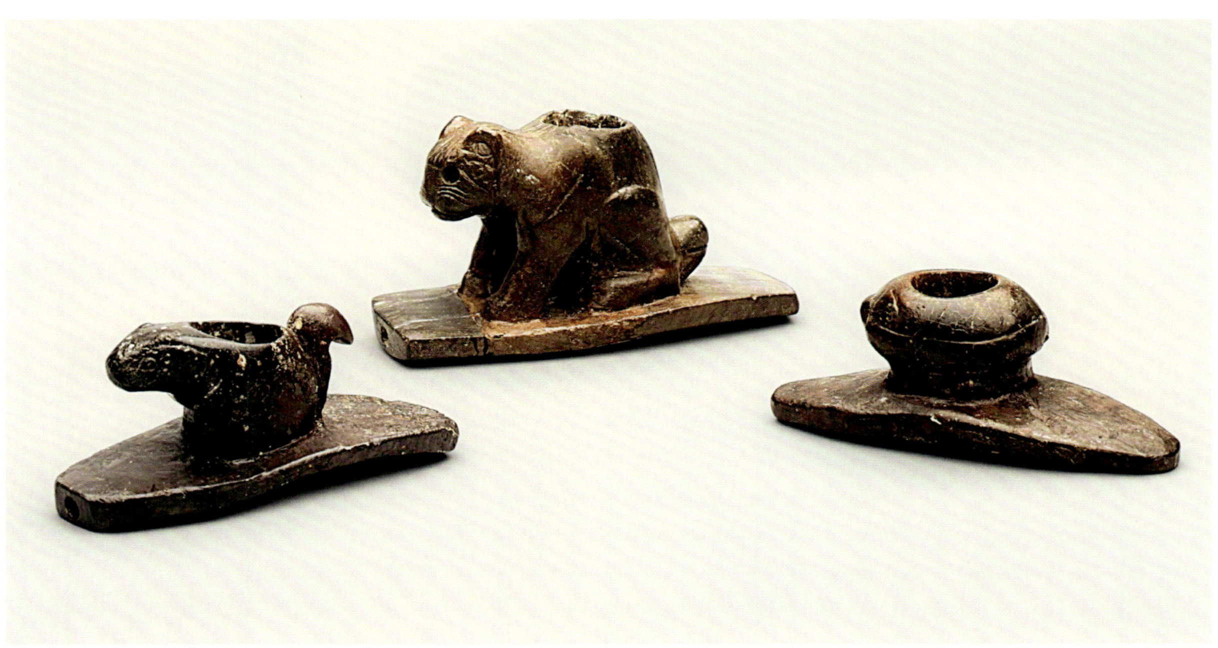

Figs. 18a–c Rodent (squirrel ?) effigy platform pipe; l. 7 cm; young feline effigy platform pipe; l. 8.75 cm; turtle effigy platform pipe; l. 7.25 cm; Hopewell culture; Ohio, Ross County, Mound City, Mound 8, A.D. 1–400; W. Blackmore Collection, The British Museum, London. Cat. nos. 68, 69, and 71.

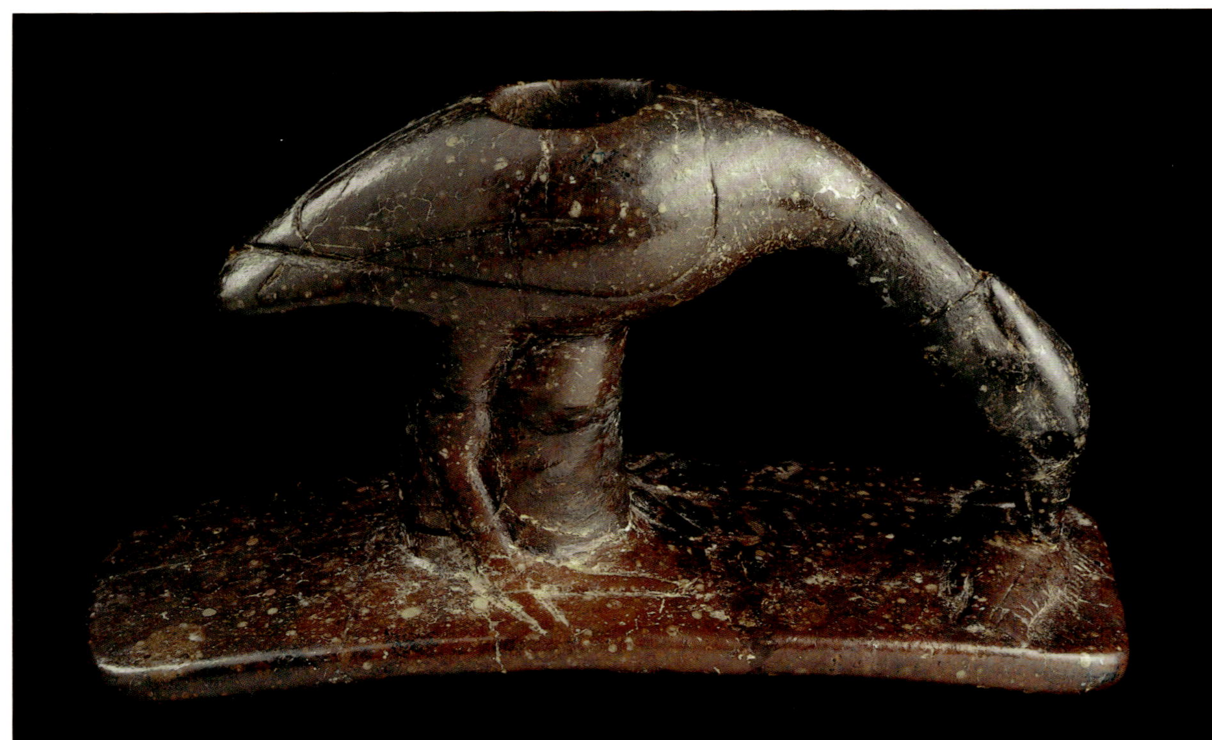

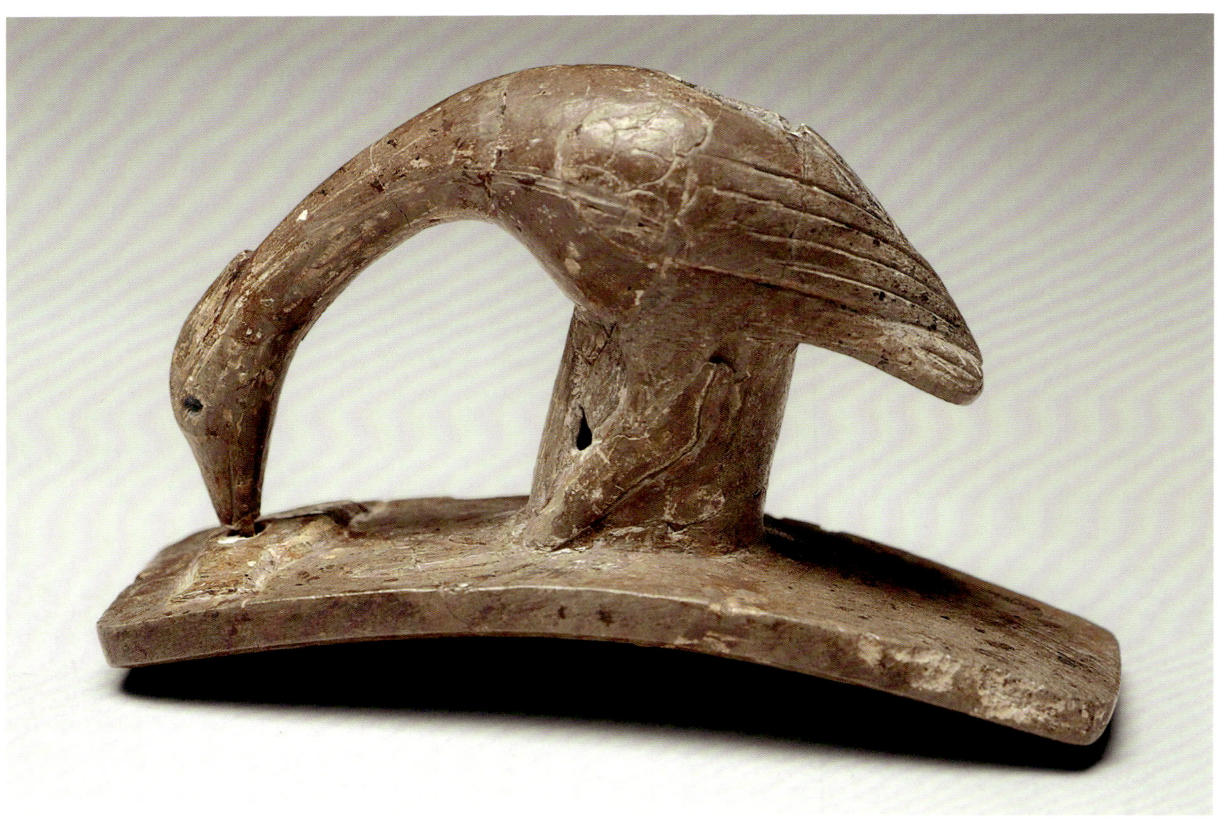

Fig. 19 Effigy platform pipe of a heron eating a fish; Hopewell culture; Ohio, Ross County, Mound City, Mound 8, A.D. 1–400; l. 9 cm; W. Blackmore Collection, The British Museum, London. Cat. no. 72.

Fig. 20 Effigy platform pipe of a heron eating a fish; Hopewell culture; Ohio, Scioto County, Tremper Mound, A.D. 1–400; pipestone, l. 9.4 cm; Ohio Historical Society, Columbus.

fact that, due to a complicated sequence of historical events, the Mound 8 group, unearthed by Ephraim Squier and Edwin Davis in 1846, ended up at the British Museum (figs. 18–19 and 21). Clearly, more than one artist was at work, although, to my eye, a single carver at Tremper and another at Mound City were responsible for most of them. A more detailed study using the Morellian method might sort out the individual hands.[13] But, clearly, a relatively small group of artists created hundreds of individual pipes closely conforming in scale, technique, style, and image, even to the extent that the Mound City and Tremper sets include pipes that virtually duplicate their effigy images in pose, attitude, and detail (figs. 19–20).

Further afield, things get even more interesting. Resident to the lower and central Illinois River valley, hundreds of miles to the west, a very different ethnic group whom archaeologists call the Havana people built smaller burial crypts on the bluffs above the river, log tombs covered with bark and eventually covered

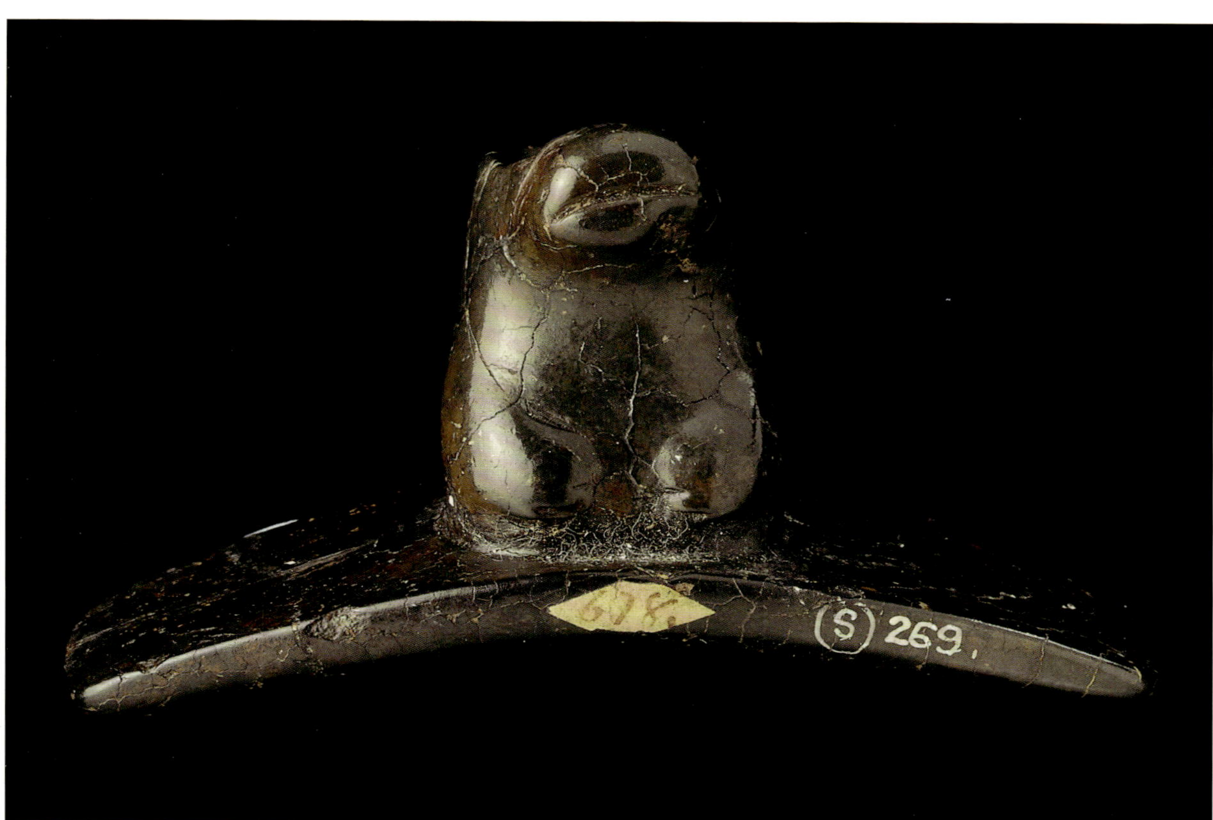

Fig. 21 Otter effigy platform pipe; Hopewell culture; Ohio, Ross County, Mound City, Mound 8, A.D. 1–400; l. 8.9 cm; W. Blackmore Collection, The British Museum, London. Cat. no. 70.

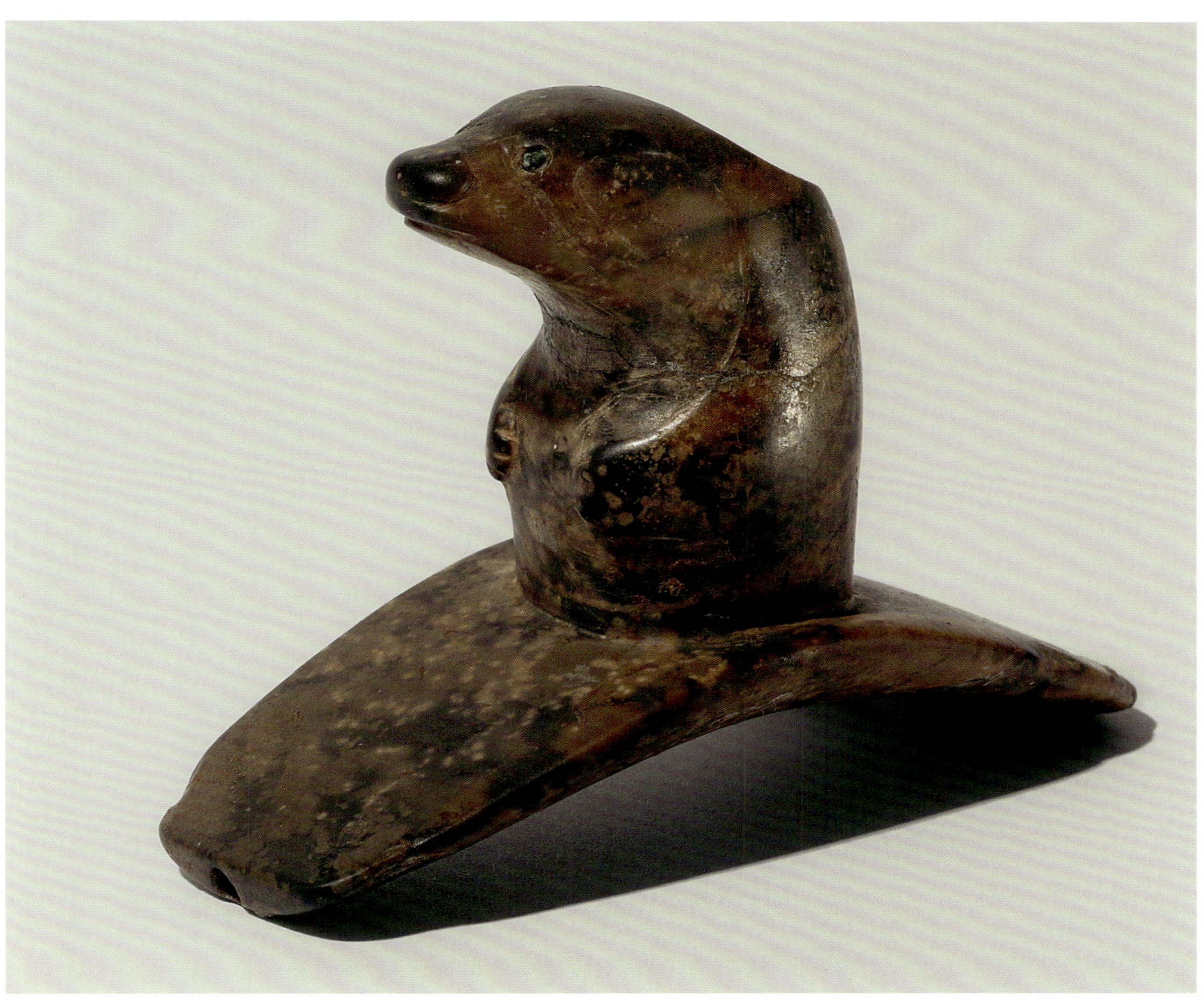

Fig. 22 Otter effigy platform pipe; Illinois, White County, Wilson site, A.D. 1–400; siliceous shale and copper, h. 6.3, l. 8.6 cm; Illinois State Museum, Springfield. Cat. no. 62.

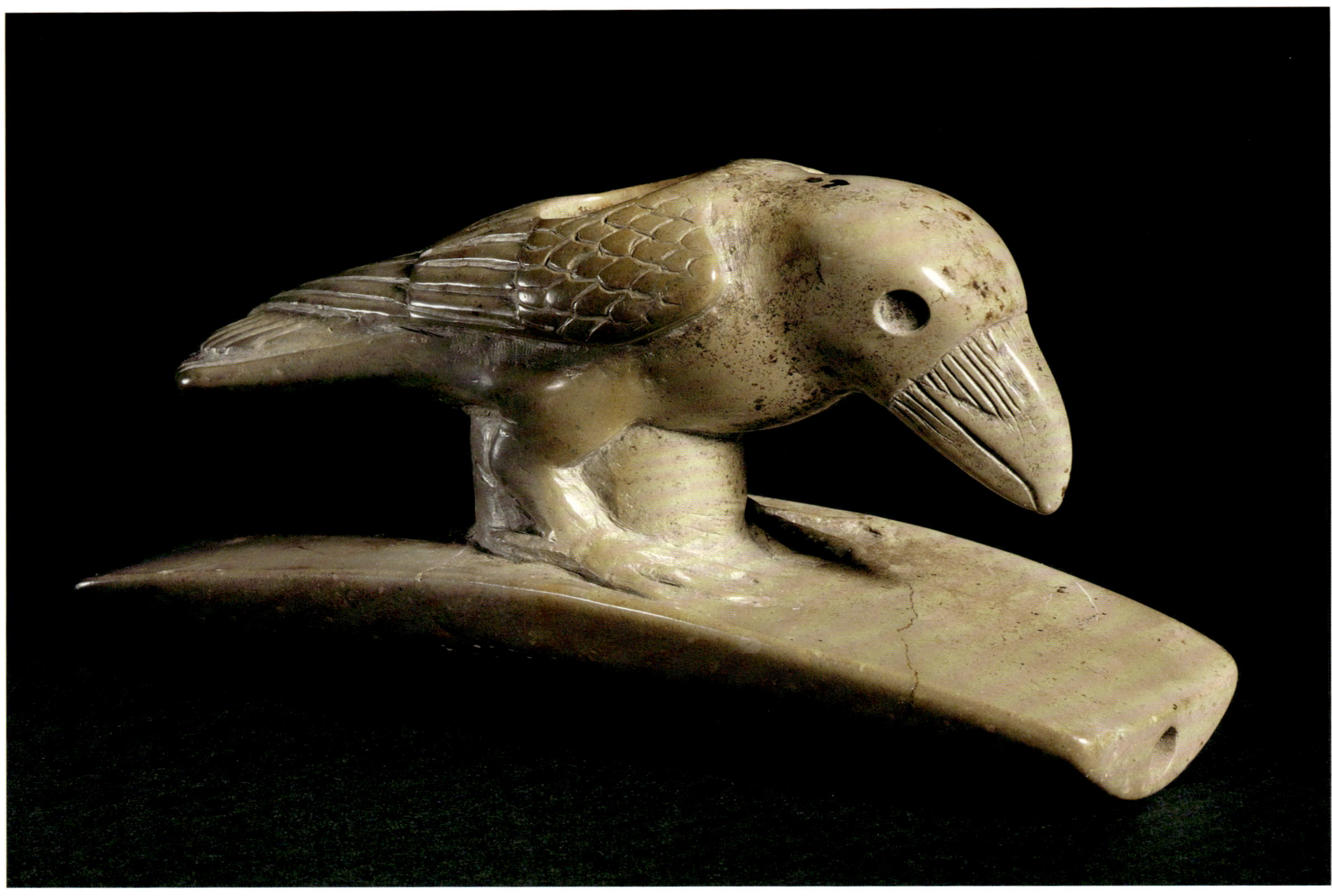

Fig. 23 Raven effigy platform pipe; Illinois, Pike County, Bedford site no. 9, A.D. 200–400; conglomerate stone, l. 10.2 cm; Gilcrease Museum, Tulsa, Oklahoma. Cat. no. 66.

with an earthen mound. Some of the dead possessed effigy platform pipes closely matching those found at the Tremper Mound and Mound City, but carved for the most part by local masters (figs. 21–22). Their neighbors in southern Illinois, known to archaeologists as the Crab Orchard people, also included effigy platform pipe owners. Individuals dispersed as far away as the Mississippi delta and the central Appalachians took effigy platform pipes with them to their tombs (figs. 1, 23–25).[14] The phenomenon cannot be explained simply as trade. Who was trading with whom? Although very possibly some pipes moved from one place to another, many are clearly local productions nevertheless closely tied by form and imagery to the larger set as a whole. If those buried at Tremper represent some kind of community of pipe owners, what is the nature of these broader relationships, stretched between mortuary sites and extended beyond ethnic boundaries: a network? a cult? a club? an organization? What kinds of words can we find to describe these relationships?

When I struggled with these questions in a catalogue essay for *Ancient Art of the American Woodland Indians*, I borrowed the expression "primitive valuables" from anthropologist George Dalton, who had coined it in an essay, as he put it, "emphasizing the importance of relations of alliance and hostility and the special role of primitive valuables in political transactions in stateless societies."[15] Although historian Francis Jennings later chided me for using this "unfortunate phrase," he put his finger on the passage that best expressed what I was trying to say: that is, that such objects "created and maintained crucial obligations among individuals, families, clans, and communities."[16] Effigy platform pipes, along with a host of other highly crafted and specialized objects, are themselves but partial manifestations of transactions that created binding obligations, transmitted exclusive knowledge, and, one presumes, granted great power and influence. Centuries later, among the far more politically stratified Mississippian chiefdoms, high-ranking families built upon this foundation by creating and exchanging objects and ornaments with esoteric imagery restricted exclusively to their social class and alluding to their sacred sources of privilege and power.

This indigenous aesthetic system, then, is one in which the formal properties of an object, those that we may admire as art or sculpture, seem inexorably tied to exclusive knowledge, privilege, and access to power. This represents a kind of Pandora's box for archaeology: if an objective of archaeological research is greater insight to the cultural meanings of artifacts and an understanding of the cultural values they represent, then what is the price of such knowledge? Assertive Native American voices have been saying for some

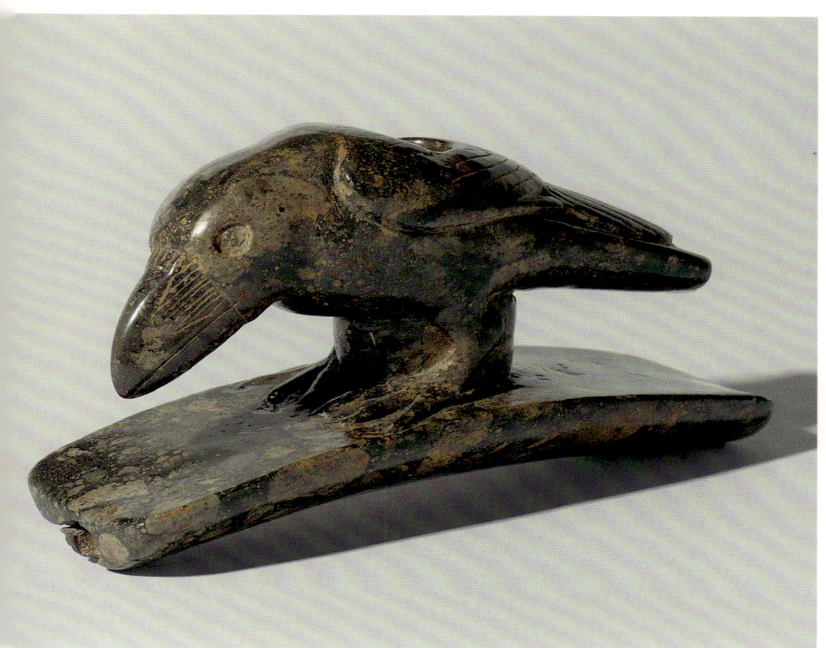

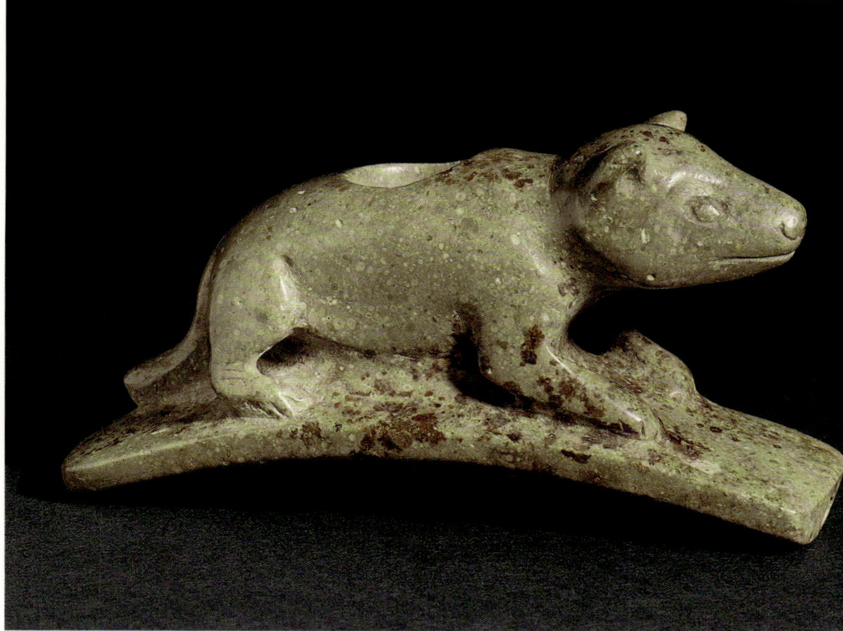

Fig. 24 Raven effigy platform pipe; Illinois, Hardin County, Rutherford Mound, A.D. 1–400; conglomerate stone, h. 6, l. 12 cm; Illinois State Museum, Springfield. Cat. no. 63.

Fig. 25 Dog effigy platform pipe; Illinois, Fulton County, Weaver site, A.D. 1–400; oolitic limestone, h. 5.2, l. 9 cm; Illinois State Museum, Springfield. Cat. no. 60.

time that when these objects were consigned to the earth with elaborate and necessary ritual, they were intended to stay there. After excavation, the social lives of these things resumed, albeit in the very different contexts of museum collections, exhibitions, and academic research. The chief benefit of the 1990 Native American Graves Protection and Repatriation Act is that it forces the acknowledgment, careful consideration, and discussion of these issues. And many of the Native people who are working as NAGPRA officials today struggle under a real and heavy burden. What are we to do with objects that were never intended to be here? Many recognize that such things cannot be restored to their former state. Who today has the knowledge and right to do so? How do we weigh the values of their educational power against the values of spiritual belief? The values these things represent stem from very different and yet pervasive aesthetic systems, each legitimate but informed by contending qualitative foundations. I often hear questions from Native acquaintances about the value of archaeological query: what is the value of the knowledge that results and to what purpose is it put? One answer is to help inform, earnestly, honestly, and respectfully, the deliberations about how we should think about these things; what purpose, under the present circumstances, can they serve; and what should become of them in the future.

Notes

1. The volume most closely associated with "New Archaeology" is Binford and Binford 1968. Howard Winters has an essay in it. For the "Classificatory-Historical" period of American archaeology, see Willey and Sabloff 1974. William A. Ritchie's work during this period is summarized in Ritchie 1965. William S. Webb's works are too numerous to mention, but I was thinking of Webb and Funkhauser 1932.
2. Webb and Snow 1945.
3. Penney 1980.
4. Winters 1969.
5. Penney 1980, p. 26.
6. Penney 1988. The catalogue of the exhibition is Brose, Brown, and Penney 1985.
7. Asch and Asch 1985.
8. Mills 1902.
9. The best documented and informed discussions of Adena artifacts in the east took place during a symposium at Ball State University in 1970. See Swartz 1971 for an edited transcripts of the papers and discussion.
10. Leuthold 1998.
11. Mills 1916.
12. Seeman 1979. An account of the discovery of the pipe cache in Mound 8 at Mound City appears in Squier and Davis 1848, pp. 152–53. Mills returned to Mound 8 in 1920, finding evidence of the cache and more pipe fragments, plus the two additional collections of pipes in Mounds 13 and 18. See Mills 1922.
13. The "Morellian method" refers to the work of the scholar of Renaissance painting, Giovanni Morelli, who developed a technique for identifying the works of Italian painters by comparing various, small details of their paintings, such as hands and ears.
14. See Penney 1980, pp. 174–91.
15. Penney 1985, p. 147; Dalton 1977, pp. 191–92.
16. Jennings 1993, pp. 64–65; Penney 1985, p. 147.

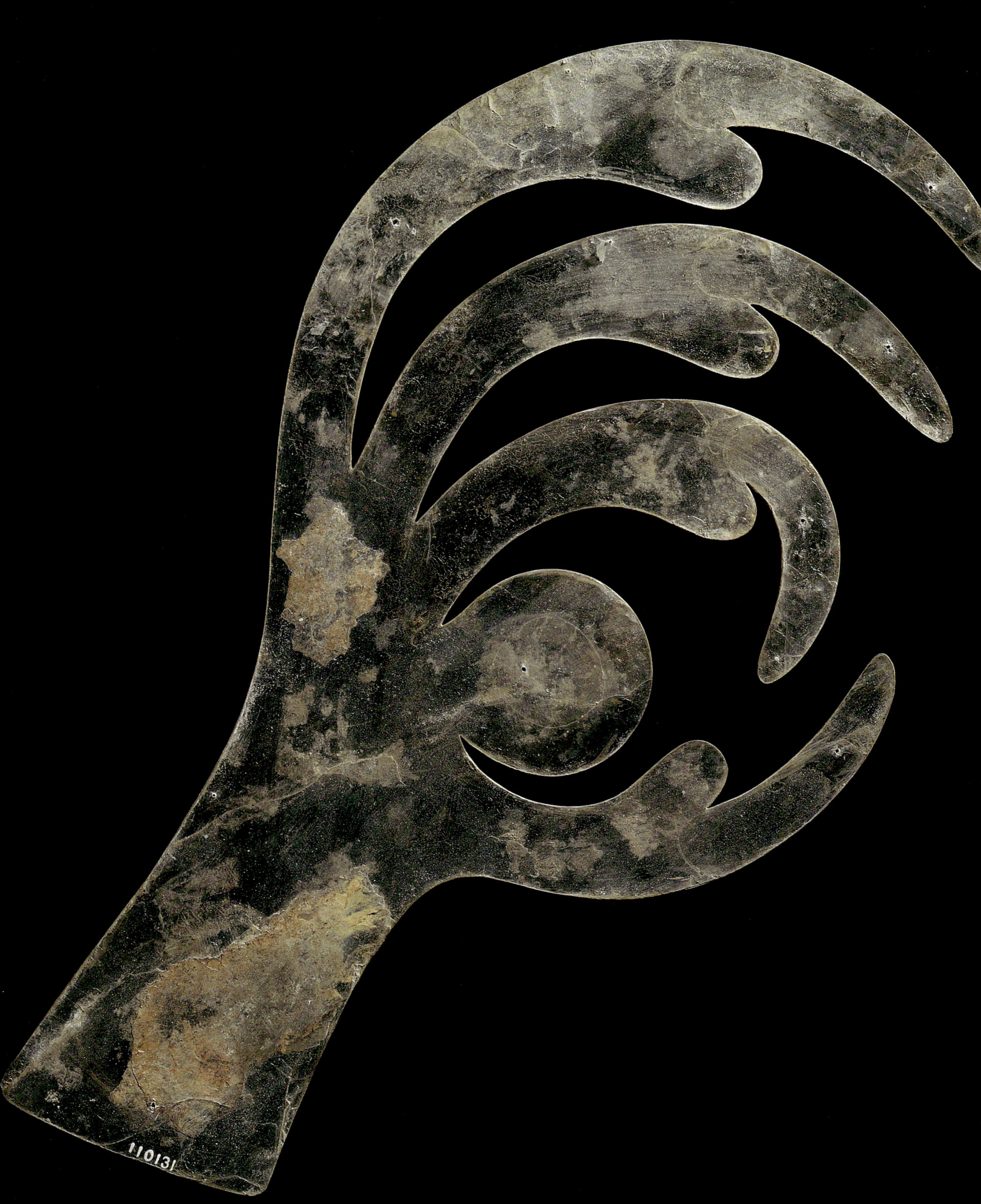
110131

Hopewell Art in Hopewell Places

Mark F. Seeman

The ancient art of the Eastern Woodlands is one of the least-studied areas of North American art. Furthermore, most of what is known pertains to the relatively recent Mississippian societies of the tenth through sixteenth centuries rather than those of the deeper past. But well before the development of Mississippian culture, peoples of great talent and ability occupied all portions of this vast region. Their artistry, which shares with Mississippian art a generally religious caste, has proven difficult to find and even more difficult to interpret. Much of this is due to the ravages of time as well as to certain cultural differences between maize-farming Mississippian societies and pre-Mississippian peoples with less intensive economies and smaller populations. Conceptually, Mississippian art is close enough in time to connect it to the religious practices and oral traditions of historical groups such as the Chickasaw, Creek, Caddo, and Osage.[1] But art of the preceding Woodland, Archaic, and Paleoindian periods in eastern North America is sufficiently removed from the present that such historical connections are exceedingly difficult to make. Mississippian art was a sacred art in the sense that it was created for ritual use in sacred places. So too was pre-Mississippian art, but the kinds of sacred places were different and, to some degree, were governed by different sensibilities or relationships among places.

Fig. 1 Bird claw cutout; Ohio, Ross County, Hopewell site, Mound 25, A.D. 1–400; sheet mica, h. 27.9 cm; The Field Museum, Chicago. Cat. no. 45. A masterpiece of Hopewell design, the flowing outline of open talons suggests the swift gesture of a bird of prey. Fine graphic quality and the precise cutout of the costly mica testify to the presence of specialist artisans employed in the making of ceremonial regalia.

The concept of a "Woodland period" was developed to clarify broad similarities in lifeways and material culture among various peoples over a thousand years ago, before the development of Mississippian societies.[2] The term "Woodland" has come to designate a two-thousand-year span of time beginning about 1000 B.C. and ending about A.D. 1000, during which the development of middle-range "tribal" societies dominated the ancient history of the region. The archaeological correlates of this process—elaborate burial programs, large-scale public works, ceramic arts, exchange networks, sedentary villages, and agriculture—lend definition to the notion of a Woodland period distinct from an earlier, Archaic period that was shaped by hunting and collecting and from a later, Mississippian period typified by intensive maize agriculture, higher population densities, and hierarchically organized political structures.

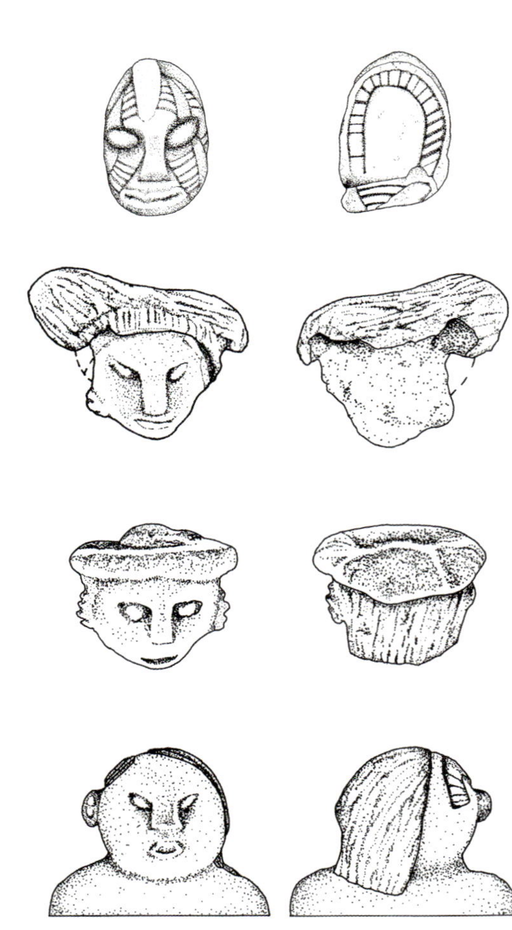

Fig. 2 Ohio River valley Hopewell clay figurines display elaborate patterns of hairstyles, as evident in these specimens from the Mann site in Posey County, Indiana. Objects depicted are in the Glenn A. Black Laboratory of Archaeology at Indiana University, Bloomington, and in the collections of Charles Lacer and Alvin Nurrenbern; drawings by Linda Spurlock.

The People

Recognized since about 1900 as a distinctive aspect of Woodland archaeology, "Hopewell," especially in the Ohio River valley, has often been viewed as the climax of the period because its artistic, constructional, and ritual efforts surpass those of earlier and later manifestations.[3] To archaeologists, the term "Hopewell" connotes either an "archaeological horizon" or an "interaction sphere," in that it displays a series of related characters—copper bicymbal earspools, metal panpipes, platform effigy pipes, zoned rocker-stamped pottery with iconographic motifs—of brief duration and of broad geographic distribution that were selectively introduced into local sequences.[4] Temporally, most scholars agree that this lasted about thirteen

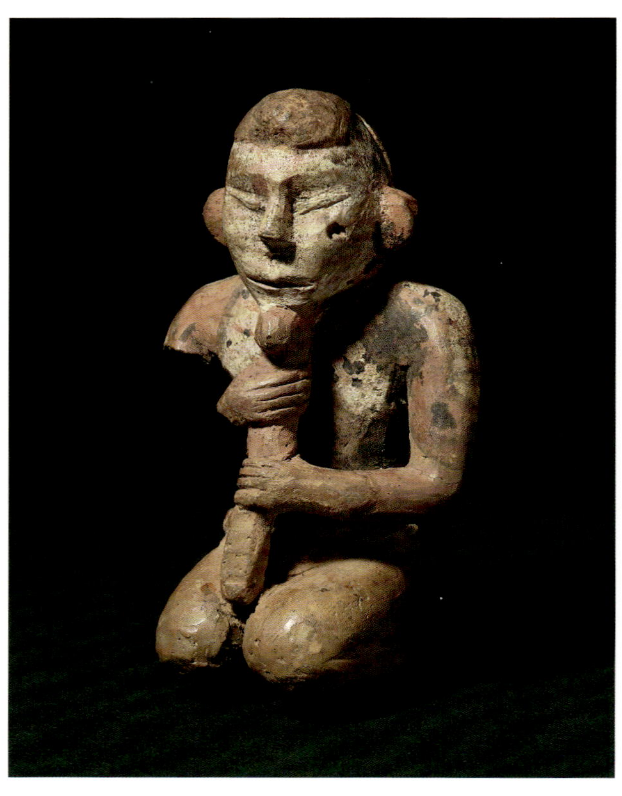

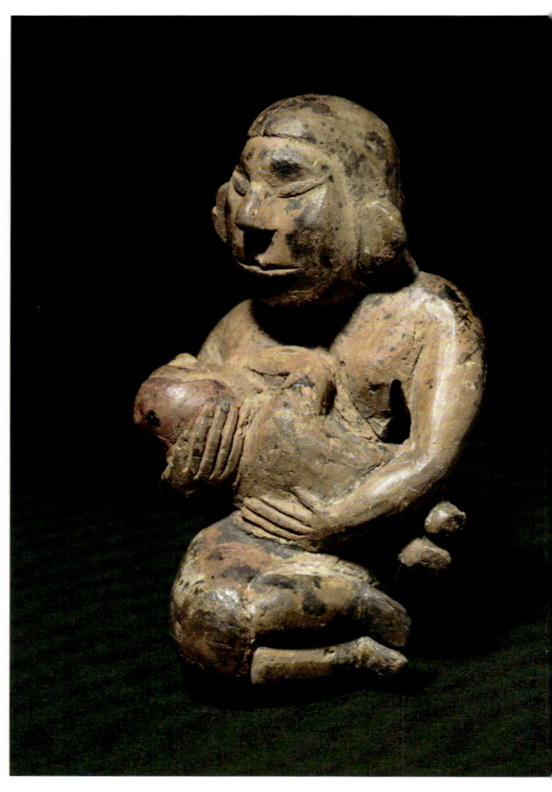

generations between A.D. 1 and A.D. 400. Spatially, Hopewell participation included much of the riverine and Great Lakes areas of the Midwest, Midsouth, and Gulf Coast. In contrast to the correlated distribution of the material symbols of the Southeastern Ceremonial Complex exchanged among Mississippian elites, Hopewell objects often show more individualistic distributions, more evidence for localized production of finished objects, and considerable contextual variability. In reference to Hopewell figurines, platform pipes, and pottery, David Penney of the Detroit Institute of Arts has shown that the origins of Hopewell symbols developed in different geographic areas before attaining broad, interregional popularity.[5] Hopewell relationships both within regions and between regions are consistent with interpretations of considerable communication, visitation, and some intermarriage, but with little institutional control.

The basic building blocks of societies participating in Hopewell relationships were individual households scattered along the major stream valleys of the midcontinent. Networks of kinship, alliance, and trade linked them together at several scales. These societies were certainly not identical; they spoke different languages, displayed different degrees of sedentary settlement, and engaged in different ritual practices. All were simpler politically than later Mississippian societies; the notions of "temple town" or "controlling elite" that have been applied to Mississippian communities were relevant to none of them. These people benefited from well-balanced diets, but they died young and were comparatively short by today's standards. Men in leadership positions, as has been identified by their prominent and expensive burial ceremonies, were taller than the average; size apparently correlated with the characteristics necessary to assume certain key roles in Hopewell society, just as it did in some Mississippian societies.[6] Such leadership roles were validated by the exchange and use of precious objects of recognized "Hopewell" form.[7]

There is no single factor that explains the increased prominence of leadership roles in Woodland societies c. A.D. 1. In many of the areas where Hopewell participation was most developed—the Ohio River valley, the Illinois River valley, and the upper Tennessee River valley—an increased involvement with food production and associated population concentration in certain favorable areas—for example, the lower Illinois valley, the Wabash River lowland, or the confluence of the Scioto River and Paint Creek—would seem to support an interpretation based upon subsistence intensification in these rich environs. In western Illinois, there was a dramatic, ten-fold increase in plant utilization at this time, including a new food, maize (*zea mays*).[8] But prominent people in areas for which we have no similar evidence for farming or horticulture—for example, in the mountains of northwest Georgia, the swamps of Louisiana, or the forests of central Ontario—were also actively using Hopewell valuables, albeit on a smaller scale. The prominence of material symbols in all of these areas supports the view that Hopewell societies were prestige-goods economies and that the use of such objects was necessary for social reproduction.[9]

In the Ohio valley, it has proven difficult to identify specific types of leaders from any evidence of costume and regalia found in mortuary contexts. This is due in part to the variety of individual histories and experiences that can accumulate in societies that do not have

Figs. 3–7 Five figurines; Illinois, Calhoun County, Knight Mound group, Mound 8, A.D. 200–400; painted earthenware, h. 7.5–11 cm; The Milwaukee Public Museum. Cat. nos. 47–51. These Hopewell figurines from western Illinois show variation in hairstyling and ornamentation comparable to those from the Ohio River valley.

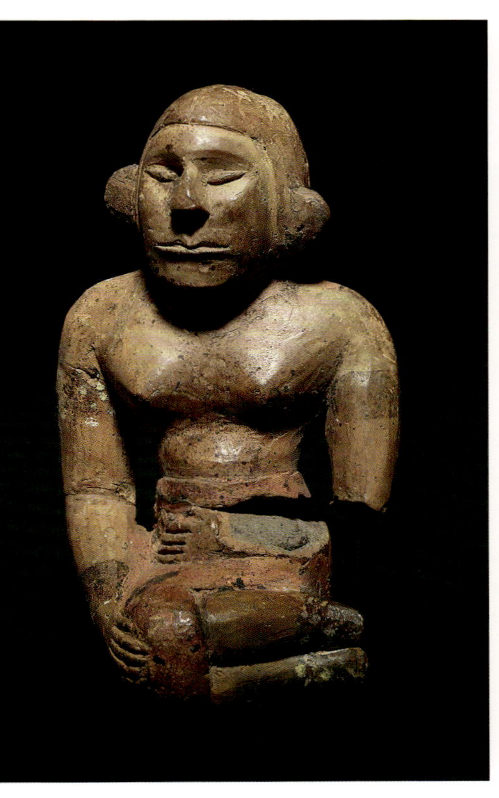

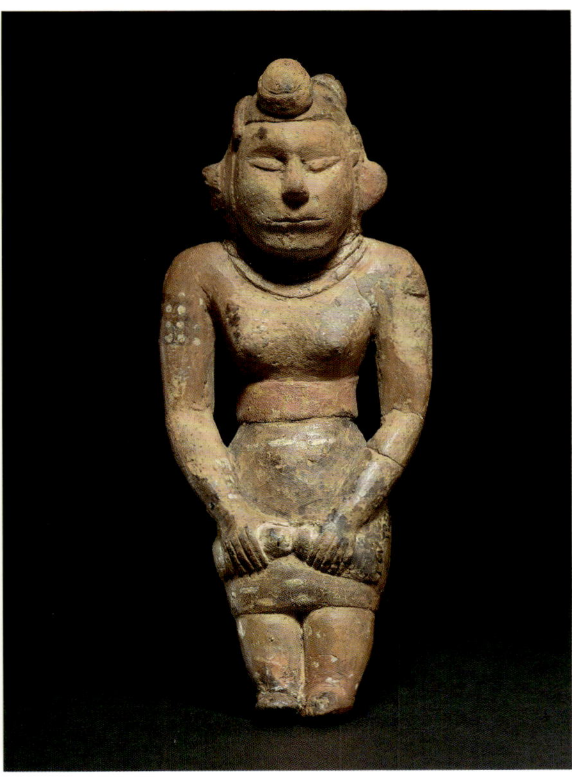

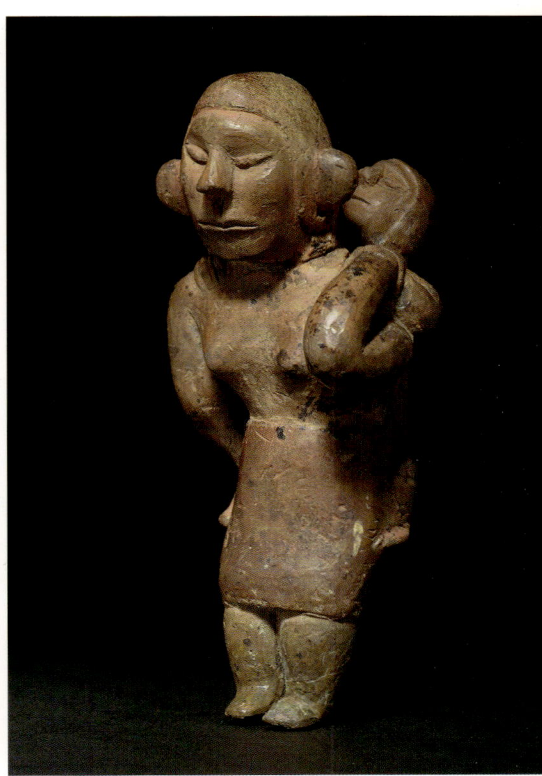

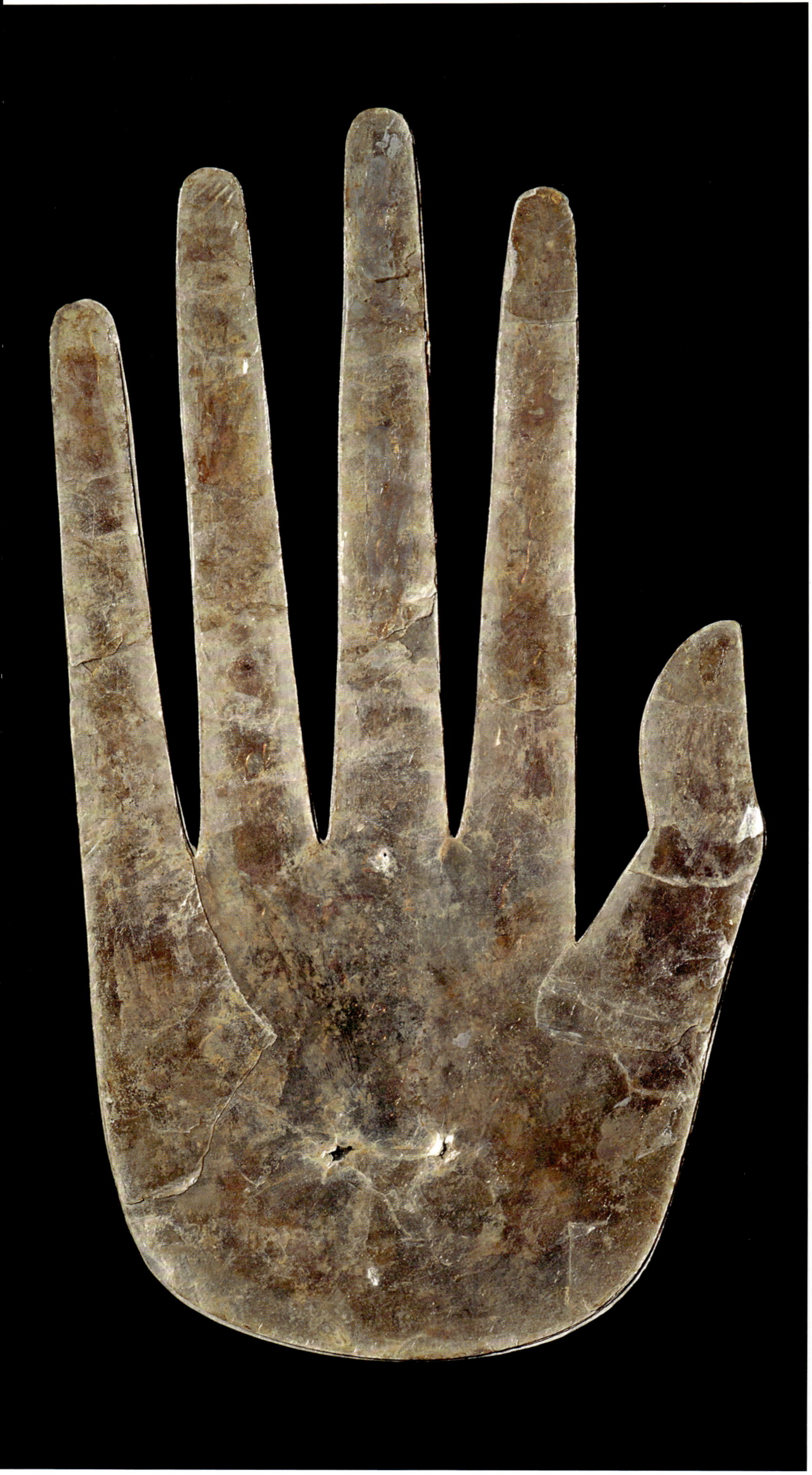

Fig. 8 Hand cutout; Ohio, Ross County, Hopewell site, Mound 25, A.D. 1–400; sheet mica, h. 29 cm; Ohio Historical Society, Columbus. Cat. no. 46. Among the most elegant icons in the art of the ancient Americas, this mica cutout hand—with its elongated fingers and the graceful curve around the heel of the palm—conveys through form and a sense of gesture a suggestion of communication between the human community and the world of spirits beyond.

Fig. 9 Human profile cutout; Ohio, Hamilton County, Turner site, Mound 3, A.D. 1–400; sheet mica, h. 18.4, w. 13 cm; Harvard University, Peabody Museum of Archaeology and Ethnology, Peabody Museum Expedition 1882, F. W. Putnam and Dr. C. L. Metz, Directors. Cat. no. 41.

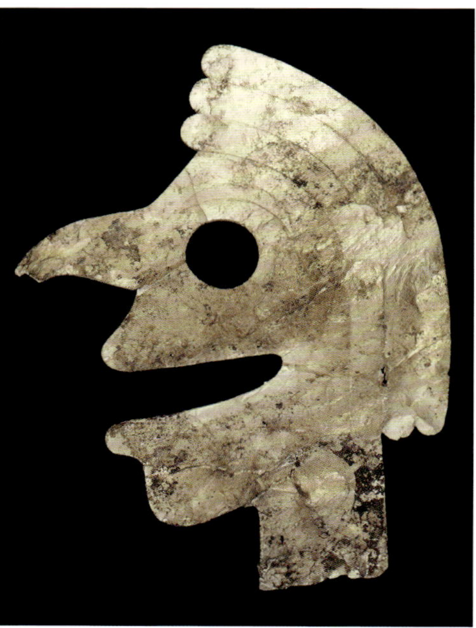

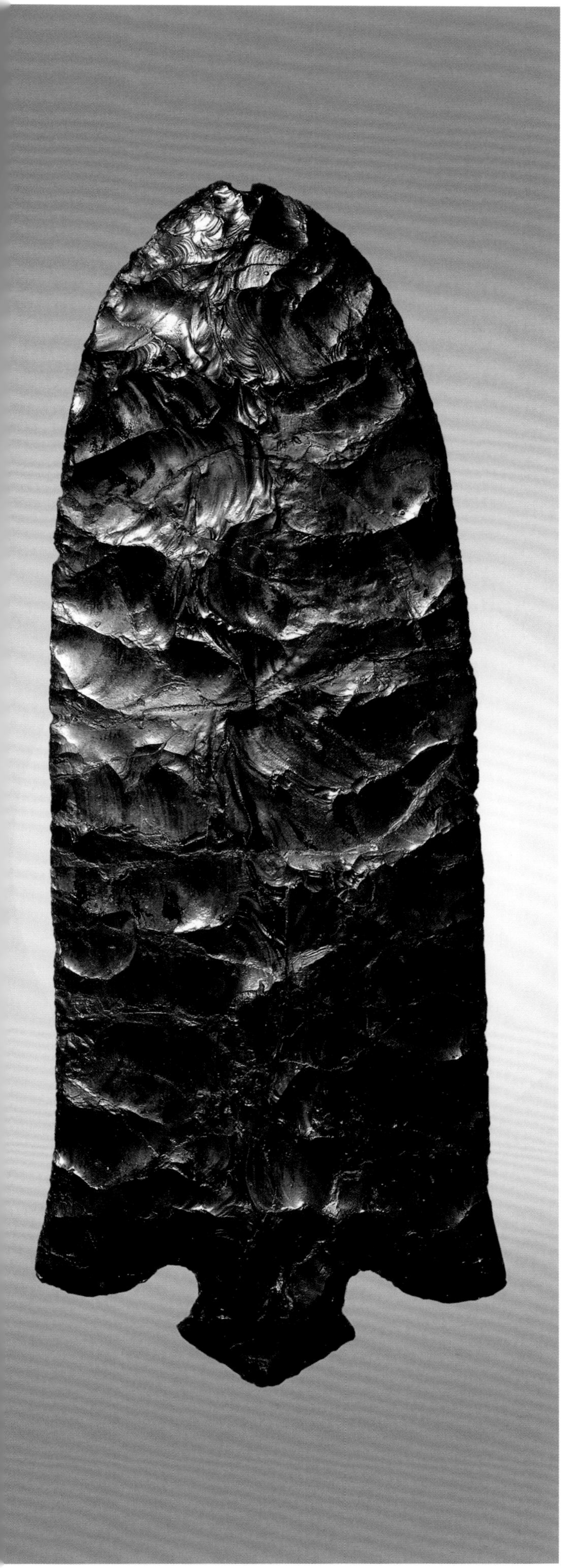

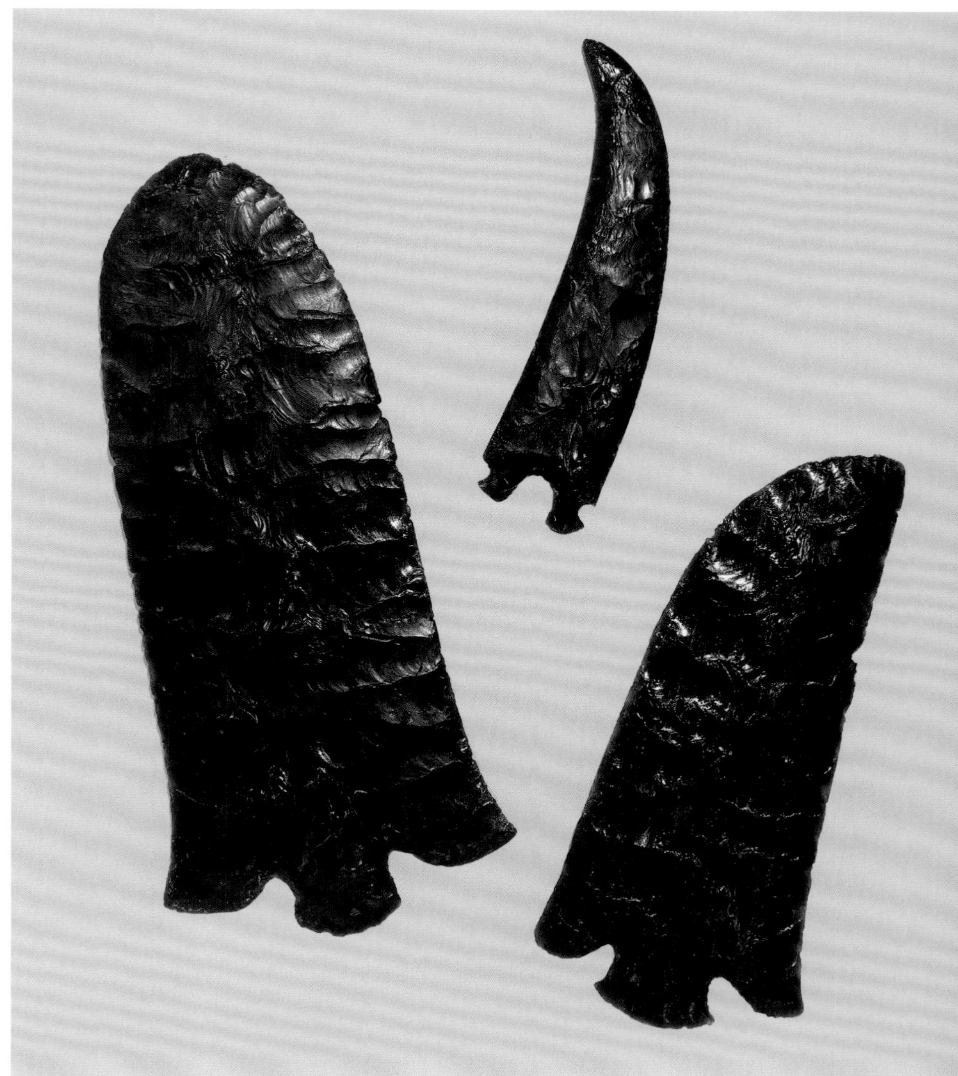

established hierarchies in which leadership is inherited. Shamanism is known to have existed for a long time in eastern North America, and leaders of this sort must have been prominent in Ohio Hopewell ritual. Indeed, Hopewell art is replete with images of men costumed as bears, great cats, deer, or composites, thus suggesting a link of shamans to animal masters in maintaining the health and nutritional well-being of the people. Historically, such individuals tended to be exceptional hunters because of their rapport with the spirit world; they supported large polygamous families and showed off their wealth and prestige with a competitive flair.[10] An indirect measure of leadership competition can be found in the elaborate pattern of hairstyles evident for both men and women in Ohio valley Hopewell societies. Pottery figurines, for example, give particular attention to the details of coiffures involving elaborate patterns of shaving, knotting, roaching, parting, braiding, and dressing (figs. 2–7). Elaborate visual statements of individual identity, honor, and beauty are clear markers of social differentiation and, correspondingly, of roles pointing toward leader-follower distinctions.

Fig. 10 Ceremonial blade; Ohio, Ross County, Hopewell site, A.D. 1–400; obsidian, h. 40.6 cm; Ohio Historical Society, Columbus. Cat. no. 36.

Fig. 11 Three ceremonial blades; Ohio, Ross County, Hopewell site, Mound 25, A.D. 1–400; obsidian, h. 27.9, 17.8, and 22.9 cm; The Field Museum, Chicago. Cat. no. 37.

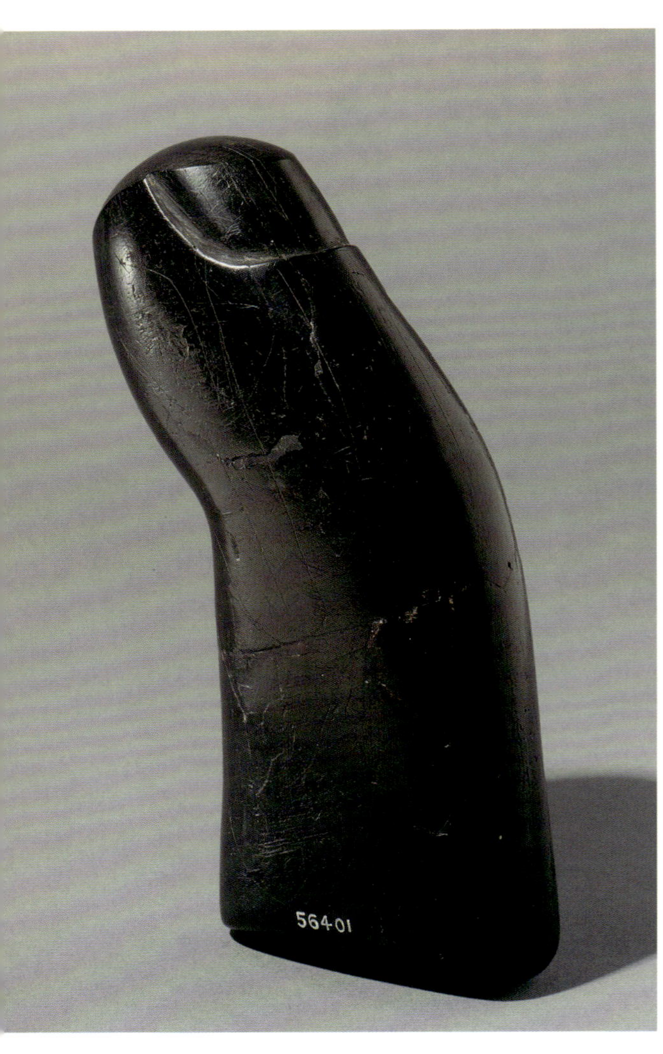

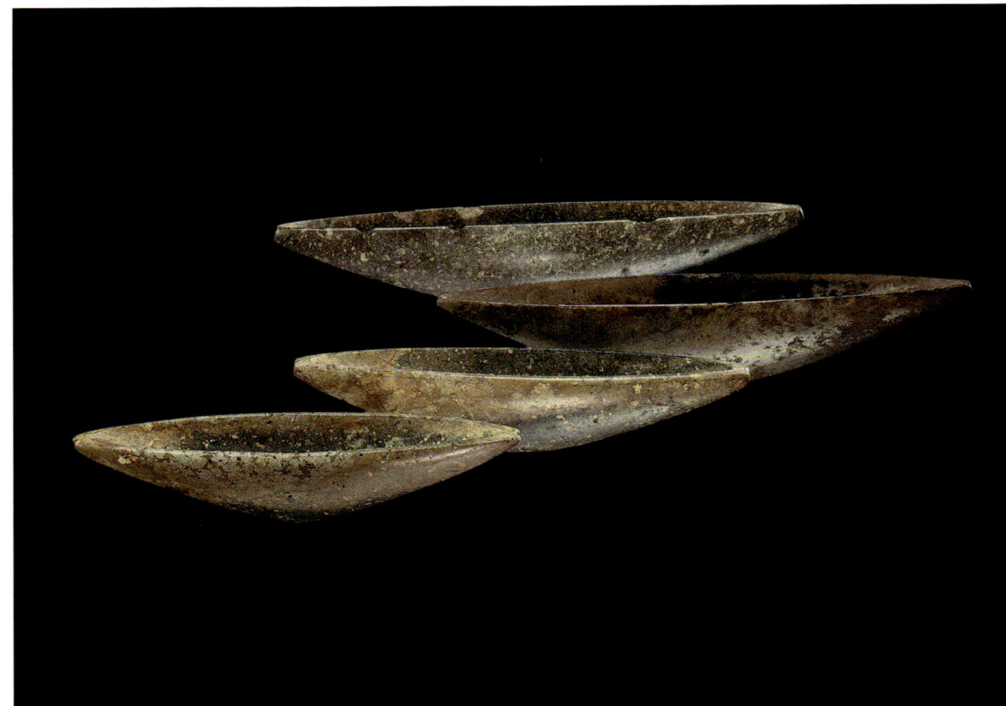

Their Gifts

Gifts between people and between people and spiritual beings were important dimensions of Hopewell life. Many of the raw materials appropriate for such exchanges—copper, marine shell, mica, red ocher pigment, galena, pipestone, pearls, and exotic flints—had held traditional value for a thousand years or more and continued to be used for such purposes into historic times (figs. 1 and 8–9). All of these materials were costly in the sense that they came from distant lands or were difficult to replace, but they were also valued because of metaphorical connections to earth, sky, and directionality. What is surprising is the tremendous increase in the use of these materials by Hopewell populations, especially those in the Ohio valley.[11] New exotic materials—especially meteoric iron, silver, chlorite, obsidian, quartz crystal, and grizzly bear canines—were also actively sought. The long-distance connections or voyages necessary to acquire these materials from the Canadian Shield, the Rocky Mountains, south Florida, or the plains of Kansas were greater than for any other time period in eastern North American archaeology. Many materials were acquired either by direct procurement or limited trading partnerships that leapfrogged across substantial intervening areas.[12] This sort of journeying expanded frames of consciousness and personal power and was a vehicle for establishing leadership credentials in many middle-range societies.[13]

Hopewell peoples used costly raw materials to make a modest set of standardized, durable forms that were used as personal adornments, costume elements, corporate property, and standards of wealth (fig. 13).[14] Simple beads of marine shell and freshwater pearls dominated this array. At the other extreme were objects of some technical complexity: highly crafted and assembled metal ear ornaments, carved effigy pipes, symbolic weapons of exaggerated style and size, or dyed and patterned textiles (figs. 10–11). Many of these objects were designed for display and easy assessment, and some, such as earspools and

Fig. 12 Effigy of a human thumb; Ohio, Ross County, Hopewell site, A.D. 1–400; cannel coal, h. 7.6 cm; The Field Museum, Chicago. Cat. no. 86.

Fig. 13 Four boatstones; Oklahoma, A.D. 1–400; greenstone, l. 15.2–25.4 cm; Smithsonian Institution, National Museum of Natural History, Washington, D.C. Cat. no. 34.

Fig. 14 Convoluted shamanic themes on bone tubes; Ohio, Ross and Hamilton counties, Hopewell and Turner sites; from Moorehead 1922, fig. 20, and Willoughby and Hooton 1922, pl. 2.

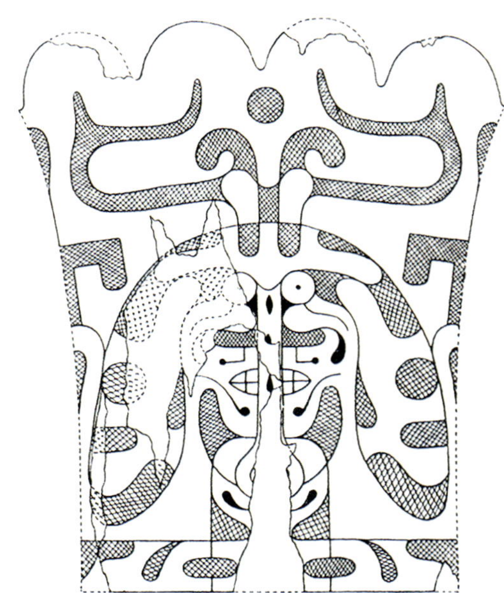

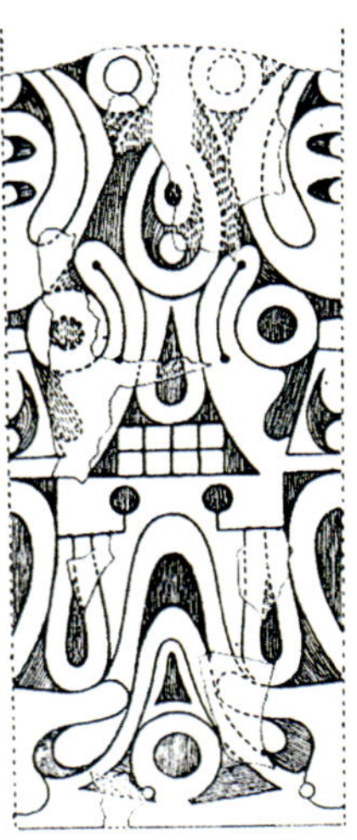

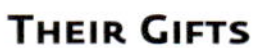

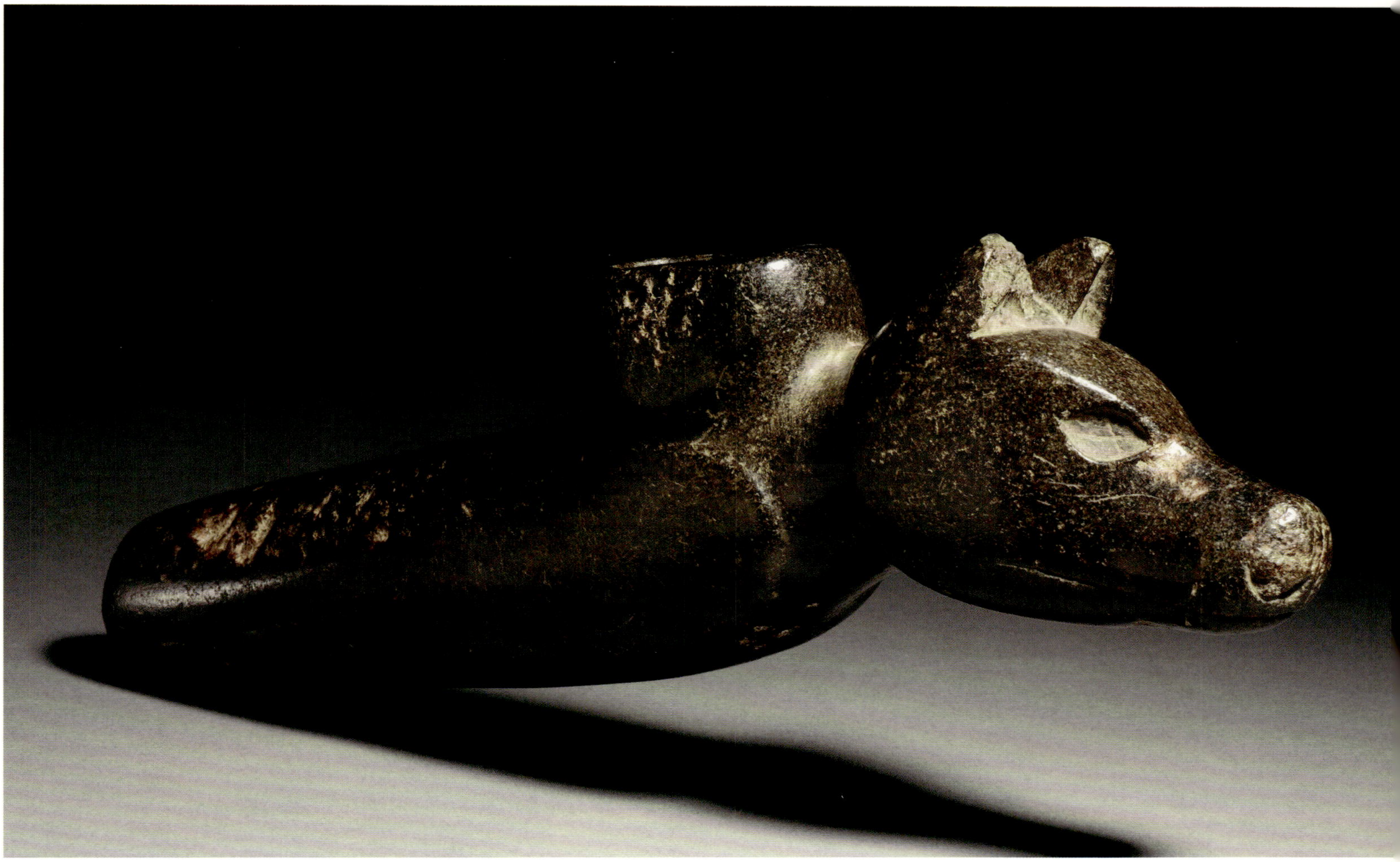

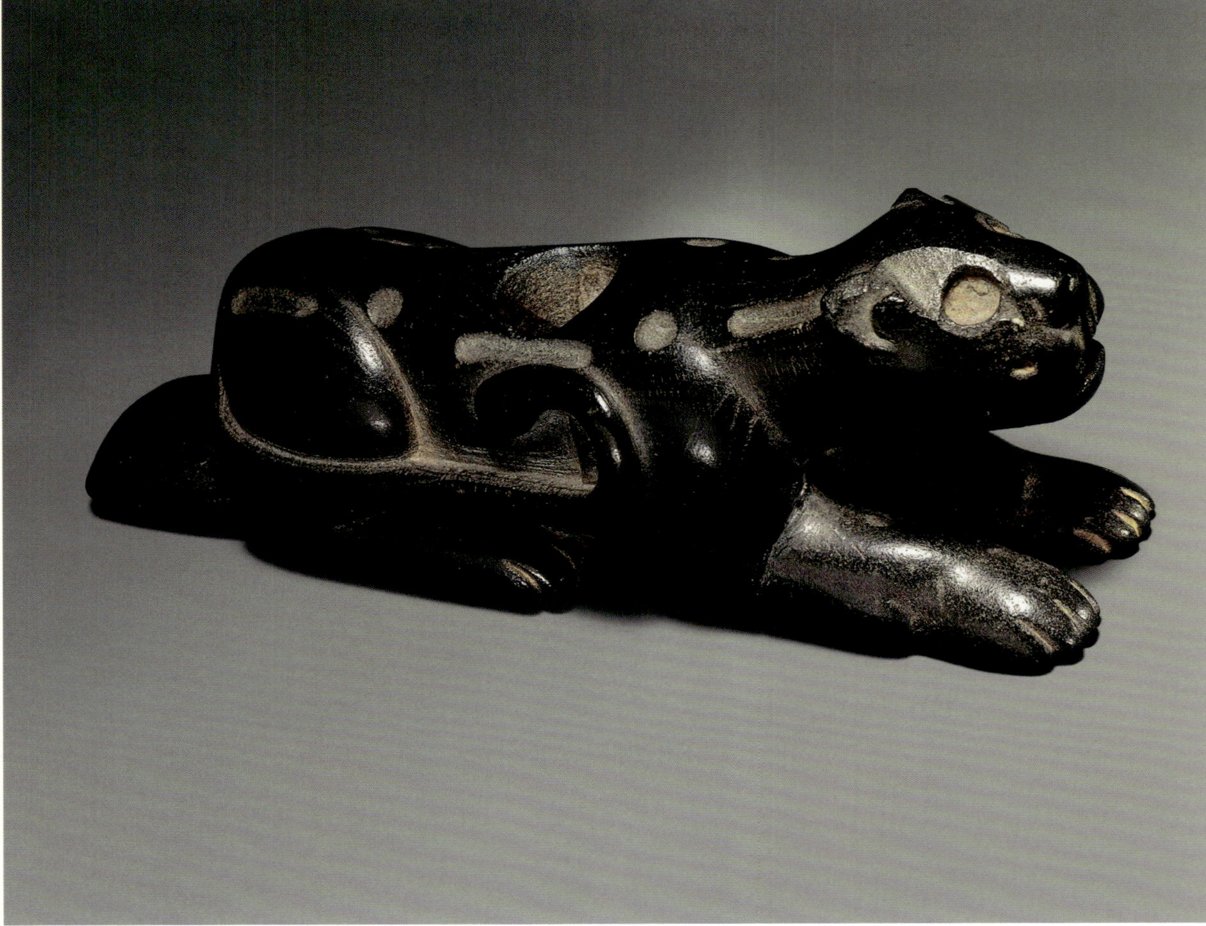

Fig. 15 Wolf effigy pipe; Copena complex; Tennessee, A.D. 1–500; steatite, l. 34 cm; Peabody Museum of Natural History, Yale University. Cat. no. 75.

Fig. 16 Panther effigy pipe; Indiana, Posey County, Mann site, A.D. 1–400; black steatite, h. 6, l. 16 cm; Anonymous loan to the Brooklyn Museum of Art. Cat. no. 81.

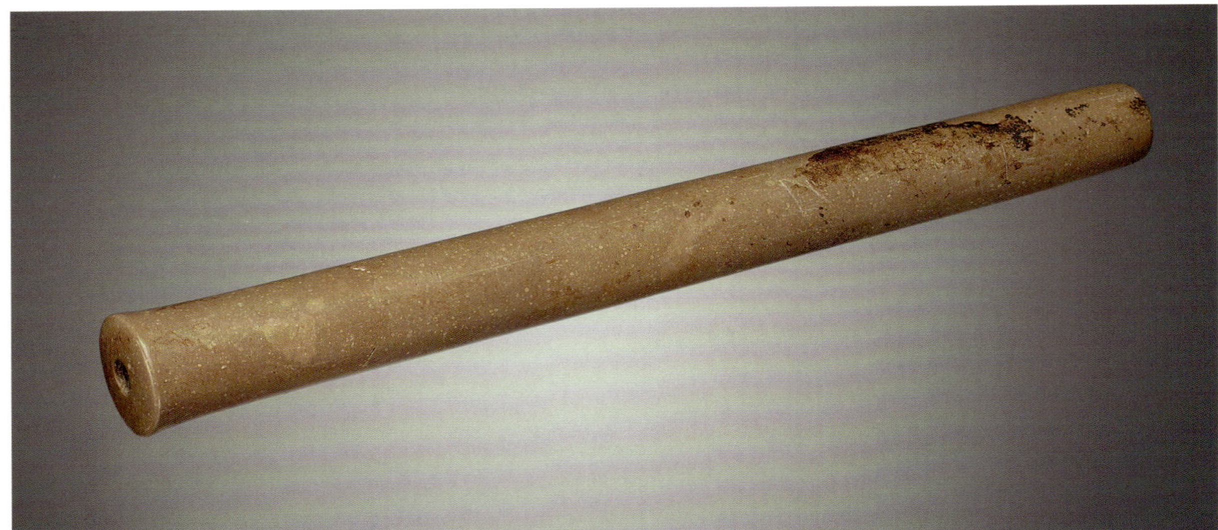

Fig. 17 Blocked-end tube pipe; West Virginia, 400 B.C.–A.D. 1; brown stone, l. 25.4 cm; Smithsonian Institution, National Museum of Natural History, Washington, D.C. Cat. no. 56.

bear canine ornaments, showed considerable stylistic variability in the details of their construction that were masked by finishing techniques that provided an outward show of conformity.[15] The primacy of the form was further emphasized by using rare materials as overlays on the visible side of certain items, varying the size dimension, and imitating common forms in novel materials, the latter often reduced to certain basic but understandable details (fig. 12). The intricacy of these manipulations, the refinement of forms, and the overt cosmological references show the development of a symbolic system of greater complexity than at any time previously in eastern North America.[16]

Hopewell artistry was distinct and recognizable. It was also highly media-specific, with no pervasive style.[17] Effigy smoking pipes and boatstones, for example, share a sculptural form emphasizing natural and accurate renditions of animal body proportions and shapes but have tight constraints with respect to the range of poses and patterns of detail (figs. 15–16).[18] The implications are that artists had opportunities to inspect one another's work carefully and were more concerned with conformity than innovation. These conventions contrast with those on incised bone tubes where foreground and background are purposely confused and animal, human, and geometric fields are combined in

Fig. 18 Hopewell ware jar; Illinois, Calhoun County, Pete Klunk site, Mound 7, A.D. 1–400; ceramic, h. 14 cm; Gilcrease Museum, Tulsa, Oklahoma. Cat. no. 88.

Fig. 19 Hopewell-related zoned jar (Alligator Bayou Stamped); Porter/Santa Rosa complex; Florida, Washington County, St. Andrews Bay, A.D. 1–400; ceramic; Smithsonian Institution, National Museum of the American Indian, Washington, D.C. Cat. no. 89.

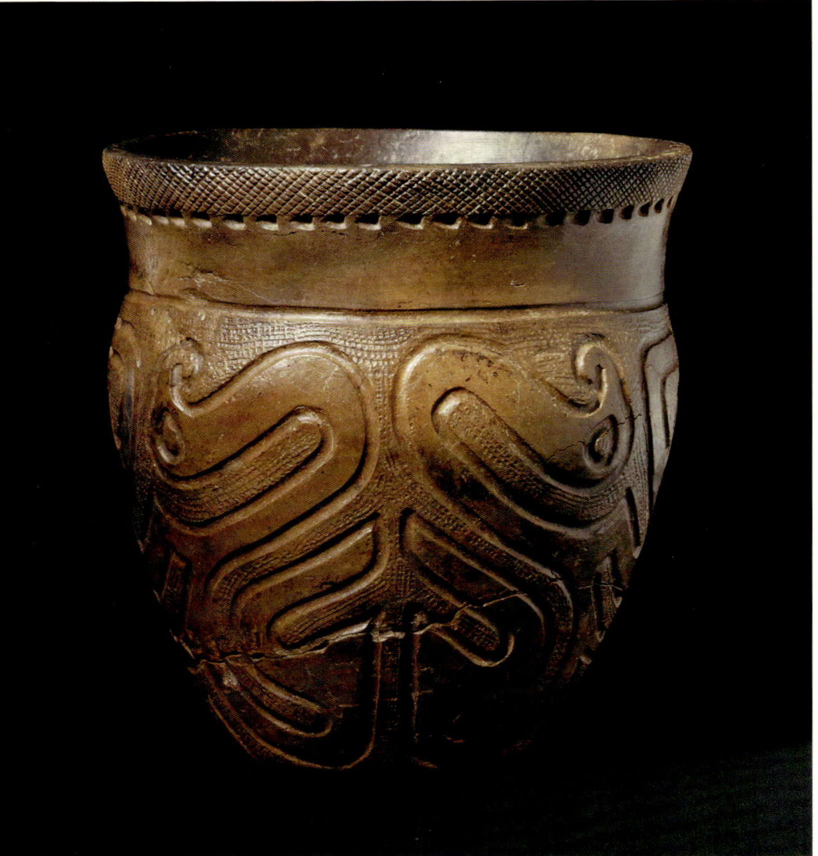

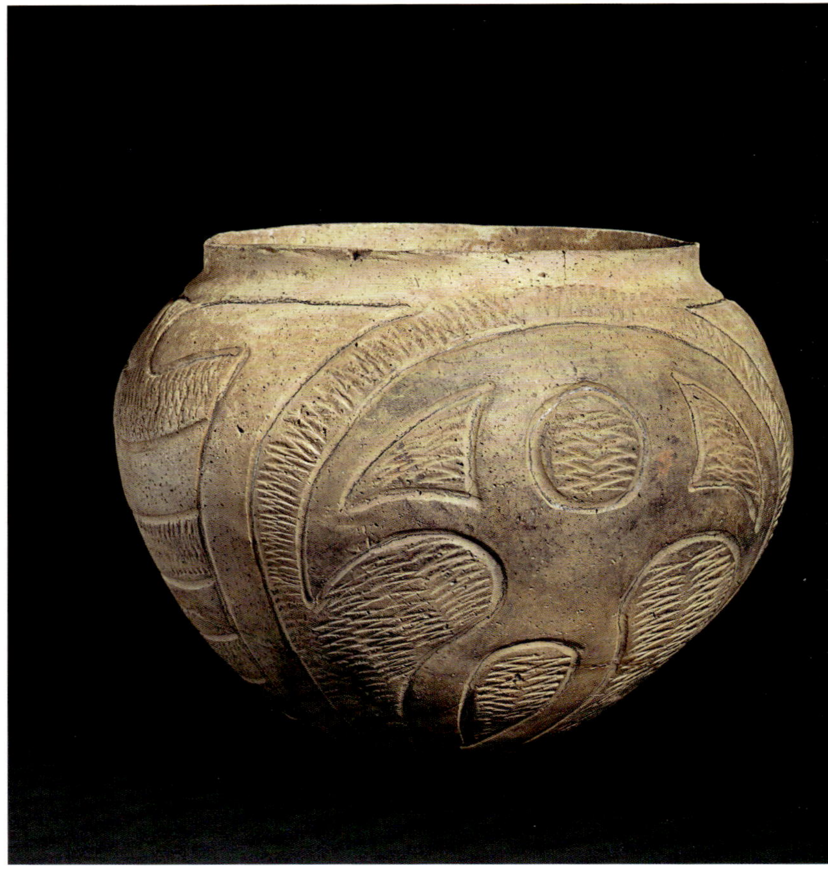

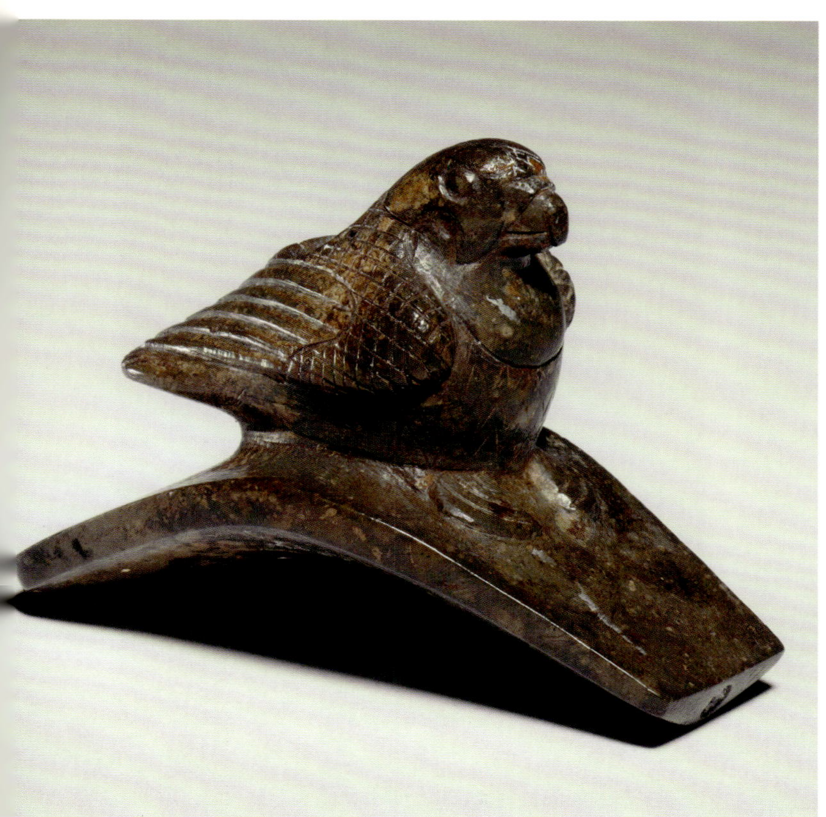

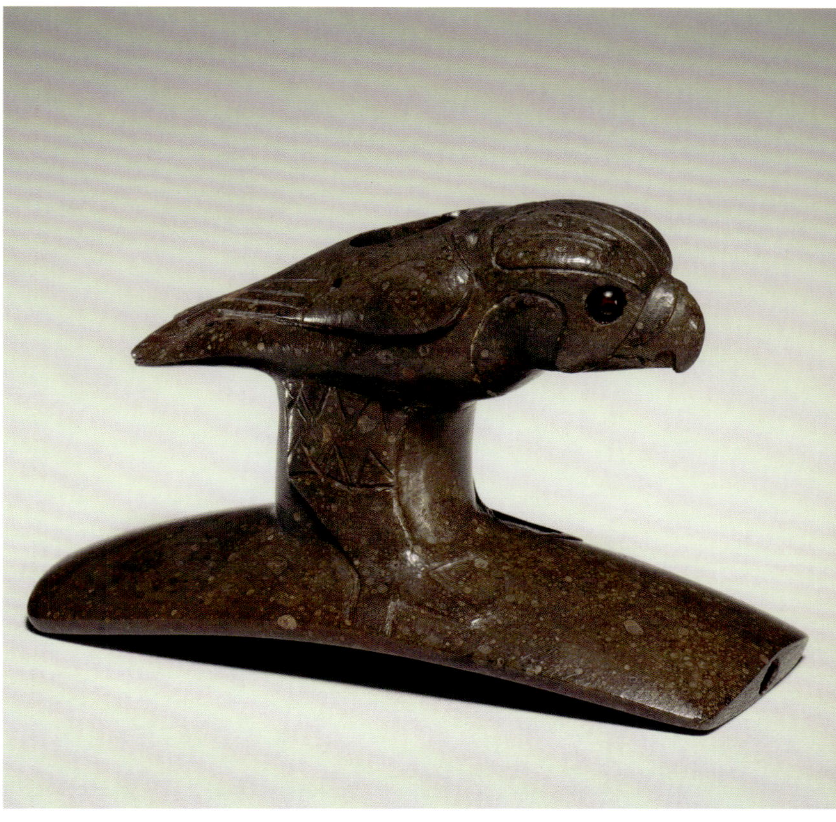

Fig. 20 Seated falcon effigy platform pipe; Havana Hopewell; Illinois, Calhoun County, Peisker site, Mound 2, A.D. 1–400; pipestone, l. 6.4 cm; Gilcrease Museum, Tulsa, Oklahoma. Cat. no. 65.

Fig. 21 Falcon effigy platform pipe; Havana Hopewell; eastern Iowa, A.D. 1–400; pipestone, l. 8.3 cm; Gilcrease Museum, Tulsa, Oklahoma. Cat. no. 64.

complex fashion (fig. 14). Similar unembellished tubes occur for thousands of years and into the period of written history, where they are associated with shamanistic healing (fig. 17).[19] Hopewell ceramics display yet different sensibilities, with considerable artistry directed toward the production of wares used primarily in ritual context. Pottery used in ritual was of finer quality than domestic ware, a convention found also in later Mississippian societies. "Hopewell ware," with its snakelike crosshatched, cambered rim bands and incised bird body motifs, is clearly iconographic in character and may portray Above World/Beneath World distinctions (figs. 18–19). Similar cosmological references occur in the decoration of later Mississippian ceramics (see also the essay by George Lankford in this volume).[20]

Animals were the dominant theme of Hopewell art. Found on a variety of media are a veritable company of animals—toads, otters, bears, redhorse suckers, squirrels, and ravens—of the sort that would have helped the Creator at the beginning of the world and at a time when animals spoke with human tongue (figs. 20–23). Hopewell animals probably were regarded as living in societies parallel to humans, and as being capable of grieving for dead relatives, accepting and receiving gifts, and having souls that transcended death. Such animals could give themselves up as food only if they or their protectors were treated with appropriate respect.[21] This kind of spiritual imagery is different from later Mississippian themes that emphasized humanized deities, agriculture, warfare, and upper and lower world distinctions.

Their Sacred Places

The production and use of Hopewell art took place in very specific places, and by implication was under the supervision of leaders affiliated with such sacred places. When the first European colonists crossed the Allegheny Mountains, they found a land filled with ancient constructions: thousands of mounds and hundreds of earthen enclosures of considerable size and, in some cases, complexity, most of which were built during the Woodland period over a thousand years ago; these were interpreted to be comparable to ancient British "barrows" or "cairns of the ancient Celts" or as "corresponding to the barbican in the system of defense of the Britons of the middle era."[22] Racial prejudice kept European settlers from considering these places to be the products of American Indian culture, and thus was born the myth of an ancient race of civilized, pre-Indian "Moundbuilders."[23] Although Cyrus Thomas and others did much to dispel the notion of something other than an Indian origin for these constructions, the lack of any real commitment was signaled by the fact that hundreds of mounds already had been destroyed by the time of his investigations in the 1880s (fig. 24).[24]

Woodland societies lived in worlds of their own creation. They not only interpreted the landscape in ways that were meaningful to them but added to it a variety of buildings, monuments, pathways, fields, and public spaces. They used fire and celt to clear substantial tracts of garden lands as early as 1000 B.C., built hundreds of mounds and earthworks by 100 B.C., and constructed elaborate ceremonial precincts covering hundreds of acres by A.D. 200. These modifications

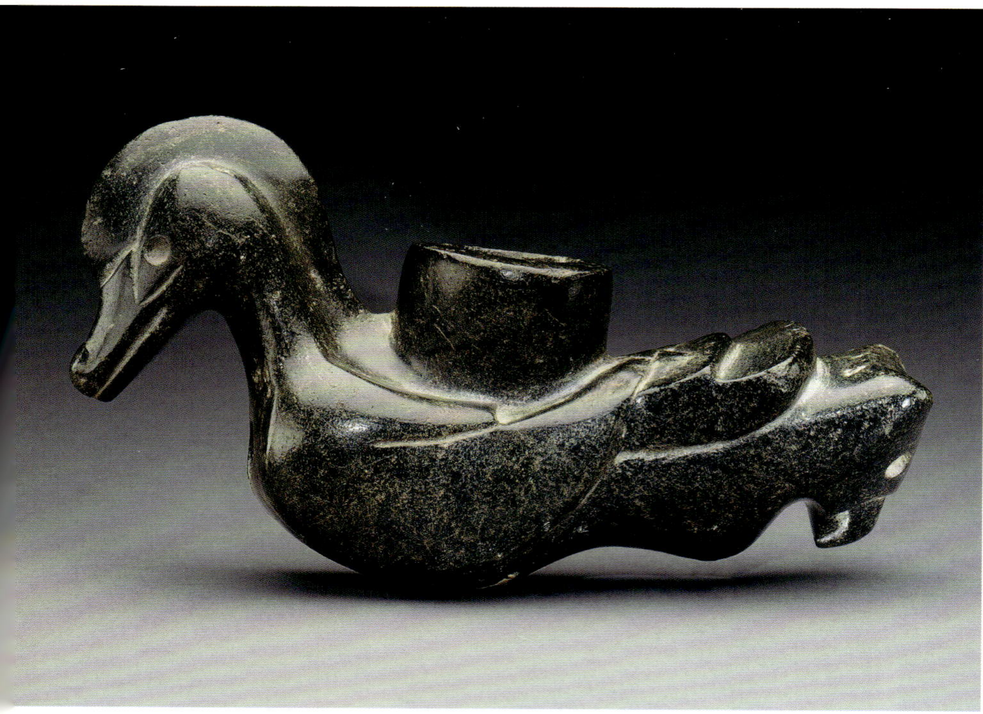

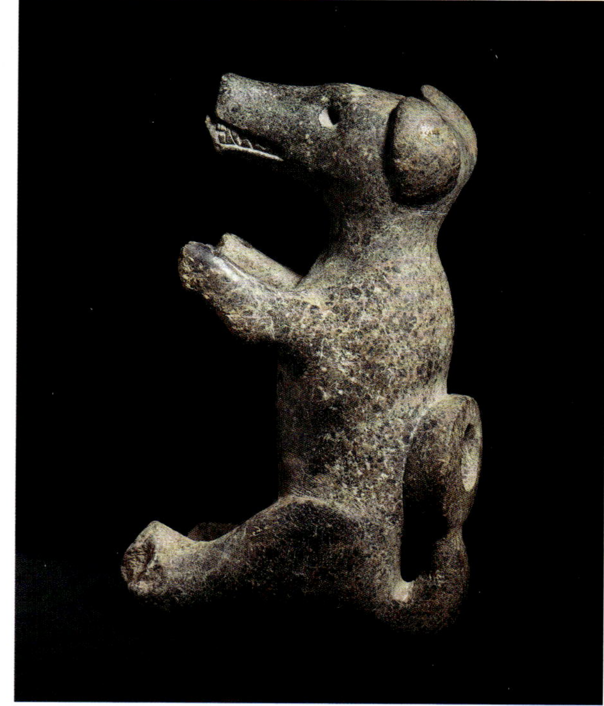

were made with distinctive conceptions of time, space, and, especially, sacredness. "Sacred place" as used here refers to those locations where public rituals were performed. A sacred place facilitated the coordination of many different household schedules and agendas. Such places were intended to focus or center spiritual power, in some cases by the recreation of particular myths or by the reestablishment of cosmic balance through purification and renewal.[25] But they were also vital forces of social history, legitimacy, and identity, as old places were reused in similar ways or new ways or rejected entirely in favor of constructing new sacred places. The High Bank Works along the Scioto River just south of Chillicothe, Ohio, at the confluence of the Scioto River and Paint Creek, provides a good example. Here can be found a variety of structural forms and juxtapositions of long-term, additive usage in earthworks of varying scale, orientation, and shape (fig. 25). The use and location of sacred places certainly affected other spatial choices, including the development of trails and pathways connecting them.[26] Importantly, for purposes of this discussion, these were the kinds of places where Woodland art was sometimes created and most often used.

Woodland sacred places were chosen with care and were more variably positioned than later Mississippian public ritual locations, which were constrained by their association with nucleated villages and alluvial farmland. Proximity to streams, springs, caves, mountains, mineral outcrops, trails; an ability to monitor celestial events against a distinct horizon; and the location of other sacred places have all been recognized as important in the selection of specific sites. Perhaps the most spectacularly sited of these Woodland sacred places is the Old Stone Fort in central Tennessee where a rock and earthen enclosure occupies the tip of a promontory at the forks of the Duck River and is flanked by twin waterfalls.[27] Nearly as commanding are the many mounds that line the edge of the 150–300-foot (46–91 m) limestone bluffs of the lower Illinois River valley.[28] The Seip-Overly complex in south-central Ohio, which orients to Copperas Mountain, a unique 350-foot-high (106 m) black shale cliff that is home to dozens of nesting vultures and that produces quartz crystals and other minerals, provides a third example of auspicious placement.[29]

Along with the choice of a site, construction too was certainly an important element of Woodland ceremonialism. Earth, sod, sand, mud, rock, and timber were used to define and redefine places, often a basketload at a time. Although the earliest mound and embankment building in eastern North America began during the Late Archaic period, the use of constructions

Fig. 22 Bird and owl effigy pipe; Virginia, Scott County, A.D. 100–600; steatite, l. 25.5 cm; Smithsonian Institution, National Museum of Natural History, Washington, D.C. Cat. no. 77.

Fig. 23 Wolf effigy pipe; Ohio, Ross County, Seip-Pricer Mound, A.D. 1–400; steatite, h. 27.9 cm; Ohio Historical Society, Columbus. Cat. no. 79.

Fig. 24 Charles Sullivan (1794–1867), *The Miamisburg Mound*; unsigned and undated; oil on canvas, 66 × 91.5 cm; Ohio Historical Society, Columbus. Large Woodland mounds and earthworks form an enduring part of the cultural landscape of the Ohio River valley. Land-use practices in the 19th century, however, along with antiquarian treasure hunting quickly destroyed many smaller constructions.

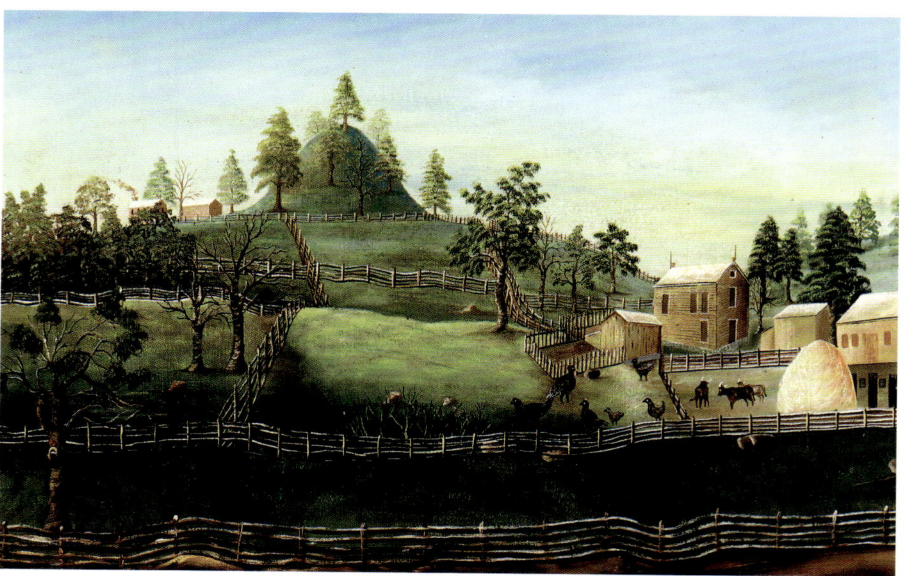

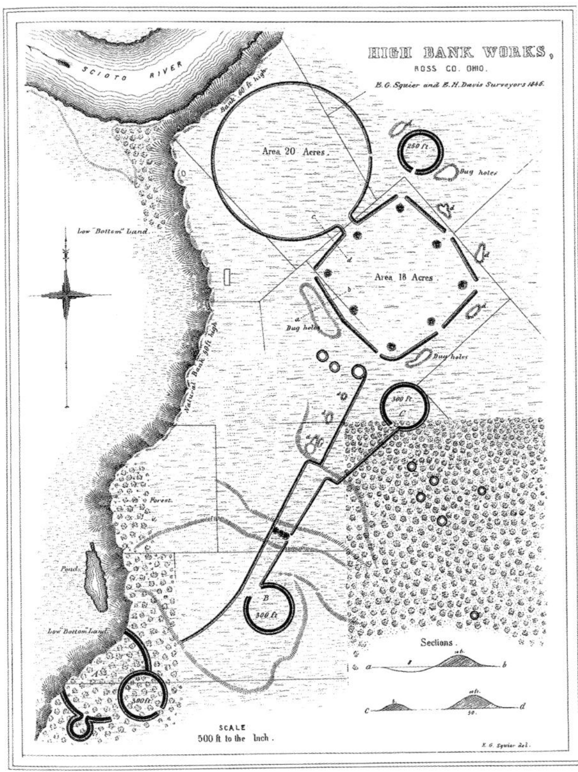

Fig. 25 Ephraim G. Squier and Edwin H. Davis, Map of High Bank Works, Ross County, Ohio; from Squier and Davis, 1848, pl. 16. Multiple elements and construction styles indicate an additive commitment to a sacred space.

to augment and define sacred places over a broad area is more characteristic of the succeeding Woodland period.[30] Beginning about 1000 B.C., these most often took the form of low mounds covering human remains. Enclosures appeared somewhat later, documented by at least 400 B.C.[31] Woodland societies living in the Ohio valley showed the most continuous commitment to these kinds of ritual places and provided the greatest degree of elaboration. The peak of complexity correlates with participation in the Hopewell complex, as it did for most regions in the Midwest and Middle South. The large scale of many of these constructions suggests that several cooperating local groups were involved, with implications for recruitment and the coordination of efforts.[32] By way of example, the impressive Newark Earthworks in Licking County, Ohio, extended over two square miles and contained construction elements over 16 feet high (5 m; see also the following essay by Bradley Lepper in this volume).[33] The less well known GE Mound in Posey County, Indiana—probably the fifth- or sixth-largest Hopewell mound ever discovered—was at least 350 feet long, 125 feet wide, and 15 feet high (106 × 38 × 4.6 m), and it represented a minimum of 166,400 bushel basket-loads of earth.[34]

Especially notable is the greater organization of the sacred places of Ohio valley Hopewell societies as compared with the sacred sites of preceding Woodland groups associated with Adena ceremonialism.[35] Not only were there larger and more diverse groups gathering to sponsor, participate, or witness ritual, but Ohio Hopewell ritual placed a stronger emphasis on display, made use of a more complex vocabulary of material goods, and occurred in a more limited area than was evident for any preceding population in the region (fig. 26). Hopewell participants were actively constructing identities in new ways. Such seemingly minor changes as abandoning practices that produced extremely high incidences of cranial deformation, making tools from different flint sources, or using platform pipes rather than tubular ones facilitated the formation of new kinds of social groups and the modification of basic boundaries (compare fig. 17 with figs. 20–21). Mound City, one of the earliest Hopewell centers, provides a case in point. During the first century A.D. and adjacent to Mount Logan in Ross County, Ohio, a fifteen-acre site was imposed into one of the densest concentrations of ritual sites in the Ohio valley. Mound City, an array of at least twenty-four mounds surrounded by a quadrilateral embankment, was a type of ritual space that was quite different from the dozens previously used in the immediate vicinity. In this case, there was continuity in the use of space for ritual purposes but a discontinuity in how the space was used. It generated site-specific patterns of placement, organization, and ceremony that imply shifting axes of cooperation and competition among regional groups and their leaders.

Community Ritual in Sacred Places

The main constructed components of Ohio Hopewell sacred places were large earthen enclosures (fig. 25; see also Lepper, figs. 1–3 and 10). The most dramatic of these were geometric in form and combined circular, oval, square, octagonal, or other elements in compositions covering hundreds of acres. Gateways and causeways provided multiple points of access and egress and also linked various elements of the whole. Since most were built on river terraces of modest elevation above

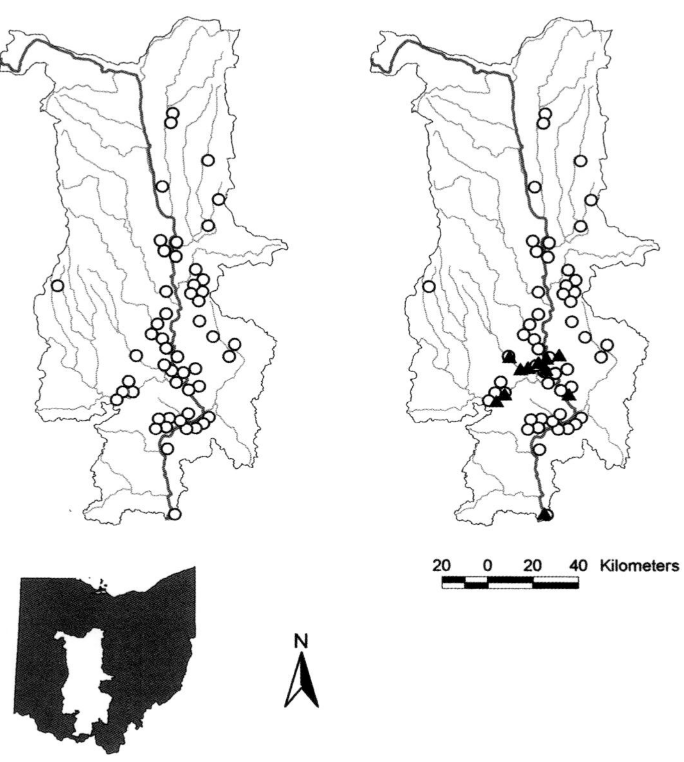

Fig. 26 Comparative distribution of large Woodland mounds in the Scioto River valley of Ohio showing spatial concentration of Hopewell ceremonialism c. A.D. 50. Large mounds are defined as more than 90 feet (27.4 m) in diameter or more than 20 feet (6.1 m) high. In this drawing, open circles reflect pre-Hopewell Woodland, and the solid triangles indicate Hopewell mounds.

the floodplain, it would have been possible to appreciate them in their entirety from nearby higher terraces or hills. These compositions could have been laid out with little more than a knotted cord, the rudiments of geometry, and a willing labor force.[36] These defined spaces were fitted into landforms in such a way that geometric principles were compromised to accommodate the primacy of place; thus, for example, portions of "circular" walls at the Baum site and Seip Earthworks, both in Ross County, follow terrace edges rather than adhering to geometric perfection (figs. 27–28). Beyond relations to place, a comparison of elemental sizes and shapes used to compose Hopewell earthworks shows a shared knowledge of how they should be. That the "square" element at seven of these sites approximated 27 acres (10.9 ha) is one of the strongest patterns of intersite consistency (fig. 29).[37] A commitment to common standards may have helped to cement intergroup relationships at some level. Investigators as early as the mid-nineteenth century compared Hopewell square embankments to the square ground or "Big House" sacred places of Muskhogean peoples of the historic Southeast.[38]

The idea that Hopewell circle-and-square earthworks were either sociograms or cosmograms has come under considerable debate. James Brown has made the case that the simple quadrilateral enclosure at Mound City is a metaphor for "houselodge," and he has emphasized the structural similarity between the domestic house form, the shape of ritual buildings at the site, and the embankment shape—thus, the entire site is a "building of buildings" (see fig. 36 in the essay by Richard Townsend in this volume).[39] Later and more complex forms were probably extensions of this principle, possibly differentiating the framework of a house from its exterior outline or possibly representing different kinds of houses.[40] The basic circle-and-square structural pairing as an iconographic module continued into Mississippian times.[41] Some Hopewell earthworks were planned so as to orient to the cardinal directions or cosmological events, such as the summer solstice or minimum north moonrise.[42] The cycling of the seasons established a rhythm for life in the Ohio valley, and it is reasonable to assume that ceremonies and ceremonial enclosures were related to such cycles so as to enhance and focus spiritual energy. Thus, Ohio Hopewell earthworks created "cosmic centers" for ritual performance.[43]

Many buildings and other wooden structures were built in and around Hopewell enclosures. Recent mechanical stripping at the Stubbs Earthworks near Morrow, Ohio, in the Little Miami River valley (prior to its destruction for the construction of a high school) revealed the remains of twenty-one wooden structures —some round, some square, some little more than lean-tos.[44] Other sites, notably Fort Ancient in Warren County, northeast of Cincinnati, suggest similar situations. Constructions of these types may represent the temporary quarters of people coming to these special places to prepare for or participate in ceremonies.

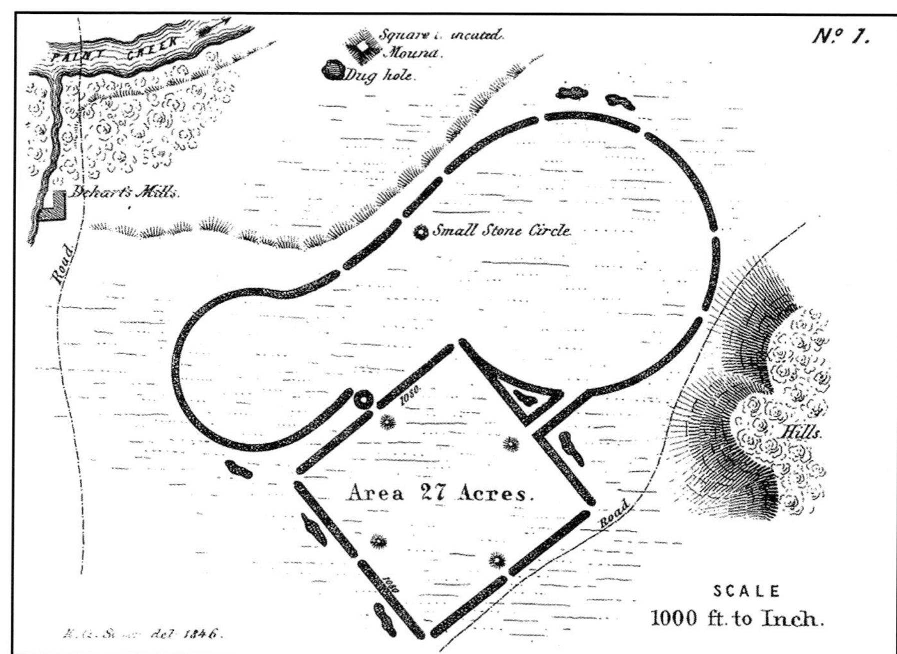

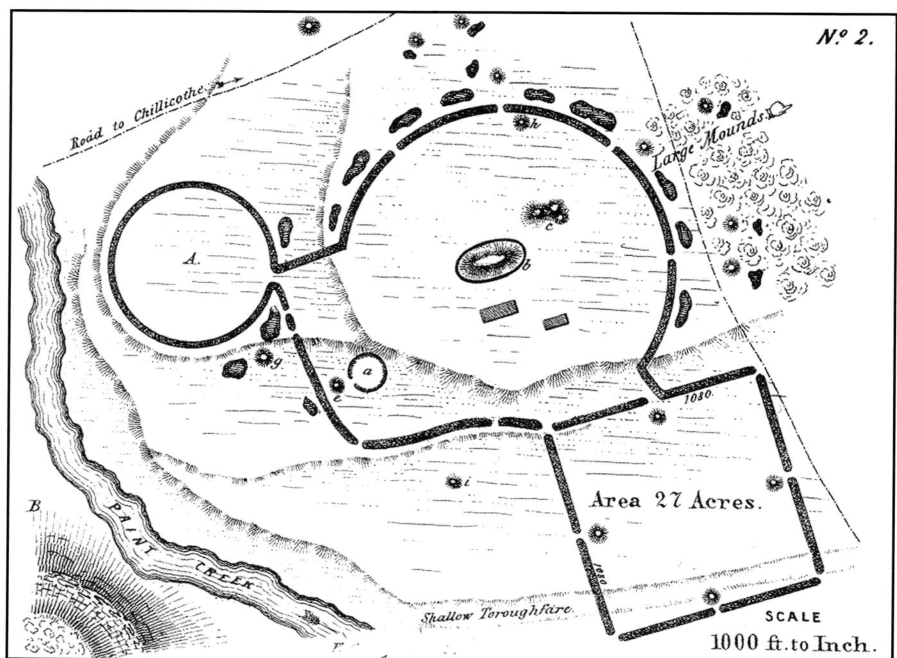

Preparation also is suggested by the discovery of blade-making concentrations associated with these earthworks, as well as debris and other remnants indicating that specialized items of obsidian, mica, quartz crystal, and other materials also were made in these places by skilled individuals.[45]

Although less clear than the evidence for craftwork and housing, other types of preparations undoubtedly took place within earthwork confines. Feasting, smoking strong tobacco, and drinking "black drink" were probably important as preparatory elements of ritual; the latter two heightened or altered consciousness and were linked substances in the practice of historic southeastern ritual.[46] The suggestion for use of the black drink in Hopewell ceremony rests, as it does for Late Woodland and Mississippian usage, on the

Fig. 27 Ephraim G. Squier and Edwin H. Davis, Map of earthworks at the Baum site on the south bank of Paint Creek west of Chillicothe, in Ross County, Ohio; from Squier and Davis 1848, pl. 21, no. 1.

Fig. 28 Ephraim G. Squier and Edwin H. Davis, Map of Seip Earthworks on the north bank of Paint Creek west of Chillicothe, in Ross County, Ohio; from Squier and Davis 1848, pl. 21, no. 2.

facing page
Fig. 29 Schematic plans of Ohio Hopewell earthen enclosures. Numbers indicate approximate enclosed acreage; from DeBoer 1997, fig. 7.

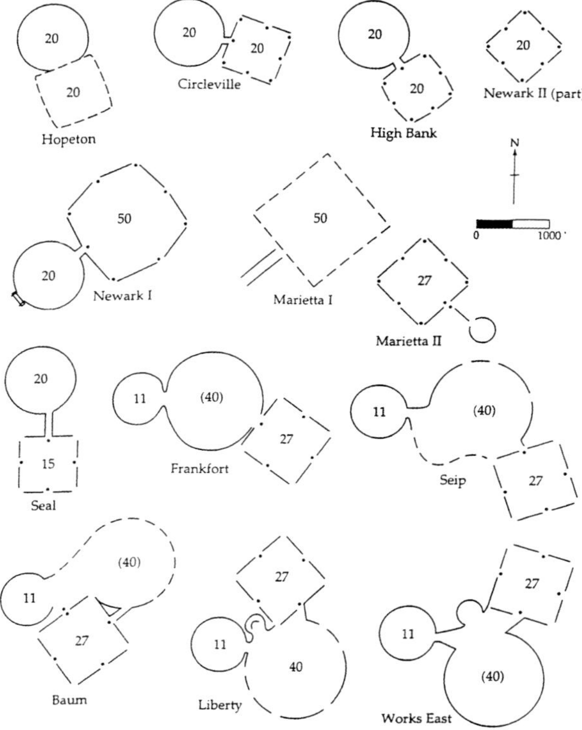

occurrence of the same sort of marine shell cups that were associated with drinking it historically.[47] Marine shell cups occur frequently in Hopewell ritual contexts, but not before. All of these preparations are consistent with situations where laymen take on what were formerly shamanistic prerogatives as aspects of community ritual.[48]

Actual rituals were centered in formal buildings and timber constructions. That they were carefully disassembled or covered with mounds is an indication of their directly sacred nature. The largest of these, the Great Circle at the Stubbs Earthworks, consisted of 172 substantial and precisely spaced posts that formed a 239-foot-diameter circle (72.9 m). Similar constructions can be found in later Mississippian contexts, suggesting a long tradition of the use of such arrangements. More numerous were substantial, generally quadrilateral buildings, although circular and compound structures also are known. This variability in building size and shape carries implications for the size and composition of groups using them. Twenty-three of these have been documented at Mound City near Chillicothe, the highest single total. The superposition of sand and clay floors, interior post structures, burned areas, deposits, and the renewal of selected features indicate that these buildings were actively used for a variety of purposes. Some appear to have been paired or were part of multiple-room compositions, suggesting that certain rituals moved between defined spaces or required complementary components.[49]

Within these shrine buildings prepared clay basins were one important type of facility (fig. 30). These were generally quadrilateral in shape, made of puddled clay, and three to six feet in length. Basins were carefully arranged on building floors in central locations. Hopewell clay basins show evidence of long use and much repair and cleaning. Broken or shattered basins were carefully cared for, and sometimes were included as portions of offerings in intact basins. In some cases, a new basin was built over the location of an old one and a new floor was prepared; four such episodes of superposition were found within Mound 5 at the Turner Earthworks site near Cincinnati.[50] Basins of this type were made to contain intense fires, and they no doubt sent up considerable plumes of smoke. Basin rituals involving the incineration of both human remains and Hopewell style objects were key features of Ohio Hopewell ceremonialism.

Early investigators referred to these Hopewell basins as "altars" because they sometimes held formally arranged artifacts, pieces of artifacts, and/or cremated remains. This was clearly a secondary function to their original purpose, but important nonetheless. Indeed, "offerings" or deposits of many kinds are associated with Ohio Hopewell ritual centers. Generally these were placed within buildings before the structures themselves were covered, but they were also placed in other areas of sites in more peripheral positions. Some were associated with mound construction itself in that they occurred as deposits above floor level. The size and composition of these offerings vary greatly, and, as James Brown has described, they often contain huge quantities of one material or another but little to reflect the broad array of Hopewell materials.[51] Such offerings have been interpreted as demonstrating the efforts of groups with particular spiritual prerogatives.[52] But the variable condition, composition, and context of Ohio Hopewell offerings suggest that they served several purposes, and the sizes of some mortuary offerings—hundreds of copper earspools or thousands of pearl beads—suggest that they were community gifts or contributions rather than the property of an individual. Much of Hopewell art occurs as components of these offerings.

Ancestral remains also were kept in these shrine buildings, often placed on small, covered, log-rimmed

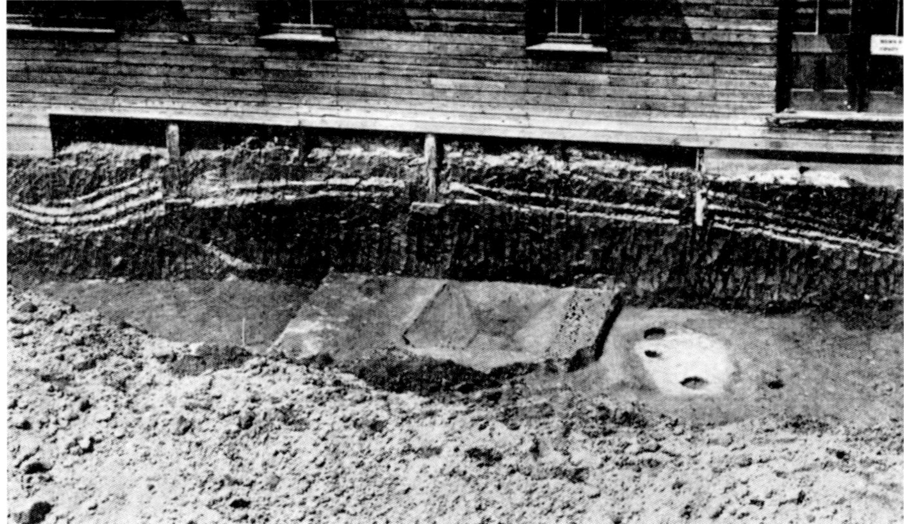

Fig. 30 Two centrally placed, superimposed basins and floors under Mound 18, Mound City, Ross County, Ohio; from Mills 1922. The four thin white layers of sand in the soil signal various stages in the completion of the mound. The entire structure was later covered by an early-20th-century building erected for Camp Sheridan, a World War I training camp.

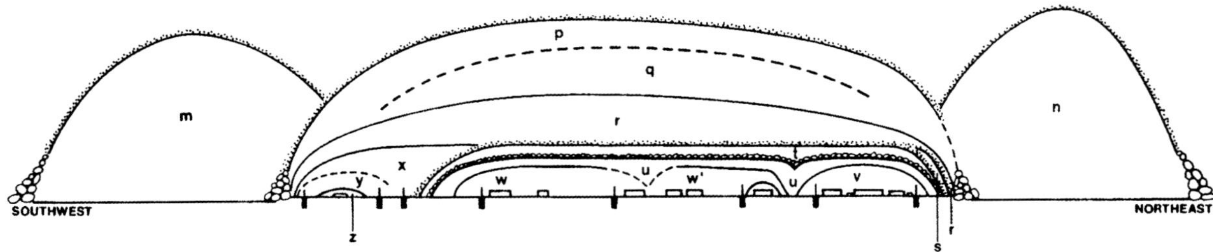

Fig. 31 Schematic cross-section of Mound 25, Hopewell site, Ross County, Ohio: m) western mound composed of general fill covered with gravel cap and large stones at base; n) eastern mound; p) uppermost layer eroded by plowing; q) major capping stratum of loam; r) major capping stratum of loam; s) side addition; t) gravel layer covering separate primary mounds; u) gravel layer joining separate primary mounds; v, w, and w') soil layers covering burnt structures; x) construction stage at 2.5–3 meters; y) stratum with burials above floor; z) small mounded covering of western burial group. Post molds projecting downward from main prepared relate to buildings. Open rectangles above floor are individual deposits of human remains and associated materials. This mound was 10 meters tall (33 feet) in 1850; from Greber and Ruhl 1989, fig. 2.14.

platforms arranged in particular spatial patterns. A large percentage of both men and women had funerary gifts placed with them or wore durable ornaments, costume elements, or weaponry.[53] These patterned arrangement of burials appear to stand for particular lineages, clans, or other corporate groups;[54] the underrepresentation of subadults and women suggests the possibility that these people were selected to represent the collective ethos of larger groups, some possibly resident outside of the immediate area.[55] Similar patterns are sometimes seen in Mississippian burial groups.[56] The placement of selected ancestral remains in designated buildings and the memorialization of this relationship by mound building carries strong implications for the construction of histories and identities. In keeping with the theme of collectivity, it must be noted that some of the carefully arranged riches associated with certain individuals—the 66 copper celts and 23 copper plates above the twin burials 260 and 261 at Hopewell Mound 25, for example—represent not so much the property of a "Big Man" as they do ancestral vehicles for the conveyance of group concerns to the other world. These kinds of elaborately staged arrangements, to the extent that they emphasize group practices and contain mythic elements, caution that a particular individual's place as "ancestor" was not necessarily identical to his or her social status at death.[57] Mortuary rituals helped to assert personal and collective identity, but they also helped to build among mourners social memories of what it meant to be a member of a community of believers. Works of art figured importantly in these representations.

The creation of a memorial mound was itself a complex process beginning even before the destruction of the buildings they were intended to cover (fig. 31). It would appear, for example, that individual burial platforms and basins were covered with timber, bark, and earth before the entire building was mantled. Once the structure was decommissioned, some or all of its segments were themselves covered with small mounds. The main body of the mound fill was then added, often taking the form of distinct strata of basket-loaded soil separated by thin layers of fine gravel or sand. A covering or berm of stone around the mound base was another aspect of mound structure. Not all mounds followed this formula, and a small minority covered no structures at all. Notable in this regard were the small mounds placed as architectural elements in many gateways and the development of a separate trajectory of platform mound construction. A few of the loaf-shaped and flat-topped mounds such as Mound 25 at the Hopewell site in Ross County, the Seip-Pricer Mound, or Mann Mound 1 in Indiana were extensive constructions and could not have been built quickly. The majority of mounds, however, were no larger than many of those built by preceding Woodland populations in the Ohio valley. What is most distinctive is not the scale of mound construction but the association with a very limited range of spatial circumstances. It was the definition and redefinition of different kinds of activities within these proscribed circumstances that determined where many Ohio Hopewell mounds would be built and where Hopewell artistry would accumulate.

Conclusions

When compared with the public ceremonialism of preceding periods, it is clear that Ohio Hopewell communities conducted their activities in less numerous but more complex sacred places. These places were located with considerable specificity and were built to symbolize and center ritual performance. They were grand constructions meant to attract spiritual powers and impress believers, and each shows a distinctive accumulated history. Some sites, such as Mound City, Hopewell, and Mann, were apparently associated with people who succeeded in operating over a broader area than others, as evidenced by the quantities of materials pertaining to extraregional contacts and the cumulative size and density of what was constructed. Processes promoting the construction of sacred places as distinct precincts within larger, nucleated villages and towns are relevant only to post-Hopewell changes in the Ohio valley.

Ohio Hopewell public ritual required considerable preparation and involved the use of both animal and ancestral symbolism. The form and context of their art make clear that the human-animal relationship was a key cosmological construct, and the spiritual imagery of their societies suggests a sense of community between people and animals and the importance of ritual in maintaining or renewing the natural cycle of fertility and well-being of both. The central themes of Hopewell art are different in focus and address a more limited range of concerns than the later Mississippian and Fort Ancient art in the Ohio valley, which emphasized humanized deities, agriculture and annual renewal, warfare, and Above World/Beneath World distinctions.

A respect for ancestral remains is strongly expressed in the ceremonies associated with the use, renewal, and covering of Ohio Hopewell public buildings and the clay basins within them. The arrangement of Hopewell ancestral remains on building floors represented membership in particular corporate groups, but it must be remembered that these were ritualized presentations and thus reflected a number of other contingencies. Ancestral rites have a long history in the Woodland period prior to the development of Ohio Hopewell, but the complex arrangement of burials, rooms, altars, mounds, and earthwork elements evident in Ohio Hopewell were of sufficient scope to suggest not only participation by larger communities than was formerly the case but also more differentiated communities, in some cases composed of complementary subgroups with distinct privileges. The scale and organization of public ritual at this time also suggest that laymen were taking on aspects of what may formerly have been strictly the prerogatives of shamans. The quantity and increased variety of objects required for display indicates on the one hand the increased social distance over which prestige was negotiated, and on the other, the fragility of relationships that constantly had to be reinforced with action. Ohio Hopewell leaders and their followers forged a delicate mix of competition and cooperation, kinship and charisma, men and women. As the numerous works illustrated here have shown, they provided a legacy of art and archaeology that is recognizably connected to the present through continuities with Mississippian practices and that supports the deep antiquity of many elements of American Indian social and religious life.

Notes

1. See, for example, Brown 1997, p. 480; Kelly 1996, p. 97.
2. Such formal contexts as the Indianapolis Conference (McKern 1939), the First Woodland Conference (Anonymous 1943), and Griffin's (1952) *Archaeology of Eastern United States* helped to refine the concept.
3. Mills 1906, p. 135; Hall 1980.
4. Willey and Sabloff 1993, pp. 204–06.
5. Penney 1988.
6. Buikstra 1976, p. 37; Powell 1992, pp. 90–91.
7. Braun 1986, pp. 122–23; Seeman 1995, p. 123.
8. Fortier 2001, p. 270; see also Smith 1992; Wymer 1997.
9. Cobb 1996, p. 256.
10. Vecsey 1983, pp. 162–64.
11. For example, in his study of galena, a lead sulfide used to make white paint, Walthall (1981, p. 11) notes an increase in use of over 600 percent from that of the preceding period. Copper, marine shell, and mica showed similar patterns of increased usage.
12. See, for example, Braun, Griffin, and Titterington 1982, pp. 88–89.
13. Helms 1988.
14. Cowan 1996; Seeman 1995.
15. Ruhl and Seeman 1998.
16. Penney 1988, p. 249.
17. DeBoer 1991.
18. See Hall 1977.
19. See, for example, Kenyon 1982, pp. 19, 48.
20. Emerson 1997a; Hilgeman 2000.
21. See Harrod 2000, pp. 24, 46.
22. Squier and Davis 1848, pp. 9, 141, 159.
23. Trigger 1989, pp. 104–07.
24. Thomas 1894.
25. Hall 1979; Buikstra and Charles 1999, pp. 214–16.
26. See, for example, Jefferies 1976, p. 50; Goad 1979, pp. 244–45; Bulter 1979, p. 156; Chapman and Keel 1979, p. 158.
27. Bacon 1980.
28. Charles 1992.
29. Seeman and Branch 2000.
30. Saunders and Allen 1994.
31. Clay 1988, p. 22; Garland and Beld 1999, p. 140.
32. Bullington 1988, pp. 223, 234.
33. Squier and Davis 1848, pp. 67–68.
34. Seeman 1995, p. 128.
35. Seeman 1992, pp. 25–29.
36. Romain 2000, pp. 32–64.
37. Ruby 1997, p. 10.
38. Squier and Davis 1848, p. 123; DeBoer 1997, pp. 228–30.
39. Brown 2004b.
40. DeBoer 1997, p. 230; see also Gartner 1996.
41. Kelly 1996, p. 111.
42. Hively and Horn 1982, 1984; Romain 2000.
43. See Brown 1997, p. 476.
44. Cowan, Sunderhaus, and Genheimer 1999; Sunderhaus, Riggs, and Cowan 2001.
45. Baby and Langlois 1979, p. 18; Griffin 1990, p. 182.
46. For feasting, see Brown 2004b; see also Knight 2001. For ritual practices involving smoking and drinking, see Hudson 1976, pp. 228, 336.
47. Brown 1996, p. 417; Milanich and Fairbanks 1980, pp. 124, 142.
48. See Hultkrantz 1967, p. 75; Fenton 1987, pp. 14–15, 29, 73–74.
49. Brown 1979, pp. 213; Brown 2004b.
50. Willoughby and Hooton 1922, p. 74.
51. Brown 2004b.
52. Greber 1996, p. 162–64; Penney 1985, p. 185.
53. Fischer 1974, p. 53; Greber 1979b, p. 34.
54. Cowan 1996, p. 136; Greber 1997, p. 215; Prufer 1964, pp. 73–74.
55. See Greber 1979a, pp. 50, 53; Hooton 1922, p. 100; Konigsberg 1985, p. 142; Prufer 1964, p. 74.
56. Steponaitis 1998, p. 40; Powell 1992, pp. 90–91.
57. Carr 1995.

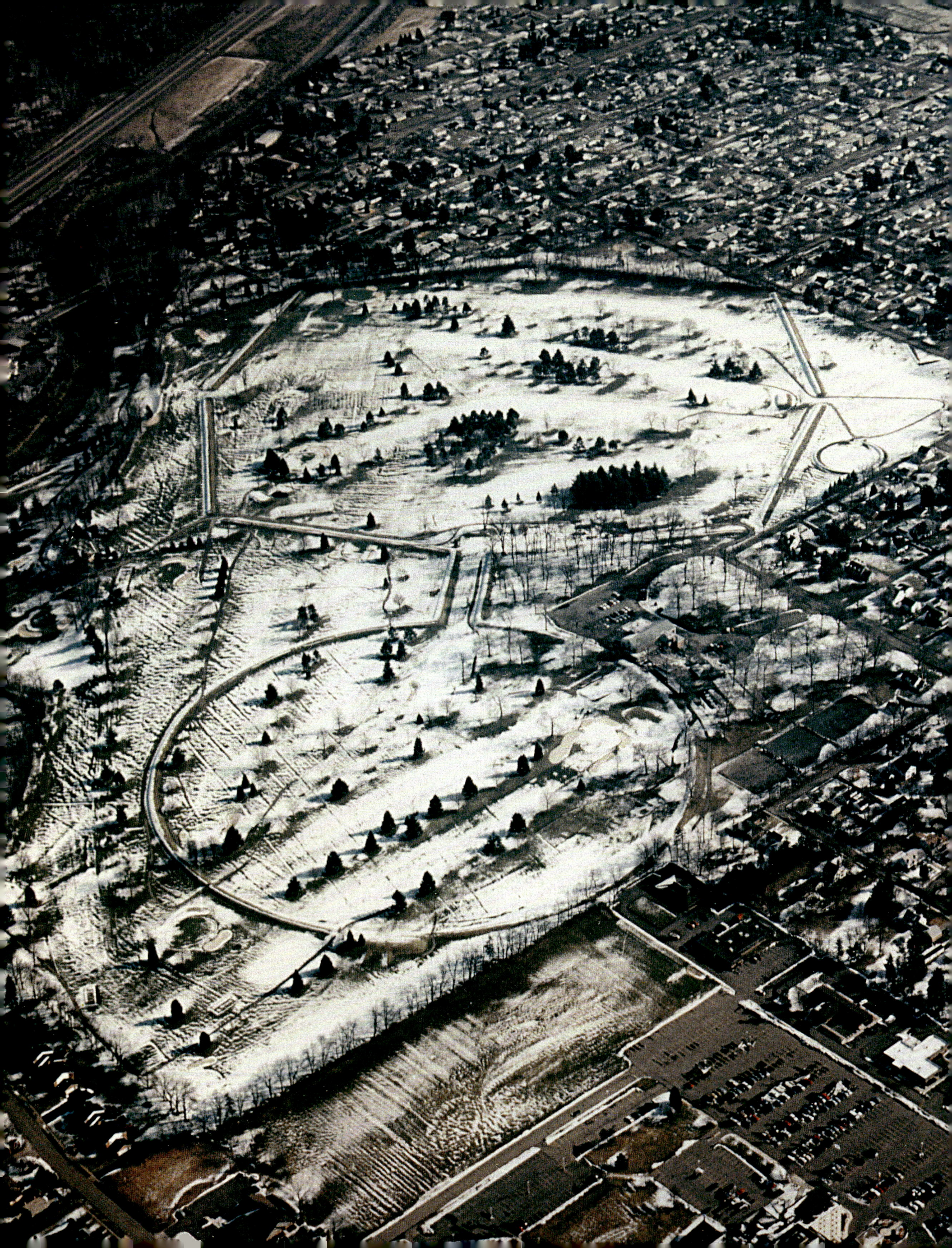

Marvels Ohio, on thy soil abound,

Fragments it puzzles Science to explain,

Of mammoth, mastodon, and Indian mound,

Temple, tomb, fortress?—still discussed in vain!

Who may the history of those bones expound?

Where do the annals of that age remain?

—Richard Henry Wilde, *Hesperia*

The Newark Earthworks

Bradley T. Lepper

Monumental Geometry and Astronomy at a Hopewellian Pilgrimage Center

The Newark Earthworks in central Ohio comprise the largest complex of monumental geometric earthen enclosures ever built by the Hopewell culture (A.D. 1–400). The site originally encompassed more than four square miles (ten square kilometers) and included two gigantic circles, an even bigger ellipse, a square, and an octagon—all connected by a network of parallel walls. In addition, there were numerous smaller circular enclosures, mounds of various shapes and sizes, a second large square just across a river to the east, and another oval earthwork encircling the highest hilltop to the south. Ephraim G. Squier and Edwin H. Davis, among the foremost of the early students of American archaeology, declared in 1848 that the works occupying this "remarkable plain" were so complicated that it was "impossible to give anything like a comprehensible description of them."[1] Yet, in spite of their magnificence, many of the earthworks were obliterated by the plow and the unrestrained growth of the city of Newark. All that remains of the wondrously labyrinthine geometry are the Great Circle, the Octagon attached to its somewhat less great circle, a small fragment of the principal square, and a few additional shreds and patches of earthworks in front yards and scattered wood lots. Squier and Davis were more or less correct in their prediction that within a few years of their publication, "the residents upon the spot" would need to refer to their map "to ascertain the character of the works which occupied the very ground upon which they stand."[2]

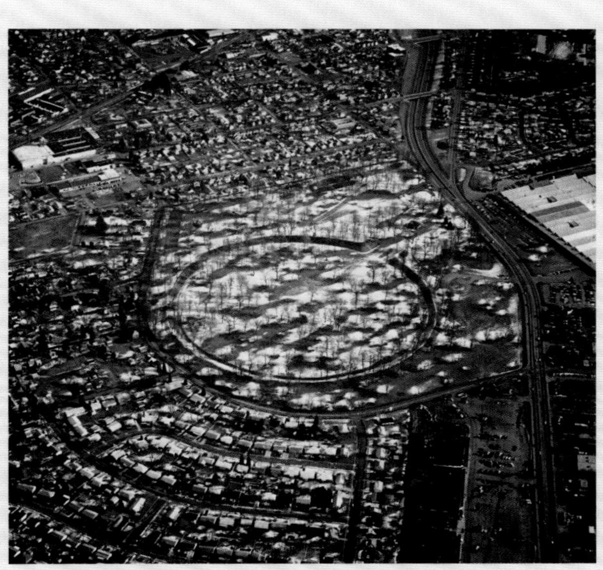

Fig. 1 View of the Observatory Circle and Octagon, part of the Newark Earthworks in Licking County, Ohio. Surveys of the ancient earthen enclosures at Newark and related sites in south-central Ohio indicate a widely shared, underlying architectural grammar and a way of connecting separate sites and prominent natural features through processional paths and long-distance alignments. In this symbolic claiming of the land, a cohesive cultural domain was affirmed.

Fig. 2 View of the Great Circle, a portion of the Newark Earthworks measuring 1,200 feet in diameter.

It is sadly revealing that the European settlers did not preserve any of these works primarily for their intrinsic historic value.[3] Instead, they survived because the citizens of Newark found ways to incorporate them into their contemporary cultural landscape. The Great Circle, for example, became the centerpiece of the county's fairgrounds beginning in 1854; and in 1893 the Octagon and its accompanying circular earthwork were rescued from encroaching potato fields to become the encampment for the Ohio State Militia. The militia abandoned the site in 1908 and the city of Newark began leasing it to the Moundbuilders Country Club in 1910. Although the Ohio Historical Society eventually acquired both sites, the Octagon has continued to be operated foremost as a private golf course (fig. 1).

An Architecture of Earth, Water, and Sky

Due to the unfortunate extent of their demolition in the nineteenth and twentieth centuries, our understanding of the Newark Earthworks is limited. We are able to reconstruct the original outlines of the earthworks from maps such as the one published by Squier and Davis in *Ancient Monuments of the Mississippi Valley*, the first volume of the Smithsonian Institution's Contributions to Knowledge series (fig. 4). In spite of the historical significance of this image, it is neither the most accurate nor the most complete. Long neglected maps by David Wyrick in 1860 and by James and Charles Salisbury, who conducted their survey in 1862, show more features and are more useful for understanding the archaeology of the Newark Earthworks (figs. 5–6). These maps reveal a complicated network of mounds and enclosures of varying shapes and sizes. When viewed in two dimensions on the page of a book, the geometric shapes look like a series of arcane glyphs that we might be able to decipher with the aid of a Hopewellian Rosetta Stone. This is, however, nothing like how the Hopewell people would have experienced the site. The Newark Earthworks were precisely sculpted and molded in accordance with architectural canons that emphasized monumental, earthen geometry enclosing vast interior spaces tied to multiple water sources and oriented to the tracks inscribed across the sky by the moon. The earthworks were not just symbols on the landscape, they were built to be a part of the landscape; and, perhaps, to allow their builders to transcend the boundaries of the terrestrial sphere (fig. 3).

facing page

Fig. 4 Ephraim G. Squier and Edwin H. Davis, Map of the Newark Earthworks; from Squier and Davis 1848, pl. 25a.

Fig. 5 David Wyrick and Joseph S. Unzicker, Map of the Newark Earthworks, c. 1860. Courtesy of the Western Reserve Historical Society, Cleveland.

Fig. 6 James and Charles Salisbury, Map of the Newark Earthworks, 1862. Courtesy of the American Antiquarian Society, Worcester, Massachusetts.

Fig. 3 View looking east over a portion of the Newark Earthworks, showing the Observatory Circle and Octagon in their alignment with the moonrise, with the Great Circle visible at upper right. Processional ways connected these principal enclosures at Newark; another long path extended southward and is thought to have led toward other earthworks near Chillicothe, Ohio, some 60 miles (96.8 km) distant. Rendering by Steven Patricia.

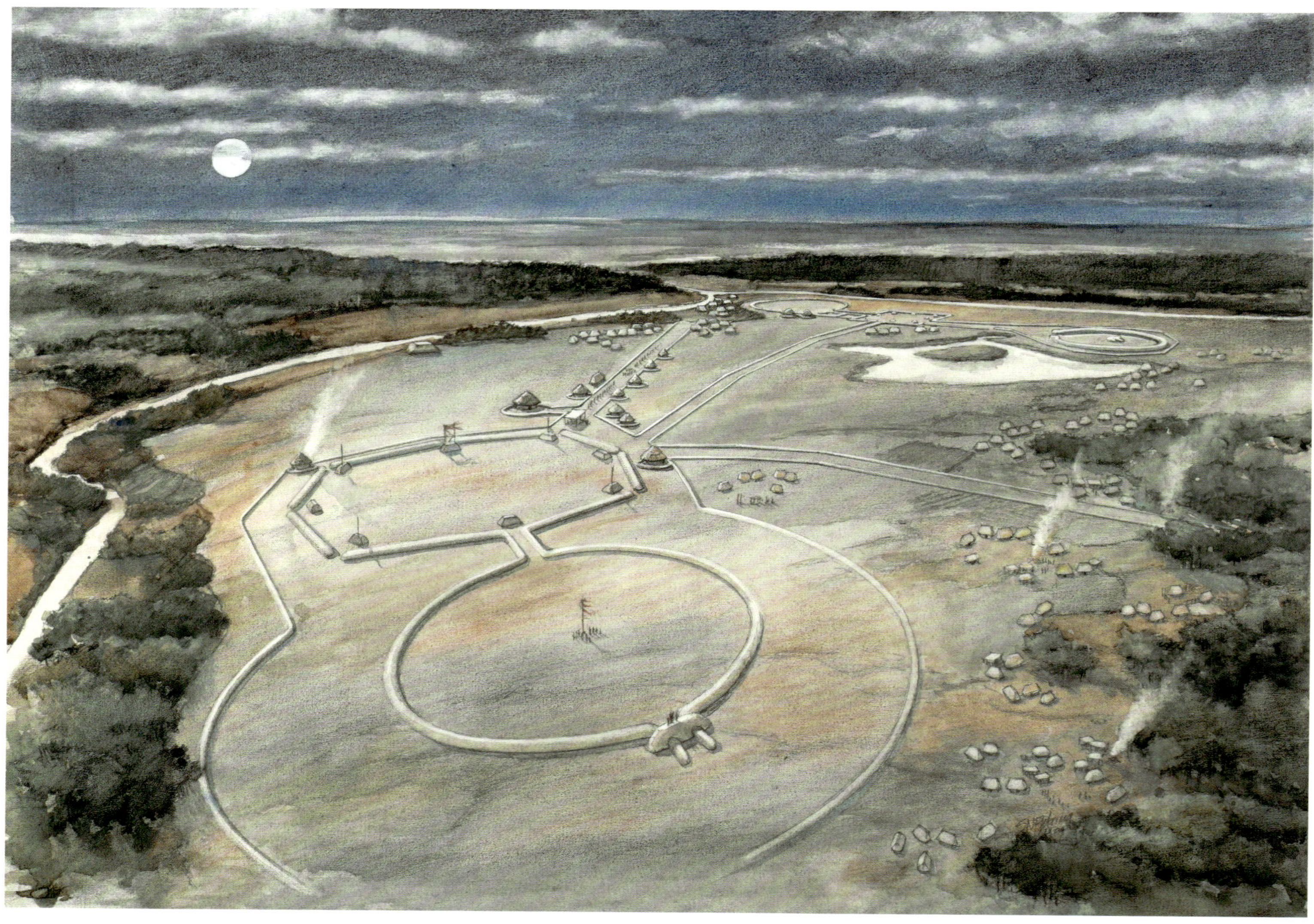

Monumental Earthen Geometry

The Great Circle is a gigantic circular enclosure measuring 1,200 feet (365.9 m) across from the crest of one wall to the opposite crest (fig. 2). The walls enclose an area of about 30 acres (12.1 ha). The circular wall varies in height from five to fourteen feet (1.5–4.3 m) with a ditch or moat at the base of the wall inside the enclosure. The ditch varies in depth from eight to thirteen feet (2.4–4.0 m) and is deepest at the entrance to the circle. The Observatory Circle, named for the unique platform mound located along its southwestern circumference, totals 1,054 feet (321.3 m) in diameter. It deviates from a perfect circle of that diameter by less than four feet (1.2 m). The walls of the attached octagonal enclosure each measure about 550 feet long (167.7 m) and range from five to six feet (1.5–1.8 m) in height. The Octagon itself encloses nearly 50 acres (20.2 ha), while the circle encloses an area of about 20 acres (8.1 ha). The principal Newark Square also was nearly geometrically perfect, with sides ranging in length from about 940 to 950 feet (286.6–289.6 m), also enclosing about 20 acres (8.1 ha).

Perhaps the best means of grasping the overwhelming scale of the Hopewellian architecture at Newark is to compare it to other, more familiar monuments. The Great Pyramid of Cheops would fit comfortably within the Newark Square and four structures the size of the Colosseum in Rome could be placed together inside the Octagon. The circle of monoliths at Stonehenge would fit within the small circular enclosure located just outside the southeastern gateway of the Octagon. The scale of this architecture is remarkable and unexpected for a culture without an urban concentration of people and a hierarchically structured society. It is difficult for us to imagine how the requisite labor was marshaled, directed, and sustained without hereditary leaders who could command the labor of masses of workers; and yet, it was. Moreover, the earthworks are not just big in scale. They also reflect a remarkably sophisticated understanding of geometry. In the early 1980s astronomer Ray Hively and philosopher Robert Horn of Earlham College carefully studied the plan of the Newark Earthworks and determined that it was not haphazard. They determined, for example, that the distance from the center of the Observatory Circle to the center of the Great Circle is six times the diameter of the Observatory Circle. The distance from the center of the Octagon to the center of the Newark Square is also six times the diameter of the Observatory Circle.[4]

William Romain has recently observed a number of geometric relationships between components of the Newark Earthworks that suggest they were conceptually integrated. The circumference of the Great Circle, for example, was nearly equal to the perimeter of the Square. Romain suggests that this reflects the geometric exercise of "squaring the circle" also found at Stonehenge and the Great Pyramid.[5] There are also examples of coincident areas at Newark. Hively and Horn observed that the total area of the Octagon is precisely double

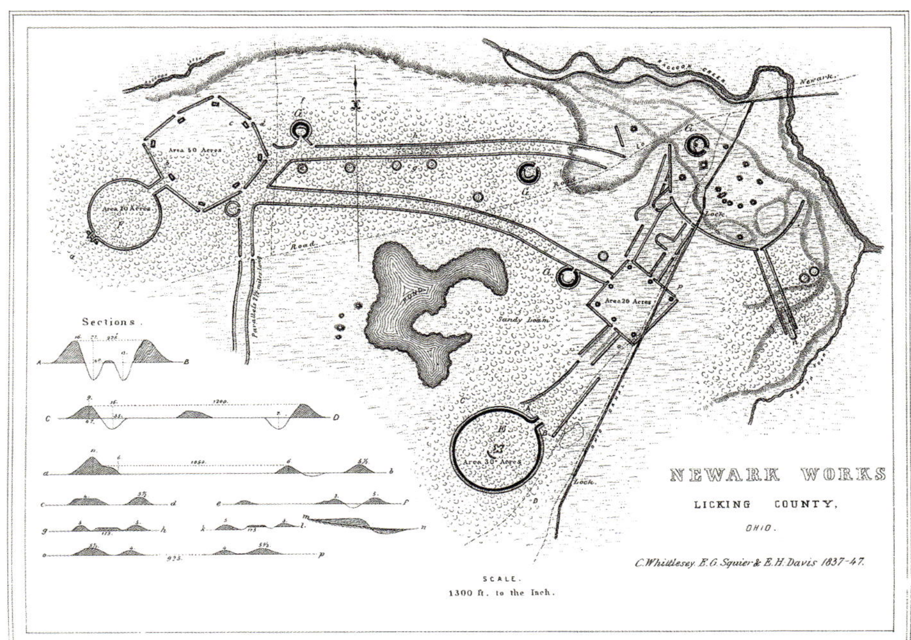

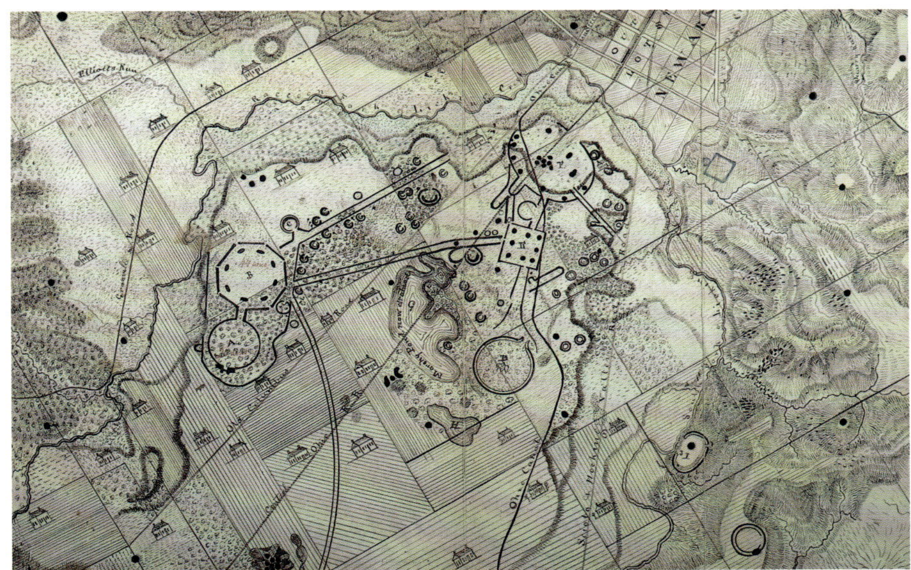

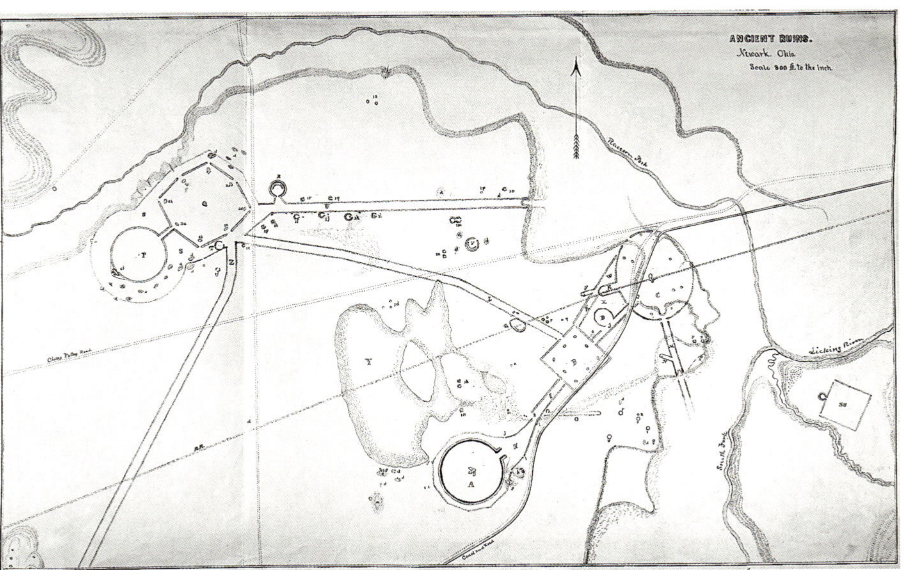

the area of the Observatory Circle and the connecting avenue. Furthermore, the area of the Square is nearly equal to that of the Observatory Circle. Finally, based on the Salisburys' estimate, the area of the elliptical enclosure nearby in Cherry Valley was approximately equal to the area of the Octagon.

Surveyor James Marshall believes he has identified what he refers to as "cryptographic" geometric forms that underlie the plans of the Newark and other Hopewellian earthworks. By drawing lines connecting the centers of each major earthwork component at a site and orienting these to the cardinal directions, Marshall has formed a variety of fundamental triangles, including a 3-4-5 right triangle relating the positions of the Observatory Circle and the Great Circle to each other. Marshall argues that the same sort of "Pythagorean" geometry ties together the Newark Earthworks with Hopewell earthwork enclosures at various sites in south-central Ohio near Chillicothe in Ross County—the Baum site, High Bank Works, Liberty Township Earthworks, and the Seip Earthworks set along Paint Creek—altogether forming the "true core of Ohio Hopewell." While Marshall's interpretations are a bit fanciful, his work in relation to Newark, combined with the observations of Hively and Horn, and Romain, implies that the site plan is not a haphazard mélange of individual earthworks connected to each other with parallel walls added during a culminating episode of construction. Instead, there is a powerful, albeit subtle, underlying system of order to which nearly every element of the site conforms.

Earthworks and Water

One of the most immediately obvious features of the Newark Earthworks, apparent in almost any map of the site is the close association of the enclosures with water. The entire complex of earthworks appears to have been built around a large pond, and streams formed the northern, eastern, and southern boundaries of the site: Raccoon Creek to the north, the South Fork of the Licking River to the east, and Ramp Creek to the south. This large pond is a central, dominating feature of what Squier and Davis called this "remarkable plain." The water level fluctuated widely in historic times. It was apparently dry for much of the period between 1800 and 1811, and its configuration changes in every map drawn from 1820 through 1862. Squier and Davis estimated that it covered more than 100 acres (40.5 ha) in 1848, which roughly corresponds to the modern distribution of poorly drained soils mapped in this area by the Soil Conservation Service. Some have supposed that the depression was a gigantic borrow pit, the result of prehistoric excavations for the earth used to build the many mounds and enclosures. But James and Charles Salisbury categorically refuted this conjecture in 1862 with their observation that drainage ditches dug through the area revealed a layer of peat with marl and shells at the bottom of the pond. This layer indicates that the pond had been there long enough for these deposits to form. The pond most likely formed at the end of the last Ice Age and therefore would have been a prominent part of the Hopewellian landscape both before and after construction of the earthworks.

The map produced by the Salisbury brothers is the most thorough and complete record of the Hopewellian achievement at Newark. Such a comprehensive plan may permit us to recover fundamental aspects of the architectural canons underlying the structure of the site. If, for example, we assume that the walls, regardless of their height, were meant to serve as physical barriers, then a complex pattern of movement through the enclosures is implicated. There were only three principal ways to enter the earthworks without climbing over an earthen wall. These three portals are framed by parallel walls extending from each of the three surrounding streams and, in at least one case to be discussed later, well beyond.

There were a few other less formalized openings and these, although more cryptic, also are closely tied to water sources. First, there was an opening in the northwestern arc of the Ellipse surrounding the Cherry Valley mounds that opened onto the second terrace of Raccoon Creek. Second, a passage in the western perimeter of the outer wall surrounding the Octagon and Observatory Circle was partially blocked by a semicircular embankment. This opening was on the edge of the high terrace overlooking Raccoon Creek, which would have provided a strategic vantage point for viewing traffic approaching Newark from the west. Third, a small but elaborate gateway in the polygonal wall that surrounded the Great Circle was located at the point where the enclosure came closest to the large pond. Another opening in this polygonal wall was located on the eastern side of the Great Circle, at a point more or less opposite the first. According to the Salisburys, it opened "at the brink of a deep basin" that always contained water.

In addition, a break in the western wall leading from the Great Circle to the Square was associated with an apparently artificial drainage feature composed of a dam that appears to have diverted the outlet of the pond through the opening in the embankment. The Salisbury brothers speculated that a tunnel carried the water beneath the surface of the enclosed passageway and on down to the South Fork of the Licking River. And, finally, the Great Circle has an interior ditch that, when observed by Caleb Atwater sometime prior to 1820, was partially filled with water. Since this is the only one of the great enclosures at Newark that has a ditch associated with it, it is likely that it served a special function. Perhaps it was intended to hold water and serve as a reflecting pool, reservoir, or water barrier. This use of natural and artificial water sources as part of the intentional sacred architecture has been observed at other Hopewell earthwork sites, including Fort Ancient, located in Warren County, northeast of Cincinnati. The ways water is used to frame ritual spaces

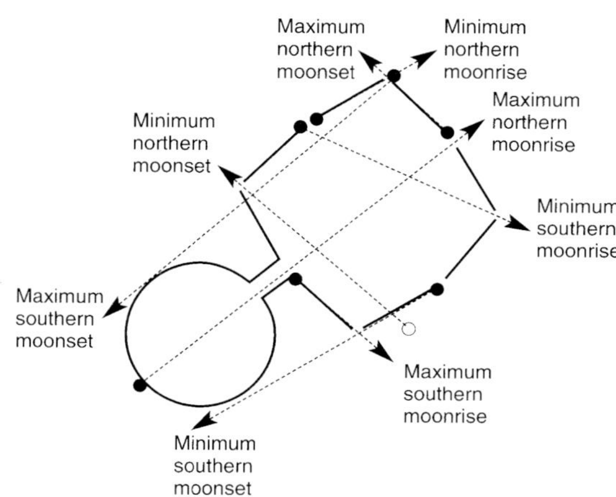

Fig. 7 Diagram showing the maximum and minimum points of the moon's rising and setting as observed from the Octagon and Observatory Circle at the Newark Earthworks; from Hively and Horn 1982.

suggests it is not simply a matter of locating these sites conveniently near drinking water or canoe routes.

Archaeoastronomy

The Newark Earthworks are a remarkable testament to the architectural and mathematical genius of the Hopewell culture, but astronomers recently have come to realize that the Hopewell builders also aligned these earthworks to the cyclical dance of the earth and moon. Hively and Horn determined that if one stands atop the Observatory Mound and looks across the circle through the parallel-walled passage leading into the Octagon and out through the Octagon's northeastern gateway, the point that you see on the horizon is where the moon rises at its most northerly extreme (fig. 7). In addition, at this complex site the intricate 18.6-year cycle of the moon can be encompassed by four points on the eastern horizon marking a maximum northern moonrise, a minimum northern moonrise, a maximum and minimum southern moonrise, and four points on the western horizon marking the corresponding moonsets.

Hively and Horn also established that the walls that form the gateway of the Great Circle are aligned to the minimum northern moonrise. Furthermore, a line that goes through the eastern and western corners of the Newark Square is oriented to those points on the eastern and western horizons that mark the midpoint of the monthly lunar cycle. And the axis of the avenue of parallel walls entering the Square from the Octagon is aligned to the minimum northern moonset. In addition to the astronomically significant alignments of particular earthworks, some individual elements of the site are oriented with respect to other elements to frame more alignments to significant moonrises. Hively and Horn showed that the axis of the Great Circle's gateway is parallel displaced from the corresponding axis in the Observatory Circle along a mean azimuth that corresponds to the maximum southern moonrise (fig. 8). The displacement of the Square with respect to the Octagon is similarly aligned to the minimum southern moonrise.[6] The Hopewell builders encoded all of these astronomical landmarks into the architecture of the Newark Earthworks. Whether or not they ever intended to use this site as an astronomical observatory, the Hopewell architects certainly succeeded in bringing some of the moon's magic down to earth.

The Archaeology of the Newark Earthworks

Burial mounds

Many people assume that all Indian mounds are ancient cemeteries, but burials at the Newark Earthworks seem largely to have been concentrated in one area, where a group of eleven conical mounds surrounded a large, irregularly shaped mound at the center of a now-demolished Ellipse. This part of the site has been called the Cherry Valley Mound group. Canal workers in 1827 dug through one of the smaller mounds while excavating for a lock and discovered a large number of burned human bones covered with varying amounts of "very beautiful transparent mica." One of the skeletons was set off from the others and was completely covered with an extravagant quantity of cut mica sheets. The total amount of mica removed from this small mound exceeded "eight or ten bushels."[7]

The principal mound of this group resembled, in some respects, the large mounds at the Tremper site in Scioto County near Portsmouth, Ohio, and the Edwin Harness Mound site at the Liberty Township Earthworks in Ross County. It was about 140 feet long, 40 feet wide, and about 20 feet high at its highest point (approximately 43 × 12 × 6 m). To the vivid imaginations of James and Charles Salisbury, its shape suggested a priest with outstretched arms. This mound was largely destroyed between 1852 and 1855, when the builders of the Central Ohio Railroad cut through it and used fill from it and the surrounding mounds to elevate the bed for the train tracks. A remnant of the largest part of the mound was not completely flattened until a rolling mill was built on the site.

A general idea of what this mound contained can be drawn from a newspaper article published more than a decade later by local antiquarian J. N. Wilson along with supplementary information collected by James and Charles Salisbury.[8] At the base of the tallest section of the mound, there was a "tier of skeletons"—their

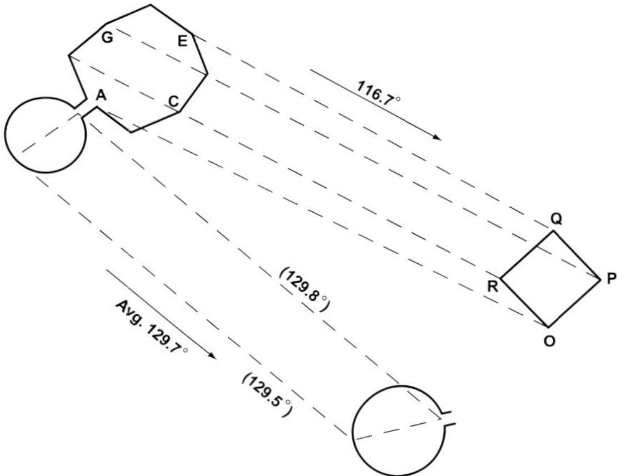

Fig. 8 Diagram of parallel-displaced relationship between the Great Circle in Newark and the Observatory Circle and between the Square and the Octagon. The azimuths of the displacements mark the extreme southernmost point of the moon's rise; drawing by Chester P. Walker after Hively and Horn 1982.

heads placed together with their feet radiating outward.[9] Wilson observed several post molds suggesting the former presence of some sort of substantial structure, or structures, possibly similar to the Great Houses uncovered at the bases of the Tremper and Harness mounds. It is now impossible to determine how these various discoveries were associated, but the burials originally may have been interred inside the wooden structure. The mound itself was said to be composed of alternating layers of black loam, blue clay, sand, and cobblestones, punctuated by periodic episodes of burning and burial. Artifacts found in association with numerous fragmentary burials included mica sheets, a copper axe, large shells, beads, and at least one drilled canine tooth of a bear.[10]

When the rolling mill was torn down in 1881 and workers began to dig the foundation for a new building in this area, they encountered another burial. This burial included a remarkable stone image of a Hopewell shaman wearing ritual regalia made from a bear's head and hide, and with an apparent decapitated human head in his lap (fig. 9).[11] Since the figurine was buried beneath the bottom of this prominent and centrally located mound, it must be from one of the oldest burials at the site. It may be an image of a particular historic personage or it may be an item of shamanic paraphernalia used in the rites and ceremonies associated with the founding of Hopewellian Newark.

Great Circle Earthworks

In 1992 archaeologists excavated a trench through the Great Circle revealing details of the structure of the embankment as well as clues to the history of the site. The base of the earthwork rests on a surface radiocarbon dated to 2110 + 80 years BP (Beta-58449), or 160 B.C. The construction of the Great Circle began sometime after this date. Microscopic remains of plants from this soil indicate that the vegetation in the area at the time the Great Circle was built was a prairie.

The profile of the embankment itself revealed a relatively simple sequence of construction. The excavators observed three principal construction episodes. Initially, the builders erected a series of small mounds on an unprepared surface. The excavation trench cut through one such mound. The archaeologists infer the presence of a circle of small mounds that would have provided the basic plan for the subsequent embankment. Next, dark brown silt loam was mounded atop the low mounds creating a circular enclosure. The builders probably obtained this dark brown earth from the interior ditch, and if so, left a gap between the ditch and the embankment to allow for the final width of the earthwork. Finally, they obtained yellow brown gravelly silt loam from deep borrow pits and piled it between the crest of the dark brown embankment and the edge of the ditch. At the completion of this work, the embankment would have been dark brown when viewed from the outside and yellow brown when viewed from inside the enclosure. Color is likely to have carried great symbolic meaning for the Hopewell people, as it did for later Eastern Woodland tribes. It is not known, however, whether these different shades of brown were significant in the presentation of the architecture, or whether it was important only that they be in their proper place beneath the sod.

At the center of the Great Circle is a group of conjoined mounds that is popularly known as Eagle Mound. It is doubtful, however, that the mound was intended to be an effigy of any sort. In 1881 Isaac Smucker stated that excavations conducted "into the center of [Eagle Mound], where the elevation is greatest, developed an altar built of stone, upon which were found ashes, charcoal, and calcinced bones."[12] Emerson Greenman, who excavated Eagle Mound in 1928 on behalf of the Ohio Historical Society, identified a series of fifty-nine post molds at the base of the mound, possibly the remains of a Great House nearly one hundred feet long by more than twenty feet wide (30.5 × 6 m). In the center of the structure there was a rectangular basin made from clay. It was similar to basins excavated at other Hopewell sites that sometimes contained cremated human remains, although Greenman recovered no human remains from Eagle Mound. The floor of the Great House was composed of successive layers of black muck, yellow clay, and red clay. The use of soils of varying color and composition reinforces the sense of a highly dynamic, ritualized, and symbolically charged architecture. Greenman documented more than fifty artifacts from these excavations, but only a handful were collected and curated. The most intriguing discoveries were two copper artifacts: a copper crescent and a stylized copper beaver effigy.

Salisbury Square

Sometime prior to 1862, the square enclosure located on the glacial terrace east of the South Fork of the Licking River was destroyed. A brickyard had been established on the site to make use of the fine clay that the Hopewell used to build the walls. During these excavations, the workers discovered "a stack of flint spears, numbering 194, about two feet below the surface" beneath one of the walls of the square. James and Charles Salisbury reported that the leaf-shaped bifaces, crafted from the local Flint Ridge flint, had been "placed points upwards in a conical pile like stacked arms, resting upon a large flat stone."[13] The careful arrangement of these artifacts and their placement beneath the corner of an earthen enclosure, suggest that they represent a ceremonial deposit.

In 1970 Marie Sunkle discovered another cache of flint artifacts in the same general vicinity. Sunkle fortuitously uncovered a pit feature containing more than 500 artifacts. These included around 120 Hopewell cores and 150 bladelets made from Flint Ridge flint, 26 projectile points, including several varieties made centuries and even millennia before the Hopewell culture, 5 ground stone artifacts, including an unfinished Adena gorget, 3 pieces of fossil coral, and other flakes

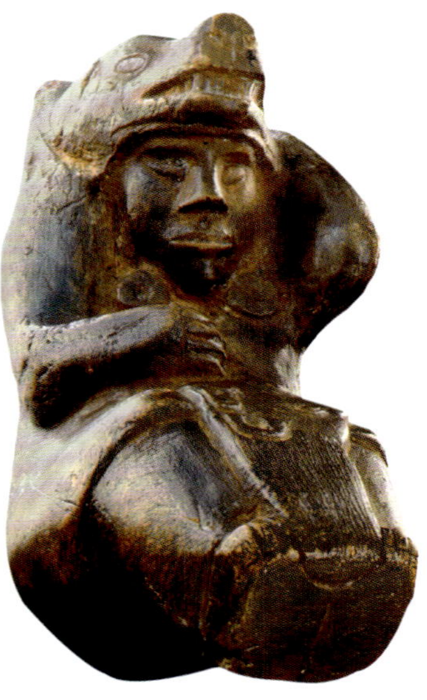

Fig. 9 Shaman wearing the head and hide of a bear; known as the Wray figurine; Ohio, Licking County, Newark, A.D. 1–400; stone, h. 16 cm; Ohio Historical Society, Columbus.

and bifaces. According to Sunkle, these artifacts had been deposited in the pit systematically with projectile points at the bottom, followed by bladelets, and then cores at the top. The care evident in the placement of these selected artifacts in a pit feature not associated with a habitation or manufacturing site, and the proximity of the pit to an earthen enclosure and another ceremonial deposit of flint tools, suggests that the Marie Sunkle cache also was a ceremonial offering.

The Great Hopewell Road

The parallel walls that extended southwestward from Newark's Observatory Circle and Octagon are conservatively judged to have reached Ramp Creek, two and a half miles away (4 km).[14] Atwater suggested in 1820 that they might be as much as 30 miles long (48.4 km). In 1862 the Salisbury brothers found that the walls did indeed continue on the opposite bank of Ramp Creek. They followed them for a total of at least six miles (9.5 km) over fields and through "tangled swamps and across streams, still keeping their undeviating course."[15] The Salisburys suggested these walls might eventually lead to Chillicothe, but apparently never traced them to their ultimate destination. The suggestion of a link to Chillicothe is notable because the Ohio Hopewell people built one other circle and octagon earthwork, High Bank Works along the Scioto River at Chillicothe—a circular enclosure, with the same diameter as Newark's Observatory Circle, connected to a much smaller octagonal earthwork (fig. 10; see also fig. 25 in the essay by Mark Seeman in this volume). The Circle and Octagon at the High Bank Works also incorporate alignments to the eight lunar rise and set points. Moreover, the main axis of High Bank Works—that is, a line projected through the center of the Circle and the Octagon—bears a direct relationship to the axis of Newark's Observatory Circle and Octagon. Although built more than 60 miles apart (96.8 km), the axis of High Bank Works is oriented at precisely 90 degrees to that of Octagon earthworks. This suggests a deliberate attempt to link these sites through geometry and astronomy from which we may infer that the Hopewell people of Newark and Chillicothe had a close relationship. Perhaps this Great Hopewell Road was a pilgrim's path like similarly long and straight roads built by the Mayan culture in Mesoamerica or the Anasazi of Chaco Canyon.[16] Hopewell people may have followed this road, and perhaps others like it, to the great earthwork centers bringing offerings of copper or mica as gifts to the supernatural powers invoked by the monumental geometry of these sacred places.

The Machinery of Ritual

The Newark Earthworks complex is the largest connected set of geometric earthworks in the Hopewell world and an avenue of parallel walls extended from that site along a trajectory that led directly to the undisputed center of Ohio Hopewell culture at modern Chillicothe. Although located 60 miles away, with few or no earthworks of prominence in the intervening territory, these centers exhibit a close relationship. Elements of the architecture of the Newark Earthworks echo discrete sites in the Scioto Valley. Newark's Observatory Circle and Octagon, for example, are obviously related to the High Bank Works south of Chillicothe. Newark, however, is unique in that these disparate forms were brought together in a singular composition. Architectural canons discernable in the plan of the site reveal fundamental aspects of the function and history of the site. The Hopewell builders carefully selected different varieties of soil to construct geometric earthworks enclosing vast interior spaces. The monumental size of the works indicates they were built to serve large numbers of people who gathered periodically here from far and wide. These pilgrims brought offerings from the ends of the Hopewell world that ultimately were buried here.

Water was a central feature in the architecture and ritual. Nearby watercourses framed the earthwork complex and a large pond was located at the center

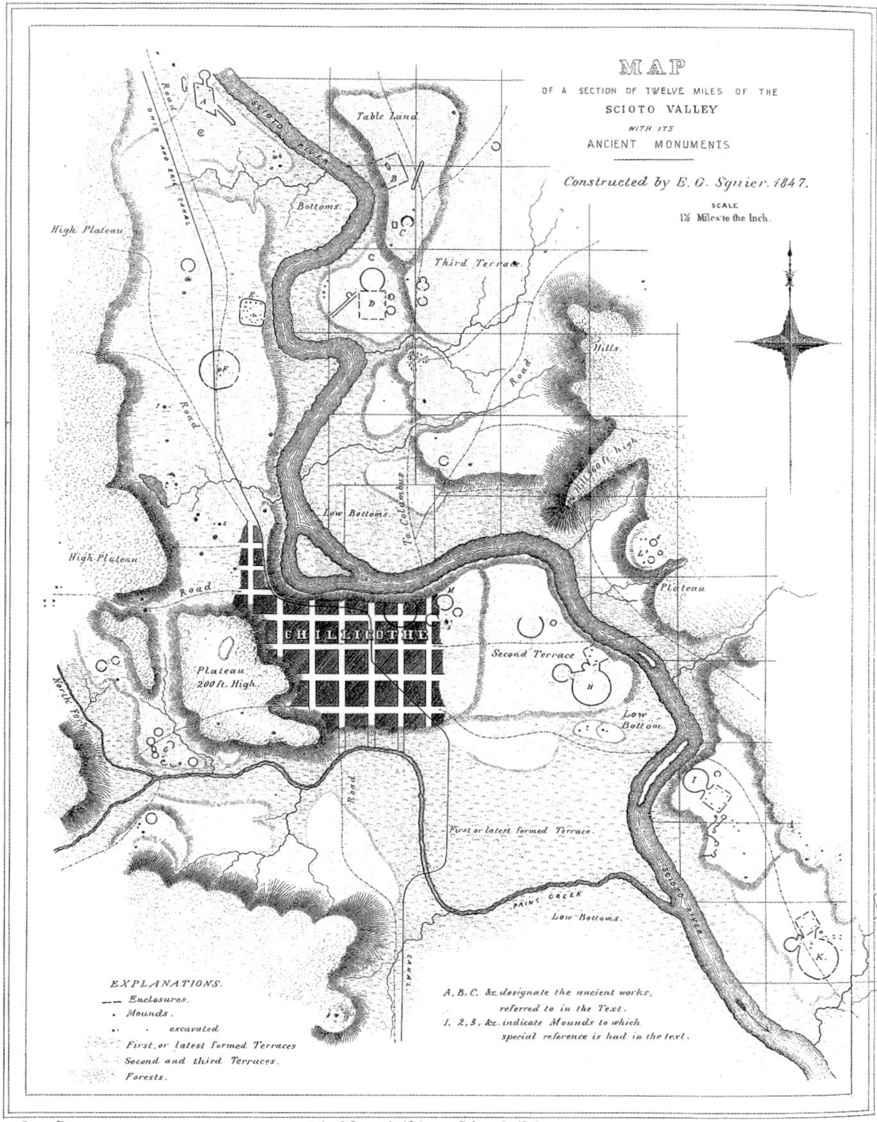

Fig. 10 Ephraim G. Squier and Edwin H. Davis, Map of the Scioto River valley at Chillicothe; from Squier and Davis 1848, pl. 2. Among the many sites included in this engraving of the Chillicothe area are, on the east side of the Scioto River, the Hopeton Works, High Bank Works, and, in the extreme southeast corner, Liberty Township Earthworks. On the west side of the Scioto River, north of Chillicothe, lies Mound City, while the East Works site is clearly represented between the old town limits and the river.

of the site. When visitors came to the earthworks, they entered from a stream along a straight and wide corridor that delivered them to an enclosure from which they could select alternative passages to other parts of the complex. Perhaps shamans or votaries conducted them from one enclosure to another in a ritualized sequence. The enclosures themselves were aligned, individually and collectively, to the intricate cycle of moonrise and moonset. This architecture was linked formally and systematically to the sky. If the earthworks occupied a prairie, as the soil beneath the Great Circle indicates, the Hopewell sky-watchers at Newark would have had a relatively unobstructed view of the celestial vault.

These facts suggest that the Newark Earthworks can be viewed not merely as arcane symbols built upon the landscape, but as a gigantic machine or factory in which energies from the three levels of the Eastern Woodland Indian's cosmos—the Upper World of the sky, the watery Underworld, and the Middle World of soil and stone—were drawn together and circulated through conduits of ritual to accomplish some sacred purpose. Perhaps they were the Hopewellian equivalent of our giant superconducting supercolliders: monumental machinery for unleashing powerful cosmic forces. A surprising implication of this interpretation is that the Newark Earthworks, the grandest architectural achievement of the Hopewell culture, were planned and built within a relatively brief span of time.

N'omi Greber of the Cleveland Museum of Natural History has criticized the simplistic assumption that each monumental Hopewellian earthwork represented a singular event, that the plan views mapped by Squier and Davis and others are simple reflections of the plans as devised by the original architects. She has argued persuasively that this was not the case at least for the Seip Earthworks south of Chillicothe. Robert Riordan of Wright State University and Robert Connolly of the University of Cincinnati (and others) have uncovered similarly impressive evidence for an evolving architecture at the Pollock Works in Greene County, Ohio, west of Cedarville and at the Fort Ancient Earthworks, respectively. On the other hand, the demonstration that several Hopewell sites changed markedly through time does not preclude the possibility that some might represent historically abrupt, singular events. It is too soon to abandon all theoretical models that consider that miles of earthen walls, mounds, "and the various wooden structures, pits, deposits, and other features of the site . . ." might be coeval, as Greber appears to suggest.[17] Greber is quite correct to state that "we must consider pace" when we examine "the true human scale probably represented by such sites," but she is wrong to imply that the pace could not sometimes be rapid.[18]

Based on the work of Connolly, Greber, Riordan, and others, I think most archaeologists would now assume that sites as large and complex as Newark were the product of generations, if not centuries, of gradual accretion. This view is based on the evidence recovered at other earthwork sites as well as from the relatively modest level of sociocultural complexity inferred for Hopewell societies based on the data from habitation sites.[19] Moreover, the diversity evident in earthwork forms at Newark and other sites has been interpreted as changing architectural traditions over time. The Great Circle, for example, has an interior ditch similar to the earthen architecture of the Adena culture (c. 800 B.C.–A.D. 100). The Observatory Circle has no ditch at all and more closely approximates a geometrically perfect circle. For these reasons, some have concluded it was built at a later date following new and improved architectural canons.

The evidence for three stages of embankment construction at the Great Circle might be seen as corroboration of the view that this earthwork was modified and enlarged by subsequent groups. The "stages" of construction, however, are not marked by any discernable soil development, suggesting that no substantial interval of time elapsed between construction "episodes." Moreover, the "stages" are not merely enlargements of the earthwork. The earliest stages presuppose the later ones, which are a logical fulfillment of the design. Finally, the different components of the Newark Earthworks seem to have complementary, or at least non-redundant, functions. The archaeological evidence, meager as it is, suggests the differences in the forms of the earthworks are related to distinctive and particular functional differences. The burial mounds of the Cherry Valley group, the interior ditch at the Great Circle, and the barrier mounds at the openings of the Octagon and Square, suggest that each enclosure had particular design requirements. For the whole "machine" to function properly, all of the individual parts had to be in place.

This is, of course, not to suggest that the site was completely devoid of earthworks or ritually significant activity prior to the construction of the principal earthworks, nor that all moundbuilding activity ceased with the realization of the original program of construction. The site must have been in use for a long period of time and the individual mounds in the Cherry Valley mound group may have accumulated over an extended period. Certainly, the large, central mound appears to have been built up through successive episodes of use as indicated by the alternating layers of burning and burial. The Eagle Mound Great House also may have been used repeatedly before its culminating ritual destruction and burial. But the overall configuration of earthworks may have been largely established at the beginning of the Hopewell occupation of this "remarkable plain."

An alternative interpretation is that the order, or system, is a creation of modern analysts. The earthworks were built by episodic accretion, more or less haphazardly, and only coincidentally exhibit the sorts of mathematical and astronomical configurations attributed to them. Given the coherence of the overall plan, however, this interpretation seems unlikely. Another alternative is that the plan was conceived originally by a person or group and then executed over a period of generations. But if the plan, with all its geometrical precision and astronomical complexity, was conveyed and followed across such a span of time, then there must have been a system of record-keeping or information transmittal coupled with social mechanisms capable of sustaining such a multigeneration project. Neither of these necessary, but not necessarily sufficient, capacities is known for the Hopewell culture.

Clearly, the Newark Earthworks site remains a great mystery, subject to many different interpretations. The scale of monumental architecture is comparable to what traditional models of social and cultural evolution suggest should arise from a more urban, agriculturally based society with institutionalized and hierarchical leadership. The Hopewell culture is characterized by small, scattered hamlets with some swidden agriculture, and little evidence of powerful hereditary leaders. That these people could have created the Newark Earthworks at all is wonderful; that they might have done so within a generation is incredible. Such a radical interpretation must be supported by more evidence before it can be sustained, but the alternative interpretations seem equally outlandish. It is unfortunate that so much of the Newark Earthworks complex has been destroyed by the growth of the modern city of Newark. That so much of this ancient wonder has been preserved, however, will make it possible for future archaeological research to answer these questions as well as others that we have not yet thought to ask.

Notes

1. Squier and Davis 1848.
2. Squier and Davis 1848, p. 71.
3. It should be noted, however, that some more enlightened citizens did attempt to save the earthworks. According to Samuel Haven, Daniel Webster, "our distinguished statesman," desired to have the Newark Earthworks "preserved in perpetuity at the national charge" (Haven 1870, p. 41). Had Webster succeeded, these "beautiful specimens of the moundbuilders' art" would have become America's first National Park.
4. Hively and Horn 1982, p. S9.
5. Romain 2000.
6. Hively and Horn 1982, pp. S9, S15.
7. *The Advocate* [Newark, Ohio] 1827.
8. Wilson 1868.
9. Salisbury and Salisbury 1862, p. 12.
10. Lepper 1998a, p. 121.
11. Dragoo and Wray 1964; Mason 1882.
12. Smucker 1881, p. 266.
13. Salisbury and Salisbury 1862, p. 27.
14. Squier and Davis 1848, p. 70; pl. 25.
15. Salisbury and Salisbury 1862.
16. Lepper 1995; Lepper 1996; Lepper 1998a.
17. Greber 1997, p. 209.
18. Greber 1997, p. 209.
19. For example, Dancey and Pacheco 1997b.

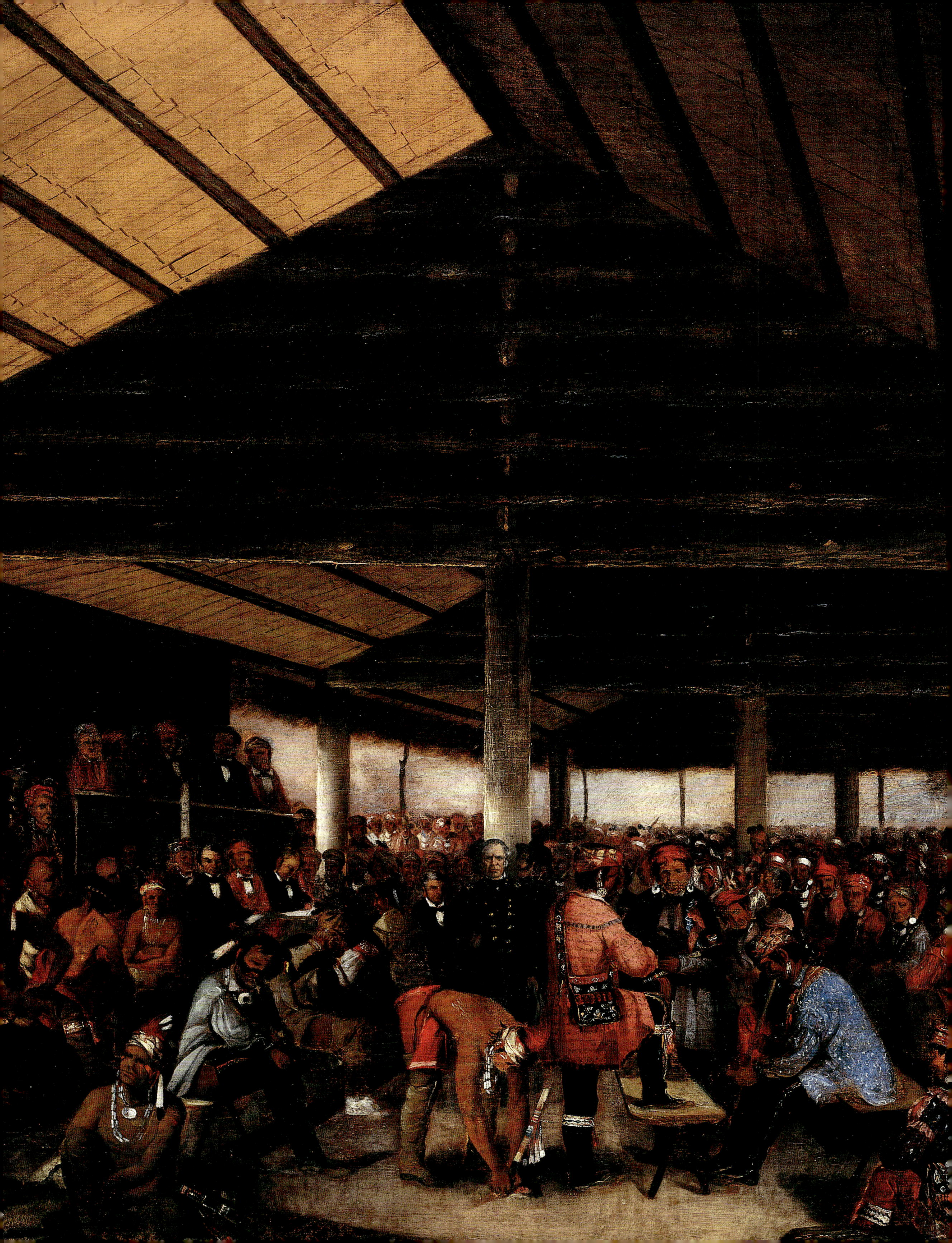

Continuity and Change in Mississippian Civilization

Garrick Bailey

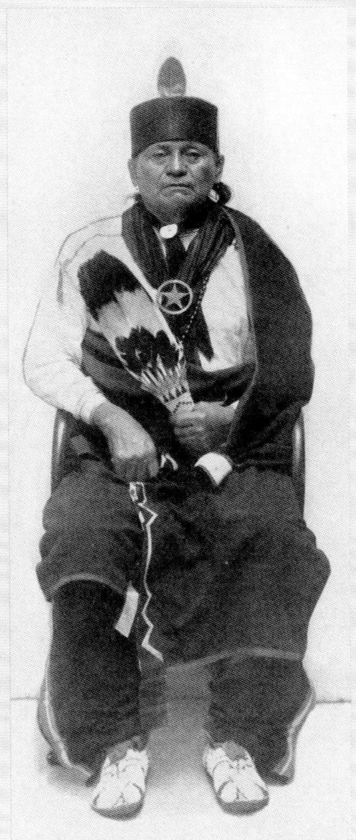

Fig. 1 John Mix Stanley (American; 1814–1872), *International Indian Council (Held at Tahlequah, Indian Territory, 1843)* (detail), 1843; oil on canvas, 80 × 102.9 cm; Smithsonian American Art Museum, gift of the Misses Henry, 1985.66.248,934B. See fig. 8.

Fig. 2 Portrait of Saucy Calf; from La Flesche 1939, pl. 11.

In 1910 Omaha anthropologist Francis La Flesche recorded Saucy Calf singing the songs and reciting the ritual prayers used in his clan's portion of the sacred songs of the *Wa-xo'-be* rite of the Osages (figs. 2–3). Saucy Calf's version of the four-day-long rite consisted of ninety songs, six long ritual prayers, and seven symbolic ritual acts called *we'-ga-xe*. Like all Osage clan priests, Saucy Calf used a tally stick to assist as a memory aid, notched in various places along both of its flat sides. On one side there were fifty-one notches representing the sacred "seven songs," and on the other thirty-nine notches of the sacred "six songs." The notches were further clustered in groups of between one and twelve notches, with each notch representing a specific song, and each cluster a set of related songs. As Saucy Calf sang the songs and recited the prayers he moved his finger along the notches on the stick to keep track of where he was in the sequence. Several times during the recording La Flesche noticed that the old priest passed over a notch without singing a song. When LaFlesche asked about the missing songs, Saucy Calf replied that he should not concern himself about those songs, for the ones he had forgotten were of "no particular importance."[1]

The Exploration of North America

Compared to the Spanish, the English and French were slow in establishing permanent settlements in North America and even slower in penetrating

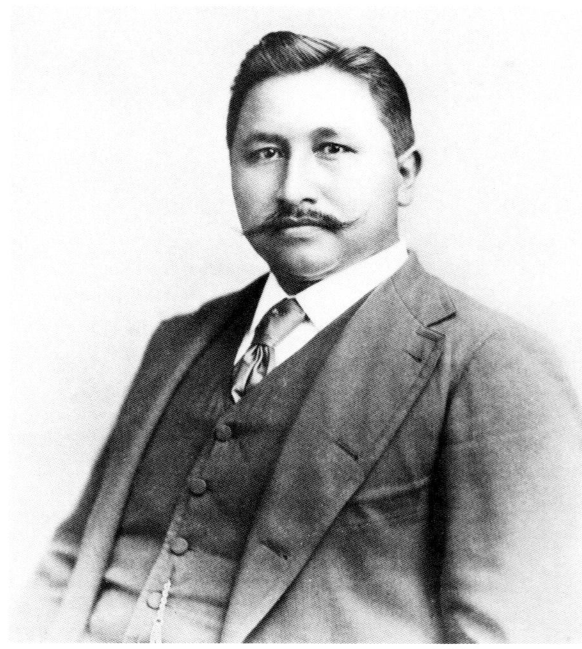

Fig. 3 Ethnologist and Omaha tribe member Francis La Flesche (1857–1932) served with the Bureau of Indian Affairs from 1881 to 1910 and from 1910 to 1929 with the Bureau of American Ethnology, for which institution he produced major studies of the Omaha (with Alice C. Fletcher) and the Osage.

the vast interior of the continent. In 1605 French settlers finally succeeded in founding a permanent settlement on the mainland at Port Royal, in present-day Nova Scotia. Two years later the English finally arrived at Jamestown, more than one hundred years after Columbus and almost ninety years after Cortez had conquered Mexico. In the decades that followed, additional English settlements were established along the Atlantic coastline. Only cautiously and reluctantly did these English farmers inch inland toward the Appalachian Mountains. Even the more adventuresome French fur traders were slow to explore the interior. It was not until 1682 that René-Robert Cavelier, Sieur de La Salle, descended the Mississippi to its mouth (fig. 4). It would be almost a generation later, in 1700, before English traders, traveling overland from Charleston, would stand on the banks of this same river. Probably few if any members of these parties of explorer-traders realized that they were not the first Europeans to travel over these trails and waterways. Almost 150 years earlier, Hernando de Soto and his men had marched and fought their way from the western coast of what is now Florida, north into South Carolina and Georgia and west to the Mississippi (fig. 5).[2]

To the French and English traders, missionaries, and soldiers who explored the Mississippi River valley and Gulf Coast during the eighteenth century, the area appeared to be a vast wilderness. It was a region of great forests, parklands, and prairies, cut by broad, rich river valleys and relatively few native inhabitants. The tribes of the region lived in widely scattered small villages, supporting themselves by hunting and by planting corn, beans, and squash. They had no metal. Their tools of clay, stone, wood, horn, and bone, though nicely fashioned and functional, rarely demonstrated any exceptional skill. They clothed themselves in animal skins, usually decorated in quills or paint. Their only architecture was their simple, semipermanent dwellings, lightly constructed of poles and covered by mats, bark, mud, hides, or thatch. Although leadership in these communities was frequently hereditary, the leaders had more influence than authority, and most decisions were reached by community consensus. Although many of the Europeans of the time came to idealize them as "noble savages," they were nonetheless uncivilized savages in their eyes.

The Natchez

In French Louisiana during the early 1700s, there was one native people, the Natchez, so totally different from the other tribes of the colony that they seemed out of place.[3] Although numbering only about 3,500 people, their main village, called Grand Village, their way of life, and their style of leadership sharply distinguished them from their neighbors. The center of Grand Village consisted of a large plaza with artificial earthen mounds at either end. Atop one of these mounds was a temple, 30 feet long and slightly narrower, with high, mud-plastered walls and a pitched roof adorned with carved wooden figures of birds. The interior of the temple was divided into two rooms. In the first room was the sacred eternal fire, symbolic of the sun, and a coffin containing the bones of last ruler, or Great Sun. In the back room were other ritual objects and coffins containing the bones of earlier rulers. Atop the other mound was a house, 25 feet deep and 45 feet wide, which was the home of the reigning Great Sun. Eight large houses at ground level were occupied by members of the ruling family; behind these were smaller houses where the other members of the village lived.

The Natchez were divided into four classes: the Suns, the Nobles, the Honored People, and the Commoners. Although some aspects of Natchez social organization are ambiguous, certain things are clear. The Suns,

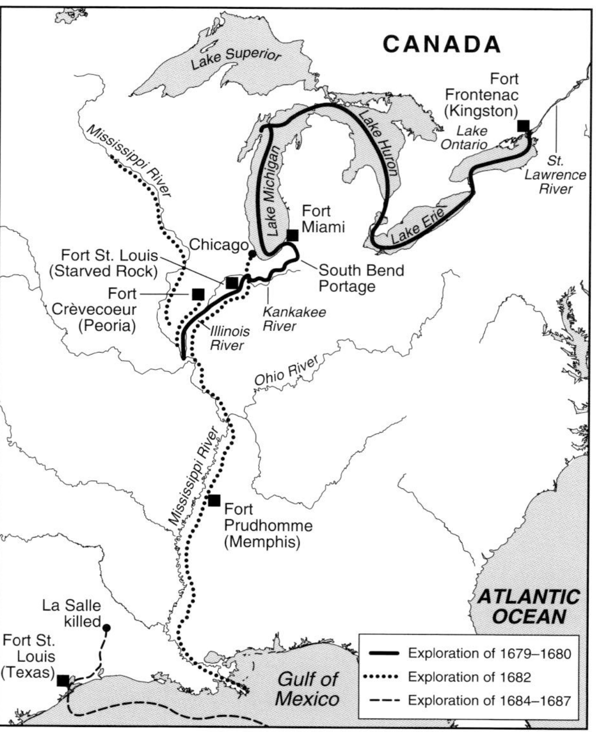

Fig. 4 Map of the eastern half of North America showing the path of French explorer René-Robert Cavelier, Sieur de La Salle (1643–1687). Starting in 1679, La Salle voyaged from the Great Lakes down the Mississippi River to the Gulf of Mexico, leading France to claim the entire Mississippi River valley under the name of Louisiana.

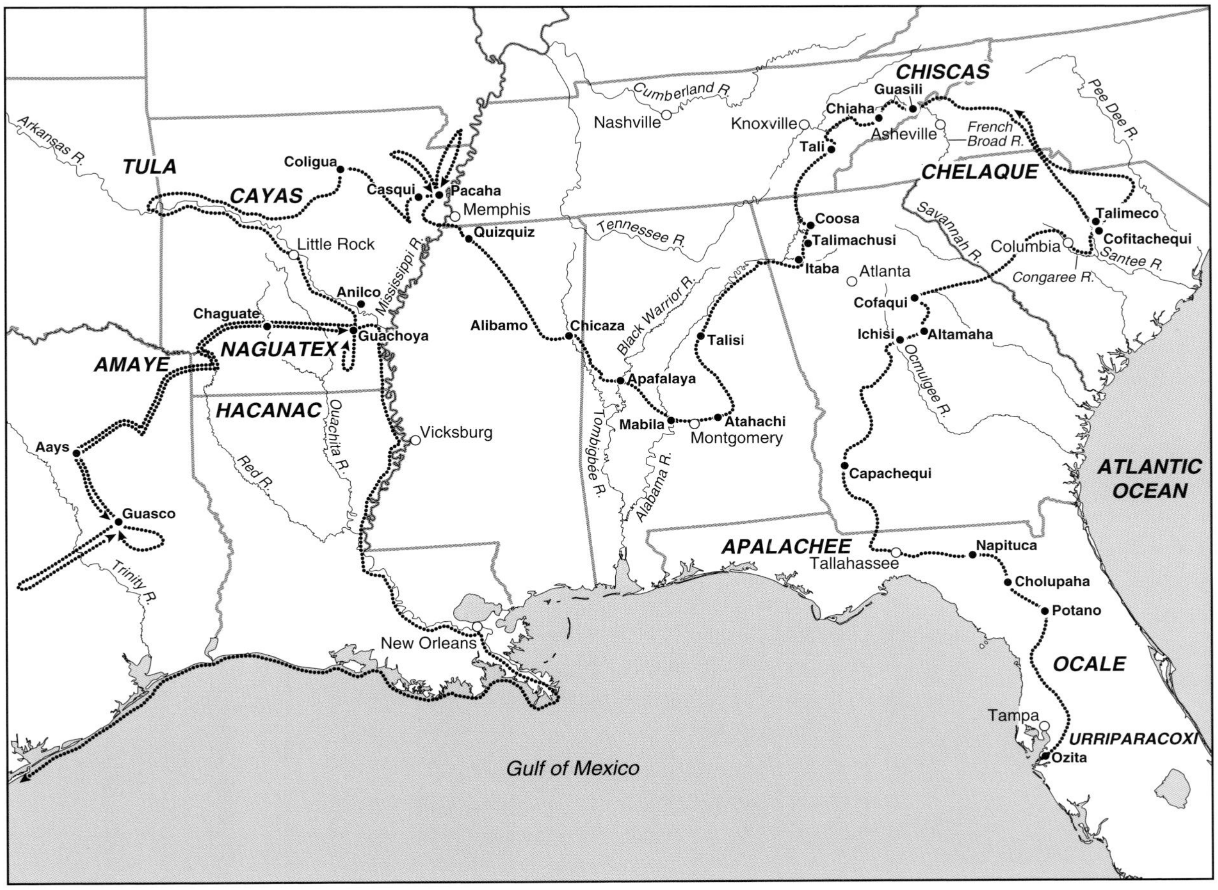

Fig. 5 Map of the Southeast showing the path of Spanish explorer Hernando de Soto (1496–1542) from 1539 to 1543; after Hudson 1997.

occupying the apex of the Natchez social pyramid, belonged to a lineage in which membership was ascribed matrilineally. All members of the Sun lineage married Commoners. All children of Sun mothers were members of the Sun lineage and it was the eldest male child of one of these women who filled the office of the Great Sun. On the other hand, all children of Sun men, including those of the Great Sun himself, belonged to the Noble class. The Honored People class was composed of individuals who were more distantly related to the Sun lineage or who had been elevated to this position for their services to the Great Sun. These three classes formed a ruling elite, whose members had rights and privileges that distinguished them from each other as well as the Commoners below them. For instance, only men of the ranking classes could wear black breechcloths and only women of these classes could wear feather-covered mantles. Tattooing was likewise limited to the members of these classes.

The greatest distinctions, however, were allocated to the Great Sun and the members of his lineage. The Great Sun was considered divine, a god-king on earth, and both the political and religious leader of the society. The line of succession was clear; the eldest son of the eldest sister of the reigning Great Sun would succeed his uncle. The authority of the Great Sun over his people, unlike the leaders of neighboring peoples, was absolute, and he could and did at times put individuals to death for even trivial offenses. He had a number of personal retainers and slaves to serve him. When he traveled he was carried in a canopied litter on the backs of eight servants. The people had to speak to him from a distance, bowing and facing him. When they left his presence they had to back away from him.

Possibly the greatest distinction between members of the Sun lineage and the others was not their treatment in life but in death. At the death of any of the members of the lineage, their spouses were sacrificed to accompany them spiritually. When more important members of the lineage died, even greater numbers of people were killed. In 1725, at the burial of Tattooed Serpent, the war leader and younger brother of the Great Sun, eight men and women, including his two wives, were ritually sacrificed. In addition, a family of Commoners strangled one of their children out of respect.

Unlike any other people in French Louisiana, the Natchez fascinated the French settlers and explorers who wrote about them. Nevertheless, in a series of wars between 1716 and 1731, the French destroyed the Grand Village and the Natchez way of life altogether.

Who Were the Moundbuilders?

In the waning decades of the eighteenth century, following the American Revolution, English-speaking settlers began flooding the Appalachian Mountains and the Ohio and Tennessee river valleys. As they cleared the forests to establish towns, they began exposing first hundreds and then thousands of vast earthworks and temple and burial mounds. Digging into these mounds, early archaeologists began to uncover finely fashioned pots and stone and even metal figures and tools. The size and numbers of these earthworks and the quality of the goods contained in their burials left no doubts in the minds of these amateur archaeologists that they had discovered a great and unknown civilization. The question was, who were these people?

Few settlers thought that the local Indian peoples were related to the builders of these earthworks. The construction of these mounds required engineering skills, strong leadership, and large numbers of laborers working over long periods of time—all of which the native tribes currently lacked. Neither did the native craftspeople have the technical skills needed to produce the impressive grave goods found in the mounds. Finally, the native peoples of the region did not construct mounds, nor did any of them have oral traditions relating to these earthworks. Among the many theories concerning the moundbuilders, one idea that gained wide acceptance posited a highly civilized "Lost Race" whom the contemporary Indians had earlier destroyed. Through most of the nineteenth century this controversy over the moundbuilders would rage in the academic community. Only in the 1890s did research show that the ancestors of the native Indians had indeed constructed these great earthworks.

The World De Soto Found

In 1539 Hernando de Soto and six hundred Spanish soldiers landed at Tampa Bay, the largest and best-equipped army of conquistadors ever organized in Spanish America. Unlike the English and French who came later, De Soto and his men did not find a vast uninhabited wilderness. The valleys they traveled were densely populated, with towns that were not merely larger versions of the dependent farm villages that surrounded them, but the political and religious centers of powerful chiefdoms. Many were simple chiefdoms, such as the Natchez, with a single divine-chief, a central town, and a series of dependent villages. Still others were paramount chiefdoms, in which numerous simple chiefdoms—by alliance or conquest—were dependent and subordinate to a central more powerful figure. The largest and the most powerful of the paramount chiefdoms De Soto encountered was Coosa. According to their accounts, they marched for six days through dependent villages before nearing the capital itself. The dependent chiefdoms and villages of Coosa stretched for four hundred miles along a northeast-southwest axis, from the upper Tennessee River in eastern Tennessee, through northwest Georgia to the Coosa and Alabama rivers in central Alabama.[4]

The capital towns of these chiefdoms were basically similar in plan to that of the Grand Village of the Natchez: open plazas surrounded by large mounds, on top of which were elaborate temples or houses of the rulers. One of the most impressive of the temples was at Talomeco (or Talimeco), in present-day South Carolina (others say near Augusta, Georgia):

> More than a hundred paces long and forty wide; the wall were high . . . and the roof was very high and steeply pitched. . . . On the roof . . . had been placed many shells. . . . the inner side on top because of its greater luster. . . . Near the [large] door(s) were twelve giant figures carved from wood, such faithful imitations of life. . . . had [they] been in the most famous temples of Rome . . . [they] would have been esteemed and valued for their grandeur and perfection.
>
> The upper part of the temple about the walls was adorned like the roof outside with periwinkles and shell . . . with skeins between them made of strings of pearls and seed pearls hanging from the roof. . . . On the floor against the walls . . . were the chests that served as sepulchers, in which were the bodies of the [chiefs] . . . and their sons and brother and nephews. . . . No others were buried in that temple. . . . Exactly one vara above each chest was a statue carved from wood. . . . This was a portrait taken while living of the deceased man or woman.[5]

The Spanish chronicler also noted that other rooms held wooden chests filled with pearls, white deerskins, and weapons of various types.

The native leaders they encountered did not rely on influence and consensus, but like the Great Sun of the Natchez were apparently divine rulers with absolute authority and power. When the expedition reached the banks of the river separating them from the town of Cutifachiqui (or Cofitachequi), a woman chief "came from the town in a carrying chair in which certain principal Indians carried her to the river. She entered a canoe with an awning at the stern and on the bottom of which was already spread a mat for her and above it two cushions one on top of the other, on which she seated herself."[6] Perhaps the most spectacular meeting was with the paramount chief of Coosa, who "came out to welcome [De Soto] . . . in a carrying chair carried on the shoulders of his principal men, seated on a cushion, and covered with a robe of marten skins. . . . He wore a crown of feathers on his head; and around about him were many Indians playing and singing."[7]

Had any early archaeologists accompanied De Soto, it would not have taken them almost a century to determine that the moundbuilders were ancestors of the native Indian tribes. Had any of the French authors who wrote about the Natchez accompanied De Soto, they would not have thought them to be unusual in the least. They would have realized that the Natchez were merely the last surviving Mississippian chiefdom.

The Collapse of the Mississippian Chiefdoms

In less than one hundred and fifty years, the towns and cities that De Soto and his men saw and conquered were gone. Unknowingly, De Soto himself witnessed the fate that was soon to befall these chiefdoms. At Talomeco they found an abandoned town of five hundred houses, its fields chock-full with weeds. They were told that a few years earlier the town had been struck by a pestilence that had killed many of the people and caused the survivors to flee. Some iron tools found at the deserted town showed that these people had already come in contact with Europeans, most likely the Spanish settlers at San Miguel de Guadalupe, a coastal settlement founded in 1526 and abandoned the following year.[8]

It was not until the 1960s that scholars began to recognize the role that the introduction of Old World diseases had played in the history of the Americas. The Spanish and other Europeans introduced into the New World a host of diseases for which the native peoples had no natural immunities: smallpox, malaria, measles, yellow fever, influenza, pneumonic plague, bubonic plague, and many more. Generations of exposure to these diseases had created some natural immunity in European populations, but in the Americas they took the form of "virgin-soil" epidemics. Having no natural immunities, Mississippian peoples were far more vulnerable to virulent epidemics. In 1738 an outbreak of smallpox killed half of the Cherokee. Twenty years later about half of the Catawba died from the same disease, and in the 1830s it felled almost half of the Plains Indians. But the problem was not one of single epidemics, but one of recurring outbreaks, generation after generation.[9] The combined effects were catastrophic: from a possible population of a million or more, we can estimate that by the late eighteenth century the core group of Mississippian peoples numbered less than 150,000.[10]

These epidemics not only destroyed most of the population of these chiefdoms but also wreaked havoc with their cultural institutions and political structures as well. At times whole generations within these societies must have been destroyed, leaving gaps in the lines of succession and in the process of transmitting cultural knowledge. Deaths within the ruling lineages would have created conflicts and disputes between surviving members over who should fill the leadership positions. The most important cultural and sacred knowledge was known only by select members of priesthoods, and their deaths undoubtedly left important gaps in the orally transmitted, collective knowledge of the society. Similarly, highly skilled craftspeople would have died without passing on their skills and technical knowledge. Even in communities where these principal figures survived, the base populations may have been too small to support the complex superstructure of such chiefdoms.

Mississippians of the Postcontact Era

In a general sense all of the farming peoples of eastern North America from the eastern edge of the Great Plains to the Atlantic Coast and from the Great Lakes to the Gulf of Mexico were "Mississippian peoples." The area in which this civilization reached its highest levels of development and intensity, however, was far more restricted. The core area of Mississippian civilization was in the Mississippi valley and the valleys of its major tributaries, the Ohio, the Tennessee, the lower Missouri, the lower Arkansas, and the lower Red River, together with the coastal plain along the Gulf. The postcontact peoples of this area were the descendants

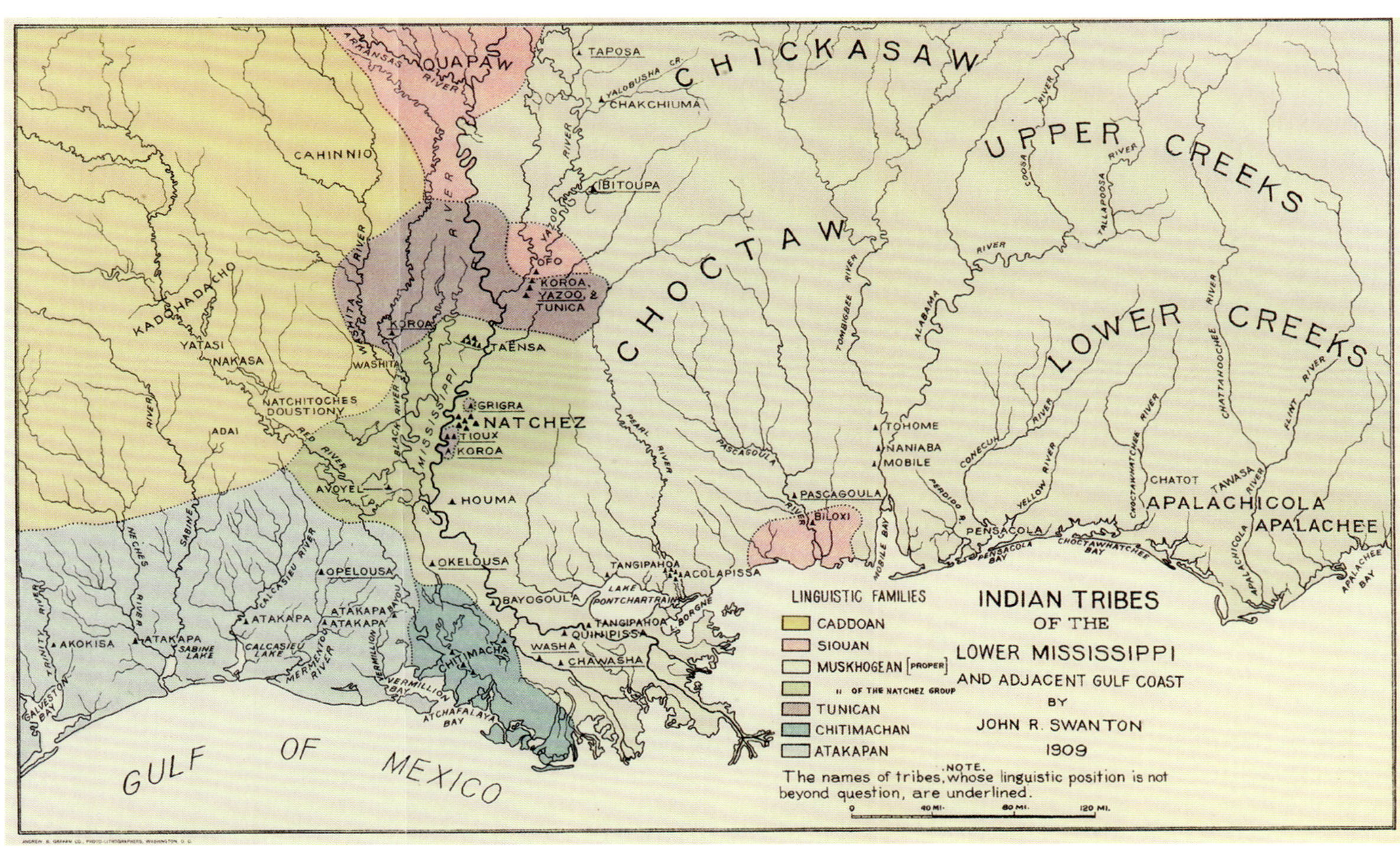

Fig. 6 Map of Indian tribal regions of the lower Mississippi and adjacent Gulf Coast; from Swanton 1911.

of the peoples most directly linked to the development of the great Mississippian chiefdoms (fig. 6). They were the true Mississippians.

The Mississippians were not a single group of people; in fact, linguistically, they were extremely diverse. Concentrated in the upper Mississippi valley and the lower Missouri and Arkansas valleys were the Dhegiha and Chiwere Siouan-speaking peoples (the Osage, Kansa, Omaha, Ponca, Quapaw, Otoe, Missouri, Ioway, and Winnebago). South and west of these Siouan speakers were Caddoan speakers (the historic Wichita, Caddo, and Pawnee). In the Ohio valley were the central Algonquian peoples (the historic Kickapoo, Shawnee, Sauk, Fox, Peoria, Illini, Wea, and Miami). East of the Mississippi River and south of the Tennessee, and stretching to the Gulf and Atlantic coasts was a region primarily occupied by Muskhogean peoples (the Choctaw, Chickasaw, and the so-called Muskogee/Creek), a highly diverse grouping that encompassed Hitchiti-, Apalachee-, Alabama-, and Koasati-speaking people. Widely scattered through this same region were other linguistically distinct groups, some of whom were linguistic isolates, such as the Natchez, Yuchi, and Timucua, while others spoke Iroquoian languages (the Cherokee) and other Siouan languages (the Biloxi, Ofo, and Catawba). South of the Arkansas River and west of the Mississippi (fig. 6), most of the peoples spoke an Atakapan language (the Chitimacha and Tunica).[11]

Except for the Timucua and Apalachee in northern Florida who had been conquered and missionized by the Spanish at the turn of the seventeenth century, most of the Mississippian peoples only came into continuous contact with Europeans in the last decades of the seventeenth century. In the late 1600s French and English fur and hide traders began expanding the range of their trade networks west and south, until by the early 1700s virtually all of these peoples were being visited by traders with some regularity.

The fur and hide trade refocused the lives of these tribes, as an ever-expanding array of trade goods quickly became necessities. Of greatest initial interest were guns and metal goods such as knives, tomahawks, axes, awls, scissors, needles, files, saws, iron kettles, and brass buckets. As the trade continued, however, still other goods became important: trade blankets, cloth, beads, yarn, ribbon, and silver jewelry. Trade had both positive and negative effects on these tribes. Guns and metal tools made their lives easier and more productive whether they were hunting, farming, or performing daily tasks about the village. Blankets, cloth, beads, yarn, and ribbon changed their style of dress and many other aspects of their material lives.[12] At the same time, trade also greatly increased intertribal warfare.

While all of these tribes had contact with either French or English traders by the early 1700s, some had a more regular and dependable supply than others. This was particularly critical in the case of guns, parts for which wore out quickly or broke. The use of guns also required a steady supply of lead balls, European gunflints, and gunpowder. Differences in the volume and regularity of trade quickly disrupted the prevailing balances of power within the region.

To acquire trade goods, the tribes had first to produce something to trade. The main trade item of native groups were fur and hides: deer and elk hides, bear skins, and the pelts of highly valued smaller animals such as fox, beaver, otter, martin, weasel, wolf, and wildcat. The over-hunting of these animals in the traditional hunting areas soon resulted in the better-armed and thus more powerful tribes expanding their hunting ranges at the expense of weaker tribes.

The major cause of conflict, however, was the Indian slave trade. Both the French and English traders encouraged the tribes to raid for captives, whom they could then trade as slaves. Raiding for captives and the expansion of hunting territories were complementary. Although the Indian slave trade began in the late 1600s and persisted into the early nineteenth century throughout the entire area, the intensity of slave warfare varied greatly from one region to the next and from one time period to the next. The tribes who suffered the most were the Caddoan-speaking peoples on the Arkansas and the missionized Timucua in northern Florida. The severity of these raids began to subside by the mid-eighteenth century, when the villages of the Caddoan-speaking peoples along the Arkansas had been abandoned due to raids by their Siouan neighbors. The survivors had fled: the Wichita south to the Red River, and the Pawnee north to the Platte.[13] In Florida, the Indian mission villages had been destroyed and the Timucua were on the verge of extinction.[14]

In 1763 following the English victory over the French at Quebec, French Louisiana was divided. The English claimed the portion east of the Mississippi, and the Spanish the portion west of the river. In that same year King George III issued a proclamation that drew a new boundary line down the crest of the Appalachians. English colonists would not be allowed to settle west of this line in the territory that had been French Louisiana. This legal barrier to the westward expansion of the settlements was not to last long, however, as the American Revolution and independence quickly erased this barrier.[15]

Manifest Destiny and the Indians

Even before the Revolution was over, small groups of settlers began to venture beyond the Appalachian Mountains. At the end of the Revolution, this trickle became a torrent. During the Colonial period the leading tribes of the region had—to varying degrees of success—attempted diplomatically to play the English, French, and Spanish against one another. With the Americans the problem was very different. Many of the tribes had sided with the British during the Revolution. They were now left virtually on their own to face the hostile American settlers who wanted their land.

Scattered, and increasingly outnumbered by American settlers, many tribes began to fragment. Starting in 1787 the Spanish government of Louisiana had officially started to encourage these tribes to migrate.[16] By 1797 there were already small settlements of Shawnee, Peoria, Illini, Miami, Kickapoo, and Sauk on the lower Missouri.[17] In 1802, five hundred families of Shawnee, Miami, Chickasaw, Cherokee, and Peoria were reported living on the St. Francis River in eastern Arkansas.[18] While most fled westward across the Mississippi to Spanish Louisiana, some communities of Muskogee/Creek fled south to Spanish Florida to join their kinsmen already there, later becoming known as the Seminole.

Others turned to the British, now in Canada, for support. Relying on promises of British aid, the Miami in 1794 attempted to fight, only to be crushed at the Battle of Fallen Timbers. Realizing that the individual tribes were too small to resist successfully, the Shawnee chief Tecumseh visited the Choctaw, Creek, and other tribes to urge a united opposition to the American onslaught. While he was still visiting tribes in the South, American troops had advanced on his main village in Indiana. The ensuing Battle of Tippecanoe—though a draw—proved a defeat for Tecumseh. The next year, the War of 1812 broke out. Tecumseh, the Shawnees, and their northern allies joined the British forces in Canada. In the South, encouraged by British agents in Florida, most of the Muskogee/Creeks rebelled and destroyed Fort Mims. Tecumseh was killed at the Battle of the Thames in the fall of 1813, and in the following spring the Muskogee/Creeks were defeated at the Battle of Horseshoe Bend, with the loss of eight hundred men. With these defeats, the power of the tribes east of the Mississippi was broken.[19]

As president, Thomas Jefferson realized that he faced two problems on the western frontier. White farmers were filling the land beyond the Appalachians so rapidly that they would soon be in need of additional land to settle. The other question concerned what to do with the native Indian population. One of the arguments in support of the purchase of Louisiana in 1803 was that it could be used as a home for the eastern tribes. Jefferson suggested to the Chickasaw in 1805 and to the Choctaw in 1808 that they should move west of the Mississippi. Neither group agreed at the time. In 1808 one group of Cherokee leaders did agree to exchange the lands held by their followers for new lands in the West, but most of the Cherokees remained in their homelands. The process of piecemeal relocation of small groups of eastern Indians continued through the 1820s.[20]

In 1830 Congress passed the Indian Removal Act, creating the idea of an Indian frontier in the West. Under the provisions of this act, treaties were to be negotiated with the remaining tribes to exchange their lands east of the Mississippi for new lands in the West. The government would provide funds and transport for their removal. By fair means or foul, treaties were negotiated, and one by one, voluntarily or by force, the tribes were removed to their new homes.[21] By 1839 almost 75,000 Indians—not counting those who died along the way—had been removed over the "Trails of Tears" (see fig. 8 in Kent Reilly's interview with Joyce and Turner Bear).[22] Not all were removed. Some families and small groups hid out in the mountains or forests and tried to be inconspicuous. The only group successfully to resist removal were the Seminole. It took the government three wars to decide that it was

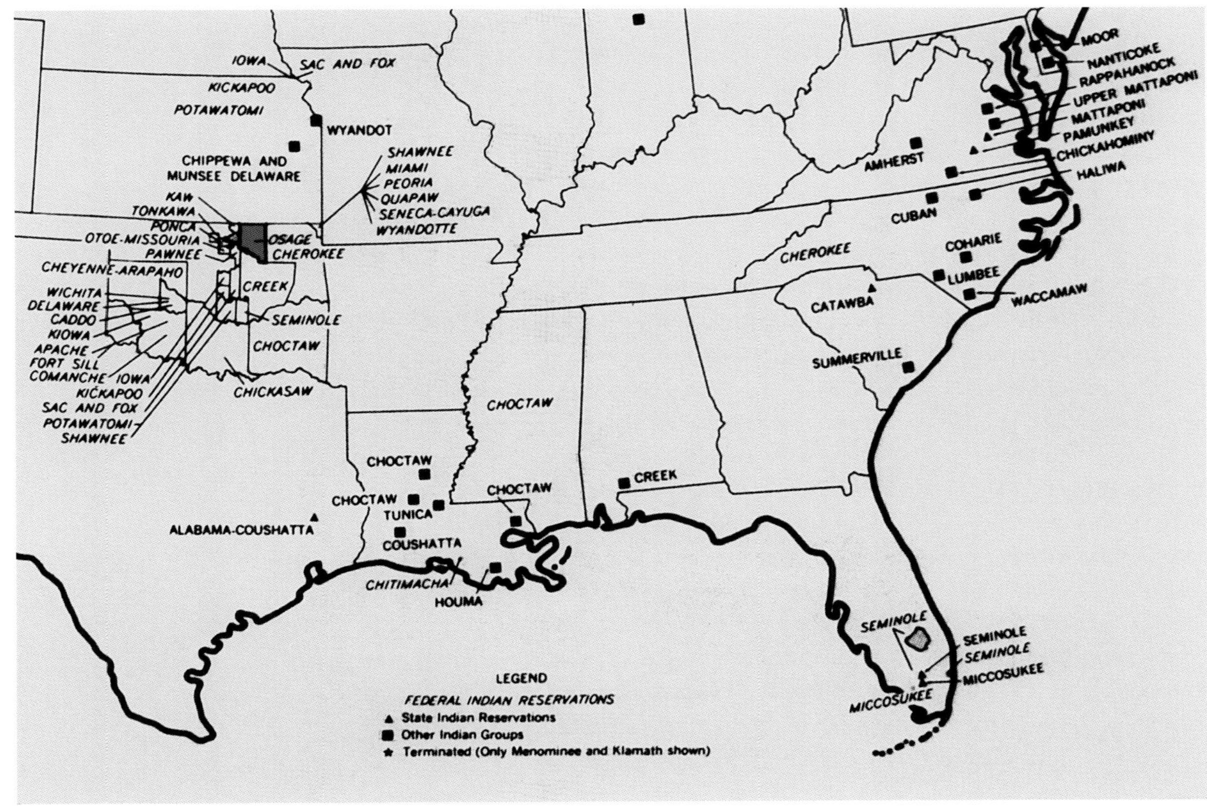

Fig. 7 Map of the greater southeastern United States showing Indian lands and communities; from Taylor 1972, p. 175.

best just to ignore the Seminole and let them remain in the swamps of southern Florida.

The new home for these displaced peoples was the so-called Indian Territory, the eastern edge of which was described by a line drawn north from the Red River to the Missouri River, and then north up the west bank of the Missouri—the present eastern boundaries of Kansas and Oklahoma. The eastern tribes were given new reservations here, where it was thought that these tribes could live forever, isolated from and unmolested by white settlers (figs. 1 and 8). Yet, in the 1850s, as pressure from white settlers for still more farmland increased, the federal government redefined and reduced the size of the Indian Territory. Only the southern part, present-day Oklahoma, would remain Indian Territory, and the government began negotiating treaties with tribes to move outside this reduced area.

After the Civil War, under pressure to make still more land available for settlement, the government again changed its Indian policy.[23] Recognizing that white settlers wanted access to virtually all of the land in the United States, a totally new policy was developed toward the Indians. There would be no reservations, no tribal governments, as there would soon be no Indians. As one Commissioner of Indian Affairs summarized it, "the American Indian was to become the Indian American."[24] Thus, in the last decades of the nineteenth century, the government began the process of attempting to destroy the Indian communities and their cultures to promote the assimilation of Indians into the general society.

There were three main facets to this new policy, the most important of which was the passage of the General Indian Allotment Act of 1887, designed to destroy Indian community life and tribal governments. The act provided for the abolishment of the communal ownership of reservation land by giving title in fee simple to individual Indians. Tribal governments would be dissolved, as would reservations, with any surplus land being opened for non-Indian settlement. To destroy Indian culture, the government turned to education and the courts. Instead of being ignored or left to missionaries, Indian education was now seen as a priority by government officials: it was to be one of the main tools by which Indian culture was to be destroyed. Boarding schools were to be established and Indian education made mandatory for school-age children. In these schools, separated from their families, Indian students would not be allowed to speak their native language, wear their native clothing, or practice their native religion. Isolated from their families and communities often for years at a time, Indian children were indoctrinated with Western cultural beliefs and values.[25] In the words of Captain Pratt, the head of Carlisle Indian School, the purpose of Indian education was to "kill the Indian to save the man."[26]

Finally, using Courts of Indian Offenses, the Department of the Interior developed its own criminal code to be applied to Indians, prohibiting, for example, "certain old heathen and barbarous customs." Hair codes were adopted on some reservations and certain burial practices, dances, and religious ceremonial were outlawed on others. Violators were punished with fines or even imprisonment.[27] These courts, according to the Department of the Interior, were "educational and disciplinary instrumentalities, by which the government . . . is endeavoring to improve and elevate the condition of these dependent tribes."[28] By the early twentieth century, the policies designed to assimilate and acculturate the Indians were fully operative and this governmental program of forcibly assimilating the American Indians into mainstream America persisted until the late 1960s.

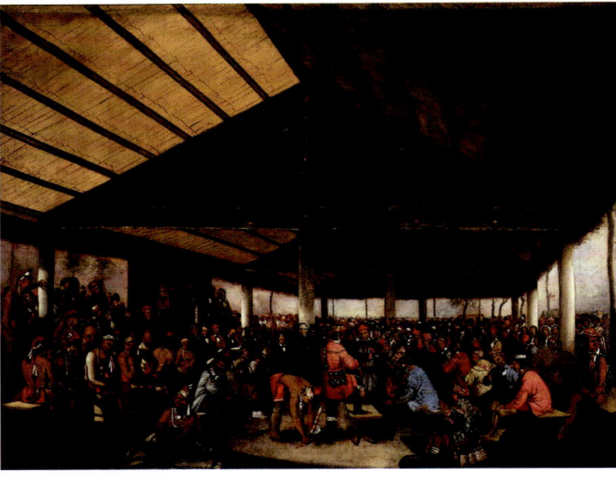

Fig. 8 John Mix Stanley (American; 1814–1872), *International Indian Council (Held at Tahlequah, Indian Territory, 1843)*, 1843; oil on canvas, 80 x 102.9 cm; Smithsonian American Art Museum, gift of the Misses Henry, 1985.66.248,934B.

The Mississippians Today

Few peoples in the world have been subject to such socially and culturally destructive forces as the Mississippian peoples. Over the past five hundred years these tribes have seen most of their population destroyed by recurrent epidemic diseases and wars. They have witnessed their traditional way of life vanish and have been subjected to the assimilationist policies of an overwhelmingly powerful dominant society determined to destroy their identities, communities, and culture. Yet in spite of these destructive forces, more than one hundred thousand descendants of the Mississippian peoples still remain active members of socially cohesive and culturally distinct tribal communities, most of which today are widely dispersed and far removed from their original homelands (fig. 7). The greatest concentration of these communities is in Oklahoma, where the Cherokee, Choctaw, Chickasaw, Muskogee/Creek, Seminole, Yuchi, Natchez, Quapaw, Miami, Peoria, Shawnee, Kickapoo, Sac and Fox, Ioway, Otoe-Missouri, Osage, Kansa, Ponca, Caddo, Pawnee, and Wichita are located. To the north in Nebraska and Kansas, there are communities of Kickapoo, Ioway, Sac and Fox, Winnebago, Omaha, and Ponca. Far to the south are the Kickapoo in northern Mexico, the Alabama-Coushatta in east Texas and Louisiana, and the Seminole and Miccosukee in Florida. Only a small number of these communities still survive in what were their historic homelands, the North Carolina Cherokee, the Mississippi Choctaw, the Alabama

Creek, the Miami in Indiana, the Ho-Chunk (Winnebago) in Wisconsin, the Mesquakie (Fox) in Iowa, the Catawba in South Carolina, and the Chitimacha, Tunica, Houma, and Choctaw communities in Louisiana.[29]

The Mississippian peoples were never a culturally homogeneous group. Five hundred years of exposure and adaptation to European peoples and culture has dramatically changed their lives and cultures. Today there is even greater social and cultural variability both within and between the members of these communities than at any time in the past. In most communities the traditional language is on the verge of extinction, if not already extinct. In very few communities do any members still live in traditional dwellings or retain much in the way of traditional material culture in their daily lives. In these respects, most members of the community are virtually indistinguishable from their non-Indian neighbors. And even those cultural characteristic that are identified as "traditional" or "Indian"—such as styles of traditional dress, food, and dances—actually evolved during the historic period. While most of the "traditional" cultural practices of these communities reflect historic borrowings and adaptations from Europeans, within each of these communities there are still some tangible links to their Mississippian past. Many communities still use songs, prayers, and sacred objects to practice religious rituals and ceremonies that have continued unbroken from those of their Mississippian ancestors. In still other communities, certain craft items such as basketry, carving, and leatherwork show direct linkage to their early ancestors. Continuity is also frequently found in their social institutions. Clan systems, which long predate European arrival in the Americas, still function within many of these communities. While most of the modern communities are the result of the fusion and fragmentation of earlier communities during the historic period, some communities themselves show direct continuity with communities that existed long before contact. While these communities have maintained certain tangible social and cultural characteristics and practices that are directly derived from those of their Mississippian ancestors, the greatest continuity is found in the less tangible expressions of their culture.

Mississippian civilization did not consist solely of mound complexes, finely crafted objects, villages, cities, and divine rulers. The true core of Mississippian civilization was not found in the tangible expressions of their culture but rather in their way of viewing the world and the role of human beings. Among other things, it was a world that valued social relationships over material goods. It was a world that valued each individual, while at the same time viewing the life of an individual as having meaning and purpose only within the context of serving the community. It is in this unique worldview that one finds the true continuity in Mississippian culture and the cohesive force that has kept and continues to keep their communities dynamic and viable.

The songs of the *Wa-xo'-be* and associated rituals have long been forgotten by the Osage people. Yet just as Saucy Calf remembered those songs that were of "importance," so do the Osage people today still remember those things that are important. The underlying ideas, cultural values, and social norms expressed in these songs and rituals are still very much alive today, though now imbedded in new sociocultural practices and institutions. So it is with the other communities as well. Even though the lives of the members of these communities today appear very different from those of their ancestors, they still view the world and the role of humans in the same basic way as did their Mississippian ancestors. They have retained those things that are of true importance.

Notes

1. La Flesche 1930, p. 678; see also Bailey 1995, pp. 80, 220–21.
2. See Billington 1960, pp. 15–102.
3. For a summary account of the Natchez, see Oswalt 2002, pp. 421–22.
4. See Smith 2000, pp. 34–49.
5. Quoted in Clayton, Knight, and Moore 1993, vol. 2, pp. 298–99, 301–02.
6. Quoted in Clayton, Knight, and Moore 1993, vol. 1, p. 82.
7. Clayton, Knight, and Moore 1993, vol. 1, p. 92.
8. Clayton, Knight, and Moore 1993, vol. 2, p. 298; Smith 2000, pp. 83–84.
9. Crosby 1976; see also Dobyns and Swagerty 1983; Thornton 1987; and Verano and Ubelaker 1992.
10. Estimate of precontact populations vary widely; see Thornton, Warren, and Miller 1992. The figure of 150,000 is based on the tribal estimates of Mooney as given in Kroeber 1939, pp. 138–41.
11. See Kroeber 1939 and Goddard 1996, pp. 4–10.
12. For a summary of effects of the fur and hide trade on material life, see Chandler 1973.
13. Bailey 1973, pp. 33–45.
14. Hudson 1976, pp. 435–36.
15. Billington 1960.
16. Kinnaird 1949, vol. 3.
17. Nasatir 1952, vol. 2, p. 529.
18. Foreman 1936, p. 28.
19. See Horsman 1988.
20. See Prucha 1988 and Strickland 1982, pp. 74–81, for brief general accounts; and Foreman 1936 for more specific data concerning the immigrant tribes west of the Mississippi during this period.
21. See Prucha 1988; Strickland 1982, pp. 81–92; and Foreman 1932, Foreman 1933, and Foreman 1946.
22. See Farnham 1906, p. 121, for a partial census by tribe.
23. See Hagan 1988; and Strickland 1982, pp. 127–43.
24. Quoted in Strickland 1982, p. 139.
25. Strickland 1982, pp. 139–41; and Szasz 1974, pp. 8–15.
26. Quoted in Oswalt 2002, p. 46.
27. See Strickland 1982, p. 141.
28. Quoted in Strickland 1982, p. 251.
29. This listing is based on Taylor 1972, pp. 226–45. There are still other small Indian communities that are not included in this listing.

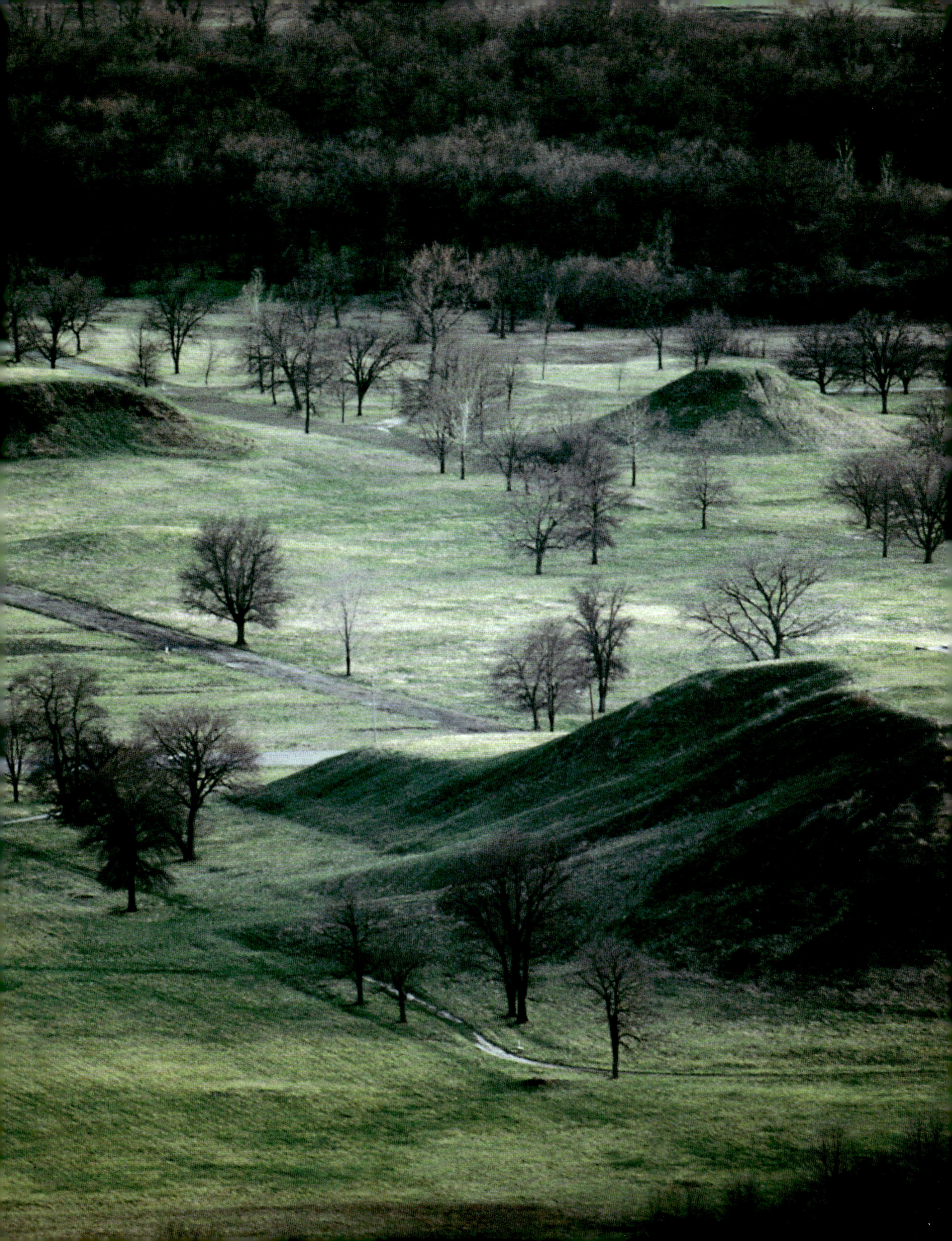

The Cahokia Site and Its People

Robert L. Hall

Fig. 1 View looking southwest over Monks Mound and the grand ceremonial plaza of Cahokia in St. Clair County, Illinois.

Introduction

When Hernando de Soto's band of adventurers crossed the southeastern United States in 1539–43, they witnessed the living, vibrant cultures of moundbuilding American Indians (see fig. 5 in the essay by Garrick Bailey). Unlike settlers in the nineteenth century, these Spaniards had no need to invent a mythical race of moundbuilders to account for the earthen monuments they beheld, because the leaders of the Natchez Indians they met in Mississippi lived in mound-top lodges and honored their ancestors in mound-top temples and did so well into the 1700s. One such temple belonging to the Natchez was visited by a Dutch-born planter, Le Page du Pratz, who portrayed its appearance and described its contents in 1758.[1] This active mound culture was one of the last recorded in the U.S.

If a traveler of Du Pratz's day had ventured farther north up the Mississippi River and into the Illinois country, he would have soon found himself in the colonial settlement of Cahokia, a French village named for the Cahokias, a branch of the Illiniwek or Illinois Indian nation. Beyond French Cahokia, he would have encountered Cahokia Creek where it enters the Mississippi River, and following the creek eastward toward the bluffs, this traveler would before long have come to a towering, man-made mountain of earth with a commanding view of the Mississippi bottomland—a massive construction that could have been visible an hour before actually arriving at its foot. This earthen monument

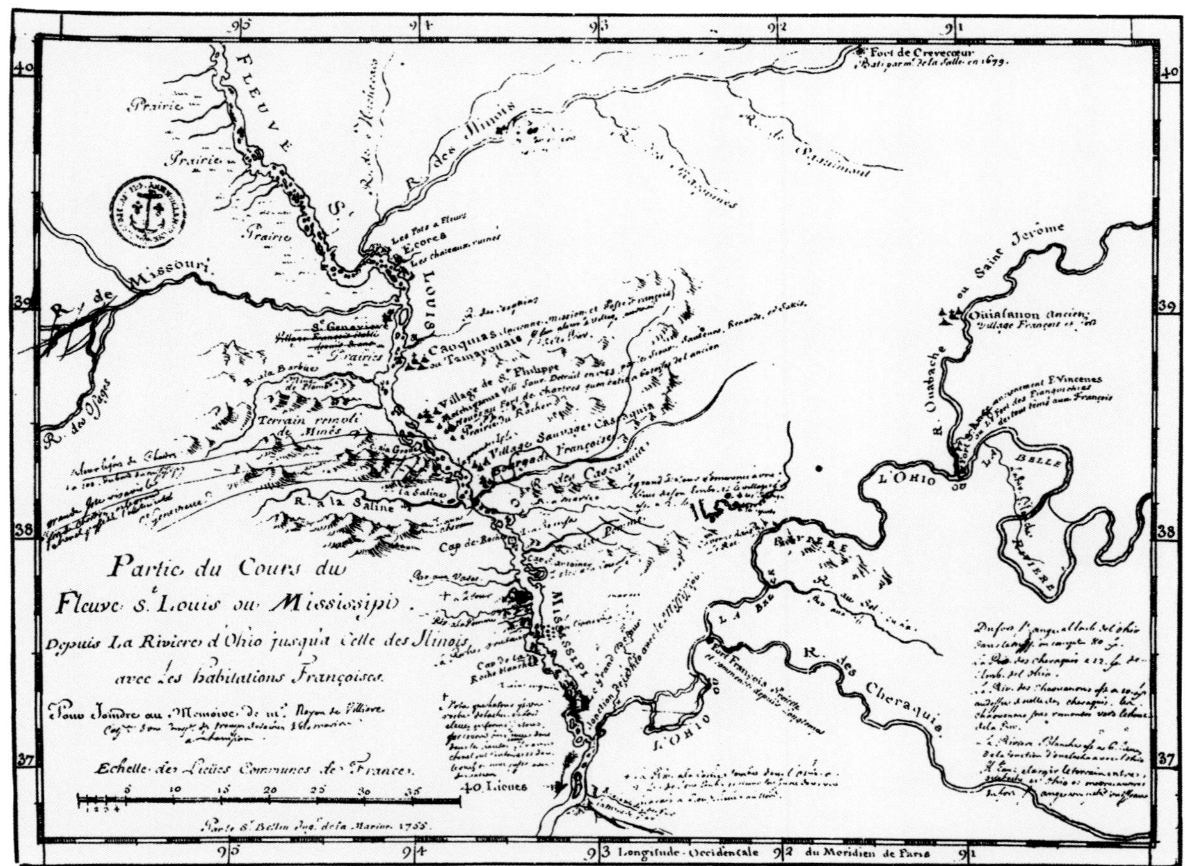

Fig. 2 French map of Illinois region, produced by Jacques Nicolas Bellin in 1755 (with later manuscript corrections) to accompany a memoir by the French captain Pierre Joseph de Neyon de Villiers. This map charts the Ohio, Mississippi, Missouri, and Illinois rivers, as well as settlements of the Kaskaskia, Cahokia, and Tamaroa Indians.

would become known generations later as Monks Mound (fig. 1). From its summit, close to a thousand years ago, a native-born lord could survey the inner precincts of a domain that extended beyond the power of human sight to see. There was no greater prehistoric temple platform in the Americas north of Mexico than Monks Mound. Borrowing a name with local roots, archaeologists have called the Monks Mound location Cahokia.

The American Bottom

France ceded control of the Cahokia area to Great Britain in 1763. When, twenty years later, Britain herself lost control of the Cahokia area to the United States, former colonists began to settle the extensive flood plain east of the Mississippi and opposite St. Louis. The American Bottom—as this region has long been called—was a wide and well-defined natural area of easily cultivated soils and marshy lakes, begotten when the Mississippi River changed its course from century to century and left relics of itself along its former course.[2] During the French regime, a mission station had been built on Monks Mound itself, ministering to the Cahokia-Illinois Indians from 1735 to 1752 (fig. 2).[3]

The name Monks Mound comes not from this French mission, which included a chapel on a terrace of Monks Mound, but from a later establishment of Trappist monks who lived at the foot of Monks Mound

Fig. 3 Karl Bodmer (Swiss; 1809–1893), *Prehistoric Indian Mounds Opposite St. Louis*, n.d.; ink over pencil on paper, 27.3 × 41.3 cm; Joslyn Art Museum, Omaha, Nebraska. Bodmer accompanied Prince Maximilian of Wied-Neuwied on a expedition across North America and made these sketches of Monks Mound at Cahokia in the early 1830s.

Fig. 4 Karl Bodmer, *Trappists Hill Opposite St. Louis*, n.d.; pencil and ink on paper, 25.4 × 31.8 cm; Joslyn Art Museum, Omaha, Nebraska.

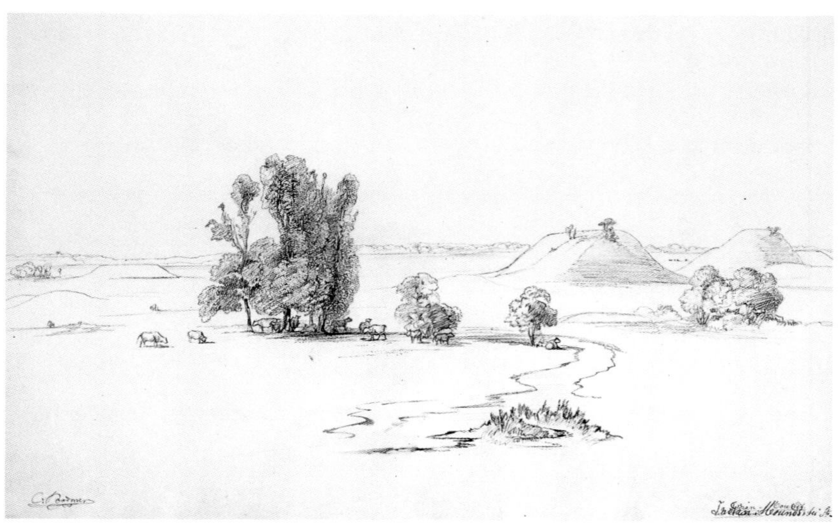

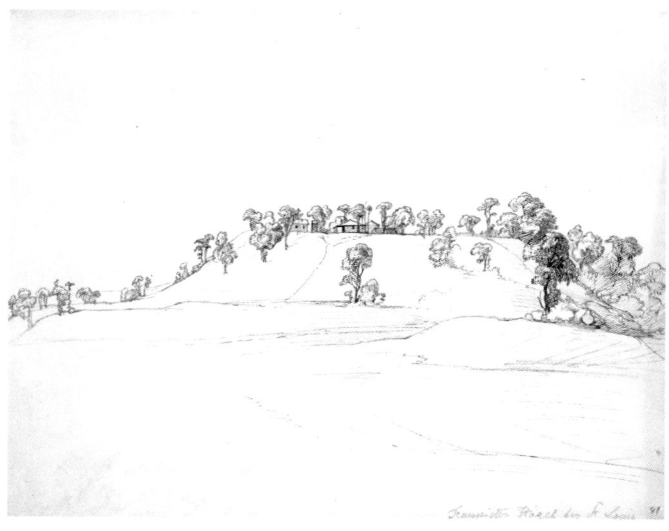

from 1809 to 1813 (figs. 3–4). This settlement existed well after American control of the area was established. In recent decades, excavations by archaeologists from the University of Wisconsin–Milwaukee have uncovered not only the foundations of the 1735 mission chapel but also an adjacent cemetery for native converts, all on a single lower terrace of Monks Mound.[4] It is all the more surprising then that despite more than a century of European and American occupation of the American Bottom, it was not until 1808 that anyone interpreted the particular environs of the Cahokia site as a scene of ancient human activity (fig. 5).

While running a government survey line across a portion of the Cahokia location in 1808, a land surveyor named John Messinger jotted in his field notes, "Twenty four or more of those mounds in Sight at one View . . . All covered with Simtoms of ancient Ruins."[5] Messinger correctly estimated the height of Monks Mound to be 100 feet (30.5 meters) from top to bottom, but he greatly underestimated its footprint. Covering an area equal to a dozen football fields, Monks Mound was constructed of earth raised basketful by basketful over the level of the flood plain to the height of a ten-story office building. Early in the twentieth century, efforts to preserve the Cahokia mounds were hampered by the reluctance of geologists advising the state government to recognize that the mounds were anything more than just natural features of the Mississippi flood plain—that they were in fact products of Indian construction. Instead, geologists considered them to be erosional remnants of a river terrace of some bygone era.

At the beginning of the twentieth century there was no professional archaeology program in Illinois, but nonetheless the mounds of the Mississippi valley were the subject of increasing interest to professional archaeologists elsewhere and to many with serious antiquarian interests locally. Less than a century after John Messinger's brief observations, it was already clear that the Cahokia site was not only one of a number of mound centers in the American Bottom and adjacent areas but also grander in scale than any site of similar character anywhere in North America. Numerous mound centers were identified: the Lunsford-Pulcher site located south of Cahokia near Dupo, Illinois; an East St. Louis mound center on the banks of the Mississippi west of Cahokia; the mound center on the opposite shore that gave St. Louis its early nickname of Mound City; the Mitchell Mounds north of Cahokia; and the Emerald Mound group, located southeast of Cahokia near Lebanon, Illinois. More than two hundred mounds have survived in the greater St. Louis area, serving as material reminders of the local achievements of a stage of cultural development that archaeologists have called Mississippian.[6]

The Mississippian Period

The Mississippian or Temple Mound period in the eastern United States was characterized by the emergence of sedentary societies based on maize agriculture with a ranked or layered social order that was governed by a leadership believed to have been perceived as semi-divine. Their ideologies were artfully expressed in the symbols incorporated in their engraved shell ornaments and other manufactures, and in settlements formally organized around plazas flanked by one or more earthen platform mounds surmounted by temples, council houses, or chiefly residences. Mississippian towns were often protected by palisaded perimeters. This specific pattern of traits was typical of hundreds of bottomland communities up and down the Mississippi River and

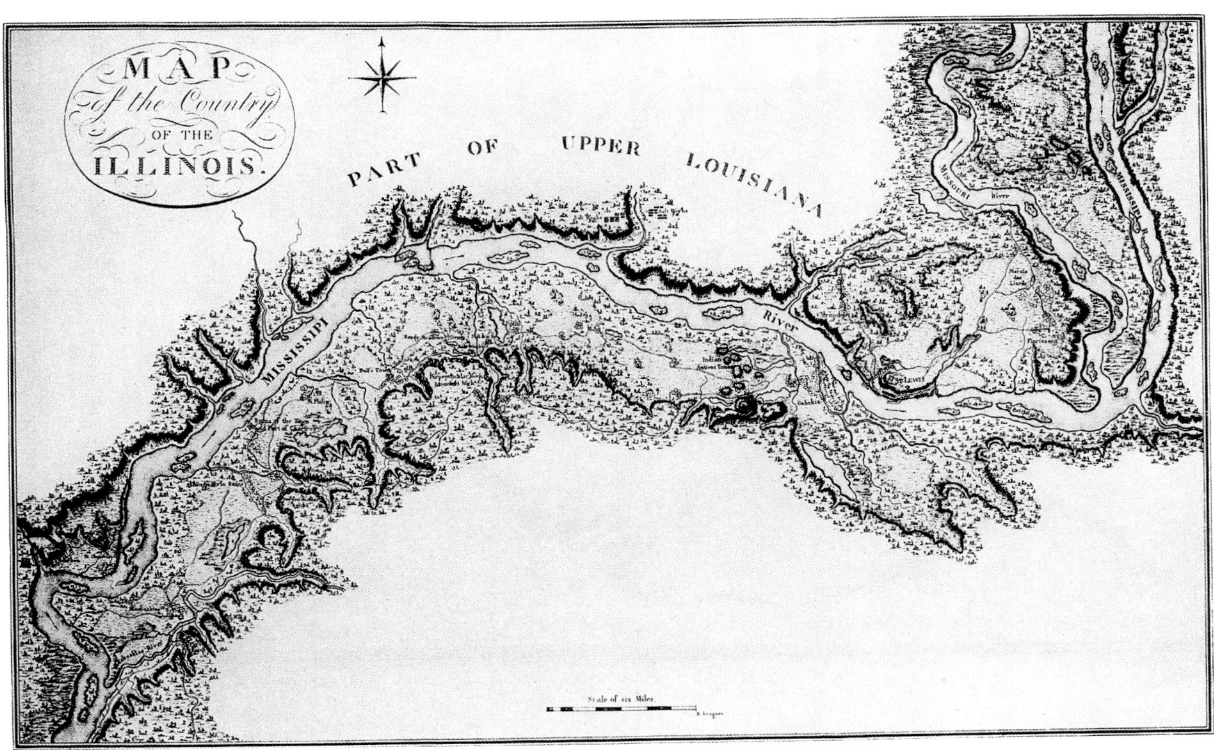

Fig. 5 Early map of the Mississippi River near Cahokia, based on a French survey by General Georges-Henri-Victor Collot in 1796 and published in French and English in Paris in 1826. This map, oriented with west at the top, shows the confluence of the Mississippi and Missouri rivers at right, the Kaskaskia River at far left, and includes the location of "Indian Antient Tombs," now identified by archaeologists as the Lunsford-Pulcher site in St. Clair County, Illinois. Although the early mission village of Cahokia is indicated on this map, Monks Mound and the other mounds that constituted the great Mississippian-period settlement only a short distance away do not appear on this survey.

throughout the Southeast. Archaeologists date the beginning of the Mississippian period to around A.D. 1000 and have calculated its ending to the mid-1500s in the South and the mid-1600s in the Midwest, depending upon when Spanish and French contacts occurred.

In outlying areas, social organization was more egalitarian, economies more a mix of hunting and gardening, and settlements more prone to relocation two or three times in a generation. This, in fact, was the character of much Indian village life in the subsequent post-contact period with certain exceptions such as the Natchez. During the 1500s in the southeastern United States, European diseases rapidly diminished the populations of native peoples. Consequently, the amount of arable land available per capita became so great that competition for resources was reduced. A societal organization of the Mississippian pattern was no longer a necessary or sustainable way to manage human relations in the smaller, surviving communities. In the central and northern Mississippi valleys there was an earlier episode of apparent depopulation of Mississippian centers, Cahokia included. This depopulation took place around 1400, more than a century before the first Spanish landfall on this continent, so European diseases accidentally introduced by the Spanish cannot have been the explanation.

The Cahokia Site and Its Organization

Broadly defined to include the nearby East St. Louis mound group, the Cahokia site stretches over 10 miles (16 km) of rich bottomland from the banks of the Mississippi River eastward almost to the bluff line at Collinsville (see figs. 20–21 in the essay by James Brown). What we know of prehistoric Cahokia comes almost entirely from the investigations of archaeologists and allied scientists from over a score of universities, colleges, museums, and cooperating agencies. Cahokia's ancient residents left no written records and no native peoples possess oral traditions that specifically identify Cahokia or even recognize its existence. Indeed, Cahokia had already been abandoned by its builders three centuries before Father Jacques Marquette and explorer Louis Jolliet passed through the St. Louis area in 1673. Indians who lived at the site from time to time during those three centuries lived in the shadows of mounds whose function belonged to an earlier era.

To judge from its commanding size, Cahokia must certainly have been a destination of religious pilgrimages and political embassies. To this might be added commercial missions, except that the Cahokians' economic exchange beyond the American Bottom more likely took the form of reciprocal gift giving between elites rather than market transactions. There would, of course, have been many opportunities for lower-level, private bartering in the background between retainers of the elite.

The Cahokia site proper, excluding the East St. Louis and other outlying mound centers, occupied an area of 5–6 square miles (16 square km).[7] To a foreign visitor the most obvious characteristic of the site would have been

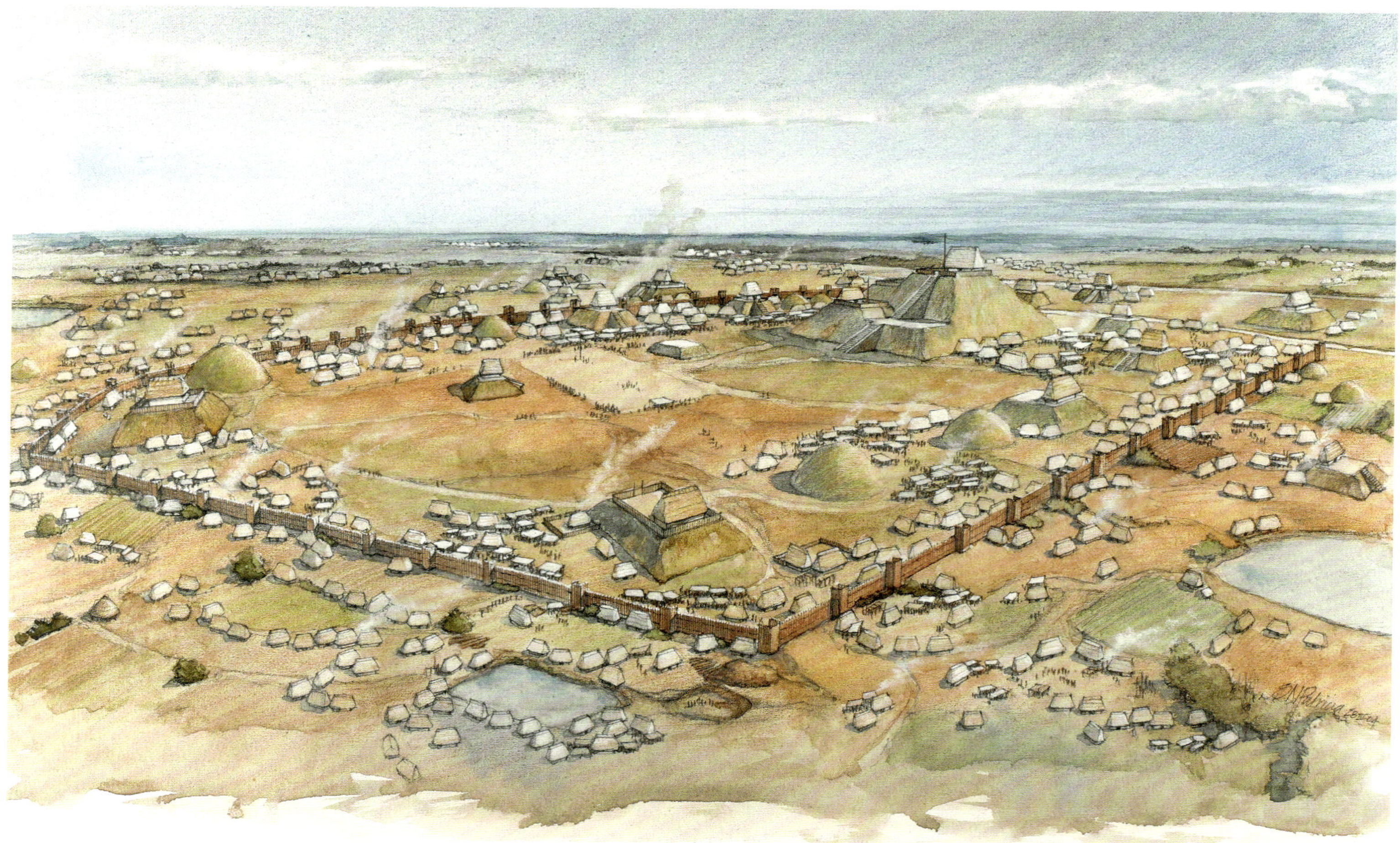

Fig. 6 View looking northwest across the ceremonial and residential center of Cahokia, the largest Mississippian settlement with approximately 100 mounds in the immediate area; rendering by Steven Patricia.

the hundred and more earthen mounds, most of them platforms on which would have been constructed lodges and temples framed with vertical pole walls and capped with gabled and thatched roofs. If the late-surviving Natchez temple can be used as a model, carvings of birds in heroic proportions would have stood silently on the ridgepoles of some structures. Monks Mound and the Grand Plaza fronting it formed the inner sanctum or inner city of Cahokia, and amounted to the prehistoric Illinois equivalent of a Vatican City in the heart of Rome. The Grand Plaza was an artificially filled and leveled square that contained and was flanked by smaller mounds (fig. 6).[8] In its day the Grand Plaza was probably the scene of Indian games that had ritual importance beyond their entertainment value.

Cahokia's inner sanctum was enclosed by a palisade of vertical logs with bastions or defensive towers set at intervals.[9] East, west, and north of this defined area, there were other major plazas with their own flanking mounds and structures.[10] Domestic dwellings, sweat lodges, drying racks for pumpkin rings and maize, and facilities for their storage would have been scattered throughout the site.

Three thousand feet (one kilometer) west of Monks Mound, a ward of domestic habitations was cleared and in its location was erected the first of a series of monumental circles of wooden columns that have come to be known as sun circles or "woodhenges." One woodhenge that has recently been partially reconstructed for visitors to Cahokia was originally 410 feet (125 meters) in diameter and consisted of forty-eight vertical log posts evenly spaced around the perimeter and a central pole.[11] South of Monks Mound's Grand Plaza and palisade, evidence has been found of another post circle of similar description in a ritual area discovered during the excavation of what archaeologists have labeled as Mound 72 of the numbered Cahokia mounds.[12] Within this mound itself archaeologist Melvin L. Fowler of the University of Wisconsin-Milwaukee found in 1967 the burial of a principal figure of the Cahokia hierarchy laid out on a bed of 20,000 flat shell beads arranged in the shape of a falcon.[13] Also found in the same mound were funerary offerings (fig. 7) and the graves of scores of many individuals believed to have been human sacrifices, including fifty-three young women and, nearby, four men beheaded and buried side by side.[14]

Cahokia Chronology

Archaeologists have divided the history of the Cahokia site during the Mississippian period into a series of phases: Lohmann (1050–1100), Stirling (1100–1200), Moorehead (1200–1275), Sand Prairie (1275–1350), and Oneota (1350–1650). Each phase is defined by its diagnostic pottery types, its distinctive domestic and public architecture, its level of sociopolitical integration, and its relationship to neighboring peoples. In the two centuries preceding the Lohmann phase, for example, Indian populations in the American Bottom lived in a number of small, independent, nucleated settlements based on hunting, fishing, gathering, gardening, and maize cultivation, with dwellings surrounding a small open area or courtyard. This courtyard often contained a central pole flanked by four pits that may have stored sacred corn and other seeds that had ritual significance to the whole village rather than to individual households. Viewed from the perspective of its origins, this way of life belonged to the terminal centuries of the Woodland period that preceded the Mississippian period. Viewed from the perspective of its destiny, this maize-farming, courtyard-centered, village life helped to define a period that John Kelly has called Emergent Mississippian.[15] It foreshadowed the later pattern of large temple towns with major plazas.

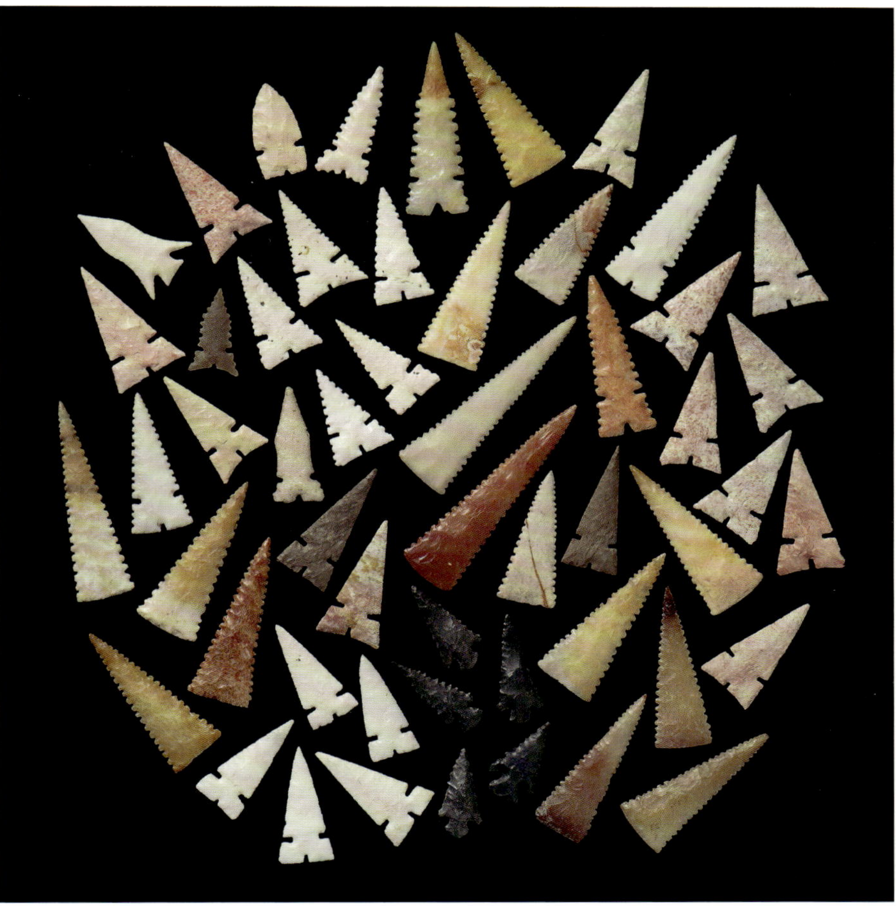

Fig. 7 Cache of projectile points; Illinois, St. Clair County, Cahokia, Mound 72, C. A.D. 1000; chert, l. 3.0–6.5 cm; Illinois State Museum, Springfield. Cat. no. 195.

In the beginning of the Lohmann phase there was a major change in community structure. Cahokia became a center of social, religious, and political power of such strength that individual families were able to populate the outlying countryside in what amounted to family farmsteads without fear of attack.[16] The sovereignty of the Cahokia leadership was expressed in major public works such as the first post circle or circles, the enlarging of Monks Mound, and the practice of human sacrifice in ritual dramas related to agricultural fertility and the mourning of elite personages, such as was found in the excavation of Mound 72. Monks Mound appears to have been constructed in a series of fourteen stages starting just before the Lohmann and continuing through the Lohmann and Stirling phases: that is, begun just before 1050 and completed around

1200.[17] During the Lohmann phase there is evidence of interaction with the lower Mississippi valley and indications of influence in matters of religious beliefs and practices from state-level societies in Mexico. One example of such influence was the introduction of World Renewal and World Centering rituals calling for human sacrifice.[18]

The Stirling phase witnessed Cahokia's widest cultural influence. Cahokians' contacts beyond Cahokia during the Stirling phase are evidenced by examples of a distinctive pottery type called Ramey Incised (fig. 8).[19] This pottery is found as scattered imports or local copies from the middle Missouri River valley in the northwest to the Wabash River valley in the east and northward into Minnesota and Wisconsin. Much of the same area was occupied during the seventeenth century by Indians speaking languages of the Siouan family (to be discussed below).[20]

While Cahokia was in its Stirling phase, a distinctive, new, agriculturally based culture called Oneota was maturing in Wisconsin alongside the marshy borders of the Mississippi River and among the lakes and streams of southeastern Wisconsin. Oneota ceramic decoration came to be replete with elements and derivations of a falconine thunderbird theme that had deep roots in Wisconsin as a common form of Woodland period "effigy" mounds, which were burial mounds of animal form.[21] This ceramic motif resembled falcons that appeared on embossed or repoussé sheet copper plates in the fully developed Southeastern Ceremonial Complex (SECC).[22]

During Cahokia's Moorehead phase, ground-level public buildings became larger, but there was a reduction in the total population along with some apparent need to protect the inner city from domestic or foreign enemies. Energy was diverted from constructing or enlarging mounds to maintaining the palisade around the Cahokia center, with exceptions like Mound 34.[23] Evidence from excavations in Mound 34 show that Cahokia played a seminal role at this time and before in the development of the iconography of the SECC found in southeastern sites such as Etowah in Georgia, Moundville in Alabama, and Spiro in Oklahoma (see the essay by James Brown in this volume).[24]

During the Sand Prairie phase at Cahokia, residences were built in former ritual precincts and public areas and Cahokia ceased to be a hegemonic cultural force. The latest Sand Prairie ceramics from Cahokia have much in common with those of the contemporary Crable site, some 100 miles (160 kilometers) north of Cahokia and the last surviving town and phase of Cahokia-related Mississippian culture in the central Illinois River valley. Crable was heavily influenced by its Oneota neighbors and vice versa to an extent that ethnic mixture is likely.[25] That is, Crable possibly became a multitribal town like so many known in Illinois and the Midwest during the postcontact period.

By the time Cahokia was abandoned around 1350 and Crable no later than 1450, the Mississippian pattern of life in Illinois directly influenced by the Cahokia model had ended. As a cultural force in the northern Mississippi valley, Cahokia had been replaced by the Oneota model now spreading widely across the same area.[26] The difference was that for the Cahokia interaction there was a single center for the diffusion of material and ideas controlled by an elite. Cultures of the Oneota pattern were more egalitarian; each participating band and village shared the same level of power and influence. There were no temple mounds in Oneota and no great plazas. Nor is there any evidence of human sacrifice. A new uniformity of style spread across the upper Midwest through exchange and peaceful communications. The intergroup relationships during this period of Oneota interaction were probably made possible by networks of fictive kinship that were created by symbolic adoptions.[27]

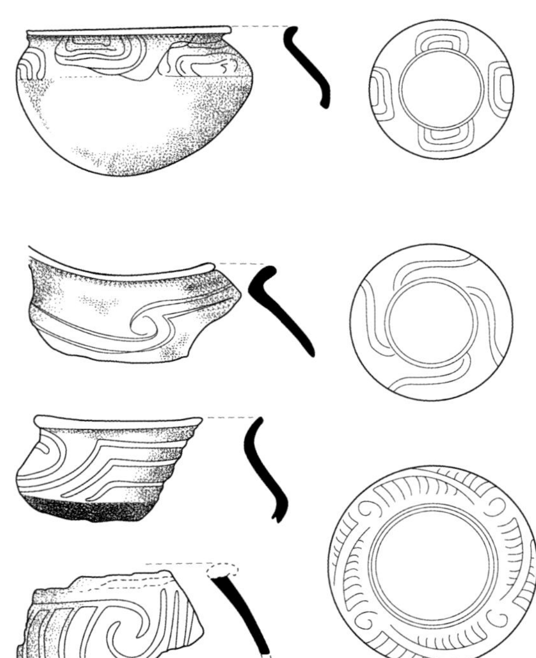

Fig. 8 Ramey Incised pottery of the type found at Cahokia; drawing by Elizabeth Reese Baloutine after Dick 1955.

After 1350 the American Bottom became a cultural backwater, but the Cahokians were not there to witness it. By this time most were well away from Cahokia, some undoubtedly on their way to acquiring a new guise as Oneotans. Other Oneotans made a desultory entrance into the American Bottom, but they never constituted a major presence.[28] Finally, to return where we began, the known occupants of the Cahokia area during the period of documentary history were largely representative of the Illinois Indian nation along with, of course, the newly arrived French and later English and American settlers.

Pole Ceremonialism

One of the most unexpected and most unique structural features of the Cahokia site was surely the sequence of post circles that have come to be called sun circles or woodhenges. These features have usually been associated only with observations of the sun (fig. 9). Certainly one of their functions was to serve as sighting posts for solar calendars when viewed from near the center posts. The distance from the equinox sunrise position on the horizon to either solstice sunrise position at the latitude of Cahokia is very close to 30 percent, which is one-twelfth of the horizon arc. Each of the six woodhenges has a number of poles that is exactly divisible by twelve in the pattern shown in table 1.

Warren L. Wittry discovered the original five woodhenges west of Monks Mound in 1961.[29] Subsequently Melvin L. Fowler demonstrated the presence of a sixth woodhenge at the location of Mound 72, south of Monks Mound.[30] Mound 72 included the burial of an elite individual and, as such, supports an understanding of why woodhenges were constructed as complete circles. The woodhenges defined a sacred area in the form of a cosmogram or image of the universe. The perimeter was a conflation of the circle of the horizon with that of the ecliptic or apparent path of the sun around the earth. In other words, woodhenges were a representation on one plane of the obliquely intersecting planes of the horizon and the ecliptic. The quadrants of the circle presumably represented seasons, as has been documented in Pawnee and Sioux belief.[31] The central pole functioned as an observation station for the woodhenges when used as solar horizon calendars, but in its cosmological role the central pole symbolized the Cosmic Axis, which was also seen as a Spirit Trail, a route to the hereafter.[32]

The woodhenges served community functions, or at least functions related to the top levels of Cahokia society. Among the Caddoan Hasinai of Texas, for example, post circles were constructed as part of the mourning ritual for important religious leaders.[33] Single posts with pennants attached were a common feature of mourning rites in the midcontinental United States. The Choctaw embellished such poles with a spiral of vines to aid the spirit in its climb to the next world,[34] which may have been a more general practice at one time. While living among the Timucua Indians of Florida in 1564–65, Jacques Le Moyne de Morgues sketched a row of seven tall poles on top of which were attached war trophies in the form of human arms, legs, and scalps (see fig. 26 in the essay by David Dye in this volume; see also fig. 10).[35] Each of these poles was wrapped with one or two ropes or vines that formed a pattern like that of the vines attached to Choctaw mourning poles. If this Choctaw and Timucua practice

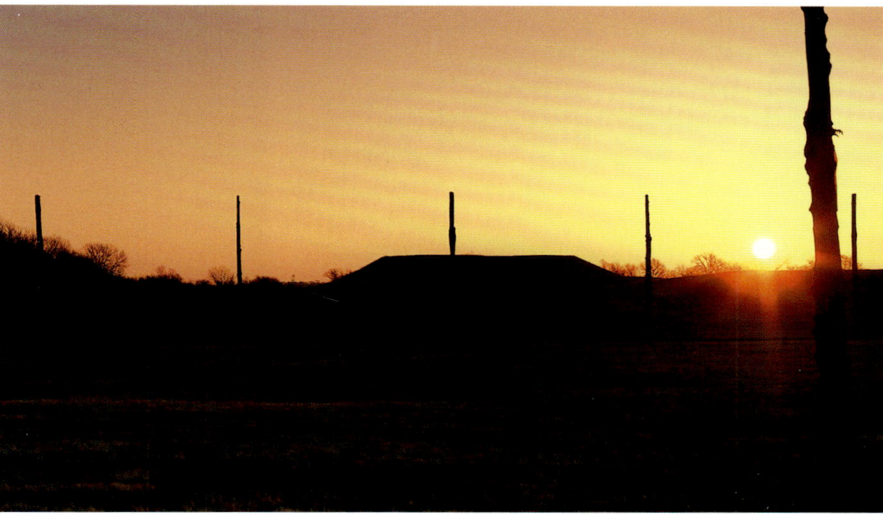

Fig. 9 View looking east toward Monks Mound across the reconstructed woodhenge at Cahokia.

Table 1 The Cahokia Woodhenges

Woodhenge	Posts	Radius (in feet)
I	24	120
II	36	204
III	48	205
IV	60	238
V*	72	233
Mound 72	48	207

*Only the sunrise arc was present for Woodhenge V. The number of posts given is that which the woodhenge would have had if it had been complete, based on the spacing of the posts.

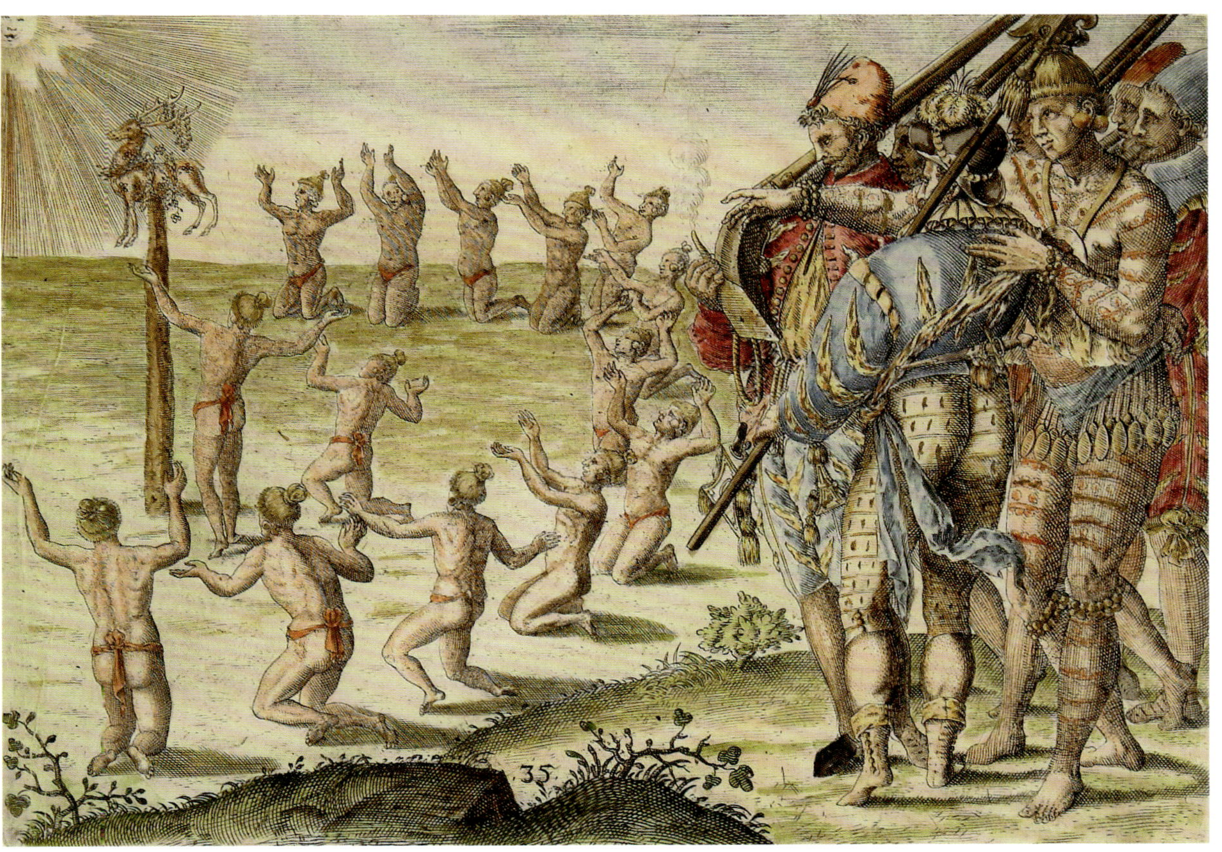

Fig. 10 Theodor de Bry (Flemish; 1528–1598), after an original painting of 1564 by Jacques Le Moyne de Morgues (French; c. 1533–1588), *Offering the Skin of a Stag to the Sun*, 1591; from *America*, 1st ed. (Frankfurt-am-Main, 1591), pt. 2, pl. 35; Rucker Agee Map Collection, Birmingham Public Library, Alabama. Cat. no. 279. This engraving by De Bry records the ritual offering to the sun of a stag's hide atop a ceremonial pole, while other members join their chief and shaman in chants of celebration.

has an expression within the SECC, it could relate to the spirally striped poles seen on engraved shells that are as yet unexplained.

The camp circles of the Osage and Omaha tribes are also known to have served as cosmograms—images of the universe. Tipis spaced along the north half were those of sky-associated clans and those along the south half were those of earth- and water-associated clans.[36] As in the case of the woodhenges, a camp circle cosmogram can be understood as a flattening together of the ecliptic plane with that of the horizon. The Osage and Omaha association of north with sky rather than earth is a Mesoamerican perception and is a clue to some past cultural influence from Mexico. In Mesoamerica the sun can be seen in the northern half of the sky at midday during part of every summer, so north was logically associated with "up" and south with "down." The sun is never seen in the northern half of the sky at midday anywhere in the United States, so it was south that was more logically associated with the sky, as in the symbolism of the Medicine Lodge ceremony of the Great Lakes area.[37]

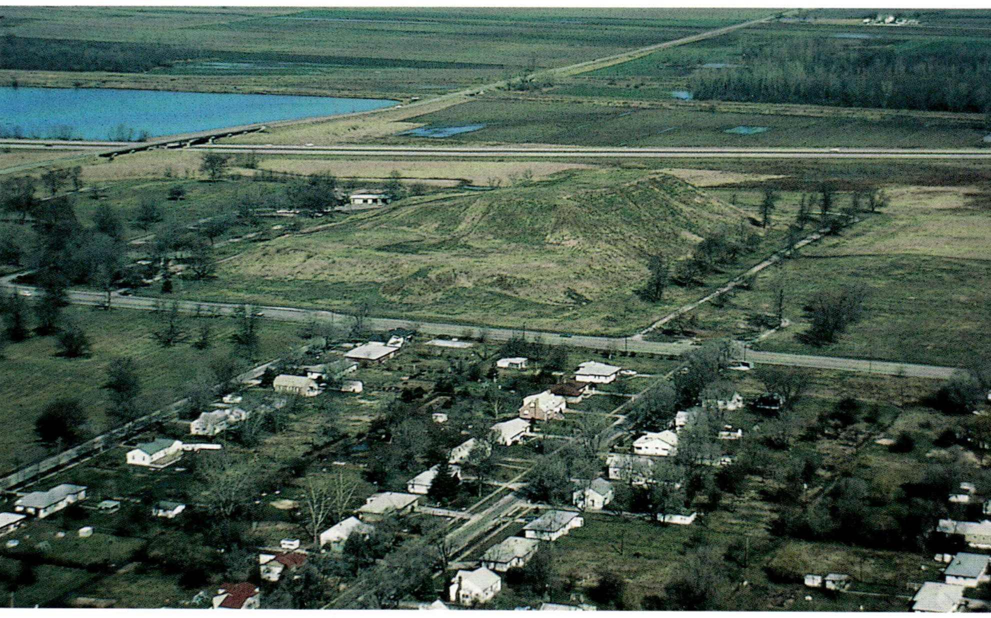

Fig. 11 This aerial view of Cahokia, taken around 1970, shows the housing development that had encroached upon the site between East St. Louis and Collinsville, Illinois, since the 1920s and that was finally removed in the 1980s.

The Cahokia Countryside

Most of the archaeological investigations at the Cahokia site have consisted of salvage excavations that rescued cultural resources from threats posed by highway construction, commercial and residential development, agricultural activity, capital improvements at the Cahokia Mounds State Historic site, and the erosion of mounds and pathways (fig. 11). One product of this salvage work was the discovery of the Cahokia woodhenges and the subsequent generation of a phase chronology for Cahokia anchored to radiocarbon dates.[38] The woodhenges were major discoveries and so important that their finding led shortly to the rerouting of a major section of what is now Interstate 255. Originally scheduled to pass through Cahokia west of Monks Mound, I-255 was moved to the east and beyond the limit of the Cahokia site. This shift protected the integrity of Cahokia itself, but it threatened other smaller sites that then had to be excavated archaeologically to preserve the information they contained.

Among the smaller sites affected by the relocation of the highway were two referred to by archaeologists as BBB Motor site and the Sponemann site, but a few miles east of Cahokia. In their day these settlements constituted two of many ceremonial and civic nodes within a network of farmsteads in the rural Cahokia countryside. Mark Mehrer has described nodal farmsteads as centering on "households that specialized in hosting community activities" and "homes of locally prominent families who were part-time ceremonial specialists but who produced their own food."[39]

A consideration of nodal households within their communities of scattered farmsteads reveals exactly what one would expect of a society whose religion was centered on a variety of ceremonial bundles, pipes, and other sacred objects in the care of a kin group elder, the leader of a dream society, or the officer of a warrior society. In other words, the Cahokia countryside was organized very much like many Indian communities of the postcontact period, and, in fact, very much like many Indian communities of the present day. The community comprised a social infrastructure with the potential for existing independently of Cahokia's "high church" leadership when the opportunity arose.

Thomas Emerson has argued that such nodal farmsteads were locations where the religious and civil power of the Cahokia elite maintained contact with an otherwise widely scattered farming sector of the total Cahokia society.[40] The specialized nature of these nodes is inferred from such evidence as their physical layouts and the material remains recovered, including a series of sculptures made of a red fireclay called "flint clay" that was mined in an area west of St. Louis.[41]

Excavations at the BBB Motor site uncovered two sculptures known as the Birger and Keller figurines (see figs. 16–17 in the essay by Kent Reilly in this volume).[42] Excavations at the nearby Sponemann site resulted in the discovery of three other sculptures, the Sponemann, Willoughby, and West figurines.[43] The subjects are all female and appear to represent different aspects of a goddess related to fertility in nature and agriculture. This and other evidence points to the existence in the Cahokia community of "a fertility, world renewal, mortuary complex that dominated rural Cahokian religious beliefs and rituals" and survived in part as the annual Busk or Green Corn ceremony widely practiced during the postcontact period in the Southeast.[44]

Who Were the Ancient Cahokians?

Cahokia was the product of one or more American Indian peoples whose modern descendants should be familiar in name and story, but who were they? The candidates can first be grouped by major language stock or family. One of these, the Algonquian family,

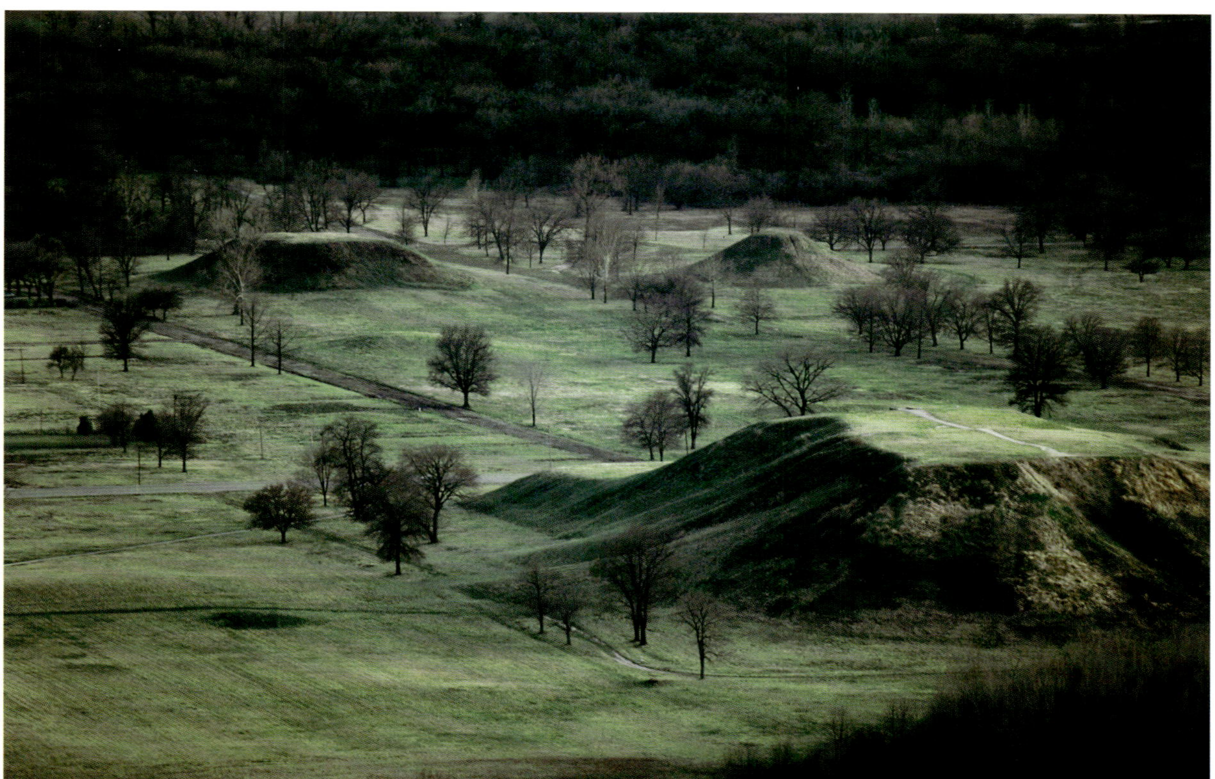

Fig. 12 View of Cahokia, taken in 1992, looking southwest over Monks Mound, the Grand Plaza, and two other, well-preserved mounds, numbers 59 and 60, known as Round Top and Fox Mound, respectively.

was present in historic times in the American Bottom in the person of the Kaskaskia, Cahokia, Peoria, Tamaroa, and Mitchigamea branches of the Illinois nation. Contrary to earlier beliefs, the evidence of archaeology today indicates, however, that the Illinois nation did not enter their namesake state early enough to have participated in the Mississippian development at Cahokia.[45]

A second family of contenders would be tribes of the Muskhogean language family, which includes the Choctaw, Chickasaw, and Creek among others. Although no Muskhogean tribe is known to have lived in Illinois at any time, Muskhogean speakers descend from people who undoubtedly did have a way of life of the Mississippian pattern centuries ago in the southeastern United States. Another factor mitigating against a Muskhogean ethnic identification for Cahokia, however, is that after the initial rise of the Cahokia polity, Cahokia's external relations were largely to the north, northwest, and west of Cahokia into areas of Illinois and other states almost exclusively Siouan in language, making Siouan speakers themselves more likely candidates.

Another possible ethnic association with Cahokia would be the Caddoan family. At the time of European contact, Caddoan speakers lived in villages spread through the Plains from Texas north to South Dakota. It is unlikely that Caddoans ever occupied Cahokia, yet Cahokians must have interacted with Caddoan speakers. The evidence for this association includes engraved shellwork and fireclay sculptures manufactured at Cahokia but found in Oklahoma at prehistoric sites presumed to have been ethnically Caddoan, as well as projectile points in styles typical of the Caddoan area found among offerings of arrows buried with the elite personage of Mound 72 at Cahokia.[46]

The area Caddoans occupied constituted a natural route for influences coming from Mexico toward the Cahokia area. Such a route would have paralleled any that followed the Mississippi River north from the Gulf of Mexico. A "scaffold sacrifice" by arrows once performed by the Skiri band of the Caddoan-speaking Pawnees was unquestionably of Mesoamerican origin, but it is not known whether it was transmitted directly from Mexico through the Plains or was received by the Pawnees from a Mississippian center like Cahokia as a secondary center of diffusion.[47] A related practice of scaffold execution by arrows, for example, was observed among the Natchez Indians in Mississippi in the early 1700s.[48]

The Siouan language family takes its name from the Sioux proper or from the Dakota, whose branch of the Siouan family was once distributed from northwestern Wisconsin across Minnesota into the Dakotas and Canada. More immediately to the north and west of Cahokia in historic times were the Winnebago or Ho-Chunk and the closely related Iowa, Oto, and Missouri tribes. These last three are usually grouped as the Chiwere Sioux or just as the Chiweres. There is little doubt that ancestors of the Chiwere-Winnebago interacted at some level with Cahokia. They were the immediate neighbors of the large Mississippian temple towns of the central Illinois valley that comprised a sequence of important outlying manifestations of Cahokia Mississippian influence.[49] The cultural relationship of Chiwere-Winnebago speakers and Oneota culture to Cahokia Mississippian has been a matter of speculation for many years.[50]

A division of the Siouan family that is more likely to have included actual participants in the Cahokia development is the Dhegiha or Dhegiha Sioux. Dhegiha speakers include today's Omaha, Ponca, Kansa, Osage, and Quapaw tribes. When first encountered by Europeans, the Dhegihas lived west of the Mississippi River from Arkansas to Iowa with the Osage being closest geographically to Cahokia. One Dhegiha tradition describes the lower Ohio valley as the starting point for Dhegiha migrations. The Quapaw are not known to have ever lived in the Cahokia area; tradition and history place the Quapaw's original and later homes well south of Cahokia. On the other hand, Osage-Kansa and Omaha-Ponca traditions move the balance of the Dhegihas through the greater Cahokia area at one time in their histories, although it is difficult to determine when this shift occurred.[51] The Osage and Kansa are said to have lived together as one people for a while on the Missouri River, after which they followed separate tributaries of the Missouri toward their historically known territories of residence in western Missouri and Kansas. The Omaha and Ponca similarly lived together as one people when following the Missouri River upstream into northwestern Iowa and southeastern South Dakota. There the Ponca separated from the main body of the Omahas.[52]

A second tradition gives a common origin for the Omaha and the Chiwere-Winnebago north of the Great Lakes.[53] This and the preceding tradition are not contradictory when examined in their contexts. The Siouan language family as a whole is believed to have originated in the lower Ohio and central Mississippi valley area sometime before 500 B.C.[54] Traditions of Dhegiha roots in the area of the central Mississippi valley could thus have had a basis in historical memory, albeit one lacking a timescale useful to archaeology. Traditions of an origin in the far north have their basis in mythological origins associated with a Seven Stars constellation, which could have been the Big Dipper.

This constellation has seven main stars and is seen in the night sky seemingly north of the Great Lakes. Knowing such mythological connections, one can understand the importance of sevens in much Siouan social organization—Seven Council Fires and seven tribes in Sioux origins, seven bands in Teton (Western Sioux) social organization, a Council of Seven Chiefs and/or Seven Pipes among the Omahas, Iowas, and Otos, and the Hidatsa association of their Dog Soldier societies with the seven stars of the Big Dipper.[55]

The Cahokia Diaspora

Societies with a Mississippian level of sociopolitical organization remained alive and healthy in the deep South until the sixteenth century and the advent of European diseases to which they had no resistance. In the lower Tennessee and Ohio valleys and in the central Mississippi valley, including Cahokia, Mississippian settlements and temple towns were abandoned about 1400 leaving behind what Stephen Williams has called the Vacant Quarter.[56] The same phenomenon occurred in the central Illinois valley, where there is no archaeologically visible Indian occupation for two centuries after 1450.

After A.D. 1200 bison hunting was becoming more visible in the archaeological record among the village farming cultures of the Missouri valley and in the prairie margins of the Plains. By 1300–1400 Indian populations along the upper Mississippi River were being drawn toward the Plains to take advantage of this resource, thereby reducing the population pressure around Mississippi valley centers such as Cahokia.[57] In time bison became numerous enough to provide an economic resource for Indians east of the Mississippi in Illinois, although not until the 1600s.

Coupled with factors that could have given Cahokians an area into which to move were factors that would have allowed them to take advantage of the opportunity presented. Studies of maize show that toward the end of Cahokia's Mississippian occupation, Cahokians were using increasing amounts of an eight-rowed corn that is known to have had many advantages over the Midwestern twelve-row corn that until then had been cultivated in the American Bottom. With a shorter growing season and greater drought resistance, the eight-rowed Northern flint corn was an ideal crop for areas west of the well-watered American Bottom. It was also the crop of choice for all tribes of the Midwest when the post-contact period dawned.[58]

Rather than thinking of the disappearance of Cahokia as its downfall or collapse, with all the negative associations of those words, one may more positively consider it as a successful readaptation permitted by "a serendipitous concurrence of events permitting resettlement outside of the circumscribing confines of riverine bottomland environments."[59] Why, for example, "should the abandonment of Cahokia be represented as a collapse or death rather than as a well-considered trade-off for new options available to Indians of the time, successfully leading to ways of life familiar from later history?"[60]

There is much to be said for seeking the inheritors of Cahokia's cultural legacy west of the Mississippi among Dhegiha speakers, specifically among the Omaha, Ponca, Osage, and Kansa, with more to be learned from studying the beliefs and cultural backgrounds of the Chiwere-Winnebago. There has long been speculation that at least some sites of Oneota culture in Kansas, Missouri, and Nebraska were Dhegiha in origin.[61] Interacting with preexisting Oneota peoples to the north and coming to resemble them in matters of style and economic adaptation, Cahokia Mississippians may prove to have become Oneota.

Before Cahokia, the highest recognized level of sociopolitical integration in the American Bottom was the courtyard-centered agricultural hamlet whose inhabitants were probably members of a single lineage. The rise of Cahokia led to the creation of a new fabric of rural society that apparently outlived Cahokia itself and survived in the form of large multiclan tribes like those of the Dhegiha and Chiwere-Winnebago—egalitarian in outlook yet complexly integrated in matters of religion and social roles. Thomas Emerson has suggested that "the creation of an organized stable rural population" may have paradoxically been a factor in the disintegration of Cahokia's central authority.[62]

The overarching civil and religious authority of Cahokia's central government must have provided a political environment that enabled the integration of scattered rural households. Once supported by an ideology that sanctioned human sacrifice, Cahokia's central authority under the direction of its ruling elite could have been found redundant during the Moorehead phase and dispensable during the Sand Prairie phase. It would not have been a disorganized, revolting peasantry that left the American Bottom. Rural Cahokians must have been pre-adapted to cooperative life in multiclan tribal villages like those found in the Midwest during the postcontact period.

Notes

1. Le Page du Pratz 1972, pp. 333, 338.
2. Kelly 1990b, pp. 113–15.
3. Walthall and Benchley 1987.
4. Walthall and Benchley 1987.
5. Messinger 1808.
6. Griffin 1952b, pp. 361–64; Milner 1998, pp. 2–3.
7. Fowler 1989; Fowler 1997.
8. Dalan 1993.
9. Fowler 1989, p. 198, fig. 10.1.
10. Brown and Kelly 2000, fig. 3; Chappell 2002, frontispiece and fig. 42; Pauketat 1998a, fig. 1.2
11. Wittry 1969; Wittry 1996.
12. Fowler et al. 1999, pp. 141–59.
13. Fowler 1991, fig. 17; Fowler et al. 1999, p. 132, fig. 1.7.
14. Fowler et al. 1999, fig. 6.6.
15. Bareis and Porter 1984; Kelly 1990a; Kelly 1990b; Milner 1998, p. 20.
16. Milner 1991, p. 33; Pauketat and Emerson 1997.
17. Reed, Bennett, and Porter 1968.
18. Hall 1999; Hall 2000; Hall 2001.
19. Stoltman 1991.
20. Hall 1991, figs. 1.4, 1.5; Springer and Witkowski 1982, fig. 1.
21. Benn 1995.
22. Benn 1989, figs. 4a, 7d; Hall 1991, fig. 1.6; Link 1975.
23. Milner 1998, pp. 147–50, 171.
24. Brown and Kelly 2000.
25. Esarey and Conrad 1998.
26. Hollinger and Benn 1998, fig. 1.
27. Hall 1987.
28. Jackson 1998.
29. Pauketat 1998a, p. 17; Wittry 1969; Wittry 1996.
30. Fowler et al. 1999.
31. Walker 1980, p. 54; Wittry 1996, p. 33, n. 3.
32. Hall 1998, pp. 61–62, 63.
33. Bolton 1987, p. 156; Demel and Hall 1998, p. 219.
34. Swanton 1946, pl. 89.
35. Wittry 1996, p. 30, fig. 3.3.
36. Fletcher and La Flesche 1972; Fowler et al. 1999, p. 183, fig. 15.2.
37. Hall 1997b.
38. Fowler and Hall 1972; Fowler and Hall 1975.
39. Mehrer 1995, p. 166.
40. Emerson 1995, p. 435.
41. Milner 1998, p. 101; Emerson and Hughes 2000.
42. Emerson 1982.
43. Jackson, Fortier, and Williams 1992.
44. Emerson 1995, p. 9; Witthoft 1949.
45. Esarey and Conrad 1998, pp. 55–56; Grantham 1993.
46. Brown and Kelly 2000; Emerson et al. 2002; Fowler et al. 1999, pp. 108, 114–15.
47. Hall 1997a, pp. 86–94.
48. Le Page du Pratz 1972, fig. on p. 355; Swanton 1946, pl. 83.
49. Conrad 1991.
50. Griffin 1960; Griffin 1995.
51. Fletcher and La Flesche 1972, pp. 37–41; Ridington and Hastings 1997, pp. 44–47 and fig. 5; Vehik 1993; Yelton 1998.
52. Henning 1993; Ridington and Hastings 1997, p. 53.
53. Dorsey and Thomas 1907.
54. Springer and Witkowski 1982.
55. Hall 1993, pp. 28–29; Hall 1997a, pp. 181 n. 8, 182 n. 18; Walker 1980, pp. 115, 296 n. 25.
56. Milner 1998, p. 173; S. Williams 1990.
57. Boszhardt 2000; Hall 1991; Henning 1998.
58. Hall 1991, pp. 22–25 and table 1.1; Hall 2001.
59. Hall 2001.
60. Anonymous reviewer cited in Chappell 2002, p. 78.
61. Chapman 1952; Henning 1998; Wedel 1959; Yelton 1998;
62. Emerson 1995, pp. 447–48.

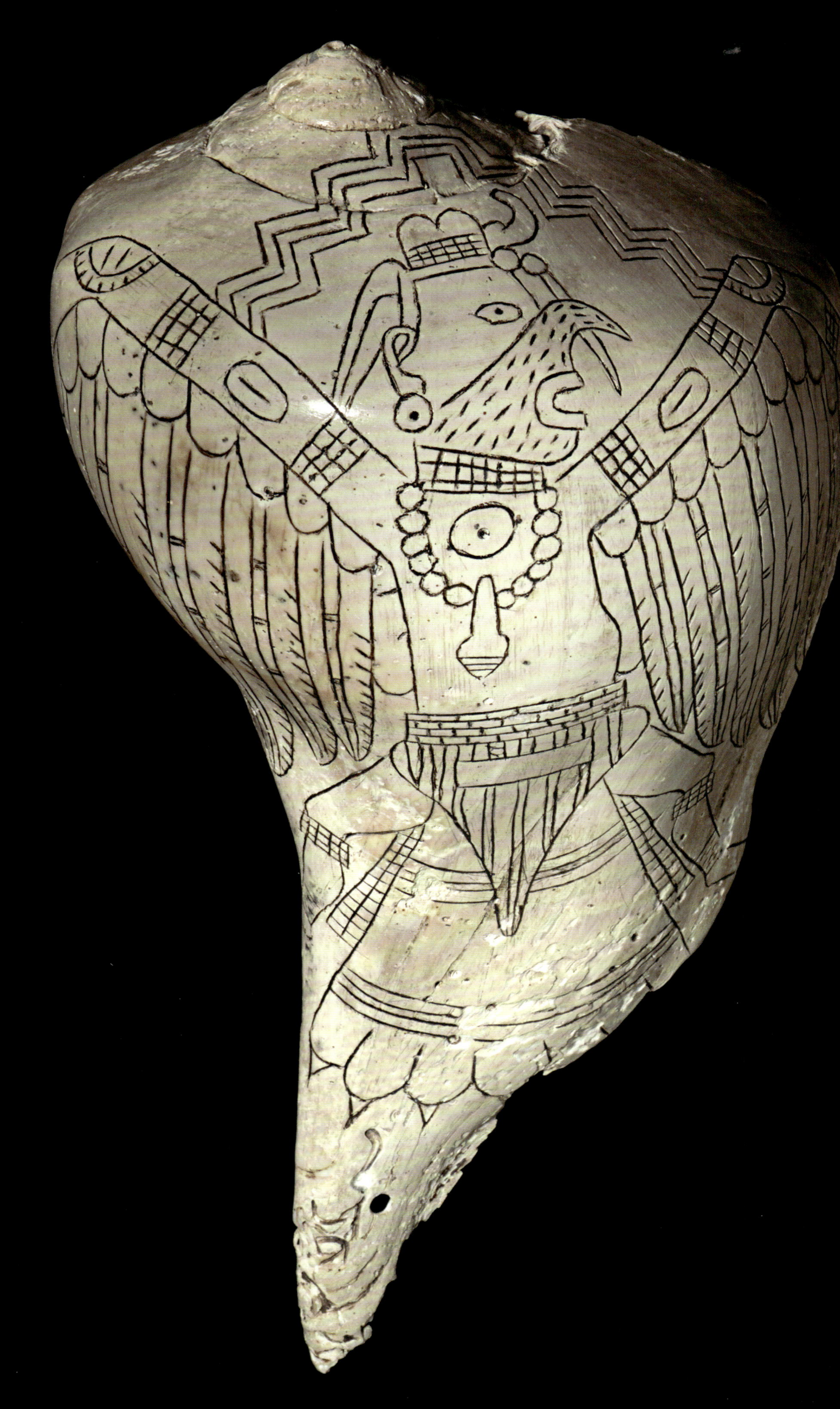

The Cahokian Expression

James A. Brown

Creating Court and Cult

In 1884 archaeologist John Rogan discovered two thin, beautifully embellished copper plates at the ancient town site of Etowah, near Cartersville, Georgia, while excavating one of its three major mounds (see figs. 1 and 11 in the essay by Adam King in this volume). The thinness of these plates, beaten from nuggets of natural copper, combined with the refined and detailed tooling of a naturalistic image of a costumed warrior, struck Cyrus Thomas of the Bureau of American Ethnology in Washington, D.C., as belonging to an entirely different league than previously known craft work and consequently totally unprecedented in the archaeology of the Eastern Woodlands.[1] The range of artwork then known did not approach the degree of artistic refinement exhibited by these copper sheets. What Thomas could not have realized is that under the auspices of the Bureau, Rogan's digging into the summit of Mound C had divulged the presence of an ancient, precontact period of sophisticated craft work in copper, marine shell, and stone carving in the Southeast. In keeping with contemporary attitudes Thomas saw no connection with postcontact crafts.

The plates that Rogan found have since become benchmark artifacts of what we now call the Southeastern Ceremonial Complex (SECC), a set of specialized ritual imagery from the Mississippian period in which thematically important animal and human figures are rendered according to specific stylistic conventions of representation. Thanks to advances in archaeological scholarship, these embossed plates are widely acknowledged to

Fig. 1 Engraved whelk shell depicting Birdman; Craig B style; Oklahoma, LeFlore County, Spiro, Craig Mound, A.D. 1200–1400; marine shell, l. 33 cm; Smithsonian Institution, National Museum of the American Indian, Washington, D.C. Cat. no. 125. The regalia depicted on this warlike figure of Birdman also appears on figures identified as the hero Morning Star or Red Horn.

have been made by indigenous peoples, and their connections to postcontact artwork have become easier to trace. For instance, such figural imagery persisted into postcontact time, and plates of copper themselves continue to be regarded as sacred by Muskhogean-speaking peoples. The historical antecedents of the SECC are likewise indigenous. Archaeologically, key features of the symbolic repertoire can be demonstrated to reach back into the Late Woodland period. All told, between roughly 1200 and 1400, the SECC has a history firmly seated within the Eastern Woodlands of North America, and nowhere else.[2] Within the East, historical connections among the SECC participants are more difficult to discern, but a good start can be made toward such a history by identifying the specific art styles associated with the Complex.

The Southeastern Ceremonial Complex

SECC objects have been principally identified through details of imagery. After a long history in which abstract, nonfigural designs were virtually universal, figural depictions of SECC themes became prominent around 1200. The dominating image is the Birdman, a warrior figure with falcon markings who brandishes a mace or axe (King, fig. 1), or alternatively rolls a chunkey stone (fig. 2). Birdman figures are also frequently shown wearing the bilobed arrow in his headdress (see fig. 44 in the essay by Richard Townsend) or holding other specific objects. On the Rogan plates just such elaborate ornaments project from the Birdman's hair. Identical copper-headed hairpins have been found at the heads of individuals buried both at Etowah and at Moundville in western Alabama. The same maces (see figs. 10–11 in the essay by David Dye) and axes (see Dye, figs. 27–29) held in the hands of the Birdman, along with items of dress and other objects associated with this figure, have been found within the Complex as well.[3]

The level of workmanship exhibited is another identifying attribute of the SECC. As Cyrus Thomas acknowledged, the level of artistry these objects display transcends the level of skill incorporated in household crafts. During the period when the highly crafted work associated with the SECC flourished, a very productive maize-based farming economy supported substantial populations and a degree of social and political complexity not seen in the postcontact period. But the era that gave rise to the SECC came to an end through political instability sometime after 1400, well before European contact. Although he understood the significance of individual objects from Etowah, the rise and decline of this precontact cycle of cultural complexity in the Mississippian period was something that Thomas, who died in 1910, never became aware of, nor could he, from the evidence available to him, have imagined its possibility.

An Archaeological Perspective on History

Within fifty years of the first discoveries, numerous examples of similar copper repoussé plates turned up over a wide swath of the greater Southeast—from the

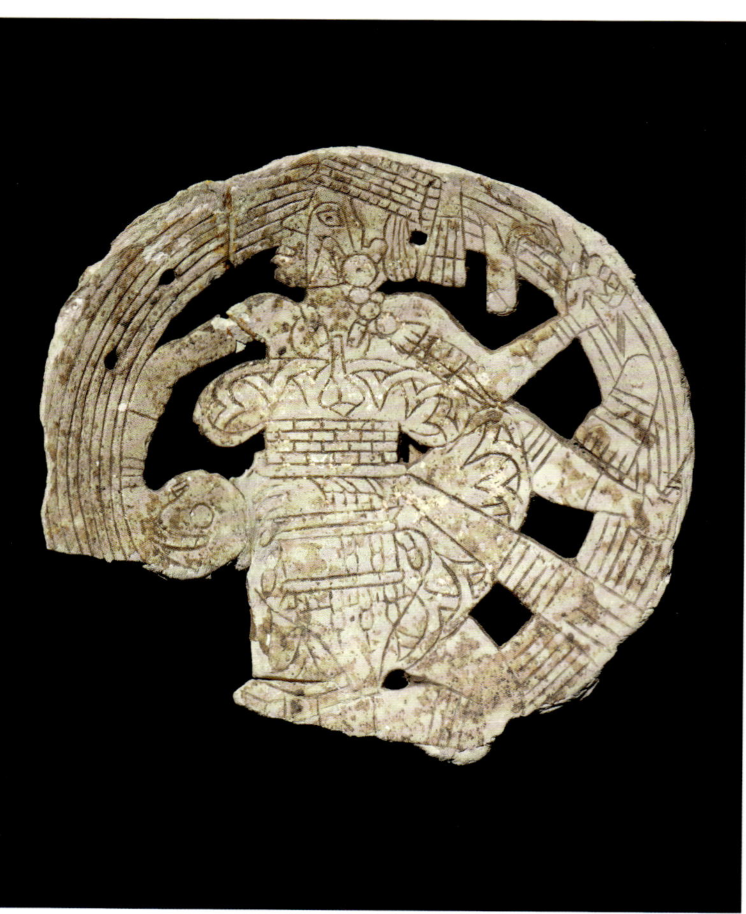

Fig. 2 Engraved shell gorget depicting a chunkey player; Classic Braden style; Missouri, Perry County, St. Marys, A.D. 1200–1350; marine shell, diam. 10.6 cm; Peabody Museum of Natural History, Yale University. Cat. no. 140. The Classic Braden style is represented here by the fine-line graphic detail of the inventory of ritual paraphernalia and the figure's dynamic, swastika-like pose. The round chunkey stone is held in his right hand.

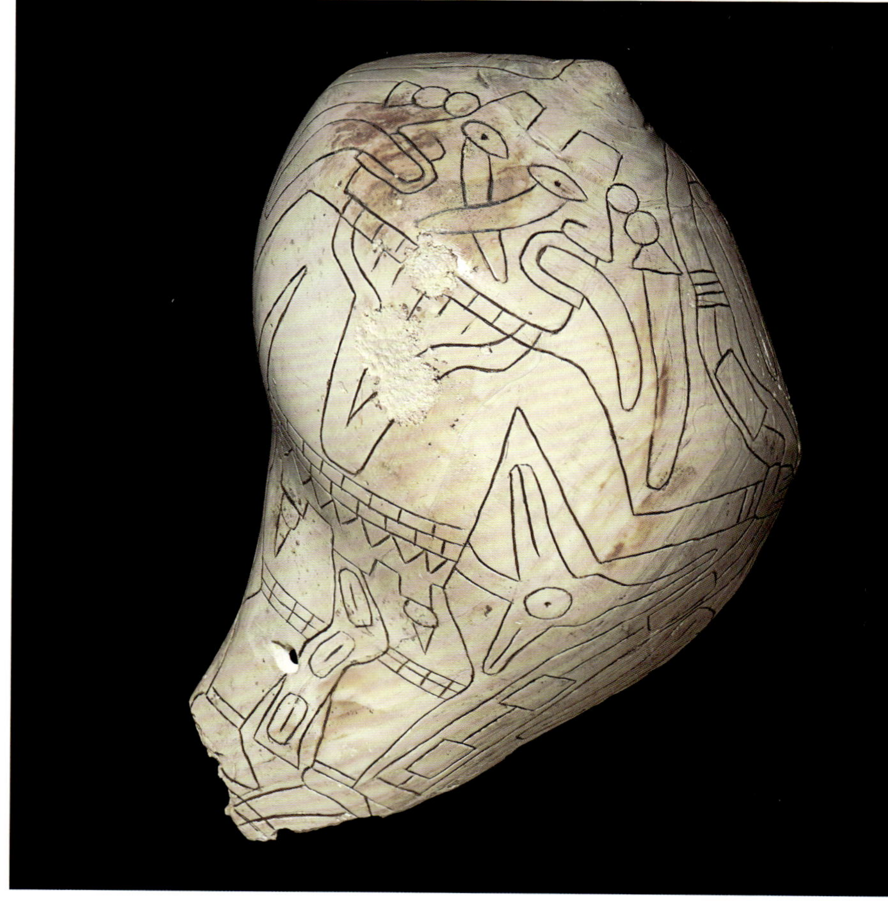

Fig. 3 Engraved whelk shell depicting Birdman; Craig C style; Oklahoma, LeFlore County, Spiro, Craig Mound, A.D. 1200–1400; marine shell, l. 29.2 cm; Smithsonian Institution, National Museum of the American Indian, Washington, D.C. Cat. no. 133. The Craig-style variants (A, B, and C) are characterized by simplified, schematic outlines and larger figures covering the surface area. The ritual figure shown here wears a two-faced mask.

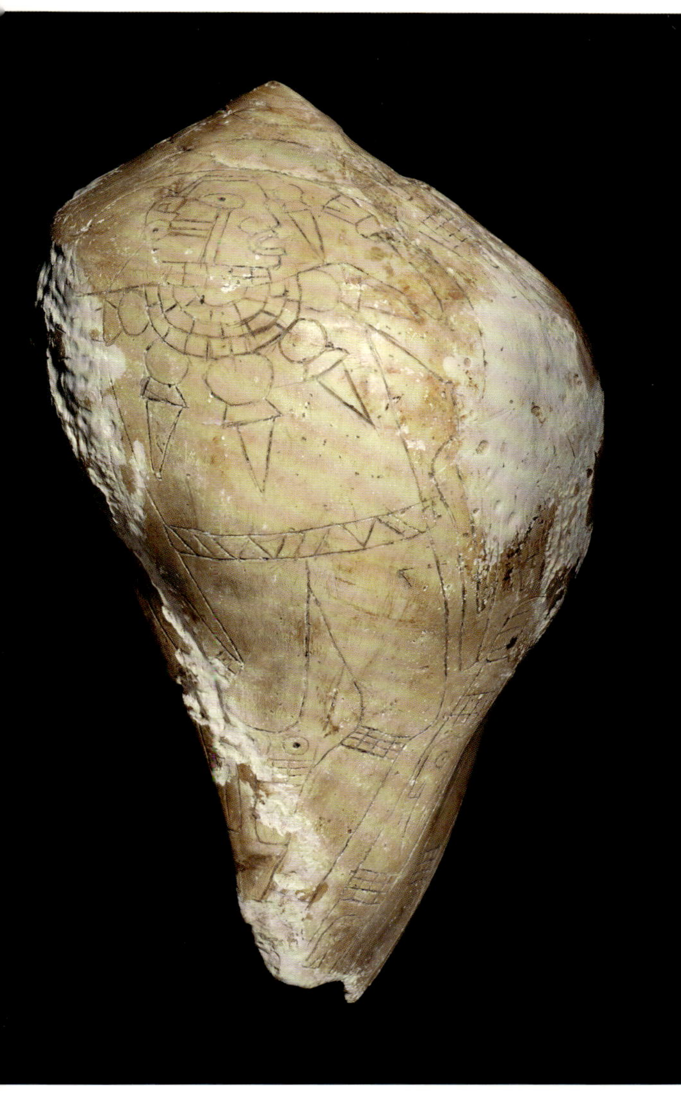

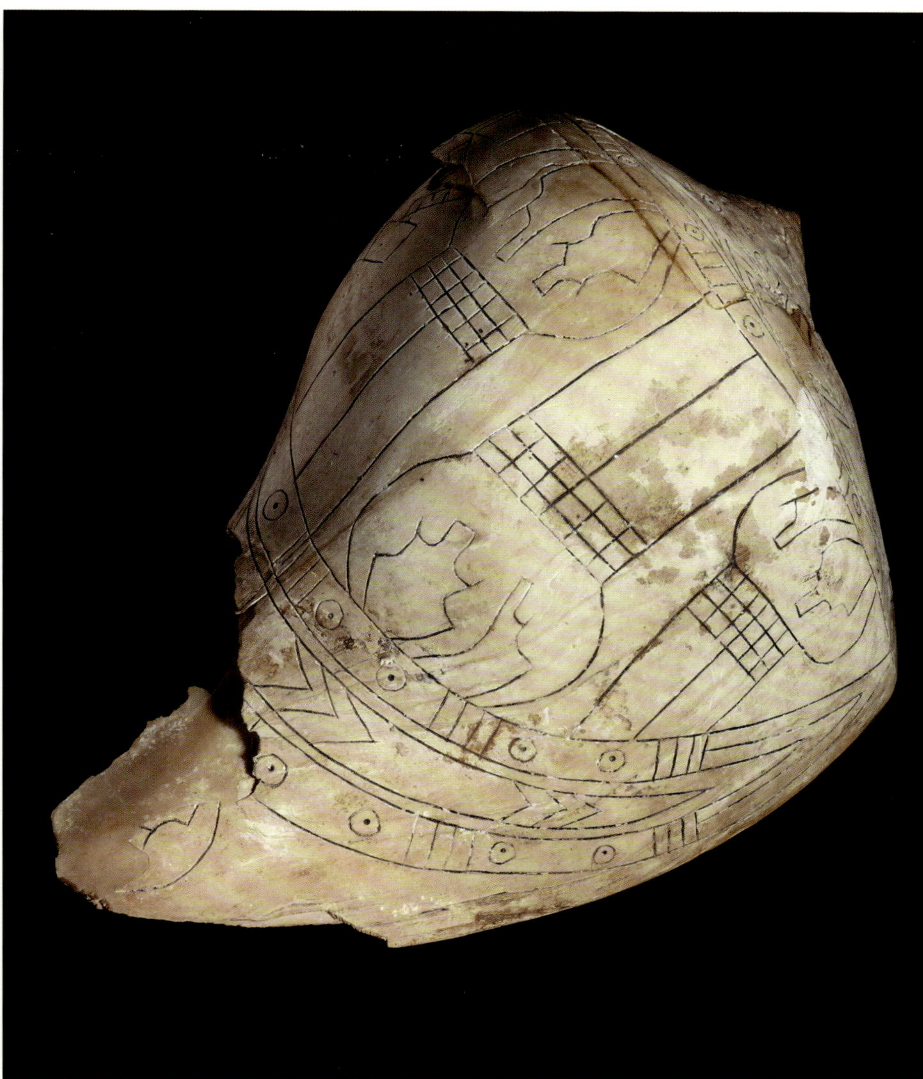

east coast of Florida to eastern Oklahoma. Even the locations where SECC material was concentrated are widely spaced. The geographical spread was so vast that it raises the question of just which culture or cultures were responsible for creating them.[4] Certainly the existence of three concentrations at the centers of Etowah, Moundville, and Spiro, Oklahoma, has complicated this question and deepened the mystery of authorship. The entire complex has sometimes been visualized solely from the perspective of one or another source. At best, each of these source areas has contributed its own distinctive style, named Hightower (see Dye, fig. 6), Hemphill (see fig. 12 in the essay by George Lankford), and Craig (figs. 3–6; see also figs. 4–6 in the essay by Kent Reilly), respectively.[5] While each is an important center in its own right, none of these three can be defended as the source of the most ubiquitous style of all—that known as the Classic Braden, so famously epitomized by John Rogan's copper plates. That honor goes to a fourth site—Cahokia, in southern Illinois—the one site whose developmental role in the emergence of the Classic Braden style can be sustained. The stylistic precursors of Classic Braden reside in the Midwest where they have chronological priority centuries before the appearance of the Complex throughout the Southeast.[6] The figural subject matter likewise has roots in the prairies of the Midwest. In fact, a "Generalized Braden" style has a presence in stone sculpture, on the walls of rock shelters and caves, and on the surfaces of pottery and other materials dated to the ninth to twelfth centuries. The deployment of the human figure, as seen specifically in the Birdman of the Rogan plates, comes from this

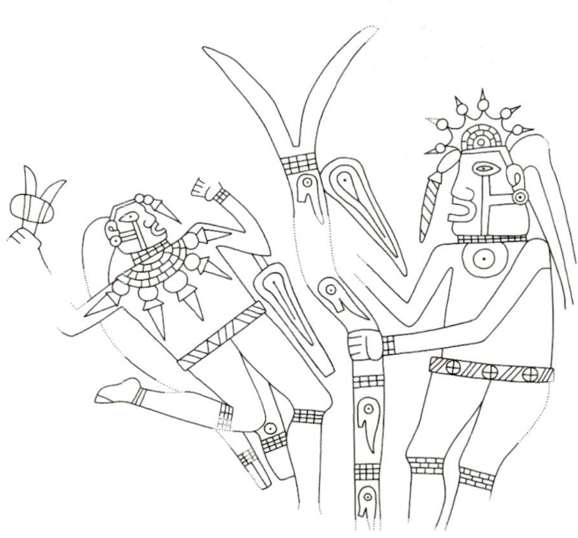

Fig. 4 Engraved whelk shell with two figures confronting a serpent staff (see fig. 6, below); Craig C style; Oklahoma, Le Flore County, Spiro, Craig Mound, A.D. 1200–1400; marine shell, l. 31.1 cm; University of Arkansas Museum, Fayetteville. Cat. no. 132.

Fig. 5 Engraved whelk shell with snake and talons motif; Craig C style; Oklahoma, LeFlore County, Spiro, Craig Mound, A.D. 1200–1400; marine shell, l. 34.3 cm; University of Arkansas Museum, Fayetteville. Cat. no. 136.

Fig. 6 Drawing of the engraved whelk shell with two figures confronting a serpent staff shown in fig. 4; from Phillips and Brown 1984, pl. 309.

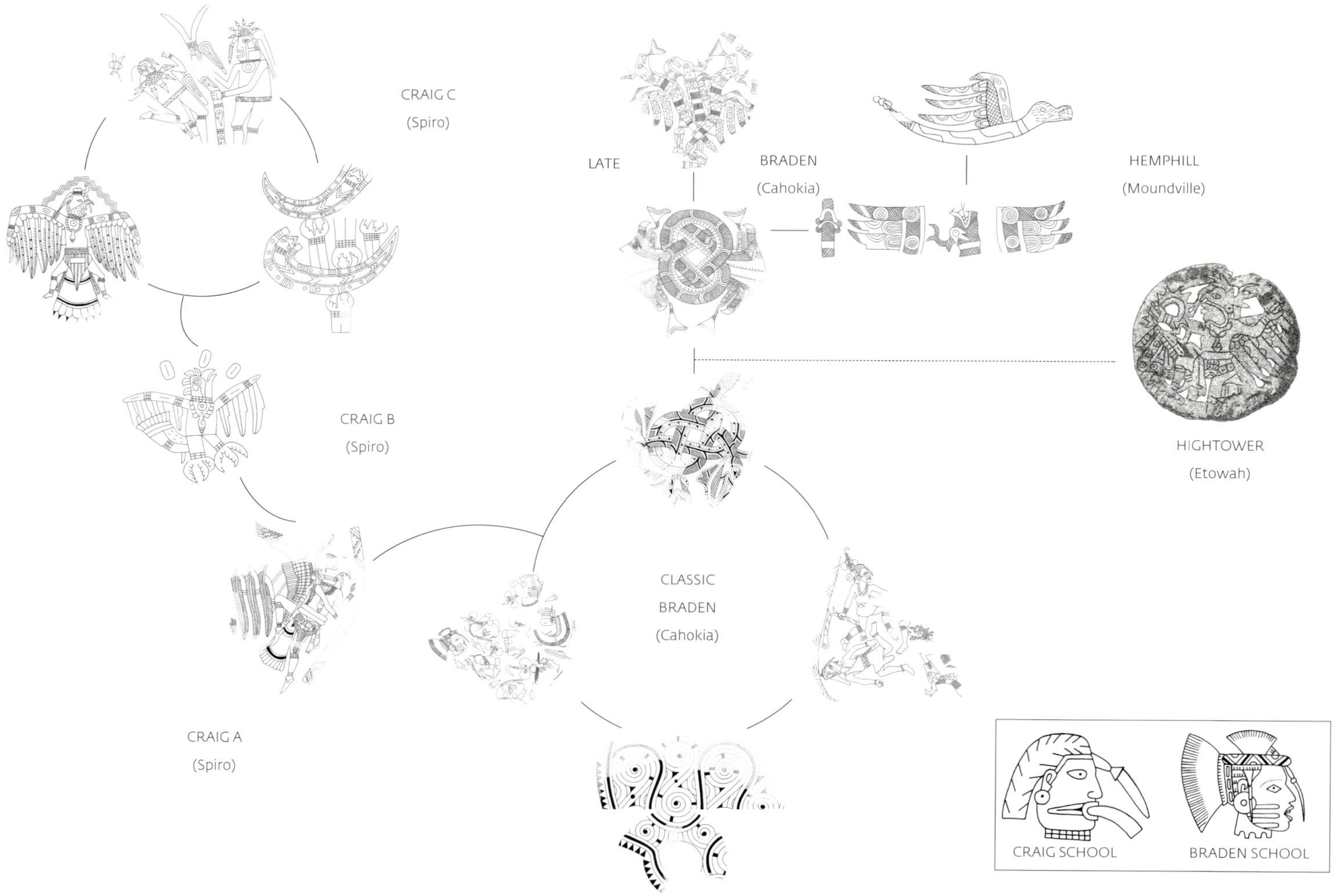

CRAIG C
(Spiro)

LATE BRADEN
(Cahokia)

HEMPHILL
(Moundville)

CRAIG B
(Spiro)

HIGHTOWER
(Etowah)

CLASSIC
BRADEN
(Cahokia)

CRAIG A
(Spiro)

CRAIG SCHOOL

BRADEN SCHOOL

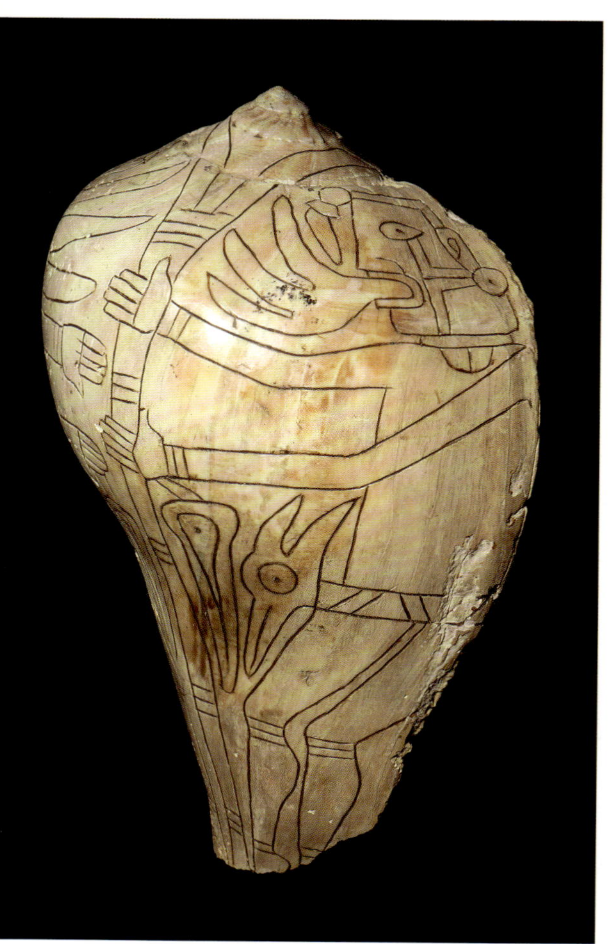

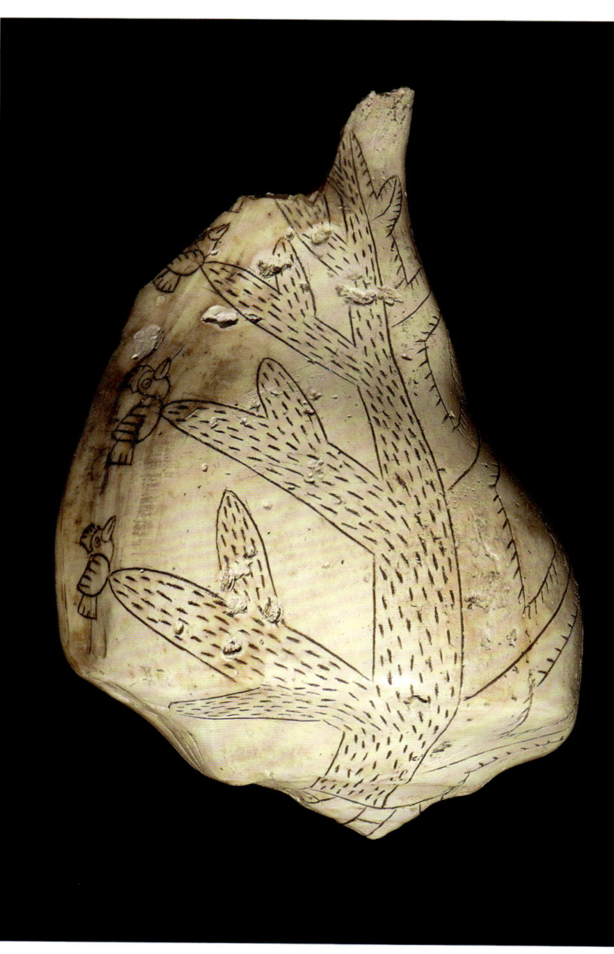

Fig. 7 Projected development of Braden, Craig, Hemphill, and Hightower styles.

Fig. 8 Engraved whelk shell with paired figures confronting a serpent staff or pole; Craig C style; Oklahoma, LeFlore County, Spiro, Craig Mound, A.D. 1200–1400; marine shell, l. 29.9 cm; Smithsonian Institution, National Museum of the American Indian, Washington, D.C. Cat. no. 134.

Fig. 9 Engraved whelk shell with "Tree of Fur and Feathers" motif; Craig B style; Oklahoma, LeFlore County, Spiro, Craig Mound, A.D. 1200–1400; marine shell, l. 26.7 cm; Smithsonian Institution, National Museum of the American Indian, Washington, D.C. Cat. no. 130.

facing page

Fig. 10 Engraved whelk shell depicting intertwined, two-headed serpents; Late Braden style; Oklahoma, LeFlore County, Spiro, Craig Mound, A.D. 1200–1400; marine shell, l. 38.1 cm; University Arkansas Museum, Fayetteville. Cat. no. 123.

Fig. 11 Chunkey Player effigy pipe, with chunkey stone in right hand and chunkey sticks in left; Oklahoma, Muskogee County, A.D. 1100–1200; flint clay, h. 21.6 cm; St. Louis Science Center. Cat. no. 94.

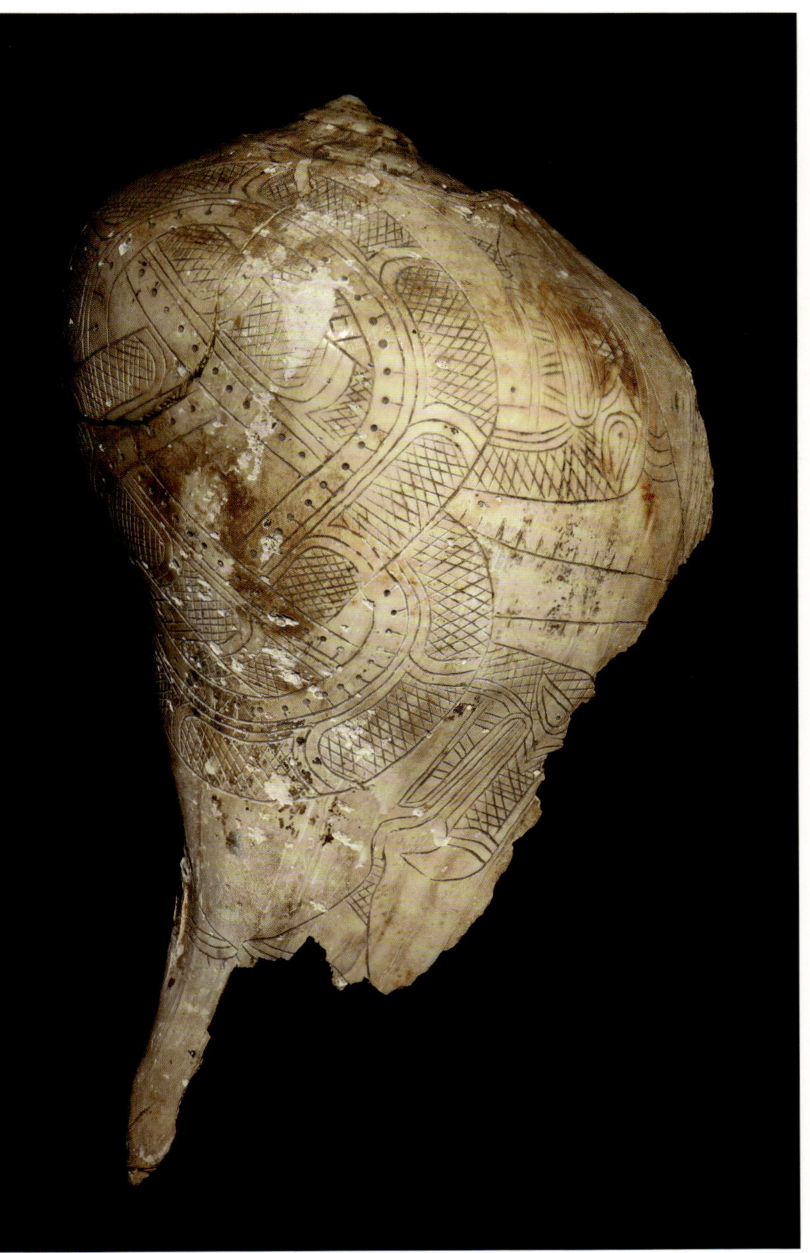

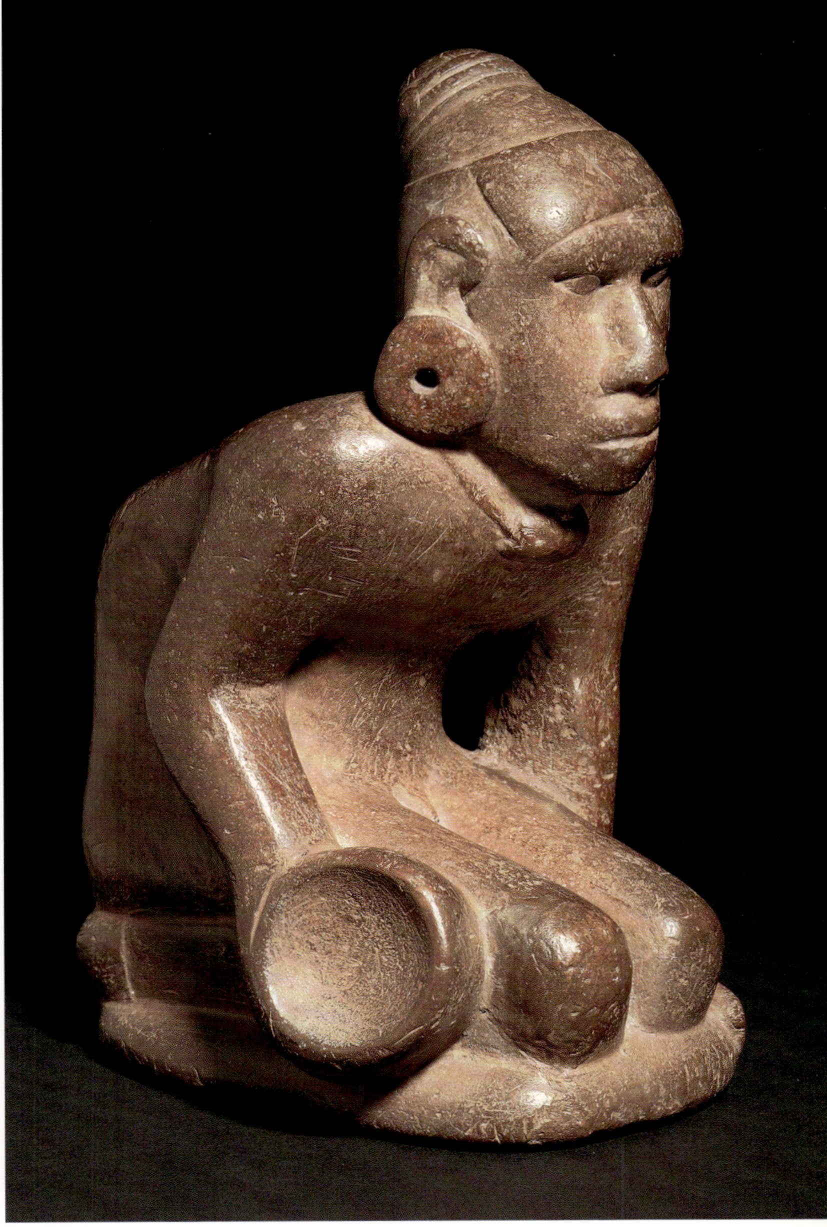

practice of using human and animal figures to express epochal narratives.

In the absence of a complete chronology of relevant archaeological contexts, the origins and spread of the Complex can be clarified by a genealogy of southeastern art styles. Sketchy though this genealogy might be, the available radiocarbon datable contexts strongly support the following model (fig. 7). If one were to suppose that the Classic Braden style at Cahokia represented the trunk of a style tree, its direct descendant, Late Braden, would lie on the central branch (fig. 10). The major side branch would delineate the Craig stylistic sequence (Craig A, B [fig. 1; see also Townsend, figs. 42–43], and C [figs. 3–6 and 8]) centered in the Caddoan area of Arkansas, Louisiana, Oklahoma, and Texas, and preeminently associated with the Spiro site. The Hightower and the Hemphill styles from Etowah and Moundville, respectively, appear to be branches as well. Thematic content rather than stylistic mannerisms compel us to consider a connection of the latter two to the Braden style sequence.[7]

Midwestern figural representation is not the only indication of Cahokia's ideological presence in the cult centers of the Southeast. Ritual equipment such as the chunkey stone (figs. 11 and 12–19) and instruments of power such as the bilobed-arrow headdress are transmitted there as well. In this conceptualization, the interconnections among the high art styles of the respective towns make better sense if the Classic Braden style, which represents a iconographic fusion at a special moment in the history of Cahokia, is conceived of as a major source of inspiration for the regionally based Craig, Hemphill, and Hightower styles of Spiro, Moundville, and Etowah.

Cult and Icon at Cahokia

Cahokia's complexity was due in part to its size. It was a major center of ritual activity, which in the Americas

page 110

Fig. 12 Chunkey stone; Georgia, Oostanaula Valley, Popes Plantation, c. A.D. 1300; stone, diam. 13.5 cm; American Museum of Natural History, New York. Cat. no. 167.

Fig. 13 Chunkey stone; Georgia, Lowndes County, c. A.D. 1300; conglomerate stone, diam. 11 cm; American Museum Natural History, New York. Cat. no. 172.

Fig. 14 Chunkey stone, A.D. 1200–1400; greenstone, diam. 11.4 cm; Smithsonian Institution, National Museum of Natural History, Washington, D.C. Cat. no. 169.

Fig. 15 Chunkey stone; Missouri/Tennessee, A.D. 1300–1400; quartz, diam. 12.7 cm; James and Elaine Kinker Collection, Midwest. Cat. no. 166.

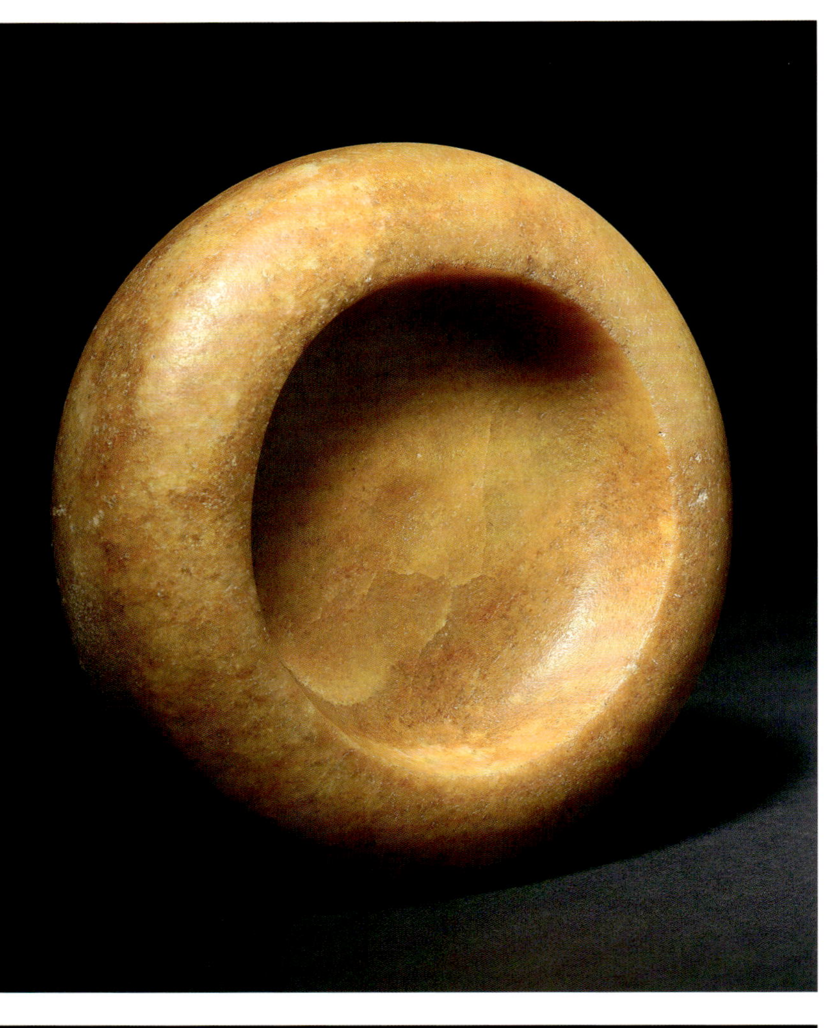
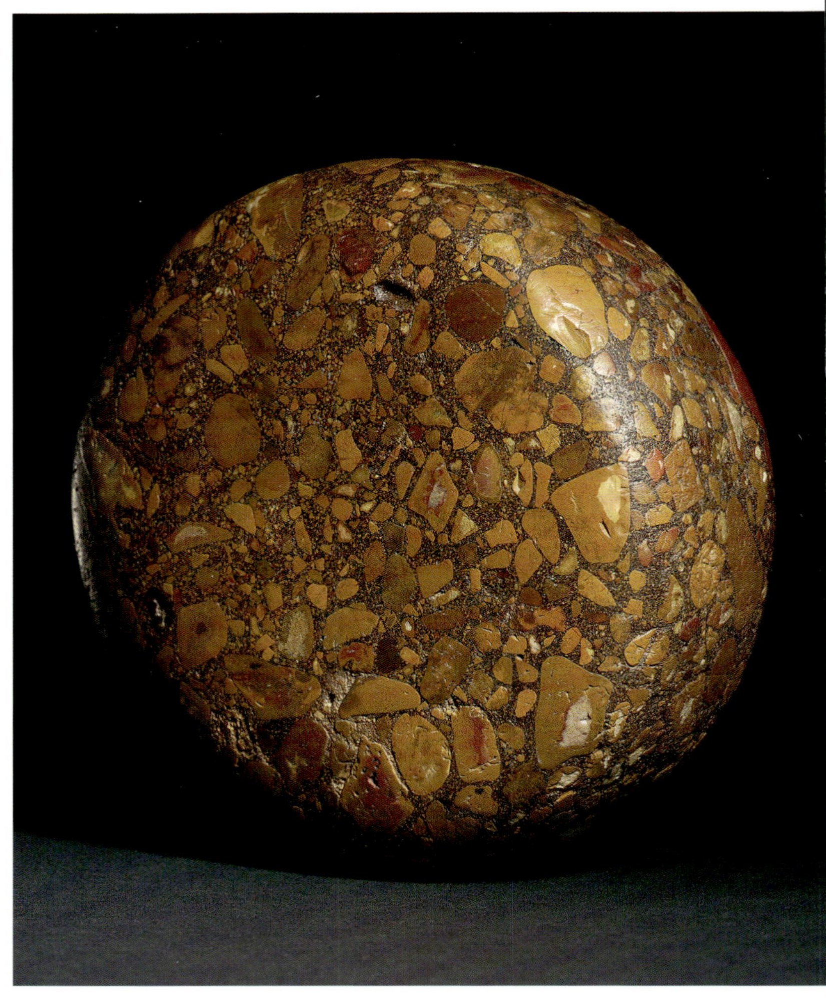
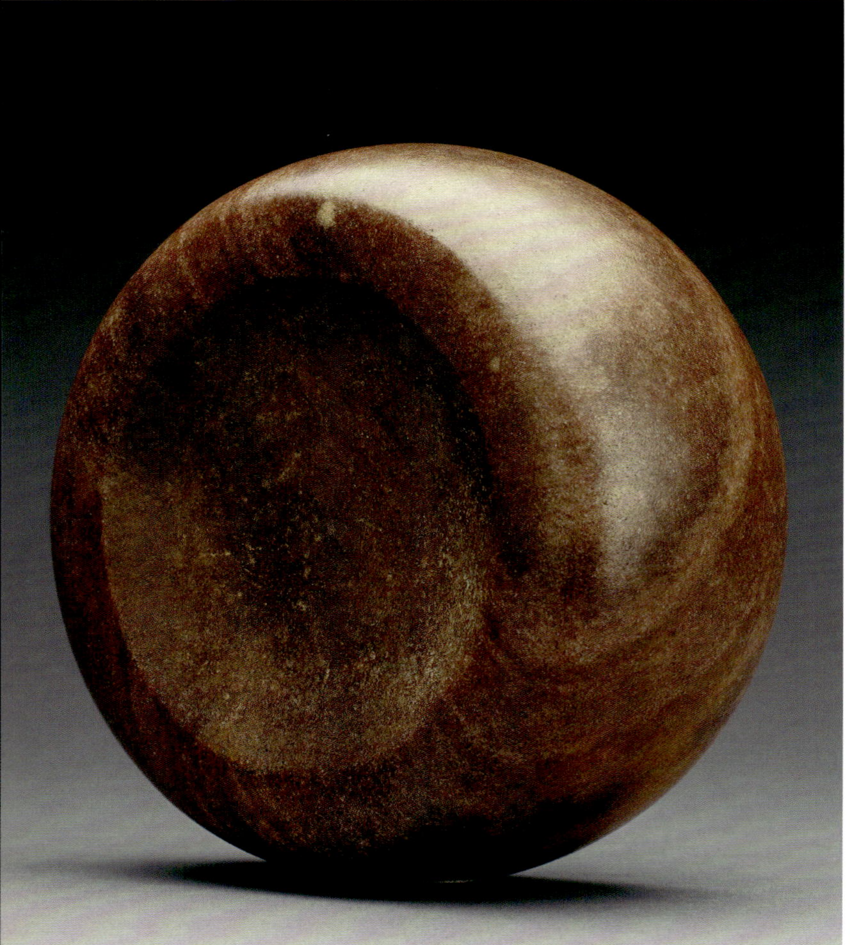
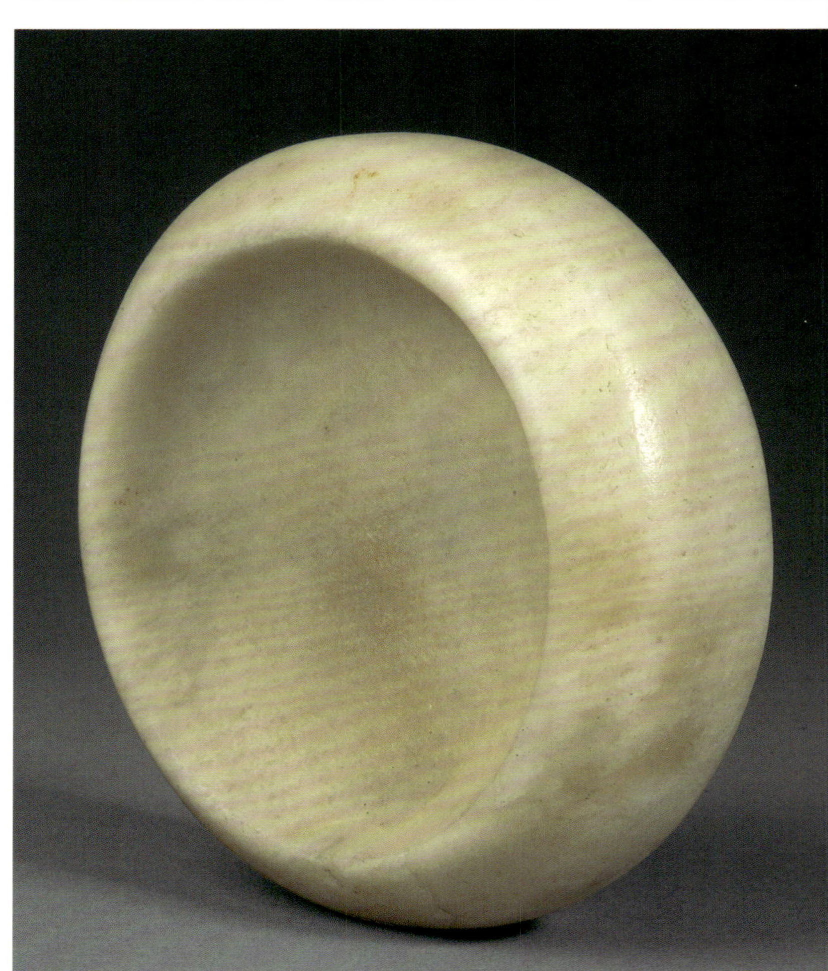

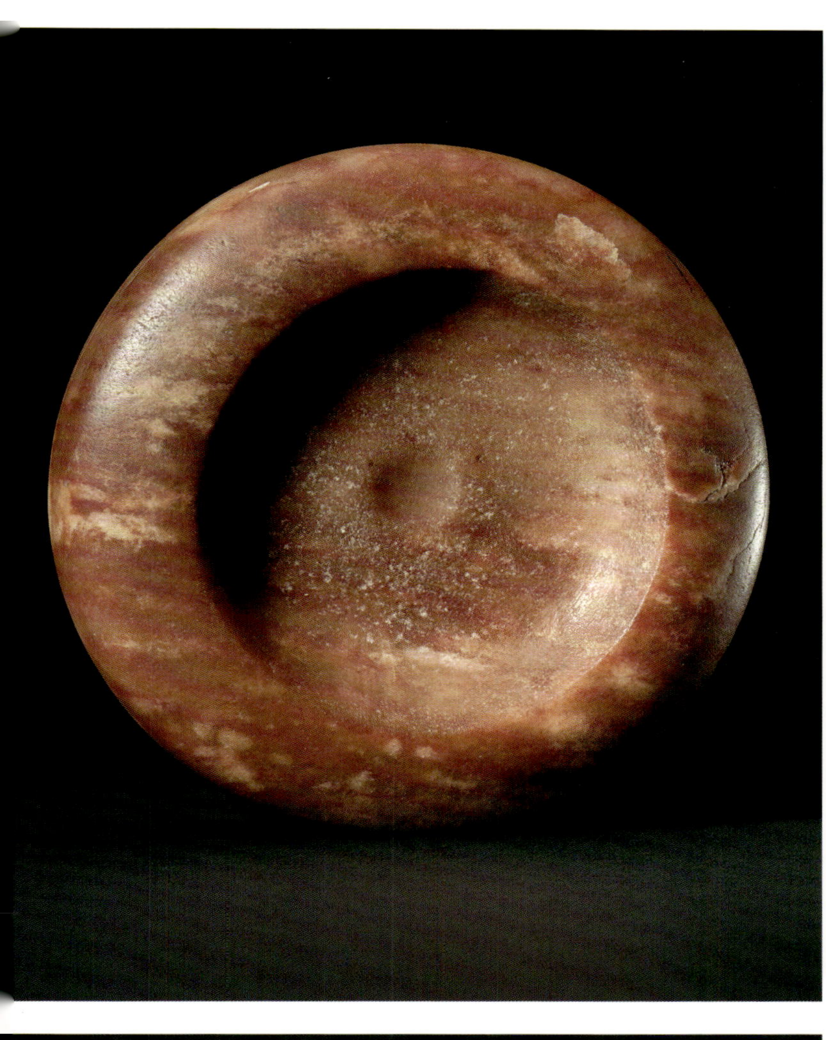

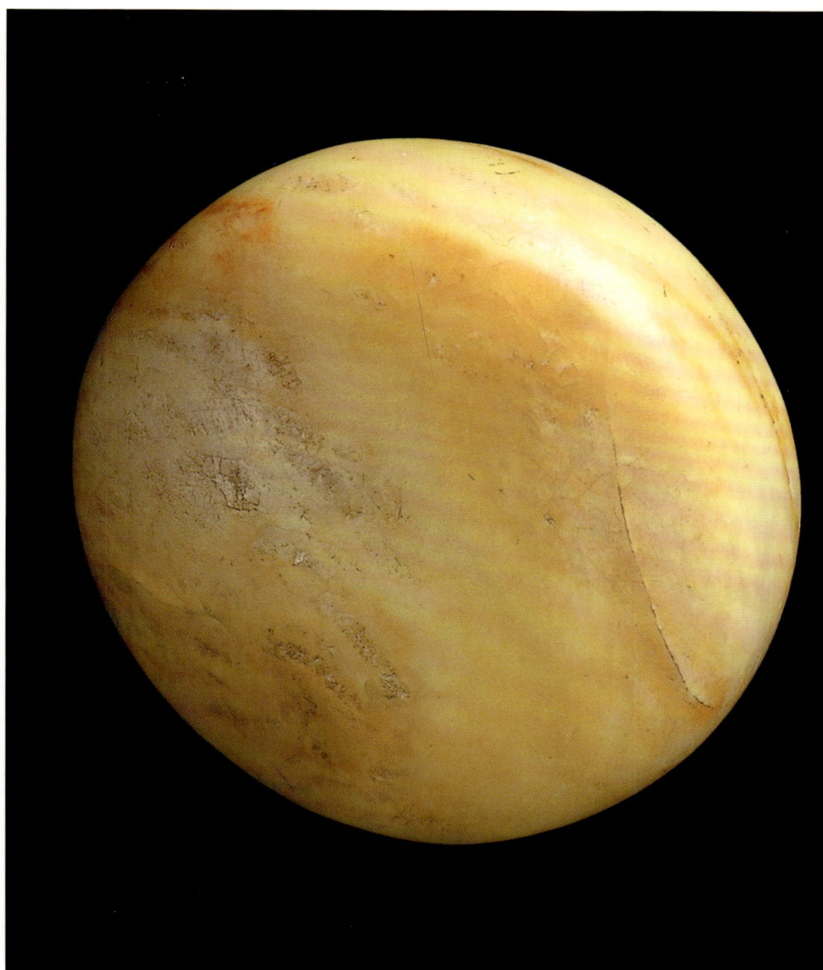

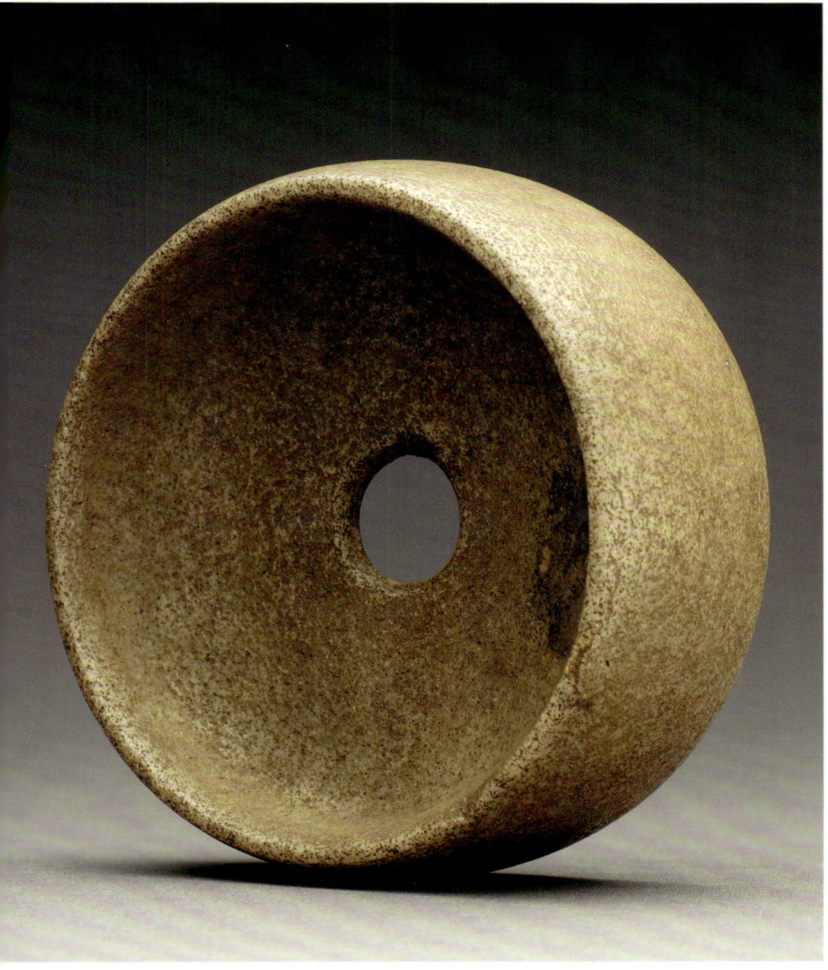

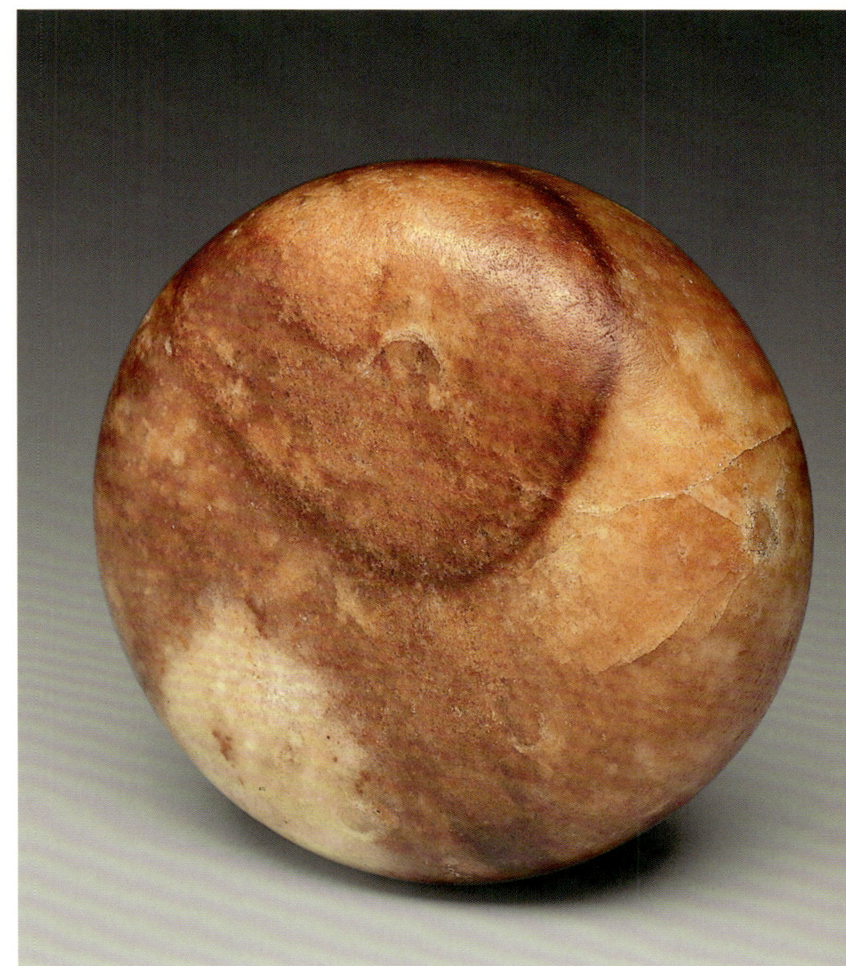

is frequently connected with highly refined craft production. Relatively early in Cahokia's history, a large-scale ceremonial layout was established with a complex ritual architecture. Around 1050 a preexisting village was transformed by the creation of a monumental mound and plaza arrangement. Cahokia attained a maximal size of 10 square kilometers (3.9 sq. miles) early in its history as a regional center. No other subsequent center achieved anywhere near this size.[8] Four large plazas were laid out in the cardinal directions around a centrally located platform mound of colossal size (fig. 20). Although yet to attain its final height of 30.5 meters (100 ft.), Monks Mound had already become the largest mound north of the Valley of Mexico.[9]

Even during a period of occupational retrenchment after 1200, a substantial town remained. The plaza east of Monks Mound, where occupation of this period is concentrated, encompasses an area of 7 hectares (17.3 acres) surrounded by 13 to 18 mounds. A minor member of this group is Mound 34, from which a quantity of engraved shell cup material has been recovered. On its own this quarter of the site constitutes a substantial town site by southeastern standards.[10] In all, Cahokia's preeminence spanned three centuries, but Cahokia was not the sole such center in the American Bottom region. Others included the Pulcher site—a group of ten mounds approximately 24 kilometers (15 miles) south of Cahokia—as well as other mound groups in East St. Louis and the St. Louis area (fig. 21). These political centers competed for followers. Over time Cahokia was the most successful, but it was never completely able to exclude other centers, even after 1200.[11]

The Braden Style—Cahokia's Contribution

As stated above, the subtly embossed Rogan plates exemplify what I call the Classic Braden style. The name "Braden" itself originated with Philip Phillips, who assigned it to one of the two major schools of art in his masterful analysis of the large and important corpus of engraved shells uncovered at the Spiro site in eastern Oklahoma.[12] Classic Braden compositions emphasize a balanced placement of masses rather than a spatial composition indicative of activities. Anatomical details of both human and animal forms are depicted in what the Western art canon would characterize as a naturalistic style and have precise body part ratios. An emphasis on balance is illustrated by the transformations that

page 111

Fig. 16 Chunkey stone; Missouri, Mississippi County, Wolf Island, A.D. 1000–1600; stone, diam. 15.9 cm; Gilcrease Museum, Tulsa, Oklahoma. Cat. no. 168.

Fig. 17 Chunkey stone; Arkansas, Crittenden County, Beck site, A.D. 1300–1500; kaolin, diam. 14 cm; Private collection, Missouri. Cat. no. 171.

Fig. 18 Chunkey stone; Tennessee, A.D. 1200–1400; stone, diam. 7.6 cm; Smithsonian Institution, National Museum of Natural History, Washington, D.C. Cat. no. 170.

Fig. 19 Chunkey stone; Arkansas, Mississippi County, A.D. 1200–1600; quartzite, diam. 7.6 cm; Private collection, Missouri. Cat. no. 173.

Chunkey game players rolled the stones as bets were made and arrows were shot or long poles were thrown to mark where players thought the stones would stop. Clearly prized and fashioned of the most beautiful and costly material, chunkey stones were requisite items among the Mississippian elite.

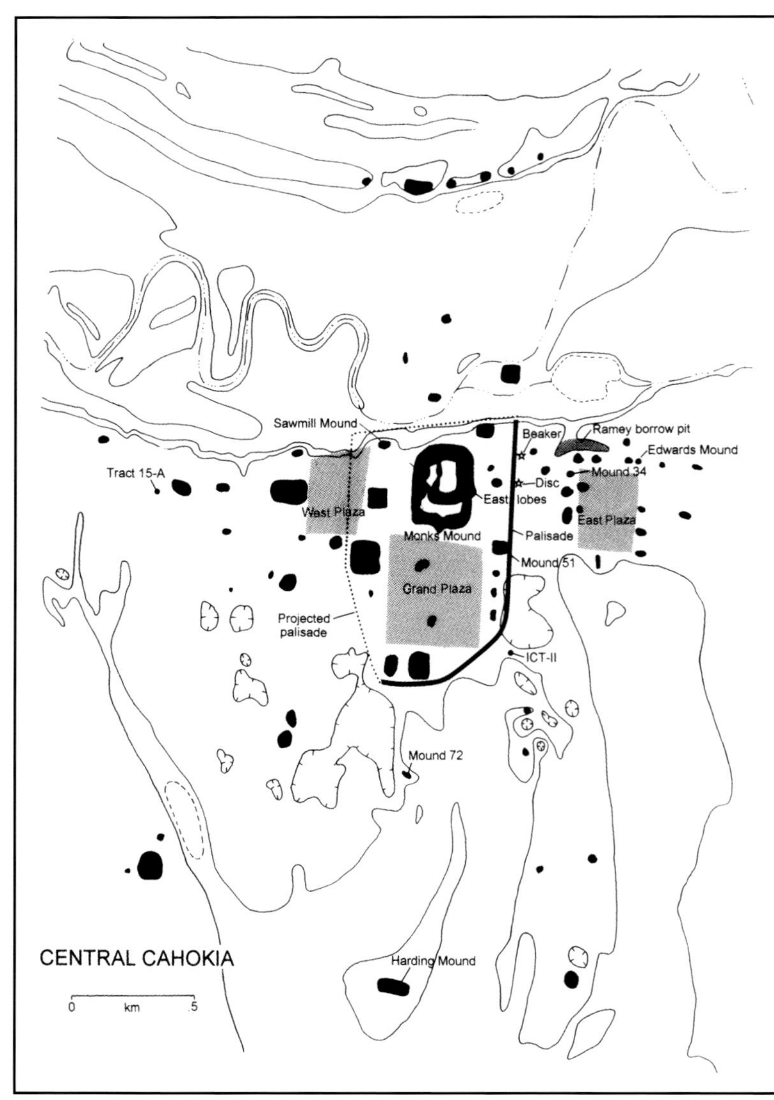

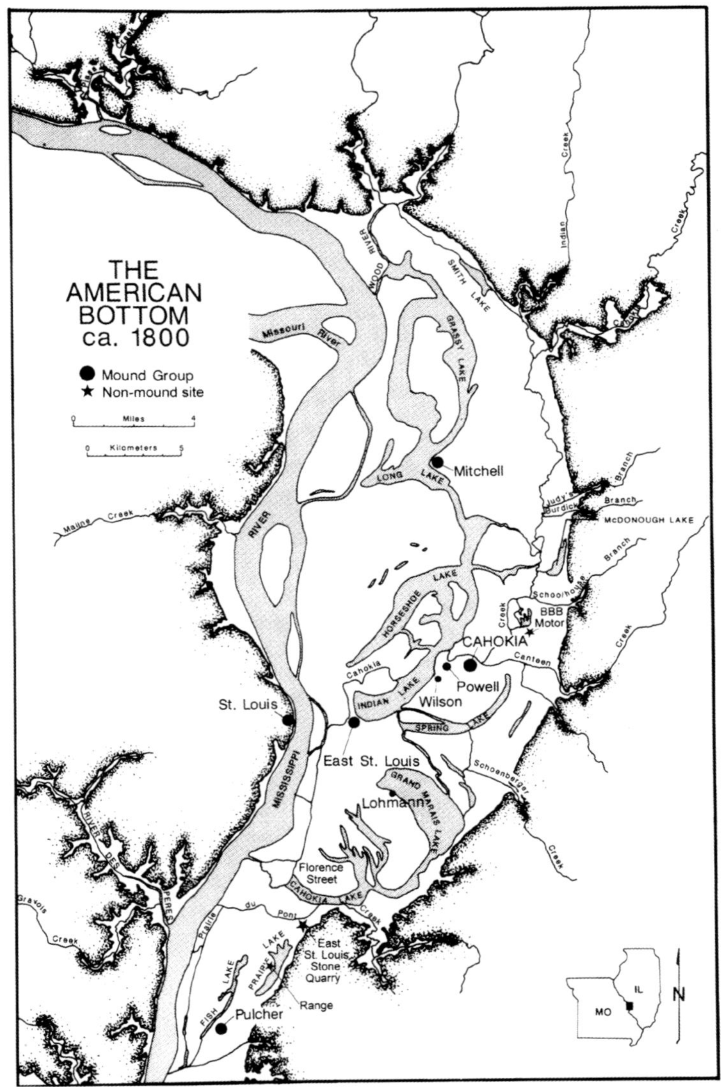

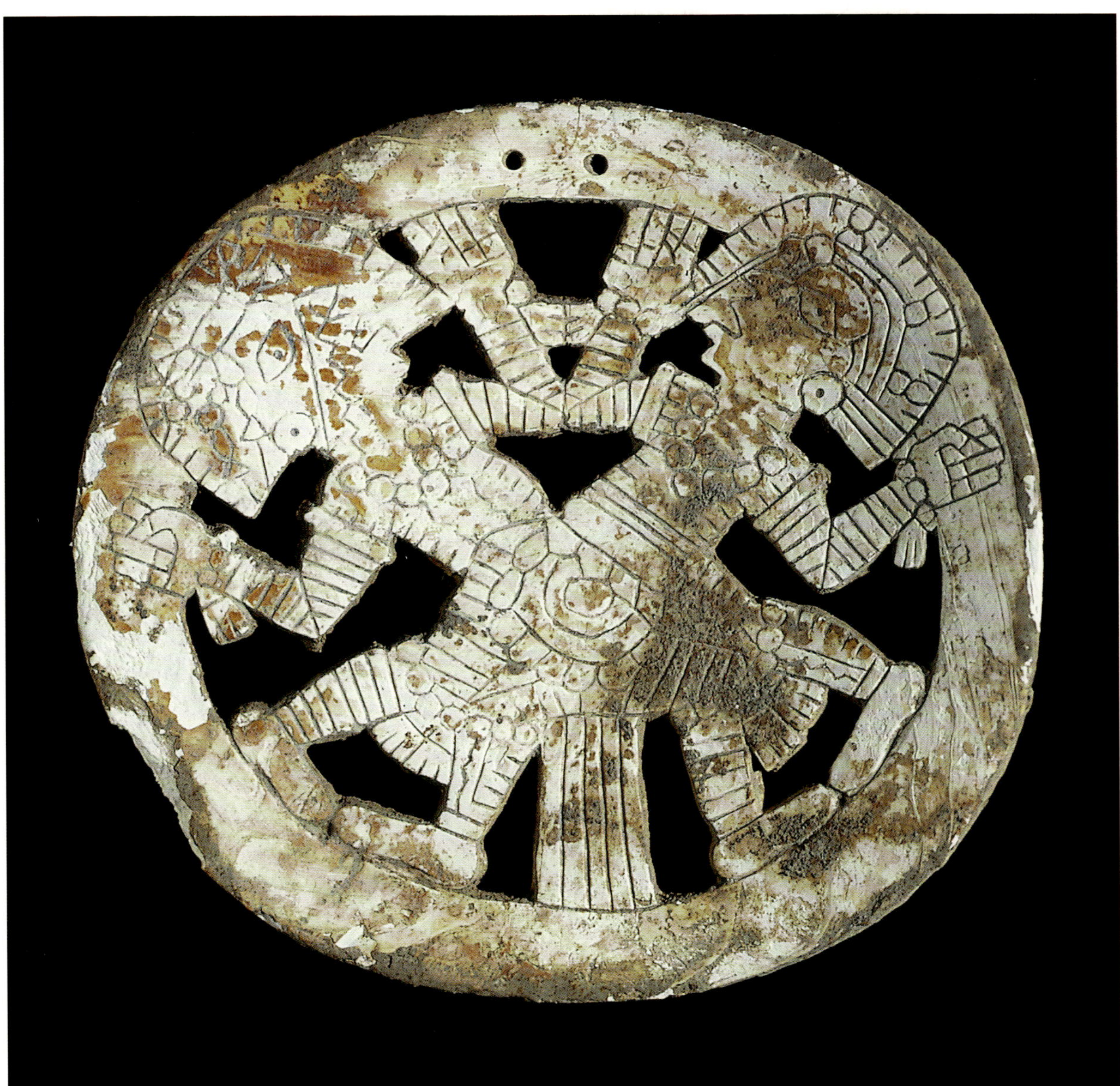

Fig. 22 Engraved shell gorget with pair of figures; Cartersville type, Late Braden style; Tennessee, Sumner County, Saundersville site, A.D. 1200–1400; marine shell, diam. 11.5 cm; Dr. Arthur Cushman Collection, Old Hickory, Tennessee. Cat. no. 139. With bold, graphic genius, the artist who engraved this gorget juxtaposed a pair of gesturing performers in an angular, spokelike composition within the encompassing circle.

take place in specific subject matter. For instance, the realistically knotted amphisbaena snake of the early Classic Braden is replaced in its later development in the Late Braden style by a deliberate reorientation of the heads with respect to the knot in order to achieve a more balanced composition (figs. 7 and 10). Of these balanced forms, the vertically compressed St. Andrews cross is one of the preferred symmetrical arrangements, and it can be represented by the Cartersville type of gorgets excavated at Etowah and one found in middle Tennessee (fig. 22). The eight embossed copper plates found in Malden, Missouri, and now part of the Wulfing Collection of Washington University in St. Louis, also nicely exemplify Late Braden style (figs. 23–25).[13] The open "hawk beak," or "snarling," mouth is diagnostic, and the crenellated diagonal line across the face, reminiscent of the gap-toothed upper jaw line of the agnathous (jawless) head, is equally distinctive.[14]

Cahokia and the surrounding area have a unique history, with experimentation in ritual imagery that centuries later would become important SECC themes. The Birdman theme, for example, was expressed very early in rock art.[15] At Picture Cave in Warren County, Missouri, just west of St. Louis, Carol Diaz-Granados has identified the Birdman with the Long-Nosed God maskette (see figs. 19–20 in her essay in this volume).[16] This and other figural images were drafted in both Classic Braden and not-so-classic Braden-like work as early as A.D. 1100. Thereafter, many more examples of Classic Braden rendering show up on different media, particularly on pottery.[17] The severed head imagery seen on the Rogan plate has been found scratched on pottery, and the highly distinctive T-bar element of what has been called the Akron Grid motif—after an engraved shell cup found near Akron, Arkansas (fig. 26)—was engraved on a duck head mounted on a pottery bowl that clearly predates the numerous examples of this motif on marine shell cups from Spiro, Oklahoma.[18]

The earliest dated evidence for the Long-Nosed God maskettes and the stone roller used in the chunkey game is to be found in the Cahokia area. During the 1100s a distinctive treatment emerged in some of the better-executed flint clay figurines, indicating the activity of a specific workshop and perhaps a single

facing page

Fig. 20 Map of the central Cahokia area showing the principal mounds, ceremonial plazas, and projected palisade; from Brown and Kelly 2000, fig. 3.

Fig. 21 Map of the American Bottom, c. 1800, showing principal mound groups and other nonmound archaeological sites; from Brown and Kelly 2000, fig. 2.

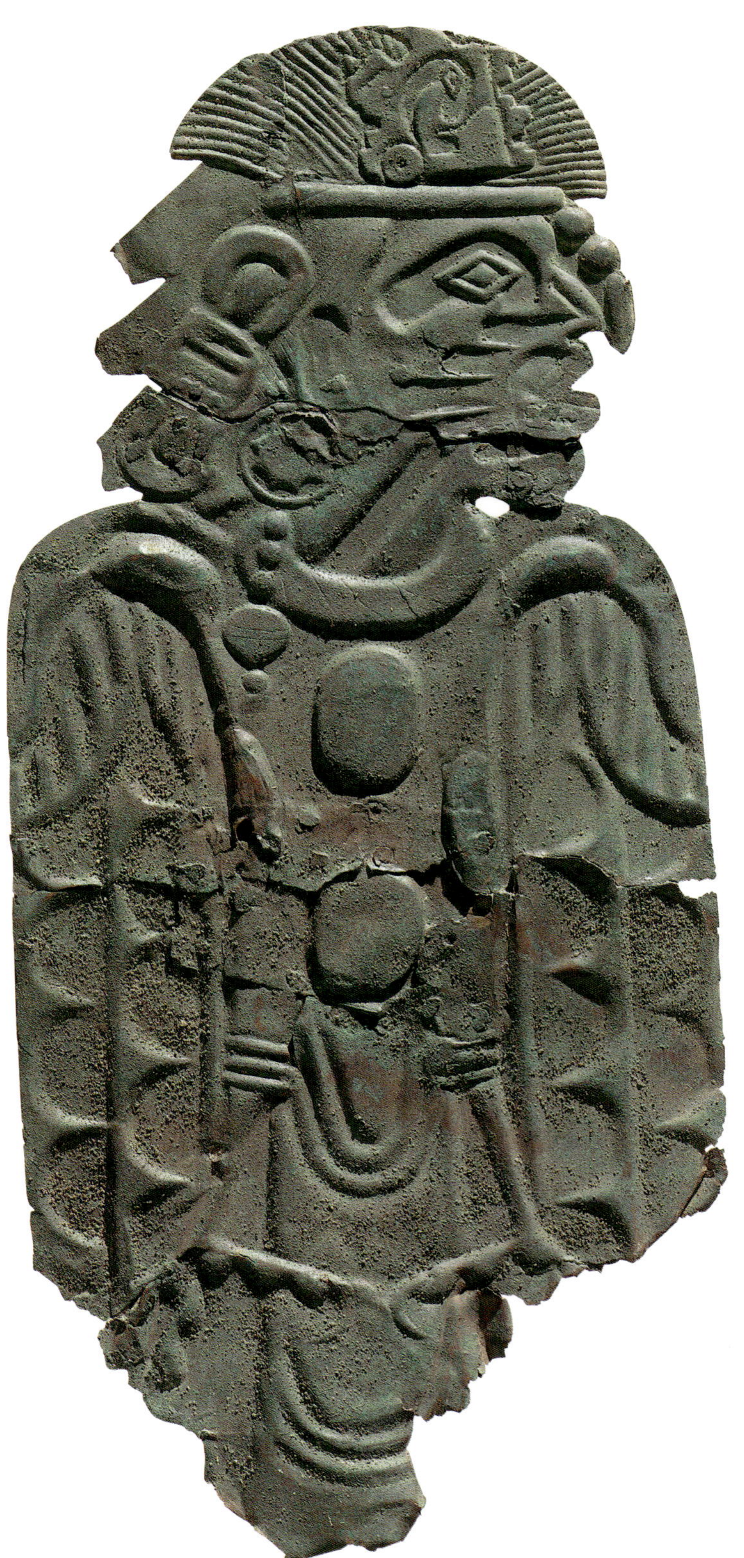

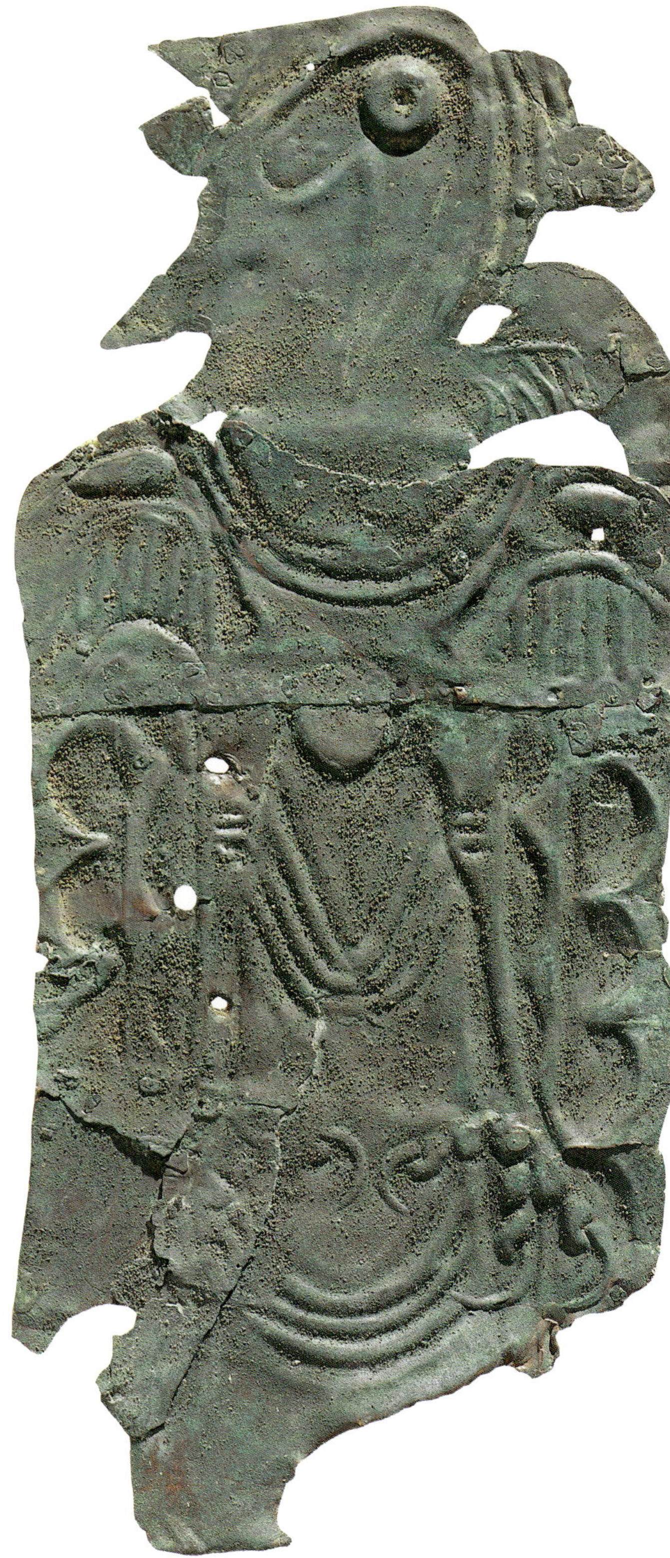

sculptor. Certain figural pipes that exemplify this stylistic coherence—the same rounded oblong platform, for instance—include the Grizzly Man from Spiro (see Reilly, fig. 18) and the Crouching Man from Shiloh, Tennessee (see Reilly, fig. 15). These large figures have substantial portions of their mass carved away. Together with the figure of Birdman or Morning Star (see Reilly, figs. 13a–b), they exhibit the same characteristic handling of the forearm that may well be the signature trait of a single master carver.[19]

Thus, Classic Braden engraving appeared on marine shell after previous expression on pottery of local manufacture. Some of these compositions show combinations that did not persist later. In other words, certain representations made it into, and became diagnostic elements of, the canonical repertoire of

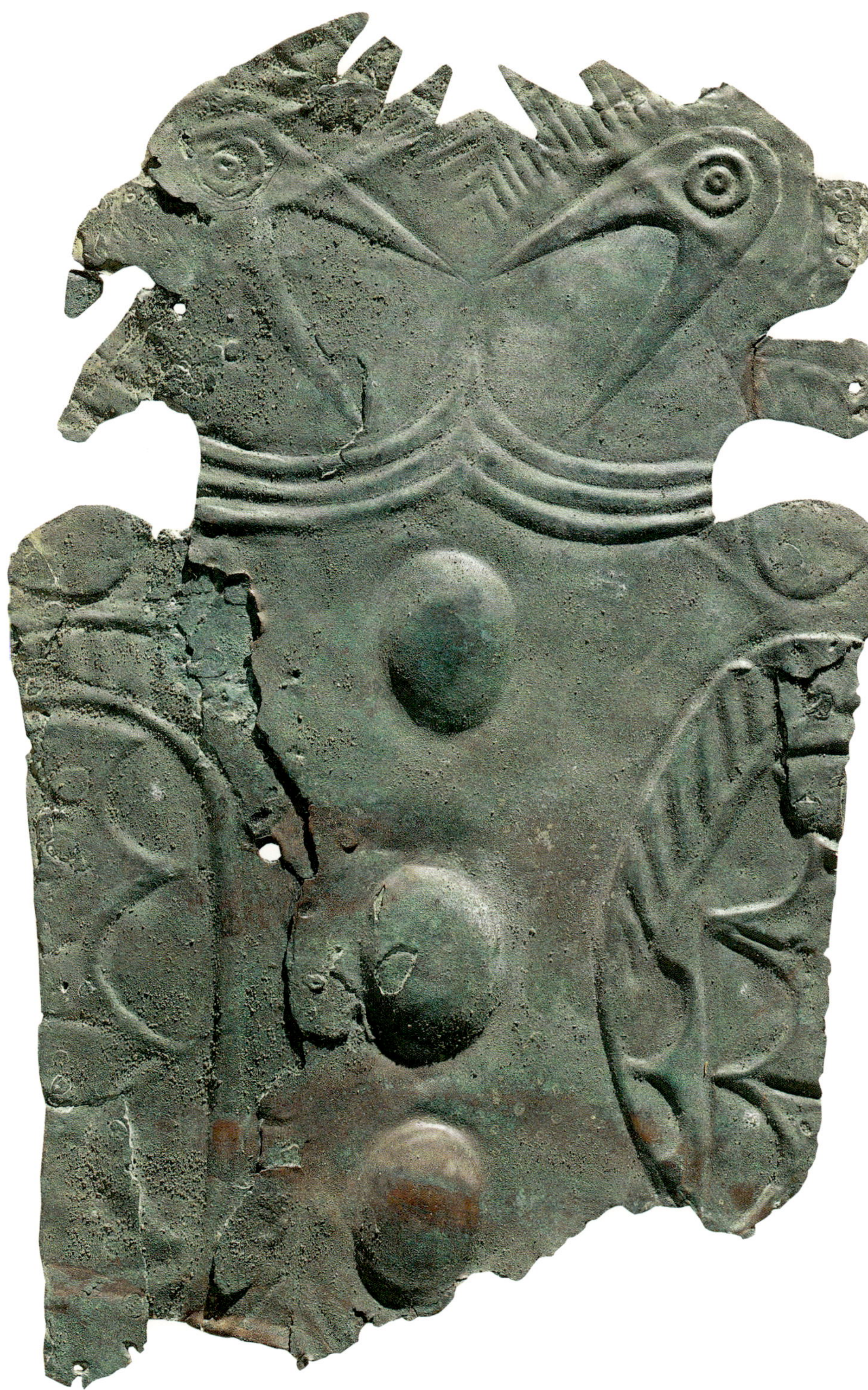

Fig. 23 Copper repoussé plate depicting Birdman; Late Braden style; Missouri, Dunklin County, Malden, Baldwin Farm, A.D. 1200–1400; copper, h. 29.9 cm; Washington University Gallery of Art, St. Louis; Gift of J. Max Wulfing, 1937. Cat. no. 112. This Birdman figure wears paraphernalia variously associated with warriors and, most notably, with the culture hero Morning Star or Red Horn (see also figs. 1 and 11 in the essay by Adam King in this volume).

Fig. 24 Copper repoussé plate depicting a falcon; Late Braden style; Missouri, Dunklin County, Malden, Baldwin Farm, A.D. 1200–1400; copper, h. 31.1 cm; Washington University Gallery of Art, St. Louis; Gift of J. Max Wulfing, 1937. Cat. no. 113.

Fig. 25 Copper repoussé plate depicting a double-headed falcon; Late Braden style; Missouri, Dunklin County, Malden, Baldwin Farm, A.D. 1200–1400; copper, h. 26.7 cm; Washington University Gallery of Art, St. Louis; Gift of J. Max Wulfing, 1937. Cat. no. 114. The craftsmanship evident in these and related copper plaques reveals a technical and graphic expertise developed in specialized, court-sponsored workshops.

the thirteenth century. Examples include fragments of shell engraving in Mound 34 bearing the Akron Grid motif.[20] The appearance of this canonical style took place around 1200 during a period of momentous change at Cahokia.[21] In sum, Cahokia has a record of early development leading to the formation of the SECC of the thirteenth century with the crystallization of style and iconography. No evidence for this distinctive midwestern imagery appears at Etowah, Moundville, and Spiro before 1200.

Southern Iconography at Cahokia

The history of the figural tradition in the Midwest, however, is only part of the picture, for coexisting with it is a widespread deployment of scrolls, swirls, and related abstractions on fineware bowls and the

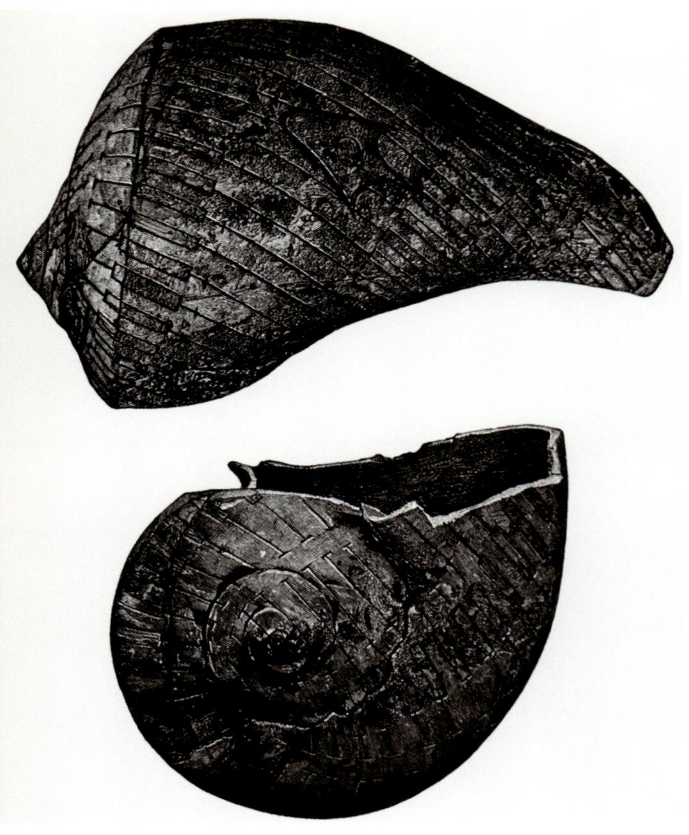

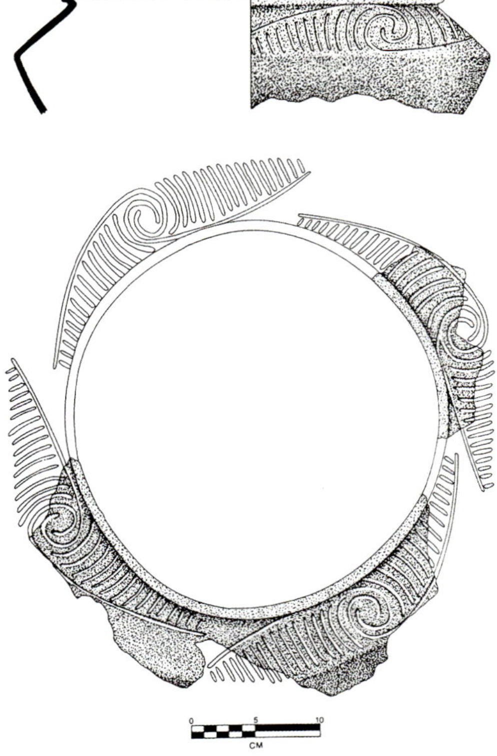

Fig. 26 Engraved whelk shell with Akron Grid motif; Arkansas, Independence County, Akron; from Thomas 1894.

Fig. 27 Ramey Incised vessel illustrating the deployment of ritually significant motifs surrounding a central opening; from Holley 1989, fig. 47. Such vessels are typical of Cahokia.

below

Fig. 28 Copper repoussé plate depicting forked-eye-surrounds and concentric circles; Oklahoma, LeFlore County, Spiro, Craig Mound, A.D. 1100–1200; copper, h. approx. 34 cm; Smithsonian National Museum of the American Indian, Washington, D.C. Cat. no. 115.

shoulders of fineware jars that are clearly of southern origin.[22] This abstract iconographic language was widespread throughout the greater Southeast, where it had considerable antiquity. At Cahokia the figural tradition was brought together with this geometric symbolism sometime around 1200 (figs. 27–29). One shell cup in particular epitomizes this iconographic imposition, for in it the dominant image of a Birdman is shown dancing into the starry heavens—as represented by an arc of annular elements within a band (fig. 30).[23] Surrounding this composition is a running border of arrows. This border is not a simple edge decoration, but can be readily visualized as representing the same thing as similar bands of running elements on shouldered fineware jars. Whereas the jar orifices presented an open space when viewed from above, the corresponding center of the aforementioned shell cup is occupied by a complex visual theme. This domination of the central space by a figure is a theme repeated many times over in other cases.[24]

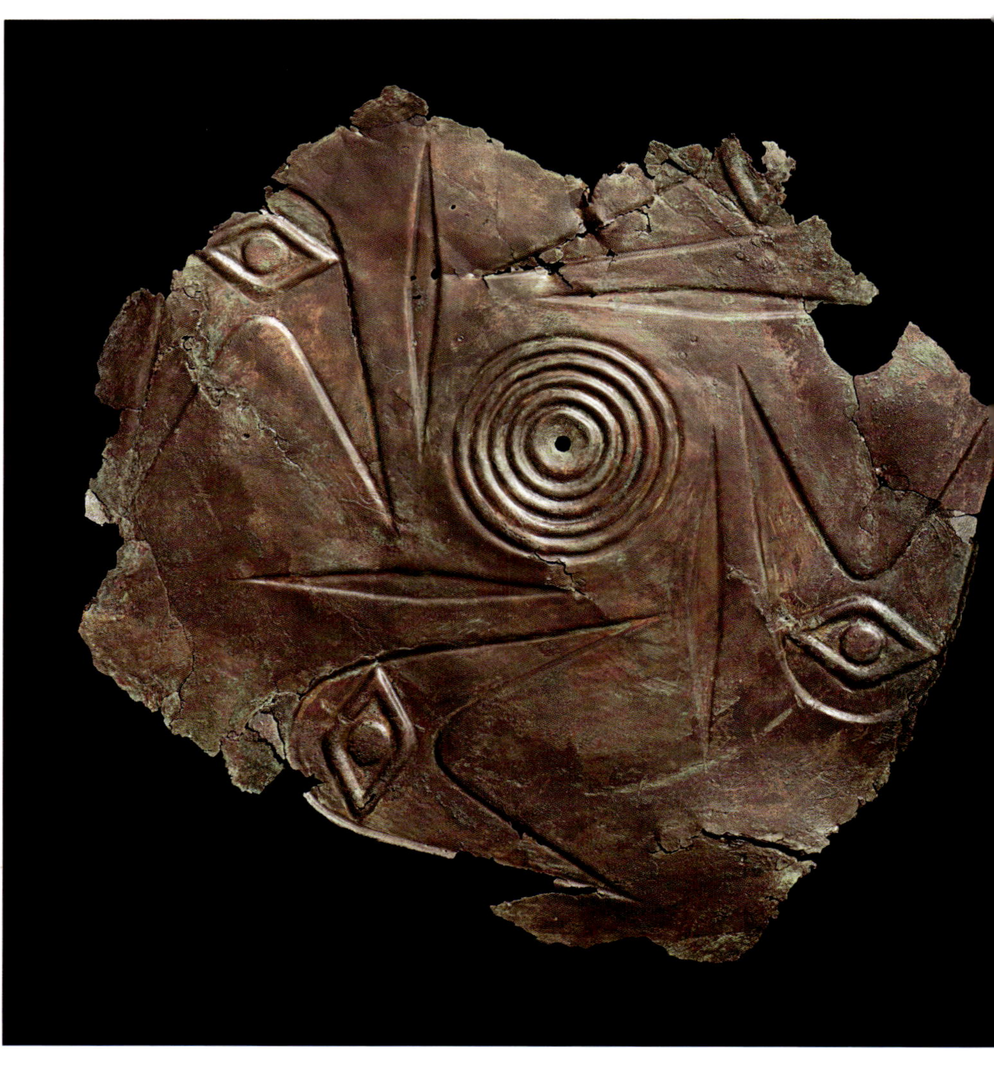

More commonly, however, Classic Braden figural imagery ignored centering symbolism altogether. The conjunction cited above was short-lived and presumably represents a point in time when the patrons of the figural tradition initiated an appropriation of the commonly held rituals that were referenced by these ceramics. Later in the thirteenth century, the motifs on the fineware bowls were transferred to the rims of plates. Thus, the two traditions merged at a crucial juncture in the formation of Classic Braden iconography, only to separate thereafter. A clear distinction was

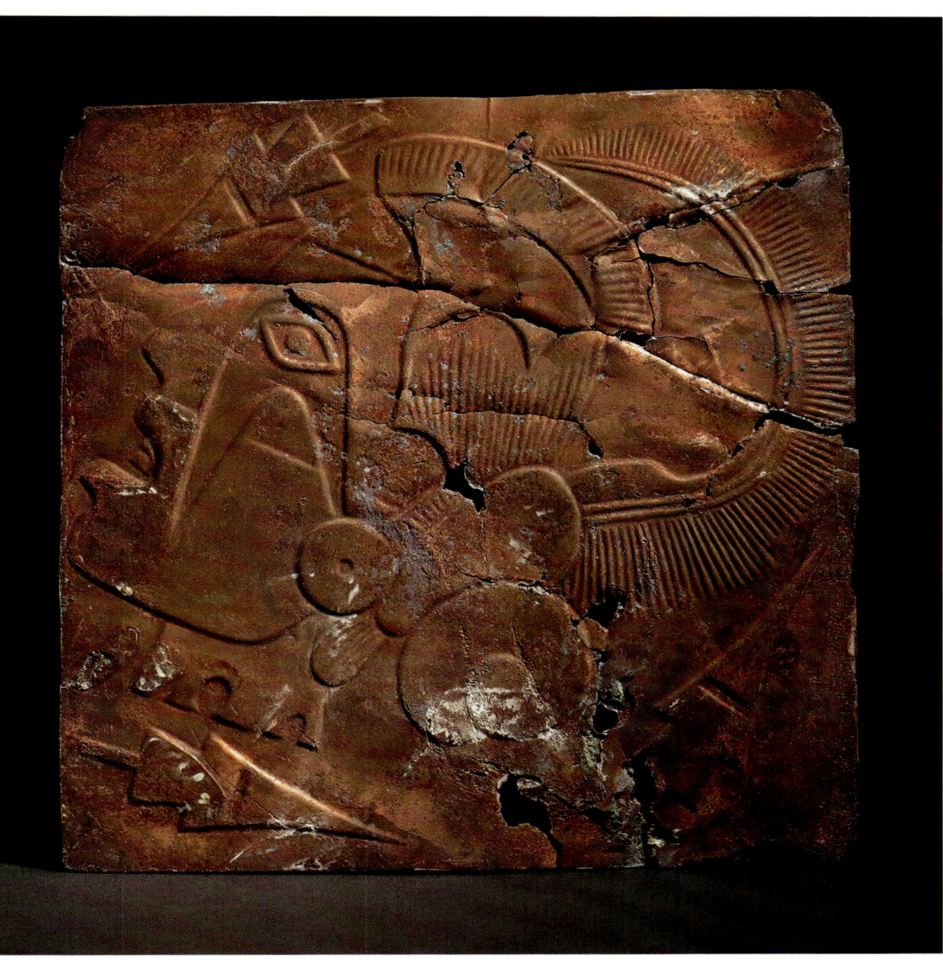

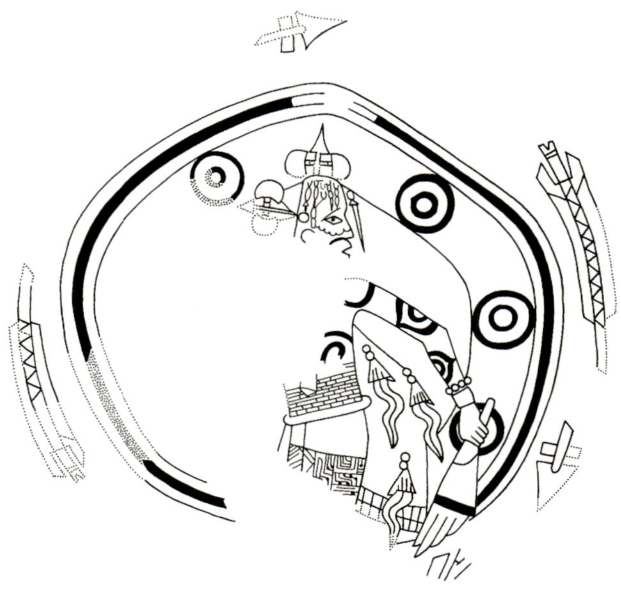

Fig. 29 Copper repoussé plate depicting a severed head surrounded by running arrowheads; Oklahoma, LeFlore County, Spiro, A.D. 1100–1200; copper, h. 30.5 cm; Ohio Historical Society, Columbus. Such tokens of military triumph would have been awarded and displayed as trophies and emblems of office for high-ranking warriors and commanders.

Fig. 30 Drawing of an engraved whelk shell showing Birdman rising within an arc of annular elements surrounded by running arrows; Classic Braden style; Oklahoma, LeFlore County, Spiro, Craig Mound, A.D. 1200–1400; from Phillips and Brown 1978, pl. 19.

subsequently maintained between the elite-controlled exclusivity of the Classic Braden and the inclusive, uncontrolled iconography of the plates.

Craft Specialization at Cahokia

The SECC encompassed a number of highly crafted objects that were made, used, and disposed of in exclusive contexts such as grave offerings, ritual observance, or display before eventual interment. These objects represent the readily identified, high end of ritual performance that we can assume extended into everyday life. Above all they can be regarded as an embodiment of spiritual power. Chiefly elites had a strong incentive to invest resources in visual symbolism: the more goods produced and the more intense the artistic achievement, the greater the impression of their accumulated power. Any retrenchment in elite investment and support could only have led to a decline in artistic skills.

A community of artists was necessary to sustain any artistic vision and a body of elite supporters was required to patronize these artists on a reliable basis. Each of these SECC styles became the product of many years of sustained practice by a small, intimate group of craft workers who acquired their skills through lengthy apprenticeship starting from a young age. Few precontact localities had the requisite productive surplus to support the kind of craft flow implied by the craft worker's control over delicate engraved lines. The skill level evinced by Classic Braden engraving could only come with decades of training.[25] For this reason the number of regionally based styles remained limited to those polities—such as Cahokia during the twelfth and thirteenth centuries—that could sustain a support system for craft workers over a period of decades.

The conditions for craft production were underway in the 1100s. The production of stone figures manifested varying levels of skill, but one workshop from this field of experimentation that was particularly gifted in producing engraved shell cups and shell gorgets can be regarded as creating a canonical iconography. More individualized approaches to shell cup engraving were left to the unsophisticated workshops with less work experience. Nevertheless, essential to these conditions for craft production was an economic surplus. Its deployment is represented in the debris of exotic raw materials found archaeologically on the living floors of the larger and presumably wealthier households. These households, according to Mary Beth Trubitt, had greater access to hard-to-acquire goods.[26] Shell bead production, for instance, was associated with these larger, presumably wealthier households. Under these circumstances elites can be recognized as dominating a particular portion of communal ritual in order to maintain it solely for themselves. Ritual expression that hitherto everyone had participated in now had a portion that had become the exclusive domain of a priestly elite.[27]

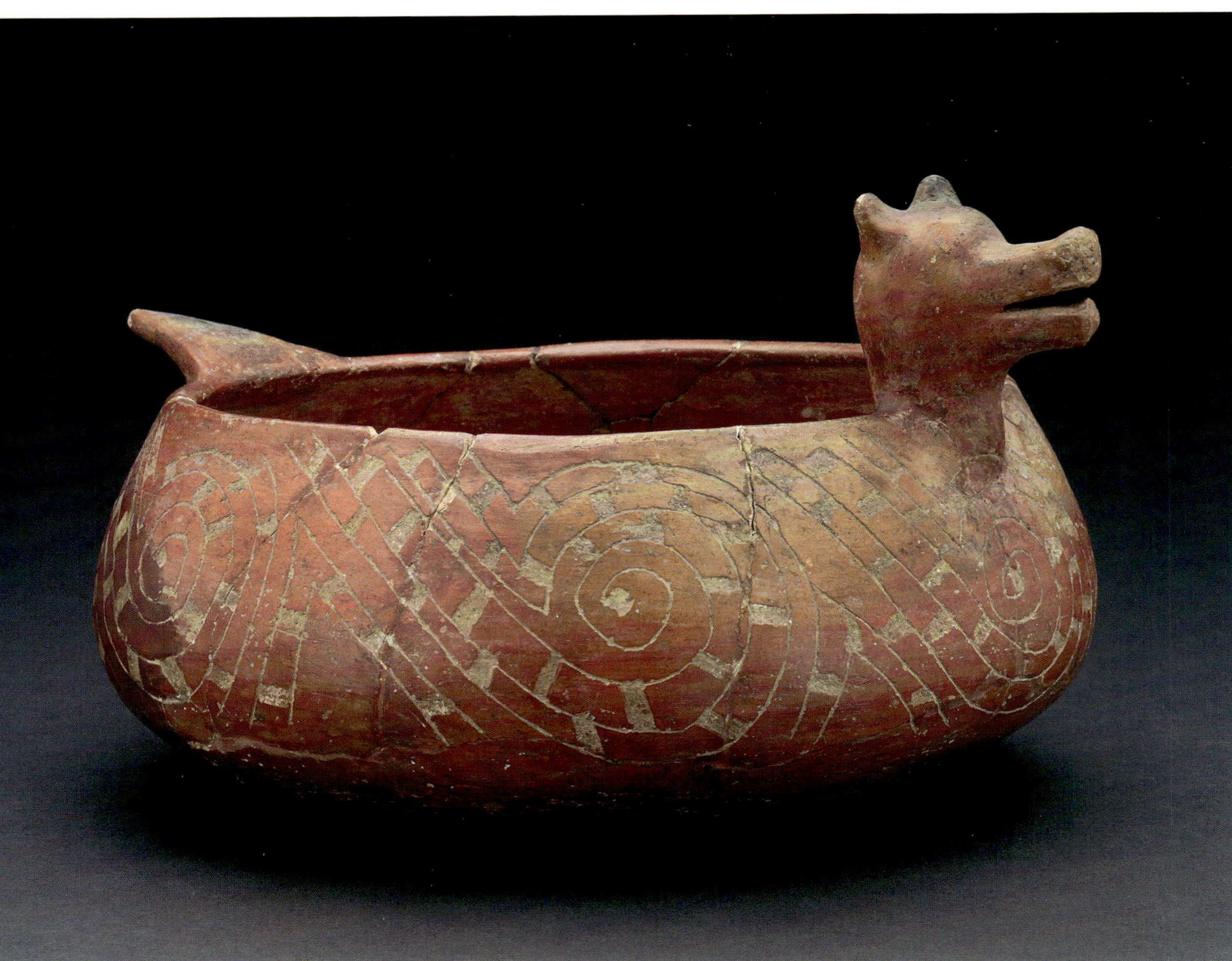

Fig. 31 Underwater Panther effigy vessel with engraved swirls of the blocked-line motif; Illinois, Fulton County, Shryock site, c. A.D. 1200; ceramic, h. 7.5, diam. 20 cm; Illinois State Museum, Springfield. Cat. no. 252.

Birdman

These exclusive contexts in which precious objects display the Southeastern Ceremonial Complex convey only an abstract sense of their visual and material distinctiveness. To move beyond this formalism one must have a conception of what these images portray: specifically, in the mythic narrative of the Morning Star, an allegorical figure who plays a central role in ensuring the triumph of life over death, day over night, summer over winter.[28] Who then is this central cult figure of the Birdman?[29] Recall that the two copper plates that John Rogan found were none other than outstanding examples of this image accompanied by a bilobed arrow and brandishing a knobbed club in one hand and a severed head in the other, along with other articles of costumery. Many attributes of the hawk are prominent in these depictions, including the raptorial beak, the forked-eye-surround, and the angel-like wings and tail. The bird is so strongly identified with this personage that in some cases the falconine image takes over at the expense of the human (figs. 23–25). In later depictions even the human mouth takes on the appearance of a raptor's open beak.

How is it that the Birdman assumed a centrality in ancient belief and became the dominant image of the SECC? Certainly, the falcon image readily evokes its renowned hunting behavior—aerial dives that strike larger birds out of the air and render their dazed bodies easy prey to feeding on the ground. One could hardly conceive of a more striking model for a spirited, swift, and daring attack. But is the Birdman as aggressive a killer as this bird itself? The answer to this question brings to bear a richer set of images than one merely of success in battle and is cosmologically more complete—a cult figure representing an allegory with deeper significance. For chiefs aspiring to power on the back of an appropriate ideology, the allegorical narrative that holds Morning Star at its center is a prize worth controlling. And we could put a name and a whole ritual narrative to this figure by considering the myths and cosmological beliefs of Southern Siouan-speaking peoples, the ancestors of whom are highly likely to have lived at Cahokia and in neighboring communities of the eastern prairies. Today these peoples are collectively the Kansa, Omaha, Osage, Ponca, and the Quapaw.[30] Among them, and most conspicuously documented among the Osage, the central figure of the falcon (generally just a hawk) is identified with the Morning Star deity.

Opposing Morning Star is the Great Serpent in its many guises. This deity sometimes bears wings, sometimes stands alone, and sometimes is combined with the image of a puma. When the three elements are combined—snake, puma, and bird wings—it is called a "piasa" (see Townsend, fig. 10). In Southern Siouan cosmological conceptions this deity represents the lower world, night, and death. Morning Star represents the capacity for rebirth; the Great Serpent exercises discretion over the timing of death. Each controls aspects of fertility: Morning Star controls the generation of human life and the Serpent/puma the generation of plant and animal life.[31]

Cultural Transfer to the South

Whereas figural representations have a long history at Cahokia and throughout the eastern prairies of the Midwest, the same cannot be said for the greater Southeast. Prior to the thirteenth century, human and animal imagery was almost absent from iconography.[32] Although nonfigural iconography dominated the prethirteenth-century Eastern Woodlands, it had a particularly strong representation in the Deep South where it had become established well before the Mississippian period. For instance, the shoulders and sides of carinated bowls bear continuous bands of curvilinear motifs (figs. 27 and 31). Concentric designs and chains of scrolls, swirls, and other curvilinear elements are emphasized on engraved marine shell cups and the shoulders of pottery vessels. The continuous chain of these curvilinear motifs is echoed later by a parallel circuit of overlapping logs in the log crib motif. A version is present on pottery and is a theme of a particular type of shell gorget (see Lankford, fig. 2).[33] This subject is logically a reference to the New Fire ceremony that I find plausible to have begun around 1050.[34] Pottery bowls, shell cups, and copper plates bear motifs of the arrow, arrowheads, and forked-eye-surround that evoke the theme of Birdman without calling into existence any figural representation (fig. 28; see also Dye, figs. 12–13). Lastly, iconography emphasizes the "centering" theme of collective representation, in which concentric rings dominate the centers of composite designs.

Midwestern items began to appear in the southern latitudes of the Deep South and Caddo country in the twelfth century and intensified during the thirteenth. Early examples consist of red flint clay figures, Long-Nosed God maskettes, and a limited number of examples of Braden-style shellwork and copperwork.[35] A different set dominated the thirteenth century. Prominent among these are the Classic Braden shell cups, shell gorgets, and copper repoussé plates. This appearance of Midwestern iconography in the South is too selective to be the product of ordinary trade. They suggest the appearance of a specific cult, because these precious objects contain too much power to be treated as objects of ordinary trade. New cultural practices are indicated by the advent of open plates of locally made ceramic fineware in which the rim is decorated with sunburst and related motifs. Another is the emergence of spin-off art styles, best exemplified by the Craig style localized in the Caddoan region.

The Cult-Bringer

The scale and depth of the local response to the interaction with Cahokia reminds us that Cahokia's actions may have had an impact upon certain southern towns decisive enough to shape their subsequent history. It is hardly accidental that the period of Cahokian impact is about the same for each of our three SECC centers.[36] The proximity of Cahokia to Spiro, Moundville, and Etowah signals a special relationship that nearby cultures did not enjoy. The three host territories have had a radically different history of material culture, each with deep roots in their respective regions. In each of these southern centers, special copper objects have been found that constitute a kind of ceremonial or cult paraphernalia. Heading the list is the bilobed-arrow head ornament (see Townsend, fig. 44; Dye, fig. 1). Following this is the repoussé copper plaque and the sacred scalp, which takes the form of a "heart-shaped apron" for an early period of gifting to Spiro (see fig. 6 in the essay by Chester Walker). Relationships to Etowah and Moundville took place when the "oblong gorget" form represented the sacred scalp. Spiro was the recipient of the largest number of Classic Braden-style copper plates, followed by Etowah and then Moundville.

Copper bilobed arrows, copper plumes, and the repoussé copper plaques are all prominently displayed in Birdman imagery. The carefully documented contexts of many of these pieces at Etowah testify to their display on the head or worn in the hair. The copper plaques have been assigned to a Cahokian source because the images have been executed in the Classic Braden style. At least one of the bilobed headdresses found by Warren K. Moorehead during his excavations at Etowah in the mid-1920s can be assigned to the same source. The lobes bear delicately incised Birdman profiles of Classic Braden style.[37] The prominence with which these objects are ornamented with Birdman imagery has been communicated in an unambiguous manner in highly exclusive contexts in the few graves where their burial context has been carefully reported. Furthermore only a select group of sites—Etowah, Moundville, and Citico, Tennessee—have yet to produce these ceremonial objects at all.

The exchange of copper plates is key to this political connection between Cahokia and its regional satellites (fig. 32). The subject matter of the Birdman plates encapsulates all of the qualities important for elite leaders to control. Hence it is logical to presume that the individuals with whom these plates were interred had rights to their exclusive use and that their claim overrode all others. Significantly, at the time of their burial these plates were not only exotic—having been introduced to Etowah from Cahokia—but also antiques.[38] Furthermore their disposal in the summit of the first cycle mantle points to their interment as part of the ceremonies that ritually closed the mound as it then stood.

The donor relationship has some precedence in the legendary history of Muskhogean cultures. Antonio Waring has described how the foundational importance of the cult-bringer is recorded in Muskhogean legend:

> Their final religious integration came after that [after the Coweta and Kasihta had settled at Ocmulgee Fields in central Georgia], according to their own accounts, and this is the period in which their stories refer to the Culture-bringers and the copper plates. These Culture-bringers lived with them and eventually died as ordinary mortals carrying to their graves much flashy ceremonial material.[39]

It does not matter whether this legend expresses a historically specific event or is a conflation of a string of such events. The notion of a cult-bringer elevates the archaeological evidence into our historical consciousness.

Spiro, Moundville, and Etowah

The response of Etowah, Moundville, and Spiro to the impact of Cahokia was exemplified materially in radically different ways.[40] Spiro, which started receiving precious goods from Cahokia in the twelfth century, was also the most influenced by Cahokian ideology.[41] Throughout the following century Cahokian objects, including not only pottery and arrowheads but also flint clay sculptures, copper Long-Nosed God maskettes, chunkey stones, engraved shell cups, gorgets, and copper plaques in both the Classic and Late Braden styles appeared at Spiro. The sheer quantity of copper repoussé plates, engraved shell cups, and gorgets in the Classic Braden style (see Dye, figs. 23–24) and in the later Late Braden style underscores the fact that Spiro was the recipient of a substantial Cahokian gift exchange over a period of many generations. A remarkable series of objects include different phases in the Braden stylistic development. Given this sustained relationship to Cahokia, it should not be surprising that instances of cultural emulation should be found. The pattern of reuse of engraved shell cups at Spiro confirms this assessment.[42] The practice of engraving the polished exteriors of whelk shells was adopted for the purpose of making ceremonial cups. The shell craft was extended to gorget production in the same style, as well as to a few repoussé copper plates.[43] This Craig style (Craig A) initially was so close to Classic Braden in form and subject matter as to make its distinction difficult.

Etowah and Moundville had different relationships to Cahokia. The range of Cahokian objects at Etowah is very narrow and is restricted to copper paraphernalia and to some engraved shell gorgets. At the Etowah site Classic Braden had already morphed into Late Braden when Classic Braden Birdman plates were exchanged around 1275.[44] But the timing of these gifts is so close to the beginning of important new uses of the mortuary mound location as to suggest that the contact was essential if not crucial to the social and political events after about 1275. The Birdman ideology was central to local politics. Selected graves held examples of the copper plaques, plumes, sacred scalps, and bilobed-arrow headdresses. Shell gorgets prominently displayed the Birdman, but incorporating a moth symbol according to Vernon Knight and Judith Franke that was foreign to Cahokia (see fig. 13 in the essay by Vincas Steponaitis and Vernon Knight).[45] The local Hightower style owes little to Classic Braden. Nor does it owe anything to the Late Braden Cartersville shell gorgets that were found in contemporary graves at Etowah.

Moundville has a relationship to Cahokia that is similar to Etowah's although the extant copper and marine shell materials are even fewer in number. Birdman plates are not in evidence at Moundville, although the same copper paraphernalia found at Etowah is. The local Hemphill style has a wider range of themes in common with Late Braden; therefore, a stylistic connection with Late Braden seems plausible, although the transitional steps are not evident.

Both the local Hightower and Hemphill styles (see Steponaitis and Knight, fig. 6, and Lankford, fig. 12) are likely to have been inspired by Late Braden, although the iconographic connections are the most obvious, as in the Birdman's presence in the Hightower style. In contrast, the Classic Braden style was well represented in marine shell and copper at Spiro, only in copperwork at Etowah, and only in one engraved shell fragment from Moundville.

The earliest version of the Craig A style bears close resemblance to Classic Braden; its later development into Craig B and finally Craig C diverge so strongly in

Fig. 32 Copper repoussé plate depicting two dancing Birdman figures (?); Classic Braden style; Illinois, Union County, Upper Bluff Lake, A.D. 1100–1200; copper, h. 27.9 cm; Smithsonian Institution, National Museum of Natural History, Washington, D.C. Cat. no. 118. The significance of the descending, ropelike motif is unknown.

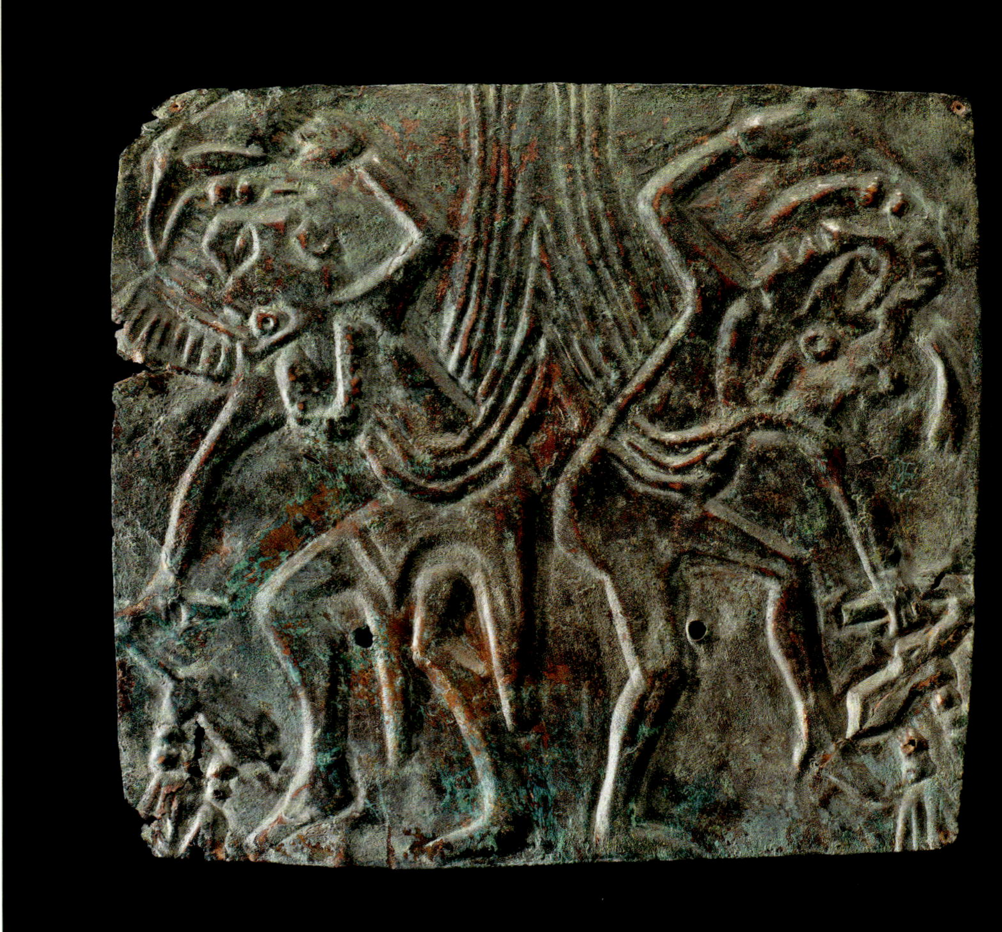

theme, compositional organization, and deployment of engraved line as to leave no question that an independent artistic model had taken root in this area. In contrast, only a shell gorget style (Hightower) was stimulated by Cahokian contact at Etowah. In the case of Moundville, neither a cup nor a gorget style was established. Instead a strong focus was placed on the engraving of pottery vessels.

In sum, different sites had very different relationships to Cahokia. Cahokian ideology had a stronger impact on the Caddoan beliefs at Spiro than it had at the other two centers. In ritual-related objects Spiro was inspired to produce a local form of shell engraving on marine shell cups and gorgets, as well as a few pieces of copper repoussé. For Etowah and Moundville the relationships were relatively short-term and largely confined to the late thirteenth century. Finally, the amount and diversity of material from Cahokia differed quite fundamentally.

Conclusion

Serious study of style in the SECC has led to insights into the developmental histories of specific styles, each of which is tied to a particular source region. The creation of a canonical iconography of Birdman imagery and other important mythic figures at Cahokia has a seminal place in the history of these SECC styles. The Classic Braden style developed and elaborated at Cahokia fundamentally defined the SECC, and it was as well the instrument for the dissemination of the Birdman iconography in at least three spin-off styles, one of which owes its stylistic formation to Classic Braden.

The timing, the place, and the cultural circumstances leading to the creation of the Complex's imagery are known, at least in its essential outlines. The period in question is the centuries leading up to 1200; the place is Cahokia; and the context in which the SECC arises as a distinctive artistic entity the moment that chiefs exercised control over an ideologically potent cult. Their patronage of the kind of artistic excellence that is manifested in the objects of the Complex can be regarded as a fitting instrument for the grip they achieved on exclusive powers.

The donor relationship between Cahokia and key town sites in the Southeast is clearly indicated by the impact that large numbers of highly crafted items had upon Spiroan culture. It inspired a local high art and created a surplus of wealth in ritual goods that resulted in their interment in graves at the principal regional site. At each site where Cahokian goods have been uncovered a similar relationship can be inferred (fig. 33). New cultural forms were inspired by the exchange, and these forms led to the rise and consolidation of cultural regions within the greater southeastern area that produced a heritage passed down to the time of European contact.

The location and timing puts the formulation of the SECC outside of the heart of the Deep South where Etowah, Moundville, and other political centers were located. Cahokia lies well to the north at the margins of the Eastern Prairies in the Mississippi River valley. Ironically, this northern location places the beginnings of the SECC more distant than ever from the high cultures of Mesoamerica where scholars have usually cast their eyes for sources of ritual complexity. The identification of Cahokia as the place where the figural theme of the SECC originated and developed casts a telling perspective on the SECC as a subject of interest for twenty-first-century observers. Consider what the complex would have been called had our knowledge emanated from findings first and primarily from Cahokia.

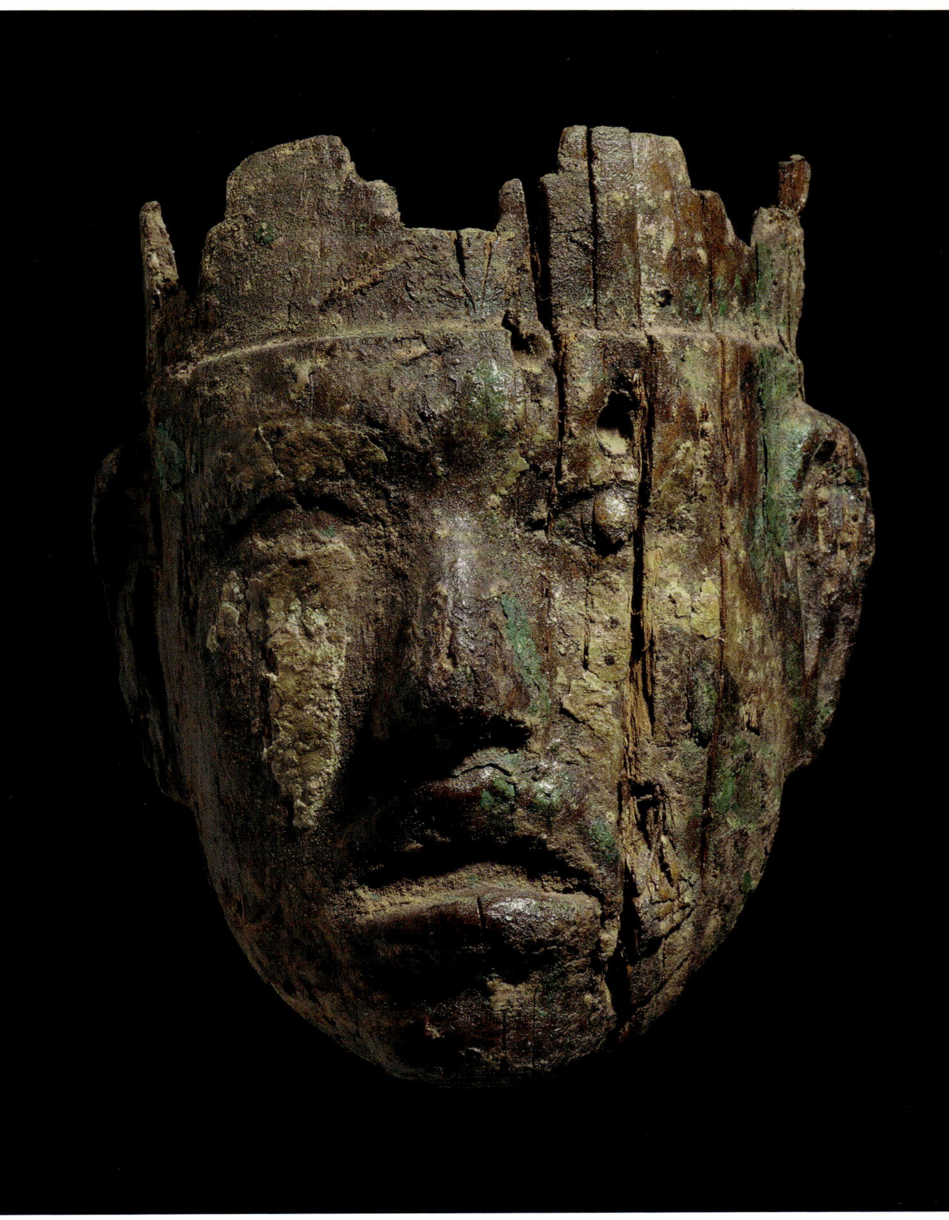

Fig. 33 Wooden maskette; Illinois, Fulton County, Emmons site, A.D. 1200–1350; red cedar, 11.9 × 9.9 × 5.5 cm; Illinois State Museum, Springfield. Cat. no. 273. This maskette would have originally been sheathed in copper and affixed to a headdress or another item of ritual regalia.

Notes

1. Actually this is an overstatement by Thomas (1887, p. 105; 1894, p. 703) because William Holmes (1883, p. 308) had reacted similarly to the Potter gorget from the Cairo lowland. In 1880 W. B. Potter published this engraved shell artifact from his own collection (Phillips and Brown 1978, pp. 176–77).

2. During this discovery period when archaeologists had a poor conception of when SECC objects originated, they were so struck by the unprecedented quality of these objects that they dabbled with the idea that the SECC was the result of an outpouring of religious expression in reaction to contact with Europeans. The SECC was thought to be the visual component of a nativistic movement that was a cultural reaction to the presence of European might on the shores of the Gulf and Atlantic (Waring and Holder 1945). Radiocarbon dating soon put to rest the times of these sites in relation to European contact. Widespread application of carbon-14 dating, together with more meticulous excavation, disclosed a long history at each of these sites in which the involvement with the SECC took place in the 13th and 14th centuries (Brown and Kelly 2000).

3. An additional but relatively unexplored presence are the traces that past activities on the off-mound archaeological record. For instance, deposits of rocks, minerals, plants, and animal remains in pits connected with feasting can be thought of as cultic components potentially complementary to the ritual objects of the Southeastern Complex (Kelly et al. n.d.; Pauketat et al. 2002).

4. Moundville and Etowah are separated by 200 miles. Citico and Hixon, Tennessee, among many others, extended the distribution northward and Lake Jackson, Florida, to the south. They form a relatively compact distribution compared with the Spiro outlier 450 miles to the west. Cahokia is separated from Spiro, Moundville, and Etowah by 350, 430, and 450 miles, respectively. The distribution of relevant shell art—both figural and abstract—is much greater, easily encompassing Cahokia (Brain and Phillips 1996).

5. The principle was initially argued in Krieger 1945. Hightower is drawn from the analysis of Muller 1989; Hemphill from Steponaitis 1983a; Craig from Phillips and Brown 1978.

6. Brown and Kelly 2000; Diaz-Granados et al. 2001.

7. Details in the treatment of snakes early in the Hemphill style has been shown by Schatte (1997) to have correspondences with Late Braden shell engraving.

8. In decreasing order, Cahokia has a maximum extent of 1000 ha; Moundville 150 ha; Spiro 33 ha; and Etowah 21 ha (Milner 1998, p. 109; Morgan 1980).

9. Notes on comparative size: Monks Mound alone has a basal area [measuring 316 by 241 m (Morgan 1980, p. 49)], a footprint so to speak, of about 7.6 ha, about 40 percent greater than the over 5.3 ha of the Great Pyramid of Egypt (Morgan 1980, pp. 52, 142).

10. See Kelly 1997 and the relevant area covered in *The Cahokia Atlas*, where these mounds are included in his Ramey Group (Morgan 1980, p. 52; Fowler 1997, pp. 194, 198). John Kelly's survey research argues for the 1200–1275 period age for this plaza as well as occupation to the east (Kelly et al. n.d.).

11. The history of nearby competitive centers is documented in Kelly 2002, and the persuasive political environment has been advanced in Beck 2003 and Beck n.d.

12. Here I have modified his concept by labeling Phillips's Braden A as Classic Braden, to which I have joined Jon Muller's (1989) Eddyville gorget style, the Birdman plates from Etowah, and certain examples of the Cahokia-type flint clay figurines. Phil Phillips (Phillips and Brown 1978, pp. 187–90; Brain and Phillips 1996) noted the strong similarity of these repoussé coppers to Braden A but preferred to erect a separate Etowah copper style instead, with the implication that the plates were an Etowah craft product because of their priority at this site—just as Braden A shell cups had come to be regarded as a Spiro craft product from the same principle of numerical preponderance (Brown 1989).

13. Phillips's Braden B shellwork and Phillips's Bellaire cat pipe style also exemplify Late Braden; see Brain and Phillips 1996, p. 386. Brain and Phillips (1996, pp. 50–1) drew attention to the St. Andrews cross arrangement of bodies in the Cartersville gorget type. Earlier, Phil Phillips (Phillips and Brown 1978) had demonstrated how the St. Andrews cross design was an important organizational principle in Late Braden (Phillips's Braden B). George Kubler (1962) would see the Late Braden as a saturation of a particular group of class forms whose inception arose around 1200 and persisted into the fourteenth century.

14. Brown 2005b.

15. This thesis has been elaborated in detail by Brown and Kelly 2000. Radiometric dates of the Picture Cave paintings have extended the age to at least A.D. 1000 (Diaz-Granados and Duncan 2000; Emerson et al. 2002; and Diaz-Granados et al. 2001). The Braden style does not encompass the numerous examples of cross-in-circle imagery, some of which have an early, independently occurring distribution (e.g., objects found in Key Marco, Florida). The Bennett log-crib gorget style can be placed in the same category.

16. Diaz-Granados et al. 2001.

17. Brown 1989; Brown and Kelly 2000, figs. 8a–d, 9a; Emerson 1989, pp. 78–80, fig. 10; Emerson 1995; and Phillips and Brown 1978, p. 172.

18. Of prime importance is the appearance of the Akron Grid, first on a duck head adorno and then on two pieces of engraved shell from later contexts at Mound 34. The ceramic instance is from a locally produced bowl found in an impeccable context at a housing tract. This and the tattooed duck head effigy adorno confirm that this diagnostic Braden signature trait is tied to Stirling and Moorehead phase Cahokia. If one wanted to challenge this association, one need only refer to the famous Gottschall tattooed stone sculptured head to confirm the very early, Midwestern provenience of this Braden trait.

19. The "Grizzly Man" figurine turned into pipe (Spiro Craig Mound provenience B99-3) combines features of dwarfism (hunched back and enlarged head with prominent bossing on the sides of the forehead) with an open, tooth-filled, snarling mouth, and a pair of hair knots that Richard Zurel (2002) has shown to be signature markers of the grizzly bear in frontal view.

20. Brown and Kelly 2000; Phillips and Brown 1978, p. 171, pl. 15. A summary of known examples from Stirling and Moorehead phase contexts at Cahokia is summarized in Brown and Kelly 2000.

21. Beck n.d.; Trubitt 2000.

22. See Emerson 1997b. These abstract designs led many archaeologists to deny local manufacture at all and to insist—despite the local shell-tempered paste of many pieces—that they derived from the Caddoan area. Also belonging to this southern tradition of abstract iconography are a number of shell cups, which Phillips called the "pottery style" and assigned to Braden A; a few copper repoussé plates known from Spiro and Mt. Royal, Florida; and one block-lined motif and thirteen cups and cup fragments (Phillips and Brown 1978, pls. 46–52). The Rayed, Concentric Barred Oval, and Davis Rectangle seem

to belong to the Geometric group. See Burnett 1945 and Moore 1894 for examples of the copper plates.

23. Spiro shell cup 19 (Phillips and Brown 1978).

24. Specifically in the copper plates in which the warrior head is surrounded by a running band of arrowheads (Brown 1996).

25. Brown n.d.

26. Trubitt 2000.

27. This elite-sponsored cult shared much content with the collectively oriented communal cults. As a consequence they may not be as easily segregated from one another as I have asserted here. In particular, both draw upon a pre-1200 ideology to be found on engraved pottery, embossed copper plates, engraved marine shell cups, and gorgets made in the preceding century. This is a time at Cahokia when a stockade was constructed around the central plaza as an exclusionary step, and a projection (or first terrace) was constructed off the main Monks Mound facing the plaza. This projection can be interpreted as the location of priestly intercessors between the sacred posers on the summit of the mound and the populace assembled in the plaza below.

28. Other deities were the subject matter for depiction of the stone figures. But after 1200 iconography becomes dominated by the Birdman and his cosmological adversary—the puma or snake.

29. I realize that the gender of the term Birdman is contested, but I have retained Phil Phillips's terminology (Phillips and Brown 1978) because I adhere to a position articulated in a recent paper that the falcon-marked figure stands for the male procreative principle (Brown 2005a).

30. The findings at Cahokia enlarge the geographical dimensions of the SECC many miles to the north. With this expansion other ethnic groups—the Dhegiha branch of the Siouan-speaking population—are brought into consideration through old association with the Prairie Plains.

31. This pattern is seen in the gifts of the falcon in the Osage legend of the patient warrior (La Flesche 1939, pp. 9–11), and the gifts of the puma/snake in the Pawnee legend of Owl Medicine (Dorsey 1904, pp. 206–07).

32. Weeden Island effigy vessels are a notable exception.

33. Sullivan 2001.

34. Brown 2004a; Knight 1997.

35. Emerson et al. 2003. Grant Mound and Mount Royal sites in eastern Florida belong to this early cultural horizon of widespread interaction that includes Spiro and Gahagan, Louisiana (Williams and Goggin 1956).

36. The Plaquemine culture of the Lake George site in Mississippi is another example.

37. Brain and Phillips (1996, p. 136) show how similar the heads are to the copper plate from Upper Bluff Lake (see fig. 32) and to the Castalian Springs shell gorget and the Lightner shell cup (no. 20) from Spiro.

38. A plate from Moorehead's Burial 86 illustrates how exotic the Classic Braden Birdman plates were to Etowah. Willoughby (1932, p. 39) called it "the crudest and probably one of the oldest portrait plates found with these burials" (Brain and Phillips 1996, pp. 142–43). Not only have two plates from different sources joined together, but no attention was paid to the articulation of their artwork. Indeed, the traces of repoussé figures are inscrutable because the embossing has been partly rubbed away (Byers 1962, fig. 3). The very use of older plates nearly devoid of intelligible design shows that artistic involvement was virtually absent at the moment of the new plate's creation. This is not an attitude in harmony with Etowah as the creative source of the Birdman in repoussé. It fits more appropriately with an external source of creation and places Etowah as sole recipient of repoussé work in the Classic Braden style. The Rogan plates, however, are not mere holdovers within the Early Wilbanks phase time span. These plates contain an archaism in the form of the so-called heart-shaped apron. A large range of depictions shows that the alleged article of costume suspended from the Birdman belt is nothing less than a full scalp complete with headdress (Brown 2005a and Brown 2005c). Its evolutionary replacement in the form of the "oblong pendant" was found in a contemporary stone box grave (Moorehead no. 76). It takes the form of a large oblong sheet copper pendant, albeit with four roundels instead of the usual one (Brain and Phillips 1996, p. 142; Willoughby 1932). To further drive home the point that these Classic Braden–style plates were out of place chronologically, a Late Braden Cartersville gorget was found in a contemporaneous grave (Rogan's f) (King 2003a; Thomas 1894). This gorget type is representative of an evolved form of Braden (Brown 2005b). The conspicuousness of the mace in the Rogan plates tells us that these plates were heirlooms when they were buried. Stone mace implements are absent from the Etowah gravelots, or for that matter contemporary ones in Moundville II deposits. The Etowan mace-form copper badges are clearly derivative from functional clubs. They are hypertrophic in form and are commonly modified with a key-shaped cutout outline on one side. Maces are not the emblematic warrior's invariant weapons. One of the copper Birdman plates from Lake Jackson displays the handle of an axe in place of the mace (Jones 1982). See also the Douglas gorget (Phillips and Brown 1978).

39. Waring 1968b, p. 93.

40. But this newfound appreciation for the historical time depth of the SECC at each of the major SECC sites has put off the outstanding issue—and that is the reason for the coordinated appearance of so much material. Not only do the same images appear repeatedly, but they also have the appearance of having been created in the same workshop. Just what was the way in which specific imagery and associated artifacts were generated in so many widely separated places at around the same time? If Europeans were not the catalyst for artistic expression, we are still left with the matter of whether a single source is represented. If not, then a unified process has to be identified that is applicable to each and every site. Comparable Classic Braden figural work found elsewhere has been dated to the previous century. The Cahokia Mound 34 context for Classic Braden engraved shell cup fragments is 1280± 200 (uncorrected) (M-635) (Brown and Kelly 2000). A repoussé plate from Spiro has an AMS date on associated organics of 1160–1280 corrected (Brown and Rogers 1999). Both of these dates lie comfortably close to 1275, the estimated beginning date for the Early Wilbanks phase (King 2003a).

41. Early input was documented by the appearance of "bell-shaped" polished chert axe heads of Kaolin chert (Brown 1996).

42. Phil Phillips stated that: "Taken strictly at face value the results [of a review of reuse patterns] would indicate that Craig A is later than Braden A, possibly to the point of overlapping with Braden B; that Craig B is later than Braden A (which is no surprise), or even later than Braden B; and that Craig C is later than Braden B" (Phillips and Brown 1978, p. 38). A later assessment affirms this appraisal with additional information (Phillips and Brown 1984, pp. vi–xiii, xvi).

43. Brown and Rogers 1989.

44. Brown 2005c.

45. Knight and Franke 2005.

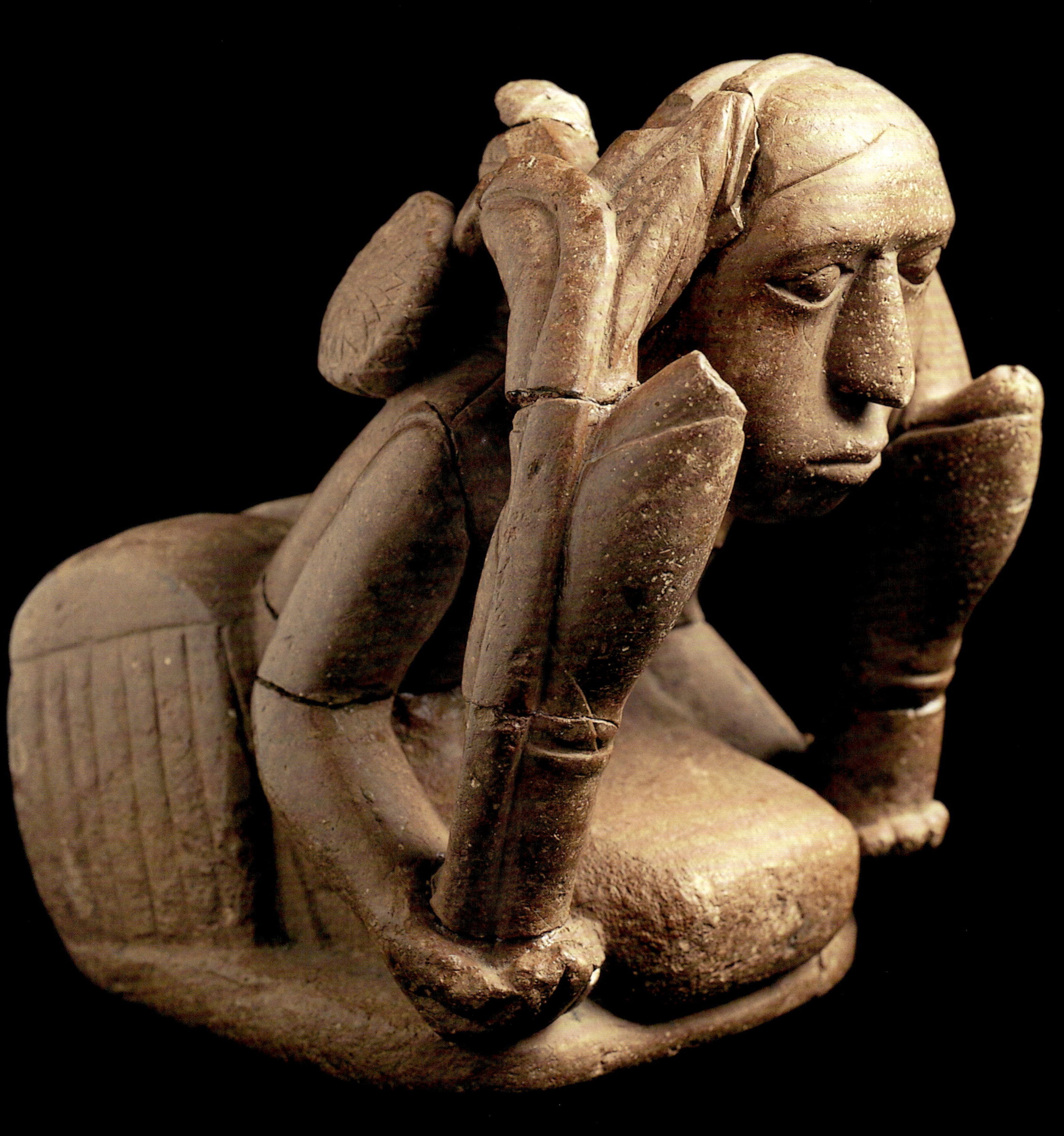

People of Earth, People of Sky

F. Kent Reilly III

Visualizing the Sacred in Native American Art of the Mississippian Period

Art and ritual provided the symbolic and metaphorical means by which the people of the Mississippian world visualized their spiritual relationships with the supernatural. Mississippian art—or, more specifically, what I shall argue is the art of a Mississippian Art and Ceremonial Complex (MACC)—often displayed an encoded symbolic system that portrayed the locations and inhabitants of a perceived, yet unseen, reality. The MACC possessed a complex symbolic language with important political and social functions. It not only visualized the sacred and portrayed ritual activity, but also manifested the religious vision of the many Native American peoples who occupied North America from the Rocky Mountains to the Atlantic Ocean and from the Great Lakes to the Gulf of Mexico for a period of more than 700 years.[1] During the last fifteen years a number of important concepts have gained acceptance concerning the function and production of Mississippian art (see, for example, the essays by James Brown and George Lankford in this volume). A review of these points of understanding will provide us an excellent starting place for any interpretation of the specifics of Mississippian-period iconography.

Fig. 1 Effigy pipe of a kneeling female figure holding maize and sunflower plants; Arkansas, Desha County, A.D. 1100–1200; flint clay, 18 × 18 × 14 cm; Dr. Kent and Jonnie Westbrook Collection, Little Rock, Arkansas. Cat. no. 102. This effigy pipe—excavated in Arkansas but probably sculpted in Illinois at Cahokia—portrays the female personification of Corn Mother, the provider of plants and horticultural skills. Maize stalks grow from her outstretched hands and sunflowers lie upon her back. The imagery of Corn Mother, Our Grandmother, and related female deities is recognizable in tribal mythology even today, as wives of the hero Red Horn or Morning Star.

Some General Understandings about Mississippian Art

When first posited almost sixty years ago, the interpretation of Mississippian iconography focused on an organizational phenomenon labeled the Southeastern Ceremonial Complex (SECC).[2] In recent years, however, I have become convinced that the term Mississippian Art and Ceremonial Complex (MACC) would more accurately describe the artistic output of the Mississippian period, its multiethnic complexity, and its broad geographical spread, particularly in light of identifications related to style regions outside the southeastern United States. Nonetheless, I still find the designation of a "complex" a useful tool in discussing this body of artwork, because it emphasizes that Mississippian art not only possesses an aesthetic quality, but also communicates the visualization of both belief and ritual activity. The MACC identifier is also useful because it provides a more flexible temporal and geographical framework for the several art styles that compose the complex. The SECC label remains useful because it accurately designates a specific time frame (A.D. 1300–1500) and a more limited geographical distribution within the larger category of the MACC.

Style distinctions are readily apparent in the MACC.[3] Within these styles, however, the themes are conservative and relatively limited. This multiplicity of styles with conservatism in theme can be explained by the fact that if individual artists had arbitrarily manipulated the way a supernatural location or actor was represented, then the attributes of that location or deity might no longer be ascertainable. Thus, the purpose of the art might not only have gone undiscerned, but might even have been lost. This does not mean, of course, that all MACC art is readily accessible. In fact, MACC art is populated with bizarre zoomorphic images. As Vernon J. Knight has argued, "The rise of this inventive imagery is bound up with the struggle of emerging Mississippian elites to consolidate power by exhibiting a positive control over a scarce commodity, namely, esoteric knowledge" (fig. 3).[4] Examining the extensive corpus of ethnographic material collected in the eighteenth, nineteenth, and early twentieth centuries reveals continuities between MACC images and symbols on the one hand and ethnographic information on the other. Ongoing research has decoded some elements, symbols, and motif sets within the fascinating symbol system of the MACC. From these ethnographic sources, we can better understand the cosmological placement of certain anthropomorphic and zoomorphic figures represented on objects that were created in various MACC styles, such as Braden, Craig, Hemphill, and Hixon (Hightower).

The religious system expressed through the MACC is inherently Native American in that it focuses on an animated cosmological vision. The sources of Mississippian-period art have great time depth and, in fact, are the conceptual legacy of the preceding Late Archaic- and Woodland-period cultures.[5] Specifically, many of the Mississippian symbols first appeared in the artistic production of the Middle Woodland–period Hopewell Interaction Sphere (see the essays by Mark Seeman and Bradley Lepper in this volume).

This religious system is expressed through an overarching creation myth or cosmogony composed of at least three overlapping mythic cycles and ritual components: the Morning Star Cycle, the Earth and Fertility Cycle, and the Path of Souls.[6] Ethnographic and iconographic evidence strongly indicates that many Native American mythic sagas shared narrative episodes, and that they can, in fact, be best understood as chapters in a single, all-embracing creation cycle. One may conceive of the relationship among these overlapping mythic cycles much as an environmental scientist perceives overlapping environmental zones. The transitional area where zones overlap—what ecologists call an ecotone—possesses the most wide-ranging biodiversity. Analogously, the area where these mythic cycles overlap, in effect, constitutes a religiously charged ecotone in which various Mississippian cosmogonic beliefs thrive. Aspects of these three mythic cycles unquestionably survive today in the traditional beliefs

The Mississippian Art and Ceremonial Complex falls into several temporal periods:

A.D. 900–1100: The MACC develops out of the art of the earlier Hopewell Interaction Sphere.

A.D. 1100–1200: A quantity of recognizable MACC material in the media of copper, flint clay, and shell is produced in the Greater Braden style. A stylistic argument, which a limited amount of archaeological data supports, suggests a possible Cahokian origin for this material and for the Greater Braden style.*

A.D. 1200–1300: MACC Greater Braden material is found in several geographical areas of the Eastern Woodlands. An elite exchange mechanism accounts for the distribution of this material. The Greater Braden material inspires many MACC regional styles. Despite the links among Greater Braden–style objects and the MACC, over time several MACC elements, symbols, motif sets, and zoomorphic figures cross style boundaries and are adapted in several of the emerging stylistic regions. These stylistic regions may correspond to Mississippian-period linguistic, ethnic, and political regions.

A.D. 1350–1500: Much of the Greater Braden and Missouri flint clay heirloom material is removed from the active Mississippian artistic corpus as these ritual objects are cached after some 150 years of ritual use. During this same period, essential MACC symbols migrate from the media of copper, shell, and stone to the more readily available medium of clay. The reason for this transference may be the collapse of earlier elite exchange systems. Clay vessels bearing many aspects of MACC symbolism are frequently used as mortuary items.

* Brown and Kelly 2000; Brown 2005b.

and religious rituals of certain contemporary Native American groups.

The MACC Cosmological Model

Much of the iconography of this Mississippian-period Art and Ceremonial Complex focused on cosmology and the supernaturals who inhabited the cosmos. Just as a modern map can convey both geographical and cultural functions, so the art of this MACC reflects a coherent vision of an observed, ideologically generated, cosmic model. The Mississippian cosmic model encompassed real, knowable locations, whether in this physical realm or in the extraphysical reality of the Otherworld.

The Native American universe of the Mississippian period, in which ideological as well as historical action occurred, was a three-leveled configuration composed of the Above World or Overworld (i.e., the sky), the Middle World, and the Beneath World or Underworld (fig. 2). A central axis connected all these levels, and it could take the form of a center pole or a sacred tree, often a cedar. Many Native American peoples also perceived the Above World and the Beneath World as subdivided into tiers or levels. In all of these models, each tier was home to specific deities who could travel among cosmic levels. Also deeply embedded in this trilevel cosmology was the dynamic concept of dualistic oppositions. This notion—as fundamental as gravity is to our world vision—expresses the tension of the natural balanced against the supernatural, or of the Above World poised against the Beneath World. The practitioners of this living but ancient religious system accessed sacred power through deities of this trilevel universe, as well as through animals and the spirits of their ancestors. In Native American belief, both contemporary and ancient, animals shared the earth with humans and nourished them. But animals possessed preternatural powers that humans lacked, and in many instances they were crucial actors in cosmogonic tales.[7] In the Mississippian and later Native American world, ritual and ceremony were the means to access these cosmic powers.

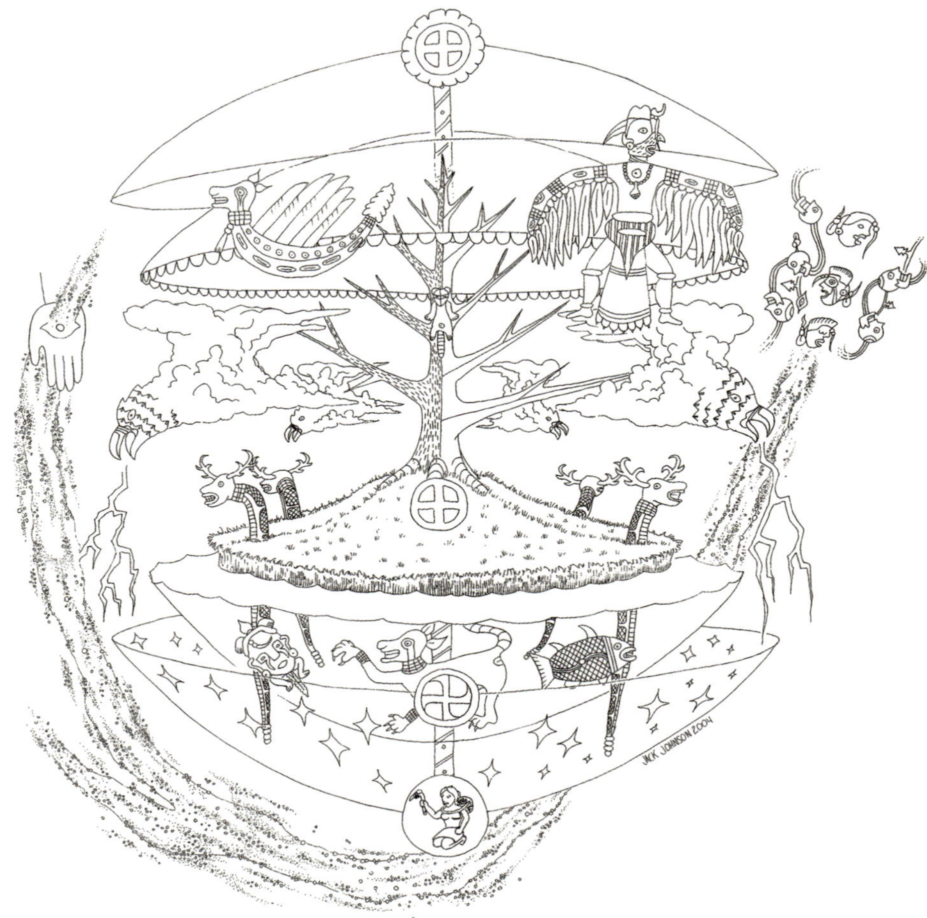

Fig. 2 Hypothetical model of the Native American cosmos; drawing by Jack Johnson.

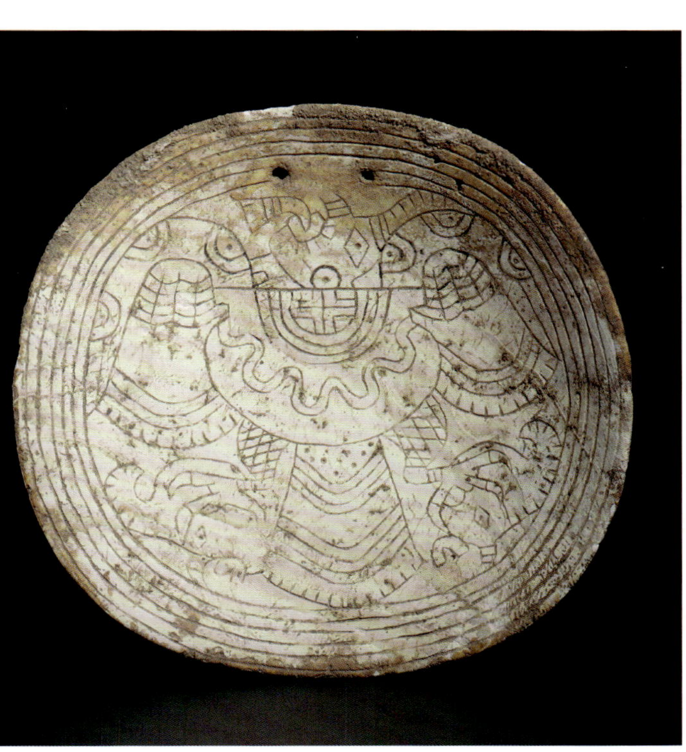

Fig. 3 Engraved shell gorget with Birdman vessel and severed heads; Arkansas, Craighead County, A.D. 1200–1400; marine shell, diam. 12.1 cm; Tommy Beutell Collection. Cat. no. 143.

In the ethnographic sources that documented the beliefs of later Native American peoples, the perceived rotation of the sky was interpreted as the edge of the stony sky vault moving up and down at the edge of the earth's horizon, much as the lip of a spinning bowl makes contact with the top of a table.[8] When the sky vault manifested itself as the night sky, it contained the celestial path that we know as the Milky Way. Along this celestial, starry path, the dead journeyed as they traveled to the realm of the Otherworld.[9] Also located in the night sky was the lodge of the female lunar deity, a goddess who likewise carried both Middle World and Underworld connotations. The creation force, often identified as a solar deity, had its home in the day sky. The Thunderers too inhabited the day sky, as did the lords of wind and lighting, who were identified as falcons or other birds of prey. These deities were also associated with the cardinal directions. Furthermore, the Thunderers constantly opposed the Underworld powers. The Middle World of humankind was likewise

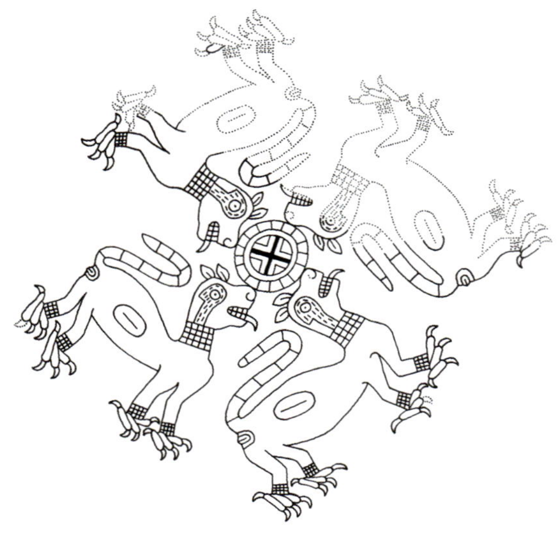

oriented by cardinal or semicardinal directions and was perceived as either floating on the surface of a primordial sea, or resting on the back of a turtle that floated in such an ocean. The guardians of the Middle World stilled the rocking motion of the earth that was caused by the movement of the primordial ocean. Iconographically, this steadying of the earth's surface was achieved by knotted ropes suspended from the sky or by four serpents driven into the earth itself.

The Underworld was, in fact, an underwater realm, entered from the Middle World through caves, lakes, rivers, and streams, and from the Overworld by following the Path of Souls. The lord of this watery domain was the Underwater Panther or piasa.[10] This legendary zoomorphic supernatural possessed the attributes of both panther and snake. In some ethnographic accounts, four piasas existed, each associated with its own cardinal or intercardinal direction. As an Underwater Panther using its thrashing tail, the piasa could stir the surface of lakes and rivers into dangerous waves and whirlpools. As a winged and horned serpent, it was both a constellation and a major component of the Path of Souls (see fig. 13 in the essay by George Lankford in this volume).[11] In two examples from the corpus of the shell engravings unearthed near Spiro, Oklahoma, four piasas surround cross-in-circle motifs. In the first engraved example, each piasa takes the form of an Underwater Panther equipped with a whiplike, segmented tail; a segmented border, highly reminiscent of these segmented tails, surrounds this cross-in-circle motif (fig. 4). The second engraving depicts four winged or celestial rattlesnakes that also surround a cross, which is itself enclosed in concentric circles (figs. 5–6). In some instances, concentric circles have been shown to function as symbolic locatives indicating the night sky.[12] As George Lankford has argued in his essay in this volume, these two sets of piasa images surely depict different forms of the same supernatural, as it acts in both the Beneath World and the Above World. These two shell engravings present striking evidence that certain supernaturals can cross the boundaries among cosmic levels, and they encode little-understood cosmic beliefs of Mississippian-period Native Americans. For instance, where did the night sky, with its specific celestial actors, originate? Where did the day sky go at sunset? Perhaps these engraved piasas display the cosmological concept that, in fact, the night sky was perceived as a visualization of the Beneath World.

Fig. 4 Drawing of an engraved whelk shell from the Craig Mound at Spiro, Oklahoma, showing four Underwater Panthers or piasas surrounding a cross-in-circle motif; Craig B style; from Phillips and Brown 1984, pl. 228.

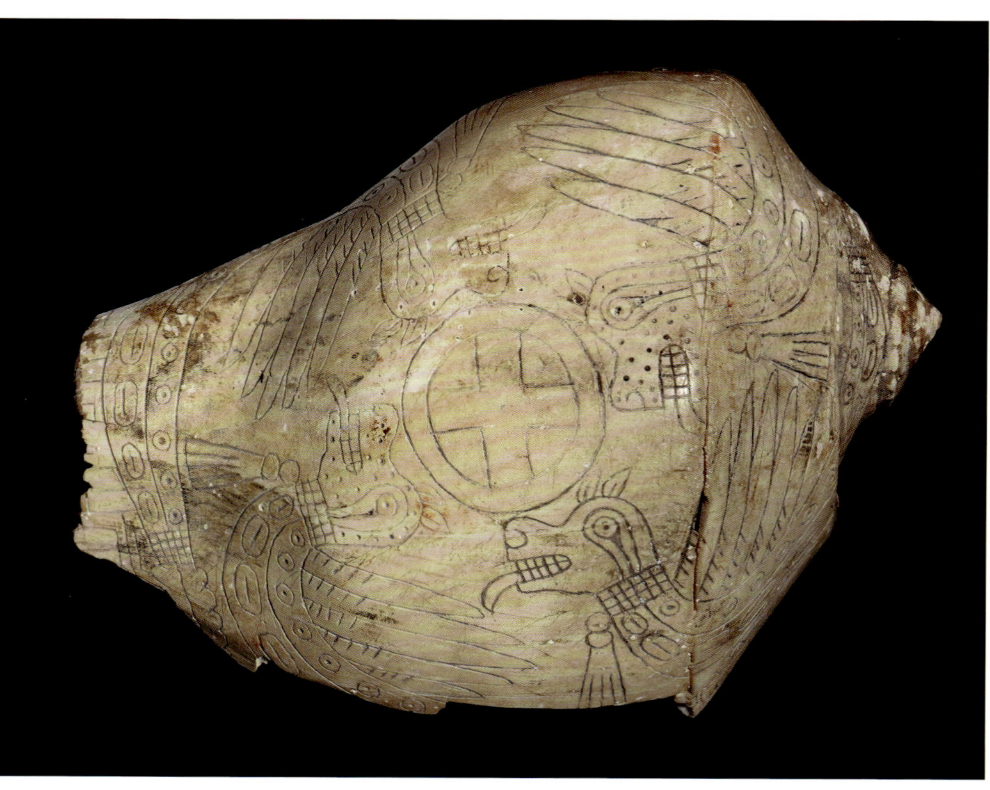

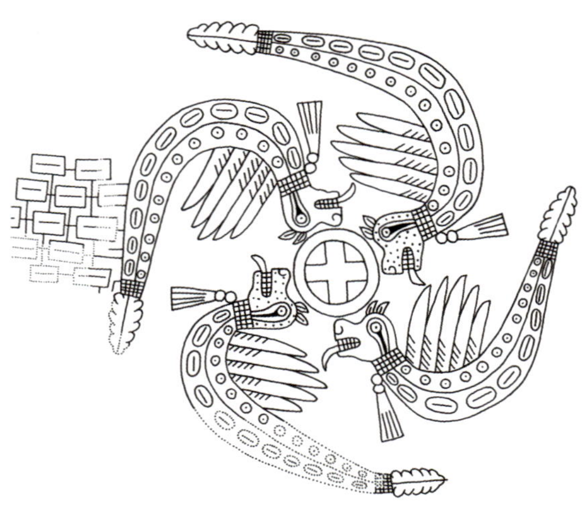

Fig. 5 Engraved whelk shell with four winged serpents surrounding a cross-in-circle motif; Craig B style; Oklahoma, LeFlore County, Spiro, Craig Mound, A.D. 1200–1350; marine shell, l. 21.6 cm; University of Arkansas Museum, Fayetteville. Cat. no. 127.

Fig. 6 Drawing of the four winged serpents engraved on the shell shown in fig. 5; from Phillips and Brown 1984, pl. 229.

Mississippian-period art illustrates that the various supernaturals, heroes, and gods who inhabited the multiple tiers of the universe were depicted artistically in three categories: anthropomorphs, zoomorphs, and natural beings (i.e., plants and animals). Although specific supernaturals are identified through equally specific symbol and pictorial sets, these same supernaturals can cross category boundaries by assuming the motifs and symbols of other supernaturals. These apparent category boundaries are not always clearly defined. Such manipulation of categories could have signaled transformations, as well as travels among different cosmic realms.

Needless to say, anthropomorphic representations clearly are human. Nonetheless, they can carry ritual and animal aspects in the form of costume details that help identify certain attributes of their supernatural natures. Zoomorphic images occasionally display human aspects, but their overall composition is not naturalistic. The primary forms of these zoomorphs derive from particular animals—felines, spiders, snakes, and birds of prey. The body parts of these animals, however, are combined in such surprising ways that they could not be mistaken for natural creatures: they are indeed supernaturals. Images of animals usually are linked with anthropomorphic and zoomorphic representations. Specifically, creatures such as raccoons appear as costume details or ritual bundles. Birds of prey representations provide an exception: at first glance, they appear to depict real animals, but a close examination usually reveals supernatural attributes.

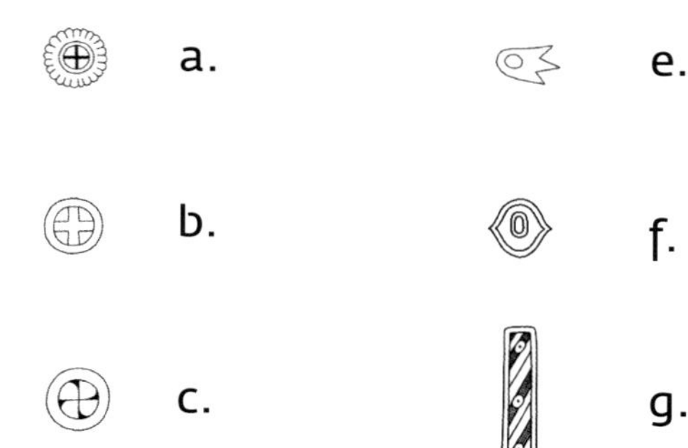

Fig. 7a-h Six common motifs on engraved whelk shells from the Craig Mound at Spiro, Oklahoma: a) petaloid motif; b) cross-in-circle; c) swastika-in-circle; d) forked-eye-surround; e) eye-surround with three prongs; f) ogee motif; g) striped-center-pole motif; h) trilobed motif; from Phillips and Brown 1978.

Symbolic Keys to the Cosmic Map: A Brief Catalogue of Identified Motifs

Symbols are necessary in order to construct and read maps, cosmic or otherwise. Most maps contain keys or legend blocks that interpret, for the map reader, the symbolic information from which that map is constructed. Our understanding of the map key that explains the meaning of Mississippian art, symbolism, and allegorical landscape derives from the archaeological, ethnographic, and iconographic information recorded from the North American colonial period to the present. Many of the symbols currently being interpreted derive from a particular artistic corpus documented in the critically important volumes of the *Pre-Columbian Shell Engravings from the Craig Mound at Spiro, Oklahoma*, compiled and interpreted by Philip Phillips and James Brown.[13] In addition, certain interpretations have come through the structural analysis of engraved stone and clay objects, from the sites of Etowah, Georgia, and Moundville, Alabama, as well as the corpus of what is now called Walls-phase engraved pottery (see the essay by Chester Walker in this volume). Several of the symbols and motifs revealed by the structural method function as place signs, or locatives, to identify the cosmic realm within which the action of the overall composition unfolds. A limited number of these symbols function as connecting agents, portals, or gateways between the natural and supernatural oppositions inherent in the multitiered Native American cosmos.

The meaning of several symbols, motifs, and motif sets are understood with enough certainty that they surely belong within the cosmic key or legend block for the MACC. Among these symbols that I will describe here are the wing and petaloid motif set, the cross-in-circle motif set, and the striped-panel or striped-center-pole motifs, as well as the several forked-eye-surrounds, the various forms of the ogee or portal symbols, and the trilobed motif (figs. 7a–h). Several of these motifs and symbols are associated with anthropomorphic and zoomorphic figures who display the wing motif, and when a supernatural bears a wing motif, that figure is clearly in the Above World. The repeated petal-like design—derived from downy avian feathers—that often accompanies the wing also cues the viewer that the figurative action takes place in the Above World (fig. 7a). As a multivalent symbol, this petaloid motif can function both as a ground-line or frame, or cartouche.[14] In addition, one particular shell engraving in the Craig style strongly suggests that beyond its general function as an Above World locative, the petaloid motif can

Fig. 8 Drawing of an engraved whelk shell; Craig A style; Oklahoma, Spiro, Craig Mound, A.D. 1200–1400; from Phillips and Brown 1984, pl. 164. This shell depicts a figure wearing a bellows-shaped apron, holding a staff banded with animal skins, and walking atop an arc formed with the petaloid motif.

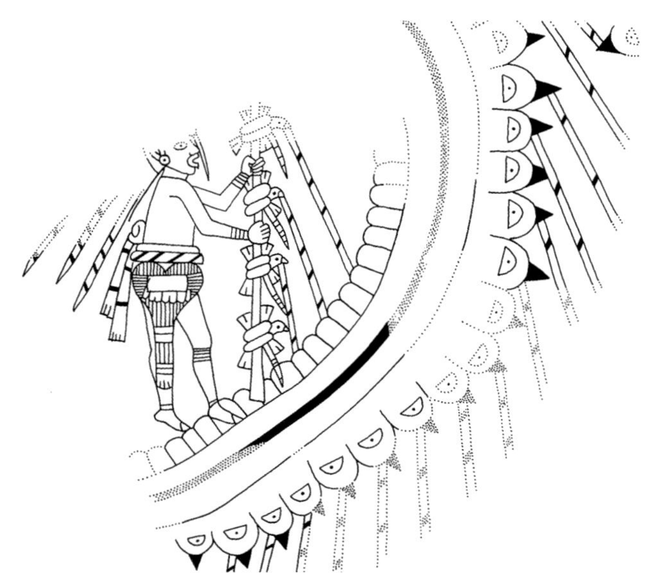

specifically designate the Path of Souls or Milky Way (see fig. 8).

Certainly among the most important symbol sets in the MACC are those that function as locatives specifying which cosmic level is being depicted; this is especially true of those based on the cross-in-circle motif, which carries solar attributes and visually expresses the sacred fire that exists in the Middle World (fig. 7b). It also symbolizes the sacred fire that lies at the heart of much of the early historic era and contemporary religious system of the Native Americans of the Eastern Woodlands. When expressed as a cross-in-circle with a petaloid surround (fig. 7a), this specific variant seems to identify the Above World, as well as the phenomena and supernaturals who occupy this celestial space. Likewise, as George Lankford has suggested, the swastika-in-circle motif (fig. 7c) also functions as a locative, but the cosmic realm it identifies is the Beneath World or Underwater realm.

In my opinion, in its several variants the forked-eye-surround (figs. 7d–e) has been the symbol that most readily lends itself to interpretation based almost solely on internal evidence from the MACC symbolic corpus, without relying on ethnographic analogy. If an anthropomorphic or zoomorphic creature was depicted with a forked-eye-surround, the wearer was understood to exist in the celestial, or Above World, realm (fig. 7d). If the forked-eye-surround was equipped with three prongs instead of two (fig. 7e), then the wearer undoubtedly inhabited the Beneath World. This certainly appears to be the case on a Late Mississippian ceramic bottle, on which two horned rattlesnakes are distinguished by separate eye configurations (see fig. 9; see also Lankford, fig. 18). In another forked-eye example, the lower fork is rendered as an undulant or wavy variant, often placed on copperwork avian images; such undulations very possibly represent lightning emanating from the eyes of the Thunderers (fig. 10). Other categories of eye-surrounds are unforked, and these too surely convey their own specific cosmological information, which awaits further study of their iconographic functions.

The ogee symbol, in its several aspects, marked the portals between the different levels of the Native American cosmos (fig. 7f). Internal artistic evidence demonstrates that the ogee's origin is linked to the Otherworld and to serpents, which in some instances carry ogees as body markings. Certain MACC ritual objects and costume paraphernalia bear the ogee symbol, signaling their ritual function as portals between realms. The beautifully executed quartzite disk in the McClung Museum at the University of Tennessee, for example, bears an ogee on one side and displays a petaloid motif surrounding the reverse (see figs. 15a–b in the essay by Adam King in this volume). Unquestionably, these symbols visually cued viewers that the palettes played a role in celestial rituals. The ogee on the obverse surface designates the opening between the Above World and other cosmic levels. The two

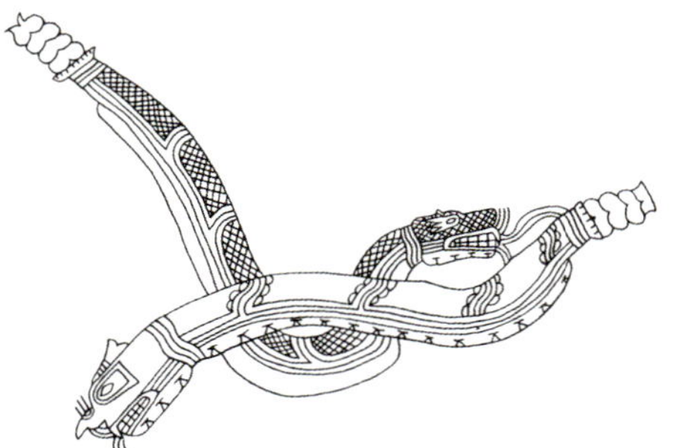

Fig. 9 Drawing of intertwined horned serpents from a vessel known as the Centi pot, found at the Chucalissa site near Memphis; from Phillips and Brown 1978, p. 200, fig. 261.

serpents carved on the Moundville disk (see fig. 1 in the essay by Vincas Steponaitis and Vernon Knight in this volume) are intertwined to form an ogeelike portal that surrounds a hand-and-eye motif. Currently, the hand-and-eye motif is interpreted as one of the portals or doorways to the Path of Souls (see the essay by George Lankford).

During the later Mississippian period, a specific category of engraved, long-necked ceramic bottles carries both ogee symbols and entwined-snake-ogee symbols as its predominant surface design. These bottles are engraved so that their necks emerge through the ogee symbol. In other words, such bottles were designed so that when they are tilted to pour out their contents, the liquid literally gushes forth from the ogee or symbolic portal. This interpretation allows us to

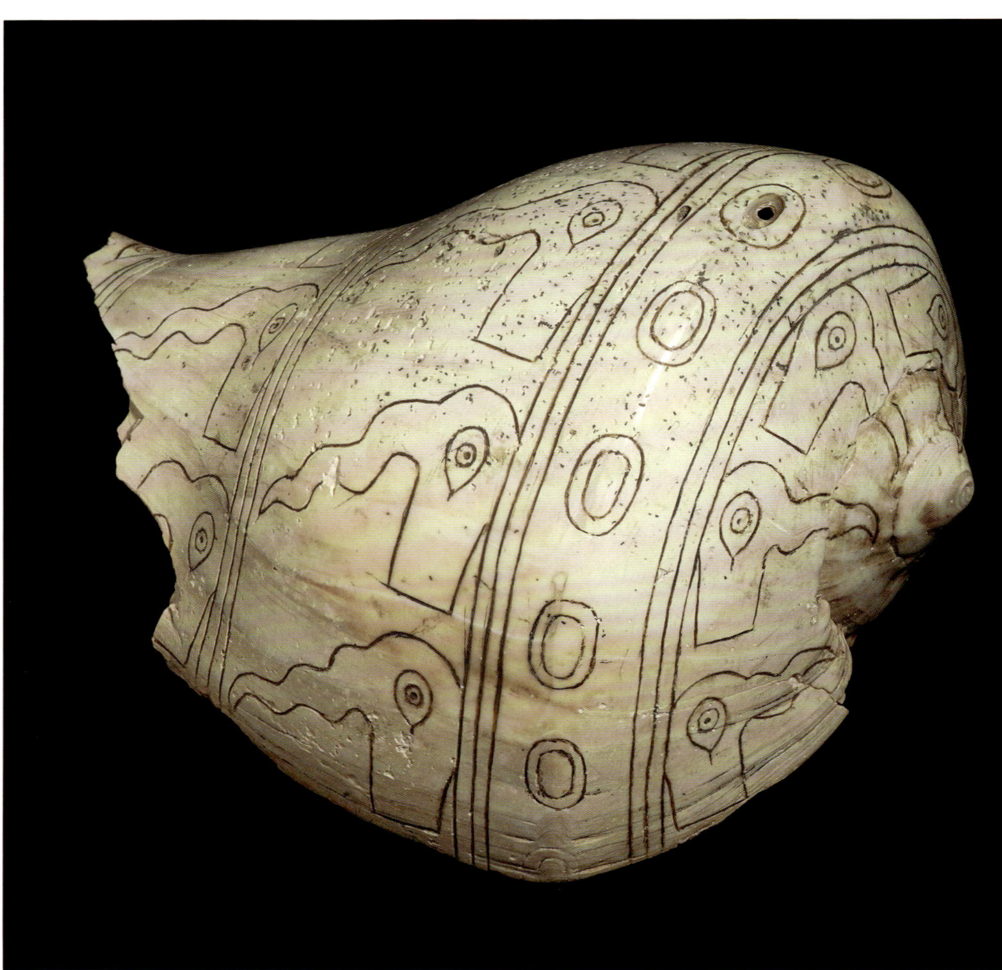

Fig. 10 Engraved whelk shell with droopy-eye-surrounds; Craig B style; Oklahoma, LeFlore County, Spiro, Craig Mound, A.D. 1200–1400; marine shell, l. 26.4 cm; Smithsonian Institution, National Museum of the American Indian, Washington, D.C. Cat. no. 129.

understand at least one important fact about the contents of these bottles: the liquid contained within was understood as a ritual "medicine" that had originated in the Otherworld.

Another critical symbol set in the MACC cosmological key is the striped-panel or striped-center-pole motif (see fig. 7g), both of which belong to a set of representations that signify the cosmic axis. While we do not know the color of the stripes on the center-pole, ethnographic evidence suggests that the stripes would have been alternating bands of red and white.[15] The striped center-pole is often ornamented with objects such as anthropomorphic heads and raccoon-skin bundles. The striped center-pole and its accoutrements form part of the Mississippian-period ritual vocabulary that clearly and directly links the ritual objects used by early-post-contact-period Native Americans with those their contemporary descendants still ritually employ.

These same artists also produced two-dimensional objects that possess the three-dimensional quality of Mississippian flint clay figurines. In Western art we use a vanishing-point perspective in order to impart to two-dimensional images the optical illusion of three dimensions. Yet one may gain just such a critically enlightening visual effect by constructing three-dimensional models based on the two-dimensional renderings in MACC art.[16] For example, within the corpus of Mississippian shell gorgets or medallions, in many instances the circular design that frames the imagery is often an unadorned double line (see figs. 21–22 in the essay by Adam King). In effect, the artists have created a scene whose action unfolds on top of, and within, these double- or multiple-lined circular frames. Shell gorgets are the perfect artifact category to introduce the multiple-horizons technique of structural investigation. The advantage of using a multiple-horizons technique of model-building lies in creating a visual field in which an oval orientation—perhaps designating a dance circle—can be shown with a vanishing-point perspective, while the individual representations contained within the circle then assume the effect of a nearly three-dimensional profile. Thus we understand the figure from our own vantage as three-dimensional beings; by standing them up, so to speak, we can perceive them on the plane of the groundline. In other words, the two-dimensional surface plane of the shell medallion, on which the scene is carved, may achieve a three-dimensional visualization by applying the Western technique of creating a model with a cut-out-and-fold-up technique. Another benefit of such modeling is the recovery of specific ritual moments within Mississippian ceremonies. By applying the cut-out-and-fold-up technique, the framing double-line border in fact assumes the shape of a ceremonial dance circle. Within this circular boundary, two individuals in profile may perform a ritual dance, on either side of a bundled and ornamented center-pole (fig. 11).

In the Greater Braden style, the trilobed motif functions as a serpent marking (fig. 7h). It also appears on the bodies of multicomposite zoomorphic supernaturals, such as the intertwined serpents (amphisbaena version), the Underwater Panther or piasa creature on one of the Perrault pipes in the Milwaukee Public Museum (fig. 12), and on the serpent-bird head rising from the exquisite diorite vessel from Moundville (see Steponaitis and Knight, fig. 18). All this strongly suggests that the trilobed motif identified those supernaturals who possessed the ability to move from the Beneath World into the celestial or Above World realms. Thus, the trilobed motif functions specifically as a locative identifying this multilevel cosmic ability of a particular set of supernaturals who can cross or transcend realms.

Some Anthropomorphic Cosmic Inhabitants

With these motifs and variants as our keys to the cosmic map, we may now possibly identify a few of the gods and heroes who populated the Mississippian cosmic landscape. The most dramatic of these representations are to found in the small corpus of statuettes carved from Missouri flint clay. Most of these statuettes appear to have been produced at Cahokia during the Stirling phase, A.D. 1050–1150.[17] Many, but not all, of the statuettes, however, were reworked later as pipes, sometime after the Cahokian Stirling phase. In my opinion, the MACC artistic corpus should include not only the copper, shell, and stone objects created in the Greater Braden style, but also most of these three-dimensional figurines.[18]

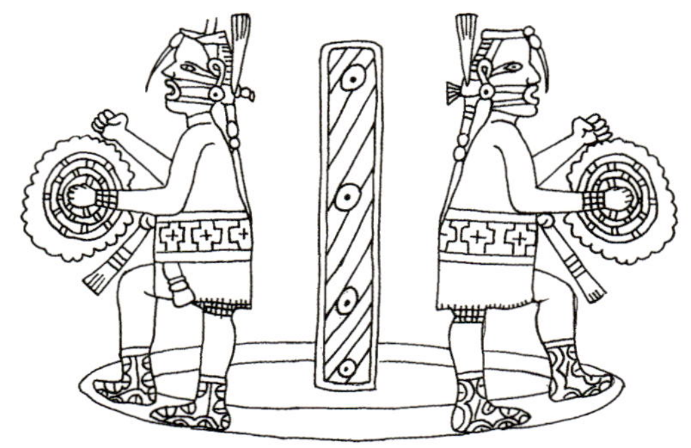

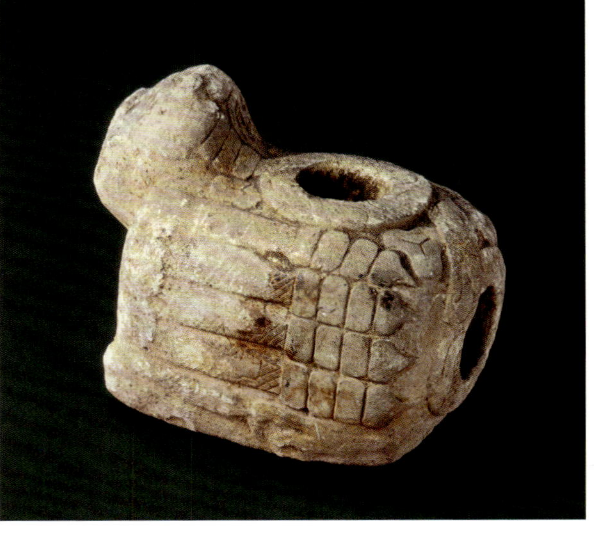

Fig. 11 A three-dimensional visualization of an engraved shell gorget from the Craig Mound at Spiro, Oklahoma, showing two dancing figures on either side of a striped center-pole; drawing by Jack Johnson.

Fig. 12 Underwater Panther effigy pipe; Bellaire style; Mississippi, Adams County, Emerald Mound, near Natchez, A.D. 1250–1450; formerly in the Perrault Collection; Glendon limestone, 16 × 12.3 × 8.9 cm; Milwaukee Public Museum. A trilobed motif appears between the pipe bowl and the insertion hole for the pipe stem.

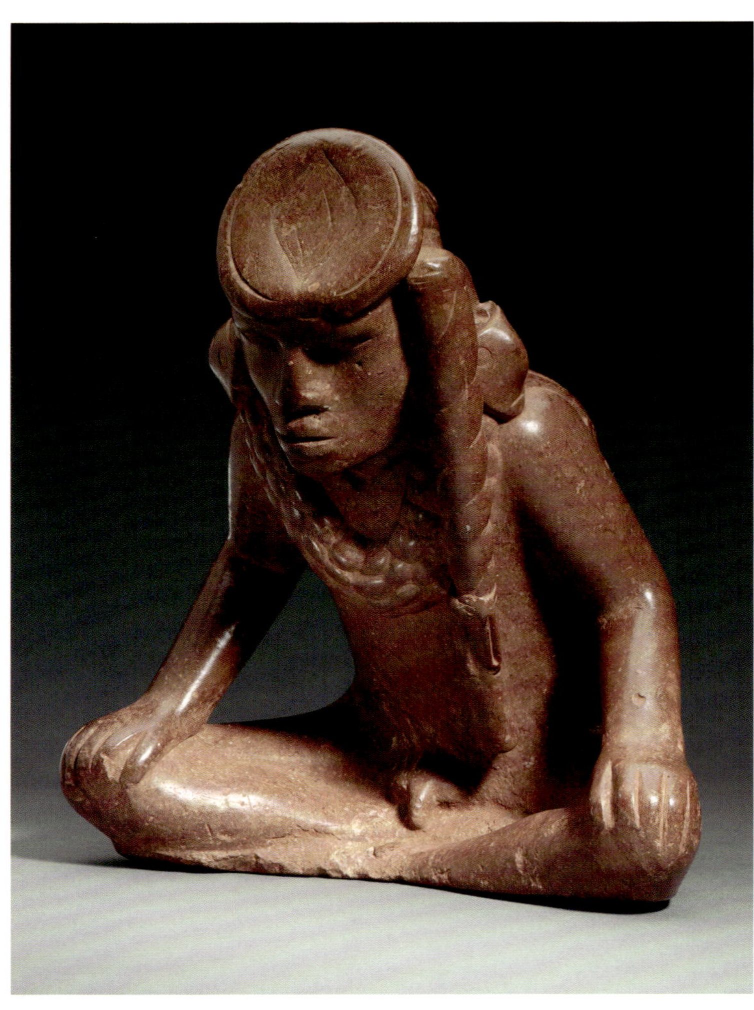

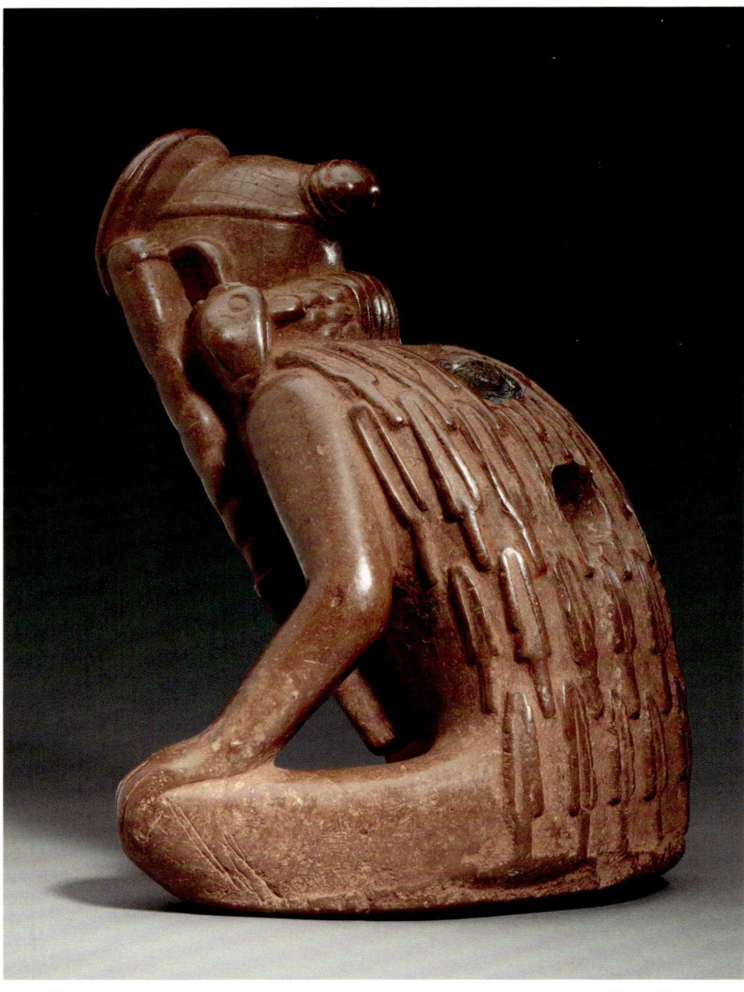

Recent scientific research has demonstrated clearly that the source of the flint clay from which these statuettes were carved is in southeastern Missouri not far from Cahokia.[19] Interestingly, this flint clay source is in the same location as several dramatic Mississippian rock art sites (see the essay by Carol Diaz-Granados in this volume). These compelling statuettes fall into three categories: human female and human male figures and animal representations. With one exception, the female figures have come from the environs of Cahokia. On the other hand, the male and zoomorphic figures have been found throughout the Eastern Woodlands, with a large number concentrated in the Caddoan area of Oklahoma.

In a recent iconographic study, Thomas Emerson has illustrated that many of the statuettes display shamanic attributes such as transformation.[20] Assuredly, the statuettes also portray experiences derived from the overlapping mythic cycles that defined the Mississippian cosmic vision. Like Classic-period Maya art, the art of MACC in general and of the flint clay statuettes in particular focused on "the continuous sequence of ritual experience."[21] Specifically, the statuettes seem to focus on the progression or episodic nature of the ritual and cycle, and therefore readily lend themselves to sequential ordering. Indeed, when we consider the known flint clay figurines as a corpus, we are viewing a cast of supernatural performers interacting upon the primeval cosmic stage! If the flint clay figurines are seen as representations of primordial deities and heroes, then a closer examination reveals that individually they most likely portray specific characters from the Morning Star mythic cycle. If my interpretation is correct, then in principle we may apply the narrative sequence of the myths to the iconography of the short-lived phenomenon of Cahokian flint clay figurines. This allows us to group the iconography into tableaux of individual, significant episodes within specific cycles. The key to unlocking this episodic sequence is our current understanding that the greatest of the flint clay figurines—the seated figure of a Resting Warrior, found in Spiro—is Morning Star, identifiable by his long red braid of hair and his distinctive earrings rendered as stylized heads (figs. 13a–b and 14).

If the Resting Warrior from Spiro depicts Morning Star, then at least some of the other figurines also probably represent characters from the Morning Star Cycle. In fact, we should think of them as freeze-frame highlights of episodes in this myth cycle. What are some of Morning Star's key episodes?[22] In the cycle, Morning Star, the youngest of ten brothers, identifies his persona by the epithet He-Who-Is-Hit-with-Deer-Lungs. As such, Morning Star conceals his supernatural powers from his family. Yet, in another episode, Morning Star reveals himself to his brothers and his people, proclaiming that he is Red Horn or He-Who-Wears-Human-

Figs. 13a–b Effigy pipe of a seated male figure; known as the Resting Warrior and identified as Morning Star or Red Horn in related legendary accounts; Oklahoma, LeFlore County, Spiro, site 34LF46, A.D. 1100–1200; flint clay, h. 22.5 cm; University of Arkansas Museum, Fayetteville. Cat. no. 92.

Fig. 14 Long-Nosed God ear ornament; Illinois, St. Clair County, Booker T. Washington site, A.D. 1100–1200; shell, h. 3.8 cm; Gilcrease Museum, Tulsa, Oklahoma. Cat. no. 121. The figure of Red Horn (figs. 13a–b) wears a pair of such ornaments, described in Winnebago mythology as "little faces with winking eyes."

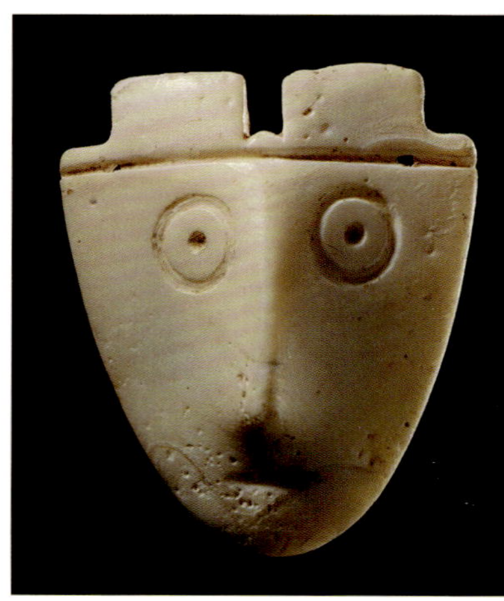

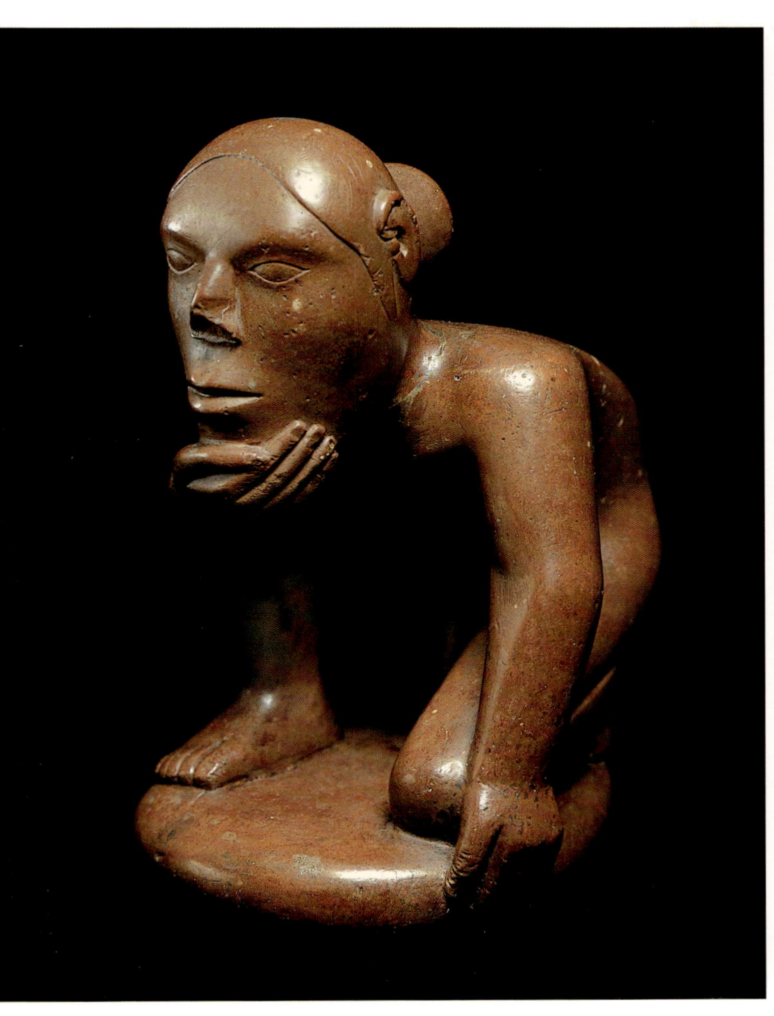

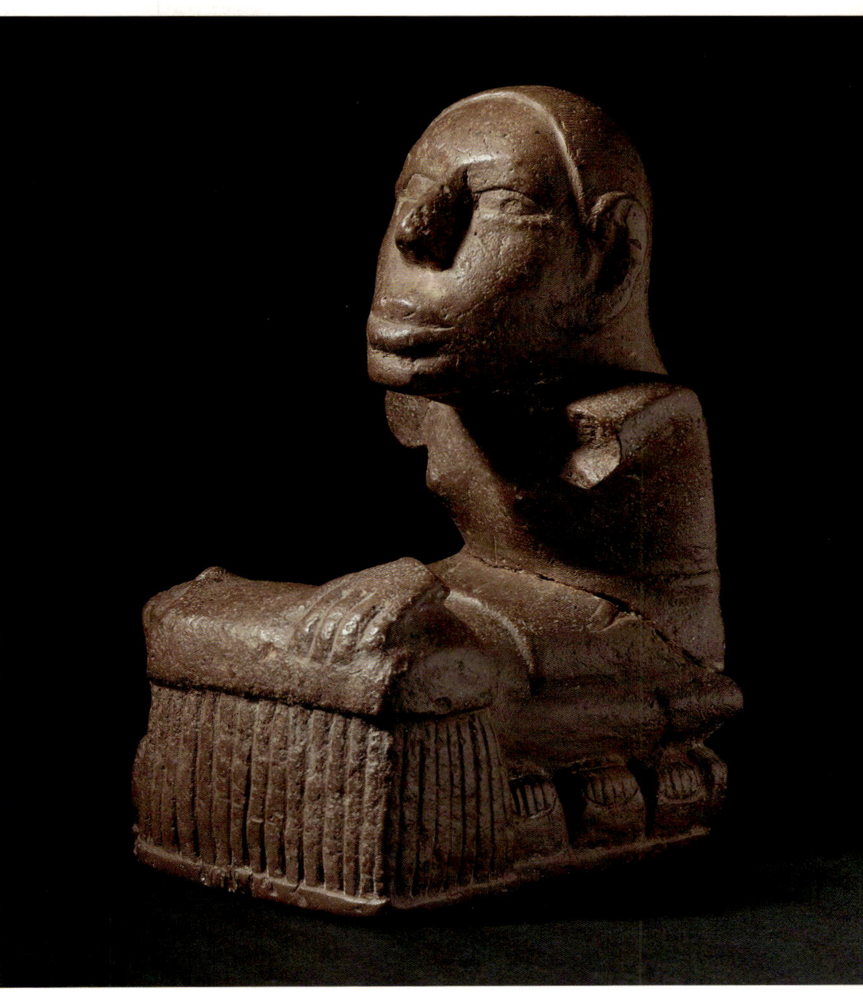

Heads-in-His-Ears. In the next episode he goes to battle and takes war trophies. Later in the story, He-Who-Wears-Human-Heads-in-His-Ears and his companions defeat the giants in a ball game. As trophies, he then takes the giant chieftainess and a human woman to wife. But in another contest with the giants, Morning Star and his companions are defeated and killed, only to be resurrected later through the heroic efforts of his two sons. After cheating death and a series of other adventures, the companions of Morning Star eventually return home, resuming their animal forms, visually to represent aspects of the animal powers.

These highlights in no way capture the scope and complexity of the Morning Star myth. This selection merely sketches a brief outline for ordering the sequence of flint clay figurines in the following statuette/episode sequence. First, the unrevealed Morning Star is personified by unclothed statuettes (to be unclothed is to lack identifying attributes) such as the Crouching Man pipe found at the Shiloh mounds in Tennessee (fig. 15). Next, as mentioned, the Resting Warrior pipe from Spiro represents the revealed Morning Star. Third, in the National Museum of the American Indian collection, the Conquering Warrior pipe shows Morning Star armed and taking a head as war trophy (see figs. 16a–b in the essay by David Dye in this volume). Fourth, the kneeling figure of a man holding a deer and a rattle—commonly called the Grizzly Man—may well represent the leader of the giants (fig. 18), while the Chunkey Player pipe in the St. Louis Science Center portrays Morning Star as a game-player (see fig. 11 in the essay by James Brown in this volume).

With their pervasive themes of fertility and ritual power, two statuettes surely depict the wives of Morning Star, even as they possess the attributes of an important deity who survives today in the ceremonialism of a Native American group formerly located east of the Mississippi River. The first of these, the Westbrook figurine, was discovered at a site near the confluence of the Arkansas and Mississippi rivers, several hundred miles south of Cahokia (fig. 1). Nevertheless, the material from which it is modeled, as well as its overall form and style, leaves little doubt that this beautifully made figurine was created in a Cahokian workshop, regardless of how it eventually arrived at its point of discovery.[23] This figurine represents the earth and lunar deity in her aspect as the Corn Mother, the provider of plants and the horticultural arts to humankind—an important focus of the religion of Native Americans of the Eastern Woodlands. As a Mississippian-period representation of this Corn Mother complex, the Westbrook figurine shares several attributes with other female figures discovered in the area of Cahokia who have been identified as artifacts from the same complex.[24] The Westbrook figurine appears to emerge from a lidded basket that actually may be a sacred bundle associated with the

Fig. 15 Crouching Man effigy pipe; Tennessee, Hardin County, Shiloh Indian Mounds National Historic Landmark, Shiloh National Military Park, A.D. 1100–1200; Missouri flint clay, h. 20.3 cm; United States National Park Service, Shiloh National Military Park. Cat. no. 96. Excavated in 1899, this ceremonial pipe was probably a trade item from Cahokia. This finest of Mississippian sculptural figures is composed of a sophisticated interplay of vertical and oblique angular lines, concave and convex shapes, and spherical, cylindrical, and circular forms within a basic, cubical block.

Fig. 16 Kneeling female effigy; known in archaeological literature as the Keller figurine; Illinois, Madison County, BBB Motor site, near Collinsville, A.D. 1100–1200; flint clay, h. 14 cm; University of Illinois, Illinois Transportation Archaeological Research Program. Cat. no. 101.

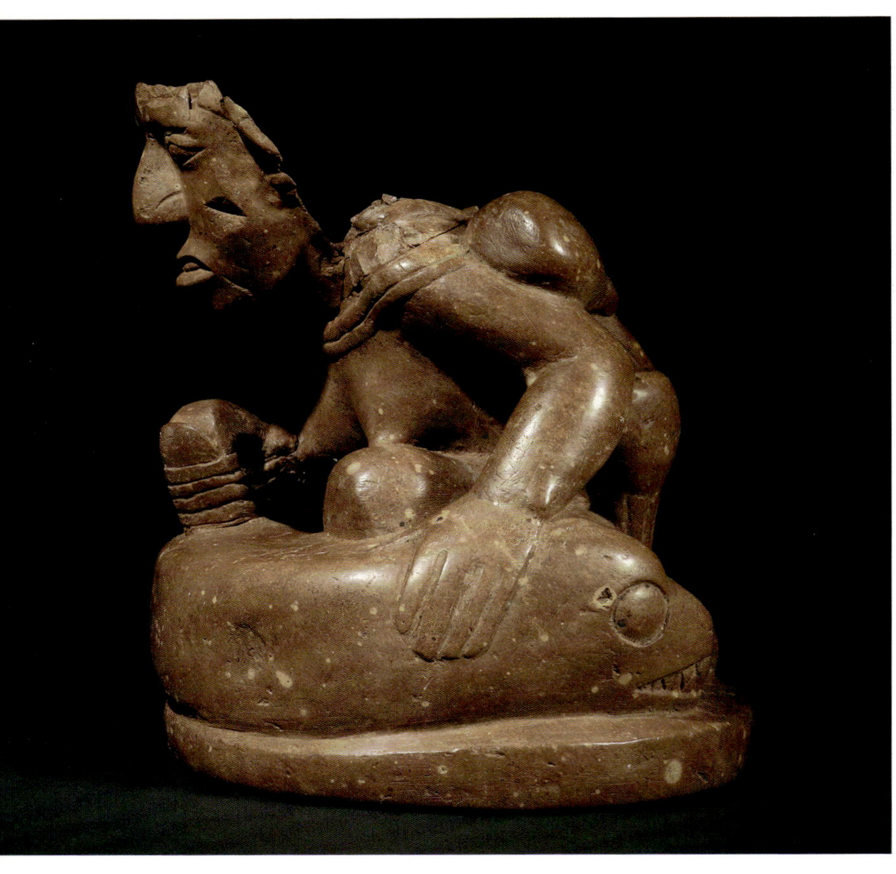

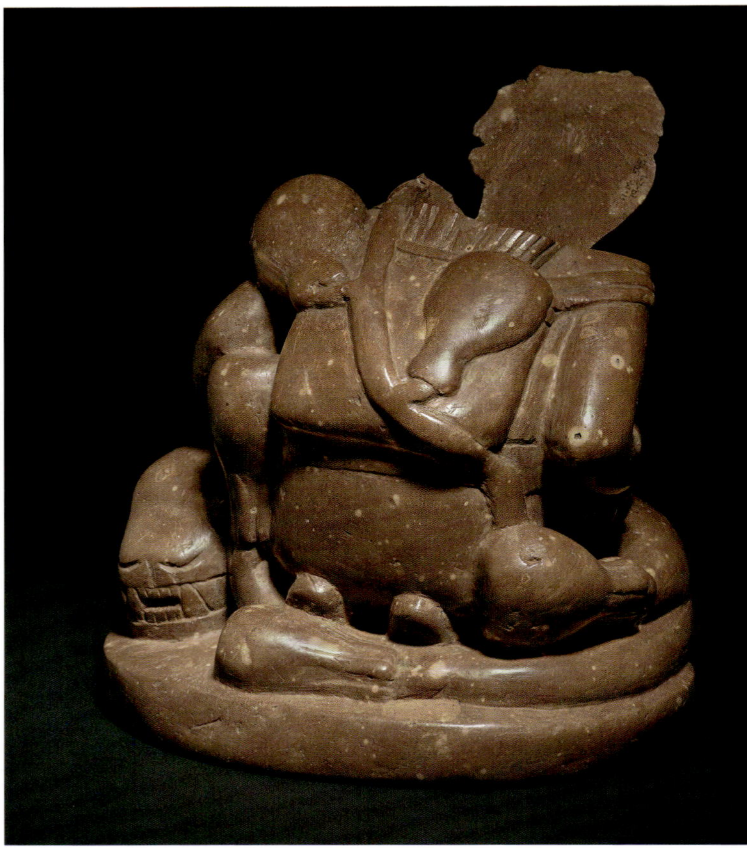

Corn Maiden cult. The fact that this basket or sacred bundle is identical to the object touched by the hands of the Keller figurine (fig. 16) serves to link closely the Westbrook figure with the larger corpus of Cahokian female figurines described by Emerson. Unlike the Keller figurine, however, the Westbrook Corn Mother leans forward, resting her open and upturned palms beside her knees. From her open palms, maize and sunflower plants grow forth; they are not held in clenched fists. These intertwining plants wrap around the back of her head. Her kneeling posture is identical to the depiction of another female figure, the fragmented work known as the Birger figurine.

The Birger figurine, discovered by Thomas Emerson only a few miles from Cahokia, is also an artifact of the same earth and fertility cult that includes the Corn Maiden (figs. 17a–b).[25] In the case of this female figurine, however, the theme focuses on Otherworld powers rather than on vegetative ones. This beautifully executed female figure hoes the back of a serpentlike creature. A close examination of the serpent reveals specific features—notably, its teeth and prominent snout—that visually link it to numerous piasa images in the shell engravings unearthed at the famous archaeological site of Spiro, Oklahoma. In addition, the tail of this Cahokian version of the piasa is split. Robert Hall has pointed out that this split tail is also a physical attribute of the Pawnee water serpent (i.e., piasa) housed in Chicago's Field Museum.[26] At an annual ceremony, the Pawnee medicine men would construct a large, three-dimensional model of their version of the piasa. This three-dimensional, sixty-foot image would encircle the interior of a ceremonial earth lodge.[27] Similarly, the Birger piasa forms a single coil that surrounds the female figure. The position of the coiled piasa vis-à-vis the female figure strongly suggests that the piasa is functioning as an ogeelike portal from which the female figure emerges.

Out of the split tail of the piasa on the Birger figurine grow gourds and vines, literally climbing up the back of the hoeing female figure. Emerson has noted that gourds are the source of shamans' rattles and in several mythic sequences they function as soul containers.[28] Robert Hall, drawing on the work of George A. Dorsey, has noted that the pebbles in the Pawnee rattle symbolized the souls of priests who journeyed to the garden of the Morning Star along a road that was symbolized by the handle of the rattle.[29] The female figure also carries a pack on her back. This pack may well be a ritual bundle. The Birger female figure and her accoutrements strongly suggest that she is manifesting a specific female deity known as Our Grandmother or Old-Woman-Who-Never-Dies.[30]

C. F. Voegelin, in his famous study of the Shawnee description of this deity, stated that her personal name is revealed as Cloud.[31] The Cloud Woman, sometimes described as a giantess with gap-teeth, is the source of communal ritual, ritual accoutrements, prophecy, and ceremonial dances. She may also be one of the major actors on the Path of Souls, where she is known to keep a sweat lodge and administer healing medicines, as well as the mother of the Corn Mother, whom she created.[32] Furthermore, Cloud Woman is vested with lunar and aquatic symbolism.[33]

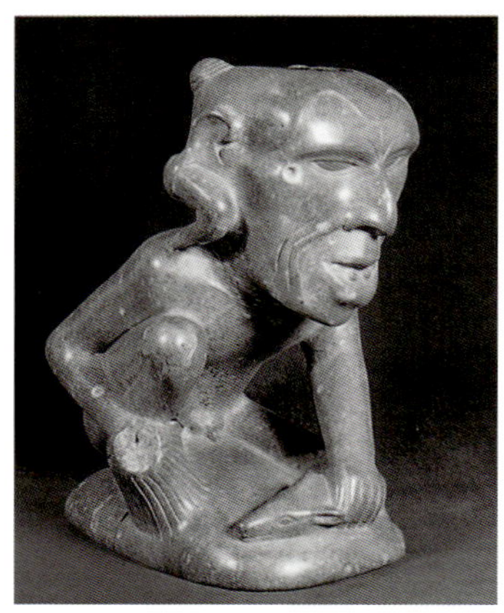

Figs. 17a–b Effigy figurine of a mythical woman, possibly Our Grandmother or Old-Woman-Who-Never-Dies, hoeing an earth-serpent; known in archaeological literature as the Birger figurine; Illinois, Madison County, BBB Motor site, near Collinsville, A.D. 1100–1200; flint clay, h. 14 cm; University of Illinois, Illinois Transportation Archaeological Research Program. Cat. no. 100.

Fig. 18 Effigy pipe of a crouching man holding a deer and rattle; known in archaeological literature as Grizzly Man or the Kneeling Rattler; Oklahoma, LeFlore County, Spiro, Craig Mound, A.D. 1100–1200; flint clay, h. 20.3 cm; Sam Noble Museum of Natural History, University of Oklahoma, Norman.

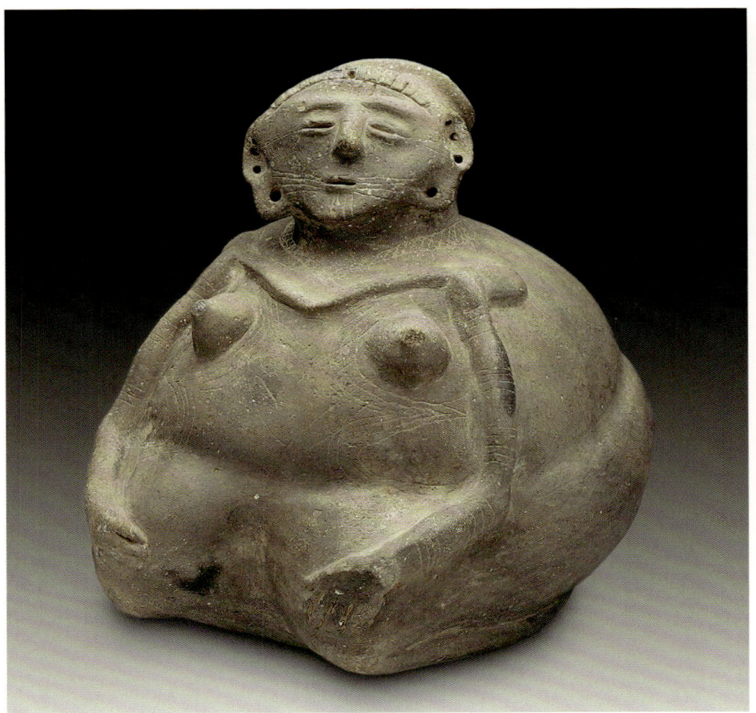
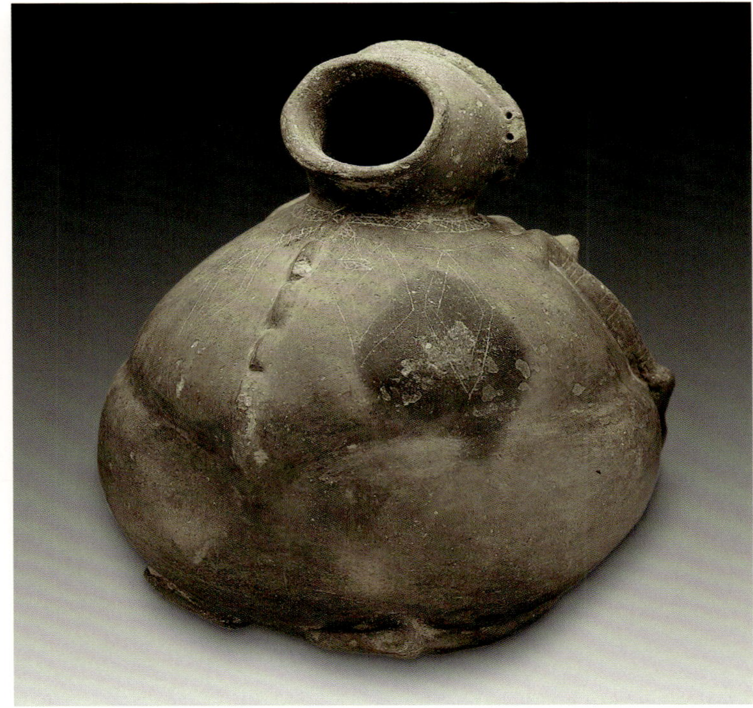

The image of Cloud Woman as Our Grandmother, or Old-Woman-Who-Never-Dies, certainly survived the apparently short production span of these Cahokian flint clay statuettes. In the later Mississippian period (after A.D. 1500), she was portrayed as an old woman in the form of a clay vessel. One of these vessels shows Old-Woman-Who-Never-Dies equipped with a necklace of intertwined ogeelike serpents similar to the configuration on the Moundville palette (figs. 19a–b). The head of this female clay figure emerges from the intertwined snake coil in much the same way as the whole figure of the Birger female emerges from the looped, coiled piasa. Certainly the Westbrook and Birger figurines provide excellent examples of thematic overlapping among Mississippian-period mythic cycles. The two MACC figures, however, also form a female deity dyad that still resonates in the belief systems of small groups of traditional Native Americans.

Finally, returning to our episodic sequence, the frog effigy pipe from East St. Louis, now in the Illinois State Museum, perfectly illustrates the episode in which the companions of Morning Star return home, resume their animal forms, and visually manifest the animal powers (fig. 20), as one might judge from its appearance elsewhere (fig. 21). Perhaps, in time, other existing fire clay figures such as the human effigy pipe from the Gilcrease Museum (fig. 22) and the kneeling figure pipe from the Beutell Collection (fig. 23) will also be incorporated into this episodic sequence. The fact that many of these figurines functioned as pipes and that they were found far

Figs. 19a–b Seated female effigy vessel; known as Old-Woman-Who-Never-Dies; Arkansas, A.D. 1500; ceramic; Arkansas State University Museum, Jonesboro.

Fig. 20 Frog effigy pipe; Illinois, St. Clair County, East St. Louis, A.D. 1100–1200; Missouri flint clay, h. 13, l. 14.5 cm; Illinois State Museum, Springfield. Cat. no. 98.

Fig. 21 Frog vessel; Arkansas, Lee County, Clay Hill site, A.D. 1000–1300; ceramic, h. 15.2 cm; Gilcrease Museum, Tulsa, Oklahoma. Cat. no. 254.

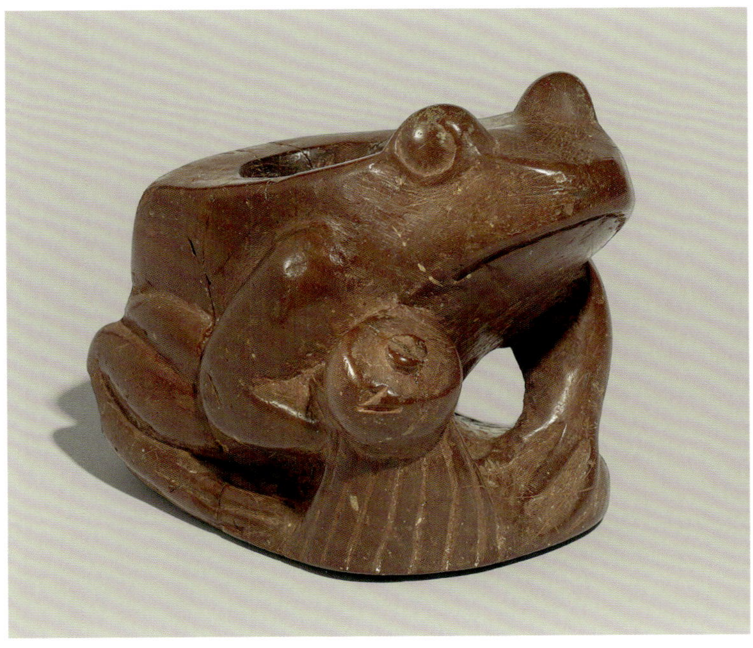
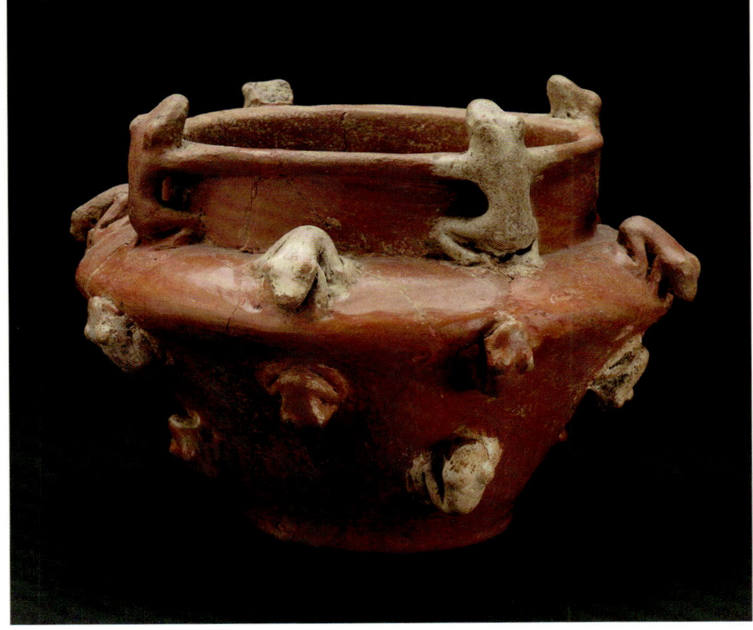

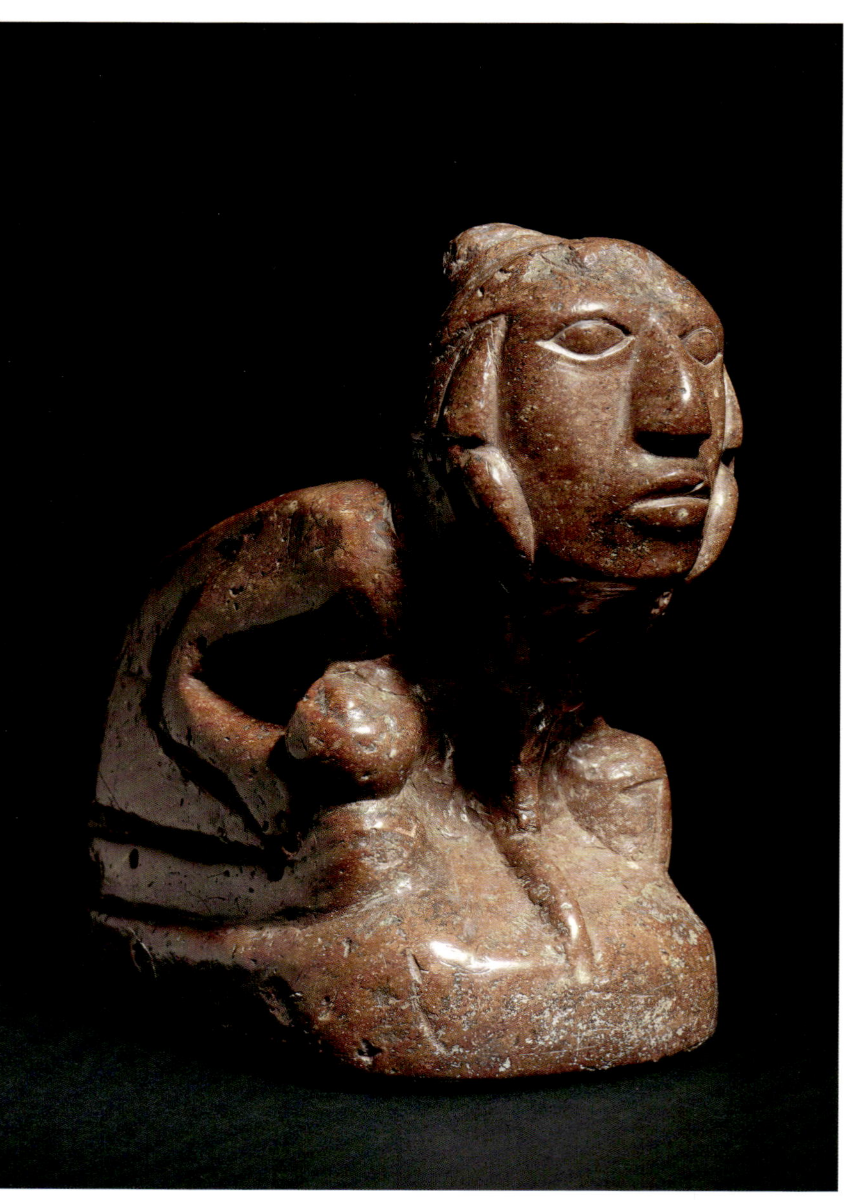

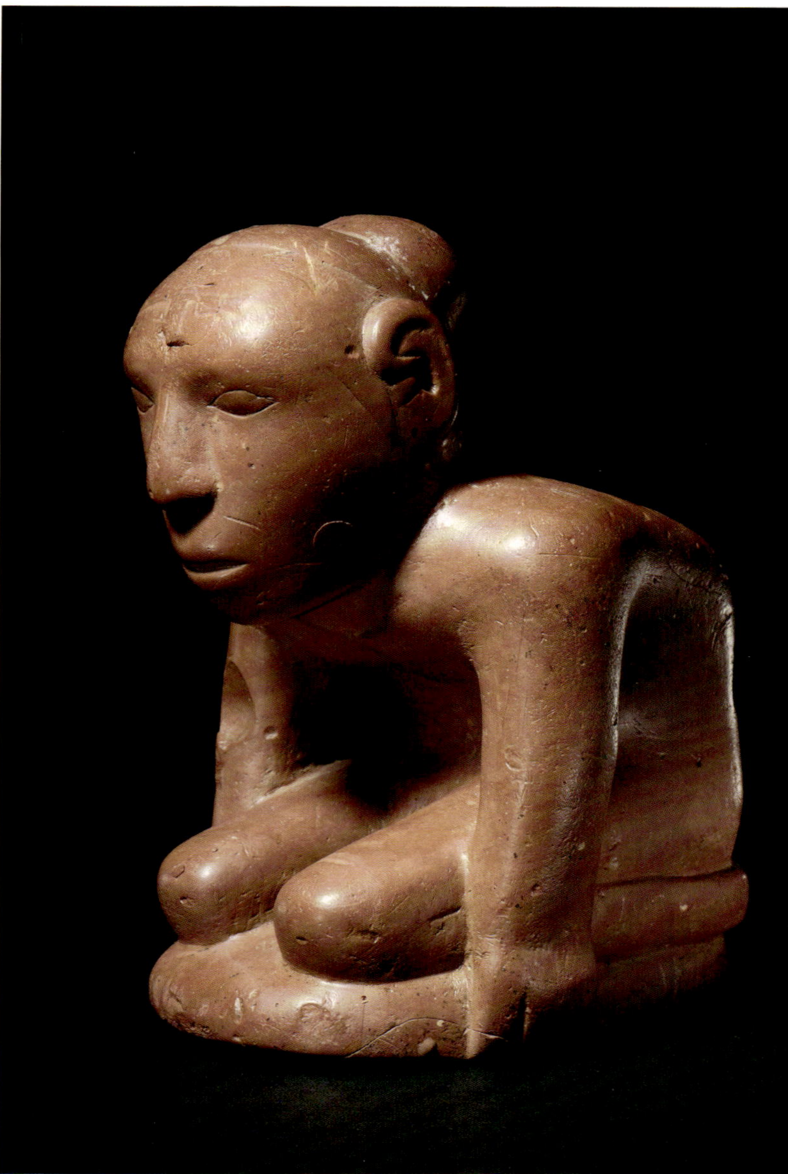

Fig. 22 Human effigy pipe; Illinois, Madison County, Piasa Creek Mound, A.D. 1100–1200; flint clay, h. 20.3 cm; Gilcrease Museum, Tulsa, Oklahoma. Cat. no. 97.

Fig. 23 Kneeling figurine effigy pipe; Kentucky, Ballard County, Twin Mounds site, A.D. 1100–1200; flint clay, h. 17.8 cm; Tommy Beutell Collection. Cat. no. 95.

from Cahokia, their point of origin, strongly suggests that these pipes may have functioned in ways similar to the historic-period calumet ceremonies.[34]

If what I have posited here is essentially correct, then Cahokian and other Mississippian elites clearly seem to have applied episodes from the Morning Star mythic cycle to their iconographic representations in order to charter their own authority as being sanctioned supernaturally. Perhaps, through the act of retooling these flint clay figurines into pipes and distributing them to certain, select outlying elites, the rulers of Cahokia were visually and ritually "adopting" other groups by transferring objects that expressed commonalities of belief, thus strengthening long-distance alliances. Certainly these rites of adoption were central to the ritual life of almost all the Native Americans of the Eastern Woodlands in colonial and historic times.[35] This process of distributing power-invested objects rippled through the distant elites, who possessed Cahokian pipe figurines and used them to charter their own legitimacy. By controlling, manipulating, and sharing these mythically charged symbols, they drew the supernatural powers of Cahokia unto themselves![36]

Conclusion

As I have illustrated in this discussion, the art and symbolism of the MACC visually manifested Native American religious and ideological systems. If other researchers and I are correct in these interpretations, early in the Mississippian period, artists developed a canon of visual expression with which to synthesize and codify the rhythms of the natural and the supernatural realms with great variety and breathtaking effect. Later on, emerging elites in other areas of the Eastern Woodlands adopted and encoded the surviving aspects of this artistic canon and its symbolic systems to manifest and validate their rank. The elite dance and medicine societies, with their attendant ceremonies, provided the initiates and, in some instance, the public with a meaningful mythical display through which their special status was ceremonially presented, mutually acknowledged, and publicly validated. The art and symbolism of the MACC, derived from a Woodland-period matrix, conveyed to their people the supernatural power and prestige inherent in the cosmos itself, which they purported to control.

Today, among surviving Native American traditional communities, rituals are performed and beliefs are held that are analogous to those of their Mississippian-period ancestors. The art and symbolism of the MACC, though embodying certain aspects of contemporary Native American belief, were, in effect, status objects for elite consumption. Such objects and symbols identified both owners and ritual manipulators as controllers of the ongoing processes of the natural and supernatural order. In some ways both holder and artist, through these works of art, step forward to be acknowledged by the art objects themselves before a contemporary audience. The fact that we can now appreciate both the aesthetic and symbolic value of these works of art is a testament to the fact that, as Robert Hall has written, "Cultural objects and preserved traditions can tell stories beyond count when they are approached like respected elders and their mysteries sought out."[37]

Notes

1. See Lankford 2005b.
2. Waring and Holder 1945.
3. Muller 1966 and Muller 1989.
4. Knight 1989, p. 206.
5. Berlo and Phillips 1998, p 79.
6. Emerson 1989; Emerson 1982; Lankford 2005b; Knight, Brown, and Lankford 2001.
7. Harrod 2000.
8. Dorsey 1893; Mooney 1900, p. 256; Schutz 1975, pp. 85–88.
9. Lankford 2005b.
10. Lankford 2005c.
11. Lankford 2005c.
12. Knight, Brown, and Lankford 2001, p. 137.
13. Phillips and Brown 1978.
14. Reilly 2005b.
15. Lankford 1993.
16. Reilly 2005a and Reilly 2005b.
17. Emerson 1997a.
18. Emerson et al. 2003; Emerson and Hughes 2000.
19. Emerson et al. 2003; Emerson, personal communication September 2003; Emerson and Hughes 2000.
20. Emerson 2003, pp. 142–43.
21. Schele and Miller 1986, p. 38.
22. Radin 1948.
23. Emerson, personal communication September 2003.
24. Emerson 1997a and 1997b; Emerson 1989; Emerson 1982.
25. Prentice 1986; Emerson 1982.
26. Hall, personal communication October 2003.
27. Linton 1923, pp. 67–69.
28. Emerson 2004; Lankford 1987, p. 214; Gayton 1953, pp. 272–73; Hultkrantz 1957, p. 54.
29. Hall 1985, p. 186.
30. Prentice 1986.
31. Voegelin 1936.
32. Voegelin 1936, pp. 7–8.
33. Schutz 1975, p. 497.
34. Hall 1997a.
35. Hall 1997a.
36. The transference of SECC symbolism from one set of media to others may also reflect a "cultic shift" as well as the breakdown of Mississippian centralized authority (see Knight and Steponaitis 1998a). In effect, it is now believed that the elites' political controls—which had successfully used art to charter and validate their power—gave way to a more publicly accessible, and perhaps less politically centered, vision. The likely cultic shift tends to be more preoccupied with the myths and rituals of death, adoption, the afterlife, and the otherworldly journey or the "Path of Souls" (see the essay by George Lankford in this volume and Lankford 2005c). The right to display and access the supernatural power generated through MACC symbolism now passed to the initiated members of dance and medicine societies that even today play prominent roles in the ritual life of contemporary Native Americans (Grim 1983).
37. Hall 1997a, p. 171.

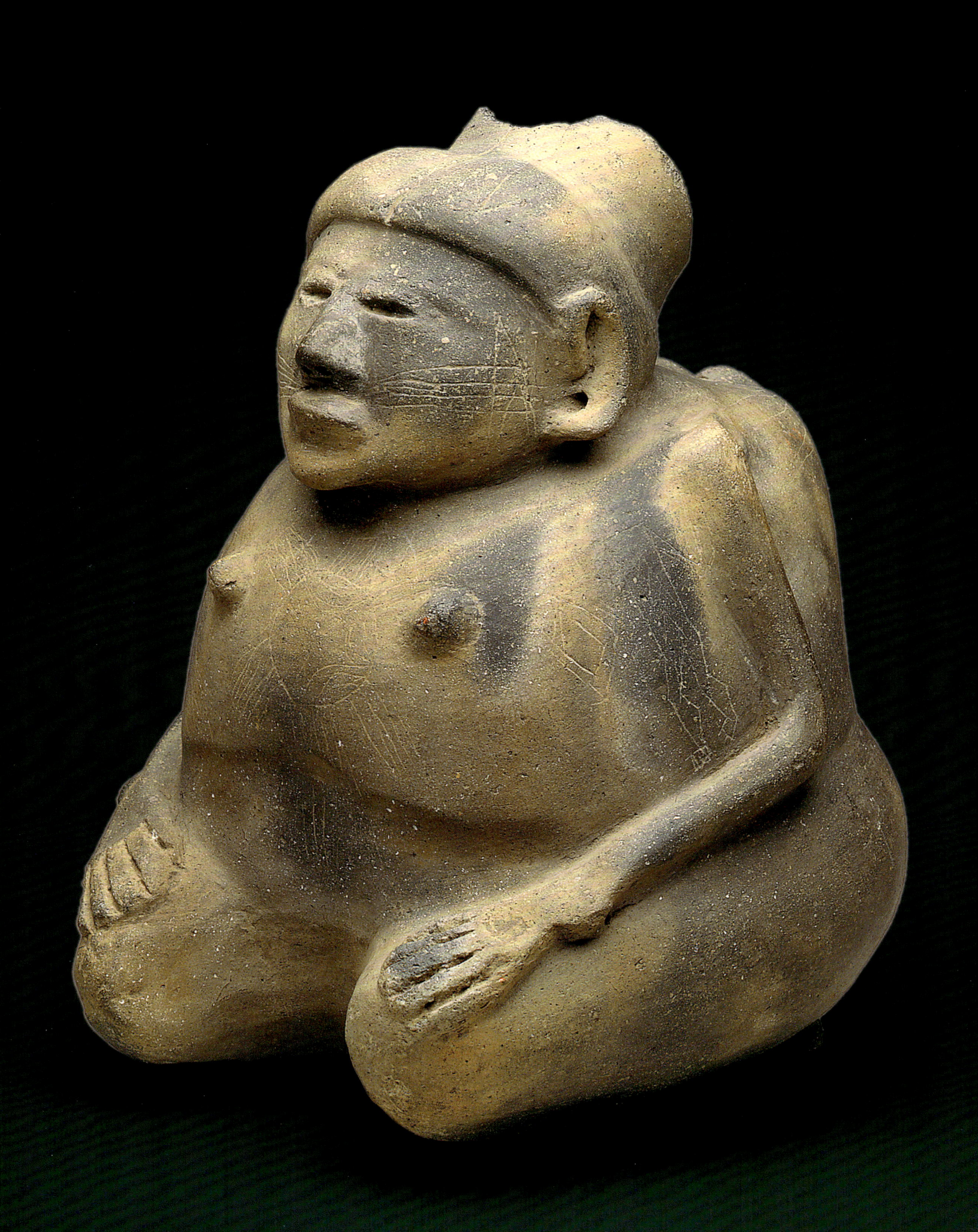

In myths that deal with the creation of the earth, with the contention of man against strange monsters that controlled the animals, with the interdependence of various forms of life, and with the persistent mystery of death we find the idea of permanence, of length of days, of wisdom acquired by age, to be symbolized by the rock or stone . . .

—Fletcher and La Flesche, *The Omaha Tribe*, vol. 1

Marking Stone, Land, Body, and Spirit

Carol Diaz-Granados

Rock Art and Mississippian Iconography

Prologue

The landscape was different back then. It belonged to Wa-Ko^{n}-da, "the mysterious creative power that brings into existence all living things."[1] The landscape, including the mountains, rivers, trees, flowers, grass, clouds, and even the winds, was deemed sacred. Everything that was put here by Wa-Ko^{n}-da was respected by the American Indian populations, including those residing in the Mississippi and eastern Missouri river valleys, particularly the Osage and their relations: the Kansa, Omaha, Ponca, and Quapaw. The Osage believed all of the cosmos, both the visible and the invisible, to be animated by a sacred force, an energy called Wa-Kon, "holy."

All things embodied Wa-Ko^{n}-da, but stone was especially venerated because it was here first. It was called Inyan by the Osage's northern relatives. Inyan was wise; Inyan was revered; Inyan was the father of all. Inyan was imbued with such power that people would go to the stone for comfort, and pray to the sacred stone to be healed, supplicate it for favors, and consecrate it with symbols encoded with meaning. They would either carve or paint images onto the stone, or carve and then fill them with red or black pigment. The imagery included birds, bird tracks, various animals, animal tracks, serpents, human figures, feet, and hands. Other markings included geometric forms such as circles, concentric circles, cross-in-circles, squares, lines, the pit-and-groove, and cup marks.

Fig. 1 Kneeling female effigy vessel; Arkansas, A.D. 1350–1500; ceramic, h. 15.2 cm; The Detroit Institute of Arts, Founders Society Purchase, Lynn W. and Stanley R. Day Fund. Cat. no. 260. This vessel may be an image of the female earth deity Our Grandmother or Old-Woman-Who-Never-Dies. (See also fig. 10; in addition, see figs. 19a-b in the preceding essay by Kent Reilly.)

The requisite force inherent in the landscape was even more plentiful at sacred places. Mountains were patently majestic and awe inspiring. Caves and rock shelters were understandably alluring sites for ritual activity. These places were deemed holy for various reasons: in these locations religious rites took place, epiphanies were experienced, unique bits of nature were found, or unusual natural phenomena such as lightning strikes occurred. Lightning would periodically strike the cedar trees in the Ozark glades, transforming these glades into sacred places. The low-lying boulders were carved with motifs and story panels to honor the supernatural ancestors who brought special wonders, such as lightning, to the Middle World from the Upper World of the cosmos.

This great force also tended to concentrate and flow through the great axis or tree that held together and helped form the cosmos of the Upper World, Middle World, and Lower World. This force flowed through the Milky Way or "Great Road" and was reflected on earth by the Mississippi and Missouri rivers. In fact, much of the Upper World was reflected in the Middle World landscape, both figuratively and literally (fig. 2). The pathways of spiritual energy formed both the natural divisions of the cosmos and the planes that were traversed by supernatural beings who controlled those natural forces and who could move between the levels of the cosmos.

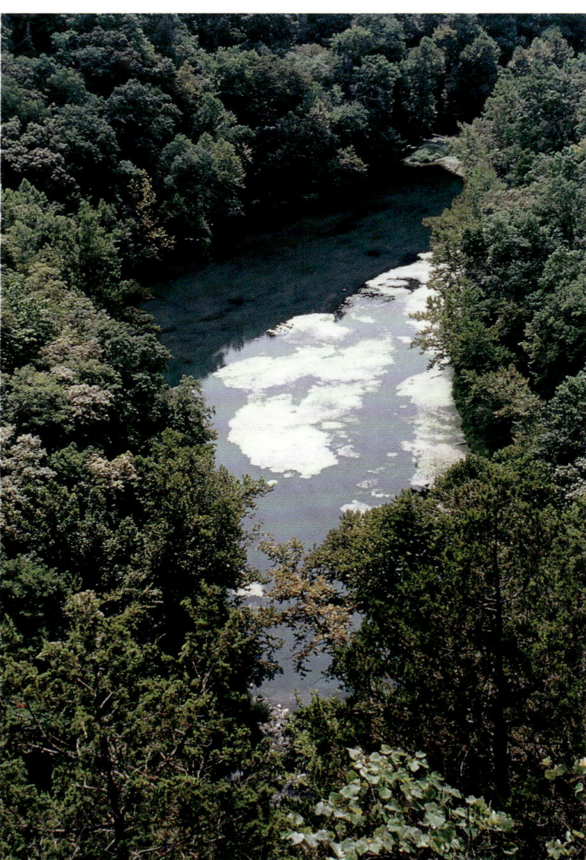

Fig. 2 The landscape of the Middle World reflecting the Upper World is seen in a natural spring in Camden County, Missouri—the heart of original Osage territory.

Introduction

Petroglyphs (carvings on stone) and pictographs (drawings or paintings on stone), collectively and commonly referred to as "rock art," are a widespread phenomenon. Basic principles informing these relationships between human society and the natural environment are ancient and analogous to systems well known among prehistoric populations around the world going as far back in time as the Upper Paleolithic in Europe. There are also networks of sacred places across North America, notably in the Southwest, where pictographs and petroglyphs form a specially developed tradition: in the mountains of Baja, California; near the confluence of the Pecos River and the Rio Grande in Texas; as well as in New Mexico and Arizona. In eastern North America we see rock art along the coast of Maine, in the upper reaches of the Ohio River, into Pennsylvania, along the Tennessee River, in Kentucky and Arkansas, and south into Alabama. A major area of such activity in North America occurs within the Mississippi River valley, particularly in eastern Missouri and southwestern Illinois (fig. 3), in an area radiating out from the prehistoric urban center of Cahokia (and the confluence of the Mississippi and Missouri rivers), where there is a conspicuous density of these ancient carvings and drawings. The rock art comprises motifs and imagery that were used to define the cosmos, understand natural phenomena, honor supernatural beings such as mythical heroes, heroines, or the deified forces of nature, and manage complex social groups in Mississippian societies. Birdman and Dancing Warrior motifs, maces, bilobed arrows, ogees, and other markings placed on boulders, bluffs, rock shelters, and cave walls have their counterparts in artifacts and artifact decoration, as well as in ancient and early historic tattooing. These motifs, many of them identified with the Southeastern Ceremonial Complex (SECC), altered and rendered sacred the landscape, pottery, shell objects, human bodies—anything they adorned. Such symbols served as devices to remember and relate oral traditions, manipulate power, and breach portals of the Upper, Middle, and Lower worlds. In the networks of sacred places, religion, economy, and history are fused together in the way people connect to the landscape. Title to the land is claimed by affirming a relationship

Fig. 3 Photograph of a petroglyph site in Monroe County, Illinois, with an incised hand. The limestone slab that bears this motif is 40 cm high and 74.9 cm across.

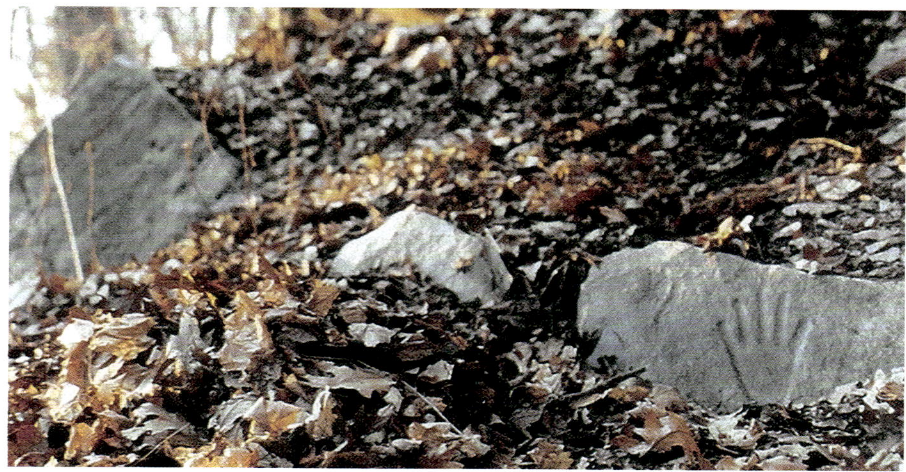

that stems from the time of genesis—the mythical origins of things. This essay explores these rock art images, their artifactual counterparts, their Mississippian iconography, and how they comprise a symbolic and supernatural ownership of the land.

The Setting

The Missouri River valley, particularly in the area of the confluence of the Missouri and Mississippi rivers, was a crossroads of concentrated activity as well as a region of bountiful resources (see fig. 21 in the essay by James Brown in this volume). It is not surprising that precontact populations in this region flourished and expanded. The prehistoric peoples had everything they needed right here: an abundance of potable water, plentiful game, trees, wild nuts, and berries that supplied all the necessary resources for a growing population on both sides of the central Mississippi River valley. Moreover, the rivers provided a crossroads for trade activity and economic gain with connections reaching across the vast Mississippian basin. The westernmost Mississippian sites cluster around this confluence, an area of extremely fertile soil. Areas of this sort are not all that common, so they were prized and protected by those groups who could garner control. The principal sites of Cahokia in Illinois and the now-demolished Mound City group across the Mississippi River in present-day St. Louis attest to the size and complexity these prehistoric urban centers reached around A.D. 1150–1200.

By looking at the imagery on precontact cultural materials coming out of southeastern Missouri and southwestern Illinois—regardless of the modern state political boundaries—we can better understand the distribution of symbolic Mississippian motifs. The motifs that were of importance to the Mississippian people in this particular area are evident in the rock art record, which fortunately remains in situ. Portable cultural materials can move or may be traded, but the imagery found in the rock art—the petroglyphs and pictographs—remains in place right where it was created long ago. These rock art sites were unquestionably sacred places of ritual activity, whether involving a lone individual, specially designated groups, or priests and holy persons, both men and women, who communicated with forces of the invisible worlds.

Much of the same Mississippian imagery found in the portable works of art, including the shell cups and gorgets, pottery, stone objects, and hammered copper ornaments, widely distributed in the Cahokian orbit from Oklahoma to Florida, is also reflected in the prehistoric petroglyphs and pictographs. The carved and painted motifs intensified the consecration of a sacred stone and its environs with symbols of power, bravery, competition, fertility, and birth. The images served as mnemonic devices to recount oral traditions of clan origins, creations stories, special events, feats of supernatural beings, and trickster tales. In this way, the site is claimed and made particular to a specific group or society.

The assortment of Mississippian and SECC motifs provides a partial listing of the icons observed in Missouri rock art.[2] Jon Muller has noted in the past that the Ceremonial Complex symbolic elements and the local styles in which they are rendered do not always mesh.[3] It is true that styles have a way of changing much faster than the icons that are being used and depicted in a variety of media—on pottery, in hammered copper, on shell, and in the rock art. In addition, primary symbols can change meaning either over time or over space—or both. But the contrary should also be stated. That is, many of the symbolic forms seen in rock art can likewise retain their meaning across time and space. The same applies to basic oral traditions that endure for centuries, possibly millennia. Thus we see the longevity of many visual symbolic elements paralleling components in the imagery of ancient oral traditions found in recent ethnographic literature. For example, the vulva form retains a universality not only geographically but also chronologically (see fig. 11). A sampling of the most typical versions, namely the U-shaped or horseshoe-shaped motifs, are not unlike those seen at sites around the world. They are known to represent what could be considered an encoded,

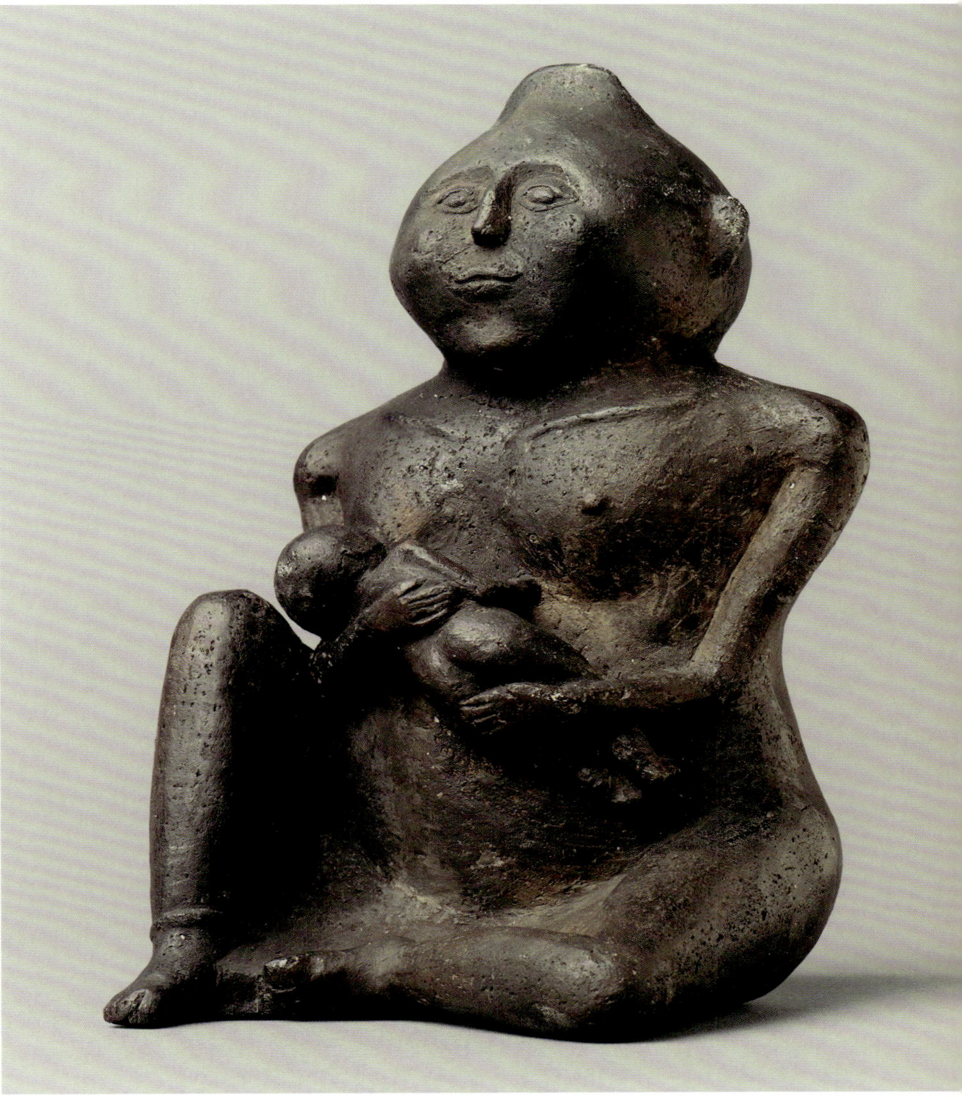

Fig. 4 Nursing mother effigy bottle; Illinois, St. Clair County, Francis Simonim Farm, A.D. 1200–1400; ceramic, h. 15.2 cm; St. Louis Science Center. Cat. no. 270.

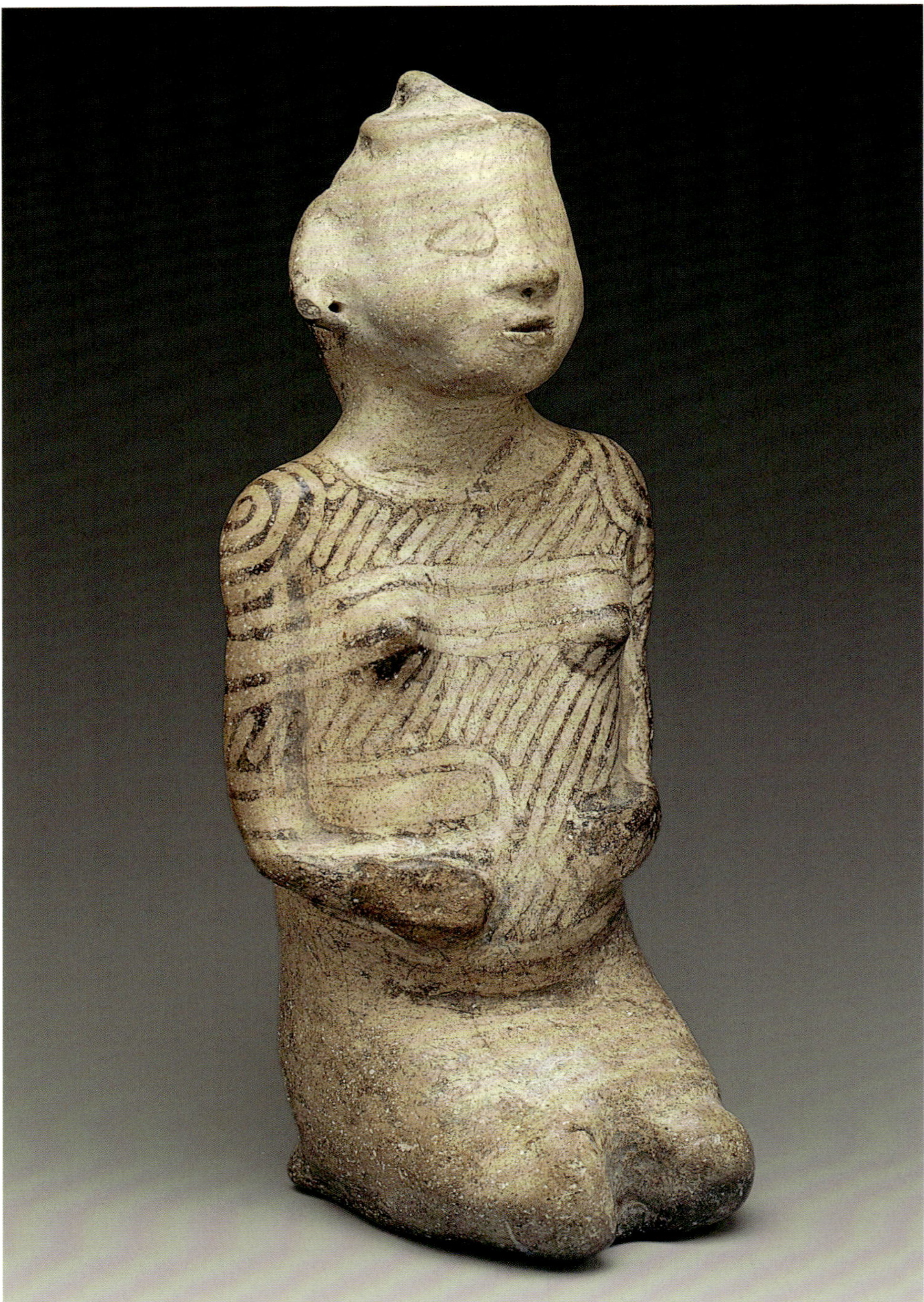

Fig. 5 Kneeling female figurine with tattoos; Tennessee, Smith County, rock shelter by the Cumberland River; ceramic, h. 22.9 cm; Dr. Arthur Cushman Collection, Old Hickory, Tennessee. Cat. no. 269.

shorthand symbol for the ever-present and powerful female deity who figures strongly in the cosmological domain, as a personification of the regenerative powers of the earth (fig. 4).

Themes in Missouri Rock Art

Supernatural beings were represented on stone by motifs that indicated their status and placement in the cosmos. Their paraphernalia and symbols of power, and even the supernaturals themselves, were depicted. But more often, possibly out of respect, these supernaturals were symbolized by icons representing a facet of their identity (such as a mace or bilobed arrow). Just as these supernatural elements are identified metaphorically by symbolic markings etched, tattooed, or painted on otherwise naturalistic contexts, so do their ritual representatives—the priests, ceremonial impersonators, and others connected to their cults, or even whole tribes of other social groups—mark or tattoo their bodies to affirm this spiritual bond. Symbolic markings include the falconine eye, concentric circles on shoulders, and other motifs on chests, arms, and hands (fig. 5). Because supernaturals cannot die—nor can their progeny's spirits die—they are constantly reborn from the earth's vulva in an unending cycle.

The Birdman or hawk theme is basic to Mississippian and SECC art (see Brown, fig. 1). Although the importance and place of the Birdman theme found at Cahokia is not equally manifest west of the Mississippi, there are nevertheless a substantial number of birds linked to this theme represented in eastern Missouri rock art. Avian forms at sites in nine eastern Missouri counties

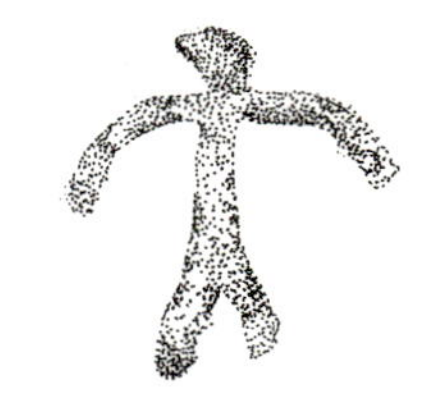

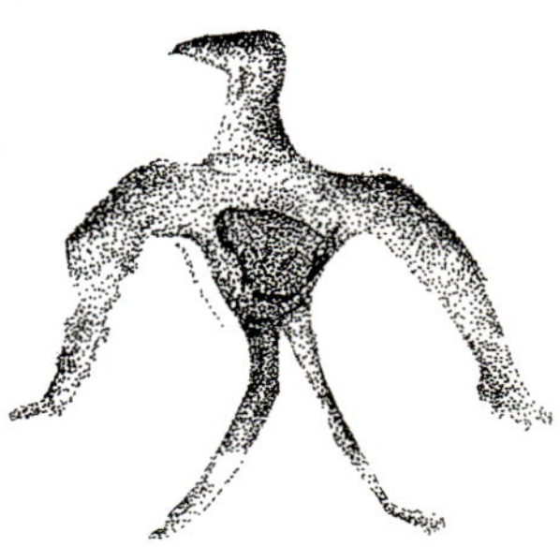

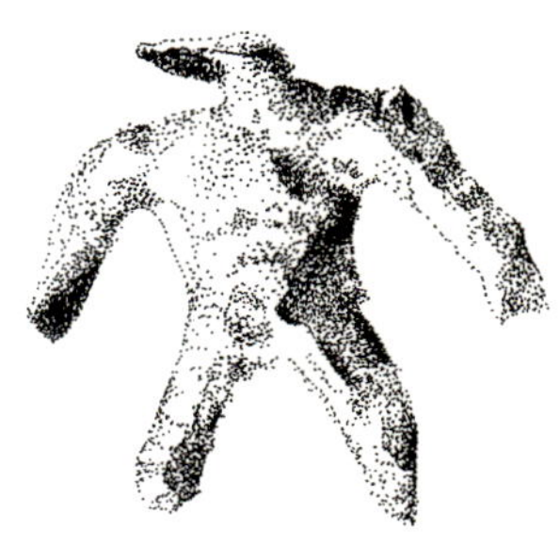

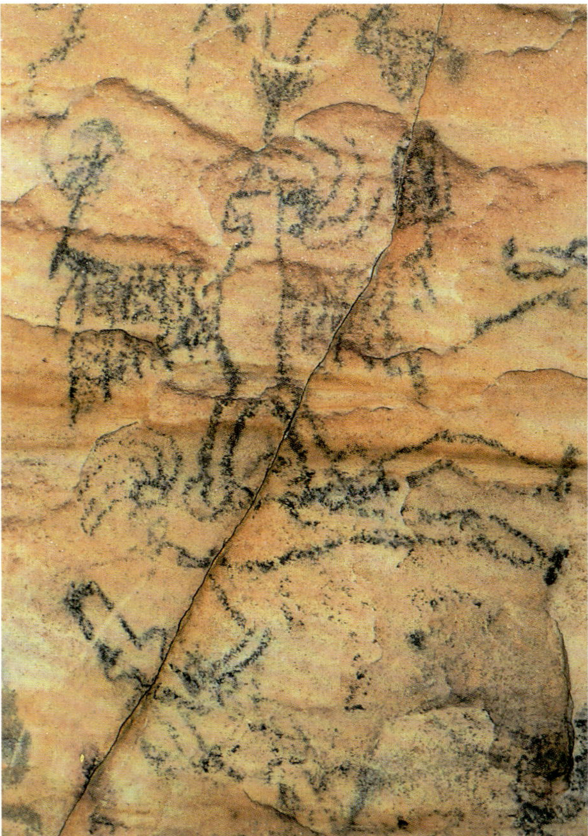

Fig. 6 Various avian motifs, including: Rocky Hollow bird with bifurcated tail feathers; Birdman petroglyph at the Peene-Murat site in Gasconade County, Missouri; and Birdman petroglyph at the Maddin Creek Ridge site in Washington County, Missouri; drawing by Gigi Bayliss.

Fig. 7 A detailed pictograph at Picture Cave I in Warren County, Missouri, shows a victorious Bird-man holding a mace and standing over a supine figure.

form a concentration radiating out from the Cahokia area. The bird is the most frequently depicted icon in rock art both north and south of the Missouri River, with the Birdman theme evident in a selection of these depictions. Those with bifurcated tails are also considered possible depictions of Birdmen. Some portrayals are rendered more "man-like" than others (fig. 6), and some are unmistakable in that they derive from the high prototypes depicted in shell carvings or copper plaques associated with the metropolitan workshops of Cahokia itself (fig. 7). These birds were often placed in conjunction with other Mississippian motifs; a possible rock altar or table at the Three Hills Creek site, for example, has a bird with a cross-in-circle in its beak (figs. 8–9). The image is one of many in a palimpsest covering the eroded surfaces of the rock. The entire monument likely functioned in an altarlike manner for the display of ritual bundles; a cedar grove close by, undoubtedly once more extensive, had formed the hallowed setting.

The vulvar motif, significant because it is likely the symbolic representation of a female deity, is also manifest in portable objects, particularly in pottery. This female character, depicted in pottery form, is certainly *not* a tuberculosis-ridden woman as previously thought, but rather the Old Woman who is revered and respected, the Siouan Old-Woman-Who-Never-Dies; she is the mother of all things in the heavens and the Middle World, also known as the Corn Mother or Earth Mother, depending on the group, location, and associated oral tradition (figs. 1, 4, and 10).

The contemporary Osage, some of whom practice the Big Moon Peyote religion, select a sacred location on which to erect a structure incorporating a vulvar-shaped altar referred to as the Earth.[4] This altar is also referred to as Morning Star's grave. Morning Star is a supernatural figure, the eldest son of the "Old Woman" (earth) and "First Man" (Sun), and he is sometimes referred to as a "Hawk." Configurations and additions to the altar represent various symbols including the sun, steps to heaven, the morning star, "and Christ's

Figs. 8–9 The petroglyph panel at the Three Hills Creek site in St. Francois County, Missouri, shows a bird image with a cross-in-circle motif at its beak, seen here in a photograph of a rock altar or table and a detailed drawing by Gigi Bayliss.

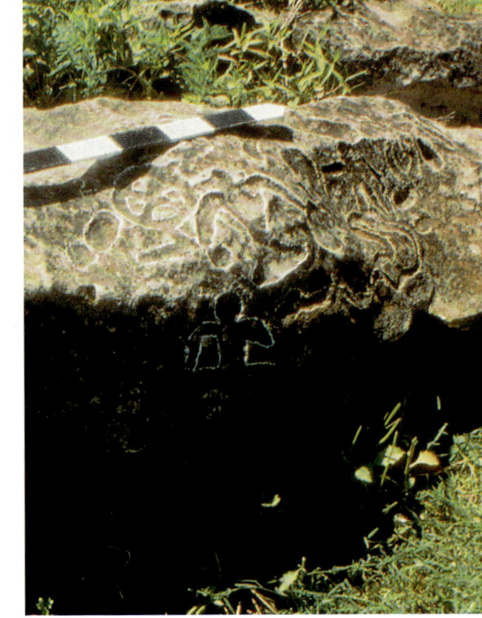

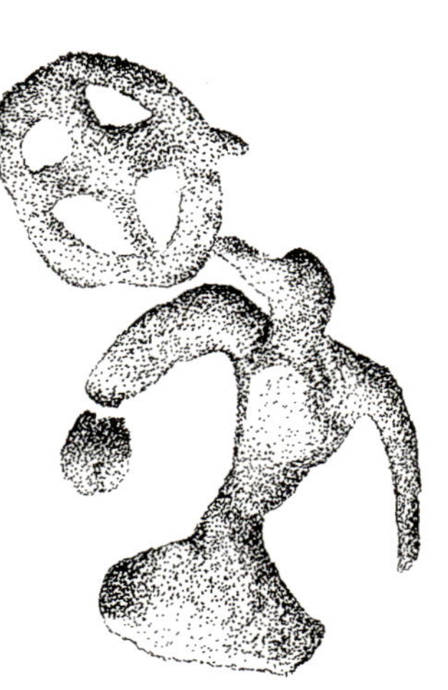

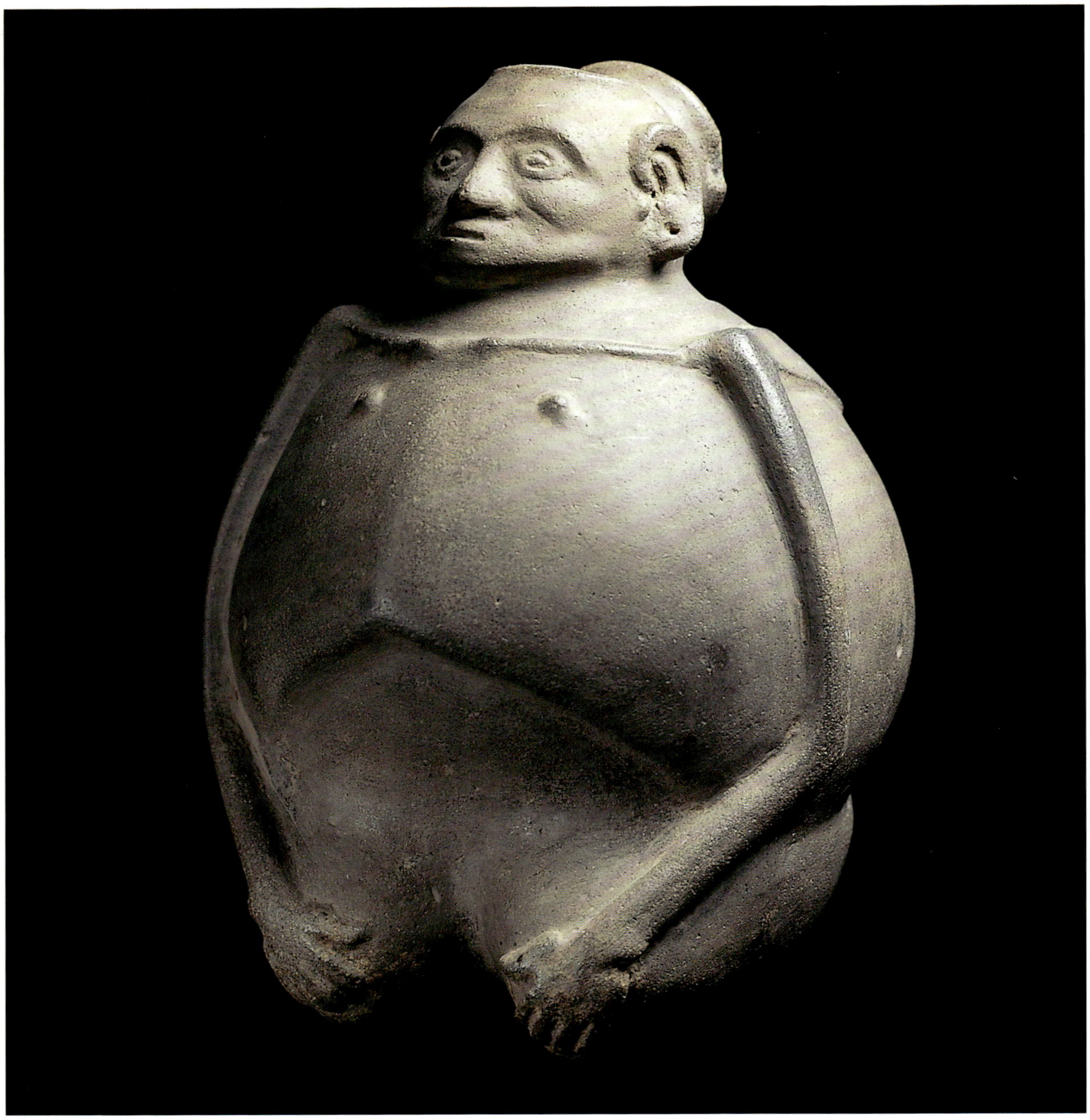

Fig. 10 Vessel in the form of a kneeling female figure; Bell Plain type; Arkansas, Crittenden County, Bradley site, c. 1300–1500; shell-tempered ceramic, h. 20.3 cm; Private collection, Missouri. Cat. no. 261.

footprints as he stood for the Ascension."[5] The Peyote or Native American Church religion, a syncretism of indigenous and Christian beliefs, originated in Mexico and was widely adopted in the United States toward the end of the nineteenth century and remains widely practiced today among many tribes.

Although the Old Woman deity is portrayed in pottery, it is readily conceivable that the most stylized way to symbolize her on rock is simply via the essential vulvar motif, which is seen in abundance on rock boulders on the west side of the Mississippi River in this same region (fig. 11). In the known oral traditions, she is the magical, shape-shifting character who can turn herself into a young doe; she makes corn by scraping her thighs; and she is the grave as well as the birthplace of Morning Star. The snakes are her husbands.[6] She is the figure who gives birth to several supernatural beings according to a variety of oral traditions. She is the one to whom people pray for fertility in food crops as well as for game animals. In the rock art, we see her associated with her messengers—the birds. The birds carry prayers to her when they migrate south in the fall. And the birds herald the arrival of the growing season with their return in the spring. So it is not

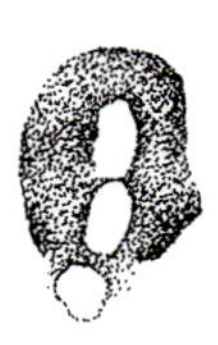
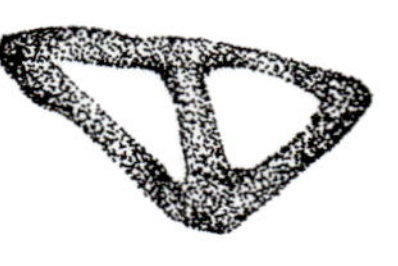
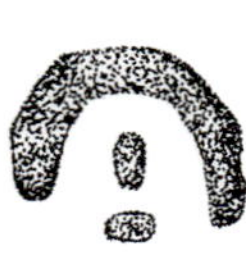
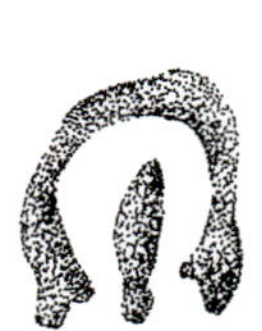
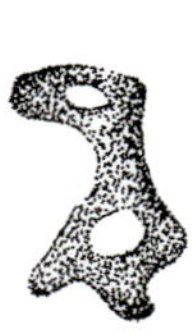
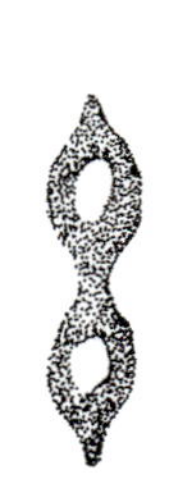

Fig. 11 A sampling of the vulvar motifs found in Missouri petroglyphs; drawing by Gigi Bayliss.

surprising to see the bird and vulvar motifs or cosmic earth signs such as the cross-in-circle, depicted in close proximity (fig. 9).

The Mace

The war club or mace, as it is often called, is an essential part of Dhegiha Sioux war bundles—the woven rush bags that contained a preserved hawk and provided a spiritual bridge between Sioux warriors and Morning Star, Hawk, or the Great Star that sits in the daytime sky.[7] All warriors carried war clubs as the principal weapon for close quarter, hand-to-hand fighting among precontact Woodland and Prairie peoples (fig. 12). The war club or mace plays a prominent role in rock art imagery along the Missouri and Mississippi rivers. It is depicted at a minimum of nine sites—sometimes in multiples. At a site south of the rivers' confluence, it is carved together with "the four stones of the hearth in the house of mystery" (fig. 13). In this house, warriors made medicine and magically aided their war expeditions, slaying their enemies in spirit before the actual events.[8] The mace is also seen in conjunction with another widespread image—the Dancing Warrior—whose frequent occurrence testifies to the profound influence of the Southeastern Ceremonial Complex. The Dancing Warrior pictograph at Rattlesnake Bluff (fig. 14) can be compared in stance and basic profile to the famous Rogan copper plates from Etowah, Georgia

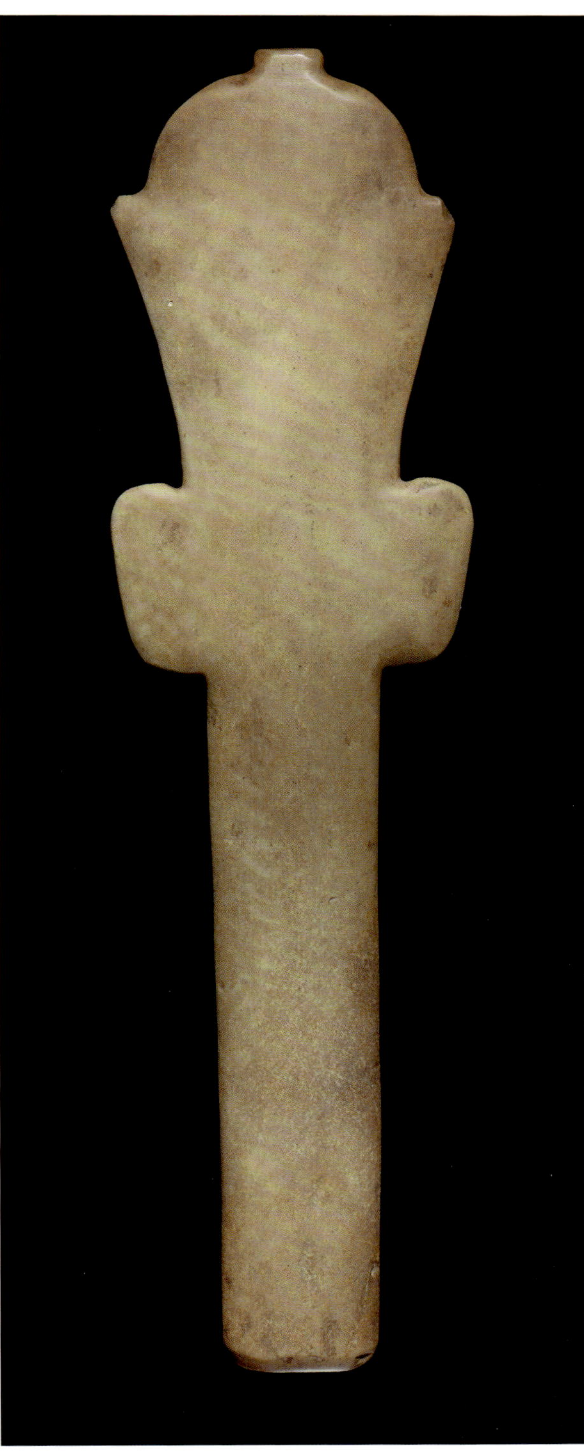

Fig. 12 Ceremonial mace; Oklahoma, LeFlore County, Spiro, A.D. 1200–1350; stone, l. 25.4 cm; Gilcrease Museum, Tulsa, Oklahoma. Cat. no. 185.

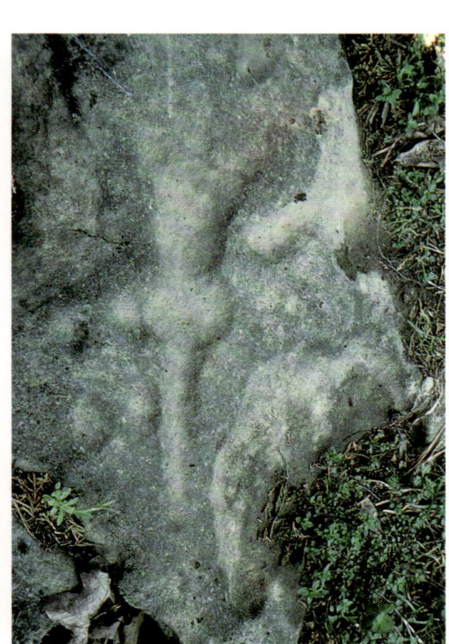

Fig. 13 Mace petroglyph at Washington State Park, Site B, Washington County, Missouri.

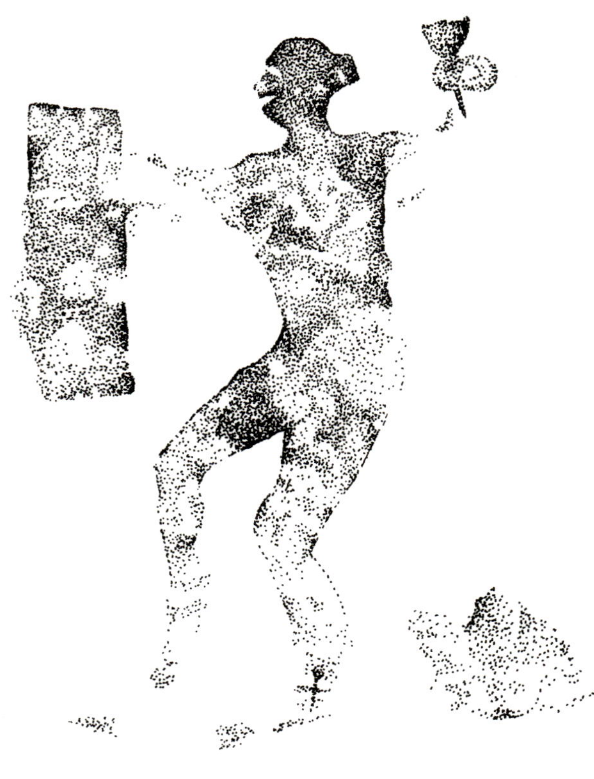

Fig. 14 Dancing Warrior at Rattlesnake Bluff site, located above the Little Bourbeous River in Franklin County, Missouri (on private property); drawing by Gigi Bayliss.

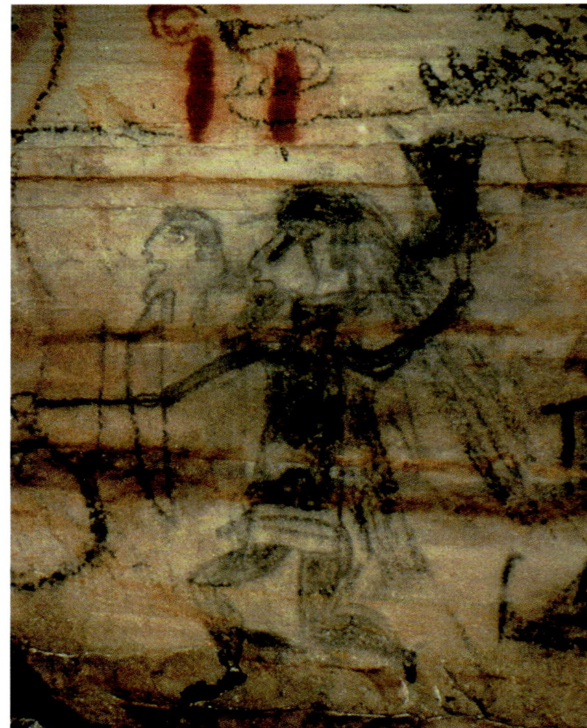

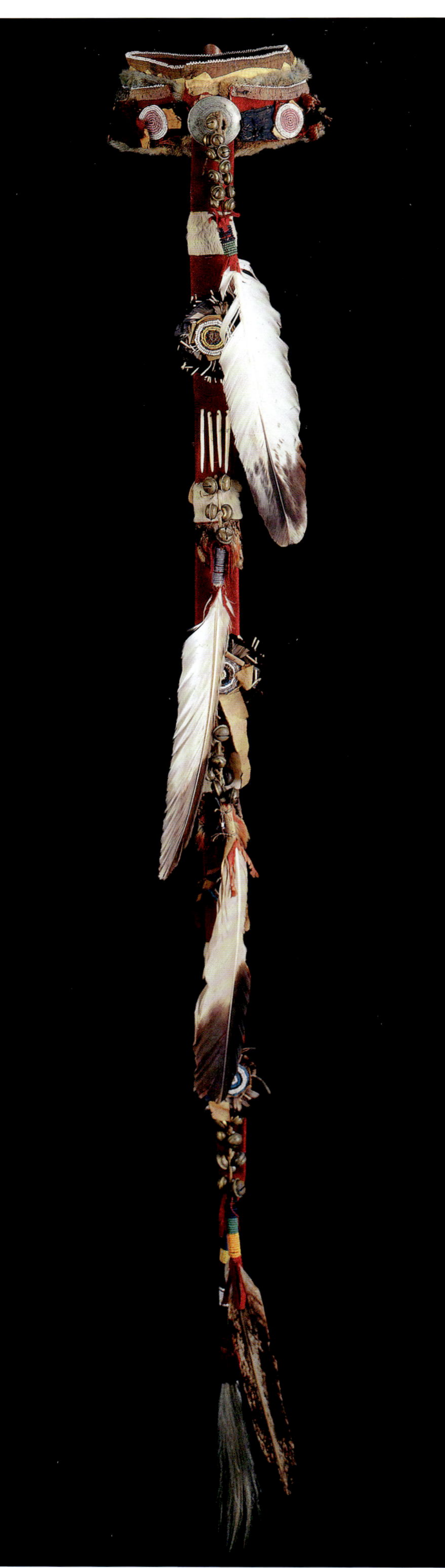

Fig. 15 Pictograph panel of the Black Warrior at Picture Cave I in Warren County, Missouri.

Fig. 16 Osage headdress, 18th/19th century; hide, otter fur, feathers, beads, metal, shell, bird beak, and pigment, 121.9 × 20.3 cm; The Osage Tribal Museum, Library, and Archives; Osage Reservation, Oklahoma.

(see figs. 1 and 11 in the essay by Adam King in this volume); it is also depicted on shell gorgets (see fig. 1 in the essay by David Dye).

This iconic image of a warrior in war regalia brandishing a mace above his head is also present in two pictographs at Picture Cave I: one of the Black Warrior, the other of the Giant. The Black Warrior pictograph is a large figure measuring 50 centimeters in height (19¾ in.). It is drawn in black outline with some black, filled areas (fig. 15). The hands and feet are completely drawn, unlike the cave's two other main figures in which the ankles trail off. The face is in profile showing a falconine eye-marking. A second, almost identical face is drawn in front of the first, which could indicate either a redrawing or correction, or a spirit emerging as a war cry from his open mouth. There is a mace in one raised hand and a bow with a cruciform arrow in the other. This lively, charging figure is rendered naturalistically with the emblematic sash of a warrior society and a drum-shaped hat. The carefully drawn hat or headdress is a specific type that survived into historic times, as seen in an example of an Osage military headdress from the late eighteenth to early nineteenth century (fig. 16). The headdress has a trailer with feathers and horsetail tassels representing scalps, while the head band features ivory-billed woodpecker scalps with the upper beaks still attached and lined with thin, hammered copper. This avian detail, seen also in Spiro shell gorgets, speaks of a standardized association between ivory-billed woodpeckers and emblems of warriors.

The character called the Giant at Picture Cave I is depicted with a textile or hide wrapping embellished with nested, semicircular motifs, and carrying a small, trilobed mace in the left hand (fig. 17). The face, with a falconine eye-marking, is drawn in profile with an

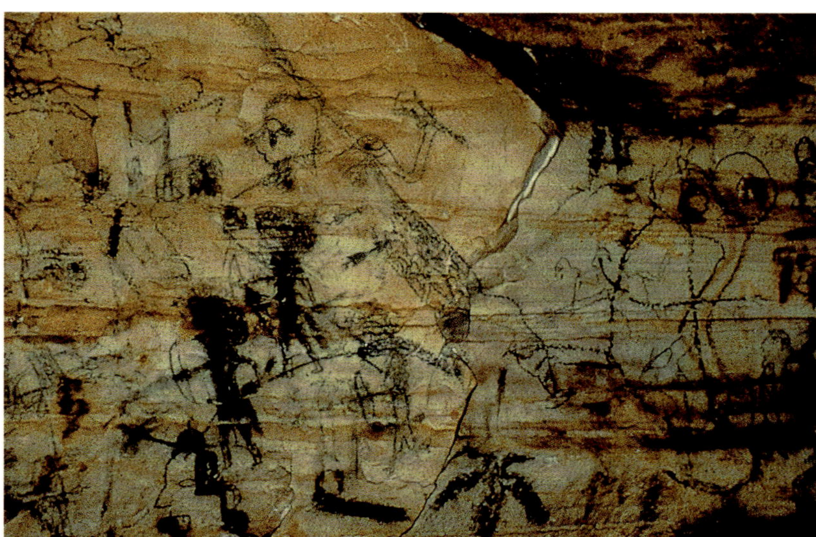

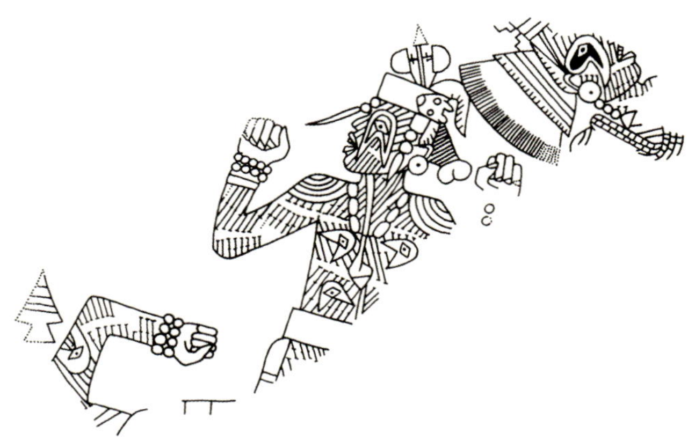

Fig. 17 Pictograph panel of the Giant at Picture Cave I in Warren County, Missouri. The figure is 75 centimeters in height.

Fig. 18 Drawing of an engraved shell cup showing a figure with shoulder tattoos of concentric circles; Classic Braden style; Oklahoma, LeFlore County, Spiro, Craig Mound, A.D. 1200–1350; from Phillips and Brown 1978, pl. 6.

occipital hair bun and a single upright feather. Concentric circles appear on the shoulder of the figure, most probably representing a tattoo. The significance of this shoulder marking has been variously considered as a symbol of the sun, water, a hawk, or an eye. The motif is relatively common Classic Braden–style figures from Cahokia (fig. 18).[9] Originally identified and labeled by Phillips and Brown (1978) with regard to Spiro engraved shell, the Braden style is most noted by its use of realistic facial profiles and body proportions.

We can, to some degree, generalize that carving a stone with symbols consecrated it and distinguished it from others. In some cases it rendered the stone otherworldly in that it could "grant favors" if properly supplicated. "The stone symbolized the steadfast power of Wa-Ko^{n}-da, the permeating life of all nature, and so was possessed with 'power to receive supplications'. . . . Therefore to it man turned for protection and help when beset by distress of body or mind."[10] Because stones, both large ones in fields and small ones used in the sweat lodge, were used for supplicatory and other spiritual purposes, it is understandable that once altered with sacred symbols, the stone was imbued with the power to transmit messages to the spirits of other worlds. The stone was a part of the Middle World; to consecrate it transformed it into a part of the Upper or Lower worlds. It became an intermediary between humans of the Middle World and the powerful supernatural beings dwelling in the Upper and Lower worlds.

Just as the stone was marked and consecrated, tattooing was employed as a means to consecrate the human body. Tattooing, such as the one seen on the shoulder of the Giant at Picture Cave, or on the youthful body of a female figurine (fig. 5) appears to have a long tradition—at least one thousand years—according to the date for the pictograph.[11] Tattooing presumably occurred in conjunction with a rite of passage, for example, upon coming of age, assuming a certain office, following a war exploit, or as another signature of honor or identity. Once tattooed, the individual bearing the markings was thus consecrated.

The act of rendering an individual of prominence holy or special was not unlike that of marking the sacred stone. Tattoos were marks of honor. They served as a means of group identity and were believed to promote longevity. Osage men were tattooed with the wing feathers of a hawk on their upper bodies, and some war captains also had war pipes tattooed on their chests. The war pipe motif indicated that they were a keeper of the sacred war bundle or pack. These tattoos protected them and gave them the power to incite fear and to triumph over their enemies. Elderly women of the Isolated Sacred Earth Clan, consorts of leaders, wore the spider motif on their hands to commemorate how the spider aided Morning Star in his journey through the sky.[12]

Another manner in which an individual was symbolically changed or made sacred was with the addition of a special pair of ear ornaments. The Long-Nosed God maskettes seen in copper are portrayed at a Missouri pictograph site in the white shell version (figs. 19–20). At 30.6 centimeters in height (12 in.), this pictograph is the clearest, most delicately rendered drawing in the cave, complete with iconographic details. It is also the only one rendered by incised lines filled with white pigment, a technique more often seen on terminal late Woodland or developmental Mississippian artifacts such as pipes, discoidals, and other gaming pieces. This detailed and naturalistic style of incising does not emphasize the feet and hands, which trail off, but rather emphasizes facial features rendered in profile and body painting. The striped face and body are a common metaphorical reference to the personification of Morning Star, Sun, or related celestial phenomena.

With scientific analyses, it is possible to date at least a portion of the pictographs of this western Mississippian rock imagery. Pigment samples were taken from five of the pictographs at Picture Cave I and dated by accelerator mass spectrometry (AMS) to approximately A.D. 1025. In particular, the panel with the Giant was most revealing in terms of diagnostic motifs: complex clothing elements and paraphernalia, including the

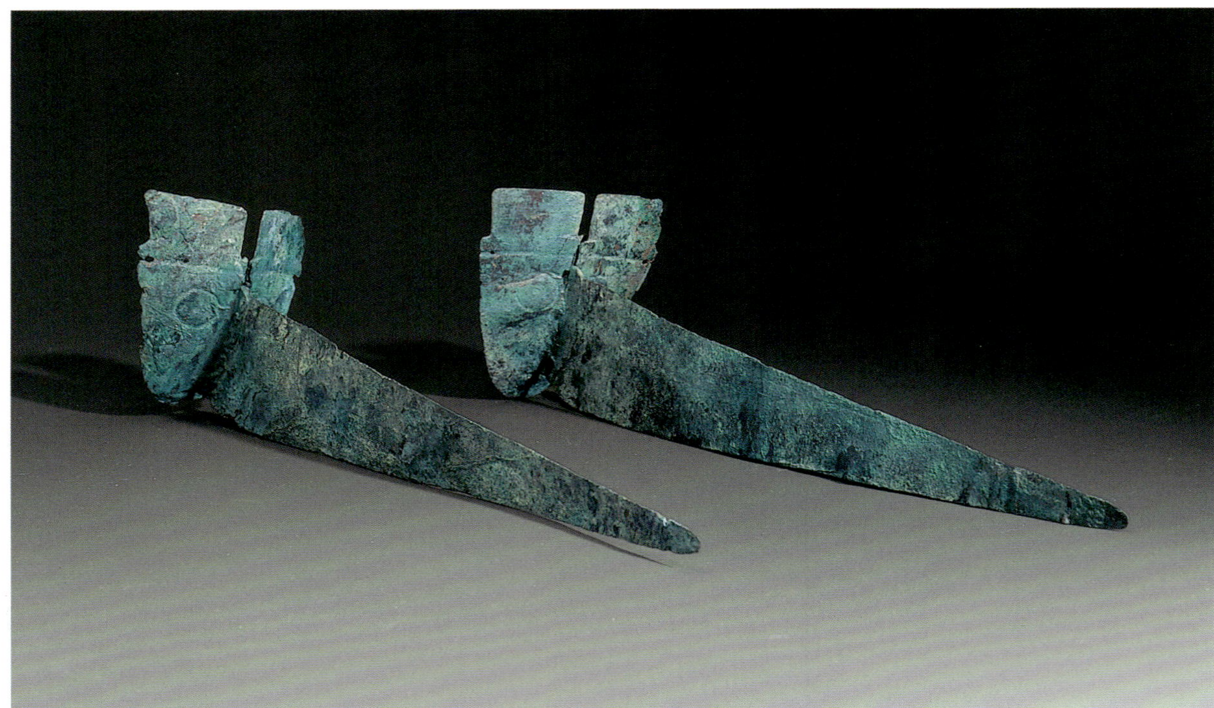

Fig. 19 Long-Nosed God maskette ear ornaments; Illinois, Meppen Mound site, A.D. 1000–1400; copper, l. 22.4, 22 cm; Charles L. Adam Family Collection, Missouri. Cat. no. 119.

Fig. 20 Close-up of Morning Star pictograph panel in Picture Cave I, showing white shell maskette ear ornament. This is the only known example of the use of white pigment in parietal rock art in the Midwestern region.

mace, the occipital hair bun, the single feather, the falconine eye-marking, and the body wrap with its nested semicircles, are all related to the Mississippian Southeastern Ceremonial Complex time period.

The Bilobed Arrow

The bilobed-arrow motif is well represented in eastern Missouri rock art. Depicted at a minimum of five eastern Missouri sites, this symbol has been found archaeologically on shell cups, painted on pottery, and in the form of a hammered copper repoussé plaque, worn as a headdress by the Morning Star or Red Horn character (see King fig. 1 and fig. 44 in the essay by Richard Townsend). Although there is no bilobed-arrow headdress in the Morning Star (or He-Who-Wears-Human-Heads-in-His-Ears) panel at Picture Cave I, there is a side view of a probable ogee plaque, stuck with five arrows at his forehead or forelock (see fig. 20). This could represent an earlier version of the same headdress iconography, later represented by the copper repoussé plaque presumably depicted at Maddin Creek (fig. 21). At another site we see the close juxtaposition of the bilobed-arrow rulership symbol, the petaloid cross-in-circle cosmogram, and the female ogee symbol (fig. 22).[13] The same eye-marking appears on the head of a diorite effigy bowl from Moundville (see fig. 18 in the essay by Vincas Steponaitis and Vernon Knight).

No artifacts were collected during the many trips to record the pictographs in the dark zone of Picture Cave. Unfortunately, local collectors had cleaned out the cave floor long before it came to the attention of professional archaeologists. One collector, however, claims to have gathered both Cahokia points and Mississippian pottery at the site. On a survey in the early 1990s, a small collection of pottery fragments was gathered by archaeologists Patty Jo Watson and George Crothers from surface debris within the cave. Items included both Late Woodland limestone-tempered sherds and a body sherd of St. Claire Polished Plain, an early Mississippian pottery type found along the Mississippi River just south of Cahokia. This latter type is dated to approximately A.D. 1050, connecting with the time period for the general Braden style of shell engraving. Picture Cave I was obviously a ritual site. Because of its Long-Nosed God maskette, maces, falconine eye-markings, and Birdman images, the cave is assigned a tentative date range of A.D. 900 to 1400, which fits with the Mississippian period, and appears to extend into a slightly earlier developmental period that encompasses proto-Mississippian Southeastern Ceremonial Complex iconography.

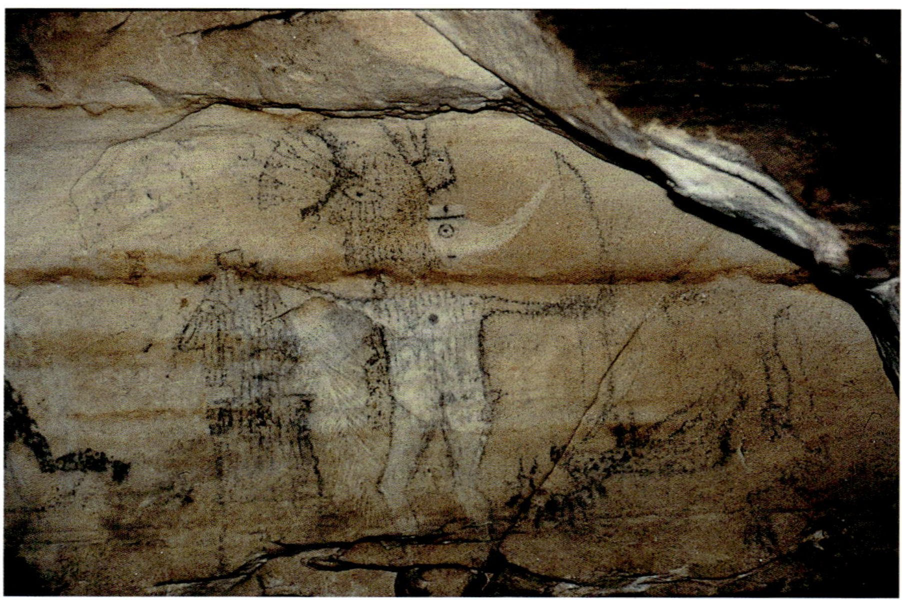

Conclusion

The petroglyphs and pictographs of the central Mississippi and Missouri river valleys not only have brought to light the abundance of Mississippian imagery available for comparative studies and analysis, but also serve to support links to the surviving ethnographic information from Dhegihan-speaking groups who occupied the general region. This rock art has brought into a more solid context the union of various motifs from the Cahokian sphere. It has also helped to identify places on the landscape that were undoubtedly sacred to the prehistoric people of this region. This is a decisive step forward with regard to the interpretation of these and other related symbolic arts from the Eastern Woodlands.

Scholars concerned with the interpretation of the visual arts have learned that "what we see is not always what we get," but this is the nature of all symbolic arts: what may appear or be taken as a Middle World representation is more likely a reference to a supernatural being from the Upper World or Lower World. In certain instances, one need only observe the character's paraphernalia to gain insight into which otherworldly supernatural is being portrayed. The mere fact that rock art has been found in caves and rock shelters, where ritual activity took place, reflects the magico-religious realm of the basic tripartite cosmos.

These supernatural beings acted as guiding spirits and could be benevolent as well as malevolent characters to be revered or feared. They arose from the sacred, natural environment and its resources—the very elements of the landscape itself: caves, rocks, waters, the sun, the cycle of fertility and growth. Hence, as the locations varied, so did the identifying symbolic imagery. In the Mississippian world the signs, symbols, deities, and heroes were those seen in the art of Cahokia. Such patterns may also be seen in other time periods of the ancient Midwest and South. Indeed, similar ways of marking and consecrating the landscape occur elsewhere throughout the ancient Americas. These practices were deeply ingrained in the worldviews of the American Indians and arose out of a deep awareness of and respect for the landscape and its gifts.

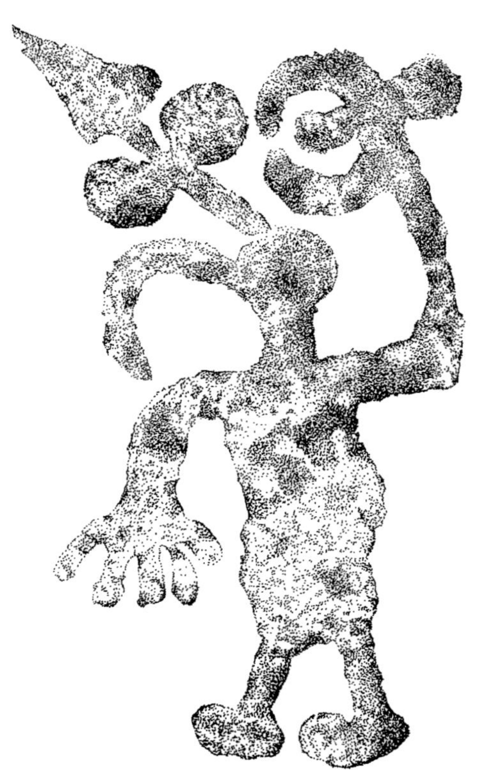

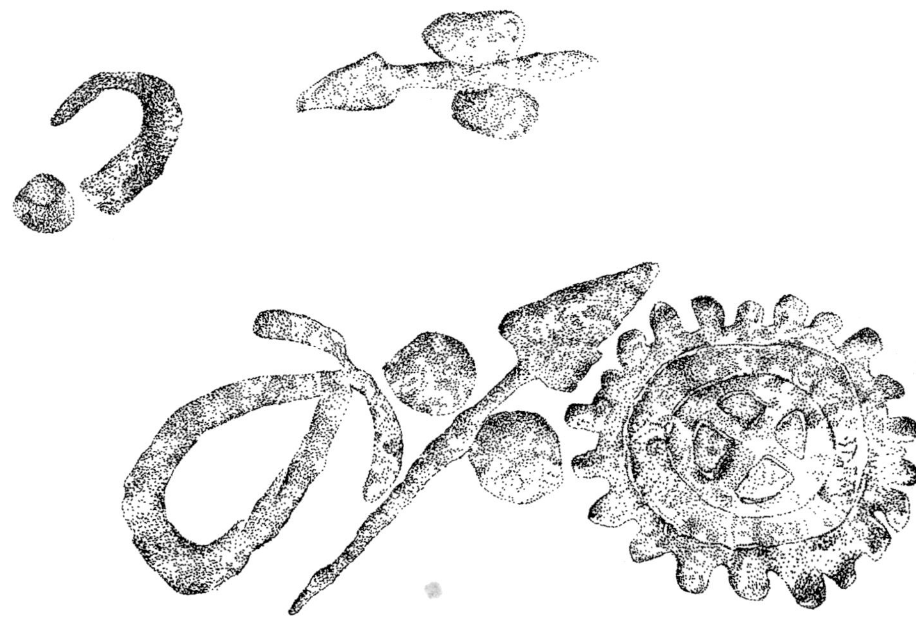

Fig. 21 This petroglyph of a Morning Star figure with a bilobed-arrow headdress is part of a petroglyph panel carved on an exposed rock escarpment at the Maddin Creek site in Washington County, Missouri; drawing by Gigi Bayliss.

Fig. 22 This petroglyph panel at the Maddin Creek site shows the juxtaposition of bilobed arrows, petaloid cross-in-circle motif, vulva form, and a type of eye marking or ogee symbol also found in the iconography at Moundville, Alabama; drawing by Gigi Bayliss.

Notes

1. La Flesche 1932, pp. 193–94.
2. Waring and Holder 1945, Fundaburk and Foreman 1957, Muller 1966, and Muller 1989, among others.
3. Muller 1989.
4. Swan 1999, p. 26; Mathews 1961, p. 744.
5. Swan 1999, p. 31; Mathews 1961, p. 744.
6. Bowers 1992, p. 372.
7. La Flesche 1932, pp. 365, 393.
8. La Flesche 1932, pp. 385–86.
9. Phillips and Brown 1978, p. 148.
10. Fletcher and La Flesche 1992 [1911], p. 587.
11. The pigments in this figure were dated by Accelerator Mass Spectrometry to 940±80 b.p. See Diaz-Granados et al. 2001 for details of the pigment dating project at Picture Cave I.
12. Fletcher and La Flesche 1992 [1911], pp. 219–21; and Mathews 1961. Both attest to the importance of tattoos among the Osage. A forthcoming chapter by Duncan and Diaz-Granados (University of Alabama Press, 2004) also discusses tattooing.
13. All of these motifs are portrayed in a single image along with an AMS date for this figure of an uncalibrated 940±80 YBP (years before present). Diaz-Granados et al. 2001.

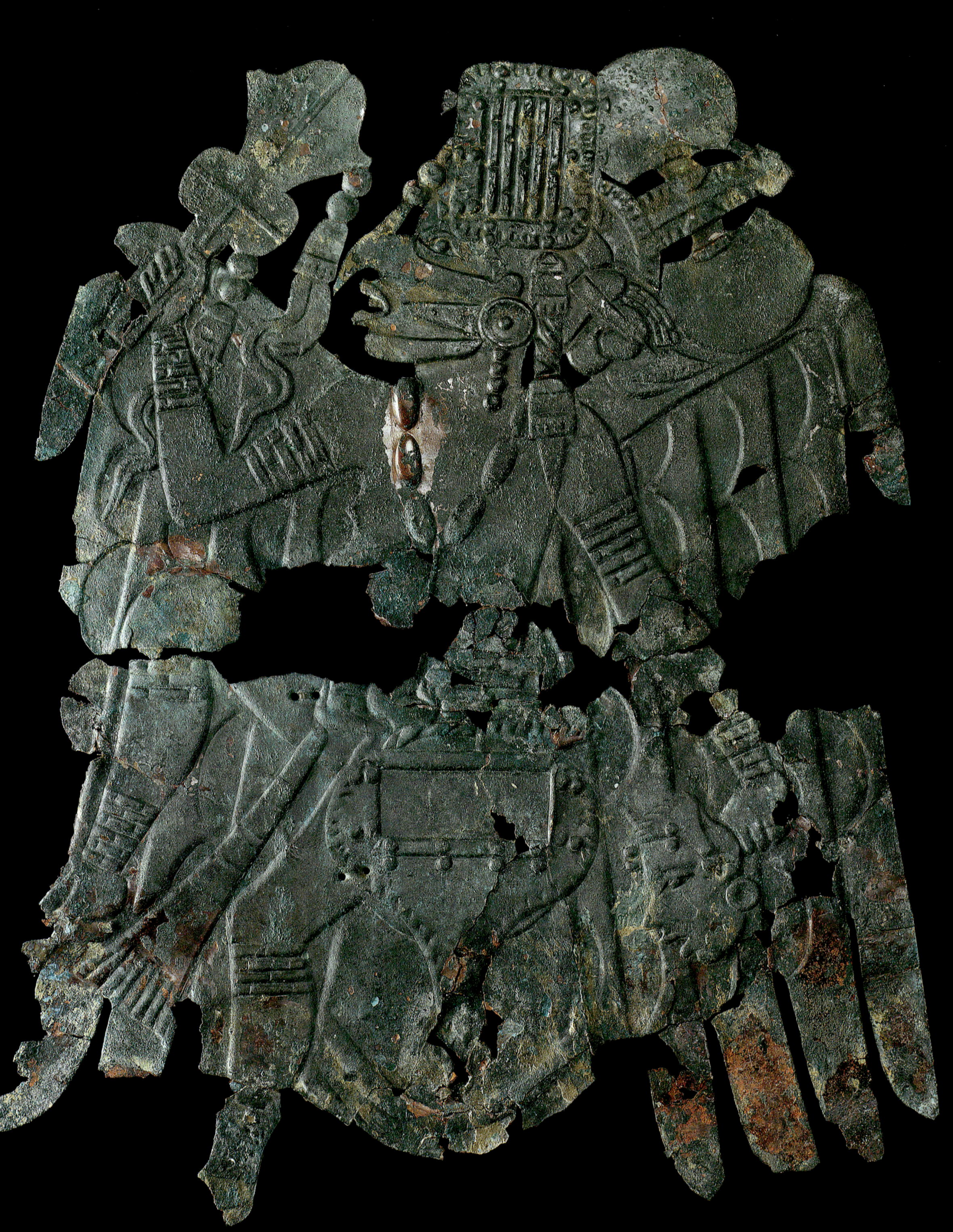

It seems a monument of the past ages, venerable in its antiquity, solemn, silent, and yet not voiceless—a remarkable exhibition of the power and industry of a former race.

—Colonel Charles Whittlesey

Power and the Sacred

Adam King

Mound C and the Etowah Chiefdom

Fig. 1 Copper repoussé plate depicting Birdman; one of the two so-called Rogan plates; Georgia, Bartow County, Etowah, Mound C, 13th century; copper, h. 27.9 cm; Smithsonian Institution, National Museum of Natural History, Washington, D.C. Cat. no. 110. This heirloom copper repoussé plate is of Cahokian origin but was recovered as part of the regalia of an Etowah chief. The image incorporates the Birdman theme with specific symbols of the cultural hero Red Horn (note his long braid of hair, a symbolic horn), He-Who-Is-Hit-with-Deer-Lungs (note the bilobed-arrow headdress); the hero is also named Morning Star in various accounts. As the figure dances in triumph, he brandishes a mace in his right hand and dangles a trophy head from his left. This plaque would have served as an emblem of office awarded a chieftain, and would have accompanied him as a sign of his strength among the ancestral spirits.

The Etowah site, located in the northwestern corner of Georgia, still inspires the same sense of wonder and mystery that it invoked in Colonel Charles Whittlesey, a nineteenth-century geologist and amateur archaeologist.[1] Etowah, with its complex arrangement of large mounds and plazas, is one of the most impressive Mississippian centers in the Deep South (fig. 2). Even more impressive is the collection of finely crafted and often elaborately decorated ceremonial objects recovered from the site's burial mound, Mound C. These objects have long been recognized as part of a widespread complex of artistic styles, ceremonial objects, and ritual themes collectively called the Southeastern Ceremonial Complex (SECC).[2] These SECC goods are examples of native craftsmanship that deserve to take their rightful place among the artistic achievements of humankind. In addition, they constitute an integral part of a cultural record that, as Whittlesey intimated so long ago, can tell us a great deal about the history of Etowah and its inhabitants. That history is long and complex, and Mound C and the sacred artifacts it contained played a key role in the rise and fall of this important Mississippian center.

Etowah and Its Archaeological History

Archaeological investigations began at Etowah in 1884 and have continued sporadically up to the present time, resulting in the investigation of a large portion of the site and its major features. All of the mounds with

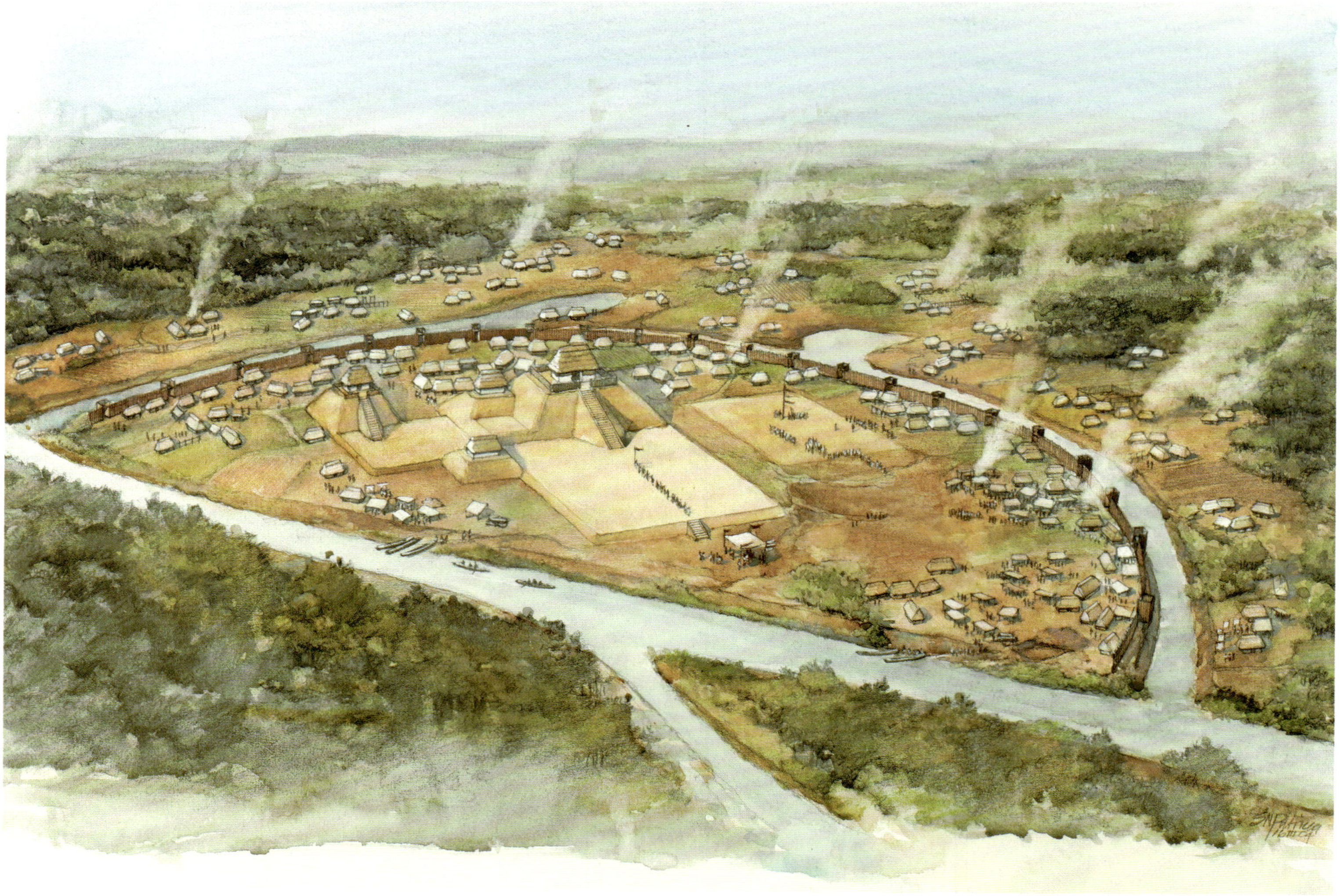

Fig. 2 View looking northwest over Etowah; rendering by Steven Patricia.

the exception of Mound F have been examined at some level, and those areas between Mounds B and C, as well as between Mounds A and D, have been systematically tested.[3] Block excavations have been conducted on the west side of Mound B, in the immediate vicinity of Mound C, in several locations east of Mound A, and at the edge of the palisade ditch.[4] The area between Mounds D, E, and F and the palisade ditch has been systematically surface collected, but no excavations have been conducted.[5] The large areas to the north and west of Mound A have never been investigated.

The Etowah site is a large, multimound Mississippian-period town located on the Etowah River in Bartow County, Georgia (figs. 2 and 4). During its periods of occupation, a total of six known earthen mounds were constructed at the site; archaeologists have designated these as Mounds A through F. Mound A is the largest measuring over 19 meters (62 ft.) in height. It has a prominent ramp projecting from its eastern side, as well as a lower terrace attached to its southern side. Mounds B and C are each large, flat-topped pyramidal mounds measuring 7 and 6 meters tall (23 and 20 ft.), respectively. Of the two, only Mound C originally had a ramp, which also projected from its eastern flank. The smallest mounds at the site (D, E, and F) are rectangular to oblong platforms that each stand about 3 meters (10 ft.) high. To the south, the site is bordered by the Etowah River, but on all other sides it is surrounded by a series of borrow pits connected by a large ditch. According to Lewis H. Larson, Jr., who conducted his first excavations at Etowah in the mid-1950s, there was once a palisade with bastions located just inside of the ditch, suggesting that the site was fortified at one time.[6] This ditch encloses 22 hectares (54.3 acres)

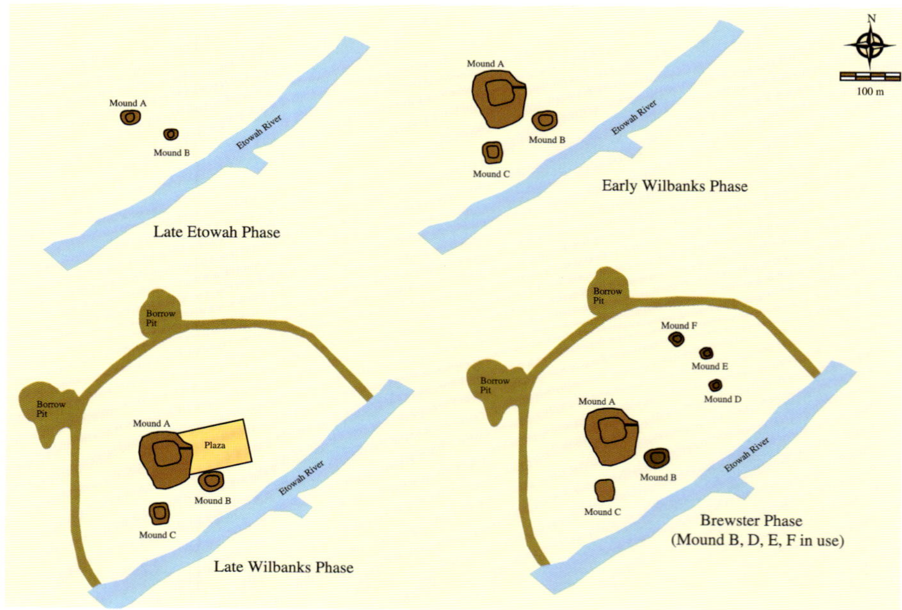

Fig. 3 Changes in the Etowah site plan from A.D. 1100 to 1550.

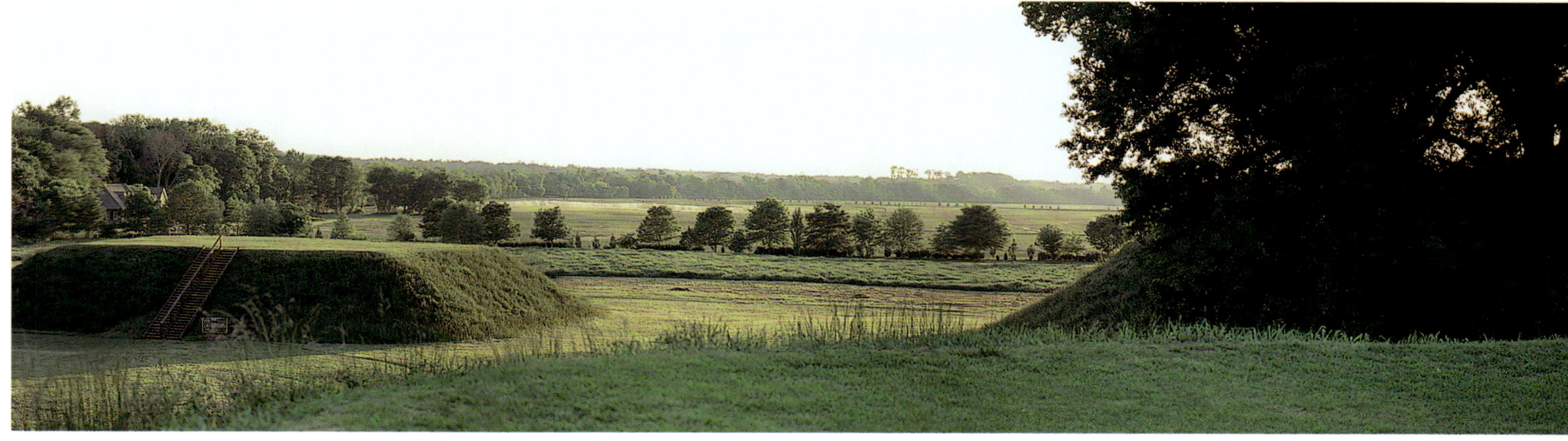

Fig. 4 Panoramic view of Etowah.

and extended to the river on both sides before it was partially filled for agricultural purposes.

A Brief History of the Etowah Site

All told, over a century of archaeological investigations have been conducted at Etowah.[7] Although a great deal has been examined at the site, most of the investigations have focused on the mounds and the areas immediately adjacent to them. As a result, much more is known about the history of the mounds and areas that have been discovered to be the burial sites of elite members of the community than about non-elite and residential portions of the site. Despite these problems, enough data has been collected to allow for a fairly complete reconstruction of Etowah's occupational sequence (see chronological chart, p. 12).

The Mississippian-period occupation of Etowah began roughly one thousand years ago, during which time this modest place contained at most one small mound, a series of large public buildings, and possibly a small plaza. The evidence for mound construction is limited and consists of circumstantial evidence that construction may have begun on Mound A.[8] Given the clear connection between platform mounds and their role in serving the needs of Mississippian leaders, the presence of a mound at Etowah suggests it functioned as the capital of a chiefdom. Furthermore, the lack of other mound centers in the Etowah River valley shows that Etowah was the only such capital in the valley. By the Late Etowah phase (A.D. 1100–1200), however, Etowah was joined by two other modest centers to the east along the river. At Etowah itself construction presumably continued on Mound A, and there is direct evidence that construction had begun on Mound B (fig. 3).[9] The similarity in the sizes of these three centers in the valley and the distances separating them argue for each being the capital of an independent, simple chiefdom.

Sometime after 1200, all three of the simple chiefdoms in this valley collapsed. No occupations have been recorded either through settlement survey or extensive testing at the valley's known political centers for the period from roughly 1200 to 1250.[10] In fact, data suggest a population exodus that brought a temporary end to chiefdoms in the Etowah River valley. People returned after 1250, however, and the Etowah site flourished once again. A boom in monumental construction occurred during the Early Wilbanks phase (A.D. 1250–1325), with Mound B being significantly enlarged and most of the huge Mound A being constructed (fig. 3). It is of particular significance that this is also the phase when construction began on Mound C, with three stages being added. As noted above, Mound C served as a mortuary facility for Etowah's elite, and many of the burials placed in it contained grave offerings exhibiting characteristic SECC traits. While this build-up was occurring at the site, a similar construction boom occurred in the immediate vicinity of Etowah (fig. 5). As many as five secondary centers were established in close proximity to Etowah—east, south, and

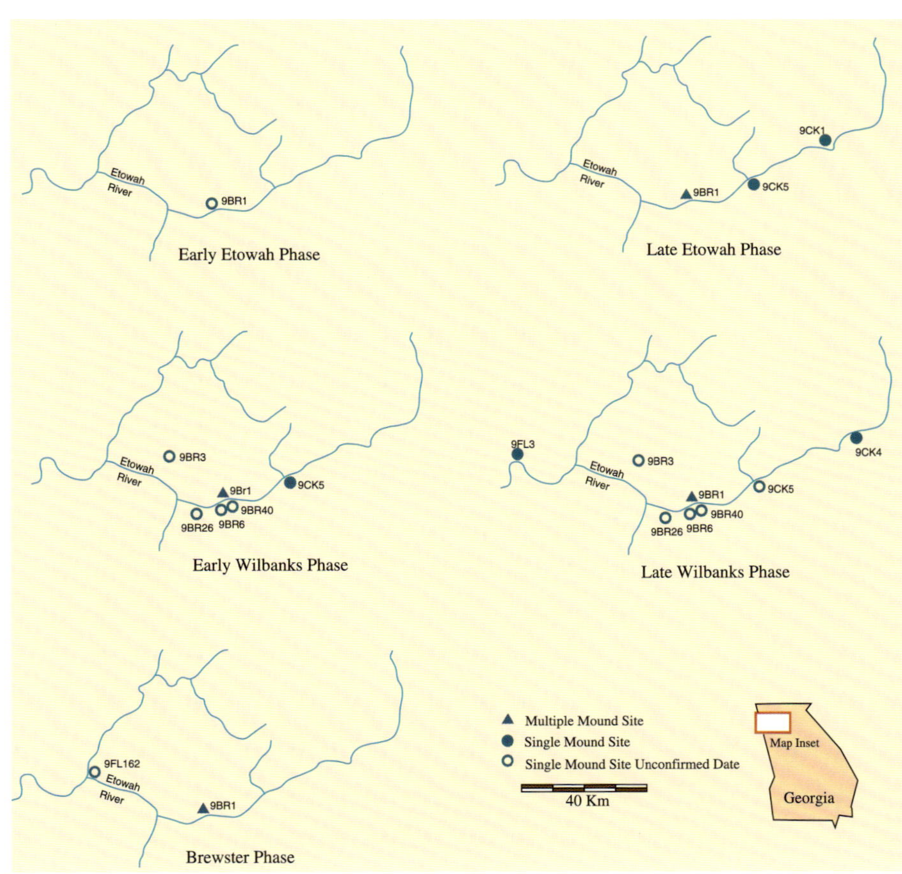

Fig. 5 Map showing the development of chiefdom capitals in the Etowah River valley from Early Etowah phase (A.D. 1000–1100) through the Brewster phase (A.D. 1475–1550). The presence of five single-mound sites in near proximity to Etowah during the Early Wilbanks phase (A.D. 1250–1325) indicates that Etowah was the dominant center of a complex chiefdom.

northwest—suggesting that Etowah had become the capital of a complex chiefdom and the clear center of power in the region.

During the Late Wilbanks phase (A.D. 1325–1375), Etowah itself became even more formalized and impressive (fig. 3). Construction continued on the mounds, as the final stages were added to Mounds A, B, and C. In addition, the area east of Mound A was converted from a residential zone to a plaza with a paved surface surrounded by a low rock wall; a palisade and an associated ditch that together encircled the site were also completed. As in the previous phase, Mound C continued to function as a mortuary facility for elite members whose graves contained elaborate arrays of SECC goods.

Activities in the rest of the valley indicate that Etowah remained an important center of power in the region. In addition to the five single-mound centers that had developed within 22 kilometers (13.8 miles) of Etowah, most likely functioning in some way as secondary centers in a complex chiefdom administrative hierarchy, two other, new, single-mound centers appeared during this phase, located at either end of the Etowah valley (fig. 5). While it is difficult to know for certain, it seems likely that these communities were under the political influence of Etowah as well. Yet, before the end of the fourteenth century, Etowah and all other mound centers in the valley were abandoned, perhaps pointing to yet another valley-wide collapse of chiefdoms. Fortunately, in the archaeological record of Etowah, there are a few clues as to how this second abandonment may have come about. First, it appears that the palisade constructed in the Late Wilbanks phase burned. While it is possible to envision an accidental burning of the palisade caused by lightning or Etowah's inhabitants, it seems more plausible that the palisade was burned intentionally—possibly as part of an armed attack.

Fig. 6 Seated male and kneeling female figures; Georgia, Bartow County, Etowah, Mound C, A.D. 1325–1375; marble, h. 61 and 55.9 cm; Etowah Indian Mounds State Historic Site, Georgia Department of Natural Resources, Atlanta. Cat. nos. 107–08. Recovered from a pit in front of Mound C, where they were hastily deposited following the destruction of the temple above, the pair leans slightly forward with wide, staring eyes, their upright torsos seemingly charged with tension and energy. They may represent a primordial pair from a creation myth or, perhaps more likely, lineage ancestors.

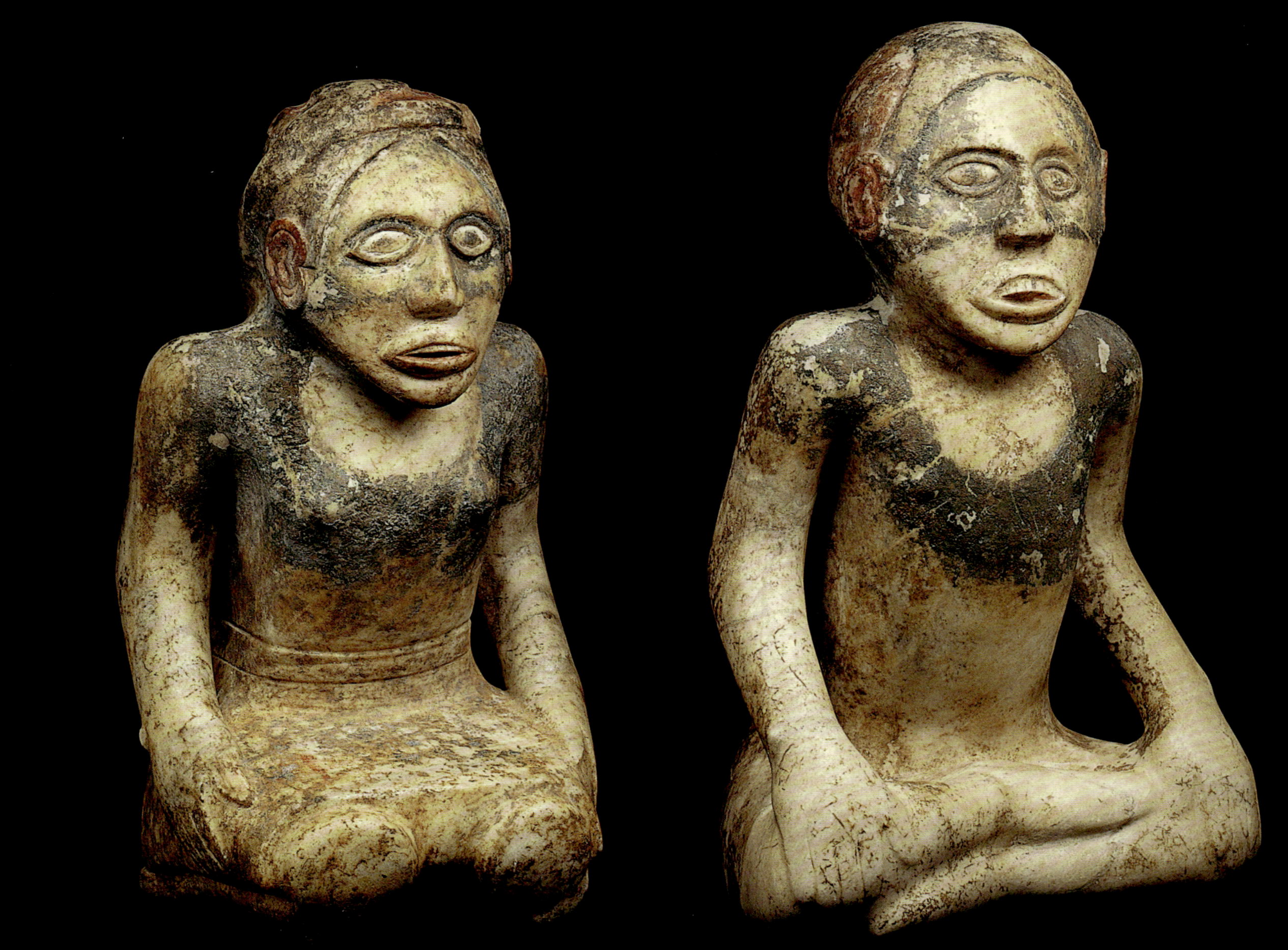

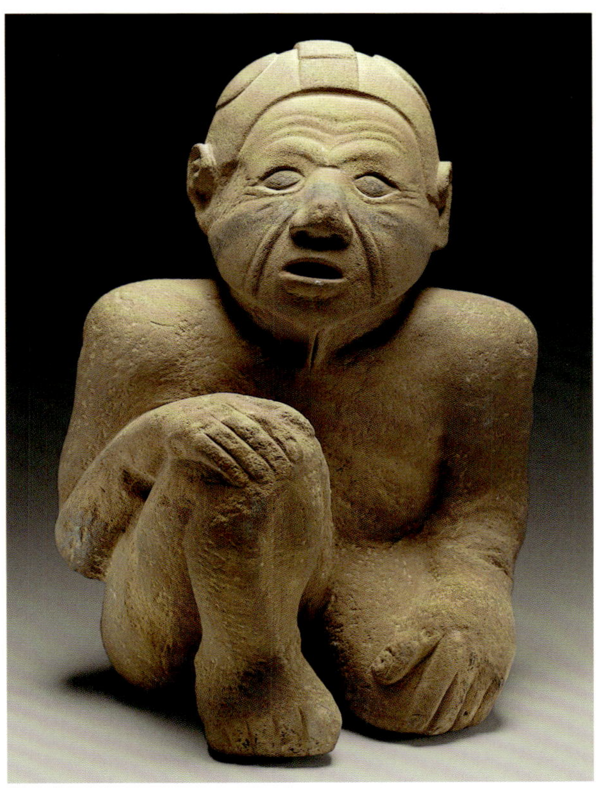

Fig. 7 Kneeling ancestor effigy; Tennessee, Wilson County, Sellers Farm site, A.D. 1000–1450; sandstone, h. 46.2 cm; Frank H. McClung Museum, University of Tennessee, Knoxville. Cat. no. 106. The middle-aged, highly individual features and somewhat quizzical expression of this effigy are testimony of portraiture. The simplified limbs and torso suggest that the figure was meant to be clothed in a robe or mantle.

The final mortuary activities conducted at Etowah's Mound C may provide more details about this series of events.[11] One of the last burials interred in the mound, labeled by Lewis Larson as Burial 15, contained two painted marble statues of seated male and female figures (fig. 6), as well as the scattered remains of four individuals and associated grave goods. Statues like those found in Burial 15 are generally considered to be representations of chiefly ancestors, in some cases even representing the founders of chiefly lineages (see figs. 7 and 8a–b).[12] If this is the case at Etowah, then the burial of the statues marks a symbolic end to the site's ruling lineage. As Larson described the burial, the statues were jumbled one on top of the other and the human remains and grave goods were scattered about the floor of the tomb. One might interpret from their position that the statues were buried in a hurry or under some duress, and that that duress may have been the threat of armed attack. Immediately above Burial 15 Larson recorded a scattering of human remains and burial items that continued up the ramp to the summit of Mound C. Ethnohistoric accounts include descriptions of invading armies sacking sacred mortuary temples, and, certainly, the materials Larson found on the ramp at Mound C could very well be the remains of one such rampage. While the evidence is largely circumstantial, it appears that Late Wilbanks-phase Etowah met a violent end.

People did not again return to Etowah until the end of the fifteenth century, just before the coming of Hernando de Soto and his troops (see the essay by Garrick Bailey in this volume). During this Brewster-phase occupation of the site (1475–1550), its inhabitants built the three small mounds (D, E, and F) and also reused the summit of Mound B (fig. 3).[13] Etowah again became the capital of a simple chiefdom and was likely joined in the river valley by a second polity to the west that was centered at the confluence of the Etowah and Oostanaula rivers. At this time, Etowah comes into

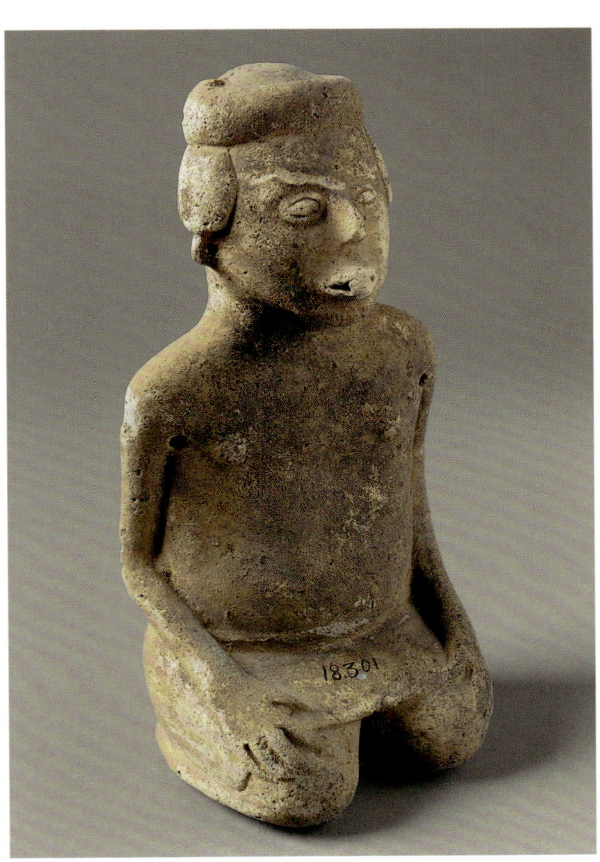

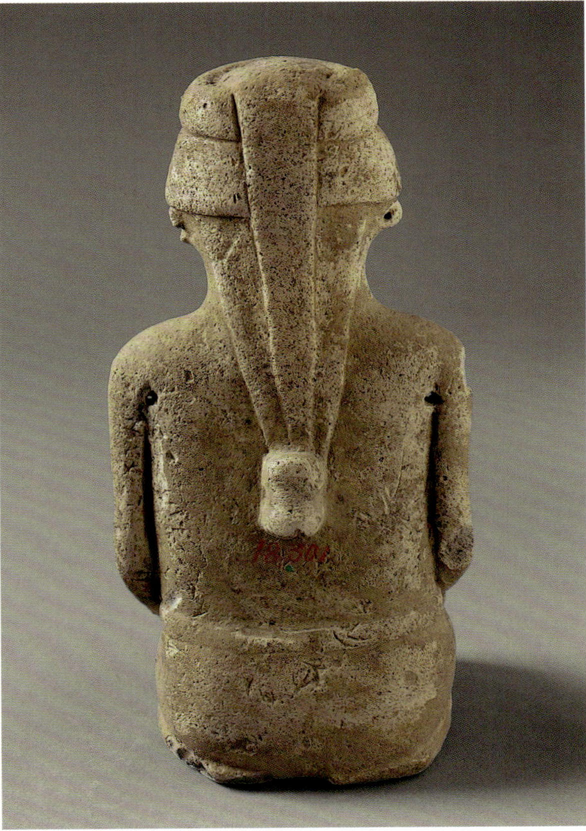

Figs. 8a–b Kneeling human effigy figurine; Tennessee, Davidson County, Nashville, Hayes Farm, A.D. 1000–1450; ceramic, h. 22.2 cm; Harvard University, Peabody Museum of Archaeology and Ethnology, Peabody Museum Expedition 1878–79, Edwin Curtiss, Director. Cat. no. 268.

written history as the town of Itaba, visited by De Soto in August 1540.[14] Ample evidence of that visit has been found in the Brewster-phase village investigated by Larson, including such items as an iron celt and an iron spike, fragments of chain mail, and a sword hilt and portions of a European-style rotary quern.[15] At that time, De Soto made little of Itaba except to say that it was a subject town in the larger, paramount chiefdom of Coosa.

Apparently when people returned to Etowah, the political landscape was different than it had been a century before. Etowah's collapse had created a political vacuum in northern Georgia that was eventually filled by another mound center that archaeologists have named Little Egypt, located to the north of Etowah on the Coosawattee River.[16] By 1540 the shift in the center of power was completed as De Soto found the Little Egypt site to be the capital of the powerful chiefdom of Coosa, which, like Etowah before it, held sway over much of the region. By the time Etowah was reoccupied during the Brewster phase, its inhabitants were latecomers on the regional political scene and, despite the site's past greatness, they were destined to become subjects of the paramount chief Coosa.[17]

The depopulation and social disruption caused by the initial Spanish incursions and later attempts to colonize the Southeast fundamentally altered the native political and social landscape. By the close of the sixteenth century, Mississippian chiefdoms disappeared from the Etowah valley for the last time. According to Marvin T. Smith, populations in northwestern Georgia, decimated by disease, coalesced and moved down the Coosa River drainage into Alabama and ultimately became part of the Creek Confederacy.[18]

Mound C, the Sacred, and Power

As the history I have just recounted indicates, Mound C was built and used entirely during the Middle Mississippian period (A.D. 1250–1400). That history also shows that this was a key time in the developmental sequence of Etowah, for it was during the Early and Late Wilbanks phases that the site was dramatically enlarged and became the dominant center in northern Georgia. The archaeology of Mound C and the SECC goods found within the mound provide some valuable insights into this critical period in Etowah's history. Before exploring what Mound C can tell us about Etowah's rise to regional prominence, however, it is important to understand a little bit about the history of Mound C itself, which has been completely excavated and now stands reconstructed at the site. Three separate investigators completed excavations during three distinct investigations, beginning with John P. Rogan in 1884 for the Bureau of Ethnology in Washington, D.C.; followed by Warren K. Moorehead in 1925 through 1927 sponsored by the R. S. Peabody Foundation; and finally Lewis H. Larson, Jr., who completed excavation of the mound between 1954 and 1961 for the Georgia Historical Commission.[19]

John Rogan's early excavations, working under the supervision of Cyrus Thomas, focused on a small area of the mound's summit, where he recorded eleven burials. Rogan was the first to discover the remarkable nature of the burial goods contained within Mound C. Among his discoveries were two embossed copper plates, known as the Rogan plates, depicting the Birdman motif, identified in James Brown's essay in this volume as Morning Star (figs. 1 and 11). As might be expected, Rogan's recording and recovery techniques were quite incomplete by today's standards, so the information available from that work is limited. Warren Moorehead's later investigations effectively removed all of the summits of Mound C, recording an additional 111 graves. These burials contained a remarkable collection of sacred objects, including, among other things, shell gorgets, stone blades, stone celts, and a variety of copper headdress pieces (figs. 25–27). Unfortunately,

facing page
Fig. 11 Copper repoussé plate depicting Birdman; one of the two so-called Rogan plates; Georgia, Bartow County, Etowah, Mound C, 13th century; copper, h. 27.9 cm; Smithsonian Institution, National Museum of Natural History, Washington, D.C. Cat. no. 111.

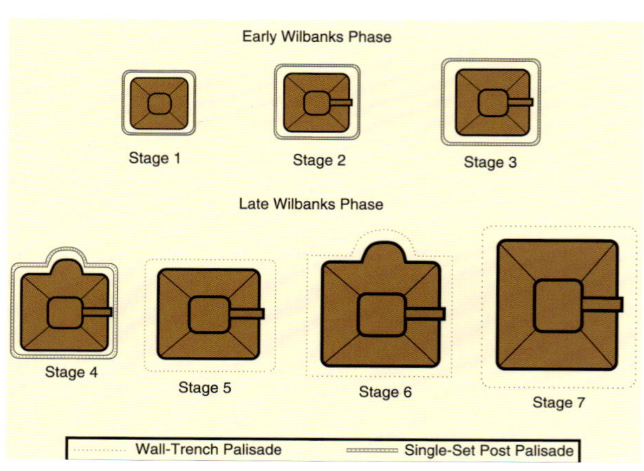

Fig. 9 Construction stages of Mound C.

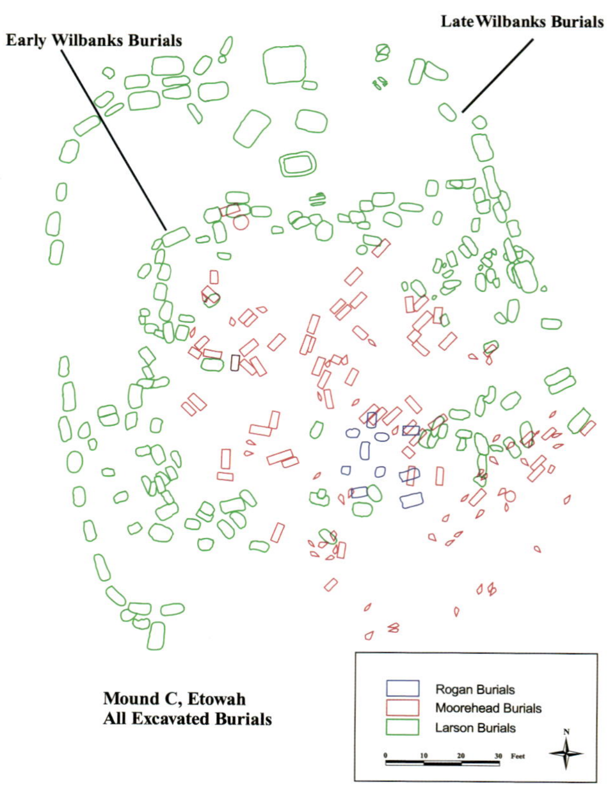

Fig. 10 Composite plan of various excavations at Mound C, showing Late Wilbanks phase burials, A.D. 1325–1375. This illustration does not show all of the burials excavated by Lewis Larson.

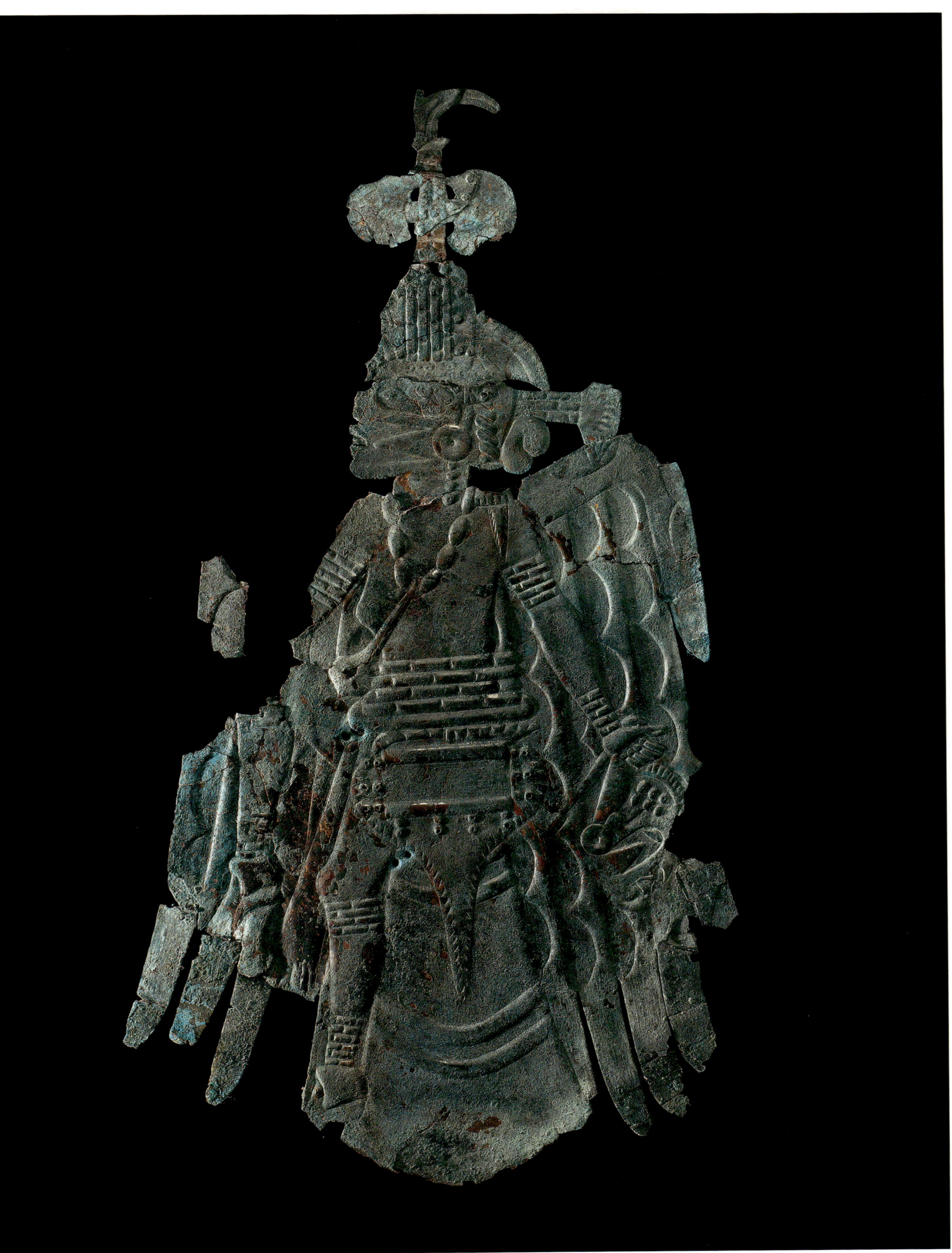

Moorehead's recording and recovery techniques were only marginally better than those of his predecessor.

When Lewis Larson began his work at Mound C, he was faced with a remnant, the summits of which and part of its inner core had been removed by the unsystematic digging of Rogan and Moorehead. Despite these difficult conditions, Larson's careful excavations recorded invaluable information about Mound C and its now famous mortuary record, which lay largely undisturbed along the flanks and base of the mound. All told, Larson recorded an additional 244 burials, many with impressive collections of SECC goods. Most famous among Larson's discoveries were the two painted marble statues from Burial 15 shown in figure 6.

Based largely on the information collected by Larson, I have argued that Mound C was built in seven stages, each associated with some mortuary activity (fig. 9). The first three stages, which date to the Early Wilbanks phase, were built and used with a high degree of regularity. In each instance, a mound stage was constructed and it was surrounded by a palisade wall. Burials either took the form of simple pits or stone-lined tombs, and were placed into the summit and flank of each stage. The richest burials apparently were placed into the summits. During the Late Wilbanks phase, four new stages were added, and, as before, each was surrounded by a palisade wall. The practice of placing graves in the mound summits was abandoned and the most elaborate burials were placed along the northern periphery of each stage and covered with a mound of earth, creating a small lobe.[20] Burials took the form of simple pits and log-lined tombs.

While this general construction sequence seems fairly clear, it has proven difficult to associate all burials with individual construction stages. This problem has thwarted efforts to analyze the Mound C mortuary record fully, and it can be attributed directly to the recording and recovery techniques used by Rogan and Moorehead. Despite this problem, Larson collected enough information to distinguish Early from Late Wilbanks graves in Mound C. The Early Wilbanks-phase burials were placed into the mound's summits and along the flanks in close association with the Early Wilbanks-phase palisade wall trenches. The Late Wilbanks burials were found in the lobe areas, as well as in a single, clearly identifiable ring around the final construction stages (fig. 10).

The Sacred and Power

The meaning behind the symbolic themes and ritual objects present in the Southeastern Ceremonial Complex, including those things found in Mound C, have been the subject of considerable scholarly inquiry. Some notions about their meaning have been around for a long time, while others have only been developed fairly recently largely through an iconography working group headed by Kent Reilly of Texas State University (see his essay in this volume).[21] One thing that seems to be clear, however, is that most, if not all, of the SECC goods recovered from Mound C reference the supernatural world in some way.[22] That supernatural cast is suggested by the frequent depiction of clearly supernatural beings or other elements of the supernatural world. For example, one of the most commonly represented supernatural beings in the Etowah corpus is the Morning Star or Birdman.[23] Examples are found in engraved shell, particularly in the anthropomorphic theme of what are called Hightower-style gorgets, and in embossed copper, quintessentially in the Rogan plates.[24] That the Birdman is not of this world is demonstrated by his (or her) possession of clearly both human and raptor physical characteristics.

Also common are depictions that seem to reference the notion that the cosmos was made up of three worlds: the Sky World (or Overworld), This World (Middle World), and the Underwater World (also called Underworld or Beneath World).[25] This worldview was commonly held during the early historic period throughout the East. George Lankford has posited that the turkey-cocks theme of the Hightower-style shell gorgets found in Mound C and elsewhere in the Tennessee River valley (fig. 12) depicts all three worlds viewed from the side (see also fig. 4 in his essay in this volume).[26] Similarly, it has long been argued that the circle-and-cross motif—one of a number of cruciform designs such as is seen in a shell gorget in the Peabody Museum at Harvard University (fig. 13)—is a representation of This World, historically conceived of as a flat disk held up at the cardinal directions by ropes reaching the

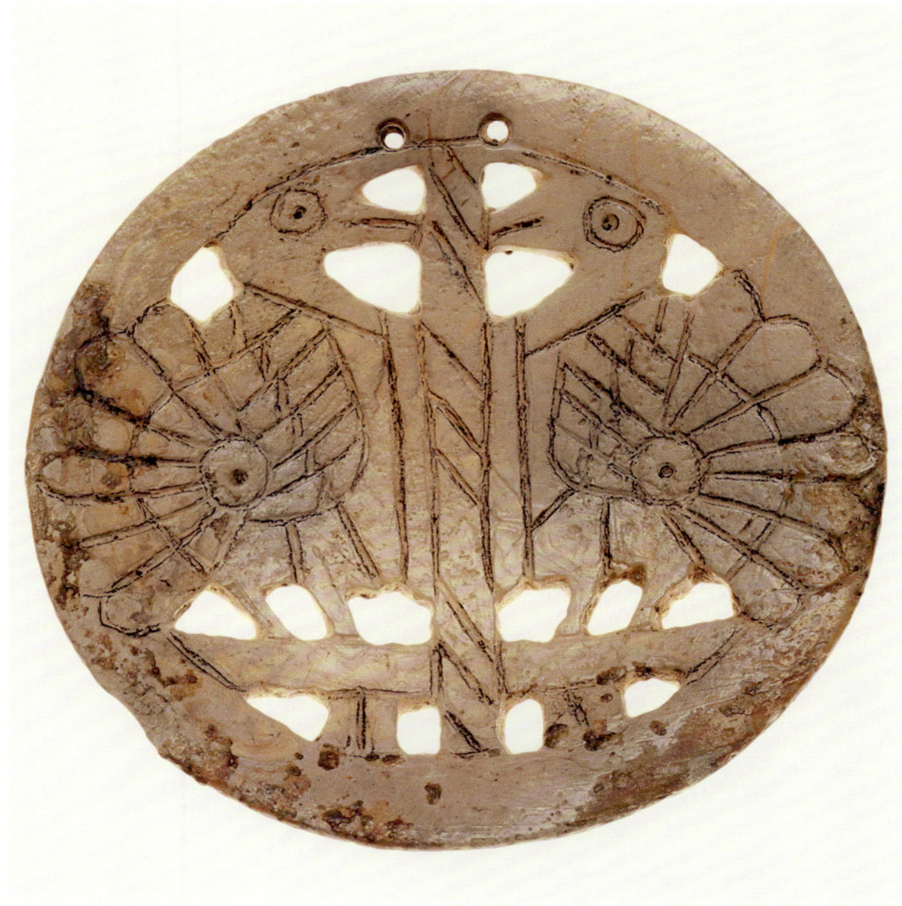

Fig. 12 Engraved shell gorget with turkey-cocks; Hightower style; Tennessee, Hamilton County, Hixon site; marine shell, diam. 7 cm; Frank H. McClung Museum, University of Tennessee, Knoxville, no. 618/1Ha3.

facing page

Fig. 13 Engraved shell gorget with cross-in-circle design; Georgia, Columbia County, Stallings Island Mound, A.D. 1250–1450; marine shell, diam. 7.6 cm; Harvard University, Peabody Museum of Archaeology and Ethnology, Peabody–Claflin Expedition 1929, Mr. and Mrs. C. B. Cosgrove, Directors. Cat. no. 147.

Fig. 14 Engraved shell gorget with triskele design; Tennessee, Williamson County, Fisher-Reams site, Gray's Farm, A.D. 1000–1450; marine shell, diam. 8.6 cm; Harvard University, Peabody Museum of Archaeology and Ethnology, Peabody Museum Expedition 1878, F. W. Putnam, Director. Cat. no. 148.

Figs. 15a–b Disc with ogee motif and scallop design; Arkansas, Arkansas County, Almond Farm site, 1000–1450; quartzite, diam. 35 cm; Frank H. McClung Museum, University of Tennessee, Knoxville. Cat. no. 154.

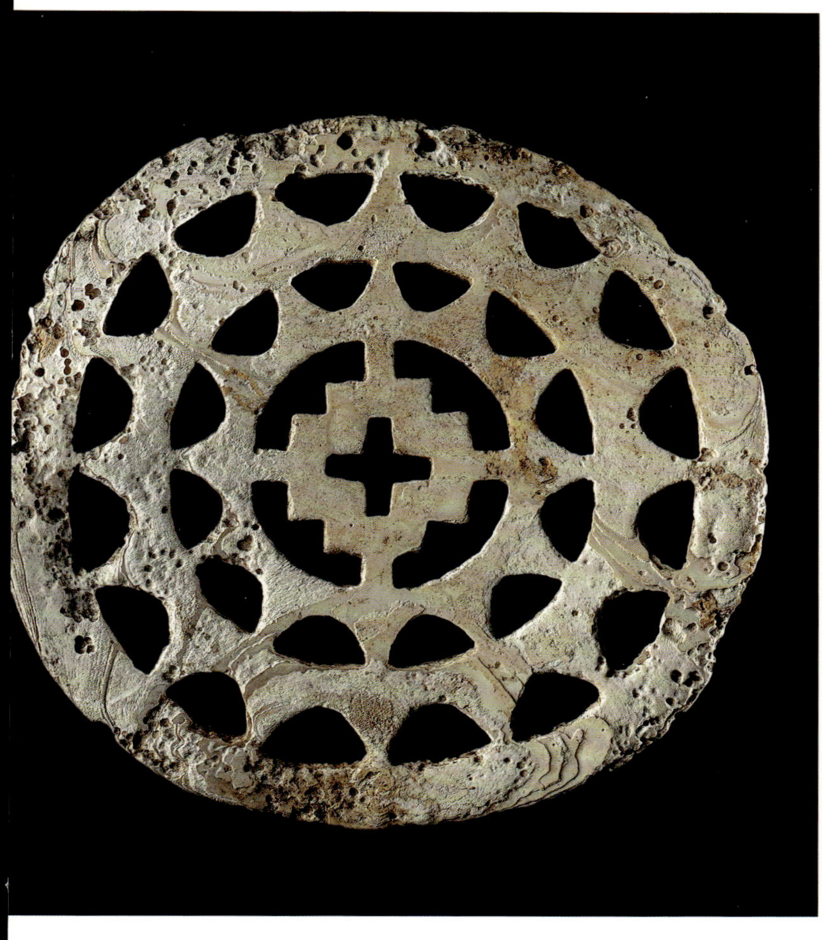

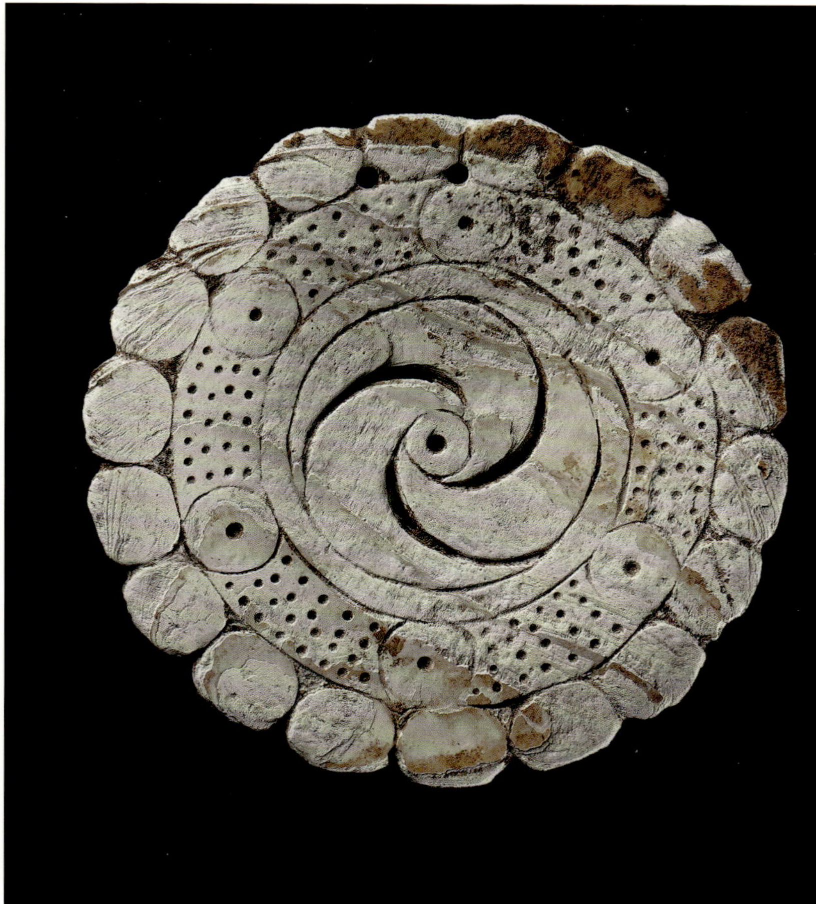

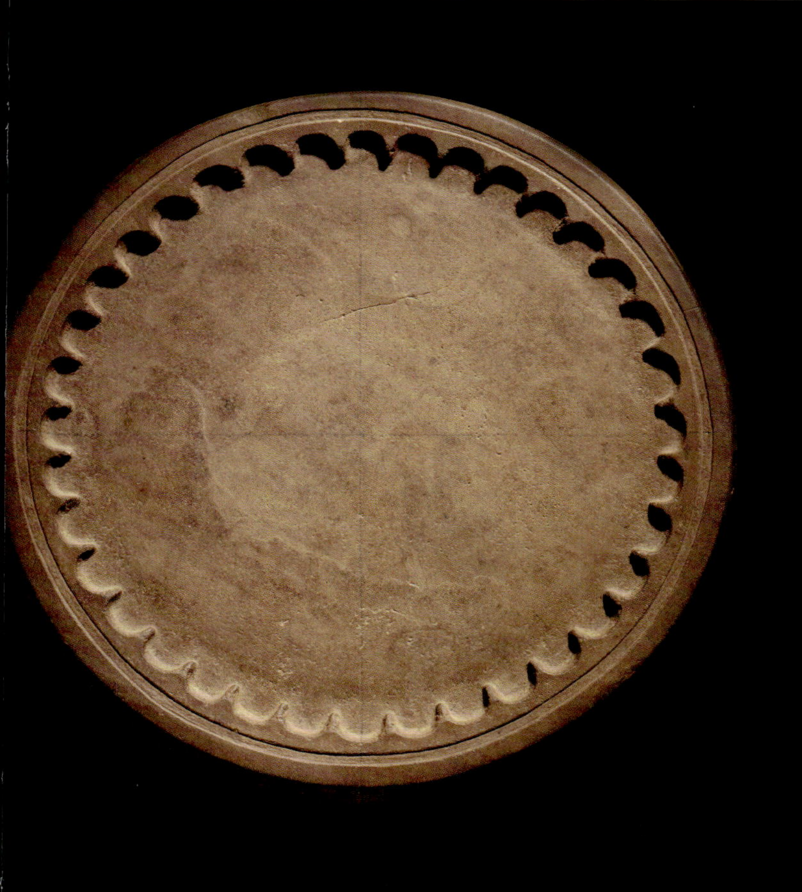

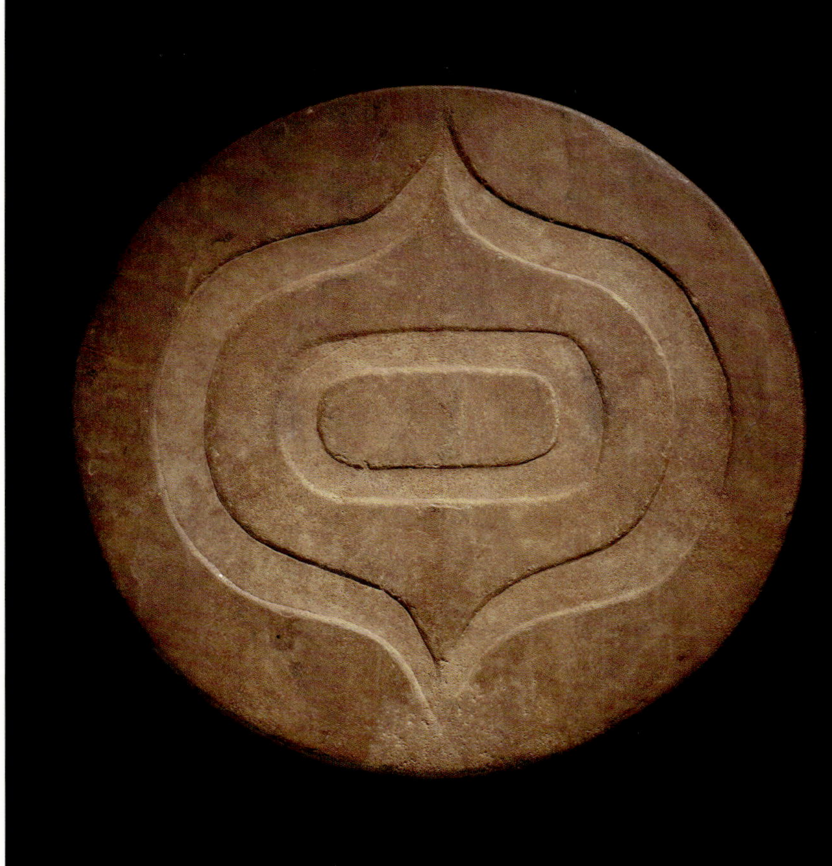

Sky World.[27] Lankford has also suggested that the triskele motif—the central element in another shell gorget in the Peabody/Harvard collection (fig. 14)—is a signifier of the Beneath World.[28] Finally, Kent Reilly and David Dye have argued that the ogee motif—depicted only in copper at Etowah, but found elsewhere in ceramic and stone (figs. 15a–b)—represents a portal through which the different levels of the cosmos could be accessed.

Even the warfare clearly alluded to in the Mound C corpus of art is likely linked to the supernatural world. Warfare allusions can be found in the apparent depictions of combat and its aftermath represented on shell gorgets and embossed copper plates (see the essay by David Dye in this volume). As already noted, however, the individuals engaged in combat appear to be supernaturals themselves. Military references likely are present also in the numerous depictions of birds of prey (generally presumed to be falcons) and related eye, wing, and tail elements. Historically, birds of prey, specifically the falcon, were associated with warfare, and many of these raptor elements occur as physical attributes of supernatural beings.[29] Finally, warfare also seems to be referenced through specific kinds of objects that James A. Brown has called socio-technic warfare-related artifacts.[30] These objects represent weaponry in the form of maces, celts, and blades that were clearly made to be displayed and not used in actual combat (see Dye, figs. 10–11 and 19–20). As with the allusions to falcons, many of the same kinds of socio-technic weapons found in Mound C graves also are shown in the hands of supernaturals. While these references to warfare were almost certainly connected to the qualities and accomplishments of the individuals who possessed them, they likely also draw their meaning from combat and warrior figures of the supernatural world.[31]

If these interpretations are correct, then most if not all of the ritual objects and symbolic themes present in the SECC of Mound C likely reference the supernatural world, either through depictions of inhabitants of those worlds or of events that occurred and continue to occur in them.[32] Therefore, at some level the SECC goods interred in Mound C were sacred objects connected to the supernatural. As Mary Helms has argued, at least some of that connection to the supernatural world comes not just from the representations they exhibit or the forms they take, but also from the fact that they were made of non-local materials or were decorated in clearly foreign styles.[33]

When burial treatment in Mound C is examined, it becomes clear that individuals were buried with these sacred symbols often as parts of regalia.[34] Even more interesting, perhaps, is the fact that among those interred in the mound were individuals whose mortuary goods display at least some of the same symbols and objects associated with the Birdman image depicted on the Rogan plates. Not only did individual elites possess these symbols as parts of their uniforms or regalia, at least some appear to have been dressed as, and possibly representing, known supernaturals. Clearly, concrete connections to the supernatural world were key to the maintenance and reproduction of elite status at Etowah in the Middle Mississippian period. These very symbols and possibly even claims to descent from particular supernatural beings were important sources of power for Etowah's ruling elites.

Even more intriguing is the possibility that at least some of the SECC goods buried in Mound C graves reference a mythology that was not even local to northern Georgia and were, indeed, over a century old when they were finally buried in Mound C. James Brown continues to construct a compelling case that some of the embossed copper plates and cutouts in Mound C burials are decorated in the Classic Braden style (see the essay by James Brown in this volume).[35] These Braden items are exemplified by the Rogan plates. Although the Braden style was first defined by the study of objects from the Craig Mound at Spiro, Oklahoma, Brown and John Kelly have put forth the idea that the Braden-style school originated as a formal style during the Early Mississippian period in the American Bottom and possibly even at Cahokia.[36] Furthermore, using an internal chronology for the Braden style, Brown has argued that at least some of the Braden pieces at Etowah were made early in the history of that style, making them antiques by the time they were buried in Mound C.[37] Thus, these data suggest that when Etowah reached its political peak, its leaders relied upon a foreign symbolic set that no doubt referenced a foreign mythology to justify their place in a ranked social order. That foreign style and

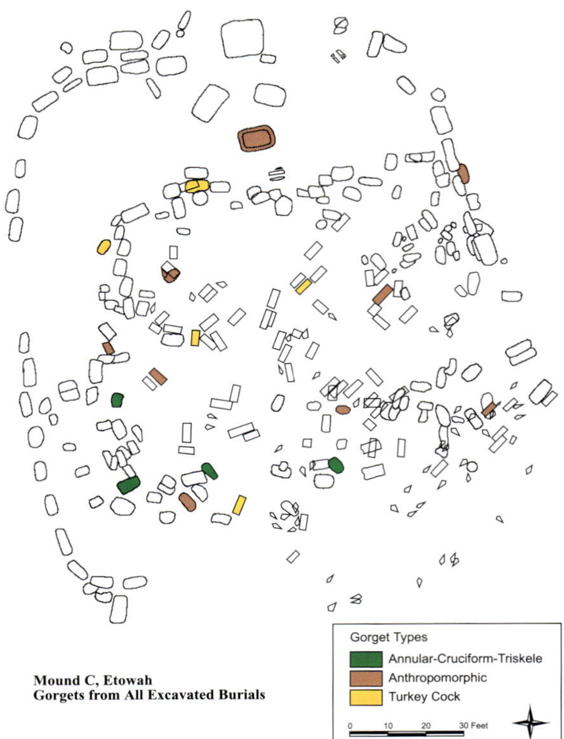

Fig. 16 Distribution of annular, triskele, cruciform, turkey-cocks, and anthropomorphic gorgets at Mound C, Etowah. This illustration does not show all of the burials excavated by Lewis Larson.

Figs. 17a–e Five gorget types represented in burials in Mound C at Etowah: a) annular; b) triskele; c) cruciform; d) turkey-cocks; and e) anthropomorphic; drawings by Elizabeth Reese Baloutine.

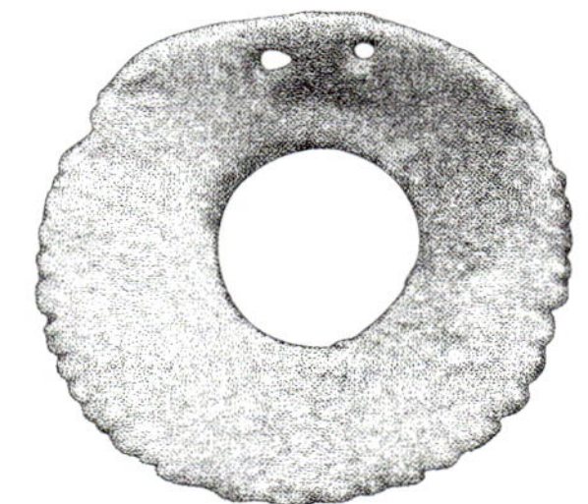

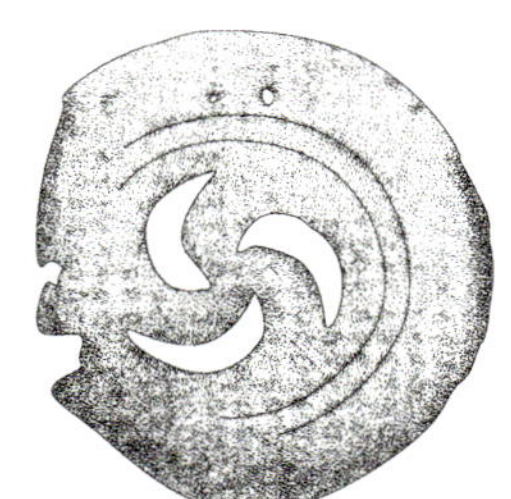

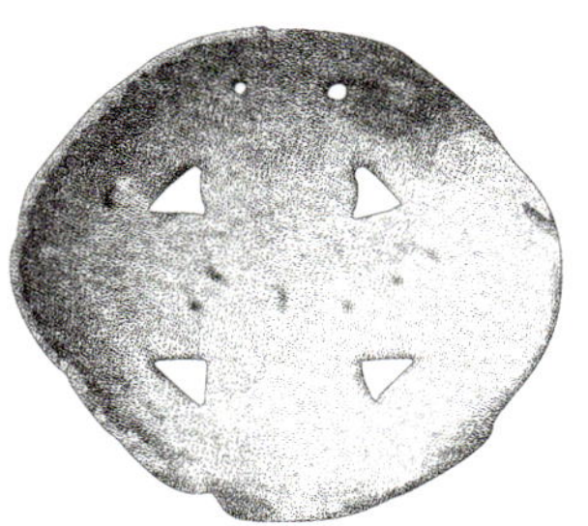

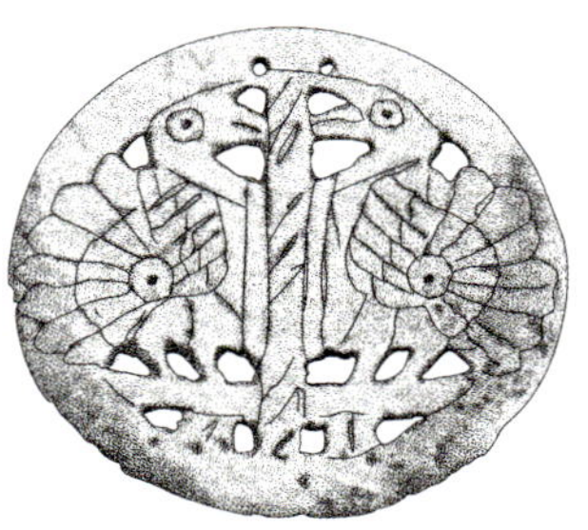

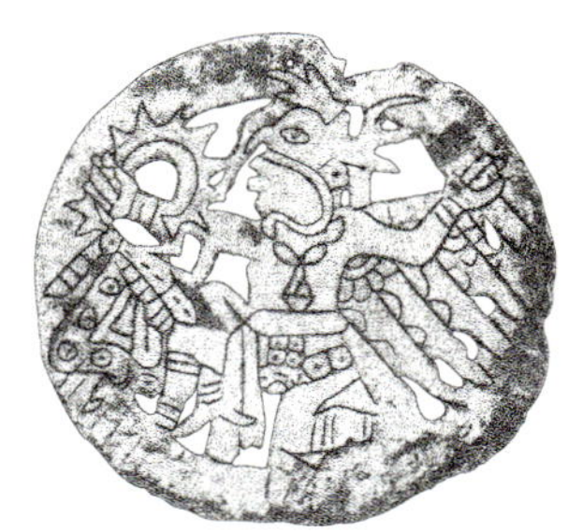

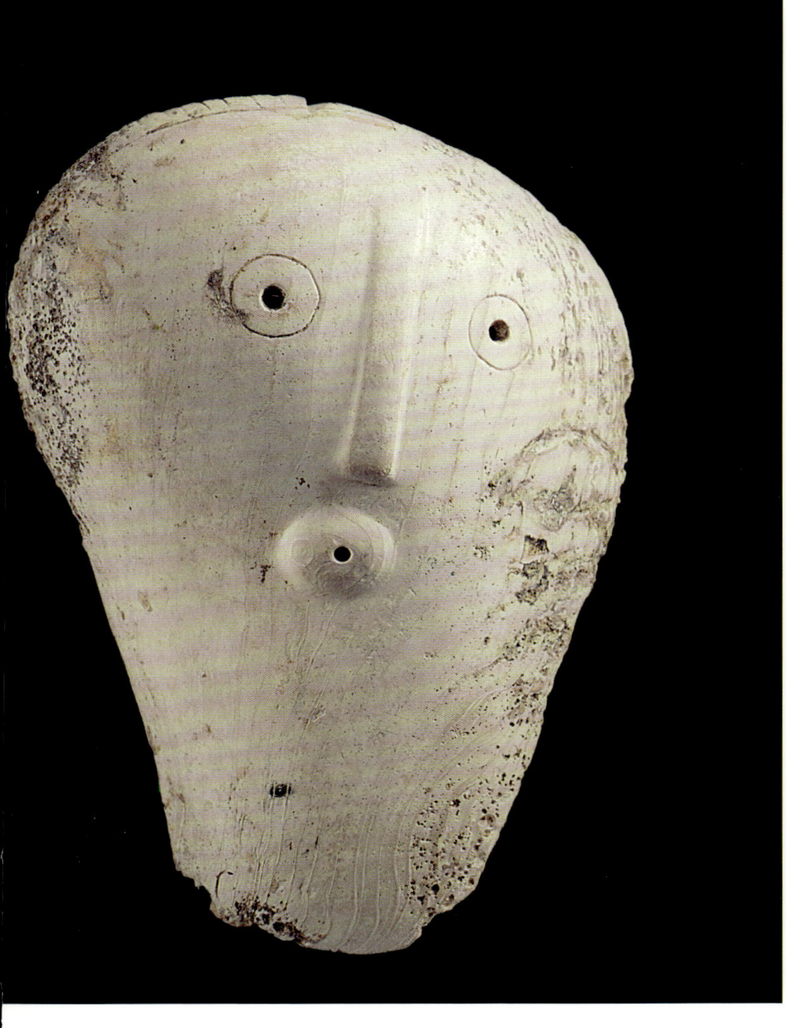

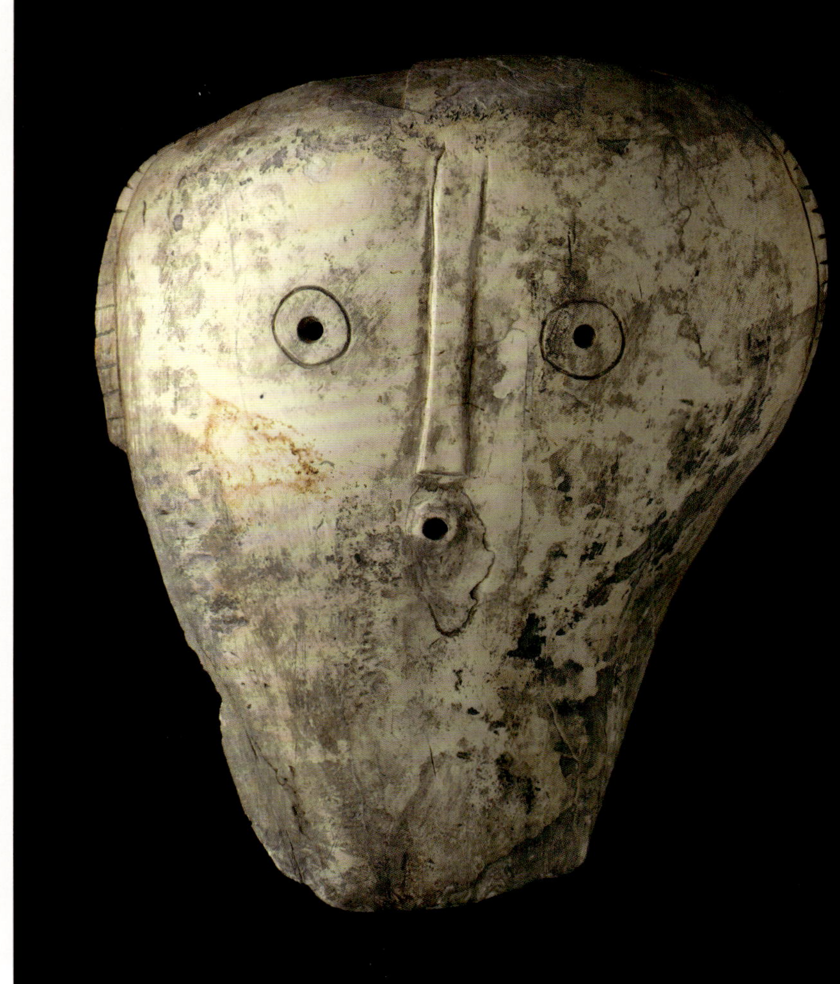

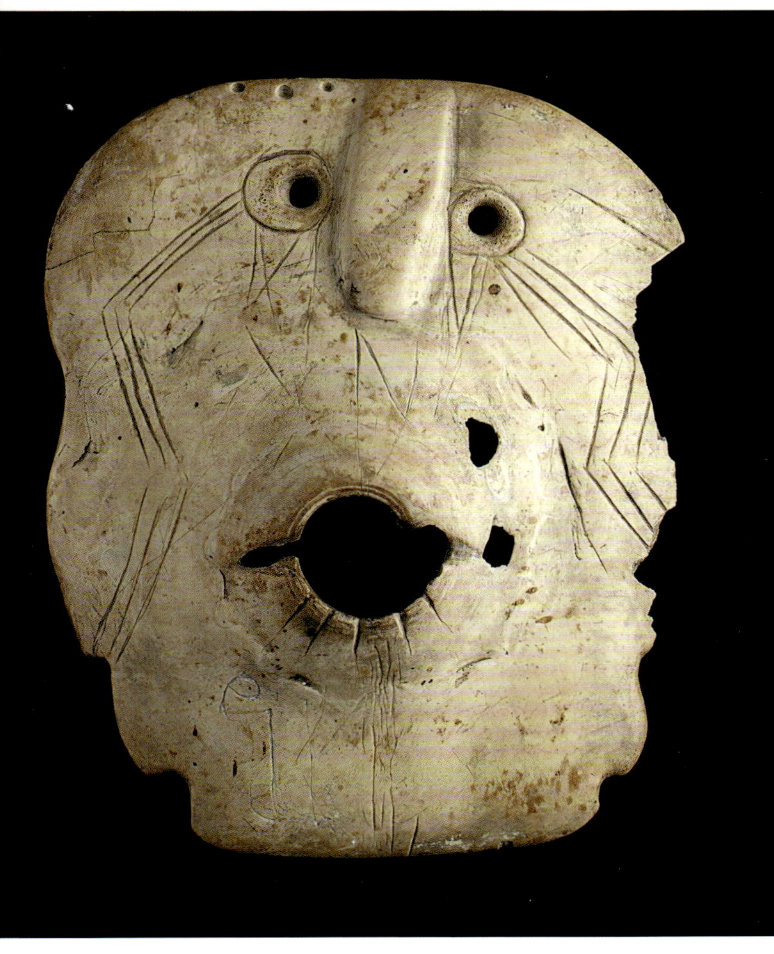

Fig. 18 Engraved shell mask; Tennessee, Knox County, Brakebill Mound, 14th century; marine shell, h. 20.3 cm; Harvard University, Peabody Museum of Archaeology and Ethnology, Peabody Museum Expedition 1869, Rev. E. O. Dunning, Director. Cat. no. 153.

Fig. 19 Engraved shell mask; Tennessee, Monroe County, Toco Mound, 13th/14th century; marine shell, h. 15.2 cm; Smithsonian Institution, National Museum of Natural History, Washington, D.C. Cat. no. 152.

Fig. 20 Engraved shell mask; unknown origin, 13th/14th century; marine shell, h. 15.2 cm; Smithsonian Institution, National Museum of Natural History, Washington, D.C. Cat. no. 151.

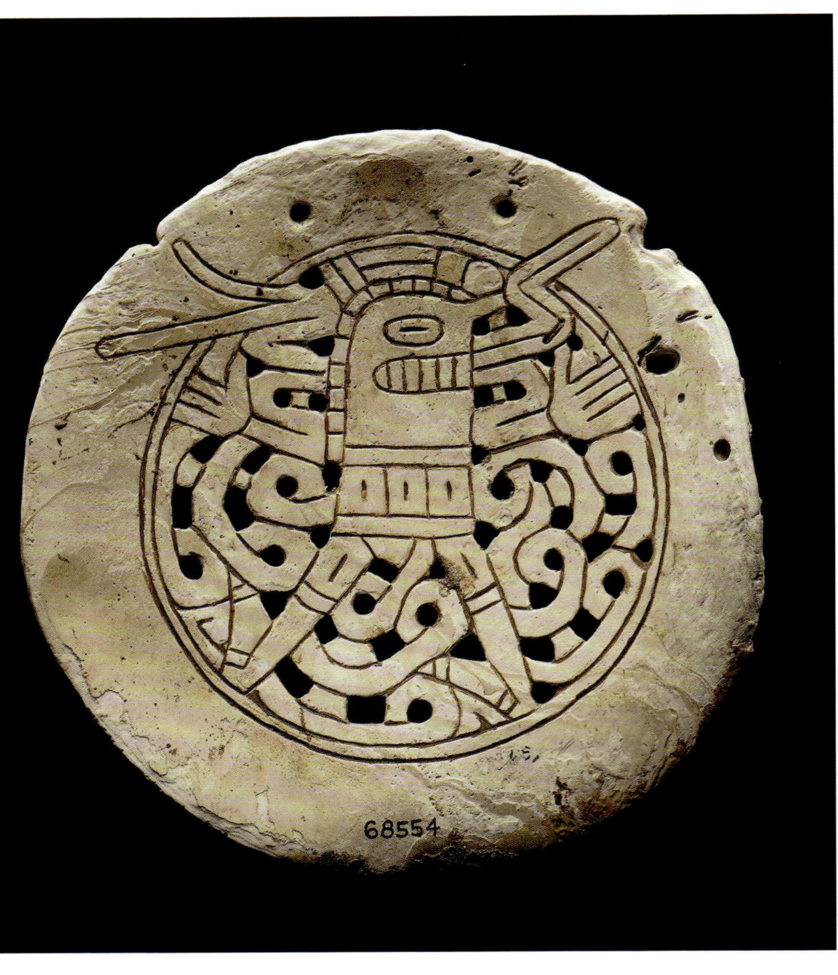
68554

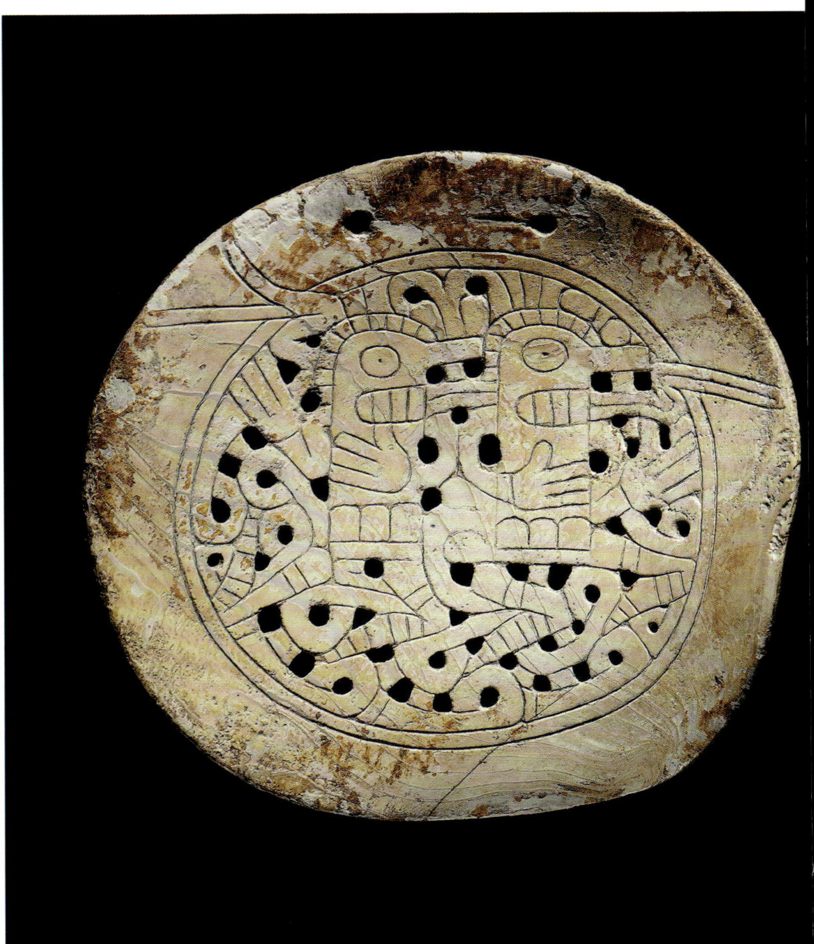

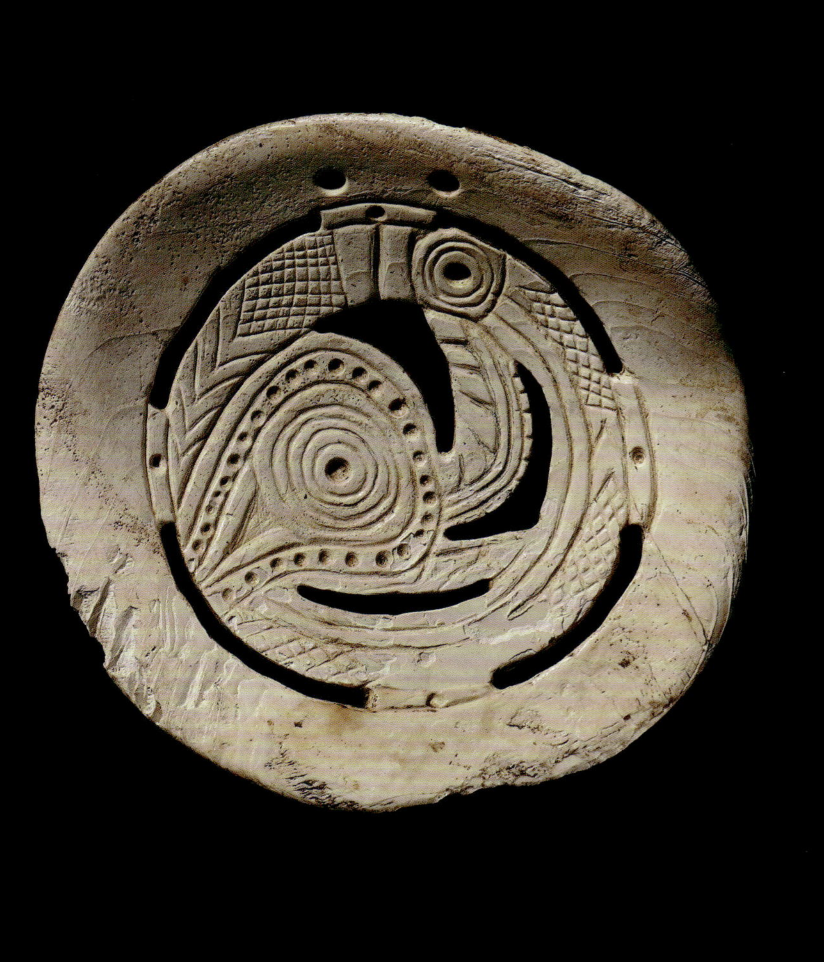

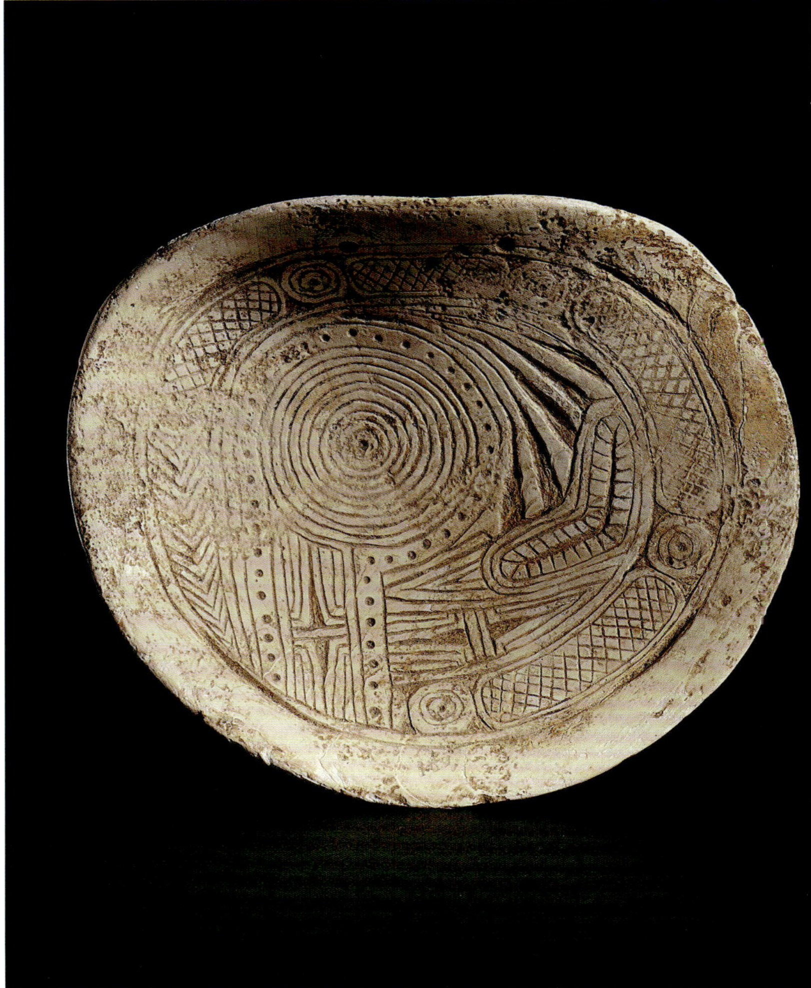

mythology served to charter the power of Etowah's Middle Mississippian elites, and it was all the more compelling because of its association with what I suspect was largely a mythological place in the Mississippian world: Cahokia.

The Organization of Elite Status

While stylistic content conveys the chartering of elite status, the use of space in Mound C provides clues about the organization of Etowah's ranking system. Lewis Larson and later Jeffrey Brain and Philip Phillips have noted that the final ring of burials at Mound C seems to contain discrete groupings or at least gaps that suggest the presence of groupings.[38] Brain and Phillips have argued that distinct clusters of burials were positioned at the each of the corners of Mound C as well as in the two lobes appended to its northern side (see fig. 10).

In an attempt to see whether similar kinds of groupings existed during the Early Wilbanks phase, I recently examined the distribution of shell gorgets in Mound C (fig. 16). Three of the themes or sets of themes in the mound present clearly identifiable distributions that lead me to posit a spatial organization to the Early Wilbanks burials as well. Both the turkey-cocks theme of the Hightower style and the grouping of the shell gorgets exhibiting the annular, triskele, and cruciform themes attest that different burial clusters were placed in quadrants of Mound C (figs. 17a–d). I suspect these groupings might represent corporate kin groups or some other kind of sodality. The anthropomorphic theme of the Hightower style crosscuts these groupings and likely represents another kind of status (fig. 17e). Therefore, in the Early Wilbanks phase there may have been four groupings of burials, each focused on a quadrant of the mound, instead of five groupings seen in the Late Wilbanks phase.

Undoubtedly as more artifact forms and classes are included in these distributions, the patterns will become more complex. Nevertheless, both the spatial arrangement of burials and the distribution of shell gorgets suggest that there were distinct groupings of burials in Mound C. This result implies that elite status at Etowah in the Middle Mississippian period was not limited to members of a single extended family, as might be expected of the classic conical clan model. Instead elite status comprised a series of what I envision to be kin-based corporate groups, possibly ranked with respect to one another. Crosscutting those groups were other kinds of status categories or possibly even sodalities like dance and medicine societies.

Mound C and the Rise and Fall of Etowah

Taken together and placed in the larger context of the history of Etowah as a chiefdom capital, these elements of the archaeological record of Mound C provide some interesting insights into Etowah's rise to regional dominance. First, we can recall that Etowah's reemergence during the Wilbanks phases was preceded by a period of abandonment, so its quick rise to prominence began with a reoccupation of the site and a reestablishment of a ranked social structure. Clearly one of the keys to social and political power in this new polity was the demonstration of connections to the supernatural world through the possession and manipulation of non-local, elaborately decorated, and supernaturally charged SECC goods.

The critical nature of these mortuary goods likely also helps explain why people returned to Etowah after A.D. 1250 and why the site became such an important place. It is well understood that SECC goods were exchanged widely across the Southeast and that they likely moved "down the line" within elite-dominated exchange networks. Brown and colleagues have identified one such network through which both finished goods and important raw materials moved during the Middle Mississippian period.[39] The Etowah River valley would have been a key node in the network as materials passed from centers in the Piedmont into the Ridge and Valley province and ultimately into the Tennessee River drainage. Leaders and their followers returned to Etowah to participate in that developing exchange network. If Brown's identification of the Classic Braden style in objects unearthed at Etowah and the style's connections to the American Bottom withstand further scrutiny, then the leaders who returned to Etowah did so with a foreign and potentially very compelling charter for their power.

The typical conception of a Middle Mississippian–period chiefdom is a polity that is socially and politically dominated by a single chief and his or her immediate family. But the distributions of shell gorgets and the spatial arrangement of burials suggest instead that the highest ranks of Etowah's society during the Wilbanks phases were dominated by members of several corporate groups, probably kin based, whose membership was crosscut by other kinds of non-kin sodalities.

The emphasis on sources of power derived from external networks may also help explain the potentially violent end suffered by the Etowah polity just as it had reached its peak. Richard Blanton and his colleagues have put forth the idea that the kinds of strategies used by Etowah's leaders during the Wilbanks phases create competitive political landscapes, as they encourage factionalism in local polities and competition among leaders in wider networks.[40] These strategies involve a focus on externally derived sources of power and well-defined hierarchical ranking structures that exclude most members of society from sharing in the benefits of power. The sheer number of SECC goods recovered from Etowah's Mound C suggest that its leaders were major players in the exchange of such goods. Within this competitive landscape, a center of power like Etowah would have been a target for attack from other regional players as well as susceptible to internal political unrest.

Thus, while it is apparent that Etowah was indeed an important place on the Mississippian landscape, it

Fig. 21 Engraved shell gorget with single figure; Spaghetti style; unknown origin, A.D. 1000–1450; marine shell, diam. 17.8 cm; The Field Museum, Chicago. Cat. no. 149.

Fig. 22 Engraved shell gorget with double dancers; Spaghetti style; Tennessee, Hamilton County, Dallas site, A.D. 1000–1450; marine shell, diam. 17.2 cm; Frank H. McClung Museum, University of Tennessee, Knoxville. Cat. no. 150.

Fig. 23 Engraved shell gorget with rattlesnake design; Brakebill style; Tennessee, Roane County, DeArmond site, A.D. 1000–1450; marine shell, diam. 12.3 cm; Frank H. McClung Museum, University of Tennessee, Knoxville. Cat. no. 144.

Fig. 24 Engraved shell gorget with rattlesnake design; Citico style; Alabama, Terrapin Creek, A.D. 1000–1450; marine shell, h. 12.7 cm; Museum of the Red River, Idabel, Oklahoma. Cat. no. 145.

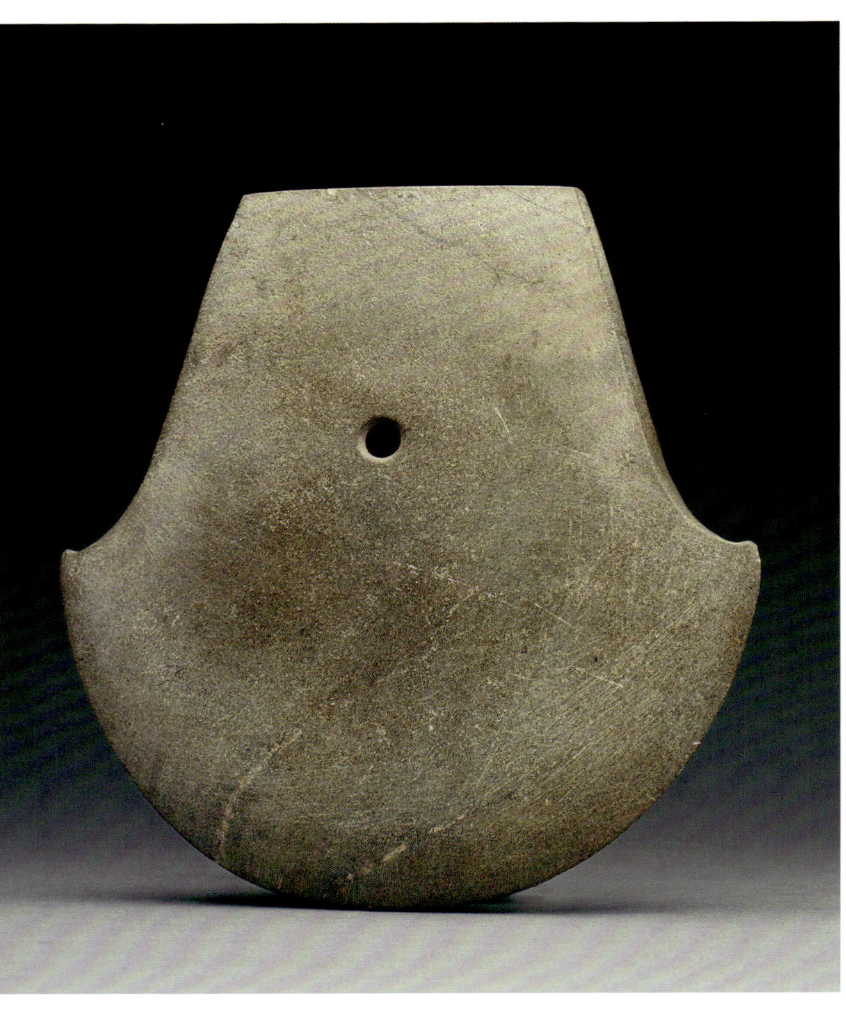

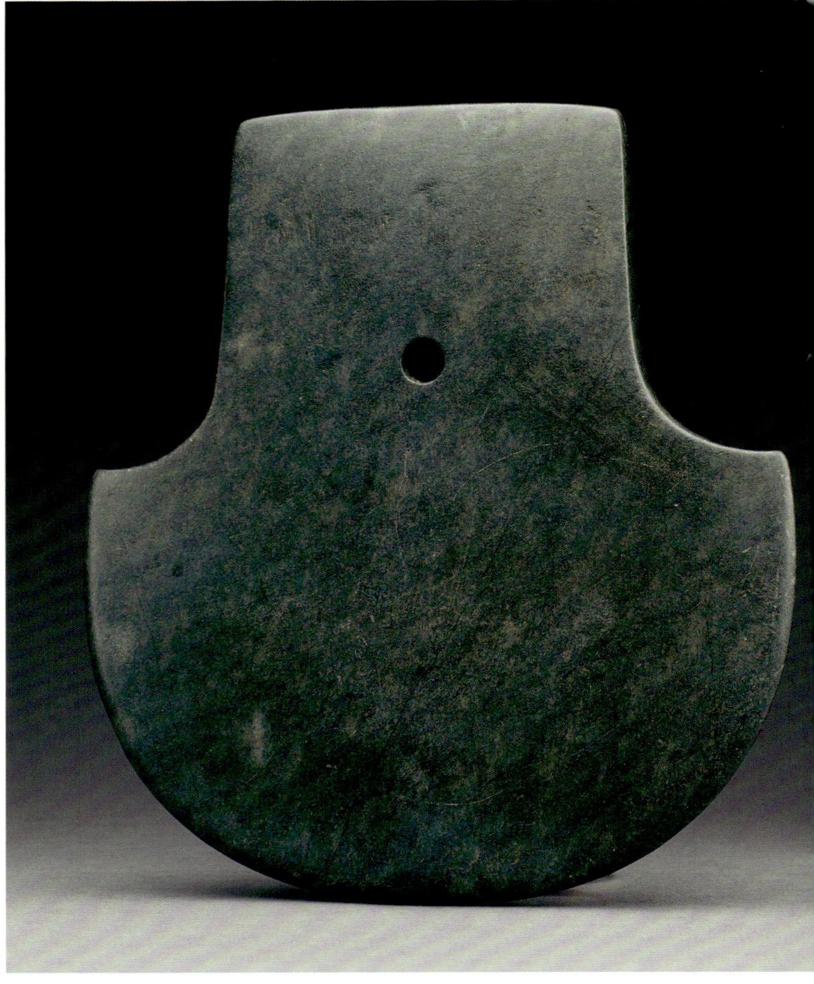

Fig. 25 Polished spud stone; Tennessee, Monroe County, McGee Farm, 13th/14th century; graystone, h. 20.3 cm; Smithsonian Institution, National Museum of Natural History, Washington, D.C. Cat. no. 179.

Fig. 26 Polished spud stone; Tennessee, Loudon County, Lenoir Mound no. 2, 13th/14th century; greenstone, h. 20.3 cm; Smithsonian Institution, National Museum of Natural History, Washington, D.C. Cat. no. 180.

Fig. 27 Spatulate baton; Georgia, 13th century; greenstone, l. 60 cm; Smithsonian Institution, National Museum of Natural History, Washington, D.C. Cat. no. 174.

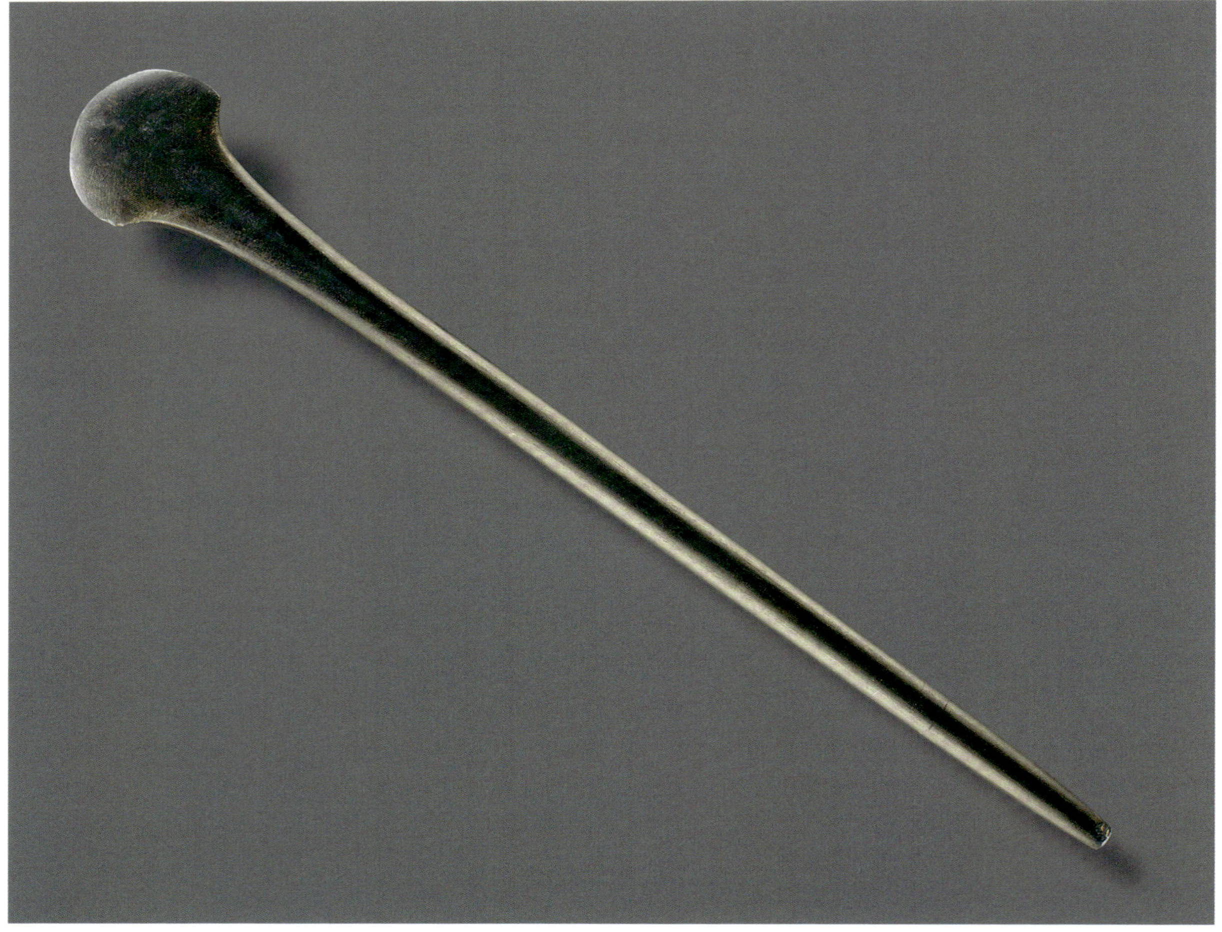

is also clear that the site's inhabitants were only able to sustain that status for a relatively brief period of time. During that short segment of Etowah's history, the vast majority of mound construction took place, the site became fortified, and its elite created for themselves a special burial place. The sacred remains placed in that burial place tell us a great deal about Etowah's quick rise to greatness and its dramatic collapse.

Elites and their followers were lured back to Etowah by the draw of the sacred power contained in the SECC goods moving through exchange networks. By tapping into these networks, Etowah's leaders fashioned a large and powerful polity. The same strategy that brought power to Etowah's leaders also sowed the seeds of their demise by creating a political landscape where competition for exclusive access to sources of power was common. These circumstances left Etowah susceptible to attack from the outside, while the presence of multiple corporate groups in the elite ranks also left the site vulnerable to internal factional disputes. The end result was a rather dramatic and apparently violent end to Etowah's short reign in northern Georgia.

This collapse did not just impact Etowah, however, for at about the same time, other large polities across northern Georgia also fell apart, creating a fragmented and politically decentralized landscape. While the sacred realm undoubtedly remained a source of power in Mississippian society, it is clear that elaborate and supernaturally charged objects and symbols, once exclusively controlled by elites, became more widely available. Most prominent of these materials are the engraved shell gorgets with rattlesnakes and the spaghetti men of the Williams Island style, and the shell facemasks (figs. 18–24). More often than not, these gorgets and masks are found in contexts suggesting that they were not markers of elevated status, but instead functioned as some indicator of horizontal statuses like kin groupings, dance and medicine societies, or other social sodalities.[41] Apparently with the collapse of Etowah and other large chiefdoms, leaders not only lost their political control, but also lost their exclusive control over the power of the sacred that was so critical to Etowah's rise to prominence.

Notes

Interpretations regarding the meaning of Mississippian symbolism presented in this paper were formed in large part through my interactions with the participants of the workshop on Mississippian iconography hosted by Kent Reilly at Texas State University in San Marcos. George Wingard expertly and tirelessly drafted the line drawing figures, while Farrah L. Brown developed GIS data for the Mound C burials and produced the resulting distribution maps.

1. Cited in Thomas 1894, pp. 296–98.
2. Galloway 1989.
3. Kelly and Larson 1957; King 1991, King 1995, and King 1996; Larson 1971; Moorehead 1932b; Thomas 1894. On Mounds A and D, and the area between Mounds B and C, see Sears 1958.
4. King 2001, Larson 1971, and Larson 1972.
5. Morgan R. Crook, personal communication 1995; King 1996, pp. 136–40.
6. Larson 1972.
7. For a fuller accounting of those excavations, see King 2003a.
8. See King 2003b.
9. King 1995.
10. Hally and Langford 1988; King 1996; Southerlin 1993.
11. Larson 1971.
12. Brown 1976; Knight 1986.
13. King 1995 and King 1996.
14. DePratter, Hudson, and Smith 1985.
15. Brain and Phillips 1996; Larson, personal communication 1995.
16. Hally, Smith, and Langford 1990.
17. King 1999.
18. Smith 1987, Smith 1989, and Smith 2000.
19. For the early excavations, see Thomas 1894 and Moorehead 1932b. On Larson's work at Etowah, see Brain and Phillips 1996; Larson 1971 and Larson 1989; King 1996.
20. See Larson 1971; King 2003a.
21. For early studies of the SECC, see, for example, Willoughby 1932; Waring and Holder 1945; Waring 1968a; and Brown 1976. For Reilly's iconography study team, see Reilly and Garber 2005.
22. See Knight, Brown, and Lankford 2001.
23. See Brown 2005a.
24. For the Hightower style gorgets, see Muller 1989, fig. 6.
25. Hudson 1976; Lankford 2005a.
26. Lankford, personal communication 2004; Lankford 2005a.
27. Again, see Hudson 1976; Lankford 2005a.
28. Lankford 2002.
29. Hudson 1976.
30. Brown 1976.
31. Knight, Brown, and Lankford 2001.
32. Knight, Brown, and Lankford 2001.
33. Helms 1994.
34. Larson 1971.
35. Brown 2005a; Brown and Kelly 2000.
36. On Spiro objects and the Braden style, see Phillips and Brown 1978. For more recent treatment, see Brown and Kelly 2000.
37. Brown 2005c; Brown and Kelly 2000.
38. Larson 1971; Brain and Phillips 1996, pp. 169–70.
39. Brown, Kerber, and Winters 1990.
40. Blanton et al. 1996.
41. Hatch 1976; Smith and Smith 1989.

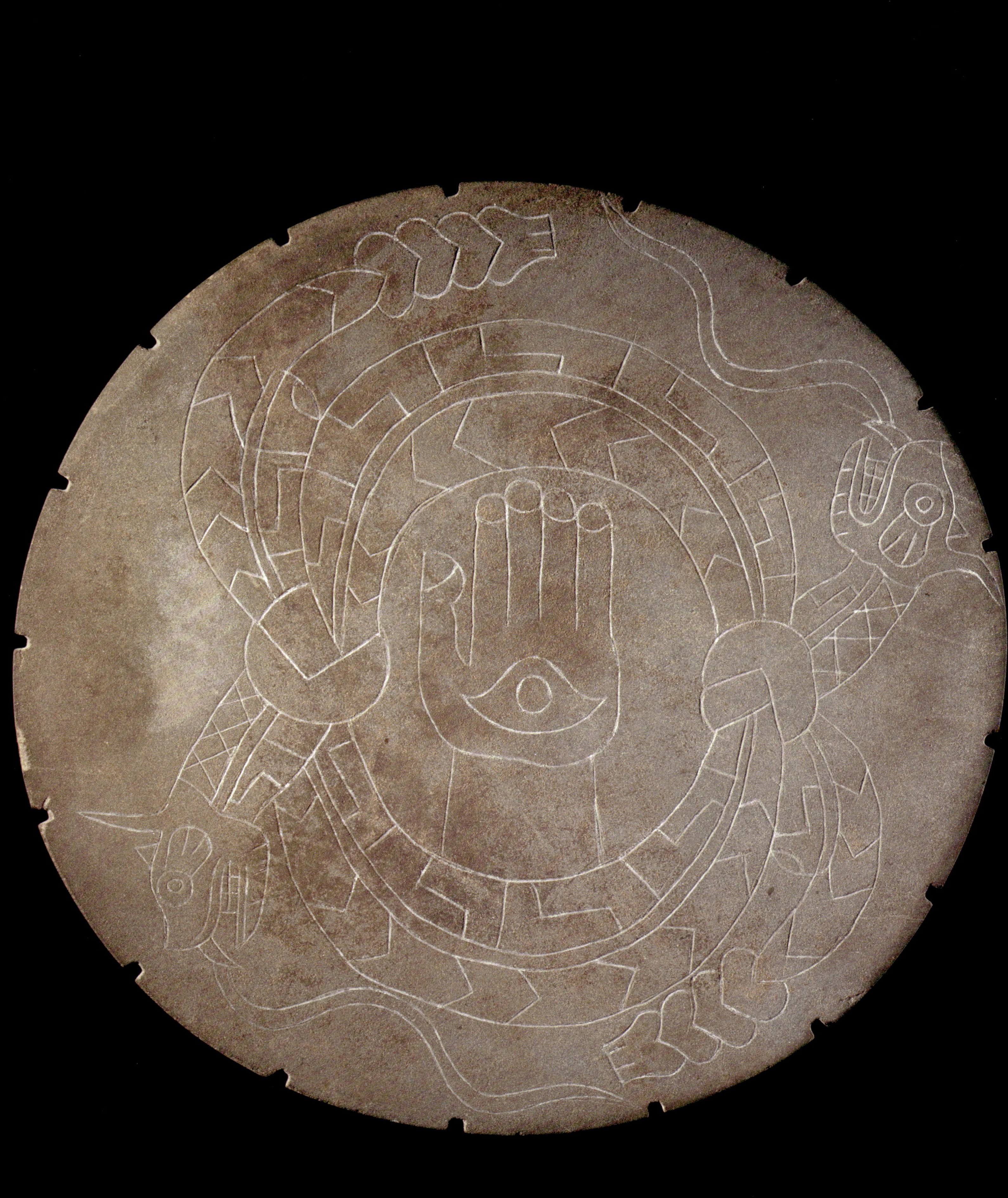

Moundville Art in Historical and Social Context

Vincas P. Steponaitis and Vernon J. Knight, Jr.

Fig. 1 Engraved circular palette with hand-and-eye motif and intertwined serpents; known in archaeological literature as the Rattlesnake Disk; Alabama, Tuscaloosa and Hale counties, Moundville, A.D. 1300–1450; sandstone, diam. 31.9 cm; Alabama Museum of Natural History, University of Alabama, Tuscaloosa. Cat. no. 155. Research is revealing that the mysterious imagery of this disk formed part of a system of cosmological signs connecting the Moundville leaders to their ancestors and the forces of nature.

Moundville in its prime was one of the largest civic-ceremonial centers in the Mississippian world, surpassed in monumental grandeur only by the great Cahokia site near modern St. Louis. Situated on the banks of the Black Warrior River in western Alabama, this site was founded around A.D. 1100, grew to regional prominence soon after 1200, and continued to be occupied until about 1600. Through most of that time it served as the political and religious capital of a powerful chiefdom. Among its residents were important political officials, priests, aristocrats, and their many retainers. It served as a place for ceremonies and rituals, including funerals, for much of the surrounding countryside. And in this context it produced and amassed a remarkable corpus of representational art—used as ornaments, regalia, symbols of power, ceremonial implements, and decorations on pottery. Indeed, this corpus remains one of the "big three" from the Mississippian world—the others being from Spiro, Oklahoma, and Etowah, Georgia—and has always played a key role in discussions of Mississippian art.

History

As its name suggests, Moundville's architecture was dominated by pyramidal mounds arranged around a large, rectangular plaza (figs. 2–5). Nowadays, twenty of these mounds are well preserved, but once there were at least thirty. At one time the site was protected by a bastioned palisade or defensive wall. The area outside the plaza and within this wall was a residential zone that, at its maximum, may have housed some one thousand people. At its largest extent, this town covered some 75 hectares (185 acres).[1] Most of the earthen mounds were rectangular and had flat summits that originally supported elaborate wooden structures: public buildings and the residences of chiefs. Some of the mounds were quite large. Mound A, in the center of the plaza, covers .8 ha (2 acres) and is 6 meters (20 ft.) tall. Mound B, at the northern end of the plaza, is about 90 meters square at the base and 17 meters high (295 ft. square × 56 ft.). The labor invested in building these earthworks was enormous.

Ethnohistorical parallels suggest that Moundville was originally built as a sociogram—an architectural depiction of a social order based on ranked clans.[2] Paired groups of mounds along the plaza's edge were associated with specific clans, arranged according to social power and prestige. The highest ranking clans were situated along the northern edge of the plaza, and the ranks decreased progressively as one moved along both sides of the plaza to the south. Thus, it is not surprising that the largest mounds and the most elaborate burials were found at the site's northern end.

A century of excavations at Moundville, coupled with decades of scholarship focused on the collections yielded by these excavations, has resulted in a reasonable understanding of the site's history, at least in broad outline.[3] The underlying chronology is based on five ceramic phases, each 100–150 years long, that span the period from A.D. 1000 to 1650 (see chronological chart, p. 12).[4] Here we present a brief social history of this period, as prelude to our discussion of Moundville's art.[5]

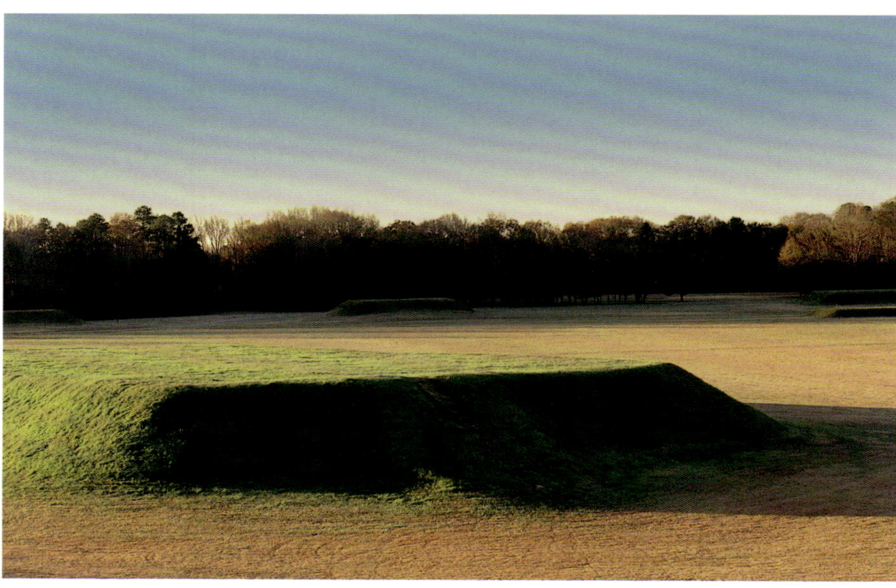

Fig. 2 View of Moundville, Tuscaloosa and Hale counties, Alabama.

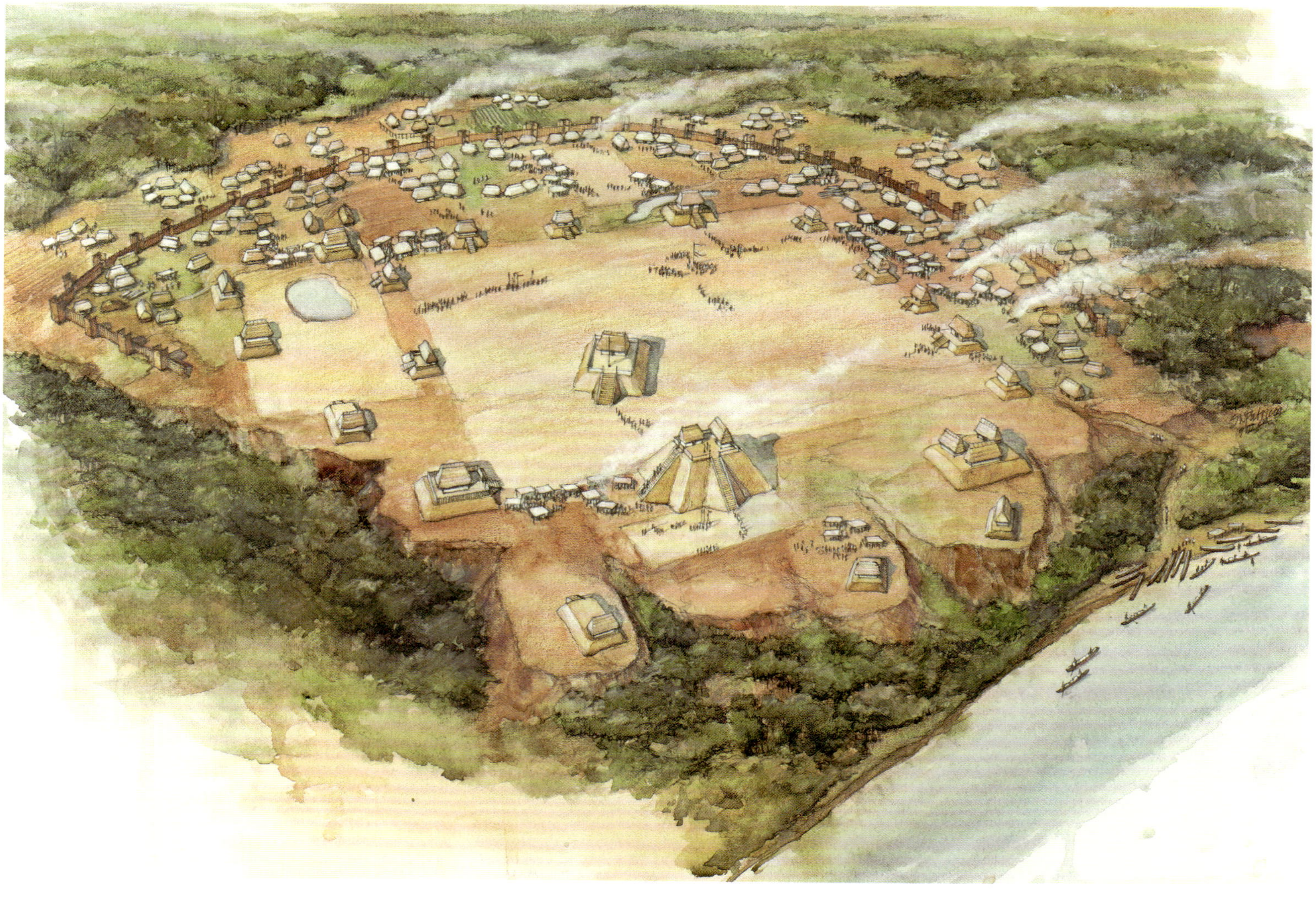

Fig. 3 View looking south over Moundville as it may have appeared in the 13th century; rendering by Steven Patricia.

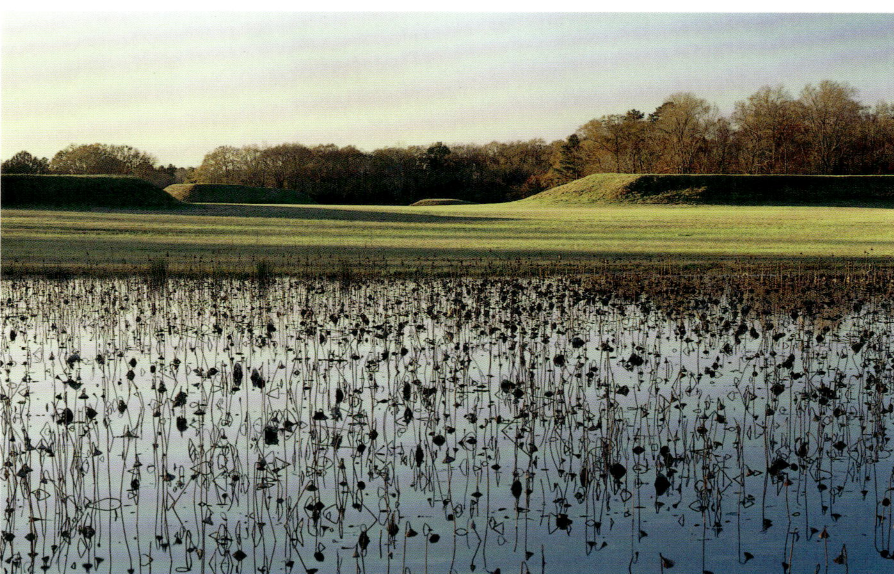

Fig. 4 View of Moundville, Tuscaloosa and Hale counties, Alabama.

The eleventh century A.D. was a time of conflict in this part of the South. Archaeological evidence suggests endemic warfare, coupled with occasional food shortages. People lived in hamlets and villages, densely clustered in certain areas, with large buffer zones between clusters. These settlement clusters must have constituted autonomous political units—perhaps groups of related towns—that from time to time made war against each other. People at this time did not build mounds, and their burials showed few signs of social inequality. One gets the sense that political centralization was minimal. In this setting occurred two important economic changes that set the stage for later political developments.

The first of these changes was a rapid intensification of farming. In addition to the traditional wild staples of deer and hickory nuts, people began to eat maize in ever-increasing amounts. At A.D. 1000, maize was an insignificant part of the diet, hardly detectable in the archaeological record. A century later maize was ubiquitous and a major part of the diet. This rapid shift to a more agricultural economy ameliorated local food shortages, made possible denser concentrations of people, and, perhaps most importantly, created a source of wealth that could be mobilized and manipulated for political ends. Equally important at this time was an upsurge in local craft production, particularly in the manufacture of shell beads. These beads were sewn onto garments that were worn as regalia at ceremonial occasions. They were also undoubtedly a source of wealth. We suspect that this increase in craft production was fueled mainly by ambitious individuals and families who were competing economically and socially for prestige.

These trends culminated, shortly after A.D. 1100, in the first material signs of political centralization: two small mounds were constructed on the Moundville terrace, accompanied by a large, dispersed community of households stretched out along the terrace's edge. Clearly, Moundville had emerged as a center of political and ceremonial activity in the region, although still modest in scale. This pattern continued until about 1200 or shortly thereafter, when Moundville was suddenly transformed into a major regional center. A new, monumental plan was conceived and imposed on the landscape. A huge central plaza was laid out and leveled by cutting away high spots and filling in depressions. Some twenty new mounds were then built around the plaza's edge, formerly dispersed houses were relocated to the margins of this ceremonial precinct, and the entire settlement was fortified by a massive wall. Thus the sociogram described earlier came into being. A powerful individual or family, whose name we shall never know, took a particular vision of the social order and literally shaped its representation into the earth, thereby creating one of the grandest centers in the Mississippian world. The construction of this center clearly signaled, to all who saw it, the emergence of a great chiefdom, ruled by aristocrats whose power in the region was unrivaled. A number of smaller mound centers, subsidiary to Moundville, were also built in the region at this time.

Around A.D. 1300 the character of the Moundville center changed once again. Archaeological signs of this change were several: (*a*) the resident population at Moundville substantially declined, as people relocated to outlying settlements; (*b*) the number of burials interred at the site increased dramatically; and (*c*) the defensive palisade was dismantled and never rebuilt. Moundville stopped being a fortified, densely populated town, and instead became a "vacant" ceremonial center, inhabited principally by elite families, ritual specialists, and retainers. As residential precincts at Moundville were emptied, they were turned into cemeteries where people from outlying settlements were brought for burial. Indeed, the absence of cemeteries at contemporary outlying sites suggests that Moundville became a necropolis, the principal place of burial for much of the region's population.

The increasing physical separation of elites from commoners at Moundville was also accompanied by

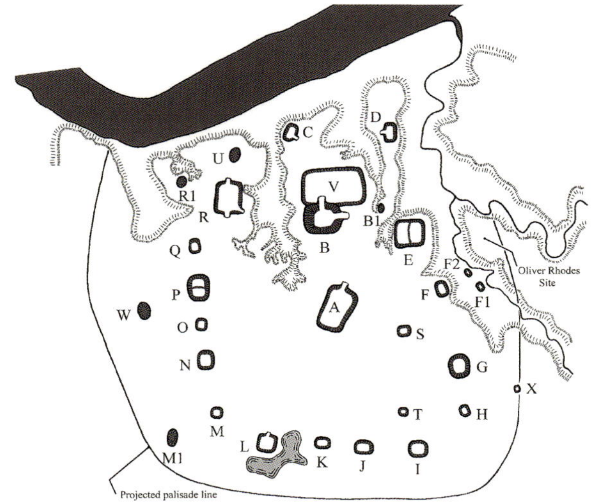

Fig. 5 Plan of Moundville.

an increasing symbolic separation. During the fourteenth century some of the most elaborate elite burials were placed in Mounds C and D, accompanied by beautifully crafted copper and shell regalia. We see this as a time when the power of Moundville's chiefs was expressed most clearly in ritual, and may well have reached its zenith in practice. Subsequent centuries saw Moundville's gradual decline. By 1400 most of the mounds along Moundville's southern flank were no longer in use, and over the next century, most of the remaining mounds were "decommissioned." By 1450 the truly elaborate burials were no longer being made, and the scale of mortuary activity across the site was greatly reduced. A few mounds were still occupied and used in the 1500s, and by 1600 the site was no longer inhabited.

Throughout this period people continued to live in the Black Warrior region, so Moundville's decline was not a matter of regional abandonment. Quite the contrary, for, as the political and religious importance of Moundville diminished, that of other, smaller mound centers in the region seemed to increase. Mounds at these outlying centers became larger, and at least two of these outlying centers were marked by the appearance of cemeteries of the kind that had formerly been found only at Moundville. Initially, Moundville's decline signaled not so much a disappearance, but a redistribution of political and religious power in the region, as outlying centers gradually became more autonomous. But by 1600 all the mound centers were gone, leaving only villages with few material signs of chiefly power.

In sum, Moundville emerged as a political and religious center in the twelfth century; became a fortified, densely populated town in the thirteenth century; and evolved into a less-populated ceremonial center in the fourteenth and fifteenth centuries, which, among other things, served as a necropolis, a special place of burial for the dead from the surrounding countryside. Most of the elaborate representational art that has survived archaeologically at Moundville dates to the last of these periods, which correspond to the late Moundville II and early Moundville III phases in the ceramic chronology (A.D. 1300–1450).

Representational Art

Broadly speaking, the artifacts considered here fall into two classes. One consists largely of work in stone, marine shell, and copper—mostly ritual items (such as pipes and palettes) and regalia (such as gorgets, headdress elements, ear disks, and beads). These were generally found in elite contexts, associated with high-ranking individuals or with places where such individuals carried out their public or ritual activities. The other class consists of engraved or painted pottery decorated with representational motifs. Such pottery initially was used only in elite contexts, but by the late fourteenth century also started to appear more broadly, both in non-elite burials at Moundville and at outlying sites.

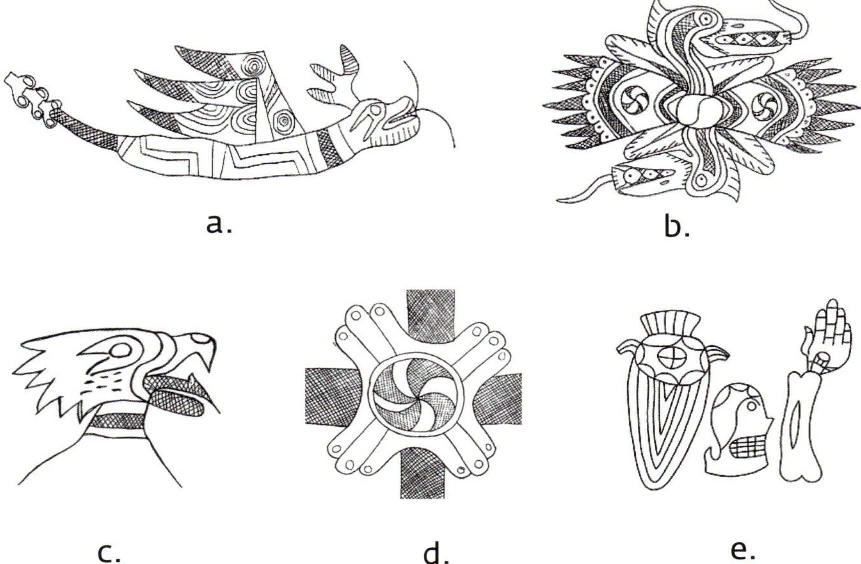

Figs. 6a–e Common themes on Hemphill-style pottery from Moundville: a) winged serpent; b) crested bird; c) raptor; d) center symbols and bands; e) trophy; from Moore 1905, figs. 9, 147, and 152; Moore 1907, figs. 5 and 8.

In the sections that follow we describe Moundville's art, organized into categories based on material and function. We also consider evidence of provenance, that is, whether particular items were locally produced or imported. As James Brown has persuasively argued,[6] the assemblage of elaborately crafted objects found archaeologically at any major Mississippian site is likely to contain items from multiple, geographically dispersed sources. Such "stylistically mismatched assemblages" can only be sorted out by tackling questions of provenance. Here, we make such discriminations based on both geological and stylistic evidence. Needless to

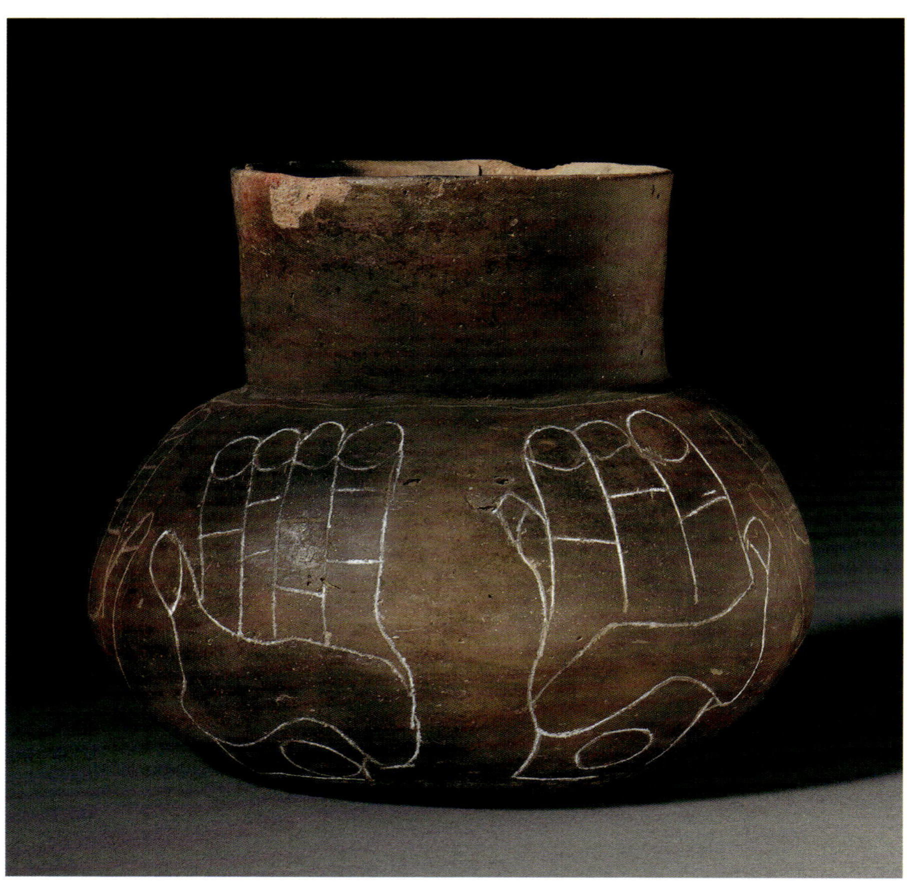

Fig. 7 Jar with incised hands; Alabama, Tuscaloosa and Hale counties, Moundville, Rhodes site (northeast of Mound F), A.D. 1300–1450; ceramic, h. 16.6 cm; Alabama Museum of Natural History, University of Alabama, Tuscaloosa. Cat. no. 265.

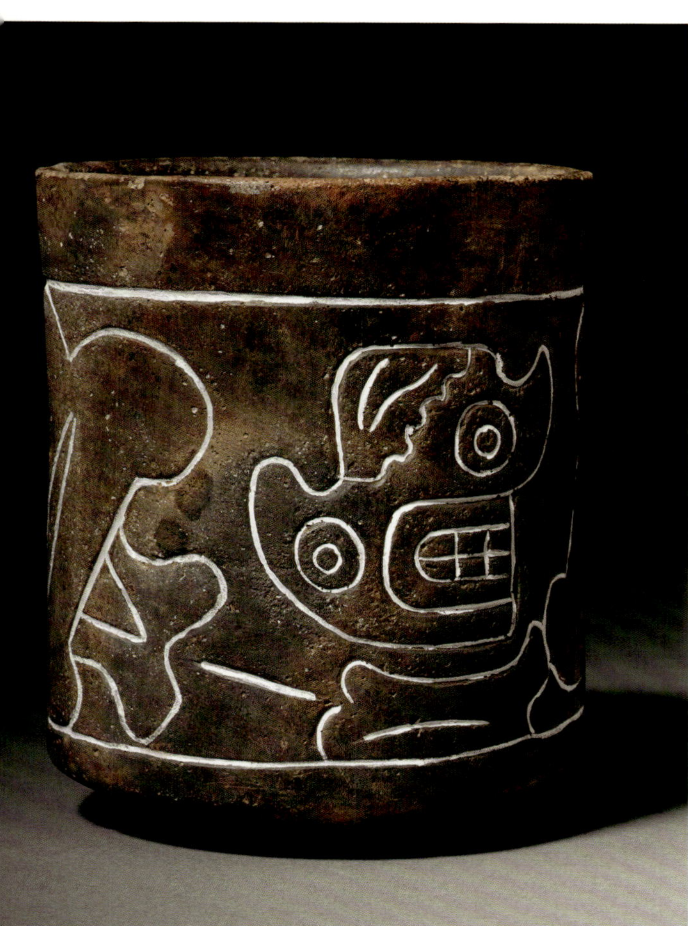

Fig. 8 Cup with incised skull motif; Alabama, Tuscaloosa and Hale counties, Moundville, southeast of Mound H, A.D. 1300–1450; ceramic, h. 11.5 cm; Alabama Museum of Natural History, University of Alabama, Tuscaloosa. Cat. no. 263.

say, our comfort in making these assessments varies according to the strength of this evidence, which differs from item to item. Even so, we believe that the available information is now sufficient to make this line of inquiry productive. While future research may refine the picture and possibly revise some of our more tentative assignments, we are confident that, at least in broad outline, these attributions will hold up under further scrutiny.

Pottery

No artifact is more ubiquitous at Moundville or has been more thoroughly studied than pottery. Typical Moundville vessels range from purely utilitarian cooking pots—mostly jars—to beautifully made serving wares—mostly bowls and bottles. The latter were often decorated with either geometric or representational designs, executed by means of engraving, incising, or painting. It is the representational work, with its evocative subject matter such as the winged serpent and the hand-and-eye motif, that has attracted the most attention as art. We admit that it is not an easy matter to draw a strict distinction between the symbolic art and the merely decorative. We suspect that at least some, if not most, of the designs that appear to us as purely geometric originally had widely understood conventional meanings. For present purposes, however, we focus on the two categories of decorated pots that show the most elaborate representational designs: the engraved wares for which Moundville is justifiably renowned, and the bichrome or polychrome painted wares.

Typologically, the engraved wares with representational designs constitute a variety called Moundville Engraved, *variety Hemphill*.[7] Such vessels are typically thin-walled bottles and bowls, which were tempered with finely ground shell, polished, and "smudged" in firing to produce a glossy black surface. Chemical studies leave no doubt that these vessels were made of local clays.[8] The engraved designs on these vessels are executed in a distinctive manner that has come to be called the Hemphill style.[9] Approximately one hundred and fifty whole or restorable vessels engraved in this style are known. Most of these pots were found as grave accompaniments, although it is clear that they were not made strictly as mortuary vessels, having been routinely used and broken in domestic settings. The Hemphill style can be distinguished from closely related engraved Mississippian pottery from the Tennessee River valley, the central and lower Mississippi valley, and the northern Gulf Coast. This style is highly conservative and is confined to a small, repetitive range of subjects drafted in accord with rather rigid artistic canons. Its subject matter, although it overlaps with that of other contemporary Mississippian centers, reflects a distinctive Moundville vision of the cosmos.

The vast majority of compositions engraved in the Hemphill style are variations on only five themes, or categories of subject matter (figs. 6a–e). The first of these is a winged serpent, depicted as having the body of a rattlesnake with either a reptilian or a mammalian head affixed with deer antlers (fig. 6a; see also fig. 12 in the essay by George Lankford in this volume). Feathered wings sprout from the back of this dragonlike creature. Second is a crested bird, typically shown in multiples knotted together in pairs around a central medallion or knot, with four birds to a vessel (fig. 6b). This bird has a long, sinuous neck, a straight beak, and a distinctive flattened head crest. The third and last of the major zoomorphic themes is a raptor, a bird of prey with a hooked beak, a serrated crest, and characteristic eye markings (fig. 6c). Unlike raptor depictions elsewhere in the Mississippian world, these birds show no signs of being combined with human features or human costume. A fourth theme is called center symbols and bands (fig. 6d), comprising a number of geometric-looking compositions that exhibit fairly obvious cosmological references by incorporating strategically placed center symbols intercepted by wide, ribbonlike bands, referencing four quarters or quadrants. Other motifs, such as three conjoined fingers, sometimes radiate outward from the center symbols at the semicardinal points. The range of motifs that can act as center symbols in these compositions include the cross-in-circle, concentric circles, the swastika, the radial T-bar, and the dimple. The fifth major category of subject matter is the so-called "trophy" theme: compositions that show, in varying combinations, a small checklist of motifs that include the human hand, the

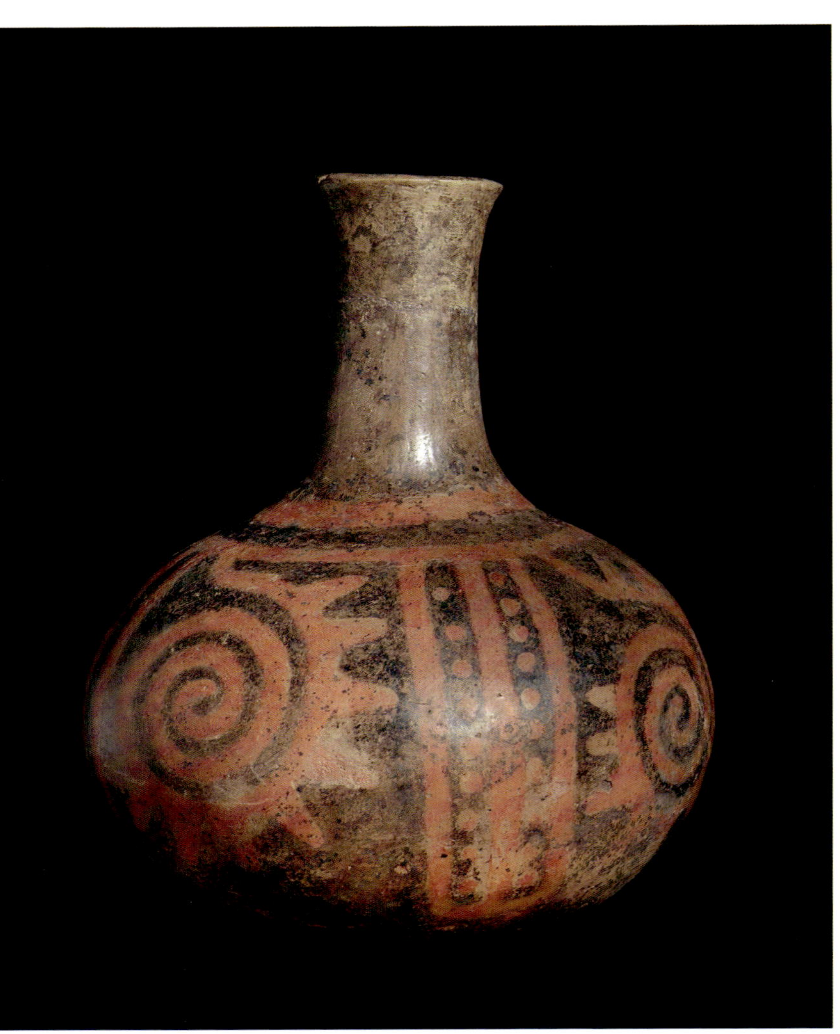

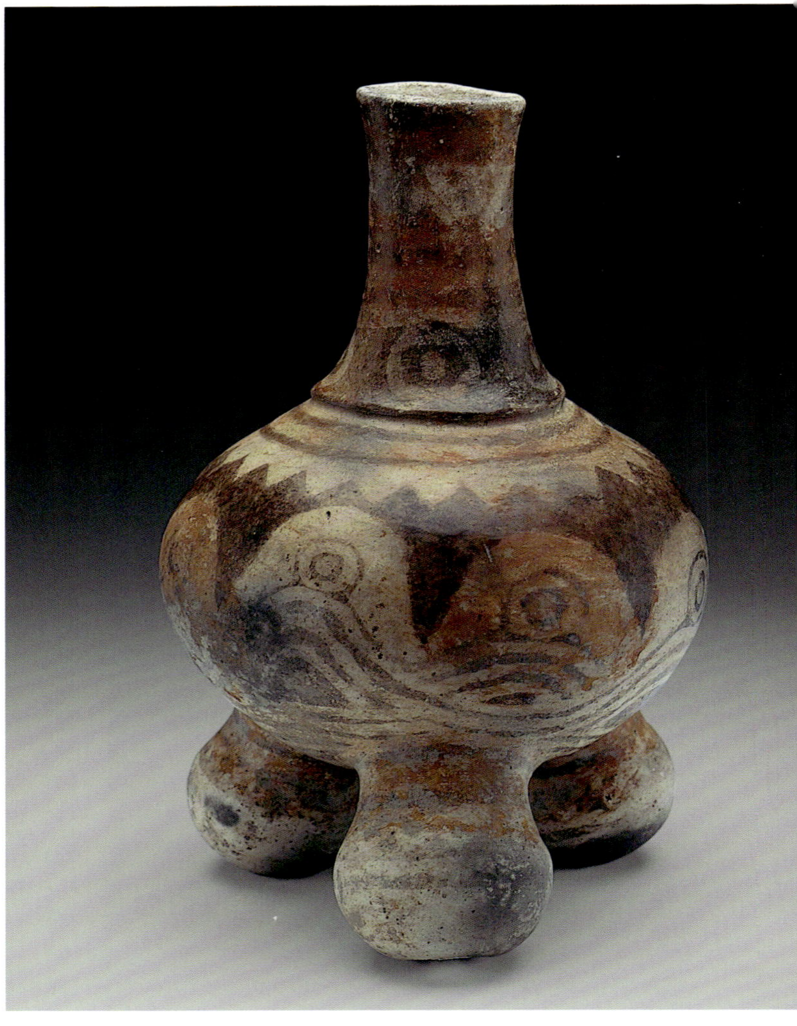

forearm bone, the skull, and the scalp stretched on a hoop (figs. 6e and 7–8). Depictions of skulls show what are arguably scalp marks at the back of the head. Occasionally the head of a raptor is included in the mix of motifs. The meaning of this set of associations has proven especially difficult to penetrate, but George Lankford has argued that most elements of this theme, together with the winged serpent and raptor, allude to the Path of Souls, a journey taken by the dead that is well documented in the Native American traditions of the Great Plains and Eastern Woodlands.[10]

Chronologically, Hemphill-style engraved pottery spans much of the fourteenth century and the first half of the fifteenth. Within this span there were probably never more than a few potters working in this style at any one time. The total number of known vessels is not large, and duplicate vessels bearing "signature" characteristics of the same potter have been identified in several cases. The most elaborate, expertly composed, and competently drafted pieces with winged serpent and crested bird figures were made in the fourteenth century.[11] These earliest pieces are also those with the most obvious external stylistic connections, particularly with certain early Walls and late Braden style engraving from the central Mississippi valley. The style was probably originally inspired by engraving in other media and was adapted to pottery. By the fifteenth century, Hemphill engraved vessels generally show a breakdown in competency, a rather poor control of the medium, and more stylistic independence, suggesting a dispersal of potters and workshops away from the Moundville site proper and less importance attached to the engraver's skill. There is no indication that the circulation of Hemphill engraved pottery was restricted only to elites. The vessels are found in seemingly ordinary graves in all parts of the Moundville site. While these vessels are most abundant at Moundville, Hemphill-style vessels and sherds have also been found at a number of outlying sites including small farmsteads.

The second kind of pottery with representational motifs consists of bichrome and polychrome vessels painted with red, white, and/or black pigments. The first two are applied in the form of slips of colored clay, while the last is a carbon pigment often applied with a negative or resist technique. As with the engraved wares, this painted pottery also tends to be a relatively thin ware, tempered with fine shell and burnished on the exterior. Two vessel shapes dominate this category. The first is a bottle with a spherical body, usually equipped with narrow, curving "carafe" neck. The second is a terraced rectanguloid bowl, a Moundville specialty. This kind of bowl is a vertical-sided, flat-bottomed, rectangular vessel that has an eccentric rim, with one side lower than the others as if to display the vessel's

Fig. 9 Long-necked globular bottle with negative resist design; Arkansas, Scott County, A.D. 1300–1500; ceramic, h. 20.3 cm; Gilcrease Museum, Tulsa, Oklahoma. Cat. no. 230.

Fig. 10 Tripod vessel with negative resist design; Missouri, Mississippi County, A.D. 1300–1500; ceramic, h. 23.2 cm; Dr. Arthur Cushman Collection, Old Hickory, Tennessee. Cat. no. 229.

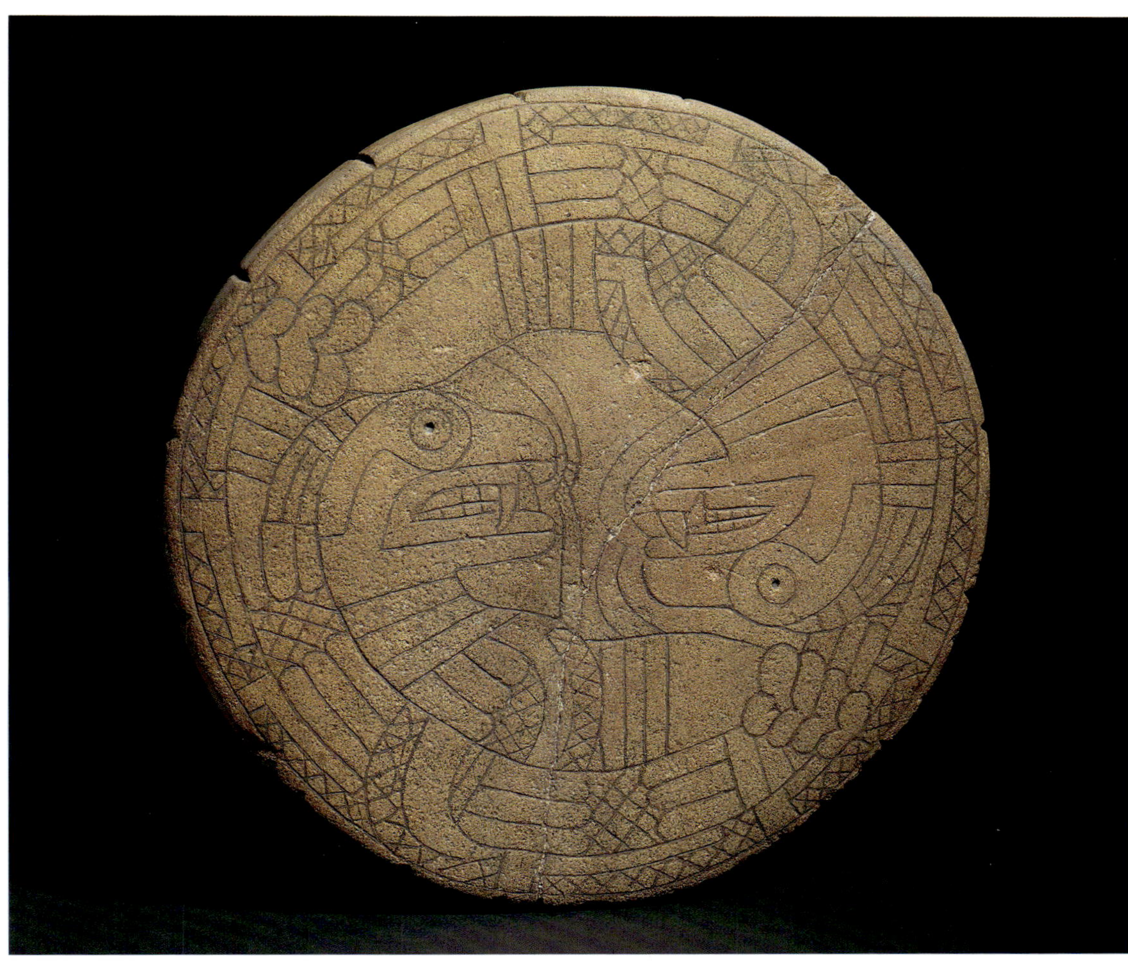

Fig. 11 Engraved circular palette with with intertwined plumed serpents; known in archaeological literature as the Issaquena Disk; Mississippi, Issaquena County, probably Grace Mounds, A.D. 1250–1500; sandstone (?), diam. 21.6 cm; Ohio Historical Society, Columbus. Cat. no. 158.

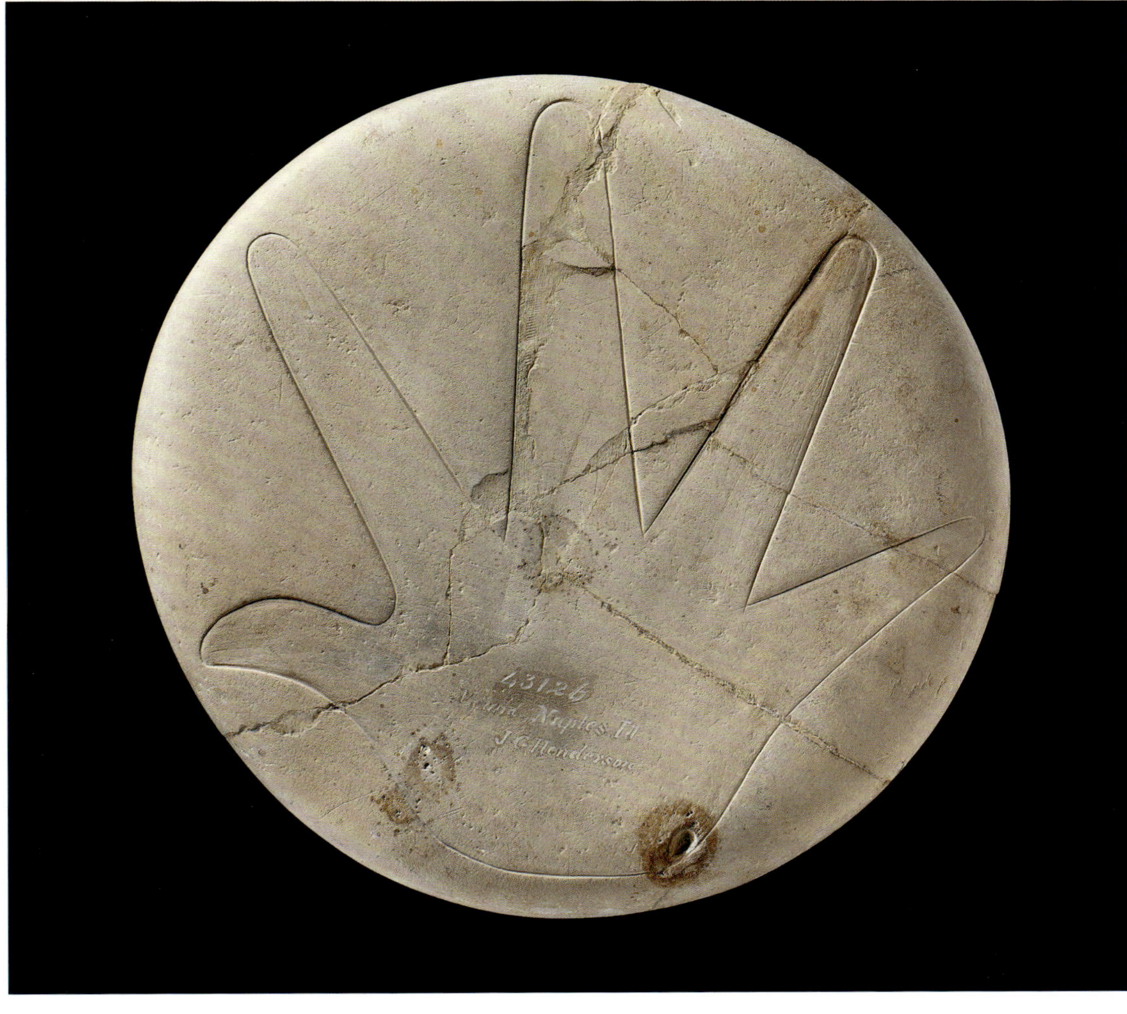

Fig. 12 Engraved circular palette with hand motif, one of the earliest examples of this type; Illinois, Naples, Winchester Mound, 100 B.C.–A.D. 300; siltstone (?), diam. 31.8 cm; Smithsonian Institution, National Museum of Natural History, Washington, D.C. Cat. no. 157. Mississippian circular palettes had precedent in the earlier Woodland tradition, as seen in this disk featuring the motif of an open hand. The simple, abstract rendering of the hand in this instance bears a resemblance to the famous Hopewell mica cutout hand from Ross County, Ohio (see Seeman essay, fig. 8).

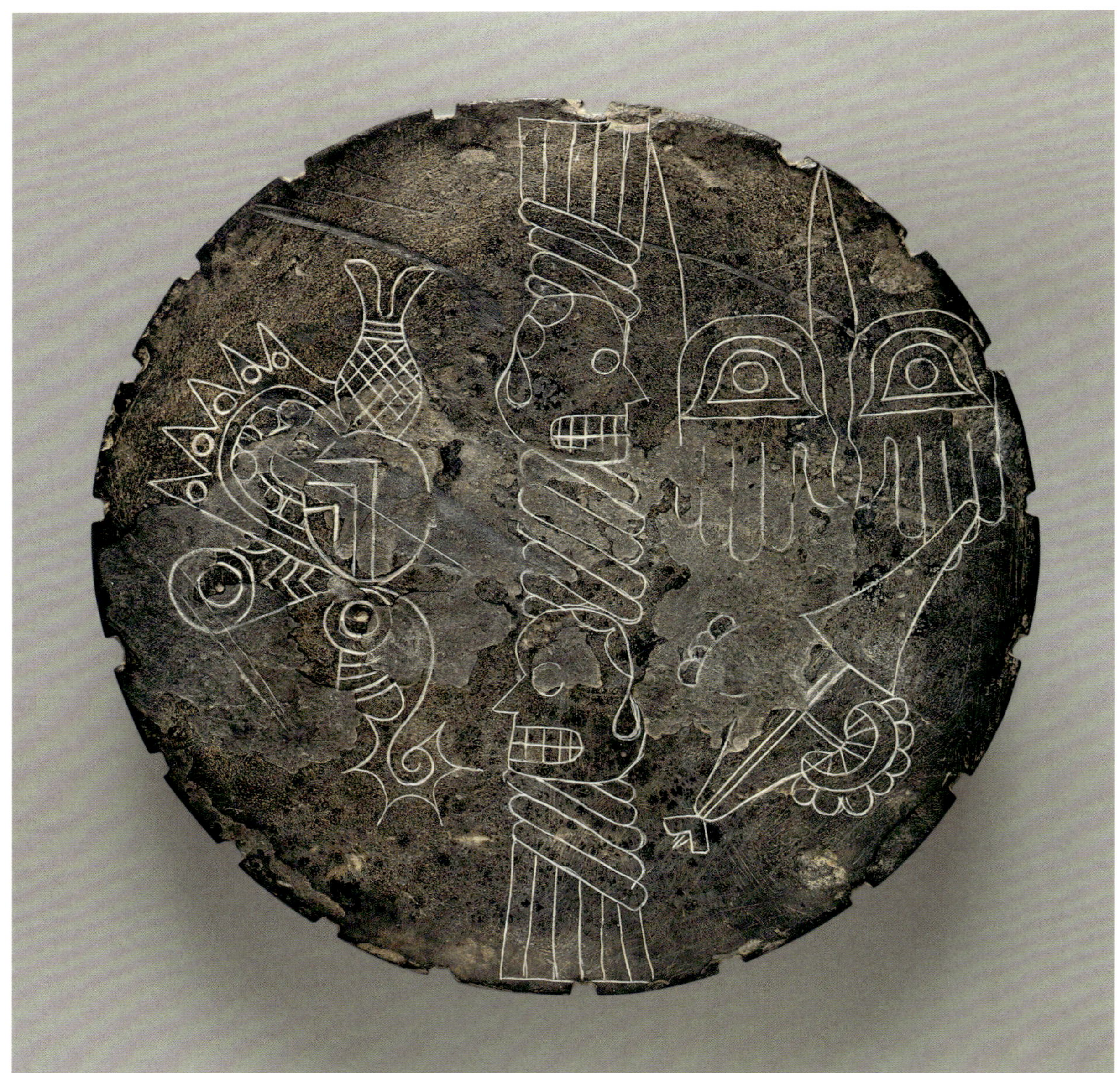

Fig. 13 Engraved circular palette; known in archaeological literature as the Willoughby Disk; Alabama, Tuscaloosa and Hale counties, Moundville, A.D. 1300–1450; shale (?), diam. 22.2 cm; Harvard University, Peabody Museum of Archaeology and Ethnology, gift of F. E. Hyde and Charles P. Bowditch, 1896. Cat. no. 156.

contents. Stylistically, much of the painted pottery found at Moundville closely resembles that found in other parts of the Mississippian world. The resemblance is particularly close with the painted pottery found along the Tennessee, Cumberland, and lower Ohio River valleys to the north of Moundville, and in the central Mississippi valley to the west (figs. 9–10). That much of this pottery, long suspected of being imported, was not made of local clays has recently been borne out by chemical provenance studies.[12] Yet these same chemical studies show that some painted pots were made locally as well, including terraced rectanguloid bowls and designs duplicated in Moundville copper and stone pendants. The negative-painted pottery, whether locally made or acquired from external sources, circulated only in restricted contexts. Such vessels often ended up as grave goods in elite cemeteries at the Moundville site, and neither negative-painted vessels nor sherds are so far known from any of the sites in Moundville's hinterlands.

Stone Palettes

Although notable examples of decorated stone palettes have been unearthed in other contexts—including one from Mississippi with plumed serpents now in the Ohio Historical Society collection (fig. 11) and one of impressive size with an engraved hand design at the Smithsonian Institution (fig. 12)—it is safe to say that such palettes constitute another distinctive Moundville artifact. Dozens of complete specimens and hundreds of fragments have been found, more than at any other Mississippian site. These palettes are typically circular, about 20–30 cm (8–12 in.) in diameter, and 1–2 cm thick; a few rectangular examples of comparable size are also known.[13] They are incised with designs on one or both sides and usually show patches of red, white, or black—traces of distinctively colored minerals that were placed on these flat surfaces.[14] We suspect these palettes were used as ritual furniture, portable altars on which medicines and other supernaturally powerful mixtures were prepared.

The vast majority of the palettes at Moundville are made of a fine, gray, micaceous sandstone that occurs in great abundance at outcrops only 30 km (18.8 miles) north of the site.[15] So there can be little doubt that these artifacts were made locally. The obverse face of the palette is usually decorated with a notched or scalloped edge and concentric lines drawn parallel to the rim. This simple design shows clear iconographic parallels to the scalloped edge and multilinear band often found on copper gorgets.[16] The palette's reverse face is usually undecorated, but the few known exceptions to this pattern are iconographically spectacular. One such exception is the aptly named Rattlesnake Disk, which is decorated on the reverse with a masterfully executed design showing two horned rattlesnakes knotted together into a circle (fig. 1). This ophidian circle, in turn, surrounds a hand—a symbolic portrayal of a portal into the celestial realm.[17] A second exception is the Willoughby Disk, made of a dark gray, shale-like stone (fig. 13). Although the specific geological source of its material has yet to be identified, it is consistent with the kinds of rocks that occur nearby and our best current guess is that this palette was made locally as well.[18] Its reverse face is covered with a mélange of motifs: a central rope-like element bearing two skulls, flanked on one side by two hands and a bilobed arrow, and flanked on the other side by a curious creature with the spiral proboscis and wing of a moth.[19] The meaning of this mélange is not at all clear, but iconographic elements are all ones that occur in some form on local pottery (the engraved and painted wares discussed earlier) and are consistent with local styles. These stylistic links strengthen our suspicion that the Willoughby Disk was decorated by a Moundville artist, despite its atypical raw material.

Stone Pendants

A specialty of Moundville's lapidary work is the production of small, tabular, engraved stone pendants. Fashioned from thin stone of uniform thickness, these pendants were shaped, polished, and engraved to represent standard symbols. In most though not all cases the material of manufacture is a blood-red, fine-grained ferruginous stone. Although this material has not yet been securely identified geologically, tabular rock of similar appearance has been noted in the superficial geology of the upper Coastal Plain hills only a short distance from Moundville. At any rate it is abundantly clear that the manufacture of these pendants was local, in that partially finished blanks, partially engraved specimens, and specimens bearing evidence of having broken during manufacture have all been found at the Moundville site, along with a majority of the finished specimens.[20] Blanks and unfinished specimens show that the stone was first ground to a uniform thickness, then sawn into shape by a groove-and-snap technique. Edges and surfaces were then polished, fenestrations and suspension holes were drilled, and the outer surface

Fig. 14 Oblong pendant with swastika and hand-and-eye motif; Alabama, Tuscaloosa and Hale counties, Moundville, southwest of Mound M, A.D. 1250–1500; stone, h. 9.8 cm; Alabama Museum of Natural History, University of Alabama, Tuscaloosa.

Fig. 15 Oblong pendant with rayed circle, ogee, and hand-and-eye motif; Alabama, Tuscaloosa and Hale counties, Moundville, south of Mound D, A.D. 1250–1500; copper, h. 13 cm; Smithsonian Institution, National Museum of the American Indian, Washington, D.C., no. 17/3107; from Moore 1907, fig. 101.

Fig. 16 Hair ornament; Alabama, Tuscaloosa and Hale counties, Moundville, Mound H, A.D. 1250–1500; copper, h. 16 cm, with bone pin; Smithsonian Institution, National Museum of the American Indian, Washington, D.C., no. 17/0147.

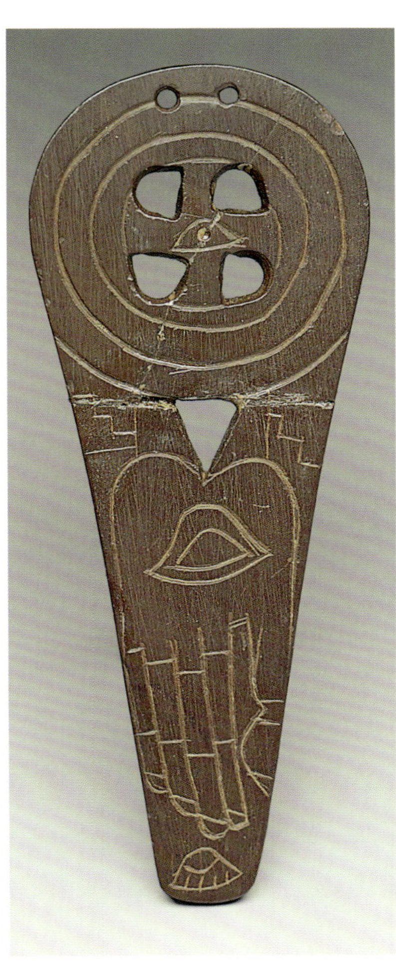

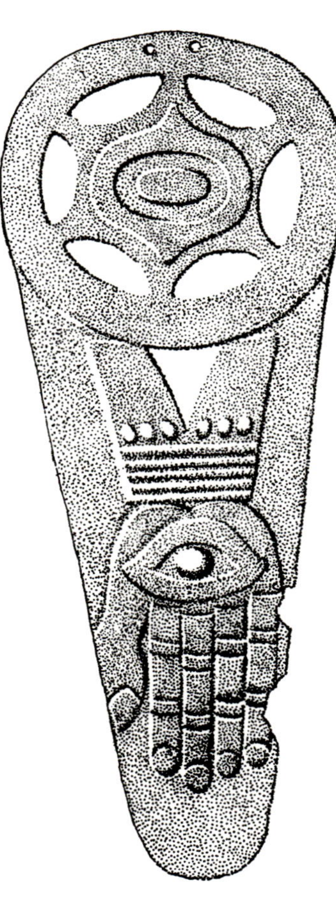

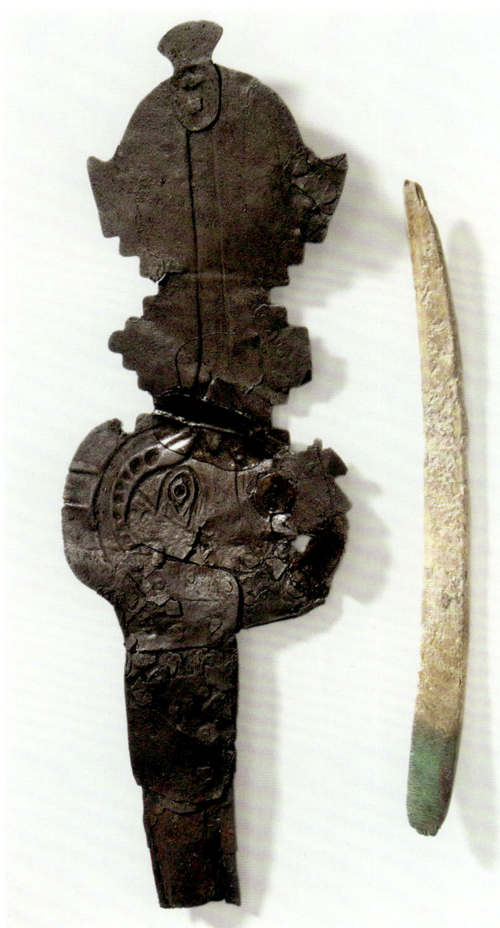

was engraved. No such production evidence has been found at any of the other sites in Moundville's hinterland, and, to date, only one site in Moundville's hinterland has yielded an example. Two other sites, one in the Tennessee River valley and the other in the Tombigbee valley, have produced one specimen apiece, both no doubt originating at Moundville.[21]

The most common type, the oblong emblem (fig. 14), is a design of central importance to Moundville iconography, shared with other media including sheet copper and negative painted pottery.[22] This design's original prototype is an older Mississippian motif consisting of a human scalp stretched on a frame, which also shows up as an item of regalia called the "bellows-shaped apron" in the literature.[23] Here the design has become conventionalized over time beyond immediate recognition of its scalp prototype. As translated in time and space into Moundville art, the design had become an independent emblem, and the upper and lower registers were now fields for a standard set of locally important motifs. As with the corresponding copper artifacts, the upper register of the oblong stone pendants is occupied by either of two circular motifs: the rayed circle or the swastika-in-circle. The lower register may be blank, or may contain the hand-and-eye motif with the fingers downward, plus terrace motifs. Extraneous "eyes" may appear in either the upper or lower register.

Copper Ornaments

Moundville's decorative arts include copper in a variety of forms, including items of regalia cut from sheet copper, copper-clad wooden ornaments, and copper-bladed axes made for display.[24] All were manufactured of native copper, that is, relatively pure nuggets that were cold-hammered into thin sheets and cut into the desired shapes. Native copper occurs naturally in many parts of eastern North America, but nowhere close to Moundville. Trace-element studies suggest that most of the copper found at Moundville came from geological sources in the southern Appalachian Mountains, while some came from sources near the Great Lakes.[25] In this case, however, the source of the raw material bears little relationship to where a particular artifact was crafted, as native copper from many sources circulated widely across the Mississippian world, and was turned into artifacts at many different places. Thus, conclusions on the place of manufacture must currently rest on the grounds of style, iconography, technology, and distribution. It seems clear that at least some copper-working was done at the Moundville site, as sheet-copper scrap has been found in midden contexts, particularly where there is other evidence of craft activity, as at Mound Q.[26] It is also likely on the basis of stylistic and distributional evidence that some copper artifacts at Moundville were imported from other Mississippian chiefdoms.

Let us first discuss the copper objects we believe were made locally at Moundville. Among the items strongly correlated with elite burials at Moundville are gorgets of embossed sheet copper, doubly perforated for suspension along one margin.[27] They occur in only two shapes, circular and oblong. Like their more diminutive stone counterparts, the oblong gorgets feature a circular upper register that contains either a cutout swastika-in-circle or a scalloped circle motif (fig. 15). The circular gorgets, which tend to possess embossed concentric circles around the outer margin, share the same two motifs, the swastika and scalloped circle, as their central elements. Thus, all but one of the 32 known specimens fall into a scheme of only four possibilities: oblong with swastika-in-circle, oblong with scalloped circle, circular with swastika, and circular with scalloped circle.

Among these copper gorgets by far the most common type is oblong, with the upper register containing a cutout swastika enclosed by two embossed concentric circles, and a lower register containing a cutout triangle. It seems highly important that this design is the most frequently seen in copper at Moundville, that it has almost exact stylistic counterparts in other media known to be of local Moundville manufacture, and that the design, as executed in this style, is extremely rare outside of Moundville. Its combination with a hand-and-eye motif is again precisely duplicated in local stonework. These circumstances in our opinion render it unlikely that the oblong copper gorgets found at Moundville, and by extension the circular copper gorgets, were made at any other Mississippian center. Indeed this set of copper gorgets, or more precisely the iconography they convey, is the closest thing we can find to local emblems identifying Moundville's elites. In this connection it is revealing that this small package of elite symbols has so little in common with the iconography shown on Hemphill style engraved pottery, which is also indigenous to Moundville, but has a very different pattern of circulation.

It is useful to contrast these gorgets with other copper items at Moundville which are less common but which do have close, if not exact, external counterparts at other Mississippian centers. There are, for example, hair ornaments from Moundville made of embossed sheet copper which have a riveted socket at one end, made to receive a bone or bison-horn hairpin (fig. 16). One complete specimen is in the form of a curving feather notched on one side, another is in the shape of a key-sided mace, and a third is in the form of a bilobed arrow.[28] All three forms are immediately recognizable as closely identified with elite burials at Etowah and related sites. Although we are not aware of any detailed stylistic study of these artifact forms, the Moundville hair ornaments seem to us to conform stylistically to published examples from Etowah.[29] At the Moundville-related Lubbub site has been found a sheet copper plate bearing an embossed falcon that is unquestionably realized in the "Etowah copper style" as named by Philip Phillips and James Brown. In fact an exact duplicate is known from northern Georgia.[30] There is, in sum, evidence of an important copper connection between Moundville and certain eastern sites, including Etowah, that previously has been

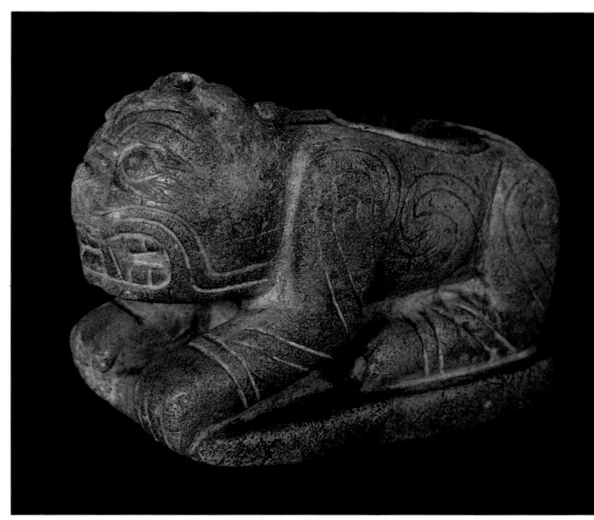

underappreciated. Many of the artifacts in Moundville's copper inventory were probably fabricated in that area.

Stone Effigy Pipes

Moundville has yielded an array of massive effigy pipes made of stone, one of the biggest assemblages of such pipes in the Mississippian world. These pipes depict both animal and human forms in the round. They typically have two conically drilled holes connected by a narrow passage: a bowl in the top to contain the substance (presumably tobacco) being smoked, and a hole in the side to receive a stem. Four of these pipes are examples of the Bellaire style.[31] As is typical of the style, they depict a piasa—a supernatural being that combines the features of a cat, a snake, and a bird, and sometimes a human or a deer.[32] The Moundville specimens have a distinctly feline head and body and an unusually long, snakelike tail that runs up the creature's back and curls around the pipe's bowl (fig. 17).[33] Ethnographic and folkloric evidence leaves little doubt that this being was the "Great Serpent," a denizen of the Beneath World in the Mississippian cosmos.[34] All four of these pipes are made of a cream-colored limestone, which, based on distinctive fossils visible in the surface, has been identified as a type called Glendon limestone. Large outcrops of this rock occur near Vicksburg, Mississippi. Based on geological, stylistic, and distributional evidence, a strong case can be made that the Glendon limestone pipes were made in the lower Mississippi valley and imported to Moundville.[35]

Another effigy pipe worthy of note is made of red flint clay and shows a squatting man with no clothing.[36] The raw material has been mineralogically linked to sources in eastern Missouri, and the pipe is of a style believed to have been made during the twelfth century in or near Cahokia (see the essay by Kent Reilly in this volume).[37] Like the others just discussed, this pipe is unquestionably an import.

Stone Effigy Bowls

Items in this category are rare, but they include two of the best known and most beautifully crafted objects at Moundville. Based on their shape and decoration, they seem to be elaborated versions of the ceramic effigy bowls that are relatively abundant at Moundville. They may even have been used for similar purposes. A clue as to what these purposes may have been comes from the journal of Paul du Ru, a French Jesuit who traveled to Louisiana in 1700. Describing the temple in a Taensa village, he wrote:

> At the door of this temple one sees only elders lamenting and shouting, cantors praying, people bearing offerings, and all with an extraordinary orderliness and restraint. Among other things there are six large wooden bowls with handles, of which one represents the tail of a swan and the other the neck, which are filled with [maize] flour and carried solemnly to the temple. The Athenian virgins did not carry their baskets of flowers to the temple of Juno with greater dignity.[38]

Except for the material, his description of the bowls in which offerings were made fits well the stone effigy bowls from Moundville.

First and foremost is a spectacular vessel (fig. 18), carved from a massive piece of dark green, metamorphosed diorite, which the excavator called "a triumph of aboriginal endeavor, the 'Portland vase' of prehistoric art in the United States."[39] The object so praised is a very large hemispherical bowl, some 30 cm in diameter and 16.5 cm high (11¾ × 6½ in.), decorated with a band of incised parallel lines just below the lip—the same design that is usually found on ceramic effigy bowls. Rising another 12 cm above the rim on one side is the gracefully curving neck and head of a creature that was originally identified as a wood duck. Superficially, the head does indeed resemble that of a duck, but a closer examination in light of current understandings of Mississippian iconography leads to a very different conclusion regarding the creature's identity:

> The neck is serpentine and of a length far out of proportion to that of any actual duck. This neck, moreover, is crosshatched and bears a trilobate motif on the back, not to be found on any living bird. In Braden style art the trilobate motif has snake associations. The design surrounding the eyes is teardrop shaped. This combination of details, along with the crest of the bird, align it strongly with the amphisbaena, a double-ended knotted snake monster in Classic Braden style engraved shell art at the Spiro site. We suspect . . . that the artisan of the diorite bowl intended not an ordinary wood duck, but rather a monstrous supernatural, one partaking of both snake and bird in its cognized form.[40]

The geological source of this metamorphosed diorite is still unknown, but it could be somewhere in the southern Appalachian Mountains. At this point we are unwilling to say whether the artifact was locally made or imported.

A companion to the stone vessel just described is another large bowl, 23 cm in diameter and 10 cm

Fig. 17 Piasa effigy pipe; Bellaire style; Alabama, Tuscaloosa and Hale counties, Moundville, A.D. 1300–1500; limestone, h. 10.2 cm; Tennessee State Museum, Nashville, Gates P. Thruston Collection of Vanderbilt University.

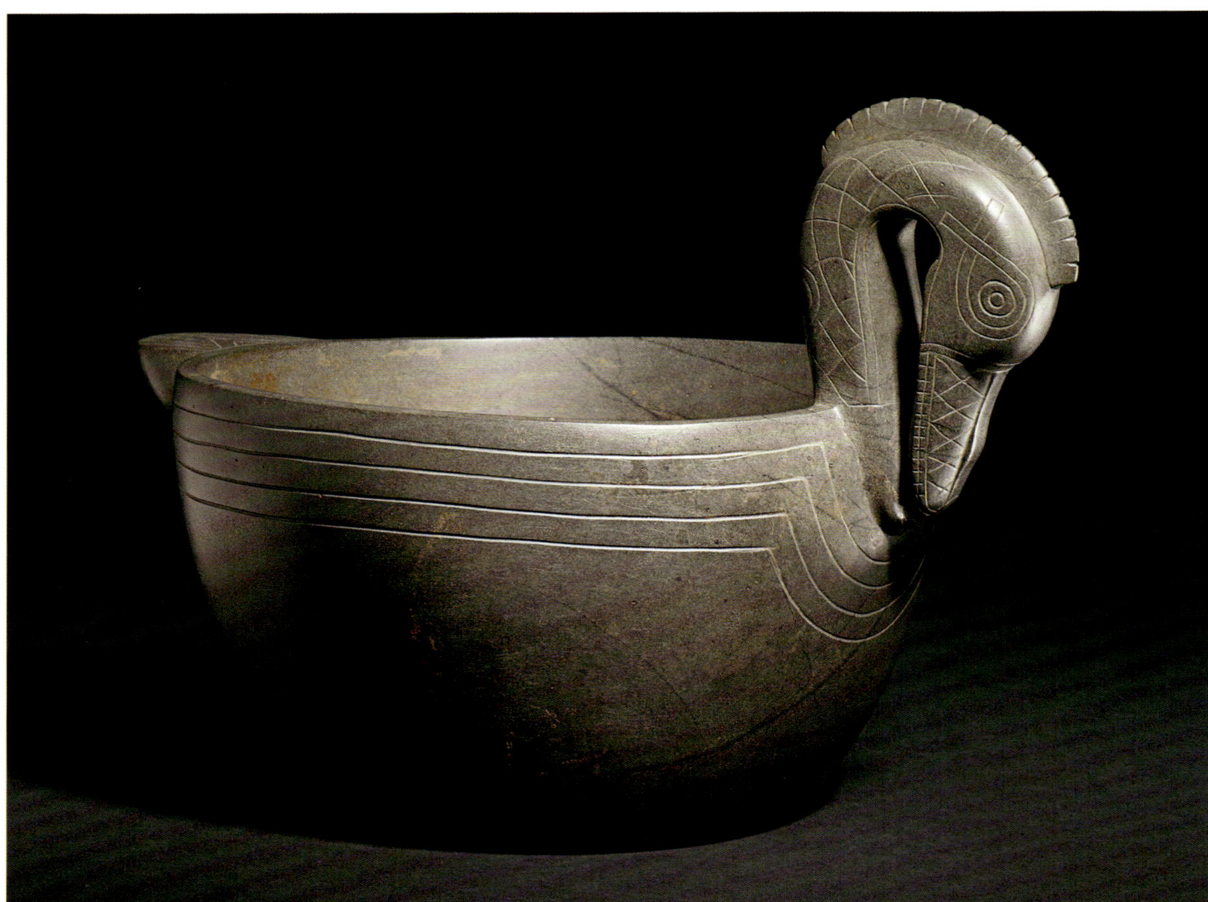

Fig. 18 Bowl with serpent/bird effigy; Alabama, Tuscaloosa and Hale counties, Moundville, north of Mound R, A.D. 1250–1500; altered diorite, h. 16.5, diam. 30 cm; Smithsonian Institution, National Museum of the American Indian, Washington, D.C. Cat. no. 160.

high (9 × 4 in.), that also portrays a subject with avian features (figs. 19–20).[41] On this piece the neck emerges from the side of the rim and curves horizontally an eighth of the way around the circumference, where the tip of the beak meets the rim once again. The vessel's exterior is incised with lines showing feathers, wings, and talons in the round. Lines on the head and below the neck of the creature suggest the fleshy wattle and feathered "beard" of a wild turkey. But it also has features—an unusually long neck, two trilobate elements (incised on the neck), and the concentric semicircles (incised on the legs)—that iconographically mark serpents.[42] In other words, this bird can only be a supernatural one. The raw material is a limestone very different from the Glendon limestone often seen in the effigy pipes, and its source is unknown.

Marine Shell Ornaments and Cups

In contrast to other Mississippian centers, the medium of engraved marine shell was of only minor importance in Moundville's artistic repertoire. Well-appointed, elite burials at the site, while rich in copper, tend to lack engraved shell artifacts. That is not to say that marine shell per se is rare at Moundville, as strands of simple marine shell beads are common accompaniments of elite burials. As for engraved shell art, however, there are on record only eight shell gorgets and three shell cup fragments, among the 3,022 documented burials from the site.[43] Despite their relative infrequency, those gorgets and cup fragments that do occur at Moundville are of much interest, because they exhibit a variety of styles having external connections.

The shells themselves originated in the Gulf of Mexico, but, just as with copper, knowing the source of the material tells us little about where these artifacts were crafted, as raw shell circulated widely across the Southeast and was worked in many places. Nevertheless, it can safely be said that the majority of such artifacts at Moundville are nonlocal. This is most clearly the case with the engraved shell cup fragments, all three of which have stylistic counterparts at the distant Spiro site in the west.[44] The best example of these shell cups is a fragment showing portions of at least two elaborately dressed individuals.[45] The style of depiction is unmistakably Classic Braden as designated by James Brown (see his essay in this volume), a style indigenous to the central Mississippi valley and one elsewhere dated considerably earlier than the context of the find at Moundville.[46]

Engraved shell gorgets from Moundville are a highly diverse lot from the standpoint of style and subject matter. Some are obvious examples of documented styles having centers of distribution elsewhere, most prominently the central Tombigbee River valley to the west and the middle Tennessee area to the north.[47] A striking gorget found by Clarence B. Moore in 1905 depicts a supernatural piasa, in this case part panther and part human, with perhaps some bird and serpent components as well (fig. 21).[48] In this piece, while the style is unrecognizable, its foreign origin is nonetheless

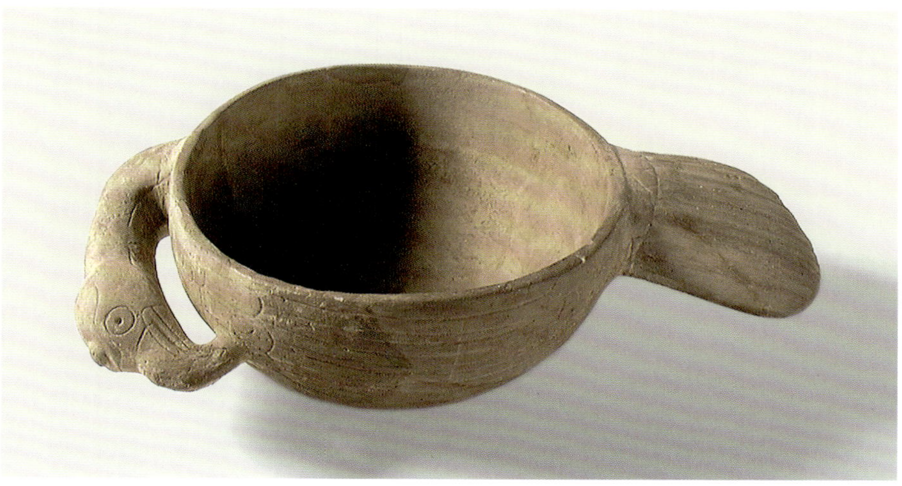

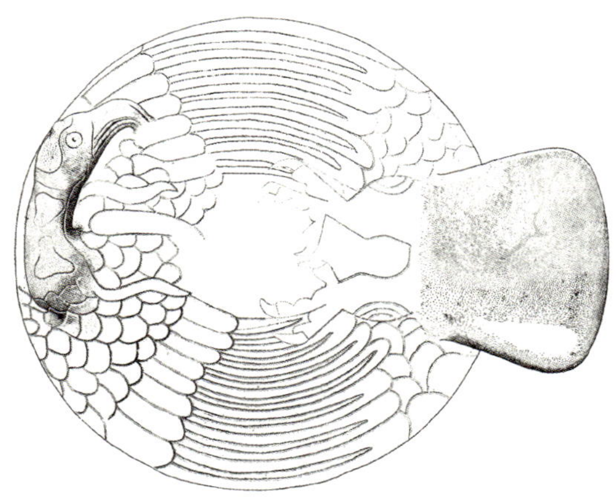

style is unrecognizable, its foreign origin is nonetheless apparent. The subject matter, for one thing, is patently non-Moundvillian, being much more at home in the Mississippi valley. Human-animal composites in general are not among the subjects of local Moundville art. The depiction of the panther is otherwise known only in the stone Bellaire-style pipes that are independently sourced as nonlocal. The details of the depiction reinforce this assessment. At the hip of the figure is the object known as the "bellows-shaped apron" in the literature; at the neck is a whelk columella pendant, also a staple Mississippian image duplicated in actual costumery at other sites. Neither subject is known at Moundville, however, other than in this unique piece.

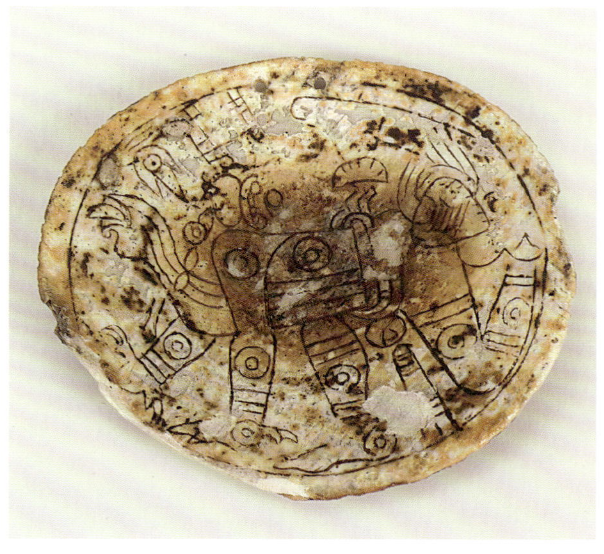

Styles and Social Context

Now that we have reviewed the various categories of objects found at Moundville, it remains for us to view this assemblage in broader perspective. Let us begin by sorting out the objects that we believe to be nonlocal. Perhaps the clearest examples are the Bellaire-style pipes, almost certainly made in the lower Mississippi valley, and the flint clay human-effigy pipe, probably crafted in or near Cahokia. Other likely imports include some (but not all) of the polychrome painted pots, and a great variety of items made of copper and shell that tend to be exceptional at Moundville but have close stylistic counterparts in other regions.

Once the "clutter" of these nonlocal items is stripped away, we are left with a numerically larger, but stylistically more coherent group of items that were almost certainly made locally, in or near Moundville. It would be incorrect to say that these items constitute a single style. Rather, we recognize several related styles, which are manifested in different kinds of objects. The best known of these local styles is the Hemphill style of engraved pottery. Many of these pots show considerable wear, as though they were used for a long time before being broken or buried.[49] It is reasonable to infer that they were used in ritual; whether they were also used as domestic serving vessels is still unclear. When buried as offerings, such pots are not confined to elite graves or cemeteries, but are found in seemingly ordinary graves in all parts of the Moundville site.[50] Although Hemphill style pots and sherds are concentrated at Moundville, they are not confined to this major site. They have also been found at a number of outlying sites, including small farmsteads.[51] We infer from these facts that Hemphill was a "public" style, which was accessible to, and used by, a broad cross section of Moundville society.

A second category of local items—copper gorgets and pendants, stone gorgets, stone palettes, painted pottery, and stone bowls—had distributions that were much more limited and were probably used mainly by the society's elite. These comprise what we call the "restricted" sphere of Moundville art. The pendants and gorgets in particular show a remarkable homogeneity in style, so much so that we suspect they were emblematic of a particular social status or sodality, such as a dance or medicine society. The palettes, painted pots, and stone bowls, on the other hand, likely had different meanings and uses. We suggest that these items, together with the imported massive effigy pipes, were ritual paraphernalia—objects used in ceremonies and personal ritual, only by select practitioners who had the necessary knowledge and training.

Taking an even broader view, we also see a thematic unity that crosscuts the "public" and "restricted"

Fig. 19 Bowl with serpent/bird effigy; Alabama, Tuscaloosa and Hale counties, Moundville, south of Mound D, A.D. 1250–1500; limestone, h. 10, diam. 23 cm; Smithsonian Institution, National Museum of the American Indian, Washington, D.C., no. 17/0020.

Fig. 20 Drawing of the incising on the underside of the limestone bowl shown in fig. 19; from Moore 1907, fig. 79.

Fig. 21 Engraved shell gorget with piasa; Alabama, Tuscaloosa and Hale counties, Moundville, northeast of Mound C, A.D. 1250–1500; marine shell, diam. 7.6 cm; Smithsonian Institution, National Museum of the American Indian, Washington, D.C., no. 17/1042.

is manifested by a strong predominance of motifs and themes that have meanings connected with death and the Beneath World.[52] Specifically, we point to the following patterns: the dominance of the swastika, a symbol associated with the underworld, as the central motif on the local pendants and gorgets made of copper and stone; the frequent appearance of the hand motif, which was seen by Indian peoples as a portal to the Path of Souls traversed by the dead; and the frequent appearance of serpents and feline piasas—alternate incarnations of the Great Serpent, widely regarded by Indians in the Eastern Woodlands as master of the Beneath World and protector of the realm of the dead.

This iconographic emphasis fits perfectly with what we know about Moundville's history at the time this art was being made and used: in the fourteenth and fifteenth centuries, Moundville was a necropolis, a place where the dead were brought for burial from throughout the surrounding region. It is reasonable to speculate that at least some of the priests and chiefs who lived at Moundville had a special connection with the Beneath World. It is also possible that Moundville itself may have been seen as a propitious point of entry to the Path of Souls, which would explain the iconographic emphasis on the hand motif. In either case, such beliefs would have provided powerful ideological support for the social and political power wielded by Moundville's elite residents.

It is interesting to note that depictions of the Great Serpent differ consistently between the public and the restricted spheres at Moundville. In the public sphere, which largely consists of Hemphill pottery, the Great Serpent is always shown as a winged rattlesnake, the wing being a locative that iconographically places this being in the sky—the Above World in the Indian cosmos. Depictions of Great Serpent on other artifacts at Moundville are quite different. The creature may be shown in feline or serpentine form—as in the Bellaire pipes and stone palettes, respectively—but it never appears with wings. This was the Great Serpent as it might be encountered in the Beneath World, a potentially dangerous place with which only individuals having the requisite knowledge and spiritual power dared to communicate. It is not surprising, therefore, that these wingless depictions appear exclusively on artifacts in our restricted sphere, that is, on ritual paraphernalia that were probably kept in sacred bundles and used only by ritual specialists or priests—some of whom may also have been Moundville's chiefs.

Also striking is the thematic distinctiveness of Moundville's art when compared to that of other Mississippian centers. For example, human figural representations are plentiful at Spiro and Etowah, but virtually absent at Moundville. Conversely, the hand motif, so prevalent at Moundville, is rare at Spiro and absent at Etowah. Also, unlike elsewhere in the Mississippian world, no shrine figures have ever been found in the Moundville region.[53] Taken together, these differences point up the fact that there never existed a single Southeastern Ceremonial Complex. Rather, the art and iconography of the Mississippian world comprised a set of regional complexes that shared certain themes and motifs, but at the same time retained a distinctiveness that was rooted in local history, as well as the various social and ritual contexts in which the objects were used.

Notes

Many of the ideas presented in this paper were developed at meetings of the Mississippian Iconographic Workshop at Texas State University in San Marcos. We thank Kent Reilly for inviting us to these meetings and wish to acknowledge the stimulating discussions and ideas prompted by all the participants, but especially those who have taken part in the Moundville working groups: Jim Brown, Jim Garber, Bob Hall, Mary Helms, George Lankford, Shirley Mott, Clay Shultz, and Ken York. We are also grateful to Steve Williams for his comments on an earlier draft and to Pat Galloway for translating the passages from Father du Ru's journal that are quoted herein.

1. Knight and Steponaitis 1998a, pp. 2–6; Steponaitis 1998.
2. Knight 1998.
3. For a history of scholarly work at Moundville, see Peebles et al. 1981 and Knight and Steponaitis 1998a, pp. 1–9. For a collection of articles that summarize current knowledge about the site, see Knight and Steponaitis 1998b.
4. The published chronology for Moundville, based on uncalibrated radiocarbon dates, places the span of each phase as follows: West Jefferson, A.D. 900–1050; Moundville I, 1050–1250; Moundville II, 1250–1400; Moundville III, 1400–1550; and Moundville IV (formerly Alabama River), 1550–1650 (Steponaitis 1983a; Knight and Steponaitis 1998a). Recently, Knight, Konigsberg, and Frankenberg (1999) have revised these spans using more dates, which have been both corrected for isotopic fractionation and calibrated for fluctuations in atmospheric carbon. This more sophisticated analysis has yielded a new set of calendrical spans: West Jefferson, A.D. 1020–1120; Moundville I, 1120–1260; Moundville II, 1260–1400; Moundville III, 1400–1520; and Moundville IV, 1520–1650. In effect, the two earliest phases have been shortened and their starting dates have been moved about a century later than previously estimated, while the three latest phases have been left more or less the same. This revised chronology is the one we have adopted for present purposes.
5. Our historical account is abstracted from a more complete synthesis that has been published elsewhere; see Knight and Steponaitis 1998a, pp. 10–25 and references therein. The calendrical chronology, however, has been altered as explained in the preceding note.
6. Brown 1989.
7. Steponaitis 1983a, pp. 54–63, 317–18.
8. Neff et al. 1991.
9. The parameters of the Hemphill style have recently been worked out in a series of master's theses written under the direction of Vernon J. Knight: see Lacefield 1995, Schatte 1997, and Gillies 1998.
10. Lankford 2005c.
11. Lacefield 1995; Schatte 1997.
12. Neff et al. 1991; cf. Steponaitis, Blackman, and Neff 1996.
13. For illustrations and discussion of these palettes see Moore 1905; Moore 1907; Webb and DeJarnette 1942; Mellown 1976, pp. 9–10; Krebs et al. 1986, pp. 48, 52, 102. Specifically excluded from this category are two artifacts, also made of fine micaceous

sandstone, that are decorated but irregularly shaped. We refer to these as "tablets" and suspect that they are functionally different from the palettes. One is illustrated by Moore (1907, fig. 89, upper left) and the other by Knight (1992, fig. 14).
14. Moore 1905, pp. 145–47; Moore 1907, p. 392.
15. See Whitney, Steponaitis, and Rogers 2002. Sites with abundant debris consisting of this sandstone occur near the outcrops, but this debris cannot as yet be definitively tied to the manufacture of the elaborate palettes found at Moundville (cf. Johnson and Sherard 2000).
16. For example, compare fig. 19 with fig. 25 in Moore 1905.
17. For previously published illustrations and descriptions of the Rattlesnake Disk, see Moore 1905, pp. 134–37; Mellown 1976, p. 9; Krebs et al. 1986, p. 48. The case for interpreting the hand as a portal has been made by Lankford 2005c (see also the essays by George Lankford and Kent Reilly in this volume).
18. For previously published illustrations and descriptions, see Moore 1905, pp. 131–34; Mellown 1976, p. 9.
19. Franke 1998; Knight and Franke 2005.
20. Webb and DeJarnette 1942, p. 58.2; Steponaitis 1983b, p. 138; Knight 2002, p. 116.
21. The Tennessee valley specimen comes from Seven Mile Island (1Lu21) in the Pickwick Basin (Webb and DeJarnette 1942, pl. 58.2). The other example was found at Wildcat Bend (22Lo558) in the central Tombigbee valley (Rucker 1974, pp. 85–86, pl. 4c).
22. Mellown 1976, p. 11; Krebs et al. 1986, p. 50; Marcoux 2000, pp. 57–58, figs. 7–8.
23. Brown 2005c.
24. For examples, see the numerous specimens illustrated in Moore 1905 and Moore 1907.
25. Goad 1978; see also Hurst and Larson 1958, Rapp et al. 2000.
26. Knight 2002, pp. 117–18; Markin 1997; Scarry 1995, p.83.
27. McGhee-Snow 1999.
28. The first two types are described and illustrated by Moore (1905, pp. 162–63, 198, figs. 45, 105); the bilobed-arrow ornament is unpublished and resides in the collections of the Alabama Museum of Natural History.
29. See the relevant observations and comparisons in Brain and Phillips 1996, pp. 308, 329, 373.
30. Descriptions of and commentary on the Lubbub plate can be found in Jenkins 1982, pp. 130–32, fig. 22; Jenkins and Krause 1986, p. 97, fig. 26c; Brain and Phillips 1996, p. 285. For an extended discussion of the "classic Etowah" copper style, see Phillips and Brown 1978, pp. 185–93. More recently, Brain and Phillips (1996, pp. 368–71) have assigned the Lubbub plate to their "Wulfing style," which also has strong representation at Etowah. The Georgia counterpart of the Lubbub plate was found at the Shinholser site; see M. Williams 1990, fig. 35, pp. 232–33; Williams 1994, fig. 5, p. 189.
31. Brain and Phillips 1996, pp. 384–88.
32. Phillips and Brown 1978, pp. 140–43.
33. See published examples in Thruston 1890, fig. 84; Moore 1905, figs. 1–3, 165, 166; Mellown 1976, p. 12; Krebs et al. 1986, p. 104; Cox 1985, pl. 6; Scarry 1995, fig. 86.
34. Lankford 2005b.
35. Steponaitis and Dockery 1997.
36. Moore 1905, figs. 131–32.
37. Emerson et al. 2003, pp. 300–301.
38. Translated by Patricia K. Galloway from the original manuscript, which resides in the Newberry Library (Ayer MS 262, pp. 64–65). In French, the key passage reads: *"six grandes Ecuelles de bois dont une ance represente la queue d'un cigne et une autre le col qu'on remplit de farine. . . ."* The word *ecuelle* typically refers to a bowl with two handles, and *ance* is simply an alternate spelling of the word *anse*, meaning handle. The one previously published translation of this passage is unsatisfactory, in that it inexplicably leaves out the mention of handles (see du Ru 1934 [1700], p. 42).
39. Moore 1905, p. 238.
40. Knight, Brown, and Lankford 2001, pp. 133–34, internal references omitted.
41. Moore 1907, figs. 76–79.
42. Phillips and Brown 1978, p. 149, 156.
43. Brain and Phillips 1996, p. 296.
44. Brain and Phillips 1996, pp. 298–99.
45. Moore 1905, fig. 34.
46. Brown 2005b.
47. Brain and Phillips 1996, p. 301.
48. Moore 1907, fig. 98.
49. Good examples of Hemphill sherds from mound contexts are documented by Knight (1995, 2002); sherds from off-mound residential areas at Moundville are described by Steponaitis (1983a); and whole vessels from burials are illustrated by Moore (1905, 1907). The heavy wear that sometimes occurs on these vessels is evident in published photographs (e.g., Moore 1907, fig. 60) and has been observed by the authors in the collections they have studied.
50. See, for examples, the descriptions in Moore 1905 and 1907.
51. DeJarnette and Peebles 1970, pp. 98–101; Mistovich 1986, pp. 75–77.
52. These meanings have been persuasively reconstructed in a series of seminal papers by George Lankford. For his arguments concerning the swastika, see Lankford 2002; for the Path of Souls, see Lankford 2005c; for the Great Serpent, see Lankford 2005b. Although the Great Serpent was commonly viewed as master of the underworld (or, in Lankford's terms, the "Beneath World") and protector of the realm of the dead, it is not clear whether these two places were regarded as the same. In many of the stories that Lankford (2005c) cites, the realm of the dead is described as being "in the south," without reference to any specific layer in the Native cosmos. A few stories locate the realm of the dead in the Above World, and at least one places it "beneath the earth-disk," which seems to imply the Beneath World.
53. For comparative material from Spiro and Etowah, see Moorehead 1932a, Phillips and Brown 1978, Brown 1996, and Brain and Phillips 1996. Although the hand motif is absent at Etowah proper, it is engraved on the Wilbanks monolithic axe, which is said to have been found in the same region (Williams 1968, pp. 78–80). Yet here the exception proves the rule, for the engraving on this artifact seems stylistically out of place. As Phillips and Brown put it, the design on this axe "shows Spiroan and Moundville affinities in approximately equal strength, with Etowah—only twenty miles away—scarcely represented" (1978, p. 193). A thorough discussion of Mississippian shrine figures can be found in Brown 2001.

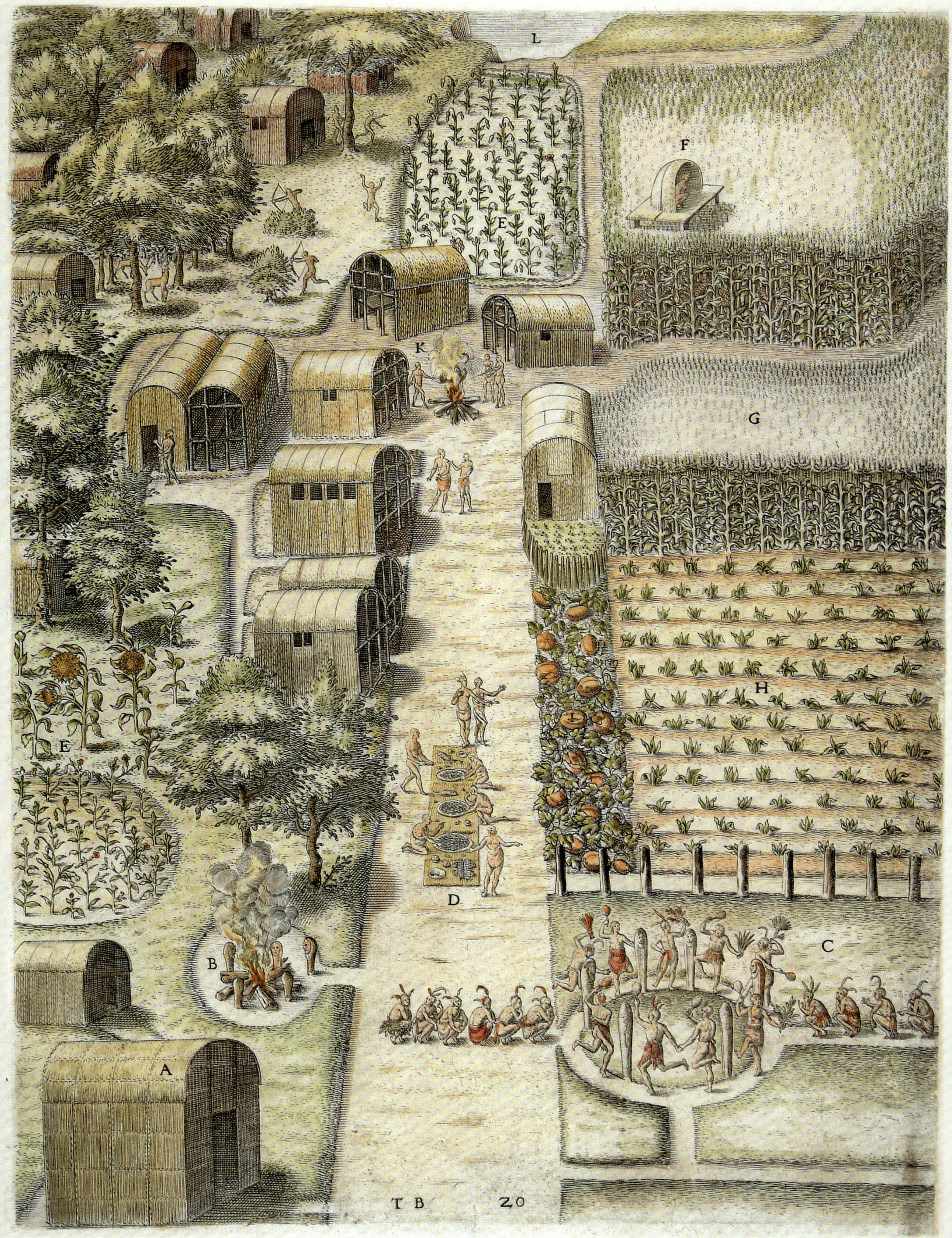
L
F
E
K
G
H
E
D
B
C
A
T B
20

Thoughts on the Preservation of Traditional Culture

F. Kent Reilly III

An Interview with Joyce and Turner Bear

Fig. 1 Theodor de Bry (Flemish; 1528–1598), after an original watercolor by John White (English; fl. 1585–1593), *The Town of Secota*, 1590; from *America*, 2nd ed. (Frankfurt-am-Main, 1600), pt. 1, pl. 20; Rucker Agee Map Collection, Birmingham Public Library, Alabama. Cat. no. 283. Englishman John White helped establish a colony at Roanoke Island, Virginia, in 1585 and made numerous watercolors of flora, fauna, and Native American communities along the coast. These drawings were engraved for publication by De Bry and were published in Frankfurt, Germany, in a ten-volume compilation of travel literature issued between 1590 and 1618.

December 28, 2002

Kent Reilly: The 1940s and 1950s took a terrible toll on the cultural and linguistic survival of Native Americans throughout the United States. There were specific efforts by both state and federal agencies to suppress Indian identity. In particular, elementary school programs were structured so that Native American languages could not be spoken by students. What do you think the overall effect of that educational system has been in terms of Creek culture and of Native American culture in general?

Turner Bear: Schools weren't the only ones responsible for stifling American Indian culture. It was already ingrained in the general population that we were going to educate our students in English only. I was born and reared in the traditional culture from birth to the first grade, attending the ceremonial programs, participating in the taking of traditional medicines, and in the eating of food. I participated in all the social functions that involved a lot of Native Americans and so I had a full understanding of the culture. Also, the Creek language I learned from my family. But, when I started first grade, Mom and Dad said, "Son, you're not going to speak the Creek language anymore." I asked why not, and they replied, "You're going to a white school and if you're going to succeed in a white school you're going to learn and speak only English." Right there it seemed like the suppression came from my own family, so I didn't speak the language any more. Some of my parents' Creek friends, however, did speak Creek to one another, which I could understand. Sometimes my parents would run me outside, saying, "You don't need to be back there listening, go out and play." But sometimes I would sneak back into the house and stand behind the door and listen to what they were saying. So that was my experience with the Native American language.

KR: You mentioned that once you went to school you no longer participated in the rituals. Did you have a sense that you were losing something by going to this school?

TB: No, at the time I felt that I didn't lose anything. Nor did I realize that this loss was a very important experience in my life. But as I got older and out into the non-Indian world I began to realize that there was something missing. But I didn't take the time to examine or analyze what was missing.

KR: Joyce, you are the Historic Preservation Officer for the Muscogee Nation, and Turner, you have a long and distinguished career teaching in secondary and higher education. You both grew up in the post–World War II era. As you got older, how did government restrictions on learning the language and participating in rituals affect you personally?

Joyce Bear: In my family, we were learning the language, even though it was never taught in the schools. We were exposed to the language at home or at church. I was raised in a Christian home, yet it was always taught to my parents that worshiping the Creator was different from the traditional culture of our southeastern people. Nevertheless, missionaries in our churches spoke the Creek language, which, oddly enough, is the key to preserving the whole culture of our Nation because traditional life is conducted in our language. If we don't preserve that language, we will lose our culture; we'll lose so much of the heritage and the traditions of our tribe.

KR: Turner, you mentioned that in school you quit participating in ceremonies. When did you begin participating in ceremonies again?

TB: In our home town we were the only Indian family in a population of about 2,500 and everyone knew we were Indian and I didn't have any difficulty with that. As I began to advance in the educational system, I began to realize that we didn't project the image of being Indian; we were considered to be just like any other student in school. In retrospect, I realize that the federal government was trying to unite all the ethnic groups or races in the United States to speak one language—English—as if one language spoken by all groups would unite the country. The federal government policy was the melting pot theory. But American Indian languages are not compatible with this form of unification because each tribe speaks its own language. Native Americans realize that this was something we do not want to do—we do not want to give up our language.

KR: What types of family traditions, languages, stories, etc., did you hear?

TB: I heard various family traditions, of course, my family being full-bloods [i.e., one who has never intermarried with non-Indians]. We participated in the traditions of the ceremonial grounds, where occasionally I would go with my parents. They upheld the values of the American Indian families. But as far as resisting the forces of assimilation, I think inwardly my parents had already accepted assimilation because that was one of the ways the federal government was trying to work. We look at assimilation as part of the government's policies. From early colonial times to the present, the first things they were trying to do were to isolate and segregate. When those two strategies weren't working, they developed the policy of removal from the southeastern part of the United States where the Muscogee peoples had been located. (This led to the Trails of Tears as described in Garrick Bailey's essay in this volume.) Finally they developed a policy for assimilating the American Indian into the national society.

KR: May I ask you what tribal town you belonged to when you were growing up?

Fig. 2 George Catlin (American; 1796–1872), *Ball Play of the Choctaw–Ball Up*, 1834–35; oil on canvas; 49.5 × 69.9 cm; Smithsonian Museum of American Art, gift of Mrs. Joseph Harrison, Jr., 1985.66.428.

Fig. 3 Native American students at the Hampton Institute in Virginia, founded in 1868, were taught to play baseball as part of their assimilation into American culture. Identified in this photograph are, back row, William Harrison (Winnebago), Alfred Powless, Jesse Cornelius (Oneida), another member of the Powless family, and Amos Reed; front row, Albert Ninham, Corey LaFlesche (Omaha); and another member of the Ninham family.

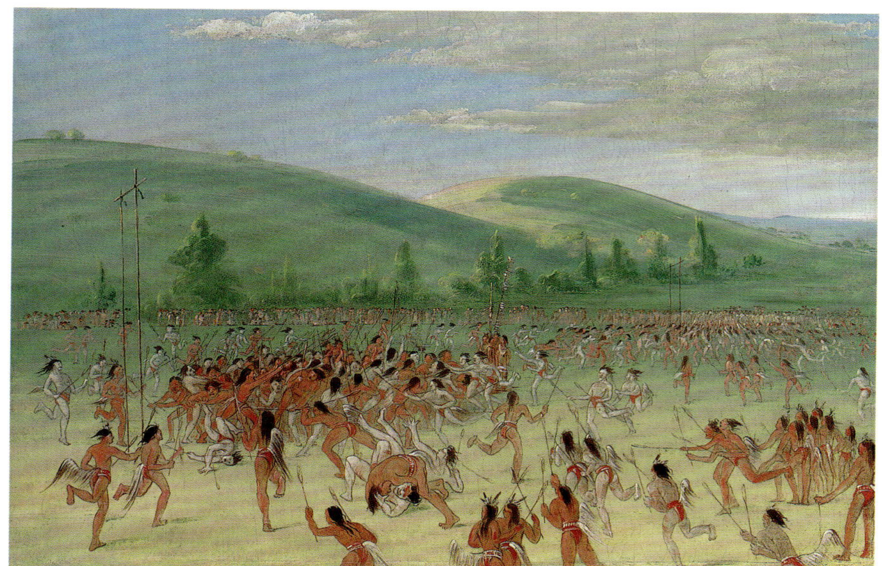

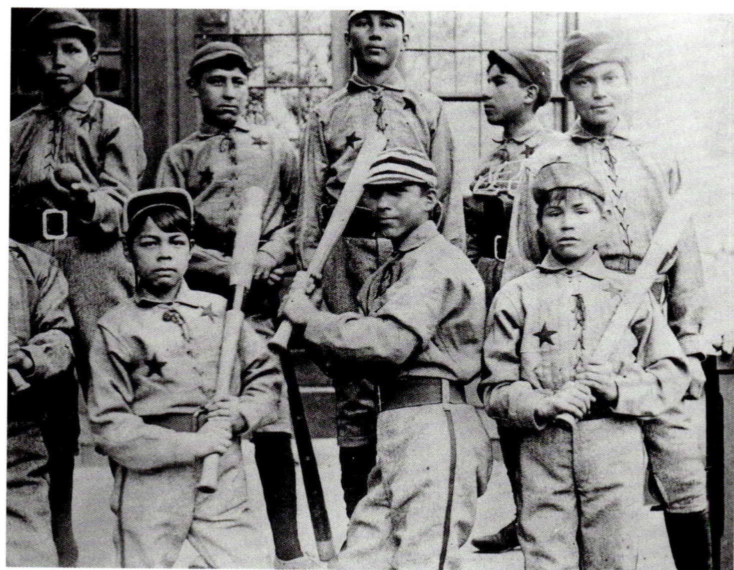

TB: I belonged to the Eufaula; we called it Ufalagee. I think nowadays they call it Ufala Canadian, but it was originally Ufalagee, which is no longer active as I knew it. When I was young, they still had the fire, but it's not active as far as a ceremonial ground.[1]

JB: In the other part of the Muscogee Nation where I grew up, at Coweta the traditional fires had gone out years ago, so my family pretty much assimilated. My father went to boarding school at four years old, my mother went to boarding school at seven years old and so consequently they were educated in the non-Indian way. When we five children came along, we also were assimilated right along with them at school. Nevertheless, at home we spoke the language and had foods that were prepared in the traditional way. A lot of our environment, the way we grew up, was still in the traditional way. But we crossed over a threshold every morning when we boarded the school bus and attended the public school. But we always knew we were Creek Indians. We lived just like anyone else, yet we always knew we were different.

KR: Do you remember when you went to your first ceremony?

JB: I wasn't allowed to go to a ceremonial until I was a grown woman. It was because Christian missionaries taught my father that to attend the ceremonial dances was against the Christian religion. We were definitely discouraged from participating in ceremonial life at the fires. It wasn't until years later, when I was a grown woman, that I realized I had learned of other Indian cultures but had never been allowed to learn about my own. That's when I started getting more and more interested. I started attending some of the ceremonial grounds to learn, because I knew no one else in my family was. And I felt someday that my grandchildren or my nieces or nephews would want to know about traditional Creek culture. Some things can not be learned out of a book; some things have to be taught from generation to generation, and so that's why I started to get more and more involved. It wasn't really until about twenty years ago when I married Mr. Turner Bear that I started to learn more because of his family. I saw how I had been deprived of learning my own culture and about my own people.

KR: What tradition, what township would you have belonged to, even though the fires were out? And what township do you participate in today?

JB: I am a member of the Luchvpokv, which is the Turtle Town, and it came from Alabama, our mother taught us that, and we knew what clan we are, the Ahalakvlke, which is the Sweet Potato clan. I always knew that, but yet we were not allowed to participate in their ceremonies because we were encouraged to go to the Christian churches instead.

KR: I'd like to ask both of you, Turner and Joyce, what role can tribal-supported education play in the preservation of Muscogee culture today?

TB: Tribes can play a very, very important role in education of their respective tribal members. Who else knows more about us than our own tribal government? We need to learn more about our own culture because it's up to those who have educated themselves and become more knowledgeable about the culture to feed it back to the uneducated. In a sense our elders were deprived of a full education whether they realize it or not. We've had so many academics write about our Native or American Indian people that what these people learn about Indians comes from scholars, especially non-Indian academicians, when our own people want to write about ourselves and determine what we want to tell the general public.

JB: I believe that of course our tribe needs to listen more and more to our people who have actually lived and helped preserve the culture. These people still attend ceremonial grounds and still go to the Poskelv [Green Corn—New Fire] every summer. Language is entwined with the culture and the traditions. You have to admire the people who are still in our Nation and have hung on to these traditions with such great strength, preserving it for the rest of us. You're not going to get it in public school, although now we do have a K–3 introduction to the language and the curriculum already developed within forty-two of the public schools within the Muscogee Nation boundaries. But it's not mandatory to take the language classes. I believe the language is going to be preserved with the Head Start program here in our own Nation and also from our tribal centers teaching adults at night. Parents can reinforce the language that's being taught today while their children are still very young.

TB: For the preservation of the tribe, I've always emphasized that we need the language, we need the culture, but most importantly, we need our Medicine People.[2] These three important things will keep us continuing as a Muscogee Nation. Our Medicine People have saved more knowledge of the tribe than any other tribal members. In learning the medicine ways, they start from birth to the time they have, in a sense, their own practice at the ceremonial grounds. Our Medicine Men believe in holistic medicine and people of our tribe and nation still go to them for help or advice.

As far as preserving Muscogee culture, we need more involvement by our tribal members in the ceremonial grounds and participation in the dances. How are new generations going to learn, if they are slowly getting away from the practice of the ceremonial grounds? A lot of time I think this causes problems among our young people because they think that education or knowledge of our tribe should be instinctive and instantaneous, but with Indian culture you have to live it, eat it, swallow it, and smell it.

As we become more knowledgeable about our own culture, and as we teach young people about it and have them participate in the ceremonial grounds, they will develop a higher appreciation of their heritage.

A lot of young people participating in the Stomp Dances [traditional social dances] on Saturday nights are hungry for something that they're not getting in a formal education, to support their need for more knowledge about our own people. We need to fill that gap. A lot of times, too, our young people are brought up with the notion that you can either be white or you can be Indian. And yet to make a choice is wrong because they can accept both value systems and work with them and take which is best, or they can combine the values for their personal benefit.

KR: Do either of you have additional comments to make about the survival of traditional Muscogee culture in a consumerist and government-dominated world?

JB: I can remember when I was growing up there were a lot of things, especially during World War II, that we had to assimilate. We lived on a small vegetable farm and we were pretty much self-supporting. Mother had government ration stamps to pay for sugar or coffee at the grocery store, but they really weren't available even to buy. My father found a bee tree in the woods and got the honey to substitute for sugar. He also traded vegetables to a man who lived about forty-five miles away who had a sorghum mill. We are a part of the land and we believe that the land is part of us. In order to survive we always go back to the land. As I said, we were farmers, and we went hunting for small game like rabbits and squirrels. We went into the forest for mushrooms, wild greens, nuts and berries, and wild plums; this is what we ate along with the vegetables that we grew in our farms. We went back to ways of living as hunter-gatherers in order to survive through that period of time (see figs. 1, 4–7).

TB: I would like to interject my thoughts here about how government influences and policies affected the American Indian. They have affected us in a sometimes subtle way, as if we were their children, you could say. They forcibly removed us to Oklahoma, yes, but then, after a period of years, the government again intervened by supervising our financial business. For example, my dad had some money, yet every time he needed it he had to talk to the Bureau of Indian Affairs office in Muskogee. We lived in a community about twenty-three miles south of Muskogee and when we came to hard times, my dad would go up to the area office and ask for the funds he had in his special account. As Indians we had what we called an individual Indian money account with Bureau of Indian Affairs who managed these funds. I know in some cases they'd say, no, you can't have it or you used up all your money, or what are you going to use this money for? It shouldn't have been their concern, but that's the way they treated individual Indian money account holders. So, the federal government really influenced us: they educated our children, put them in boarding schools, and if you look at it, whoever's handing out the money usually has the control. The government has control of the Native American population and the American Indian governments, and the only way we are going to get away from that is for our own tribal governments to assert ourselves and manage our own money. This new financial sovereignty will give the American Indian tribes a chance to become autonomous and not remain dependent upon the federal government and their policies.

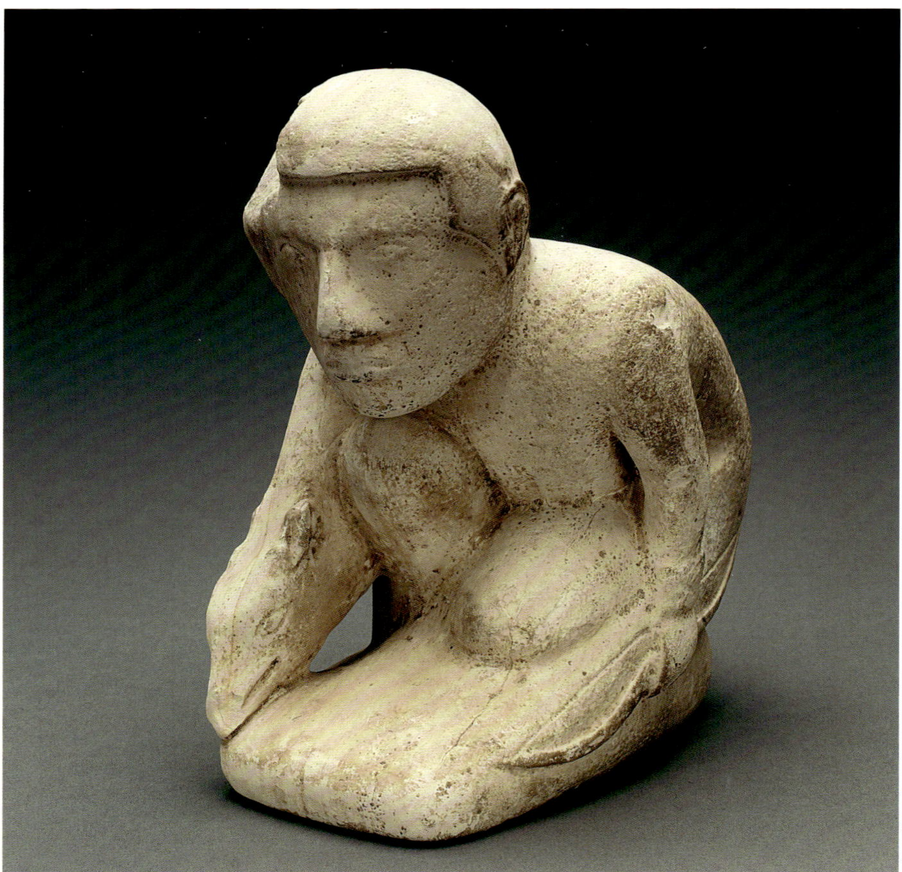

Fig. 4 Crouching hunter effigy; Missouri, 13th century; limestone, h. 17.8 cm; Smithsonian Institution, National Museum of Natural History, Washington, D.C. Cat. no. 105.

KR: Moving to questions associated with the exhibition, people talk about the symbols and these Mississippian art objects as metaphors. It's generally accepted that metaphors are unique to the language of the system in which they exist. If that is true, then can the art objects and symbols displayed in this exhibition serve as an impetus to both the Native American educational systems in general, and the Muscogee educational systems, specifically, for language preservation and also for language survival?

JB: I surely believe they will. This exhibition will show Muscogean people what their ancestors created. The objects themselves are also magnificent records of the ways that they were created. These ways have now been lost. A perfect example are the Etowah marble effigies: how did they carve those without the modern tools that we have today? How did they smooth out that marble? What other kinds of stories do these objects tell, in addition to their symbolism?

KR: Do you think that this exhibition might stimulate interest in learning the Muscogee language?

JB: I definitely do. We're already seeing this interest in language expressed in our monthly newspaper. Just about three months ago we began including a page not only in Muscogean language but also in the Yuchi language. There's just the one page, but it has stimulated so much curiosity that people want to know what it says. We've had numerous inquiries about language classes.

TB: American Indians and the general population will be interested in the contribution of the American Indians to American society today. This would promote self-esteem and will encourage our young people to know more about their American Indian heritage. Also, it would point out the ways in which American Indians influenced the United States of America in becoming a country. For instance, there's evidence that in inventing our type of democratic government, the founders looked to the league of the Iroquois as well as to the Greeks of Athens. The Muscogee Creeks were known for their diplomacy and they could survive and exist with all nations. When nations that they dealt with wanted to take over Creek country, the Muscogee Creeks were able to use diplomacy to settle arguments. In their own private cultures today they have documents settling controversies within their own Creek boundaries.

KR: During our preparatory meetings for this exhibition, in Oklahoma and in the Art Institute of Chicago, we have emphasized that the exhibition should be of value to Native Americans and non-Native American communities. During these discussions there have been agreements and disagreements about the meaning of Native American history and the specific aspects of their culture. Turner, in what way, in your opinion, will the exhibition serve as a sounding board for public discussions of these very important perceptions?

TB: I taught Native American and American history in high school, and every time the opportunity presented itself I would try to interject Indian history into American history because American history includes Indian history. And yet our curriculum specialists and our educators have been reluctant to recognize this. I think that they want to see that this country was developed exclusively by Americans, which does not give the due recognition to the Native Americans. Yet without our understanding of the environment and how to produce food goods, the non-Indians would not have survived at the beginning. The Mayflower landed on Indian shores (Plymouth, Mass.) without adequate food supply or time to plant crops. Consequently they were wholly dependent upon Native Americans. And Native Americans, wanting to take care of our fellow man, helped them to survive that first harsh winter. Even in our own state we have Oklahoma history, but it's not about the Indian history and it's not detailed. In eastern Oklahoma everyone thinks, well, I've been around the Indians, I've been reared with the Indians, I've eaten with them and I know all about them. But they don't, and as a result of not knowing, a lot of times I think we still have differences. To understand and appreciate works of art that were produced by the American Indians, descriptions of the objects in this exhibition should be very simple in order to reach the broadest possible audience.

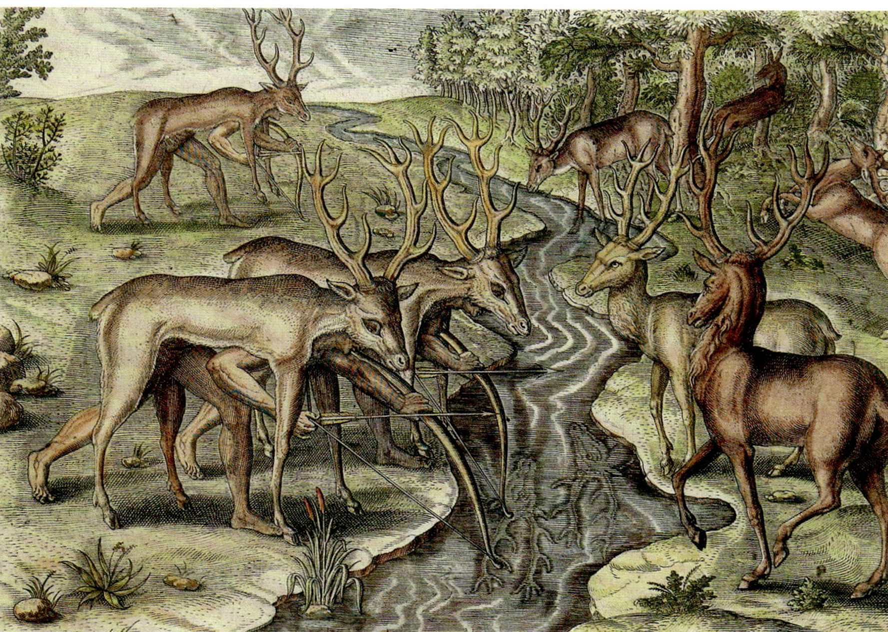

Fig. 5 Theodor de Bry, after an original painting of 1564 by Jacques Le Moyne de Morgues (French; c. 1533–1588), *Hunting Deer*, 1591; from *America*, 2nd ed. (Frankfurt-am-Main, 1609), pt. 2, pl. 25; Rucker Agee Map Collection, Birmingham Public Library, Alabama. Cat. no. 277. Artist Jacques Le Moyne accompanied a French expedition to Florida in 1564 under the direction of René de Laudonnière, and there recorded many practices of the Timucua Indians that were later engraved and published by De Bry.

JB: This exhibition is going to show that there was a civilization here on this continent long before Europeans ever appeared. It's also going to show that we were a civilization and we had our own governments, we had our own way of life. The history of this continent started a long, long time ago. The exhibition is going to make our tribal people realize that we are descendants from a wonderful and great culture. Our ancestors built imposing pyramids in the southeastern part of the United States, up in the Mississippi River valley, and all the way up into the Ohio valley. Beautiful art forms also came from there. Our people were great artists. Our people were great leaders in their own right. Visitors will gather a different understanding from how Hollywood has always portrayed the American Indian people.

KR: Currently there are certain Native American religious restrictions on the display and handling of ancient objects that may have associations with the honored dead. How can these objects be respectfully handled and displayed in our exhibition so that they become the voices of those honored ancestors, speaking and educating modern populations?

TB: Our American Indian restrictions have been handed down from century to century. We promote these restrictions in modern Creek culture because there are certain things that we do with our deceased. I can give you an example from my own family. When my father passed away, we didn't have ceremonies, drum-beating, or other Hollywood-type depictions of how we should handle it. Instead, we just had Dad dressed in a suit, the way they were during that era. There were one or two things we did with the coffin, and there were certain rituals for the interment of the body that are widely practiced. For example, in what we call the

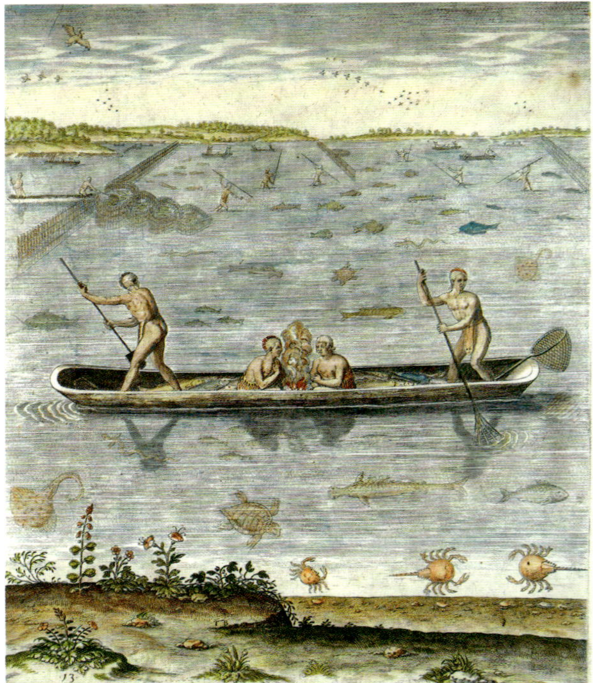

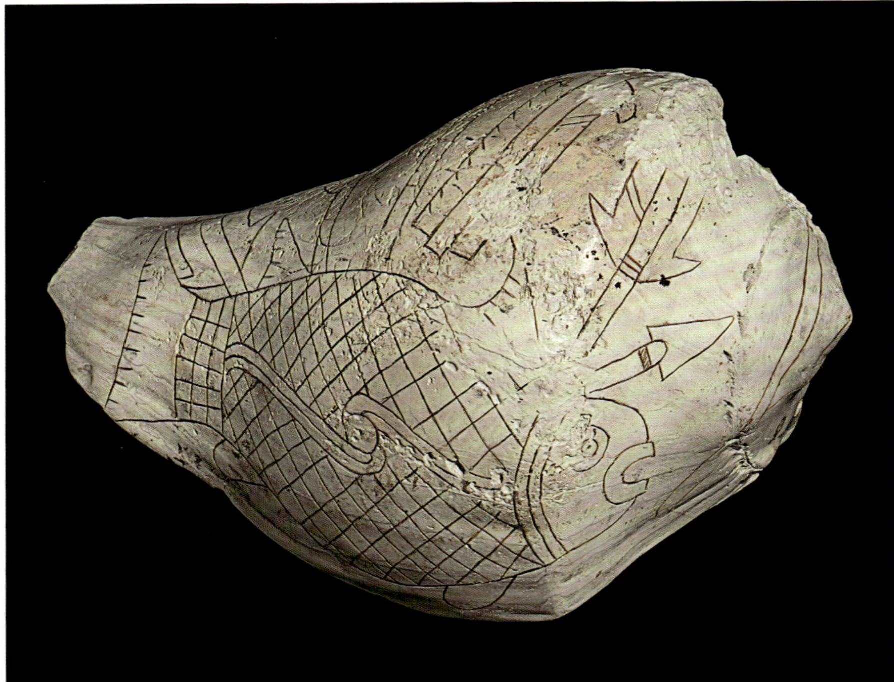

Fig. 6 Theodor de Bry, after an original watercolor by John White, *How They Catch Fish*, 1590; from *America*, 2nd ed. (Frankfurt-am-Main, 1600), pt. 1, pl. 13; Rucker Agee Map Collection, Birmingham Public Library, Alabama. Cat. no. 281.

Fig. 7 Engraved whelk shell showing fish being speared; Craig C style; Oklahoma, LeFlore County, Spiro, Craig Mound, A.D. 1200–1350; marine shell, l. 25.4 cm; Smithsonian Institution, National Museum of the American Indian, Washington, D.C. Cat. no. 137.

"hand of friendship," the mourners take shovels full of dirt and stand on the sides of the grave, and anyone can participate by taking a handful of dirt and throwing it into the grave. Somebody behind you would step up to do the same thing until everyone participates. All the men would then help cover the grave with their shovels, taking turns when a person gets tired, until every one of the males participates.

JB: I was taught that the Milky Way is the highway to heaven, or a highway to a better place and the stars in the Milky Way are the souls. As people pass on from this life and are making a journey to somewhere else, they will need things to help them with that journey. Food that is prepared by the loved ones, friends, and family is put inside the grave, along with goods or objects that were dear to the departed. It might be an arrow point, it might be a bowl, it might be some part of their clothing. If they were a warrior, the breastplate was put in. We still do that. We still include a quilt or blanket with the body because we believe that as they are making their journey they might be tired and want to rest and so they have their blanket and they have their food and water to drink. The exhibition will respectfully explain the context of these objects, noting what they are and how they were used. Explanations with privileged information will be left mainly to our Medicine People, because they are the ones who have that knowledge. Other information belongs strictly to women and they can't talk about some of this. The man's role is similarly privileged.

KR: How does the proposed exhibition reinforce your personal connection to the distant history of the Muscogee people? How does it underscore your commitment to the preservation and advancement of knowledge about Muscogee heritage?

JB: When our people were forcibly removed into Indian Territory (Oklahoma) in the 1830s on what we call the infamous "Trails of Tears" (fig. 8), we brought the culture and traditions of the old Mississippian world with us. We never forgot our ancient homelands in the southeastern part of the United States. I remember as a child my mother used to talk about huge mounds that were in Georgia and Alabama, which were referred to as the "Old Homelands," and she would say, those are our ancestors—the "old folks" or the "old people." My mother was born in 1910 and only had about a tenth-grade formal education, but yet she knew about them because she was taught through oral tradition. And to me there is a connection between seeing this exhibition and something that my mother had told us about, that her mother told her, and her mother had told her, and it was passed down through the generations. And so it has connected me, as a modern person in the twenty-first century, that I'm a descendant from those who built the mounds. Mother used to say she wished she could go back to Georgia and see the mounds. I descend from the old people who made these works of art and this exhibition is making it more realistic to me, opening my eyes. I'm gaining much more honor, more respect, and knowledge about who my people are. It's showing me that I come from kings and queens, and my bloodlines are just as strong and as pure as we see in old European culture. I'm really excited about going back to those old stories that I heard as a child and making that connection to the distant past.

TB: Either my family was not very knowledgeable about the old Southeast culture, or they thought somebody else might tell me about it—kinfolk who came from there perhaps; but I was not aware of it. As I've grown older, however, I have done some research and have

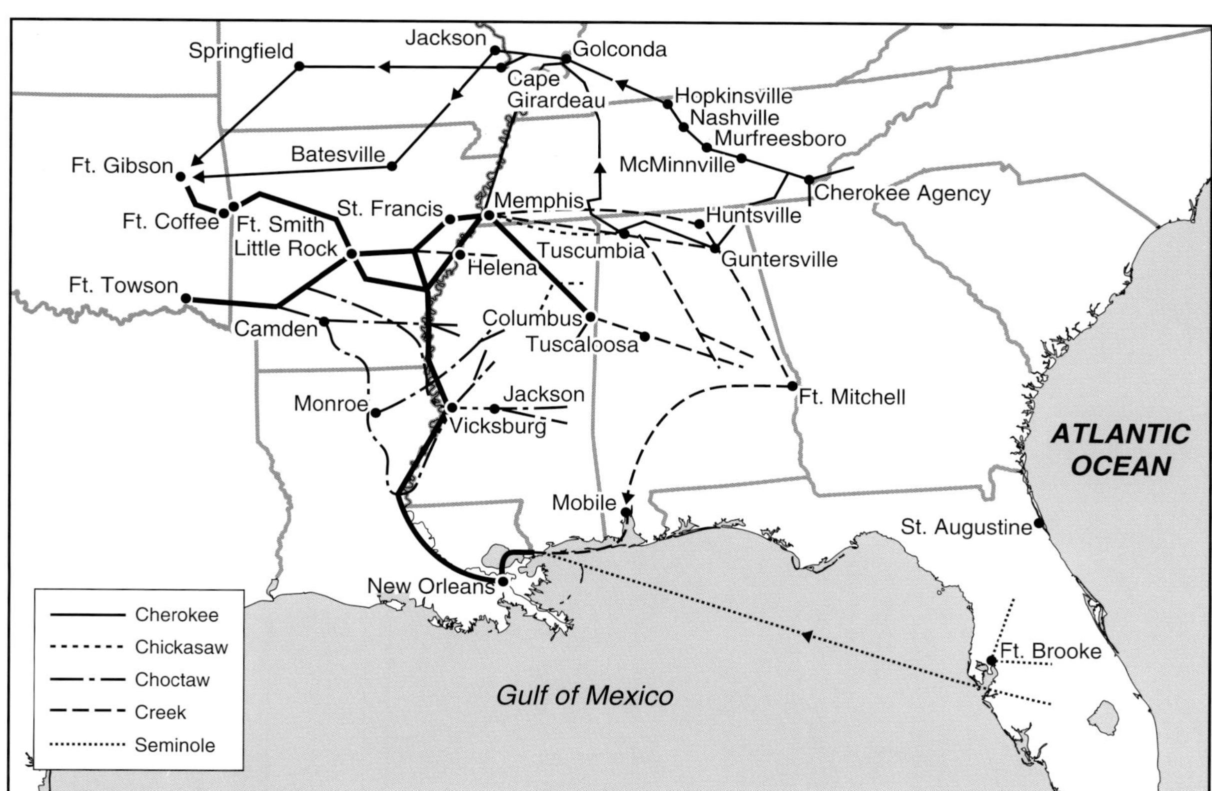

Fig. 8 Map of the Trails of Tears, showing the paths of forced removal of five Native American tribes—Cherokee, Choctaw, Chickasaw, Creek, and Seminole—from their homelands in the Southeast to present-day Oklahoma: Choctaw in 1831–33; Creek, 1836–37; Chickasaw and Cherokee, 1835–38; and Seminole, 1859.

developed more interest. This interest developed when I was working for the Cherokee Nation. We had East Cherokee and West Cherokee council meetings in which all the departments would get together and talk about shared problems. One year, on the way to Cherokee, North Carolina, Joyce suggested going to see the mounds at Ocmulgee National Monument near Macon, Georgia. I reluctantly agreed but there my eyes were opened. These mounds, located in historically Creek country, were akin to the Egyptian pyramids, or to those of the Yucatan peninsula, and others in Mesoamerica. Yet they were located here within our borders. I was intrigued and inspired to learn about the civilization they represented. Like Joyce, I was very impressed that we belonged to that culture. We had studied Greek, Roman, Egyptian, Mesopotamian, and Chinese civilizations in American schools, and here was something just as unique. Yet the mounds were not getting the recognition they deserved. So I decided that I wanted to learn more. As Preservation Officer in the Muscogee Nation, Joyce is now developing programs to promote the culture to our people here in Oklahoma. She helped charter buses so that our own elderly, middle aged, or young people could see the Ocmulgee and other mounds. These visits have stimulated more interest and curiosity. And now periodically, various groups from Muscogee Nation go to see these ancient sites. Educators should promote the Art Institute's exhibition as an opportunity to learn about an ancient civilization in the United States the public knows little about. By recognizing that American Indians created that culture, people will begin to realize and accept how much we have really contributed to our collective society.

I would like for this exhibition to develop a curiosity among Native American people. There's always the curiosity about where did I come from as an Indian? What did I participate in? And what about my ancestors? I know I have ancestors that lived in the Southeast, but did they create these art objects as a way of communicating with us? Because I think all individuals at some time or another in their life will question, "What am I going to leave for my kids?" Just as they see what these ancestors have left for us. I think that this should serve as an impetus for my own Muscogee people, just as for the Caddo and all other Indian tribal communities, to want to learn, study, and interpret what our elders know so that we can transmit this knowledge to younger generations.

Notes

1. The ceremonial ground "fire" is rekindled every year and symbolizes the life of the community and the world around it.
2. Medicine Men are the priests, curers, and preservers of traditional practices. They are trained in ceremonial prayers and language.

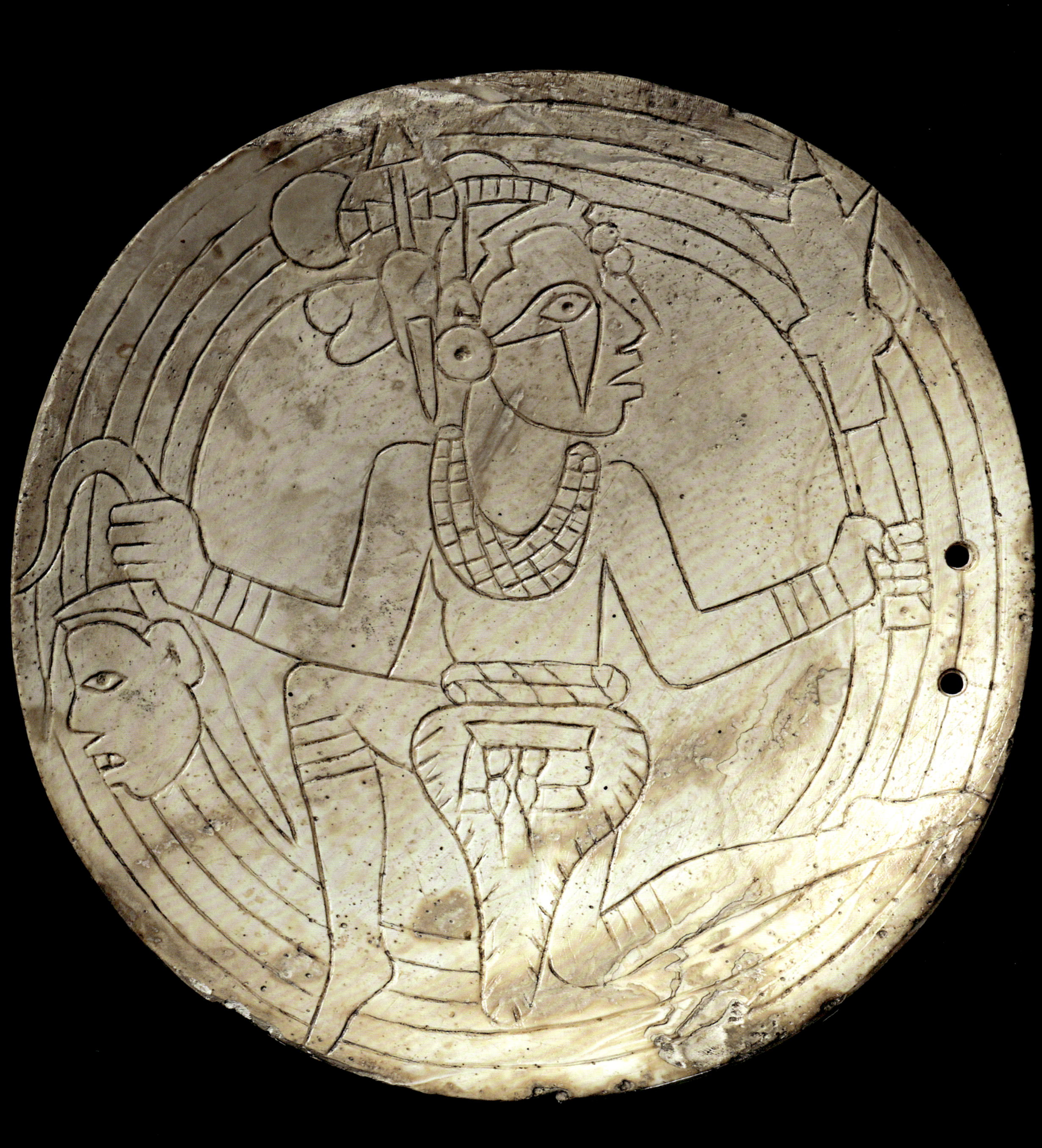

Art, Ritual, and Chiefly Warfare in the Mississippian World

David H. Dye

Fig. 1 Engraved shell gorget with supernatural warrior holding a severed head and mace; Tennessee, Sumner County, Castalian Springs site, A.D. 1250–1350; marine shell, diam. 9.7 cm; Smithsonian Institution, National Museum of the American Indian, Washington, D.C. Cat. no. 142. The swastika-like figural pose on this gorget illustrates an artistic convention used to express dynamic action. Worn as a badge of rank and office, the image testifies to the deeds required for the advancement of warriors.

On a hot summer night in the mid-fourteenth-century Southeast, a chief prepares for a raid on his enemies. The forest is quiet and still as his warriors solemnly approach their fortified capital at the lake's edge. The Sacred Warrior, the priestly leader of the war party, and his war commanders assemble in the great plaza or square ground that lies between the chief's mound at one end and the temple that holds the remains and treasures of the chief's ancestors at the other. With arrows nocked in their bows, four principal warriors stand guard at the cardinal directions of the square ground, a sacred space that is assuredly a recreation of the cosmic landscape. Large platters of food have been prepared and the warriors begin to eat, breaking their four-day fast. They gorge on venison to give them speed and agility, and the meat of a white dog to enhance their fidelity to the war commanders and their loyalty to the Sacred Warrior.

The warriors have fasted apart from their families, drinking the war medicine that has been brewed from the roots of button snakeroot. The war priests have transformed this once-profane liquid into a sacred medicine in ceremonial jars engraved and painted with sacred cosmic symbols of the world above them and the world beneath. The warriors have bathed in the nearby lake to cleanse, purify, and sanctify themselves for the dangerous and violent work ahead. They and their weapons are painted red and black, the colors of war and death; the symbols portray each warrior's cosmic affiliations and the divine sources of their power. The heads of the

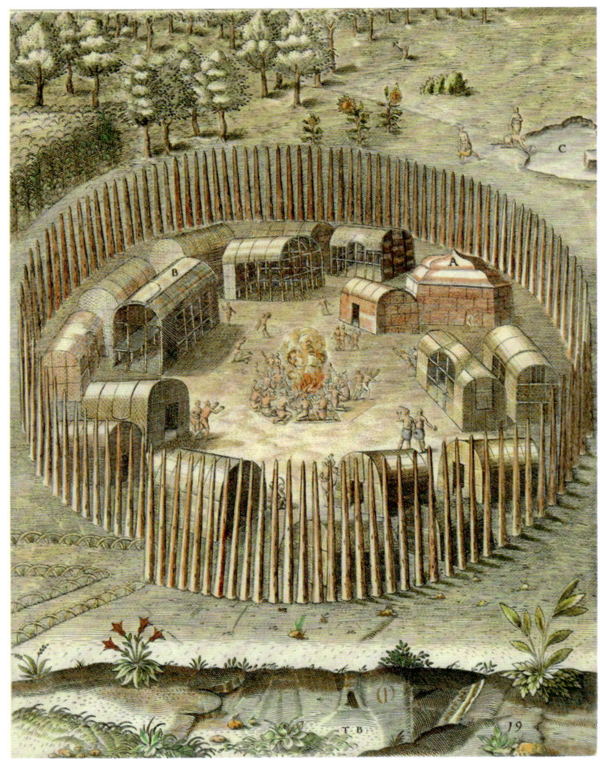

Fig. 2 Theodor de Bry (Flemish; 1528–1598), after an original watercolor by John White (English; fl. 1585–93), *The Town of Pomeiock*, 1590; from *America*, 2nd ed. (Frankfurt-am-Main, 1600), pt. 1, pl. 19; Rucker Agee Map Collection, Birmingham Public Library, Alabama. Cat. no. 282. Englishman John White recorded various Native American settlements along the Virginia coast at the time of his efforts to establish a colony at Roanoke Island in 1585. This print, engraved and published by De Bry, shows an assembly around the sacred fire in the palisaded town of Pomeiock.

clans carry their war medicine bundles, while one of the sacred war commanders bears on his back the great sacred shrine—a wooden box that contains the paraphernalia necessary for them to continue the purifying war rituals en route to the enemy.

The great war chief wears a feathered headdress attired with copper arrows and miniature war clubs. Wearing the regalia of combat, including hawk and turkey feathers in their hair roaches and scalp locks, the warriors proudly recite their war honors, counting them with the slender willow tally sticks before the people of the town. Having proclaimed their past heroic deeds, and wearing protective amulets made from the peregrine falcon, black bear, turkey, ivory-billed woodpecker, mountain lion, and timber rattlesnake, they strike with fury and vengeance the spiral-striped war pole—a symbolic axial conduit between the Sun and the sacred fire. They dance the war dance and sing their death songs.

Beseeching the Sun, the Thunderers, the celestial heroic supernaturals, and a host of local spirits for divine aid, protection, and power, the warriors offer oaths of allegiance to their leaders as they quietly fade into the enveloping forest. The sacred fire, the earthly representation of the Sun, slowly dies as a new dawn emerges at the crimson horizon. The chief greets the Sun, the primary celestial divinity and the one to whom they will offer the war trophies and prisoners upon their return.

As the Morning Star, the great mystic warrior, rises in the eastern horizon, each warrior is imbued and sanctified by the brilliant celestial being who promises success in combat. The participants again proclaim their fidelity, courage, and power to the Sun and other celestial supernaturals, the Thunderers, and their military leaders. Each warrior's thoughts are now raised to the great cosmic forces of the universe in supplication to the spirits who will provide power and protection. They feel the achievement of balance and purity and the divine aid granted them for their mission. They now have sufficient strength to hold and wield the powers bestowed upon them by the awesome forces of the Above World and the Beneath World in their avowed effort to combat the ferocious and destructive powers of their adversaries. Some of the visionary warrior priests in the war party have journeyed along the Path of Souls to the realm of the dead in search of divine weapons and power. With the use of sacred, spiritual weapons they have had violent confrontations with powerful antagonists, such as Underwater Panthers, the Great Serpent, the Old-Woman-Who-Never-Dies, and the Raptor, in order to return with weapons and the gifts of esoteric knowledge, sacred weapons, and purifying rituals. The Sacred Warrior leads them from the world of their families toward the inevitable confrontation with death.[1]

In the sixteenth century Spanish and French explorers witnessed scenes of Mississippian preparations for war similar to the one described above. Flemish engraver Theodor de Bry's 1590–91 copper plates illustrate European perceptions of these stages of war rituals (figs. 2–4; see also figs. 5, 14, and 26).[2] French colonizers described and illustrated deliberations on important affairs such as warfare, and documented the ceremonies performed before an expedition went against the enemy and on their return from combat. Preparations prior to military campaigns included war feasts and declarations of war. The French colonists saw chiefs heading their warrior militias and their consultation with priests on the chances of success in combat. They witnessed the order of march of the military expeditions, the way in which towns were fortified, and how they were set on fire by their enemies. They

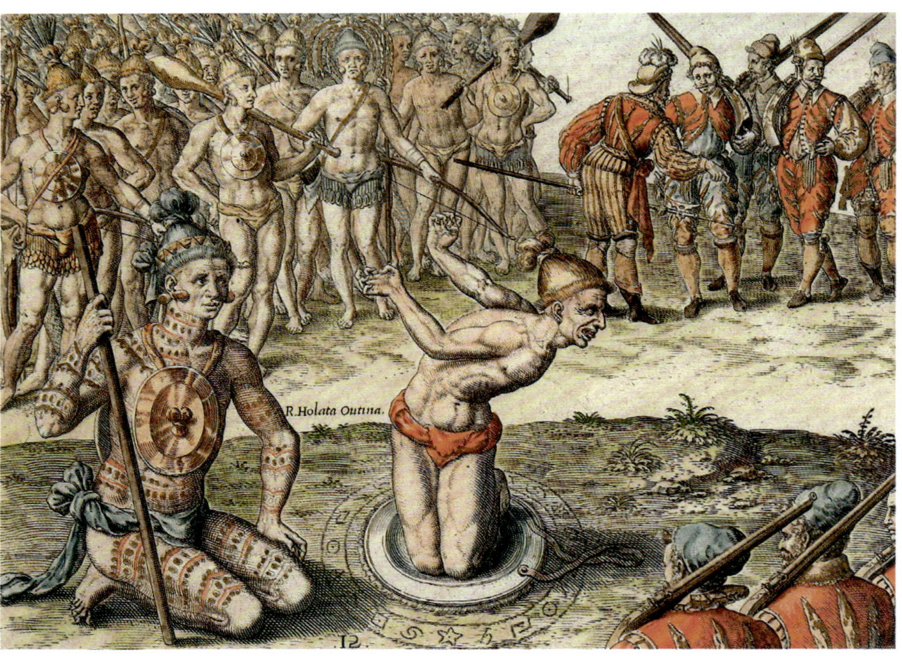

Fig. 3 Theodor de Bry, after an original painting of 1564 by Jacques Le Moyne de Morgues (French; c. 1533–1588), *Outina Consults a Sorcerer*, 1591; from *America*, 2nd ed. (Frankfurt-am-Main, 1609), pt. 2, pl. 12; Rucker Agee Map Collection, Birmingham Public Library, Alabama. Cat. no. 274. Artist Jacques Le Moyne documented a French expedition to Florida in 1564 led by René de Laudonnière and their stay among the Timucua Indians. This engraving by De Bry shows Chief Outina consulting a shaman about his battle plans against a neighboring enemy.

also observed how warriors treated their slain enemies, the exhibition of trophies, and the ceremonies conducted after a victory and the thanks given to the Sun.

The daily rhythms of work and play bound the Mississippian people, through kinship, social responsibilities, and ritual obligations, into a tightly knit, enduring social fabric (fig. 5). But the never-ending threat of political violence permeated every fiber of this fabric. Conflict was a major and constant concern of Mississippian life. The heavily fortified towns constructed across the Southeast and Midwest—with their palisaded walls, bastions, and dry moats—and the emphasis on heroic combat in Mississippian art and ritual bear mute witness to the stark reality of this conflict. Warfare rituals were a fundamental part of the invocation to spiritual powers for successful military operations, and such rituals emphasized authority, unity, purpose, organization, and the appropriate behavior required of warriors in their desire for success.

Chiefly warfare spread rapidly throughout the midcontinent at the end of the first millennium A.D., transforming and transformed by the rapidly evolving Mississippian chiefdoms. At the heart of Mississippian warfare lay intense rivalries among chiefs.[3] Chiefly political struggles for survival were predicated on a cycle of dramatic ceremonies hosted by these chiefs and conducted by their sacred war priests. Chiefly elites used ritual attire and ceremonial paraphernalia to communicate symbolically to the participants and audience alike the efficacy of their abilities to draw upon otherworldly domains. Rulers who gained access to the supernatural realm by ritual performance achieved success in warfare in this world.

Conflict touched all aspects of daily life and was reflected in myths, ceremonies, and rituals that integrated the course of their lives with the forces of the Middle World, the celestial Above World, and the watery Beneath World. Archetypal dramas, played out in ritual, were central elements in the iconography of Mississippian warfare. The conspicuous images of combat scenes, weaponry, trophy taking, and human sacrifice are prominent in Mississippian art and document the triumphs of archetypal mythic heroes over their foes, including otherworldly guardians and supernatural monsters (fig. 7).[4] The desire of warrior chiefs to reinforce and legitimize their social status was fundamentally linked to imagery, myths, and rituals that showcased their military exploits. This ancient Native American belief system was based on the spiritual powers of the Above World and the Beneath World for the successful operation of warfare in the Middle World. Warrior priests, for example, invoked the forces of the cosmos for their aid and protection, and actively conducted warfare to defend themselves, gain war honors, and emulate the behaviors of the archetypal warrior heroes.

Throughout the Mississippian world local art styles varied, but the theme of combat was widespread and always a central element. Why did Mississippian elites employ combat scenes in their artwork? How did these scenes function within Mississippian society? Why were some scenes chosen over others for representation? And what meaning might these scenes have held for the Mississippian elite? In answering these questions we will explore the idea that Mississippian combat artwork was created to function as a vital and integral element in connecting the living community with the Otherworld where all-powerful forces resided. Human images depicted in ritualistic poses, while grounded in reality, portrayed the archetypal and represented a mythic model that could be replicated in ritual and warfare. The Mississippian system of combat imagery and thought was part of the ancient stratum of Native American belief and symbolism, and indeed was widely shared among the peoples of the Western Hemisphere. These rituals and systems of beliefs connected warriors, their towns, and their chiefs and war

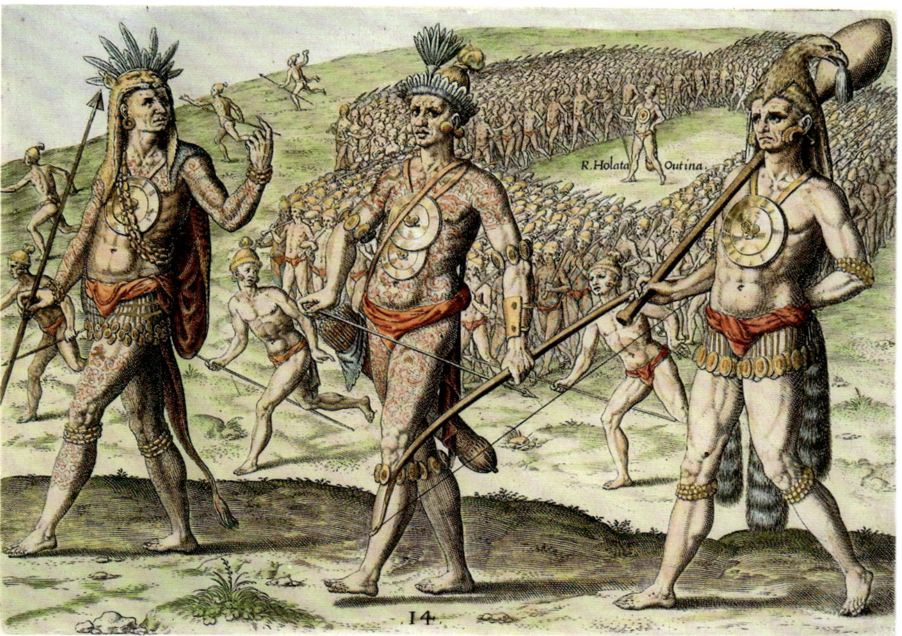

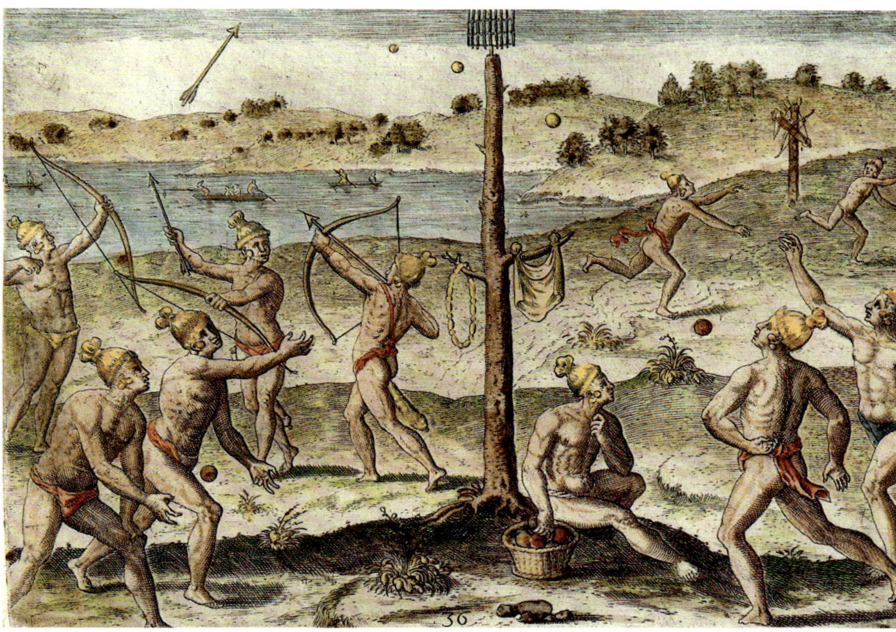

Fig. 4 Theodor de Bry, after an original painting of 1564 by Jacques Le Moyne de Morgues, *Outina's Order of March*, 1591; from *America*, 1st ed. (Frankfurt-am-Main, 1591), pt. 2, pl. 14; Rucker Agee Map Collection, Birmingham Public Library, Alabama. Cat. no. 275. Here chief Holata Outina is depicted at the center of his organized ranks of troops in their march against Saturiba, leader of his enemies.

Fig. 5 Theodor de Bry, after an original painting of 1564 by Jacques Le Moyne de Morgues, *Exercises of the Youths*, 1591; from *America*, 1st ed. (Frankfurt-am-Main, 1591), pt. 2, pl. 36; Rucker Agee Map Collection, Birmingham Public Library, Alabama. Cat. no. 280. Young warriors are depicted here playing a native ball game and practicing their skill with the bow and arrow.

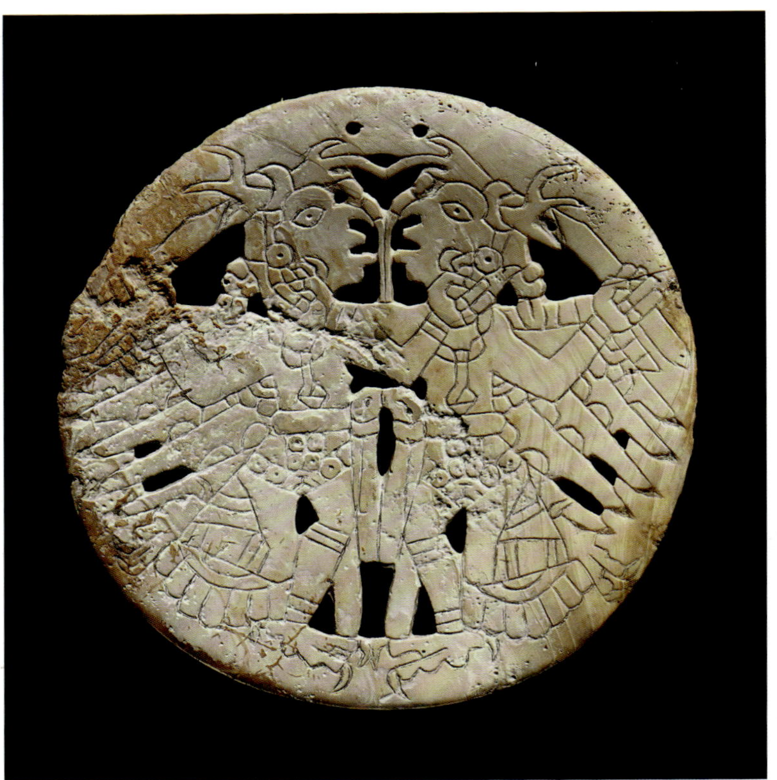

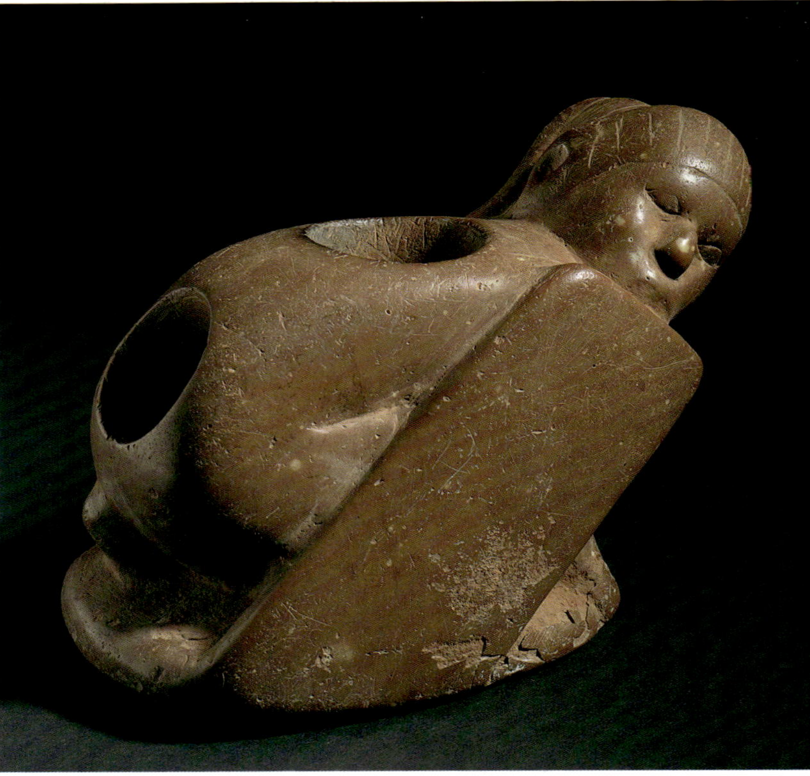

Fig. 6 Engraved shell gorget with two figures engaged in mortal combat; Hightower style; Tennessee, Hamilton County, Hixon site, A.D. 1250–1350; marine shell, diam. 11.5 cm; Frank H. McClung Museum, University of Tennessee, Knoxville. Cat. no. 141. This gorget may also represent two ritually attired figures engaged in a war dance.

Fig. 7 Crouching warrior effigy pipe; Illinois, Jackson County, Guy Smith Village site, A.D. 1100–1200; flint clay, h. 9.5 cm; University of Illinois, Illinois Transportation Archaeological Research Program. Cat. no. 99.

priests with a fundamental cosmological order and the powers of the Above World and Beneath World.

Mississippian Warfare Art

The most dramatic and detailed illustrations of Mississippian warfare art were created in a broad band extending from eastern Tennessee to eastern Oklahoma and from central Illinois to northern Florida between approximately A.D. 1200 and 1400.[5] Major political and ceremonial centers throughout this area have yielded figural combat art in three key artifact genres: repoussé sheet copper plates, engraved marine shell cups, and engraved marine shell gorgets. Each of these artifact genres represents a core component of the Southeastern Ceremonial Complex, consisting of complexly articulated and highly conspicuous images connected to the warrior elite. This figural art incorporates scenes of dramatic combat, featuring axe-, mace-, sword- or falchion-wielding supernaturals dressed in ritual regalia in aggressive postures and engaged in archetypal and celebratory smiting scenes.

A thirteenth-century shell gorget from the upper Tennessee River valley, for example, depicts two heroic figures brandishing long flint swords (falchions), while attempting to decapitate each other at the articulation of the mandible and cranium with raptor talon effigy bifaces (fig. 6). They wear antler headdresses with raccoon pelt hindquarter bindings and pendant necklaces displaying a columella—the central shaft or axis at the heart of a marine whelk. Their waistbands support kilts decorated with circles, radial t-bars, and a long tassel. They have knotted hair buns and disc-style earspools, and their arms and legs bear protective bands. Their taloned feet and petaloid-marked wings establish without a doubt that this scene occurs in the celestial Above World. The actual combat regalia depicted in these figural scenes—swordlike flint bifaces and raptor talon effigy bifaces—have been recovered from mortuary contexts at the great Mississippian political centers. War priests or chiefs dressed in the personae of celestial supernatural heroes may have enacted key archetypal dramas in which they recreated the great cosmic order or they may have represented individuals buried in the personae of great supernatural warrior heroes with their celestial accoutrements.

When Antonio J. Waring, Jr., and Preston Holder first described the Southeastern Ceremonial Complex (SECC) in 1945, they envisioned a list of traits grouped under four headings: motifs, god-animal representations, ceremonial objects, and costume regalia.[6] They thought of the trait complex as a symbol system that was internally coherent and of brief duration. The core of the complex therefore centered on the god-animal representations and their ceremonial regalia, including both weaponry and "costumes." Those responsible for the origin of the complex were believed to have been Muskhogean speakers of the Deep South. Archaeological work over the last fifty years, however, has suggested that the SECC is not so much a uniform style or set of images, as it is a mosaic of divergent styles stemming from several ethnic and linguistic groups, each with contrasting regional variations in style, genre, and thematic content.[7] These regional expressions are now known to have undergone a long history of local development. On the other hand, these regional developments were undoubtedly related historically and functionally, although the origin of the SECC now appears to have been seated in the Midwest

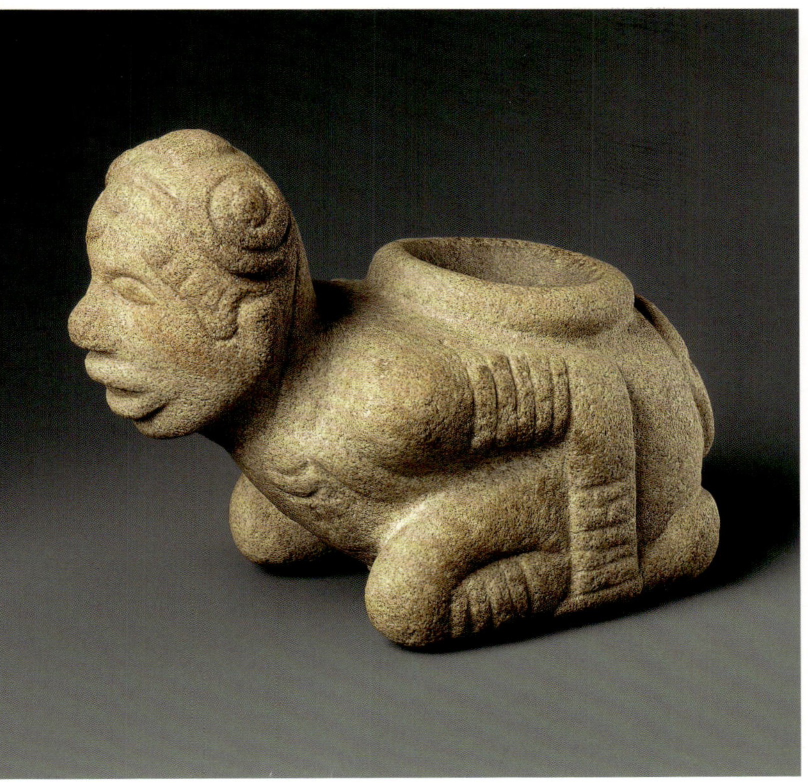

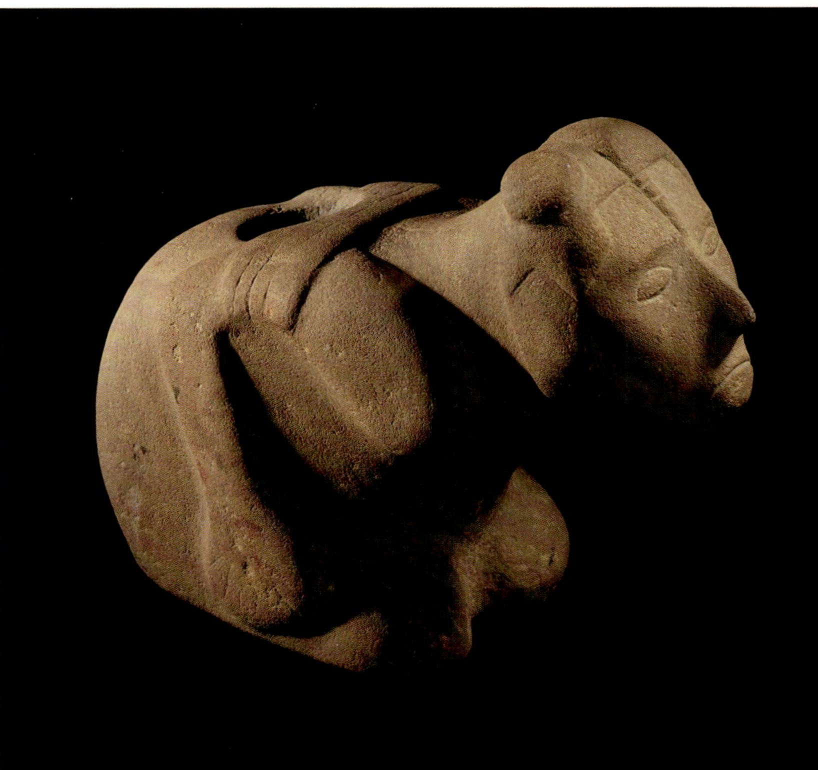

Fig. 8 Kneeling prisoner effigy pipe; Mississippi, A.D. 1400–1500; stone, h. 12.2, l. 17 cm; Henry L. Batterman Fund and the Frank Sherman Benson Fund, Brooklyn Museum of Art. Cat. no. 103.

Fig. 9 Bound captive effigy pipe; Arkansas, A.D. 1200–1500; stone, h. 19.1, l. 22.9 cm; Museum of Red River, Idabel, Oklahoma. Cat. no. 109. Deprived of all signs of rank and status, prisoners such as the two shown here are tied in humiliating poses.

among Siouan-speaking peoples, rather than in the Muskhogean Southeast, and to have spread out in the early thirteenth century in a dominant style known to archaeologists as the Braden style.[8]

The Classic Braden style illustrates the universal concern with death and the resurrection of life. The basic principles of life and death are played out in the archetypal dramas recorded in Braden figural art.[9] For example, a primary myth whose central message is reincarnation is the Twin hero myth cycle. In this myth one twin who is civilized adheres to the basic tenets of society, while the other, uncivilized twin opposes society. The civilized boy is associated with thunder and can bring his wild brother back to life. He has arrows in a sacred bundle which have great power and are used in healing and resurrecting the dead. Wild boy is also a Thunderer who can cause lightning. In one story wild boy is decapitated and replaces his own head with a rattle, becoming a rattle head. The ritual death and reviving of the Twins is an important mythic theme and is based on the power of the sacred medicine bundle and its ability to heal and resurrect, a pervasive idea tied to the reincarnation of elite individuals and powerful, heroic mythic characters. The sacred Twins portray a duality of opposing forces that must be balanced and maintained in order to remain in harmony with the cosmos.

The Mississippian warrior scenes, perhaps based to some degree on mythic episodes such as the Twins myth cycle, reflect a concern with the illustration of the heroic myths that charter or validate combat (figs. 8–9). While one of the two captives shown here wears protective bands on his arms and legs and braided hair buns, both prisoners display a beaded forelock. The figural imagery of the Mississippian world is one of mythic heroes existing in the dawn time, in interaction in a tiered cosmos of the Beneath World, the Middle World, and the Above World.[10]

The Mississippian hero warrior theme is expressed in the Braden style throughout the Southeast and Midwest in figural art. Perhaps the most famous examples of this theme are the graceful repoussé copper plates recovered at the Etowah site in northwestern Georgia in the late nineteenth century by John P. Rogan on behalf of archaeologist Cyrus Thomas (see figs. 1 and 11 in the essay by Adam King in this volume). In this celebratory smiting scene a supernatural warrior, perhaps the mythic Morning Star, brandishes in his right hand a forked tail war club, adorned with two beaded tassels, while grasping a severed human head by the hair bun with his left hand. The arms and legs of this celestial hero are adorned with protective bands, and his feet are covered by leather moccasins. He has a forked-mouth-surround and ellipsoidal eye-surrounds. As he looks across his right shoulder we see him in mid dance step. His complex headdress includes copper or mica sheets in the form of circular discs, a rectangular, copper forehead plaque, and a bilobed arrow. His left ear sports a circular disk with attached pearls or shell beads. He has a stiffened, beaded forelock with two large, marine shell beads tied to its base. A columella whelk shell pendant, the quintessential emblem of the warrior hero, hangs from a shell necklace. He wears a scalp lock-shaped pouch—much like a Scottish sporran—as a container for his scalp lock trophies. A long, fringed tassel hangs from his woven waistband. The elaborate wing feathers, decorated with petaloid designs, denote the location of the action as the Above

World. The priestly warrior regalia represented by the Rogan plates allow us to see the accoutrements in vogue among elites in the thirteenth century.

The Rogan plates also illustrate the sophistication and complexity of copper figural art that portrays the archetypal combat scene. While depicting a supernatural warrior hero, replete with ritual regalia, they provide the basis for warrior priests to recreate the cosmos through archetypal myths. The ritual regalia signifies the sacred and potent persona of the supernatural and his bestowal of power to his earthly charge, who may then possess this artwork and have it buried with him to designate his chiefly status.

Ritual and Chiefly Warfare

Warfare characterizes most chiefdoms, and Mississippian chiefdoms were no exception.[11] With the evolution of chiefly society and the rise of warrior chiefs, warfare became a way for a chief to extend influence over neighboring chiefdoms, not for the conquest of land, but as a way to expand one's financial and political base and to defend it against the aggressive actions of other chiefs. Warfare, in part, was directed at the competition over the flow of wealth objects so necessary for chiefly political authority and legitimacy. Within the first centuries of Mississippian development, warfare had become endemic; towns became fortified with palisades, bastions, and moats. By the early thirteenth century, figural art portraying combat and weapons as accoutrements of ritualized aggressive action appeared (figs. 10–11). Figural art rapidly became crucial to the rituals of warfare as priestly warriors gained increasing authority over warfare ceremonies connected with combat.

Chiefly warfare is based on social ranking and hierarchy. Prior to Mississippian chiefdoms, tribal forms of social organization emphasized achieved leadership positions. With the rise of chiefdoms specific offices were inherited and filled by elites. Thus, opportunities for warfare offices gave rise to greater command structures and were accordingly marked by insignias and badges of office, based on war honors. Graded positions of warriors could then be effectively organized and deployed by warrior chiefs.[12]

Purity was critical to success in warfare and was achieved and maintained when the proper rules were observed, including separation. Consequently, pollution occurred when separation failed. Warriors had to overcome pollution in order to hold the spiritual powers. Balance, as important as purity, was based on the notion that the cosmos consisted of parts that were in opposition to each other.[13] For example, the forces of the Above World were opposed to the forces of the Beneath World. Balance was upset when one force prevailed over the other. The denizens of the Above World, such as the Thunderers and raptors, were held to be in deadly conflict with the monsters, piasas, and serpents of the Beneath World. Mississippian ritual specialists sought power and divine aid from these powerful cosmic forces by seeking the support of supernatural ones.

Ritual became an effective means for warrior chiefs and their councils of elites both to legitimize these positions and to establish and maintain social authority. Art, as an important component of symbolic rituals, was a public symbol that emphasized the status of male warriors and indicated a broadly shared warrior ideology. The Mississippian world shared an extensive

Fig. 10 Ceremonial mace; southeastern Kentucky, A.D. 1200–1300; Dover flint, h. 27.9 cm; Tennessee State Museum, Nashville, Gates P. Thruston Collection of Vanderbilt University. Cat. no. 186.

Fig. 11 Ceremonial mace; Oklahoma, LeFlore County, Spiro, A.D. 1200–1300; stone; Smithsonian Institution, National Museum of the American Indian, Washington, D.C. Cat. no. 187. The standardization of the implements and emblems of authority and power across an immense and ethnically diverse region is a mark of the Late Mississippian world.

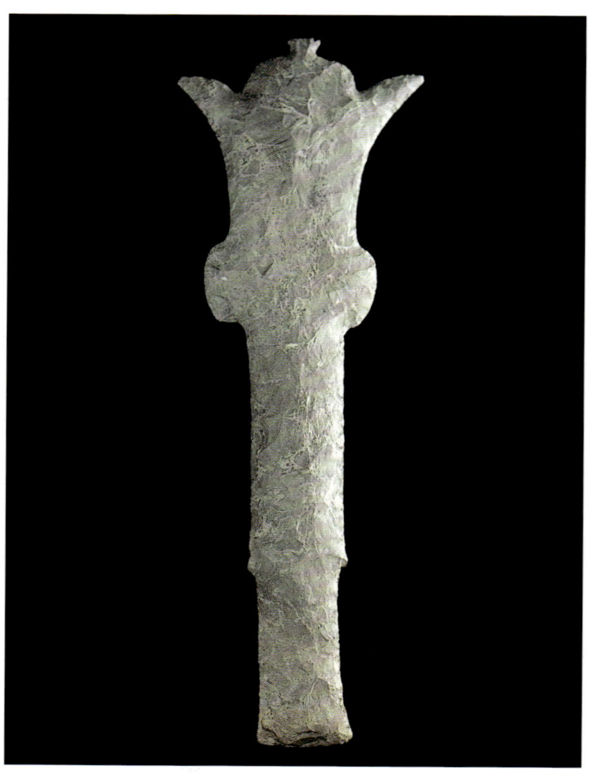

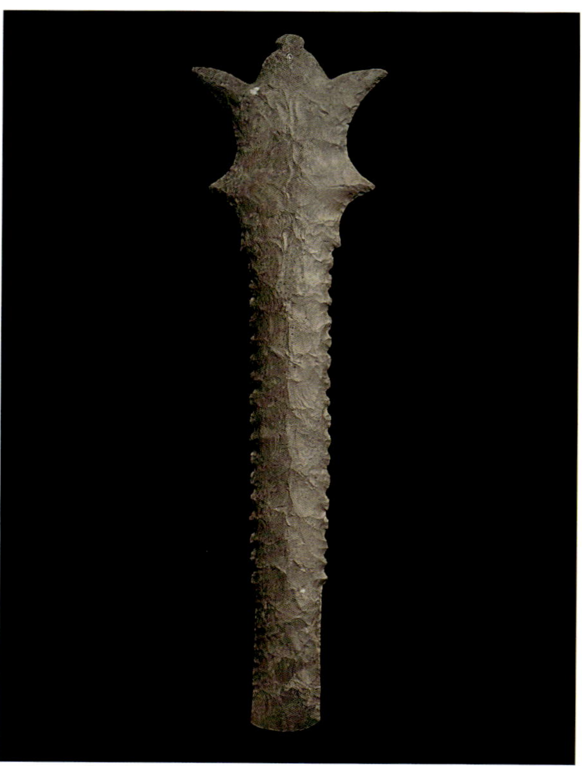

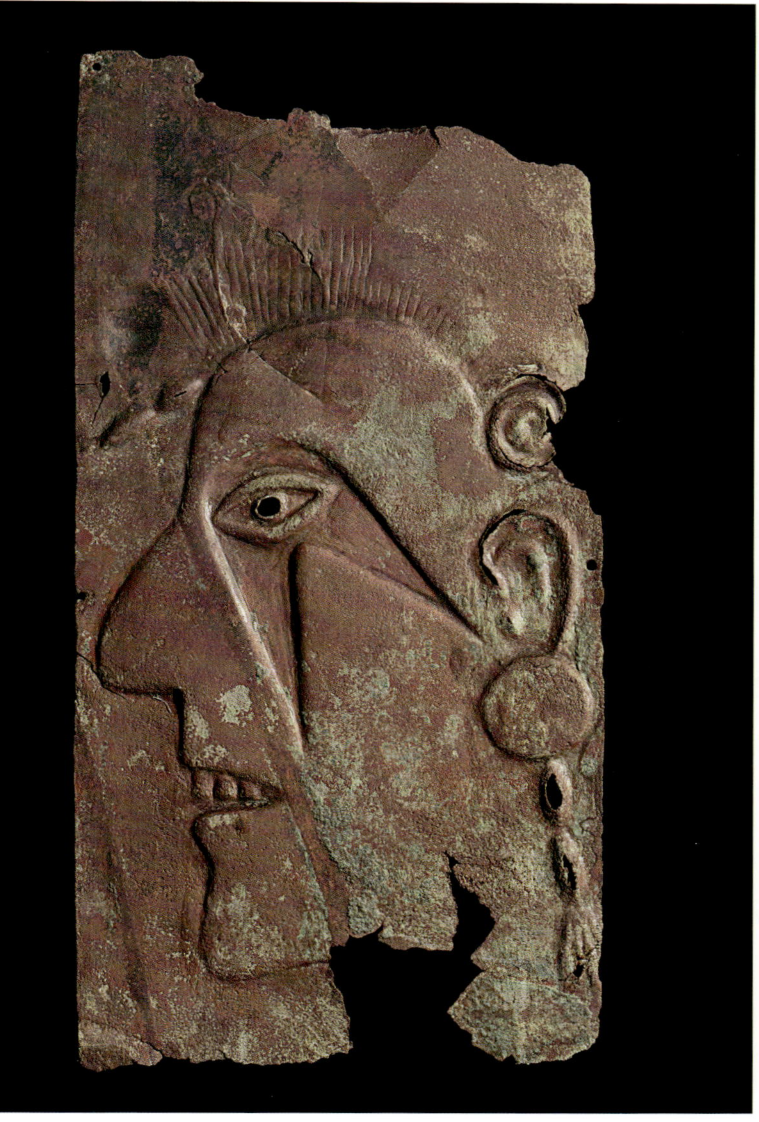

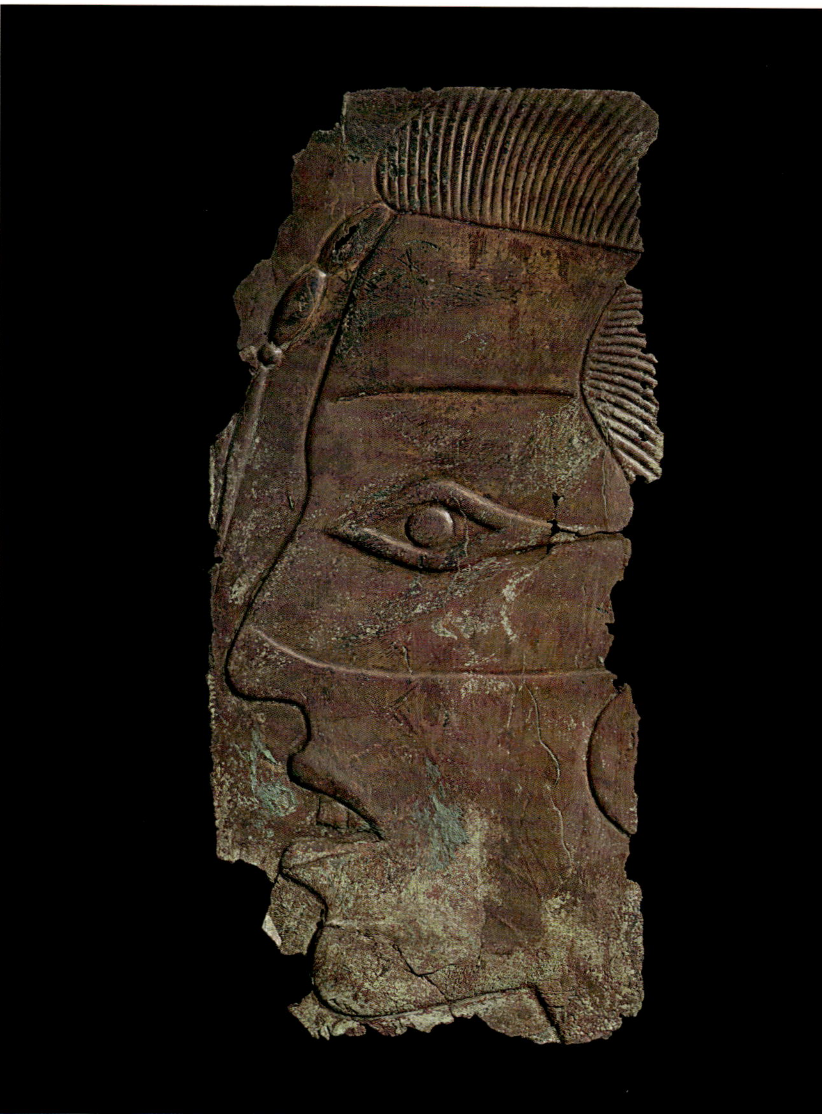

Figs. 12–13 Copper repoussé plates; Oklahoma, LeFlore County, Spiro, Craig Mound, A.D. 1200–1300; copper, h. 24.2, 22.5 cm; Smithsonian Institution, National Museum of the American Indian, Washington, D.C. Cat. nos. 116–17.

figural imagery associated with combat that emphasized the portraiture of the ideal warrior hero, as can be seen in copper plates from the Craig Mound in Spiro, Oklahoma, uncovered in 1933 (figs. 12–13). These rites are linked to a well-developed custom of feasting and gift exchange, forming part of the larger network of religious, political, and economic activities.[14]

The Mississippian people had major ceremonies that illustrate the belief system associated with warfare, the rites of passage for warriors, and the rituals associated with achieving purity and balance.[15] The three stages of rites of passage are based on the separation, transition, and reincorporation of the warrior with society.[16] In the rite of passage rituals associated with warfare, warriors were separated from their normal activities in order to undergo the transition to various levels of instruction in the group's culture, duties, and responsibilities. Each increase in status included new obligations and was marked by public conferment of badges, honors, and insignia of rank. Upon successful completion of military activities, warriors would be reincorporated or renewed in their social standing in order to rejoin the larger group. Such junctures in social roles and changes in military status were ceremonially marked. For instance, individuals might be presented with war titles or war honors based on their success and accomplishments in a raid or in battle. The separation and reincorporation ceremonies often involved large communal events held in the town plaza or in a public building atop one of the great mounds where war titles and war honors, advancement in rank, name changes, badges of office, and the initiation of warriors and chiefs would be proclaimed. To varying degrees these transitions may have been modeled on mythic archetypes established by the doings of deities, heroes, or natural forces.

Repetition and formal correctness were important in Mississippian warfare rituals. Rituals were associated directly with the conduct of warfare, including precombat, combat, and postcombat events, and there were others for the rites of initiation for warriors as they advanced through the various ranks from the lowest warrior to the most exalted chief. Included in these rituals were the funerals of warriors and their treatment at death.

While these rituals have basic differences, they all share the fundamental ceremonial structure of maintaining purity, avoiding pollution, and carrying out ritual responsibilities. Aids in these practices included physical and social separation, smoking tobacco, dancing, fasting, abstinence from sex and sleep, the consumption of emetic war medicines, and the use of prophylactic amulets (fig. 14). Success in warfare was believed to be directly related to the strictness with which these rituals were observed and to the bestowal of power from the Above World. Shell cups and ceramic vessels were integral paraphernalia for such ceremonies because they could serve as devices to transform mundane ingredients into potent medicines. The engravings on ceramic vessels may have served to transform generic, profane mixtures into specific, sacred war medicines (see fig. 8 in the essay by Vincas Steponaitis and Vernon Knight in this volume).[17] The different death or war trophy motifs—human head, scalp lock, forearm bones, etc.—may have denoted specific varieties of the war medicine to be used for various occasions or purposes. For example, the various locales used as portals or stations along the Path of Souls, especially those where combat or mortal altercation took place, may have required different configurations of the "war" medicine. The motifs on shell or ceramic containers may have served to concoct various brands of medicine. Combat in the Otherworld also appears to have been an important mechanism for warrior heroes in their quest for power and knowledge. Likewise, the dead may have required potions to combat the fearsome obstacles along the Path of Souls or in the realm of the dead.

Often violence was carried out in the reenactment of the great mythic struggles of the heroic warrior figures who battled the forces of the cosmos in order to maintain the balance between the cosmic powers (fig. 15). The raptor in the stone pipe shown here is clearly a supernatural who possesses human hands that hold a human head trophy. Although the specific story is unknown, the supernatural raptor may be a celestial being who charters trophy-taking behavior.

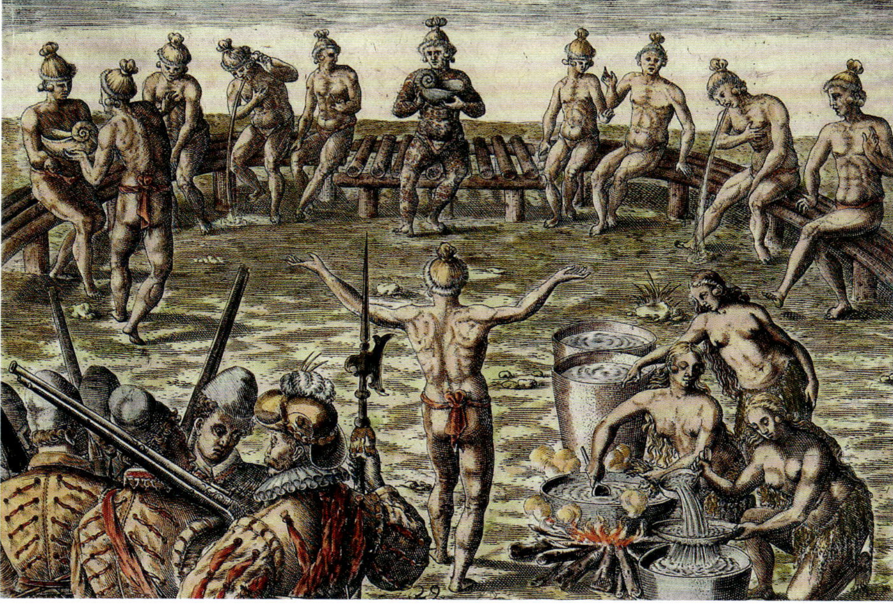

Fig. 14 Theodor de Bry, after an original painting of 1564 by Jacques Le Moyne de Morgues, *A Council of State*, 1591; from *America*, 1st ed. (Frankfurt-am-Main, 1591), pt. 2, pl. 29; Rucker Agee Map Collection, Birmingham Public Library, Alabama. Cat. no. 278. Warriors, shown in this print consuming a powerful ritual drink, prepared for battle by fasting and cleansing themselves before partaking of potent, and often emetic, war medicines.

The Osage have stories of falcons who have given human supplicants martial powers, but in return the warriors must take human trophies in remembrance of the celestial falcon's generosity.[18] Iconography was critical to combat rituals because the iconic symbols made concrete the worldview of the ruling elite and their ideological charter, which established the warrior in relation to cosmic forces. Iconography becomes the material form of the ruling elites' mythic claims to ideological power; it is the lynchpin of their chiefly and priestly authority.

Chiefs and priestly warriors possessed sacred powers. Their authority was based on myths that established their reigns and the supernaturals who recognized them as divine. Chiefs competed for access to and control over powerful systems of esoteric knowledge and combat objects that imbued them with the sacred powers bestowed by supernaturals. Much of the competitive arena of chiefdoms involved struggles over varying sources of power. Chiefs as generalized leaders acted as economic managers, war leaders, ritual specialists, and political statesmen. Public ceremonial events, such as warfare rituals, were strictly prescribed in form, participation, and sequence, and had to be repeated on a regular basis to be effective. Ceremonial events could be restricted by limiting the number of those who participated and the expense incurred in hosting the ceremony. Large-scale ceremonies incorporating feasts required war leaders who were capable of mobilizing labor and resources to finance such events.

Components or ingredients of ritual events include the participation of military specialists, who may demonstrate martial arts with combat weapons[19] and perform dramatic events, including torture and human sacrifice.[20] An example of ritual sacrifice is depicted in the Conquering Warrior figurine from Spiro (figs. 16a–b). Manufactured at Cahokia during the twelfth century A.D. from locally available red Missouri flint clay,[21] the figure was later drilled for use as a pipe, suggesting

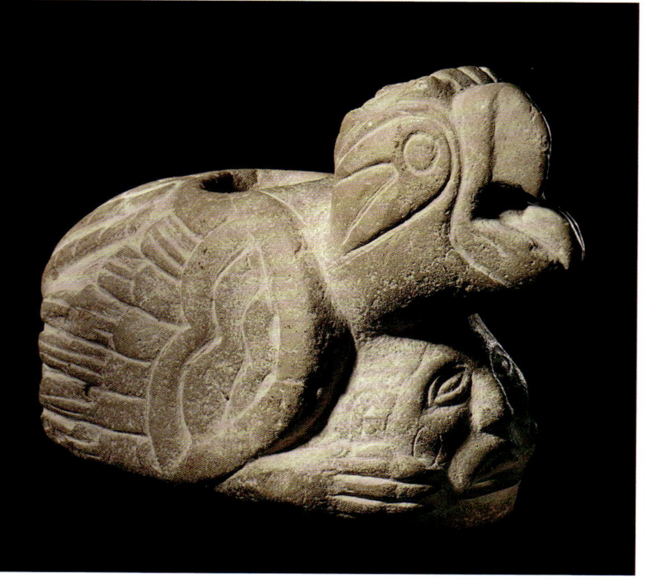

Fig. 15 Hawk and human head effigy pipe; Mississippi, Washington County, Winterville site, A.D. 1200–1300; stone, h. 12.1 cm; Gilcrease Museum, Tulsa, Oklahoma. Cat. no. 104.

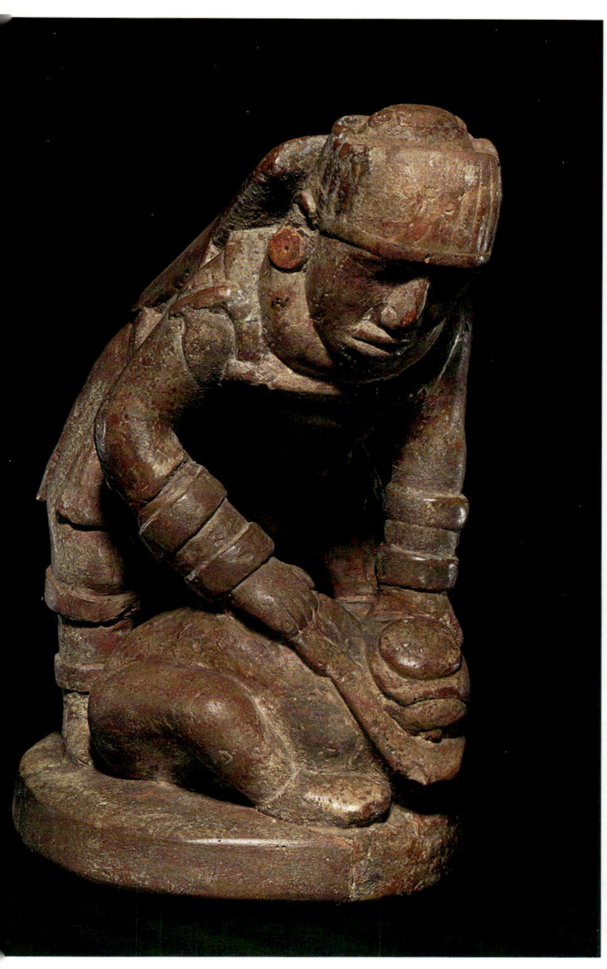

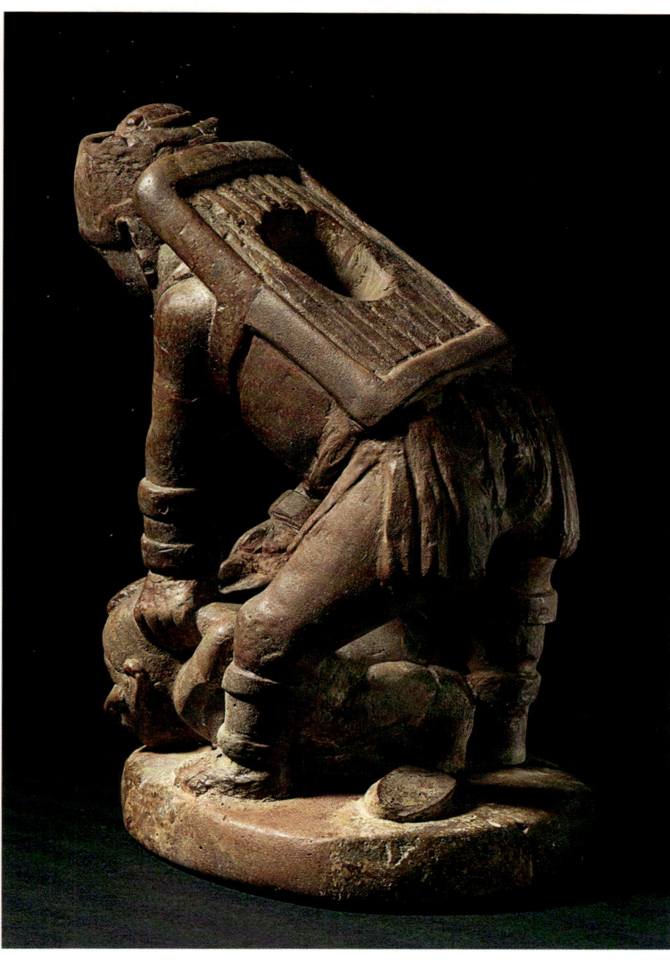

Figs. 16a–b Conquering Warrior effigy pipe; Oklahoma, LeFlore County, Spiro, A.D. 1100–1200; flint clay, h. 24.8 cm; Smithsonian Institution, National Museum of the American Indian, Washington, D.C. Cat. no. 93. This effigy pipe portrays the decapitation of a captive. Details of costume and pose are faithfully and naturalistically sculpted, as are the gruesome details of the execution.

Fig. 17 Raptor talon effigy; Tennessee, Humphreys County, Duck River, near Waverly, A.D. 1250–1350; stone, l. 26.7 cm; Gilcrease Museum, Tulsa, Oklahoma. Cat. no. 192.

Fig. 18 Raptor talon effigy; Tennessee, Humphreys County, Duck River, A.D. 1250–1350; stone, l. 12.1 cm; Private collection. Cat. no. 191.

a change in ritual use. The figurine depicts a warrior engaged in decapitating a victim. The warrior, with a topless broad, flat headband, thick round neck collar, and perforated earspools, is wearing a kilt and heavy, protective arm and leg bands. His chest and back are protected by distinctive form of heavy, flat shieldlike body armor, connected by a harness. His hair bun is secured with a long pin. In his right hand he clutches a talon-shaped war club, while he pins the victim in place with his left hand. This pipe constitutes some of our best information for the ritual regalia of a warrior priest.[22]

Symbolic objects, including copper plates, shell gorgets, shell cups, statuary/pipes, sociotechnic weapons, and pottery, act as ideal signifiers of social position and social relationships. Public symbols in the form of ceremonial paraphernalia and ritual attire often define political office and rank. The widespread use of hypertrophic weapons indicates that a broadly shared warrior ideology existed throughout much of the Mississippian world, as evident in a group of objects from the Duck River in Tennessee (figs. 17–22). The manufacture of these finely crafted items required leadership, coordination, skilled labor, and access to scarce resources. Symbolic weapons and the mounds and plazas that served as stages for ceremonial cycles were central to the functioning of the chiefly and priestly lineages, as were the temples where ritual implements were curated.[23]

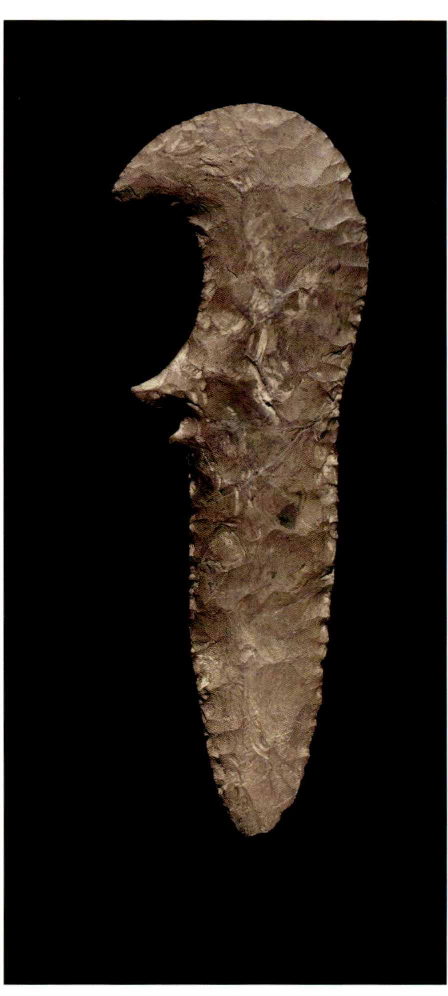

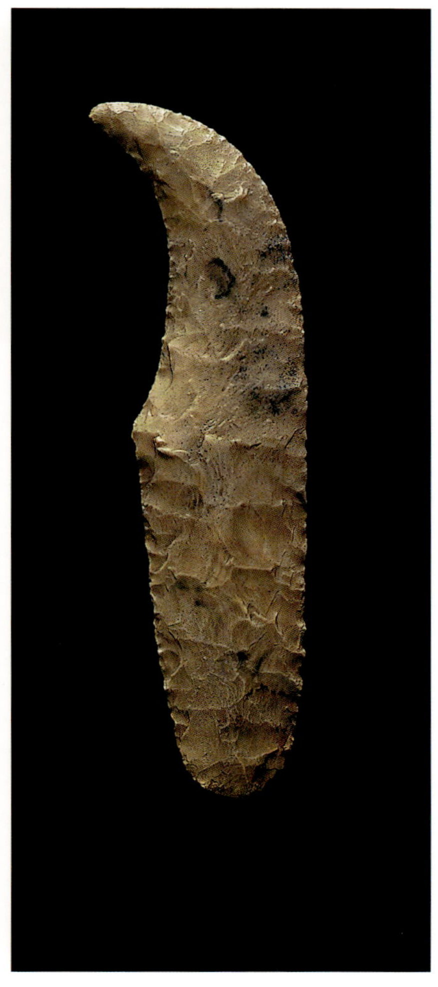

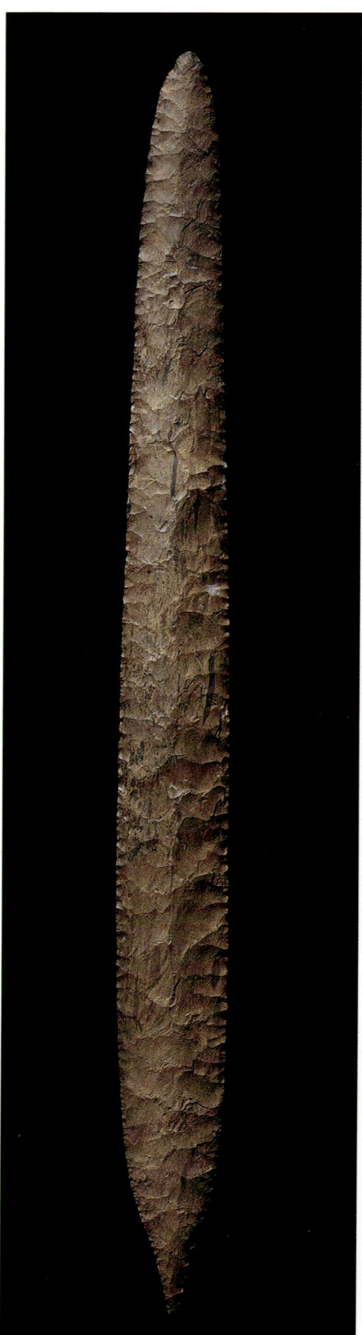

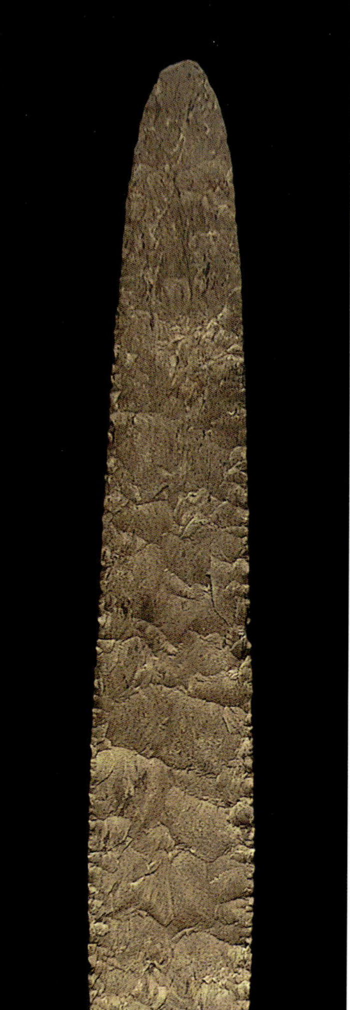

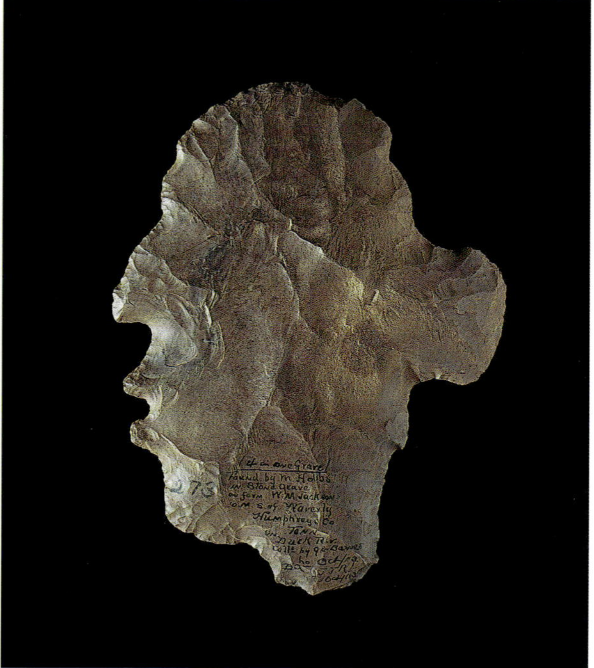

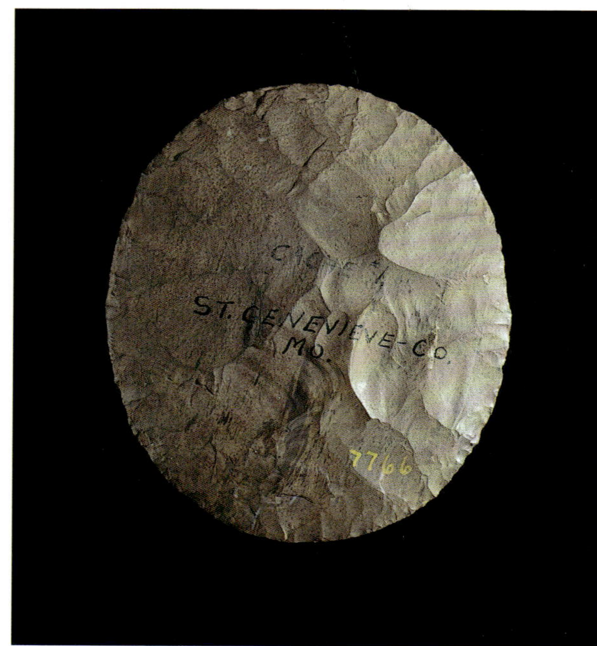

Just as purity involved the avoidance of pollution and the maintenance of balance between cosmic forces, so it required a set of ritual paraphernalia, including whelk shell cups, ceramic bottles, and other regalia. One component of achieving power and purity may have been the recreation of the mythic charter based on an archetypal heroic warrior in large public events. A shell gorget from Sumner County, Tennessee, for example, appears to depict Otherworld activities by a supernatural (fig. 1). The head of the dancing or running figure on this gorget is adorned with a prominent forked-eye-surround, earspools, and a beaded forelock. The high, crested, feather headdress has a bilobed-arrow hair ornament piercing a knotted hair bun (see also fig. 44 in the essay by Richard Townsend in this volume). The figure's neck is surrounded by a multiple-strand shell necklace. This imposing figure holds in his left hand a crown-form mace and, in his right, a human head lifted by a strand of hair from an unraveled hair bun. The woven belt supports a bellows-shaped apron that reveals two forelocks attached to the scalps hidden within. Woven or plaited bands protect the arms and legs.

For the great chiefs and priests, warfare was an important source of religious and political authority. Chiefs and war priests may have gained authority through their warrior status, even though they were born into office. Their success in defending their communities and the surrounding territory from attack would have been proof of their sacred authority. They were esteemed as accomplished fighters, and they organized and led wars of succession that determined who ruled. They fashioned wars of conquest that helped expand

Fig. 19 Sword; Tennessee, Humphreys County, Link site, A.D. 1250–1350; Dover chert, l. 55.9, w. 4.7 cm; Frank H. McClung Museum, University of Tennessee, Knoxville. Cat. no. 189.

Fig. 20 Chipped stone blade; Tennessee, Humphreys County, Duck River, near Waverly, A.D. 1250–1350; l. 37.5 cm; Private collection. Cat. no. 190. This blade is one of six found in a stone box burial.

Fig. 21 Profile of a human head; Tennessee, Humphreys County, Duck River, near Waverly, A.D. 1250–1350; stone, h. 17.8 cm; Private collection. Cat. no. 194.

Fig. 22 Chipped stone disk; Missouri, Ste. Genevieve County, A.D. 1250–1350; diam. 8.9 cm; Private collection. Cat. no. 193.

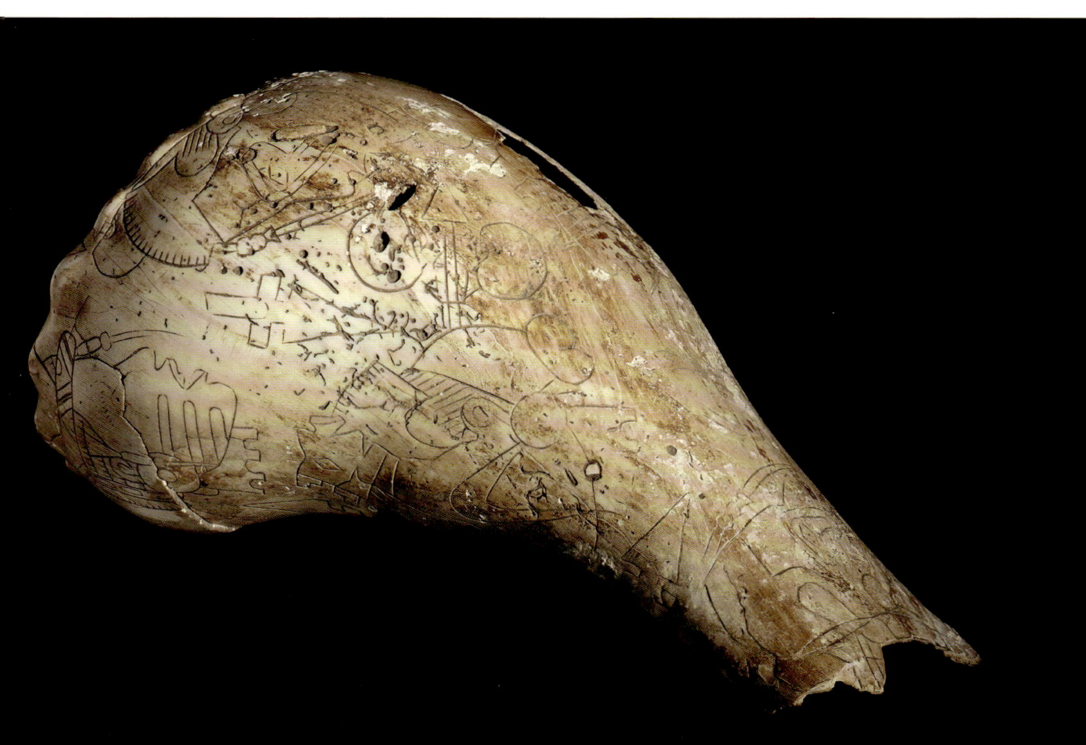

Fig. 23 Engraved whelk shell with warriors' heads motif; Classic Braden style; Oklahoma, LeFlore County, Spiro, Craig Mound, A.D. 1200–1350; marine shell, l. 28 cm; University of Arkansas Museum, Fayetteville. Cat. no. 122.

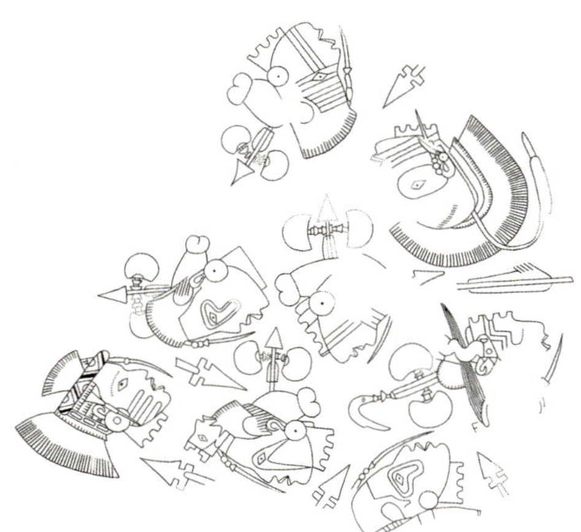

Fig. 24 Drawing of the engraved whelk shell shown in fig. 23; from Phillips and Brown 1978, pl. 17.

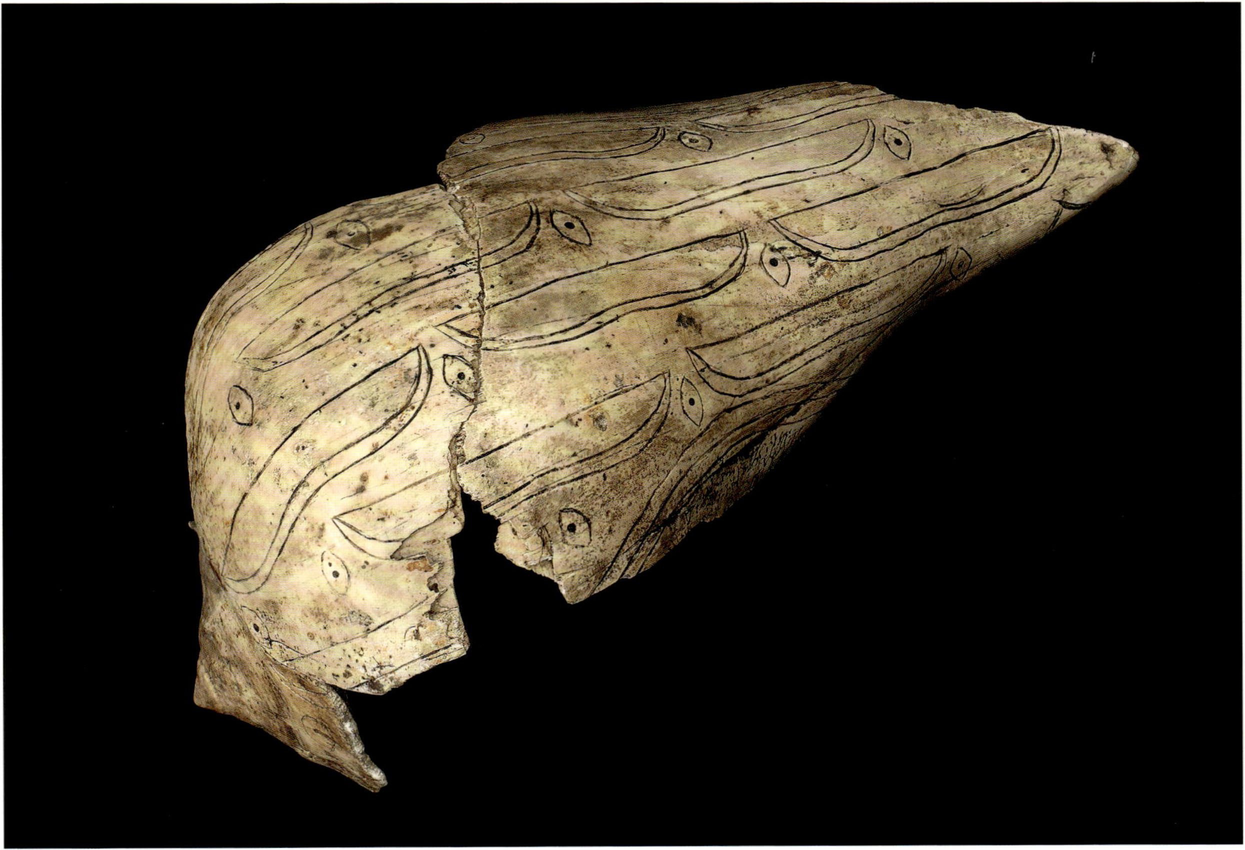

Fig. 25 Engraved whelk shell with bows and eyes motif; Craig B style; Oklahoma, LeFlore County, Spiro, Craig Mound, A.D. 1200–1350; marine shell, l. 20.3 cm; Smithsonian Institution, National Museum of Natural History, Washington, D.C. Cat. no. 131.

the chiefly domain. Powerful chiefs controlled men and surplus resources. Chiefs were generalized leaders and much of the competitive arena of chiefdoms involved fights over sources of power. Ideas, values, stories, and myths were transformed into a physical reality that could take the form of ceremonial events and symbolic objects. One of the two shell cups shown here from Spiro, for example, undoubtedly depicts the beheading of supernaturals (figs. 23–24). Mortal combat and decapitation are suggested by the eight skillfully and gracefully engraved heads depicted here with their serrated necks, the prominent arrowheads, and the agnathic or jawless head regalia. The other shell displays motifs of bows interspersed with eyes. Such symbolic images on engraved shell would have had a mythic theme.

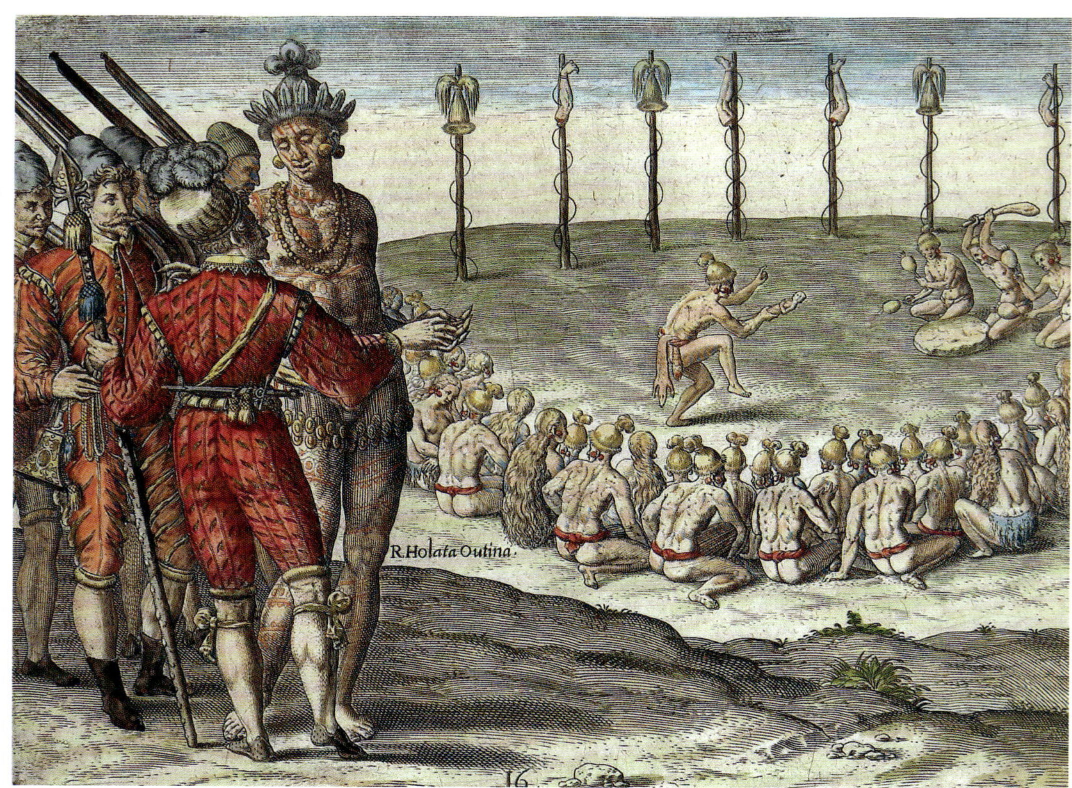

Fig. 26 Theodor de Bry, after an original painting of 1564 by Jacques Le Moyne de Morgues, *Trophies and Ceremonies after a Victory*, 1591; from *America*, 2nd ed. (Frankfurt-am-Main, 1609), pt. 2, pl. 16; Rucker Agee Map Collection, Birmingham Public Library, Alabama. Cat. no. 276. Chief Holata Outina's forces celebrate a victory by arraying their war trophies—severed limbs and scalps—on ceremonial poles and attending to the shaman's chants with a sculpted effigy, while others beat time with clubs and rattles.

Fig. 27 Monolithic axe; Oklahoma, LeFlore County, Spiro, Craig Mound, A.D. 1300–1400; stone, l. 36.8 cm; Gilcrease Museum, Tulsa, Oklahoma. Cat. no. 181.

Trophies of War

Human war trophies began to be portrayed in iconographic form by the thirteenth century A.D., being integrated into elite rituals associated with warfare and chiefly office.[24] Mississippian elites incorporated war trophies and combat weaponry as a dominant theme of the chiefly cult organization (figs. 26–29).[25] The connection of war trophy symbolism with elites and the chiefly pursuit of war honors reinforced the role of warfare in confirming honor and prestige upon those individuals who gained preeminent political and ritual positions, in part, through demonstrated personal military success and efficacy. Mississippian warfare trophy imagery is manifested as costume elements, regalia, badges, insignia, ritual paraphernalia, pottery motifs, and symbols of elite office. Symbolic human trophies consist of the representation of dismembered body parts, including scalp locks, severed heads, hands, etc., that were engraved, modeled, and painted on pottery vessels; combat weaponry; marine shell cups and gorgets; ironstone pendants; copper gorgets and pendants; and exotic chipped stone bifaces (figs. 30–31). In addition, human statuary, marine shell gorgets, and repoussé sheet copper plates were crafted to portray individuals attired in ritual paraphernalia, and engaged in smiting scenes or dismemberment activities. Their aggressive stances include brandishing martial weapons, donning scalp pouches as ritual regalia, beheading bound captives with flint blades, and grasping severed human heads by the scalp lock.

War trophies served as symbols of military victories and demonstrations of prowess in warfare, reflecting elite status and military rank when included as burial

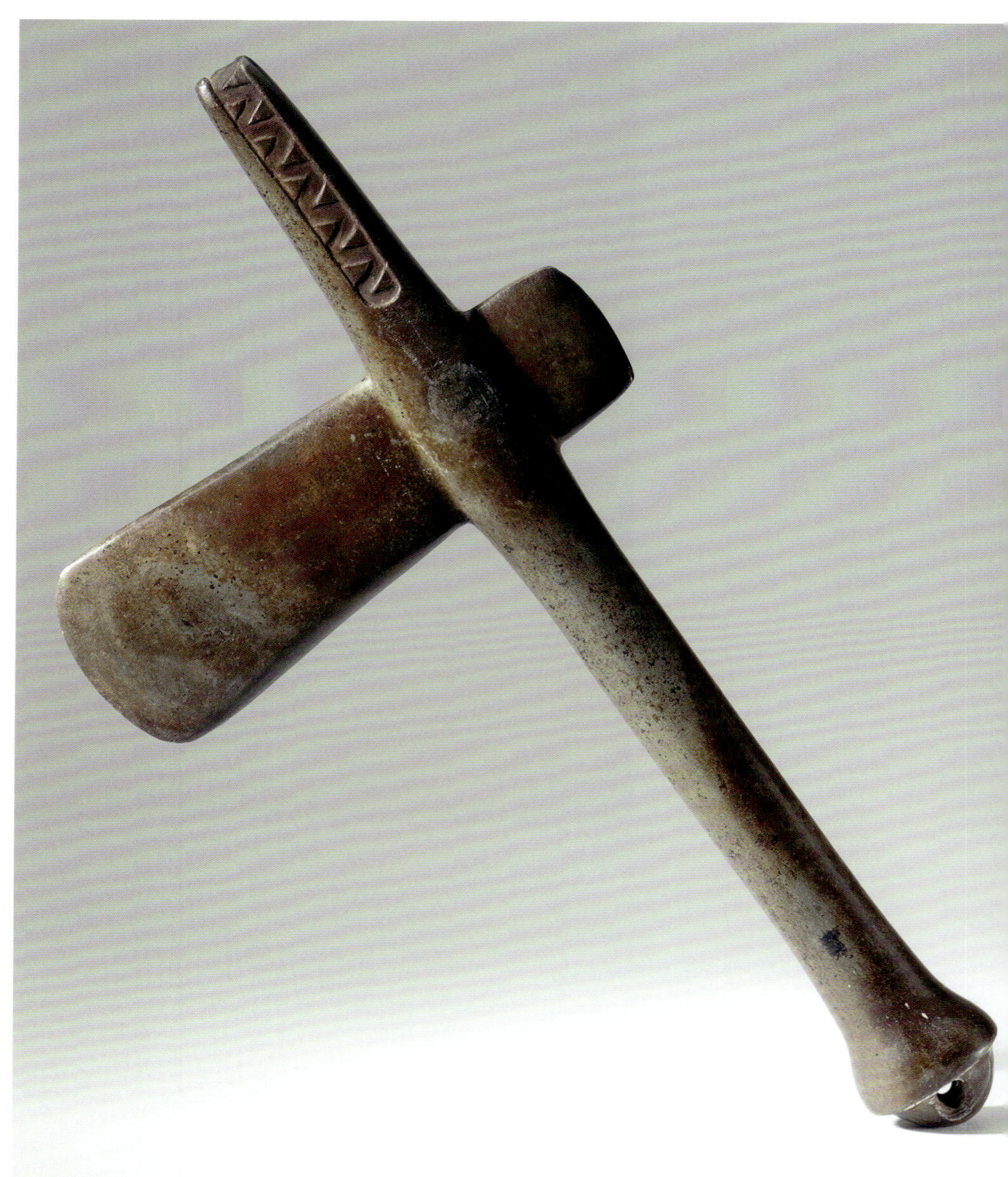

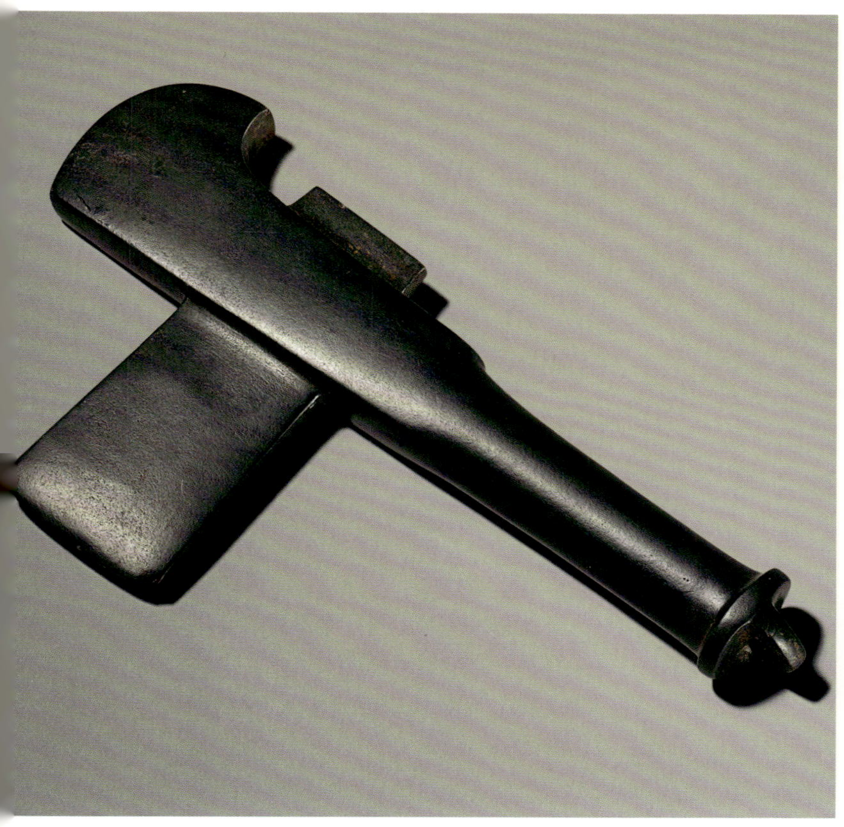

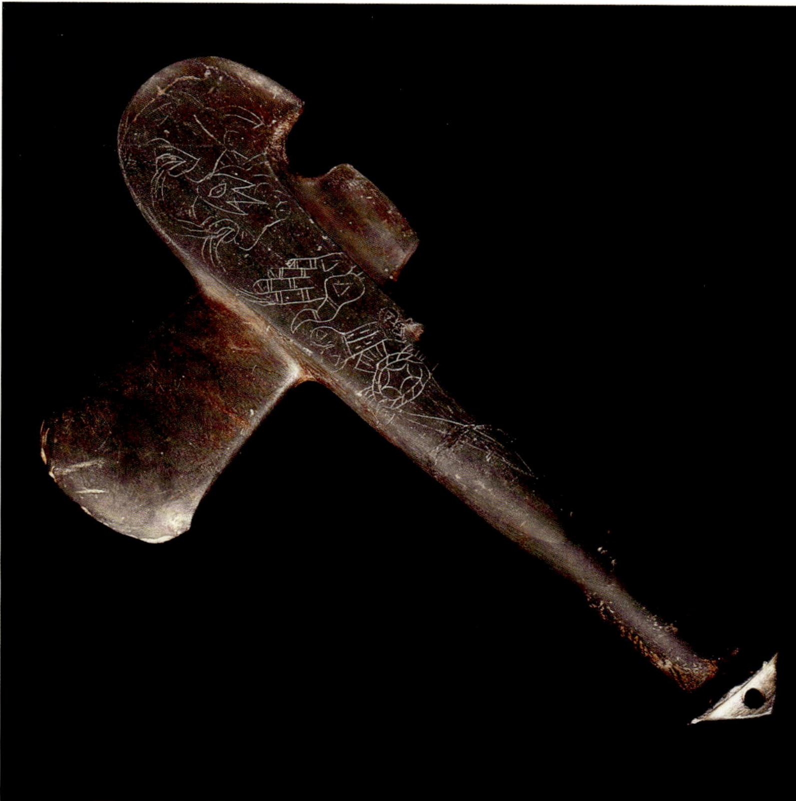

Fig. 28 Monolithic axe; Alabama, Tuscaloosa and Hale counties, Moundville, A.D. 1300–1450; stone, l. 29.5 cm; Smithsonian Institution, National Museum of the American Indian, Washington, D.C. Cat. no. 183.

Fig. 29 Monolithic axe; Georgia, Cherokee County, A.D. 1300–1400; greenstone, l. 35.6 cm; Smithsonian Institution, National Museum of Natural History, Washington, D.C. Cat. no. 184.

accompaniments. Human body parts were believed to contain the essence, soul, or spirit of the person killed. The trophy then becomes a representation of the whole, linking the spirit of the victim with the captor.[26] Chiefs acquired power from the acquisition, storage, and display of war trophies. Warfare provided chiefs not only with opportunities to augment and sanctify their chiefly authority and expand their rule, but also to gain war honors through the possession of war trophies. Demonstrations of personal inner power were critical to chiefly governance. A political leader's power, innate efficacy, and greatness was often measured by the number of war trophies he possessed. Dismembered body parts could accompany the dead as burial accompaniments in the form of actual human body parts or as symbolic and iconographic forms.

Warrior cult imagery, including weaponry, death, trophy taking, and dismemberment are prominent in scenes of combat, decapitation, and human sacrifice on marine shell cups and gorgets, ceramic vessels, and copper plates, documenting the triumphs of archetypal, mythical, otherworldly heroes in combat against races of giants, otherworldly guardians, and supernaturals (see figs. 23–25 in the essay by James Brown in this volume).[27] Weaponry and regalia found in elite burials mirror what was portrayed on the Birdman copper plates and marine shell gorgets, which portray supernatural heroes. Certain charter myths may have been used to reinforce key social features of ritual and status concerning warfare, representing a mythic model that could be replicated in rituals with the chiefly or priestly actors using weaponry and trophies and further replicated in the geopolitical world.

Individuals in tribal and chiefdom societies sought recognition as great warriors based on their personal achievements through the possession of human trophies.[28] In Mississippian chiefdoms the acquisition, public display, and hoarding of trophies was vital for the functioning of chiefly office. The association between trophies and chiefly office was manifested in their public display, the quantities of trophies earned, and their use as prestige items, symbolizing a chief's military might. These trophies, or their iconographic representations, were wealth markers, status emblems, and rank signifiers.

In ritual dramatizations scalps were often treated as if they were the enemy. For example, an Osage priest would wrap a scalp around the middle of a war club, and, holding the club aloft, strike the scalp that is wound around the club with a war medicine bundle. This symbolic act formed a drama representing a warrior going forth to strike and overcome the enemy; such an act implies that a courageous warrior, armed with this club, would be able to overcome the enemies of his tribe.[29]

War trophies were sought for a number of reasons: to seal alliances, achieve success in battle, and obtain war honors, which could then be used for political, social, and religious advancement. Trophies could be used to connect the spirit of slain enemies with relatives in order for the slain enemy to accompany deceased relatives on their journey along the Path of Souls or spirit trail. Trophy imagery thus became one of the key powers for warriors in their connection with ancestors and deities, and the celestial realm. Myths that promoted and legitimized trophy-taking behavior

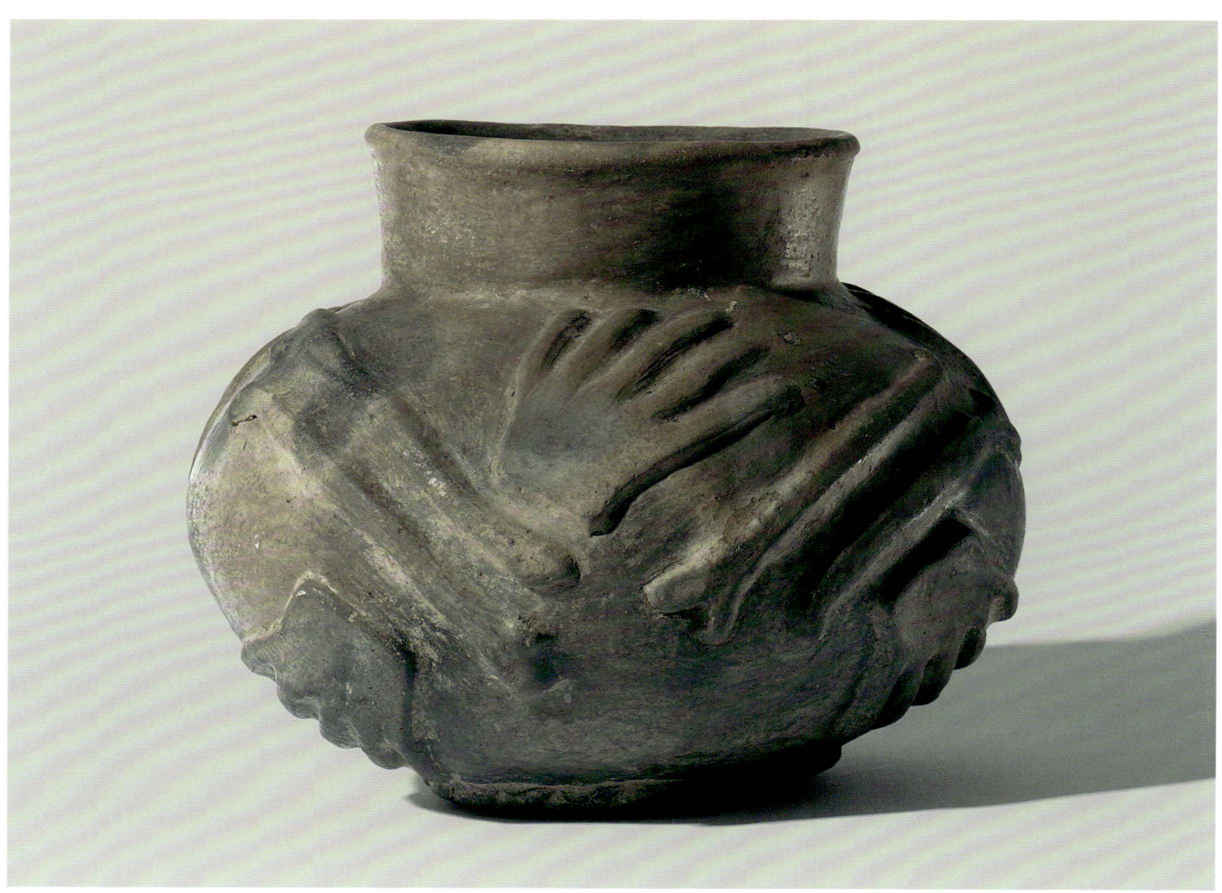

Fig. 30 Vessel with bones and hand motifs; Bell Plain type; Tennessee or Arkansas, A.D. 1350–1450; ceramic, h. 15.2 cm; The Field Museum, Chicago. Cat. no. 259.

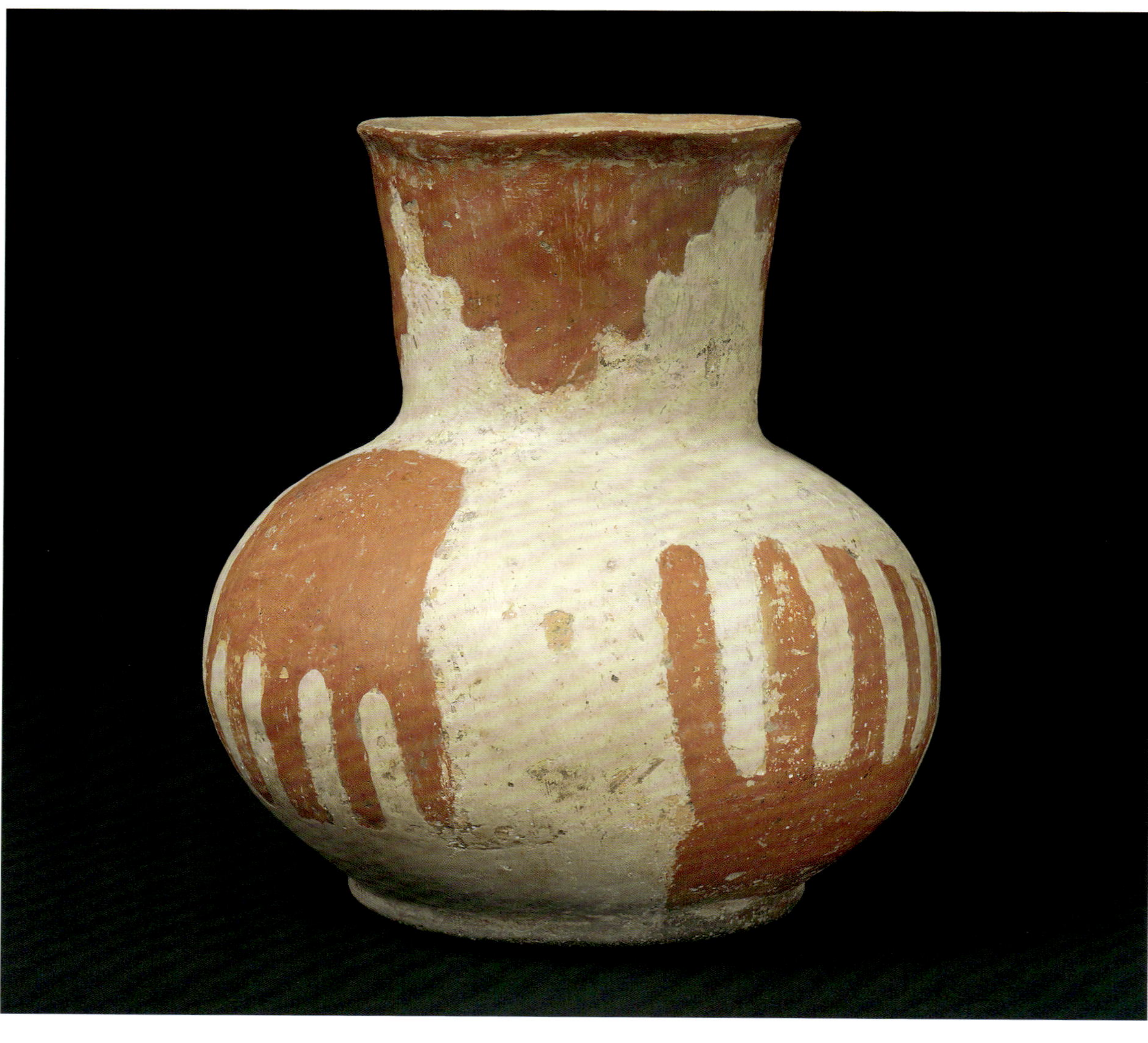

Fig. 31 Wide-necked jar with human hand design; Nodena Red and White type; Arkansas, Poinsett County, A.D. 1350–1450; ceramic, h. 17.8 cm; James and Elaine Kinker Collection, Midwest. Cat. no. 232.

in the Mississippian world may have been widespread. Elements of these charters survived into the nineteenth century, especially on the eastern Great Plains, and they bear remarkable similarities, suggesting that many Eastern Woodland polities and cultures in the recent past shared a common cosmology. By the late fourteenth century, however, much of the Mississippian world had changed, bringing about the demise of the great lords of the Southeast, the cessation of their struggle for dominion over geopolitical worlds, and the end of the remarkable variety of combat iconography that has been examined and illustrated here.

Notes

1. This fictional narrative introduction is based on recent archaeological, iconographic, and ethnohistorical information concerning ritual and warfare in the Mississippian world. See Anderson 1994; Dye 1995; Dye 2005; Hudson 1976; Hudson 1997; King 2003a; Milner 1999; Swanton 1946.
2. Theodor De Bry based his engravings of Florida's Timucuan Indians on the observations and paintings of Jacques Le Moyne de Morgues, a member of the Laudonnière expedition of 1564. See Fundaburk 1969; Hulton 1977; Lorant 1965; Milanich and Milbrath 1989.
3. Anderson 1994; Dye 1995.
4. Knight, Brown, and Lankford 2001.
5. Brown 2005b.
6. Waring and Holder 1945.
7. Knight, Brown, and Lankford 2001.
8. Brown and Kelly 2000; Brown 1989; Brown 2005b.
9. Brown 2005b.
10. Knight, Brown, and Lankford 2001.
11. Earle 1997.
12. Reyna 1994.
13. Hudson 1976; Churchill 1996.
14. Dye 1995; Knight 2001.
15. Hudson 1976; Swanton 1946; Tregle 1975; Williams 1930.
16. Dye 2005.
17. Dye 2005; Lankford 2005c.
18. La Flesche 1939, p. 11.
19. Van Horne 1993.
20. Knowles 1940.
21. Emerson 2003.
22. Brown 1996.
23. Brown 2001.
24. Dye 2004.
25. Brown 1985; Knight 1986.
26. Hall 1997a; Hall 2000.
27. Knight, Brown, and Lankford 2001.
28. Redmond 1994.
29. Bailey 1995.

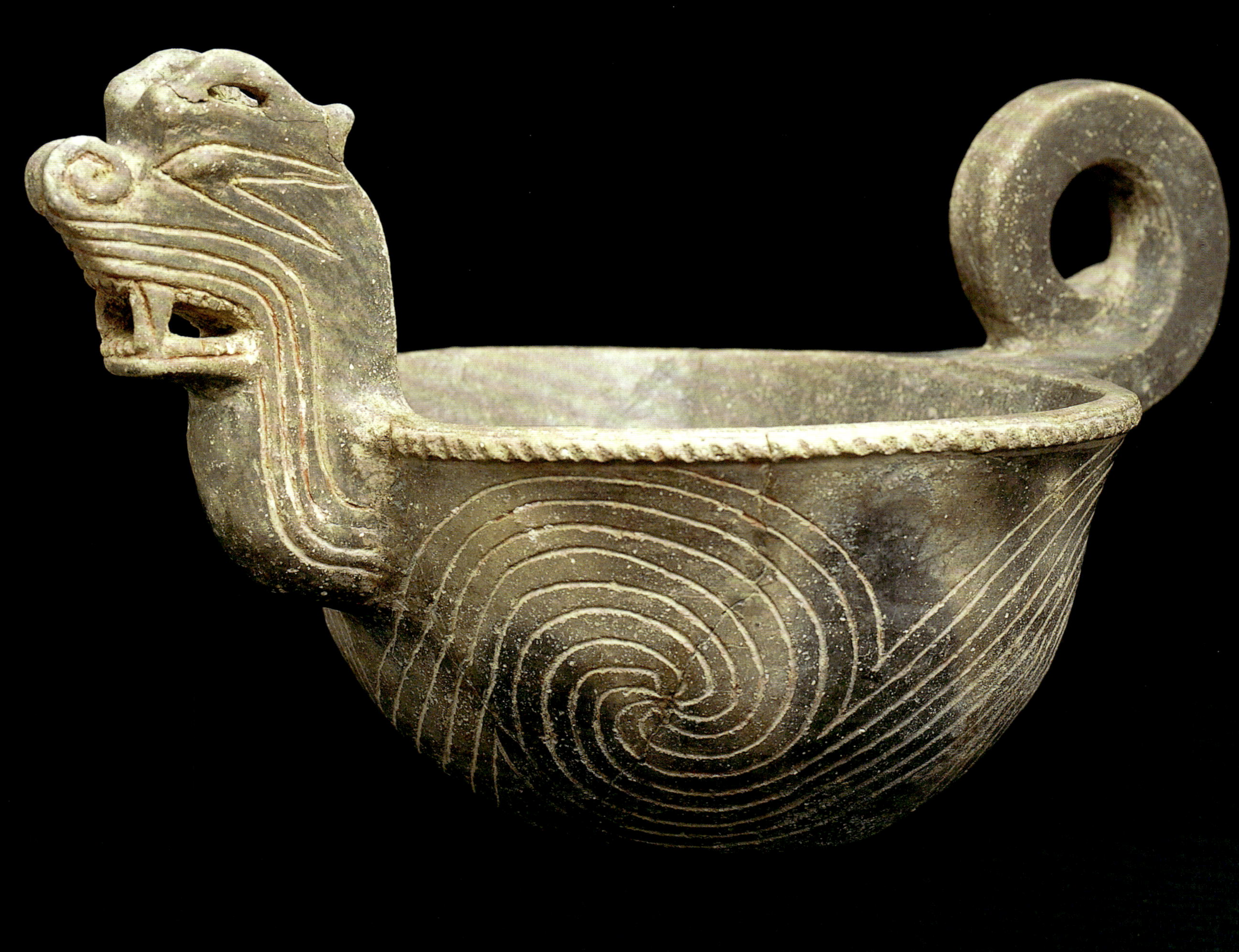

Life is not possible without an opening toward the transcendent; in other words, human beings cannot live in chaos.

—MIRCEA ELIADE, *THE SACRED AND THE PROFANE*

World on a String

George E. Lankford

SOME COSMOLOGICAL COMPONENTS OF THE SOUTHEASTERN CEREMONIAL COMPLEX

Refusing to live in chaos means that humans must necessarily be creators of order.[1] It is presumed that human beings always seek that order in the real world, so that the order that they establish—on the ground, in their social organizations, and in their behavior—is a reflection of the greater, cosmic order in which humanity is embedded. However it is perceived, the great cosmos is fundamentally one that humans did not create. Yet, as participants in it, they may legitimately recreate it and manipulate it. They may also symbolize it in words, in song, in ritual, in architecture, and in visual images.

Societies based upon scientific knowledge are tempted to be scornful of prescientific forms of cosmic understanding, objecting that "the world is not really that way." Such an attitude, of course, is rooted in a compulsion to make cosmic understanding a pure reflection of the great Cosmos, as if that is of primary significance to human beings desperately trying to live well in the face of chaos. All attempts to create cosmos may be said to have two things in common, regardless of the level of their creators' ability to sense and measure the great Cosmos—their goal of providing a sense of transcendence and the power to use it, and their inability to describe it or symbolize it adequately. Despite the inadequacy, the best expression of all humanity's striving for cosmos may be the relatively small set of artistic images the countless generations have produced.

Fig. 1 Great Serpent/Underwater Panther vessel; Arkansas, A.D. 1300–1500; ceramic, h. 17.2, l. 32.4 cm; Dr. James F. Cherry Collection, Fayetteville, Arkansas. Cat. no. 250.

One of the outstanding forms of cosmic art comes from people who lived in eastern North America during the twelfth through fourteenth centuries. An extensive collection of art pieces that they created—from many different peoples, different locations, and different cultures—has received several labels during the last century. Names once applied to this body of artifacts, such as Death Cult, Buzzard Cult, and Southern Cult, have been replaced by Southeastern Ceremonial Complex (SECC), but there are difficulties with that label as well.[2] It is probably more accurate to call it a Southeastern Artistic Complex, for that title at least emphasizes the known fact: that there was an extraordinary explosion of the creation of artwork during these centuries. Ritual and sociological understandings of the art pieces, like the symbolic and philosophical dimensions, are matters of debate and hypothesis construction. The art itself, however, is simply there, mutely testifying to its beauty and power long after its creators and social framework have died.

Microcosms

It has long been suggested by archaeologists, anthropologists, and other interpreters of these art forms that some of the symbols refer to the cosmology of the Native Americans, and that appears to be a reasonable interpretation of an important portion of the corpus.[3] The formal nature of some of the compositions argues that there are one or more structural principles at work in the design. When it becomes apparent that many of the elements that make up these complex designs are also used independently and in other designs, then it seems likely that each element has a meaning of its own. If the designs are cosmological in nature, then the individual elements probably represent particular parts of the cosmic structure. The cosmic structure itself is known fairly well from ethnographic narratives and myth collections, for Native Americans shared an understanding of the organization of the world that continued late into the postcontact period.[4] Generally, the cosmos is described as organized in layers, with the bottom layer consisting of a vast body of water, presumably contained in something solid. This Beneath World (or Underwater World) is matched by the celestial Above World (or Overworld). The earth where humans and four-legged creatures live—the Middle World (or what some have called This World)—is a disk floating on the water, and thus is the dividing line and meeting ground for the two opposing worlds and their inhabitants. Beyond this basic understanding shared throughout the Eastern Woodlands, the tribal groups maintained their own detailed traditions, with manifold variation. In applying ethnographic information to the interpretation of the SECC iconography, it is difficult to know which details were relevant for the creators of the prehistoric art forms. As a result, the knowledge of several ethnic groups will be presented in the following discussion, since, despite the differences in detail, there is general agreement on the cosmic structure in eastern North America.[5]

Two designs in particular invite us to consider a cosmological interpretation, for it seems reasonable to read them as microcosms, or images of total cosmic structure made very small. In the case of these two examples, they are small indeed, because they are both gorgets, or small circular decorations intended to be strung on a string or a leather thong and worn around the neck. The raw material of these gorgets is shell cut from large whelk shells of several varieties, probably from the Gulf of Mexico, and the design on both has been cut into the shell, an engraving process that is very difficult to accomplish using flaked stone tools on hard shell. Yet these designs were done in multiple copies, on shell gorget after shell gorget, with little variation and by more than one artist.

These gorget designs have been named for the locations where early examples were found by archaeolo-

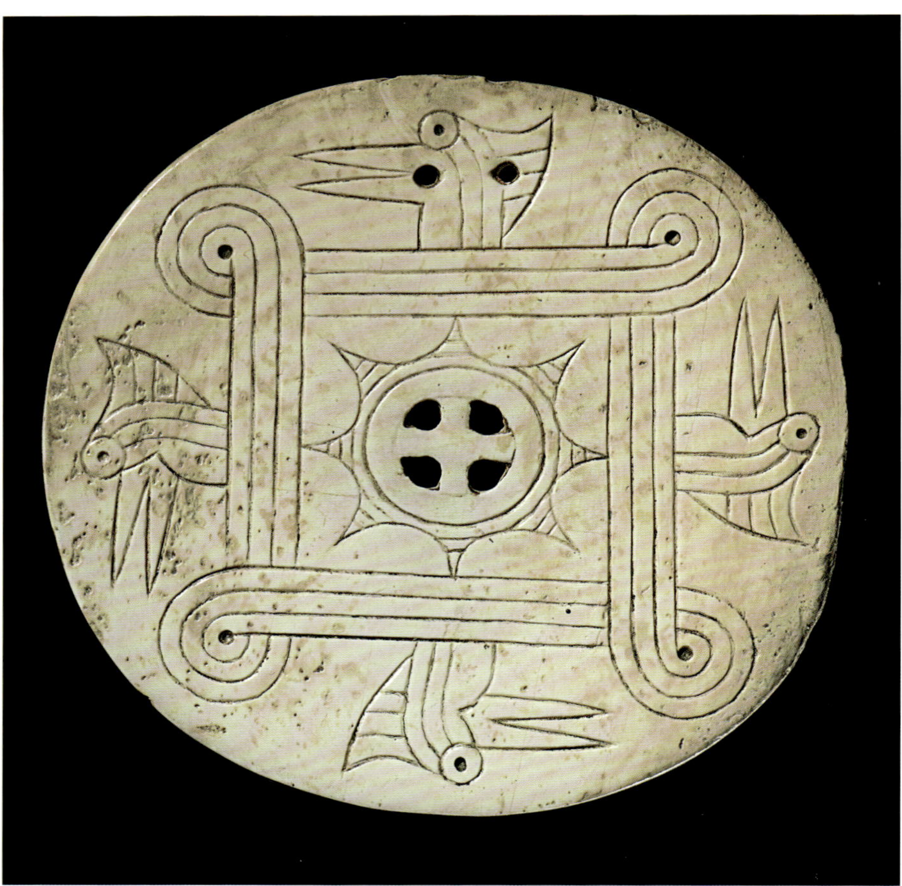

Fig. 2 Engraved shell gorget; Cox Mound style; Tennessee, Sumner County, Castalian Springs site, A.D. 1000–1400; marine shell, diam. 8.5 cm; Smithsonian Institution, National Museum of the American Indian, Washington, D.C. Cat. no. 138.

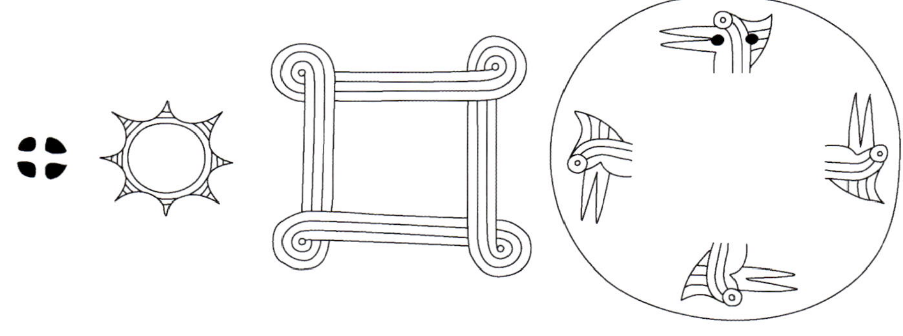

Fig. 3 Drawing of the five elements in a Cox Mound gorget: cross, sun, looped square (guilloche), crested birds (woodpeckers), and circle; drawing by Elizabeth Reese Baloutine.

gists and treasure hunters. The two that I am considering here—the Cox Mound–style and the Hixon-style gorgets—are named after two sites in the upper Tennessee River valley in eastern Tennessee.[6] Their designs are elegant (figs. 2 and 4). For analytical purposes it is useful to break down both designs into their elements. Taking the Cox Mound design first, we can identify five distinct elements (see fig. 3). The central element, the cross, has been identified by James H. Howard as directly cognate to the four-log fire that burns at the center of the Muskogee (Creek) square ground, which is the summer architectural equivalent of the council house.[7] The location of the town council meetings, the square ground is clearly a cosmogram in its own right. The center is marked by the four-log hearth—oriented to the four cardinal points—on which burns a sacred fire that is annually extinguished and rekindled ceremonially in order to purify the fire and restore its closeness to its celestial source, the sun.

It is the sun that is unmistakably the second element in the Cox Mound cosmogram, consisting of a circle and rays. Its position surrounding the fire-cross suggests that what is intended is a three-dimensional image rather than the obvious two-dimensional one. The sun is in its celestial position, the zenith of the cosmos, directly above the fire on the earthly plane. It is significant that there is ethnographic information that the fire is indeed the earthly representative of the Sun, which is the celestial representative of the chief divinity. The southeastern accounts describe careful attention to preserving the purity of the fire, including the institution of taboos and the selection of specialists who must tend the fire throughout the year.[8]

The third element of the composition is the looped square. In the square ceremonial ground of the Muskogee (Creek), the square is composed of the "beds" in which the chiefs, elders, and warriors sat to deliberate on the affairs of the town or on earthly concerns (fig. 5). Thus, if the correspondence with the gorget symbolism continues, then the looped square represents the earth. This connection is supported by the mythic accounts from a wide variety of Eastern Woodland peoples that the earth-disk is supported by water creatures. The specific identification of these creatures may range from turtles to water spirits, but all are inhabitants of the Beneath World. The most probable direct referent is the Central Algonquian peoples' view of four water serpents that form the foundation of earth floating on the water. The cardinal directions (and variants) are responsible for stabilizing the four supports, but a Winnebago variant of this mythic narrative speaks of four serpents used by the character called the Breathmaker as stakes to nail the earth to the foundations of the Beneath World itself. From these details it is a simple step to identify the square as consisting of four serpents, interlocked at the cardinal directions where they receive stability.

This identification of the looped square as an artistic symbol raises an interesting problem, for it pulls into

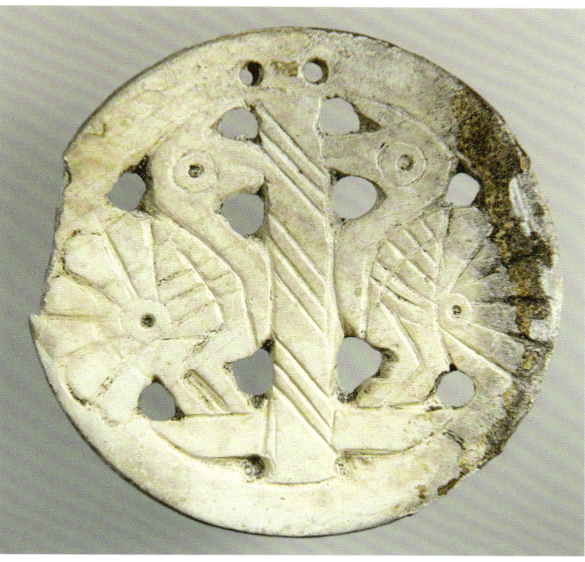

Fig. 4 Engraved shell gorget with turkey-cocks; Hixon style; Tennessee, Hamilton County, Hixon site, A.D. 1000–1400; marine shell, diam. 14.6 cm; Frank H. McClung Museum, University of Tennessee, Knoxville, no. 508/1Ha3.

the collection of art forms that clearly belong to the SECC a large number of prehistoric pots that, despite their different locations and ceramic treatments, are characterized by a common incised or engraved design. Called a guilloche, this design, when looked at from above the mouth of the pot, is recognizable as the looped square (fig. 6). Its presence on the pottery argues that these pots—constituting a great body of additional artistic material in the SECC corpus—are themselves microcosmic in design.[9]

The fourth element is a set of four birds that are distinguished by a straight feather crest and a straight pointed bill. These crested birds are frequently encountered in other artistic constructs, but in the Cox Mound gorgets they are categorizable as birds of the four directions, probably identifiable as the Winds or the

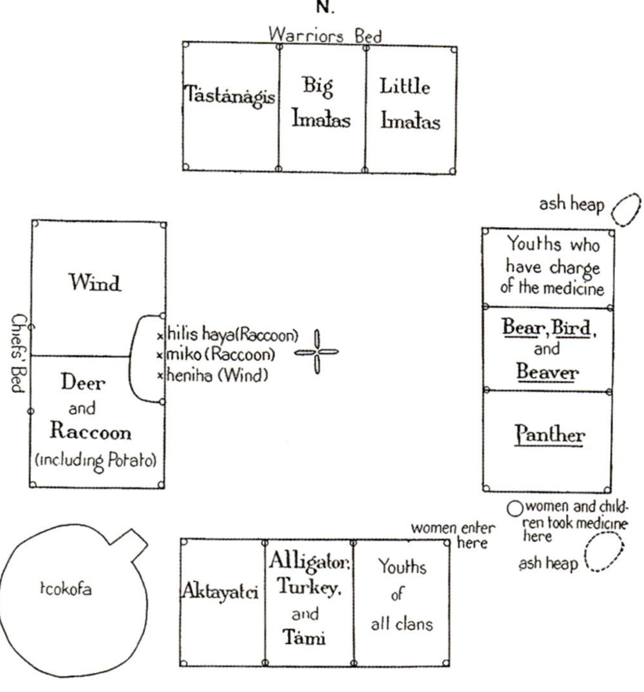

Fig. 5 Plan of the Kealedji square ground, a traditional Creek ceremonial site in eastern Oklahoma, as recorded by John R. Swanton of the Bureau of American Ethnology; from Swanton 1928, p. 251.

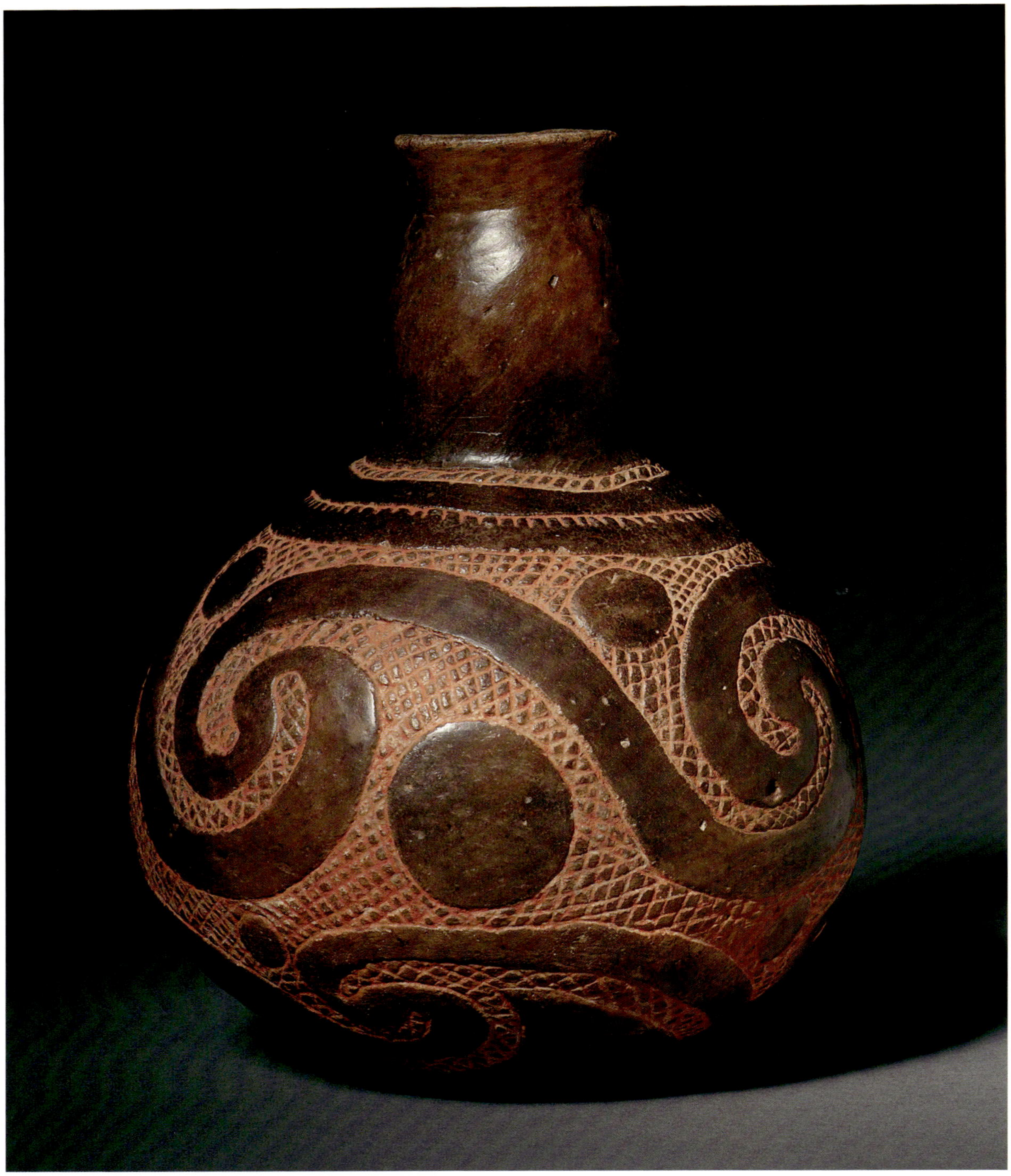

Fig. 6 Globular bottle; Hodges Engraved type; Caddoan; southwestern Arkansas, A.D. 1400–1700; ceramic, h. 24.8 cm; Museum of the Red River, Idabel, Oklahoma. Cat. no. 203.

Thunders of myth. It should be noted that the images of the Thunder powers in art of the Southeast are more varied than are depictions of the standard Thunderbird of other sections of North America. The fifth and final element of the Cox Mound-style gorget is the circle of the rim itself, which would in this design represent the horizon circle of the cosmos, the edge of the waters of the Beneath World. The circle is also the edge of the shell on which the engraved portion of the design rests, and the shell material itself is a part of the message, since shell is a gift of the Beneath World powers. All together, the shell and its engraved forms, though two-dimensional in execution, form a three-dimensional image, a model of the cosmos (fig. 7).

The Hixon-style gorget has also been found at several Tennessee sites, but not at the *same* sites as the Cox Mound gorgets. Nonetheless, it too appears to be a microcosm, though from a different perspective: the cosmos as seen from the side rather than from above. A few hints will enable a reader to work out the correspondences. First, the Sun-fire column, the mythic axis mundi or center of the world, becomes an actual vertical column, usually characterized as a pole with spiral stripes and dotted circles (fig. 4). The looped square becomes a flat horizontal line (representing a geometric plane) across the bottom of the pole. On it stand the four crested birds, here reduced to two by artistic necessity. These two figures have traditionally been

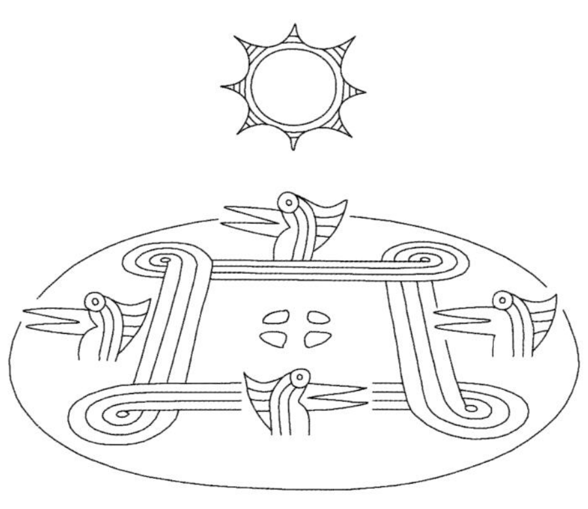

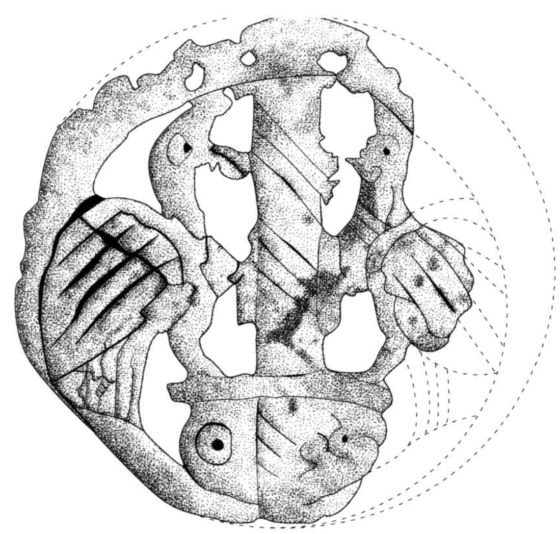

Fig. 7 Representation of a Cox Mound gorget in three dimensions; drawing by Elizabeth Reese Baloutine.

Fig. 8 Drawing of an engraved shell gorget with turkey-cocks; Hixon style; Georgia, Bartow County, Etowah, Mound C; marine shell, diam. 5.1 cm; Peabody Museum, Phillips Academy, Andover, Massachusetts; drawing by Elizabeth Reese Baloutine.

seen as turkeys, because of the spread tails visible in some of the Hixon-style gorgets (which are thus called "turkey-cocks gorgets"). In this microcosmic interpretation, the crested bird is not understood to be a naturalistic turkey, and this distinction opens a more intriguing iconographic possibility. There are other gorget styles that feature humanlike figures who have in their extended hands feather fans that are almost identical to the "turkey tails" in the Hixon variant.[10]

The compositional parallel between these two examples suggests that the artists of the Hixon style were kenning with known images. If the meaning of the figures with the feather fans were already known, the artistic imitation of the fans on the crested birds—surely a form of artistic play—might be revealed to have a surprising depth of meaning. Currently this meaning is not known, but it seems important to recognize that kenning may also have been part of the iconographic repertoire available to the SECC artists. In the Hixon side view, the Beneath World can no longer be symbolized by the shell and the edge of the gorget as it was in the Cox Mound style, and it is replaced by some curved lines beneath the horizontal line of earth. A comparison of different artistic renderings of these curved lines reveals that they are the rims of a pot on which rests the earth disk, as shown on a gorget unearthed from Mound C at the Etowah site in northwestern Georgia (fig. 8; see also the essay by Adam King in this volume). The pot is presumably the container for the waters of the Beneath World, and the image is doubly suggestive when we recall the placement of the looped square or guilloche around the mouth of the microcosmic ceramic pot.

Thus, these two gorget designs alone—the Cox Mound and Hixon—suggest the basic cosmological ideas and their artistic rendition by prehistoric Native Americans. They can be admired for their elegance and their execution, for Native artists have taken various symbols and melded them in these remarkable images of a unified microcosm. Yet these elements are also free to be utilized in other designs, and they can stand alone. Such preliminary hints of the cosmological repertoire of the SECC iconographers enable a viewer to appreciate the artistic ability of the engravers, both in compositional skill and in execution. They also strongly indicate that the visual art of these artisans is far beyond mere representation and is to be seen as part of their mental world of complex cultural symbolism.

A Path in the Above World

If the entire cosmos can be conveyed in an elegantly simple image, then it stands to reason that images could designate specific portions of the cosmos as well. The reason for wishing to do so is clear: the cosmos was not a neutral architectural notion, but a map of where power was located. Humans were understood to live in the Middle World surrounded by powerful forces that needed to be placated, sought after, and negotiated with for usable power. Any image of the cosmos or any portion of it was thus likely to be seen as a powerful object in its own right. In human life, individuals and social groups such as lineages or lodges were likely to have been befriended and given power by a particular entity inhabiting a particular part of the cosmos. Thus it was useful to be able to use the iconographic code to denote cosmic affiliation.

One example of the more limited cosmic segment expressed in the art of the Native cultures of the Southeast is the Path of Souls, which runs across the night sky.[11] The Above World of course consists of the diurnal duality of day and night, and each should be depicted in art. We have already seen the day represented in the Sun-fire axis of the Hixon-style gorgets, but we have not yet encountered the night world. The primary figure in the night sky, even though modern people might find it a bit surprising because of the difficulty of seeing its starry expanse, is the Milky Way. It dominates the night sky, and its movements are a bit eccentric, for it appears to change its directional orientation through time.

Culturally, for the Native American peoples of the Eastern Woodlands, the Milky Way was the path traversed by the souls of the dead. In fact, this metaphor is almost universally present in the ethnographic literature of historic period tribes. If it were to be taken as a literal description of the journey after death, whether for all people or selected groups such as religious specialists (the tribes differed on this), then the night sky becomes a landscape that must be understood in detail. The details of its geography would be enshrined in myth, as a guidebook for the future postmortuary journey, and would probably take the form of some key iconographic images.

There is such a myth, and it is virtually universal, despite variations, throughout the Eastern Woodlands and Plains. It tells of men who visit the realm of the dead and return with the knowledge. Their journey involves walking west (like the dead) and leaping over a river or a chasm that is marked by the "rising and falling sky." They walk the Path of Souls and along the way have various adventures, including a confrontation with one or more figures who judge the quality of the soul and determine which fork of the path should be taken. The confrontation may be violent, as when dogs must be dealt with, but eventually the men meet the guardians of the village of souls, where they are entertained. An "Orpheus" version of this myth continues with the gaining, then losing, of a dead soul. The "journey to the sky" version ends with the return of the men with gifts.[12]

One of the images that may reflect elements of the mythic understanding of the geography of the Above World is the hand-and-eye symbol that is geographically widespread and reproduced in many media in the SECC art forms (fig. 9). The ethnographic information to support the interpretation of this motif as representing a particular location on the Path of Souls is limited to a small group of people, but it is possible that the belief they have maintained was much more widespread in prehistoric times. The essential background information for the interpretation of the art motif is that one of the Twin heroes, who had gone above through a hole in the sky, cut off the hand of a sky chief and hung it in the sky where he had tried to block the portal. The stars that compose the sky chief's hand may be familiar to many readers as components of the Greek constellation Orion. This constellation, known explicitly today by the Mandan, Hidatsa, Crow, and Lakota as a Hand, is adjacent to the Milky Way. More to the point, it sets precisely in the west, just before the Milky Way falls like a wall below the horizon (fig. 10). The Hand constellation with its galactic "fuzzy star" (the "eye") is thus situated to be a portal into the sky, an entry point onto the Path for the souls that have moved west to reach that conjunction of the portal, the beginning of the Path of the Milky Way, and the edge of the earth disk.

The motion of the Hand portal as it falls below the horizon also explains a motif found in the widespread Native American "Orpheus" myth. As suggested above, travelers seeking to go to the realm of the dead must leap across a chasm and through a "rising and falling sky" portal; those who fail to make the jump correctly fall to their doom. The brief moment the Hand-and-eye is on the horizon is all the time that is available for that leap, and the artistic image is an apt illustration of the phenomenon that confronts the souls of the dead.

Other adventures of the souls on the Path are told in the myths, and these too may correlate with stars on the Milky Way and with images in the SECC corpus, but such points of connection have not yet been identified. There is one, however, that might be mentioned, since it points up an important aspect of the meaning of the SECC iconographic corpus.[13] In the Path of Souls mythology there is usually one—sometimes more than one—antagonist whom the soul must confront. Since the outcome of the encounter frequently is understood to determine the direction of the soul beyond that point, on one branch of the Path or another, the star Deneb, located exactly at the point at which the Milky Way divides, is the likely celestial referent for the antagonist (fig. 11).

Fig. 9 Bottle with ogee and hand-and-eye motifs; Alabama, near Mobile, A.D. 1300–1500; ceramic, h. 15.9 cm; Harvard University, Peabody Museum of Archaeology and Ethnology, Museum Purchase 1946. Cat. no. 266.

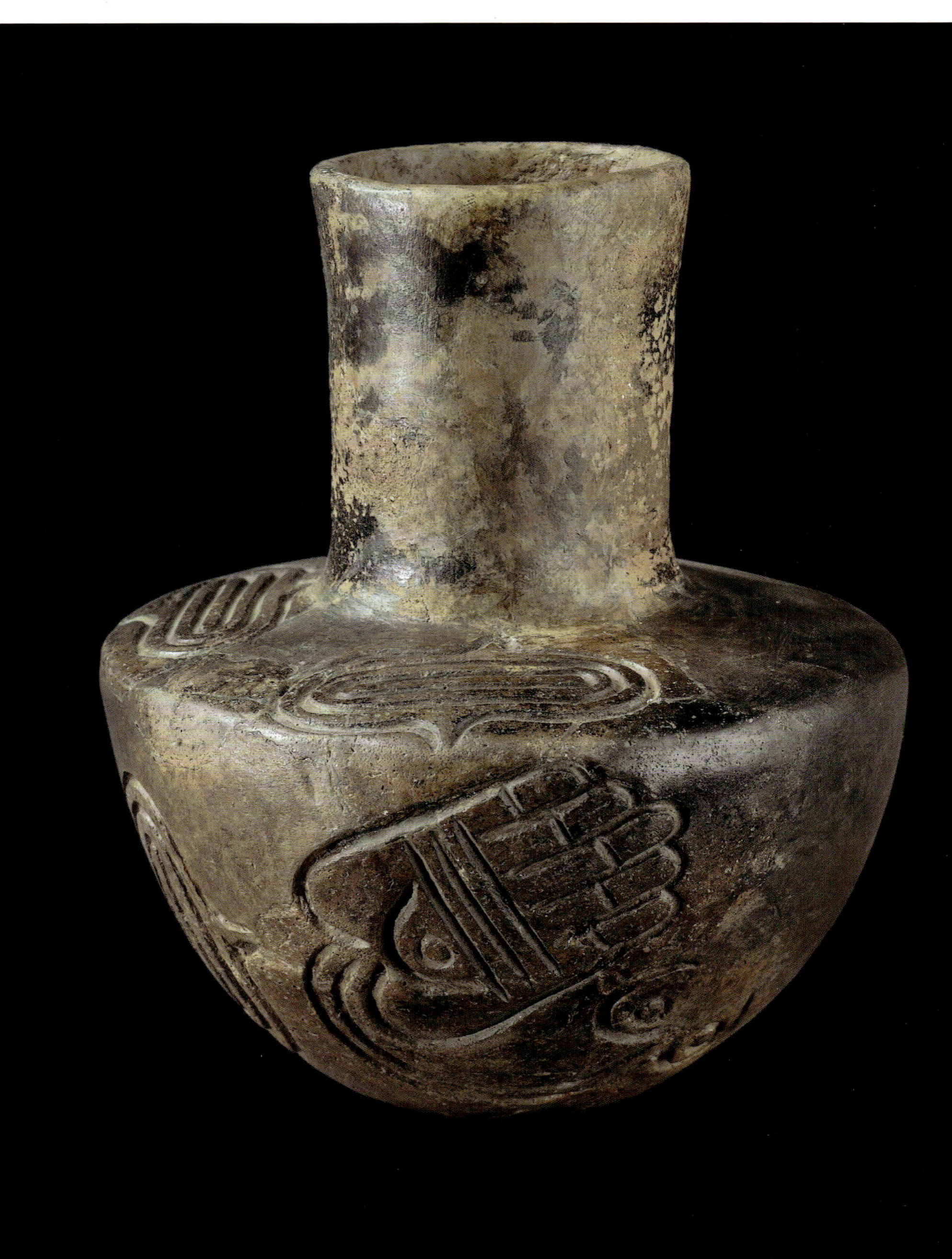

Frequently in Native American myths the antagonist takes the form of an old woman, an old man, or a dog. Among a small group of southeastern peoples (notably the Alabamas and Seminoles), however, the antagonist is an eagle, and the deceased is equipped with a knife to aid the soul in its fight. The eagle fits this star pattern nicely, because Deneb is but one of the stars of the Greek constellation Cygnus (the Swan), which might easily be seen as a different bird. An interesting aspect of this small group of Muskhogean speakers who see the antagonist as a bird is that they are likely candidates for descendants of the prehistoric people of Moundville, the largest Mississippian mound site in the Southeast, located near Tuscaloosa, Alabama (see the essay by Vincas Steponaitis and Vernon Knight in this volume). Engraved pottery uncovered at Moundville bears the SECC images interpreted as mortuary symbols. This site has also produced a group of similar pots on which are found engraved raptors, distinctive birds characterized by a curved beak and a jagged feather crest (see fig. 6c in the essay by Steponaitis and Knight).

These raptors, although they appear similar to raptors found in other contexts at many other sites that have yielded SECC materials, seem at Moundville to be restricted to this mortuary use. If this reading of the situation is correct, then it emphasizes an important fact about iconographic meanings—that is, that they may be site-specific, even though the symbol itself is widespread. It appears that at Moundville the raptor, regardless of its meaning at Etowah or elsewhere in the Mississippian world, refers to the eagle that confronts the dead on the Path of Souls. The localization of symbols adds another dimension of complexity to the interpretation of the SECC corpus, and it raises questions about the nature of the spread of the art complex and the relation of the art to the belief systems at the various sites.

Yet another Path of Souls figure is found on the engraved pottery of Moundville: this is a horned serpent with wings, an image that has traditionally raised the possibility of Mesoamerican influence in the Eastern Woodlands, since the winged serpent inevitably calls to mind Quetzalcóatl (fig. 12; see also Steponaitis and Knight, fig. 6a). It is quite possible, however, to interpret this Moundville image without reference to Mesoamerica. The difficulty lies in the wing on the horned serpent, for there is no ethnographic lore about a winged serpent in the Eastern Woodlands that would offer justification for such an image. Yet, if the wing is understood to be a locative element—an indicator of the location of the figure to which it is attached—rather than a descriptive one, then an entirely new interpretation of the Moundville serpent emerges. In this interpretation, the wing merely indicates that the horned serpent pictured is found in the sky, that it is, in fact, a constellation. It is worth noting that one of the Moundville raptor pots shows a raptor head connected to a wing virtually identical to that of the serpent, an image for which the locative explanation works equally well. In this view, the horned serpent, even though it appears in the sky, is not really at home there. Since the figure is only a temporary visitor in the sky, one that really belongs to the waters of the Beneath World, the focus of this examination needs to be moved from the celestial realm.

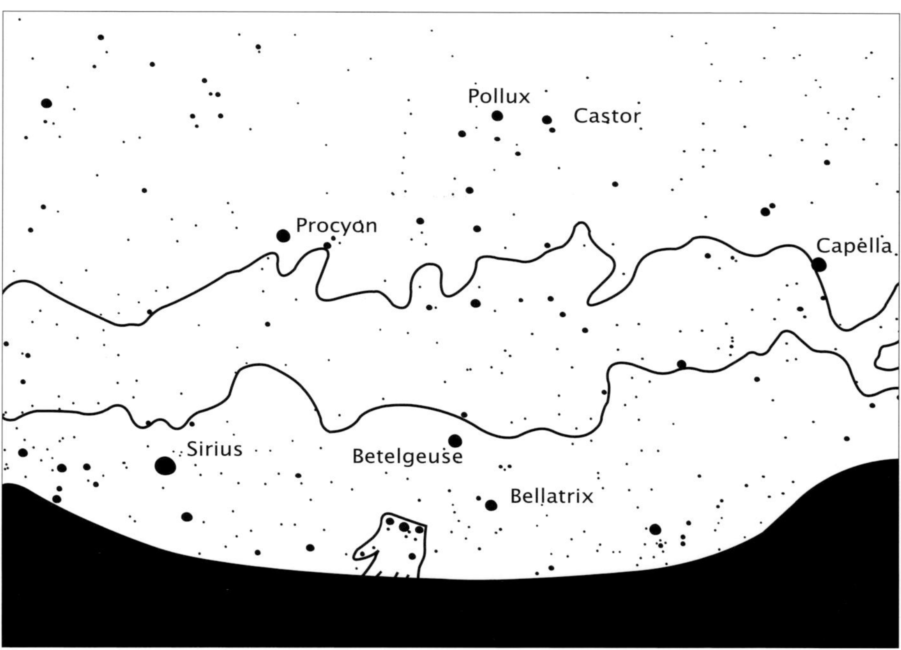

Fig. 10 Representation of the Hand constellation just before it falls below the western horizon; several of its stars also appear in the constellation Orion.

The Beneath World

There are ethnographic references to a serpent in the southern sky who is master of the realm of the dead—the Pawnees are the most precise in their treatment of this myth, but there are others whose versions confirm its authenticity.[14] At the southern end of the Milky Way a very bright constellation lies across the Path. Known in the Greek tradition as Scorpius or the Scorpion, this same configuration may easily be interpreted as a serpent (fig. 13). Scorpius has a bright red, first-magnitude star as its "eye," the star Antares, a phenomenon that matches the ethnographic information about the Great Serpent, master of the Beneath World, who has a red eye or red jewel on its head.

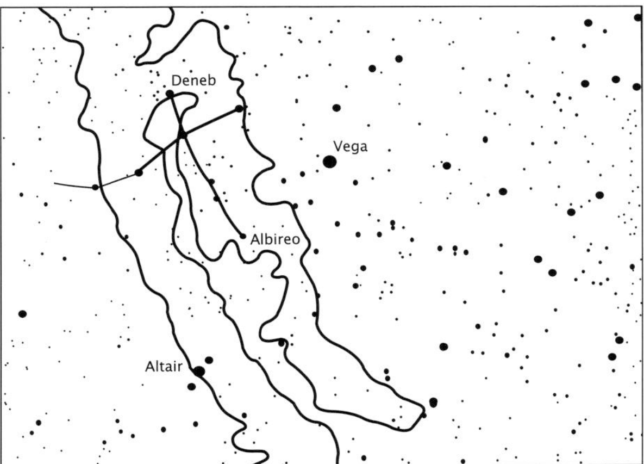

Fig. 11 The star Deneb in the constellation Cygnus stands at the dividing point of the Milky Way.

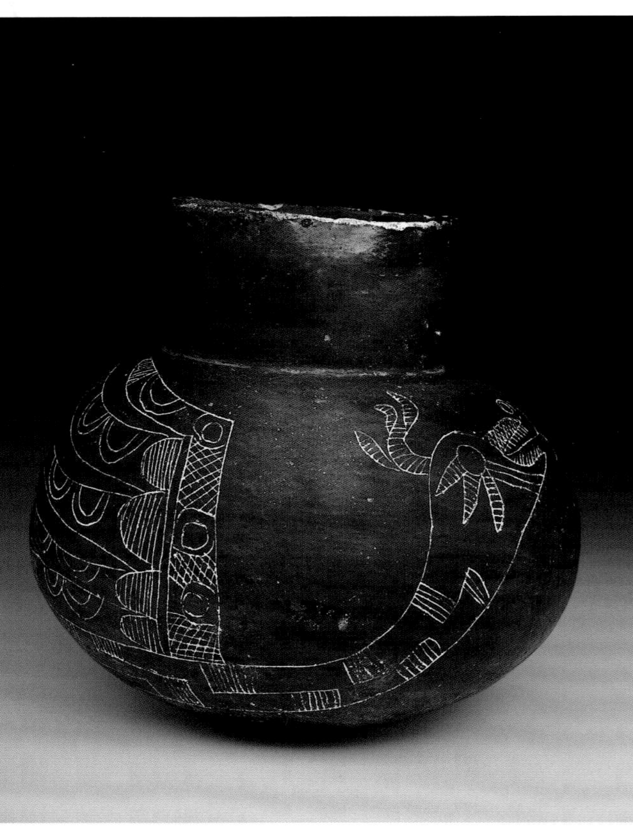

This widely known figure is characterized in myth primarily as a Horned Underwater Serpent, and it is associated culturally with great shamanistic power and also with witchcraft (fig. 14). Among the Central Algonquian peoples the Great Serpent, in its alternate form of the Underwater Panther, was the founder of the Midé Society, a lodge for people of power. Native doctors, if courageous and fortunate, received power from the Great Serpent, power that was made concrete by substances from the body of the Beneath World creature—parts of a horn, red powder from the jewel on the head, copper or shell from the scales. This figure is virtually a universal one in the Eastern Woodlands, even though its names and appearances vary greatly from tribe to tribe.

In Native American myths, the Great Serpent is diametrically opposed to the Above World, particularly to the Thunders, so it is a surprising anomaly that the Great Serpent also appears in the sky. That journey occurs primarily during the summer months, when the seasonal tilt allows the southernmost constellations to rise higher above the southern horizon. At that time the major constellation visible in the southern sky is Scorpius, which lies across the Milky Way. It is no coincidence that most tribal groups share a taboo on the telling of myths during this time, for it is thought that the Great Serpent will hear the humans talking about the sacred mysteries and will take offense, sending serpents and other dangerous antagonists into the village to punish them. Although only the Pawnee explanation of the taboo has been recorded, the taboo itself was widespread in eastern North America.

In the light of this ethnographic lore, it is an easy matter to see the Moundville winged serpent as the icon for the Great Serpent in its celestial journey, with its connection to the realm of the dead and the Path of Souls indicated by its presence on engraved pottery that is largely decorated with the icons of death.[15] Thus there appears to be no reason to invoke Quetzalcóatl to explain the SECC appearances of the winged serpent. The Great Serpent in the art is equated with the Great Serpent who is so ubiquitous a figure in the ethnographic literature, the master of the Beneath World.

With this emphasis on the importance of the Beneath World's influence on human affairs and its role in a cosmic dualism—Above World versus Beneath World—it might be anticipated that there would be an icon in the art corpus that would serve as a locative or shorthand sign for the Beneath World. And, indeed, it appears that there is one. Again, focused at Moundville, but not limited to that site, is a simple image found both individually and in many different compositional contexts. The image is referred to as a swastika, because it consists of a cross with the ends of the arms bent (see Steponaitis and Knight, figs. 6d and 14).[16] None of the examples uses a right angle as the conclusion of the arms, however, so any similarity to swastikas from India or Germany is misleading.

Comparison of its appearances in the various compositions reveals that the swastika substitutes for a limited number of other images, primarily a small cross in a circle, concentric circles, and a dot. The one thing all of the compositions have in common is that the location of the swastika is the center of the design, as are the motifs for which it can substitute. In the light of the discussion above on the microcosmic role of certain SECC designs, it seems clear that the center of the design refers to the center of the cosmos, the axis mundi, which was seen earlier in its Sun-fire mode. In the Hixon gorget design, however, the columnar axis

Fig. 12 Engraved bottle with winged serpent; Hemphill style; Alabama, Tuscaloosa and Hale counties, Moundville, south of Mound D, A.D. 1300–1450; ceramic, h. 24.1 cm; Alabama Museum of Natural History, University of Alabama, Tuscaloosa. Cat. no. 264.

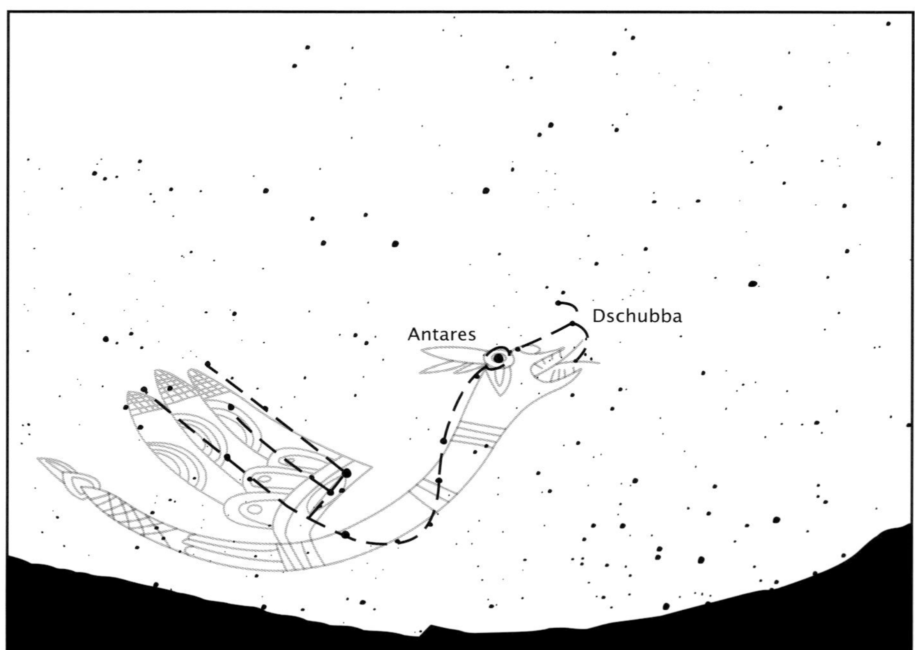

Fig. 13 Constellation of Scorpius or the Scorpion, showing the winged serpent.

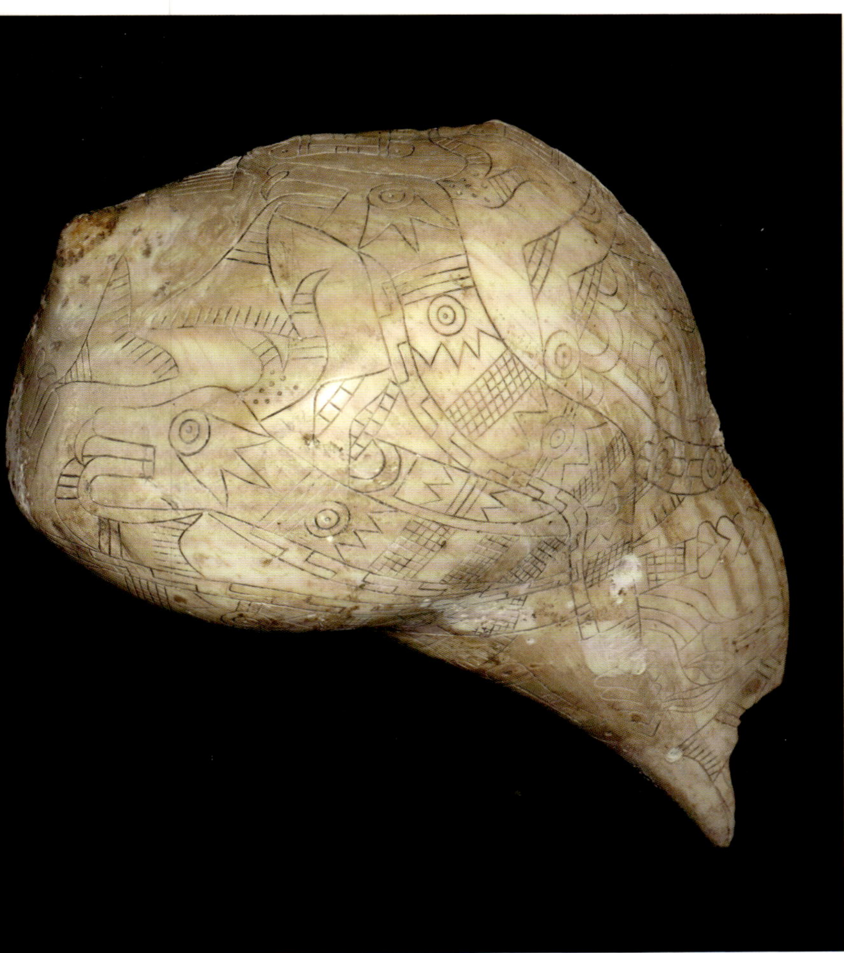

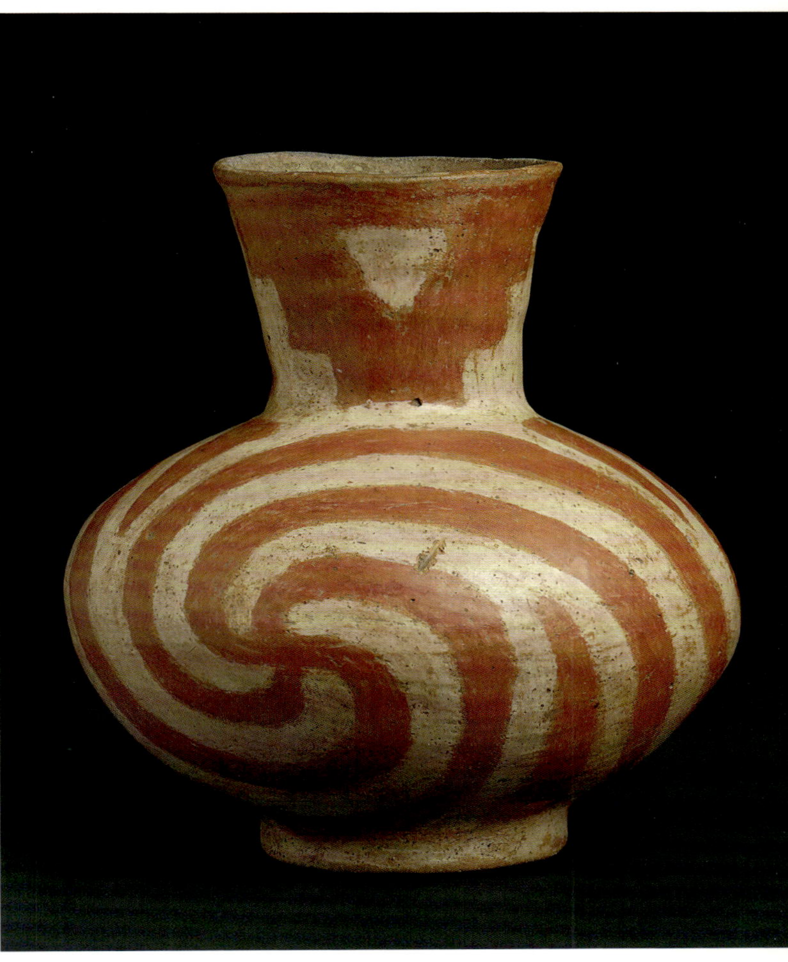

Fig 14 Engraved whelk shell with horned serpent motif; Late Braden style; Oklahoma, LeFlore County, Spiro, Craig Mound, A.D. 1200–1350; marine shell, l. 22.9 cm; University of Arkansas Museum, Fayetteville. Cat. no. 124.

Fig. 15 Wide-necked bottle with curvilinear swastika design; Nodena Red and White type; Arkansas, Poinsett County, Scott site, A.D. 1350–1450; ceramic, h. 25.4 cm; James and Elaine Kinker Collection, Midwest. Cat. no. 233.

penetrates through the earth-disk and into the Beneath World (see fig. 4). The lower portion of the axis cannot appropriately be called the Sun-fire column, since it also serves as a central axis for the water world.

If the axis is likened to an elevator shaft, then it may be considered a set of portals that can offer access to each of the levels of the cosmos, at least to those who are able to move through the axis, such as religious visionaries. What is needed iconographically, then, is a set of signs for each of the levels, so that the viewer of the art can read which level is being emphasized in any particular design. This hypothesis would explain why there can be alternate signs for the center. The rayed circle seems to be a solar sign; the cross has been identified as a fire symbol, and therefore a Middle World emblem. The swastika thus seems a likely candidate for a sign for the Beneath World (see also fig. 15).

This interpretive solution receives support from two different sources, one of which is the appearance of the swastika on the tail of crested birds on Moundville pottery (see Steponaitis and Knight, figs. 6b and 6d). On the surface, it would appear that this example would supply a counterargument, since we have already identified the crested birds as creatures between the Middle World and the Above World. In Muskhogean myth, however, there is a provocative motif in which a bird (specifically, a woodpecker) receives its tail stripes because its tail hangs down in the water at dawn.[17] The episode, whatever its more esoteric meaning might be, is thus coded in the SECC art as a bird's tail with a swastika on it—the watery tail.

The other source of support is from the Walls Focus of the Mississippi valley in the Memphis area, a source of pottery with remarkable similarities to Moundville. There are several known effigy pots bearing the heads and tails of the Great Serpent (figs. 1 and 16). They are generally known as "cat monster" pots because the heads are in the form of the Underwater Panther, but it should be remembered that the two forms—serpent and panther—are part of the same spectrum of images for the master of the Beneath World (see also fig. 18). Several of the effigy pots bear a swastika in a circle, and it shows up once on the very head of the creature (fig. 17). These occurrences make the conclusion unavoidable, that the swastika is closely associated with the Beneath World.

Conclusion

It is worth noting here that these examinations of iconographic usage from Moundville—the Path of Souls images, the Great Serpent, the swastika—have inadvertently pointed to an emphasis on the Beneath World at that important site. This observation becomes even more significant when it is realized that many of the swastikas from Moundville are in the form of copper gorgets, so numerous that they appear to be emblems peculiar to the people of Moundville. This iconographic characterization of Moundville leads to

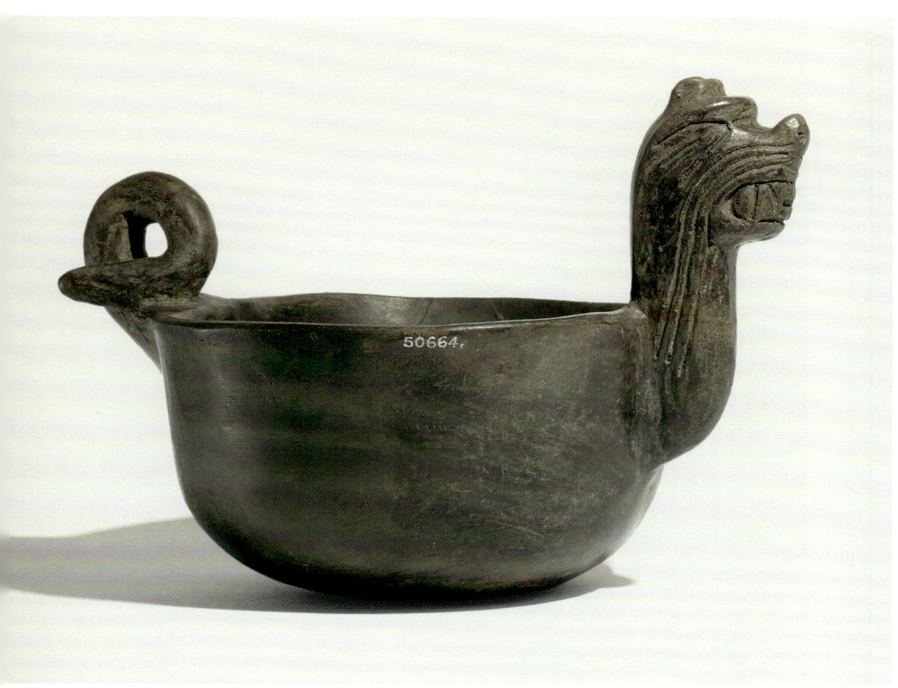

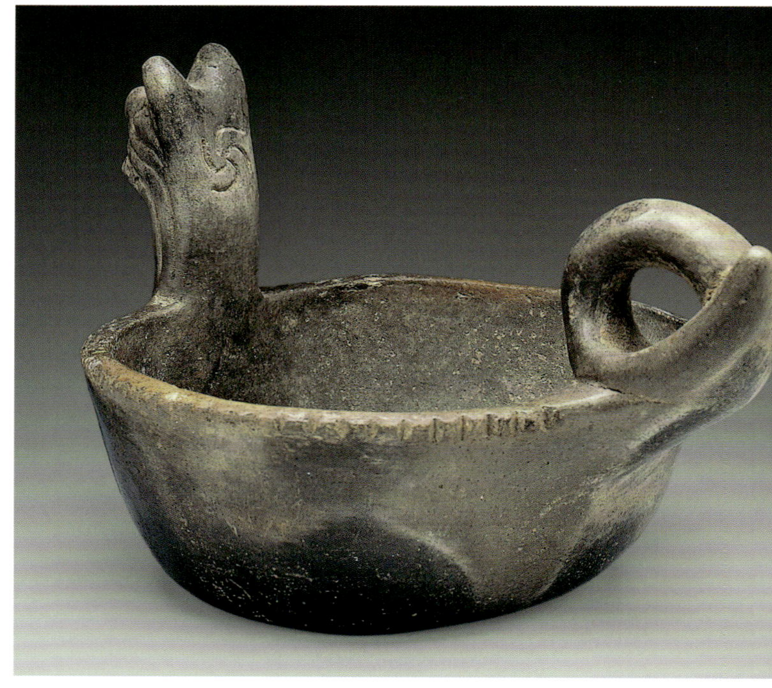

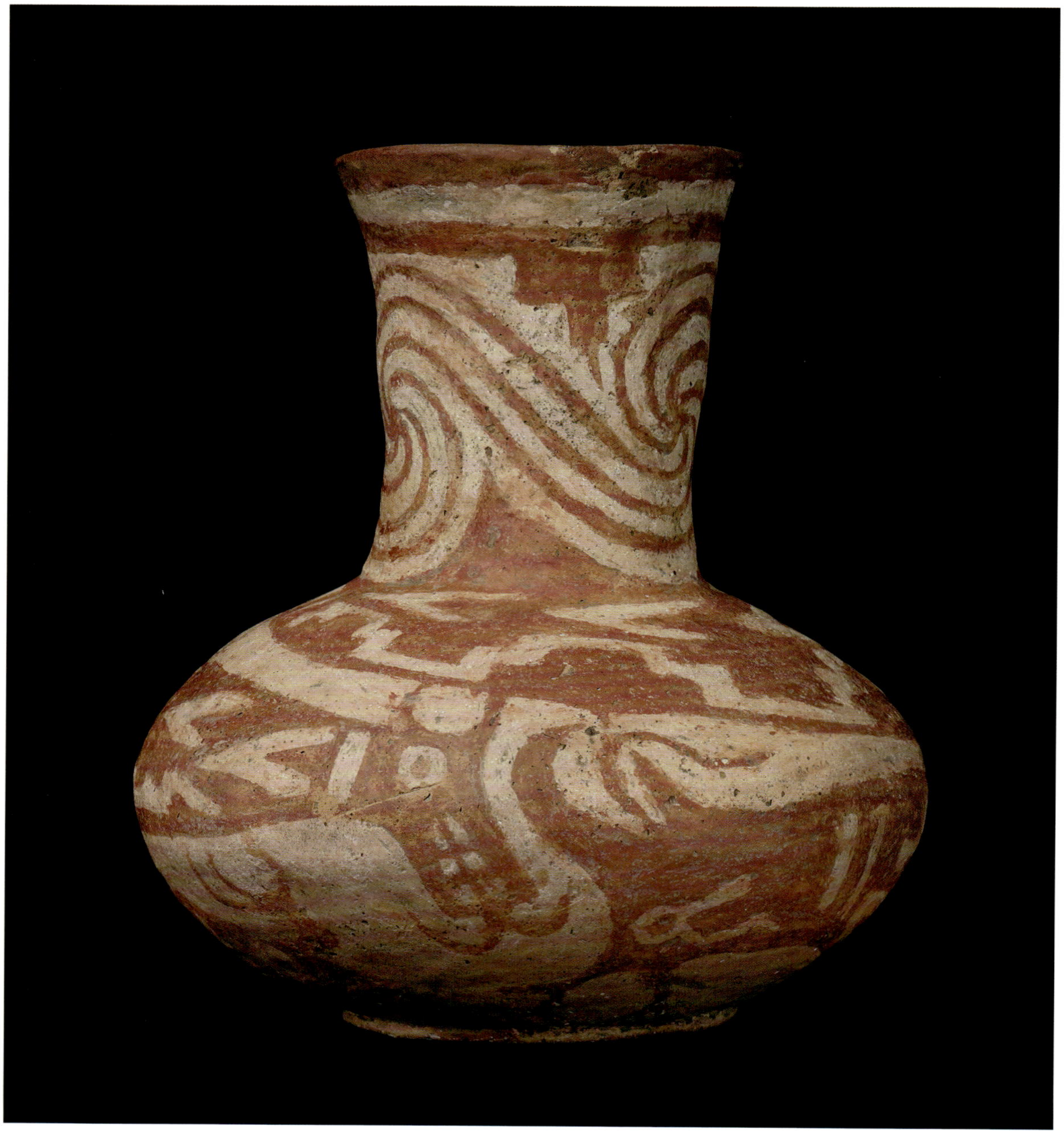

Fig. 16 Great Serpent/Underwater Panther vessel; Arkansas, A.D. 1300–1500; ceramic, h. 20.3, l. 24.1 cm; The Field Museum, Chicago. Cat. no. 251.

Fig. 17 Great Serpent/Underwater Panther vessel, with swastika on back of head; Arkansas, Crittenden County, Belle Meade site, A.D. 1300–1500; ceramic, h. 21 cm; Pink Palace Museum, Memphis.

Fig. 18 Bottle with Great Serpent/Underwater Panther; Nodena Red and White type; Arkansas, Mississippi County, Lacy site, A.D. 1300–1500; ceramic, h. 24.1, w. 20.3 cm; Tommy Beutell Collection. Cat. no. 227.

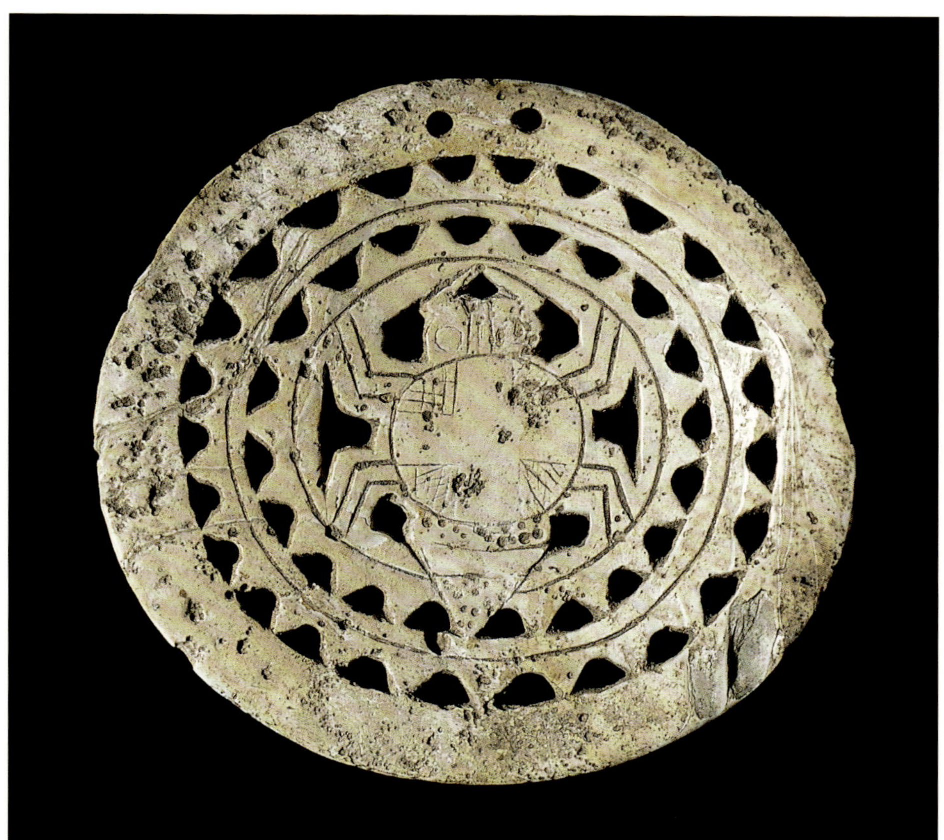

Fig. 19 Engraved shell gorget with water spider motif; Tennessee, c. A.D. 1400; marine shell, diam. 10.2 cm; Tennessee Historical Society Collection, Tennessee State Museum, Nashville. Cat. no. 146.

a provocative speculation: that the Moundville polity had a special relationship to the Beneath World that was not shared by other sites. At Etowah, for example, likely to be one of the ancestral sites of the Upper Creeks, there are few examples of the swastika and Great Serpent, although there was a strong emphasis on microcosms, Above World symbols, and celestial garb for chieftains (a theme totally lacking at Moundville). This may be only informed speculation, but it at least seems a plausible way to think about the artistic differences between the two sites. Future research may uncover peculiar emphases at other sites, thus strengthening this tentative suggestion that one of the major ways of localizing the SECC iconography was to claim portions of it as emblems of the local elite and their town (see figs. 18 and 19 for examples of possibilities).

In a more general way, it seems a fair conclusion to point out that many of the prehistoric peoples who produced these SECC art forms used them as tools or wore them as regalia, perhaps as decorations, perhaps as identifiers or rank indicators. Whatever the precise meaning and function of these images, the reality was that human beings wore upon their bodies symbols of the cosmos, a practice that surely linked them to the larger reality in which they understood themselves to be participants. Just who was able to wear a specific cosmic indicator and who was able to wear the whole microcosm will likely never be known. Even so, it seems clear that many people went to their graves, and beyond, still wearing the world on a string.

Notes

1. This has been a much-explored realm of the history of religions, one excellent example of which is Eliade 1959.
2. See Knight, Brown, and Lankford 2001 for an examination of the difficulties in isolating the phenomena for study and identifying the presuppositions that students bring to that endeavor.
3. See especially Willoughby 1932, Howard 1968, and Phillips and Brown 1978.
4. For introductions to the southeastern materials, see Hudson 1976 and Lankford 1987.
5. A more extensive discussion of the microcosmic iconography of these two gorget styles is scheduled to appear in Lankford 2005a.
6. Brain and Phillips 1996.
7. See especially the discussion in Howard 1968.
8. Swanton 1928; Hudson 1976.
9. For a provocative treatment of this sort of pottery, see Pauketat and Emerson 1991.
10. See the Rhoden style gorget in Brain and Phillips 1996, p. 61, Okla-Lf-S850.
11. For details and references for the Path of Souls interpretation, see Lankford 2005c.
12. Hultkrantz 1957; Lankford 2005c.
13. See Lankford 2000 for details of this argument.
14. For details and references for this topic, see Lankford 2005b.
15. Information on Moundville pottery is found in Steponaitis 1983a.
16. This argument is expanded in Lankford 2002.
17. Lankford 1987, pp. 109–10.

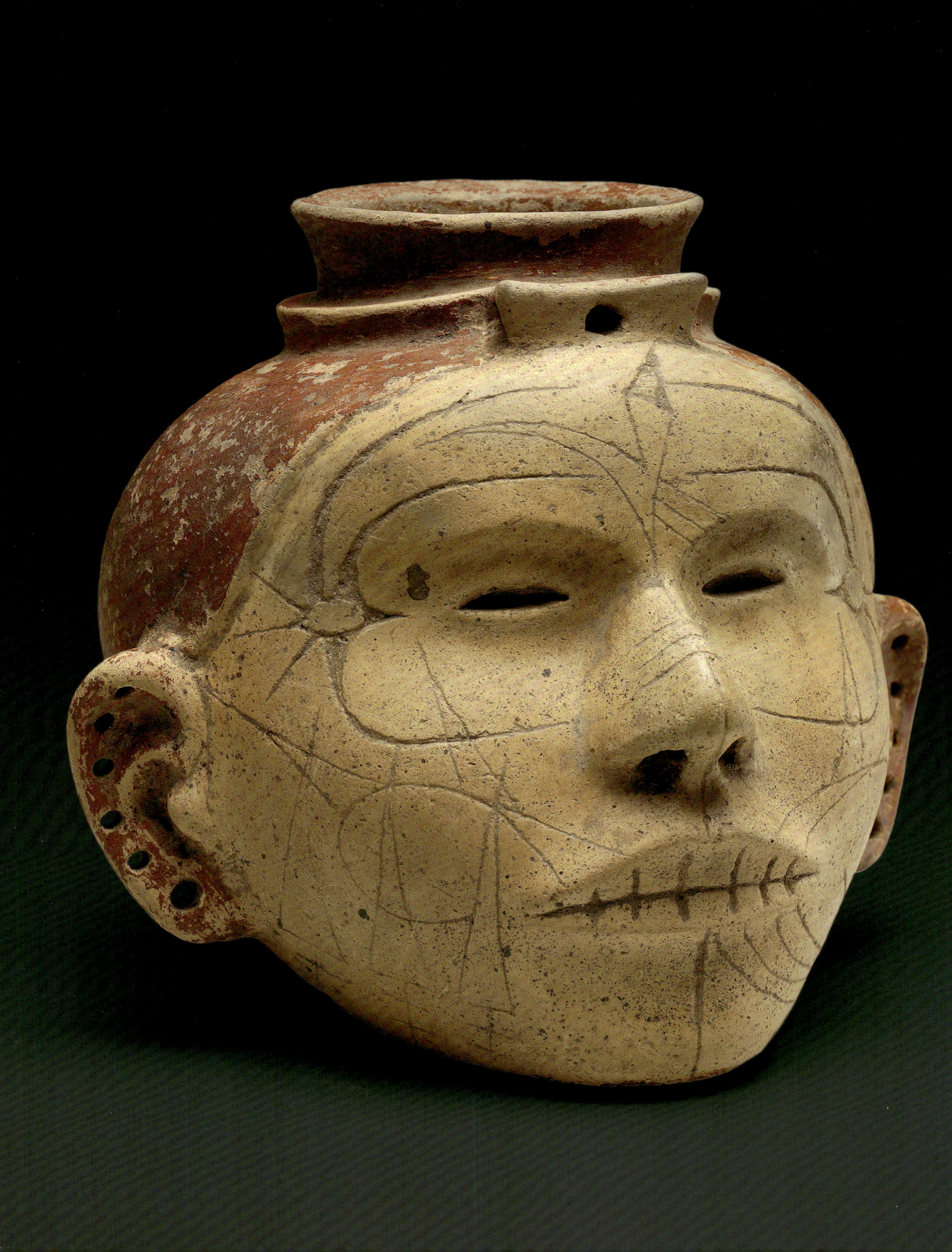

Prehistoric Art of the Central Mississippi Valley

Chester P. Walker

Fig. 1 Human head effigy vessel; Carson Red on Buff type; Arkansas, A.D. 1350–1550; ceramic, h. 15.9 cm; The Nelson-Atkins Museum of Art, Kansas City, Missouri, the Donald D. Jones Fund for American Indian Art. Cat. no. 245. Naturalistic, well-modeled, individualized features speak of portraiture in this widespread ceramic tradition. The tattoos on the face of this vessel display many design elements common to this art form. The "grappling hook" or avian eye-surrounds are quite common on head vessels and can also be seen on some seated figures from the same region (see fig. 8). The pronounced tab above the forehead is perforated and was probably used to attach ritual regalia. The vessel's earlobes and nose septum are also perforated and more than likely were used to dress the effigy vessel for ritual use.

The central Mississippi valley of the fourteenth and fifteenth centuries was a vast landscape of dissected alluvial hills, horseshoe-shaped swamps and backwaters, and massive meandering rivers and streams. In 1542 when the members of Hernando de Soto's *entrada* crossed the Mississippi River, there was a complex cultural mosaic of chiefdoms ripe with political alliances and factions. The cultural landscape seems to have consisted of ceremonial centers with various types of mounds, densely populated towns—many of which were enclosed in defensive walls or earthworks—and small farming communities.[1] The central Mississippi valley of the Late Mississippian period was also an era of transition with great artistic innovation and experimentation. The elaborate sculptural works in stone, delicately embossed copper plates, and shells carved with enigmatic designs identified with the classic Southeastern Ceremonial Complex (SECC) that have been found at sites like Moundville, Etowah, and Spiro, are not present in the central Mississippi valley in great quantity.[2] Instead the area produced several brilliantly sculpted, painted, and engraved ceramic traditions.

The diversity of the imagery engraved or embossed on the shell and copper artwork of the classic SECC continued into the late prehistoric period on some engraved pottery traditions, such as Walls Engraved, a pottery tradition local to the central Mississippi valley and distributed around the area of present-day Memphis, which consisted of imbricate

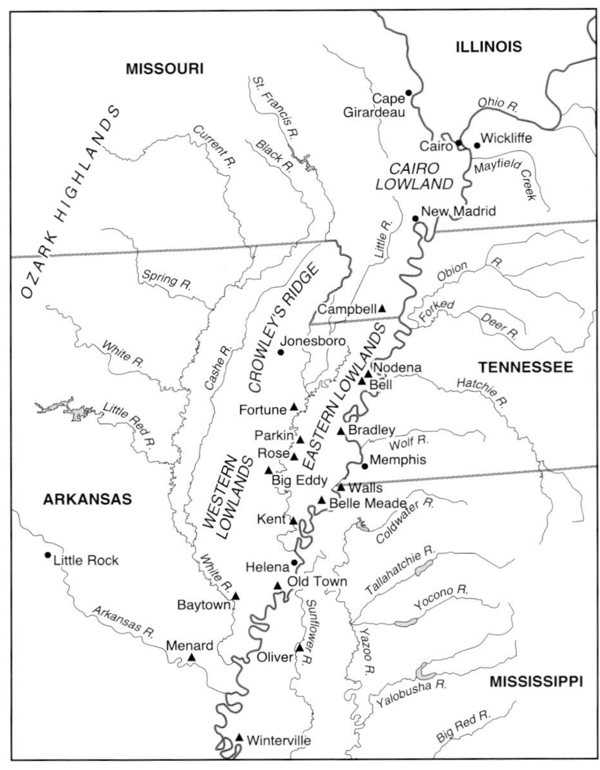

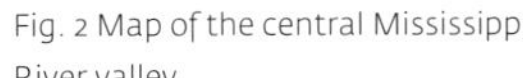
Fig. 2 Map of the central Mississippi River valley.

designs on the interiors of bowls and of zoomorphic and scroll designs on the exterior of vessels.[3] Many of these designs and forms, however, take on a dramatically different and minimal appearance on polychrome painted and effigy vessels.

One of the most striking ceramic traditions of the region is the various types of polychrome-painted ceramics. Generally speaking, painted wares from the central Mississippi valley consist of combinations of red and white; red, white, and black; solid red; or red and buff, and they are referred to by archaeologists as Nodena Red and White, Avenue Polychrome, Larto Red, and Carson Red on Buff, respectively. These painted wares, often referred to as Quapaw ceramics, are believed to be the products of the southern Siouan group who settled parts of southwestern Arkansas sometime during late prehistoric times.[4] There is no doubt that Quapaw artists sculpted and painted ceramics with elaborate forms and earthy colors; however, these painted ceramic traditions were most likely cross-cultural in origin or perhaps a part of a multicultural, Late Mississippian trade network that extended from the upper central Mississippi valley to the flood plains of the Red River (fig. 2).

The artists of the central Mississippi valley were obviously inspired by natural forms, paying much attention to the globular body and slender tapering necks of gourds, and they painted bottles with interlocking scrolls, stylized swastikas, repetitive circular bands, and expressive iconographic motifs, conveying the contrast between red and white dualities that persist in many of the folktales throughout the southern tribes. This red and white symbolism represents the distinction between peace and war, the celestial world and the subterranean or underwater realm, and light and dark.[5]

The swastika appears interwoven with mythic human forms in representational scenes of the Underworld (see the preceding essay by George Lankford in this volume). During the Late Mississippian period, this symbol is eloquently abstracted on the globular bodies of long-necked bottles (see Lankford, fig. 15), offering a condensed symbolic expression of the cosmos. The cosmic duality is completed with the interlocking terrace or stair-step motif painted around the long, cylindrical carafe neck of the vessel. It has been suggested that the terrace motif originated in the Southwest and is a general signifier of the cloudy celestial realm.[6] Artists employed this cosmic dualism over and over again. Its symbolism has also been suggested to extend to the contents of the vessels in that liquids poured from the vessel metaphorically transcend the cosmic realms,[7] an act that was perhaps even used to empower the individual performing the ritual by putting them in direct control of the cosmos.[8]

Another example of vessels expressing the general theme of cosmic order can be seen in a Nodena Red and White carafe-necked bottle (see fig. 31 in the essay by David Dye in this volume). Once again the red and white theme is paired with symbols of cosmic geography: the terrace on the neck and an additional symbol of the celestial realm located on the body. A series of alternating hand motifs suggest a comparison to the hand-and-eye symbols found throughout the Southeast and most famously at Moundville. George Lankford convincingly argues in the preceding essay that the hand-and-eye motif symbolizes the beginning of the journey to the Otherworld along the Path of Souls.

Other bottles have different treatment of their carafe necks, suggesting a closer association with their subtle gourdlike form. The bodies containing patterns of intertwined scroll motifs creating S-shaped designs have narrow constricting or slightly flaring necks painted in solid red (figs. 3–4). Executed with striking proportions and flowing lines these bottles are masterpieces in form and design. Many of these abstract symbols are excitingly unique to the Late Mississippian period; others show signs of cross-cultural interaction. One Quapaw vessel decorated with oblong images painted in red and white (fig. 5) can be easily compared to a pattern sometimes engraved on Caddo vessels.

The red-and-buff-colored motif of a star superimposed on a circle and triangle composite shape appears in the earlier art styles on many different media and forms with complex iconographies (fig. 6). Several scholars have noted a general trend of Underworld symbolism associated with this image, which is largely believed to be a stylized scalp lock.[9] The bodies of these painted wares are repeatedly seen with generalized cosmic references suggesting a symbolic geography connected to far-reaching histories, folktales, and ideas of space and placement.

One of the more dramatic scenes painted on bottles from this region depicts two serpentlike creatures intertwined in a complex pattern with an implicit cosmic

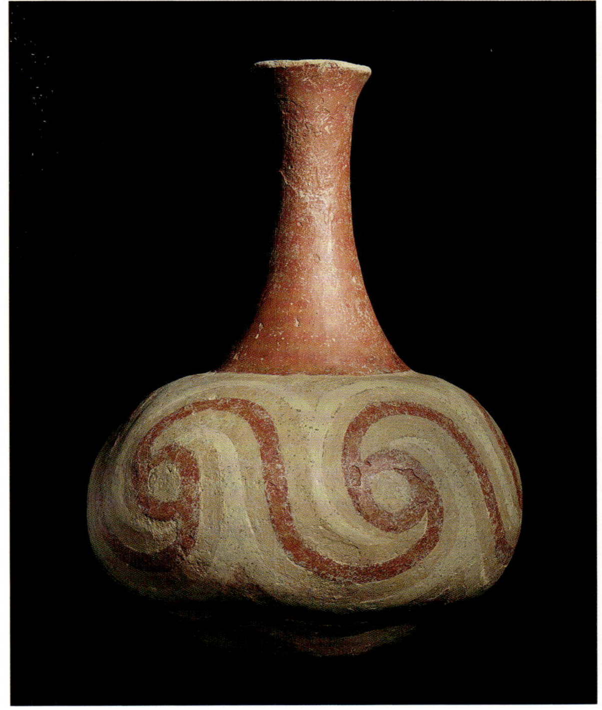

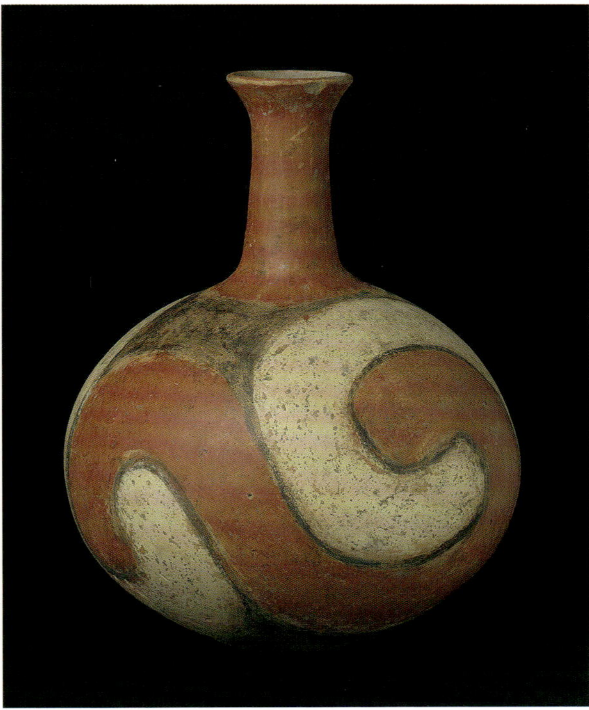

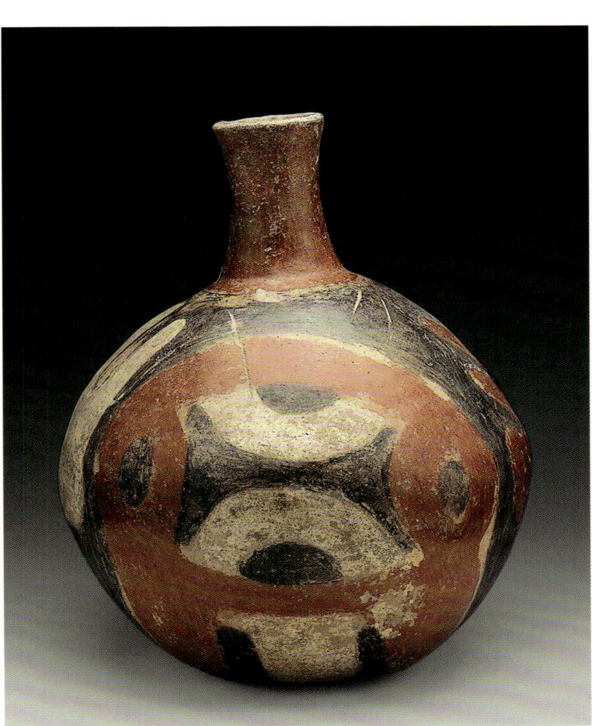

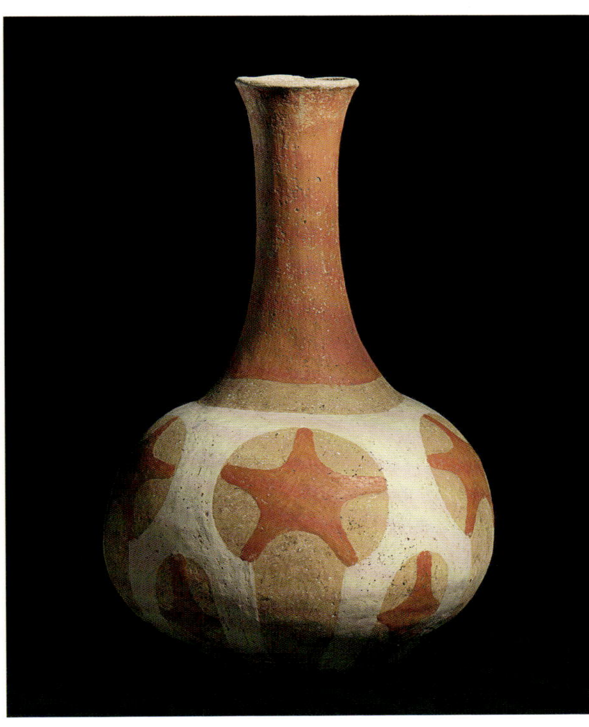

Fig. 3 Long-necked globular bottle with interlocking scrolls; Nodena Red and White type; Arkansas, Chicot County, near Halley, A.D. 1300–1500; ceramic, h. 22.2 cm; Gilcrease Museum, Tulsa, Oklahoma. Cat. no. 228. Swirling patterns in red, white, and buff color, alluding to water or ritual drinks, are a hallmark of diverse local styles in the middle Mississippian region.

Fig. 4 Long-necked globular bottle with interlocking scrolls; Avenue Polychrome type; Arkansas, A.D. 1300–1500; ceramic, h. 27.9 cm; James and Elaine Kinker Collection, Midwest. Cat. no. 231.

Fig. 5 Long-necked globular bottle; Avenue Polychrome type; Mississippi, Coahoma County, A.D. 1500–1700; ceramic, h. 27.9 cm; Private collection, Missouri. Cat. no. 234.

Fig. 6 Long-necked globular bottle with scalp lock motif; Nodena Red and White type; Arkansas, Arkansas County, Menard Mound site, A.D. 1300–1500; ceramic, h. 24.1 cm; Smithsonian Institution, National Museum of the American Indian, Washington, D.C. Cat. no. 226. This elegant, finely proportioned vessel displays an abstract, repetitive design representing trophy scalps stretched in a starlike pattern within a circular hoop; trailing hair is indicated by the buff-colored keyhole shapes.

connotation (see Lankford, fig. 18). These two creatures, composites of serpents with bird beaks and antlers, are quite familiar to Native American folklore from the Southeast and the Great Plains. Known by many names, such as the piasa, the Underwater Panther, or the Great Serpent, this creature—as Kent Reilly has discussed in his essay earlier in this volume—is expressed artistically with great variation. The serpentlike or catlike creature was a feared and sometimes violent beast that transcended the celestial, terrestrial, and underwater realms and was often encountered along mythic journeys of conquest and exploration.

There is considerable variation in the complexity of the design on carafe-neck bottles. This particular Nodena water monster vessel depicts a unique blending of Above World and Underworld symbolism poetically along the same panel. The celestial terrace motif is cautiously executed between the scrolls of the repetitive "lazy S" design that flows around the vessel with a wavelike motion. Two intertwined creatures appearing in the main panel of the vessel have curious differences in their markings and postures, yet the similarities between this painted scene and the famous Centi pot from the Chucalissa site near Memphis are remarkable (see Reilly, fig. 9). Again, Reilly has argued that the piasa creature has the ability to take on different expressions and, in the case of the Chucalissa design, that the intertwined creatures personify both the

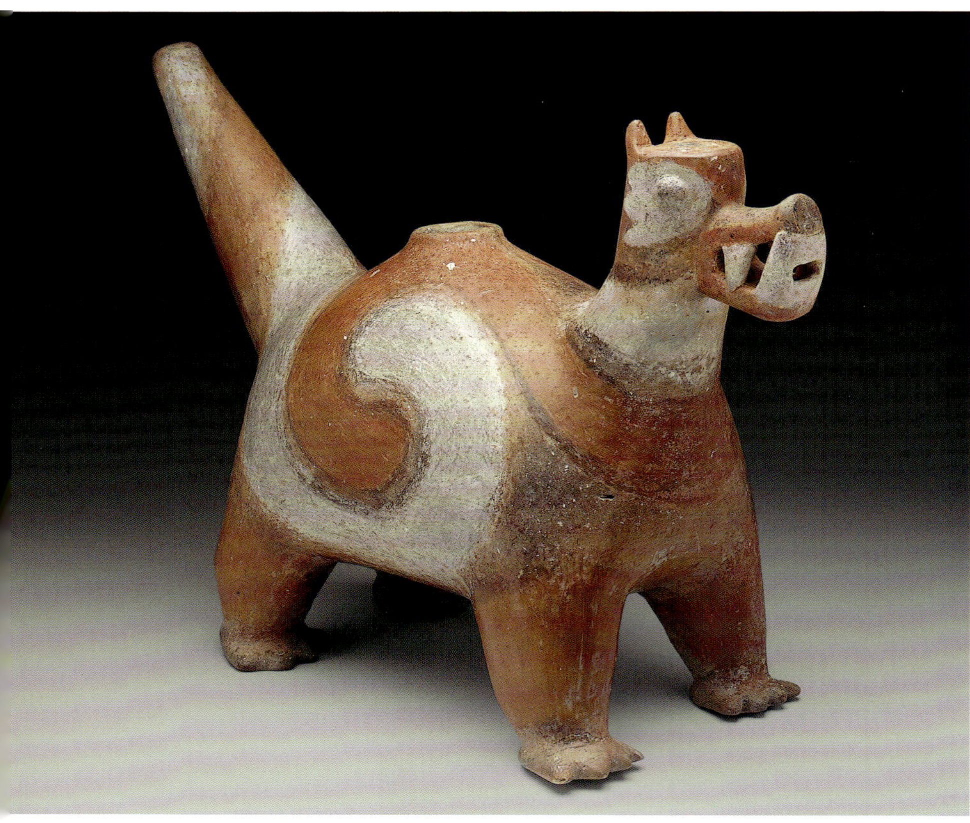

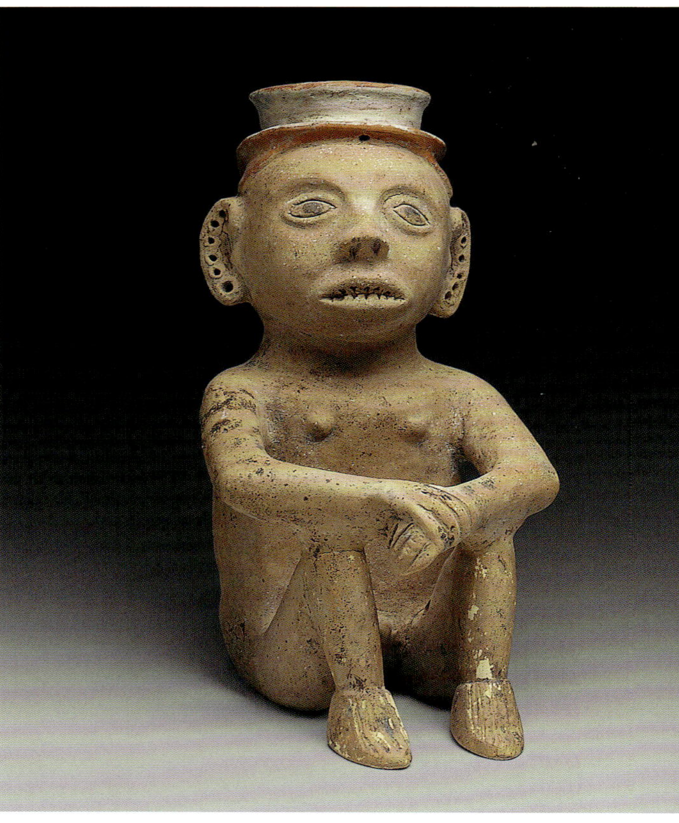

piasa of the celestial Above World and the piasa of the Underworld.

The piasa theme is the subject of several different iconic scenes and designs displayed on ceramics throughout the central Mississippi valley. This image is sometimes painted, as noted on the vessel above, and was also captured in the round. Examples from the Field Museum and from a private collection depict the piasa as an Underwater Panther (see Lankford, figs. 1, 16, and 17). Variations on the rim-rider vessel form that are quite common to the Memphis area, these figural bowls have twisted tails and curiously pug noses and, as seen in two of these examples, forked-eye-surrounds, suggesting a distant link to the classic SECC. The second piasa has swirling scrolls suggestive of water incised on the body of the bowl, further implicating the piasa's connection to the Underwater Panther. The piasa theme can also be seen as a four-legged animal, commonly mistaken for a dog, as in a red and white painted vessel (fig. 7).

One of the most notable thematic complements to the Late Mississippian artistic corpus of the central Mississippi valley is the large number of naturalistic, "real world" effigies that appear molded in clay. Thematically, the iconography of the classic SECC is believed to relate almost entirely to otherworldly events and supernatural actors.[10] This was not the case for ceramic art from the central Mississippi valley where a wide variety of "real world beings" including humans, deer, fish, frogs, and possums, as well as shells and gourds, were depicted with varying degrees of realism (figs. 8–13). Two vessels from private collections show spotted deer animated in naturalistic postures with attentive, lifelike expressions (figs. 9–10). One stands with raised ears, posed as if it were just startled, the other crouches in a watchful, but relaxed posture. Both of these deer exemplify the nexus of the "natural world" and the Nodena style with globular bodies and stemmed tails quoting other Nodena vessel forms showing affinities to gourd effigies and "teapot" vessels. Another vessel from a private collection is, among the vessels presented here, the most closely related in form to an actual gourd (fig. 14). This "gadrooned" vessel was a common form in the central Mississippi valley, shown here with a long flaring neck, fluted body, and pronounced base. Gourds were an integral part of ritual life and it is certainly no accident that the general shape of the gourd was abstracted and worked into many of the ceramic styles over considerable periods of time. Another vessel style unique to this part of the South is called a "teapot" by archaeologists, although they were probably used for some kind of medicine and not actually for tea (fig. 15). These vessels are common to the Carden Bottoms region of the middle Arkansas River valley, a region famous for its ceramic diversity that was perhaps a cultural borderland between the central Mississippi valley to the northwest and the Caddo groups to the east, west, and south.[11] Red and white interlocking swirls carefully outlined in black are painted on both sides of the body of this teapot, extending up the "spout" of the vessel.

An interesting vessel form found throughout the central Mississippi and Tennessee River valleys is an effigy type known informally as the "hunchback"—grotesque statues of emaciated mythic beings (see figs. 1 and 10 in the essay by Carol Diaz-Granados). Their form is an

Fig. 7 Underwater Panther effigy vessel; Avenue Polychrome type; Arkansas, Crittenden County, Young site, A.D. 1300–1550; ceramic, h. 24.1 cm; Dr. Arthur Cushman Collection, Old Hickory, Tennessee. Cat. no. 237. Vessels such as this one are often referred to as "dog pots" by archaeologists and collectors who note their superficial similarities to canines. Yet iconographic clues such as various types of eye-surrounds and elaborately painted patterns associate these creatures with the supernatural realm.

Fig. 8 Seated human effigy vessel; Arkansas, A.D. 1300–1500; ceramic, h. 23.2 cm; Dr. James F. Cherry Collection, Fayetteville, Arkansas. Cat. no. 262. Seated human effigies in the Pecan Point style have a similar (if not identical) distribution to head effigy vessels. Although not as common as the head pots, these human effigies can be found with perforated ears, noses, and forehead knobs, and sometimes have facial tattoos identical to those on the head vessels.

facing page, top
Fig. 9 Crouching deer effigy vessel; Nodena Red and White type; Arkansas, Lee County, Lipsky site, A.D. 1500–1700; ceramic, l. 39.4 cm; Private collection, Missouri. Cat. no. 238.

Fig. 10 Deer effigy vessel; Nodena Red and White type; Arkansas, White County, Little Red River; ceramic, h. 25, l. 30 cm; Dr. Kent and Jonnie Westbrook Collection, Little Rock, Arkansas. Cat. no. 236.

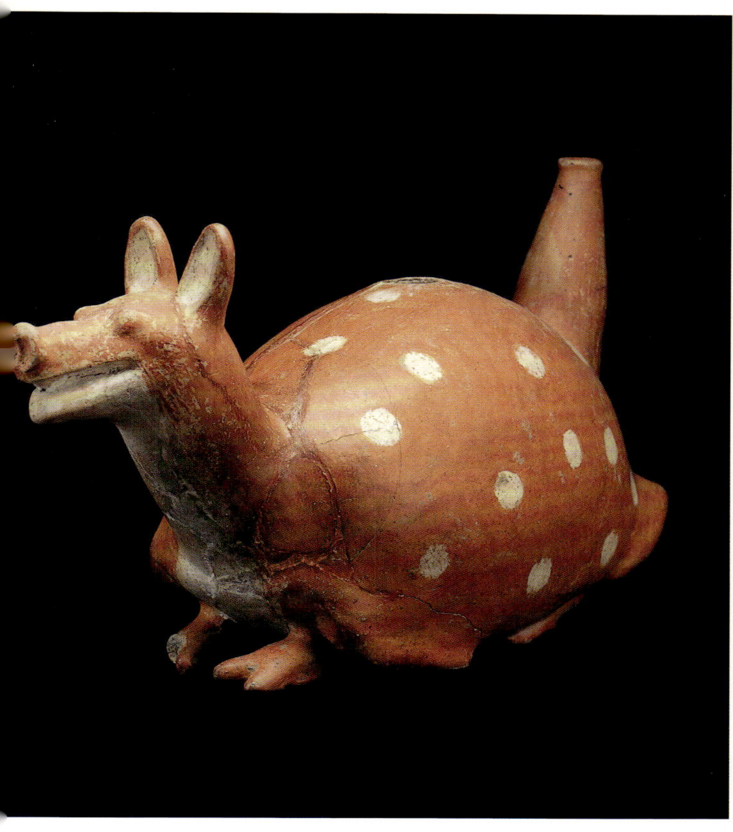

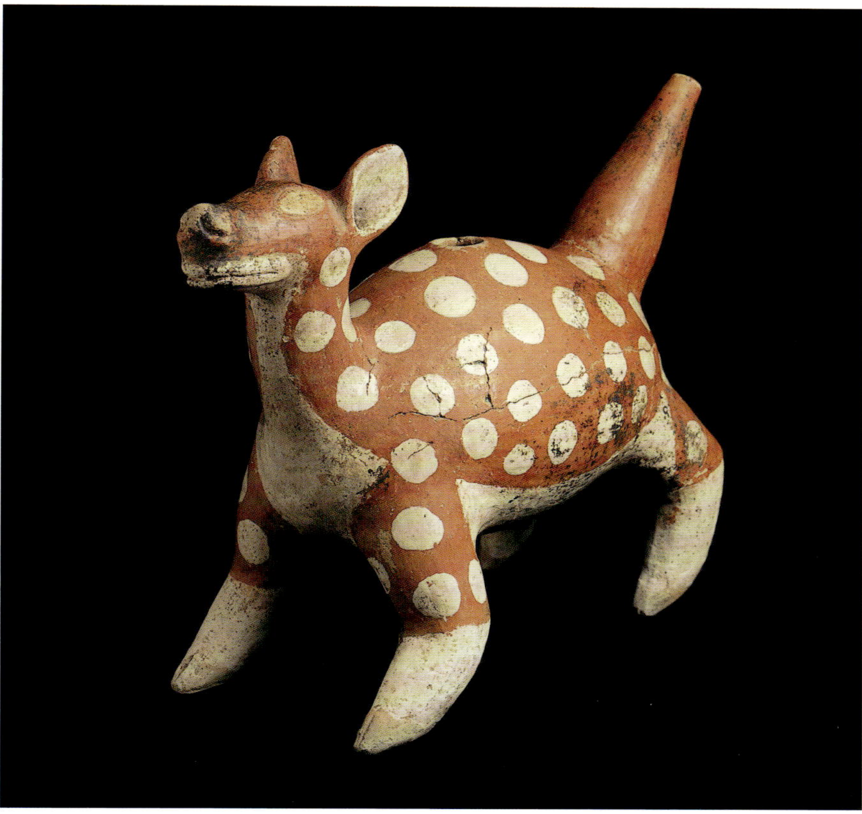

interesting use of a sub-globular gourdlike shape that can be seen on earlier gourd effigy pots (see cat. no. 258), including a constricted head with the orifice on the back, as seen on the possum effigy mentioned above (fig. 12).

Gourd-shaped vessels painted with images of the human head provide an interesting transition to another well-known ceramic style of the central Mississippi valley. One vessel depicts a dead or trancing human in negative resist painting (fig. 16). Possibly in the act of shamanic trance or transformation, this individual has the three-pronged forked-eye-surround, an element of the piasa of the Underworld, as well as the so-called death grin, an element of head vessels, which we will see examples of later. In contrast, the "Screaming Man" shows a disembodied head painted in classic red and white, with a crenulated neckline starkly indicating its decapitation (fig. 17). This artistic convention was widespread in the shell carvings of the classic SECC and intentionally sets this object apart from portraits of leaders or mythic heroes (see Dye, fig. 1).

Another familiar ceramic style from the central Mississippi valley is represented by small sculpted head effigy bottles that ironically exhibit lifelike portraits of dead individuals, many of which are variations of the Nodena Red and White style discussed above. Head portrait vessels provide a clear contrast to the classic SECC, which contains no naturalistic portraiture.[12] These vessels all show varying signs of death and decay. On many vessels the lips are pulled back exposing the

Fig. 11 Fish effigy jar; Bell Plain type; Arkansas, Crittenden County, Beck site, A.D. 1200–1400; shell-tempered ceramic, w. 27.9 cm; Private collection, Missouri. Cat. no. 255.

Fig. 12 Bottle with possum head effigy; Arkansas/Missouri, A.D. 1200–1400; ceramic, h. 15.2 cm; James and Elaine Kinker Collection, Midwest. Cat. no. 256.

Fig. 13 Frog effigy jar; Bell Plain type; Arkansas, Mississippi County, Blytheville, A.D. 1200–1400; ceramic, h. 19.1, l. 26.7 cm; Smithsonian Institution, National Museum of the American Indian, Washington, D.C. Cat. no. 257.

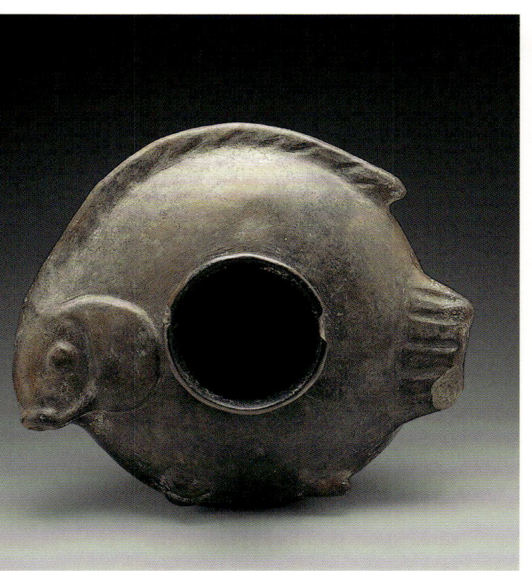

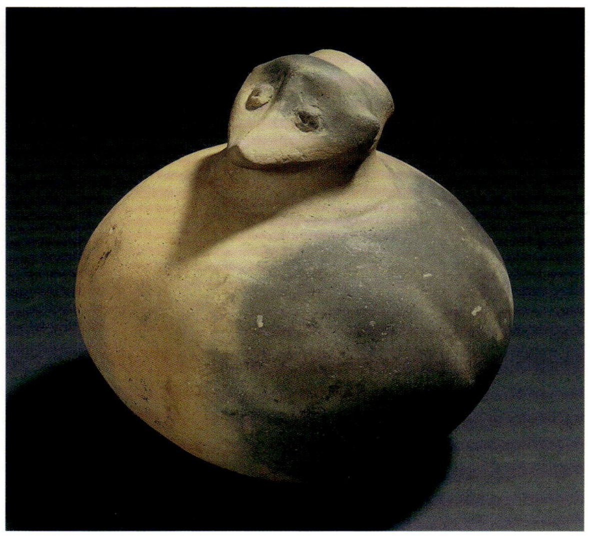

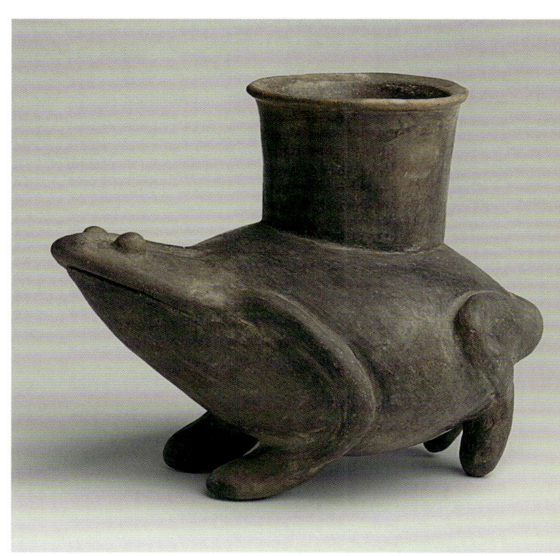

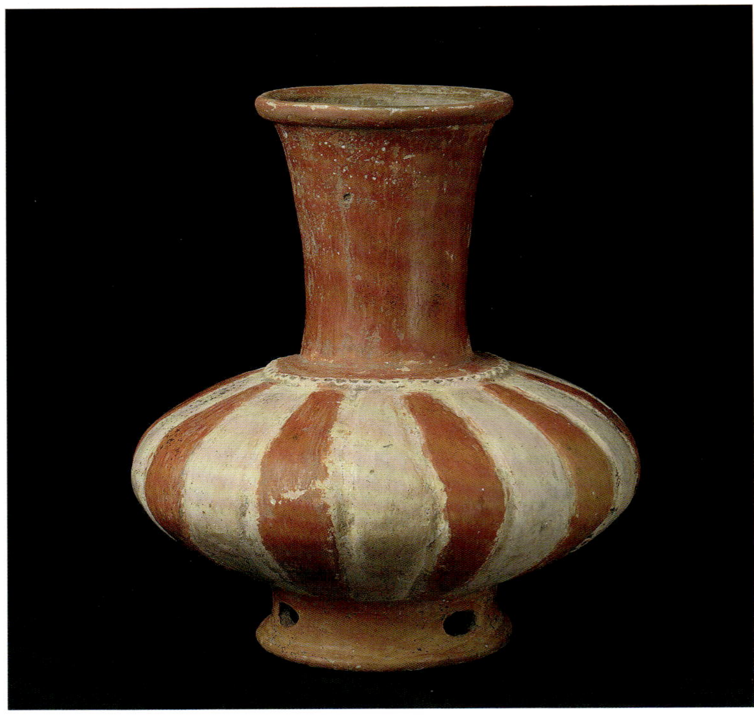

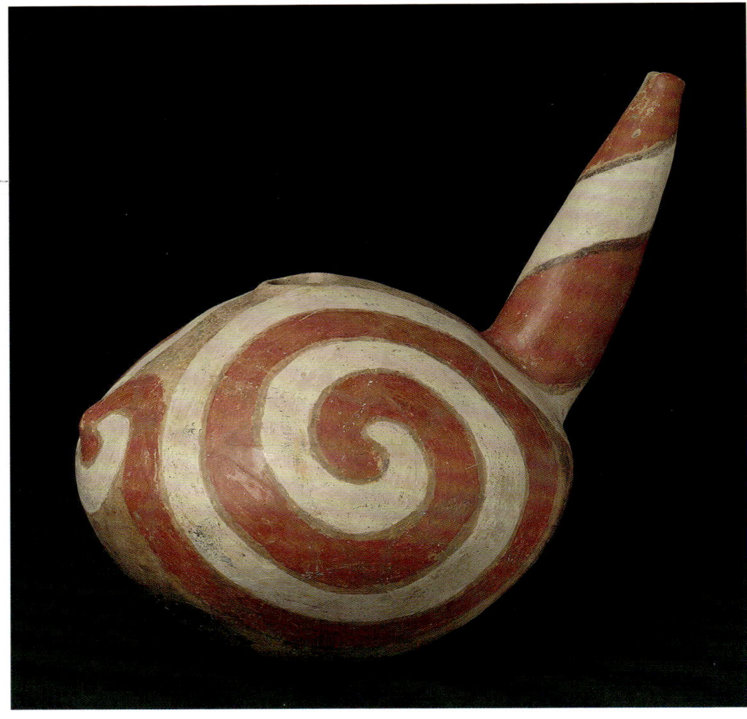

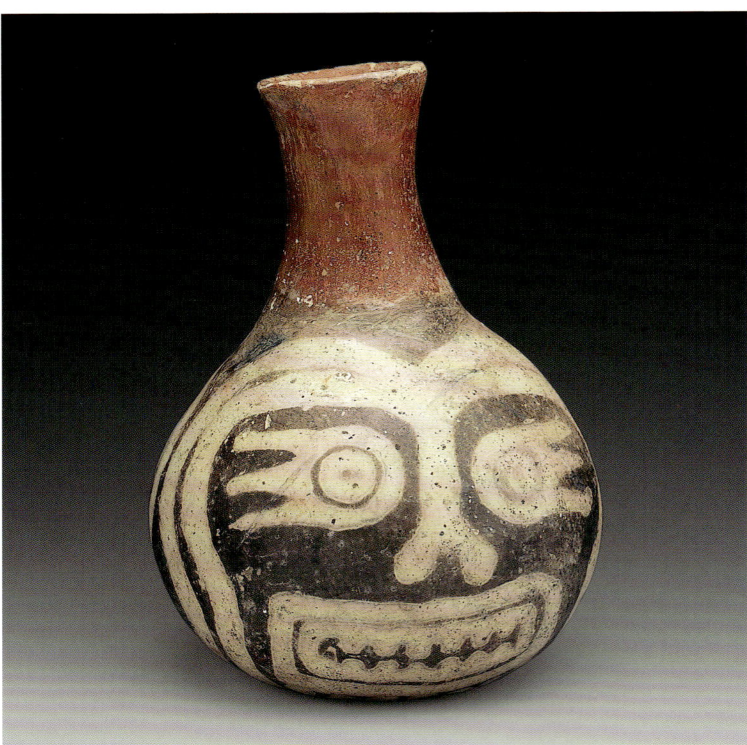

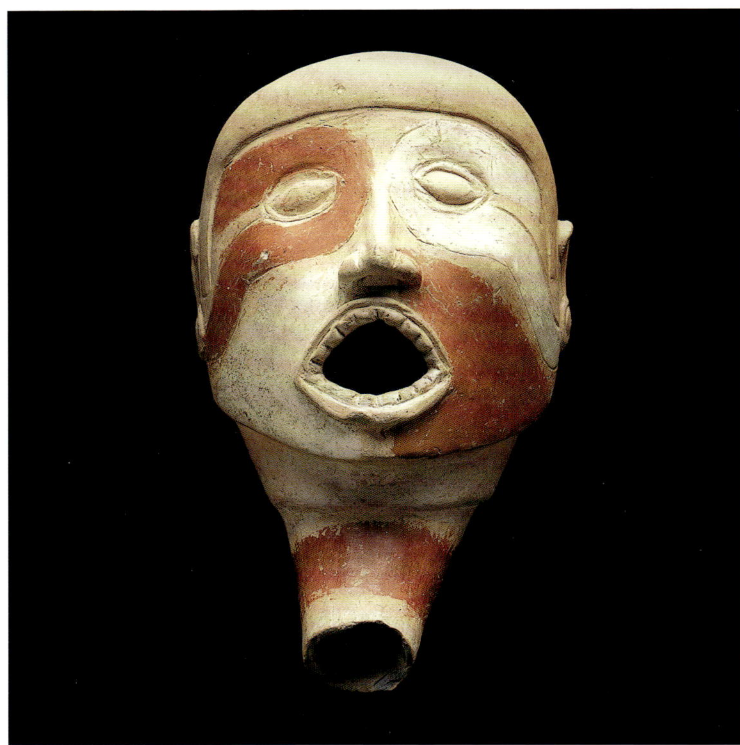

individual's teeth in an expression called a death grin. Other signs of death include deeply sunken eye sockets that give the vessels a lifeless gaze. Often described as the artistic hallmark of the Mississippian period, head vessels display considerable variation in both style and form and have captivated the imagination of archaeologists and others for more than a century.

Archaeologist James Griffin defined the "Pecan Point variant," named after the Pecan Point site in northeastern Arkansas, as the style of head vessel truest in form to the human head. The Pecan Point variant includes vessels in which the sculptural form takes precedent over the form of the vessel—in other words where the vessels are more "headlike" than "bottlelike."[13] As far back as William Henry Holmes's canonical 1886 study, *Ancient Pottery of the Mississippi Valley*, it has been noted that these vessels represent the "classic" expression of this art form.[14]

Variations in form exist even within Griffin's Pecan Point style. It is obvious that the head vessels, as we shall see, are of the highest quality. There are, however, many expedient replicas that were produced prehistorically. These replicas do not have the same attention to detail, nor do they truly capture the lifeless expression of death that can be seen in what could be called "Prime Objects."[15]

Pecan Point head vessels are distributed over a limited geographic area with the majority of vessels found within a fifty-mile radius; there are, however, a few outliers to this core cluster.[16] Griffin has suggested that head vessels were made around the time of European invasion.[17] This designation is supported both archaeologically and stylistically: first, the majority of head vessels have been found on sites with components dating to this time period; and second, head vessels are associated with Late Mississippian to protohistoric ceramic wares. Unfortunately, there is little radiometric evidence confirming the dates of this art form.[18]

Ever since Holmes first described head vessels in the late nineteenth century, speculation about their meaning and function has encompassed a wide range of interpretations, including descriptions of the vessels as death masks, as portraits of long-past ancestors, as decapitated heads of war captives, or as sculptures of important individuals.[19] Holmes observed that the facial features of the vessels were precisely executed in both technique and character, and suggested that the artists were creating individual portraits.[20] He linked the vessels to mortuary rituals:

> In one section of the Mississippi Valley we find small mortuary receptacles made to represent the human face as it appears after death. So unusual is the shape that we are justified in assuming that the vessels were made exclusively for mortuary use and consignment to the tomb. They are too small to have contained bones, and we can only surmise that they were intended to contain food, drink, or other kinds of offerings.[21]

Holmes recorded elaborate engraving on the face of a vessel from the Pecan Point site (fig. 18), describing the left eye-surround as resembling a grappling hook and the right eye as being covered by a comblike pattern.[22] He cautiously suggested that these engravings have the same function as modern Native American tattoos. He also observed that all the head vessels were manufactured from local clay and thus did not indicate long-distance exchange. Like many of his other theories about the art and artifacts from the Southeast, Holmes's ideas have largely stood the test of time. Head vessels are unequivocally related to mortuaries and are still widely believed to represent portraits of leaders or ancestors.[23]

Many head vessels bear traces of wear in places that could be attributed to their ritual use. The rims of many head vessels are severely battered and their bases also show signs of continued use. Numerous vessels have perforated earlobes and septums, which no doubt could be employed to adorn the objects for ritual use. In some cases ear perforations were broken and redrilled prehistorically. These wear patterns suggest continued use in a ritual context. We can only speculate about their precise ritual function, but the dramatic sculptural form of head vessels demands attention. They are reminiscent of the examples from the classic SECC, where sculptures of ancestors were placed in temples and used by elites for legitimizing their claims to power. Perhaps head vessels served a similar purpose at a less grandiose level, for instance, in establishing charters of providential shrines for lesser elites.

Since Holmes's study, however, there has been a considerable increase in the number of recovered vessels, and it has become apparent that a complex vocabulary of symbols existed from which the artist could choose. It has become increasingly evident that head vessels were not just simple portraits of passed leaders, but perhaps were idealized portrayals of leaders taking on the roles of mythic actors. This theory is illustrated by the series of pots I call the "Four Winds cluster" (figs. 19–22). All four vessels clearly represent the same being or individual and were all probably created by the same artist. Vessels from the Field Museum in Chicago and from the University of Arkansas Museum are identical stylistically and iconographically (figs. 19–20). They both depict a rounded face with strong bulging cheeks and sunken closed eyes. A half-moon-shaped tattoo is incised around their clinched teeth showing the ever-present death grin. Vertical lines are incised across their chins and chevron bands radiate from the eyes back to their perforated ears. On the foreheads of both vessels is a circle with lines incised in the four cardinal directions, a symbol commonly referred to as the Four Winds when it appears on Native American art of the Southwest.

The next pot in this sequence depicts the same individual described above (fig. 21). The facial proportions are identical, as is its lifeless expression. On both sides of its clenched teeth, straight lines are incised across its cheeks. Another set of lines traverse the sides of its face running from the forehead to the sides of its chin,

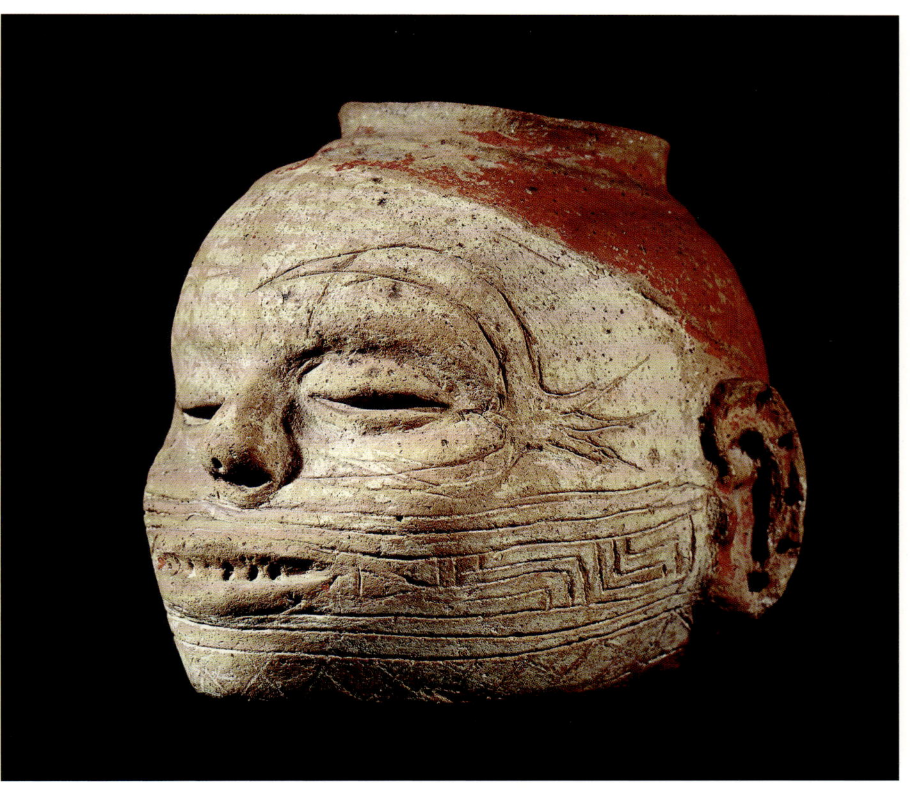

Fig. 18 Human head effigy vessel; Carson Red on Buff type; Pecan Point style; Arkansas, Poinsett County; Pecan Point site, A.D. 1350–1550; ceramic, h. 17.8 cm; Smithsonian Institution, National Museum of Natural History, Washington, D.C. Cat. no. 247. This was one of the first head vessels discovered. The incised designs on the face of such vessels probably represent tattoos. On this vessel, the design on the lower portion of the face is similar to the Davis Rectangle, a motif named for its presence on Caddoan ceramics from the George C. Davis site in eastern Texas.

facing page

Fig. 14 Long-necked gadrooned bottle; Nodena Red and White type; Arkansas, Mississippi County, Chickasawba site, A.D. 1200–1400; ceramic, h. 20.3 cm; James and Elaine Kinker Collection, Midwest. Cat. no. 225.

Fig. 15 "Teapot" bottle with interlocking scrolls; Avenue Polychrome type; Arkansas, Phillips County, A.D. 1200–1400; ceramic, l. 25.4 cm; James and Elaine Kinker Collection, Midwest. Cat. no. 235.

Fig. 16 Long-necked globular bottle with mask motif; Arkansas, Mississippi County, A.D. 1200–1400; ceramic, h. 21.6 cm; Private collection, Missouri. Cat. no. 239.

Fig. 17 Spouted head vessel; Nodena Red and White type; Arkansas, White County, Little Red River; ceramic, h. 15, l. 23 cm; Dr. Kent and Jonnie Westbrook Collection, Little Rock, Arkansas. Cat. no. 240.

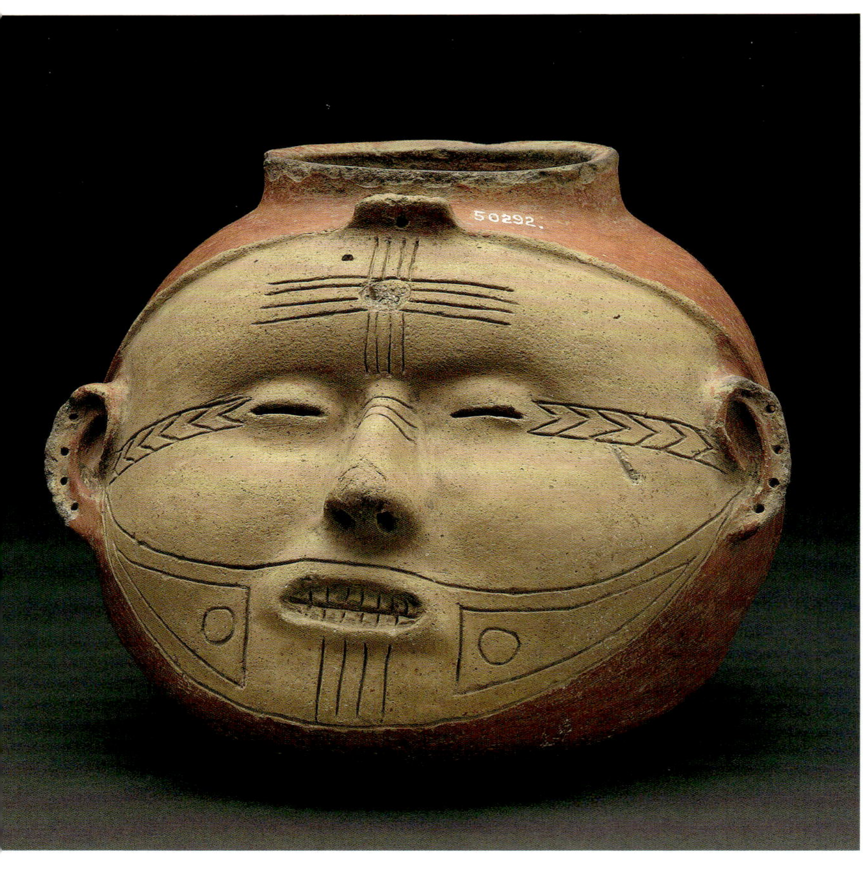

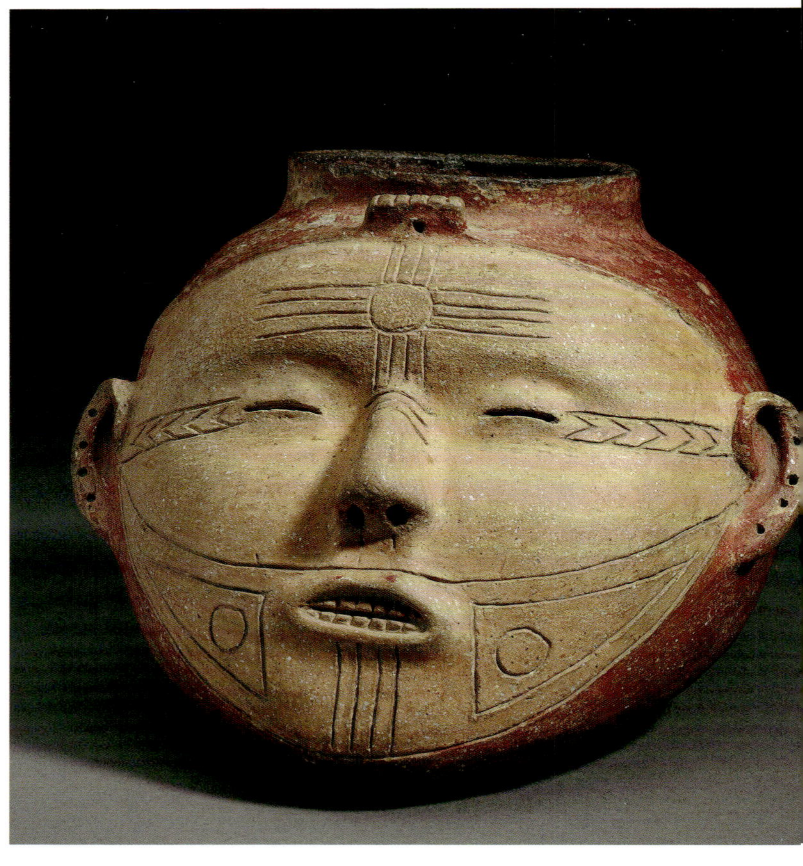

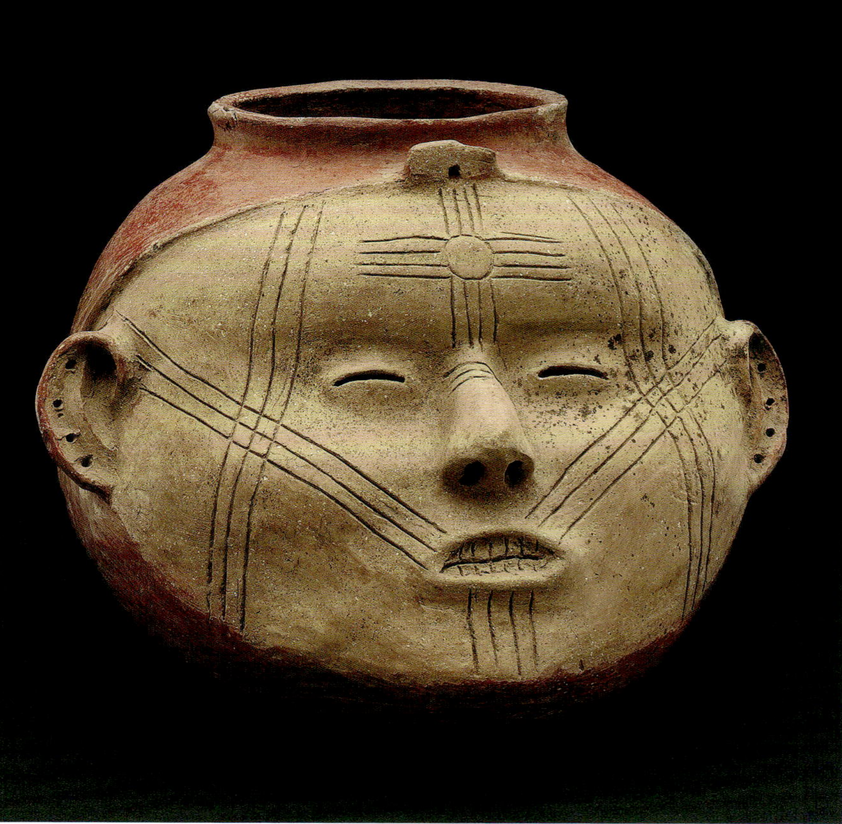

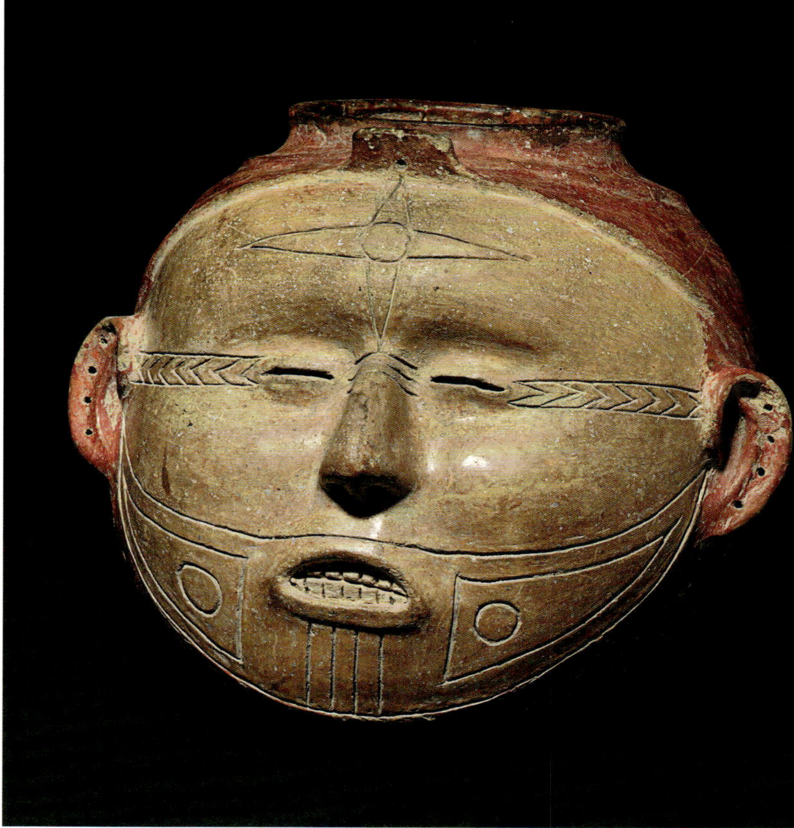

Employing a generalized facial type, the artist from this workshop stressed tattoo markings for differentiation. All four vessels, recovered from separate locations, commemorate the same individual or persons from the same group or place.

Fig. 19 Human head effigy vessel; Carson Red on Buff type; Pecan Point style; Arkansas, Cross County, A.D. 1350–1550; ceramic; The Field Museum, Chicago. Cat. no. 242.

Fig. 20 Human head effigy vessel; Carson Red on Buff type; Pecan Point style; Arkansas, Crittenden County, Bradley Place, A.D. 1350–1550; ceramic, h. 15.2 cm; University of Arkansas Museum, Fayetteville. Cat. no. 243.

Fig. 21 Human head effigy vessel; Carson Red on Buff type; Pecan Point style; Arkansas, St. Francis County, Big Eddy site, A.D. 1350–1550; ceramic, h. 15.2 cm; Private collection. Cat. no. 241.

Fig. 22 Human head effigy vessel; Carson Red on Buff type; Pecan Point style; Kentucky, McCracken County, A.D. 1350–1550; ceramic; Smithsonian Institution, National Museum of the American Indian, Washington, D.C.

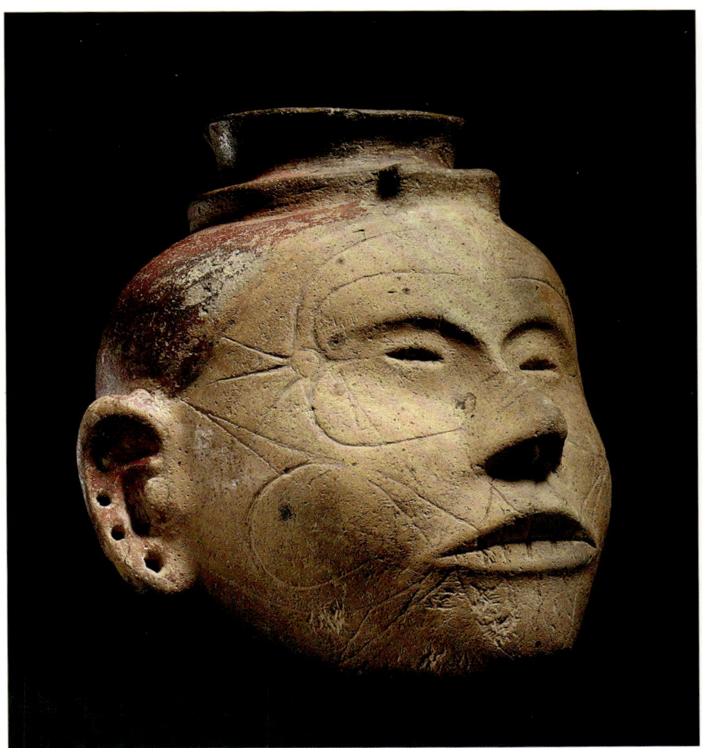

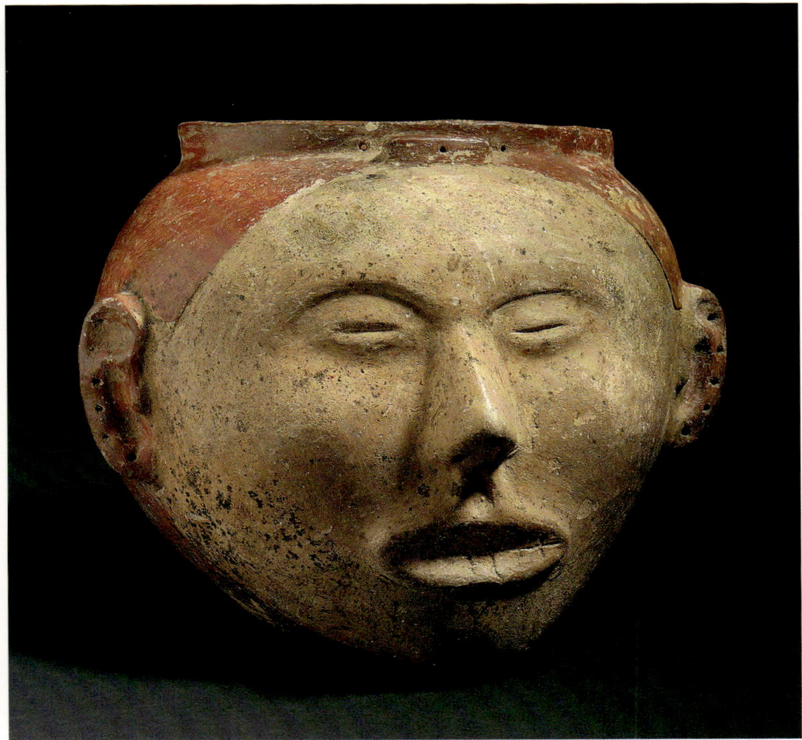

creating an X-shaped intersection high on its strong pronounced cheekbone. Its chin has similar lines incised vertically and the Four Winds symbol is incised in familiar fashion in the center of the forehead.

The fourth object completing the sequence is from the Smithsonian Institution's National Museum of the American Indian (fig. 22). This vessel is identical in all proportions, expression, and iconography to the first two vessels described, except that the Four Winds symbol in the center of its forehead has been replaced with a star. This Four Winds star is not a common iconographic motif associated with the earlier ceremonial complex, but it continues to appear in late-nineteenth-century regalia of various tribes of the Great Plains, especially the Pawnee.

These four vessels are probably all portraits of the same individual taking on different ritual personifications of mythical beings, a function that would not be unique to the Four Winds vessels: two other head vessels also depict portraits of the same individual, and again were probably sculpted by the same artist (figs. 1 and 23). Both of these vessels have strong facial features

The range of facial types, individual ages, markings, and even hints of personalities are vividly and spontaneously expressed to a degree rarely seen in the ancient art traditions of the Americas.

Fig. 23 Human head effigy vessel; Carson Red on Buff type; Pecan Point style; Arkansas, Mississippi County, Matlock site, A.D. 1350–1550; ceramic, h. 15.2 cm; University of Arkansas Museum, Fayetteville. Cat. no. 244.

Fig. 24 Human head effigy vessel; Carson Red on Buff type; Pecan Point style; Missouri, Pemiscot County, Campbell site, A.D. 1350–1550; ceramic, h. 15.2 cm; James and Elaine Kinker Collection, Midwest. Cat. no. 249.

Fig. 25 Human head effigy vessel; Carson Red on Buff type; Pecan Point style; Arkansas, Poinsett County, Fortune Mound, A.D. 1350–1550; ceramic, h. 19.1 cm; Harvard University, Peabody Museum of Archaeology and Ethnology, Peabody Museum Expedition 1879–1880, Edwin Curtiss, Director. Cat. no. 248.

Fig. 26 Human head effigy vessel; Carson Red on Buff type; Pecan Point style; Arkansas, Poinsett County, Shawnee Village site, A.D. 1350–1550; ceramic; Hampson Museum State Park, Arkansas. Cat. no. 284.

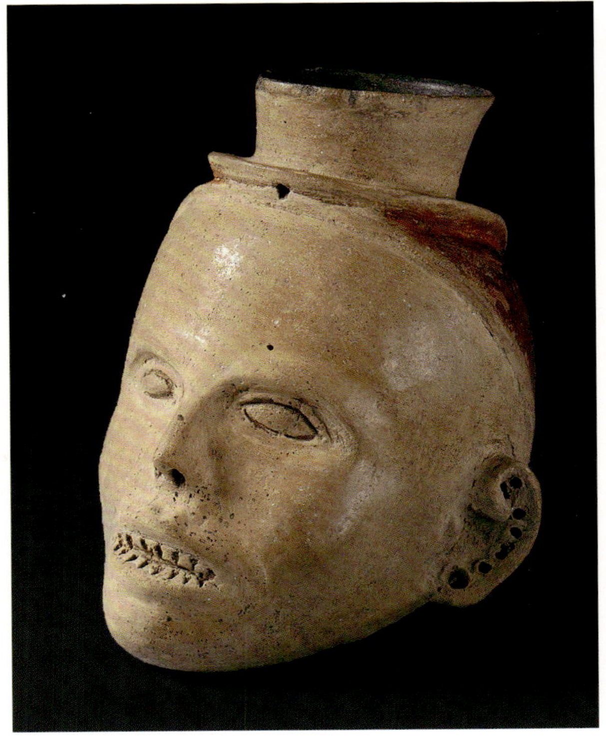

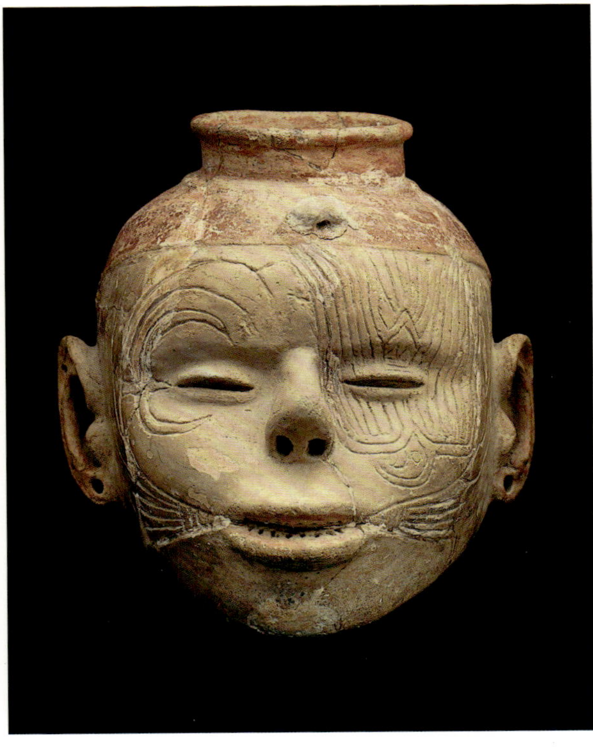

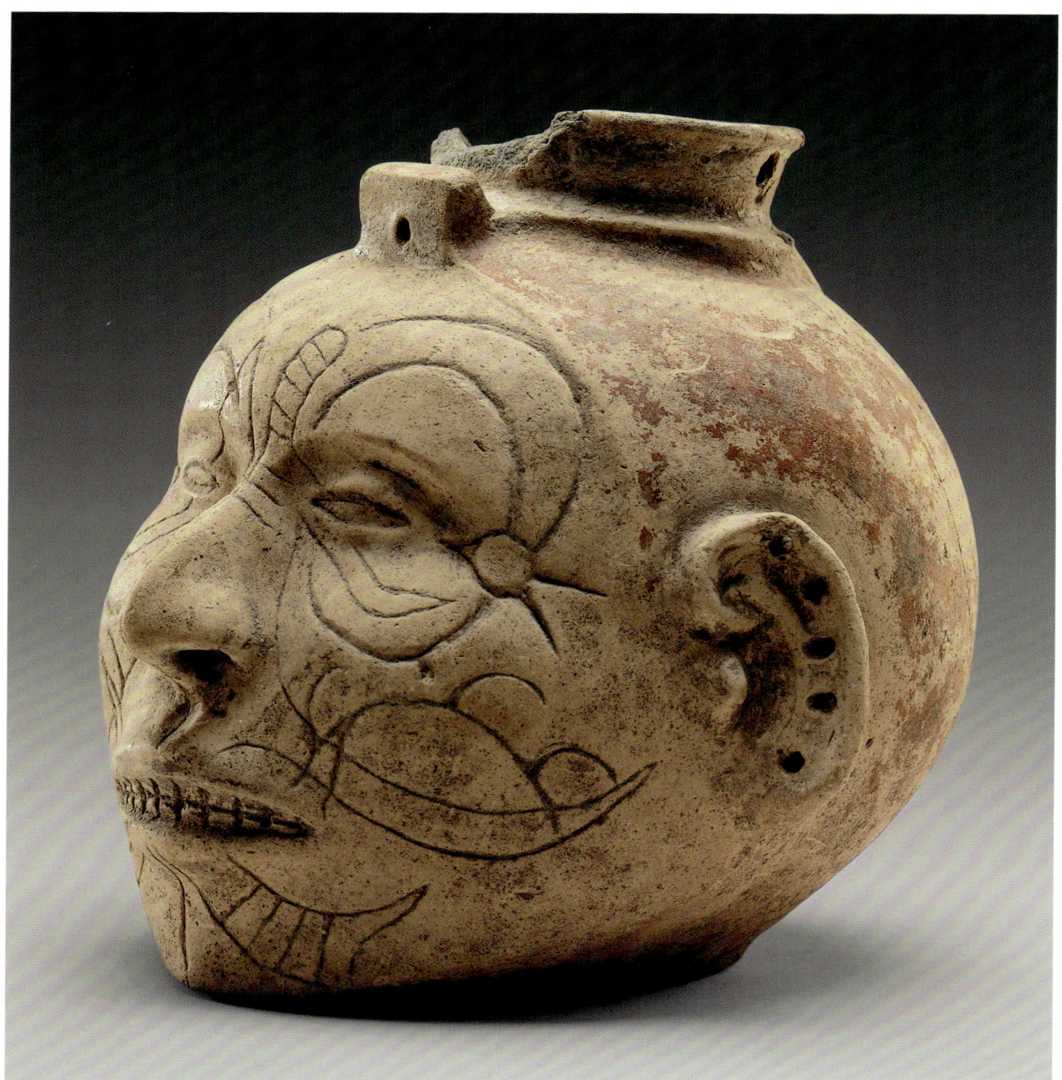

Fig. 27 Human head effigy vessel; Carson Red on Buff type; Pecan Point style; Missouri, Pemiscot County, Campbell site, A.D. 1350–1550; ceramic, h. 16.2 cm; The Detroit Institute of Arts, Founders Society Purchase with funds from the Mary G. and Robert H. Flint Foundation. Cat. no. 246. This head effigy vessel was found at the Campbell site (23PM5) in extreme southeastern Missouri. The artists of the Campbell site produced more head vessels than have been discovered at any other site. Some scholars even speculate that this site was in fact the city of Pacaha, mentioned in the De Soto narratives.

with pronounced cheek and upper facial structure and slender, elegant jaw lines. The lifeless, empty eye sockets and the overpowering death grin dominate the expressions.

The tattooing of these two pots is wonderfully unique. Both pots have eye-surrounds with the "grappling hook" shape that Holmes described years ago, yet each pot has different designs incised around its clinched teeth. The University of Arkansas piece has whiskerlike triangles radiating from its mouth, while the other pot has a complex abstract design of curving lines and arching triangles.

Head vessels with elaborate tattoos were not the only ones that were created in sets. A large group of at least six head vessels are remarkably similar and with the exception of simple vertical lines on some of their chins, they are devoid of elaborate facial tattooing.[24] Only one vessel from this group is shown here (fig. 24),[25] but it can serve to illustrate the structural range of this art form. The well-known head vessel from the Peabody Museum at Harvard University (fig. 25), which also has at least one counterpart, shows one of the best examples of the death grin. It is worth mentioning that these serial clusters all belong to the Pecan Point style, and that as the art form was distributed and expediently copied, it lost some of its original function and symbolic representation.

There are other head vessels tattooed and scarred with motifs that have interesting artistic ties with the greater Southeast. An example from the Smithsonian's National Museum of Natural History was actually one of the first head vessels described by Holmes (fig. 18). This vessel has the famous Davis Rectangle motif incised on its lower face (see Brown, fig. 30). This motif has been found engraved on Caddo ceramics from east Texas as early as A.D. 1000 and has a complex history of appearing on pottery at Cahokia and Moundville as well as on engraved, Braden-style shell cups excavated from Spiro.[26] This is yet another artistic quotation illustrating the complexity and continuity of the art styles of the precontact Southeast.

Other clear-cut iconographic ties to the classic SECC can be noted in an example from the Hampson Museum (fig. 26). This vessel (still needing extensive conservation work) shows the Birdman image diving across the vessel's left eye. James Brown has successfully linked the Birdman theme to the Morning Star cycle. This thematic connection suggests a possible association between the Morning Star ritual cycle and head vessels (see Brown's discussion of the Birdman in his essay in this volume). This proposes a curious situation in which head vessels could be seen as a Late Mississippian extension of the flint clay statuary discussed by Kent Reilly in this volume. The well-known head vessel from the Detroit Institute of Arts (fig. 27) has no strong artistic comparison to the figural imagery of the SECC, even though it is clearly linked stylistically to the Hampson Museum Birdman piece. It has been suggested that the tattooed image on this pot is a stretched animal pelt; the evidence for this argument, however, remains uncertain.[27]

The late prehistoric ceramic art from the central Mississippi valley illustrates a dramatic shift in Native American expressive culture. The exact reasons artists stopped using imported exotic materials such as copper and shell and instead intensified and expanded upon preexisting ceramic traditions are not fully understood. Is it is obvious, however, that the Late Mississippian period was a time of change and artistic innovation. It was a time when new artistic solutions were being formed despite epic cultural disruption and change.

Notes

1. Morse and Morse 1983; Dye and Cox 1990; McNutt 1996; and O'Brien and Dunnell 1998.
2. Knight, Brown, and Lankford 2001.
3. Dye 1998, pp. 95–98.
4. Hoffman 1993.
5. Lankford 1993.
6. On the vessel's origins in the Southwest, see Phillips and Brown 1978. This design had a very limited distribution in the shell carvings from the classic SECC. The most well known example is on the Birdman cup from Spiro, Oklahoma, which is currently at the National Museum of the American Indian (see fig. 1 in the essay by James Brown in this volume).
7. Reilly, personal communication, 2001.
8. Pauketat and Emerson 1991.
9. Knight, Brown, and Lankford 2001.
10. Knight, Brown, and Lankford 2001.
11. Perttula 1992, pp. 138–41.
12. Knight, Brown, and Lankford 2001.
13. Benson 1951.
14. Holmes 1886, pp. 407–08.
15. Kubler 1962.
16. Mills 1968, p. 3.
17. Griffin 1952, p. 137.
18. Dr. James Cherry obtained a calibrated date of approximately 1400–1440 (SMU sample number 2157) from a human bone sample in direct association with a head vessel from the Belle Meade site in Arkansas.
19. Walker 2001; Dye 2004; and Holmes 1886.
20. Holmes 1992 [1903], p. 97.
21. Holmes 1992 [1903], pp. 39–40.
22. Holmes 1992 [1903], pp. 96–98.
23. Walker 2000a; Walker 2000b; Walker 2001; and Brown 1991.
24. Mills 1968, pp. 13–15, reports that three of these vessels are in public collections and three others are in private collections.
25. Walker 2000a.
26. Brown and Kelly 2000.
27. Walker 2000a.

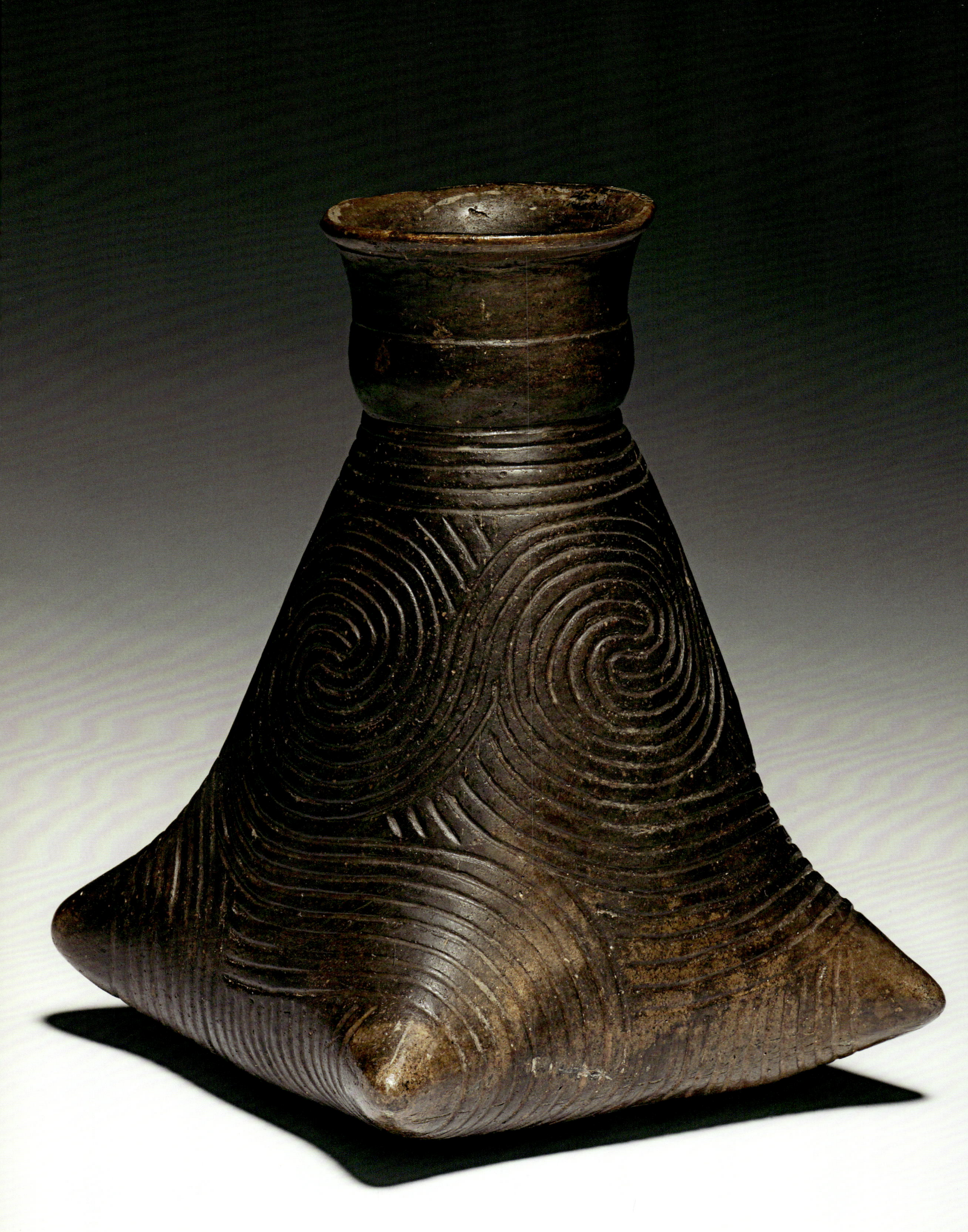

The Ancient Art of Caddo Ceramics

Richard F. Townsend and Chester P. Walker

Fig. 1 Water jar; Keno Trailed type; Caddoan; Louisiana, Ouachita Parish, A.D. 1600–1800; ceramic; h. 14.6 cm; Smithsonian Institution, National Museum of the American Indian, Washington, D.C. Cat. no. 215. Monochrome color and abstract geometric patterns adapted to specific vessel shapes distinguish classic Caddo ceramics from those of their neighbors.

Fig. 2 Map of the Caddo area of Arkansas, Louisiana, Oklahoma, and Texas.

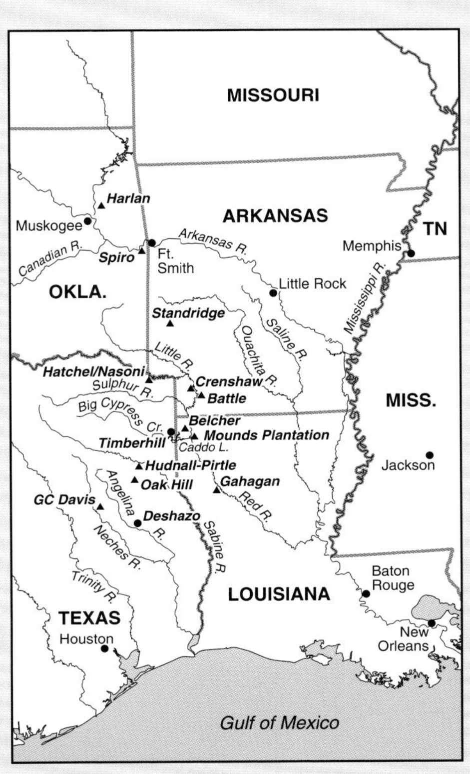

In Search of a Cultural Memory

When in early June 1991 Jereldine Redcorn and her friends in the Caddo Culture Club visited the Museum of the Red River in Idabel, Oklahoma, she saw for the first time a collection of beautifully shaped black and red earthenware bowls, bottles, jars, and other containers, elegantly burnished and finely engraved with abstract linear designs. These vessels had been recovered from archaeological sites widely distributed in old Caddo homelands, along the Red River between Texas and Oklahoma, in southwestern Arkansas and northwestern Louisiana, and down into neighboring east Texas (see fig. 2). Some pieces came from ancient graves; others were found in large earthen mounds that once supported the houses of rulers; still others were unearthed from the sites of temples, domestic structures, and old refuse middens. Hundreds of related pieces are also presently held in numerous public and private collections, but for the Caddo Culture Club visitors this Museum of the Red River collection was an astonishing revelation: here was evidence of an ancestral aesthetic achievement, as well as a view into the deep history of their people, stretching back hundreds, perhaps even thousands, of years, of which they had little knowledge. Although Jereldine Redcorn and her friends had grown up in the 1940s and 1950s in the vicinity of the small town of Binger, Oklahoma, where the Caddo tribal headquarters is located, and from time to time had attended communal cultural events led by traditional singers and dancers, this was still in the period when the United States government's policy of assimilation dominated Indian schooling, suppressing the use of Native American languages and limiting traditional forms of cultural expression. Archaeological investigations had been carried out in the old Caddo lands for decades, and historians were examining and publishing the Spanish and French colonial descriptions of Caddo chiefdoms of the sixteenth, seventeenth, and eighteenth centuries and later documents of the American period, but there had been little motivation or incentive to communicate this knowledge to the community in Binger, where the tribe had been forced to resettle during the nineteenth century.

So compelling were the impressions of the pottery in the Museum of the Red River that in the weeks and months that followed, Jereldine began searching for a direct approach to the ancient art of Caddo ceramics as well as to tribal history. As there was no active pottery making among the various tribes now residing in Oklahoma, she began to learn from other sources. Her brother had some experience as a potter, and he taught her the basic techniques of hand-building vessels; archaeologist friends recommended books and pictures of Caddo ceramic decoration and forms; and her husband, Charles, helped to develop the arduous process of firing. In due course her expertise became more intuitive, and her finely made vessels began to be sought by collectors, museums, and individuals with an interest in Native American art and culture (fig. 3). For Jereldine Redcorn, the process of making pottery has been intimately bound with a developing sense of rapport with her cultural patrimony.

Although severed from their ancestral homelands, resettled, and dispersed among other tribes—their culture drained of much of its ancient power and originality and hardly more than a shadow of its old self—the Caddo tribe today exhibits a new, perceptible spirit of inquiry, a quest for recovering and rebuilding the unique, never entirely lost, sense of being Caddo. In this search for lifelines between past and present, the art of Caddo ceramics is one of the significant elements in recovering the larger pattern of cultural identity. As we shall see in tracing the historical evolution of this remarkable artistic tradition, there is reason to believe that the internal bond between art, culture, and society was an active element for maintaining Caddo continuity for some nine hundred years.

The anthropologist and historian John R. Swanton, a prolific author with the Smithsonian Institution's Bureau of American Ethnology during the first half of the twentieth century, wrote with special interest on the Indians of the southeastern United States. He noted, "In Caddo ceramics the art of the Southeast easily reached its apex, for while there are specimens of pottery from the middle Mississippian region and Moundville which show as high technical excellence, there are none that, upon the whole, exhibit equal artistic feeling."[1] Yet this tradition, and the history of the people who made it, remains little known in the realm of public knowledge. It was only with the Caddo Treaty with the U.S. in 1835 that tribal displacement was set into motion. The formation of the Texas Republic in 1846 and the advent of Americans seeking tribal land intensified this process. The Caddo also attracted little broad public attention, for they never participated in the fierce and dramatic Indian wars that took place on the High Plains from the late 1860s to the 1880s. As the pattern of Caddo society and cultural evolution emerges from archaeological explorations, ethnohistorical texts, and surviving tribal customs, language, and lore, a picture appears of a people with a culture of remarkable stability and an art deeply rooted for hundreds of years in the Red River valley and adjacent regions.

The Caddo, in fact, were the westernmost of the Mississippian peoples, participating in that extended cultural sphere, yet distinct in that they were never entirely subject to the great fluctuations of economic, political, and religious power that stemmed from Cahokia in the late eleventh and early twelfth centuries and accompanied the fourteenth- and fifteenth-century rise and fall of Moundville, Etowah, and related seats of paramount chiefdoms in the Southeast. The nature of Caddo connections with the important fourteenth-century Mississippian center at Spiro, Oklahoma, on the Arkansas River north of the heartland region, remains a much-debated matter, for the stable rhythm and consistency of life in the core Caddo lands seem not to have been radically interrupted or substantially altered until the catastrophic disruptions brought on by epidemic diseases, foreign invasions, and the final removal to Oklahoma. This essay aims to sketch the development of the Caddo ceramic tradition and to explore its significance in maintaining the long cultural

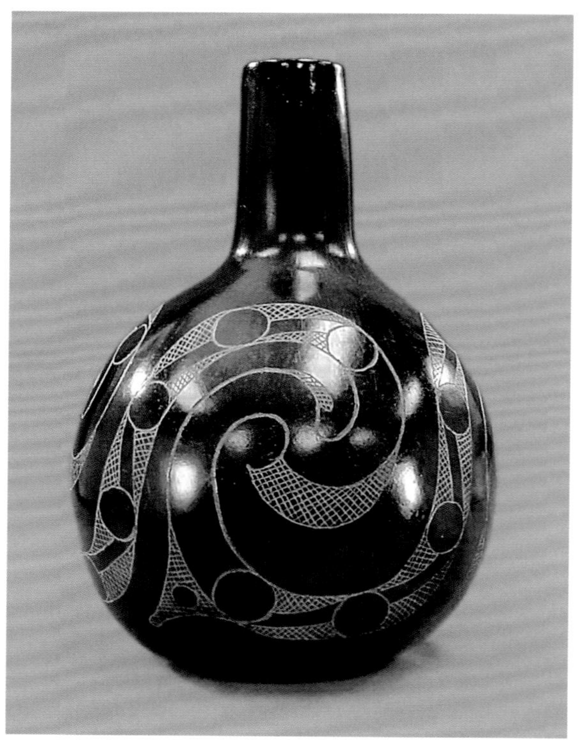

Fig. 3 Jereldine Redcorn (American, born 1939). Long-necked globular bottle, 1996; Hodges Engraved type; Caddoan; ceramic, h. 20, diam. 13 cm; Kerza and Elton Prewitt Collection. Jereldine Redcorn has been successful in replicating many different ancient Caddoan ceramic styles. This vessel is a replica of a type of ware that archaeologists have named Hodges Engraved, made from about A.D. 1400 to 1700.

tradition. This is not only a matter of describing the external forms, ornamentation, symbolism, and functions of the vessels, and pointing to differences between them and the arts of their neighbors; it is also an attempt to identify the internally willed, positively identified motivations and decisions of the Caddo to shape the ways of their materials and aesthetic expressions. If the originality of the tradition is to be defined, it is perhaps this internal creative purpose that most needs explaining.

Historical Sources

Our approach to the art of the archaeological vessels must first consider basic information concerning Caddo culture and society. For this we shall briefly review descriptions by the Spanish and French missionaries, soldiers, and administrative authorities. Their reports are often highly biased and selective, yet they offer an outline of a cultural fabric and society that can be linked to the archaeological record, providing a context for considering the formal developments, functions, and expressive purposes of the ceramic tradition.

The Spanish were the first to mention the Caddo. Garcilaso de la Vega, born in Peru of Inca and Spanish parents, interviewed members of Hernando de Soto's expedition throughout the Southeast in 1539–42 and chronicled their disastrous adventure. Shortly after De Soto's death in Arkansas from illness, exhaustion, and depression, his successor in command, Luis de Moscoso, led the army across the forested lowlands in a southwesterly direction. Local chieftains and captive guides, terrified of the dangerous intruders, urged them on toward the Red River with stories of a fertile land and wealthy, well-ordered communities. East of the river, the first Caddo settlement they came to was called Amaye. This was followed by Naguatex—the most populous and prosperous settlement of all the various Caddo "provinces" the Spanish were to encounter. The expedition passed through other Caddo communities, plundering granaries in passing; but here as elsewhere on their long route of war and pillage they found no gold, no silver, nor any empires to conquer such as those of the Aztecs or Incas. Presently they departed, returning to the Mississippi River where they embarked, eventually to reach Mexico City.

More than a hundred years were to pass before the Caddo were reported again. In 1650 Diego Castillo and Fernando Martín, leaders of an expedition sent out to explore the west Texas plains from the Spanish province of New Mexico, learned from local Jumano Indians of the Tehias, a distant trading people to the east. Soon thereafter another report reached Governor Cruzate in New Mexico, alluding to the "Great Kingdom of the Tejas," twenty days travel toward the east. The term *tehias* in Caddo means "friends," spelled in Spanish orthography as Tejas or Texas. Yet it was the Frenchman René-Robert Cavelier, Sieur de La Salle, who first reached the Caddo with his party in 1685 and again in 1686. A member of La Salle's group, Father Anastasius Douay, described the settlement of Asinais, one of the Caddo tribes of east Texas, as one of the largest and most populous he had yet seen in America:

> It was at least twenty leagues long, not that it is evenly inhabited, but in hamlets of ten or twelve cabins, forming cantons, each with a different name. Their cabins are fine, forty or fifty feet high, of the shape of beehives. Trees (center poles) are planted in the ground and branches (a ring of small poles) are united above and covered with grass. The beds are arranged around the cabin, three or four feet from the ground; the fire is in the middle, each cabin holding two families.

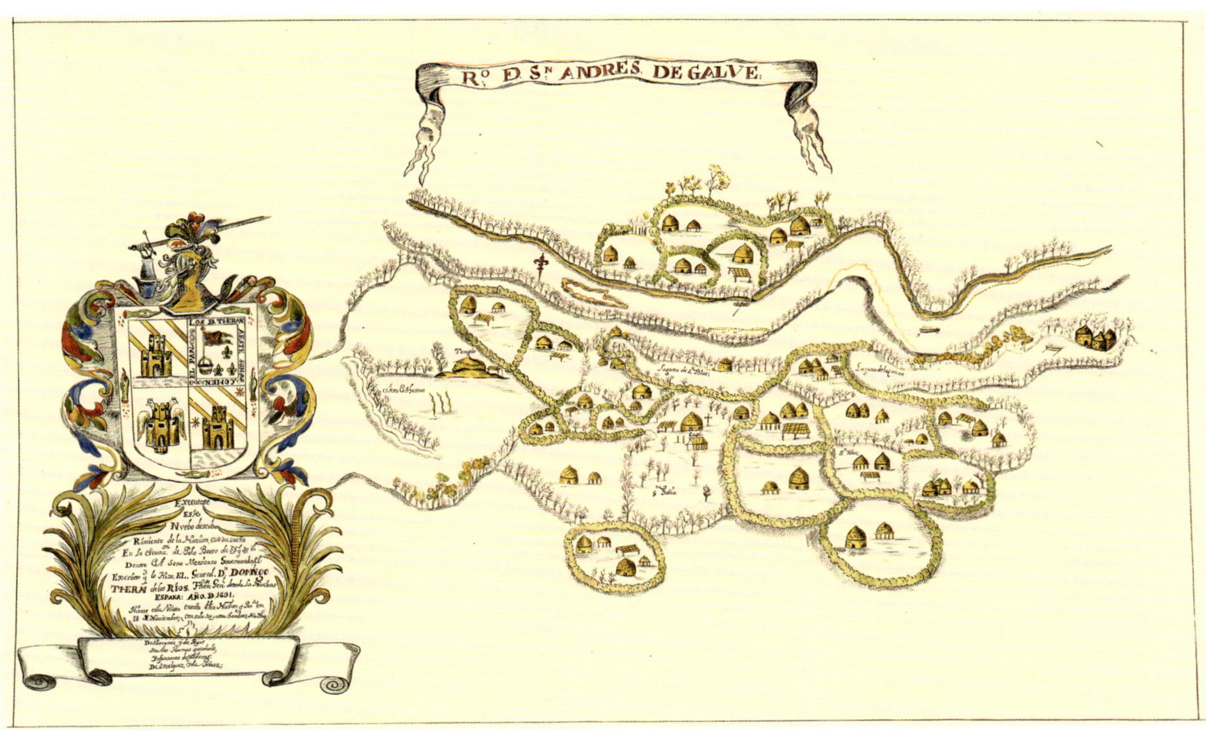

Fig. 4 Map of Upper Nasoni, a principal Caddo town, as documented in a 1691 report to Domingo Terán de los Ríos, the governor of Coahuila, Mexico; Bexar Archives, courtesy of the Barker Texas History Center, General Libraries, University of Texas at Austin. Archaeologists now refer to this town as the Hatchel-Mitchell-Moore complex.

This was a dominant Caddo settlement pattern—an extended, open series of hamlets and individual beehive-shaped houses with outlying structures, strongly contrasting with the stockaded towns, villages, and ceremonial centers elsewhere in the Southeast. Father Douay's account and that of La Salle's pilot, Henri Joutel, offer much valuable information about the hierarchical Caddo society, agriculture, and customs. News of French interest in this frontier bordering the Spanish dominions spurred the formation of an expedition, departing from Coahuila, Mexico, in 1689, and led by Francisco de Leon and Father Damian Massanet. Massanet's effusive report of the Caddos and his positive outlook on the prospect of their conversion to Christianity next prompted the viceregal government in Mexico City to sponsor a major colonizing effort. Massanet returned with Father Francisco Casañas in 1690 to establish the mission San Francisco de los Tejas on the banks of the Neches River. Casañas wrote an extensive report that remains today one of the chief sources on the Caddo. His recommendation to establish seven missions inspired the governor of Coahuila, Domingo Terán de los Ríos, to launch a major expedition in 1691. It eventually reached north as far as Cadohadacho, a major "province" on the Great Bend of the Red River. Terán's map of a principal town, now known archaeologically as the Hatchel-Mitchell-Moore complex, illustrates the cellular pattern previously described by Douay in another location (fig. 4). The community extended in open fashion along the banks of the river, and individual plots with their houses and outlying structures were surrounded by fields bordered by trees and brush. Archaeological explorations at the Hatchel site have revealed a settlement hierarchy, with evidence of special structures such as temples, council houses, and a few oversized "elite residences." Some of these residences were built upon sizeable earthen mounds, one of the largest of which supported a major structure, following the Mississippian custom. Other Caddo archaeological sites show that such mounds were sometimes arranged around an open plaza, although the rule was that buildings and mounds were more irregularly disposed than neatly laid out, in the manner of Cahokia or Moundville. Terán's map also reveals the importance of farming, in that houses and outbuildings were scattered among fields and gardens. Maize was the basic crop, introduced from Mexico around A.D. 800 but not acquiring wider importance until some three or four centuries later. Two kinds of maize were planted: "little corn," ripening in summer, and "great corn," harvested in the fall. It is likely that the diffusion of maize was also accompanied by religious observances in the annual ritual cycle, such as the Green Corn ceremony or the celebration of the first fruits of the season, and was also tied to ceremonial rites of the New Fire and the worship of the sun, and to the harvest rite in the fall. At such times of year families, kinfolk, friends, and allies were reunited for feasting, smoking tobacco, drinking yaupon tea, dancing, ball game playing, and courtship. Important crops included varieties of beans, squash, pumpkins, sunflowers, and other domesticated plants, as well as the European watermelons and peaches. This diet added to the products of fishing, hunting, and the gathering of hickory nuts, walnuts, pecans, acorns, and other wild plants and fruits in their season.

The Spanish observers mentioned above and others who followed in the late seventeenth and early eighteenth centuries—such as Father Isidro Felix de Espinosa and Father Juan Augustin de Morfí—as well as the nineteenth century American John Sibley and others, also described the structure of Caddo society. The *xinesí*, or high priest, lived in a special precinct; his house was a large, grass-covered structure often located close by the fire temple, within which burned a perpetual fire. This fire was fed by logs arranged in the cardinal directions. The *xinesí* was charged with the ritual obligation to keep the fire going, for it was believed that death and catastrophe would ensue if it were allowed to die. Smaller fires were also kept in lesser communities watched over by lesser priests. The *xinesí* connected the Caddo to the realm of the supernatural, principally to Cadi Ayo, the principal god-creator, via sacred twins, the Coninisí, whose invisible spirits dwelled in one or two small house-temples near the *xinesí*'s residence. The *xinesí* also decided when to schedule the first-fruits ceremonies, harvest, and naming ceremonies. The Caddo towns were politically autonomous, with their own religious and civil chiefs, and probably conducted their own independent cycle of ceremonies, though they conformed to a shared pattern of social and religious behavior.

Below the *xinesí* was ranked the *caddi*, or principal man (the civil chief), who inherited his rank from father to son; the *canahas*, or village elders, made important political decisions, held diplomatic ceremonies, conducted councils of war, and held calumet-smoking ceremonies for important people. The *tammas* were subordinate officials who enforced proper behavior and saw to it that the *caddi*'s decisions were obeyed. The *connas*, or medicine men, were curers and healers who conducted a series of lesser rituals. Caddo society thus had a strong sense of order, procedure, and place, but the powers of chiefs were probably somewhat limited, the people retaining a great measure of independence, valuing their kin and clan ties more than collective tribal allegiances. Descent was traced through the mother's line, and clans traced descent to a common ancestor through the female line. Clans were named after an animal such as the bison, bear, or raccoon, or after one of the forces of nature such as the sun, thunder, etc. Clans were also socially ranked, with leaders tending to be chosen from the highest ranked clans. In broad terms, the Caddo thus reflected a regional form of the overarching Mississippian pattern.

The Ceramic Tradition

Several Spanish and French explorers, missionaries, and administrators remark on the Caddo use of pottery. Massanet and Father Francisco Hidalgo, for example, spoke of very large earthen pots like water jars, used only in making maize gruel *atole*, and other sizeable containers for carrying and preserving things. Espinosa, describing a communal house-raising, wrote of the custom of householders feeding the participants, noting a variety of vessels:

> During all the time people are working, the householders are busy preparing the food for everybody, having previously provided quantities of deer meat and many pots of ground corn, which in this section of the Indies they call *atole*. They then serve the food from the captains down to the smallest, in order, abundantly and carefully, because they have earthen vessels, some large and some small, in which to serve the old and the young. This done, the crowd scatters and goes home much pleased.

Andre Penicault was another who took care to describe Caddo customs.

> They are neat enough in their manner of eating: they have separate pots for each thing that they cook, that is to say, the pot which is for the meat is not used for the fish.

From this we are given a sense of the specialization of vessels, as one might speak of tureens, soup bowls, salad plates, dinner plates, and the like in a formal dinnerware service. Espinosa identified incense burners for fat and tobacco in use in the tribal temples, and also described wooden animal effigies. There is reason to believe that ceramic versions of these effigies were also made, for some have survived whereas the wooden ones have not.

> Near this house (the Fire Temple) there are two other small houses about a gunshot distant. They call them the houses of the two *coninicís*. These, they say, are two boys or small children whom their captain sent from *chachao ayo*, the sky, for the purpose of discussing their problems with them. They pretend that these children were in these houses until a little more than two years ago, according to some. . . . In these houses there are two little chests about three palm lengths long, and raised upon a wooden altar with four little forked poles with curious covers of plaited reed. . . .
>
> In the company of another priest I found that inside these chests there were four or five little platters or vessels of black wood like circular shields, all curiously worked and having four feet. Some represented little ducks, having the head and tail of a duck. Others had the head and tail of an alligator or lizard. In addition to these there were many feathers of various shapes and colors.

These and other scattered references in the seventeenth- and eighteenth-century reports thus indicate that

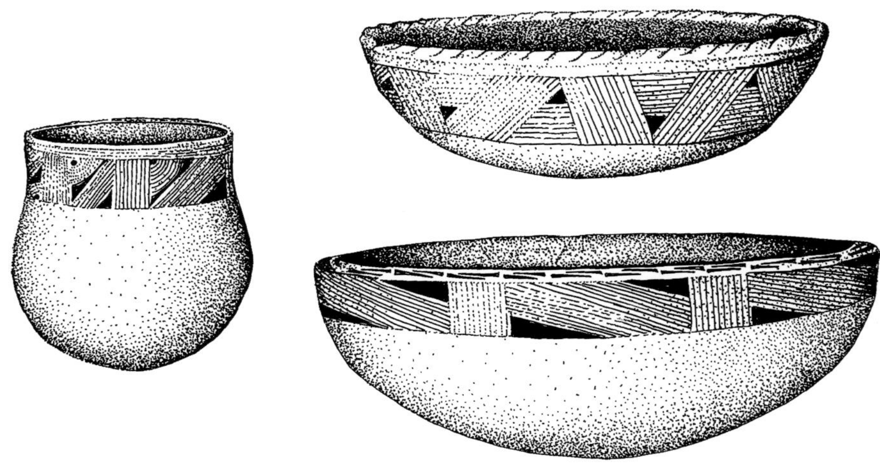

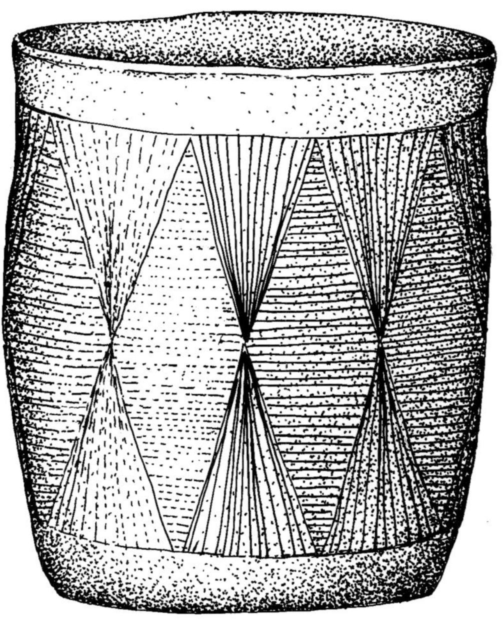

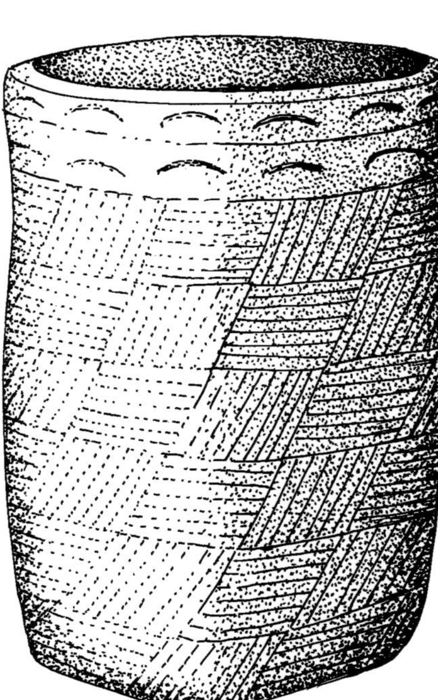

Fig. 5 Three vessels of the Holly Fine Engraved type; Caddoan; Texas, Cherokee County, George C. Davis site, A.D. 900–1300; drawing by Gigi Bayliss after Suhm and Jelks 1962, pl. 39.

Fig. 6 Two vessels of the Dunkin Incised type; Caddoan; Texas, Cherokee County, George C. Davis site, A.D. 900–1300; drawing by Gigi Bayliss after Suhm and Jelks 1962, pl. 19.

ceramic vessels were well differentiated for a variety of uses in Caddo domestic and ceremonial life. In the process of excavating, modern archaeologists have found that bowls, bottles, and jars were filled with food and placed beside the deceased for their journey in the afterlife. Such offerings suggest that memories and associations attached to the objects were projected by the living into the domain of the dead.

The types of Caddo ceramics are numerous, with many local variations over a nine-hundred-year period; therefore, in this brief review, we must be selective. The earliest distinctive Caddo ceramic tradition developed between the eighth and ninth centuries out of several earlier ceramic practices that generally consisted of large utilitarian wares made with a sandy paste. Dramatic changes in vessel forms and decoration, the development of a distinct Temple Mound complex,[2] and increasing signs of social inequity have all led archaeologists to believe that major changes in social, political, and religious organization occurred during this time. Attempting to explain why this transition took place, researchers have advanced many scenarios. Did colonists from other parts of the Southeast move into the region and settle the uninhabited areas, forcing the existing populations out or even assimilating them into a structured Caddoan hegemony? Or did the local populations gradually change their life ways, adapting to their cultural and environmental surroundings? Archaeology is now indicating that perhaps all of these processes happened throughout the Caddoan region.

The earliest Caddo pottery (c. 900–1300) shows affinities in shape and decoration with forms of basketry (fig. 6). Vessels of this kind, named Dunkin Incised, are primarily cylindrical, the sides straight or slightly convex, with flat bottoms, some of which are squared at the corners in a distinctly basketlike manner. There are also wide shallow bowls with short vertical upper rims, and deep containers with rounded lower bodies and tall, somewhat everted rims. Surface decoration is achieved by linear incising and fingernail punctuations;

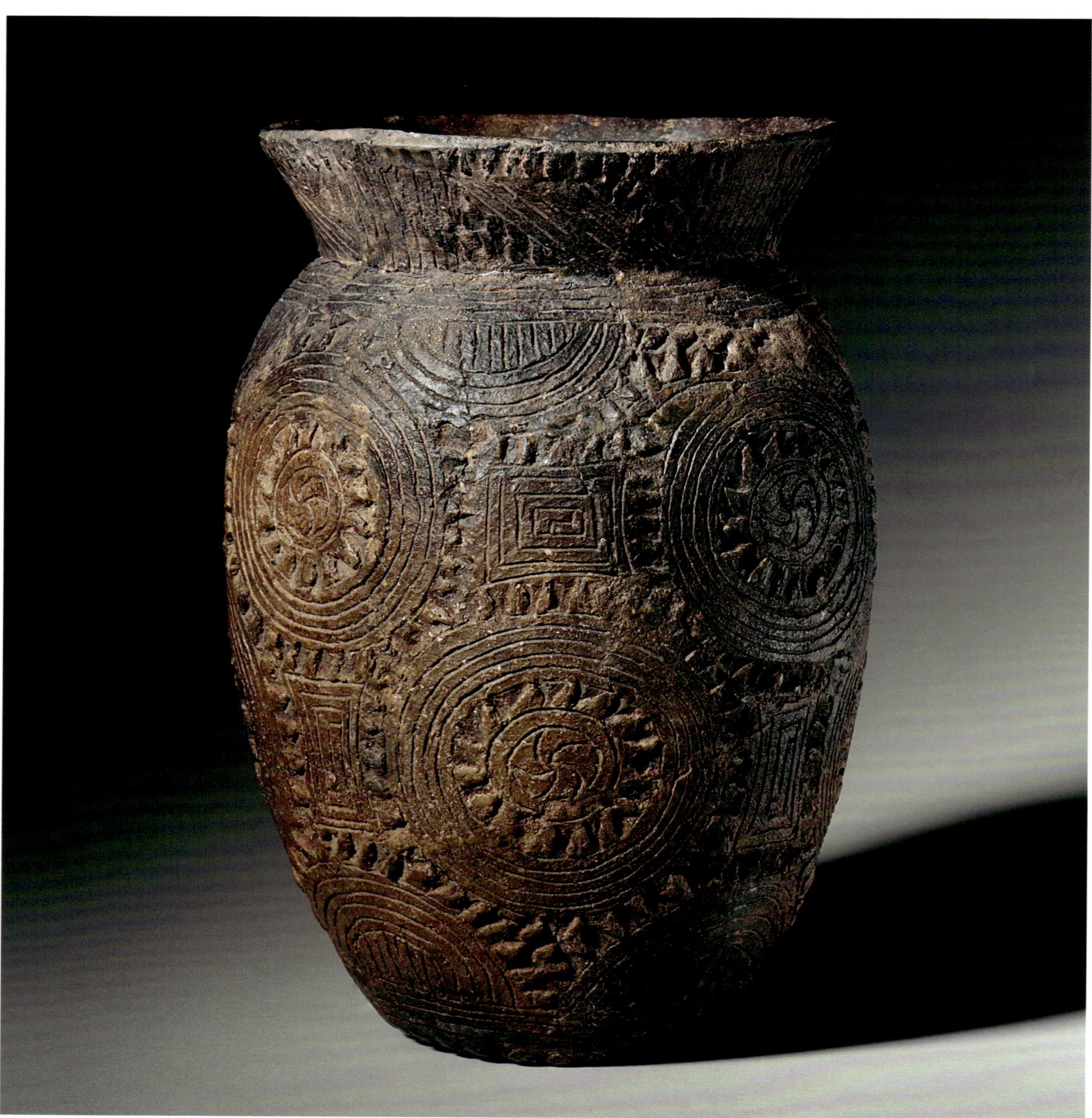

Fig. 7 Vessel; Haley Complicated Incised type; southwestern Arkansas, A.D. 1000–1400; ceramic, h. 22.9 cm; Museum of the Red River, Idabel, Oklahoma. Cat. no. 196. The flaring neck on this vessel suggests that it is a late example of the Haley Complicated Incised type.

facing page, top

Fig. 8 Engraved whelk shell showing a ritual figure with a shell necklace and raccoon; Oklahoma, LeFlore County, Spiro, Craig Mound, A.D. 1200–1400; marine shell, h. 30.5 cm; Museum of the Red River, Idabel, Oklahoma, gift of Kent Westbrook, M.D. Cat. no. 135. Although this cup was not included in Philip Phillips and James A. Brown's monumental study (1978 and 1984) of engraved shell from the Spiro site, this cup can be placed in the large group of cups exhibiting Craig C style. Some of the most interesting features of this cup are the carrot-shaped appendage used here in place of a beaded forelock and the bellows-shaped apron worn by the ritually attired figure.

patterns replicate the appearance of basketry weaves with overall matlike quadrangular interweaving, and sets of parallel lines arranged in repetitive triangles or diamonds, sometimes leaving the lower part of the vessel plain. A second type of early pottery, Holly Fine Engraved, features wide shallow bowls, and also bottles deriving from the shapes of gourds (fig. 5). These bowls, having rounded bottoms with narrow vertical rims or shoulders, are termed "carinated" and are decorated with very fine engraved lines in sets running in zigzaglike patterns, and occasionally quarter-circle units. Another design motif features circles framed by overlapping rectilinear bands forming a quadrangle. Such design units are repeated around the vessel body in sets of three or four. A third type of pottery, Kiam Incised, is distinguished by large jars with slightly everted rims, decorated with encircling bands of horizontal lines; the surfaces of globular jars tend to be covered in overall patterns of fingernail punctuations or fine vertical striations. From the outset, Caddo potters thus employed abstract motifs and regular geometric shapes that suggest the transference of artistic possibilities from earlier basket weaving and decoration into the field of ceramics.

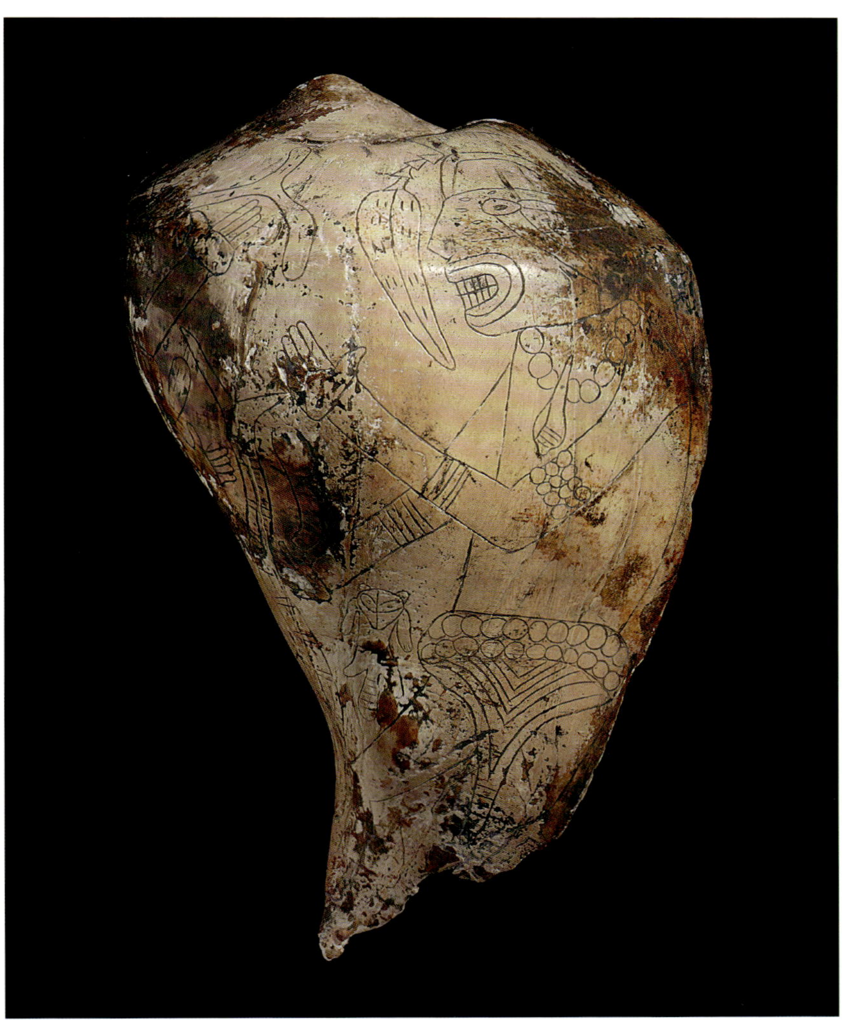

Between roughly 1300 and 1700 a wider range of fine decorative effects was achieved, embracing highly burnished areas and engraved motifs. New shapes appeared, including small-bodied bottles with cylindrical necks, reflecting the shapes of gourds. Haley Engraved pottery, as it is called, often suggests the replication of gourd painting with engraved linear scrolls, double-back meanders, and chevrons in symmetrical units repeated two, three, or four times around the vessel body. More complex forms and decorative effects were achieved on small jars with outflaring rims, and jars with rims raised in four prominent peaks, their surfaces covered with incised concentric circles, scrolls, and parallel lines; small areas could also be filled with stick punctuations, and surfaces divided with appliquéd fillets running vertically and diagonally (fig. 7).

At this juncture we must interrupt the narrative by referring to objects from the important archaeological site of Spiro, Oklahoma, c. 900–1400, and its curious disjunction with the Caddo ceramic art we have been describing. Works of art and related furnishings recovered from burials in the Craig Mound at Spiro have been referred to repeatedly in other chapters of this book as projections of a formal and symbolic system originating in Cahokia (see, for example, the essay by James Brown). These objects represent an extension of courtly and religious paraphernalia belonging to a powerful Cahokian aristocratic elite who were almost certainly seeking bonds with ruling lineages of other societies for the purpose of forming military, trading, and religious alliances. These relationships would have been legitimized by ritual, marriage, and the exchange of goods and privileges. Yet the problem of explaining the presence of the objects at Spiro and the ethnic affiliation of the rulers remains a much-debated issue. Spiro is therefore called a "Caddoan" site, the general term embracing the Caddo proper and also other speakers of Caddoan languages such as the Wichita or the Kichai, whose traditional homelands lie upstream from Spiro along the Arkansas River (more distantly, the Pawnee and the Arikara of the Great Plains also speak Caddoan languages). An alternate theory holds that the rulers of Spiro may have been of Tunica origin—traders from lands in the middle lower Mississippi.[3] The issue is inconclusive. In any event, it is a curious fact that the

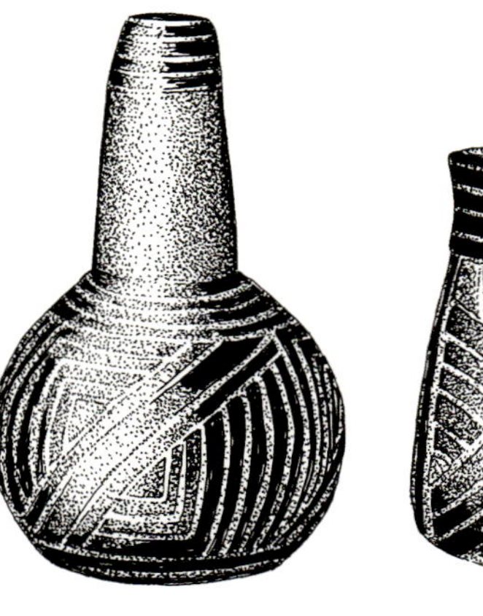

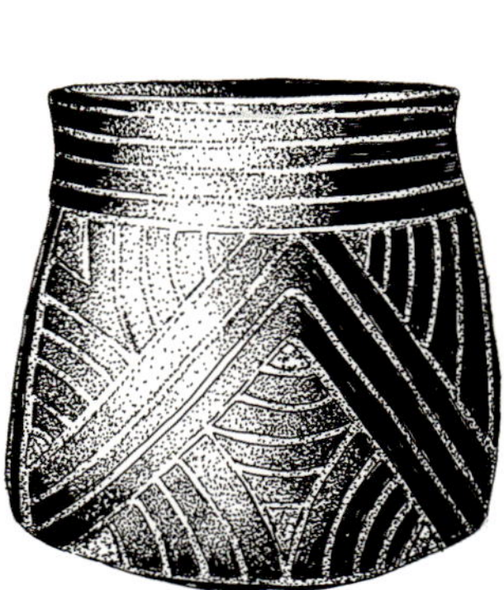

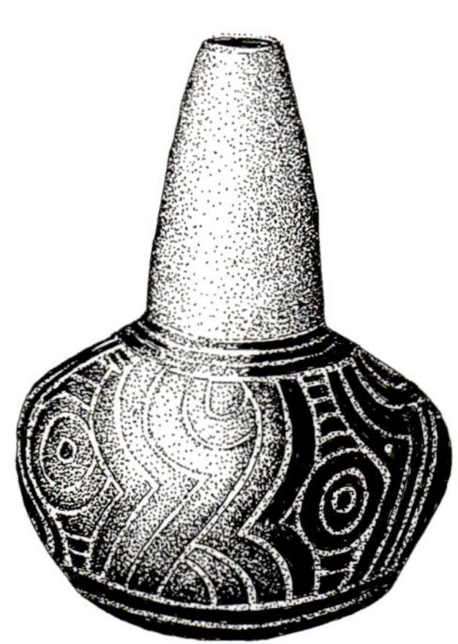

Fig. 9 Three vessels of the Spiro Engraved type; Caddoan; Oklahoma, LeFlore County, Spiro, Craig Mound, A.D. 900–1400; drawing by Gigi Bayliss after Suhm and Jelks 1962, pl. 74.

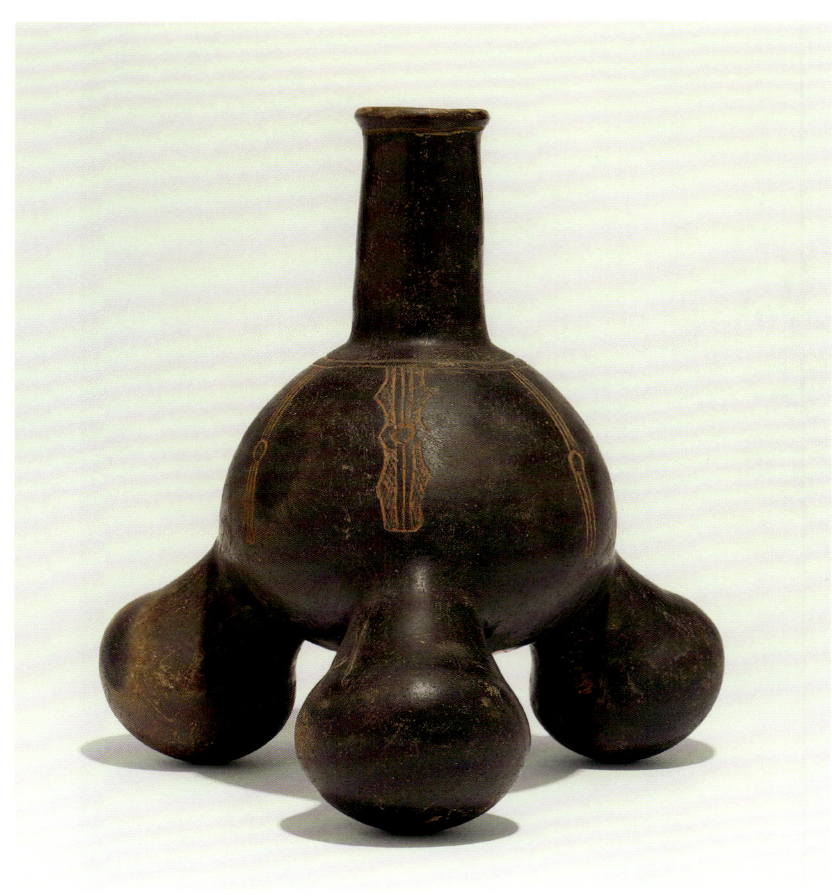
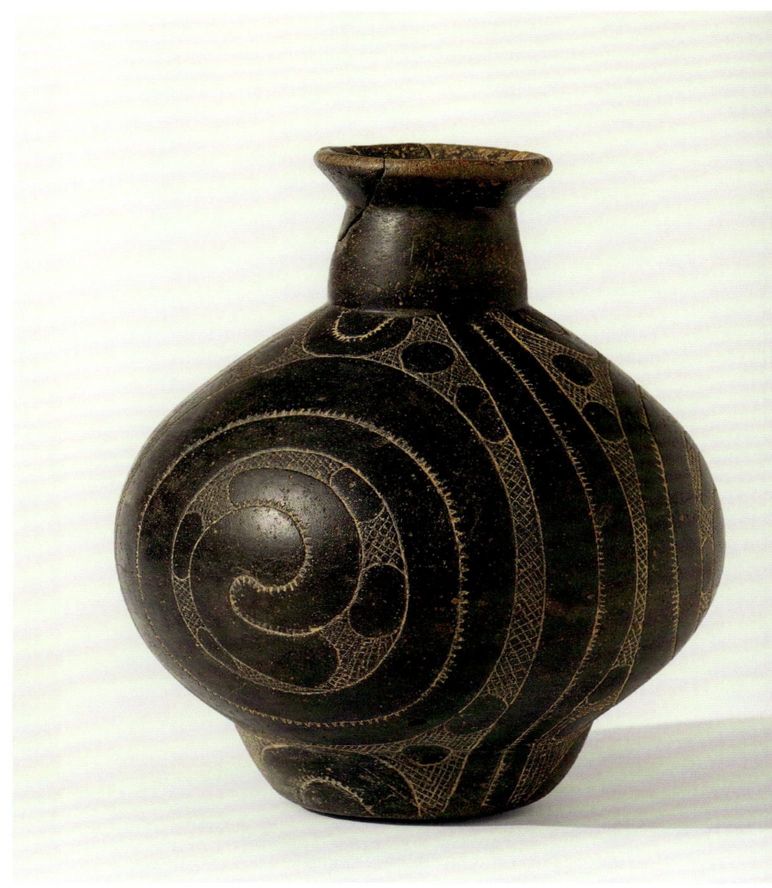
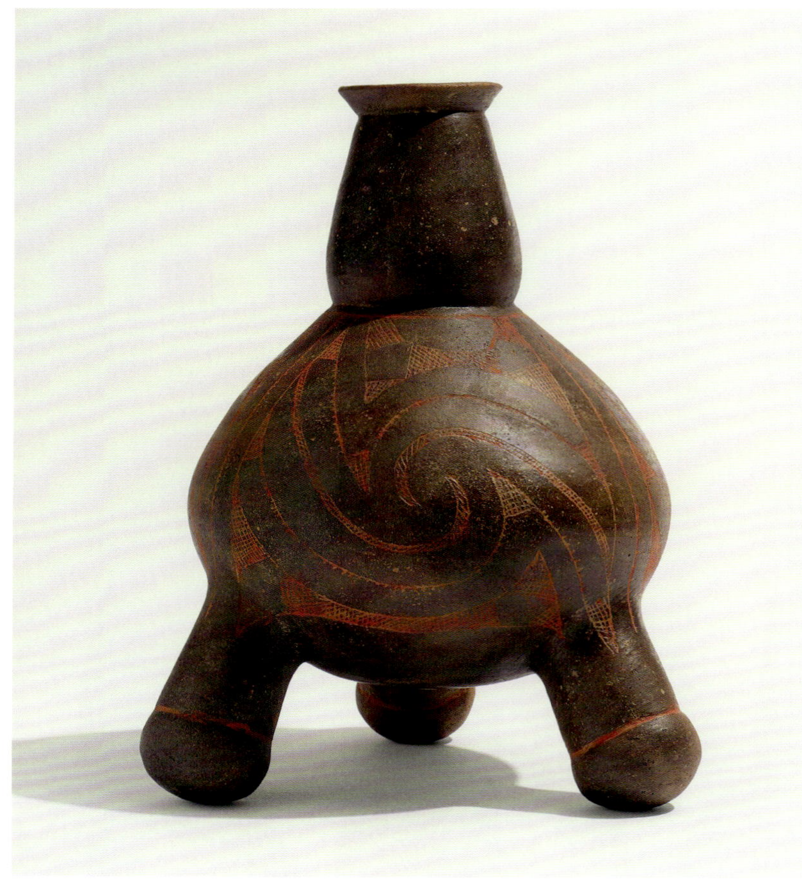
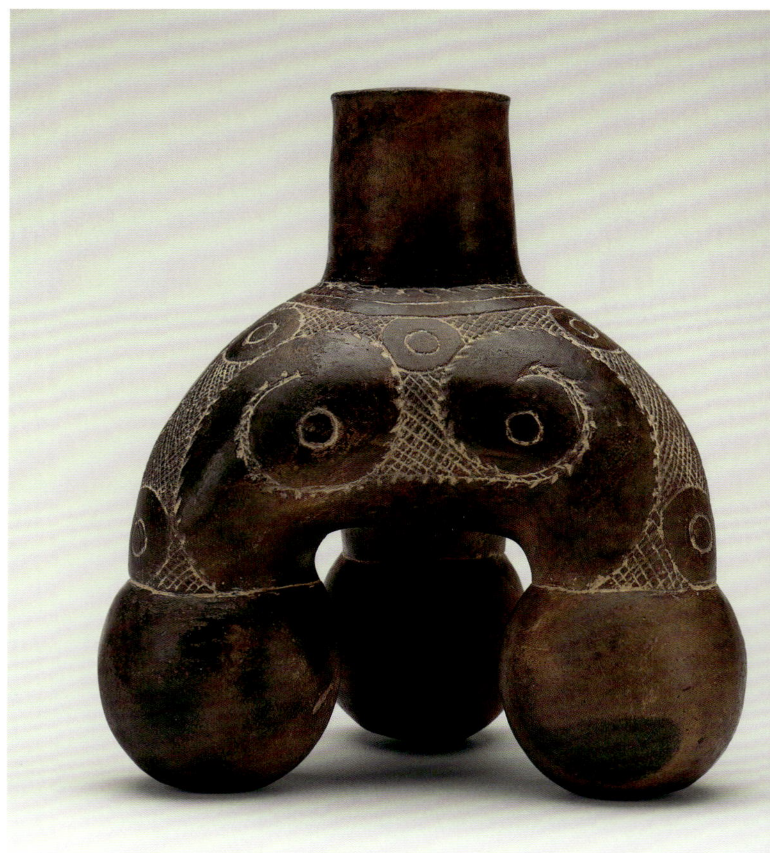

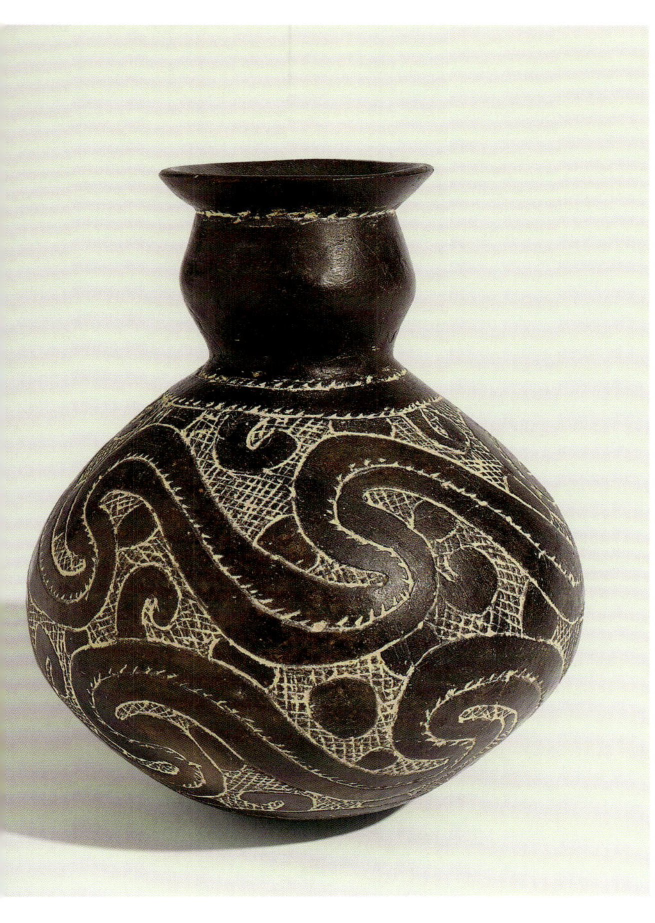

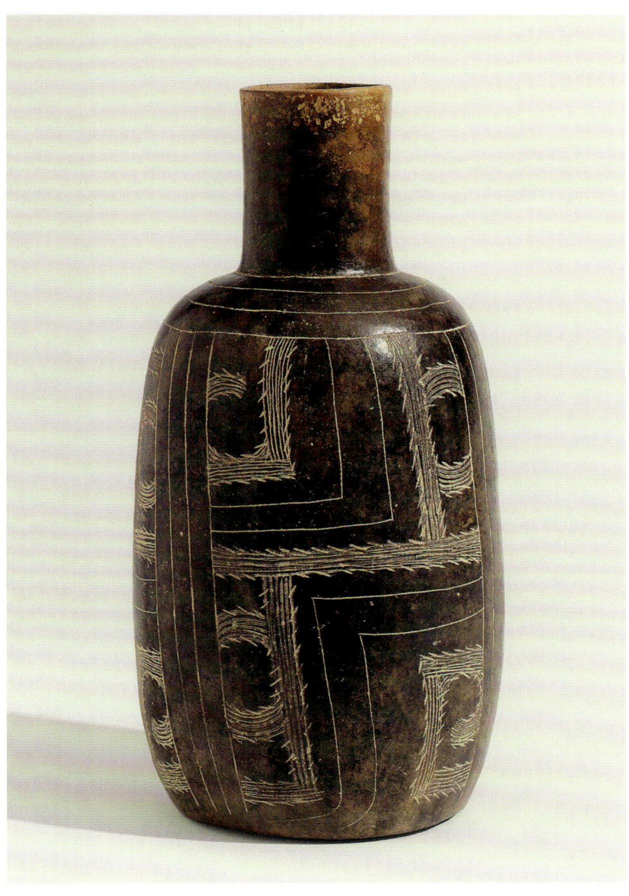

Fig. 10 Burnished tripod bottle; Blakeley Engraved type; Caddoan; Arkansas, A.D. 1400–1500; ceramic, h. 25.4 cm; James and Elaine Kinker Collection, Midwest. Cat. no. 207.

Fig. 11 Engraved jar with protuberant footing; Hodges Engraved type; Caddoan; Arkansas, A.D. 1400–1700; ceramic, h. 20.3 cm; James and Elaine Kinker Collection, Midwest. Cat. no. 205.

Fig. 12 Engraved jar; Hodges Engraved type; Caddoan; Arkansas, A.D. 1400–1700; ceramic, h. 14 cm; James and Elaine Kinker Collection, Midwest. Cat. no. 204.

Fig. 13 Engraved cylindrical bottle; Hodges Engraved type; Caddoan; Arkansas, A.D. 1400–1700; ceramic, h. 25.4 cm; James and Elaine Kinker Collection, Midwest. Cat. no. 199.

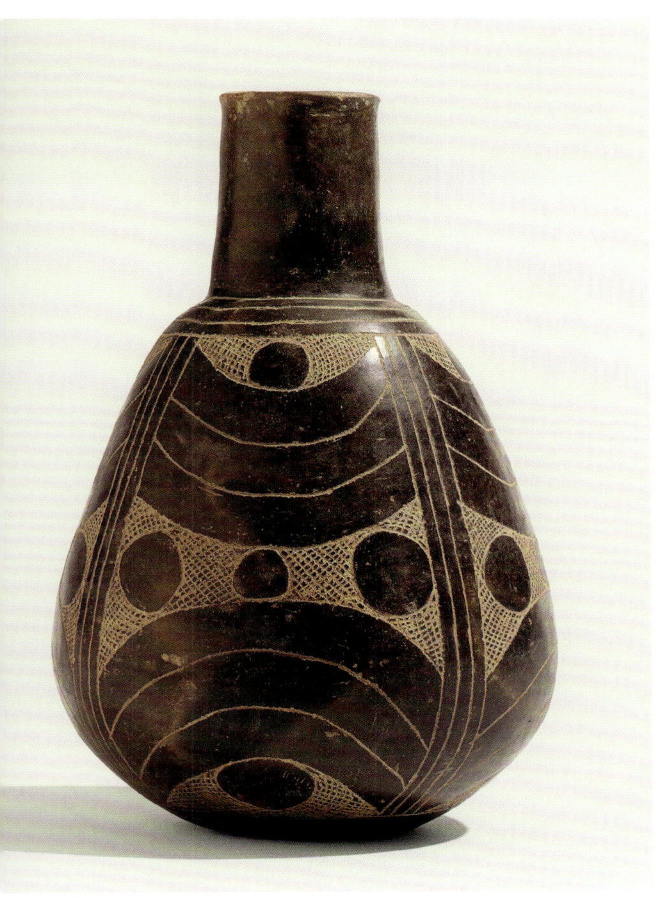

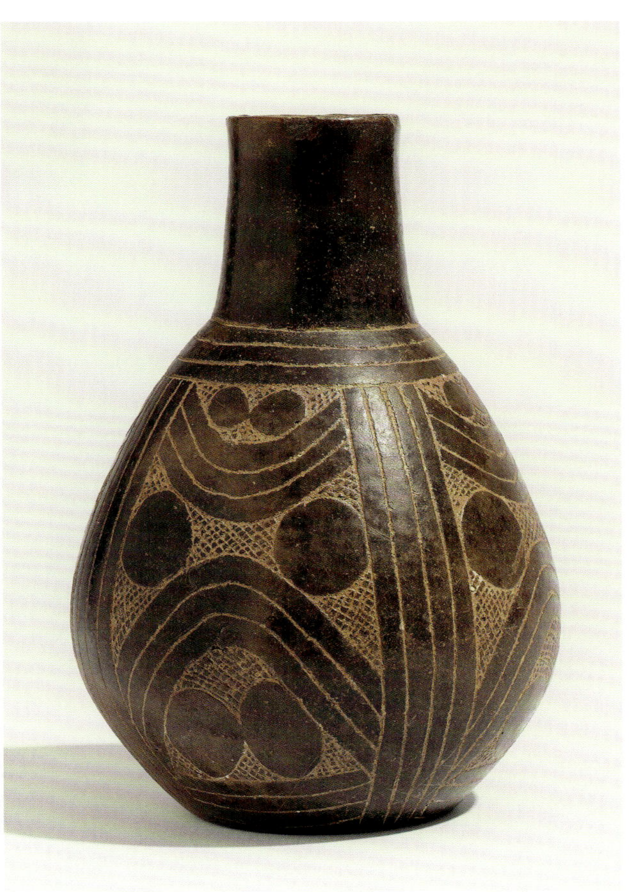

Fig. 14 Engraved tripod bottle; Hodges Engraved type; Caddoan; Arkansas, A.D. 1400–1700; ceramic, h. 25.4 cm; James and Elaine Kinker Collection, Midwest. Cat. no. 208.

Fig. 15 Engraved tripod vessel; Hodges Engraved type; Caddoan; southwestern Arkansas, A.D. 1400–1700; ceramic, h. 20.3; Museum of the Red River, Idabel, Oklahoma. Cat. no. 206.

Fig. 16 Engraved egg-shaped bottle; Hodges Engraved type; Caddoan; Arkansas, A.D. 1400–1700; ceramic, h. 21.6 cm; James and Elaine Kinker Collection, Midwest. Cat. no. 200.

Fig. 17 Engraved egg-shaped bottle; Hodges Engraved type; Caddoan; Arkansas, A.D. 1400–1700; ceramic, h. 17.8 cm; James and Elaine Kinker Collection, Midwest. Cat. no. 201.

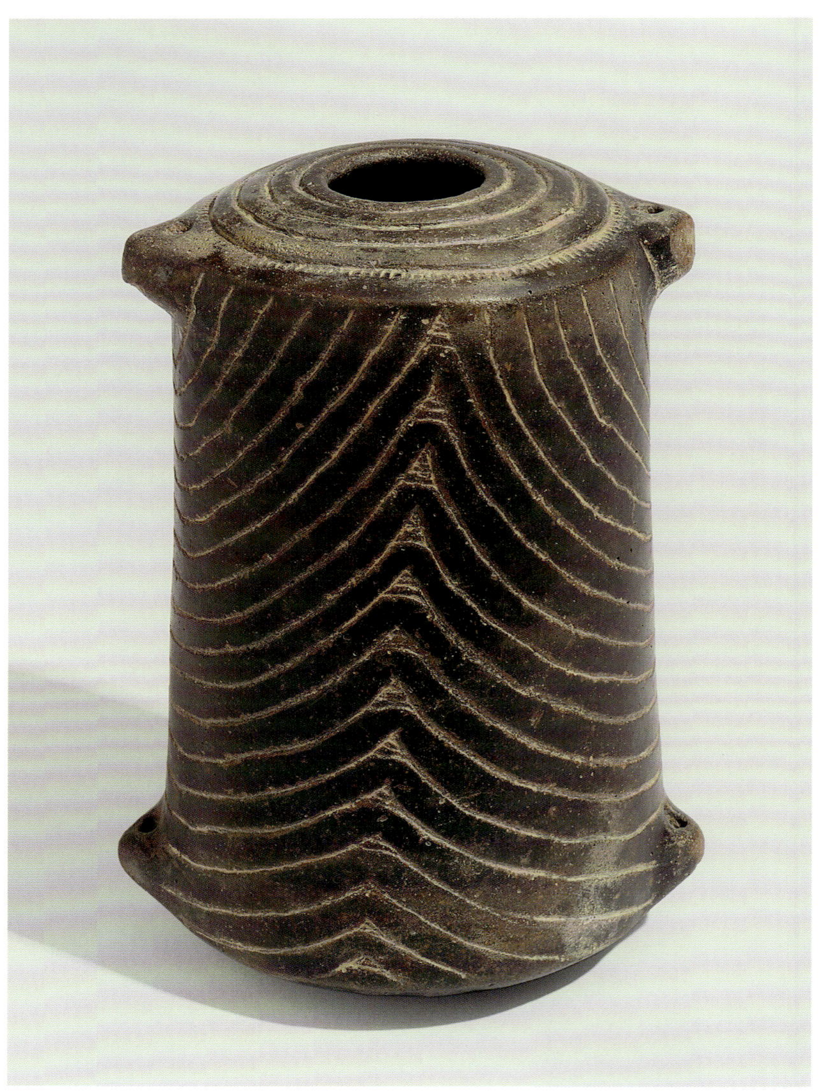

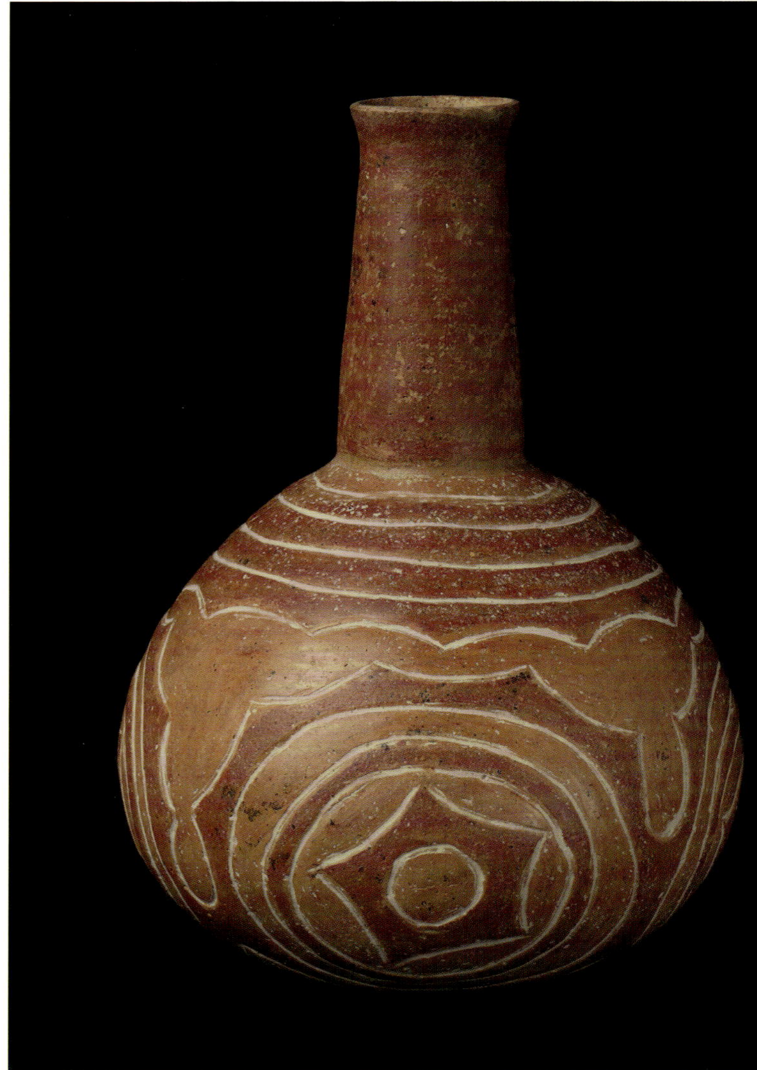

figurative, highly representational imagery that is seen on engraved whelk shells found in the Craig Mound at Spiro (fig. 8) was not accepted into the core artistic repertoire of the Caddo. Their ceramics continued with no significant figurative diversification, as shown by Spiro Engraved, a type of pottery strongly embedded in the Caddo tradition (fig. 9), widely distributed from eastern Oklahoma to the Red River valley and adjacent parts of Texas, c. 900–1450. Gourd-shaped bottles, slightly tapered cylindrical containers, and vessels with rounded bottoms and squared upper rims are predominant shapes. The surfaces are highly burnished and engraved with wide stripes composed in scrolls, diagonal and straight bands, recurved bands and chevrons, and semicircles, quarter-circles, or concentric squares. Such boldly minimalist geometric patterns draw upon the earlier decorative language of Holly Fine Engraved of roughly A.D. 900–1300, continuing the mainline Caddo tradition.

During and after the artistic heyday of Spiro between 1250 and 1370, termed the "Copper Dominated Horizon,"[4] Caddo ceramics continued a florescence with the appearance of Blakeley Engraved and Hodges Engraved, c. 1400–1700, building upon the decorative solutions of earlier forms and related local variants (figs. 10–19). Bottles with spool-shaped spouts, tripod vessels, nesting vessels with upper and lower chambers, and globular, conical, and carinated bowls are covered with overall engraved designs. Among the prominent ornamental motifs are meandering scrolls, scrolls that double back sharply, sometimes pinched in at a narrow neck; crosshatched, negative spaces often surrounding burnished dots, semicircular bands, or interlocking curves; and major decorative units often flowing around the vessel in an uninterrupted pattern, or maybe separated into compartments by broad vertical bands. Red or white pigments may be rubbed across surfaces to enrich visually the shallow relief. The effigy vessels that also appear at this time are surely related to the wooden effigy forms kept in the two houses of the mythical twins as described by Espinosa. These ceramics are unlike the naturalistic models of contemporary Nodena tradition: although the animal forms are recognizable, they are entirely subordinated to the vessel shape and decorative program (figs. 20–21). Turtles, alligators, fish, bears, and quadruped figures with open spouts instead of identifiable heads are embellished with the kinds of geometric designs seen on all other vessels of this period. Restrained and elegant shapes also appear, such as cylindrical bottles with chevron

Fig. 18 Engraved cylindrical jar; Means Engraved type; Caddoan; Arkansas, A.D. 1400–1500; ceramic, h. 20.3 cm; James and Elaine Kinker Collection, Midwest. Cat. no. 216.

Fig. 19 Engraved redware bottle; Caddoan; Arkansas, A.D. 1400–1700; ceramic, h. 20.3 cm; James and Elaine Kinker Collection, Midwest. Cat. no. 197. Unlike ceramics from the central Mississippi River valley, Caddoan ceramics rarely feature surface painting. This bottle is a unique object displaying the use of red paint by a Caddoan artist.

facing page, bottom

Fig. 22 Seed jar with fire clouds; Caddoan; Arkansas, Grant County, Saline River, A.D. 1400–1500; ceramic, h. 26.7 cm; Gilcrease Museum, Tulsa, Oklahoma. Cat. no. 217.

Fig. 23 Seed jar with fire clouds; Caddoan; Arkansas, A.D. 1400–1500; ceramic; Princeton University. Cat. no. 219.

Fig. 24 Seed jar with fire clouds; Caddoan; Arkansas (?), A.D. 1400–1500; ceramic; Princeton University. Cat. no. 218.

patterns, and the minimal ovoid cylindrical seed jars, ornamented only with abstract fire-clouds (figs. 22–24). Boldly inventive shapes were created as well, such as an oval stirrup-spout bottle, one of the masterpieces of Caddo art (fig. 25). Yet even here one finds that the running triangular decoration has precedent in the Holly Engraved ceramics of centuries before, and the shape itself is an elaboration of possibilities inherent in other traditional forms.

Other notable variants of 1600–1800 include vessels of the Keno Trailed style. In general the shapes are conventional bottles and globular vessels, but they display a unique decorative technique (fig. 26).[5] This is achieved by incising a broad line impressed with a blunt stylus, in endless combinations of straight, curved, or parallel lines fitted close together to cover the vessel body. Scrolls, spirals, guilloches, meanders, concentric circles, and arcs are among the common motifs. Two of the finest known Caddo pieces come out of this Keno Trailed variant. The first is a three-part bottle, deriving its form from the nesting of three carinated bowls, the shoulders of each tier decorated with incised parallel lines and scrolls, contrasting with plain burnished undersides (see fig. 7 in the essay by Stacey Halfmoon in this volume). The second famous bottle is of tapered conical shape, with four corners protruding markedly from the slightly curving bottom (fig. 1). This is an exaggeration of a basketrylike form first seen centuries earlier in Dunkin Incised. We shall close this brief review with the magnificent, large redware and blackware containers from the period between 1300 and 1700. Avery Engraved features the largest of Caddo vessels. The most common forms are tapered, conical shapes decorated with a broad band of scrolls, incised into the hard surface by post-firing (fig. 27). More complex vessels with high outward-flaring rims, carinated shoulders and curved bottoms, also display decorative designs with concentric, banded semicircular motifs repeated four times around the vessel, plain lines alternating with ticked lines, narrow bands with large spurs, and various combinations (fig. 28). There are reversed S-shapes and a familiar assortment of spirals, whorls, scrolls, circles, and disks outlined by cross-hatching, in a range of pleasing designs.

Conclusions

Caddo pottery showed remarkable continuity over a span of approximately nine hundred years. It is a strongly defined tradition, outstanding in the Mississippian world for its inventive, finely made forms. There is a marked tendency for artistic activity to follow in well-established channels of expression, the limits of which were undoubtedly socially determined. Yet this conservative tendency also allowed artists of marked originality, operating within the established canon, constantly to succeed in creating new local variations, overriding conventional boundaries with new reaches of aesthetic activity. Nevertheless, even the most adventurous masterpiece works invariably reflect possibilities afforded by the accepted tradition.

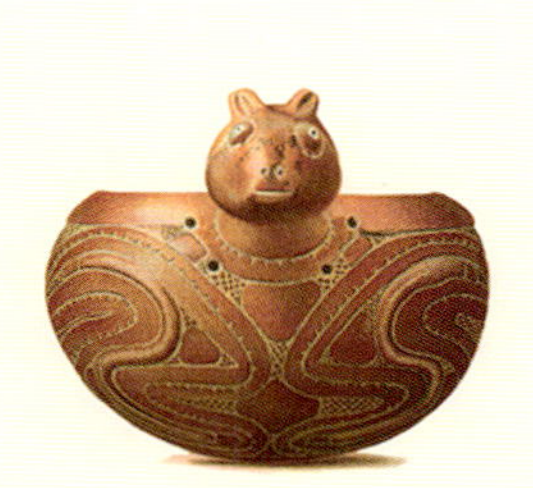

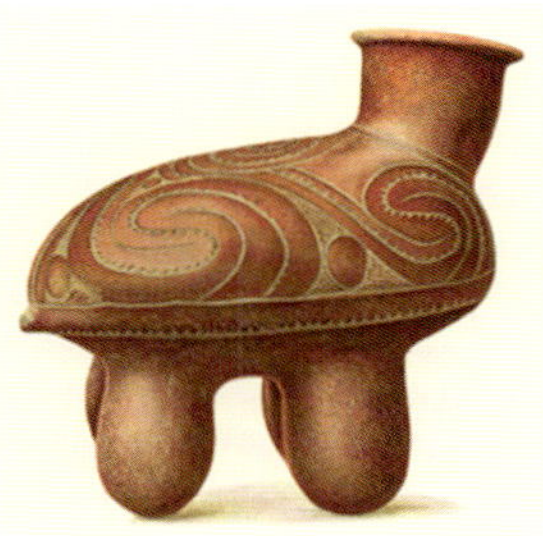

Fig. 20 Animal effigy vessel; Hodges Engraved type; Caddoan; Louisiana, Ouachita Parish, Glendora Plantation, A.D. 1680–1750; from Moore 1909, pl. 1.

Fig. 21 Animal effigy vessel; Hodges Engraved type; Caddoan; Louisiana, Morehouse Parish, Keno Place, A.D. 1680–1750; from Moore 1909, pl. 7.

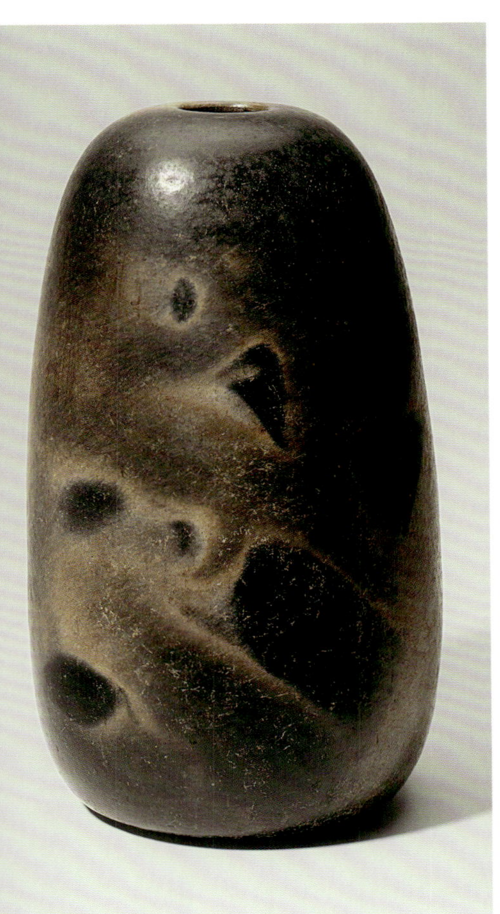

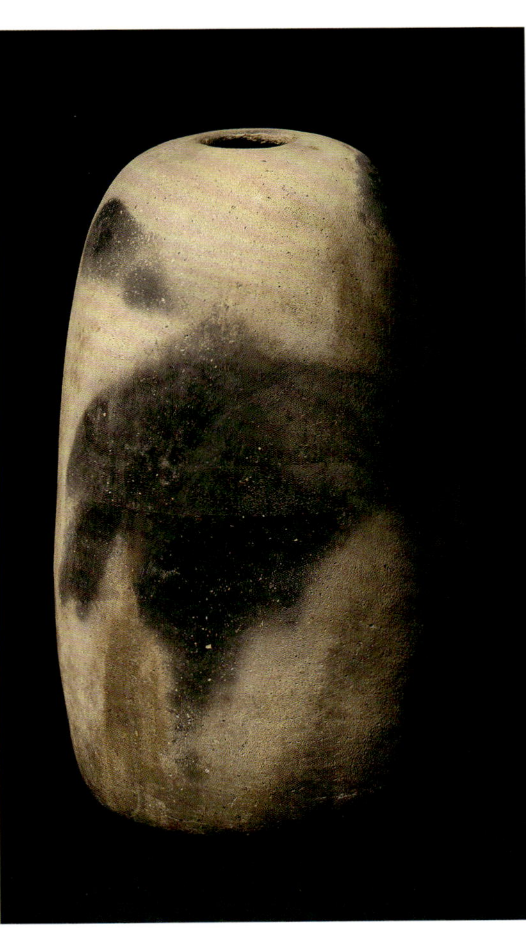

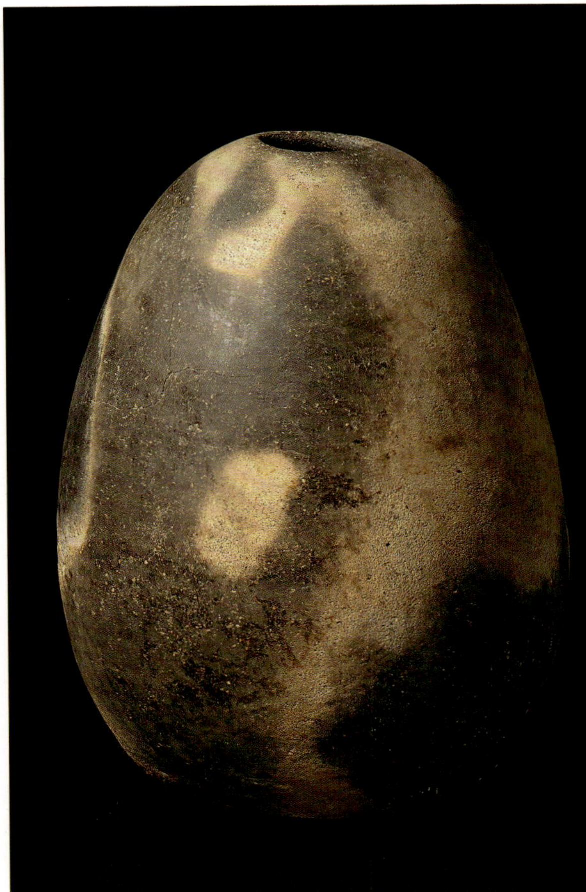

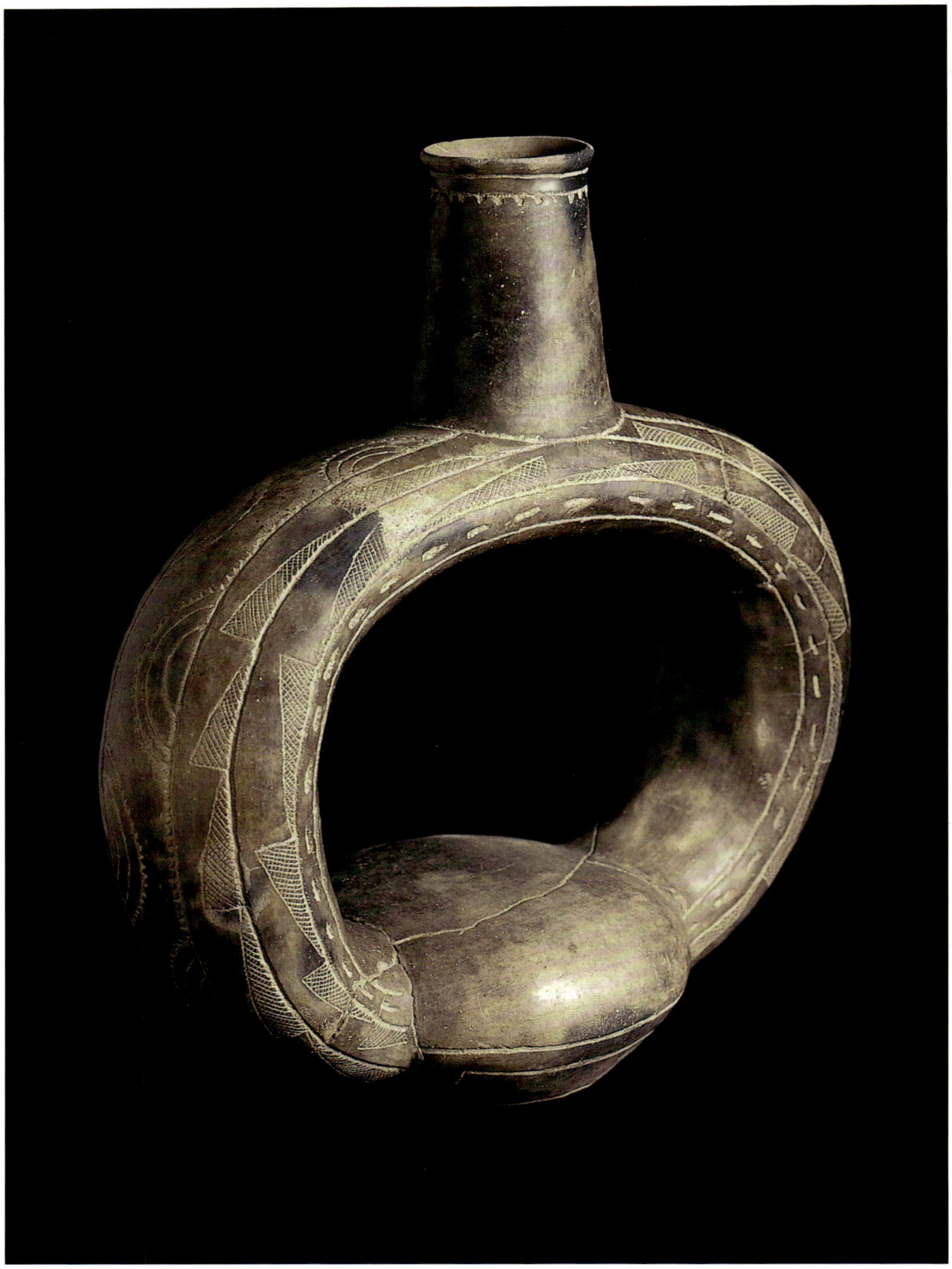

Fig. 25 Stirrup spout bottle; Hodges Engraved type; Caddoan; Arkansas, Clark County, A.D. 1300–1700; ceramic, h. 32, w. 28 cm; Dr. Kent and Jonnie Westbrook Collection, Little Rock, Arkansas. Cat. no. 212.

Caddo ceramic art played an ongoing, determining role in the maintenance of a distinctly Caddo identity. The fact that its abstract vocabulary of shapes and decorations rejected the figurative narrative imagery stemming from Cahokia is important to note. The Caddo example contrasts markedly with the art of Moundville, Etowah, and other traditions across the central Mississippi valley.

While the Caddo resisted influence from other figurative art styles, there are several occasions where these other traditions from the greater Southeast incorporated elements of Caddo ceramic design into their own formal vocabularies. This is perhaps the most recognizable with the so-called Davis Rectangle motif, seen on some Cahokian ceramics and incorporated into effigy vessels from the central Mississippi valley as well as Braden-style shell cups from Spiro (see fig. 30 in the essay by James Brown in this volume).[6] In addition, there are examples on shell cups engraved in the Craig style from Spiro with curvilinear designs that surely are derived from Caddo ceramic sources. It may well be the case that Caddo artisans were employed in the workshops of Cahokia. Archaeological work has also made great strides showing the vast distribution of Caddo ceramics across the Great Plains and the Deep South,[7] indicating that Caddo wares were valued and sought by their neighbors.

Abstraction in Caddo ceramic art is not the simplified rendering of some outward reality. It is a reality in itself, with its own structural rules. The syntax of Caddo form and decoration may be broadly characterized in three categories. First, the visible units of design—scrolls, meanders, hatchings, etc.—are articulated so as to unify decorated and plain areas

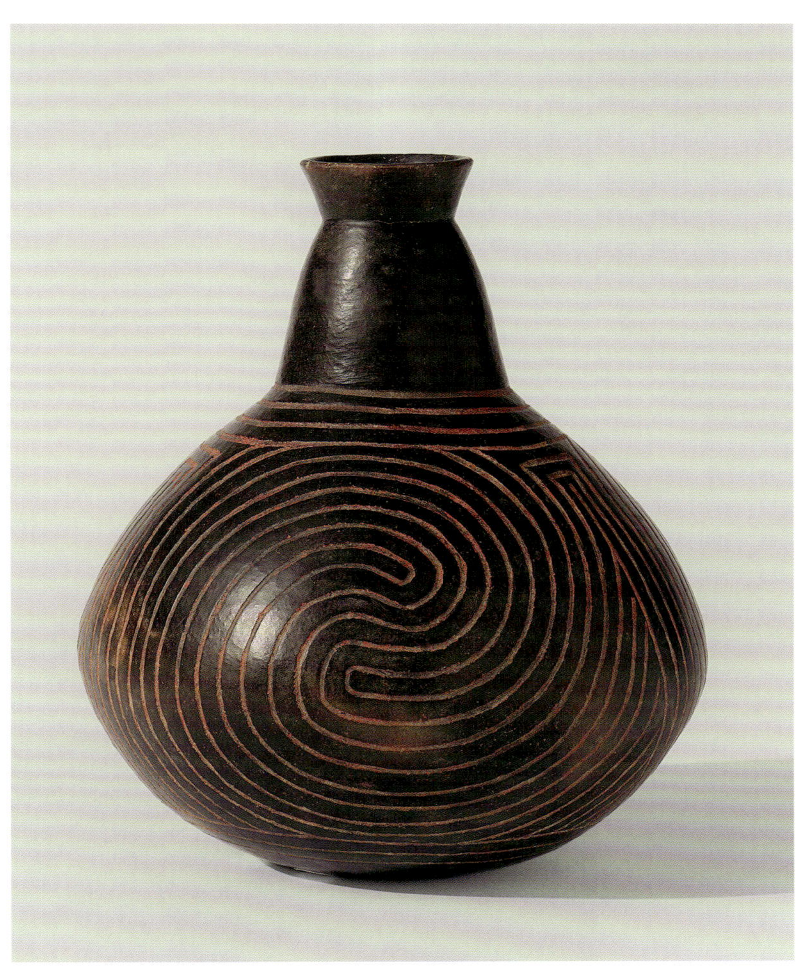

Fig. 26 Engraved bottle; Keno Trailed type; Caddoan; Arkansas, A.D. 1600–1800; ceramic, h. 20.3 cm; James and Elaine Kinker Collection, Midwest. Cat. no. 213.

Fig. 27 Round-bottomed flared vessel; redware, Taylor Engraved type; Caddoan; Arkansas, A.D. 1500–1700; ceramic, h. 25.4 cm; James and Elaine Kinker Collection, Midwest. Cat. no. 223.

Fig. 28 Wide-necked vessel; redware, Avery Engraved type; Caddoan; Arkansas, A.D. 1300–1700; ceramic, h. 27.9 cm; James and Elaine Kinker Collection, Midwest. Cat. no. 221.

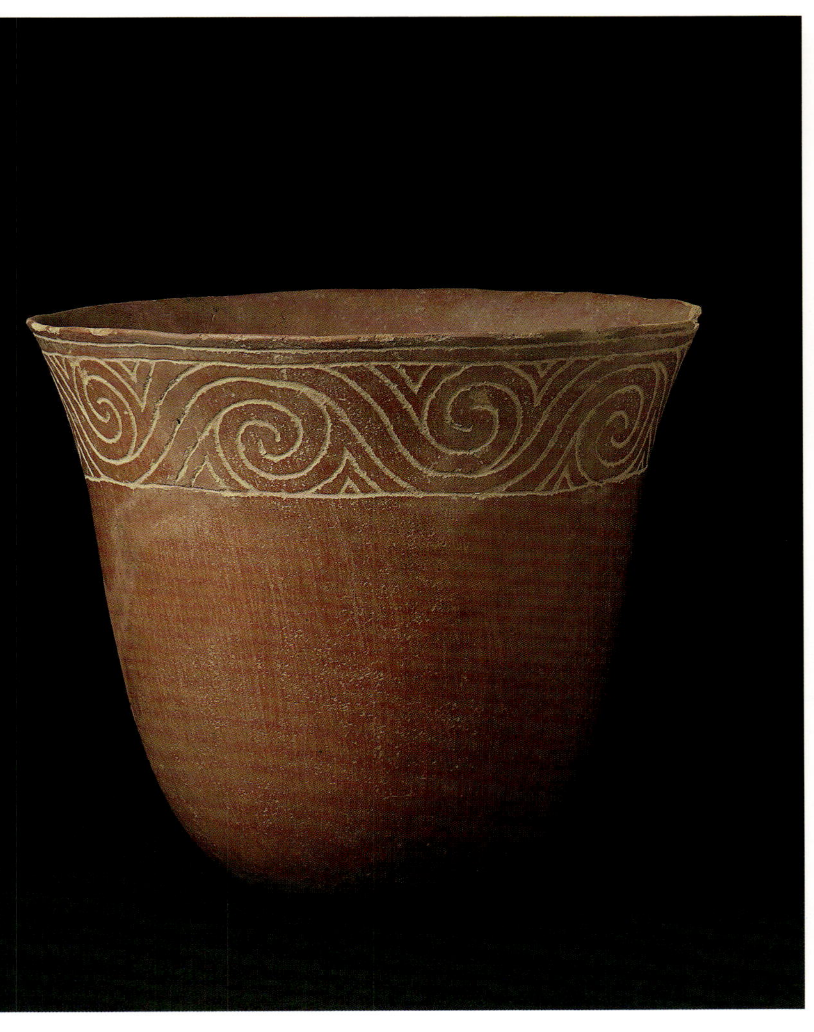

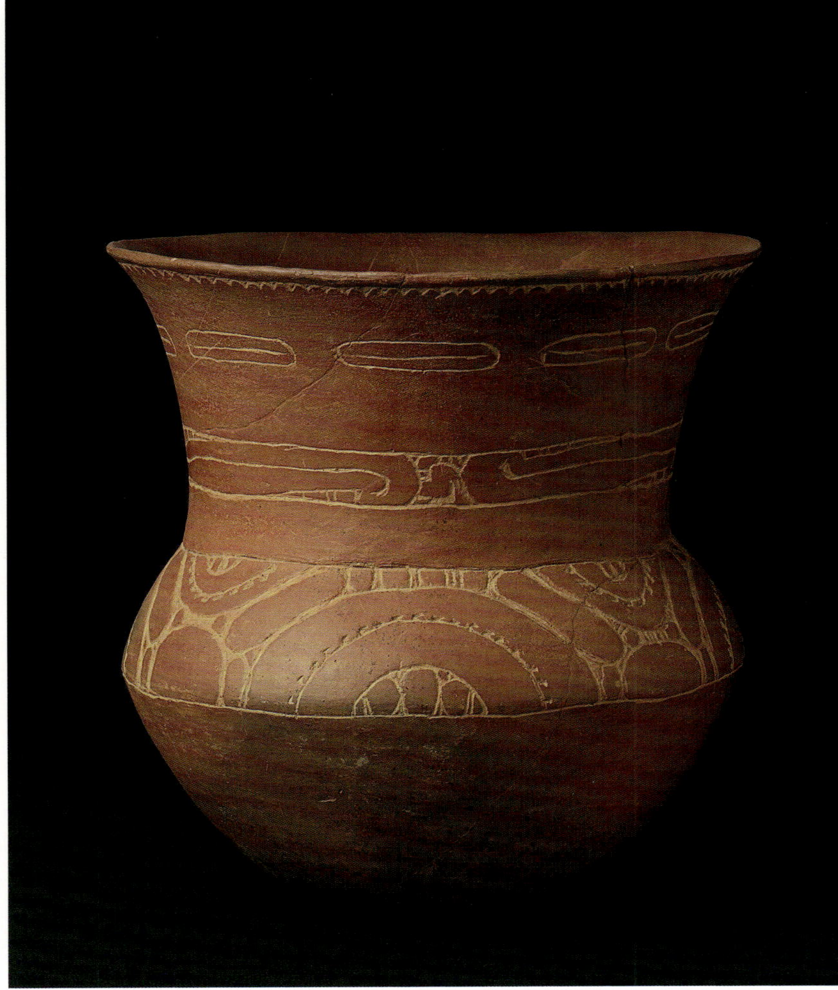

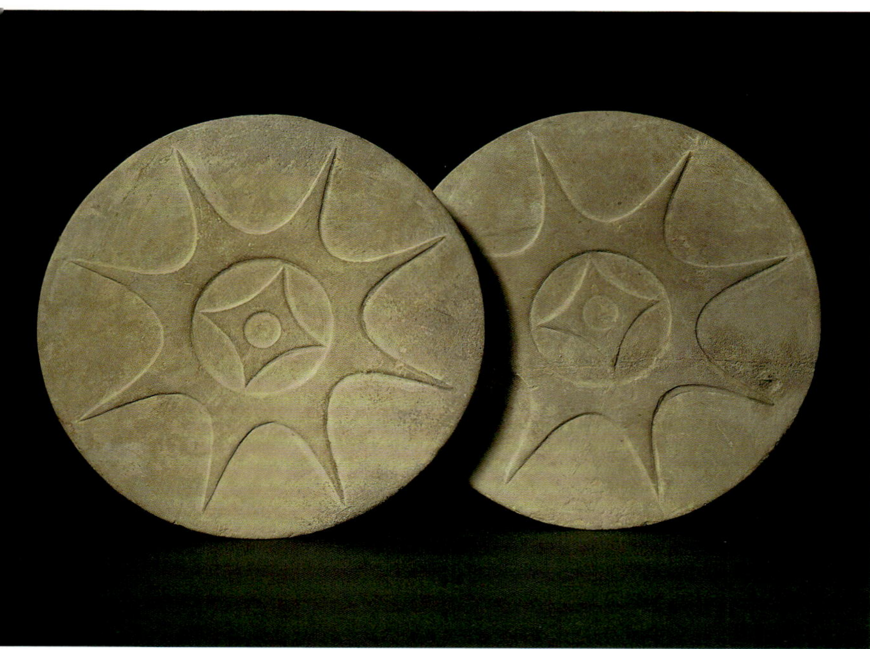

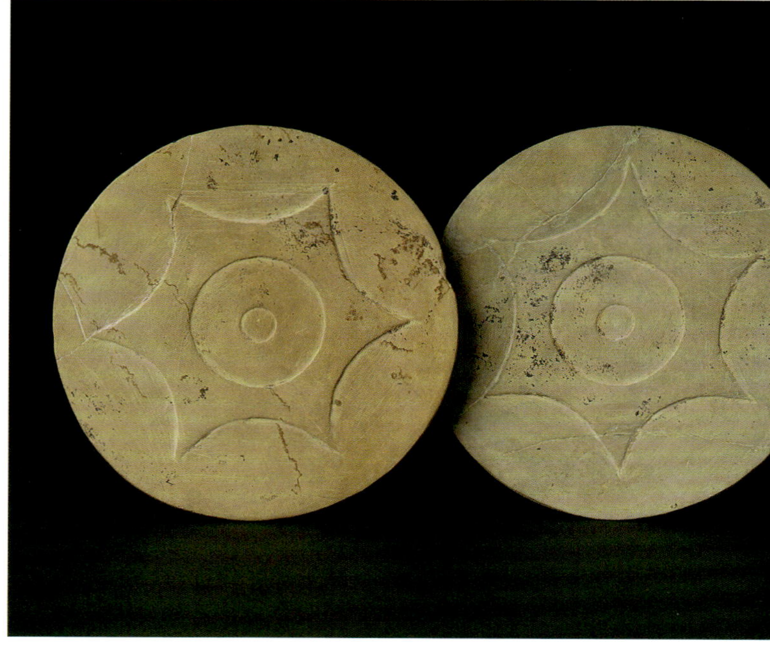

in integrated patterns. The most striking examples of decoration virtually cover whole vessel surfaces in a way that fuses positive and negative areas. Second, the decoration can best be defined in terms of organic relationships between forms, rather than a sum of discrete, mechanically connected units. These relationships are expressed in abstract, geometric terms that make the decorative programs unsuitable for representational forms. Third, the geometric shapes of vessels evolve with considerable variety, and the layout of complex design units tends to follow symmetries of two, three, and four appearances around the vessel forms. An important aspect of this abstract patterning is that the more complex units do not necessarily contain within themselves a logical end to the overall design, but tend instead to favor an overall flow.

Is there a symbolism to these works? With figural elements excluded, save for the abstract animal effigy vessels and very rare human head pots, is it possible to identify a Caddo symbolic program? Scrolls and related curvilinear designs may have aquatic associations, as they clearly do in Nodena wares of the middle Mississippi River valley, yet the fact that such motifs appear so ubiquitously on such a wide range of Caddo vessels, and are unaccompanied by composite, metaphoric creatures or other storytelling figures, argues against such fixed symbolic associations. There are also occasional star motifs that may be emblematic, carrying connotations of rank, as they do on Spiro earspools (figs. 29–31). But here, too, their occurrence on different types of Caddo vessels seems to dissolve the idea of rigorously prescribed associations. Still another motif, the Davis Rectangle, occurs on early wares and may be traced in a succession of types, and it even appears as a tattoo mark on a Nodena portrait vessel (see fig. 18 in the preceding essay by Chester Walker in this volume). Could this be a sign of Caddo social identity, an emblem of clan or rank? No clear answer can now be presented. Finally, we have seen that animal imagery has a restricted field: while none of the usual Mississippian allegorical, composite creatures appear, the ducks, lizards, and alligators mentioned by Espinosa, and other animals abstractly portrayed by Caddo vessels, do point to the persistence of another form of religious symbolism expressing associations with the sky, the earth, and the waters.

In the general absence of figural imagery or a prescribed, encompassing system of symbols, Caddo vessels are therefore unlikely to have carried conventional meanings of the kind associated with specific historical events, allegorical themes, or legendary happenings. Therefore we must look to other, more intrinsic aspects

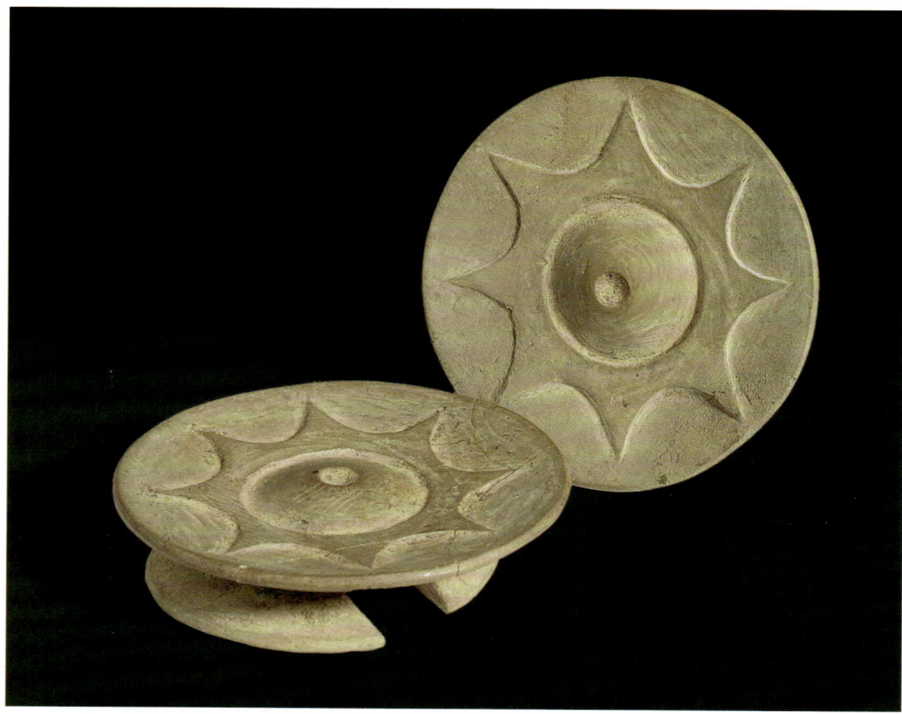

Fig. 29 Pair of earspools, 8-pointed star motif; Oklahoma, LeFlore County, Spiro, A.D. 1200–1400; stone, diam. 10.2 cm; Anthony Patano Collection, Chicago. Cat. no. 162.

Fig. 30 Pair of earspools, 6-pointed star motif; Oklahoma, LeFlore County, Spiro, A.D. 1200–1400; stone, diam. 8.9 cm; James and Elaine Kinker Collection, Midwest. Cat. no. 164.

Fig. 31 Pair of earspools, 8-pointed star motif; Oklahoma, LeFlore County, Spiro, A.D. 1200–1400; stone, diam. 5.7 cm; James and Elaine Kinker Collection, Midwest. Cat. no. 163.

of meaning. There is meaning in the visual autonomy of abstract decoration and shape—the coherent force of an imaginative design. In addition to these formal qualities, the vessels also surely carried a field of fluctuating cultural associations, mental images, and sentiments that attach themselves to valued objects, giving them properties beyond their immediate, practical functions, in assisting cultural memory. We have seen, from the earliest period when basketry patterns were first imitated, to the creation of the late masterpiece bottles, that Caddo potters were habituated to look to past authority while moving into the future. From mother to daughter, generation to generation, the makers of vessels advanced their art while constantly reviewing, selecting, and recasting earlier motifs. This conservative drift points to an effort to unify and order experience through an intuitive dialogue between the past and the present. Caddo pottery served a range of utilitarian purposes, but beyond holding water, *atole*, and different foods, it was part of the highly visible paraphernalia of communal festivals, diplomatic meetings, governmental proceedings, and ritualistic events, and also accompanied the departed on their journey to in the domain of the dead. Ceramic art was prized as a valued part of the cultural fabric, and can be said to have played a considerable role in prompting memory and recognition of social and spiritual connections, prerogatives, obligations, values, and mores.

Throughout its long history this art had the recurring power to evoke itself and to provide a structure for recollection. It was tied to the sense of being Caddo, and, as the Caddo Culture Club members and others have now discovered, it is again renewing this ancient function.

Notes

1. John R. Swanton's *Source Material on the History and Ethnohistory of the Caddo Indians*, Smithsonian Institution, Bureau of American Ethnology, Bulletin 132, was published in 1942. This volume is an extensive compendium of primary and secondary sources on the Caddo Indian groups. Swanton summarized and presented works from many chroniclers, explorers, bureaucrats, and historians, including works by Garcilaso de la Vega, Father Francisco Casañas, Diego Castillo, Father Anastasius Douay, Father Isidro Felix de Espinosa, Father Francisco Hidalgo, Henri Joutel, Francisco de Leon and Father Damian Massanet, Fernando Martín, Father Juan Augustin de Morfi, Andre Penicault, Domingo Terán de los Ríos, and John Sibley. This compendium, recently reprinted in 1996 by the University of Oklahoma Press, is still considered one of the most valuable sources on the subject and remains widely in use by Caddo scholars. All references throughout this essay to the above-mentioned writers have been drawn from Swanton's *Source Material* and will not be cited individually.
2. There was a burial mound tradition in the Caddo area perhaps as early as 100 B.C., although it was notably different from the Temple Mound tradition of later Caddo times; see Schambach 1997.
3. Schambach 1990.
4. James Brown and John Kelly (2000, p. 477) have discussed this time period as the "Copper Dominated Horizon" at Spiro (Spiro III phase). It is argued that during this time period the majority of the representational art was produced that was later interred in the "Great Mortuary" in the Craig Mound around 1400. Brown and Kelly argue that this horizon is represented at Moundville during the Moundville II phase, at Etowah during the Early and Late Wilbanks phases, and at Cahokia during the Sand Prairie phase.
5. Earlier forms of trailed vessels are found in Foster Trailed-Incised, but there is no stylistic connection between the two wares.
6. See Brown and Kelly 2000, p. 490, fig. j.
7. See Perttula, Hawley, and Scott 2001; Steponaitis, Blackman, and Neff 1996.

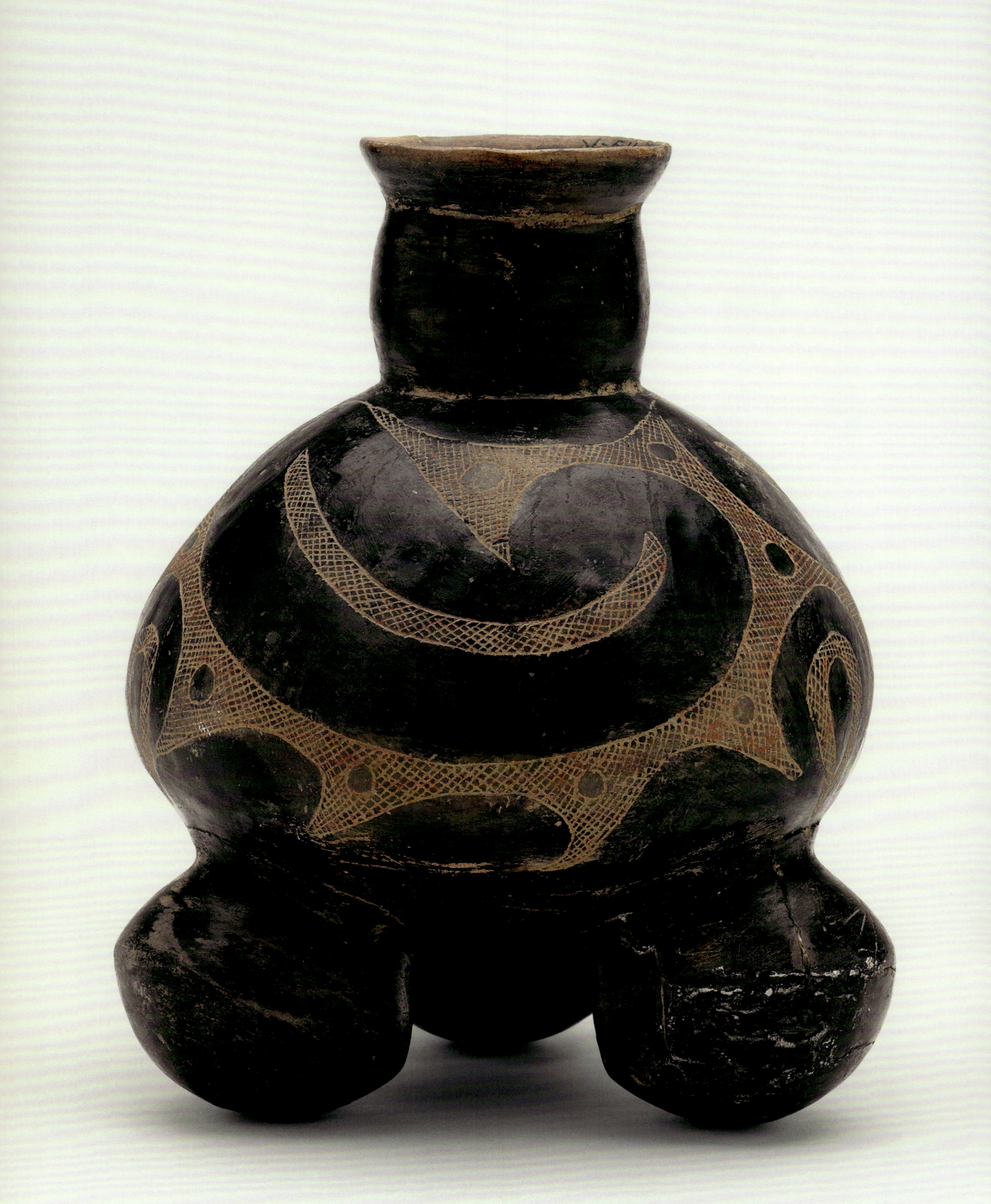

Every piece of real art,

made for the sake of making real art,

is a declaration of love and guts.

—T. C. Cannon (Kiowa/Caddo painter and poet)

Caddo Art

A Personal Perspective

Stacey Halfmoon

As a Caddo person with a true love of my tribal family and my heritage, I have a perspective of Caddo art that is a personal one and by no means reflects that of any majority group, tribal or non-tribal. I feel fortunate to have had some unique, personal experiences in relation to the art of my ancestors, and I am honored and obligated to share these experiences.

First, I want to address how to define Caddo art. What makes a work of art distinctly Caddo? The answer largely depends on who is doing the defining. Is Caddo art simply art created by a Caddo person? Surely it must be more than that; otherwise any person of Caddo descent with even minimal artistic skills would be creating Caddo art. Most would agree that to qualify as Caddo art the object or creation must conform to some agreed-upon notions of design, form, function, geographic origin, and other definitive cultural markers and criteria. But whose conceptions are we using and who defines the criteria?

Caddoan people find art and beauty everywhere: in the way a wisp of smoke rises and curls and carries one's blessings to the creator or in the soft hooting of an owl, delivering a message from the unseen world. Living art surrounds our every waking moment; it cannot be contained in an autonomous artifact. Caddo art is also created and alive under the sparkling stars and around the glowing fire while the ancient Fish Dance and Bell Dance are being performed; it is alive in every perfectly timed step of moccasined feet as they gently tap out the rhythm of the Turkey

Fig. 1 Tripod bottle; Hodges Engraved type; Caddoan; Arkansas, Garland County, Ouachita River, Kimes Place, A.D. 1400–1700; ceramic, h. 19.7 cm; Gilcrease Museum, Tulsa, Oklahoma. Cat. no. 210.

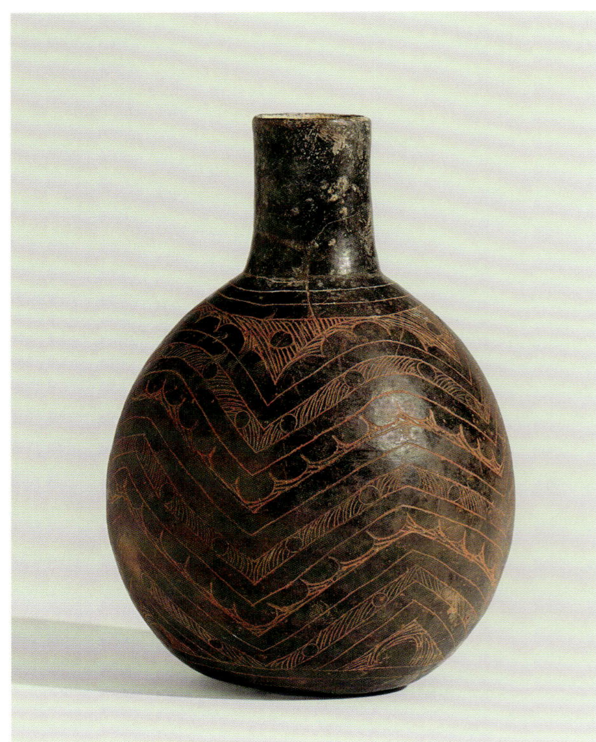

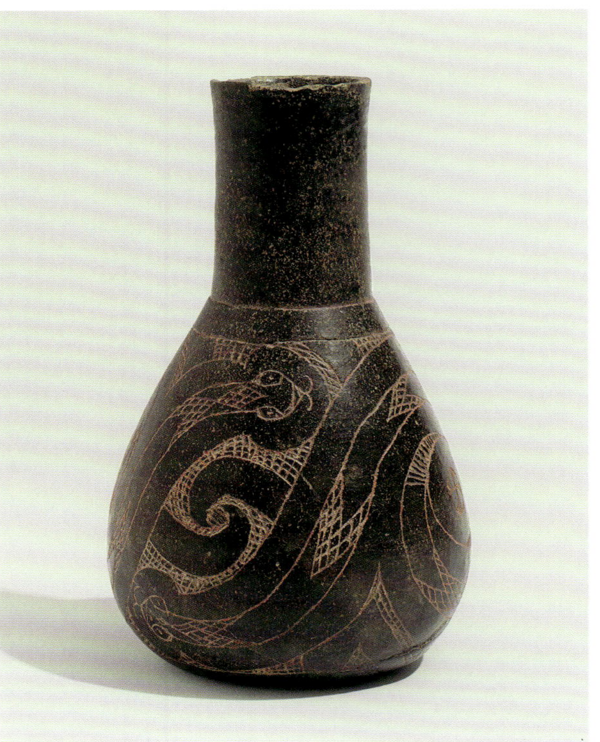

Fig. 2 Engraved bottle with chevron bands and petaloid motifs, hematite rubbed; Caddoan; Arkansas, A.D. 1200–1500; ceramic, h. 20.3 cm; James and Elaine Kinker Collection, Midwest. Cat. no. 202.

Fig. 3 Engraved egg-shaped bottle with interlocking serpent design; Caddoan; Arkansas, A.D. 1200–1500; ceramic, h. 20.3 cm; James and Elaine Kinker Collection, Midwest. Cat. no. 198.

Dance on the red earth; it is alive in the sway of the women's shawls as they move in perfect time with the beat of the drum; it is alive in the harmonies and the rise and fall of the men's voices as they sing the songs of our ancestors. All of these examples of living art are artistic and cultural masterpieces.

True art does not reside in an object but is only reflected through objects. It is my belief that an artifact or a piece of art becomes powerful and alive when life and spirit are breathed into it by a person or people. Caddo art was never created just to hang on a wall. It was functional art, intended to be used for some utilitarian purpose (water bottle, cooking pot, food bowl, seed jar; see figs. 1–9), for personal adornment (necklace, earspools), or for protection, hunting, and warfare (weapons, arrows, spears). Yet many of these objects were designed with such delicate care and beautiful design that they were highly valued as trade items by other tribes and villages; they were considered worthy to accompany the deceased in elite burials; and they continue to be valued by many, including looters who dig them up for unlawful sale.

While scholars of art may understand this connection of spirit and culture more openly, archaeologists are trained to view objects as technological or sociological clues only. Archaeologists may have a different approach to what defines art and what distinguishes an artistic masterpiece from an artifact. To many scholars, students, and others, Caddo art indeed resides in the form of archaeological artifacts. Ancient artifacts created by my tribal ancestors are considered to be the most representative and definitive pieces of "Caddo" art, although they are more often referred to as "artifacts" than as "art" or "artworks." I am not sure that pieces of art—artifacts from archaeological sites dating back hundreds to thousands of years—have ever been viewed solely as artwork, although surely that is what they are. The use of the term "artifact" diminishes any personal connection, history, or spirit contained within a piece, taking away the human element that is as embedded in the object as are the natural materials with which it is made. Artifacts to me seem to imply clues only, pieces of a puzzle to be studied, labeled, and placed in a box. Perhaps they can be pieced back together to get a glimpse of a brilliant image from another place and time. Or perhaps they can help us to understand how a particular piece was made and with that knowledge we can create again.

But how can we define art from a period and cultural context that was lost hundreds of years ago? Most connections to this cultural heritage were lost to my people

Fig. 4 Scalloped-rim vessel; Caddoan; northeastern Texas, A.D. 1200–1400; ceramic, h. 12.1, w. 24.1 cm; Museum of the Red River, Idabel, Oklahoma. Cat. no. 224.

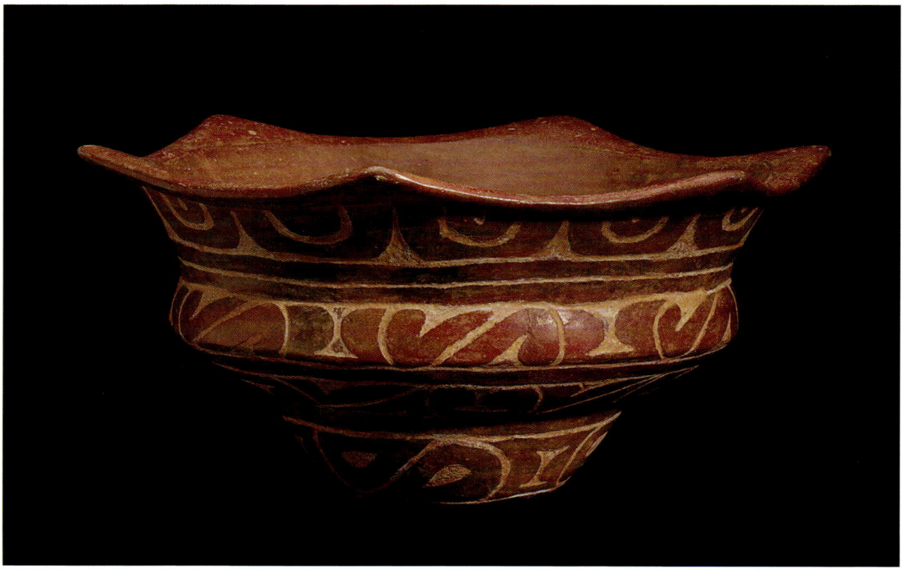

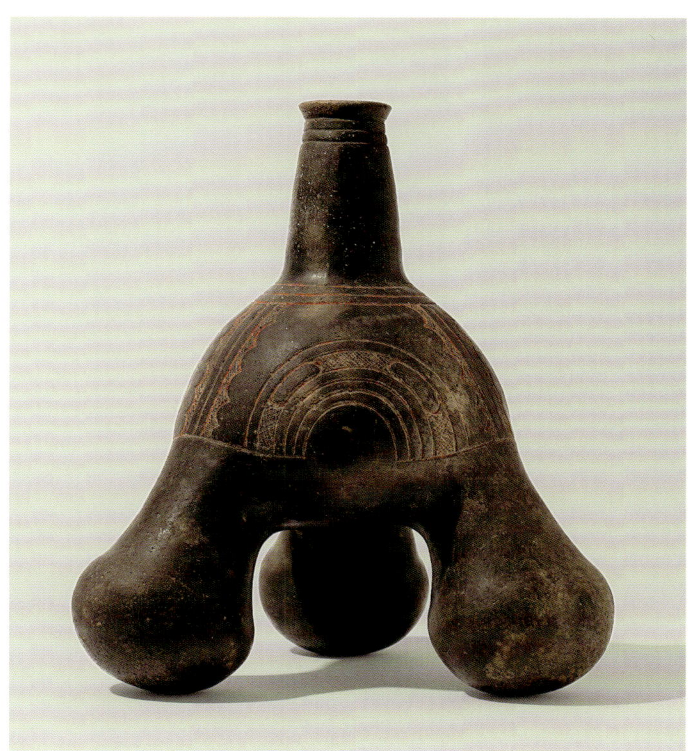

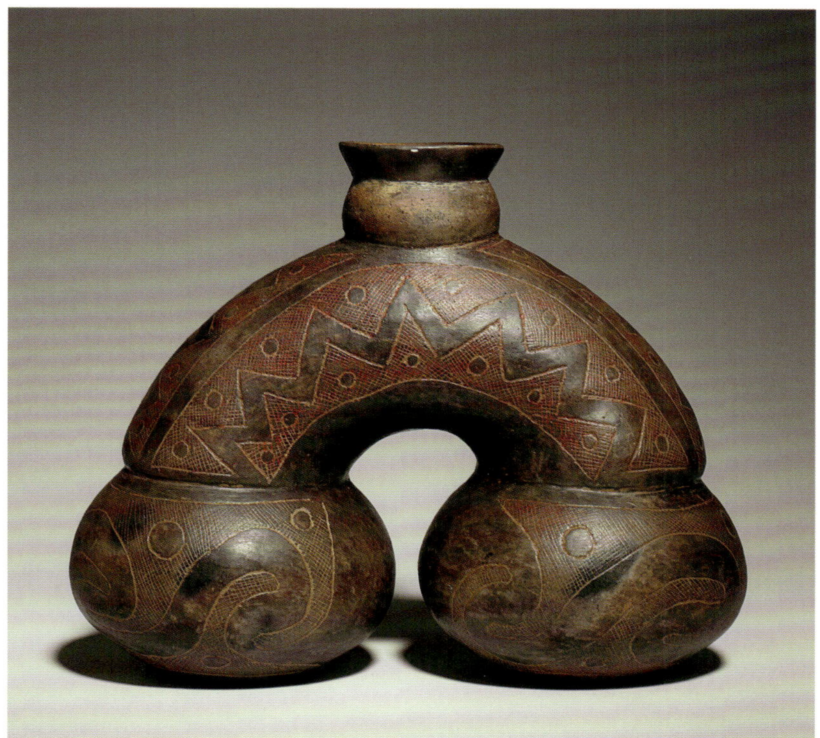

Fig. 5 Tripod bottle with arched band designs; Caddoan; Arkansas, A.D. 1400–1700; ceramic, h. 27.9 cm; Anthony Patano Collection, Chicago. Cat. no. 209.

Fig. 6 Engraved double bottle; Hudson Engraved type; Caddoan; Arkansas, Yell County, Fourche River, Podo Place, A.D. 1500–1700; ceramic, h. 16.2, w. 20.3 cm; Gilcrease Museum, Tulsa, Oklahoma. Cat. no. 211.

for many reasons, including environmental changes, European expansion, loss of land, forced removals, and disease. We cannot apply our own modern terms and definitions of art to that which was created in an entirely different cultural context. And yet we cannot help but continue to define it by our own modern terms and thinking. How can a modern interpretation ever compare to understanding the pieces, the styles, the symbols, the function, and the meanings in their own, original context? Yet archaeologists (usually non-Indian and non-Caddo people), who engage in modern, scientific analysis as standard practice, study Caddo artifacts and identify their uses, functions, forms, and symbols largely in theoretical frameworks.

How can descendants of those who made these objects respond to this objective, scientific inquiry? How does a modern Caddo feel when holding and seeing what they are told is a beautiful Caddo artifact or piece of pottery? Holding an object that was created by one's ancestors hundreds of years ago will most likely be different for each person depending on how they have been raised, and what their values are. When honored with the opportunity to hold and see my ancestors work, I feel reverence for the piece and am humbled by the vast cultural and environmental knowledge of my ancestors to understand how to make such artwork; I feel the sacredness of the pieces and am frightened at holding something I don't fully understand; I am in awe of their talent and am proud that I am related by blood to these intelligent, artistic people who are being studied by so many. Yet at the same time I feel disconnected from the past and from my heritage and sad that I have to learn about my culture and history while standing in a storeroom or laboratory wearing latex gloves. Finally, I feel very angry at being kept apart from my heritage and angry at seeing my ancestors themselves relegated to boxes. Angry, sad, and proud—these are some of my reactions to the situation.

Can there ever be a true, current understanding of ancient Caddo artwork? Perhaps that goal is something Caddo people, archaeologists, anthropologists, linguists, and artists all share. But I think Caddo people more than anyone else yearn to understand the past in its own context—for ourselves and our children—and we wish that we had never been removed from our traditional homelands. We all certainly strive for that understanding and learn much about ourselves in doing so. Although our motivations stem from different sources, this shared longing for understanding can serve to unite Caddo people with archaeologists, anthropologists, artists, and historians. After all, Caddo history is American history; Caddo art is American art.

The discussion of Caddo art would be incomplete without a discussion of repatriation. The passage of the Native American Graves Protection and Repatriation Act (NAGPRA) in 1990 has created a new reality and new opportunity for tribes, tribal members, and tribal governments. The new laws are changing the way Native American human remains and cultural objects are being treated by the institutions and museums that currently hold them. It is also amending historic wrongs by requiring the return of Native American human remains to their tribal descendants. For the first time in history, repatriation laws acknowledge tribal people's authority to make decisions about the objects originally created by them and for their uses.

I became involved with repatriation and the cultural objects of my tribe in 1994. Looking back on how it all happened, it now seems like much more than coincidence. That year I had just graduated from the

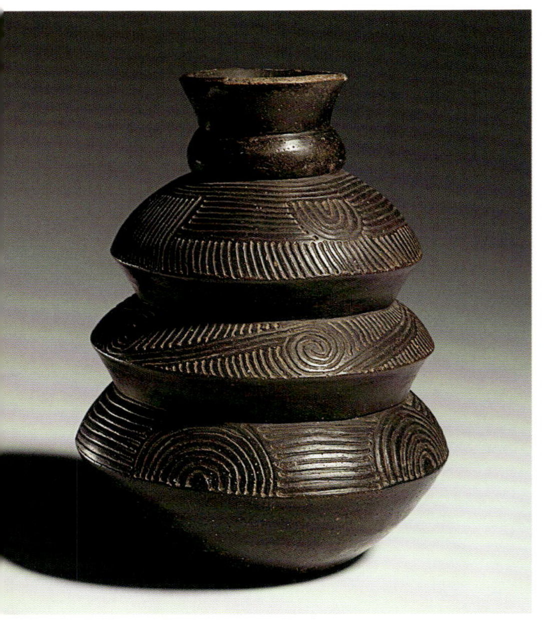

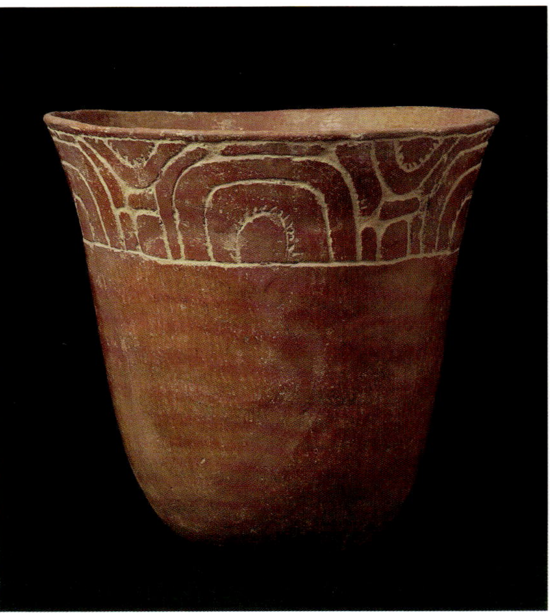

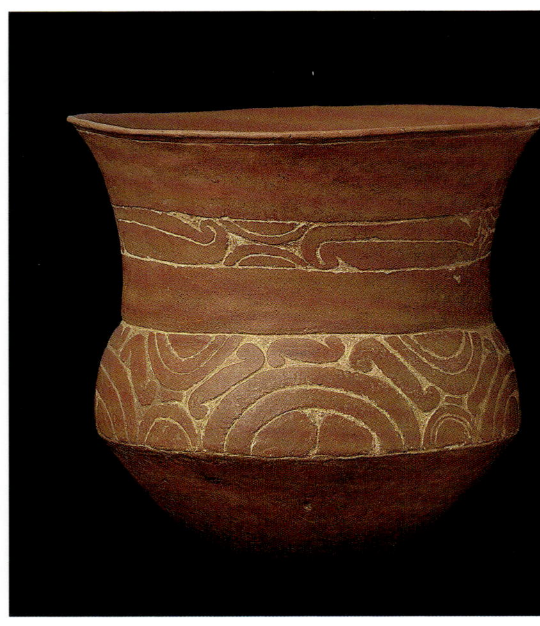

University of Oklahoma with a bachelor's degree in anthropology. I had found the study of culture to be of great interest and I delighted in my course work. Despite warnings such as "What are you ever going to do with an anthropology degree?" I continued to pursue my degree. Upon graduation I wasn't sure where my career would take me, but with a young daughter and a newborn son in tow, I wasn't too worried about it yet. I ended up relocating to Cordell, a small town in rural Oklahoma, which I didn't realize at the time was about forty miles from the Caddo tribal headquarters. The Caddo tribe was seeking to hire staff as part of its newly formed repatriation program, eventually hiring me.

It was only at that point in my life, at age twenty-four, that I began to comprehend the gravity of the situation. With NAGPRA's passage, a new door was opened for American Indians, and Alaskan and Hawaiian natives. This law required a reporting process for human remains, funerary objects, and sacred objects belonging to or originating from Native American groups. For the first time ever, tribes were learning what was held in the storage facilities and displayed on the shelves and in the galleries of federally funded museums and federal agencies.

With the assistance of Caddo author and historian Mary Cecile Elkins Carter, the Caddo tribe was the first in the state of Oklahoma to receive a NAGPRA grant from the National Park Service. As inventories of human remains, associated funerary objects, sacred objects, and objects of cultural patrimony (groupings for NAGPRA purposes) began pouring in from all over the United States, I discovered that the creations and belongings of my ancestors were still in existence and were actually being held by non-Indian entities and organizations.

Not only were the objects of my ancestors in these museums, but so were the human remains of my people, my grandfather's ancestors. Initially humiliated, angry, and powerless, I was shocked that my ancestors were lying in boxes on shelves in storerooms. I wept tears of sadness as I stood in storage facilities and curatorial labs, overwhelmed by the sheer insult. I felt ashamed that my people were treated like museum artifacts. What made my people different and deserving to be treated with so little respect—the subject of prodding and probing and scientific research? Students received master's degrees and doctorates by studying the remains of our people and had never even introduced themselves to tribal members. How many fingers and hands had probed these poor, helpless dead, unable to defend themselves with their only descendants hundreds of miles away, unable to protect them. Yet there were too many objects and too many human remains for our tribe even to begin to take on—to repatriate—or rebury.

These are overwhelming feelings for an individual to have. I remain torn between the values that were cultivated in me by my grandparents and the understanding of the reasoning behind museology and scientific analysis. It leaves me with an extremely difficult opposition to reconcile.

Because of the Repatriation Act, I was able to learn firsthand about the art created by Caddo people. My eyes have seen the beauty of clay molded, etched, and fired by the hands of my people. I have admired the loops, curves, dashes, hoops, and fingernail imprints; the suns and the stars. I have yearned in my heart to see what they saw—to understand the designs and symbols the same way they did. What did they mean? I have been inspired by the sheer beauty and skill of my people. They were famous pottery makers, jewelry makers, salt makers, mound builders, corn growers, and the makers of untold numbers of traditions.

These art pieces were direct links to an art formed and mastered over thousands of years. How could my heart not feel the connection and not take pride in their skill, knowledge, and grace? How could I not feel frustrated at the fact that non-Caddo people so easily

Fig. 7 Water vessel; Keno Trailed type; Caddoan; Arkansas, Yell County, Carden Bottoms, A.D. 1500–1700; ceramic, h. 17.8 cm; Smithsonian Institution, National Museum of the American Indian, Washington, D.C. Cat. no. 214.

Fig. 8 Engraved vessel with rayed concentric oval motif; Avery Engraved type; Caddoan; Arkansas, A.D. 1300–1700; ceramic, h. 22.9 cm; James and Elaine Kinker Collection, Midwest. Cat. no. 222.

Fig. 9 Engraved vessel with arched bands and "lazy S" motifs; Avery Engraved type; Caddoan; Arkansas, A.D. 1300–1700; ceramic, h. 27.9 cm; James and Elaine Kinker Collection, Midwest. Cat. no. 220.

discarded the human remains and so carefully prized the objects? It has always been strange to me—that separation of object from person. Yet it seemed as though museums were more interested in the objects than their creators. I know that these are generalizations, but they reflect some of my earliest impressions. We know so little about the ancient worldview of the Caddo at that time and these objects are indeed how they speak to us.

The Caddo tribe has battled with some of the most difficult decisions people could ever be asked to make. Some of the inquiries the NAGPRA office received are:

- "Can we study the remains of your people?"
- "Can we take a few grams of bone for research? This research can help your people."
- "Can we keep the pottery for future generations, although we understand it came from one of your ancestor's burial?"
- "Can you bless the vessel so it will bring no harm upon those who keep it from the ground?"
- "Do you want these Caddo human remains even though we don't know where all the funerary objects went and we don't know where the bones come from?"
- "Do you want to come and rebury the remains that were dug up many years ago?"
- "Do you want to come and help us dig up your people? It is to protect the archaeological site."

These are some of the questions that have been asked of us and of tribal members, religious leaders, and tribal government leaders. So many difficult questions for a people who are still grappling with recovery from a harsh removal. It was only one hundred and fifty years ago that our ancestors—great-grandmothers and great-grandfathers—were forcibly removed to Oklahoma. It is not some ancient past that is no longer remembered. It was only yesterday in our tribal memory. We have still not recovered from losing our beloved homelands, our medicinal knowledge, our traditional religion and government, and major portions of our culture. We have not recovered from having to live on rations instead of being able to plant, harvest, and hunt the foods we ate for thousands of years. Our bodies are still paying the price of living on a foreign diet. In addition, we are still suffering from inadequate hospitals and health care, both of which were promised to us in exchange for our lands. We have not fully recovered from boarding schools, Catholic schools, and lack of schools.

And now, after all of these years and the separation from our ancestors' culture and lifeways, we are supposed to know inherently how to answer these complicated ethical questions? What is the right thing to do? Where are all the elders to guide us to these decisions? How I have longed for the time when the answers would be sure and quick-coming. In a different cultural world, before there was any debate about what is culturally right and what is wrong, that knowledge was shared by all, and it was easy to answer these questions. But maybe there was never a time like that. Maybe it's foolish to think that there was a perfect place in time where culturally everything was intact.

Before European contact my people lived their lives the way they chose for thousands of years. It may not have been perfect, as they, too, tried to understand the world around them and develop answers for their questions about the world: how it began, who made it, how it works, what is right, what is wrong, what is good, what is bad, what is the afterlife like. But they did indeed develop answers, and they came into beautiful synchronicity with their environment and the world around them. For generations, they passed down this knowledge. As new religious beliefs were introduced from other cultures and distant lands, new ideas were adopted into the current belief system. Perhaps that is exactly what happened with what is now called the Mississippian moundbuilding period.

We may never know and we cannot go back to a time when things were surer than today, when we all ask each other, what is right? What is traditional? How do you say this or that Caddo word correctly? What did the old Caddos used to do? An elder once told me that to try to save the language was a pointless endeavor because that world is gone. The time when our people spoke to each other only in their tongue is no longer the reality for our tribe—why fight it? I agree that world is gone, but I will not allow myself to believe that there is no bright future for the Caddo people, who have changed and adapted many times and will continue to do so. We now stand on the shoulders of those ancestors who suffered and fought to keep Caddo traditions alive. The repatriation legislation has enhanced our ability to move forward while understanding our past. Although this newfound access to our physical culture is continually a painful reminder of what we lost, it is also beginning to fill the void created by our disturbing past. The ancient burial mounds and the rediscovered pieces of Caddo pottery are painful reminders of what we lost and yet at the same time they are also powerful reminders of what we can have again.

Note

I would like to thank my Caddo family, near and far, new and old, for inspiring me to write about these experiences. I would also like to thank those who fought diligently for the passage of the Native American Graves Protection and Repatriation Act. Lastly, I express my sincere appreciation to those scholars of Caddo cultural history and archaeology whose work has enlightened the Caddo people.

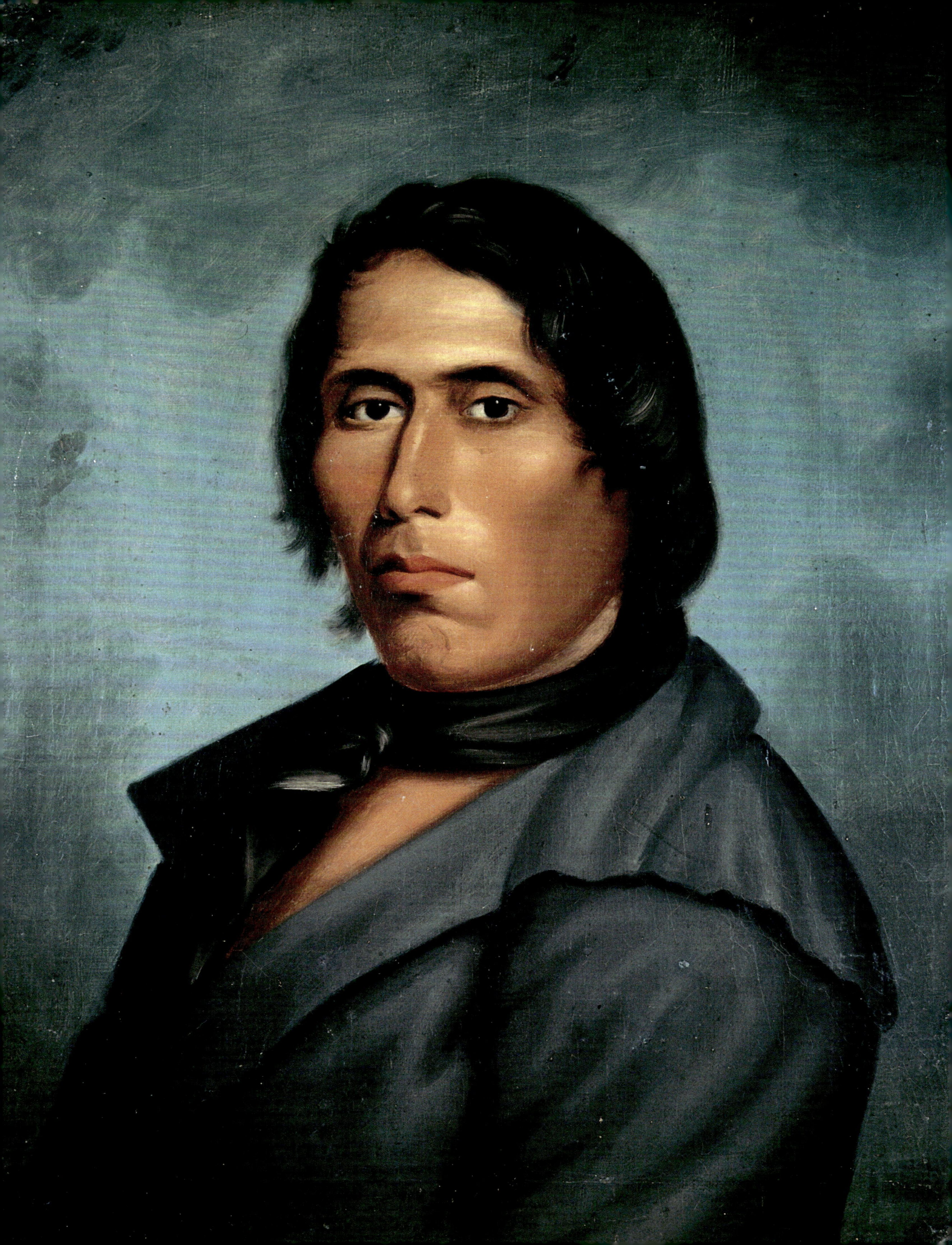

The Bread Dance

A Shawnee Ceremony of Thanks and Renewal

Ruthe Blalock Jones

Fig. 1 Portrait of Tecumseh (1768–1813) by an unknown artist; The Field Museum, Chicago.

In late spring, when the dogwood begins to bud, some say when the dogwood blossom is the size of a squirrel's ear, a Shawnee council meeting is held to talk about the Bread Dance. According to our tribal traditions, the Bread Dance is the most important event in Shawnee life, ceremonial or otherwise.[1] The ceremony represents the hunt, planting, and harvest, annually retelling the male and female roles in planting, germination, and new life. Attendance or participation is a part of being Shawnee.

These annual rites of seasonal passage stem from ancient traditions, and were carried by our people from their original homeland in western Pennsylvania across the Allegheny Mountains to Ohio and Indiana, and on to Kansas before being admitted into Indian Territory in Oklahoma. The Shawnee bands who signed land agreements with the British government and the neighboring Delaware and Mingo tribes in 1765 (fig. 2) lived primarily by hunting and gathering with some agriculture in small villages throughout western Pennsylvania. As pressures from the incoming European migrations increased, the Shawnee migrated across the Alleghenies and the Ohio River divide eventually to settle in central Ohio. Shawnee villages were established around the ancient squares, circles, and conical mounds of the Adena and Hopewell ruins, built some two thousand years earlier. But these new settlements were not to be permanent. During the time of contention between the British and the French

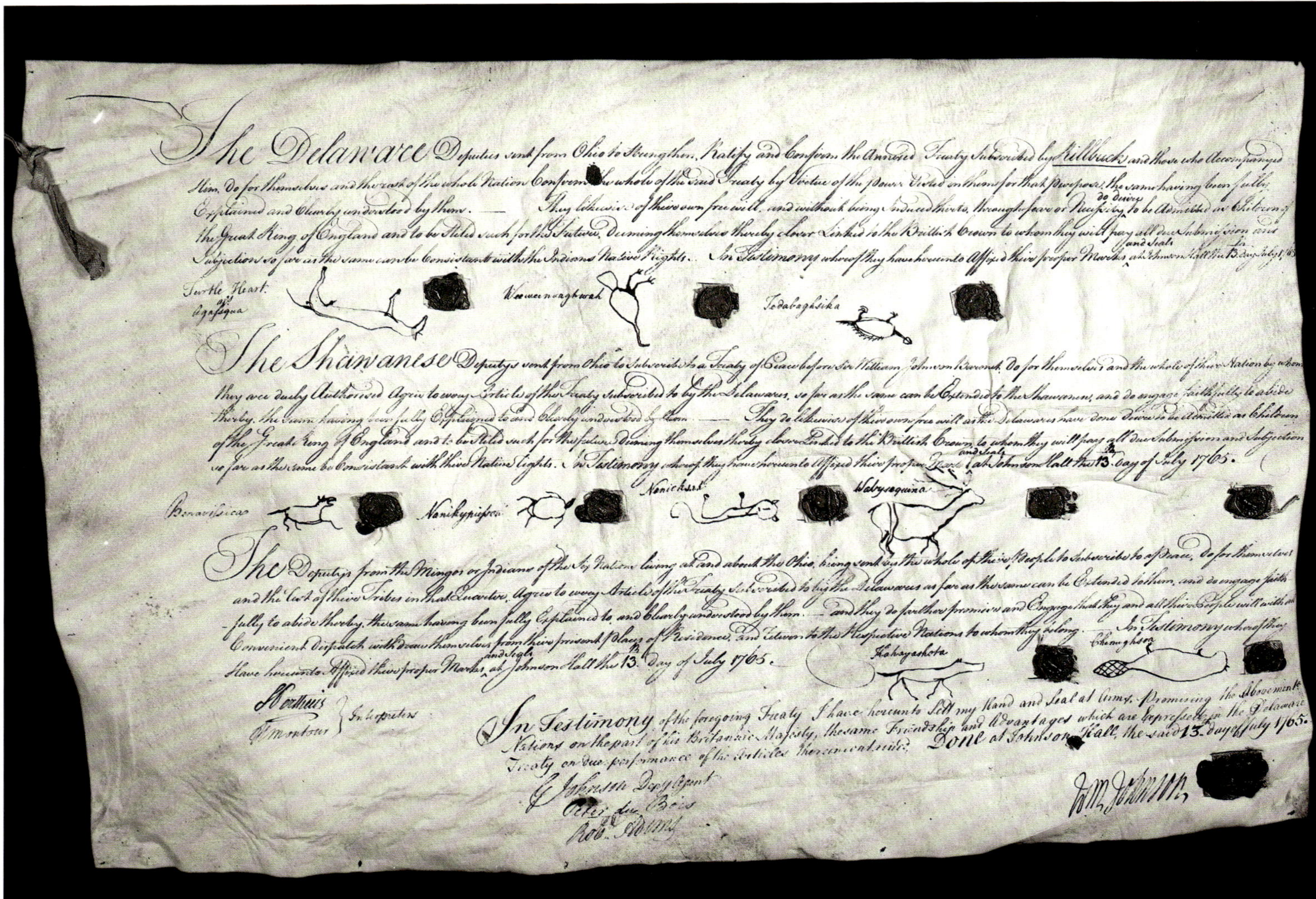

The Delaware Deputies sent from Ohio to Strengthen, Ratify and Confirm the Annexed Treaty Subscribed by Killbuck and those who Accompanyed Him, do for themselves and the rest of the whole Nation Confirm the whole of the said Treaty by Virtue of the Power Vested on them for that Purpose, the same having been fully Explained and Clearly understood by them. — They likewise of their own free will, and without being induced thereto, through fear or Necessity do desire to be Admitted as Children of the Great King of England and to be Stiled such for the Future, Deeming themselves thereby closer Linked to the British Crown to whom they will pay all due Submission and Subjection so far as the same can be Consistent with the Indians Native Rights. In Testimony whereof they have hereunto Affixed their proper Marks and Seals at Johnson Hall the 13 day of July 1765

Turtle Heart

The Shawanese Deputys sent from Ohio to Subscribe to a Treaty of Peace before Sir William Johnson Baronet, do for themselves and the whole of their Nation by whom they are duly Authorised Agree to every Article of the Treaty Subscribed to by the Delawares, so far as the same can be Extended to the Shawanese, and do engage faithfully to abide thereby, the same having been fully Explained to and Clearly understood by them. — They do likewise of their own free will as the Delawares have done desire to be Admitted as Children of the Great King of England and to be Stiled such for the future, deeming themselves thereby closer Linked to the British Crown to whom they will pay all due Submission and Subjection so far as the same be Consistent with their Native Rights. In Testimony whereof they have hereunto Affixed their proper Marks and Seals at Johnson Hall the 13 day of July 1765.

The Deputys from the Mingoes or Indians of the Six Nation living at and about the Ohio, being sent by the whole of their People to Subscribe to a Peace, do for themselves and the Rest of their Tribes in that Quarter, Agree to every Article of the Treaty Subscribed to by the Delawares as far as the same can be Extended to them, and do engage faithfully to abide thereby, the same having been fully Explained to and Clearly understood by them. — and they do further promise and Engage that they and all their People will with all Convenient dispatch withdraw themselves from their present Places of Residence, and Return to their Respective Nations to whom they belong. — In Testimony whereof they Have hereunto Affixed their proper Marks and Seals at Johnson Hall the 13 day of July 1765.

Montour } Interpreters

In Testimony of the foregoing Treaty I have hereunto Sett my Hand and Seal at Arms, Promising the Abovementioned Nations on the part of his Britannic Majesty, the same Friendship and Advantages which are expressed in the Delaware Treaty on due performance of the Articles therein contained. Done at Johnson Hall, the said 13 day of July 1765.

G Johnson Dep. Agent

Wm Johnson

Fig. 2 Treaty between Shawnee, Delaware, and Mingo Indians and Great Britain, signed in 1765; Smithsonian Institution, National Museum of American Indian, Washington, D.C., N39369.

for control of North America, our leaders established treaties and alliances with the British. But after the success of the American Revolution, as settlers again began pouring into the valley of the Ohio River, new pressures for this land and its resources began mounting (fig. 3). After 1805 the Shawnee prophet Tenskwatawa (fig. 4) and his brother, Chief Tecumseh (fig. 1), were preaching an Indian religious revival—a return to a distinctly Indian way of life. Tecumseh's emissaries traveled far and wide, arguing forcefully for political unity among the tribes. But as the War of 1812 between the British and Americans approached, some tribes elected to remain neutral, some joined the Americans, while others fought on the side of the British. Tecumseh led many into battle, but after the British and Indian defeat at the Battle of the Thames in 1813 and Tecumseh's death, Indian resistance in the Midwest effectively came to an end. Eventually the Shawnee were forced to move first to Kansas and then to present-day Oklahoma.[2]

Historians have documented the migration of three main groups or bands of Shawnee from Ohio to Indiana and Kansas prior to their settling in Indian Territory in Oklahoma. Of these groups, the Eastern Shawnee, a mixed band of Senecas and Shawnees, now located in Ottawa County near Miami, Oklahoma, moved to Indian Territory from Ohio following the 1830 Indian Removal Act. The smallest of the Shawnee bands, the Eastern Shawnee do not have a ceremonial ground and are closely related to the Seneca.[3] They are governed by the Miami Agency office of the Bureau of Indian Affairs.

The Loyal or Cherokee Shawnee, also called the Kansas Shawnee, moved to Indian Territory in 1869. They were called "loyal" because they sided with the Union during the Civil War. Their tribal offices are located in Miami, Oklahoma, while their ceremonial headquarters is in White Oak, near Vinita, in Craig County, Oklahoma. Listed on the Cherokee Tribal Roll in 1869, the Cherokee Shawnee always retained their identity as Shawnees. The tribe separated from the Cherokees and received federal recognition as the Shawnee Tribe of Oklahoma in 2000. They are also known as the White Oak Shawnee.

The Absentee Shawnee were so named because they were "absent" from Kansas shortly before the Cape Girardeau Treaty of 1825. The Absentee Shawnee are the largest of the three bands and have retained more of their culture and ceremony than the others. With tribal offices in Shawnee, Oklahoma, and ceremonial grounds near Little Axe, Oklahoma, they are under the jurisdiction of the Anadarko area office of the Bureau of Indian Affairs.

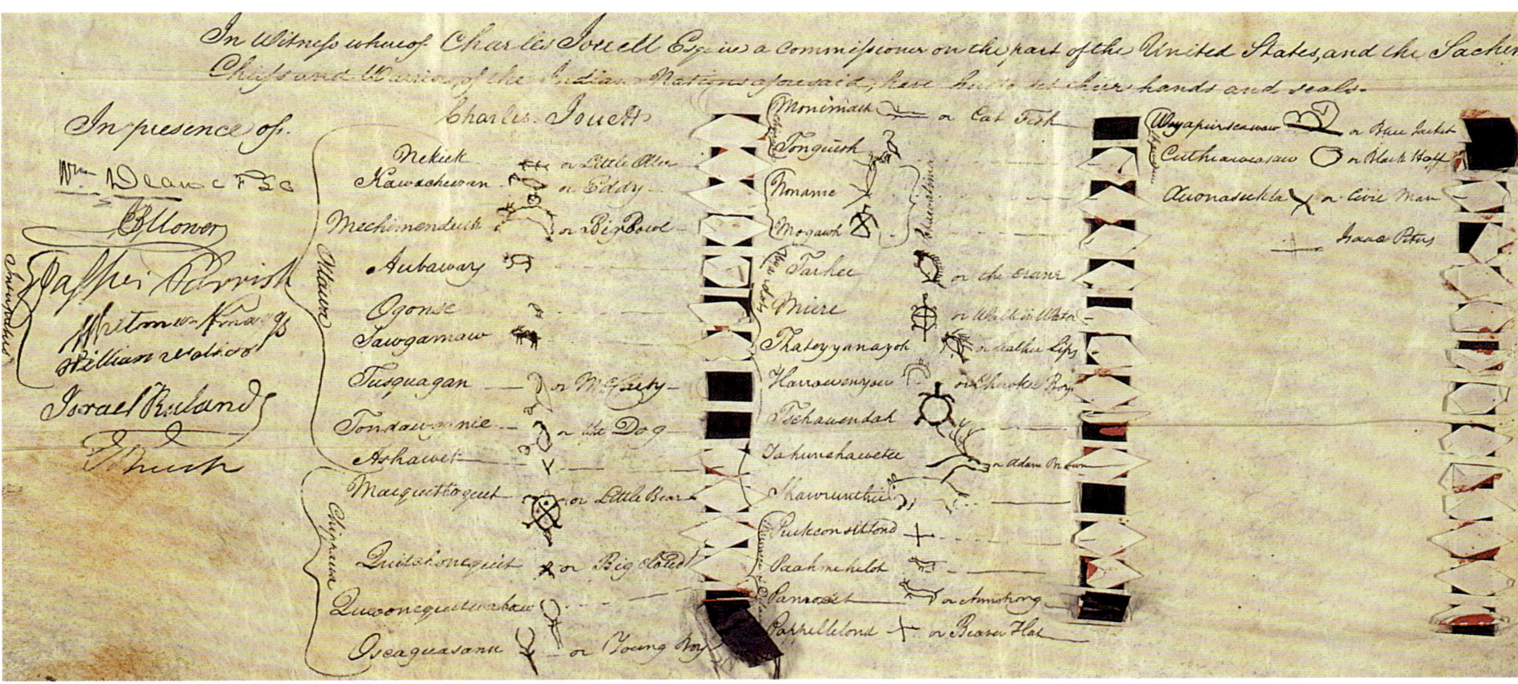

In Witness whereof Charles Jouett Esq. is a Commissioner on the part of the United States, and the Sachems Chiefs and Warriors of the Indian Nations aforesaid, have hereunto set their hands and seals.

In presence of.

Charles Jouett

Fig. 3 Treaty signed at Fort Industry (Toledo) in 1805 between the United States and Shawnee, Potawatomi, Wyandot, Chippewa, and other Indians for the release of lands south of Lake Erie; National Archives and Records Administration, Washington, D.C. (RG 11, Indian Treaty no. 45).

The Bread Dance

Throughout all these travels, trials, removals, and wars, annual ceremonial dances have endured in maintaining our sense of tribal continuity and historical sense of integrity to our people. Both the Absentee and the Shawnee (or White Oak Shawnee) have retained most of their ceremonial cycles, with the Absentees being the most traditional. Both bands begin the year with the spring Bread Dance, followed by the Green Corn Dance and the fall Bread Dance. A fourth dance, the Buffalo Dance, is sometimes held in White Oak following the fall Bread Dance, and sometimes it is a part of the fall Bread Dance. I do not know the reason for this, except that the Absentees have retained the hunt as a part of the Bread Dance and the White Oaks have not.

Like many native American people, it is not Shawnee custom to discuss the ceremonies or other tribal rituals with outsiders. Photography, videotaping, and audiotaping of the ceremonies are not allowed. Shawnees say, "We don't want other people to hear our songs; the songs are so pretty they will copy them." Nevertheless, a small, privately printed booklet outlining the ceremonies of the Loyal Shawnee for use by tribal members was published by Velma Nieberding in *The Chronicles of Oklahoma* in 1964. Compiled by elder Shawnee women in the 1950s, this booklet provides much of the information presented here. I will confine my essay to ceremonies of the White Oak Shawnee, as that is the tribe to which I belong (fig. 1). Speaking from a feminine perspective, I am very conscious of the high regard and honor that is accorded Shawnee women.

Called by women, planning meetings for the Bread Dance that I have attended have occurred at the beginning of the week in the early morning. These meetings set in motion a series of clearly defined events that mark the seasonal transitions to which the cycles of Indian life were traditionally linked. The leader, or Queen Bee, calls the meetings, although, due to the Queen Bee's frail health, her daughter has lately carried out these duties. There are several older women in the group. It is very unusual for any of these positions or seats to be reassigned except in case of death. In earlier times, they were probably decided according to clan. Today, with fewer participants and fewer still who know the rules and customs, the seats—so named because the women sit at certain places on the log benches in the ceremonial ground—have more or less remained within the same families.

Among the Shawnees, one's name identifies his or her clan. Names were formerly given by an elder family

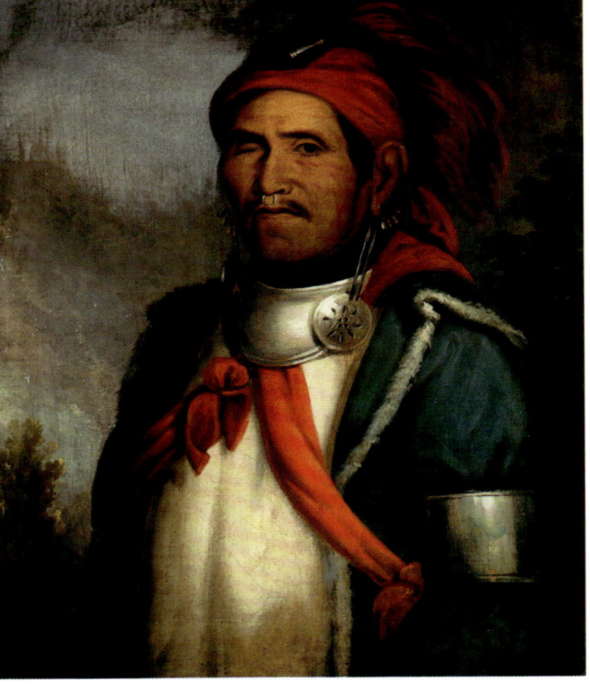

Fig. 4 Henry Inman, after Charles Bird King, *Portrait of Tenskwatawa, the Prophet* (1775–1837); oil on canvas, c. 1830; Smithsonian Institution, National Portrait Gallery, Washington, D.C., 82.71. Tenskwatawa was Tecumseh's brother and a major leader of Shawnee and allied tribal resistance on the side of the British against the Americans during the War of 1812 in the "dark and bloody ground" of Ohio.

member or a close family friend, and one's siblings would be of the same clan. At White Oak today, some names are given to balance numbers within the clans. Most names at White Oak are given by the Queen Bee, who is the official name-giver. The general rule of keeping one's tribal practices and beliefs private applies even from group to group within the Shawnee, and even as we will see, between men and women within a given community. For instance, I do not know how names are given among the Absentee Shawnee. According to one historian, one's clan was the same as that of the person who named you.[4] Clans were associated with kinship and dictated rules of courtship and marriage, according to which one did not date or marry within the clan, as that would have been considered incest.

After the time for the spring or fall Bread Dance is determined, the women set a date within the next two weeks to set up camp. Following this will be several days of preparation for the dance. These preparations afford us an opportunity to begin to step away from our daily routines, allowing time to renew friendships and enter the spirit of community. On the first day we skin the corn that will be made into meal for the bread. The Queen Bee and her designated helpers, called Bushels, lead the women and other volunteers. Meanwhile, men are directed to the heavy work of chopping firewood, building and maintaining the fire, carrying water, and lifting heavy cooking pots. The corn is first boiled in water with lye and ashes and then set out to dry before being ground into coarse meal the following day. Lye and ashes are used to help soften the corn grains, in a method of preparation that goes back thousands of years, ultimately originating in Mexico where corn was first domesticated. In the old days, it took several women all day to pound corn in wood mortars with log pestles to make the cornmeal. I remember my grandmother coming to our house to use my mother's corn pounder. In my childhood memory, it seems that my grandmother worked outside nearly an entire day pounding her corn. As a concession to modern convenience, tribal members now use an electric grinder that only takes a few minutes to create the cornmeal.

As the ceremonial day draws closer, chosen members of the tribe make the sacred ceremonial hoop. I have never observed the construction of the hoop, although I have been present at the ceremonial ground and have observed its placement overhead, above the dance leaders, or hung in a tree for the duration of the festival. The old men and women adorn the hoop with seeds of corn, beans, squash, and animal fur. This ritual of adorning the hoop is not open to everyone. The items are placed in a specific order and prescribed words are spoken. At a certain time, the hoop will be placed over the heads of the two selected lead dancers.[5] Next, the hoop is hung in a specially designated place until the conclusion of the dance, when it will be taken down and dismantled.

As preparations unfold, on an afternoon or early evening, twelve women and twelve men dancers are

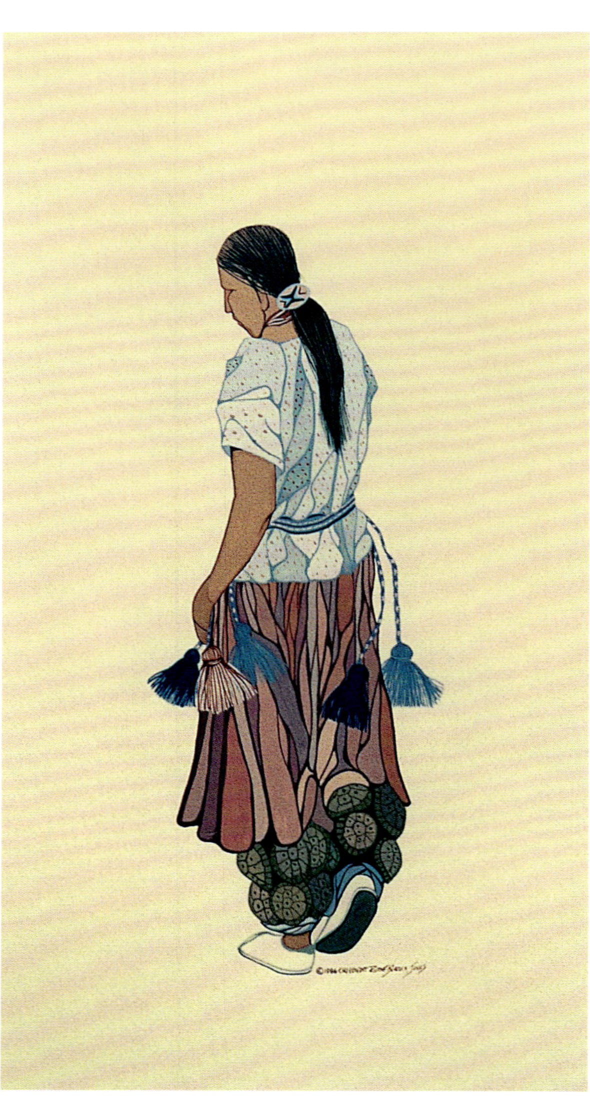

Fig. 5 Ruthe Blalock Jones (American, born 1939), *Shell Shaker*, 1986; gouache on paper, 35.6 × 25.4 cm; Collection of the artist.

chosen to represent the various tribal clans. Although in earlier times the dancers were probably all chosen at this time, today, because people live farther away from the ceremonial ground, only the first few dancers are selected on this opening day. The rest will be chosen on the actual day of the dance as people begin arriving, some from faraway towns in other states. Each female dancer is asked if she will be dancer number so and so. She answers "yes, *n'yweh*" (thank you). When all the women dancers are chosen, each is told a number of breads she will be responsible for making, according to the order in which they were chosen. The most important dancer, the lead dancer, is selected from a bird, turtle, or "spring" clan in the spring ceremony, to represent new life and planting. In the fall ritual, the female dance leader is chosen from a clan with the name of a furred animal, as thoughts are directed toward the hunt and winter. This seasonal division of summer versus winter and its connection to the structure of society is a very old pattern of traditional Shawnee life, as it is among many other indigenous people of North America and ancient Mexico as well. It is an honor to be chosen to be a dancer. I have led the dances, and my daughter and granddaughter have also been dancers. I am very proud of them for carrying on our Shawnee traditions (fig. 5).

Following the selection of the dancers, there is a ball game between the men and women in the spring. In the fall, there is a seed game. The losers of each season assume the obligation to provide the wood for the ceremonials. The ball game is played between two upright poles that the Queen Bee's helpers, the Bushels, place in the ground. Women and girls are allowed to run and throw the ball, while the men may not touch the ball with their hands, and instead can only kick the ball. Everyone is allowed to tackle, block, wrestle, tickle, or otherwise stop an opponent in any way. In this free-for-all, the game can be rough, and many players have experienced scrapes, sprains, and broken bones. Sometimes an elder woman will be given the ball and allowed to score and, out of respect, no one will touch her, although some good-natured mock shoving or butting may occur. Concealing the ball in her skirt or apron, she will invariably be allowed to walk to the goal and toss or roll the ball through the posts. The game is followed by supper held in the various family camps. In the old days, there were public social dances popularly called "Stomp Dances" around the fire each night of the festival, but today they only occur on the night of the Bread Dance.

After having been chosen, the women dancers meet to make the ceremonial bread. Once again, the men are called upon to build and maintain the fire for the women amid a lot of banter and teasing. When the fire is ready, the Bushels and their assistants heat cast iron Dutch ovens in which the bread will be baked. They will have already cooked beans and pumpkin on the fire. Now the elder women and the chosen dancers begin to make bread in a well-established routine. First, the Queen Bee and Bushels mix the prepared cornmeal with the bean or pumpkin soup. The lead dancer makes the first bread and adds her clan mark. Others continue until all the special ceremonial bread has been made from the three traditional vegetable staples. After this is done, biscuits are made. Finally, the breads are put away until the dance on Saturday. During this time, men have also been carrying out their own private rituals, which women are not supposed to know about.

Once all of these preparations are completed, we all enjoy a "rest day." Some campers remain at the grounds the entire time, just like in the old days, although today they tend to stay in motor homes, campers, or very modern tents. Electricity is available at the White Oak grounds and the White Oak tribe has been criticized by other more traditional tribes for being "white man-ized" in providing this amenity, which allows the campers to have fans, coffeemakers, and other appliances if they so desire. Many other campers, however, elect to live as close to the old ways as possible, rejecting the option of modern conveniences. This is the only time of the year when certain special foods are prepared and served. It is a time of visiting, of physical and spiritual renewal as people and ways of the past are remembered through favorite foods, songs, stories, and personal reminiscences. Shawnees are thankful to have come through the winter to attend another Bread Dance.

During this time the grounds are readied for the dance. Weeds, brush, and grass are cut. Fallen timber is picked up, roads are cleared and graded, and gravel or rocks added to fill holes, and so on. Wood is cut and stacked. Repairs may also be made to the log benches around the ceremonial ground.

At the White Oak Bread Dance, alcohol is not allowed. One approaches the dance area through the designated men's or women's entrances, never stepping over the log benches. Women or girls who are menstruating may not participate and should not be on the grounds. These rules are ways that Shawnees show respect for the sacredness of the dance ground and ceremony.

The next step of the ceremony begins when the women dancers who are not camping, and who live or stay nearby are told to be at the grounds early. Once again, the men will have made a fire. This time, the women cook meat that will be shared with all who have come to participate. At White Oak, purchased or donated beef is used. There is no one alive who remembers the ancient custom of the ritual hunt, although it is still practiced among the Absentee Shawnees. The women are required to bring their own knives to cut up the meat. The lead dancer places the first piece into the pot of boiling water, and after the meat has all been cooked, it is removed from the kettle and corn is cooked in the broth.

After this, the women make dumplings. They mix hot water with the already prepared cornmeal, shaping the dough into slightly flattened balls and dropping them into the boiling broth. Other shapes may also be made. Again, the lead dancer makes the first dumpling and places it in the cook pot. When the beef, corn, and dumplings are cooked, it is time to get ready for the dance.

Excitement and anticipation now rise as the women go to their various cars and camps to dress for the dance. The wearing of traditional dress is vital to the process of reinforcing our sense of collective memory and identity as a people. As in the preparation of food, there is a simple but binding set of rules for the design and making of the dancers' attire. Women at White Oak wear long cotton skirts and aprons decorated with bands of ribbon at the bottom, and a mandatory pocket. Otherwise, the women's dress may vary; they may wear a long-sleeved blouse with a bertha collar adorned with silver buttons. Others wear ribbon shirts or any Indian-style blouse with ribbon trim. The blouse fabric may match or contrast with the skirt. Proper Shawnee ceremonial dresses are torn, not cut, and are completely sewn by hand. The sewing and all work on the dress must be done in the morning. Despite these guidelines, in modern times many dresses are in fact made on electric sewing machines. Women may wear strings of beads, beaded medallion necklaces, and a neck scarf. Some wear capelike beaded collars. They usually wear

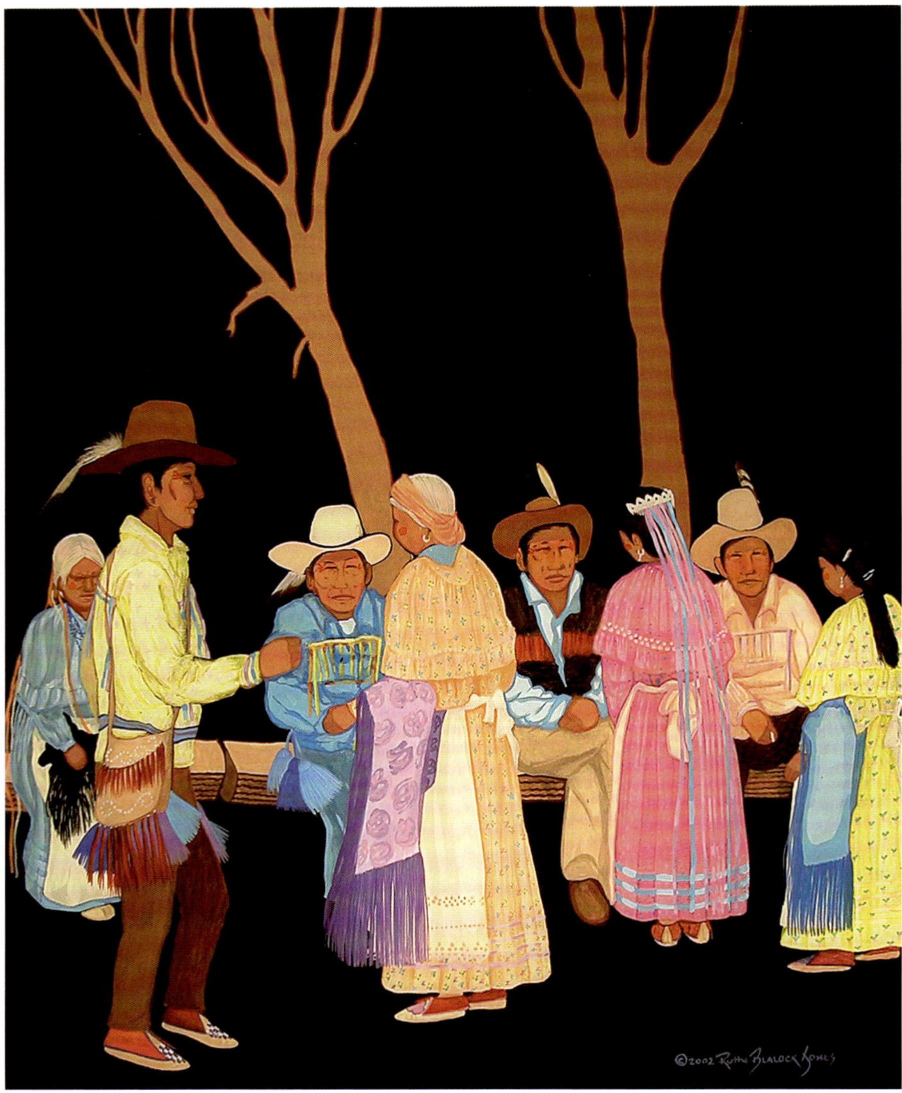

Fig. 6 Ruthe Blalock Jones, *Shawnees at the Ceremonial Ground*, 2002; acrylic on canvas, 76.2 × 61 cm; Private collection.

earrings, and some favor necklaces or other jewelry featuring a turtle, wolf, horse, chicken, or other clan symbol. Some wear a silver hair comb with long ribbon streamers. A few wear moccasins, but most do not. Shawls are carried. Such attire reflects various historical influences, from moccasins to Colonial and nineteenth-century styles, both of European and Indian sources. Such ceremonial dresses are not worn at the secular, social powwow festivals or to other events and places. They wear other outfits considered more suitable for such occasions.

The dance is now ready to begin. The men dancers and singers assemble in the dance ground and take their places (fig. 6). The men wear Shawnee shirts with pleats and ribbons. Some wear moccasins and yarn belts and hats with feathers. The men and women have separate entrances and assigned seating in the dance ground. The women Bushels arrange a cloth covering the center ground. The male Bushels bring pots of soup and baskets of beef and place them on the cloth as a focal point of the ceremonial setting, where the culminating dances are about to unfold.

Meanwhile, the various women dancers meet where the breads were stored. The Bushels line them up according to their given number, and paint a single round red spot on each woman's cheek. The breads are distributed among the dancers, and at a signal from the men, the dancers all follow the older women into the dance ground in a single-file procession. As each woman places her breads on the cloth, the men quietly voice their approval. When all the breads have been placed, the women and the Queen Bee take their positions in the dance ground. All the remaining dancers and Bushels follow.

Concurrently, the men dancers will also have been painted, as well as the singers and the old men. The drummer will already have made his preparations by tying a skin cover across the top of a handheld water pot, the "water drum." The men will also paint the drum.

A speaker selected for his dignity and eloquence now stands up to welcome everyone and to thank them for coming. He admonishes everyone to be on their best behavior and carry out the dances so that Kokomthena (the Shawnee grandmother deity) will look down and be pleased with the Shawnee people. The speaker or a designate will offer prayer.

The singers begin to the tapping of the water drum. The first set of dances is for women only. Next are songs for the men. The women join in the dance in a line outside the men's circle. Although I do not know what the songs are about, some are combinations of repetitive rhythmic sounds, while others have Shawnee words. Old songs of different types are sung, always in a prescribed order; no new songs are made.

There will be *kokeki*, or cluster dance songs, in which the women stand and sway in front of the singers. They also sing with the men. At a certain point in the song, the drumbeat changes and the women begin to dance.

The final dance is the Pumpkin Dance. It is faster and more spirited than the previous dances. It is usually led by a man and a woman other than the dance leaders. The man carries a turkey wing. Everyone who is able joins in this dance. These great communal dances produce a strong sense of physical and emotional bonding and shared excitement; coordinated rhythmic movement, the sounds of the chorus, and the visual delight of the brilliantly colored attire all contribute to the feeling of solidarity and cohesion.

After the Pumpkin Dance, the Bushels distribute the food, which has now been hallowed. The male dancers, singers, and old men receive the bread. The women receive the beef and a few of the biscuits. They take containers to receive corn soup and dumplings. After the dancers have been served, the campers and audience may bring containers until the food is gone and everyone adjourns for supper.

It is beginning to get dark after a long day. Some men arrived before daybreak to build the fire. Some women have been there since shortly after to fix breakfast for them. Yet now another more publicly inclusive event, the Stomp Dance, will begin (fig. 7). The first leaders will be the men dancers, singers, speaker, old men, and so on. The women will dance, after which the drum will be taken out of the dance ground and ceremonies are concluded. The Stomp Dance continues until daybreak.

We all look forward to the process and the various steps of this highly meaningful event. In their long preparations and prescribed sequence of events, such ritual gatherings as these dances remove participants from the pressures of daily life and allow for another rhythm or pace that gives time for reflection and conviviality and brings about a sense of renewal in the fabric of Shawnee life. The outer appearance of the ceremonial sequence may appear simple to an outsider—the gathering of food and firewood; the preparations that follow; the donning of traditional dress; the placement of the food; the procession, speeches of welcome, and prayer to Kokomthena; the gestures and movement and sounds of the dance; the distribution of food and the concluding Stomp Dance—all unfold in a time of cyclic, seasonal renewal, suggesting that the ongoing patterns of Shawnee life form part of a larger order that reaches back through our long history.

I have been attending the White Oak ceremonies ever since I can remember. My father participated and he was also a Stomp Dance leader. My mother was a shell shaker. I remember being put to bed in the car many times as our parents danced until morning. I was allowed to stay up as long as I danced. My younger brother and sister would be asleep on the seats in the car, so I always lay down on the floor of the car on the center hump. Some of my fondest memories are of drifting off to sleep to the sound of Stomp Dance songs from the dance ground. Our mother always had ample provisions for the night.

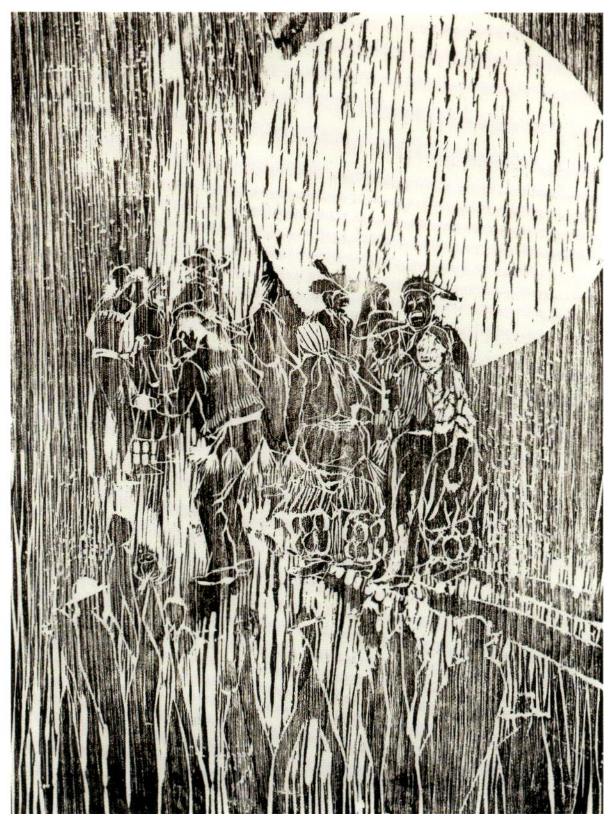

Fig. 7 Ruthe Blalock Jones, *Oklahoma Stomp Dance*, 1986; woodblock print on rice paper, 61 × 45.7 cm; Collection of the artist.

The next morning there is a ball game. The adult players usually bet an article against the other side. Because money is not wagered, other objects such as handkerchiefs, scarves, ribbons, hats, and aprons may be bet.

These are some memories of the most important Shawnee ceremonial, the Bread Dance. Just as my ancestors did, I participate with pride, and I am prouder still that my children and their children are learning and carrying on our traditions.

Notes

1. Howard 1981.
2. For general background on Shawnee history, see Mahon 1988 and Horsman 1988.
3. Nieberding 1964.
4. Alford and Drake 1936.
5. Howard 1981.

Catalogue of the Exhibition

Cat. no. 1 Double-edged bannerstone; Tennessee, Madison County, 5800–4000 B.C.; banded claystone, h. 4.6, w. 10.3 cm; T. W. McGuire Collection. Townsend essay, fig. 18.

Cat. no. 2 Bowtie bannerstone; Iowa, 5000–3000 B.C.; porphyry granite, h. 8.7, w. 11.6 cm; Tommy Beutell Collection, B151. Townsend essay, fig. 17.

Cat. no. 3 Reel-shaped bannerstone; Ohio, Ross County, D. J. Jones Farm, south of Bourneville on Paint Creek, 5000–3000 B.C.; banded slate, h. 7.5, w. 13.5 cm; Edward Harvey Collection, California. Townsend essay, fig. 19.

Cat. no. 4 Double-cresent bannerstone; Ohio, Auglaize County, 3000–1000 B.C.; banded slate; Smithsonian Institution, National Museum of the American Indian, Washington, D.C., 6/6386.

Cat. no. 5 Notched ovate bannerstone; Michigan, c. 4800 B.C.; banded slate, h. 12.7 cm; Steve and Susan Hart Collection, Huntington, Indiana. Townsend essay, fig. 25.

Cat. no. 6 Notched ovate bannerstone; Ohio, Union County, along Bokes Creek, c. 4800 B.C.; banded slate, h. 14.5, w. 8.3 cm; Edward Harvey Collection, California. Townsend essay, fig. 21.

Cat. no. 7 Bannerstone; Florida, Suwannee River, c. 4500 B.C.; granite, h. 11.4, w. 10.2 cm; Tommy Beutell Collection. Townsend essay, fig. 22.

Cat. no. 8 Bannerstone; Indiana, c. 3000 B.C.; carnelian, l. 7.6 cm; Smithsonian Institution, National Museum of Natural History, Washington, D.C., A9099.

Cat. no. 9 Bannerstone; Tennessee, Montgomery County, c. 3000 B.C.; carnelian, w. 14 cm; Gilcrease Museum, Tulsa, Oklahoma, 6123.908.

Cat. no. 10 Bottle-shaped bannerstone; Kentucky, Union County, c. 3000 B.C.; ferruginous quartz, h. 8.6, w. 6.4 cm; Maury Meadows Collection, Bethany, Missouri. Townsend essay, fig. 20.

Cat. no. 11 Two atlatl hooks and weights; Indiana, Spencer County, Crib Mound, c. 3000 B.C.; saddleshaped bannerstone; claystone, l. 7 cm; antler atlatl, l. 18.1 cm; saddle-shaped bannerstone; banded claystone, l. 7.6 cm; antler atlatl, l. 21 cm; David Lutz Collection, Newburgh, Indiana. Townsend essay, fig. 23.

Cat. no. 12 Cache of three bannerstones (two hooked type; one hourglass-shaped); Indiana, Spencer County, Rockport site, c. 2300 B.C.; gneiss, l. 10.5 cm; gneiss, l. 9 cm; granite, l. 9.5 cm; David Lutz Collection, Newburgh, Indiana. Townsend essay, fig. 24.

Cat. no. 13 Saddle-shaped bannerstone; Indiana, Posey County, c. 2000 B.C.; quartz, h. 7.2, w. 5.4 cm; T. W. McGuire Collection.

Cat. no. 14 Hourglass-shaped bannerstone; Indiana, Daviess County, near Plainville, c. 2000 B.C.; ferruginous quartz, h. 8.7, w. 5.9 cm; Maury Meadows Collection, Bethany, Missouri. Townsend essay, fig. 14.

Cat. no. 15 Hourglass-shaped bannerstone; Kentucky, Christian County, c. 2000 B.C.; carnelian, h. 11.4 cm; Gilcrease Museum, Tulsa, Oklahoma, 6123.902. Townsend essay, fig. 15.

Cat. no. 16 Hourglass-shaped bannerstone; Arkansas, Desha County, Boltwier, c. 2000 B.C.; ferruginous quartz, h. 9.5, w. 7.5 cm; Bobby Onken Collection. Townsend essay, fig. 16.

Cat. no. 17 Human figure; Louisiana, West Carroll Parish, Bayou Maçon, Poverty Point; 1500–700 B.C.; ceramic, h. 5.1 cm; Gilcrease Museum, Tulsa, Oklahoma, 5424.5739.

Cat. no. 18 Parakeet effigy bead; Arkansas, Lafayette County, Badlow Creek, J. T. Lee site, c. 3000 B.C.; red jasper, l. 6 cm; Gilcrease Museum, Tulsa, Oklahoma, 6123.2964. Townsend essay, fig. 3.

Cat. no. 19 Axe head, Nebo style; Missouri, Andrew County, south of Savannah, c. 2000 B.C.; porphyry, l. 24.1 cm; Maury Meadows Collection, Bethany, Missouri. Townsend essay, fig. 26.

Cat. no. 20 Plummet stone; Louisiana, West Carroll Parish, Bayou Maçon, Poverty Point; 1500–700 B.C.; hematite, l. 8.9 cm; Gilcrease Museum, Tulsa, Oklahoma, 6123.2658.

Cat. no. 21 Plummet stone engraved with bird motif; Louisiana, West Carroll Parish, Bayou Maçon, Poverty Point; 1500–700 B.C.; red jasper, l. 8.9 cm; Gilcrease Museum, Tulsa, Oklahoma, 6123.2596.

Cat. no. 22 Birdstone; Georgia, Floyd County, near Rome, 1500–1000 B.C.; greenstone, l. 12 cm; American Museum of Natural History, New York, 2/2068CAT1869-90-81. Townsend essay, fig. 11.

Cat. no. 23 Birdstone; Ohio, Wood County, southeast of Grand Rapids, 1500–1000 B.C.; greenstone, l. 20.8 cm; American Museum of Natural History, New York, DN/601CAT1901-39. See p. 6.

Cat. no. 24 Birdstone; Ohio, 1500–1000 B.C.; stone, l. 14.5 cm; Peabody Museum of Natural History, Yale University, 257753.

Cat. no. 25 Birdstone; Ohio, 1500–1000 B.C.; stone, l. 16 cm; Peabody Museum of Natural History, Yale University, 257754. Townsend essay, fig. 13.

Cat. no. 26 Birdstone; Ohio, 1500–1000 B.C.; stone, l. 8.9 cm; Gilcrease Museum, Tulsa, Oklahoma, 6124.1155. Townsend essay, fig. 12.

Cat. no. 27 Two rectangular gorgets; Illinois, Brown County, Hemphill site, 1000–500 B.C.; quartz, l. 15.9, 14.9 cm; Gilcrease Museum, Tulsa, Oklahoma, 6123.1208–09. See p. 9.

Cat. no. 28 Wolf skull mask; Ohio, Logan County, 500 B.C.; l. 22.9 cm; Ohio Historical Society, Columbus, A3816/1. Townsend essay, fig. 32.

Cat. no. 29 Wilmington tablet; Adena culture; Ohio, Clinton County, Sparks Mound, 400 B.C.–A.D. 1; sandstone, w. 12.4 cm; Ohio Historical Society, Columbus, A3490/210. Penney essay, fig. 2.

Cat. no. 30 Berlin tablet; Adena culture; Ohio, Jackson County, 400 B.C.–A.D. 1; sandstone, w. 14.3 cm; Ohio Historical Society, Columbus, A340/1. Penney essay, fig. 3.

Cat. no. 31 Low tablet; Adena culture; West Virginia, Wood County, 400 B.C.–A.D. 1; sandstone, l. 12.1 cm; Ohio Historical Society, Columbus, A3800/1. Penney essay, fig. 4.

Cat. no. 32 Human effigy pipe; Ohio, Ross County, Adena Mound, 100 B.C.–A.D. 100; pipestone, h. 20 cm; Ohio Historical Society, Columbus, A1200/10. Townsend essay, figs. 41a–b.

Cat. no. 33 Effigy of a mythic horned animal; Ohio, Hamilton County, Turner site, Mound 3, A.D. 1–400; petrified wood, h. 7.6, l. 25.4 cm; Harvard University, Peabody Museum of Archaeology and Ethnology, Peabody Museum Expedition 1882, F. W. Putnam and Dr. C. L. Metz, Directors, 82-35-10/29685. Townsend essay, fig. 9.

Cat. no. 34 Four boatstones; Oklahoma, A.D. 1–400; greenstone, l. 15.2–25.4 cm; Smithsonian Institution, National Museum of Natural History, Washington, D.C., A448677. Seeman essay, fig. 13.

Cat. no. 35 Engraved shell gorget with feline and hawk; Fairfield style; Texas, Bell County, near Oenaville, A.D. 300–700; marine shell, diam. 14 cm; Smithsonian Institution, National Museum of the American Indian, Washington, D.C., 22/75/74. Townsend essay, fig. 8.

Cat. no. 36 Ceremonial blade; Ohio, Ross County, Hopewell site, A.D. 1–400; obsidian, h. 40.6 cm; Ohio Historical Society, Columbus, A283/322C. Seeman essay, fig. 10.

Cat. no. 37 Three ceremonial blades; Ohio, Ross County, Hopewell site, Mound 25, A.D. 1–400; obsidian, h. 27.9, 17.8, and 22.9 cm; The Field Museum, Chicago, 31.56808, 31.56777, and 31.56782. Seeman essay, fig. 11.

Cat. no. 38 Cache of 32 bifacial blades; Illinois, Tazewell County, near Mackinaw, Hopewell, A.D. 1–400; Burlington chert, l. 12.7–13.5 cm; Illinois State Museum, Springfield, 803/676 series. Townsend essay, fig. 27.

Cat. no. 39 Scroll ornament; Ohio, Hamilton County, A.D. 1–400; copper, w. 21 cm; Harvard University, Peabody Museum of Archaeology and Ethnology, Peabody Museum Expedition 1882, F. W. Putnam and Dr. C. L. Metz, Directors, 82-35-10/19898. Penney essay, fig. 9.

Cat. no. 40 Ornamental deer ear; Ohio, Ross County, Hopewell site, Mound 25, A.D. 1–400; copper, l. 50.8 cm; The Field Museum, Chicago, 31.56165. Penney essay, fig. 8.

Cat. no. 41 Human profile cutout; Ohio, Hamilton County, Turner site, Mound 3, A.D. 1–400; sheet mica, h. 18.4, w. 13 cm; Harvard University, Peabody Museum of Archaeology and Ethnology, Peabody Museum Expedition 1882, F. W. Putnam and Dr. C. L. Metz, Directors, 82-35-10/30002.1. Seeman essay, fig. 9.

Cat. no. 42 Serpent effigy; Ohio, Hamilton County, Turner site, Mound 3, A.D. 1–400; sheet mica, river pearl, and pigment, w. 35.6 cm; Harvard University, Peabody Museum of Archaeology and Ethnology, Peabody Museum Expedition 1882, F. W. Putnam and Dr. C. L. Metz, Directors, 82-35-10/29683. Penney essay, fig. 7.

Cat. no. 43 Atlatl effigy; Ohio, Ross County, Hopewell site, Mound 25, A.D. 1–400; sheet mica; The Field Museum, Chicago, 31.56451. Penney essay, fig. 6.

Cat. no. 44 Headless torso; Ohio, Ross County, Hopewell site, Mound 25, A.D. 1–400; sheet mica, h. approx. 20.3 cm; The Field Museum, Chicago, 1579.110133. Penney essay, fig. 5.

Cat. no. 45 Bird claw cutout; Ohio, Ross County, Hopewell site, Mound 25, A.D. 1–400; sheet mica, h. 27.9 cm; The Field Museum, Chicago, 1579.110131. Seeman essay, fig. 1.

Cat. no. 46 Hand cutout; Ohio, Ross County, Hopewell site, Mound 25, A.D. 1–400; sheet mica, h. 29 cm; Ohio Historical Society, Columbus, A283/294. Seeman essay, fig. 8.

Cat. nos. 47–51 Five figurines; Illinois, Calhoun County, Knight Mound group, Mound 8, A.D. 200–400; painted earthenware, h. 7.5–11 cm; The Milwaukee Public Museum, A50673A–E/17562. Seeman essay, figs. 3–7.

Cat. no. 52 Seated female figurine; Hopewell culture; Illinois, Jackson County, Twenhafel site, A.D. 200–400; ceramic, h. 8 cm; Illinois State Museum, Springfield, 803/630. Penney essay, fig. 10.

Cat. no. 53 Kneeling male figurine; Ohio, Hamilton County, Turner site, Mound 4, A.D. 1–400; ceramic, h. 8.3 cm; Harvard University, Peabody Museum of Archaeology and Ethnology, Peabody Museum Expedition 1882, F. W. Putnam and Dr. C. L. Metz, Directors, 82-35-10/29687. Penney essay, fig. 11.

Cat. no. 54 Seated figurine; Hopewell culture; Illinois, Schuyler County, LaMoine River, A.D. 200–400; stone; Private collection. Not in exhibition.

Cat. no. 55 Human face effigy; Kentucky, Gallatin County, Warsaw, 200 B.C.–A.D. 400; stone, h. 25.4 cm; Smithsonian Institution, National Museum of the American Indian, Washington, D.C., 6/397. See p. 4.

Cat. no. 56 Blocked-end tube pipe; West Virginia, 400 B.C.–A.D. 1; brown stone, l. 25.4 cm; Smithsonian Institution, National Museum of Natural History, Washington, D.C., A398407. Seeman essay, fig. 17.

Cat. no. 57 Blind wolf pipe; Tennessee, Macon County, A.D. 1–400; steatite, l. 56.5 cm; Willis Family Collection. Townsend essay, fig. 39.

178

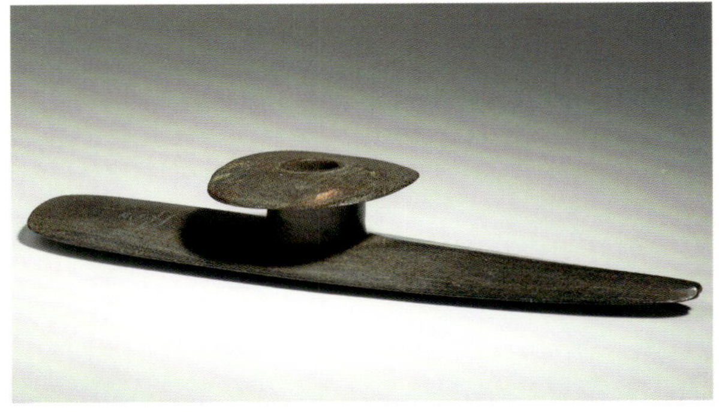

59

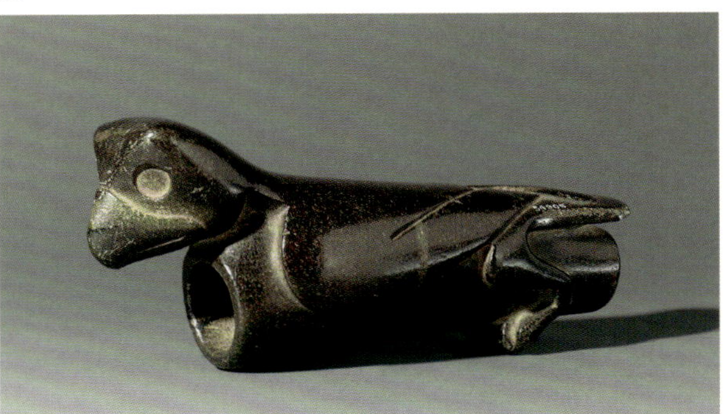

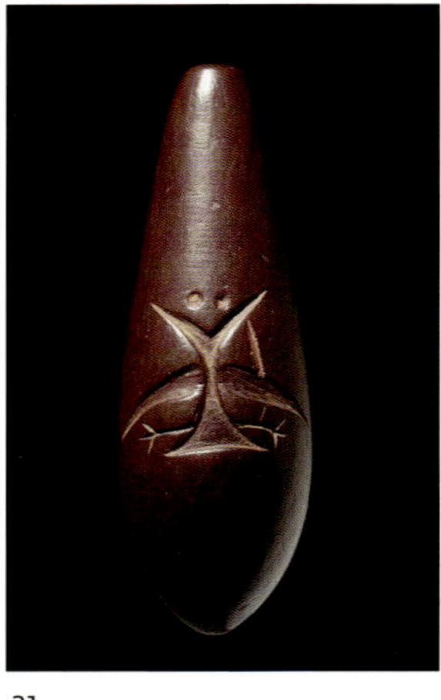
21

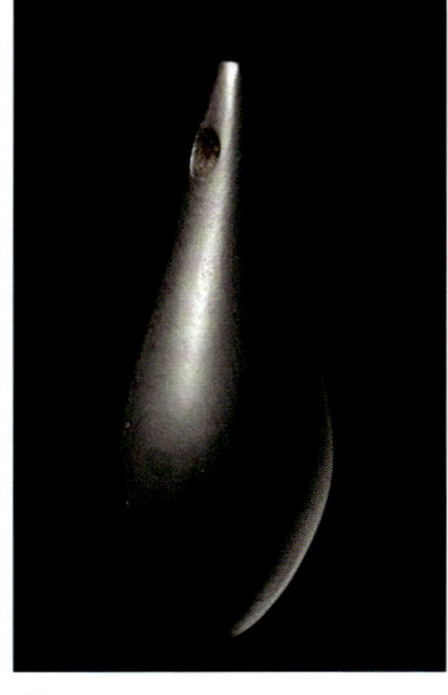
20

Cat. no. 58 Wolf tube pipe; Tennessee, Williams Island, 4th century; greenstone, l. 23.2 cm; Smithsonian Institution, National Museum of Natural History, Washington, D.C., AL1017. Townsend essay, fig. 40.

Cat. no. 59 Raptor effigy pipe; Ohio (?), 200 B.C.–A.D. 500; steatite, l. 20.3 cm; The Field Museum, Chicago, 662.54905.

Cat. no. 60 Dog effigy platform pipe; Illinois, Fulton County, Weaver site, A.D. 1–400; oolitic limestone, h. 5.2, l. 9 cm; Illinois State Museum, Springfield, 806/039. Penney essay, fig. 25.

Cat. no. 61 Hawk effigy platform pipe; Illinois, Naples, A.D. 1–400; pipestone, h. 8.6, l. 11 cm; Anonymous loan to the Brooklyn Museum of Art, L49.3.1. Townsend essay, fig. 37.

Cat. no. 62 Otter effigy platform pipe; Illinois, White County, Wilson site, A.D. 1–400; siliceous shale and copper, h. 6.3, l. 8.6 cm; Illinois State Museum, Springfield, 814/515. Penney essay, fig. 22.

Cat. no. 63 Raven effigy platform pipe; Illinois, Hardin County, Rutherford Mound, A.D. 1–400; conglomerate stone, h. 6, l. 12 cm; Illinois State Museum, Springfield, 814/510. Penney essay, fig. 24.

Cat. no. 64 Falcon effigy platform pipe; Havana Hopewell; eastern Iowa, A.D. 1–400; pipestone, l. 8.3 cm; Gilcrease Museum, Tulsa, Oklahoma, 6124.1144. Seeman essay, fig. 21.

Cat. no. 65 Seated falcon effigy platform pipe; Havana Hopewell; Illinois, Calhoun County, Peisker site, Mound 2, A.D. 1–400; pipestone, l. 6.4 cm; Gilcrease Museum, Tulsa, Oklahoma, 6125.1142. Seeman essay, fig. 20.

Cat. no. 66 Raven effigy platform pipe; Illinois, Pike County, Bedford site no. 9, A.D. 200–400; conglomerate stone, l. 10.2 cm; Gilcrease Museum, Tulsa, Oklahoma, 6124.1141. Penney essay, fig. 23.

Cat. no. 67 Beaver effigy platform pipe; Illinois, Pike County, Bedford site, A.D. 200–400; pipestone, river pearl, and bone, l. 11.1 cm; Gilcrease Museum, Tulsa, Oklahoma, 6124.1140. Penney essay, fig. 1.

Cat. nos. 68, 69, and 71 Rodent (squirrel ?) effigy platform pipe; l. 7 cm; young feline effigy platform pipe; l. 8.75 cm; turtle effigy platform pipe; l. 7.25 cm; Hopewell culture; Ohio, Ross County, Mound City, Mound 8, A.D. 1–400; W. Blackmore Collection, The British Museum, London, S219, S259, and S271. Penney essay, figs. 18a–c.

Cat. no. 70 Otter effigy platform pipe; Hopewell culture; Ohio, Ross County, Mound City, Mound 8, A.D. 1–400; l. 8.9 cm; W. Blackmore Collection, The British Museum, London, S269. Penney essay, fig. 21.

Cat. no. 72 Effigy platform pipe of a heron eating a fish; Hopewell culture; Ohio, Ross County, Mound City, Mound 8, A.D. 1–400; l. 9 cm; W. Blackmore Collection, The British Museum, London, S234. Penney essay, fig. 19.

Cat. no. 73 Double goose pipe; Ohio, Ross County, Hopewell site, Mound 17, A.D. 1–400; steatite, l. 16.5 cm; Ohio Historical Society, Columbus, 283/110. Penney essay, fig. 14.

Cat. no. 74 Owl effigy pipe; Illinois, Shawneetown, A.D. 700–1200 steatite, h. 23.5, l. 18 cm; Peabody Museum of Natural History, Yale University, 003865. Townsend essay, fig. 38.

Cat. no. 75 Wolf effigy pipe; Tennessee, Copena complex, A.D. 1–500; steatite, l. 34 cm; Peabody Museum of Natural History, Yale University, 003697. Seeman essay, fig. 15.

Cat. no. 76 Raptor effigy pipe; Tennessee, Coffee County, A.D. 600–900; steatite, l. 18.4 cm; Smithsonian Institution, National Museum of the American Indian, Washington, D.C., 7757. Penney essay, fig. 15.

Cat. no. 77 Bird and owl effigy pipe; Virginia, Scott County, A.D. 100–600; steatite, l. 25.5 cm; Smithsonian Institution, National Museum of Natural History, Washington, D.C., A211243. Seeman essay, fig. 22.

Cat. no. 78 Raven effigy pipe; Hopewell culture; Tennessee, Cumberland County, A.D. 1–400; steatite, h. 9.2, l. 34.3 cm; Tommy Beutell Collection, P348. Penney essay, fig. 17.

Cat. no. 79 Wolf effigy pipe; Ohio, Ross County, Seip-Pricer Mound, A.D. 1–400; steatite, h. 27.9 cm; Ohio Historical Society, Columbus, 957/20. Seeman essay, fig. 23.

Cat. no. 80 Bird and fish effigy pipe; Ohio, Ross County, Hopewell site, Mound 25, A.D. 1–400; steatite, l. 6 cm; The Field Museum, Chicago, 31.56750. Penney essay, fig. 13.

Cat. no. 81 Panther effigy pipe; Indiana, Posey County, Mann site, A.D. 1–400; black steatite, h. 6, l. 16 cm; Anonymous loan to the Brooklyn Museum of Art, L49.5. Seeman essay, fig. 16.

Cat. no. 82 Six-fingered-hand pipe; Ohio, A.D. 1–400; greenstone, l. 15.2 cm; Smithsonian Institution, National Museum of Natural History, Washington, D.C., A97433. Penney essay, fig. 12.

Cat. no. 83 Pipe; Virginia, Pulaski County, A.D. 600–900; stone, l. 38.7 cm; Smithsonian Institution, National Museum of the American Indian, Washington, D.C., 18/2785.

Cat. no. 84 Ovoid platform pipe; Smithsonian Institution, National Museum of Natural History, Washington, D.C., A326619.

Cat. no. 85 Beetle effigy; Michigan, Kent County, Converse Mounds, A.D. 200–500; carved antler, l. 7.6 cm; Harvard University, Peabody Museum of Archaeology and Ethnology, Gift of Capt. W. L. Coffinberry, John H. Strahan, and F. H. Weatherby, 1885, 85-51-10/38841.

Cat. no. 86 Effigy of a human thumb; Ohio, Ross County, Hopewell site, A.D. 1–400; cannel coal, h. 7.6 cm; The Field Museum, Chicago, 31.56401. Seeman essay, fig. 12.

Cat. no. 87 Elongated bird head; Florida, Brevard County, Turkey Creek Mound, south of Melbourne, A.D. 200–500; greenstone, l. 13.6 cm; American Museum of Natural History, New York, DN/749CAT1901-39. Penney essay, fig. 16.

Cat. no. 88 Hopewell ware jar; Illinois, Calhoun County, Pete Klunk site, Mound 7, A.D. 1–400; ceramic, h. 14 cm; Gilcrease Museum, Tulsa, Oklahoma, 5424/4702. Seeman essay, fig. 18.

Cat. no. 89 Hopewell-related zoned jar (Alligator Bayou Stamped); Porter/Santa Rosa complex; Florida, Washington County, St. Andrews Bay, A.D. 1–400; ceramic; Smithsonian Institution, National Museum of the American Indian, Washington, D.C., 17/3755. Seeman essay, fig. 19.

Cat. no. 90 Vessel; Weeden Island culture; Florida, Taylor County, Fish Creek, A.D. 400–900; ceramic, h. 16.8, w. 17.2 cm; Tommy Beutell Collection, V455.

Cat. no. 91 Castellated vessel; Weeden Island culture; Florida, Levy County, Fowler's Landing, A.D. 400–900; ceramic, h. 13.4, w. 16.5 cm; Smithsonian Institution, National Museum of the American Indian, Washington, D.C., 17/1459.

Cat. no. 92 Effigy pipe of a seated male figure; known as the Resting Warrior and identified as Morning Star or Red Horn in related legendary accounts; Oklahoma, LeFlore County, Spiro, site 34LF46, A.D. 1100–1200; flint clay, h. 22.5 cm; University of Arkansas Museum, Fayetteville, 47-2-1. Reilly essay, figs. 13a–b.

Cat. no. 93 Conquering Warrior effigy pipe; Oklahoma, LeFlore County, Spiro, A.D. 1100–1200; flint clay, h. 24.8 cm; Smithsonian Institution, National Museum of the American Indian, Washington, D.C., 21/4088. Dye essay, figs. 16a–b.

Cat. no. 94 Chunkey Player effigy pipe, with chunkey stone in right hand and chunkey sticks in left; Oklahoma, Muskogee County, A.D. 1100–1200; flint clay, h. 21.6 cm; St. Louis Science Center, 12X83. Brown essay, fig. 11.

Cat. no. 95 Kneeling figurine effigy pipe; Kentucky, Ballard County, Twin Mounds site, A.D. 1100–1200; flint clay, h. 17.8 cm; Tommy Beutell Collection, P336. Reilly essay, fig. 23.

Cat. no. 96 Crouching Man effigy pipe; Tennessee, Hardin County, Shiloh Indian Mounds National Historic Landmark, Shiloh National Military Park, A.D. 1100–1200; Missouri flint clay, h. 20.3 cm; United States National Park Service, Shiloh National Military Park. Reilly essay, fig. 15.

Cat. no. 97 Human effigy pipe; Illinois, Madison County, Piasa Creek Mound, A.D. 1100–1200; flint clay, h. 20.3 cm; Gilcrease Museum, Tulsa, Oklahoma, 6125.18913. Reilly essay, fig. 22.

Cat. no. 98 Frog effigy pipe; Illinois, St. Clair County, East St. Louis, A.D. 1100–1200; Missouri flint clay, h. 13, l. 14.5 cm; Illinois State Museum, Springfield, 800/519. Reilly essay, fig. 20.

Cat. no. 99 Crouching warrior effigy pipe; Illinois, Jackson County, Guy Smith Village site, A.D. 1100–1200; flint clay, h. 9.5 cm; University of Illinois, Illinois Transportation Archaeological Research Program, A3419. Dye essay, fig. 7.

Cat. no. 100 Effigy figurine of a mythical woman, possibly Our Grandmother or Old-Woman-Who-Never-Dies, hoeing an earth-serpent; known in archaeological literature as the Birger figurine; Illinois, Madison County, BBB Motor site, near Collinsville, A.D. 1100–1200; flint clay, h. 14 cm; University of Illinois, Illinois Transportation Archaeological Research Program. Reilly essay, figs. 17a–b.

Cat. no. 101 Kneeling female effigy; known in archaeological literature as the Keller figurine; Illinois, Madison County, BBB Motor site, near Collinsville, A.D. 1100–1200; flint clay, h. 14 cm; University of Illinois, Illinois Transportation Archaeological Research Program. Reilly essay, fig. 16.

Cat. no. 102 Effigy pipe of a kneeling female figure holding maize and sunflower plants; Arkansas, Desha County, A.D. 1100–1200; flint clay, 18 × 18 × 14 cm; Dr. Kent and Jonnie Westbrook Collection, Little Rock, Arkansas. Reilly essay, fig. 1.

Cat. no. 103 Kneeling prisoner effigy pipe; Mississippi, A.D. 1400–1500; stone, h. 12.2, l. 17 cm; Henry L. Batterman Fund and the Frank Sherman Benson Fund, Brooklyn Museum of Art, 37.2802PA. Dye essay, fig. 8.

Cat. no. 104 Hawk and human head effigy pipe; Mississippi, Washington County, Winterville site, A.D. 1200–1300; stone, h. 12.1 cm; Gilcrease Museum, Tulsa, Oklahoma, 6125.1206. Dye essay, fig. 15.

Cat. no. 105 Crouching hunter effigy; Missouri, 13th century; limestone, h. 17.8 cm; Smithsonian Institution, National Museum of Natural History, Washington, D.C., A99343. Reilly, Bear, and Bear interview, fig. 4.

Cat. no. 106 Kneeling ancestor effigy; Tennessee, Wilson County, Sellers Farm site, A.D. 1000–1450; sandstone, h. 46.2 cm; Frank H. McClung Museum, University of Tennessee, Knoxville, 1/1Wl1. King essay, fig. 7.

Cat. nos. 107–08 Seated male and kneeling female figures; Georgia, Bartow County, Etowah, Mound C, A.D. 1325–1375; marble, h. 61 and 55.9 cm; Etowah Indian Mounds State Historic Site, Georgia Department of Natural Resources, Atlanta. King essay, fig. 6.

Cat. no. 109 Bound captive effigy pipe; Arkansas, A.D. 1200–1500; stone, h. 19.1, l. 22.9 cm; Museum of Red River, Idabel, Oklahoma, HL6718. Dye essay, fig. 9.

Cat. no. 110 Copper repoussé plate depicting Birdman; one of the two so-called Rogan plates; Georgia, Bartow County, Etowah, Mound C, 13th century; copper, h. 27.9 cm; Smithsonian Institution, National Museum of Natural History, Washington, D.C., A91117. King essay, fig. 1.

Cat. no. 111 Copper repoussé plate depicting Birdman; one of the two so-called Rogan plates; Georgia, Bartow County, Etowah, Mound C, 13th century; copper, h. 27.9 cm; Smithsonian Institution, National Museum of Natural History, Washington, D.C., A91113. King essay, fig. 11.

Cat. no. 112 Copper repoussé plate depicting Birdman; Late Braden style; Missouri, Dunklin County, Malden, Baldwin Farm, A.D. 1200–1400; copper, h. 29.9 cm; Washington University Gallery of Art, St. Louis; Gift of J. Max Wulfing, 1937, WU3679. Brown essay, fig. 23.

Cat. no. 113 Copper repoussé plate depicting a falcon; Late Braden style; Missouri, Dunklin County, Malden, Baldwin Farm, A.D. 1200–1400; copper, h. 31.1 cm; Washington University Gallery of Art, St. Louis; Gift of J. Max Wulfing, 1937, WU3682. Brown essay, fig. 24.

Cat. no. 114 Copper repoussé plate depicting a double-headed falcon; Late Braden style; Missouri, Dunklin County, Malden, Baldwin Farm, A.D. 1200–1400; copper, h. 26.7 cm; Washington University Gallery of Art, St. Louis; Gift of J. Max Wulfing, 1937, WU3680. Brown essay, fig. 25.

Cat. no. 115 Copper repoussé plate depicting forked-eye-surrounds and concentric circles; Oklahoma, LeFlore County, Spiro, Craig Mound, A.D. 1100–1200; copper, h. approx. 34 cm; Smithsonian National Museum of the American Indian, Washington, D.C. Brown essay, fig. 28.

Cat. nos. 116–17 Copper repoussé plates; Oklahoma, LeFlore County, Spiro, Craig Mound, A.D. 1200–1300; copper, h. 24.2, 22.5 cm; Smithsonian Institution, National Museum of the American Indian, Washington, D.C., 20/699 and 20/700. Dye essay, figs. 12–13.

Cat. no. 118 Copper repoussé plate depicting two dancing Birdman figures (?); Classic Braden style; Illinois, Union County, Upper Bluff Lake, A.D. 1100–1200; copper, h. 27.9 cm; Smithsonian Institution, National Museum of Natural History, Washington, D.C., A88142 Brown essay, fig. 32.

Cat. no. 119 Long-Nosed God maskette ear ornaments; Illinois, Meppen Mound site, A.D. 1000–1400; copper, l. 22.4, 22 cm; Charles L. Adam Family Collection, Missouri. Diaz-Granados essay, fig. 19.

Cat. no. 120 Swallow-shaped gorget; Algonquin; New Hampshire, Manchester, Amoskeag Falls, A.D. 1500–1600; copper, h. 24.1 cm; Harvard University, Peabody Museum of Archaeology and Ethnology, Gift of A. Lawrence Lowell, 1933, 33-54-10/1536.

Cat. no. 121 Long-Nosed God ear ornament; Illinois, St. Clair County, Booker T. Washington site, A.D. 1100–1200; shell, h. 3.8 cm; Gilcrease Museum, Tulsa, Oklahoma, 9025.450. Reilly essay, fig. 14.

Cat. no. 122 Engraved whelk shell with warriors' heads motif; Classic Braden style; Oklahoma, LeFlore County, Spiro, Craig Mound, A.D. 1200–1350; marine shell, l. 28 cm; University of Arkansas Museum, Fayetteville, 37-1-4. Dye essay, fig. 23.

Cat. no. 123 Engraved whelk shell depicting intertwined, two-headed serpents; Late Braden style; Oklahoma, LeFlore County, Spiro, Craig Mound, A.D. 1200–1400; marine shell, l. 38.1 cm; University Arkansas Museum, Fayetteville, 37-1-17. Brown essay, fig. 10.

Cat. no. 124 Engraved whelk shell with horned serpent motif; Late Braden style; Oklahoma, LeFlore County, Spiro, A.D. 1200–1350; marine shell, l. 22.9 cm; University of Arkansas Museum, Fayetteville, 37-1-20. Lankford essay, fig. 14.

Cat. no. 125 Engraved whelk shell depicting Birdman; Craig B style; Oklahoma, LeFlore County, Spiro, Craig Mound, A.D. 1200–1400; marine shell, l. 33 cm; Smithsonian Institution, National Museum of the American Indian, Washington, D.C., 18/9121. Brown essay, fig. 1.

17

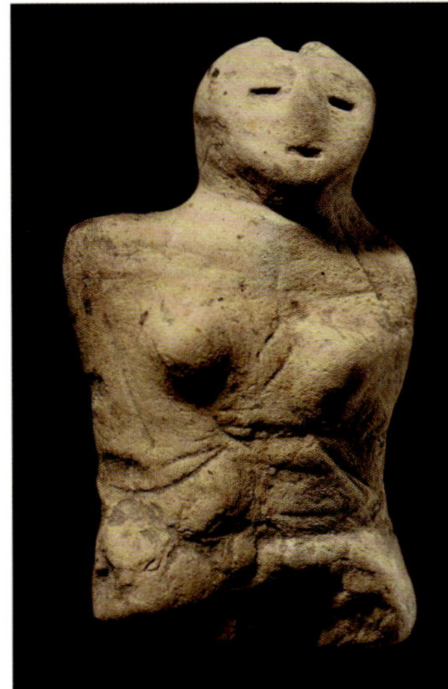

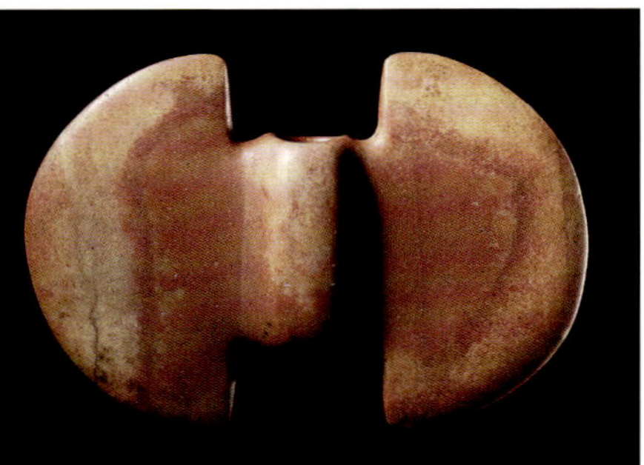

9

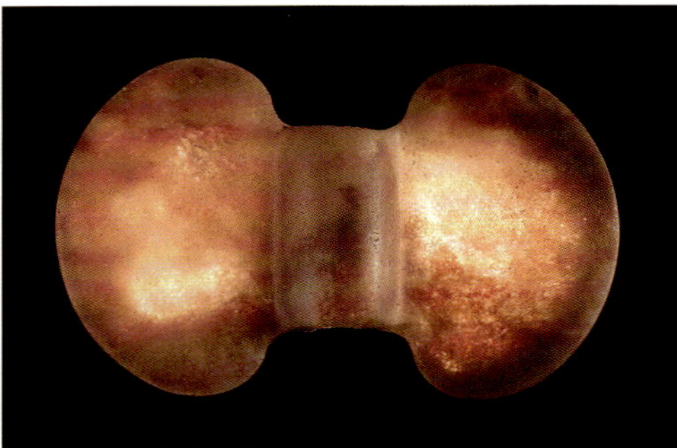

8

Cat. no. 126 Engraved whelk shell with two intertwined snake-men; Craig B style; Oklahoma, LeFlore County, Spiro, Craig Mound, A.D. 1200–1400; marine shell, l. 33 cm; Smithsonian Institution, National Museum of the American Indian, Washington, D.C., 18/9083. Townsend essay, fig. 42.

Cat. no. 127 Engraved whelk shell with four winged serpents surrounding a cross-in-circle motif; Craig B style; Oklahoma, LeFlore County, Spiro, Craig Mound, A.D. 1200–1350; marine shell, l. 21.6 cm; University of Arkansas Museum, Fayetteville, 37-1-39. Reilly essay, fig. 5.

Cat. no. 128 Fragment of an engraved whelk shell with an Underwater Panther or piasa; Craig B style; Oklahoma, LeFlore County, Spiro, Craig Mound, A.D. 1200–1400; marine shell, h. 19.7 cm; University of Arkansas Museum, Fayetteville, 37-1-43. Townsend essay, fig. 10.

Cat. no. 129 Engraved whelk shell with droopy-eye-surrounds; Craig B style; Oklahoma, LeFlore County, Spiro, Craig Mound, A.D. 1200–1400; marine shell, l. 26.4 cm; Smithsonian Institution, National Museum of the American Indian, Washington, D.C., 18/9119. Reilly essay, fig. 10.

Cat. no. 130 Engraved whelk shell with "Tree of Fur and Feathers" motif; Craig B style; Oklahoma, LeFlore County, Spiro, Craig Mound, A.D. 1200–1400; marine shell, l. 26.7 cm; Smithsonian Institution, National Museum of the American Indian, Washington, D.C., 18/9120. Brown essay, fig. 9.

Cat. no. 131 Engraved whelk shell with bows and eyes motif; Craig B style; Oklahoma, LeFlore County, Spiro, Craig Mound, A.D. 1200–1350; marine shell, l. 20.3 cm; Smithsonian Institution, National Museum of Natural History, Washington, D.C., A448818. Dye essay, fig. 25.

Cat. no. 132 Engraved whelk shell with two figures confronting a serpent staff; Craig C style; Oklahoma, Le Flore County, Spiro, Craig Mound, A.D. 1200–1400; marine shell, l. 31.1 cm; University of Arkansas Museum, Fayetteville, 37-1-40. Brown essay, fig. 4.

Cat. no. 133 Engraved whelk shell depicting Birdman; Craig C style; Oklahoma, LeFlore County, Spiro, Craig Mound, A.D. 1200–1400; marine shell, l. 29.2 cm; Smithsonian Institution, National Museum of the American Indian, Washington, D.C., 18/9122. Brown essay, fig. 3.

Cat. no. 134 Engraved whelk shell with paired figures confronting a serpent staff or pole; Craig C style; Oklahoma, LeFlore County, Spiro, Craig Mound, A.D. 1200–1400; marine shell, l. 29.9 cm; Smithsonian Institution, National Museum of the American Indian, Washington, D.C., 18/9123. Brown essay, fig. 8.

Cat. no. 135 Engraved whelk shell showing a ritual figure with a shell necklace and raccoon; Oklahoma, LeFlore County, Spiro, Craig Mound, A.D. 1200–1400; marine shell, h. 30.5 cm; Museum of the Red River, Idabel, Oklahoma, gift of Kent Westbrook, M.D., 91.11.5. Townsend and Walker essay, fig. 8.

Cat. no. 136 Engraved whelk shell with snake and talons motif; Craig C style; Oklahoma, LeFlore County, Spiro, Craig Mound, A.D. 1200–1400; marine shell, l. 34.3 cm; University of Arkansas Museum, Fayetteville, 37-1-45. Brown essay, fig. 5.

Cat. no. 137 Engraved whelk shell showing fish being speared; Craig C style; Oklahoma, LeFlore County, Spiro, Craig Mound, A.D. 1200–1350; marine shell, l. 25.4 cm; Smithsonian Institution, National Museum of the American Indian, Washington, D.C., 18/9308. Reilly, Bear, and Bear interview, fig. 7.

Cat. no. 138 Engraved shell gorget; Cox Mound style; Tennessee, Sumner County, Castalian Springs site, A.D. 1000–1400; marine shell, diam. 8.5 cm; Smithsonian Institution, National Museum of the American Indian, Washington, D.C., 15/855. Lankford essay, fig. 2.

Cat. no. 139 Engraved shell gorget with pair of figures; Cartersville type, Late Braden style; Tennessee, Sumner County, Saundersville site, A.D. 1200–1400; marine shell, diam. 11.5 cm; Dr. Arthur Cushman Collection, Old Hickory, Tennessee, AC476. Brown essay, fig. 22.

Cat. no. 140 Engraved shell gorget depicting a chunkey player; Classic Braden style; Missouri, Perry County, St. Marys, A.D. 1200–1350; marine shell, diam. 10.6 cm; Peabody Museum of Natural History, Yale University, 002751. Brown essay, fig. 2.

Cat. no. 141 Engraved shell gorget with two figures engaged in mortal combat; Hightower style; Tennessee, Hamilton County, Hixon site, A.D. 1250–1350; marine shell, diam. 11.5 cm; Frank H. McClung Museum, University of Tennessee, Knoxville, 566/1HA3. Dye essay, fig. 6.

Cat. no. 142 Engraved shell gorget with supernatural warrior holding a severed head and mace; Tennessee, Sumner County, Castalian Springs site, A.D. 1250–1350; marine shell, diam. 9.7 cm; Smithsonian Institution, National Museum of the American Indian, Washington, D.C., 15/853. Dye essay, fig. 1.

Cat. no. 143 Engraved shell gorget with Birdman vessel and severed heads; Arkansas, Craighead County, A.D. 1200–1400; marine shell, diam. 12.1 cm; Tommy Beutell Collection, SH355. Reilly essay, fig. 3.

Cat. no. 144 Engraved shell gorget with rattlesnake design; Brakebill style; Tennessee, Roane County, DeArmond site, A.D. 1000–1450; marine shell, diam. 12.3 cm; Frank H. McClung Museum, University of Tennessee, Knoxville, B76-1/3RE12. King essay, fig. 24.

Cat. no. 145 Engraved shell gorget with rattlesnake design; Citico style; Alabama, Terrapin Creek, A.D. 1000–1450; marine shell, h. 12.7 cm; Museum of the Red River, Idabel, Oklahoma, 43077. King essay, fig. 24.

Cat. no. 146 Engraved shell gorget with water spider motif; Tennessee, c. A.D. 1400; marine shell, diam. 10.2 cm; Tennessee Historical Society Collection, Tennessee State Museum, Nashville, 4.203.2. Lankford essay, fig. 19.

Cat. no. 147 Engraved shell gorget with cross-in-circle design; Georgia, Columbia County, Stallings Island Mound, A.D. 1250–1450; marine shell, diam. 7.6 cm; Harvard University, Peabody Museum of Archaeology and Ethnology, Peabody-Claflin Expedition 1929, Mr. and Mrs. C. B. Cosgrove, Directors, 29-78-10/A7505. King essay, fig. 13.

Cat. no. 148 Engraved shell gorget with triskele design; Tennessee, Williamson County, Fisher-Reams site, Gray's Farm, A.D. 1000–1450; marine shell, diam. 8.6 cm; Harvard University, Peabody Museum of Archaeology and Ethnology, Peabody Museum Expedition 1878, F. W. Putnam, Director, 78-6-10/15916. King essay, fig. 14.

Cat. no. 149 Engraved shell gorget with single figure; Spaghetti style; unknown origin, A.D. 1000–1450; marine shell, diam. 17.8 cm; The Field Museum, Chicago, 727.68554. King essay, fig. 21.

Cat. no. 150 Engraved shell gorget with double dancers; Spaghetti style; Tennessee, Hamilton County, Dallas site, A.D. 1000–1450; marine shell, diam. 17.2 cm; Frank H. McClung Museum, University of Tennessee, Knoxville, 767/8HA1. King essay, fig. 22.

Cat. no. 151 Engraved shell mask; unknown origin, 13th/14th century; marine shell, h. 15.2 cm; Smithsonian Institution, National Museum of Natural History, Washington, D.C., A448743. King essay, fig. 20.

Cat. no. 152 Engraved shell mask; Tennessee, Monroe County, Toco Mound, 13th/14th century; marine shell, h. 15.2 cm; Smithsonian Institution, National Museum of Natural History, Washington, D.C., A115566. King essay, fig. 19.

Cat. no. 153 Engraved shell mask; Tennessee, Knox County, Brakebill Mound, 14th century; marine shell, h. 20.3 cm; Harvard University, Peabody Museum of Archaeology and Ethnology, Peabody Museum Expedition 1869, Rev. E. O. Dunning, Director, 69-32-10/2238. King essay, fig. 18.

Cat. no. 154 Disc with ogee motif and scallop design; Arkansas, Arkansas County, Almond Farm site, 1000–1450; quartzite, diam. 35 cm; Frank H. McClung Museum, University of Tennessee, Knoxville. King essay, figs. 15a–b.

Cat. no. 155 Engraved circular palette with hand-and-eye motif and intertwined serpents; known in archaeological literature as the Rattlesnake Disk; Alabama, Tuscaloosa and Hale counties, Moundville, A.D. 1300–1450; sandstone, diam. 31.9 cm; Alabama Museum of Natural History, University of Alabama, Tuscaloosa, MI922. Steponaitis and Knight essay, fig. 1.

Cat. no. 156 Engraved circular palette; known in archaeological literature as the Willoughby Disk; Alabama, Tuscaloosa and Hale counties, Moundville, A.D. 1300–1450; shale (?), diam. 22.2 cm; Harvard University, Peabody Museum of Archaeology and Ethnology, gift of F. E. Hyde and Charles P. Bowditch, 1896, 96-11-10/48122. Steponaitis and Knight essay, fig. 13.

Cat. no. 157 Engraved circular palette with hand motif; Illinois, Naples, Winchester Mound, 100 B.C.–A.D. 300; siltstone (?), diam. 31.8 cm; Smithsonian Institution, National Museum of Natural History, Washington, D.C., A43126. Steponaitis and Knight essay, fig. 12.

Cat. no. 158 Engraved circular palette with intertwined plumed serpents; known in archaeological literature as the Issaquena Disk; Mississippi, Issaquena County, probably Grace Mounds, A.D. 1250–1500; sandstone (?), diam. 21.6 cm; Ohio Historical Society, Columbus, A14/23. Steponaitis and Knight essay, fig. 11.

Cat. no. 159 Fish-shaped pendant, Missouri, Pemiscot County, Campbell site, A.D. 1400–1650; red jasper, l. 6.4 cm; Private collection, Missouri.

Cat. no. 160 Bowl with serpent/bird effigy; Alabama, Tuscaloosa and Hale counties, Moundville, north of Mound R, A.D. 1250–1500; altered diorite, h. 16.5, diam. 30 cm; Smithsonian Institution, National Museum of the American Indian, Washington, D.C., 16/5232. Steponaitis and Knight essay, fig. 18.

Cat. no. 161 Concentric circle earspools; Oklahoma, LeFlore County, Spiro site, A.D. 1200–1350; stone and copper, diam. 7.6 cm; Gilcrease Museum, Tulsa, Oklahoma, 6125.3979a–b.

Cat. no. 162 Pair of earspools, 8-pointed star motif; Oklahoma, LeFlore County, Spiro, A.D. 1200–1400; stone, diam. 10.2 cm; Anthony Patano Collection, Chicago. Townsend and Walker essay, fig. 29.

Cat. no. 163 Pair of earspools, 8-pointed star motif; Oklahoma, LeFlore County, Spiro, A.D. 1200–1400; stone, diam. 5.7 cm; James and Elaine Kinker Collection, Midwest. Townsend and Walker essay, fig. 31.

Cat. no. 164 Pair of earspools, 6-pointed star motif; Oklahoma, LeFlore County, Spiro, A.D. 1200–1400; stone, diam. 8.9 cm; James and Elaine Kinker Collection, Midwest. Townsend and Walker essay, fig. 30.

Cat. no. 165 Pair of earspools; Oklahoma, LeFlore County, 13th century; stone; Smithsonian Institution, National Museum of Natural History, Washington, D.C., A448691.

Cat. no. 166 Chunkey stone; Missouri/Tennessee, A.D. 1300–1400; quartz, diam. 12.7 cm; James and Elaine Kinker Collection, Midwest. Brown essay, fig. 15.

Cat. no. 167 Chunkey stone; Georgia, Oastenaulla Valley, Popes Plantation, c. A.D. 1300; stone, diam. 13.5 cm; American Museum of Natural History, New York, 2/90CAT1869-90-81. Brown essay, fig. 12.

Cat. no. 168 Chunkey stone; Missouri, Mississippi County, Wolf Island, A.D. 1000–1600; stone, diam. 15.9 cm; Gilcrease Museum, Tulsa, Oklahoma, 6125.959. Brown essay, fig. 16.

Cat. no. 169 Chunkey stone, A.D. 1200–1400; greenstone, diam. 11.4 cm; Smithsonian Institution, National Museum of Natural History, Washington, D.C., A448678. Brown essay, fig. 14.

85

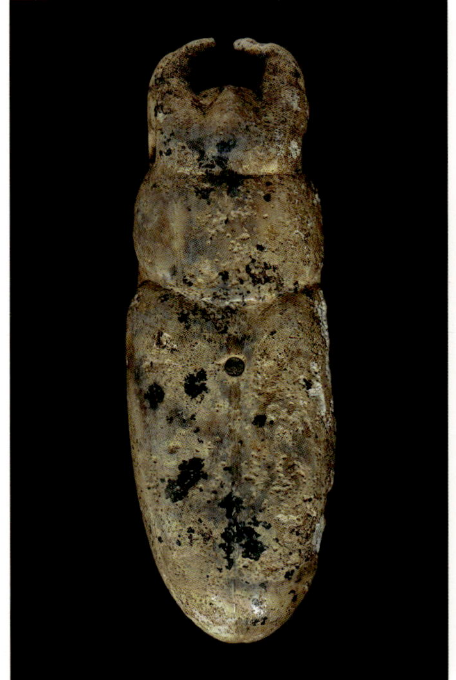

120

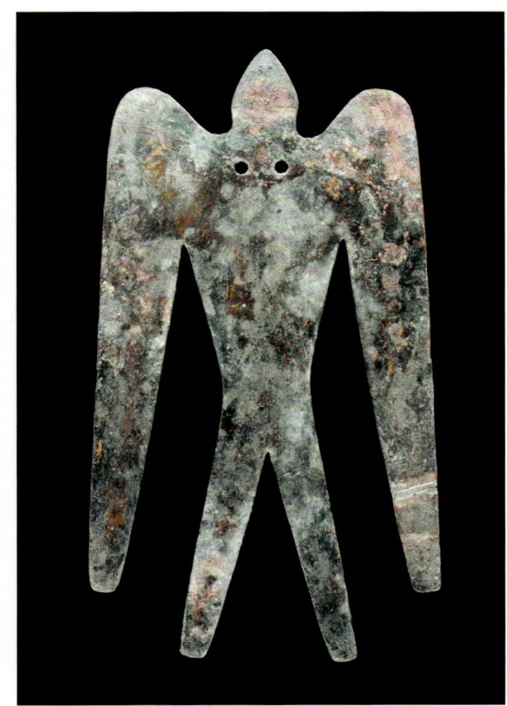

Cat. no. 170 Chunkey stone; Tennessee, A.D. 1200–1400; stone, diam. 7.6 cm; Smithsonian Institution, National Museum of Natural History, Washington, D.C., A388051. Brown essay, fig. 18.

Cat. no. 171 Chunkey stone; Arkansas, Crittenden County, Beck site, A.D. 1300–1500; kaolin, diam. 14 cm; Private collection, Missouri. Brown essay, fig. 17.

Cat. no. 172 Chunkey stone; Georgia, Lowndes County, c. A.D. 1300; conglomerate stone, diam. 11 cm; American Museum Natural History, New York, 2/1770CAT1869-90-81. Brown essay, fig. 13.

Cat. no. 173 Chunkey stone; Arkansas, Mississippi County, A.D. 1200–1600; quartzite, diam. 7.6 cm; Private collection, Missouri. Brown essay, fig. 19.

Cat. no. 174 Spatulate baton; Georgia, 13th century; greenstone, l. 60 cm; Smithsonian Institution, National Museum of Natural History, Washington, D.C., A170832. King essay, fig. 27.

Cat. nos. 175–76 Two ceremonial celts; Illinois, Madison County, Cahokia, and Tennessee, Hardin County, A.D. 1100–1500; stone, l. 37.5, 39.4 cm; Tommy Bryden Collection, Springfield, Illinois. Townsend essay, figs. 29–30.

Cat. no. 177 Spatulate Pipe with lizard motif; West Virginia, 13th century; greenstone, l. 25.4 cm; Smithsonian Institution, National Museum of Natural History, Washington, D.C., A440179.

Cat. no. 178 Ovoid pipe with broad rim; Tennessee, McMinn County, William Moore Farm mound, near Athens, c. A.D. 1200; greenstone, l. 32.5 cm; American Museum of Natural History, New York, T/720CAT1891-93-29.

Cat. no. 179 Polished spud stone; Tennessee, Monroe County, McGee Farm, 13th/14th century; graystone, h. 20.3 cm; Smithsonian Institution, National Museum of Natural History, Washington, D.C., A116035. King essay, fig. 25.

Cat. no. 180 Polished spud stone; Tennessee, Loudon County, Lenoir Mound no. 2, 13th/14th century; greenstone, h. 20.3 cm; Smithsonian Institution, National Museum of Natural History, Washington, D.C., A173545. King essay, fig. 26.

Cat. no. 181 Monolithic axe; Oklahoma, LeFlore County, Spiro, Craig Mound, A.D. 1300–1400; stone, l. 36.8 cm; Gilcrease Museum, Tulsa, Oklahoma, 6125.1781. Dye essay, fig. 27.

Cat. no. 182 Monolithic axe; Caddoan; Oklahoma, LeFlore County, Spiro site, A.D. 1200–1350; stone, l. 33 cm; Gilcrease Museum, Tulsa, Oklahoma, 6125.18910. Townsend essay, fig. 28.

Cat. no. 183 Monolithic axe; Alabama, Tuscaloosa and Hale counties, Moundville, A.D. 1300–1450; stone, l. 29.5 cm; Smithsonian Institution, National Museum of the American Indian, Washington, D.C., 17/891. Dye essay, fig. 28.

Cat. no. 184 Monolithic axe; Georgia, Cherokee County, A.D. 1300–1400; greenstone, l. 35.6 cm; Smithsonian Institution, National Museum of Natural History, Washington, D.C., A317614. Dye essay, fig. 29.

Cat. no. 185 Ceremonial mace; Oklahoma, LeFlore County, Spiro, A.D. 1200–1350; stone, l. 25.4 cm; Gilcrease Museum, Tulsa, Oklahoma, 6125.18906. Diaz-Granados essay, fig. 12.

Cat. no. 186 Ceremonial mace; southeastern Kentucky, A.D. 1200–1300; Dover flint, h. 27.9 cm; Tennessee State Museum, Nashville, Gates P. Thruston Collection of Vanderbilt University, 82.100.318. Dye essay, fig. 10.

Cat. no. 187 Ceremonial mace; Oklahoma, LeFlore County, Spiro, A.D. 1200–1300; stone; Smithsonian Institution, National Museum of the American Indian, Washington, D.C., 20/7099. Dye essay, fig. 11.

Cat. no. 188 Ceremonial blade; Oklahoma, LeFlore County, Spiro site, A.D. 1200–1400; Kaolin flint, l. 33.7 cm; Bobby Onken Collection. Townsend essay, fig. 45.

Cat. no. 189 Sword; Tennessee, Humphreys County, Link site, A.D. 1250–1350; Dover chert, l. 55.9, w. 4.7 cm; Frank H. McClung Museum, University of Tennessee, Knoxville, 2/35. Dye essay, fig. 19.

Cat. no. 190 Chipped stone blade; Tennessee, Humphreys County, Duck River, near Waverly, A.D. 1250–1350; l. 37.5 cm; Private collection. Dye essay, fig. 20.

Cat. no. 191 Raptor talon effigy; Tennessee, Humphreys County, Duck River, A.D. 1250–1350; stone, l. 12.1 cm; Private collection. Dye essay, fig. 18.

Cat. no. 192 Raptor talon effigy; Tennessee, Humphreys County, Duck River, near Waverly, A.D. 1250–1350; stone, l. 26.7 cm; Gilcrease Museum, Tulsa, Oklahoma, 6125.1562. Dye essay, fig. 17.

Cat. no. 193 Chipped stone disk; Missouri, Ste. Genevieve County, A.D. 1250–1350; diam. 8.9 cm; Private collection. Dye essay, fig. 22.

Cat. no. 194 Profile of a human head; Tennessee, Humphreys County, Duck River, near Waverly, A.D. 1250–1350; stone, h. 17.8 cm; Private collection. Dye essay, fig. 21.

Cat. no. 195 Cache of projectile points; Illinois, St. Clair County, Cahokia, Mound 72, c. A.D. 1000; chert, l. 3.0–6.5 cm; Illinois State Museum, Springfield, 1967-86 and 1970-45. Hall essay, fig. 7.

Cat. no. 196 Vessel; Haley Complicated Incised type; southwestern Arkansas, A.D. 1000–1400; ceramic, h. 22.9 cm; Museum of the Red River, Idabel, Oklahoma, HL3485. Townsend and Walker essay, fig. 7.

Cat. no. 197 Engraved redware bottle; Caddoan; Arkansas, A.D. 1400–1700; ceramic, h. 20.3 cm; James and Elaine Kinker Collection, Midwest. Townsend and Walker essay, fig. 19.

Cat. no. 198 Engraved egg-shaped bottle with interlocking serpent design; Caddoan; Arkansas, A.D. 1200–1500; ceramic, h. 20.3 cm; James and Elaine Kinker Collection, Midwest. Halfmoon essay, fig. 3.

258

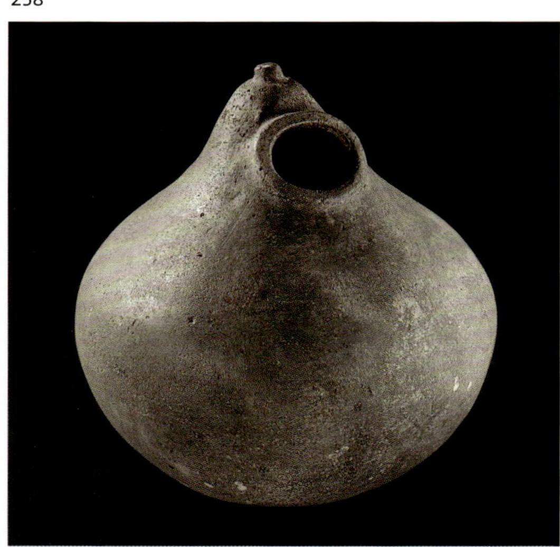

91

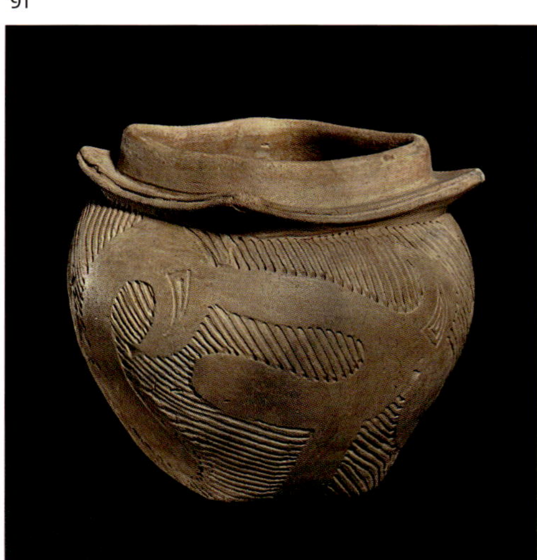

267

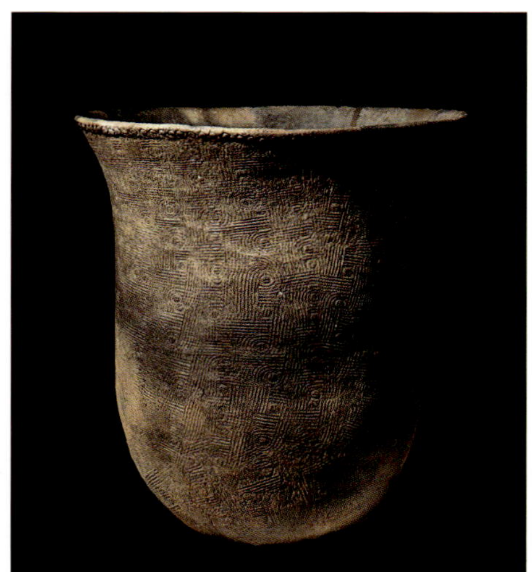

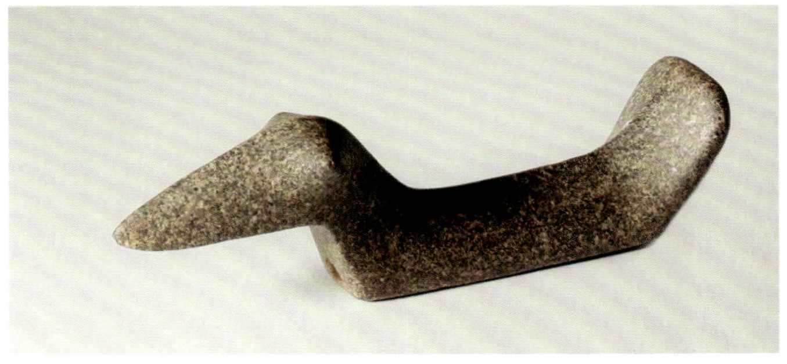

24

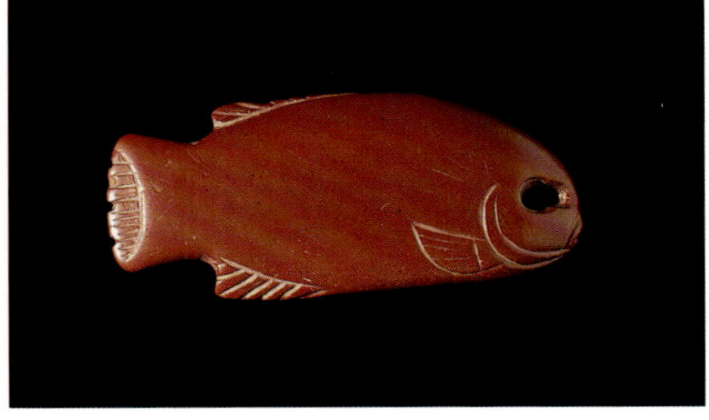

159

Cat. no. 199 Engraved cylindrical bottle; Hodges Engraved type; Caddoan; Arkansas, A.D. 1400–1700; ceramic, h. 25.4 cm; James and Elaine Kinker Collection, Midwest. Townsend and Walker essay, fig. 13.

Cat. no. 200 Engraved egg-shaped bottle; Hodges Engraved type; Caddoan; Arkansas, A.D. 1400–1700; ceramic, h. 21.6 cm; James and Elaine Kinker Collection, Midwest. Townsend and Walker essay, fig. 16.

Cat. no. 201 Engraved egg-shaped bottle; Hodges Engraved type; Caddoan; Arkansas, A.D. 1400–1700; ceramic, h. 17.8 cm; James and Elaine Kinker Collection, Midwest. Townsend and Walker essay, fig. 17.

Cat. no. 202 Engraved bottle with chevron bands and petaloid motifs, hematite rubbed; Caddoan; Arkansas, A.D. 1200–1500; ceramic, h. 20.3 cm; James and Elaine Kinker Collection, Midwest. Halfmoon essay, fig. 2.

Cat. no. 203 Globular bottle; Hodges Engraved type; Caddoan; southwestern Arkansas, A.D. 1400–1700; ceramic, h. 24.8 cm; Museum of the Red River, Idabel, Oklahoma, HL2374. Lankford essay, fig. 6.

Cat. no. 204 Engraved jar; Hodges Engraved type; Caddoan; Arkansas, A.D. 1400–1700; ceramic, h. 14 cm; James and Elaine Kinker Collection, Midwest. Townsend and Walker essay, fig. 12.

Cat. no. 205 Engraved jar with protuberant footing; Hodges Engraved type; Caddoan; Arkansas, A.D. 1400–1700; ceramic, h. 20.3 cm; James and Elaine Kinker Collection, Midwest. Townsend and Walker essay, fig. 11.

Cat. no. 206 Engraved tripod vessel; Hodges Engraved type; Caddoan; southwestern Arkansas, A.D. 1400–1700; ceramic, h. 20.3; Museum of the Red River, Idabel, Oklahoma, HL1263. Townsend and Walker essay, fig. 15.

Cat. no. 207 Burnished tripod bottle; Blakeley Engraved type; Caddoan; Arkansas, A.D. 1400–1500; ceramic, h. 25.4 cm; James and Elaine Kinker Collection, Midwest. Townsend and Walker essay, fig. 10.

Cat. no. 208 Engraved tripod bottle; Hodges Engraved type; Caddoan; Arkansas, A.D. 1400–1700; ceramic, h. 25.4 cm; James and Elaine Kinker Collection, Midwest. Townsend and Walker essay, fig. 14.

Cat. no. 209 Tripod bottle with arched band designs; Caddoan; Arkansas, A.D. 1400–1700; ceramic, h. 27.9 cm; Anthony Patano Collection, Chicago. Halfmoon essay, fig. 5.

Cat. no. 210 Tripod bottle; Hodges Engraved type; Caddoan; Arkansas, Garland County, Ouachita River, Kimes Place, A.D. 1400–1700; ceramic, h. 19.7 cm; Gilcrease Museum, Tulsa, Oklahoma, 5425.629. Halfmoon essay, fig. 1.

Cat. no. 211 Engraved double bottle; Hudson Engraved type; Caddoan; Arkansas, Yell County, Fourche River, Podo Place, A.D. 1500–1700; ceramic, h. 16.2, w. 20.3 cm; Gilcrease Museum, Tulsa, Oklahoma, 5125.1523. Halfmoon essay, fig. 6.

Cat. no. 212 Stirrup spout bottle; Hodges Engraved type; Caddoan; Arkansas, Clark County, A.D. 1300–1700; ceramic, h. 32, w. 28 cm; Dr. Kent and Jonnie Westbrook Collection, Little Rock, Arkansas. Townsend and Walker essay, fig. 25.

Cat. no. 213 Engraved bottle; Keno Trailed type; Caddoan; Arkansas, A.D. 1600–1800; ceramic, h. 20.3 cm; James and Elaine Kinker Collection, Midwest. Townsend and Walker, fig. 26.

Cat. no. 214 Water vessel; Keno Trailed type; Caddoan; Arkansas, Yell County, Carden Bottoms, A.D. 1500–1700; ceramic, h. 17.8 cm; Smithsonian Institution, National Museum of the American Indian, Washington, D.C., 5/6318. Halfmoon essay, fig. 7.

Cat. no. 215 Water jar; Keno Trailed type; Caddoan; Louisiana, Ouachita Parish, A.D. 1600–1800; ceramic; h. 14.6 cm; Smithsonian Institution, National Museum of the American Indian, Washington, D.C., 17/3248. Townsend and Walker essay, fig. 1

Cat. no. 216 Engraved cylindrical jar; Means Engraved type; Caddoan; Arkansas, A.D. 1400–1500; ceramic, h. 20.3 cm; James and Elaine Kinker Collection, Midwest. Townsend and Walker essay, fig. 18.

Cat. no. 217 Seed jar with fire clouds; Caddoan; Arkansas, Grant County, Saline River, A.D. 1400–1500; ceramic, h. 26.7 cm; Gilcrease Museum, Tulsa, Oklahoma, 5125.168. Townsend and Walker essay, fig. 22.

Cat. no. 218 Seed jar with fire clouds; Caddoan; Arkansas (?), A.D. 1400–1500; ceramic; Princeton University. Townsend and Walker essay, fig. 24.

Cat. no. 219 Seed jar with fire clouds; Caddoan; Arkansas, A.D. 1400–1500; ceramic; Princeton University. Townsend and Walker essay, fig. 23.

Cat. no. 220 Engraved vessel with arched bands and "lazy S" motifs; Avery Engraved type; Caddoan; Arkansas, A.D. 1300–1700; ceramic, h. 27.9 cm; James and Elaine Kinker Collection, Midwest. Halfmoon essay, fig. 9.

Cat. no. 221 Wide-necked vessel; redware, Avery Engraved type; Caddoan; Arkansas, A.D. 1300–1700; ceramic, h. 27.9 cm; James and Elaine Kinker Collection, Midwest. Townsend and Walker essay, fig. 28.

Cat. no. 222 Engraved vessel with rayed concentric oval motif; Avery Engraved type; Caddoan; Arkansas, A.D. 1300–1700; ceramic, h. 22.9 cm; James and Elaine Kinker Collection, Midwest. Halfmoon essay, fig. 8.

Cat. no. 223 Round-bottomed flared vessel; redware, Taylor Engraved type; Caddoan; Arkansas, A.D. 1500–1700; ceramic, h. 25.4 cm; James and Elaine Kinker Collection, Midwest. Townsend and Walker essay, fig. 27.

Cat. no. 224 Scalloped-rim vessel; Caddoan; northeastern Texas, A.D. 1200–1400; ceramic, h. 12.1, w. 24.1 cm; Museum of the Red River, Idabel, Oklahoma, HL5607. Halfmoon essay, fig. 4.

Cat. no. 225 Long-necked gadrooned bottle; Nodena Red and White type; Arkansas, Mississippi County, Chickasawba site, A.D. 1200–1400; ceramic, h. 20.3 cm; James and Elaine Kinker Collection, Midwest. Walker essay, fig. 14.

Cat. no. 226 Long-necked globular bottle with scalp lock motif; Nodena Red and White type; Arkansas, Arkansas County, Menard Mound site, A.D. 1300–1500; ceramic, h. 24.1 cm; Smithsonian Institution, National Museum of the American Indian, Washington, D.C., 17/4177. Walker essay, fig. 6.

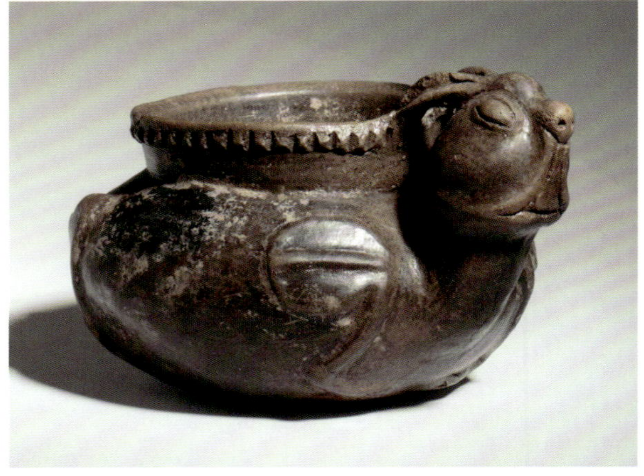

253

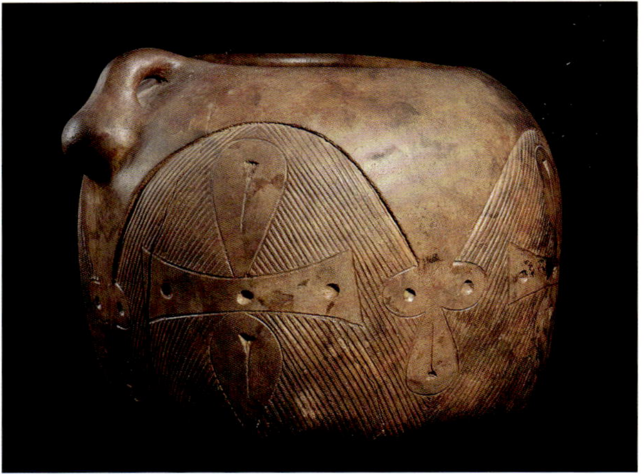

90

Cat. no. 227 Bottle with Great Serpent/Underwater Panther; Nodena Red and White type; Arkansas, Mississippi County, Lacy site, A.D. 1300–1500; ceramic, h. 24.1, w. 20.3 cm; Tommy Beutell Collection. Lankford essay, fig. 18.

Cat. no. 228 Long-necked globular bottle with interlocking scrolls; Nodena Red and White type; Arkansas, Chicot County, near Halley, A.D. 1300–1500; ceramic, h. 22.2 cm; Gilcrease Museum, Tulsa, Oklahoma, 5425.2559. Walker essay, fig. 3.

Cat. no. 229 Tripod vessel with negative resist design; Missouri, Mississippi County, A.D. 1300–1500; ceramic, h. 23.2 cm; Dr. Arthur Cushman Collection, Old Hickory, Tennessee, AC875. Steponaitis and Knight essay, fig. 10.

Cat. no. 230 Long-necked globular bottle with negative resist design; Arkansas, Scott County, A.D. 1300–1500; ceramic, h. 20.3 cm; Gilcrease Museum, Tulsa, Oklahoma, 5425.69. Steponaitis and Knight essay, fig. 9.

Cat. no. 231 Long-necked globular bottle with interlocking scrolls; Avenue Polychrome type; Arkansas, A.D. 1300–1500; ceramic, h. 27.9 cm; James and Elaine Kinker Collection, Midwest. Walker essay, fig. 4.

Cat. no. 232 Wide-necked jar with human hand design; Nodena Red and White type; Arkansas, Poinsett County, A.D. 1350–1450; ceramic, h. 17.8 cm; James and Elaine Kinker Collection, Midwest. Dye essay, fig. 31.

Cat. no. 233 Wide-necked bottle with curvilinear swastika design; Nodena Red and White type; Arkansas, Poinsett County, Scott site, A.D. 1350–1450; ceramic, h. 25.4 cm; James and Elaine Kinker Collection, Midwest. Lankford essay, fig. 15.

Cat. no. 234 Long-necked globular bottle; Avenue Polychrome type; Mississippi, Coahoma County, A.D. 1500–1700; ceramic, h. 27.9 cm; Private collection, Missouri. Walker essay, fig. 5.

Cat. no. 235 "Teapot" bottle with interlocking scrolls; Avenue Polychrome type; Arkansas, Phillips County, A.D. 1200–1400; ceramic, l. 25.4 cm; James and Elaine Kinker Collection, Midwest. Walker essay, fig. 15.

Cat. no. 236 Deer effigy vessel; Nodena Red and White type; Arkansas, White County, Little Red River; ceramic, h. 25, l. 30 cm; Dr. Kent and Jonnie Westbrook Collection, Little Rock, Arkansas. Walker essay, fig. 10.

Cat. no. 237 Underwater Panther effigy vessel; Avenue Polychrome type; Arkansas, Crittenden County, Young site, A.D. 1300–1550; ceramic, h. 24.1 cm; Dr. Arthur Cushman Collection, Old Hickory, Tennessee, AC642. Walker essay, fig. 7.

Cat. no. 238 Crouching deer effigy vessel; Nodena Red and White type; Arkansas, Lee County, Lipsky site, A.D. 1500–1700; ceramic, l. 39.4 cm; Private collection, Missouri. Walker essay, fig. 9.

Cat. no. 239 Long-necked globular bottle with mask motif; Arkansas, Mississippi County, A.D. 1200–1400; ceramic, h. 21.6 cm; Private collection, Missouri. Walker essay, fig. 16.

Cat. no. 240 Spouted head vessel; Nodena Red and White type; Arkansas, White County, Little Red River; ceramic, h. 15, l. 23 cm; Dr. Kent and Jonnie Westbrook Collection, Little Rock, Arkansas. Walker essay, fig. 17.

Cat. no. 241 Human head effigy vessel; Carson Red on Buff type; Pecan Point style; Arkansas, St. Francis County, Big Eddy site, A.D. 1350–1550; ceramic, h. 15.2 cm; Private collection. Walker essay, fig. 21.

Cat. no. 242 Human head effigy vessel; Carson Red on Buff type; Pecan Point style; Arkansas, Cross County, A.D. 1350–1550; ceramic; The Field Museum, Chicago, 146.50292. Walker essay, fig. 19.

Cat. no. 243 Human head effigy vessel; Carson Red on Buff type; Pecan Point style; Arkansas, Crittenden County, Bradley Place, A.D. 1350–1550; ceramic, h. 15.2 cm; University of Arkansas Museum, Fayetteville, 32-74-129. Walker essay, fig. 20.

Cat. no. 244 Human head effigy vessel; Carson Red on Buff type; Pecan Point style; Arkansas, Mississippi County, Matlock site, A.D. 1350–1550; ceramic, h. 15.2 cm; University of Arkansas Museum, Fayetteville, 31-35-3. Walker essay, fig. 23.

Cat. no. 245 Human head effigy vessel; Carson Red on Buff type; Arkansas, A.D. 1350–1550; ceramic, h. 15.9 cm; The Nelson-Atkins Museum of Art, Kansas City, Missouri, the Donald D. Jones Fund for American Indian Art, 2003.11. Walker essay, fig. 1.

Cat. no. 246 Human head effigy vessel; Carson Red on Buff type; Pecan Point style; Missouri, Pemiscot County, Campbell site, A.D. 1350–1550; ceramic, h. 16.2 cm; The Detroit Institute of Arts, Founders Society Purchase with funds from the Mary G. and Robert H. Flint Foundation, 1986.43. Walker essay, fig. 27.

Cat. no. 247 Human head effigy vessel; Carson Red on Buff type, Pecan Point style; Arkansas, Poinsett County; Pecan Point site, A.D. 1350–1550; ceramic, h. 17.8 cm; Smithsonian Institution, National Museum of Natural History, Washington, D.C., A91298. Walker essay, fig. 18.

Cat. no. 248 Human head effigy vessel; Carson Red on Buff type; Pecan Point style; Arkansas, Poinsett County, Fortune Mound, A.D. 1350–1550; ceramic, h. 19.1 cm; Harvard University, Peabody Museum of Archaeology and Ethnology, Peabody Museum Expedition 1879–1880, Edwin Curtiss, Director, 80-20-10/21542. Walker essay, fig. 25.

Cat. no. 249 Human head effigy vessel; Carson Red on Buff type; Pecan Point style; Missouri, Pemiscot County, Campbell site, A.D. 1350–1550; ceramic, h. 15.2 cm; James and Elaine Kinker Collection, Midwest. Walker essay, fig. 24.

Cat. no. 250 Great Serpent/Underwater Panther vessel; Arkansas, A.D. 1300–1500; ceramic, h. 17.2, l. 32.4 cm; Dr. James F. Cherry Collection, Fayetteville, Arkansas. Lankford essay, fig. 1.

Cat. no. 251 Great Serpent/Underwater Panther vessel; Arkansas, A.D. 1300–1500; ceramic, h. 20.3, l. 24.1 cm; The Field Museum, Chicago, 146.50664. Lankford essay, fig. 16.

Cat. no. 252 Underwater Panther effigy vessel with engraved swirls of the blocked-line motif; Illinois, Fulton County, Shryock site, c. A.D. 1200; ceramic, h. 7.5, diam. 20 cm; Illinois State Museum, Springfield, 819/849. Brown essay, fig. 31.

Cat. no. 253 Rabbit vessel; Caddoan; Arkansas, Mississippi County, A.D. 1000–1600; ceramic, h. 10.2 cm; Gilcrease Museum, Tulsa, Oklahoma, 5425.867.

Cat. no. 254 Frog vessel; Arkansas, Lee County, Clay Hill site, A.D. 1000–1300; ceramic, h. 15.2 cm; Gilcrease Museum, Tulsa, Oklahoma, 5425.2631. Reilly essay, fig. 21.

Cat. no. 255 Fish effigy jar; Bell Plain type; Arkansas, Crittenden County, Beck site, A.D. 1200–1400; shell-tempered ceramic, w. 27.9 cm; Private collection, Missouri. Walker essay, fig. 11.

Cat. no. 256 Bottle with possum head effigy; Arkansas/Missouri, A.D. 1200–1400; ceramic, h. 15.2 cm; James and Elaine Kinker Collection, Midwest. Walker essay, fig. 12.

Cat. no. 257 Frog effigy jar; Bell Plain type; Arkansas, Mississippi County, Blytheville, A.D. 1200–1400; ceramic, h. 19.1, l. 26.7 cm; Smithsonian Institution, National Museum of the American Indian, Washington, D.C., 5/6528. Walker essay, fig. 13.

Cat. no. 258 Gourd-shaped vessel; Missouri, Mound XIV, A.D. 1300–1500; ceramic, h. 19.1 cm; Harvard University, Peabody Museum of Archaeology and Ethnology, gift of Dr. George J. Engelmann, 1895, 95-21-10/48675.

Cat. no. 259 Vessel with bones and hand motifs; Bell Plain type; Tennessee or Arkansas, A.D. 1350–1450; ceramic, h. 15.2 cm; The Field Museum, Chicago, 146.50723. Dye essay, fig. 30.

Cat. no. 260 Seated female effigy vessel; Arkansas, A.D. 1350–1500; ceramic, h. 15.2 cm; The Detroit Institute of Arts, Founders Society Purchase, Lynn W. and Stanley R. Day Fund, 1991.115. Diaz-Granados essay, fig. 1.

Cat. no. 261 Vessel in the form of a kneeling female figure; Bell Plain type; Arkansas, Crittenden County, Bradley site, c. 1300–1500; shell-tempered ceramic, h. 20.3 cm; Private collection, Missouri. Diaz-Granados essay, fig. 10.

Cat. no. 262 Seated human effigy vessel; Arkansas, A.D. 1300–1500; ceramic, h. 23.2 cm; Dr. James F. Cherry Collection, Fayetteville, Arkansas. Walker essay, fig. 8.

Cat. no. 263 Cup with incised skull motif; Alabama, Tuscaloosa and Hale counties, Moundville, southeast of Mound H, A.D. 1300–1450; ceramic, h. 11.5 cm.; Alabama Museum of Natural History, University of Alabama, Tuscaloosa, SEH9. Steponaitis and Knight essay, fig. 8.

Cat. no. 264 Engraved bottle with winged serpent; Hemphill style; Alabama, Tuscaloosa and Hale counties, Moundville, south of Mound D, A.D. 1300–1450; ceramic, h. 24.1 cm; Alabama Museum of Natural History, University of Alabama, Tuscaloosa, 1932.3.5. Lankford essay, fig. 12.

Cat. no. 265 Jar with incised hands; Alabama, Tuscaloosa and Hale counties, Moundville, Rhodes site (northeast of Mound F), A.D. 1300–1450; ceramic, h. 16.5 cm; Alabama Museum of Natural History, University of Alabama, Tuscaloosa, 1930.2.308. Steponaitis and Knight essay, fig. 7.

Cat. no. 266 Bottle with ogee and hand-and-eye motifs; Alabama, near Mobile, A.D. 1300–1500; ceramic, h. 15.9 cm; Harvard University, Peabody Museum of Archaeology and Ethnology, Museum Purchase 1946, 46-61-10/27872.1. Lankford essay, fig. 9.

Cat. no. 267 Jar, Georgia, Chatham County, Ossabaw Island, A.D. 1200–1400; ceramic, h. 41.9 cm; Smithsonian Institution, National Museum of the American Indian, Washington, D.C., 17/4486.

Cat. no. 268 Kneeling human effigy figurine; Tennessee, Davidson County, Nashville, Hayes Farm, A.D. 1000–1450; ceramic, h. 22.2 cm; Harvard University, Peabody Museum of Archaeology and Ethnology, Peabody Museum Expedition 1878–79, Edwin Curtiss, Director, 79-4-10/18301. King essay, figs. 8a–b.

Cat. no. 269 Kneeling female figurine with tattoos; Tennessee, Smith County, rock shelter by the Cumberland River; ceramic, h. 22.9 cm; Dr. Arthur Cushman Collection, Old Hickory, Tennessee, AC882. Diaz-Granados essay, fig. 5.

Cat. no. 270 Nursing mother effigy bottle; Illinois, St. Clair County, Francis Simonim Farm, A.D. 1200–1400; ceramic, h. 15.2 cm; St. Louis Science Center, 8X65. Diaz-Granados essay, fig. 4.

Cat. no. 271 Kneeling human-feline effigy figure; Florida, Collier County, Key Marco, A.D. 1400–1500; wood, h. 15 cm; Smithsonian Institution, National Museum of Natural History, Washington, D.C., A240915. Townsend essay, fig. 34.

Cat. no. 272 Deer mask; Oklahoma, LeFlore County, Spiro, Craig Mound, A.D. 1200–1400; red cedar and marine shell, 29.2 × 15.9 cm; Smithsonian Institution, National Museum of the American Indian, Washington, D.C., 18/9306. Townsend essay, fig. 1.

Cat. no. 273 Wooden maskette; Illinois, Fulton County, Emmons site, A.D. 1200–1350; red cedar, 11.9 × 9.9 × 5.5 cm; Illinois State Museum, Springfield, 824/444. Brown essay, fig. 33.

Cat. no. 274 Theodor de Bry (Flemish; 1528–1598), after an original painting of 1564 by Jacques Le Moyne de Morgues (French; c. 1533–1588), *Outina Consults a Sorcerer*, 1591; from *America*, 2nd ed. (Frankfurt-am-Main, 1609), pt. 2, pl. 12; Rucker Agee Map Collection, Birmingham Public Library, Alabama. Dye essay, fig. 3.

Cat. no. 275 Theodor de Bry, after an original painting of 1564 by Jacques Le Moyne de Morgues, *Outina's Order of March*, 1591; from *America*, 1st ed. (Frankfurt-am-Main, 1591), pt. 2, pl. 14; Rucker Agee Map Collection, Birmingham Public Library, Alabama. Dye essay,

83

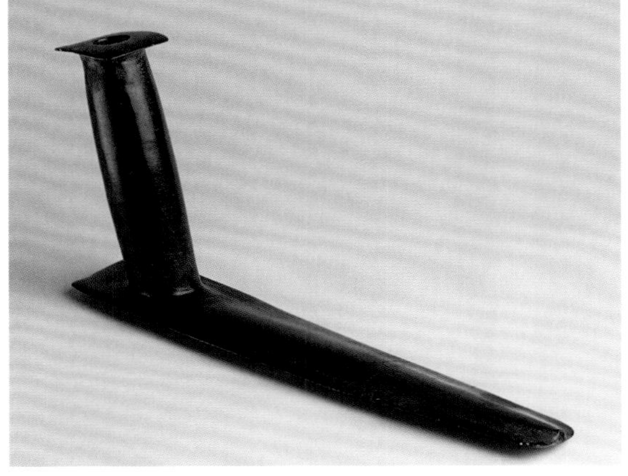

84

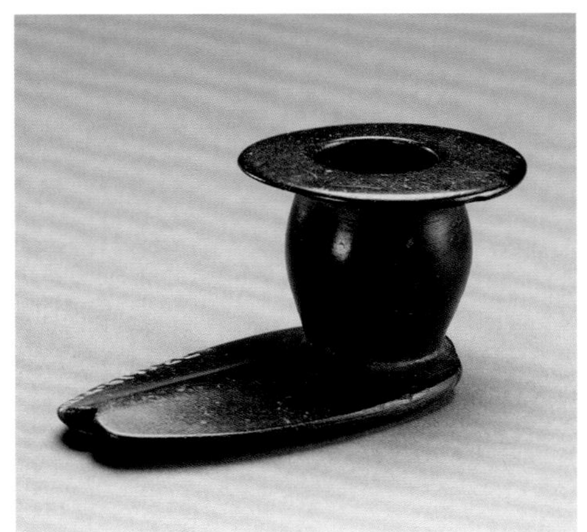

177

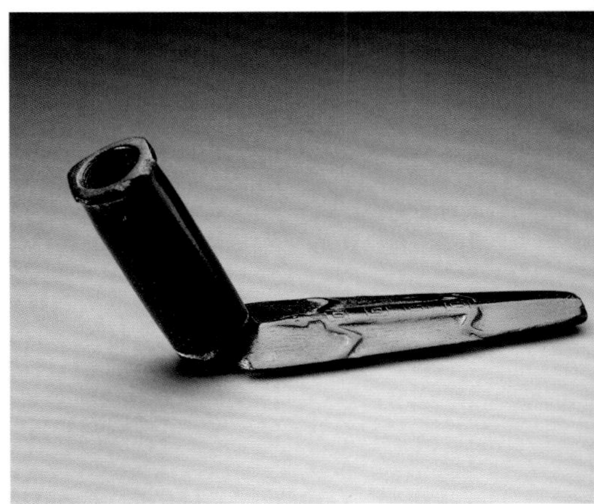

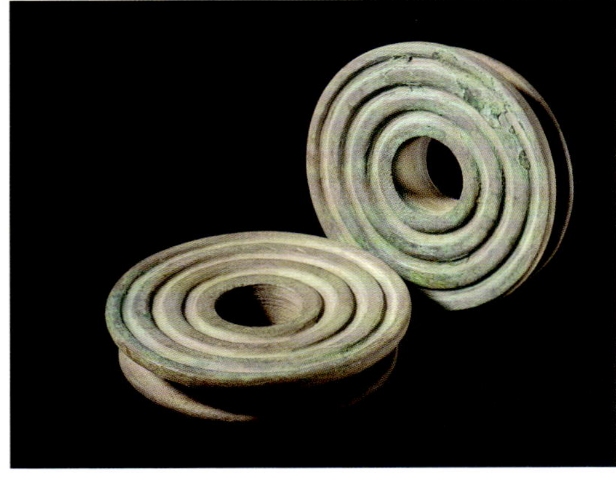

161

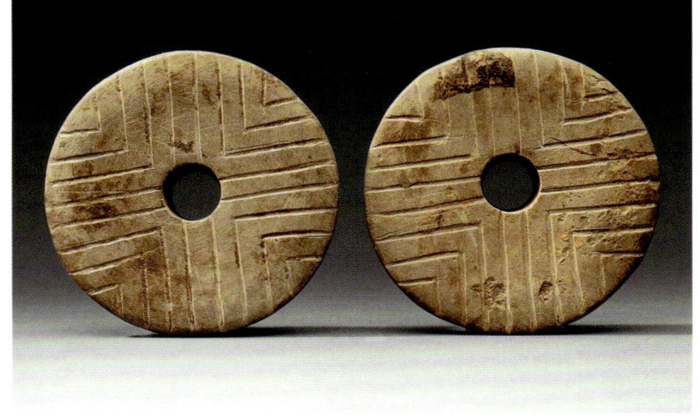

165

fig. 4.

Cat. no. 276 Theodor de Bry, after an original painting of 1564 by Jacques Le Moyne de Morgues, *Trophies and Ceremonies after a Victory*, 1591; from *America*, 2nd ed. (Frankfurt-am-Main, 1609), pt. 2, pl. 16; Rucker Agee Map Collection, Birmingham Public Library, Alabama. Dye essay, fig. 26.

Cat. no. 277 Theodor de Bry, after an original painting of 1564 by Jacques Le Moyne de Morgues, *Hunting Deer*, 1591; from *America*, 2nd ed. (Frankfurt-am-Main, 1609), pt. 2, pl. 25; Rucker Agee Map Collection, Birmingham Public Library, Alabama. Reilly, Bear, and Bear interview, fig. 5.

Cat. no. 278 Theodor de Bry, after an original painting of 1564 by Jacques Le Moyne de Morgues, *A Council of State*, 1591; from *America*, 1st ed. (Frankfurt-am-Main, 1591), pt. 2, pl. 29; Rucker Agee Map Collection, Birmingham Public Library, Alabama. Dye essay, fig. 14.

Cat. no. 279 Theodor de Bry, after an original painting of 1564 by Jacques Le Moyne de Morgues, *Offering the Skin of a Stag to the Sun*, 1591; from *America*, 1st ed. (Frankfurt-am-Main, 1591), pt. 2, pl. 35; Rucker Agee Map Collection, Birmingham Public Library, Alabama. Hall essay, fig. 10.

Cat. no. 280 Theodor de Bry, after an original painting of 1564 by Jacques Le Moyne de Morgues, *Exercises of the Youths*, 1591; from *America*, 1st ed. (Frankfurt-am-Main, 1591), pt. 2, pl. 36; Rucker Agee Map Collection, Birmingham Public Library, Alabama. Dye essay, fig. 5.

Cat. no. 281 Theodor de Bry, after an original watercolor by John White (English; fl. 1585–93), *How They Catch Fish*, 1590; from *America*, 2nd ed. (Frankfurt-am-Main, 1600), pt. 1, pl. 13; Rucker Agee Map Collection, Birmingham Public Library, Alabama. Reilly, Bear, and Bear interview, fig. 6.

Cat. no. 282 Theodor de Bry, after an original watercolor by John White, *The Town of Pomeiock*, 1590; from *America*, 2nd ed. (Frankfurt-am-Main, 1600), pt. 1, pl. 19. Dye essay, fig. 2.

Cat. no. 283 Theodor de Bry, after an original watercolor by John White, *The Town of Secota*, 1590; from *America*, 2nd ed. (Frankfurt-am-Main, 1600), pt. 1, pl. 20; Rucker Agee Map Collection, Birmingham Public Library, Alabama. Reilly, Bear, and Bear interview, fig. 1.

Cat. no. 284 Human head effigy vessel; Carson Red on Buff type; Pecan Point style; Arkansas, Poinsett County, Shawnee Village site, A.D. 1350–1550; ceramic, h. 17.5 cm; Hampson Museum State Park, Arkansas. Walker essay, fig. 26.

4

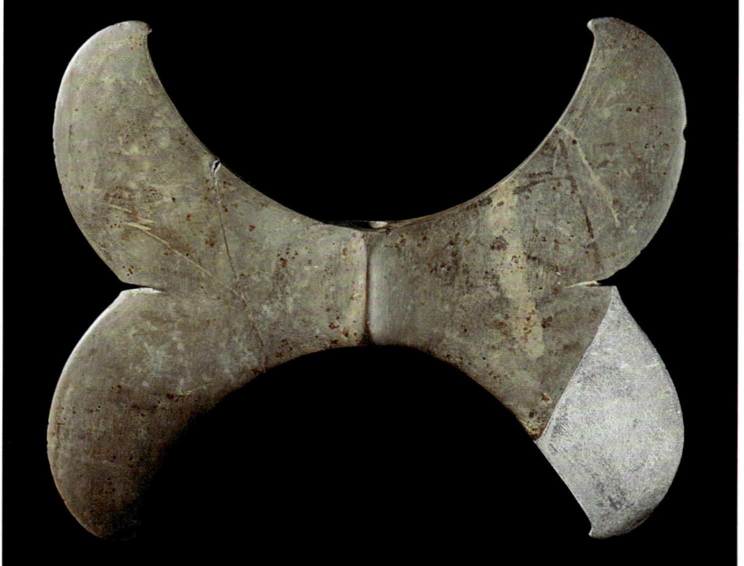

13

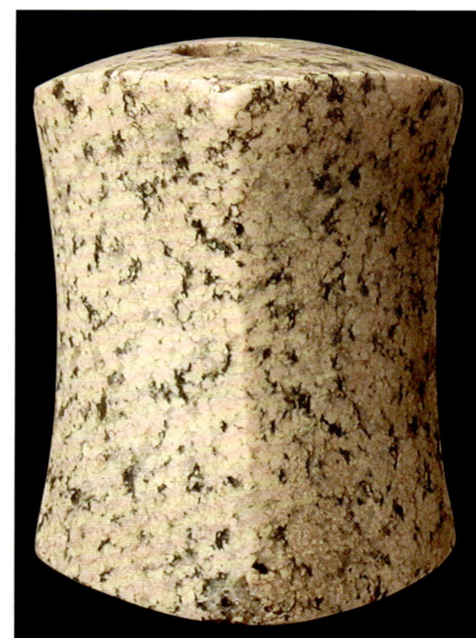

Bibliography

The Advocate [Newark]. 1827. Antiquities of Ohio. *The Advocate* [Newark, Ohio], March 29, 1827.

Ahler, Steven R., ed. 2000. *Mounds, Modoc, and Mesoamerica: Papers in Honor of Melvin L. Fowler*. Illinois State Museum, Scientific Papers, vol. 28.

Alford, Thomas Wildcat, and Florence Drake. 1936. *Civilization and the Story of the Absentee Shawnee*. University of Oklahoma Press, 1979.

Anderson, David G. 1994. *The Savannah River Chiefdoms: Political Change in the Late Prehistoric Southeast*. University of Alabama Press.

Anonymous. 1923. Stone Disc. *Arrow Points* [Monthly Bulletin of the Alabama Anthropological Society] 7, no. 6, p. 118.

Anonymous. 1943. Report on the First Archaeological Conference on the Woodland Pattern. *American Antiquity* 8, pp. 393–400.

Asch, David L., and Nancy B. Asch. 1985. Prehistoric Plant Cultivation in West-Central Illinois. In *Prehistoric Food Production in North America*, edited by R. J. Ford, pp. 149–203. University of Michigan Museum of Anthropology Anthropological Papers, no. 75.

Atwater, C. 1820. Description of the Antiquities Discovered in the State of Ohio and Other Western States. *Archaeologia Americana* 1, pp. 105–267.

Baby, Raymond S., and Suzanne M. Langlois. 1979. Seip Mound State Memorial: Nonmortuary Aspects of Hopewell. In Brose and Greber 1979, pp. 16–18.

Bacon, Willard S. 1980. Factors in Siting a Middle Woodland Enclosure in Middle Tennessee. *Midcontinental Journal of Archaeology* 18, pp. 245–81.

Bailey, Garrick A. 1973. *Changes in Osage Social Organization 1673–1906*. University of Oregon Anthropological Papers, no. 5.

———. 1995. *The Osage and the Invisible World: From the Works of Francis La Flesche*. University of Oklahoma Press.

Bareis, Charles J., and James W. Porter, eds. 1984. *American Bottom Archaeology: A Summary of the FAI-270 Project Contribution to the Culture History of the Mississippi Valley*. University of Illinois Press.

Bastien, Joseph W. 1978. *Mountain of the Condor: Metaphor and Ritual in an Andean Ayllu*. West Publishing Co.

Beck, Robin A., Jr. 2003. Consolidation and Hierarchy: Chiefdom Variability in the Mississippian Southeast. Forthcoming in *American Antiquity*.

———. n.d. If You Build It, They Will Come: Persuasive Politics and Domination at Moundville and Cahokia. Unpublished manuscript.

Becker, Marshall. 1975. Moieties in Ancient Mesoamerica. *American Indian Quarterly* 2, no. 3.

Benn, David W. 1989. Hawks, Serpents, and Bird-Men: Emergence of the Oneota Mode of Production. *Plains Anthropologist* 34, no. 125, pp. 233–60.

———. 1995. Woodland People and the Roots of Oneota. In *Oneota Archaeology Past, Present, and Future*, edited by William Green, pp. 91–139. Report 20, Office of the State Archaeologist, University of Iowa.

Benson, S. Natalie. 1951. The Head Vases of the Arkansas-Missouri Region—Their Art and Archaeology in Relation to Culture Complexes in the Southeast. Master's thesis, Columbia University.

Berlo, Janet C., and Ruth B. Phillips. 1998. *Native North American Art*. Oxford University Press.

Billington, Ray Allen. 1960. *Westward Expansion: A History of the American Frontier*. Macmillan.

Binford, Sally R., and Lewis R. Binford, eds. 1968. *New Perspectives in Archaeology*. University of Chicago Press.

Blanton, R. E., G. M. Feinman, S. A Kowalewski, and P. N. Peregrine. 1996. A Dual-Processual Theory for the Evolution of Mesomerican Civilization. *Current Anthropology* 37, no. 1, pp. 1–14.

Bolton, Herbert Eugene. 1987. *The Hasinais: Southern Caddoans as Seen by the Earliest Europeans*. University of Oklahoma Press.

Boszhardt, Robert F. 2000. Turquoise, Rasps, and Heartlines: The Oneota Bison Pull. In Ahler 2000, pp. 361–73.

Bowers, Alfred W. 1992. *Hidatsa Social and Ceremonial Organization*. University of Nebraska Press.

Brain, Jeffrey P., and Philip Phillips. 1996. *Shell Gorgets: Styles of the Late Prehistoric and Protohistoric Southeast*. Peabody Museum Press.

Braun, David P. 1986. Midwestern Hopewell Exchange and Supra-local Interaction. In *Peer Polity Interaction and Sociopolitical Change*, edited by C. Renfrew and J. Cherry, pp. 117–26. Cambridge University Press.

Braun, David P., James B. Griffin, and Paul F. Titterington. 1982. *The Snyders Mounds and Five Other Mound Groups in Calhoun County, Illinois*. University of Michigan Museum of Anthropology, Technical Reports in Archaeology, no. 8.

Brose, David S., James A. Brown, and David W. Penney. 1985. *Ancient Art of the American Woodland Indians*. Harry N. Abrams and The Detroit Institute of Arts.

Brose, David S., and N'omi Greber, eds. 1979. *Hopewell Archaeology: The Chillicothe Conference*. Kent State University Press.

Brown, James A. 1976. The Southern Cult Reconsidered. *Midcontinental Journal of Archaeology* 1, no. 2, pp. 115–35.

———. 1979. Charnel Houses and Mortuary Crypts: Disposal of the Dead in the Middle Woodland Period. In Brose and Greber 1979, pp. 211–19.

———. 1981. The Search for Rank in Prehistoric Burials. In *The Archaeology of Death*, edited by R. Chapman, I. Kinnes, and K. Randsborg, pp. 25–37. Cambridge University Press.

———. 1983. Spiro Exchange Connections Revealed by Sources of Imported Raw Materials. In *Southeastern Natives and Their Pasts: A Collection of Papers Honoring Dr. Robert E. Bell*, edited by Don G. Wyckoff and Jack L. Hofman, pp. 129–62. Oklahoma Archaeological Survey, Studies in Oklahoma's Past, no. 11.

———. 1985. The Mississippian Period. In Brose, Brown, and Penney 1985, pp. 93–145.

———. 1989. On Style Divisions of the Southeastern Ceremonial Complex—A Revisionist Perspective. In Galloway 1989, pp. 183–204.

———. 1991. The Falcon and the Serpent: Life in the Southeastern United States at the Time of Columbus. In *Circa 1492: Art in the Age of Exploration*, edited by Jay A. Levenson, pp. 529–34. National Gallery of Art and Yale University Press.

———. 1996. *The Spiro Ceremonial Center: The Archaeology of Arkansas Valley Caddoan Culture in Eastern Oklahoma*. 2 vols. Museum of Anthropology, University of Michigan.

———. 1997. The Archaeology of Ancient Religion in the Eastern Woodlands. *Annual Reviews in Anthropology* 26, pp. 465–85.

———. 2001. Human Figures and the Southeastern Ancestor Shrine. In *Fleeting Identities: Perishable Material Culture in Archaeological Research*, edited by Penelope Ballard Drooker, pp. 76–93. Occasional Paper 28. Center for Archaeological Investigations, Southern Illinois University, Carbondale.

———. 2003. The Cahokia Mound 72Sub1 Burials as Collective Representation. In *A Deep-Time Perspective: Studies in Symbols, Meaning, and the Archaeological Record*, edited by John D. Richards and M. L. Fowler. *The Wisconsin Archeologist* 84, nos. 1 and 2.

———. 2004a. Exchange and Interaction to A.D. 1500. In William C. Sturtevant, ed., *Handbook of North American Indians*, vol. 14, *Southeast*. Smithsonian Institution.

———. 2004b. Mound City and Issues in the Developmental History of Hopewell Culture in the Ross County Area of Southern Ohio. Forthcoming in *Essays in Honor of Howard D. Winters*, edited by Anne-Marie Cantwell and Lawrence Conrad. Illinois State Museum, Scientific Papers.

———. 2005a. On the Identity of the Birdman of the Southeastern Ceremonial Complex. Forthcoming in Reilly and Garber 2005.

———. 2005b. The Greater Braden Style of the Southeastern Ceremonial Complex. Forthcoming in Reilly and Garber 2005. Expanded and revised version of a paper presented at the 56th Annual Meeting of the Southeastern Archaeological Conference, Pensacola, Florida.

———. 2005c. Chronological Implications of the Bellows-Shaped Apron. Forthcoming in *Chronology, Iconography, and Style: Current Perspectives on the Social and Temporal Contexts of the Southeastern Ceremonial Complex*, edited by Adam King. University of Alabama Press. First presented at the 57th Annual Meeting of the Southeastern Archaeological Conference, Macon, Georgia.

———. n.d. The Invention of an Art Style as an Instrument of Elite Control in the Mississippian Southeast. Forthcoming in *The Moorehead Phase Revisited*, edited by James A. Brown and John E. Kelly.

Brown, James A., and John E. Kelly. 2000. Cahokia and the Southeastern Ceremonial Complex. In Ahler 2000, pp. 469–510.

Brown, James A., R. A. Kerber, and H. D. Winters. 1990. Trade and the Evolution of Exchange Relations at the Beginning of the Mississippian Period. In *The Mississippian Emergence*, edited by Bruce D. Smith, pp. 251–80. Smithsonian Institution Press.

Brown, James A., and J. Daniel Rogers. 1989. Linking Spiro's Artistic Styles: The Copper Connection. *Southeastern Archaeology* 8, pp. 1–8.

———. 1999. AMS Dates on Artifacts of the Southeastern Ceremonial Complex at Spiro. *Southeastern Archaeology* 18, pp. 134–41.

Bullington, Jill. 1988. Middle Woodland Mound Structure: Social Implications and Regional Context. In *The Archaic and Woodland Cemeteries at the Elizabeth Site in the Lower Illinois Valley*, edited by D. Charles, S. Leigh, and J. Buikstra, pp. 218–41. Kampsville Archeological Center, Research Series, vol. 7. Center for American Archeology.

Buikstra, Jane E. 1976. Hopewell in the Lower Illinois Valley: A Regional Approach to the Study of Human Biological Variability and Prehistoric Behavior. Northwestern University Archeological Program.

Buikstra, Jane E., and Douglas K. Charles. 1999. Centering the Ancestors: Cemeteries, Mounds, and Sacred Landscapes of the Ancient North American Midcontinent. In *Archaeologies of Landscape*, edited by W. Ashmore and A. B. Knapp, pp. 201–28. Blackwell Publishers.

Burnett, E. K. 1945. The Spiro Mound Collection in the Museum. *Contributions of the Museum of the American Indian, Heye Foundation*, vol. 14, pp. 1–47.

Butler, Brian M. 1979. Hopewellian Contacts in Southern Middle Tennessee. In Brose and Greber 1979, pp. 150–56.

Byers, Douglas S. 1962. The Restoration and Preservation of Some Objects from Etowah. *American Antiquity* 28, pp. 206–16.

Carr, Christopher. 1995. Mortuary Practices: Their Social, Philosophical-Religious, Circumstantial, and Physical Determinants. *Journal of Archaeological Method and Theory* 2, pp. 105–200.

Chandler, Milford G. 1973. Art and Culture. In *Art of the Great Lakes Indians*, pp. xv–xxvi. Flint Institute of Art.

Chapman, Carl H. 1952. Culture Sequence in the Lower Missouri Valley. In Griffin 1952a, pp. 139–51.

Chapman, Jefferson, and Bennie C. Keel. 1979. Candy Creek-Connestee Components in Eastern Tennessee and Western North Carolina and Their Relationship with Adena-Hopewell. In Brose and Greber 1979, pp. 157–62.

Chappell, Sally A. Kitt. 2002. *Cahokia: Mirror of the Universe*. University of Chicago Press.

Charles, Douglas K. 1992. Woodland Demographic and Social Dynamics in the American Midwest: Analysis of a Burial Mound Survey. *World Archaeology* 24, no. 2, pp. 175–97.

Churchill, Mary C. 1996. The Oppositional Paradigm of Purity Versus Pollution in Charles Hudson's *The Southeastern Indians*. *American Indian Quarterly* 20, no. 4, pp. 563–89.

Clay, R. Berle. 1988. Peter Village: An Adena Enclosure. In *Middle Woodland Settlement and Ceremonialism in the Mid-South and Lower Mississippi Valley*, edited by R. Mainfort, pp. 19–30. Mississippi Department of Archives and History, Archaeological Report No. 22.

Clayton, Lawrence A., Vernon J. Knight, Jr., and Edward C. Moore 1993. *The De Soto Chronicles: The Expedition of Hernando de Soto to North America in 1539–1543*. 2 vols. University of Alabama Press.

Cobb, Charles R. 1996. Specialization, Exchange, and Power in Small-Scale Societies and Chiefdoms. *Research in Economic Anthropology* 17, pp. 251–94.

Conrad, Lawrence A. 1991. The Middle Mississippian Cultures of the Central Illinois Valley. In *Cahokia and the Hinterlands: Middle Mississippian Cultures of the Midwest*, edited by Thomas E. Emerson and R. Barry Lewis, pp. 119–56. University of Illinois Press.

Cowan, C. Wesley. 1996. Social Implications of Ohio Hopewell Art. In Pacheco 1996, pp. 130–48.

Cowan, Frank L., Ted S. Sunderhaus, and Robert A. Genheimer. 1999. Notes from the Field, 1999: More Hopewell "Houses" at the Stubbs Earthwork Site. *OAC Newletter* 11, no. 2, p. 11.

Cox, Stephen D., ed. 1985. *Art and Artisans of Prehistoric Middle Tennessee*. Tennessee State Museum.

Crosby, Alfred W. 1976. *The Columbian Exchange: Biological and Cultural Consequences of 1492*. Greenwood Press.

Dalan, Rinita. 1993. Landscape Modification at the Cahokia Mounds Site: Geophysical Evidence of Culture Change. Ph.D. diss., University of Minnesota.

Dalton, George. 1977. Aboriginal Economies in Stateless Societies. In *Exchange Systems in Prehistory*, edited by Timothy K. Earle and Jonathan E. Ericson, pp. 191–212. Academic Press.

Dancey, William S., and Paul J. Pacheco, eds. 1997a. *Ohio Hopewell Community Organization*. Kent State University Press.

———. 1997b. A Community Model of Ohio Hopewell settlement. In Dancey and Pacheco 1997a, pp. 3–40.

DeBoer, Warren R. 1991. The Decorative Burden: Design, Medium, and Change. In *Ceramic Ethnoarchaeology*, edited by W. Longacre, pp. 144–61. University of Arizona Press.

———. 1997. Ceremonial Centres from the Cayapas (Esmeraldas, Ecuador) to Chillicothe (Ohio, USA). *Cambridge Archaeological Journal* 7, pp. 225–53.

DeJarnette, David L., and Christopher S. Peebles. 1970. The Development of Alabama Archaeology: The Snow's Bend Site. *Journal of Alabama Archaeology* 16, no. 2, pp. 77–119.

Demel, Scott J., and Robert L. Hall. 1998. The Mississippian Town Plan and Cultural Landscape of Cahokia, Illinois. In *Mississippian Towns and Sacred Spaces*, edited by R. Barry Lewis and Charles Stout, pp. 200–226. University of Alabama Press.

DePratter, C. B., C. M. Hudson, and M. T. Smith. 1985. The Hernando de Soto Expedition: From Chiaha to Mabila. In *Alabama and the Borderlands: From Prehistory to Statehood*, edited by Reid Badger and Lawrence A. Clayton, pp. 108–211. University of Alabama Press.

Diaz-Granados, Carol, and James R. Duncan. 2000. *The Petroglyphs and Pictographs of Missouri*. University of Alabama Press.

Diaz-Granados, Carol, Marvin W. Rowe, Marian Hyman, James R. Duncan, and John R. Southon. 2001. AMS Radiocarbon Dates for Charcoal from Three Missouri Pictographs and Their Associated Iconography. *American Antiquity* 66, no. 3, pp. 481–92.

Dick, George C. 1955. Incised Pottery Decorations from Cahokia. *The Missouri Archaeologist* 17, no. 4, pp. 36–48.

Dobyns, Henry F., and William R. Swagerty. 1983. *Their Number Become Thinned: Native American Population Dynamics in Eastern North America*. University of Tennessee Press in cooperation with the Newberry Library Center for the History of the American Indian.

Dorsey, George A. 1904. Traditions of the Skidi Pawnee. *Memoirs of the American Folk-Lore Society*, vol. 8. Houghton Mifflin.

Dorsey, James O. 1893. The Rising and Falling of the Sky in Souian Mythology. *American Anthropologist* o.s. 6, p. 64.

Dorsey, James O., and Cyrus Thomas. 1907. Iowa. In *Handbook of American Indians North of Mexico*, part I, edited by Frederick W. Hodge, pp. 612–14. Bulletin 30. Bureau of American Ethnology, Smithsonian Institution. Reprinted in 1975 by Rowman and Littlefield.

Dragoo, Don W., and Charles F. Wray. 1964. Hopewell Figurine Rediscovered. *American Antiquity* 30, pp. 195–99.

Duncan, James R., and Carol Diaz-Granados. 2000. Of Masks and Myths. *Midcontinental Journal of Archaeology* 25, no. 1, pp. 1–26.

du Ru, Paul. 1934. *Journal of Paul du Ru, Missionary Priest of Louisiana. February 1 to May 8, 1700*. Translated and annotated by Ruth Lapham Butler. Caxton Club, Chicago. Reprinted in 1997 by Ye Galleon Press.

Dye, David H. 1995. Feasting with the Enemy: Mississippian Warfare and Prestige-Goods Circulation. In Nassaney and Sassaman 1995, pp. 289–316.

———. 1998. An Overview of Walls Engraved Pottery in the Central Mississippi Valley. In *Changing Perspectives on the Archaeology of the Central Mississippi Valley*, edited by Michael J. O'Brien and Robert C. Dunnell, pp. 80–98. University of Alabama Press.

———. 2004. Scalplocks, Forearms, and Severed Heads: War Trophy Behavior in the Midcontinent. Forthcoming in *Biocultural Studies of Warfare*, edited by Maria O. Smith. University of Alabama Press.

———. 2005. Ritual, Medicine, and the War Trophy Theme in Southeastern Iconography. Forthcoming in Reilly and Garber 2005.

Dye, David H., and Cheryl Anne Cox, eds. 1990. *Towns and Temples along the Mississippi*. University of Alabama Press.

Dye, David H., and Camille Wharey. 1989. Exhibition Catalog. In Galloway 1989, pp. 321–382.

Earle, Timothy. 1997. *How Chiefs Come to Power: The Political Economy in Prehistory*. Stanford University Press.

Echo-Hawk, Roger. 2000. Ancient History in the New World: Integrating Oral Traditions and the Archaeological Record in Deep Time. *American Antiquity* 65, pp. 267–90.

Eliade, Mircea. 1959. *The Sacred and the Profane*. Translated by Willard R. Trask. Harcourt, Brace, and Co.

———. 1964. *Shamanism: Archaic Techniques of Ecstasy*. Translated by Willard R. Trask. Princeton University Press.

Emerson, Thomas E. 1982. *Mississippian Stone Images in Illinois*. Illinois Archaeological Survey, Inc., Circular No. 6.

———. 1989. Water, Serpents, and the Underworld: An Exploration into Cahokian Symbolism. In Galloway 1989, pp. 45–92.

———. 1995. Settlement, Symbolism, and Hegemony in the Cahokian Countryside. Ph.D. diss., University of Wisconsin.

———. 1997a. *Cahokia and the Archaeology of Power*. University of Alabama Press.

———. 1997b. Cahokian Elite Ideology and the Mississippian Cosmos. In Pauketat and Emerson 1997, pp. 190–228.

———. 2003. Materializing Cahokian Shamans. In *Southeastern Archaeology* 22, no. 2, pp. 135–54.

Emerson, Thomas E., and Randall E. Hughes. 2000. Figurines, Flint Clay Sourcing, the Ozark Highlands, and Cahokian Acquisition. *American Antiquity* 65, no. 1, pp. 79–101.

Emerson, Thomas E., Randall E. Hughes, Mary R. Hynes, and Sarah U. Wisseman. 2002. Implications of Sourcing Cahokia-Style Flint Clay Figurines in the American Bottom and the Upper Mississippi River Valley. *Midcontinental Journal of Archaeology* 27, pp. 309–38.

———. 2003. The Sourcing and Interpretation of Cahokia-Style Figurines in the Trans-Mississippi South and Southeast. *American Antiquity* 68, pp. 287–313.

Erdoes, Richard, and Alfonso Ortiz, eds. 1984. *American Indian Myths and Legends*. Pantheon Books.

Esarey, Duane, and Lawrence A. Conrad. 1998. The Bold Counselor Phase of the Central Illinois River Valley: Oneota's Middle Mississippi Margin. *The Wisconsin Archeologist* 79, no. 2, pp. 38–61.

Farnham, Thomas J. 1906. *Travels in the Great Western Prairies, the Anahauc and Rocky Mountains and the Oregon Territory* (1843). 2 vols. Arthur A. Clark Co.

Fenton, William N. 1987. *The False Faces of the Iroquois*. University of Oklahoma Press.

Fischer, Fred W. 1974. Early and Middle Woodland Settlement, Subsistence, and Population in the Central Ohio Valley. Ph.D. diss., Washington University, St. Louis.

Fletcher, Alice C., and Francis La Flesche. 1972 [1911]. *The Omaha Tribe*. 2 vols. University of Nebraska Press. Originally published as the Twentieth-seventh Annual Report of the Bureau of American Ethnology, 1905–1906, Smithsonian Institution, 1911.

Foreman, Grant. 1932. *Indian Removal: The Emigration of the Five Civilized Tribes of Indians*. University of Oklahoma Press.

———. 1933. *Advancing the Frontier, 1830–1860*. University of Oklahoma Press.

———. 1936. *Indians and Pioneers: The Story of the American Southwest before 1830*. Rev. ed. University of Oklahoma Press.

———. 1946. *The Last Trek of the Indians*. University of Chicago Press.

Fortier, Andrew C. 2001. *The Dash Reeves Site: A Middle Woodland Village and Lithic Production Center in the American Bottom*. American Bottom Archaeology, FAI-270 Reports, vol. 28. University of Illinois Press.

Fowler, Melvin L. 1989. *The Cahokia Atlas: A Historical Atlas of Cahokia Archaeology*. Illinois Historic Preservation Agency, Studies in Illinois Archaeology, no. 6.

———. 1991. Mound 72 and Early Mississippian at Cahokia. In *New Perspectives on Cahokia: Views from the Periphery*, edited by James B. Stoltman, pp. 1–28. Monographs in World Archaeology, no. 2. Prehistory Press.

———. 1997. *The Cahokia Atlas: A Historical Atlas of Cahokia Archaeology*. Revised edition. Illinois Transportation Archaeological Research Program, University of Illinois.

Fowler, Melvin L., and Robert L. Hall. 1972. *Archaeological Phases at Cahokia*. Illinois State Museum, Research Series, Papers in Anthropology, no. 1.

———. 1975. Archaeological Phases at Cahokia. In *Perspectives in Cahokia Archaeology*, edited by M. Fowler, pp. 1–14. Illinois Archaeological Survey Bulletin No. 10.

Fowler, Melvin L., Jerome Rose, Barbara Vander Leest, and Steven R. Ahler. 1999. *The Mound 72 Area: Dedicated and Sacred Space in Early Cahokia*. Illinois State Museum, Reports of Investigations, no. 54.

Franke, Judith A. 1998. The Birdman and the Insect. *The Living Museum* 60, no. 2, pp. 6–9.

Fundaburk, Emma L. 1969. *Southeastern Indians, Life Portraits: A Catalogue of Pictures, 1564–1860*. Scarecrow Reprint.

Fundaburk, Emma Lila, and Mary Douglass Fundaburk Foreman, eds. 1957. *Sun Circles and Human Hands: The Southeastern Indians—Art and Industry*. Privately printed.

Galloway, Patricia, ed. 1989. *The Southeastern Ceremonial Complex, Artifacts and Analysis: The Cottonlandia Conference*. University of Nebraska Press.

Garland, Elizabeth B., and Scot G. Beld. 1999. The Early Woodland: Ceramics, Domesticated Plants, and Burial Mounds Foretell the Shape of the Future. In *Retrieving Michigan's Buried Past: The Archaeology of the Great Lakes State*, edited by J. Halsey, pp. 125–46. Cranbrook Institute of Science, Bulletin 64.

Gartner, William G. 1996. Archeoastronomy as Sacred Geography. *The Wisconsin Archeologist* 77, pp. 128–50.

Gayton, A. H. 1953. The Orpheus Myth in North America. *Journal of American Folklore* 48, pp. 263–93.

Gibson, Jon L. 2000. *The Ancient Mounds of Poverty Point: Place of Rings*. University Press of Florida.

Gibson, Jon L., and Philip J. Carr. 2004. *Signs of Power: The Rise of Cultural Complexity in the Southeast*. University of Alabama Press.

Gillies, Judith L. 1998. A Preliminary Study of Moundville Hemphill Representational Engraved Ceramic Art Style. Master's thesis, University of Alabama.

Goad, Sharon I. 1978. Exchange Networks in the Prehistoric Southeastern United States. Ph.D. diss., University of Georgia.

———. 1979. Middle Woodland Exchange in the Prehistoric Southeastern United States. In Brose and Greber 1979, pp. 239–46.

Goddard, Ives. 1996. Introduction. In William C. Sturtevant, ed., *Handbook of North American Indians*, vol. 17, *Languages*, edited by Ives Goddard, pp. 1–16. Smithsonian Institution.

Grantham, Larry. 1993. The Illini Village of the Marquette and Jolliet Voyage of 1673. *The Missouri Archaeologist* 54, pp. 1–20.

Greber, N'omi B. 1979a. Variations in Social Structure of Ohio Hopewell Peoples. *Midcontinental Journal of Archaeology* 4, pp. 35–78.

———. 1979b. A Comparative Study of Site Morphology and Burial Patterns at Edwin Harness Mound and Seip Mounds 1 and 2. In Brose and Greber 1979, pp. 27–38.

———. 1983. *Recent Excavations at the Edwin Harness Mound, Liberty Works, Ross County, Ohio*. MCJA Special Paper No. 5. Kent State University Press.

———. 1996. A Commentary on the Contexts and Contents of Large and Small Ohio Hopewell Deposits. In Pacheco 1996, pp. 150–73.

———. 1997. Two Geometric Enclosures in the Paint Creek Valley: An Estimate of Possible Changes in Community Patterns through Time. In Dancey and Pacheco 1997a, pp. 207–29.

Greber, N'omi B., and Katharine C. Ruhl. 1989. *The Hopewell Site: A Contemporary Analysis Based on the Work of Charles C. Willoughby*. Westview Press.

Griffin, James B., ed. 1952a. *Archeology of Eastern United States*. University of Chicago Press.

———. 1952b. Culture Periods in Eastern United States Archeology. In Griffin 1952a, pp. 352–64.

———. 1960. A Hypothesis for the Prehistory of the Winnebago. In *Culture in History: Essays in Honor of Paul Radin*, edited by Stanley Diamond, pp. 809–65. Columbia University Press.

———. 1990. Review of *The Hopewell Site: A Contemporary Analysis Based on the Work of Charles C. Willoughby*. *Ohio History* 99, pp. 180–83.

———. 1995. A Search for Oneota Cultural Origins: A Personal Retrospective Account. In *Oneota Archaeology Past, Present, and Future*, edited by William Green, pp. 9–18. Report 20, Office of the State Archaeologist, University of Iowa.

Grim, John A. 1983. *The Shaman: Patterns of Religious Healing among the Ojibway Indians*. University of Oklahoma Press.

Haas, Jonathan. 1982. *The Evolution of the Prehistoric State*. Columbia University Press.

Hagan, William T. 1988. United States Indian Policies, 1860–1900. In William C. Sturtevant, ed., *Handbook of North American Indians*, vol. 4, *History of Indian-White Relations*, edited by Wilcomb E. Washburn, pp. 51–65. Smithsonian Institution.

Hall, Robert L. 1977. An Anthropocentric Perspective for Eastern United States Prehistory. *American Antiquity* 42, pp. 499–518.

———. 1979. In Search of the Ideology of the Adena-Hopewell Climax. In Brose and Greber 1979, pp. 258–65.

———. 1980. An Interpretation of the Two-Climax Model of Illinois Prehistory. In *Early Native Americans: Prehistoric Demography, Economy, and Technology*, edited by D. Browman, pp. 401–62. Mouton.

———. 1985. Medicine Wheels, Sun Circles, and the Magic of World Center Shrines. *Plains Anthropologist* 30, no. 109, pp. 181–93.

———. 1987. Calumet Ceremonialism, Mourning Ritual, and Mechanisms of Inter-Tribal Trade. In *Mirror and Metaphor: Material and Social Constructions of Reality*, edited by Daniel W. Ingersoll, Jr., and Gordon Bronitsky, pp. 29–43. University Press of America.

———. 1991. Cahokia Identity and Interaction Models of Cahokia Mississippian. In *Cahokia and the Hinterlands: Middle Mississippian Cultures of the Midwest*, edited by Thomas E. Emerson and R. Barry Lewis, pp. 3–34. University of Illinois Press.

———. 1993. Red Banks, Oneota, and the Winnebago: Views from a Distant Rock. *The Wisconsin Archeologist* 74, pp. 10–79.

———. 1997a. *An Archaeology of the Soul: North American Indian Belief and Ritual*. University of Illinois Press.

———. 1997b. Comment on Warren DeBoer's "Ceremonial Centres from the Cayapas (Esmeraldas, Ecuador) to Chillicothe (Ohio, USA)." *Cambridge Archaeological Journal* 7, no. 2, pp. 241–42.

———. 1998. A Comparison of Some North American and Mesoamerican Cosmologies and Their Ritual Expressions. In *Explorations in American Archaeology: Essays in Honor of Wesley R. Hurt*, edited by Mark G. Plew, pp. 55–88. University Press of America.

———. 1999. Sacred Fire Symbolism and World Renewal. Paper presented at the 56th Annual Meeting of the Southeastern Archaeological Conference, Pensacola, Florida.

———. 2000. Sacrificed Foursomes and Green Corn Ceremonialism. In Ahler 2000, pp. 245–53.

———. 2001. Exploring the Mississippian Big Bang at Cahokia. Paper presented at the symposium "A Pre-Columbian World: Searching for a Unitary Vision of Ancient America," Dumbarton Oaks, Washington, D.C.

Hally, David J., and J. B. Langford, Jr. 1988. *Mississippi Period Archaeology of the Georgia Valley and Ridge Province*. University of Georgia, Laboratory of Archaeology Series, Report 25, Department of Anthropology, University of Georgia.

Hally, David J., Marvin T. Smith, and J. B. Langford, Jr. 1990. The Archaeological Reality of De Soto's Chiefdom of Coosa. In *Columbian Consequences*, vol. 2, *Archaeological and Historical Perspectives on the Spanish Borderlands East*, edited by David H. Thomas, pp. 121–38. Smithsonian Institution Press.

Harrod, Howard L. 2000. *The Animals Came Dancing: Native American Sacred Ecology and Animal Kinship*. University of Arizona Press.

Hatch, James W. 1976. Status in Death: Principles of Ranking in Dallas Culture Mortuary Remains. Ph.D. diss., Pennsylvania State University.

Haven, S. F. 1870. Report of the Librarian. *Proceedings of the American Antiquarian Society* 27 (April), pp. 39–41.

Helms, Mary W. 1988. *Ulysses' Sail: An Ethnographic Odyssey of Power, Knowledge, and Geographical Distance*. Princeton University Press.

———. 1994. Chiefdom Rivalries, Control, and External Contacts in Lower Central America. In *Factional Competition and Political Development in the New World*, edited by Elizabeth M. Brumfiel and John W. Fox, pp. 55–60. Cambridge University Press.

Henning, Dale R. 1993. The Adaptive Patterning of the Dhegiha Sioux. *Plains Anthropologist* 38, 146, pp. 253–64.

———. 1998. Oneota: The Western Manifestations. *The Wisconsin Archeologist* 79, no. 2, pp. 238–47.

Hilgeman, Sherri L. 2000. *Pottery and Chronology at Angel*. University of Alabama Press.

Hively, Ray, and Robert Horn. 1982. Geometry and Astronomy in Prehistoric Ohio. *Archaeoastronomy* 4, S1–S20. Supplement to vol. 13, *Journal for the History of Astronomy*.

———. 1984. Hopewellian Geometry and Astronomy at High Bank. *Archaeoastronomy* 7, S85–S100. Supplement to vol. 15, *Journal for the History of Astronomy*.

Hoffman, Michael P. 1993. Identification of Ethnic Groups Contacted by the de Soto Expedition in Arkansas, pp 132–42. In *The Expedition of Hernando de Soto West of the Mississippi, 1541–1543*, edited by Gloria A. Young and Michael P. Hoffman. University of Arkansas Press.

Holley, George R. 1989. *The Archaeology of the Cahokia Mounds ICT-II: Ceramics*. Illinois Historic Preservation Agency.

Hollinger, R. Eric, and David W. Benn. 1998. Oneota Taxonomy: Addressing Considerations of Time, Space and Form. *The Wisconsin Archeologist* 79, no. 2, pp. 1–8.

Holmes, William H. 1883. Art in Shell of the Ancient Americans. In *Second Annual Report of the Bureau of Ethnology, 1880-1881*, Smithsonian Institution, pp. 185–305.

———.1886. Ancient Pottery of the Mississippi Valley. In *Fourth Annual Report of the Bureau of Ethnology, 1882–1883*, Smithsonian Institution, pp. 361–436.

———.1992 [1903]. Aboriginal Pottery of the Eastern United States. In *The Archaeology of William Henry Holmes*, edited by David J. Meltzer and Robert C. Dunnell. Smithsonian Institution Press. Originally published in *Twentieth Annual Report of the Bureau of American Ethnology, 1898–1899*, Smithsonian Institution, 1903, pp. 1–201.

Hooton, Earnest A. 1922. The Skeletal Remains. In *The Turner Group of Earthworks, Hamilton County, Ohio*, edited by C. Willoughby and E. Hooton, pp. 99–132. Papers of the Peabody Museum of American Archaeology and Ethnology, vol. 8, no. 3. Harvard University.

Horsman, Reginald. 1988. United States Indian Policies, 1776–1815. In William C. Sturtevant, ed., *Handbook of North American Indians*, vol. 4, *History of Indian-White Relations*, edited by Wilcomb E. Washburn, pp. 29–39. Smithsonian Institution.

Howard, James H. 1968. *The Southeastern Ceremonial Complex and Its Interpretation*. Memoir of the Missouri Archaeological Society, no. 6.

———. 1981. *Shawnee! The Ceremonialism of a Native Indian Tribe and Its Cultural Background*. Ohio University Press.

Hudson, Charles. 1976. *The Southeastern Indians*. University of Tennessee Press.

———. 1997. *Knights of Spain, Warriors of the Sun: Hernando de Soto and the South's Ancient Chiefdoms*. University of Georgia Press.

Hultkrantz, Ake. 1953. *Conceptions of the Soul among North American Indians*. Ethnographical Museum of Sweden, Stockholm.

———. 1957. *The North American Indian Orpheus Tradition: A Contribution to Comparative Religion*. Ethnographical Museum of Sweden, Stockholm.

———. 1967. *The Religions of the American Indians*. Translated by Monica Setterwall. University of California Press.

Hulton, Paul H. 1977. *The Works of Jacques le Moyne de Morgues: A French Huguenot Artist in France, Florida, and England*. 2 vols. British Museum Publications.

Hurst, Vernon J., and Lewis H. Larson, Jr. 1958. On the Source of Copper at the Etowah Site, Georgia. *American Antiquity* 24, no. 2, pp. 177–81.

Jackson, Douglas K. 1998. Settlement on the Southern Frontier: Oneota Occupations in the American Bottom. *The Wisconsin Archeologist* 79, no. 2, pp. 93–116.

Jackson, Douglas K., Andrew C. Fortier, and Joyce A. Williams. 1992. *The Sponemann Site 2: The Mississippian and Oneota Occupations*. American Bottom Archaeology FAI-270 Site Reports. University of Illinois Press.

Jackson, John B. 1972. *American Space: The Centennial Years, 1865–1876*. W. W. Norton.

Jefferies, Richard W. 1976. *The Tunacunnhee Site: Evidence of Hopewell Interaction in Northwest Georgia*. Anthropological Papers, no. 1. University of Georgia.

Jenkins, Ned. J. 1982. *Archaeology of the Gainesville Lake Area: Synthesis*. Archaeological Investigations in the Gainesville Lake Area of the Tennessee-Tombigbee Waterway, vol. 5. Report of Investigations 23. Office of Archaeological Research, University of Alabama.

Jenkins, Ned J., and Richard A. Krause. 1986. *The Tombigbee Watershed in Southeastern Prehistory*. University of Alabama Press.

Jennings, Francis. 1993. *The Founders of America: From the Earliest Migrations to the Present*. W. W. Norton.

Johnson, Hunter B., and Jeff L. Sherard. 2000. Domestic Sandstone Artifact Production. In *Archaeology at Pride Place (1Tu1): Its Position in the Moundville Chiefdom*, edited by Hunter B. Johnson. Manuscript on file, Office of Archaeological Research, University of Alabama.

Jones, B. Calvin. 1982. Southern Cult Manifestations at the Lake Jackson Site, Leon County, Florida: Salvage Excavation of Mound 3. *Midcontinental Journal of Archaeology* 7, pp. 3–44.

Keegan, John. 1996. *Fields of Battle: The Wars for North America*. Alfred A. Knopf.

Kelly, A. R., and L. H. Larson. 1957. Explorations at the Etowah Indian Mounds near Cartersville, Georgia: Seasons 1954, 1955, 1956. *Archaeology* 10, no. 1, pp. 39–48.

Kelly, John E. 1990a. Range Site Community Patterns and the Mississippian Emergence. In *The Mississippian Emergence*, edited by Bruce D. Smith, pp. 67–112. Smithsonian Institution Press.

———. 1990b. The Emergence of Mississippian Culture in the American Bottom Region. In *The Mississippian Emergence*, edited by Bruce D. Smith, pp. 113–52. Smithsonian Institution Press.

———. 1996 Redefining Cahokia: Principles and Elements of Community Organization. *The Wisconsin Archeologist* 77, pp. 97–119.

———. 1997. Stirling-Phase Sociopolitical Activity at East St. Louis and Cahokia. In Pauketat and Emerson 1997, pp. 141–66.

———. 2002. The Pulcher Tradition and the Ritualization of Cahokia: A Perspective from Cahokia's Southern Neighbor. *Southeastern Archaeology* 21, pp. 136–48.

Kelly, John E., James A. Brown, and Jenna M. Hamlin. n.d. Mound 34 Revisited: Early Evidence of the Southeastern Ceremonial Complex at Cahokia. Unpublished manuscript.

Kenyon, W. A. 1982. *The Grimsby Site: A Historic Neutral Cemetery*. Royal Ontario Museum.

King, Adam. 1991. Excavations at Mound B, Etowah: 1954–1958. Master's thesis, University of Georgia.

———. 1995. *Steps to the Past: 1994 Archaeological Excavations at Mounds A and B the Etowah Site (9Br1), Bartow County, Georgia*. The Georgia Department of Natural Resources, Atlanta.

———. 1996. Tracing Organizational Change in Mississippian Chiefdoms of the Etowah River Valley, Georgia. Ph.D. diss., Pennsylvania State University.

———. 1999. DeSoto's Itaba and the Nature of Sixteenth Century Paramount Chiefdoms. *Southeastern Archaeology* 18, no. 2, pp. 110–23

———. 2001. *Excavations at Mound B, Etowah: 1954–1958*. University of Georgia, Laboratory of Archaeology Series, Department of Anthropology, Report 37.

———. 2003a. *Etowah: The Political History of a Chiefdom Capital*. University of Alabama Press.

———. 2003b. Over a Century of Explorations at Etowah. *Journal of Archaeological Research* 11, no. 4, pp. 279–306.

Kinnaird, Lawrence, ed. 1949. *Spain in the Mississippi Valley, 1765–1794*. 3 vols. Annual Report for the American Historical Association for 1945.

Kirchoff, Paul. 1952. Meso-American. In *Heritage of Conquest: The Ethnology of Middle America*, edited by Sol Tax, pp. 17–30. Free Press.

Knapp, A. Bernard, and Wendy Ashmore. 1999. Archaeological Landscapes: Constructed, Conceptualized, Ideational. In *Archaeologies of Landscape*, edited by W. Ashmore and A. B. Knapp, pp. 1–30. Blackwell Publishers.

Knight, Vernon James, Jr. 1986. The Institutional Organization of Mississippian Religion. *American Antiquity* 51, pp. 675–87.

———. 1989. Some Speculations on Mississippian Monsters. In Galloway 1989, pp. 205–210.

———. 1992. Evidence for the Dating of Mounds A, B, P, R, and S, Moundville. Paper presented at the 51st Annual Meeting of the Southeastern Archaeological Conference, Lexington, Kentucky.

———. 1995. Chronology and Use of Public Architecture at the Moundville Site: Excavations in Mounds R, F, G, and E. Unpublished report submitted to the National Science Foundation in fulfillment of award number 9220568.

———. 1997. Some Developmental Parallels between Cahokia and Moundville. In Pauketat and Emerson 1997, pp. 229–47.

———. 1998. Moundville as a Diagrammatic Ceremonial Center. In Knight and Steponaitis 1998b, pp. 44–62.

———. 2001. Feasting and the Emergence of Platform Mound Ceremonialism in Eastern North America. In *Feasts: Archaeological and Ethnographic Perspectives on Food, Politics, and Power*, edited by M. Dietler and B. Hayden, pp. 311–33. Smithsonian Institution Press.

———. 2002. Chronology and Use of Public Architecture at the Moundville Site: Excavations in Mound Q. Unpublished report submitted to the National Science Foundation in fulfillment of award numbers 9220568 and 9727709.

Knight, Vernon James, Jr., ed. 1996. *The Moundville Expeditions of Clarence Bloomfield Moore*. University of Alabama Press.

Knight, Vernon James, Jr., James A. Brown, and George E. Lankford. 2001. On the Subject Matter of Southeastern Ceremonial Complex Art. *Southeastern Archaeology* 20, no. 2, pp. 129–41.

Knight, Vernon J., Jr., and Judith A. Franke. 2005. Identification of a Moth/Butterfly Supernatural in Mississippian Art. Forthcoming in Reilly and Garber 2005.

Knight, Vernon J., Jr., Lyle W. Konigsberg, and Susan R. Frankenberg. 1999. A Gibbs Sampler Approach to the Dating of Phases in the Moundville Sequence. Unpublished manuscript.

Knight, Vernon J., Jr., and Vincas P. Steponaitis. 1998a. A New History of Moundville. In Knight and Steponaitis 1998b, pp. 1–25.

———, eds. 1998b. *Archaeology of the Moundville Chiefdom*. Smithsonian Institution Press.

Knowles, Nathaniel. 1940. The Torture of Captives by the Indians of Eastern North America. *Proceedings of the American Philosophical Society* 82, pp. 151–225.

Koningsberg, Lyle W. 1985. Demography and Mortuary Practice at Seip Mound One. *Midcontinental Journal of Archaeology* 10, pp. 123–48.

Krebs, W. Phillip, Polly Futato, Eugene M. Futato, and Vernon J. Knight, Jr. 1986. *Ten Thousand Years of Alabama Prehistory*. Bulletin 8. Alabama State Museum of Natural History.

Krieger, Alex D. 1945. An Inquiry into Supposed Mexican Influence on a Prehistoric "Cult" in the Southern United States. *American Anthropologist* 47, pp. 483–515.

Kroeber, A. L. 1939. *Cultural and Natural Areas of Native North America*. University of California Publications in American Archaeology and Ethnology, vol. 38. University of California Press.

Kubler, George. 1962. *The Shape of Time: Remarks on the History of Things*. Yale University Press.

Lacefield, Hyla L. 1995. *A Preliminary Study of Moundville Engraved Pottery*. Master's thesis, University of Alabama.

La Flesche, Francis. 1930. *The Osage Tribe: Rite of the Wa-xo'-be*. In Forty-fifth Annual Report of the Bureau of American Ethnology, 1927–1928, Smithsonian Institution, pp. 529–833.

———. 1932. *A Dictionary of the Osage Language*. Bulletin 109. Bureau of American Ethnology, Smithsonian Institution.

———. 1939. *War Ceremony and Peace Ceremony of the Osage Indians*. Bulletin 101. Bureau of American Ethnology, Smithsonian Institution.

Lankford, George E. 1987. *Native American Legends*. August House.

———. 1993. Red and White: Some Reflections on Southeastern Symbolism. *Southern Folklore* 50, pp. 54–80.

———. 2000. The Raptor on the Path. Paper presented at the 57th Annual Meeting of the Southeastern Archaeological Conference, Macon, Georgia.

———. 2002. The Swastika and the Center. Paper presented at the 59th Annual Meeting of the Southeastern Archaeological Conference, Biloxi, Mississippi.

———. 2005a. Some Cosmological Motifs in the Southeastern Ceremonial Complex. Forthcoming in Reilly and Garber 2005.

———. 2005b. The Great Serpent in Eastern North America. Forthcoming in Reilly and Garber 2005.

———. 2005c. The "Path of Souls": Some Death Imagery in the Southeastern Ceremonial Complex. Forthcoming in Reilly and Garber 2005.

Larson, Lewis H., Jr. 1957. An Unusual Wooden Rattle from the Etowah Site. *Missouri Archaeologist* 19, no. 4, pp. 6–11.

———. 1971. Archaeological Implications of Social Stratification at the Etowah Site, Georgia. In *Approaches to the Social Dimensions of Mortuary Practices*, edited by James A. Brown, pp. 58–67. Society for American Archaeology, Memoir 25.

———. 1972. Functional Considerations of Warfare in the Southeast during the Mississippi Period. *American Antiquity* 37, pp. 383–92.

———. 1989. The Etowah Site. In Galloway 1989, pp. 133–41.

Le Page du Pratz, Antoine S. 1972. *The History of Louisiana*. Baton Rouge: Claitor's Publishing Division. Reprint of the London edition of 1774, a translation of *Histoire de la Louisiane*, published in Paris in 1758.

Lapham, I. A. 1855. *The Antiquities of Wisconsin*. Smithsonian Institution Press.

Lepper, Bradley T. 1995. Tracking Ohio's Great Hopewell Road. *Archaeology* 48, no. 6, pp. 52–56.

———. 1996. The Newark Earthworks and the Geometric Enclosures of the Scioto Valley. In Pacheco 1996, pp. 225–41.

———. 1998a. The Archaeology of the Newark Earthworks. In *Ancient Enclosures of the Eastern Woodlands*, edited by L. Sullivan and R. Mainfort, pp. 114–34. University Press of Florida.

———. 1998b. Ancient Astronomers of the Ohio Valley. *Timeline* 15, no. 1, pp. 2–11.

———. 1999. *People of the Mounds: Ohio's Hopewell Culture*. Guidebook on the Hopewell culture prepared for Hopewell Culture National Historical Park, National Park Service, revised and reprinted.

Lepper, Bradley T., and J. B. Gill. 2000. The Newark Holy Stones. *Timeline* 17, no. 3, pp. 16–25.

Lepper, Bradley T., and R. W. Yerkes. 1997. Hopewellian Occupations at the Northern Periphery of the Newark Earthworks: The Newark Expressway Sites Revisited. In Dancey and Pacheco 1997a, pp. 175–205.

Leuthold, Steven. 1998. *Indigenous Aesthetics: Native Art, Media, and Identity*. University of Texas Press.

Lindauer, Owen, and John H. Blitz. 1997. Higher Ground: The Archaeology of North American Platform Mounds. *Journal of Archaeological Research* 5, no. 2, pp. 169–207.

Link, Adolph W. 1975. A Bird Motif on a Mississippian Pot. *The Minnesota Archaeologist* 34, no. 3–4, pp. 71–83.

Linton, Ralph. 1923. *Annual Ceremony of the Pawnee Medicine Men*. Field Museum of Natural History, Chicago.

Lorant, Stefan. 1965. *The New World: The First Pictures of America*. Duell, Sloan and Pearce.

Lutz, David L. 2000. *The Archaic Bannerstone: Its Chronological History and Purpose from 6000 B.C. to 1000 B.C.* Newburgh, Indiana: D. L. Lutz.

Mahon, John K. 1988. Indian-United States Military Situation, 1775–1848. In William C. Sturtevant, ed., *Handbook of North American Indians*, vol. 4, *History of Indian-White Relations*, edited by Wilcomb E. Washburn, pp. 144–62. Smithsonian Institution.

Marcoux, Jon Bernard. 2000. Display Goods Production and Circulation in the Moundville Chiefdom: A Mississippian Dilemma. Master's thesis, University of Alabama.

Markin, Julie G. 1997. Elite Stoneworking and the Function of Mounds at Moundville. *Mississippi Archaeology* 32, no. 2, pp. 117–35.

Marshall, James A. 1996. Towards a Definition of the Ohio Hopewell Core and Periphery Utilizing the Geometric Earthworks. In Pacheco 1996, pp. 210–20.

Mason, O. T. 1882. Stone Image Found in Ohio. *American Naturalist* 16, no. 2, p. 154.

Mathews, John Joseph. 1961. *The Osages: Children of the Middle Waters*. University of Oklahoma Press.

McGhee-Snow, Katherine. 1999. Preliminary Results of the Analysis of the Copper Assemblage Recovered from Moundville. Paper presented at the 56th Annual Meeting of the Southeastern Archaeological Conference, Pensacola, Florida.

McKern, Will C. 1939. The Midwest Taxonomic Method as an Aid to Archaeological Study. *American Antiquity* 4, pp. 301–13.

McNutt, Charles H., ed. 1996. *Prehistory of the Central Mississippi Valley*. University of Alabama Press.

Mehrer, Mark W. 1995. *Cahokia's Countryside: Household Archaeology, Settlement Patterns, and Social Power*. Northern Illinois University Press.

Mellown, Robert O. 1976. *The Art of the Alabama Indians*. The University of Alabama Art Gallery.

Messinger, John. 1808. Field Notes for South Edge of Town 9 North, Range 3 West, of the Third Principal Meridian, dated Saturday, January 9th. In *Illinois Land Records, Original Field Notes* 12, 76. Illinois State Archives.

Milanich, Jerald T., and Charles H. Fairbanks. 1980. *Florida Archaeology*. Academic Press.

Milanich, Jerald T., and Susan Milbrath. 1989. *First Encounters: Spanish Explorations in the Caribbean and the United States, 1492–1570*. University of Florida Press.

Mills, Lawrence. 1968. Mississippian Head Vases of Arkansas and Missouri. *The Missouri Archaeologist* 30, pp. 1–83.

Mills, William C. 1902. Excavation of the Adena Mound. *Ohio Archaeological and Historical Quarterly* 10, pp. 452–79.

———. 1906. Baum Prehistoric Village. *Ohio Archaeological and Historical Quarterly* 15, pp. 45–136.

———. 1916. Explorations of the Tremper Mound. *Ohio Archaeological and Historical Quarterly* 25, pp. 262–398.

———. 1922. Exploration of the Mound City Group. *Ohio Archaeological and Historical Quarterly* 31, pp. 423–584.

Milner, George R. 1991. American Bottom Mississippian Culture: Internal Developments and External Relationships. In *New Perspectives on Cahokia: Views from the Periphery*, edited by James B. Stoltman, pp. 29–47. Prehistory Press.

———. 1998. *The Cahokia Chiefdom: The Archaeology of a Mississippian Society*. Smithsonian Institution Press.

———. 1999. Warfare in Prehistoric and Early Historic Eastern North America. *Journal of Archaeological Research* 7, no. 2, pp. 105–51.

Mistovich, Tim S. 1986. *Excavations at Sites 1Tu265 and 1 Tu423, Oliver Lock and Dam, Tuscaloosa, Alabama*. Report of Investigations 51. Office of Archaeological Research, University of Alabama.

Mooney, James. 1900. Myths of the Cherokee. In *Nineteenth Annual Report of the Bureau of American Ethnology, 1897–1898*, Smithsonian Institution, part 1, pp. 3–548.

Moore, Clarence B. 1894. Certain Sand Mounds of the St. John's River, Florida, Part I. *Journal of the Academy of Natural Sciences of Philadelphia* 10, no. 1.

———. 1905. Certain Aboriginal Remains of the Black Warrior River. *Journal of the Academy of Natural Sciences of Philadelphia* 13, pp. 125–244.

———. 1907. Moundville Revisited. *Journal of the Academy of Natural Sciences of Philadelphia* 13, pp. 337–405.

———. 1909. Antiquities of the Ouachita Valley. *Journal of the Academy of Natural Sciences of Philadelphia* 14, pp. 1–170.

Moorehead, Warren King. 1911. *The Stone Age in North America*. 2 vols. Houghton Mifflin.

———. 1922. *The Hopewell Mound Group of Ohio*. Field Museum of Natural History Anthropological Series 6, no. 5, pp. 73–184.

———. ed. 1932a. *Etowah Papers*. Yale University Press, for the Phillips Academy, Andover. Reprinted as *Exploration of the Etowah site in Georgia: The Etowah Papers* in 2000 by University Press of Florida.

———. 1932b. Description of Excavations, Mound C, First Season. In Moorehead 1932a, pp. 68–87.

Morgan, William N. 1980. *Prehistoric Architecture in the Eastern United States*. MIT Press.

Morse, Dan F., and Phyllis Morse. 1983. *The Archaeology of the Central Mississippi Valley*. Academic Press.

Muller, Jon. 1966. Archaeological Analysis of Art Styles. *Tennessee Archaeologist* 22, no. 1, pp. 25–39.

———. 1979. Structural Studies of Art Styles. In *The Visual Arts: Plastic and Graphic*, edited by Justine Cordwell, pp. 139–211. Mouton.

———. 1987. Salt, Chert, and Shell: Mississippian Exchange and Economy. In *Specialization, Exchange and Complex Societies*, edited by Elizabeth Brumfiel and Timothy Earle, pp. 10–21. Cambridge University Press.

———. 1989. The Southern Cult. In Galloway 1989, pp. 11–26.

———. 1995. Regional Interaction in the Later Southeast. In Nassaney and Sassaman 1995, pp. 317–40.

———. 1997. Review of Brain and Phillips: Shell Gorgets: Styles of the Late Prehistoric and Protohistoric Southeast. *Southeastern Archaeology* 16, pp. 176–78.

———. 1999. Southeastern Interaction and Integration. In *Great Towns and Regional Polities in the Prehistoric American Southwest and Southeast*, edited by Jill E. Neitzel, pp. 143–58. University of New Mexico Press.

Myer, William E. 1922. Recent Archaeological Discoveries in Tennessee. *Art and Archaeology* 14, no.3, pp. 141–50.

Nasatir, A. P., ed. 1952. *Before Lewis and Clark: Documents Illustrating the History of the Missouri, 1785–1804*. 2 vols. St. Louis Historical Documents Foundation.

Nassaney, Michael S., and Charles R. Cobb. 1991. Patterns and Processes of Late Woodland Development in the Greater Southeastern United States. In *Stability, Transformation and Variation: The Late Woodland Southeast*, edited by M. S. Nassaney and C. R. Cobb, pp. 285–322. Plenum Press.

Nassaney, Michael S., and Kenneth E. Sassaman, eds. 1995. *Native American Interactions: Multiscalar Analyses and Interpretations in the Eastern Woodlands*. University of Tennessee Press.

Neff, Hector, Michael D. Glascock, Katherine Stryker, Vincas P. Steponaitis, and Paul D. Welch. 1991. Chemical Characterization of Moundville Pottery. Manuscript on file, Research Reactor Center, University of Missouri.

Nieberding, Velma. 1964. Shawnee Indian Festival: The Bread Dance. *Chronicles of Oklahoma* 42, p. 3.

O'Brien, Michael J. and Robert C. Dunnell, eds. 1998. *Changing Perspectives on the Archaeology of the Central Mississippi Valley*. University of Alabama Press.

Ortiz, Alfonso. 1969. *The Tewa World*. University of Chicago Press.

Oswalt, Wendell H. 2002. *This Land Was Theirs: A Study of Native Americans*. 7th edition. McGraw-Hill/Mayfield.

Pacheco, Paul J., ed. 1996. *A View from the Core: A Synthesis of Ohio Hopewell Archeology*. Ohio Archaeological Council.

Pauketat, Timothy R. 1996. The Place of Post-Circle Monuments in Cahokian Political History. *The Wisconsin Archeologist* 77, pp. 73–83.

———. 1998a. *The Archaeology of Downtown Cahokia: The Tract 15a and Dunham Tract Excavations*. Studies in Archaeology No. 1, Illinois Transportation Archaeological Research Program, University of Illinois.

———. 1998b. Refiguring the Archaeology of Greater Cahokia. *Journal of Archaeological Research* 6, no. 1, pp. 45–89.

Pauketat, Timothy R., and Thomas E. Emerson. 1991. The Ideology of Authority and the Power of the Pot. *American Anthropologist* 93, pp. 919–41.

———, eds. 1997. *Cahokia: Domination and Ideology in the Mississippian World*. University of Nebraska Press.

Pauketat, Timothy R., Lucretia S. Kelly, Gayle J. Fritz, Neal H. Lopinot, Scott Elias, and Eve Hargrave. 2002. The Residues of Feasting and Public Ritual at Early Cahokia. *American Antiquity* 67, no. 2, pp. 257–79.

Paz, Octavio. 1990. *In Search of the Present: Nobel Lecture, 1990*. Translated by Anthony Stanton. Harcourt, Brace, Jovanovich.

Peebles, Christopher S. 1987. Moundville from 1000 to 1500 A.D. as Seen from 1840 to 1985 A.D. In *Chiefdoms in the Americas*, edited by Robert D. Drennan and Carlos A. Uribe, pp. 21–41. University Press of America.

Peebles, Christopher S., and Susan Kus. 1977. Some Archaeological Correlates of Ranked Societies. *American Antiquity* 42, pp. 421–48.

Peebles, Christopher S., Margaret J. Schoeninger, Vincas P. Steponaitis, and C. Margaret Scarry. 1981. A Precious Bequest: Contemporary Research with the WPA-CCC Collections from Moundville, Alabama. In *The Research Potential of Anthropological Museum Collections*, edited by Anne-Marie Cantwell, James B. Griffin, and Nan A. Rothschild, pp. 433–47. New York Academy of Sciences.

Penney, David W. 1980. The Adena Engraved Tablets: A Study of Art Prehistory. *Midcontinental Journal of Archaeology* 5, no. 3, pp. 3–38.

———. 1985. Continuities of Imagery and Symbolism in the Art of the Woodlands. In Brose, Brown, and Penney 1985, pp. 147–98.

———. 1988. Hopewell Art. Ph.D. diss., Columbia University.

Perryman, Margaret. 1966. Stone Effigy Figures from Georgia. *Tennessee Archaeologist* 22, pp. 40–42.

Perttula, Timothy K. 1992. *The Caddo Nation: Archaeological and Ethnohistoric Perspectives*. University of Texas Press.

Perttula, Timothy K., Marlin F. Hawley, and Fred W. Scott. 2001. Caddo Trade Ceramics. *Southeastern Archaeology* 20, no. 2, pp. 154–73.

Phillips, Philip, and James A. Brown. 1978. *Pre-Columbian Shell Engravings from the Craig Mound at Spiro, Oklahoma*. Part 1. Peabody Museum Press.

———. 1984. *Pre-Columbian Shell Engravings from the Craig Mound at Spiro, Oklahoma*. Part 2. Peabody Museum Press.

Polhemus, Richard R. 1987. *The Toqua Site-40Mr6-A Late Mississippian, Dallas Phase Town*. University of Tennessee, Department of Anthropology, Report of Investigations, no. 41.

Powell, Mary Lucas. 1992. In the Best Health? Disease and Trauma among the Mississippian Elite. In *Lords of the Southeast: Social Inequality and the Native Elites of Southeastern North America*, edited by A. Barker and T. Pauketat, pp. 81–97. American Anthropological Association, Archeological papers, no. 3.

Prentice, Guy. 1986. An Analysis of the Symbolism Expressed by the Birger Figurine. *American Antiquity* 5, no. 12, pp. 239–66.

Prucha, Francis Paul. 1988. United States Indian Policies, 1815–1860. In William C. Sturtevant, ed., *Handbook of North American Indians*, vol. 4, *History of Indian-White Relations*, edited by Wilcomb E. Washburn, pp. 40–50. Smithsonian Institution.

Prufer, Olaf H. 1964. The Hopewell Complex of Ohio. In *Hopewellian Studies*, edited by Joseph R. Caldwell and Robert L. Hall, pp. 35–83. Illinois State Museum, Scientific Papers, vol. 12.

Ponziglione, Paul M., S. J. 1897. The Osages and Father John Schoenmakers, S.J. *Interesting Memoirs Collected from Legends, Traditions and Historical Documents*. Manuscript on file, Midwest Jesuit Archives, St. Louis, Missouri.

Radin, Paul. 1948. Winnebago Hero Cycles: A Study in Aboriginal Literature. *Indiana University Studies in Anthropology and Linguistics*, Supplements to the *International Journal of American Linguistics* 14, no. 3.

Rapp, George, James Allert, Vanda Vitali, Zhichun Jing, and Eiler Henrickson. 2000. *Determining Geologic Sources of Artifact Copper: Source Characterization Using Trace Element Patterns*. University Press of America.

Redmond, Charles L. 1978. *The Rise of Civilization*. W. H. Freeman Company.

Redmond, Elsa M. 1994. *Tribal and Chiefly Warfare in South America*. Museum of Anthropology, University of Michigan.

Reed, Nelson, John W. Bennett, and James W. Porter. 1968. Solid Core Drilling of Monks Mound: Technique and Findings. *American Antiquity* 33, no. 2, pp. 137–48.

Reilly, F. Kent, III. 1995. Art, Ritual, and Rulership in the Olmec World. In *The Olmec World: Ritual and Rulership*, edited by Jill Guthrie, pp. 27–46. Princeton University Art Museum and Harry N. Abrams.

———. 1999. A Proposed Function for the Bi-Lobed Arrow Motif. Paper presented in Iconography and Mississippian Archaeology: The Function of Symbols within the Southeastern Ceremonial Complex, Plenary Symposium, 60th Annual Meeting of the Southeastern Archaeological Conference, Pensacola, Florida.

———. 2000.The Striped Pole Motif and the Ritual Construction of Cosmic Order in the Southeastern Ceremonial Complex. Paper presented in Recovering Meaning from the Symbols and Imagery of the Southeastern Ceremonial Complex, 57th Annual Meeting of the Southeastern Archaeological Conference, Macon, Georgia.

———. 2002. The Symbolic Function of Locatives within the Motif Sets of Walls Engraved Pottery. Paper presented at the 59th Annual Meeting of the Southeastern Archaeological Conference, Biloxi, Mississippi.

———. 2005a. Craig Style Gorgets. Forthcoming in *Chronology, Iconography, and Style: Current Perspectives on the Social and Temporal Contexts of the Southeastern Ceremonial Complex*, edited by Adam King. University of Alabama Press.

———. 2005b. The Petaloid Motif: A Celestial Location in the Shell Art of Spiro. Forthcoming in Reilly and Garber 2005.

Reilly, F. Kent, III, and James F. Garber, eds. 2005. *Studies in Mississippian Iconography*, vol. 1. University of Texas Press.

Reyna, Stephen P. 1994. A Mode of Domination Approach to Organized Violence. In *Studying War: Anthropological Perspectives*, edited by S. P. Reyna and R. E. Downs, pp. 29–65. Gordon and Breach.

Ridington, Robin, and Dennis Hastings. 1997. *Blessing for a Long Time: The Sacred Pole of the Omaha Tribe*. University of Nebraska Press.

Ritchie, William A. 1965. *The Archaeology of New York State*. Natural History Press.

Romain, William F. 2000. *Mysteries of the Hopewell: Astronomers, Geometers, and Magicians of the Eastern Woodlands*. University of Akron Press.

Ruby, Bret J. 1997. The Mann Phase: Hopewellian Community Organization in the Wabash Lowlands. Paper presented at the 62nd Annual Meeting of the Society for American Archaeology, Nashville.

Rucker, Marc D. 1974. *Archaeological Survey and Test Excavations in the Upper-Central Tombigbee River Valley: Aliceville-Columbus Lock and Dam and Impoundment Areas, Alabama and Mississippi*. Report to the U.S. Department of the Interior, National Park Service, submitted by the Department of Anthropology, Mississippi State University.

Ruhl, Katherine C., and Mark F. Seeman. 1998. The Temporal and Social Implications of Ohio Hopewell Copper Ear Spool Design. *American Antiquity* 63, pp. 651–62.

Salisbury, James H., and Charles B. Salisbury. 1862. Accurate Surveys and Descriptions of the Ancient Earthworks at Newark, Ohio. Manuscript on file, American Antiquarian Society, Worcester, Massachusetts.

Saunders, Joe W., and Thurman Allen. 1994. Hedgepeth Mounds, an Archaic Mound Complex in North-Central Louisiana. *American Antiquity* 59, pp. 471–89.

Scarre, Chris. 1999. *Seventy Wonders of the Ancient World*. Thames and Hudson.

Scarry, C. Margaret. 1995. *Excavations on the Northwest Riverbank at Moundville: Investigations of a Moundville I Residential Area*. Report of Investigations 72. Office of Archaeological Services, University of Alabama.

Schambach, F. F. 1990. The Place of Spiro in Southeastern Prehistory: Is It Caddoan or Mississippian. *Southeastern Archaeology* 9, no. 1, pp. 67–69.

———. 1997 The Development of the Burial Mound Tradition in the Caddo Area. *Journal of Northeast Texas Archaeology* 9, pp. 53–72.

Schatte, Kevin E. 1997. Stylistic Analysis of the Winged Serpent Theme at Moundville. Master's thesis, University of Alabama.

———. 1997. Moundville's Winged Serpents: An Analysis of Style. Paper presented at the 54th Annual Meeting of the Southeastern Archaeological Conference, Baton Rouge, Louisiana.

Schele, Linda, and Mary Ellen Miller. 1986. *The Blood of Kings: Dynasty and Ritual in Maya Art*. Kimbell Art Museum.

Schnell, Frank T., Vernon J. Knight, Jr., and Gail S. Schnell. 1981. *Cemochechobee: Archaeology of a Mississippian Ceremonial Center on the Chattahoochee River*. University Presses of Florida.

Schroedl, G. F., and C. C. Boyd, Jr. 1991. Late Woodland Period Culture in East Tennessee. In *Stability, Transformation, and Variation: The Late Woodland Southeast*, edited by M. S. Nassaney and C. R. Cobb, pp. 69–90. Plenum Press.

Schutz, Noel Williams. 1975. The Study of Shawnee Myth in an Ethnographic and Ethnohistorical Perspective. Ph.D. diss., Indiana University.

Swartz, B. K., ed. 1971. *Adena: The Seeking of an Identity*. Ball State University.

Sears, W. H. 1958. *Excavations at Etowah*. Manuscript on file, Department of Anthropology, University of Georgia.

Seeman, Mark F. 1979. *The Hopewell Interaction Sphere: The Evidence for Interregional Trade and Structural Complexity*, Indiana Historical Society Prehistory Research Series 5, no. 2.

———. 1992. Woodland Traditions in the Midcontinent: A Comparison of Three Regional Sequences. In *Long-Term Subsistence Change in Prehistoric North America*, edited by Dale R. Croes, Rebecca Hawkins, and Barry L. Isaac, pp. 3–46. JAI Press.

———. 1995. When Words Are Not Enough: Hopewell Interregionalism and the Use of Material Symbols at the GE Mound. In Nassaney and Sassaman 1995, pp. 122–43.

Seeman, Mark F., and James L. Branch. 2000. The Mounded Landscapes of Ohio: Hopewell Patterns and Placements. Paper presented at the Hopewell at the Millennium Conference, Alton, Illinois.

Shetrone, Henry C. 1926. Explorations of the Hopewell Group of Prehistoric Earthworks. *Ohio Archaeological and Historical Publications* 35, pp. 1–227.

Smith, Bruce D. 1984. Mississippian Expansion: Tracing the Historical Development of an Explanatory Model. *Southeastern Archaeology* 3, no. 1, pp. 13–32.

———. 1992. *Rivers of Change: Essays on Early Agriculture in Eastern North America*. Smithsonian Institution Press.

Smith, Marvin T. 1987. *Archaeology of Aboriginal Culture Change in the Interior Southeast: Depopulation during the Early Historic Period*. University Press of Florida.

———. 1989. Aboriginal Population Movements in the Early Historic Period Interior Southeast. In *Powhatan's Mantle: Indians of the Colonial Southeast*, edited by P. H. Wood, G. A. Waselkov, and M. T. Hatley, pp. 135–49. University of Nebraska Press.

———. 2000. *Coosa: The Rise and Fall of a Southeastern Mississippian Chiefdom*. University Press of Florida.

Smith, Marvin T., and Julie Barnes Smith. 1989. Engraved Shell Masks in North America. *Southeastern Archaeology* 8, pp. 9–18.

Smith, Theresa S. 1995. *The Island of the Anishnaabeg: Thunderers and Water Monsters in the Traditional Ojibwe Life-World*. University of Idaho Press.

Smucker, I. 1881. The Mound-builders' Works near Newark, Ohio. *American Antiquarian* 3, no. 4, pp. 261–70.

Southerlin, B. G. 1993. Mississippian Settlement Patterns in the Etowah River Valley Near Cartersville, Bartow County, Georgia. Master's thesis, University of Georgia.

Springer, James W., and Stanley R. Witkowski. 1982. Siouan Historical Linguistics and Oneota Archaeology. In *Oneota Studies*, edited by Guy E. Gibbon, pp. 69–83. University of Minnesota, Department of Anthropology.

Squier, Ephraim G., and Edwin H. Davis. 1848. *Ancient Monuments of the Mississippi Valley*. Smithsonian Institution, Smithsonian Contributions to Knowledge, vol. 1.

Steponaitis, Vincas P. 1983a. *Ceramics, Chronology, and Community Patterns: An Archaeological Study at Moundville*. Academic Press.

———. 1983b. The Smithsonian Institution's Investigations at Moundville in 1869 and 1882. *Midcontinental Journal of Archaeology* 8, no. 1, pp. 127–60.

———. 1998. Population Trends at Moundville. In Knight and Steponaitis 1998b, pp. 26–43.

Steponaitis, Vincas P., M. James Blackman, and Hector Neff. 1996. Large-Scale Patterns in the Chemical Composition of Mississippian Pottery. *American Antiquity* 61, no. 3, pp. 555–72.

Steponaitis, Vincas P., and David T. Dockery III. 1997. The Geological Source of the Emerald Effigy Pipes and its Implications for Mississippian Exchange. Paper presented at the 54th Annual Meeting of the Southeastern Archaeological Conference, Baton Rouge, Louisiana.

Stoltman, James B. 1991. Cahokia as Seen from the Peripheries. In *New Perspectives on Cahokia: Views from the Periphery*, edited by James B. Stoltman, pp. 349–54. Prehistory Press.

Strickland, Rennard, ed. 1982. *Felix S. Cohen's Handbook of Federal Indian Law*. Bobbs-Merrill.

Suhm, Dee Ann, and Edward B. Jelks, eds. 1962. *Handbook of Texas Archeology: Type Descriptions*. Texas Archeological Society and Texas Memorial Library.

Sullivan, Lynne P. 2001. Dates for Shell Gorgets and the Southeastern Ceremonial Complex in the Chickamauga Basin of Southeastern Tennessee. *Frank H. McClung Museum Research Notes no. 19*.

Sunderhaus, Ted S., Rodney Riggs, and Frank L. Cowan. 2001. The Smith Site: A Small Hopewell Site Overlooking the Stubbs Earthworks. *OAC Newsletter* 13, no. 2, pp. 5–12.

Swan, Daniel C. 1999. *Peyote Religious Art: Symbols of Faith and Belief*. University Press of Mississippi.

Swanton, John R. 1911. *Indian Tribes of the Lower Mississippi Valley and Adjacent Coast of the Gulf of Mexico*. Bulletin 43. Bureau of American Ethnology, Smithsonian Institution.

———. 1928. *Social Organization and Social Usages of the Indians of the Creek Confederacy*. In Forty-second Annual Report of the Bureau of American Ethnology, 1924–1925, Smithsonian Institution, pp. 23–472.

———. 1929. *Myths and Tales of the Southeastern Indians*. Bulletin 88. Bureau of American Ethnology, Smithsonian Institution.

———. 1942. *Source Material on the History and Ethnohistory of the Caddo Indians*. Bulletin 132. Bureau of American Ethnology, Smithsonian Institution.

———. 1946. *The Indians of the Southeastern United States*. Bulletin 137. Bureau of American Ethnology, Smithsonian Institution.

Szasz, Margaret. 1974. *Education and the American Indian: The Road to Self-Determination, 1928–1973*. University of New Mexico Press.

Taylor, Theodore W. 1972. *The States and Their Indian Citizens*. Bureau of Indian Affairs, United States Department of the Interior.

Thomas, Cyrus. 1887. Burial Mounds of the Northern Sections of the United States. In Fifth Annual Report of the Bureau of Ethnology, 1883–1884, Smithsonian Institution, pp. 3–119.

———. 1894. *Report on the Mound Explorations of the Bureau of Ethnology*. In Twelfth Annual Report of the Bureau of Ethnology, 1890–1891, Smithsonian Institution, pp. 3–730.

Thornton, Russell. 1987. *American Indian Holocaust and Survival: A Population History Since 1492*. University of Oklahoma Press.

Thornton, Russell, Jonathan Warren, and Tim Miller. 1992. Depopulation in the Southeast after 1492. In Verano and Ubelaker 1992, pp. 187–95.

Thruston, Gates P. 1890. *The Antiquities of Tennessee and the Adjacent States, and the State of Aboriginal Society in the Scale of Civilization Represented by Them*. Cincinnati: The R. Clarke Company.

Townsend, Richard. 1979. *State and Cosmos in the Art of Tenochtitlan*. Studies in Pre-Columbian Art and Archaeology, no. 20. Dumbarton Oaks.

———. 1992. Landscape and Symbol. In *The Ancient Americas: Art from Sacred Landscapes*, edited by Richard F. Townsend, pp. 29–49. The Art Institute of Chicago and Prestel Verlag.

Tregle, Joseph G., Jr., ed. 1975 [1774]. *The History of Louisiana*. London: T. Becket. Facsimile reprint, 1975, Louisiana State University Press.

Trigger, Bruce G. 1989. *A History of Archaeological Thought*. Cambridge University Press.

Trubitt, Mary Beth. 2000. Mound Building and Prestige Goods Exchange: Changing Strategies in the Cahokia Chiefdom. *American Antiquity* 65, no. 4, pp. 669–90.

Van Horne, Wayne W. 1993. The Warclub: Weapon and Symbol in Southeastern Indian Societies. Ph.D. diss., Department of Anthropology, University of Georgia.

Vann Gennep, Arnold. 1960. *The Rites of Passage*. Translated by Monika Vizendon and Gabrielle L. Caffee. University of Chicago Press.

Vecsey, Christopher. 1983. *Traditional Ojibwa Religion and Its Historical Changes*. The American Philosophical Society, Memoirs 152, Philadelphia.

Vega, Garcilaso de la. 1951. *The Florida of the Inca*. Translated by John G. Varner and Jeannette J. Varner. University of Texas Press.

Vehik, Susan C. 1993. Dhegiha Origins and Plains Archaeology. *Plains Anthropologist* 38, no. 146, pp. 231–52.

Verano, John W., and Douglas H. Ubelaker, eds. 1992. *Disease and Demography in the Americas*. Smithsonian Institution Press.

Vogt, Evon A. 1969. *Zinacantan: A Maya Community in the Highlands of Chiapas*. Harvard University Press.

Voegelin, C. F. 1936. The Shawnee Female Deity. *Yale University Publication in Anthropology* 10, pp. 3–21. Yale University Press.

Walker, Chester P. 2000a. Head Vessels and the SECC: An Iconographic Interpretation. Paper presented in an invited symposium at the 57th Annual Meeting of the Southeastern Archaeological Conference, Macon, Georgia.

———. 2000b. Stylistic Analysis of Incised Head Vessels of the Southeastern United States. Master's thesis, University of Memphis.

———. 2001. Emblems of Rank and Membership: Tattooing in the Archaeological and Ethnohistoric Record. Paper presented in an invited symposium at the 12th Biennial Conference of the Native American Art Studies Association, Portland, Oregon.

Walker, James R. 1980. *Lakota Belief and Ritual*, edited by Raymond J. DeMallie and Elaine A. Jahner. University of Nebraska Press.

Walthall, John A. 1981. *Galena and Aboriginal Trade in Eastern North America*. Illinois State Museum, Scientific Papers, vol. 17.

Walthall, John A., and Elizabeth D. Benchley. 1987. *The River L'Abbe Mission*. Studies in Illinois Archaeology no. 2. Illinois Historic Preservation Agency.

Waring, Antonio J., Jr. 1968a. The Southern Cult and Muskhogean Ceremonial. In Williams 1968, pp. 30–69.

———. 1968b. The Southern Cult Revisited. In Williams 1968.

Waring, Antonio J., Jr., and Preston Holder. 1945. A Prehistoric Ceremonial Complex in the Southeastern United States. *American Anthropologist* 47, no. 1, pp. 1–34.

Watson, Virginia D. 1950. *The Wulfing Plates: Products of Prehistoric Americans*. Washington University Studies, n.s., no. 8.

Webb, William S., and David L. DeJarnette. 1942. *An Archeological Survey of Pickwick Basin in the Adjacent Portions of the States of Alabama, Mississippi and Tennessee*. Bulletin 129. Bureau of American Ethnology, Smithsonian Institution.

Webb, William S., and W. D. Funkhauser. 1932. *Archaeological Survey of Kentucky*. University of Kentucky Reports in Archaeology and Anthropology, vol. 2.

Webb, William S., and Charles E. Snow. 1945. *The Adena People*. University of Kentucky Reports in Archaeology and Anthropology, vol. 6.

Wedel, Waldo R. 1959. *An Introduction to Kansas Archeology*. Bureau of American Ethnology Bulletin 174. Smithsonian Institution.

Whitney, Cynthia, Vincas P. Steponaitis, and John J. W. Rogers. 2002. A Petrographic Study of Moundville Palettes. *Southeastern Archaeology* 21, no. 2, pp. 227–34.

Willey, Gordon R. 1973. Mesoamerican Art and Iconography and the Integrity of the Ideological System. In Ignacio Bernal et al., *The Iconography of Middle American Sculpture*, pp. 153–62. The Metropolitan Museum of Art.

Willey, Gordon R., and Jeremy A. Sabloff. 1974. *A History of American Archaeology*. Thames and Hudson.

———. 1993. *A History of American Archaeology*. 3rd edition. W. H. Freeman.

Williams, Mark. 1990. *Archaeological Excavations at Shinholser (9BL1): 1985 and 1987*. Publication 4. LAMAR Institute, Watkinsville, Georgia.

———. 1994. Growth and Decline of the Oconee Province. In *The Forgotten Centuries: Indians and Europeans in the American South, 1521–1704*, edited by Charles Hudson and Carmen Chaves Tesser, pp. 179–96. University of Georgia Press.

Williams, Samuel C., ed. 1930 [1775]. *Adair's History of the American Indian*. Promotory Press.

Williams, Stephen, ed. 1968. *The Waring Papers: The Collected Works of Antonio J. Waring, Jr.* Peabody Museum of Archaeology and Ethnology, Harvard University.

Williams, Stephen. 1990. The Vacant Quarter and Other Events in the Lower Valley. In Dye and Cox 1990, pp. 170–80.

Williams, Stephen, and John M. Goggin. 1956. The Long Nosed God Mask in Eastern United States. *The Missouri Archaeologist* 18, no. 3, pp. 1–72.

Willoughby, Charles C. 1932. Notes on the History and Symbolism of the Muskhogeans and the People of Etowah. In Moorehead 1932a, pp. 7–67.

Willoughby, Charles C., and Earnest A. Hooton. 1922. *The Turner Group of Earthworks, Hamilton County, Ohio*. Papers of the Peabody Museum of American Archaeology and Ethnology, Harvard University, vol. 8 no. 3.

Wilson, J. N. 1868. Mounds near Newark. *Isaac Smucker Scrap Book*, pp. 69–71. Manuscript on file, Granville Public Library, Ohio.

Winters, Howard D. 1969. *The Riverton Culure: A Second Millenium Occupation of the Wabash Valley*. Illinois State Museum and the Illinois Archaeological Survey, monograph 1.

Witthoft, John. 1949. *Green Corn Ceremonialism in the Eastern Woodlands*. Occasional Contributions from the Museum of Anthropology, University of Michigan, no. 13

Wittry, Warren L. 1969. An American Woodhenge. In *Explorations into Cahokia Archaeology*, edited by Melvin L. Fowler, pp. 43–48, Illinois Archaeological Survey, Bulletin 7.

———. 1996. Discovering and Interpreting the Cahokia Woodhenges. In *The Ancient Skies and Sky Watchers of Cahokia: Woodhenges, Eclipses, and Cahokian Cosmology*, edited by Melvin L. Fowler, pp. 26–35. Special issue of *The Wisconsin Archeologist* 77, nos. 3 and 4.

Wymer, Dee Anne. 1997. Paleoethnobotany in the Licking River Valley, Ohio: Implications for Understanding Ohio Hopewell. In Dancey and Pacheco 1997a, pp. 41–84.

Yelton, Jeffrey K. 1998. A Different View of Oneota Taxonomy and Origins in the Lower Missouri Valley. *The Wisconsin Archeologist* 79, no. 2, pp. 268–83.

Zurel, Richard. 2002. Signature Theory and Meaning of Hopewell Icons. Paper given at the 48th Annual Meeting of the Midwest Archaeological Conference, Columbus, Ohio.

Contributors

Richard F. Townsend is Curator of the Department of African and Amerindian Art at the Art Institute of Chicago. He received his Ph.D. in art history from Harvard University in 1975 and has taught at the University of Nebraska and the University of Texas in Austin. Dr. Townsend's publications include *The Aztecs* (Thames and Hudson, 1992), and he was the editor of and a contributor to two other Art Institute exhibition catalogues, *The Ancient Americas: Art from Sacred Landscapes* (1992) and *Ancient West Mexico: Art and Archaeology of the Unknown Past* (1998).

Garrick Bailey received his Ph.D. from the University of Oregon and is a professor of anthropology at the University of Tulsa. He has worked extensively with the Osage Indians and is the author of *The Osage and the Invisible World* (University of Oklahoma Press, 1995) and coauthor of *Art of the Osage* (Saint Louis Art Museum and University of Washington Press, 2004). In 2000, Dr. Bailey was named one of three academics to serve on the NAGPRA review committee by Secretary of the Interior Bruce Babbitt.

Joyce Bear is Cultural Preservation Officer of the Muscogee (Creek) Nation. A well-known speaker, she was Director of Indian Education Programs of Wagoner Public Schools, Oklahoma, and is currently a consultant on NAGPRA issues with state and federal agencies, museums, and libraries. Ms. Bear was also a consultant for the 1999 exhibition *Native Lands: Indians and Georgia* at the Atlanta History Center.

Turner Bear received his degrees in education from Northeastern State University and the University of Oklahoma, and he served as the first president of the Oklahoma Indian Higher Education Scholarship Administrators Association, and as Higher Education Program Director of the Cherokee Nation of Oklahoma. He was an education consultant for *Native Lands: Indians and Georgia*, an exhibition funded by the National Endowment for the Humanities.

Archaeologist **James A. Brown** received his doctorate from the University of Chicago in 1965 and teaches in the Department of Anthropology at Northwestern University, Evanston, Illinois. Dr. Brown has excavated at the Cahokia site, and he is especially known as an authority on style and meaning in the Southeastern Ceremonial Complex. Among his numerous publications is the monumental, two-volume work *Pre-Columbian Shell Engravings from the Craig Mound at Spiro, Oklahoma* (Peabody Museum Press, 1978 and 1984), coauthored with Philip Phillips, a landmark of Mississippian iconographic studies.

Carol Diaz-Granados received her Ph.D. from the Department of Anthropology at Washington University in St. Louis, where she continues as a Research Associate. Dr. Diaz-Granados has been a leader in the charting and interpretation of Native American petroglyphs and pictographs. Her principal study, *The Petroglyphs and Pictographs of Missouri*, coauthored with James R. Duncan (University of Alabama Press, 2000), is the foremost work in this field.

The recipient of a Ph.D. in anthropology from Washington University in St. Louis, **David H. Dye** is a professor at the University of Memphis. In addition to his work on warfare iconography and ritual, he is well known for his research in the ancient and early historic Southeast and has conducted major excavations in the central Mississippi valley. He coedited *Towns and Temples along the Mississippi* with Cheryl Anne Cox (University of Alabama Press, 1990).

Stacey Halfmoon is Assistant Native American Liaison, Department of Defense, Office of the Deputy Undersecretary of Defense (Installations and Environments). Ms. Halfmoon received her B.A. in anthropology from the University of Oklahoma in 1993. As a member of the Caddo Nation of Oklahoma, she has served as a NAGPRA officer for cultural preservation projects.

Robert L. Hall is Professor Emeritus of Anthropology at the University of Illinois at Chicago and Adjunct Curator Emeritus of Plains and Midwestern Archaeology and Ethnology at the Field Museum, Chicago. His special interests include the evolution and diffusion of religious practices in Pre-Columbian North America, archaeoastronomy, and the history of Indian-white relationships. He received a doctorate in anthropology from the University of Wisconsin–Madison in 1960 and is the author of *An Archaeology of the Soul: North American Indian Belief and Ritual* (University of Illinois Press, 1997).

Ruthe Blalock Jones is an educator and artist, and a member of the Delaware, Shawnee, and Peoria nations. She received her B.F.A. in painting from the University of Tulsa and a master's degree from Northeastern State University, Tahlequah, Oklahoma. She is currently Associate Professor of Art and Director of the Art Department at Bacone College in Muskogee, Oklahoma.

Adam King is an archaeologist with the Savannah River Archaeological Research Program of the University of South Carolina. He received his doctorate in anthropology from Pennsylvania State University in 1996, and his most significant publication to date is entitled *Etowah: The Political History of a Chiefdom Capital* (University of Alabama Press, 2003). Dr. King has closely defined the occupational sequences at this extremely important Mississippian site and has pioneered the recognition of Etowah's network of connections.

Vernon J. Knight, Jr., teaches in the Department of Anthropology at the University of Alabama, Tuscaloosa. The recipient of a Ph.D. from the University of Florida, Gainesville, Dr. Knight is one of the two leading experts on Moundville in central Alabama. *Archaeology of the Moundville Chiefdom*, coedited with Vincas P. Steponaitis (Smithsonian Institution Press, 1998), represents the latest and most complete summary and analysis of information about this major Mississippian site.

Folklorist **George E. Lankford** is one of the few such scholars who have developed a professional interest in the myths and legends of the Southeast. The author of *Native American Legends* (August House, 1987), he received his Ph.D. from Indiana University, Bloomington, in 1975 and teaches at Lyon College in Batesville, Arkansas. He has also written extensively on late prehistoric and early colonial Native American culture in the region, and has projected this information into an understanding of the Mississippian past.

Bradley T. Lepper is Curator of Archaeology at the Ohio Historical Society in Columbus. He received his doctorate in anthropology from Ohio State University in 1986 and is the site archaeologist for the major Hopewellian ceremonial center at Newark, Ohio. He is well known for his advocacy of a "Hopewellian road" leading southwest from the Newark Earthworks toward other mound groupings at Chillicothe, Ohio, and he has written extensively on archaeology of the Midwest.

Curator **David W. Penney**, Chief Curator of the Detroit Institute of Arts, is one of the few historians of Native American art with training in the archaeology of the Eastern Woodlands. Dr. Penney received his degree form Columbia University, and he was the organizing curator of the 1985 exhibition *Ancient Art of the American Woodland Indians,* the first exhibition devoted entirely to the art and archaeology of the ancient Midwest and Southeast. He is a coauthor, with George C. Longfish, of *Native American Art* (Hugh Lauter Levin Associates, 1994).

F. Kent Reilly III teaches in the Department of Anthropology at Texas State University in San Marcos. His Ph.D. in Latin American studies is from the University of Texas. In addition to his work on Olmec iconography, Dr. Reilly has a longstanding interest in Mississippian art and culture. He is a leading advocate of developing a new understanding of Mississippian cultural heritage through an analysis of architecture and art complemented by archaeological and ethnographic information.

Mark F. Seeman is a professor in the Department of Anthropology at Kent State University in Ohio. A leader in the field of Ohio Hopewell archaeology, he completed his Ph.D. in anthropology at Indiana University, Bloomington. Dr. Seeman's recent work has focused on mapping lines of sight connecting major ceremonial precincts and processional ways to outlying mounds, lesser sites, and significant topographical features and astronomical events. He has also written about the smybolic articulation of the land in Hopewell times.

Vincas P. Steponaitis is a professor in the Department of Anthropology, University of North Carolina–Chapel Hill, and Director of UNC's Research Laboratories of Archaeology. He received his doctorate in anthropology from the University of Michigan in 1980. One of the two leading authorities on Moundville, he is coeditor with Vernon J. Knight, Jr., of *Archaeology of the Moundville Chiefdom* (Smithsonian Institution Press, 1998).

Timmy Thompson is Traditional Cultural Advisor in the Cultural Preservation Office of the Muscogee (Creek) Nation. He has enjoyed a successful professional career in mechanical and engineering drafting. In addition, Mr. Thompson has long been a leader in the religious life of the Muscogee (Creek) Nation, having filled such offices as Assistant Medicine Man, Second Chief of the Hickory Ceremonial Ground, and, since 1991, Medicine Man.

Chester P. Walker is a Ph.D. candidate in the Department of Anthropology and Archaeology, University of Texas at Austin. Highly knowledgeable in the archaeology of the middle Mississippi area, Mr. Walker has conducted excavations in several locations in Tennessee and Texas, often in connection with salvage projects, and has written the technical reports on these excavations. He received his master's degree from the University of Memphis.

Photography Credits

Unless otherwise stated, all photographs of works of art appear courtesy of the lenders. The following credits apply to all images for which separate acknowledgment is due. Many of the images in this catalogue are protected by copyright and may not be available for further reproduction without the permission of the owner, lending institution, or copyright holder. Credits have been arranged according to the order in which they appear in the catalogue.

1, 2–3, 4, 6, 9, 14, 17b, 20, 21tr, 21bl, 21bc, 22c, 23tl, 23br, 25b, 26tl, 27tr, 31l, 31r, 32t, 42, 44l, 44r, 45, 46l, 46r, 47tr, 48l, 49bl, 49br, 50l, 50r, 51t, 53b, 54, 55l, 55r, 56, 58bl, 58br, 59l, 59c, 59r, 60t, 61l, 61r, 62tl, 64bl, 64br, 65l, 65r, 66tr, 97, 104, 106r, 107tl, 107tr, 108bl, 108br, 109l, 109r, 110 tl, 110tr, 110br, 111tl, 116b, 117l, 118, 121, 127b, 128bl, 130b, 132tl, 132tr, 132b, 133tr, 134tl, 134tr, 135bl, 135br, 136tl, 136tr, 141, 145l, 159bl, 159br, 162tl, 162tr, 162bl, 162br, 166, 170b, 171, 172tl, 173t, 178, 188tr, 190, 194l, 194r, 195r, 196r, 197l, 197r, 198b, 199tl, 199tr, 199bl, 200tl, 201tl, 202b, 203l, 204t, 204b, 207t, 210, 215l, 215r, 216tl, 216b, 221tl, 221tr, 221br, 223bc, 223br, 224tl, 224tr, 226tl, 226tr, 226bl, 226br, 227tl, 227tr, 230, 236, 237t, 238tl, 238tr, 238bl, 238br, 239tl, 239tr, 239bl, 239br, 240l, 240r, 241bl, 241bc, 241br, 243t, 243bl, 243br, 244tl, 244tr, 244b, 246, 248tl, 248tr, 248b, 249l, 249r, 250l, 250c, 250r, 261l, 261r, 262l, 262r, 263, 264l, 266c, 266r, 268l, 268r, 269l, 270tl, 270bl: © 2002 by John Bigelow Taylor, N.Y.C. 7: © Michael Heizer. 13, 84b, 85, 189, 220, 231: © by Mapping Specialists, Madison, Wisconsin. 17t, 74, 96, 152t, 168b: © 2004 by Steven Patricia. 18t, 27b, 72, 73:© by Richard W. Pirko. 19, 30t, 36, 99t, 111tr, 111br, 113, 124, 133tl, 135t, 142, 144t, 148t, 153t, 154, 155t, 168t, 169t, 172tr, 175l, 196l, 199br, 200tc, 200tr, 200br, 206, 214t, 216tr, 217, 221bl, 222tl, 222tr, 223tl, 223tr, 223bl, 224bl, 224br, 227br, 242, 267r: © 2004 by David H. Dye, University of Memphis. 21br, 29br, 63t, 106l, 267l: © 2003 by the Peabody Museum of Natural History, Yale University; photography by John Bigelow Taylor, N.Y.C. 22t, 22b, 23tr, 25tr, 34: © by John Pafford. 23cl, 23cr, 232bl, 270br: © by Ed Harvey and Terry McGuire. 24t, 24b: © 2004 The Art Institute of Chicago; photography by Bob Hashimoto, Department of Imaging. 25tl, 28: © 1985 by The Detroit Institute of Arts; photography by Dirk Bakker. 26c, 26r: © by Pete Bostrom, Troy, Illinois. 30b, 49t, 62tr, 64t, 66tl, 110bl, 111bl, 120, 150, 157, 161tr, 161b, 164tl, 164tr, 164b, 173b, 186, 201b, 203r, 225, 264r, 269c, 269r, 270tr © 2004 by Smithsonian Institution, National Museum of Natural History; photography by D. E. Hurlbert. 32b, 107b, 108t, 117r, 128t, 128br, 129t, 129b, 130t, 147r, 201tr: from Philip Phillips and James A. Brown, *Pre-Columbian Shell Engravings from the Craig Mound at Spiro, Oklahoma*, vols. I–VI. Peabody Museum Press. Copyright by the President and Fellows of Harvard College. 38: © 2003 by F. Kent Reilly III. 39: © 2003 by Richard F. Townsend. 66b, 78: © by Ohio Historical Society. 67b: © by Mark F. Seeman. 69t: courtesy of the *Cambridge Archaeological Journal*. 75c: courtesy of the Western Reserve Historical Society, Cleveland, Ohio. 75b: courtesy of the American Antiquarian Society, Worcester, Massachusetts. 82, 90, 184l: © by Smithsonian American Art Museum. 84t: from the 27th Annual Report of the Bureau of American Ethnology, Smithsonian Institution. 92, 101: © by Alex S. MacLean/Landslides. 94t, 95: from Sara Jones Tucker and Wayne C. Temple, *Indian Villages of the Illinois Country*, Illinois State Museum, Springfield (Atlas 1942; Supplement 1975). 99b, 182, 187tr, 188tl, 192t, 192b, 193t, 193b, 198t, 202t: © by Rucker Agee Map Collection, Birmingham Public Library, Birmingham, Alabama; photography by George Smith. 100: courtesy Cahokia Mounds State Historic Site. 127t, 131t: © by Jack Johnson. 131b: © by Milwaukee Public Museum; photography by Joanne Peterson. 138, 228: © 1992 by The Detroit Institute of Arts. 140t, 143tr, 143bl, 145tr, 146l, 147l, 148b: © by Carol Diaz-Granados. 140b: from *Prehistoric American* 36, no. 2 (2002); photography by E. A. Kassly. 147r: © by The Saint Louis Art Museum; photography by David Ulmer. 152b, 153b, 156l: drawings by George Wingard, courtesy of Adam King. 156r, 160t: drawings by Farrah L. Brown, courtesy of Adam King. 169b: courtesy of Vincas P. Steponaitis and Vernon J. Knight, Jr. 175r, 179tl, 179b, 254: © by Smithsonian Institution, National Museum of the American Indian, Washington, D.C. 184br: © by Smithsonian Institution, National Anthropological Archives, Washington, D.C., negative 54799. 213t, 213b, 214b: drawings by Chester P. Walker. 218: © by The Nelson-Atkins Museum of Art, Kansas City, Missouri; photography by Jamison Miller. 232: courtesy of Dr. Steve Black and www.texasbeyondhistory.net; photography by Sharon Mitchell. 252: © by The Field Museum, Chicago; photography by Ron Testa.

Index

Numbers in **bold** refer to pages with illustrations.

Above World, 127, 128, 129, 130, 131, 180, 192–96, 198, 208, 211, 212, 221, 222. *See also* Upper World
accelerator mass spectometry (AMS) dating, 147
Adena culture, 18, **18**, 30, **31**, 44, 45, 67; artifacts of, 45–49
Adena Mound, **31**, 47
Akron Grid motif, 113, 115, **116**
Alabama language, speakers of, 88
Algonquian languages, speakers of, 88
Amaye, 233
American Bottom region, 94, 95, 97, 102, 112, **112**, 141, 160, 163
Ancient Art of the American Woodland Indians, 45, 54
Ancient Monuments of the Mississippi Valley (Squier and Davis), **18**, **29**, **67**, **68**, 73, 74, **75**, **79**
animal imagery, 129
Antares, 213, **214**
anthropomorphic imagery, 126, 129, 131
Apalachee language, speakers of, 88
Archaic period, 17, 66
Arikara, 237
Arkansas River, 232, 237; middle valley of, 222
artifacts and aesthetics, 49–50, 54–55
Asinais, 233–34
assimilation, federal policy of, 19, 184, 186
astronomical orientation, 68, 77, **77**
Atakapan language, speakers of, 88
atlatls, 24, **24**; weights, **21**, 22, **22–25**, 26. *See also* bannerstones; birdstones; boatstones
Atwater, Caleb, 76, 79
axe head, 25, **25**
axes, 26, **26**, **202**, **203**

bannerstones, **22–23**, 24, **24**, 25, **25**, **264**, **270**
baton, **164**
Battle of Fallen Timbers, 89
Battle of Horseshoe Bend, 89
Battle of the Thames, 89, 254
Battle of Tippecanoe, 89
Baum site, 68, **68**, 76
BBB Motor site, 100
Bellin, Jacques Nicolas, map by, **94**
bellows-shaped apron, 176, 179, 200, **236–37**
Beneath World, 127, 128, 130, 131, 158, 160, 177, 180, 192–96, 198, 208–10, 213–15. *See also* Underwater World (Underworld)
Big Moon Peyote religion, 143, 144
bilobed-arrow motif, **33**, 33–34, 106, 109, 118, 119, 140, 142, 148, **149**, **174**, 175, 195, 200
Biloxi, 88
Binford, Lewis, 43
Birdman, **104**, 106, **106**, 107, 113, 114, **114–15**, **117**, 118–19, **120**, 121, 127, 140, 142–43, **143**, 148, 156, 158, 160, 203, **227**, 228; and Morning Star cycle, 228. *See also* Morning Star; Red Horn
bird motifs, **56**, **107**, 130, 143, **143**, 144, 146; crested, **208**, 209, **209**, 210; falconine imagery, **114–15**, 118, 147, 160; raptors, 196, 198, 213; and the Winds, 209
birdstones, **6**, **21**, **267**
Birger figurine, 100, 134, **134**, 135
Black Warrior pictograph, 146, **146**
Black Warrior River, 167
blades, 25, **25**, 26, **34**, **61**
Blanton, Richard, 163
Boas, Franz, 48
boatstones, **62**, 64
Bodmer, Karl, 94; *Prehistoric Indian Mounds Opposite St. Louis*, 94; *Trappists Hill Opposite St. Louis*, 94
bow, **201**; and arrow, 146
Braden style, **106**, 107, **108**, 109, **109**, 112–15, **113**, **114–15**, 116–17, **117**, 119, **120**, 126, 131, 147, 148, 160, 163, 172, 177, 195, **201**, **215**, 242
Brain, Jeffrey, 163
Breathmaker, 209
British Museum, 52
Brown, James A., 68, 69, 129, 160, 163, 170, 176, 228, 236
Bureau of American Ethnology, 105, 156, 232
Bureau of Indian Affairs, 154, 186
Buzzard Cult, 208

Caddo, 57, 88, 90, 222, 228; art, 247–51; ceramics, 231–45, **230**, **232**, **235–43**, **246**, **248**, **249**, 250, **250**; ceremonial dances, 247; history, 232, 236; myths, 33; and removal to Indian Territory, 232, 251; and repatriation, 49, 250, 251; settlements, 233–34; social structure of, 234; and Temple Mound tradition, 236; and understanding of tribal past, 251
Caddoan language, speakers of, 88, 101, 237
Caddo Culture Club, 231, 245
Cadi Ayo, 234
Cahokia, 18, **19**, **92**, 93–103, **96**, 112, **112**, 131, 133, 160, 167, 198, 237; abandonment of, and diaspora, 98, 102–03; and Birdman theme, 107, 112–17, 142–43; and Braden style, 107–09, 112–15; ceramic production at, 98, 115–16; compared to Oneota culture, 98; connections to Etowah, Moundville, and Spiro, 119–21; craft specialization at, 117; depopulation at, 96, 102; description of site, 96–97, 112; Grand Plaza of, 97, **101**; grave goods at, 97; human sacrifice at, 97, 98; and Indian tribes, as modern descendants, 100–02; modern encroachment at, **100**; Monks Mound at, **19**, **92**, 94, **100**, **101**, 112; Mound 34, 98, 112, 115; Mound 72, 97, **97**, 99, 101; and nearby sites, 100; palisade at, 97; phases of development of, 97–98; and pole ceremonialism, 98–100; and rock art, 140, 142–43, **142**, **143**, 147, 148, 149; and the Vacant Quarter, 102; woodhenges at, 97, 98–99, **99**; woodhenges and cosmic axis, 99; woodhenges, as cosmogram, 99, 100
Cahokia (Indians), 93, 94, **94**, 101
Campbell site, **227**, **228**
camp circles, as cosmograms, 100
Carden Bottoms, 222, **250**
Carter, Mary Cecile Elkins, 250
Casañas, Francisco, 234
Castillo, Diego, 233
Catawba, 87, 88, 91
Catlin, George, *Ball Play of the Choctaw—Ball Up*, **184**; *Blackfoot Medicine Man, Performing His Mysteries over a Dying Man*, **27**, 28
caves, 140
celts, 26, **26**
ceramic (artifacts), **48**, **58–59**, **64**, **118**, 130, **135**, **138**, **141**, **142**, **144**, **155**, **170**, 171–72, **171**, **172**, **204**, **206**, **210**, **212**, **214–16**, 219–20, **224–28**, **230**, 231–45, **232**, **235–43**, **248–50**, **263**, **266**, **268**; Alligator Bayou Stamped, **64**; Avenue Polychrome, 220, **221**, **222**; Avery Engraved, 241, **243**, **250**; Bell Plain, **204**, **223**; Blakeley Engraved, **238**, 240; Carson Red on Buff, **218**, 220, **225**, **226**, **227**, 228; "cat monster," 215; "dog pots," 222, **222**; Dunkin Incised, **235**, 236, 241; headpots, **218**, 222, **225–28**; Haley Complicated Incised, **236**, 237; Hemphill, 171, 179, 180, **214**;

ceramic (artifacts) *(continued)*
Hodges Engraved, **210**, **232**, **238–39**, 240, **241**, **242**, **246**; Holly Fine Engraved, **235**, 237, 240, 241; Hopewell ware, **64**; Hudson Engraved, **249**; Keno Trailed, **230**, 241, **243**, **250**; Kiam Incised, 237; Larto Red, 220; Means Engraved, **240**; Nodena Red and White, **204**, **215**, **216**, 220, **221**, **223**, **224**, 244; Pecan Point, **222**, 224, 225, **225**, **226**, **227**, **228**; Quapaw, 220; redware, **240**; Spiro Engraved, **237**, 240; Taylor Engraved, **243**
ceremonial objects, **25**, **26**, 33, **34**, **47**, **56**, **61**, **145**, 167, 169, 219–20, **219**
charter myths, 203, 205
Cherokee, 33, 87, 88, 89, 90, **189**
Chickasaw, 33, 57, 88, 89, 90, 101, **189**
chiefdom capitals, 18, 86, 153, 154, 156, 163, 167, 169, 191, 193, 196, 219; and paramount chiefdoms, 18, 232
Chippewa, 255
Chitimacha, 88, 91
Chiwere Siouan language, speakers of, 88
Chiwere Sioux, 101
Chiwere-Winnebago, 101, 102, 103
Choctaw, 33, 88, 89, 90, 91, 99, 101, **184**, **189**
Chucalissa site, **130**, 221
chunkey game, 112; stones, 106, **106**, 109, **109**, **110–11**, 112
Chunkey Player pipe, **109**, 133
Citico site, 119
Cloud Woman, 134, 135
Clovis points, 17
Collot, Georges-Henri-Victor, map from survey by, **95**
columella, **104**, **106**, 194, **194**, 195
concentric circle motifs, **116**, 119, 142, 146, **147**, 241
Connolly, Robert, 80
Conquering Warrior pipe, 133
Coosa, 86, 156
Coosa River, 86, 156
Coosawattee River, 156
copper (artifacts), 33, **33**, **47**, 113, **114–15**, **116–17**, 119, **120**, 141, **148**, **150**, 156, **157**, 160, **175**, 176–77, 194, 195, **197**, 199, 215, **265**
Copperas Mountain, 66
Copper Dominated Horizon, 240, 245 n
Corn Maiden, 134
Corn Mother (Earth Mother), 30, **124**, 125, 133, 134, 143
cosmogony, 126
cosmogram, 68, 209
cosmology, Native American, 65, 126, 127–28, **127**, 129, 130, 208, 209, 211
cosmos, Native American, 21–22, 80, 139, 140, 149, 158, 196, 207, 211, 220. *See also* Above World; Beneath World; Middle World
Crable site, 98
Crab Orchard people, 54
Craig Mound, **14**, **32**, **104**, **106**, **107**, **108**, **109**, **117**, **128**, 129, **129**, **130**, **188**, 197, **197**, **201**, **215**, 237, **237**, 240. *See also* Spiro
Craig style, **21**, 32, **104**, **106**, 107, **107**, **108**, 109, 119, 120–21, 126, **128**, 129, **129**, **130**, **188**, **201**, **236–37**, 242
Creek Confederacy, 156
cross-in-circle motif, 21, 128, **128**, 129, **129**, 130, 143, **143**, 144, 148, **149**, 158, **159**
Crothers, George, 148
Crouching Man pipe, 114, 133, **133**
Crow, 212
Cumberland River valley, 174
cups (whelk shell), **21**, **32**, **104**, **106**, **107**, **108**, **109**, 113, **116**, 117, **117**, 121, **128**, **129**, **130**, **188**, 198, **198**, 200, 201, **201**, **215**, **237**
Cutifachiqui (Cofitachequi), 86
Cygnus, 213, **213**

Dalton, George, 54
Dalton points, 17
Dancing Warrior, 140, 145, **145**
Davis, Edwin H. *See* Squier, Ephraim G.
Davis, George C., site, 225, **235**
Davis Rectangle, 225, **225**, 228, 242, 244
De Bry, Theodor, **99**, **182**, **187**, **188**, 192, **192**, **193**, **198**, **202**
decapitation, 201, **201**, 202, 203, 223
De Laudonnière, René, 187, 192
Delaware, 253, 254
Deneb, 212, 213, **213**
De Soto, Hernando, expedition of, 18, 84, **85**, 86, 93, 155, 156, 219, 233
Dhegiha Siouan language, speakers of, 88, 102
Dhegiha Sioux, 102, 103, 144, 149
Diaz-Granados, Carol, 113
diseases, effect of epidemic, 87, 96
dismemberment, 202, **202**, 203
distribution of gorgets at Mound C, Etowah, **160**
distribution of large Woodland mounds in the Scioto River valley, **67**
Dorsey, George A., 134
Douay, Anastasius, 233, 234
Duck River, 66, 199
Du Ru, Paul, 177
Dye, David H., 160

earrings, 132, **132**
earspools, 58, 62, 194, 200, **244**, **270**
Earth and Fertility Cycle, 126
Earth Mother. *See* Corn Mother
East Works, **79**
Edwin Harness Mound, 77
effigy bead, **17**
effigy figures: animal, **17**, **21**, 28, **28**, **50**, **265**, **267**; human, 4, **28**, 33, **48**, **58–59**, **62**, 138, 141, **142**, **154**, **155**, **186**, **263**
effigy mounds, **27**, **29**, 30, 98
effigy pipes: animal, **29**, **30**, 43, 49, 50–55, **50**, **51**, **52**, **53**, **54**, **55**, **63**, 64, **65**, **66**, **131**, 135, **135**, 177, **177**, 198, **261**; human, **31**, 46, **49**, **109**, **124**, **132**, **133**, **134**, **136**, **194**, **195**, **198**, **199**
effigy vessels: animal, 240, **241**; deer, 222, **223**; fish, **223**; frog, **223**; human figure, **135**, **138**, **141**, **144**, **222**; human head, **218**, 222, 223, 224, 225–27, **225–28**, 228; possum, 223, **223**; rabbit, **268**; Underwater Panther, **118**, **206**, **216**, **222**
Emerald Mound group, 95
Emergent Mississippian period, 97
Emerson, Thomas, 100, 103, 132, 134
Espinosa, Isidro Felix de, 234, 235, 240, 244
Etowah, 18, **36**, 105, 107, 120, 129, 151–65, **152**, **153**; burials at, 106, 153–56, 158, 160, **160**, 163, 165; as chiefdom capital, 153, 154, 163; collapse of, 153, 155, 165; construction of, 153–54; copper plates from, **150**, 156, **157**, 195; description of, 152–53; excavations at, 151–52; as mortuary facility, 153, 154, 155, 163; Mound A, 152, 153, 154; Mound B, 152, 153, 154; Mound C, 105, 151, 152, 153, 154, 155–56, **156**, 158, 160, 163, 211; Mounds D, E, and F, 152; palisade at, 152, 154, 158; periods of abandonment, 153, 154, 155, 163; sculpture from, **154**, 155. *See also* Rogan plates
Etowah, phases of occupation, **153**; Brewster, 155, 156; Early Wilbanks, 153, 156, 158, 163; Late Etowah, 153; Late Wilbanks, 154, 156, 158
Etowah River, 156
exchange networks, 165
eye-markings, 142, 146, **146**, 147, 148. *See also* eye-surrounds
eye-surrounds, 129, **129**, **130**, 195, 219, 222, 225; forked, **106**, **114**, **115**, **116**, **117**, 118, 119, 129, **129**, 130, **147**, **170**, **191**, **197**, **198**, 200, **201**, **206**, 222; grappling hook, **218**, 219, 225, **225**, **227**, 228, **228**; three-pronged, 129, **129**, 130, **130**, **177**, **179**, **203**, **215**, **222**, 223, **224**
farming, 18, 59, 97, 100, 102, 106, 169, 219, 234
flint clay figurines, 100, **109**, 113–14, 119, 131, 132, **132**, 133, **133**, **134**, 135, 136, **136**, 177, 198, **194**, **199**
Fort Ancient, 68, 71, 76, 80
Fortune Mound, **227**
Four Winds motif, 225, **226**, 227
Fowler, Melvin L., 97
Fox, 88, 90
frogs, symbolism of, 22

G E Mound, 67
Georgia Historical Commission, 156
Giant, 146, 147, **147**
Glendon limestone, 177, 178
gorget (copper), **265**
gorgets (shell), 33, **106**, **113**, **127**, 131, 156, **159**, 178–79, **190**, 194, **194**, 200, 202, 208–09, **208**, **209**, **211**; annular, **160**, 163; anthropomorphic, **160**, 163; Brakebill style, **162**; Cartersville style, **113**; Citico style, **162**; Cox Mound style, **208**, 209–10, **211**; cruciform, **160**, 163; Fairfield style, **20**; Hightower style, 121, 158, 194, **194**; Hixon style, 209, **209**, 210–11, **211**, 214; piasa, 178–79, **179**; rattlesnake, **162**, 165; Spaghetti style, **162**, 165; triskele, **159**, **160**, 163; turkey-cocks theme, 158, **158**, **160**, 163, **209**, 211, **211**; water spider, **217**; Williams Island style, 165
gorgets (stone), **9**
Grave Creek Mound, **18**
grave goods, 33, 153, 154, 155, 156, 158, 160, 163, 165, 170, 174
Great Hopewell Road, 79
Great Serpent, 118–19, 177, 180, 192, **206**, 213, 214, 215, **216**, 221. *See also* Underwater Panther
Great Sun, 84–85
Greber, N'omi, 80
Greenman, Emerson, 78
Griffin, James, 224, 225
Grizzly Man, 114, 133, **134**
guilloche motif, 209, 211, 241
Gulf Coast, 171

hair bun, 147, 148, 194, 195, **195**
Hall, Robert, 134, 137
Hampton Institute, **184**
hand-and-eye motif, 130, 171, **174**, **175**, 176, 212, **212**, 220
Hand (constellation), 33, 212, **213**
hand motif, 33, **60**, **140**, **173**, 180, 204, 220
Hariot, Thomas, 33
Hatchel-Mitchell-Moore site, **233**, 234
Havana people, 52
Heizer, Michael, *Effigy Tumuli: Water Strider, Frog, and Catfish*, **7**
Helms, Mary, 160
Hemphill style, 107, **108**, 109, 120, 126, **170**, 171, 172, 179, 180
He-Who-Is-Hit-with-Deer-Lungs, **33**, 34, 132
He-Who-Wears-Human-Heads-in-His-Ears, 132–33, **132**, 133, 148
Hidalgo, Francisco, 235
Hidatsa, 212
High Bank Works, 66, **67**, 76, 79, **79**
Hightower style, 107, **108**, 109, 120, **194**. *See also* Hixon style
Hitchiti language, speakers of, 88
Hively, Ray, 75, 76, 77
Hixon style, 209, **209**, 211, **211**, 214. *See also* Hightower style
Ho-Chunk (Winnebago), 91, 101
Holder, Preston, 194
Holmes, William Henry, 224, 225, 228
Hopeton Works, **79**
Hopewell: art, 62–65; basins, 69, **69**, 71; ceramics, **64**, 65; ceremonialism, 70–71; cosmology, 65; culture, 18, 58–71; earthworks, **18**, **72**, 73–81, **73–75**; earthworks as cosmogram, 68; figurines, **58–59**;

gift giving, 62–65; hairstyles and prestige, **58–59**, 61; landscapes as sacred places, 65–70, 71; mound construction, 69–70, **70**; shamanism, 61, **62**; shrine buildings, 68, 69, 71
Hopewell Culture National Historical Park, 51
Hopewell Interaction Sphere, 58, 126
Hopewell site: Mound 17, **49**; Mound 25, **46**, **47**, **49**, **56**, **60**, **61**, 70, **70**
Horn, Robert, 75, 76, 77
Houma, 91
Howard, James H., 209

Illini, 88, 89
Illinois River, 52; valley, 59, 66
Indian Removal Act of 1830, 89–90, 254
Indian slave trade, 88
Indian Territory (Oklahoma), 19, 90, 188, 232, 251, 253–54
Indigenous Aesthetics: Native Art, Media, and Identity (Leuthold), 49
Inman, Henry, *Portrait of Tenskwatawa, the Prophet*, **255**
Inyan, 139
Ioway, 88, 90
Iroquoian languages, speakers of, 88
Iroquois, 187
Itaba, 156

Jackson, Andrew, 19
Jefferson, Thomas, 89
Jennings, Francis, 54
Jolliet, Louis, 96
Jones, Ruthe Blalock: *Shawnees at the Ceremonial Ground*, **258**; *Shell Shaker*, **256**; *Oklahoma Stomp Dance*, **259**
Joutel, Henri, 234

Kansa, 88, 90, 102, 118, 139
Kaskaskia, **94**, 101
Kealedji square ground, **209**
Keller figurine, 100, **133**, 134
Kelly, John E., 97, 160
Kichai, 237
Kickapoo, 88, 89, 90
Koasati language, speakers of, 88
Kokomthena, 258, 259
Kneeling Rattler. *See* Grizzly Man
Kwakiutl, 48

La Flesche, Francis, 83, **84**
Lakota, 212
landscape, 139, 140; as wilderness, 15, 16; as record, 34–35; as sacred place, 17, 65–70, 71
Lankford, George E., 130, 158, 160, 172
Lapham, I. A., **29**
Larson, Lewis H., Jr., 152, 155, 156, 158, 163
La Salle, Sieur de, René-Robert Cavelier, 84, **84**, 233
Leach, Edmund, 49
Le Moyne de Morgues, Jacques, 99, **99**, **187**, **192**, **193**, **198**, **202**
Leon, Francisco de, 234
Le Page du Pratz, Antoine S., 93
Leuthold, Steven, 49–50
Liberty Township Earthworks, 76, **79**
Little Egypt, 156
Little Miami River valley, 68
locatives, 129, 130, 213. *See also* symbolic motifs
Long-Nosed God maskette ear ornaments, 132, **132**, 147, **148**
Long-Nosed God maskettes, 147, 148, **148**
Lower World, 140, 147, 149. *See also* Beneath World
Lubbub site, 176
lunar deity, 133

mace, 26, 140, 142, 144–45, **145**, 146, **147**, 148, **196**
Maddin Creek, **143**, 148, **149**
maize, 18, 102, 106; **124**, 134, 234
Mandan, 212
Mann Mound, 70
Mann site, **58**, **63**
map of the American Bottom (Brown and Kelly), **112**
map of the Caddo area of Arkansas, Louisiana, Oklahoma, and Texas, **231**
map of the central Cahokia area showing the principal mounds (Brown and Kelly), **112**
map of the central Mississippi River valley, **230**
map of the development of chiefdom capitals in the Etowah River valley, **153**
map of the earthworks at the Baum site (Squier and Davis), **68**
map of earthworks at Crawfordsville (Lapham), **29**
map of the earthworks at Mound City (Squier and Davis), **29**
map of the eastern half of North America showing the path of La Salle, **84**
map of the greater southeastern United States showing Indian lands and communities (Taylor), **89**
map of the High Bank Works (Squier and Davis), **67**
map of Hopewell earthworks near Frankfort, Ohio (Squier and Davis), **18**
map of the Illinois region (Bellin), **94**
map of the Indian Tribal regions of the lower Mississippi and adjacent Gulf Coast (Swanton), **87**
map of the Midwest and South, **13**
map of the Mississippi River near Cahokia (Collot), **95**
map of the Newark Earthworks (Salisbury), **75**
map of the Newark Earthworks (Squier and Davis), **75**
map of the Newark Earthworks (Wyrick and Unzicker), **75**
map of the Scioto River valley at Chillicothe (Squier and Davis), **79**
map of the Seip Earthworks (Squier and Davis), **68**
map of the Southeast showing the path of De Soto (Hudson), **85**
map of the Trails of Tears, **189**
map of Upper Nasoni, a principal Caddo town, **233**
Marquette, Jacques, 96
Martín, Fernando, 233
Marshall, James, 76
mask motif, **1**, **14**, **27**, 28, **224**
masks: engraved shell, **161**, 165; wolf skull, **27**; wooden, 1, 14
Massanet, Damien, 234, 235
Maurer, Evan, 46
Maya art, 132
Mehrer, Mark, 100
Mesquakie (Fox), 91
Messinger, John, 95
Miami, 88, 89, 90, 91
mica (artifacts), **2–3**, 45, **46**, **47**, **56**, **60**
Miccosukee, 90
Middle World, 80, 127–28, 130, 140, 147, 149, 158, 193, 195, 208, 211, 215. *See also* This World
Midé Society, 214
Milky Way, 33, 127, 130, 140, 188, 211–12, 213, **213**, 214
Mills, William C., 46–47, 50
Mingo, 253, 254
Mississippian Art and Ceremonial Complex, 125–26, 129, 132, 136–37; cosmic model, **127**; styles, 126; symbolic language, 125, 129–30, 136–37; temporal periods, 126; themes, 126
Mississippian peoples: of the precontact era, 85–86; of the postcontact era, 87–88; of today, 90–91
Mississippian period, 18, 57, 95, 96; centers, 86, 151–52, 167, 194; fortified towns, 95, 193, 196; iconography, 125, 141, 193; objects as metaphors, 186
Mississippi River, 140, 141; central valley, 102, 219–29, **220**, 222
Missouri, 88, 90
Missouri River, 140, 141
Mitchell Mounds, 95
Mitchigamea, 101
Moore, Clarence B., 178
Moorehead, Warren K., 119, 156, 158
Morfí, Juan Augustin de, 234
Morning Star, 104, 114, **114**, 118–19, 125, 132, **132**, 133, 135, 143, 144, 147, 148, 156, 158, 192, 195; cycle, 126, 132, 136. *See also* Birdman; Red Horn
Moscoso, Luis de, 233
Moundbuilders, myth of, 16, 65, 85–86
Mound City, Missouri, 95, 141
Mound City, Ohio, **29**, 51, **51**, 52, **52**, **53**, 54, 67, 68, 69, **69**, **79**
mounds, 95, 152, 153, 167–68
Moundville, 18, 107, 120, 129, 167–81, **168**, **169**, 213, 214, 215, 217, 220; burials at, 106, 168, 169, 178, 179, 180; cemeteries, 169, 170, 174; as chiefdom capital, 167, 169; connection to the Beneath World, 217; connections with other sites, 176, 177, 180; decline of, 169–70; description of, 167–68; effigy bowls from, 177–78, **178**; effigy pipes from, 177, **177**; elite associations, 170, 172, 174, 176, 179, 180; hair ornaments from, 106, **175**, 176; as major regional center, 169; Mound A, 168; Mound B, 168; Mound Q, 176; Mounds, 167, 168, 169; and Muskhogean speakers, 213; as a necropolis, 169, 180; palettes, **166**, 174–75, **174**; palisade at, 167–68, 169; pendants, of copper, **175**, 176, 215; pendants, of stone, 175–76, **175**; plaza at, 169; pottery from, engraved, 170, **170**, 171, **171**, 213, 214, 215; pottery from, painted, 172, 174; ritual artifacts from, **166**, 170, 174–75, 179, 180; ritual regalia from, 170, 175–76, **175**; shell cups, 178; shell gorgets, 178–79, **179**; social status at, 179; as a sociogram, 168, 169
Moundville art, thematic motifs of: bilobed arrow, **174**, 175, 176; concentric circles, 171, 176, 214; cross-in-circle, 171, 214; dimple, 171; hand-and-eye, 171, **174**, **175**, 176; moth, **174**, 175; ogee, **175**; radial T-bar, 171; rayed circle, **175**, 176; swastika, 171, **175**, 176, 180, 214, 215; three fingers, 171
Moundville art, themes of: center symbols, **170**, 171, 214; crested bird, **170**, 171, 172, 215; raptor, **170**, 171, 213; trophy, **170**, 171–72, **171**; winged serpent, **170**, 171, 172, 180, 213, **214**
Moundville Engraved pottery, 171
Mount Logan, 67
Muller, Jon, 141
Muscogee (Creek) Nation, 37–41, 183, 184; ceremonial grounds, 37, **40**, 185; and Christianity, 38, 185; Feather Dance, **39**; Green Corn–New Fire ceremony, **38**, 185; Hickory Ground, 37, 38, 40; history, 187; language instruction, 37; removal to Indian Territory, 188; Ribbon Dance, **38**; sacred fire, 209
Museum of the Red River, 231, 232
Muskhogean language, 194; speakers of, 88, 101, 106, 213
Muskogee/Creek, 33, 57, 88, 89, 90, 101, **189**; square ground, 209, **209**

Naguatex, 233
Natchez, 19, 22, 33, 84–86, 88, 90, 93, 96; destruction of, 85; Grand Village, 84; social organization of, 84–85
Native American beliefs, 127, 193; animals in, 26, 28, 127
Native American Church. *See* Big Moon Peyote religion
Native American Graves Protection and Repatriation Act of 1990 (NAGPRA), 55, 249
Native American history, and the settlement of North America, 83–91
Native American mythic cycles, 126
Native American traditional communities, 20, 90–91, 137

Newark Earthworks, 67, **72**, 73–81, **73–75**; and archaeoastronomy, **74**, 77, **77**; burials at, 77; Eagle Mound, 78, 80; Ellipse, 73, **75**, 76, 77; and geometry, 75–76; Great Circle, **73**, **74**, 75, **75**, 76, 77, 78, 80; Observatory Circle, **72**, **74**, **75**, 76, 77, **77**, 79; Octagon, **72**, 74, **74**, **75**, 76, 77, **77**, 79, 80; Salisbury Square, 78; and stages of development, 80–81; Square, 75, **75**, 76, 77, 80; and water, 76–77
New Fire ceremony, 119
Nieberding, Velma, 255

Ocmulgee, 18
Ocmulgee National Monument, 189
Ofo, 88
ogee motif, 129, **129**, 130, 134, 135, 140, 148, **149**, **159**, 160, **175**, **212**
Ohio Historical Society, 46–47, 50, 74
Ohio River valley, 59, **59**, 67, 71, 85, 102, 174
Old Stone Fort, 66
Old Woman deity, 144. *See also* Old-Woman-Who-Never-Dies
Old-Woman-Who-Never-Dies, 134, **134**, 135, **135**, 143, 144
Omaha, 88, 90, 100, 102, 118
Oneota culture, 98, 101, 102
Oostanaula River, 155
Orion, 33, 212
Orpheus myth, 212
Osage, 57, 88, 90, 100, 102, 118, 139, 143, 146, 147, 198, 203; headdress, 146, **146**; sacred songs of, 83, 91
Otherworld, 127, 130, 131, 134, 193, 198, 200, 220
Otoe, 88, 90
Our Grandmother, 125, 134, **134**, 135, **138**, 139
Outina, Holata, **192**, **193**, 202
Overworld, 127, 128, 158, 208. *See also* Above World

Pacaha, **228**
Paint Creek, 59, 66, 76
palettes, **159**, **166**, **173**, 174–75, **174**
palisades, 95; at Etowah, 152, 154, 158; at Moundville, 167–68, 169
Path of Souls, 126, 128, 130, 134, 172, 180, 192, 198, 203, 211–12, 213, 220
Pawnee, 88, 90, 101, 213, 214, 227, 237; ceremonial earth lodge, 134
Paz, Octavio, 34
Peabody Foundation, R. S., 156
pendants, 175–76, **175**, 267
Penicault, Andre, 235
Penne-Murat site, Gasconade County, **143**
Penney, David, 59
Peoria, 88, 89, 90, 101
Perrault Collection, 131, **131**
petaloid motif, 129–30, **129**, 195
petroglyphs, 140, **140**, 141, **143**, **144**, **145**, 148–49, **149**
Phillips, Philip, 112, 129, 163, 176, 236
piasa, 22, 118, 128, **128**, 131, 134, 177, **177**, 178–79, **179**, 180, 196, 221–22, 223. *See also* Underwater Panther
pictographs, 140, 141, **143**, 145, **145**, **146**, **147**, 148–49, **148**
Picture Cave, **143**, 146, **146**, 147, **147**, 148, **148**
Pinson Mounds, 18, **18**
pipes, **261**, **269**; Bellaire style, 177, **177**, 179; blocked-end tube, **64**, Perrault Collection, 131, **131**. *See also* effigy pipes
plan of Moundville, **169**
plan of the Ocevpofv Green Corn ground (Swanton), **40**
plan of the Ocevpofv square ground in eastern Oklahoma (Swanton), **40**
plan of Pinson Mounds in Tennessee (Myer/Norton), **18**
plan of various excavations at Mound C, Etowah, **156**
plummet stones, **262**
Pollock Works, 80
Pomeiock town, 192, **192**
Ponca, 88, 90, 102, 118, 139
Potowatomi, 255
Poverty Point, 17, **17**
Pre-Columbian Shell Engravings from the Craig Mound at Spiro, Oklahoma (Phillips and Brown), **32**, **107**, **117**, **128**, 129, **129**, **130**, **147**, **201**
projectile points, 26, **97**

Quapaw, 88, 90, 102, 118, 139
Quetzalcóatl, 213, 214

raccoon motif, **237**
Ramey Incised pottery, 98, **98**, **116**
Raptor, 192
raptor talon effigies, 194, 199; imagery of, **107**. *See also* bird motifs
Rattlesnake Bluff, 145, **145**
Rattlesnake Disk, **166**, 175
Redcorn, Charles, 232
Redcorn, Jereldine, 231, 232, **232**
Red Horn, 33, **33**, 34, 104, **114**, 125, 132, **132**, 148. *See also* Morning Star
Reilly, F. Kent, III, 158, 160
rendering of Cahokia (Patricia), **96**
rendering of Etowah (Patricia), **152**
rendering of Moundville (Patricia), **169**
rendering of Newark Earthworks (Patricia), **74**
rendering of Poverty Point, **17**
Resting Warrior, 132, **132**, 133
Riordan, Robert, 80
Ritchie, William, 43
Riverton culture, 44
Roanoke Island, 192
rock art, 113, 139–49. *See also* petroglyphs, pictographs
rock shelters, 140
Rocky Hollow site, **143**
Rogan, John P., 105, 118, 156, 158
Rogan plates, 34, 105, 106, 107, 118, **150**, 156, **157**, 160, 195, 196
Romain, William, 75, 76

Sabloff, Jeremy, 43
sacred fire, 192
Sacred Warrior, 191, 192
Salisbury, Charles and James, 74, **75**, 76, 77
San Miguel de Guadalupe, 87
Saturiba, **193**
Saucy Calf, 83, **83**, 91
Sauk, 88, 89
scalp lock, 195, 202, 203, 220, **221**; pouch, 195, 202
Scioto River, 18, 51, 59, 66, **67**
Scorpius, 213, 214, **214**
scroll motif, **47**, 119, 220, 221, **221**, **224**, 241, 244
SECC. *See* Southeastern Ceremonial Complex
Secota town, **182**
seed jars, 241, **241**
Seeman, Mark, 51
Seip Earthworks, 68, **68**, 76
Seip-Overly site, 66
Seip-Pricer Mound, **66**, 70
Seminole, 89–90, **189**, 213
Seneca, 254
Serpent Mound, **27**, 30
serpents: amphisbaena, 113, 177; and the Beneath World, 196, 213, 221; horned, **130**; imagery and motifs of, 47, 107, 108, 109, 128, 130, **130**, 135, 178, 180, 213, 214, 220, 248; plumed, 22, **173**; rattlesnakes, 33, 128, **128**, **162**, 165, **166**; serpent-bird imagery, 131, 177, 178, **178**, 179, 221; serpent-raccoon imagery, 32; winged, 22, 128, **128**
serpentlike figures, 134, **134**
severed head motif, 113, **117**, 118, **127**
shamanism, **27**, 28, 30, 61, 78, **78**
Shawnee, 88, 89, 90; Absentee Shawnee, 254, 255, 256; Bread Dance, 253–59; Buffalo Dance, 255; Eastern Shawnee, 254; Green Corn Dance, 255; Loyal (Cherokee) Shawnee, 254, 255; myths, 33; Pumpkin Dance, 259; and removal to Indian Territory, 253–54; resettlements of, 253; Stomp Dance, 257, 259; treaties with the British and others, 253–54, **254**, **255**; White Oak Shawnee, 254, 255–59
shell (artifacts), 20, **21**, **32**, 97, **104**, **106**, **107**, **108**, **109**, 113, **113**, **116**, 117, **117**, 126, **127**, 128, **128**, 129, **129**, 130, **130**, **132**, 141, 156, **158**, **159**, **160**, **161**, **162**, 169, 178, 179, **179**, **188**, **190**, **194**, 200, 201, **201**, **208**, **209**, **211**, **215**, **217**, 236, **237**. *See also* cups; gorgets; masks
Shetrone, Henry C., 50
Sibley, John, 234
Siouan languages, speakers of, 88, 101
Sioux, 145; deities, 143
Sky World, 158, 160. *See also* Above World
Smith, Marvin T., 156
Smucker, Isaac, 78
social organization: dance and medicine societies, 136, 163, 165, 179; kin groups, 163, 165, 169, 234; moieties, 22; sodalities, 163, 165
social status, 163, 165, 169; artifacts and, 160, 163, 165, 169, 179–80
Southeastern Artistic Complex, 208
Southeastern Ceremonial Complex (SECC), 98, 105–07, 125, 126, 151, 180, 194, 208; as cosmic art, 208; and mortuary goods, 117, 153, 154, 156, 160, 163, 165; regional variations of, 107, 109, 120–21, 194, 222, 223; as ritual objects, 117, 158, 160, 194, 217, 225; styles of, 107, 109, 120–21, 194; symbolic motifs of, 140, 141, 142, 145, 147, 148, 158, 160, 212–13, 217; thematic content of, 113, 194, 222
Southern Cult, 208
spider motif, 147, **217**
Spiro, 18, 28, **34**, 107, 109, 112, 113, 119, 120, 121, 132, 134, 197, 201, 228, 237, 240, 242; Great Mortuary at, 134, 237, 245 n
Sponemann site, 100; figurine, 100
spud stones, **164**
Squier, Ephraim G., and Edwin H. Davis, **18**, **29**, 52, **67**, **68**, 73, **75**, 76, **79**, 80
St. Claire Polished Plain, 148
Stanley, John Mix, *International Indian Council (Held at Tahlequah, Indian Territory, 1843)*, **82**, **90**
star motif, 244, **244**
stone (artifacts), **4**, **6**, **9**, **17**, **21**, **22–26**, **29**, **30**, **31**, **34**, **42**, **44–45**, **49–55**, **61–66**, **78**, **97**, **110–11**, **131**, 141, **145**, **154**, **155**, 156, **159**, **164**, **173**, **174**, **175**, **177**, **178**, **179**, **186**, **195**, **196**, **198**, **199–200**, **202–03**, **244**, **261–62**, **264**, **267**, **269–70**
striped-center-pole motif, 129, **129**, 131
Stubbs Earthworks, 68, 69
Sullivan, Charles, *The Miamisburg Mound*, **66**
Sun-fire, symbolism of, 210, 211, 214, 215
Sunkle, Marie, 78–79
Sun, personification of, 22, 143, 147, 192, 193, 209
supernatural beings, 128, 131, 132, 140, 142, 195, 196, 198, 200
suppression of Native American culture, 19, 183, 184
Swanton, John R., **209**, 232
swastika motif, 180, 214–15, **215**, **216**, 217, 220; swastika-in-circle motif, 129, **129**, 130
symbolic motifs, 129, **129**, 139, 140, 141, 142, 158, 160, 195, 220

tablets, engraved, 44–45, **44–45**
Taensa village, 177
Talomeco (Talimeco), 86
Tamaroa, **94**, 101
tattooing, 85, 140, 142, **142**, 147, **147**, **218**, 225, **225–26**, **227**, 228, **228**, **229**
Tecumseh, 89, **252**, 254

Temple Mound complex, 236
Temple Mound period. *See* Mississippian period
Tennessee River, 18, 176, 194; valley, 59, 158, 85, 102, 171, 174, 222
Tenskwatawa, 254, **255**
Terán de los Rios, Domingo, **233**, 234
This World, 158, 160, 208. *See also* Middle World
Thomas, Cyrus, 65, 105, 106, 156, 195
Three Hills Creek site, 143, **143**
Thunderbird, 210
Thunderers, 33, 127, 130, 192, 195, 196
Thunders, 210, 214
Timucua, 88, 99, 187, 192
tobacco, 46; and smoking, 30, 46–47, 68
Tombigbee River, 176, 177
trade, 18, 19, 45, 48
trade goods, 88
Trails of Tears, 19, 89, 184, 188, **189**
treaty between Shawnee, Delaware, and Mingo Indians, and Great Britain, **254**
treaty between the United States and Shawnee, Potawatomi, Wyandot, Chippewa, and other Indians, **255**
Tremper Mound, 50–51, 52, **52**, 54; site, 77
trilobed motif, 129, **129**, 131, **131**, 177, 178, **179**
triskele motif, **159**, 160
Trubitt, Mary Beth, 117
Tunica, 88, 91, 237
Turner Earthworks, 69
Turner site, **47**, **48**, **60**
Twins myth cycle, 30, 195

Underwater Panther, 128, **128**, 131, **207**, 215, **216**, 221, 222, **222**. *See also* piasa
Underwater World (Underworld), 80, 158, 208, 220, 221, 222, 223. *See also* Beneath World
Underworld, 128. *See* Underwater World; Beneath World
University of Wisconsin–Milwaukee, 95
Unzicker, Joseph S., **75**
Upper Nasoni, 233, 234
Upper World, 80, 140, 147, 149. *See also* Above World

vanishing-point perspective, 131
Vega, Garcilaso de la, 33, 233
Visions of the People, 46
Voegelin, C. F., 134
vulvar motifs, 142, 143, 144, **144**, **149**

Wa-Ko^{n}-da, 139, 147
Walls Focus ceramics, 129, 172, 215, 219–20
war bundles, 144
warfare, 169, 191–205; artifacts related to, 160, 194, 196, **196**, 199, 202, 203; and authority, 200, 203; iconography, 160, 193, 198, 202–03, **204**; regalia, 192, 193, 194, 195, 199, 200, 202, 203; and rites of passage, 197; rituals of preparation, 191, 192, 193, 196, 197; and social status, 193, 196, 199, 202, 203; trophies, 198, 202–03, **202**
Waring, Antonio J., Jr., 119, 194
war medicines, 198
War of 1812, 89, 254, 255
Washington State Park, **145**
Watson Brake, 17
Watson, Patty Jo, 148
Wea, 88
Webb, William, 43, 44, 46
Westbrook figurine, **124**, 133, 135
West figurine, 100
White, John, **182**, **188**, **192**
Whittlesey, Colonel Charles, 151
Wichita, 88, 90, 237
Willey, Gordon, 42
Williams Island, 165
Williams, Stephen, 102
Willoughby Disk, **174**, 175
Willoughby figurine, 100
Wilson, J. N., 77–78
Winnebago, 33; cosmology of, 209
Winters, Howard, 43, 44, 45
Wittry, Warren L., 99
wood (artifacts), **1**, **14**, **28**, **121**
woodhenges, 97, 98–99, **99**; as cosmogram, 99, 100
Woodland period, 57–58
Wulfing Collection, 113, **114–15**
Wyandot, 255
Wyrick, David, 74, **75**

Yuchi, 88, 90; language, 187

zoomorphic imagery, 126, 129, 132